Wolfram Kinzig
A History of Early Christian Creeds
De Gruyter Textbook

Wolfram Kinzig

A History of Early Christian Creeds

—

DE GRUYTER

ISBN 978-3-11-031852-4
e-ISBN (PDF) 978-3-11-031853-1
e-ISBN (EPUB) 978-3-11-038215-0

Library of Congress Control Number: 2024930852

Bibliographic information published by the Deutsche Nationalbibliothek
The Deutsche Nationalbibliothek lists this publication in the Deutsche Nationalbibliografie;
detailed bibliographic data are available on the internet at http://dnb.dnb.de.

© 2024 Walter de Gruyter GmbH, Berlin/Boston
Cover image: Laurent d'Orléans, Somme le Roi, cod. Paris, Bibliothèque nationale de France,
Département des manuscrits, Français 938 (a. 1294), f. 6r, © Bibliothèque nationale de France,
ark:/12148/btv1b84478782
Typesetting: Integra Software Services Pvt. Ltd.
Printing and binding: CPI books GmbH, Leck

www.degruyter.com

To my wife, Carmen

At non formosa est! at non bene culta puella!
at, puto, non uotis saepe petita meis!
Ovid, Amores 3,7,1–2

Preface

This work was to be written in the years 2014–16 when I was on a two-year sabbatical leave, generously supported by the Volkswagen Foundation. However, when I set out to write it, I quickly realized that not only would I first have to finish my collection *Faith in Formulae*, but that some of the topics which I wished to cover in my history needed further investigation. Over the years this history kept being postponed, because the research involved proved to be so complex and extensive that I had to publish its results in separate studies and even another monograph, on the Creed of Constantinople. This additional research was made possible by a fellowship at the Heinz Heinen Kolleg of the Bonn Center for Dependency and Slavery Studies in 2020–2021 for which I am very grateful.

Only now am I able to conclude the work for the time being. Originally, I had planned a monograph of the size of J.N.D. Kelly's famous *Early Christian Creeds* which in its third edition runs to 458 pages. In the end, I have overshot that target, not least because the number of relevant sources has increased enormously over the last fifty years. Nevertheless, I hope that the book can serve both as an academic textbook and as a reference work for those who wish to find out more about specific creeds and their history. For this purpose, I have translated all Greek and Latin texts into English such that this work can also be used by those who possess no or little knowledge of these languages (although some knowledge would be preferable). I have also tried to design it in such a way that it can be used independently from *Faith in Formulae* – important creeds and credal passages are always cited in full. Some readers might have liked to see source texts cited more, but this would simply have made the book bulkier than it is already.

In writing this book I have plundered my own earlier scholarly work, especially the three volumes of *Neue Texte und Studien zu den antiken und frühmittelalterlichen Glaubensbekenntnissen*. I felt entitled to this ruthless act because much of what I have written on the subject is published in German and may not be easily accessible to an English-speaking audience. I therefore ask my German-speaking readers for indulgence for certain repetitions – however, I have brought everything up to the latest state of my knowledge, given that over the years my views on the history of the creeds have developed further. Most importantly, I no longer think that the Roman Creed as a declaratory formula stems from the fourth century or began with Marcellus of Ancyra. In addition, the discovery of a shorter version of the Creed of Constantinople which is more than a simple abbreviation of that creed forced me to reconsider its history.

The secondary literature on the subjects which I touch upon in this book is simply enormous. In order to keep footnotes to an absolute minimum, I have abstained from extensive engagement with ideas of others that deviate from my

https://doi.org/10.1515/9783110318531-202

own. Experts will notice where I disagree, and non-experts probably won't care in any case.

A book such as this by necessity leads its author unto fields usually ploughed by specialists in biblical studies, ancient history, law, art, music, papyrology, Christian liturgy, and the history of the oriental churches. When stumbling across such fields I have been comforting myself with the thought that in all probability no single person possesses the kind of comprehensive expertise which would *really* be necessary to study the subject in all its ramifications. In other words, this book could never have been written without a certain scholarly impudence. I hope my critics will take into account this predicament when pointing out my mistakes and shortcomings in areas that are not my own.

On a technical note, I have not tried to attain overall uniformity in the spelling of Latin and Greek texts. In general, I have reproduced that of the editions used, but in Latin often altered 'v' to 'u' to be as consistent as possible.

I wish to express my gratitude to a number of organizations and individuals. The Volkswagen Foundation and the Bonn Center for Dependency and Slavery Studies kindly supported sabbatical leaves which gave me sufficient room to ponder some of the problems that are dealt with in this book. Prof. Dr Dr Hubert Kaufhold (Munich) generously took the time to read my chapter about the reception of the creeds in the oriental churches, saving me from a number of blunders. Dr Matthias Simperl (Augsburg) kindly sent me his as yet unpublished doctoral dissertation on the Synod of Antioch (325) and shared valuable information regarding the textual tradition of its synodal letter. Susanna Kinzig (Tübingen) gave me good advice on reshaping the introduction and proofread some chapters with a sharp eye for inconsistencies. Dr Thomas Brüggemann (Bonn) read the chapter on Nicaea, offering some helpful suggestions. Dr Maria Munkholt Christensen (Bonn) not only read the entire book but helped me in many ways which would take too long to detail here. Nathalie Kröger (Bonn/Bordesholm) carefully went through every chapter and assisted me with preparing the manuscript for publication as well as with compiling the indexes. Johanna Schwarz (Bonn) also gave invaluable support in indexing. Thomas Jibin Abraham (Bonn) carefully proofread chapter 9. Anna-Lena Steuckart and Michael Ehret very diligently and efficiently ensured that I would not run out of books, which involved a lot of legwork to and from the many libraries in Bonn. Anke Grimm-Haddouti (Bonn) was as reliable as ever in all administrative matters.

A special word of gratitude goes to my brilliant language editor Dr Kathrin Lüddecke (Oxford) who not only turned my clumsy English into a readable book, but with her expertise in classics even pointed out some inconsistencies in my translations from Greek and Latin.

Dr Albrecht Döhnert (De Gruyter) graciously accepted considerable delays in the completion of the manuscript. The team at De Gruyter headed by Jessica Bartz and Anne Stroka (Integra Software Services) once more turned my manuscript into a wonderful book.

To all of them: *Herzlichen Dank!*

This book is dedicated to my wife, Carmen. She endured my mental and physical absence during its writing; she never complained about weekends cut short before and during the editing process; and she encouraged me and gave me comfort when I could not see the light at the end of the tunnel: *muchas gracias.*

As we approach the anniversary of the First Ecumenical Council, it is my sincere wish that this book may serve as a useful starting point for the history of the early Christian creeds, may stimulate further research on these fundamental texts, and may help in promoting ecumenical fellowship.

Oberdollendorf, Epiphany 2024
Wolfram Kinzig

Contents

Indices

Abbreviations

Most abbreviations follow Schwertner 2014.

Abbreviations of creeds

Ant[1] First creed associated with the Council of Antioch (341; FaFo § 141c; cf. below pp. 278 f.)

Ant[2] Second creed associated with the Council of Antioch (341; FaFo § 141b; cf. below pp. 271–3)

Ant[3] Third creed associated with the Council of Antioch (341); creed of Theophronius of Tyana (FaFo § 141a; cf. below pp. 276–8)

Ant[4] Fourth creed associated with the Council of Antioch (341; FaFo § 141d; cf. below pp. 280 f.)

Ath Athanasian Creed (*Symbolum Quicumque*; FaFo § 434a; cf. below pp. 39–45)

C Creed of Constantinople (381; version unspecified)

    C[1] officially adopted Creed of Constantinople (381); largely identical with the creed attested by Nestorius (cf. Kinzig, 'Zwei neuentdeckte Predigten', 2020(2022), p. 43 and below pp. 363–7)

    Note: In Kinzig, 'Zwei neuentdeckte Predigten', 2020(2022) I have also used the provisional abbreviations N[Nest] (for the fragments of the creed found in the writings of Nestorius (FaFo § 197a–g)) and N[Hom] for the creed attested in the newly discovered homilies by Nestorius and edited in this article. I have shown there that N[Nest], N[Hom], and C[1] are largely identical which is why in this book the abbreviations N[Nest] and N[Hom] are no longer used.

    C[2] not officially adopted Creed of Constantinople (381) as first attested at the Third Session of the Council of Chalcedon (451); traditionally called Nicene Creed or Nicene-Constantinopolitan Creed; in earlier literature also abbrev. NC or C (FaFo § 184e; cf. below pp. 363–7)

Eus (alleged) Creed of Caesarea as found in Eusebius (FaFo § 134a; cf. below pp. 246–8)

J Creed of Jerusalem as attested by Cyril (FaFo § 147; cf. below pp. 202 f.)

N Creed of Nicaea (325; FaFo § 135c; cf. below pp. 246–8)

    N[Ant] Antiochene revision of N) (cf. below pp. 346–9)

    N[Ant1] Antiochene revision of N as attested by Theodore of Mopsuestia (FaFo § 180a; cf. below pp. 346–9)

    N[Ant2] Antiochene revision of N as attested by Eusebius of Dorylaeum (FaFo § 198) and John Cassian (FaFo § 203; cf. below pp. 346–9)

    N[Ant3] so-called 'Nestorian Creed' (FaFo § 208; cf. below pp. 346–9)

OGS *Old Gelasian Sacramentary* (and its credal questions; FaFo § 675c, f; cf. below pp. 121 f.)

    OGS[G1], OGS*, OGS[G2] various sets of credal questions, reconstructed on the basis of OGS (cf. below pp. 123, 127, 128 f.)

R Old Roman Creed; precursor of T (cf. below pp. 145–8)

    R[M] R as attested in Greek by Marcellus of Ancyra (FaFo § 253; cf. below pp. 146 f.)
    R[M/L1], R[M/L2] reconstructions of Latin text (cf. below p. 159)

    R[R] R as attested by Rufinus (FaFo § 254b; cf. below pp. 146 f.)

    R[L] R as attested by Leo the Great (FaFo § 255g; cf. below pp. 146 f.)

R/T summary abbreviation for all creeds deriving from R (cf. below pp. 157–89)

T *textus receptus* (i.e. traditional text) of the Apostles' Creed (FaFo § 344; cf. below pp. 161 f.)

https://doi.org/10.1515/9783110318531-204

TA   *Traditio Apostolica*, ascribed to Hippolytus (cf. below p. 148)

- TA^G reconstructed Greek baptismal questions in the TA (FaFo § 89c and below pp. 151 f.)
- TA^E baptismal questions in the Ethiopic text of the TA (FaFo § 89c and below p. 150)
- TA^L baptismal questions in the Latin text of the TA (= *Fragmentum Veronese*; FaFo § 89b and below p. 150)

Further abbreviations and explanations

app. ad. l. 00	apparatus referring to line 00 in the indicated critical edition
ex.	(*saeculo*) *exeunte*, the end of a given century
in.	(*saeculo*) *ineunte*, the beginning of a given century
fl.	*floruit*, the period of an author's literary activity
olim	formerly
r.	*rexit* (reigned)
sedit	term of office of a bishop or emperor
s.	*saeculo*, indicating the century in which a manuscript was written
v.l.	*varia lectio*, variant reading in a source or manuscript

For English translations of the Bible, I have often used the *New Revised Standard Version Updated Edition* (NRSVue), as available online, for example, at URL <https://www.biblegateway.com/> (29/11/2023), while adapting quotations freely according to context.

1 Introduction: What is a Creed?

1.1 Preliminary remarks

The creeds are arguably the most influential non-biblical texts in the history of Christianity. Most people take the Apostles' Creed or the Creed of Nicaea-Constantinople (the so-called 'Nicene Creed') for granted when they recite it or hear it as part of worship. Yet these texts have an intricate history. The creeds have evolved over a period of several hundred years. The aim of this book is to shed some light upon this history. It is a fascinating tale because it touches upon the very heart of Christianity. But it is also a complex one, which is why I recommend that any reader who wishes to understand this development in its broad outline, before studying some of its aspects in more detail, start by reading the summary in chapter 20.

In this introductory chapter we will begin by asking what it actually is that we are talking about: what is a creed? The answer is more difficult than it might seem at first glance because even the names in use today for the creed, and the processes and actions that we associate with it, need some explanation.

This book's author is from Germany. Talking about the creed is pretty straightforward for him. English 'faith' is *Glaube* or *Glauben* in German. The corresponding verb is *glauben*. A creed in German is a *Glaubensbekenntnis* ('a confession of faith') or, simply, a *Bekenntnis* ('a confession'). At times, *Credo* is used which derives from the first word of the Latin creed *credo* ('I believe'). In addition, in German academic parlance the creed is also often called a *Symbol*, a term which derives from the Latin word for the creed (*symbolum*).[1] To confess the creed is *bekennen*.

In English the situation is more complicated. Again, let us begin with 'faith'. Generally speaking, 'faith' in the religious sense has no verbal form like 'faithing'[2] (although one may say that someone 'has faith (in God)'). Instead, it is 'believing': the action associated with 'faith in God' is 'to believe in God'. Curiously, however, in

---

[1] Cf. below ch. 3. Oddly, although the usage of 'symbol' for 'creed' is listed in the *Oxford English Dictionary* (cf. *Oxford English Dictionary* Online. September 2022, s.v. 'symbol, *n.*'; URL <https://doi.org/10.1093/OED/5373115799> (02/11/2023)), it is not often found in modern English. J.N.D. Kelly, in his classic account of the history of the creeds (Kelly 1972), does use 'symbol' in the sense of 'creed', but most often in the context of quoting source texts in which *symbolum* appears.

[2] However, the *Oxford English Dictionary* does list a verb 'faith' in both intransitive and transitive usage. Cf. *Oxford English Dictionary* Online. September 2022, s.v. 'faith, *v.*'; URL <https://doi.org/10.1093/OED/2365032708> (02/11/2023). A Google book search has yielded the result that 'faithing' occurs in evangelical, pastoral, and therapeutic literature in the intransitive sense of 'being in a state of faith'.

https://doi.org/10.1515/9783110318531-001

current usage the cognate noun 'belief' (again in its religious usage) is *not* simply synonymous with 'faith' but weaker in its semantic power.[3] As J.I. Packer put it:

> The word *faith* [. . .] gets the idea of trustful commitment and reliance better than *belief* does. Whereas *belief* suggests bare opinion, *faith*, whether in a car, a patent medicine, a protégé, a doctor, a marriage partner, or what have you, is a matter of treating the person or thing as trustworthy and committing yourself accordingly.[4]

'Faith' in English is an expression of loyalty and reliability and thus has a meaning similar to 'trust'. As regards its use in a religious context, the *Oxford English Dictionary* defines 'faith' as

> belief in and acceptance of the doctrines of a religion, typically involving belief in a god or gods and in the authenticity of divine revelation. Also (*Theology*): the capacity to spiritually apprehend divine truths, or realities beyond the limits of perception or of logical proof, viewed either as a faculty of the human soul, or as the result of divine illumination.[5]

It is noteworthy that the *OED* adds:

> Earlier evidence refers almost exclusively to the Christian religion, divine revelation being viewed as contained either in Holy Scripture or in the teaching of the Church.[6]

We will have to consider this observation in more detail below.

When Christians describe the content of their 'faith', such a description is called a 'creed' or a 'confession' or a 'confession of faith' (from Latin *confessio*).[7] The content of a creed is 'believed' and may be 'confessed' or, more seldom, 'professed' (from Latin *confiteri/profiteri*). However, like its Latin counterpart, the semantic field of 'confession' (and its cognate verb 'to confess') is wider than that of 'creed' and may also, for example, extend to an acknowledgement of sin or sinfulness or, before a court of law, of the truth of a statement or charge, such as 'I am

---

3 This seems to be a modern development. Until the early twentieth century, 'belief' in its religious usage was largely synonymous with 'faith' which can be seen from the fact that the Apostles' Creed could simply be called 'the Belief'. Cf. *Oxford English Dictionary* Online. September 2022, s.v. 'belief, *n.*'; URL <https://doi.org/10.1093/OED/9976740972> (02/11/2023).

4 Packer 2008, p. 26.

5 *Oxford English Dictionary* Online. September 2022, s.v. 'faith, *n.*'; URL <https://doi.org/10.1093/OED/7269017364> (02/11/2023).

6 *Oxford English Dictionary* Online. September 2022, s.v. 'faith, *n.*'; URL <https://doi.org/10.1093/OED/7269017364> (02/11/2023).

7 The distinction between 'creed' and 'confession of faith' made by Fairbairn/Reeves 2019, pp. 7–9 does not correspond to the evidence: ancient creeds are often called a *confessio fidei* in the sources. Cf. also below ch. 3.

(not) guilty'.[8] By contrast, 'creed' is primarily restricted to a 'statement of faith' (and in a transferred meaning also to a specific belief system).[9]

'Creed' derives from Old English 'crêda' which in turn derives from the first word of the Latin creed.[10] As in German, 'Credo', usually with a capital initial, is also sometimes used for 'creed'.[11] 'Believing in Christ' and 'confessing Christ' are almost synonymous, although the latter always implies some sort of verbal expression in front of someone else. This does not necessarily have to be another human, but might well be God or even the speaker themselves (in their inner heart). In other words, in my confession I may not actually be saying it out aloud, but still express a particular loyalty to and trust in a person which I am, at least in principle, able to put into words (or else my confession would be without content). Furthermore, I do not necessarily have to 'confess Christ' using the words of a *creed*: as we will see, such a confession may simply take the form of saying 'I am a Christian', or it may even be expressed without words such as when I refuse to sacrifice to the Roman gods (because in my heart I confess Christ as my only Lord). In other words, without 'faith in Christ' there can be no 'confession of Christ', but this transition from 'faith' to 'confession' may take various forms.

When we turn to the ancient languages, the Greek equivalent for 'faith' is πίστις. The cognate verb πιστεύειν ('to believe') is construed with the dative or the prepositions εἰς or ἐπί to denote the person or object whom I believe in or trust upon; with accusative case only ('to believe something'); with infinitive, sometimes an accusative and infinitive; or with an object clause introduced by ὅτι ('to believe that something is the case'). In the context of creeds πιστεύειν is generally construed with εἰς ('to believe in'). 'Confession' in Greek is ὁμολογία (rarely also ὁμολογησία and ὁμολόγησις), its cognate verb ὁμολογεῖν. 'Faith' in Latin is *fides* and later also *credulitas*, whereas 'confession' is *confessio*. As with *faith* in English, there is no cognate verb to *fides* in the religious sense we are interested in[12] – 'to believe' is *credere*. *Credere* plus dative and *credere in* plus accusative are often used synonymously, although later an explicit distinction is sometimes made.[13] In addition, we find *credere* in the sense of 'to believe that' with infinitive or with

---

8 Cf. *Oxford English Dictionary* Online. September 2022, s.v. 'confession, *n.*', 'confess, *v.*'; URL <https://doi.org/10.1093/OED/1039093600>; <https://doi.org/10.1093/OED/8113292560> (02/11/2023).
9 Cf. *Oxford English Dictionary* Online. September 2022, s.v. 'creed, *n.¹*'; URL <https://doi.org/10.1093/OED/2719317857> (02/11/2023).
10 Cf. Pogatscher 1888, p. 88.
11 Cf. *Oxford English Dictionary* Online. September 2022, s.v. 'credo, *n.*'; URL <https://doi.org/10.1093/OED/8057746962> (02/11/2023).
12 Its cognate verb *(con)fidere* ('to trust') is never used in the religious sense of 'to believe'.
13 Cf. Becker 1969, col. 828; TeSelle 1996–2002, cols. 120 f. For example, Augustine says that 'to believe in someone (*credere in eum*)' involves loving the person we believe in whereas 'to believe

accusative and infinitive or with a clause introduced by *quod*. When it comes to the creeds the vast majority of them use *credo/credimus in* plus accusative, although in later Latin the accusative is often replaced by the ablative. Which Latin nouns are used for the creeds is discussed below.[14]

*

Since the creed is always an expression of faith, to the extent that in antiquity it was even often simply called *fides* ('faith'), we must inquire into the nature of faith in Christianity. It is a much-discussed question whether religious 'faith' or 'belief' existed in antiquity before and outside Christianity.[15] 'Did the Greeks believe in their myths?' was the question that guided Paul Veyne's (1930–2022) famous monograph of the same title.[16] He answered it in the affirmative, claiming that it was possible to identify a plurality of beliefs in classical antiquity, because beliefs were an integral part of the *condition humaine*:

> How could people believe in all these legends, and did they truly believe in them? This is not a subjective question; modalities of belief are related to the ways in which truth is possessed. Throughout the ages a plurality of programs of truth has existed, and it is these programs, involving different distributions of knowledge, that explain the subjective degrees of intensity of beliefs, the bad faith, and the contradictions that coexist in the same individual. We agree with Michel Foucault on this point. The history of ideas truly begins with the historicization of the philosophical idea of truth.[17]

Denis Feeney, 'following in the path of Paul Veyne',[18] concluded that language of belief among the Romans

> is not relating to a constant kernel of agreed and revealed belief, but is part of an ongoing contestation between different forms of speech over whether and how any particular application is going to be made to stick. The criteria of truth and belief remain variable because they are radically contextual, being always produced from ever-changing conditions of dialogue.[19]

Such an argument is difficult to prove or disprove. However, in our context it may suffice to limit ourselves to the actual use of *pístis* and *fides* and cognate terms in ancient and early medieval texts. Here the evidence is fairly clear: in her

---

someone' (*credere ei*) does not, so that the demons may believe God or Christ, but do not believe 'in' him. Cf., e.g., *In Iohannis euangelium tractatus 29*, 6.

14 Cf. below ch. 3.

15 For what follows cf. also Harrisson 2013, pp. 2–8.

16 Veyne 1988 (French: 1983).

17 Veyne 1988, p. 27.

18 Feeney 2001, p. 9.

19 Feeney 2001, p. 46.

magisterial monograph on the use of faith language among non-Christians and Christians Teresa Morgan notes as a general consensus of recent scholarship 'that *pistis*, along with other lexica of belief and related concepts, plays a far less significant role in either Judaism or Graeco-Roman religions than it plays in Christianity'.[20] Or, in the words of Old Testament scholar Anja Klein, faith 'is a decidedly Christian concept'.[21] Why? I suggest there are two basic reasons: the historical nature of Christianity and Christian monotheism.

As we will see, right from the start Christians undoubtedly believed in a fairly fixed set of propositions relating to historical events: that Jesus Christ, the Son of God, had become incarnate, died, rose again, and ascended to heaven. These events were believed to have happened in the past, at a given point in time, whose chronology could be exactly determined. They began under the reign of Emperor Augustus (r. 31 BC – 14 AD) during the governorship of Publius Sulpicius Quirinius (Lk 2:2),[22] and they ended during the governorship of Pontius Pilate (r. 26–36). Indeed, Pilate was even included in the Apostles' Creed in order to underline this historicity. Augustine later spilt much ink discussing how one could believe the veracity (in the sense of factuality) of events or phenomena which one had not witnessed oneself.[23] By and large, one might argue about the precise nature or mode of the incarnation, passion, and resurrection, and the precise 'status' or 'nature' of Jesus, but there was no doubt that you could only become a member of the Christian community if you acknowledged the factuality of these events. And such acknowledgement was only possible by way of 'faith', that is, the firm conviction that these events had (in one way or another) actually happened, that they attested to the significance of the historical Jesus that was unparalleled in the human sphere (and which remained to be defined) and that would change the life of anyone who believed in their historicity.

At the same time, Jesus was associated with a God which Christians considered matchless and, therefore – regardless of his precise nature[24] – the *only* divine being. In all other ancient cults one might pledge allegiance to a particular deity who was consequently accorded due veneration, but nowhere was the existence of

---

20 Morgan 2015, p. 2.

21 Anja Klein in Klein et al. 2014, col. 690.

22 The census mentioned in Lk 2:2 may date to 6 AD. It does not matter that this dating of Jesus' birth may in fact be inaccurate, as Jesus was born during the reign of Herod the Great (who died in 4 BC; cf. Mt 2) – what matters is that people believed it to be factually accurate.

23 Cf., e.g., his treatises *Concerning Faith of Things not Seen* (*De fide rerum inuisibilium*, after 420?) and *On the Profit of Believing* (*De utilitate credendi*, 391/392). In addition, *Confessiones* 6,7.

24 The heated debates among Christians about the precise nature of their deity could make it seem to outsiders as if they believed in more than one God; for details about this debate cf. Kinzig, 'Ist das Christentum monotheistisch?', 2017.

other – although perhaps not as powerful – gods denied. The only exception was Judaism – but Judaism did not openly propagate its monotheism. Christianity was different: Christians acknowledged that there were indeed supernatural beings that were actually quite powerful, but they had no divine status – rather they were demons, out to lead the Christians astray from worshipping their god. But Christians did not stop there: they actively tried to convince non-Christians that the gods they believed in were, in truth, evil demons. Converting to Christianity was thus not to prefer one god over another, as more helpful in a certain life situation, but an 'either-or' decision. This decision was to have 'faith'. It was a decision to trust in the life-saving power of the one God of Jesus Christ that did not have to be verbalized. However, if expressed in words or corroborated by some form of action such as martyrdom, it might lead to a (public) 'confession' of the existence of one god only and of the proposition that this one god was absolutely trustworthy and was going to change one's life for the better, as he had proven in the past, be it speaking through the prophets or, recently, having himself come down to earth. This confession could be summarized in the words of a creed.

*

What, then, is a creed? Given the sheer number of texts called, or that call themselves, 'creed', any definition will be imperfect. In this book I will draw on a definition Markus Vinzent and I developed in an article back in 1999: a creed is

> a formal pledge of allegiance to a set of doctrinal statements concerning God and his relationship to his creation in general and to humankind in particular. Typically, a creed contains the words "I/we believe" or (in interrogatory form) 'Do you believe?' to which the expected answer is: 'I/we believe'. Whereas a creed's *Sitz im Leben* may vary (catechesis, liturgy, doctrinal debate), its wording usually does not. [. . .] The vast majority of creeds consists of three articles referring to the Father, the Son and the Holy Spirit.[25]

Creeds as defined here only exist in Christianity. Other religions can do without them. Thus, there are no creeds in either Greek or Roman religion.[26] The Shema Yisrael in Judaism[27] or Shahada in Islam[28] are sets of doctrinal tenets whose truth

---

25 Kinzig/Vinzent 1999, pp. 540 f. Some time ago, Michael Kohlbacher suggested a helpful 'typology of creeds' which is based on a much wider definition (Kohlbacher, Das *Symbolum Athanasianum*, 2004). At the end of the day it is a matter of personal choice what importance one attributes to the introductory phrase 'I believe/we believe'. Cf. also Gabriel 2016.

26 Cf. Harrisson 2013, p. 4.

27 Deut 6:4: 'Hear, O Israel: YHWH is our God, YHWH is one'.

28 'I bear witness that there is no deity but God, the One, there is no partner to Him, and I bear witness that Muhammad is His servant and His messenger.' There are alternative versions, depending on the tradition that is followed. Cf. Padwick 1961(1969), pp. 126–51; Wensinck 1965.

is declared, or borne witness to, in the form of propositions, but they are not creeds according to our definition.[29] *Qur'ān* 112 comes close to a creed, and some scholars have suggested that it is, as it were, a negated Nicene Creed.[30] However, unlike these formulae most Christian creeds do not state that 'this or that is true', nor that 'I believe (or we believe) that a particular proposition is true'. Rather, such doctrinal propositions are introduced by the words 'I/we believe in' and thus express a *personal relationship*. The addition of the preposition 'in' indicates that the individual's belief goes beyond assent to particular propositions and expresses both confidence in the existence and the power of the divine persons of the Trinity and in the historical truth of the Christ story (birth – passion – crucifixion – resurrection – ascension). Using the language of dogmatics one could say: confessional texts are not only about the *fides quae creditur*, the *content* of the confession, but also express a *fides qua creditur*, a *relationship* between human and God based on *faith.*

At the same time one should bear in mind that, although creeds only exist in Christianity, even many Christian groups, for example Quakers, Anabaptists, and Antitrinitarians, have rejected such formulae. Given these facts, neither the existence of creeds as such nor their trinitarian structure are self-evident but require careful consideration. In this context we will have to examine why the Christian faith came to be expressed in fixed formulae at a certain point and why this expression included assertions concerning the existence and nature of the three trinitarian persons.

When approaching the history of the creeds we must also remember that in our modern understanding 'faith' is often seen as an internalized, personal relationship to God within the individual believer. But this is quite a modern concept which owes its existence, on the one hand, to the Pietism of the late seventeenth and eighteenth centuries which emphasized the 'heart' as the seat of faith and of one's feelings (which is why we tend to associate a particular 'pious feeling' with 'faith') and, on the other hand, to the Enlightenment in whose wake the language of faith was banned from public discourse and largely 'privatized'. By contrast, in antiquity 'faith' always had both a private *and* public side. One's *personal* alle-

---

29 For Judaism cf. also Michael Satlow in Klein et al. 2014, col. 702: 'Following the H[ebrew] B[ible], rabbinic Judaism has no creed or dogma and the rabbis of late antiquity never commanded belief or faith.' Klein et al. 2014, col. 703: 'Faith and belief would become important issues in Jewish philosophy in the early Middle Ages [. . .]. From then to the present there has been a lively controversy among Jewish thinkers about the proper role of faith in Judaism, not to mention acceptable beliefs.' Admittedly, with Islam the situation is more complex. But if I am not mistaken, the emphasis of the Shahada is on 'bearing witness to' rather than 'believing/trusting in'. Cf., e.g., Hermansen 2016.
30 Cf. Sura 112 (tr. Ali Quli Qarai in Reynolds 2018, p. 937): '*Say*, "He is God, the One. God is the All-embracing. He neither begat, nor was begotten, nor has He any equal."' For discussion cf. Hoffmann 2023 and the literature quoted there. In addition, Kropp 2011.

giance to God was regularly expressed in *public*, which was initially, for reasons of safety, largely restricted to the Christian congregation, but later formed part of everyday life. Moreover, both Greek πίστις and Latin *fides* originally meant 'reliability', 'trustworthiness', or 'credit', for example in business life, so that 'faith' also had a social and even legal connotation. Hence when someone said 'I believe in' they expressed trust in, but also allegiance to a divine overlord into whose protection they had betaken themselves.

1.2 The scope of this book

Christianity, then, is a credal religion. Yet it is not easy to determine where a history of the Christian creeds should begin. With the New Testament? In the late second or early third century when the first dogmatic propositions were assembled to form a 'rule of faith'?[31] Or not before the early fourth century when the Nicene Creed was composed? In recent decades arguments for all of these beginnings have been put forward. Ultimately, it depends on what you mean by 'creed'. The creed which is most widely accepted in Christendom is the Creed of Nicaea-Constantinople or Nicene-Constantinopolitan Creed (traditionally, but inaccurately called Nicene Creed; usually abbreviated NC or C; in this book for reasons which will be explained below:[32] C^2). It is closely followed by the Apostles' Creed (hereafter: T, short for *textus receptus*[33]), which is not usually recited in orthodox churches, but even more popular in western Christianity than C^2. It may, therefore, make sense to take these two texts as something of a guideline for a description of the genre, although we must bear in mind that these creeds had a prehistory reaching back to the beginnings of Christianity and that the genre accommodated many variations and, as it were, 'borderline cases'. For example, it is doubtful if the third of the 'great' early Christian confessions in the western churches, the so-called Athanasian Creed (also: *Symbolum Quicumque*, abbrev. Ath), can be termed a creed since an actual credal formula ('I believe' or 'we believe') is missing. I will, therefore, exclude it from further investigation.[34]

Likewise, different confessions by no means had a uniform *Sitz im Leben*. Creeds were recited not only as part of worship: catechumens learned them by heart before being baptized, priests and monks chanted them during their offices, bishops suspected of heresy composed them to prove their orthodoxy. Creeds were solemnly proclaimed at synods to initiate proceedings or, having been developed at them, to

---

31 Cf. below ch. 4.4.
32 Cf. below ch. 7.
33 The abbreviation was introduced by Kattenbusch 1894, p. 189.
34 Cf. below ch. 2.3.

then conclude the meeting. Finally, under the Roman emperors of late antiquity, creeds even acquired the force of law. Orthodox and heterodox Christians alike amended existing creeds or wrote entirely new ones. Some such confessions were very brief, containing only a few lines, while others were elaborate tracts, sometimes running to several pages in modern printed editions. Confessions of faith are like kaleidoscopes: the composition of their colours constantly changes, making it difficult to discern longer-term patterns.

Therefore, how creeds came about varied according to time and place. In times of calm, older confessions were usually simply repeated. New creeds were often written when a particular individual or group felt attacked on doctrinal grounds, although often social and political factors were also involved.

Times of crisis in antiquity and the early middle ages that were prolific in producing, as well as in prompting debate about, creeds included in the east:

(1) the trinitarian controversies of the fourth century, which, by and large, were resolved at the Council of Constantinople in 381;
(2) the christological controversies of the fifth century, which reached a provisional conclusion at the Council of Chalcedon in 451;
(3) the Miaphysite controversies that followed from 451 to 553; and
(4) the Monothelete debates in the years 630 to 681.

In the west, similar crises included:

(1) the change from Homoian to Catholic Christianity in the Visigothic Kingdom in 589 and its aftermath; and
(2) the debate on adoptionism in eighth and ninth-century Spain.

However, it is important to note that, in the east, from the fourth century onwards, the dogmatic points of reference for all discussions were the Creed of Nicaea (N) and later that of Constantinople (C^2). Even though other confessions were written later, they all claimed to be interpretations or clarifications of either N or C^2. In the west, C^2 was also considered the 'dogmatic' confession. However, the (Old) Roman Confession (R) and its descendants down to the Apostles' Creed (T) were much more important in their impact on the faith and lives of believers at large, given that these were the creeds primarily used in catechetical instruction. The changes in wording which ultimately led to the transformation of R to T are not necessarily an expression of a widespread crisis; rather, for the most part they are simply variants springing from local usage.[35] It would, therefore, be erroneous to consider R and T to be two different texts.

---

35 Cf. below ch. 5.2.

By contrast, the Athanasian Creed is – as already indicated above – a strange hybrid of confession and dogmatic treatise. While it too was very influential, if I am not mistaken, it was predominately used to help educate priests, not in preaching at large (with a few exceptions).

To summarize, more confessions were produced in the east than in the west – the vast majority of creeds in the Latin Church are variants and expansions of R. The Apostles' Creed, which became the standard creed in Carolingian times, is one of these variants. By the time of Charlemagne, the development of creeds in the west had come to a close. In the east, the same had in fact already happened with the adoption of N and C^2 at the fifth and sixth sessions of the Council of Chalcedon (451), albeit that N and C^2 subsequently continued to compete for supremacy until C^2 had largely supplanted the older confession in the Greek Orthodox Church around the eighth century. (N and its Antiochene variant N^{Ant} continued to be used in certain Oriental Orthodox Churches.[36])

This overview serves to establish both the geographical and chronological extent of this work. We will begin our investigation in the New Testament, with a search for theological formulae and summaries containing, *in nuce*, propositions that are later included in the declaratory creeds of the fourth century. As we will see, these formulae and summaries could take many forms which differed from region to region. They later 'coagulated' in those fixed verbal structures that we call 'creeds'. By the early middle ages when the 'great creeds' C^2, T, and Ath had been widely accepted, the dynamic of credal production began to slacken. Therefore, this book primarily covers confessional developments in the Latin and Greek Churches from their beginnings in the first century to the early ninth century, although some attention will also be paid to credal developments outside the Roman Empire.

1.3 Some remarks on nomenclature

In what follows I will use a number of terms which, for the sake of clarity, are briefly described here:
– *Homologies* are texts that suggest *some kind* of confessional *Sitz im Leben* as defined below in chapter 4.2 or may *in some way* be related to such confessions. My wording is deliberately vague because it is a collective term for all kinds of texts that make statements about, or express veneration of, God, Christ, and the Spirit individually or collectively (such as *pístis* formulae, prayers, acclamations,

---

36 Cf. below ch. 9.

kerygmatic formulae, doxologies etc.[37]), sometimes supplemented by summaries of Christ's saving work ('christological summaries'). My use of 'homology' is, therefore, wider than that often found in previous scholarship.[38]

– *Rules of faith* are texts that ancient sources expressly called that or 'rules of truth', etc. They consist of a series of dogmatic propositions about the persons of the Trinity with similar content yet not identical in wording. In a way, they represent an intermediary stage between homologies and creeds.

– *Interrogatory creeds* (or credal interrogations/questions) are texts introduced by 'Do you believe in?', typically used at baptism to ascertain the baptismal candidate's assent to a series of faith statements as described in chapter 4.5.

– *Declaratory creeds* were written either collectively (e.g. by a committee or synod) or by individuals (often called 'private creeds'[39]).
- Collective creeds may take three forms:
  - *Local creeds* were used especially in catechesis without it being possible to identify their author or origin (similar to modern 'folk songs'). Their significance remained largely restricted to a single region. Classical examples include the Roman Creed in the first phase of its history and the Creed of Jerusalem.
  - However, occasionally the significance of a local creed did not remain restricted to one region but had an impact on credal developments in other areas or territories, such that 'daughter creeds' developed. We may call these *transregional creeds*. Many creeds in the Latin church, including the Apostles' Creed, are such 'daughter creeds' of the Roman Creed, developing from the second half of the fourth century onwards.
  - *Synodal creeds* are either documents of a dogmatic compromise or were imposed by one of the parties at an assembly of prelates. They were created to settle matters when certain doctrines regarding the Trinity were controversial. At the same time, they served to ward off

---

37 Cf. Berger 2005, pp. 290–305.

38 Cf., e.g., Vielhauer 1975(1985), pp. 23–8; Staats 1999, p. 149; Vollenweider 2017, pp. 506 f., 509 f. Cf. also Riedl 2004, pp. 89, 164 citing New Testament scholars Günther Bornkamm and Hans Conzelmann. For the background of this debate cf. also Campenhausen 1972(1979), pp. 234 f.; Böttrich 2014, p. 95 and n. 115.

39 The term 'private' creed (which may have been coined in 1770 by the Göttingen Church historian Christian Wilhelm Franz Walch (1726–1784; cf. Markschies 2013, p. 260) is not very helpful, since it suggests that such creeds were not made 'public', whereas the opposite is true: such creeds were almost always written to be made known in public for apologetic purposes (cf. Markschies 2013, p. 264). It is, therefore, more accurate to speak of 'individual' creeds.

views deemed heretical by a majority of bishops. In these cases, sometimes solemn condemnations ('anathemas') were added, specifically naming the teachings against which that creed was directed. In terms of form criticism, such anathemas do not form part of creeds since creeds containing such condemnations can also 'survive' when their anathemas are omitted (as in the case of N when it was subsequently revised and ultimately morphed into C^2). Nonetheless, if we want to understand the apologetic and legal nature of synodal creeds, the anathemas also have to be considered. Synodal creeds were often signed individually by the bishops attending the councils which drafted them.

– *Individual creeds* were often, although not exclusively, produced by bishops or presbyters in the context of synods either in order to set out and defend a particular doctrine or to demonstrate one's view as compatible with 'orthodoxy'. In both cases, their function was mostly apologetic (e.g., because a particular cleric was facing a charge of heresy). In what follows I have drawn on such creeds only if they were relevant to my overall account.

– Finally, *credal texts* are texts that are not, strictly speaking, creeds in the way defined above, but either, though taking another shape, explicitly call themselves such or integrate credal formulae into a larger theological argument. In both these instances, reference to a given creed or the quotation of credal phrases is an indication that the 'heat is being turned up'. It is often difficult to decide whether we are 'really' dealing with creeds or whether these texts should be assigned to other genres. The purpose of these texts is either apologetic or demonstrative, i.e. they serve to defend a specific doctrinal view or to set out and lend authority to a particular doctrine – purposes that are not mutually exclusive. In FaFo I included those texts from this category that the sources called creeds (i.e. which their authors/users term a *pístis/fides* or *symbolum* (*fidei*)) and/or which use the verbs *pisteúein* or *credere* to signal assent to dogmatic propositions about God and the Trinity. One particularly tricky case is the *Symbolum Quicumque*: originally it did not bear the title of creed but was only termed such at a later stage; nor does it conform to the structure of a trinitarian creed.[40] By and large, this final category plays only a minor role in the development of the genre; accordingly, in what follows most credal texts are omitted in order not to overburden my account.

---

40 Cf. below ch. 2.3.

2 A Brief History of Credal Research since Caspari

Though perhaps not usually the most riveting, overviews of previous scholarship are nonetheless indispensable. Pointing out both the achievements and the deficiencies of earlier scholarship helps both to place one's own argument in its historical context and to inform the reader as to what has stood the test of time and why certain models and theories of credal development have been discarded.

Modern research on the creed is marked by two developments resulting from the emergence of historicism, entailing as it did a strong interest both in philologically reliable editions of sources and in the application of a historical-critical method in studying these sources: first, the discovery and publication of new credal *texts* and second, building on these discoveries, the development of new *theories* regarding the historical development of the creeds once belief in the early origin of the Apostles' Creed in particular had been discredited.

By and large, modern credal research began in the second half of the nineteenth century and was mainly carried out by Anglican and Protestant scholars in Britain and Germany. This was no coincidence: at that time, discussion about the continuing validity of the theological propositions contained in the creeds had dominated the churches and academic theology in both countries, albeit for slightly different reasons. In England T, C^2 (traditionally referred to as 'Nicene'), and Ath were mentioned in the Thirty-Nine Articles of 1562. In art. VIII it is said that they 'ought throughly to be receaued & beleued. For they maye be proued by moste certayne warraunties of holy Scripture'.[1] Therefore, they formed an important part of the liturgy as prescribed in the Book of Common Prayer.[2] In Germany, the Neo-Nicene doctrine of the Trinity, as formulated at the Council of Constantinople in 381, was mentioned in the first article of the Lutheran Augsburg Confession of 1530.[3] All three creeds were later included in the collections of confessional writings of the Reformation such as the *Book of Concord* of 1580; even now pastors in the Lutheran

---

1 Articles 1563.

2 In the revised version of the Book of Common Prayer of 1662 T is said during matins and evensong (except for thirteen days of the year when it is replaced by Ath). C^2 is said or sung at the communion service.

3 Cf. Dingel 2014, pp. 92 f. (ed. Gottfried Seebaß/Volker Leppin). Strictly speaking, the *decretum Nicenae Synodi* / 'Beschluß Concilii Niceni' referred to seems to be the synodal letter of the Council of Constantinople of 382 (Council of Constantinople, *Epistula synodalis* (FaFo § 566a)).

https://doi.org/10.1515/9783110318531-002

churches, as well as in some of those Protestant churches that combine elements of Lutheranism and Calvinism, still are being ordained using this book.[4]

However, in the wake of the rise of historical-critical exegesis of the Bible the veracity of some of the tenets contained in the creeds came to be questioned, above all the virgin birth, Christ's descent to the underworld, his resurrection, and ascension. This led to wide-ranging debates among clergy, academic theologians, as well as lay people, whether or not the creeds could still be recited, had to be changed, or to be dropped altogether from daily services, baptismal and ordination rites, and from the confessional writings. The details of these debates need not concern us here.[5] What is important, however, is that in this context the historical study of the creed intensified, because liberal scholars wanted to demonstrate the historical (and hence 'relative') nature of the creeds whereas their orthodox counterparts tried to prove, with regard to T, that it went back to the times of the primitive Church and even the apostles themselves.

The anti-Modernist stance of the popes of this period largely prevented Roman Catholic scholars from undertaking such research. Doing so meant risking one's academic career, but they were also genuinely convinced such research was not needed. As the Jesuit Wilhelm M. Peitz (1876–1954) put it very succinctly in 1918:

> For catholic scholarship this question [of the origin and development of T] lacks immediate urgency. For it is less a matter of the apostolic *origin* of the *wording* than of the apostolic *content*. However, the apostolic content is warranted with certainty by the infallible magisterium.[6]

The renewed interest in the creeds and their development inspired scholars, whatever their background, to go back to the sources. New credal texts were discovered as a result of the intensified study of medieval manuscripts. Accordingly, we can observe a surge of first or improved editions of such texts between 1860 and 1930, with scholars such as Carl Paul Caspari, A.E. Burn, C.H. Turner, and Eduard Schwartz leading the field.[7] More recently, since the turn of the millennium, there has been another wave of discoveries of late antique and medieval

---

4 Cf. the critical edition of the *Book of Concord* in Dingel 2014.

5 Cf. the fundamental study of the situation in Germany by Hanna Kasparick (Kasparick 1996) and Julia Winnebeck (Winnebeck 2016). To my knowledge, no such comprehensive study exists as yet for the Church of England. Some information is found in Winnebeck 2019. For Switzerland cf. Gebhard 2003. For the wider background cf. also Staats 1999, pp. 279–93.

6 Peitz 1918, p. 555 (emphasis original).

7 On these scholars cf. below chs. 2.1 and 2.2.1.

creeds and their explanations, inspired by Susan A. Keefe of Duke University which is indeed still on-going.[8]

By and large, three major areas of research have received particular attention. Unsurprisingly, they revolve around the three major ancient creeds of Christendom: (1) the history of the Apostles' Creed which includes the Roman Creed, its ancestors, and the emergence of Christian creeds in general; (2) the history of the Nicene Creed and the Creed of Constantinople with a special emphasis on their precise origins; (3) the history of the Athanasian Creed. In what follows, I will treat each of these fields in turn, attempting to highlight some major trajectories along which scholarship has moved in the past 150 years.[9]

2.1 The Apostles' Creed and the origins of the creeds in general

2.1.1 From Caspari to Lietzmann: The age of historicism

One of the scholars who deserves pride of place in any history of the creeds is Carl Paul Caspari (1814–1892), a Norwegian Lutheran theologian of German-Jewish extraction. He was engaged in a controversy with the Danish theologian, poet, and polymath Nikolai Frederik Severin Grundtvig (1783–1872), revolving around the role and status of the creed in the interpretation of Scripture. This led him to reappraise the history of the creed, focussing largely, albeit not exclusively, on the history of T, and publishing the results in a plethora of monographs and articles from the 1860s onwards.[10] He suggested that the creeds in Marcellus' letter to Julius of Rome (FaFo § 253), in Rufinus' *Expositio symboli* (§ 254b), in the *Psalter of King Aethelstan* (§ 295), and in the codex Laudianus Gr. 35 (§ 327) represented a recension of T earlier than T itself, which he identified with the ancient creed of Rome (R).[11] Caspari assumed that local creeds had already come into existence by the second century. Because of their presumed close resemblance to each other, he believed that a basic credal pattern could be identified that went back to the apostolic age.

---

8 Cf. also below p. 30.

9 For further information cf. Vinzent 2006 who (although focussing on the research on T only) covers much of the same ground as this chapter. For individual credal texts, see the literature listed in FaFo.

10 Cf. the list in Belsheim 1897, p. 741. Details of the controversy and Caspari's response in Vinzent 2006, pp. 136–147 on which the following account is based.

11 Here he partly reproduced an argument which had already been suggested in 1647 by James Ussher, Bishop of Armagh (1581–1656); cf. Vinzent 2006, pp. 54–6.

This early creed had originated in Johannine circles in Asia Minor whence it travelled to Rome.[12] His theory proved enormously influential, although it contained a number of serious methodological flaws which were pointed out by his contemporaries.[13] Caspari never produced a full-scale history of the early creeds – but the reverberations of his ground-breaking research can still be felt in J.N.D. Kelly's account of this history.

Caspari's editions of new texts were at least as important as his studies; most of these were published in the three volumes of his *Quellen zur Geschichte des Taufsymbols und der Glaubensregel* (1866–1875) and his *Kirchenhistorische Anecdota* (1883).[14] They received wide currency because they were included in the often-quoted *Bibliothek der Symbole und Glaubensregeln der alten Kirche* in 1877, a collection of creeds whose first edition (1842) had been produced by August Hahn (1792–1863) and which was later re-issued in an extended version by his son Georg Ludwig Hahn (1823–1903), professor of New Testament and Church History at the University of Breslau (modern Wrocław).[15] Finally, a third edition with yet more texts added was published in 1897, again by Hahn jun.[16] Furthermore, Adolf (von[17]) Harnack (1851–1930) contributed an appendix entitled 'Material on the history and explication of the old Roman creed taken from the Christian literature of the two first centuries' (*Materialien zur Geschichte und Erklärung des alten römischen Symbols aus der christlichen Litteratur der zwei ersten Jahrhunderte*).[18]

However, this collection, unrivalled at the time in its comprehensive scope, did by no means meet with an entirely positive reception in the world of scholarship. One of Hahn's fiercest critics was Ferdinand Kattenbusch (1852–1935), at the time Professor of (Protestant) Systematic Theology in Gießen.[19] He considered the collection posed a 'danger to research', because its structure and chapter headings presupposed a certain view of the history of the creeds which was far from proven and in fact, in some instances, plainly false. In addition, he suggested that Hahn had not made it sufficiently clear where he had adopted the views of other scholars.[20] Nonetheless, in spite of Kattenbusch's misgivings, the Hahns' collection

---

12 Cf. Caspari 1866–1875(1964), vol. I, pp. IV–V; vol. III, p. 161; and Vinzent 2006, pp. 138–41.
13 Cf. Vinzent 2006, pp. 141–7.
14 Cf. Caspari 1866–1875(1964); Caspari 1883.
15 Cf. Hahn 1842; Hahn/Hahn 1877.
16 Cf. Hahn/Hahn 1897.
17 He was ennobled in 1914.
18 Cf. Hahn/Hahn 1897, pp. 364–90.
19 On Kattenbusch and Harnack cf. *in extenso* Vinzent 2006, pp. 152–77.
20 Cf. Kattenbusch 1894, p. 739 n. 18. Cf. also p. 957 and Kattenbusch, review of Hahn/Hahn 1897, 1897.

remained the standard reference tool for over a century in terms of the sheer number of texts it contained.

The sharpness of Kattenbusch's criticism may also have been due to a certain fear that the work of the Hahns would outstrip his own studies on the creed in scholarly importance. Kattenbusch felt great admiration for Caspari whose results he largely adopted and, like him, he had originally planned to write a history of the creeds, but – again like him – in the end failed as well. Instead, he produced an enormous study of the history of T only, comprising no less than 1471 pages in two volumes.[21] The sheer size of this work presented a serious problem of organization: Kattenbusch was simply unable to structure the mass of material available effectively. Especially in the second volume of his *opus maximum* he added a mountain of appendices and footnotes which made his work largely unreadable.

For Kattenbusch, the Roman Creed (which he abbreviated for the first time as 'R'[22]) formed the basis of all western creeds and indeed of *all* creeds. R had been drawn up as a formula in around 100, later producing a number of descendants in the western provinces that differed from each other in certain details. Furthermore, Kattenbusch claimed that the first traces of credal texts in the east were found in the third century in the area of Syria and Palestine, and that this was due to R's migration to Antioch. In subsequent centuries the standard text of T (*textus receptus*) had developed from R through the (rather haphazard) addition of further clauses.[23] Whereas Caspari had assumed this to have taken place in southern Gaul, initially, Kattenbusch believed that any such geographical attribution was impossible, though he later considered a Spanish origin.[24]

Harnack had closely collaborated with Kattenbusch during his time in Gießen. He largely agreed with his friend and colleague with regard to the existence and the great age of R, although he dated it slightly later (around 150). The Roman Creed had remained unaltered in the capital itself, but started travelling to the western provinces from the end of the second century; there it received various modifications and additions until it morphed into T (in Gaul). However, in contrast to Kattenbusch, Harnack assumed that in the east confessions had already existed prior to R, although not as yet in a fixed form, and had influenced its wording.[25] However, from the end of the third century onwards elaborate creeds were being formulated in Syria and/or Palestine, 'after the Roman Creed had be-

---

21 Cf. Kattenbusch 1894 and 1900.
22 Cf. Kattenbusch 1892, p. 7; cf. Vinzent 2006, p. 138 and n. 282.
23 Cf. Kattenbusch 1900, pp. 192–205.
24 Cf. Vinzent 2006, p. 160.
25 Cf. Harnack 1896, esp. pp. 753 f.

come known and esteemed', a process accelerated by the Arian controversy which led to 'the formation of fixed creeds' in the east.[26]

One of the fiercest critics of previous research was Johannes Kunze (1865–1927), Professor of (Protestant) Systematic Theology at Vienna and later at Greifswald. A brilliant essay written for a wider audience, published in the *Internationale Monatsschrift für Wissenschaft, Kunst und Technik* in 1914, synthesized his views, which he had detailed in a series of monographs and articles.[27] Kunze considered any attempt to reconstruct an early confessional formula a methodological error. To him the *Apostolicum* was indeed a formula, but it was one that was not yet fixed because it had not been permitted to write it down. 'Genuine records of the baptismal creed', he wrote, 'are not found until the middle of the fourth century.'[28] However, this was not to say that it did not exist. On the contrary, it even helped inform early Christian doctrine before the fourth century. At the same time, the Apostles' Creed was not in itself dogmatic. Rather, it was 'a trinitarian confessional formula from the Early Church that was brief and variable in many ways, but on the whole uniform, reproducing in terms of content and form the kerygma of the New Testament, which is in some way traced back to the apostles wherever it occurs.'[29] As such it differed from the dogmatic creeds such as C^2 and Ath. Kunze remained sceptical that the evidence permitted the reconstruction of a history of the creed prior to the fourth century and claimed that earlier credal formulae probably never existed as invariable texts. R (or T) was nothing but a variant of this orally transmitted *Apostolicum* which predated all existing credal formulae, both western and eastern, precisely because of its undogmatic character, and ultimately derived from the primitive Church.

Kunze's shrewd observations made no great impact on subsequent research. In some way, this is surprising as the conservative Lutheran had laid bare the liberal school of Church historians' methodological weaknesses: their argument rested on the overall assumption that (a) faith had been expressed in fixed formulae already at a very early stage in the development of Christianity and (b) that such formulae had a tendency to 'grow' (indeed, botanical metaphors occur quite frequently in studies of this period).[30] Therefore, it was thought that one could rediscover the oldest version of the creed by, as it were, cutting away later 'accretions', words or phrases that disturbed the 'natural flow', the 'original beauty', or

---

26 Harnack 1896, p. 749.
27 Cf. Kunze 1914. Cf. the summary of Kunze's research in Vinzent 2006, pp. 194–203.
28 Kunze 1914, col. 1315.
29 Kunze 1914, col. 1316.
30 Badcock even entitled one of his chapters 'How Creeds Grow', as if there were some kind of natural law; cf. Badcock 1938, p. 117.

the 'theological logic' of a creed. We will see later that both assumptions are ultimately untenable because they do not allow for the orality and thus fluidity of early Christian confessions and because additions to creeds (as formulae) were often made deliberately as a result of given theological challenges.

This type of research, which mirrored the rise of form criticism in biblical exegesis, reached its peak when three German scholars published a series of articles in the same volume of the *Proceedings of the Prussian Academy of Sciences* in 1919 which built on each other, suggesting that the christological section in R was a later addition to a much more primitive formula.[31] The three were Harnack, whom we have already encountered, and two younger German church historians, Karl Holl (1866–1926), also active in Berlin, and Hans Lietzmann (1875–1942), who at that time taught at Jena and later succeeded Harnack. In Lietzmann's view this original short formula was preserved with minor modifications in a papyrus originating from Dêr Balyzeh in Upper Egypt which had been edited for the first time in 1909 (FaFo § 146).[32] On the basis of this formula Lietzmann reconstructed the following primitive version of R (which was considered to have been composed in Greek, the principal language of the Roman Christians),[33] slightly modifying an earlier attempt by Harnack:[34]

Πιστεύω εἰς	(1) θεὸν	(2) πατέρα	(3) παντοκράτορα
καὶ εἰς	(4) Χριστὸν Ἰησοῦν	(5) τὸν υἱὸν αὐτοῦ τὸν μονογενῆ	(6) τὸν κύριον ἡμῶν
καὶ εἰς	(7) πνεῦμα ἅγιον	(8) ἁγίαν ἐκκλησίαν	(9) σαρκὸς ἀνάστασιν

I believe in	(1) God	(2) the Father	(3) Almighty
and in	(4) Christ Jesus	(5) his only-begotten Son	(6) our Lord
and in	(7) the Holy Spirit	(8) the holy Church	(9) the resurrection of the flesh.

The parallel pattern of three members per section was considered an expression of the skill of the (unknown) authors of this creed. Its *Sitz im Leben* was baptism or, rather, pre-baptismal catechesis. It allegedly served as the basic pattern for all credal production in east and west.

---

31 Cf. Holl 1919(1928); Harnack 1919; Lietzmann 1919(1962).
32 Cf. Vinzent 2006, pp. 190–3.
33 Cf. Lietzmann 1919(1962), p. 184.
34 Cf. Harnack 1919, p. 112.

In addition, Holl argued that the Roman version of the christological section was an interpretation of the designations 'his only-begotten Son' and 'our Lord' in the above-quoted primitive version of R, as becomes clear from the following table:

καὶ εἰς Χριστὸν Ἰησοῦν,

τὸν υἱὸν αὐτοῦ τὸν μονογενῆ,	τὸν κύριον ἡμῶν,
τὸν γεννηθέντα ἐκ πνεύματος	τὸν ἐπὶ Ποντίου Πιλάτου σταυρωθέντα
ἁγίου καὶ Μαρίας τῆς παρθένου,	καὶ ταφέντα, τῇ τρίτῃ ἡμέρᾳ ἀναστάντα
	ἐκ νεκρῶν, ἀναβάντα εἰς τοὺς οὐρανούς,
	καθήμενον ἐν δεξιᾷ τοῦ πατρός, ὅθεν
	ἔρχεται κρῖναι ζῶντας καὶ νεκρούς

'and in Christ Jesus

his only-begotten Son,	our Lord,
who was born from the Holy	who was crucified under Pontius Pilate
Spirit and the virgin Mary,	and buried; on the third day rose
	again from the dead; ascended into
	the heavens; is sitting at the right hand
	of the Father, whence he is coming
	to judge the living and the dead'

Holl described this dual construction as a product of rhetorical artistry intending to instil 'clarity' and 'confidence' in Roman Christians.[35]

Lietzmann, in turn, suggested in a later paper that the christological section of all eastern creeds likewise derived from a single basic confession which he termed O:[36]

Πιστεύω εἰς ἕνα θεόν, πατέρα	'I believe in one God, the Father
παντοκράτορα, πάντων ὁρατῶν	Almighty, Maker of all things
τε καὶ ἀοράτων ποιητήν.	both visible and invisible.
Καὶ εἰς ἕνα κύριον Ἰησοῦν Χριστόν,	And in one Lord Jesus Christ, the
τὸν υἱὸν τοῦ θεοῦ τὸν μονογενῆ.	only-begotten Son of God.
Τὸν ἐκ τοῦ πατρὸς γεννηθέντα πρὸ	Who was begotten from the Father
πάντων τῶν αἰώνων, δι' οὗ	before all ages, through whom
τὰ πάντα ἐγένετο.	all things came into being.
Τὸν [διὰ τὴν ἡμετέραν σωτηρίαν]	Who [because of our salvation]
ἐνανθρωπήσαντα, παθόντα,	became human, suffered,

---

35 Cf. Holl 1919(1928); the quotation on p. 119.
36 Cf. Lietzmann 1922–1927(1962), pp. 211 f.

καὶ ἀναστάντα τῇ τρίτῃ ἡμέρᾳ	and rose again on the third day
καὶ ἀνελθόντα εἰς τοὺς οὐρανοὺς	and ascended into the heavens;
καὶ [πάλιν] ἐρχόμενον κρῖναι	and will come [again] to judge the liv-
ζῶντας καὶ νεκρούς.	ing and the dead.
Καὶ εἰς τὸ ἅγιον πνεῦμα.	And in the Holy Spirit.'

The question as to whether all creeds were ultimately based on a Roman model (which, perhaps, derived from some ancestor from the Apostolic Age or even the apostles themselves) was, of course, a highly sensitive issue. Roman catholic scholars, for obvious reasons, tended to be sympathetic to such an idea, but Anglo-Catholic patrologists likewise were fascinated by the possible Roman origin of R. Ironically, however, as we have seen, it was liberal Protestants like Holl, Harnack, and Lietzmann who did most to develop and establish this theory. Theirs was an ingenuous idea, but there is no evidence at all that such a basic creed ever existed.[37] As we will see, the similarities between the eastern creeds can also be explained in another manner which does better justice to the evidence.[38] All in all, later generations were much more sceptical and considered the theory by Holl, Harnack, and Lietzmann as a whole too artifical to be historically accurate.[39]

By contrast, the idea that we have to distinguish between a trinitarian formula and a christological section in the early history of the creeds (the latter of which was later added to the trinitarian formula, but may previously have had a history of its own) was further developed by Johannes Haußleiter (1851–1928),[40] professor of New Testament studies in Greifswald, and the aforementioned Wilhelm Peitz.[41] Haußleiter very succinctly summarized his hypothesis as follows:

> We have to distinguish two types [of creeds]: the older type, which was initially also the dominant one in Rome, was marked by the separate position of a very brief trinitarian confession which had developed from the Great Commission [i.e. Mt 28:19] and of a more extensive confessional formula which derived from the Christ-kerygma and which formed the basis for the second article of the Apostles' Creed. The younger type emerged from the older type in that the extensive confession of Christ was inserted into the trinitarian scheme. This is the origin of the Old Roman Creed and its descendants, furthermore of the Nicene-

---

37 This might be the place to mention the study by Reinhold Seeberg, Harnack's conservative counterpart in Berlin, who thought that the first triadic creed which included a christological summary originated in Jerusalem in *c.* 140, whereas R developed in Rome in *c.* 210; cf. Seeberg 1922. On p. 26 he offers a reconstruction of this creed. Cf. also Vinzent 2006, pp. 201 f.
38 Cf. below ch. 6.
39 Cf. esp. Kelly's criticism in Kelly 1972, pp. 123–6, 197–204.
40 Cf. Haußleiter 1920.
41 Cf. above p. 14 and Peitz 1918.

Constantinopolitan Creed, of the *textus receptus* of the Apostles' Creed, etc. But the older type did not cease to re-surface in ever new adaptations. It influenced the structure of the Athanasian Creed and a great number of oriental baptismal and private creeds.[42]

Today, it is widely accepted that the extended christological section is a later insertion into an older trinitarian formula.[43]

The fame of the German patrologists could be said to have overshadowed the important contributions simultaneously made by some of their Anglo-Saxon colleagues. C.A. Swainson (1820–1887), Norrisian Professor of Divinity at Cambridge, wrote an in many ways highly innovative history of the creeds, not only describing their origins, but also the ways and contexts in which they were transmitted within the Church down to his own time. Thus he studied, for example, the role of creeds in conciliar legislation, in collections of sermons, books of devotion, and psalters, as much as their translations into other languages, not forgetting the reception of, and controversy about, the creeds in the Church of England of his day.[44] J. Rawson Lumby (1831–1895), who succeeded him from 1879, also produced a book on the creeds which had little impact on credal research, although it went through two editions.[45] Similarly, A.E. Burn (1864–1927), a distinguished English clergyman, produced monographs on T and N respectively that failed to influence the course of credal studies in any noticeable measure. By contrast, his numerous editions of credal texts are still being used today.[46]

These scholars all took notice of each other's work and were often influenced by it. However, mention must also be made of an outsider whose legacy, as regards the creeds, remained restricted to the United States: Philip Schaff (1819–1893), a native of Switzerland who, after he had trained as a theologian in Germany, emigrated in 1843 to the States where he taught Church History, first at the German Reformed Theological Seminary at Mercersburg, Pennsylvania, and (from 1870) at the Union Theological Seminary in New York. Schaff is, above all, remembered in patristic studies for his edition of the series *A Select Library of Nicene and Post-Nicene Fathers of the Christian Church* (42 vols., New York 1886–1900). However, he also developed a great interest in the normative texts of the churches, thus publishing a history of Christian creeds in three volumes in 1877 which subsequently went

---

42 Haußleiter 1920, pp. 5 f. (emphasis original).
43 Cf. Kinzig/Vinzent 1999, p. 537 and n. 12 with a list of the relevant literature. Cf. also below ch. 4.3.3.
44 Cf. Swainson 1875.
45 Cf. Lumby 1873(1880).
46 Cf. Burn 1899; Burn 1906; Burn, *Facsimiles*, 1909; Burn, *Nicene Creed*, 1909. Cf. Vinzent 2006, pp. 131–4.

through various editions and reprints.[47] Schaff's first volume gave a synthesis of the history of the creeds, aimed at a wider audience, and his second volume collected the most important texts of the Greek and Latin churches in their original language with English translations. Since Schaff had little interest in the finer details of the history of the creed such as the *Sitz im Leben* of the individual texts and the problem of their origins and transmission, his collection was mainly consulted by pastors, theologians, and historians of dogma rather than by specialists in that history.

Incidentally, Schaff was very much aware of the controversies around the Apostles' Creed in the Church of England and the Protestant churches of Germany and Switzerland. Both his wide awareness of contemporaneous developments in Europe and his ultimately pre-modern view of Church History become apparent from a telling footnote:

> It is characteristic that, while the Church of England is agitated by the question of discontinuing simply the obligatory use of the Athanasian Creed, the Protestant Churches on the Continent are disturbed by the more radical question of setting aside the Apostles' Creed for teaching what is said to be contrary to the spirit of the age. [. . .] In the Canton Zürich it is left optional with the ministers to use the Creed in the baptismal and confirmation services, or not. It is a singular fact that in the non-Episcopal Churches of Great Britain and the United States the Apostles' Creed is practically far less used, but much more generally believed than in some State Churches, where it is part of the regular worship, like the Lord's Prayer. The Anglo-American race has retained the doctrinal substance of old Catholic and evangelical Christianity, while the Churches of the Continent have been shaken to the very base by Rationalism.[48]

2.1.2 From Haußleiter to Kelly: The role of baptismal questions in the emergence of the creeds

While the lack of sufficient evidence meant the hypothesis by Holl-Harnack-Lietzmann was losing traction, another series of scholars developed a new theory about the early history of the creeds. They included Cuthbert Hamilton Turner (1860–1930), who – late in life – was appointed Dean Ireland's Professor of the Exegesis of Holy Scripture at Oxford, Johannes Brinktrine (1889–1965), Professor of (catholic) Fundamental Theology in Paderborn,[49] F.J. Badcock (1869–1944), Fellow of St Augustine's College, Canterbury,[50] and J.N.D. Kelly (1909–1997), long-time

---

47 Cf. Schaff 1877. On the history of this work cf. FaFo, vol. I, p. 26 n. 122.
48 Schaff 1877, vol. I, p. 20 n. 2. The footnote was omitted in later editions.
49 Cf. Brinktrine 1921 and Vinzent 2006, pp. 244 f.
50 Cf. Badcock 1938, pp. 17–20, 122–35.

Principal of St Edmund Hall and, in 1966, even briefly Vice-Chancellor of the University of Oxford.[51]

Turner was primarily interested in the development of ecclesiastical law. His *opus magnum, Ecclesiae Occidentalis Monumenta Iuris Antiquissima* (often abbrev. EOMIA, 1899–1939),[52] which contained editions of the canons of the early Church councils, also included important witnesses to the history of N and C^2. He had no specific interest in the history of the creeds as such, but he did publish a lecture on the *History and Use of Creeds and Anathemas in the Early Centuries of the Church* in which he drew attention to liturgical texts such as the *Old Gelasian Sacramentary* and the *Sacramentary of Gellone* as sources for credal history.[53] In the study of this and other evidence 'two fundamental facts' had to be borne in mind:

> the one, that the Creed was closely related from the first to the process of admission to membership in the Christian Society; the other, that, close as is this relation of the Creed to Baptism, there are forms that stand in a yet closer relation to the baptismal rite and appear to be at once simpler and older than the Creed – I mean the baptismal Interrogations and Responses.[54]

Based on the baptismal formula (Mt 28:19), these interrogations were trinitarian in form, but were expanded in different areas. The declaratory creed developed from these interrogations. Its *Sitz im Leben* was not the baptismal rite, but catechesis.[55] Versions of the creed spread from Rome to the eastern part of the empire. By the end of the fourth century, 'the Creed was in universal use, because it corresponded to a universal need'.[56]

Similarly, Brinktrine, who, in many ways, was sceptical regarding the historicist approach as practised by his Protestant colleagues, distinguished between the *symbolum* (which he identified with the trinitarian baptismal formula of Mt 28:19) and the credal questions which the catechumens were asked when they approached baptism. The questions derived from the baptismal formula and were, therefore, also called *symbolum*. While they initially referred only to the persons of the Trinity, their christological and pneumatological sections were later extended. Finally, the credal questions were then transformed into declaratory

---

51 Cf. Kelly 1972, pp. 30–52. On Kelly cf. Cowdrey 1999, p. 423.
52 Cf. Turner 1899–1939. A good survey of the contents of this unwieldy work is found in URL <http://www.fourthcentury.com/index.php/eomia-contents> (02/11/2023).
53 Cf. Turner, *History and Use*, 1910 (first published in 1906).
54 Turner, *History and Use*, 1910, pp. 11 f.
55 Cf. Turner, *History and Use*, 1910, pp. 17 f.
56 Turner, *History and Use*, 1910, p. 20.

creeds. In Brinktrine's view R was a perfect piece of art, whereas all other creeds that were not descendants of R were the 'attempts of beginners'.[57]

Similarly, Badcock assumed that at first candidates for baptism were required to profess faith solely in Jesus Christ, in the Lord Jesus, or in Jesus, the Son of God. The triple formula, deriving from the baptismal formula, only came into use from the middle of the second century. He traced the development of this triple formula to the east, beginning with the *Epistula Apostolorum* (which contained 'the earliest Creed known word for word').[58] The creeds then travelled from the east to Africa. In Rome candidates for baptism were originally simply asked to believe in God, Jesus Christ, and the Holy Spirit. In order to combat gnosticism these questions were gradually expanded so that by the middle of the third century a sevenfold formula had emerged. By the fourth century, an interrogatory and a declaratory form had been established. Badcock rejected the often-used evidence of the letter of Marcellus of Ancyra regarding R, since it – in his view – reflected the practice of Marcellus' own diocese, a theory which earned Badcock sharp criticism by Lietzmann.[59] Badcock considered the fully-fledged Roman Creed to have developed not before 371, when Damasus held a council in Rome to combat Homoianism.[60] He explained the resemblance between the creed of Marcellus and that of Rufinus 'by the enlargement of the Roman creed through the indirect influence of Marcellus'.[61]

This theory of the development of the earliest creeds was given its final shape in a book by J.N.D. Kelly. Kelly's monograph on *Early Christian Creeds* has dominated the field since it was first published in 1950 and, even more so, since the publication of its third edition in 1972. It has been translated into Italian, Spanish, Japanese, and German, and it has taught generations of students of theology to this day (including the present author) the essentials concerning the history of these fundamental texts of the Christian Church.

Kelly very lucidly described the creed's origin as a genre and its composition and use at synods and in worship until the early middle ages. Given the complexities of doctrinal developments in that period, this is a great achievement and the result of his endeavours a most elegant book. But Kelly's view of the history of the creeds was also far too traditionalist and monolithic. In a way, he conceptualized this history from its end, like most of his predecessors in the subject. He was

---

57 Brinktrine 1921, p. 184.
58 Cf. Badcock 1938, p. 25. I refer only to the second edition in what follows. Concerning Badcock cf. also Vinzent 2006, pp. 245–51.
59 Cf. Badcock 1938, p. 63; Lietzmann 1922–1927(1962), pp. 224 f. In addition, cf. Vinzent 2006, p. 247 n. 183.
60 Cf. Badcock 1938, pp. 142 f.
61 Badcock 1922, p. 389.

primarily interested in those creeds which, as it were, carried the day: the Creed of Constantinople and the Apostles' Creed with their precursors. This is in itself, of course, unproblematic; indeed, I largely follow the same path in this book. However, Kelly described credal history in such a way that it led *by necessity* to the formation of these specific formulae, making it clearly teleological.

Kelly agreed with Turner and Brinktrine that one had to distinguish the earlier interrogatory creeds (baptismal questions) from the (later) declaratory confessions and that the baptismal questions in turn derived from the Great Commission (Mt 28:19). Crown witnesses, so to speak, for this hypothesis were the correspondence of Cyprian, the *Old Gelasian Sacramentary*, and a reconstruction of the so-called *Apostolic Tradition*, a Church order that was attributed to Hippolytus of Rome (d. 235). It was thought to date from the early third century and contained a series of questions which were put to converts at baptism.[62] Kelly summarized his 'study of the use of creeds in connection with baptism in the first three centuries' as follows:

> Declaratory creeds of the ordinary type had no place in the baptismal ritual of the period. If in the fourth century and thereafter their role was [. . .] secondary, prior to the fourth century they had no role at all. An affirmation of faith was, of course, indispensable, but it took the form of the candidate's response to the officiant's interrogations.[63]

Kelly saw the interrogatory creed bound up with the act of baptism, whereas the longer declaratory creeds were 'a by-product of the Church's fully developed catechetical system' and closely connected with the development of the *Traditio* and *Redditio* of the creed which belonged 'to the heyday of the fully mature catechumenate, that is, to the second generation of the third century at the earliest'.[64] We will take a closer look at the details of his account of later credal development at a later point.[65]

2.1.3 Beyond Kelly: Widening the scope

Since Kelly's work, subsequent scholarship has continued to this day to develop in constant engagement with it.[66] His views on the emergence of creeds were criticized by Hans von Campenhausen (1903–1989), (Protestant) Church historian at Heidelberg University, and his pupil Adolf Martin Ritter (b. 1933), who succeeded

---

62 Cf. FaFo § 89.
63 Kelly 1972, p. 48.
64 Kelly 1972, pp. 51, 49.
65 Cf. below pp. 200 f.
66 The surveys by Pelikan 2003 and Fairbairn/Reeves 2019, written for a wider readership, do not contain any new insights regarding the period we are interested in.

his teacher in 1981. Von Campenhausen had intended to write a new history of the creeds but his deteriorating eyesight prevented him from doing so. He did, however, produce a series of preliminary studies which strongly influenced the further course of research.[67] In his extensive article on the creeds in the *Theologische Realenzyklopädie* Ritter summarized and substantiated von Campenhausen's findings, supplementing them with the results of his own research, especially on the history of C[2] (to which I will return below in chapter 2.2.2).[68]

These findings (which were widely accepted) may be summarized by four major points:[69]

(1) Initially, Christian confession is a public *act* of recognition, of trust, and of obedience, especially in situations of oppression and threat and does not consist in reciting a *formula*. Confession is what makes a person a Christian and distinguishes them from a non-Christian.[70]

(2) A distinction must be made between the rule of faith (*regula fidei*), as it occurs in Irenaeus and Tertullian, and the creed. Whereas the creed is (more or less) fixed, the rule of faith is a loose and flexible summary of the kerygma of Christ used as doctrinal norm against dissident groups (such as gnosticism).[71]

(3) Interrogatory creeds were probably not used at baptism before the third century.[72]

(4) Declaratory creeds were probably not used at baptism or during the catechumenate before the fourth century (earliest witness: Cyril of Jerusalem). Even R as attested by Marcellus of Ancyra was not yet used in a baptismal context. The emergence of a more elaborate liturgy and the mass conversions of the Church in the fourth century as a result of the toleration and gradual promotion of Christianity since Constantine are the reasons for this change at that time.[73]

(5) The declaratory creeds as a 'test for orthodoxy' have their primary *Sitz im Leben* in the (unsuccessful) attempt at settling doctrinal dissent at synods, beginning with Nicaea in 325.[74]

Reinhart Staats (b. 1937) proceeded along similar lines in his book on C[2]. He saw five *Sitze im Leben* of the earliest Christian confession: martyrdom, apologetics,

---

67 Cf. Campenhausen 1971(1979); Campenhausen 1972(1979); Campenhausen 1975(1979); Campenhausen 1976(1979).

68 Cf. Ritter 1984. A shorter English version is found in Ritter 1991.

69 For what follows cf. esp. Kinzig/Vinzent 1999, p. 539.

70 Cf. Ritter 1984, p. 400 (drawing on an earlier definition by Ferdinand Hahn).

71 Cf. Ritter 1984, pp. 402–5. On the creed as a summary of the biblical message cf. also Toom 2022.

72 Cf. Ritter 1984, p. 406.

73 Cf. Ritter 1984, pp. 407 f.

74 Cf. Ritter 1984, pp. 411 f.

worship, baptism, and the struggle against heresy. The pre-Constantinian church produced both brief homologies, which were often binitarian, and the rule of faith, but no full-fledged, fixed creeds, because 'the history of the creed as a codified and in its wording firmly fixed text' began not until the time of Constantine.[75]

Pieter Smulders SJ (1911–2000) who taught dogmatic theology in Maastricht and Amsterdam defended exactly the opposite position to von Campenhausen. Smulders not only insisted on R's venerable age, but also believed that it was even possible to reconstruct a 'pre-R Creed' with the help of the *Traditio Apostolica*.[76] Smulders summarized the results of his research as follows:

> When the Church of Rome, towards the end of the second century began to use a Creed composed of a slightly elaborated triadic pattern in combination with a Gospel summary, it borrowed the latter from an homologia of Christ's lordship in act, which was already circulating in Asia. The Creed then is not primarily intended as a summary of teaching, and much less as a polemical text or a touchstone of orthodoxy. It might be put to such uses. But its original setting was the homologia of God Father Allsovereign, of Jesus Christ his Son whom he invested with the eschatological saving lordship, and of their divine Gift, the Holy Spirit.[77]

Further research on the creeds oscillated between these two poles. Continuing on the path which had been charted by von Campenhausen and Ritter, albeit slightly changing direction, Christoph Markschies (b. 1962), Markus Vinzent (b. 1959), and I tried to show that the prehistory of the creeds needs to be largely rewritten. In fact, this school of thought has been arguing that only now it makes sense to speak of a *pre*history in a proper sense, as no declaratory creeds may have existed before the fourth century.[78] Markschies showed that the reconstructions of the *Traditio Apostolica* produced by Gregory Dix (1901–1952) and Bernard Botte (1893–1980) were based on unsound methodological assumptions and could, therefore, no longer be used for credal research, as Kelly and others had assumed. I myself have suggested that it is possible at least partly to reconstruct the interrogatory creeds of the late second and early third centuries both for northern Africa and for Rome, without falling back on the problematic *Traditio*. Finally, Markus Vinzent has explained how specific doctrinal developments at the beginning of the fourth century led, fairly abruptly, to the formulation and evolution of synodal creeds. Vinzent also claimed that R, the ancestor of T, did not predate the fourth century, but probably originated in the letter which Marcellus of Ancyra sent to Julius of Rome in 340 or

---

75 Staats 1999, p. 157.
76 Cf. Smulders 1970/1971/1980; Smulders 1975. Furthermore, cf. Vinzent 2006, pp. 280–4, 287–8.
77 Smulders 1975, pp. 420 f.
78 Cf. Kinzig/Markschies/Vinzent 1999; cf. also below p. 154.

341 (FaFo § 253), thus presenting a modified version of Badcock's theory. According to Vinzent, the creed which Marcellus had formulated in this letter (possibly using earlier baptismal questions) was partly adopted by a synod in Rome and quickly spread from there to other parts of the Latin Roman empire. At the invitation of Maurice F. Wiles (1923–2005), Vinzent and I synthesized our findings in a brief article for the centenary edition of the *Journal of Theological Studies* in 1999.[79] These theses by Markschies, Vinzent, and myself triggered an extensive scholarly discussion.[80] Some years later, Vinzent reviewed the history of research with regard to the Apostles' Creed in an extensive monograph.[81] We will have to examine his theories carefully later, because new evidence has come to light which suggests that the pre-history of R was more complicated than Vinzent (and I) assumed at that time.[82]

Among those who disagreed were Martien Parmentier (1947–2021), Gerard Rouwhorst (b. 1951), Reinhart Staats, Uta Heil (b. 1966), and Liuwe H. Westra (b. 1966). Parmentier and Rouwhorst questioned Vinzent's view that R was, in reality, a product of Marcellus of Ancyra, partly because of the wide distribution of variants of R throughout the west.[83] Staats called the idea that a private creed would have been used by the Church 'anachronistic' and the late date of R 'absurd' (without, however, substantiating reasons for his criticism).[84] More recently, Uta Heil suggested that Marcellus quoted a creed composed by the Roman synod and not vice versa.[85]

Following in the footsteps of his teachers Parmentier and Rouwhorst, Liuwe H. Westra has also remained an advocate of the traditional view regarding an early date of R and its subsequent development. His 2002 doctoral dissertation presented a large-scale reconstruction of this text's origin.[86] He defended Kelly's explanation that the Roman Creed had, by and large, come into existence in the early third century.[87] At the same time, Westra suggested a new line of research by exploring the question as to the manner in which the descendants of R from the fourth century onwards may be explained as regional variants. In addition,

---

79 Cf. Kinzig/Vinzent 1999.

80 Cf. the list of reviews in Kinzig 2021(2022), p. 130 n. 59. In addition, Peter L. Schmidt and Michaela Zelzer in Berger/Fontaine/Schmidt 2020, pp. 19 f. who agree with Vinzent.

81 Cf. Vinzent 2006.

82 Cf. Kinzig, 'Ursprung', 2022 and below ch. 5.1.

83 Cf. Parmentier/Rouwhorst 2001.

84 Staats 2011, p. 1562 and n. 27.

85 Cf. Heil 2010; cf. already Brennecke et al. 2007, p. 155 n. i.

86 Cf. Westra 2002.

87 Cf. my short review in Kinzig 2005 and Vinzent's extensive discussion in Vinzent 2006, pp. 360–94.

he edited a number of important explanations of the creed, either for the first time or in improved versions.

Thus, what came into focus were the later history of the Roman Creed and its variants throughout the Latin west and the way in which they were expounded and used. The work of Susan Keefe (1954–2012) of Duke Divinity School gave an added, important stimulus to their study. Her seminal monograph *Water and the Word* provided a new basis for research into the baptismal liturgy of the Carolingian age, both editing a large number of relevant sources and synthesizing the data gleaned from these new texts.[88] In addition, she completed two fundamental works dealing with the history of the Apostles' Creed in the early middle ages shortly before her premature death: a catalogue of Carolingian manuscripts containing creeds and credal explanations[89] and an edition of explanations of the creed culled from these manuscripts which previous scholars had partly or totally neglected.[90]

Furthermore, two books which placed a particular emphasis on theological questions relating to the confessions of faith ought to be mentioned. Frances Young's (b. 1939) *The Making of the Creeds*, first published in 1991, has become a classic in its own right. Young's interest was in the theological motives that led to the formulation of the individual clauses of the creed rather than in the overall texts as a literary genre.[91] Gerda Riedl (b. 1961) suggested a new methodological approach in her 2004 doctoral dissertation that she called 'systematic-generative', as opposed to 'historical-genetic'. In its scholarly thrust, her work was, ultimately, not very different from Young's monograph, while opening up further perspectives on the theological principles driving, and motives behind, the composition of creeds.[92]

Most recently, Peter Gemeinhardt (b. 1970) has produced two substantial articles on T and its theology. In the first he concentrates on two major clauses of the creed, i.e. Christ's descent to hell and his ascension.[93] In the second he shows that the history of the Apostles' Creed is neither unilinear nor characterized by a steady decline, as earlier scholars suggested, but by significant transformations, a confusing plurality of texts, and also sheer happenstance.[94]

My own research in recent years has likewise concentrated on the history of the creed in the west, in particular with regard to religious instruction and

---

88 Cf. Keefe 2002.
89 Cf. Keefe, *Catalogue*, 2012.
90 Cf. Keefe, *Explanationes*, 2012.
91 Cf. Young 1991. A similar approach was taken more recently in Ashwin-Siejkowski 2009.
92 Cf. Riedl 2004.
93 Cf. Gemeinhardt, 'Sphärenwechsel', 2020.
94 Cf. Gemeinhardt, 'Vom Werden', 2020.

preaching, as well as on legal and liturgical aspects. In addition, I have also published a series of new relevant source texts.[95] My 2017 collection *Faith in Formulae* which was compiled with the assistance of Christopher M. Hays makes available a great number of the sources in both their original languages and in English.[96] My most recent studies are on terminology,[97] on the pre-history of R,[98] and on the Creed of Jerusalem (J);[99] their conclusions will be summarized below.

2.2 The Creeds of Nicaea and Constantinople

2.2.1 From Hort to Schwartz

Discussion concerning the Creeds of Nicaea (N) and Constantinople (C^2; in earlier research usually abbreviated NC or C) has in recent years revolved around two major questions: (1) the origin of N and (2) the question of whether C^2 represents a revision of N or an independent creed, and if the latter, whether other *Vorlagen* may be identified.[100] F.J.A. Hort (1827–1892) published a monograph with the unassuming title *Two Dissertations* (1876), so two years before he was appointed Hulsean Professor of Divinity at Cambridge.[101] In it, he advanced the hypotheses (1) that N was an extended version of the (presumed) creed of Caesarea which Eusebius seemingly cites in the letter to his congregation after that council (FaFo § 134a) and (2) that C^2 was not a revised form of N, as had hitherto often been assumed, but a revision of the Creed of Jerusalem (J; FaFo § 147), possibly produced by Bishop Cyril in the years 362–364 for apologetic purposes, but in any case not the result of deliberations at the Council of Constantinople. One of the main pillars of (2) was the observation that Epiphanius of Salamis appeared to have quoted C^2 already in his *Ancoratus* (written in 374, hence some time *before* the Council of Constantinople).[102] Both hypotheses were accepted by Burn[103] and Harnack.[104] Harnack saw in C^2 not a revision of N, but an earlier provincial creed

---

95 Cf. esp. Kinzig, *Neue Texte I*, 2017; Kinzig, *Glaubensbekenntnis*, 2021; Kinzig, *Neue Texte III*, 2022.

96 Cf. Kinzig, *Faith in Formulae*, 2017.

97 Cf. Kinzig, 'Symbolum', *AugL*, 2021; Kinzig, 'Symbolum', *RAC*, 2021.

98 Cf. Kinzig, 'Ursprung', 2022.

99 Cf. Kinzig, 'Origin', 2022.

100 For further details cf. Kinzig, *Glaubensbekenntnis*, 2021, pp. 4–11.

101 Cf. Hort 1876.

102 Cf. Epiphanius, *Ancoratus* 118,9–12.

103 Cf. Burn 1899, pp. 76–80, 101–10; Burn 1925, pp. 29–39, 83–93.

104 Cf. Harnack 1902, pp. 14–24.

whose Nicene 'sound' had been achieved by the addition of phrases taken from N.[105] Explanation (2) also seemed to solve the conundrum as to why C^2 was never mentioned as the official creed of the council in the decades after Constantinople. Johannes Kunze elaborated this point by arguing that C^2 might in fact have been the confession used at the rushed baptism of the future patriarch Nectarius in Constantinople in the course of the council of 381, who at the time of his election to the see had been no more than a catechumen.[106]

In spite of the detailed refutation by Hans Lietzmann and J.N.D. Kelly which need not be repeated here,[107] hypothesis (1) is still being defended by some scholars today,[108] whereas hypothesis (2) – at least as far as it rested on the testimony of Epiphanius – must be considered refuted once and for all through the appearance of new textual evidence: the Church historian and orientalist Bernd M. Weischer (b. 1937) discovered that the Ethiopic translation of the *Ancoratus* does not offer C^2 but the original N, and concluded that C^2 in the Greek text must be a later interpolation.[109] (However, this by itself did not yet prove that C^2 was indeed drawn up by the council.) Even before these fairly recent developments some scholars had been sceptical of Epiphanius' testimony as proof for an early date of C^2. Among these were Badcock[110] and, most importantly, the famous editor of the *Acta Conciliorum Oecumenicorum*, Eduard Schwartz (1858–1940), Professor of Classical Philology at Munich. In Badcock's view the available evidence left no doubt 'that the Council of 381 added certain phrases to the creed of the 318 [i.e. N] against heresies which had not arisen when this was composed'.[111] Schwartz also questioned the supposed testimony by Epiphanius, while being more cautious with regard to the origin of C^2.[112] However, both scholars agreed that C^2 was the creed officially adopted at Constantinople.

---

105 Cf. Harnack 1902, p. 20.

106 Cf. Kunze 1898, pp. 32–7 and Kelly 1972, p. 312.

107 Cf. Lietzmann 1922–1927(1962), pp. 250–3; Kelly 1972, pp. 217–20.

108 Cf. Holland 1970, pp. 177–180; Simonetti 1975, pp. 83–4; Staats 1999, p. 160; Strutwolf 1999, pp. 52–3; Roldanus 2006, pp. 80 f. Pietras 2016, pp. 182 f., also seems to suggest that Eus was the basis of N (cf., however, p. 185 where he states that 'it may as well be assumed that [at Nicaea] Eusebius' formula was replaced by another [. . .] document').

109 Cf. below p. 446 n. 202.

110 Cf. Badcock 1915; Badcock 1938, pp. 186–208.

111 Badcock 1915, p. 218. Furthermore Kelly 1972, p. 313.

112 Cf. esp. Schwartz 1926, pp. 85–8.

2.2.2 Lietzmann – Kelly – Ritter

With regard to the origin of N, Kelly accepted a suggestion made by Lietzmann according to which N was based on a model originating from Syria and Palestine which was similar to, though not identical with, the Creed of Caesarea as attested by Eusebius in the famous, now lost, letter to his congregation (Eus; FaFo § 134a). This, they argued, better explained both the differences between both texts (which excluded the possibility that N had developed from Eus), but also their substantial similarities. Another representative of this Syro-Palestinian family was preserved in the Creed of Jerusalem as attested by Cyril.[113] By contrast, Harnack, having been asked to give an opinion on Lietzmann's suggestion, acknowledged that N was not based on Eus, but did not accept the Syro-Palestine theory either, because it explained neither Eusebius' testimony, according to which Eus was the basis of N, nor N's uneven structure. Instead, he suggested that N was a composite produced by a committee, using various baptismal creeds known to different delegates. 'If one imagines such a procedure', he wrote, 'then both the present version is explained and also the claim of Eusebius (and of other bishops) that the Nicene Creed was a revision of their own local creeds.'[114] Harnack's suggestion was accepted by Hans von Campenhausen, except that he considered Eusebius' 'creed' to be his own 'private' composition, rejecting Harnack's theory of Eusebius' citing a local creed.[115] In turn, Kelly thought that Harnack had misunderstood Eusebius' testimony, as the latter had never actually claimed that N was an extended version of Eus.[116] We will discuss this problem in the appropriate section below. However, I want to flag here the questions as to why the *homooúsios* was inserted into the creed, what it actually meant, and who was behind the insertion. As we will see below, there is no consensus on any of these questions.[117]

Moreover, Kelly saw it as proven that N and C^2 'are really two utterly different texts, resembling each other in a broad, general way, but to no greater extent than any other pair of Eastern formularies'.[118] However, Kelly failed to define what exactly was meant by 'difference', given that the other eastern creeds (which, incidentally, were all younger) displayed a great deal of similarity between each other. In addition, he denied that C^2 was formally adopted under its

---

113 Cf. Lietzmann 1922–1927(1962), pp. 248–59; Kelly 1972, pp. 227–30. Cf. now also Gwynn 2021, p. 101.
114 Harnack in Lietzmann 1922–1927(1962), p. 260.
115 Cf. Campenhausen 1976(1979).
116 Cf. Kelly 1972, pp. 227–30. On Eusebius' letter cf. Kelly 1972, pp. 220–6.
117 Cf. below ch. 6.4.
118 Kelly 1972, p. 304.

own name by the council fathers in Constantinople, as earlier scholars, above all the influential Eduard Schwartz, had assumed.[119] There is no mention of this, he noted, in the surviving documents of the synod and in the reports on it, on the contrary: canon 1 of the synod (FaFo § 565c) and the letter to Emperor Theodosius (§ 565b) reaffirmed the faith of *Nicaea*. Nor is there a single reference to C^2 from the period between 381 and the Council of Chalcedon in 451 in which the creed is associated with the Council of Constantinople. Rather, the standard creed and reference to this point had always been N. Nevertheless, there must have been *some* connection with Constantinople, otherwise at Chalcedon C^2 would not have been attributed to that particular council.[120]

However, in contrast to Hort and Harnack,[121] Kelly did not consider C^2 a revision of a Palestinian creed. He pointed out that we have no information that it had been presented to the fathers at Constantinople by Cyril of Jerusalem. He also objected, against Kunze (and Einar Molland),[122] that there was no direct evidence that C^2 had been the baptismal creed of Nectarius either. Kelly's basic methodological premise ('a circumstance of immense significance'[123]) consisted in the assumption – shared by others – that when the fathers spoke of the 'faith of Nicaea' it did not necessarily refer to the *text* of N; rather, this 'faith' was also seen as preserved in C^2, which is why C^2 had then also been called 'Nicene'.[124] C^2 as a whole was not the result of synodal consultations, but originated in liturgical use and had been revised in Constantinople:

> The council of Constantinople did in fact, at some stage in its proceedings, endorse and use C [= C^2], but in doing so it did not conceive of itself as promulgating a new creed. Its sincere intention, perfectly understood by contemporary churchmen, was simply to confirm the Nicene faith. That it should do this by adopting what was really a different formula from that of Nicaea may appear paradoxical to us, until we recall that at this stage importance attached to the Nicene teaching rather than to the literal wording of N. It is improbable that the council actually composed C. The whole style of the creed, its graceful balance and smooth flow, convey the impression of a liturgical piece which has emerged naturally in the life and worship of the Christian community, rather than of a conciliar artefact.[125]

---

119 Cf. the scholars enumerated in Kelly 1972, p. 313, esp. Schwartz 1926, pp. 81 f.
120 Cf. Kelly 1972, pp. 322–31.
121 Cf. above pp. 31 f.
122 For Kunze cf. above p. 32. Molland had meanwhile supported Kunze's view; cf. Molland 1970, pp. 236 f.
123 Kelly 1972, p. 323.
124 Kelly 1972, pp. 322–5.
125 Kelly 1972, p. 325.

Kelly saw the necessity for such a revision as arising from the controversy with the Pneumatomachians.[126] In the third edition of his book, he adopted a hypothesis which Adolf Martin Ritter had outlined in his groundbreaking doctoral dissertation, published in 1965.[127] According to this view C^2 was a compromise document drawn up in order to reach a consensus with those who disputed the (full) divinity of the Spirit (the so-called 'Pneumatomachians', 'Spirit-fighters'). Therefore, while the third section (on the Holy Spirit) had been expanded and the Spirit's divinity emphasized, the fathers had stopped short of explicitly including the Spirit's consubstantiality.[128] Kelly slightly disagreed with Ritter only insofar as he assumed that the council had 'adopted' C^2 (without explaining this process in more detail),[129] while Ritter suggested that the confession had never been formally endorsed after negotiations with the Pneumatomachians had broken down, although it may have been included in the Tome of the synod.[130] As far as the origin of C^2 was concerned, Ritter left it open whether C^2 was a new creed or whether the fathers at Constantinople had revised an older formula, perhaps stemming from Palestine, which they considered 'Nicene'.[131] He also thought that it was possible to detect traces of C^2 in theological writings from Constantinople onwards.[132]

2.2.3 The critics of the Ritter-Kelly hypothesis

Luise Abramowski (1928–2014), (Protestant) Church historian in Tübingen (incidentally, the first female scholar researching the creeds), remained sceptical of the Ritter-Kelly hypothesis and suggested another explanation of the origin of C^2. She thought that its basis was an extended version of N, first drawn up at a Roman Synod under Pope Damasus in around 378 which was revised at an assembly held by the followers of Meletius of Antioch in that city a year later.[133] Her hypothesis that C^2 was the creed of the Antiochene Council of 379 (or at least of Antiochene origin) found widespread agreement.[134]

---

126 On this group cf. below p. 356.
127 Cf. Ritter 1965.
128 Cf. Kelly 1972, pp. 326–31.
129 Cf. Kelly 1972, p. 331.
130 Cf. Ritter 1965, pp. 196 f.
131 Cf. Ritter 1965, p. 187.
132 Cf. Ritter 1965, pp. 195–202.
133 Cf. Abramowski 1992. With regard to the revisions at the synods in Rome and Antioch she agreed with Reinhart Staats who had made a similar suggestion; cf. Staats 1990; Staats 1999, pp. 175–9.
134 Further details in Kinzig, *Glaubensbekenntnis*, 2021, pp. 8 f.

However, Ritter rejected Abramowski's thesis, mainly because she provided no explanation as to why the explicit confession of the divinity and consubstantiality of the Holy Spirit should not have been added in Rome or Antioch (which could be better explained when one assumed, as Ritter did, that C^2 served as a basis for the well-attested negotiations with the Pneumatomachians in Constantinople). By contrast, Wolf-Dieter Hauschild (1941–2010), (Protestant) Professor of Church History in Münster, maintained that C^2 came from Constantinople and was basically N with some additions that may have originated in catechesis or which may have been inserted at the council, even though he did not completely rule out an Antiochene origin of C^2.[135]

At that point it looked as if the scholarly discussion had reached an impasse. Therefore, Volker Drecoll (b. 1968) took a step back.[136] He suggested that there had been no revision of N at a Roman council before Constantinople (*pace* Abramowski). Instead, he allowed for the possibility that the version of the creed which was attributed to Constantinople at the Council of Chalcedon (451) was not identical with the confession actually adopted by that synod. The latter version could no longer be reconstructed. By contrast, the preserved form of the creed was a revision of that 'original' creed of Constantinople which (like the 'original' creed itself) was seen as containing the 'spirit' of Nicaea and was used as local baptismal creed in that city.

Simon Gerber (b. 1967), a pupil of Reinhart Staats, described C^2 as a revision of the Antiochene creed as attested by Theodore of Mopsuestia in his doctoral dissertation on this theologian's *Catechetical Homilies*.[137] This creed, in turn, went back to the Synod of the Meletians in Antioch of 379, which likewise approved the introduction and anathemas 1–8 of the *Tomus Damasi*, subsequently also presented in Constantinople in 381.[138] In the third article of this Antiochene creed he perceived 'a concession to the Pneumatomachians' and considered the possibility that the Antiochene formulary had already been the 'basis of an orthodox-Pneumatomachian religious colloquy' before Constantinople.[139]

Reviewing Gerber's book, Adolf Martin Ritter rejected this hypothesis as well as that of Abramowski. It presupposed

'three things: 1. that C [= C^2] should be regarded as an adaptation of Theodore's creed and not vice versa; 2. that, in his *Ninth Catechetical Homily* (§ 1. 14–16), Theodore would consis-

---

135 Cf. Hauschild 1994, p. 449.
136 Cf. Drecoll, 'Wie nizänisch', 1996.
137 Cf. Gerber 2000, pp. 145–58. Cf. already Bruns 1994, pp. 33 f.
138 Cf. Gerber 2000, pp. 136–43. On the *Tomus Damasi* cf. below pp. 333 f.
139 Gerber 2000, p. 157.

tently refer to the Synod of Antioch in 379; 3. that the first part of the *Tomus Damasi* (canons 1–8) would have to be assigned to the Synod of Antioch in 379, while canon 9, together with the rest, would have to be assigned to the period after 381'.

All three assumptions were, in Ritter's view, improbable. Gerber could not explain (*ad* 1) why the oneness of the Spirit in the third section had been deleted in Theodore's creed in Constantinople. Instead, Theodore's formula as well as Constantinople's were 'independent creeds, which in the main only agreed on the fact of the (authoritative, primarily pneumatological) addition of N'. Furthermore, (*ad* 2) one could not simply ignore Theodore's assertion that the synod that supplemented N was ecumenical. Finally (*ad* 3), there was no discernible connection between canons 1–8 of the *Tomus Damasi*, which may actually have been discussed in Antioch, and the Council of Constantinople.[140]

Finally, based on a remark by Socrates,[141] Uta Heil suggested the possibility that C^2 should not be attributed to the Synod of 381, but to that of 383 when Emperor Theodosius summoned various theological groups to Constantinople demanding that they present their respective definitions of the faith. According to Heil, it was on this occasion that Nectarius of Constantinople submitted C^2, which was probably even written for that very purpose. By contrast, the Council of 381 did nothing but reaffirm N. Nectarius' creed was meant to be an interpretation of N; indeed, was later also regarded as such.[142]

In order not to bore readers unnecessarily, I will not try to demonstrate the intrinsic deficiencies of the most recent contributions to the debate, because the discovery of the authentic creed of Constantinople in 2020 has radically altered its basis as we will see in the following chapters. Instead, mention must be made of two major studies dealing with one particular problem of credal history and, indeed, of ecumenism in general, i.e. the controversy over the *filioque*. The groundbreaking monographs of Bernd Oberdorfer (b. 1961), and of Peter Gemeinhardt have in many respects modified our traditional view of this controversy and provide a sound historical basis for all future ecumenical debate. We will return to their research in the appropriate chapter.[143]

---

140 Ritter 2004, pp. 139 f. Drecoll raised a number of similar objections in his review of Gerber's book (Drecoll 2002). Drecoll still assumed that Theodore's *Catechetical Homilies* were delivered *after* Constantinople 381 and called the connection between the Antiochene synod of 379 and the *Tomus Damasi* doubtful (cols. 63 f.). He also questioned Gerber's interpretation of Theodore's ninth homily. Cf. also below chs. 6.5.11 and 6.5.12.

141 Cf. Socrates, *Historia Ecclesiastica* 5,10,21–6 (FaFo § 163c1).

142 Cf. Heil 2019.

143 Cf. Oberdorfer 2001; Gemeinhardt 2002 and below ch. 16. By contrast, the book by Siecienski 2010 offers few new insights. Cf. the review in Gemeinhardt 2012.

Finally, in a remarkable book published in 2018 Mark S. Smith (b. 1984) turned towards an area of research which had been largely neglected previously, tracing the reception of N up to the Council of Chalcedon.[144] Finally, I have suggested a new theory about the events at the Constantinopolitan Council of 381 following the discovery of a sermon by Nestorius about what must be considered the authentic creed of Constantinople (abbrev. C^1) which is similar to, but not identical with, C^2.[145]

2.2.4 Other shortcomings of Kelly's book

As we have seen, much of the discussion in recent years has been confined to German-speaking scholarship. In the Anglo-Saxon world Kelly has continued to dominate the field, although the shortcomings of his approach are obvious. For example, he never studied the reasons as to when and why N ultimately vanished, once C^2 had appeared on the scene at the Council of Chalcedon in 451. Instead, he categorically stated that the creed of the 150 fathers (C^2) quickly superseded N after Chalcedon, becoming the standard eastern creed at baptism, although the sources which he quotes by no means bear out this claim.[146]

In addition, thorough Anglican that he was, Kelly was particularly interested in the use of the creeds at synods and in liturgy, having much to say on both accounts. Yet he failed to see that the history of these formulae was determined by additional factors as well and that, conversely, it influenced other areas of Christian thought and life. In what follows, I will focus on just two of these areas.

First, Kelly largely ignored the far-reaching legal implications of credal formulae being formulated at synods. He did recognize that the *Sitz im Leben* of the creeds changed in the fourth century as a result of their increasingly synodal character. Thus he claimed that the new synodal creeds of the fourth century served as a 'test for orthodoxy', in contrast to earlier confessions and rules of faith that had not. At the same time, N was 'the first formula to be published by an ecumenical synod: consequently, it was the first which could claim universal authority in a legal sense.'[147] In other words, Kelly described the legal character of creeds only in relation to their ecumenicity. It was only by virtue of being ecu-

---

144 Cf. Smith 2018.
145 Cf. Kinzig, *Glaubensbekenntnis*, 2021, esp. pp. 93–101 and below ch. 7.
146 Details in Kinzig 2021(2022), pp. 164–184 and below ch. 8.2.
147 Kelly 1972, pp. 206 f.

menical that they could serve as a 'test of orthodoxy'. As we will see this seems to underplay what was really happening.[148]

Furthermore, he largely ignored the interplay between the emperors and the Church when it comes to the creeds. He failed to address questions such as: what was the purpose of prescribing a particular type of trinitarian faith or even a particular creed in an imperial law, as was the practice from Theodosius I onwards? Why did emperors (or their advisers) such as Justinian later even *compose* their own creeds and insert them into laws? Kelly made no mention of these texts which fit none of the traditional categories, and he took no notice of relevant scholarship by historians and legal historians, detailing the influence of Roman law and Roman institutions on the development of synods. In recent studies, this problem has received increased attention.[149]

Finally, Kelly showed little interest in what we know of religious education or in social history. The evidence available to us suggests that creeds were also carriers of religious knowledge and served to structure Christian daily life. Kelly had little to say about the creed as a tool to help impart religious knowledge to the Christian populace. His fairly narrow perspective had far-reaching consequences. In praising the theological content of the creeds, Kelly failed to see that this content was one-sided, compared to the biblical evidence: it was largely comprised of trinitarian doctrine. For instance, in T Christ's saving work was nowhere explicitly mentioned, and in C^2 only in a rather enigmatic shorthand ('who because of us humans and because of our salvation descended from the heavens'; 'was crucified for us'). This observation applies all the more to Christian ethics which was (and is) missing in the creeds in its entirety. Finally, there is almost nothing in his book about the role which the creed came to play as an increasingly 'sacred' text in the everyday life of believers.[150]

2.3 The Athanasian Creed (*Symbolum Quicumque*)

The third (and smallest) area of research concerns the Athanasian Creed (*Symbolum Quicumque*; abbrev. Ath; FaFo § 434).[151] This is a curious text which was attributed to Athanasius probably as early as the seventh century. Largely following Augustine's theology, it sets out Catholic teaching on the Trinity (sections 1–28) and on Christol-

---

148 For details cf. below ch. 6.5.
149 Cf. the literature listed in Kinzig 2021(2022), pp. 126 f. In addition, cf. below ch. 10.2.
150 Cf. below chs. 14 and 15.
151 For more information cf. Kelly 1964, pp. 3–14; Collins 1979, pp. 329–31; Iacobone 1997, pp. 19–23.

ogy (sections 29–42) in a very condensed way. At the same time, recent research has shown that its brief propositional statements reflect a type of common language found in many credal texts or trinitarian treatises of the early middle ages, so that its origin is difficult to pin down. In the early middle ages it was so popular that it, along with T and the Lord's Prayer, was inserted into psalters and sung as a canticle in the divine office.[152]

The study of Ath using a modern approach commenced in earnest[153] earlier than that of the other creeds. It was prompted by the anti-trinitarian views of controversialists in the Church of England such as Samuel Clarke (1675–1729) and John Jackson (1686–1763).[154] In 1724 the Chancellor of the Church of York, Daniel Waterland (1683–1740), a staunch defender of the Trinity, published a *Critical History of the Athanasian Creed* which subsequently went through several editions.[155] Waterland's methodology, carefully set out in the introduction, was exemplary in that it also included an investigation into the transmission of the text and its early medieval commentaries, as well as a critical edition. He did not defend the authorship of Athanasius (which by then had long been disproved), but he did advocate a fairly early composition, attributing it to Hilary of Arles, suggesting a date of 426/430. In Waterland's view 'it was drawn up for the use of the *Gallican* clergy, and especially for the Diocess, or Province of *Arles*'. 'It was esteemed', he continued, 'by as many as were acquainted with it, as a valuable Summary of the Christian Faith'.[156]

This seemed to settle the question until another controversy broke out in the Church of England in the early 1870s, this time over the liturgical use of Ath.[157] E.S. Ffoulkes (1819–1894), erstwhile Fellow and Tutor of Jesus College, Oxford, the aforementioned J. Rawson Lumby and C.A. Swainson, G.D.W. Ommanney (1819–1902), prebendary of Wells Cathedral, and once more A.E. Burn published substantial contributions to scholarship on this creed, also editing a number of early medieval commentaries relating to it.[158] As regards the mysterious origin of Ath, much depended on (1) whether one accepted the theory according to which the bipartite structure of Ath suggested that it was a composite document and (2)

---

152 Cf. also below pp. 571–3, 580, 585, 587.

153 For doubts as to the authenticity of Ath from the sixteenth century cf. Kelly 1964, pp. 3–5.

154 The background is described in Wiles 1996(2004), pp. 110–34; Ingram 2018, pp. 25–102.

155 Cf. Waterland 1724. In 1728 he published a revised and extended second edition (Waterland 1728). The latest edition, revised and corrected by J.R. King, appeared in 1870 (Waterland 1870).

156 Waterland 1728, p. 223 (emphasis in the original).

157 Cf. above p. 14 and n. 5.

158 Cf. Ffoulkes 1871; Lumby 1873(1880), pp. 186–255; Swainson 1875 (here Ath forms part of a general study of the creeds); Ommanney 1880; Burn 1896; Ommanney 1897; Burn 1918.

whether or not similarities with other texts were considered significant enough to warrant dependency in one way or another.

Ffoulkes considered it a single document and attributed its authorship to Paulinus (d. 802), Patriarch of Aquileia, whereas Lumby and Swainson favoured a 'two-source hypothesis' on the basis of the evidence available and dated Ath's final redaction to the ninth century. However, Ommanney and Burn uncovered new manuscripts and early medieval commentaries on Ath which proved that the text as it is handed down must have been written as a single document at a much earlier stage. They then suggested that it had its origin in the hotbed of early western monasticism, Lérins Abbey on the island of Saint-Honorat off the French Riviera, and that its author was either the Abbey's founder Honoratus (d. 429) or Vincent (d. before 450), who also wrote the famous *Commonitory*.[159]

Ever since Waterland it had been assumed that the author of Ath was influenced by Augustine, but Ferdinand Kattenbusch pointed out that also the reverse was possible in a detailed review of Burn's book of 1896.[160] By contrast, Friedrich Loofs suggested a scenario of gradual growth over the period 450–600 for Ath, just as in the case of R.[161]

In the following decades discussion about the origin of Ath continued unabated. Renowned catholic scholars now also joined in the debate. Karl Künstle (1859–1932), extraordinary Professor of Patristics and Church History at Freiburg im Breisgau, unsuccessfully tried to place Ath in late-fourth century Spain.[162] The Jesuit Heinrich Brewer (1861–1922), conversely, suggested Ambrose of Milan as its author who, in his view, had written it in 382/383 to summarize trinitarian orthodoxy in order to bring the Arians in Illyricum back into the fold.[163] This theory was accepted by Burn[164] and Badcock.[165] Another Jesuit scholar, Josef Stiglmayr (1851–1934), thought that he could pin down Fulgentius of Ruspe (d. 527/533) as Ath's author which would have placed the text in North Africa,[166] a theory which did not find many supporters, although it is today acknowledged that Ath also contains quotations from Fulgentius.[167]

---

159 Cf. Ommanney 1880, pp. 286–289; Ommanney 1897, p. 390 (Vincent); Burn 1918, pp. 37–42 (Honoratus).
160 Cf. Kattenbusch, review of Burn 1896, 1897, esp. cols. 143 f.
161 Cf. Loofs 1897, p. 194.
162 Cf. Künstle 1905, pp. 204–43.
163 Cf. Brewer 1909, esp. p. 130.
164 Cf. Burn 1905.
165 Cf. Badcock 1938, pp. 222–42.
166 Cf. Stiglmayr, "Quicumque", 1925; Stiglmayr, 'Vergleich', 1925; Stiglmayr 1930.
167 Cf. Drecoll 2011, pp. 387 f.

The famous Benedictine patrologist Germain Morin (1861–1946) initially also favoured a Spanish origin of Ath and dated it to the second half of the sixth century, suggesting Martin of Braga (d. 580) as a possible author. In his catalogue of famous Christian writers (*De uiris inlustribus*) Isidore of Seville (d. 636) claimed that 'Martin, the most-holy pontiff of the Monastery of Dumio, travelled by ship from the eastern lands to Galicia and there set out a rule of faith and of sacred religion (*regulam fidei et sanctae religionis*) for those Suebian tribes that had been converted from the Arian impiety to the catholic faith'.[168] Morin tentatively identified Ath with this 'rule', but ultimately thought that there was not enough evidence to be certain.[169] Later he changed his mind while he was preparing his critical edition of the works of Caesarius of Arles (d. 542), suggesting the bishop of Arles or someone from his circle, because new manuscript evidence had shown that Ath appeared at the beginning of a collection of Caesarius' sermons.[170] Thus the monastic tradition of Lérins (where Caesarius trained as a monk) once more moved into focus;[171] this proposition was further boosted by the fact that, in 1940, the Spanish Jesuit José Madoz (Moleres; 1892–1953) published a collection of excerpts from Augustine (CPL 511) which appeared to stem from the pen of Vincent and displayed close similarities with Ath.[172]

The theory of Lerinian origin found its most powerful supporter in J.N.D. Kelly. His monograph on Ath in many ways marked a caesura, as Kelly summarized the conclusions of previous research, explained the text's complicated history, and gave a very useful introduction into its theology. Finally, Kelly scrutinized the evidence for clues that would allow to solve the mystery of Ath's origin. In the end, while he definitely excluded Caesarius as its author, he did attribute authorship to someone close to the bishop of Arles. It is worth quoting the result of Kelly's careful argument in full:

> The connexion of the creed with the monastery at Lérins, its dependence on the theology of Augustine and, in the Trinitarian section, on his characteristic method of arguing, its much more direct and large-scale indebtedness to Vincent [of Lérins], its acquaintance with

168 Isidore, *De uiris inlustribus* 35,45.
169 Cf. Morin 1911, esp. pp. 350–9.
170 Cf. Morin 1932, esp. p. 219 and CChr.SL 103, pp. 20 f. In addition, Kelly 1964, pp. 35–7.
171 Lérins had already been suggested by French patrologist Joseph Tixeront (1856–1925) and Turner on the basis of an earlier article by Morin; cf. Tixeront 1903, cols. 2184–6; Turner, *History and Use*, 1910, pp. 74–7; and Morin 1901. It is a curious twist in scholarship that, in 1911, Morin maintained a Spanish origin *after* he had, in 1901, suggested the milieu of Caesarius, only to *return* to Caesarius in 1932.
172 Cf. Madoz, 'Tratado', 1940, esp. pp. 88–90. The critical edition appeared in Madoz, *Excerpta*, 1940. It was re-edited in 1985 by Roland Demeulenaere (CChr.SL 1985, pp. 199–231).

and critical attitude towards Nestorianism, and its emergence at some time between 440 and the high noon of Caesarius's activity – all these points, as well as the creed's original function as an instrument of instruction, have been confirmed or established by our studies. [. . .] When we consider its structure and rhythm, its closely knit texture and consistent tone, we must conclude that a single hand was responsible for the final draft. In the view of the present writer, while this was certainly not Caesarius, there is every probability that the creed was composed in his milieu, and quite possibly at his instigation.[173]

Since the publication of Kelly's book only a few studies dedicated to Ath deserve a mention here. In 1972 Nicholas M. Haring (1909–1982; Nikolaus Häring, a German medievalist at the University of Toronto) published an article assembling further information about the commentaries on Ath and its reception in the middle ages.[174] Roger J.H. Collins (b. 1949) summarized the state of research in his excellent 1979 article for the *Theologische Realenzyklopädie*, rejecting Kelly's hypothesis with regard to authorship and instead once more placing Ath in a Spanish context.[175]

More recent studies include Pasquale Iacobone's (b. 1959) doctoral thesis whose chief emphasis is on the reception of Ath in medieval art.[176] In a very learned article Michael Kohlbacher (b. 1959) sought parallels to the bipartite structure of Ath in eastern credal documents, suggesting that both Ath and these eastern parallels might go back to a common *Vorlage* which he located in Antioch in the fourth century.[177] However, his theory, ingenious though it is, ultimately does not hold water since the content of Ath is thoroughly western in character. Volker Drecoll once more pointed out these features and especially Ath's dependency on Augustine (which Waterland had already noticed). Drecoll called Ath a 'compilation of Augustinian tradition', produced in the period 540–630/670 for the education of clergy.[178] Christian Müller accepted Drecoll's dating in several studies of Latin translations of Athanasius and, on this basis, thought it possible 'that the text had been published under Athanasius' name from the beginning'.[179] He located its origin in Spain in the context of King Reccared's conversion from Homoianism to Catholicism (589):

---

173 Kelly 1964, p. 123.
174 Cf. Haring 1972 (cf. also the additions in Haring, 'A Poem', 1974, pp. 225–9).
175 Cf. Collins 1979.
176 Cf. Iacobone 1997.
177 Cf. Kohlbacher, Das *Symbolum Athanasianum*, 2004, esp. pp. 155 f.
178 Cf. Drecoll 2007. In Drecoll 2011, p. 389 he seems to envisage a date in the second half of the fifth century.
179 Müller 2010, p. 28. Furthermore cf. Müller 2012; Müller 2016.

Possibly, the 'Athanasian Creed' should serve as a kind of catechism, teaching the converted people the true faith. Being an 'Athanasian' work, the text would have insinuated a doctrinal change in the light of fourth century role-models, making the converts part of the 'anti-Arian' tradition established by the Alexandrian.[180]

In 2019 Hanns Christof Brennecke (b. 1947) agreed with Drecoll that Ath had been composed for the education of clergy, but, following Müller, he insisted on a Spanish origin and proposed a date of between 589 (conversion of King Reccared) and 633 (Fourth Council of Toledo).[181] By contrast, Uta Heil and Christoph Scheerer (after summarizing the debates so far) are inclined to place Ath in Francia or, more likely, Spain where it may have been written between 530 and 679.[182]

Evidently research on Ath has reached an impasse. Certain findings, such as a dependence on Augustine's theology and an attestation from *c.* 633 onwards may be considered as firmly established which narrows the date of composition down to *c.* 430–630. However, Ath's actual origin and authorship (if indeed there was a single author[183]) remain a mystery. A thorough search of existing data banks and the evolution of new electronic resources may yield more conclusive evidence in the future. In this context, both the manuscript tradition of Ath and its reception and commentaries require further investigation. Perhaps a closer study of the text's translations into the vernacular (which I have omitted here[184]) may also yield fresh evidence.

Interestingly, although pseudonymous authorship of Ath had been largely accepted in the middle ages, doubts had always existed as to whether the text should be considered a 'symbol' (creed). Thomas Aquinas (1225–1274), for example, thought it was written in the form of a doctrinal treatise rather than of a creed.[185] Early tradi-

---

180 Müller 2016, p. 213.

181 Cf. Brennecke 2019. Adolf Martin Ritter likewise sees a connection with the Fourth Council of Toledo (Ritter 2013, pp. 303–6; Ritter 2014, pp. 52–4).

182 Cf. Heil/Scheerer 2022, pp. 309–11.

183 Cf. Brennecke 2019, p. 319 n. 23, referring to Drecoll 2007, p. 41 who, however, does not deny a single originator, instead calling him a compiler rather than an original theologian (similarly, Drecoll 2011, p. 388: 'eher ein Redaktor bzw. Exzerptor als ein eigenständiger Autor'). This reflects the judgement of Turner who called the writer of Ath 'a compiler rather than a creator yet a compiler of the first order' (Turner, *History and Use*, 1910, p. 74; cf. also Ritter 2013, p. 304). Regardless of whether he is called compiler or creator, the person who wrote Ath in its present form was a learned theologian who knew how to draw together basic trinitarian and christological doctrines skillfully in a way that would be easy to remember.

184 Cf., however, below pp. 584–7.

185 Cf. Thomas Aquinas, *Summa theologiae* II-II, q1a10 ad3 (*Editio Leonina*, vol. VIII, 1895, p. 24): 'AD TERTIUM DICENDUM quod Athanasius non composuit manifestationem fidei per modum symboli, sed magis per modum cuiusdam doctrinae: ut ex ipso modo loquendi apparet.' / 'Third we must respond that Athanasius drew up a declaration of faith, not under the form of a creed, but

tion seems to agree with this assessment: the author of the prologue to the homiliary of Caesarius of Arles (probably not Caesarius himself) saw a summary of the *fides catholica* in this text, but he then presented it like a homily.[186] The Synod of Autun of c. 670 referred to it as the *fides Athanasii* and clearly distinguished it from the *symbolum* which the apostles had handed down.[187] In 966 Bishop Ratherius of Verona (887–974) admonished his clergy that they urgently ought to memorize the three-fold faith, i.e. the *symbolum* (by which he meant T), the creed sung in mass (i.e. C^2), and Ath.[188]

This reflects the usage of the earliest manuscripts: here the text initially either bore no title at all[189] or was simply called *fides catholica*, with the codex Saint Petersburg, Russian National Library, Q I 15 from the second half of the eighth century adding *Sancti Athanasii episcopi Alexandriae*.[190] In fact, as far as we know, the earliest evidence for the custom to call it a *symbolum* and to enumerate it as such together with T and C^2 stems from the twelfth century.[191]

There is, therefore, a strong argument to consider Ath not a creed at all, although its christological part uses material from T.[192] Most importantly, (a) there is no convincing evidence that it was originally intended to be recited in any liturgical context and (b) there is no 'credal link' ('I believe' / 'we believe') indicating an immediate personal involvement of the recipient (reader or hearer).[193] Therefore, it will not be given any further consideration in this book.

---

rather by way of an exposition of a certain doctrine, as appears from his way of speaking.' (tr. taken from URL <https://aquinas101.thomisticinstitute.org/st-iiaiiae-q-1#SSQ1OUTP1> (03/11/2023); altered). Cf. Ommanney 1897, pp. 41 f.; Kelly 1964, p. 1.

186 Cf. Caesarius of Arles, *Sermo 2* (cod. Z; FaFo § 656). The text of Ath begins: 'Quicumque vult salvus esse, fratres, . . . ' (CChr.SL 103, p. 20). Cf. also Kelly 1964, p. 36.

187 Cf. Synod of Autun (c. 670), canon 1 (FaFo § 581).

188 Ratherius, *Epistula 25* (MGH.B 1, p. 125, ll. 11–18): I admonish you 'urgently to memorize the faith itself, that is, the belief in God, in a three-fold manner (*ipsam fidem, id est credulitatem dei, trifarie parare memoriter festinetis*): namely [belief] according to the creed (*secundum symbolum*); that is, the "collection" of the Apostles (*collationem apostolorum*) as it is found in the corrected psalters (*Psalteriis correctis*); and that which is sung during mass; and that of St Athanasius which begins as follows: "Whoever wishes to be saved".' In thirteenth-century England Ath was even called a psalm, because it was sung as such; cf. the references in Ommanney 1897, pp. 89–91.

189 This is true for the oldest manuscript containing Ath, the cod. Milan, Biblioteca Ambrosiana, O 212 sup. from the late seventh century.

190 Cf. Turner, 'Critical Text', 1910, p. 406. On this manuscript cf. CLA 1618; TM 67783.

191 Peter Abelard (1079–1142) refers to Ath as 'Athanasius in symbolo fidei'; similarly, Anselm of Havelberg (d. 1158) and Gilbert of Poitiers (d. 1154). Cf. the references in Haring 1972, pp. 248 f.

192 Cf. esp. sections 38–9 in FaFo § 434.

193 Instead, section 1 requires the following catholic faith 'to be affirmed' (*ut teneat*) and section 42 that it is 'to be believed' (*nisi quis [. . .] crediderit*), each time using an impersonal construction.

2.4 The task ahead: Some methodological reflections

In my outline of research into the early history of the creeds I have tried to high-light some of its main points of debate. My choices have necessarily been highly eclectic: one could, of course, cite many more contributions (also important ones), dealing, for example, with the history of individual clauses of the creed or with the theological background of single confessions. Alas, this cannot be accomplished within the limited size of this work, and I must refer readers to the bibliographical references given in FaFo.[194]

When we look back over the entire 150 years of modern credal research, we can see that a new history of the creeds faces three major challenges:

- It must cope with a voluminous dossier of very heterogeneous primary sources, avoiding being bogged down by minutiae while disentangling the major threads of credal development.
- It must take into account the major theories regarding credal development as outlined in this chapter.
- It must reconcile the new evidence which has recently come to light through the efforts of Keefe, Westra, myself, and others with a general picture of the emergence and reception of the creeds that takes sufficient account of all sources available, is historically plausible, and not self-contradictory.

In what follows, I will make some methodological suggestions based on previous research which, in my view, may assist us in tackling these challenges:[195]

1. First, the question of what constitutes an 'independent' or 'autonomous' creed has caused great confusion. To illustrate the problem with an example: is it 'independence' such as (1) between different car brands (i.e. Mercedes, Volkswagen, BMW) or rather (2) further manifestations of the same model (i.e. VW Golf I, II, III etc.)? In what follows, I consider creeds as 'independent' (in the sense of (1)) if they can be derived *neither from a common* Vorlage *nor from each other (in the sense of a revision)*. Strictly speaking, such 'independence' within the same literary genre is never truly possible since *any* generic definition presupposes *some kind* of relationship of that genre's representatives to each other and thus some form of dependence; this also applies to the example of car brands: VW and BMW

---

194 Meanwhile, a history of the creeds by Fairbairn and Reeves has been published which in its patristic section ignores most of modern scholarly research. It is most puzzling that they repeatedly quote a 'protoypical Greek creed' (which is, in fact, a complete fiction by Hahn/Hahn 1897, pp. 127–31 (§ 122); cf. Fairbairn/Reeves 2019, pp. 34–36, 58–63 who follow Pelikan 2003, p. 382 f.).
195 The following reflections are based on Kinzig, *Glaubensbekenntnis*, 2021, pp. 12–15.

are still cars, despite all their differences, and are ultimately descended from the Benz *Patent Motorwagen Nummer 1* (patent motorcar number 1). Leaving aside this problem (although by no means trivial), in a strict sense, only two credal forms from among the collective confessions of antiquity were, at least initially, more widespread, namely: a western type, which exists in its earliest fixed (!) version in R, and an eastern type, whose earliest fixed version is the creed of Antioch 325 and the confession of Eusebius of Caesarea.[196] Admittedly, R, Antioch 325, and Eus also display considerable similarities, but there are strong reasons not to assume they were based on a *fixed* model, which is why we can speak of a (relative) independence in this case.

2. All western baptismal creeds are derivatives of R, as Liuwe Westra has shown;[197] all eastern creeds after 325 (with the exception of J) are revisions of or reactions to N up to the Homoian imperial creed of Niké/Constantinople (359/360), after which a movement back to N sets in.

3. As the development of R in the west towards T shows, one must always allow for local variants of the same creed. Therefore, one should not speak of 'independence' of two creeds on the basis of *individual* deviations, but only on the basis of variant *clusters*. The following variants are usually insignificant: singular πιστεύω/*credo* or plural πιστεύομεν/*credomen*, the repetition or omission of πιστεύω/*credo* or πιστεύο-μεν/*credomen* in the christological or pneumatological sections, the placement or omission of articles or conjunctions such as καί or τε/*et*, *atque*, or -*que*, or of ἐστι/*est*, and minor transpositioning of individual words.

4. Local congregational creeds in the sense of fixed formulae used at baptism are by no means given everywhere in the fourth century – contrary to what scholars have widely assumed so far.[198] In the west, the rite of the *Traditio symboli*, which presupposes such a fixation, only appears in the second half of the fourth century.[199] The creeds used in it vary in detail, but are derivatives of R rather than independent of each other. In the east, only few local creeds existed in some places in addition to the 'great' synodal creeds (that are almost all preserved[200]) up to the Council of Constantinople; and only rarely (Jerusalem) can these be connected with the practice of baptism.

---

196 This is true, although, as I will explain below, Eus itself probably was formulated ad hoc. Cf. below ch. 6.3. The creed of Jerusalem is probably a derivative of R; cf. below ch. 5.5.
197 Cf. Westra 2002.
198 Cf. above p. 26 and below p. 200.
199 Cf. below ch. 11.1.1.
200 One of the exceptions is the so-called Third Creed of Sirmium (358; FaFo § 156).

5. The assumption that a 'local creed' could have been used (for example in Constantinople 381) to express the Nicene faith clearly underestimates the normative power of N as a *formula* by the end of the fourth century and leads to new methodological problems. Occam's razor applies here: it is easier to explain C^2 as a variant of N than to regard it as an 'independent' creed whose origin would once again have to be explained by a complex hypothesis.

6. For a long time there was no terminus technicus for *symbolum* in Greek;[201] accordingly, one must carefully differentiate whether the 'faith of Nicaea' (a phrase often used in our sources) refers to a *text* or a *theological content*. Theologically speaking, the Creed of Constantinople, of course, represented the 'faith of Nicea'; however, when the sources refer to a *formula* of faith, they always mean a creed that is either identical with N or easily recognizable as a minor revision of N. Mere theological agreement is not enough. To assume that the exact wording of a creed was of secondary importance is one of the most widespread errors in credal research.[202] To counter this, it must be remembered that (a) at the councils of the fourth and fifth centuries, beginning with Antioch and Nicaea, credal formulae were signed by the bishops after long negotiations as legally binding documents (some of which then also found their way into liturgical practice) and that (b) Rufinus specifically emphasizes with regard to R that the creed in Rome had to be reproduced absolutely literally in the *Redditio symboli* in order to prevent it from being distorted by heretical formulae.[203]

7. As a result, when an author speaks of the 'creed' or 'faith of Nicaea' (in the latter case applying this to a *text*), he usually means a fixed confession which, in his subjective view, has a (more or less unmediated) historical or genealogical connection with this council. This does not mean, of course, that the text cited in each case is completely identical with N, but simply that it is a direct derivative (i.e. N^a, N^b, N^c, etc.). As we will see, the range of variation is not arbitrary.

---

201 Cf. below p. 50.
202 Cf. Gerber 2000, p. 277 citing numerous earlier publications in n. 61. In addition, Heil 2019, pp. 32 f.
203 Cf. Rufinus, *Expositio symboli* 3 (FaFo § 638): 'This [i.e. additions to the first clause], however, we have not found to be the case in the church of the city of Rome. The reason is, I imagine, that no heresy has ever had its origin there, and because they also still maintain the ancient custom that those who are about to receive the grace of baptism recite the creed in public, that is, in the audience of the faithful, and thus the hearing of those who preceded them in the faith does not permit the addition even of a single word.'

8. When our texts speak of a 'creed' or 'faith of the 150 fathers', while bringing it in connection with the Council of Constantinople in 381, it must first be assumed that it has a direct historical connection with this Council.

In terms of methodology, I will draw on form criticism[204] in what follows – despite the reservations expressed by Gerda Riedl[205] – while supplementing this approach with insights from social, institutional, theological, and liturgical history. Only a methodology that embeds the evolution of the genre of the creed in an overall view of the development of ancient Christianity can overcome certain limitations of older credal research that will be discussed below.

---

204 Cf. the classic accounts in Koch 1969 and Berger 1987. Cf. also the brief surveys in Sweeney/ Dormeyer 2014.

205 Cf. Riedl 2004, pp. 1–3. Riedl prefers a 'systematic-generative approach' (*systematisch-generativer Ansatz*). However, although I find her book very stimulating in many respects, I think that her criticism that the continuing scholarly disagreements in the history of the creeds discredit the historical-critical method as such (Riedl 2004, p. 2) misses the point regarding the achievements and limits of this method. Furthermore, form criticism deserving of the name must, of course, also keep in mind the 'context of tradition' (*Überlieferungszusammenhang*) in a wider sense and, therefore, in a way encompasses the 'systematic-generative approach' that Riedl advocates as an alternative. However, there is a difference between a theological tradition or kerygma (whose continuity is difficult to be determined and verified in historical terms) and its expression in literary texts (which always possess a certain form which can be discerned and described), as will be shown below. Having said that, I agree that Kelly's book displays certain shortcomings in this respect (cf. Riedl 2004, pp. 16–18 and elsewhere and above pp. 25 f. and ch. 2.2.4).

3 *Symbolum* and Related Terms for the Creed

I begin my study of the creeds by examining what the writers of the Early Church called the different confessions of the faith and what explanations they offered for these rather peculiar designations.[1]

Various ancient names for the creed exist. In Greek there appears to be no fixed terminology. Creeds were usually called ἔκθεσις τῆς πίστεως ('exposition of the faith') or, more often, just πίστις ('faith') or μάθημα ('lesson, learning, knowledge'[2]). Σύμβολον was not used as a term for creeds in the east until probably the fifth century, when it appears to have been introduced from the Latin (on which below). Still, even then it was rarely used in an absolute sense; instead, τῆς πίστεως ('of the faith') was added. In the west its Latin equivalents *fides* and later *credulitas* were also sometimes used. These terms, however, are not very precise designations for this specific genre and relate to content rather than to literary form.

Generally, the situation in the west is both more clear-cut and more blurred than in the east. It is more clear-cut in that creeds are called *symbolum* or (less frequently) *fides* from the time of their first appearance. Nonetheless, the origin and precise meaning of *symbolum* and how it came to be used as a technical term denoting a creed have remained something of a mystery. Consequently, this lack of certainty has already given rise to considerable speculation in antiquity.

Symbolum goes back to a Greek word, σύμβολον, which designates a 'tally', 'token', or 'seal' serving as proof of identity and also as guarantee, warrant, official document, or receipt in various contexts; the lexeme can also be used as a term for 'treaty' or 'contract', thus being partly identical with συμβολή.[3]

These meanings are also picked up by the Latin fathers. After the emergence of the genre of credal exposition towards the end of the fourth century, almost every *Explanatio symboli* includes an account of the meaning of *symbolum*. It is generally said that *symbolum* means 'token' (*indicium*) or 'contract' (*pactum*) in Latin, too. In addition, the writers often explain that *symbolum* is some kind of 'collection' (*collectio*), a meaning which is not found in the Greek usage of the term but seems to derive from a conflation of συμβολή (which could also be a contribution of some kind) and σύμβολον.

---

1 The following chapter is based on FaFo I, pp. 3–7. For more information cf. Kinzig, 'Symbolum', *Aug-L*, 2021; Kinzig, 'Symbolum', *RAC*, 2021. The relevant literature is listed in FaFo, vol. I, p. 61.
2 Cf. Lampe 1961(1984), s.v. μάθημα, B5.
3 Cf. Kinzig, 'Symbolum', *RAC*, 2021, cols. 381–3.

https://doi.org/10.1515/9783110318531-003

Nonetheless, the details pertaining to the origin of the term given in these western explanations vary widely:

(1) Ambrose[4] and Augustine[5] say that *symbola* are used by businesspeople to establish their trustworthiness and financial credibility.[6] Augustine seems to suggest that *symbolum* is closely related to or indeed identical with some kind of business contract (*pactum*). *Symbolum* here is a word or a text, but its precise character remains unclear.

(2) Peter Chrysologus calls *symbolum* a contract or treaty which is concluded between two parties in hopes of future gain; such contracts are always produced in duplicate to prevent fraud.[7]

(3) According to the anonymous author of the *Collectio Eusebiana* and Pseudo-Faustus of Riez, *symbola* are contributions made by members (*sodales*) of an association (*collegium*) towards the costs of a shared meal (here again σύμβολον = συμβολή).[8]

(4) Rufinus says that *symbolum* was a watchword to be used in times of civil war to distinguish friend from foe; for reasons of secrecy, it was not to be written down.[9] Augustine also mentions this meaning as a 'watchword' and applies it to the creed. He calls *symbolum* the 'faith and pledge of our association' (*nostrae societatis fides placita*) by which Christians recognize each other.[10]

(5) Finally, various anonymous credal expositions include an explanation according to which *symbolum* is the sum to be paid for the hire of a ship, which at the same time must be produced in the captain's presence that one has sufficient assets.[11] It is difficult to know whether this information (which may partly be based on a comment by Tertullian[12]) corresponds to historical reality.

All explanations in later sources appear to depend on the aforementioned texts.

---

4 Cf. Ambrose, *Explanatio symboli* 2 (FaFo § 15a1).

5 Cf. Augustine, *Sermo 212*, 1 (FaFo § 19a); *214*, 12 (§ 19c).

6 Ambrose seems to use *symbolum* (neuter) and *symbola* (feminine) synonymously. Peter Chrysologus may also allude to this use of *symbolum* in *Sermo 60*, 2 (FaFo § 22e1).

7 Cf. Peter Chrysologus, *Sermo 62*, 3 (FaFo § 22g).

8 Cf. *Collectio Eusebiana*, *Homilia 9*, 1 (FaFo § 30); Pseudo-Faustus, *Sermo 2*, 1 (§ 34).

9 Cf. Rufinus, *Expositio symboli* 2 (FaFo § 18). The explanation is repeated in Pseudo-Maximus, *Homilia 83* (§ 23).

10 Cf. Augustine, *Sermo 214*, 12 (FaFo § 19c); cf. also *213*, 2 (§ 19b).

11 Cf. *Sermo de symbolo* (CPL 1759) 1 (FaFo § 27a); cod. St. Gallen, Stiftsbibliothek, 40, I,1–4 (§ 43); anonymous *Apertio symboli* (§ 44); Pseudo-Jerome, *Explanatio symboli* (§ 61).

12 Cf. Tertullian, *Aduersus Marcionem* 5,1,2 (FaFo § 8b).

In earlier Christian sources *symbolum* is used in the context of baptism, but it looks as if the term does not denote an actual text in this context, but a sign such as that of the cross.[13] There is some evidence to suggest that *symbolum* denoted the baptismal interrogations from the mid-third century onward.[14] By the late fourth century there is agreement that *symbolum* designates a specific formula and that this formula is a declaratory creed.

The fathers consider *symbolum* to have the following meanings when it is used to refer to a creed:[15]

(1) a summary of the Christian faith (often relating to the legend of the apostolic origin of T; here again σύμβολον = συμβολή);[16]

(2) token:

    (a) summary of the faith;[17]

    (b) a token of recognition among Christians (e.g. in order to distinguish them from heretics or Jews) or of a true Christian (as opposed to a nominal or false Christian);[18]

    (c) a token of confession;[19]

    (d) a token of the full knowledge of truth;[20]

    (e) a reminder of the preaching of the apostles;[21] and, therefore also

    (f) a sign of, or rule for, the true (correct) faith;[22]

---

13 This is true of Tertullian, *De paenitentia* 6,12 (FaFo § 8a); Cyprian, *Epistula 69*, 7,1–2 (§ 92a) and id., *Epistula 75*, 11,1 (Firmilianus of Carthage; § 85).

14 The first extant reference where *symbolum* is used to designate baptismal interrogations is probably Cyprian, *Epistula 69*, 7 (FaFo § 92a). Cf. also Council of Arles, canon 9(8) and the *Epistula ad Silvestrum* (§ 11); Council of Laodicea, canon 7 (§ 562a).

15 Only a selection of references is listed in what follows.

16 Cf. Rufinus, *Expositio symboli* 2 (FaFo § 18); Augustine, *Sermo 213*, 2 (§ 19b); *214*, 12 (§ 19c); Nicetas, *Competentibus ad baptismum instructionis libelli* 2, frg. 5 (§ 14a); id., *De symbolo* 5,13 (§ 14b); John Cassian, *De incarnatione* 6,3 (§ 21); Fulgentius, *Contra Fabianum*, frg. 36,1 (§ 35); *Collectio Eusebiana, Homilia 9*, 1 (§ 30); Pseudo-Faustus, *Sermo 2*, 1 (§ 34); Venantius Fortunatus, *Expositio symboli* 1–2 (§ 38).

17 Numerous references in Kinzig 2011(2017), pp. 340 f. n. 54.

18 Cf. Rufinus, *Expositio symboli* 2 (FaFo § 18); Augustine, *Sermo 212*, 1 (§ 19a); *213*, 2 (§ 19b); *214*, 12 (§ 19c); Peter Chrysologus, *Sermo 57*, 16 (§ 22b); Pseudo-Maximus, *Homilia 83* (§ 23); CPL 1759, 3 (§ 27b); CPL 1762 (§ 29); Isidore of Seville, *De origine officiorum (De ecclesiasticis officiis)* 2,23(22),3 (§ 39a).

19 Cf. Isidore of Seville, *De origine officiorum (De ecclesiasticis officiis)* 2,22(21),2 (§ 39a).

20 Cf. *Expositio super symbolum* (CPL 1760) 1 (FaFo § 33).

21 Cf. Rufinus, *Expositio symboli* 2 (FaFo § 18); Isidore of Seville, *De origine officiorum (De ecclesiasticis officiis)* 2,23(22),2 (§ 39a); id., *Etymologiarum siue originum libri XX* 6,19,57 (§ 39b).

22 Cf. Rufinus, *Expositio symboli* 2 (FaFo § 18); Priscillian, *Tractatus 1*, f. 2 (§ 16a1). f. 38 (§ 16a2); Peter Chrysologus, *Sermo 61*, 2 (§ 22f1); Venantius Fortunatus, *Expositio symboli* 2–3 (§ 38); Isidore of Seville, *De origine officiorum (De ecclesiasticis officiis)* 2,23(22),2 (§ 39a).

(3) contract:
  (a) a contract of the believers with one another;[23]
  (b) a contract of the individual believer with God;[24]
(4) sign = symbol: this interpretation of *symbolum* as *signatura rei uerae* ('sign of the true thing') is found only in Priscillian.[25] The *res uera* to which the *symbolum* refers is the Holy Scripture.

Given this variety there is considerable confusion among ancient Latin authors as to why precisely the term σύμβολον/*symbolum* came to be used.

When we look at earlier religious sources, the evidence suggests that the term σύμβολον/*symbolum* was current in mystery cults as a secret sign of recognition among the members of a particular cult.[26] It could be some kind of formula, but also an object or a 'symbol' in the modern sense of the term. This custom may have been transferred to the Christian cult in the third century (yet the details remain blurred): creeds, then, mainly served to distinguish between those that were baptized and those who were not (and, consequently, were unable to recite the creed). As will be shown below, at a later date the congregation reciting the creed (following the service of the word at the beginning of the eucharist) had precisely this function, when the doors were closed to the uninitiated.[27] Given this purpose, *symbolum* in fact refers specifically to the creed used in pre-baptismal catechesis and during baptism, and hence to R and its offshoots such as T. The fact that a Greek term was used in this context points to the time when most Christians in the west were Greek-speaking. It does not primarily refer to the eastern synodal creeds such as N and C², for which the terms *fides* or *confessio fidei* is much more common.[28]

---

23 Cf. Augustine, *Sermo 212*, 1 (FaFo § 19a).
24 Cf. Nicetas, *Competentibus ad baptismum instructionis libelli* 5,13 (FaFo § 14b); Eucherius, *Instructiones ad Salonium* 2,15 (§ 20); Peter Chrysologus, *Sermo 58*, 2 (§ 22c); *59*, 1–2. 18 (§ 22d); Fulgentius, *Contra Fabianum*, frg. 36,1 (§ 35); Theodore of Mopsuestia, *Homilia catechetica 12*, 27 (§ 635b).
25 Cf. Priscillian, *Tractatus* 3 (FaFo § 16c).
26 For further details cf. Kinzig, 'Symbolum', *RAC*, 2021, cols. 383–5.
27 Cf. below p. 508.
28 Cf. also Eichenseer 1960, pp. 42–8.

4 In the Beginning: Confessing Christ without Creeds

It was said above that there were no creeds in pagan religion.[1] Yet even within the history of Christianity, the emergence of creeds is by no means a given. Christianity managed without a declaratory confession for more than two centuries. This does not mean, of course, that the faith was not confessed (and we will have to consider how this took place), only that it was not consistently done in fixed formulae. This fact may surprise the modern Christian who is used to reciting T or C[2] in worship, but it is less remarkable in the context of ancient Christendom when one considers that Christians worshipped largely without recourse to fixed forms but by extemporizing prayers and other liturgical texts until well into the fourth century.[2]

This also applies to the ritual elements of the catechumenate and to baptism itself: these rites probably varied considerably depending on local circumstances; indeed, even in the same place their wording was not yet fixed. In the first three centuries, the term 'formula' should not be understood too narrowly. In this period, 'confessions' refer first and foremost to certain confessional topoi which were still in flux in their individual formulation, albeit not arbitrary, which is why I will call them 'homologies' and 'rules of faith'. In addition, there is some evidence to suggest a certain wording of baptismal questions and, later, also of declaratory creeds, as will be shown below. However, strictly speaking, the first fixed formulae that have come down to us do not date to before the fourth century. This process of the consolidation of confessing one's faith will be traced in more detail in this part of my book.

It is also important to note that confessions always serve to draw boundaries. The statement 'I am a Christian' was required when Christianity first manifested itself in the lives of believers, when it was ritually remembered, and when Christian identity came under pressure from the outside. Unlike Islam and Judaism, Christianity has always had ritual acts of acceptance that everyone had to undergo, and which demarcated Christians from non-Christians.[3] In addition, proving one's Christian identity was a prerequisite for admission to the eucharist. Furthermore, Christian identity could be endangered when a certain form of

---

1 Cf. above p. 6.

2 Cf. Kinzig 2012(2017), p. 338 and n. 44 listing further literature. In addition, cf. Hammerstaedt/Terbuyken 1996, cols. 1258–60; Fürst 2008, pp. 10, 36.

3 Circumcision does not *per se* constitute affiliation to Judaism, since men can be Jews even if they are uncircumcised provided they are descended from a Jewish mother. In Islam, membership of the religion is acquired by birth into a Muslim family.

https://doi.org/10.1515/9783110318531-004

Christianity was challenged by another or when being a Christian in general was called into question. Finally, unlike in other ancient cults (including Judaism), discussions about the role of doctrine and the theology that developed out of them were paramount in defining Christian identity.

4.1 Believing in and confessing God or Christ in the New Testament

Turning to the Bible, our first question would be whether there are creeds in the Hebrew Bible, the Christian Old Testament. However, there appears to be a broad consensus among biblical scholars today that this is not the case.[4] The beginning of the aforementioned Shema Yisrael (Deut 6:4), affirming God's oneness and lordship, which is said as part of the Jewish morning and evening prayer services,[5] may be seen as resembling a confession of faith. But we must be careful not to project a Christian view of the creed onto ancient Jewish worship and its biblical foundation. In its original setting, in no way does the Shema Yisrael stand out as a text fulfilling a particular liturgical function such as the Christian creed. Instead, it forms part of a section that is thoroughly legal in character (as is all of Deuteronomy): Yahweh is Israel's only God and Lord; Israel must, therefore, love and fear this God: it owes allegiance to its particular divine master and must fulfill the legal obligations arising from this relationship of dependence (Deut 6:17–19). Nowhere is it explicitly *said* that faith comes into it, although the concept is based on a trust in God whose care for Israel has often manifested itself in salvation history: God's existence and lordship are simply stated as a fact that calls for a certain reciprocal behaviour on Israel's part.[6]

---

4 Cf. the literature cited in FaFo I, p. 33.

5 Cf. above p. 6 and n. 27.

6 Martin Buber has expressed this difference between Judaism and Christianity by distinguishing two types of faith (Buber 1951, pp. 34 f.): 'In the period at the beginning of Christianity there was still no other [Jewish] form of confession than the proclamation, be it in the Biblical form of the summons to the people, "Hear, O Israel", which attributes uniqueness and exclusiveness to "our" God, or in the invocation of the Red Sea song to the King recast into a statement, "It is true that the God of the world is our King". The difference between this "It is true" and the other [i.e. Christian] "We believe and know" is not that of two expressions of faith, but of two kinds of faith. For the first, faith is a position in which one stands, for the second it is an event which has occurred to one, or an act which one has effected or effects, or rather both at once. Therefore the "we" in this instance can only be the subject of the sentence. True, Israel also knows a "we" as subject, but this is the "we" of the people, which can to be sure apply to "doing" or "doing and hearing" (Exod. xxiv. 3, 7), but not to a "believing" in the sense of the creed. Where it is said of the people (Exod. iv. 31, xiv. 31) that they

Nonetheless, it would be dangerously anachronistic to overstate the chasm between knowledge and faith. In Christianity, having faith in God or Christ did not necessarily mean that the factuality of their existence was considered precarious in any way and therefore had to be ritually affirmed by reciting certain formulae. Rather, 'faith in' implied a particular personal relationship of the individual believer with the deity, as explained in chapter 1.2, which we do not find as such in the Old Testament[7] and which we must define further. In order to do so, we must now turn to the New Testament.

*

Confessing Christ was already one of the central markers of Christian identity at a very early stage. In Mt 10:32–33 Jesus is quoted as saying,

> Everyone, therefore, who will confess me before humans, I also will confess before my Father in the heavens; but whoever will deny me before humans, I also will deny before my Father in the heavens.[8]

---

believed, that simple trust which one has or holds is meant, as in the case of the first patriarch. When anybody trusts someone he of course also believes what the other says. The pathos of faith is missing here, as it is missing in the relationship of a child to its father, whom it knows from the very beginning as its father. In this case too a trusting-in which has faltered must sometimes be renewed.' I owe this reference to Böttrich 2014, p. 67 n. 23. – Previous Christian research on the Old Testament has also often termed the text of Deut 26:5–9(11) a creed (Gerhard von Rad: 'short historical creed'; cf. Rad 1938(1966), pp. 3–13; Rad 1962/1965, vol. I, pp. 121 f., 124 f., 129, 136, 138 f., 166, 176, 187, 281, 296 f., 397; vol. II, p. 358; Rad 1973, pp. 14, 19–21, 45), but, given its entirely narrative character, it seems rather flimsy to relate it to later Christian creeds, in terms of literary genre.

7 By contrast, 'Old Testament faith is centred on a bond that is unique in nature, namely the relationship between Yahweh and the people of his election, which is based on exclusivity [. . .]' (Brandscheidt 2013, 2.2). This has a strong ethical component: '"Turning to God with faith" does not mean a passive acknowledgement of God's greatness, but a way of life that challenges the entire human being in his outer and inner behaviour' (Brandscheidt 2013, 2.4). This relation of the individual to God by means of belonging to the People of Israel and the resulting imperative to act in a manner that is morally acceptable are missing in the Christian creed. Anja Klein is even more sceptical: 'Faith is a decidedly Christian concept. However, the H[ebrew] B[ible]/O[ld] T[estament] contains a few statements about the relationship between humankind to God that deal with the firm trust in him or the lack thereof' (Klein et al. 2014, col. 690). By contrast, Levin calls 'faith' 'a theological key concept from the late period of the Old Testament' which, although rare, had a broad impact on the New Testament and beyond (Levin 2018, p. 26).

8 Πᾶς οὖν ὅστις ὁμολογήσει ἐν ἐμοὶ ἔμπροσθεν τῶν ἀνθρώπων, ὁμολογήσω κἀγὼ ἐν αὐτῷ ἔμπροσθεν τοῦ πατρός μου τοῦ ἐν [τοῖς] οὐρανοῖς· ὅστις δ' ἂν ἀρνήσηταί με ἔμπροσθεν τῶν ἀνθρώπων, ἀρνήσομαι κἀγὼ αὐτὸν ἔμπροσθεν τοῦ πατρός μου τοῦ ἐν [τοῖς] οὐρανοῖς. The translation 'before others' for ἔμπροσθεν τῶν ἀνθρώπων in the *New Revised Standard Version Updated Edition* is erroneous, because the opposition is between humans (in this world) and God (in heaven), not between the confessor and 'others'.

Confessing Christ has a salvific function. Conversely, denying Christ means excluding oneself from salvation and, by consequence, from the Christian community (which is why apostasy has always been considered a mortal sin). One's 'creed' or 'confession' can be expressed in various ways in daily life, for instance, by wearing some kind of badge or symbol declaring allegiance to a particular belief, party, or community. We have some evidence that early Christians did just that. For example, Clement of Alexandria suggested that the images on signet rings suitable to be worn by Christians should be a dove, a fish, a ship, or a ship's anchor.[9] However, emblems without text can be equivocal or downright incomprehensible; in fact, Clement intentionally exploited such ambiguity to avoid Christians being identified as such for reasons of personal safety. A dove only takes on a certain given meaning for sure when accompanied by, or in some other way securely linked to, some kind of explanation. A confession, therefore, presupposes or consists in some kind of *text* explaining what one is confessing. However, what does it mean when one confesses *a person*? And why and where would Christians do that?

There is a tendency in New Testament research to declare anything a 'confession' that looks like some sort of doctrinal proposition. As a consequence, distinctions become blurred and, in the end, different people talk about different things.[10] By contrast, as we saw above, patristic scholars have tended to look for fixed confessional formulae that could be understood as 'germs' of later creeds in a kind of 'organic' approach. This approach implied a 'growth' or 'accretion' of creeds from smaller to larger confessional units, which, however, ignored the plurality of early Christianity when the core of Christian confession was still very much a matter of debate.[11] Therefore, it may be helpful to begin our inquiry into the origins of the creeds by considering those passages in the New Testament that describe the role of faith in our relation to God and Jesus Christ, as well as the precise meaning of 'confession' in the New Testament.

---

9 Cf. Clement of Alexandria, *Paedagogus* 3,59,2.
10 Cf., e.g., Wengst 1984; John Reumann in Bochinger et al. 1998, cols. 1248 f. Here 'confession' seems to be identical with 'formula' *tout court*, a confused approach. More nuanced Böttrich 2014, esp. pp. 61–4.
11 Cf. my survey of previous research above ch. 2.

4.1.1 'Believing' in God/Christ

The New Testament is full of 'faith' language:[12] there are 239 occurrences of πιστεύειν ('to believe') and 240 of πίστις ('faith'). Christian faith language builds
upon the Hebrew Bible/Old Testament and its Greek translation, the Septuagint.
In the latter, πιστεύειν is a translation of Hebrew *he'ĕmîn*[13] (Niphal of *'mn*) and
must, like the original, be translated into English as 'to trust' almost in all instances, with the object of trust (often God) supplied primarily in the dative. (Interestingly, in the Septuagint πιστεύειν is never used with εἰς.) In some instances
πιστεύειν is followed by ὅτι, expressing a proposition. However, only in Is 43:10
does it come close to a formula ('[. . .] so that you may know and believe and understand that I am'.) An interesting case is Judith 14:10 where Achior from the
house of Uzziah is converted to Judaism:

> When Achior saw all that the God of Israel had done, he believed firmly in God (ἐπίστευσεν
> τῷ θεῷ σφόδρα). So he was circumcised and was handed over to the house of Israel until
> this day.

Here trust/faith in God serves as a marker of identity: the Ammonite Achior
switches his loyalty from his people's gods to the God of the Jews. As we will see,
this use of πιστεύειν will become more prominent later.

Both the Septuagint and early Christian writings[14] also draw on the pagan
usage of πίστις and its cognates which may denote not only 'faith' and 'trust', but
also 'means of persuasion', 'confidence', 'assurance', 'trustworthiness', 'credibility',
'proof', and even 'credit' in a commercial sense. However, the standard phrases in
later creeds and credal formulae are 'I/we believe in', indicating mostly, although
not exclusively,[15] faith in the persons of the Trinity, or 'I/we believe that' a given
theological proposition is true. We must, therefore, inquire into the origins of this
particular understanding of 'faith'.

When the noun πίστις occurs in the New Testament, the object of faith is expressed either by adding the genitive or the prepositions εἰς, πρός, ἐν, or (in one
instance only[16]) ἐπί. In the majority of occurrences, the object of faith is either
God or Christ/the Lord/Jesus in various combinations. As far as I can see, nowhere

---

12 Cf. Bultmann/Weiser 1968, pp. 187 f.; Becker/Michel 1975; Lührmann 1979, cols. 64–79; Haacker
1985; Barth 1993; Konradt, 'Faith', 2014; Morgan 2015; Horn, 'Glaube – Nicht Weisheit', 2018.
13 Cf. Levin 2018, p. 9.
14 Its usage in other writings of Hellenistic Judaism and in rabbinical literature does not appear
to yield further aspects pertinent to our (limited) investigation; cf. Swanson /Satlow 2014.
15 A famous exception is C[2] which includes faith in the Church.
16 Heb 6:1 (God).

does πίστις denote a *formula* (unlike in later centuries when it can be used to denote the creed[17]); rather, it always refers to the *act of believing* (i.e. is an action noun).[18]

As regards the verb πιστεύειν, I will briefly examine those passages in the New Testament in which the lexeme is not used in an absolute sense, but with an object or person in which one believes, or with an object clause, with an infinitive, or with an accusative-infinitive phrase.

The Apostle Paul is fairly flexible in that he construes πιστεύειν with εἰς or ἐπί with the accusative.[19] In almost all these instances the object of faith is God or Jesus Christ – this is even more striking as in the pagan environment from which the New Testament emerged such faith is nowhere expressed by using πιστεύειν εἰς/ἐπί. A difference between εἰς and ἐπί appears to be that God/Christ is accompanied by a participle denoting his actions when ἐπί with the accusative is used. In fact, the participle may replace God/Christ altogether: we believe in him (i.e. God) as the one who justifies the ungodly, or by virtue of his raising Jesus from the dead.[20]

Thus Paul stands at the beginning of the fundamental idea in Christian literature that the relation between God/Christ and his worshippers is constituted through an act of faith in the saving work of God/Christ and thus in God/Christ himself as a 'person' performing such action. The apostle himself proclaimed this message, expecting it to be 'believed' by his listeners/readers. They were asked to trust the divine Saviour, but also the apostolic messenger. As Michael Wolter put it:

> [. . .] the people who gathered together because of Paul's preaching were joined together in one group by just this one characteristic, that is, that they had agreed with what Paul had said to them and also kept on agreeing.[21]

Perhaps the best example for this interplay of God's/Christ's action – its proclamation – listening – believing – confessing is found in Rom 10:8–10:

> But what does it [Scripture] say? 'The word is near you, in your mouth and in your heart' [Deut 30:14] (that is, the word of faith that we proclaim), because if you confess with your mouth that Jesus is Lord and believe in your heart that God raised him from the dead, you will be saved. For one believes with the heart, leading to righteousness, and one confesses with the mouth, leading to salvation.

---

17 Cf. above p. 50.
18 Cf. Wolter 2015, p. 71.
19 For faith in Paul cf. esp. Wolter 2015, pp. 71–94.
20 Rom 4:5 (ἐπὶ τὸν δικαιοῦντα); 4:24 (ἐπὶ τὸν ἐγείραντα).
21 Wolter 2015, p. 73.

Here the (public) 'confession' consists in the clause: 'Jesus is Lord', whereas the resurrection from the dead does not form part of the oral 'confession', rather provides the 'historical' justification for this 'confession'. As opposed to pagan myths, Christians were asked to believe in the historicity of an event involving one particular, clearly identifiable saviour figure that had taken place at a certain location and at a particular point in time and which would guarantee their future salvation. Having faith was thus being assured of a historical, but also of a divine reality.[22] This unusual way in which the Christian message was structured meant that those who sympathized with Paul's proclamation had to make a clear decision: they were expected to believe that these events had actually happened and had been brought about by the carpenter from Bethlehem or Nazareth in Palestine, because doing so was a prerequisite of their salvation. In contrast to Judaism, such salvation did not (primarily) hinge on the fulfilment of a given set of divine laws, but on choosing to believe that during the governorship of Pontius Pilate Christ had been executed by crucifixion, had been buried, and had been raised from the dead, and that unconditionally accepting these assumptions as historical fact would ultimately guarantee the believer's resurrection (Rom 6:4). This change constituted a new Christian identity within and beyond the contemporary (Jewish) divide between Jews and Gentiles (cf. Gal 5:6; 6:5).

Furthermore, some basic statements which could easily be memorized summarized the account of these historical events for the practical purpose of preaching and teaching. Paul's writings already testify to the beginning of this process which ultimately led to the formulation of creeds. Yet even where Paul includes such theological propositions, they relate to Christians trusting in some form of salvific *event* which originated in God/Christ rather than solemnly agreeing to a set of doctrinal tenets or norms in a fixed form. Thus the apostle says in Rom 6:8 that 'if we died with Christ, we believe that we will also live with him'. According to Rom 10:9 'if you confess with your mouth that Jesus is Lord and believe in your heart that God raised him from the dead, you will be saved'. 1Thess 4:14 also includes Christ's death and resurrection as an object of belief:

> For since we believe that Jesus died and rose again, even so, through Jesus, God will bring with him those who have died.[23]

Belief in these summary statements obviously implied that one also had full knowledge of the sequence of events which they summarized (such as that they happened under the governor Pontius Pilate). It is telling that, although these con-

---

22 Wolter 2015, pp. 84–94.
23 Cf. also Gal 2:20.

densed narratives formed the core of Paul's teaching about Christ, there are such differences in their wording, indicating that this basic knowledge was not yet expressed in a fixed text. This is why it is erroneous to speak of '*pístis* formulae' in these instances as earlier scholarship has done.[24]

Paul also associates 'faith' with baptism (Gal 3:26–27):

> So you are all sons of God through the faith in Christ Jesus (διὰ τῆς πίστεως ἐν Χριστῷ Ἰησοῦ), for (γάρ) all of you who were baptized into Christ (εἰς Χριστόν) have clothed yourselves with Christ.

In Paul's view, 'faith in Christ Jesus' and 'baptism into Christ' are intimately connected, although the logic of his argument (γάρ) and its metaphorical structure (descendance vs. clothing) of the verses (in which traditional liturgical formulae may be referenced[25]) remain opaque.

A similar picture emerges from the Deutero-Pauline corpus and Hebrews. They also include the statement that 'Christ is believed/trusted in' (ἐπιστεύθη, 1Tim 3:16), as well as one explaining that Paul's testimony requires faith (2Thess 1:10; cf. 2:11–12). In Hebrews it is emphasized that we must believe 'that he [God] exists and that he rewards those who seek him' (Heb 11:6). In 1 Timothy faith is also associated with 'teaching':

> If you put these [instructions] before the brothers and sisters, you will be a good servant of Christ Jesus, nourished on the words of the faith and of the sound teaching (τοῖς λόγοις τῆς πίστεως καὶ τῆς καλῆς διδασκαλίας) that you have followed' (1Tim 4:6; cf. 2Tim 1:13; 3:10).

Here faith is not just an inward 'attitude' but is expressed in 'words' and as such can be shared among each other. However, these words are no fixed formulae – instead the author seems to refer to what he wrote before (cf. 1Tim 2:1–4:4).

At the same time, in Eph 4:4 we find faith once more associated with baptism: 'one Lord, one faith, one baptism'. Unfortunately, again the precise nature of this association is not spelled out. However, the insistence on the oneness of faith suggests that 'faith' is no longer just a matter of the heart, but also outwardly *expressed* in a way which demonstrates that there is indeed unanimity in the Christian congregation.

When we turn to the remainder of the New Testament, the Johannine corpus and Acts provide the most extensive evidence for πιστεύειν/πίστις in the sense we

---

24 Cf. Horn, 'Glaube – Nicht Weisheit', 2018, pp. 44 f. referring to Vielhauer 1975(1985), pp. 9–22 and Hahn 2011, vol. II, pp. 459 f. Hahn's list of *pístis* formulae also includes Rom 1:3b. 4a; 4:24b. 25; 5:8; 1Cor 8:6; 15:3–5. These are all summaries, but not formulae (i.e. fixed sets of a sequence of words). In addition, Vollenweider 2017, pp. 506–9.
25 Cf. the discussion in De Boer 2011, pp. 242–7.

are interested in while the Synoptic Gospels add nothing new. In the Johannine writings πιστεύειν, referring to God/Christ, is construed with the dative only, or with εἰς, as well as, perhaps, once with ἐν.[26] There appears to be no discernible semantic difference. The object of faith can be God/the Father, the Son/Son of Man/Jesus Christ, or his 'name'. We also find πιστεύειν followed by propositional statements. Propositions to be believed include the claim that Jesus is the 'Holy One of God' (ὁ ἅγιος τοῦ θεοῦ; Jn 6:69), the Christ (20:31), and that he came from God.[27] Those who believe in the 'only-begotten Son (τὸν υἱὸν τὸν μονογενῆ)' 'may not perish but may have eternal life (ζωὴν αἰώνιον)' (3:16), whereas those who do not believe 'are condemned already (ἤδη κέκριται)' (3:18). Martha believes that (ὅτι) the Lord is 'the Christ, the Son of God, the one coming into the world' (11:27). Likewise, the author of 1 John underlines the importance of the belief that Jesus is the Christ (5:1) and promises that those who believe in Jesus being the Son of God will 'overcome the world' (νικῶν τὸν κόσμον; 5:5; cf. also 5:10). In a way, these postulations are more abstract than those in Paul because they primarily point to Jesus' 'nature' or 'status'. What is central here is his divine origin which lies at the heart of his messiahship, not his death and resurrection.

In the Book of Acts πιστεύειν is construed with the dative only, with εἰς, or with ἐπί plus the accusative, the object of faith being in most cases Christ. (Acts feature no instances of propositional clauses.) Missionaries such as Peter impart the message relating to these 'Christ' events of the past, a message whose veracity and accuracy must be believed (as it cannot be verified). Acts 15:7 illustrates this very well:

> After there had been much debate, Peter stood up and said to them, 'My brothers, you know that in the early days God made a choice among you, that I should be the one through whom the Gentiles would hear the message of the good news and become believers.'

The Book of Acts also refers to 'faith' several times in the context of the ritual of baptism: Simon Magus and the crowd following him, Paul's and Silas' anonymous jailor, and the *Archisynagogos* Crispus, together with many Corinthians, believe and are then baptized (the jailor and Crispus with their entire households).[28] 'Faith' is therefore a precondition of baptism which also has to be ascertained in some way by the baptizer, although Acts provides no information as to how this is done.

Finally, in 1Peter, the addressees of the letter are called 'believers in God' (πιστοὺς εἰς θεόν) who raised Christ from the dead and gave him glory.[29]

---

26 Cf. Jn 3:15; there is, however, some textual uncertainty.
27 Cf. Jn 16:27. 30; 17:8. 21; furthermore, cf. 8:42; 13:3.
28 Cf. Acts 8:12–13; 16:31–3; 18:8. Cf. also 19:4 and the secondary ending of Mark: 16:16.
29 1Pet 1:21.

Although conceding that 'the ultimate origins of Christian *pistis* [. . .] remain mysterious', Teresa Morgan observes on the basis of this rich evidence:

> What we can say with confidence is that for the Greek-speaking communities within which and for which the texts of the New Testament were written, the idea of *pistis* proved to be so rich, and so adaptable to developing understandings of the relationship between God, Christ, and humanity, together with understandings of human life and activity within that relationship, that *pistis* is everywhere involved with the early evolution of those understandings.[30]

Contrary to what one might expect, the opposition between 'believing' and 'seeing' (in the sense of visual evidence) or 'knowing' does not play a major role in the New Testament (although it can be glimpsed here and there[31]). What is more important for understanding *pístis* in the New Testament is, first, its meaning of 'trust' in the salvific historicity of the events which the Christian message relates (with important implications for the future of every individual believer), and, second, the idea that Christians invest all their hope for salvation in one particular divine person, categorically denying not only the efficacy of other gods but their very existence. In this context, Jas 2:19 provides an important clue:

> You believe that there is one God; you do well. Even the demons believe – and shudder.

Whether or not the epistle's author is being sarcastic here, he agrees with his opponent that faith language implies trust in one God/Saviour *to the exclusion of others*. Human welfare and salvation are not the result of a kind of mosaic of actions by a pantheon of gods, let alone any cooperation between them as is often found in pagan cults. Faith language is necessary because it implicitly denies the existence of other gods and, as such, establishes a shared identity for the Christian congregation.[32] Such language relates to a historical event of the utmost consequence both for the future of humankind as a whole and for every individual believer.

The evidence, then, clearly shows that belief in Christ's incarnation, death, and resurrection and their significance for humankind, which confirmed his divine origin and status, constituted the core of 'faith' in the New Testament; however, the phrasing of this propositional content has not yet been fully formalized or standardized.

---

[30] Morgan 2015, pp. 502 f.
[31] Cf., e.g., Jn 20:29; Rom 8:24; 1Cor 13:12; Heb 11:1; 1Pet 1:8.
[32] For the communal aspect cf. Morgan 2015, p. 506.

4.1.2 'Confessing' God/Christ

Rom 10:8–10 quoted in the previous section appears to indicate that there is a difference between faith in God/Christ and confessing God/Christ. In that passage both actions (ὁμολογεῖν, 'confessing'; πιστεύειν, 'believing') entail certain propositions: Christians confess that Jesus is Lord, and they believe that God raised him from the dead. Crucially, the former proposition is said out aloud. Moreover, it expresses a specific allegiance which is performed in the speech act, rather than simply involving cognitive consent. By contrast, the latter action of believing is restricted to one's 'heart'. This does not reduce it to some kind of 'feeling' or 'emotion' only, but denotes that it is an inward expression of trust in the historicity and the salvific nature of Jesus' resurrection.[33] In Paul's view these propositions are closely interlinked: Jesus is confessed as Christ *because* he was raised from the dead. In addition, it is not sufficient simply to believe quietly – Christians are expected to acclaim Jesus as the Lord in public in order to attain salvation.

Thus, the act of 'confessing' is part of the language of faith; indeed, it played a significant role in the life of the earliest Christian communities. We will, therefore, take a closer look at the use of ὁμολογία and ὁμολογεῖν in the New Testament.[34] In most cases, they denote certain spoken, public revelations, an agreement to a statement perceived as factual which is being disclosed. Ὁμολογεῖν (26 occurrences) indicates the act of utterance, whereas ὁμολογία (6 occurrences) denotes the act itself, but also the result of such action. The content of this disclosure can differ as does the context in which it is made. Sometimes this relates to a confession of sins.[35] Often it is used to express a public confession to God/Christ. In this context it comes close to 'praise' (which is the primary meaning of ἐξομολογεῖσθαι).[36] This is frequently done in a context of outside pressure: confession requires courage and may have negative repercussions,[37] but is rewarded with eternal life. This becomes clear from 1Tim 6:12–14:

---

33 Similarly, in Jn 12:42 the Jewish leaders believe, but are afraid to confess their faith in public.
34 Cf. Michel 1967, pp. 207–12, 215–17; Hofius 1991.
35 Cf. Mt 3:6; Jas 5:16; 1Jn 1:9.
36 The primary meanings of the Hebrew equivalents in the Old Testament are also both 'confession of sins' and 'praise'. The Septuagint translates yāḏāh (hiph., hith.), nāḏar, and šāḇaʿ with ὁμολογεῖν, and neḏāḇāh, neḏer, and tôḏāh with ὁμολογία. For details cf. Michel 1967, pp. 204 f.; Fürst 1975.
37 The negative repercussions are emphasized in Jn 9:22 and 12:42: the confession of Christ leads to expulsion from the synagogue.

Fight the good fight of/for the faith (ἀγωνίζου τὸν καλὸν ἀγῶνα τῆς πίστεως); take hold of the eternal life to which you were called and for which you made the good confession in the presence of many witnesses (καὶ ὡμολόγησας τὴν καλὴν ὁμολογίαν ἐνώπιον πολλῶν μαρτύρων). In the presence of God, who gives life to all things, and of Christ Jesus, who in his testimony before Pontius Pilate made the good confession (τοῦ μαρτυρήσαντος ἐπὶ Ποντίου Πιλάτου τὴν καλὴν ὁμολογίαν), I charge you to keep the commandment without spot or blame until the manifestation of our Lord Jesus Christ [. . .].

Here again 'faith' and 'confession' occur in close proximity. Both are associated with the predicate 'good'. The 'confession' may indeed be largely synonymous with the 'good fight of/for the faith'. It is an action in front of witnesses which may in actual fact be required in court.[38] To be opposed to making this confession is tantamount to denial; it may be caused by the antichrist and will be punished by God.[39]

Nonetheless, we can discern a difference between faith and confession: 'faith' precedes 'confession'. 'Faith' refers to the relation between an individual who believes and a person or proposition that is the object of belief, whereas 'confession' is always associated with the disclosure of a proposition or a fact (which may be that of believing something or other). Moreover, a proposition such as 'Jesus is Lord' or 'I am a Christian' may be 'confessed' without its 'faith' character being disclosed.

In what follows I will look first at the use of the verb ὁμολογεῖν and then at the noun ὁμολογία, going through the writings of the New Testament in roughly chronological order. The content of confession varies over time. In Paul's letters we only find the acclamation of Jesus as 'Lord'.[40] In the Johannine corpus Jesus is confessed as the Christ (the Messiah; Jn 9:22; cf. 12:42), as the Son of God (1Jn 4:15), and as the 'Christ who has come in the flesh' (1Jn 4:2; 2Jn 7[41]). The emphasis on the reality of the incarnation introduces a distinction between those who aver its truth and, therefore, possess the Spirit of God and those who deny the reality of this event. The latter are consequently called 'deceivers' and associated with the antichrist. Hans-Josef Klauck has expressed the view in his magisterial commentary on the Johannine Letters that this confession of Christ's incarnation was an extension of the 'simple' confession of Christ. He thinks that we are 'possibly wit-

---

38 Cf. also Acts 24:14.

39 The opposition confession/denial is found in Mt 10:32–33 par. Lk 12:8–9; 1Jn 2:22–23; 4:2–3. 15 Cf. also Jn 1:20; Tit 1:16.

40 Cf. Rom 10:9 (κύριον Ἰησοῦν); Phil 2:11 (here construed as a proposition with ὅτι and ἐξομολογεῖσθαι – a praise rather than a confession). Cf. also 1Cor 12:3; 2Cor 4:5.

41 Strictly speaking, οἱ μὴ ὁμολογοῦντες Ἰησοῦν Χριστὸν ἐρχόμενον ἐν σαρκί in 2Jn 7 means: 'those who do not confess that Jesus Christ is coming in the flesh'. Cf. Klauck 1992, pp. 53–6 on this problem.

nessing the emergence of a rule of faith', as members of the community or visitors 'were asked to recite the newly formulated confession in the assembly'.[42] Yet there is no evidence that we are dealing with a fixed formula here. The 'confession' referenced here may very well have been a doctrinal proposition but one that may have been expressed in various ways in an ongoing controversy within the Johannine community.

In 1 John the meanings of 'confession' and 'belief' are nearly synonymous, as we can see when we place 1Jn 4:15 and 5:5 side by side:

> God abides in those who confess that Jesus is the Son of God (ὁμολογήσῃ ὅτι Ἰησοῦς ἐστιν ὁ υἱὸς τοῦ θεοῦ), and they abide in God.

> Who is it who overcomes the world but the one who believes that Jesus is the Son of God (ὁ πιστεύων ὅτι Ἰησοῦς ἐστιν ὁ υἱὸς τοῦ θεοῦ)?

Yet in the first case the confession is made in the Christian community (cf. v. 14: 'And we have seen and testify (μαρτυροῦμεν – also a public act) that the Father has sent his Son as the Saviour of the world.'), whereas in the second passage this aspect is irrelevant to the argument.

By way of summary, we may say that whereas for Paul it suffices to 'confess Christ as the Lord' (where ὁμολογεῖν may also be understood as 'praise'), in Johannine literature the confession's theological content is more clearly defined: it contains the avowal that Jesus is the Christ who has come in the flesh and that he is the Son of God. But, again, there is no clear indication that we are dealing with any kind of formula here. In fact, sometimes ὁμολογεῖν simply means 'acknowledgment' or 'affirmation' and is then construed with the accusative case[43] or with ἐν.[44]

In other writings of the New Testament ὁμολογεῖν is also followed by propositional clauses, construed either with accusative and infinitive or with ὅτι. An interesting passage is found in the Book of Acts in Paul's speech of defence before the Governor Felix in Caesarea:

> But this I admit/confess to you (ὁμολογῶ δὲ τοῦτό σοι), that according to the way, which they call a sect (αἵρεσιν), I worship the God of our ancestors, believing everything laid down according to the law or written in the prophets (πιστεύων πᾶσι τοῖς κατὰ τὸν νόμον καὶ τοῖς ἐν τοῖς προφήταις γεγραμμένοις) (Acts 24:14).

---

42 Klauck 1991, p. 234; Similarly, Klauck 1992, p. 53.
43 Cf. 1Jn 2:23 ('[. . .] everyone who confesses (i.e. acknowledges) the Son has the Father also'). In 2:22 the 'acknowledgment' consists in the confession that Jesus is the Christ (Messiah). Furthermore 1Jn 4:3 (where the content of the acknowledgment (Jesus as the Christ in the flesh) is mentioned in the previous verse).
44 Cf. Mt 10:32 par. Lk 12:8 (ἐν ἐμοί: a saying of Jesus from the Q source).

Here it is especially obvious that 'confession' in Greek may easily carry forensic overtones (which is why the NRSVue correctly translates as 'I admit'). The content of Paul's confession in this instance is not a formula or single proposition, but the admission of a religious act (the worship of the Jewish God) and his belief in the teachings of the Hebrew Bible. In Tit 1:16 the author claims that his 'Judaizing' opponents 'confess that they know God, but they deny him by their actions'.

*

Likewise, looking at the noun ὁμολογία, the evidence is fuzzier than previous scholarship sometimes suggests. Paul uses ὁμολογία only once in the sense of 'confession of the gospel of Christ' (τῆς ὁμολογίας ὑμῶν εἰς τὸ εὐαγγέλιον τοῦ Χριστοῦ; 2Cor 9:13) in the context of his collection for the congregation of Jerusalem. In 1Tim 6:13 it is the 'good confession (= admission)' which Christ made before Pontius Pilate. Here ὁμολογία is an action noun, not a formula.

The situation is different in the Epistle to the Hebrews where the noun is used three times in such a way that Otto Michel and Dieter Fürst have suggested in their respective dictionary entries that we are dealing here with 'a fixed ὁμολογία which sums up the beliefs of the community as a living word and which has to be held fast'[45] or with the word having a 'fixed liturgical connotation'.[46] A look at the commentary on Hebrews by Craig R. Koester reveals a similar picture. He writes in relation to Heb 3:1 that a confession such as the one mentioned here 'summarized the basic conviction of a group'. In his view it is 'statements like "Jesus is the Christ" (Acts 5:42; 9:22), "Jesus is Lord" (1 Cor 12:3; 2 Cor 4:5), and "Jesus is the Son of God" (Acts 9:20; Rom 1:3–4)' that are envisaged here, which 'encapsulated the early Christian preaching that brought people to faith (cf. Heb 2:3–4)'.[47] Finally, Erich Gräßer even thinks that this represents the 'baptismal confession/creed (*Taufbekenntnis*)'.[48] If this were the case, then some kind of creed would indeed have existed in the late New Testament period, a claim which is usually denied in modern patristic scholarship on the subject.[49]

Let us take a closer look at the biblical text. Two of the mentions of ὁμολογία in question are closely related to each other (identical words in italics):

Ὅθεν, ἀδελφοὶ ἅγιοι, κλήσεως ἐπουρανίου μέτοχοι, κατανοήσατε τὸν ἀπόστολον καὶ *ἀρχιερέα τῆς ὁμολογίας ἡμῶν Ἰησοῦν*, [. . .].

---

45 Michel 1967, p. 216.
46 Fürst 1975, p. 346.
47 Koester 2001, p. 250.
48 Gräßer 1990, p. 163.
49 Cf. above ch. 2.1.3.

> Therefore, holy brothers, partners in a heavenly calling, consider *Jesus*, the apostle and *high priest* of our *confession*, [. . .] (Heb 3:1).

> Ἔχοντες οὖν ἀρχιερέα μέγαν διεληλυθότα τοὺς οὐρανούς, Ἰησοῦν τὸν υἱὸν τοῦ θεοῦ, κρατῶμεν τῆς ὁμολογίας· [. . .].

> Since, then, we have a great *high priest* who has passed through the heavens, *Jesus*, the Son of God, let us hold fast to the *confession*. (Heb 4:14).

In the first passage, the genitive case τῆς ὁμολογίας ἡμῶν may mean one of two things: either Jesus' as apostle and high priest is the addressee (or object) of 'our confession', or Jesus by virtue of being 'archpriest' somehow leads the act of confession (which is then not addressed to him but to God) in some cultic context (in which case ὁμολογία would be an action noun here). The first explanation appears intrinsically unlikely because it would be difficult to explain why the 'confession' would address Jesus as high priest or why Jesus' office of high priest would in some way be contained in the 'confession' (for which there are no parallels which is why commentators like Koester usually refer to other acclamations). Furthermore, in 4:14 it is suggested that we are 'to hold fast to the confession', *because* we have Jesus as high priest who 'passed through the heavens' and is, therefore, particularly efficient as mediator on our behalf (cf. also 5:1. 3). This strengthens our argument that Jesus' being high priest does not relate to an address or proposition contained in the confession, but rather refers to his cultic activity in the context of the believer pronouncing such confession.

A further difficulty is posed in 4:14 by the expression κρατῶμεν τῆς ὁμολογίας. What precisely does it mean when the readers are told, 'Let us hold fast to the confession'? Does it relate to some form of verbal content (such as a formula) whose veracity we are supposed steadfastly to believe? However, there is no indication that such formula (in the sense of a – more or less detailed – creed) actually existed. It is at least equally likely that we are called upon constantly to *repeat* our confession. In this case, holding fast to the ὁμολογία in 4:14 could be an action noun (in line with 3:1), denoting the (repeated) *act of confessing* which was probably done in a cultic context. In v. 16 the readers are called upon to 'approach the throne of grace with boldness (μετὰ παρρησίας), so that we may receive mercy and find grace to help in time of need'. The use of παρρησία (cf. also 3:6; 10:19. 35) suggests some kind of 'bold' speech act such as an invocation or prayer. This is strengthened by Heb 13:15:

> Δι᾽ αὐτοῦ [οὖν] ἀναφέρωμεν θυσίαν αἰνέσεως διὰ παντὸς τῷ θεῷ, τουτέστιν καρπὸν χειλέων ὁμολογούντων τῷ ὀνόματι αὐτοῦ.

Through him, [then,] let us continually offer a sacrifice of praise to God, that is, the fruit of lips that confess his name.

Here God's name is confessed in a communal speech act which (taking up Jewish sacrificial terminology) is called 'a sacrifice of praise', i.e. some kind of Christ-centred prayer or hymn.[50]

This is confirmed by the third occurrence of ὁμολογία in Hebrews (10:23):

[. . .] κατέχωμεν τὴν ὁμολογίαν τῆς ἐλπίδος ἀκλινῆ, πιστὸς γὰρ ὁ ἐπαγγειλάμενος· [. . .].

Let us hold fast to the confession of our hope without wavering, for he who has promised is faithful.

The context in which ὁμολογία is set here is replete with a clearly cultic vocabulary (cf. esp. the sanctuary mentioned in v. 19 and the purification in v. 22) which suggests a liturgical setting. However, again, nothing is said about the content of the 'confession' nor is a formula of any kind quoted. Κατέχωμεν τὴν ὁμολογίαν τῆς ἐλπίδος ἀκλινῆ is almost synonymous with κρατῶμεν τῆς ὁμολογίας in 4:14. 'Whithout wavering' (ἀκλινῆ) does not mean that the words of the confession must always be the same; rather, we are called upon to stick to the 'confession of faith' without doubting.

All in all, the ὁμολογία mentioned in Hebrews might have been one or several prayers, hymns, acclamations, and doxologies which would also account for its liturgical *Sitz im Leben*. In contrast to the πίστις,[51] there is no indication that such a homology was in any way connected with baptism.

4.1.3 Conclusions

It seems that by the end of the first century a set of core teachings about their faith had developed in Christian communities, although no elaborate creeds existed yet. The stories about Jesus were summarized in brief propositions, as well as in titles and attributes that were ascribed to him:
- Jesus is Lord (Paul)
- Jesus died and rose again (Paul)
- Through his resurrection Jesus anticipated the general resurrection (Paul)
- Jesus is the Son of God (Johannine corpus)
- Jesus is the Christ who has come in the flesh (Johannine corpus)

---

50 On the Old Testament background cf. Gräßer 1997, pp. 389–92.
51 Cf. above pp. 61 f.

Assenting to these propositions was referred to as 'faith' or 'confession', the former relating to an inward trust in and knowledge of the veracity of the salvific divine actions, the latter emphasizing the public admittance or proclamation of such a faith. Compared to later creeds, neither God nor the Holy Spirit are explicitly mentioned as the object of the faith/confession. Likewise, we find no homological statements that could be called trinitarian (although Mt 28:19, albeit not homological as such, is, of course, triadic). We will have to consider the implications of this observation in more detail later.

One might, of course, further analyze the evidence for the use of πιστεύειν and ὁμολογεῖν in the so-called Apostolic Fathers and other writings from later periods. However, we will instead now direct our attention to the objects of faith and confession. We have already discerned short theological propositions whose content is to a certain extent fluctuating. In what follows, we will see that further propositions were added to this core message in a process of crystallization. However, beforehand, we should take a closer look at the *Sitze im Leben* in which this core teaching developed.

4.2 The *Sitze im Leben* of the earliest Christian confessions

In his seminal article on 'The confession of faith in primitive Christianity', Hans von Campenhausen put forward the hypothesis that initially there were no credal formulae at all. He suggested that the requirement of confessing Christ ultimately went back to Christ himself, specifically his saying as recorded in Mt 10:32: 'Everyone, therefore, who will confess me before humans, I also will confess before my Father in the heavens.'[52] Initially the precise content of this confession had not been defined further; yet soon the name of Jesus became associated with certain christological titles, the most important being (a) 'Jesus is the Christ' and (b) 'Jesus is the Son of God'. Whereas the title of 'Christ' placed Jesus in continuity with Jewish eschatological expectation, the title of 'Son of God' took on its proper significance against a Hellenistic-pagan background.[53] The classical example for (a) is Peter's confession in Mk 8:29: 'He asked them, "But who do you say that I am?" Peter answered him, "You are the Christ/Messiah."' In its parallel in Mt 16:16 this confession was extended by the addition of (b). Von Campenhausen rigorously denied that there was a generic link between these early confessional phrases (which were expressed by individuals) and acclamations which used the title of 'Lord' (*kýrios*), as

52 Campenhausen 1972(1979), pp. 220–4. This chapter is partly based on Kinzig 2013(2017), pp. 296–303.
53 Campenhausen 1972(1979), pp. 224–6.

in his view these had their *Sitz im Leben* in communal worship.[54] However, von Campenhausen also disputed that the *Sitz im Leben* of the early Christian confessional phrases was baptism as scholars had hitherto assumed.[55] He went so far as to claim that in actual fact these phrases had no *Sitz im Leben* at all. Instead, they were, 'as it were, everywhere at home'. They formed part of a 'religious jargon' employed in 'sermons, instructions, prayers, controversies, and edifying conversations'.[56] Whereas initially such early confessional phrases had been 'signs of a courageous decision', they gradually morphed into the 'firm spiritual possession of the traditional belief of the community'.[57] The technical use of the term 'confession' in the Letter to the Hebrews is a sign of this gradual solidification.[58]

Initially, Christian communities had been able to settle controversies internally. At the turn of the first to the second century, however, the teaching of docetism which denied the physical reality of Christ's incarnation threatened the very existence of Christianity. This is why the author of 1 John emphasized the humanity of Christ (4:1–3).[59] Thus a 'third, quite polemical confession' was added to the previous two which emphasized 'the reality and the essence' of the person of Jesus. 'From now on the further dogmatic development was geared almost exclusively to such "inner-Christian" oppositions.'[60] At the same time, those espousing traditional beliefs rallied around the confession, which consequently turned into a touchstone of orthodoxy. Those whose views diverged from it were condemned. Examples of this new use can be found in 1 and 2 John, Polycarp of Smyrna, and Ignatius of Antioch.[61] Ignatius was the first to insert historical statements into the confession, statements which served to reinforce the polemical intention that was prompting such innovation. At the same time, he was the last theologian whose confession included Jesus Christ only. In their struggle against gnosticism later theologians composed a dyadic or triadic 'rule of faith', which ultimately developed into the Apostles' Creed as well as the synodal creeds of the fourth century.[62]

Despite some criticism,[63] von Campenhausen's article, supplemented by two further studies on the subject,[64] has influenced views on the origin of the early

---

54 Campenhausen 1972(1979), pp. 236 f. This view is criticized by Ritter 1984, pp. 400 f.
55 Campenhausen 1972(1979), pp. 237–43.
56 Campenhausen 1972(1979), p. 244.
57 Campenhausen 1972(1979), p. 245.
58 Campenhausen 1972(1979), pp. 245–7.
59 Campenhausen 1972(1979), pp. 250–3.
60 Campenhausen 1972(1979), p. 253.
61 Campenhausen 1972(1979), pp. 253–70.
62 Campenhausen 1972(1979), pp. 270–2.
63 Cf. above n. 54.
64 Campenhausen 1975(1979); Campenhausen 1976(1979).

Christian confessions to a considerable degree, in particular in patristic research.[65] However, in hindsight its almost evolutionary view of the credal development in the New Testament period is too neat to be quite true, although it does contain important insights into the nature of Christian confession. For example, it is difficult to imagine that the confession to Christ which made someone a Christian did not have a distinctive shape from the very beginning. (You had to know what conversion to Christ actually entailed, even if the lived experience of that act may have gone beyond what might have been possible to express in words.) In addition, von Campenhausen's reluctance to accord the confession a distinct *Sitz im Leben* does not take the difference between text and meaning sufficiently into account. One and the same text (a 'confession') may take on different meanings depending on its use in different situations, i.e. *Sitze im Leben*. If it is true that early Christian homologies were used in various circumstances (and I think it is), then we must ask what they could have meant in each of these contexts. Finally, other texts such as Jn 1 and Col 1:15–20 played a vital role in the formulation of creeds, which von Campenhausen omitted to consider in any detail.

It also appears to me that von Campenhausen slightly downplayed the significance of the confession of Christ as an act. Although it may be true that the 'primordial word (*Urwort*)' of Jesus as recorded in Mt 10:32 had left the question as to 'how such a confession could be given in a concrete situation' completely unanswered,[66] this answer would have been obvious to his early followers. The simple confession *Christianus sum*, 'I am a Christian', distinguished those Jews and Gentiles who were followers of Jesus from those who were not. This distinction took on a critical significance in terms of (a) *worship*, (b) *mission and conversion*, (c) *paraenesis and praise*, and (d) *martyrdom*.[67]

4.2.1 Worship

Since the claim that Jesus was the saviour of humankind was a *religious* one, it influenced *worship*. Affirmation of his claim had to be expressed in a cultic context, and this was no longer possible within the traditional framework. Unfortunately, we know next to nothing about early Christian worship before the second

---

65 Cf., e.g., Ritter 1984, pp. 400 f.; Staats 1999, pp. 123, 145, 149 f. In New Testament studies James Dunn's views now appear to be more influential. Cf. Dunn 2006, ch. III; John Reumann, in Bochinger et al. 1998, cols. 1248 f.

66 Campenhausen 1972(1979), pp. 223 f.

67 For what follows cf. also Staats 1999, pp. 121–42 whose observations are similar to mine, but whose conclusions differ. In addition, Cullmann 1949, pp. 18–34; Böttrich 2014, pp. 71–81.

half of the second century.[68] The most significant piece of information relevant to the present discussion stems from a famous letter the governor of Bithynia-Pontus Pliny the Younger sent to the Emperor Trajan in 111/112. In it Pliny mentions the fact that Christians came together at a fixed day before dawn in order 'to say a *carmen* responsively to Christ as to a god' (*carmenque Christo quasi deo dicere secum inuicem*).[69] *Carmen* may refer to some kind of poem like a pagan hymn in praise of gods, a cultic acclamation, or a doxology which may have been recited or chanted.[70] It does not mean that Christ was actually *called* a god – he may have been called 'Lord' (just as in Acts 4:24b–30 God is addressed as 'Lord'). Be that as it may, the worshippers felt that they belonged to Christ (whereas others, some of them close relatives, did not), and this feeling must have been verbalized in these religious gatherings by 'confessing Christ' in some way.[71] Presumably on such occasions, stories about Jesus and his followers were also told. Letters of missionaries such as Paul were read out, also helping to inculcate some basic theological tenets such as the meaning of Jesus' passion and resurrection and the nature of the Church. Concomitantly, there appear to have been attempts to exclude Christians from traditional Jewish worship, although, again, details are unknown. The condemnation of the 'heretics' in the Eighteen Benedictions (*birkat ha-minim*) will also have affected them, although probably not specifically directed against Jewish Christians.[72]

At the same time, the withdrawal of Gentile Christians from public cults did not go unnoticed. One example is the revolt of the silversmiths at Ephesus (Acts 19:21–40) where such withdrawal even had economic repercussions. The old anti-Jewish slander of misanthropy (*odium generis humani*)[73] was now levelled at the Christians, because they did not 'fit in'. In the framework of ancient Mediterranean society such 'fitting in' always implied participation in some kind of shared cultic activity.

---

68 Cf., in general, Salzmann 1994; Löhr 2003, pp. 404–35; Fürst 2008, esp. pp. 24–37; Alikin 2010; McGowan 2014.

69 Pliny, *Epistula 10,96*. For the background of this letter cf. Kinzig, *Christian Persecution*, 2021, pp. 45–9.

70 On such pagan hymns cf. Berger 1984, pp. 1149–69; Lattke 1991; Thraede 1994; Berger 2005, pp. 297–9; as regards acclamations and doxologies cf. Stuiber 1959, esp. cols. 212–15; Berger 1984, pp. 1372–5; Berger 2005, pp. 290–7; Hermut Löhr in Körting et al. 2013, cols. 1136–9.

71 Cf. Salzmann 1994, esp. pp. 196 f.

72 Cf. Kinzig, 'Nazoraeans', 2007.

73 Cf. Tacitus, *Annals* 15,44,4.

4.2.2 Mission and conversion

Unlike the Jews, who also advocated monotheism, but very much kept to themselves, the Christians were a *missionary religion* whose adherents went out into the streets to convert people to their god. In doing so, they had to explain what Christianity stood for as opposed to traditional pagan cults, and also to traditional Judaism. The *locus classicus* for Christian mission in the New Testament is, of course, Paul's speech at the Areopagus (Acts 17:16–34). For our purposes, it does not matter whether it is in fact historical or not (I do not think it is), but the scene at Athens must have carried some kind of plausibility for readers of the Book of Acts. Paul, we are told, 'argued in the synagogue with the Jews and the devout persons and also in the marketplace every day with those who happened to be there' (17:17). When he finally addressed the Epicurean and Stoic philosophers, he spoke about God as creator and as fixing a day 'on which he will have the world judged in righteousness by a man whom he has appointed' (17:31), as well as about the resurrection of the dead, themes that were to belong to the standard repertoire of early Christian creeds.

Further instruction was offered to anyone who expressed an interest in the new religion. Unfortunately, we know nothing about early Christian *catechesis*.[74] The evidence from Acts 8:12–13, 16:31–33, and 18:8 suggests that converts were probably told about Jesus, his birth, life, death, and resurrection, in catechesis just as in worship (sometimes the two *Sitze im Leben* may have been identical).[75] At some point, they will have been asked whether or not they wanted to join to the Christian community.

From the very beginning, this act of actual initiation was baptism. It would, therefore, be completely natural for baptizands to be asked whether they agreed to some of the confessional statements they had heard about in catechesis. Although we have no evidence from the first century, credal interrogations prior to baptism or during the rite of baptism itself were in all likelihood introduced early on, and we will look at them in some more detail below.[76] The baptism of the wealthy Ethiopian in Acts 8:26–40 is certainly a fictitious account. However, the secondary addition of a baptismal question that implicitly asked whether the baptizand believed in Christ as the Son of God (8:37: 'And Philip said, "If you believe with all your heart, you may." And he replied, "I believe that Jesus Christ is the

---

74 One example may be contained in chs. 1–6 of the *Didache* (early second century). Cf. Kinzig/ Wallraff 2002, esp. p. 336 and n. 12 (literature). In addition, cf. Pasquato/Brakmann 2004, esp. cols. 425–32; Metzger/Drews/Brakmann 2004, esp. cols. 506–18.
75 Cf. Salzmann 1994, p. 463.
76 Cf. below ch. 4.5.

Son of God."') reflects a reality that could be found early on. There is some evidence to suggest that these baptismal interrogations were triadic in form in some places (such as Rome).[77]

At the same time, the use of a triadic baptismal formula as well, such as that preserved in Mt 28:19 and elsewhere, seems to have been very widespread by the late first century.[78] Indeed, this formula may also have been interrogatory. It may not only have included faith in the Father, the Son, and the Holy Spirit, but may have been expanded to incorporate further statements on the Trinity, the Church, and other matters. However, one should not expect a high degree of conformity in this respect. There are indications that various forms of interrogation were being used even in a single city. Again, we will consider this in more detail below.[79]

4.2.3 Paraenesis and praise

Christians who had been baptized were expected to attend the new religion's regular gatherings where they were taught further details about their 'faith'. These instructions may not have formed part of worship, or the boundaries between 'classroom lessons' by the bishop or presbyters and cultic activities, such as liturgical chants or prayers, may have been blurred. Unfortunately, no such doctrinal instructions have come down to us from the first three centuries. (The oldest preserved homily, 2 Clement, which may have been written around 150, is ethical in character.) They were later called 'mystagogies' (that is, explanations of the mysteries of Christian religion).[80]

Nonetheless, the New Testament contains some evidence. Passages such as Rom 10:9–10 and Mt 10:32–33 par. Lk 12:8–9 suggest that exhortations firmly to hold on to one's confession even under strong outside pressure were common. 'Confessing' in this sense was not identical with warding off erroneous doctrines or false teachings about Christ.[81] Rather, 'confession' in this context was required precisely when one was ordered to deny Christ altogether. Such a denial was not a slight failure that might easily be overlooked, rather it entailed being excluded from salvation. At the same time paraenesis involving 'confession' did have more than an

---

77 Cf. below ch. 4.5.1.

78 It is mentioned in *Didache* 7,1. 3 and in Justin Martyr, *Apologia prima* 61,3 (FaFo § 104a8). Cf. also Campenhausen 1971(1979); Kinzig 1999(2017), p. 252.

79 Cf. below ch. 4.5.1.

80 Cf. below ch. 13.

81 The New Testament passages dealing with doctrinal deception (e.g. Mt 24:4. 10; 2Thess 2:2–3; 1Tim 4:1–5; Rev 13) do not use the language of 'confession'.

exhortatory function, also serving as a consolation: holding on to Christ meant that Christ would intercede for the believer in the hereafter (Mt 10:32–33 par. Lk 12:8–9).

Finally, homilies summarizing credal content could also be written in a panegyrical style, thus also taking on a homological character. A homily by Melito of Sardes (160/170?) may give us an idea of what this looked like, even if it is no mystagogy, but a praise of Easter:

> This is the one who made the heaven and the earth,
> and who fashioned man in the beginning,
> who was proclaimed through the Law and Prophets,
> who became flesh in the Virgin,
> who was hung upon a tree,
> who was buried in the earth,
> who was resurrected from the dead,
> and who ascended into the heights of the heavens,
> who sits at the right hand of the Father,
> who has authority to save everything,
> through whom the Father created everything from the beginning to the end of the ages.[82]

4.2.4 Martyrdom

Belonging to the Christian community was no walk in the park. Christians tended to be marginalized. They were subject to harassment in everyday life. Believers were even threatened with persecution and martyrdom, depending on the circumstances. A number of New Testament writings describe situations in which Christians appear to have lived under constant threat of molestation and denunciation.[83] In this context Jesus is quoted as saying,

> And I tell you, everyone who confesses me (ὁμολογήσῃ ἐν ἐμοί) before humans, the Son of Man also will confess before the angels of God; but whoever denies me (ὁ δὲ ἀρνησάμενός με) before humans will be denied before the angels of God (Lk 12:8–9; cf. Mt 10:32–33).

Alas, the historical situation into which these words were spoken is not described in any detail, nor does the passage tell us what this 'confession' entails.

However, we find a discussion about its correct interpretation in a fragment taken from the writings of Heracleon, a follower of the gnostic theologian Valentinus around the middle of the second century. Heracleon comments on Lk 12:8–9 as follows:

---

82 Melito of Sardes, *De pascha* 104 (FaFo § 107).
83 Cf. Mk 8:34–38 parr.; Mt 10:16–33; Lk 12:1–12; 2Tim 2:8–13; Rev 3:5.

The confession (ὁμολογία) is on the one hand that made in faith and conduct (ἐν πίστει καὶ πολιτείᾳ), on the other hand that made with the mouth. Therefore, confession with the mouth takes place also before the authorities (ἐπὶ τῶν ἐξουσίων), and this the multitudes incorrectly consider to be the only confession (μόνην ὁμολογίαν), for even the hypocrites can make this confession. But it will be found that this word was not spoken in general terms. For not all who are saved made the confession by mouth before departing, among whom are Matthew, Philip, Thomas, Levi, and many others. The confession by mouth is not comprehensive, but only partial (καὶ ἔστιν ἡ διὰ τῆς φωνῆς ὁμολογία οὐ καθολικὴ, ἀλλὰ μερική). What is comprehensive (and that is here meant by him [sc. Luke/Jesus]) is the confession in works and actions which correspond to faith in him (ἐν ἔργοις καὶ πράξεσι καταλλήλοις τῆς εἰς αὐτὸν πίστεως). And this confession is followed by the partial one before the authorities (ἐπὶ τῶν ἐξουσίων) if it is necessary and reason requires it. That person will make the confession by mouth who has previously confessed rightly in disposition (ὁμολογήσει γὰρ οὗτος καὶ τῇ φωνῇ, ὀρθῶς προομολογήσας πρότερον τῇ διαθέσει).

And of those who confess, he rightly said 'in me' (ἐν ἐμοί). But in the case of those who deny he added a 'me' (τὸ ἐμέ). For even if they confess him with the mouth, they deny him since they do not confess him in action (τῇ πράξει). Only those who live in conduct and action according to him confess 'in him' (μόνοι δ' ἐν αὐτῷ ὁμολογοῦσιν οἱ ἐν τῇ κατ' αὐτὸν πολιτείᾳ καὶ πράξει βιοῦντες). In their case he confesses himself, since he has grasped them, and is held by them. As a result they can never deny him. For those who are not in him deny him. For he did not say 'whoever denies in me', but 'me'. For no one who was ever in him denies him.

'Before humans' [means] both before those who are saved and before the Gentiles, before the former also by conduct, and before the latter also by the mouth (παρ' οἷς μὲν καὶ τῇ πολιτείᾳ, παρ' οἷς δὲ καὶ τῇ φωνῇ).[84]

This fragment suggests an ongoing discussion whether a true confession guaranteeing salvation might only be possible in the context of a trial or suffering for one's faith, including voluntary martyrdom. Against such a suggestion, Heracleon points out that a number of apostles were not martyred (and yet were no doubt saved), instead arguing for a more comprehensive understanding of 'confession' also encompassing an irreproachable Christian conduct. It is possible that a Christian confession in court may *not* lead to salvation if it is not accompanied by corresponding behaviour. Incidentally, Heracleon makes no mention of 'confession' at baptism or in worship.

The *Shepherd of Hermas* (s. II/1) presents a more radical argument. In his view, only a confession made at a trial that is made entirely of one's own free will is impeccable whereas a confession made under duress or after some hesitation is 'less beautiful':

---

84 Heracleon, frg. 50 (Brooke) = Clement of Alexandria, *Stromata* 4,9,71–72 (tr. URL <http://www.earlychristianwritings.com/text/heracleon.html> (Peter Kirby; 06/11/2023; altered)).

> All, he says, who were arraigned before the authority (ἐπ' ἐξουσίαν) and who did not deny during interrogation, but willingly (προθύμως) accepted suffering, are more glorious (ἐνδοξ-ότεροί) in the eyes of the Lord – their fruit is superior. But all who were cowards, and began to have doubts, and considered in their hearts whether they should deny or confess (ὁμολογήσουσι) and suffered [in the end] – their fruit is less [beautiful], because this suggestion [i.e. to deny] rose up in their hearts; for the mere suggestion that a slave might deny his own master is wicked.[85]

Christians were, therefore, expected to confess Christ willingly, even if this would lead to harsh reactions by both fellow-Jews and the Roman authorities. Harassment by Jews who did not confess Christ as their messiah is, for example, reflected in Jn 12:42–46:

> Nevertheless many, even of the authorities (ἐκ τῶν ἀρχόντων), believed in him. But because of the Pharisees they did not confess it (οὐχ ὡμολόγουν), for fear that they would be put out of the synagogue, for they loved human glory more than the glory that comes from God (ἠγάπησαν γὰρ τὴν δόξαν τῶν ἀνθρώπων μᾶλλον ἤπερ τὴν δόξαν τοῦ θεοῦ). Then Jesus cried aloud, 'Whoever believes in me believes not in me but in him who sent me. And whoever sees me sees him who sent me. I have come as light into the world, so that everyone who believes in me should not remain in the darkness.'[86]

The sequence 'arraignment before the authorities – confession – glory from/before God' is similar in both these examples. Yet in John it is specifically the *Pharisees* who are depicted as the opponents of early Christians because Christianity was making inroads into the Jewish elite, whereas in the *Shepherd* it is the *Roman* authorities. However, in the view of the author of the Gospel of John these new (and apparently influential) converts did not confess their faith openly because they feared social and religious repercussions. In our context it is unimportant whether or not the author is correct in this assumption – the tensions that arose within Judaism about the success of the Christian mission were real.[87]

Any denunciations to the Roman authorities could quickly turn into a life-threatening situation for those being reported. 'Confessing Christ' then often meant confessing him *in court*, that is being forced to account for one's beliefs. 1Tim 6:12–14 which I discussed above[88] may belong in such a context. However, the oldest testimony of a Christian specifically confessing his religion in court occurs in the *Acta Iustini*, documenting the trial of the Christian philosopher Justin and seven companions held by the *praefectus urbi* Quintus Iunius Rusticus in

---

85 *Pastor Hermae* 105 (= *Similitudo* IX,28),4. Cf. Michel 1967, p. 217.
86 Cf. also Jn 9:22.
87 Cf. Kinzig, *Christian Persecution*, 2021, pp. 9–19.
88 Cf. above pp. 64 f.

Rome around the year 165.[89] Rusticus first questioned Justin about the content of his teachings, whereupon the latter made a confession-like statement that is remarkable in many respects:

> [This is] what we piously hold regarding the God of the Christians: we consider him to be their only Demiurge of the creation of the whole world from the beginning, and [we also consider] Jesus Christ to be the servant [*or:* child] of God (θεοῦ παῖδα); he was also foretold by the prophets as the one who was to stand by humankind as a herald of salvation and a teacher of good doctrines.[90]

Justin then went on to emphasize the importance of Christ (now referring to him as the Son of God (υἱὸν θεοῦ)). Rusticus concluded the interrogation by saying, 'Are you a Christian?' (οὐκοῦν Χριστιανὸς εἶ;) to which Justin clearly answered positively, 'Yes, I am a Christian.' (Ναί, Χριστιανός εἰμι.).[91] This confession of Christ was then repeated in unison by Justin's companions.

The quoted text is noteworthy not only because the awkward formulations are reminiscent of Justin's authentic writings, but also because it is obviously based on a very ancient Christology.[92] It suggests that Christians were questioned in court about the content of their teachings so as to ascertain if the defendants were members of a known cult, and thus to determine whether they had committed a crime. According to the famous rescript by the Emperor Trajan of 111/112, the steadfast affirmation to be a Christian was sufficient grounds for execution – there was no need for any other evidence.[93]

Therefore, Christian confession in the pre-Constantinian Church often sprang from the *status confessionis*, an existential situation in which an unequivocal confession of Christ was called for in order not to betray one's religious identity and thus to commit apostasy.[94] Under interrogation the simple confession *Christianus sum* could and did result in execution. The sheer number of references in which the simple confession of being a Christian in front of the Roman magistrate decided one's fate is startling, even if we acknowledge that not all texts are as old as they claim to be.[95] These statements were then also extended to include confes-

---

89 Cf. Kinzig, *Christian Persecution*, 2021, pp. 54 f.

90 *Acta Iustini et septem sodalium* 2,5 (recension A; FaFo § 105a).

91 *Acta Iustini et septem sodalium* 3,4 (FaFo § 105a).

92 It falls back on the servant songs of Deutero-Isaiah (Is 42:1–4; 49:1–6; 50:4–9; 52:13–53:12).

93 Cf. Pliny, *Epistula 10,97* and Kinzig, *Christian Persecution*, 2021, pp. 48–9.

94 Cf. Ritter 1984, p. 400; Reinhart Staats in Bochinger et al. 1998, cols. 1249 f.; Staats 1999, pp. 123 f. On apostasy cf. Hornung 2016.

95 Cf. *Martyrdom of Polycarp* 10,1; 12,1; *Martyrdom of Ptolemaeus and Lucius* 11–13. 16–18; *Martyrdom of Carpus, Papylus, and Agathonice* 3; 5; 23; 34; *Acts of Justin* recension A and B 3,4–4,9 (cf. recension C 3,5; a whole series of confessions during interrogation by the prefect); recension B 5,7; *Letter of*

sions to God as the Creator and/or King of Heaven,[96] to Christ as the Saviour,[97] or to the Holy Trinity.[98] They also could become the starting point for long apologetic speeches, which were presumably inserted secondarily.

The sources cited above clearly demonstrate that one of the *Sitze im Leben* of Christian confession was that of the persecution the pre-Constantinian Church experienced. The simple confession of Christ later became a hallmark of the Christian martyr and was mentioned in a number of panegyrical homilies on the feasts of martyrs.[99]

4.3 The development of homological building blocks

Confessions in the form of homologies and brief summaries of the Christian faith could be and were used in very different circumstances, as we saw in the previous section.[100] As a result, they varied enormously, which is why they are so difficult to grasp. Some time ago, Markus Vinzent described the development of synodal creeds in the fourth century introducing a 'building-block model' to

---

the Churches of Lyons and Vienne in Eusebius, Historia ecclesiastica 5,1,20; Acts of the Scillitan Martyrs 10; 13; Martyrdom of Apollonius 1–2; Martyrdom of Perpetua and Felicitas 3,2; 6,4; Martyrdom of Pionius 8,2; 15,7; 16,2; 18,6; 20,7; Martyrdom of Fructuosus and Companions 2,3; Martyrdom of Dasius 6,1; 7,2; 8,2; 10,2; Martyrdom of Agape, Irene, and Chione 3,2; Martyrdom of Ignatius (Martyrium Romanum) 8,4; cf. also 1Pet 4:16; Acts of John 4, ll. 2–3 (CChr.SA 2, p. 867); Pliny, Epistulae 10,96, 3; 10,97, 1; Justin Martyr, Apologia prima 11,1; id., Apologia secunda 2,10–11; id., Dialogus cum Tryphone 35,2; 96,2; Tertullian, Ad nationes, e.g., 1,2,1; 1,3,2; id., Apologeticum, e.g., 1,4; 2–3; 49,5; id., De corona 1; Cyprian, Ad Demetrianum 13; Collectio Eusebiana, Homilia 56, 4–5; (Pseudo-)John of Damascus, Martyrdom of Artemius 24 (PG 96, col. 1273B). In addition cf. Ritter 1984, p. 400; Reinhart Staats in Bochinger et al. 1998, cols. 1249 f.; Staats 1999, pp. 123 f.; Bremmer 2017, pp. 3–12 (a list similar to that above is given on p. 9 n. 30); Bremmer 2020; and FaFo § 105.

96 Cf., e.g., Martyrdom of Apollonius 1–2; Martyrdom of Fructuosus and Companions 2,3–4; Martyrdom of Pionius 8,2–3; 16,2–4; Acts of Cyprian 1,2; Martyrdom of Dasius 7,2; Acts of Euplus B 2,5–6; Martyrdom of Ignatius (Martyrium Romanum) 8,4. Cf. Martyrdom of Crispina 1,4. 6–7; Latin Martyrdom of Phileas 3,4.

97 Cf., e.g., Martyrdom of Carpus, Papylus, and Agathonice 5; Martyrdom of Pionius 16,2–4; Acts of Euplus B 2,5–6.

98 Cf., e.g., Martyrdom of Dasius 8,2; Acts of Euplus B 2,5–6; Acts of Donatus, Venustus, and Hermogenes (BHL 2309) 2.

99 Cf., e.g., Basil of Caesarea, In sanctos quadraginta martyres 3 (PG 31, col. 512B); 4 (512C); 7 (520C); Ephraem Syrus, Sermo de martyrio sancti Bonifatii (Phrantzolas 1998, p. 192, l. 10); John Chrysostom, Homilia in sanctum martyrem Lucianum 3 (PG 50, cols. 524 f.).

100 On the terms 'homology' and 'christological summary' cf. above ch. 1.3.

which I will return below.[101] *Mutatis mutandis*, this model may also be applied to the first three centuries. We find brief theological propositions relating to the Trinity (which may or may not have been traditional at the time of their first appearance in written form) from the earliest times onwards. Similar to toy bricks, these were later assembled in various combinations into larger theological 'constructions' such as the *regulae fidei* (cf. below chapter 4.4), ultimately forming the basis of the fixed creeds of the fourth century. Confession to Christ within the aforementioned *Sitze im Leben* produced a whole range of such 'building blocks' (homologies and summaries of the Christian faith) whose content was later mostly transposed into the 'rules of faith' and creeds. Many of them are found in chapters 3 and 6 of *Faith in Formulae*. It should suffice here to highlight a few notable examples.

4.3.1 Homologies and christological summaries in the New Testament

Christians shared traditional Jewish views about God regarding his omnipotence and eternal being, his oneness, immortality, and invisibility.[102] These propositions occur most frequently in the Gospel of John and in Revelation. In John they form part of an elaborate reflection on the relationship between God and humankind and between God and his Word.[103] In the Book of Revelation God is addressed as 'almighty' (παντοκράτωρ) in a hymnic context which may reflect liturgical tradition.[104] A similar doxological statement is also found in 1Tim 1:17: 'To the King of the ages, immortal, invisible, the only God, be honour and glory forever and ever. Amen.'

God was, of course, also considered to be the creator of the world. The prologue to the Gospel of John clearly expresses this idea (Jn 1:1–3), alluding to the account of Genesis.

Problems arose when the early Christians attempted to fit Jesus' life and work into this conceptual framework. From the beginning his status was seen by most Christians as divine or, at least, closely related to the almighty creator God, for reasons which we can no longer clearly discern. However, this would, in the long term, raise the question as to what precisely this relation was.

In the view of the Apostle Paul all that mattered in this respect was to confess Christ as the Lord and to believe that God had raised him from the dead (Rom

---

101 Cf. below p. 213. On the building-block model (*Baukastenmodell*), cf. Vinzent 1999, pp. 235–40; Kinzig/Vinzent 1999, pp. 555 f.

102 Cf. the references collected in FaFo, ch. 1.2.1.–1.2.2.

103 Cf., e.g., Jn 1:18; 17:3.

104 Cf. Rev 1:8; 4:8b; 11:17; 15:3b; 16:7b; 19:6b etc.

10:9–10).[105] He did not yet expect Christians to state publicly that Christ had been resurrected[106] – it sufficed to believe it in one's 'heart'. Such confession was in itself the work of the Holy Spirit (1Cor 12:3b). In 1Cor 15:3–4 Paul enumerates the core of his teaching in a little more detail than in Rom 10:9–10: he taught the Corinthians 'that Christ died for our sins in accordance with the Scriptures, that he was buried, and that he was raised on the third day in accordance with the Scriptures'.

Paul appears to once call Christ 'God over all' (Rom 9:5), but this passage is difficult to interpret. Otherwise he carefully distinguishes between God and the 'Lord' Jesus Christ (Rom 16:27; 1Cor 8:6). God is 'Father' and creator 'from whom are all things and for whom we exist', whereas Christ is a participator in creation. He is seen as the 'one Lord' 'through whom are all things and through whom we exist' (1Cor 8:6).

In other passages Paul describes the incarnation in greater detail, thus providing additional material that creeds could and did build upon. Interestingly, the otherwise highly influential pericope Phil 2:5–11 was rarely used in credal discourse and left no trace in the classic creeds, probably because the idea that Christ had descended to take 'the form of a slave' raised all sorts of theological difficulties which made the text unsuitable to be used in credal formulae aiming at the widest possible consensus.[107] Other Pauline utterances created fewer problems. In Gal 4:4 Christ is described as God's Son, sent by the Father and born from a woman under the Law. Paul also repeatedly mentions the resurrection from the dead as a central Christian tenet.[108] In Rom 8:34 he adds Christ's sitting 'at the right hand of God'. Paul does not mention Christ's return, but in 2Cor 5:10 he does refer to the Final Judgement 'so that each may receive recompense for what has been done in the body, whether good or evil' (a passage which was later often quoted in credal texts[109]).

Repeatedly, Paul adds the Spirit and thus creates a loose series of God – Lord (Jesus Christ) – (Holy) Spirit in varying order. In these passages certain attributes and activities are associated with each respective person of the Trinity:
- 1Cor 12:4–6: varieties of gifts (that different people have) – the same Spirit; varieties of services – the same Lord; varieties of activities – the same God;
- 2Cor 13:13: grace – Lord Jesus Christ; love – God; communion – Holy Spirit.

---

105 'Faith' and the resurrection are also associated in Rom 4:24.

106 The Gospel of John makes a similar distinction: Many people in authority 'believe' in Jesus, but do not 'confess' him for fear of being put out of the synagogue (Jn 12:42).

107 Cf. Kinzig, "'Obedient unto death'", 2024 (*sub prelo*).

108 Cf. Rom 1:4; 4:24; 6:5; 8:34; 10:9; 1Cor 15:4. 12–13. 21; Phil 3:10–11.

109 On the earliest history of the proposition that Christ will come again as judge cf. Löhr 2018.

A very ornate trinitarian passage occurs in the prescript to the Letter to the Romans (1:1–4):

> Paul, a servant of Christ Jesus, called to be an apostle, set apart for the gospel of God, which he promised beforehand through his prophets in the holy Scriptures, [the gospel] concerning his Son, who was descended from David according to the flesh and was declared to be Son of God with power according to the spirit of holiness by resurrection from the dead, Jesus Christ our Lord [. . .].

Here the divine Trinity is closely interwoven with the process of the incarnation and the resurrection.

Finally, dyadic homologies might also form part of doxologies such as the one concluding the Epistle to the Romans (16:27):

> [. . .] to the only wise God, through Jesus Christ (μόνῳ σοφῷ θεῷ διὰ Ἰησοῦ Χριστοῦ), to whom be the glory forever! Amen.

However, there is manuscript evidence that this conclusion is secondary.[110]

*

The Deutero-Pauline letters contain a series of dyadic summaries, some of them quite brief (such as 1Tim 2:5–6; 6:13), others extended with additional propositions. The most important such text is Col 1:15–20:

> [15] He [*sc. the Son*] is the image of the invisible God, the first-born of all creation (εἰκὼν τοῦ θεοῦ τοῦ ἀοράτου, πρωτότοκος πάσης κτίσεως); [16] for in him all things in the heavens and on earth were created, things visible and invisible (τὰ πάντα ἐν τοῖς οὐρανοῖς καὶ ἐπὶ τῆς γῆς, τὰ ὁρατὰ καὶ τὰ ἀόρατα), whether thrones or dominions or rulers or powers – all things have been created through him and for him. [17] He himself is before all things, and in him all things hold together. [18] He is the head of the body, the Church; he is the beginning, the first-born from the dead (πρωτότοκος ἐκ τῶν νεκρῶν), so that he might come to have first place in everything. [19] For in him all the fullness of God was pleased to dwell, [20] and through him [God] was pleased to reconcile to himself all things, whether on earth or in the heavens, by making peace through the blood of his cross.

The description of the Son as God's 'image' and as 'first-born of all creation' in v. 15 was to play a central role in the trinitarian controversies of the fourth century. Likewise, the description of the universe in v. 16 was later often quoted in one form or other (e.g., in the Creed of Jerusalem[111]). Finally, v. 17 provided a biblical testimony for the idea of Christ's pre-existence. Here the summary is extended to include the Church, the (general) resurrection, and the salvation of the

---

110 Cf., e.g., Dunn 1988, pp. 912–13; Wolter 2019, pp. 503–11.
111 Cf. below p. 206.

entire creation 'through the blood of his cross' – which as such were not included in the creeds, not least, because they might have suggested a universal restoration which later became highly controversial. Clearly, this elaborate summary is a product of the author of Colossians (who in turn was copied in Eph 1:20–23).

In addition, the Deutero-Pauline corpus also contains christological summaries, again varying from brief mentions of Christ as risen from the dead (2Tim 2:8) to detailed catalogues. 1Tim 3:16 is one such longer text which mentions incarnation and ascension while omitting the passion and resurrection:

> Without any doubt, the mystery of our godliness is great:
> He was revealed in flesh,
> vindicated in spirit,
> seen by angels,
> proclaimed among Gentiles,
> believed in throughout the world,
> taken up in glory.

In 2Tim 4:1–2 the author refers to God and Christ Jesus 'who is to judge the living and the dead' as his witnesses when urging readers to proclaim the Christian message. He also mentions Christ's epiphany and his kingdom, in passing.

As in 1Cor 12:4–6 and 2Cor 13:13 specific attributes and activities are ascribed to the Trinity in Ephesians, too:

– Eph 3:14–17: glory – Father; power – Spirit; dwelling in hearts through faith – Christ;
– Eph 4:4–6: one body – one Spirit; one Lord – one faith – one baptism; one God and Father of all.

Only in the last instance do we find an association with baptism, yet not in such a way that the triadic formula as such were connected to baptism. Instead, baptism is associated with the oneness of faith and of Christ.

∗

When we turn to the synoptic gospels the most important christological formula is Peter's confession in Mk 8:29: 'You are the Christ [= Messiah]'. Both Matthew and Luke seem to have this brief homology considered insufficient, because they both extended it:

> Lk 9:20: The Christ [= Messiah] of God.
> Mt 16:16: You are the Christ [= Messiah], the Son of the living God.

In both these gospels Jesus' messiahship and his divine origin are emphasized, albeit in different ways. Matthew goes further than Luke in that process, establishing an, as it were, ontological relationship with God. The Book of Acts instead describes this relationship as a form of appointment by which God 'made (ἐποίη-σεν)' the crucified Jesus 'both Lord and Christ [= Messiah]' (Acts 2:36)[112] and calls upon Cornelius and his circle 'to preach to the people and to testify that he is the one ordained (ὡρισμένος) by God as judge of the living and the dead' (Acts 10:42). However, in none of the gospels is there any evidence to suggest that the homology 'You are the Christ' is more than Peter's individual confession.

The key text in the Johannine writings is the prologue to the Gospel of John which describes at some length not only the relationship between God and his Word but also the process of the incarnation (Jn 1:1–18). As we will see below this was no doubt one of the most influential texts with regards to the formulation of the first two articles of the creeds.[113] In particular, verses 1–5 and 14 were later quoted or alluded to over and over again:

> [1] In the beginning was the Word, and the Word was with God, and the Word was God. [2] He was in the beginning with God. [3] All things came into being through him (πάντα δι' αὐτοῦ ἐγένετο), and without him not one thing came into being. [4] In him was life, and the life was the light (τὸ φῶς) of all people. [5] And the light shines in the darkness, and the darkness did not overtake it.
> [14] And the Word became flesh (σὰρξ ἐγένετο) and dwelt among us, and we have seen his glory, the glory as of a father's only-born [son] (μονογενοῦς), full of grace and truth.

In this context it was not the Johannine logos theology which became influential (the Word is not mentioned in T, N, or C²), but (a) the divine origin of the Word/Son as the 'only-born' (cf. also 1:18; 3:16. 18; 1Jn 4:9), (b) its/his participation in the creation, (c) the Word's description as 'light', (d) the idea that the Word 'became flesh', and (e) the entire dynamic of the Word's/Son's descent as the origin and beginning of the incarnation.

This prologue in itself is, however, not a confession in the strict sense: it does not represent a public disclosure of Christian belief by an individual. It is not a 'faith text' either: readers are not asked to 'believe' in it. Rather, it is an elaborate narration – which shows that the transitions between genres are fluent because the confessions or credal texts were always based on narrations of 'historical' events.[114] By contrast, in Jn 6:69 the author of that gospel mentions a brief homology which he puts into the mouth of Simon Peter: 'We have come to believe and

---

112 Yet elsewhere he also calls him 'Son of God' (cf. Lk 22:70). Cf. also the secondary addition Acts 8:37.

113 Cf. below ch. 6.4.4. and p. 621.

114 This is even true in the case of the confession in court 'I am a Christian' (cf. above p. 79) because it presupposes the Christ story.

know that you are the Holy One of God.' This strongly resembles Mk 8:29 parr., but both Jesus' title and the wording of the homology here (πεπιστεύκαμεν καὶ ἐγνώκαμεν) differ from the synoptic version (which is why some textual witnesses have tried to harmonize the Johannine with the synoptic text). Furthermore, John also draws a sharp distinction between Peter's confession and the betrayal of Judas (vv. 70–1)[115] and, therefore, does not necessarily use a traditional liturgical invocation.[116]

Jesus' address to the Father in Jn 17 also contains a brief dyadic homology: 'And this is eternal life, that they may know you, the only true God, and Jesus Christ whom you have sent' (17:3).

*

When we turn to the remaining writings of the New Testament, Heb 1:2–3 is a most influential text:

> [. . .] but in these last days God has spoken to us by a Son, whom he appointed heir of all things, through whom he also created the ages (δι' οὗ καὶ ἐποίησεν τοὺς αἰῶνας). He is the radiance of God's glory and the express image of God's *hypóstasis* (ἀπαύγασμα τῆς δόξης καὶ χαρακτὴρ τῆς ὑποστάσεως αὐτοῦ), and he sustains all things by his powerful word. When he had made purification for sins, he sat down at the right hand of the Majesty on high [. . .].

The author first names Christ as a divine heir (clearly alluding to the relation of a Roman emperor and his sons). He then names the cooperation of God and his Son in creation and describes the relation between God and his Son as 'radiance' and 'express image', terms which were often quoted in the fourth century. He also uses the term ὑπόστασις whose precise meaning here and elsewhere in Hebrews (3:14; 11:1) is difficult to ascertain,[117] but later became one of the keywords in trinitarian theology to describe the divine persons. Again, we are dealing with a text that is, in principle, the narration of a divine 'event', but which may nonetheless easily be condensed into confessional/credal propositions.

An extended dyadic homology occurs in 1Pet 3:21–22:[118]

> Baptism, which this [sc. the great flood] prefigured, now saves you – not as a removal of dirt from the body but as an appeal to God for a good conscience (συνειδήσεως ἀγαθῆς ἐπερ-

---

115 Cf. Keener 2003(2012), p. 697.

116 In 9:22; 11:27 John also mentions the Christ confession; cf. above p. 62. Cf., in addition, 1Jn 2:22.

117 Cf., e.g., the discussion in Köster 1972(1995), pp. 585–8. Köster suggests for 1:3: 'the actuality of the transcendent reality, i.e. God' (p. 585).

118 Cf. also FaFo § 81.

ὤτημα εἰς θεόν), through the resurrection of Jesus Christ, who has gone into heaven and is at the right hand of God, with angels, authorities, and powers made subject to him.

Here the christological section mentions the resurrection, ascension, and sitting at the right hand of God. The homology is combined with a mention of baptism, but this association remains rather vague and allows no conclusions concerning baptismal practice.

The Epistle of Jude concludes with an extended dyadic homology which is, at the same time, doxological in character and as such closely resembles Rom 16:27:

> Now to him who is able to keep you from falling and to make you stand without blemish in the presence of his glory with rejoicing, to the only God our Saviour, through Jesus Christ our Lord (μόνῳ θεῷ σωτῆρι ἡμῶν διὰ Ἰησοῦ Χριστοῦ τοῦ κυρίου ἡμῶν), be glory, majesty, power, and authority, before all time and now and forever. Amen (Jude 24–25).

Here only God is called 'Saviour'; furthermore, nowhere in Jude is Christ called divine, though the transfer of the title of 'Lord' in Jude 14 implies the divine name is being transferred to him. In Jude Christ may be seen as some kind of divine mediator through whom the community can direct their praise to God.[119]

∗

Contrary to what one may think, triadic homologies which form the basis of the majority of creeds from the fourth century onwards are fairly rare in the New Testament. The few instances in the Pauline and Deuteropauline letters have been mentioned above.

Peter's address to the crowd at Pentecost as reported in Acts 2:32–33 contains another example:

> This Jesus God raised up, and of that all of us are witnesses. Being therefore exalted at the right hand of God and having received from the Father the promise of the Holy Spirit, he has poured out this that you [both] see and hear.

Here the trinitarian statement is combined with the events at Pentecost: ascension to God's right hand – promise of the Holy Spirit – outpouring.

Another passage which likewise combines the Trinity with the divine economy (passion – eschatological restoration) is found in 1Pet 3:18:

> For Christ also suffered for sins once for all, the righteous for the unrighteous, in order to bring you to God. He was put to death in the flesh but made alive in the spirit [. . .].

---

119 On the problems of interpretation cf. Bauckham 1990, pp. 29–37.

Yet the spirit which is mentioned here may not primarily refer to the 'Holy Spirit',[120] but rather to Christ's human spirit[121] because of the opposition to the 'flesh' (although there is, of course, an intimate connection between the two).

The most famous example of a triadic homology is the Great Commission in Mt 28:19:

> Go therefore and make disciples of all nations, baptizing them upon the name of the Father, the Son, and the Holy Spirit (βαπτίζοντες αὐτοὺς εἰς τὸ ὄνομα τοῦ πατρὸς καὶ τοῦ υἱοῦ καὶ τοῦ ἁγίου πνεύματος).

Here confession of the triune God and baptism seem to be closely connected, but it is not said what 'baptism upon the name' means in liturgical terms. Does it refer to a formula spoken by the priest ('I baptize you upon the name . . .') or does it refer to one or three baptismal questions: 'Do you believe in . . .?', followed by one or three baptismal immersions (with or without a formula)? All these possibilities were actually practised in the first centuries. There are good reasons to think that the words 'baptizing them upon the name of the Father, the Son, and the Holy Spirit', at least, are actually fairly late.[122] The *Didache* (110–120?) twice mentions baptism 'upon the name of the Father, the Son, and the Holy Spirit'[123] which is identical with the formula in Mt 28:19. It is a matter of debate whether the author of the *Didache* quotes the Gospel of Matthew or vice versa or whether both authors draw from a common (liturgical?) tradition.

Taken together, the New Testament evidence of a confusing plethora of statements suggests that there were many ways to express one's faith, but that the emphasis lay mostly on some kind of confession to Christ. Extended versions of these homologies could include Christ's part in creation, the descent, incarnation, crucifixion, resurrection, ascension, sitting at the right hand of the Father, parousia, and Final Judgement in varying forms, depending on context. These elements were sometimes combined with a dyadic confession. By contrast, triadic homologies are rare and by no means uniform.

However, this evidence means that when creeds came to be created one would have expected a formula centred on Christ (including some or all of the aforementioned elements) and perhaps some reference to God/the Father. Yet right from the

---

120 Cf., e.g., Feldmeier 2008, p. 201 n. 168.
121 Cf., e.g., Elliott 2000, pp. 646 f.
122 I can leave it open here whether one might consider the clause a later addition (which in the view of Ulrich Luz 'is, appropriately, scarcely advocated any more'; cf. Luz 2005, p. 617 and n. 15) or whether this points to a late date of the entire gospel (which Luz, on inconclusive evidence, dates to not long after the year 80; cf. Luz 2007, pp. 58 f.).
123 *Didache* 7,1. 3 (FaFo § 97).

beginning the 'classic' creeds start with the *Father*, describing his creative activity (which plays no prominent role in the New Testament, except for Jn 1:1–3 and Col 1:15–20). Nor is it helpful to postulate a reference to the baptismal formula, since we do not know at what point the triadic formula became widespread as part of that ritual.[124]

In the following chapters we will, therefore, consider the reasons why, in the end, a triadic/trinitarian structure was chosen for the formulation of most creeds.

4.3.2 Dyadic and triadic homologies in the second and third centuries

Dyadic and triadic homologies continued to be produced unabatedly in extracanonical literature from the late first to the third centuries. *First Clement*, probably written at the end of the first century, contains not only dyadic,[125] but also two brief triadic homologies, one emphasizing the oneness of God, Christ, and Spirit, the other affirming: 'God lives, the Lord Jesus Christ lives, and [also] the Holy Spirit'.[126]

Ode 19 of the *Odes of Solomon* (first quarter of the second century?) starts by mentioning a 'cup of milk offered to me' which the author drank 'in the sweetness of the Lord's kindness' (19,1). The cup and milk are then described as follows:

> The Son is the cup,
> and he who was milked, the Father,
> and [the one] who milked him, the Spirit of holiness.[127]

Ode 23 concludes with a passage relating to the 'great tablet that was entirely covered with writing by the finger of God' (23,21):

> And the name of the Father was upon it,
> and of the Son and of the Holy Spirit,
> to reign as king forever and ever.
> Hallelujah.[128]

---

124 Cf., e.g., the discussion in Campenhausen 1971(1979); Kinzig/Wallraff 2002, pp. 332–56; Ferguson 2009, pp. 132–8; Labahn 2011, esp. pp. 355–7; Hartman 2011; Wischmeyer 2011, esp. pp. 750 f.; Lindemann 2011, esp. pp. 774 f.; Rouwhorst 2022, col. 986. A list of triadic baptismal formulae is given in Campenhausen 1971(1979), pp. 208–12.
125 Cf. below p. 123.
126 *First Clement* 46,6; 58,2 (FaFo § 93).
127 *Odes of Solomon 19*, 2 (Lattke 2009, p. 268).
128 *Odes of Solomon 23*, 22 (Lattke 2009, p. 325).

Ode 19 may call to mind the eucharist or some kind of 'milk sacrament', but the connection is tenuous.[129] The passage from Ode 23 resembles Mt 28:19 and *Didache* 7,1. 3, but makes no explicit connection to baptism. However, neither of these passages is, strictly speaking, homological. In the first instance we are dealing with an allegory, whereas the second passage strongly resembles a doxology.

By contrast, the homologies in the *Preaching of Peter* (s. II/1?) are dyadic, primarily affirming God's transcendence and creative activity.[130] Tertullian ascribes a similar brief formula to the modalist Praxeas who is supposed to have said 'that one cannot believe [*sic*] the one God in any other way than by saying that the Father, the Son, and the Holy Spirit are one and the same'.[131]

The apocryphal *Epistle of the Apostles* from about 150 contains an extensive description of God's majesty and creative activity and goes on to mention the incarnation of the Son of God and Word 'through the holy virgin Mary'.[132] In a later passage the author describes the feeding of the five thousand. The five loaves (Mk 6:38 parr.; Jn 6:9) are then given a symbolic interpretation (my numbering):

> They are a picture [*or:* symbol] of our faith, which concerns the great Christianity,[133] which is
> (I) in the Father, the Ruler of the entire world,
> (II) in Jesus Christ our Saviour,
> (III) in the Holy Spirit, the Paraclete,
> (IV) in the holy Church,
> (V) and in the remission of sins.[134]

Here the persons of the Trinity are each given additional attributes. God: Father, omnipotence; Jesus Christ: Saviour; Holy Spirit: Paraclete. But then a fourth and a fifth element are added because the Church and the remission of sins are also object of our faith. It is a matter of debate whether this was prompted by the need to provide a symbolic interpretation of the five loaves or whether, on the contrary, a given five-fold rule of faith (or creed?) was applied to the number of the loaves.[135]

---

129 Cf. Lattke 2009, p. 270.

130 Cf. *Praedicatio (Kerygma) Petri*, frgs. 2a and 2b (Mara; FaFo § 94a, b).

131 Tertullian, *Aduersus Praxeam* 2,3 (FaFo § 110c).

132 *Epistula Apostolorum* 3(14; FaFo § 103a).

133 The passage 'which concerns the great Christianity' is textually uncertain; cf. discussion in Hills 1990, pp. 62–4.

134 *Epistula Apostolorum* 5(16; FaFo § 103b).

135 Cf. the views supporting either side cited in Hills 1990, pp. 60–5. Hills himself offers a conjecture for the difficult Ethiopic text. Instead of 'a picture of our faith which concerns the great Christianity' he reads 'a picture of our faith for baptized Christians' and concludes: 'If this is so, then

Triadic homologies are also found in the writings of Justin Martyr (d. 165). In his Roman congregation they were used both at baptism and at the eucharist, as the following passages from his *First Apology* (after 153) show:

> Then they are brought by us to a place where there is water, and they are regenerated in the same manner in which we were ourselves regenerated. For, at the name of God, the Father and Lord of the universe, and of our Saviour Jesus Christ, and of the Holy Spirit (ἐπ᾽ ὀνόματος τοῦ πατρὸς τῶν ὅλων καὶ δεσπότου θεοῦ καὶ τοῦ σωτῆρος ἡμῶν Ἰησοῦ Χριστοῦ καὶ πνεύματος ἁγίου), they then receive the washing with water [cf. Mt 28:19].[136]
>
> [. . .] in the water the name of God the Father and Lord of the universe (τὸ τοῦ πατρὸς τῶν ὅλων καὶ δεσπότου θεοῦ ὄνομα) is pronounced over the one who chooses to be born again and has repented of his sins; the one who leads to the laver the person that is to be washed invokes [God] by this name alone. For no one has the right to give a name of the ineffable God; and if anyone might dare to say that there is a name, he raves with a hopeless madness. This washing is called 'illumination' (φωτισμός) because they who learn these things are illuminated in their understandings. Anyone who is illuminated is also washed upon the name of Jesus Christ (ἐπ᾽ ὀνόματος Ἰησοῦ Χριστοῦ), who was crucified under Pontius Pilate, and upon the name of the Holy Spirit (ἐπ᾽ ὀνόματος πνεύματος ἁγίου), who through the prophets foretold all things about Jesus.[137]
>
> Then bread and a cup [of wine] mixed with water are brought to the president of the brethren; and taking them, he sends up praise and glory to the Father of the universe, through the name of the Son and of the Holy Spirit (τῷ πατρὶ τῶν ὅλων διὰ τοῦ ὀνόματος τοῦ υἱοῦ καὶ τοῦ πνεύματος τοῦ ἁγίου) [. . .].[138]

It seems that the baptismal formula used by Justin's congregation at Rome contained an extended version of Mt 28:19/*Didache* 7,1. 3. Its first element is identical in both quotations so must have run like this: ἐπ᾽ ὀνόματος τοῦ πατρὸς τῶν ὅλων καὶ δεσπότου θεοῦ ('at/upon the name of God, the Father and Lord of the universe'). Justin even provides a reason for this extension. Christians were not allowed to pronounce God's name, clearly following Jewish custom (indeed, Christians probably did not even know how to pronounce it[139]), which is why God must be described by enumerating his status and activity: he is the 'Father and Lord of the universe'.[140] It must be noted that God's fatherhood relates to the universe, not to Christ. Christ, in turn, is called 'Son' neither in the first nor in the second passage (although Justin does

---

"faith" here means, not "trust", "confidence", or the like, but "that which is believed", approximating to a "rule of faith" or "canon of truth"' (Hills 1990, p. 64).

136 Justin, *Apologia Prima* 61,3 (FaFo § 104a8).

137 Justin, *Apologia Prima* 61,10–3 (FaFo § 104a9).

138 Justin, *Apologia Prima* 65,3 (FaFo § 104a10).

139 There was considerable confusion among the Church Fathers concerning the tetragrammaton's pronunciation (by which God was not usually addressed, following Jewish custom); for details cf. Kinzig 2008.

140 Cf. also Justin, *Apologia Prima* 44,2.

call him thus in the third passage and elsewhere). Unfortunately, we do not know whether the second and third element of the triad were also extended in the actual baptismal formula, because Justin's quotations of it in his writings differ from each other. Finally, the last passage shows that triadic formulae were used not only at baptism, but also during the eucharist in doxological fashion.

Justin quotes triadic homologies quite frequently in his *First Apology*. To give one further example:

> Therefore, what sober-minded person will not acknowledge [. . .] that we are not atheists, since we worship the maker of this universe (τὸν δημιουργὸν τοῦδε τοῦ παντός). We will make known Jesus Christ, our teacher of these things, who also was born for this purpose and was crucified under Pontius Pilate (who was procurator of Judaea in the times of Tiberius Caesar); we have learned that he is the Son of the true God himself, and we hold him in the second place and the prophetic Spirit in the third, because we honour him along with the Word [*or:* according to reason, μετὰ λόγου].[141]

Justin obviously mentions Pilate in order to pinpoint the precise date of the crucifixion (and thus of Christ's activity).[142] Interestingly, he does not blame Pilate for the crucifixion which he attributes to the Jews.[143]

In the above-quoted summaries Justin says little about the Holy Spirit, except that he is 'prophetic' – a standard epithet in his writings for the Spirit speaking through the prophets – and that he 'through the prophets foretold all things about Jesus'; nor does he mention the Church or remission of sins.

A very elaborate description of the activities of God and Christ (who are in fact identified with each other) is found in the *Paschal Homily* by Melito of Sardes (160/170?). It contains the following tenets: creation of the world and of humankind – proclamation through the Law and the Prophets – virgin birth – crucifixion – burial – resurrection – ascension – sitting at the right hand of the Father – salvation – participation in the creation.[144]

Origen (d. 254) summarizes the basic teachings which all Christians are supposed to believe at the beginning of his work *On First Principles* (after 220), in his *Commentary on John* (c. 241–243), and his *Commentary on Matthew* (before 253). In *On First Principles* (which has been preserved in its entirety only in Latin in an adapted translation by Rufinus), he repeatedly calls this the 'apostolic preaching'

---

141 Justin, *Apologia Prima* 13,1–3 (FaFo § 104a2). Cf. also 6,2 (§ 104a1); 67,2 (§ 104a11).
142 Cf. also Justin, *Apologia Prima* 46,1; *Apologia Secunda* 5,6; *Dialogus cum Tryphone* 30,3; 76,6; 85,2 (FaFo § 104b3) and below pp. 97–9, 135 f.
143 Cf., e.g., Justin, *Apologia Prima* 35,6.
144 Cf. Melito, *De Pascha* 104 (FaFo § 107); the text is quoted above p. 76.

(*praedicatio apostolica*) or 'preaching of the Church' (*ecclesiastica praedicatio*).[145] This text gives not a brief rule which could somehow be memorized, but a lengthy description of a variety of doctrines that also embrace the nature of the soul, free will, the devil, the transience of the world, the divine origin of the Scriptures, the interpretation of the Law, and other topics.

By contrast, the second passage from the *Commentary of John* is more succinct. However, before we study it, we must first take a step back and look once more at a passage in the *Shepherd of Hermas* (*s.* II/1?):

> First of all, believe that there is one God [cf. Jas 2:19] who created and ordered all things [cf. Eph 3:9], brought all things into being out of nothing (ποιήσας ἐκ τοῦ μὴ ὄντος εἰς τὸ εἶναι τὰ πάντα) [cf. 2Macc 7:28; Wis 1:14], and who alone is able to contain all things, but cannot himself be contained. Therefore have faith in him and fear him; and fearing him, exercise self-control.[146]

Here God's oneness, his creative activity, and his transcendence are emphasized in a manner similar to the *Preaching of Peter*. Yet there is a new element: the creation from nothing. The passage 'that there is – out of nothing' was later quoted by Irenaeus.[147]

Origen bases the beginning of his summary in his *Commentary on John* on this quotation from the *Shepherd*, which he had already drawn upon in the abovementioned passage in *On First Principles* when he went on to describe the God of the patriarchs.[148] In the present passage, Origen immediately adds a christological as well as a pneumatological section:

> First of all, believe that there is one God [cf. Jas 2:19] who created and ordered all things [cf. Eph 3:9] and brought all things into being out of nothing [cf. 2Macc 7:28; Wis 1:14].
>
> It is necessary also to believe that Jesus Christ is Lord [cf. 1Cor 12:3 etc.] and [to believe] in all the true teaching concerning his godhead and humanity.
>
> It is also necessary to believe in the Holy Spirit and that, being free agents (αὐτεξούσιοι ὄντες), we are both punished for what we have done wrong and rewarded for what we have done well.[149]

Once again we see an extended triadic summary which, however, differs from the aforementioned examples:

---

145 Cf. Origen, *De principiis* 1 praef. 4–8, 10 (FaFo § 116a).
146 *Pastor Hermae* 26 (= *Mandatum* I),1–2 (FaFo § 100).
147 Cf. Irenaeus, *Aduersus haereses* 1,22,1 (FaFo § 109b4).
148 Cf. Origen, *De principiis* 1 praef. 4 (FaFo § 116a).
149 Origen, *Commentarii in Iohannem* 32,16,187–189 (FaFo § 116b).

> God: oneness – creation of the universe – creation from nothing;
> Jesus Christ: Lord – teaching concerning godhead and humanity;
> Holy Spirit: eschatological rewards and punishment as a result of human free will.

By contrast another summary contained in Origen's *Commentary on Matthew*, which, again, has only been preserved in a Latin translation, looks much more 'traditional' (my numbering):

> Certain people, however, do not disagree with the public and conspicuous articles (*de publicis quidem et manifestis capitulis*), for example,
> (I) concerning the one God who gave the Law and the Gospel,
> (II) or concerning Christ Jesus, the first-born of all creation (*primogenito uniuersae creaturae*) [cf. Col 1:15], who came into the world [cf. Jn 3:19] at the end of the age according to the proclamations of the prophets and took upon himself the true nature of the human flesh such that he even underwent birth from the Virgin; he accepted death on the cross, rose from the dead, and deified the human nature which he had assumed (*deificauit, quam susceperat, humanam naturam*).
> (III) Furthermore they also believe with the greatest certitude concerning the Holy Spirit, since he who was subsequently given in the apostles was himself in the patriarchs and prophets;
> (IV) and [they believe] concerning the resurrection from the dead, as the Gospel teaches, and everything that is handed down in the churches.[150]

Here the author adds to God's oneness his function as Law-giver and revealer of the Gospel. The christological section contains the following attributes of Christ: 'first-born' – virgin birth – crucifixion and death – resurrection – ascension ('deification'). As regards the Holy Spirit, Origen emphasizes the identity of the Spirit active in the patriarchs and prophets with that active in the apostles. Finally, the resurrection and the other doctrines of the Church are added at the end.

In the *Dialogue with Heraclides* (244/249) when Origen presses his interlocutor, a defender of monarchianism, as to the divine nature of Christ, the latter takes recourse to tradition (a strategy for which he is subsequently rebuked) and offers a dyadic summary:

> But we say that God is the Almighty, God unbegun, unending, encompassing the universe and being encompassed by nothing; and that his Word is the Son of the living God [Mt 16:16], God and man, 'through whom all things came into being' [Jn 1:3; 1Cor 8:6], both God according to the spirit and man according to his birth from Mary.[151]

---

150 Origen, *In Matthaeum commentariorum series* 33 (FaFo § 116c).
151 Origen, *Dialogus cum Heraclide* 2 (FaFo § 120b).

Here Heraclides mentions God's omnipotence, eternity, and transcendence which again calls to mind the *Shepherd of Hermas* (although he does not quote him verbatim). However, he then goes on to describe the Word/Son in a way which is both traditional (participation in creation, birth from Mary) and innovative: dual nature God/man. Heraclides thus blends traditional credal building blocks with his own theology, as the occasion requires.[152]

Cyprian of Carthage (d. 258) offers a dyadic summary in a letter arguing against Marcionite docetism which includes:

God: Father – Creator

Son/Christ: virgin birth – incarnation – bearing of sins – death – bodily resurrection – appearance to disciples.[153]

Adamantius, the author of an anti-gnostic dialogue (who, according to Ramelli, is perhaps identical with Origen[154]), describes his faith as follows (I quote the Latin version by Rufinus which differs from the existing Greek version and may in fact be closer to the original Greek text):

> I believe that there is one God, Creator and establisher (*creatorem et conditorem*), and his Word, consubstantial and coeternal with him (*consubstantiuum ei et coaeternum*). In the last days [cf. Heb 1:2] this Word, after having taken on human nature from the virgin Mary, was born as man, was crucified, and rose again from the dead. Likewise I also believe [*sic*] the Holy Spirit, which is coeternal with the Father and the Son. This is my faith.[155]

This is in some respects a peculiar text. On the one hand, only the Father is called 'God', whereas, on the other hand, the christological and pneumatological sections are extended in such a way that both the Word/Son (who is consubstantial with God) and the Spirit are described as coeternal with the Father. By contrast, in the existing Greek text 'God the Word' is called ὁμοούσιος (consubstantial) and 'forever existing' (ἀεὶ ὄντα). Likewise, the Spirit is *only* called 'forever existing'. Further research into the textual history of this treatise is necessary in order to explain this summary and its different versions.

The final text in this section comes from the *Tractatus tripartitus*, a document of Valentinian gnosticism which is only preserved in Coptic and may have been composed in the third century:

---

152 Two extensive credal statements which tradition ascribed to Gregory Thaumaturgus (d. 270/275) need not detain us here, because the first one, whether or not it is written by Gregory, is an elaborate individual creed describing the Trinity in highly sophisticated metaphysical language (*Confessio fidei* (FaFo § 117)), whereas the second is most certainly inauthentic (Council of Ephesus, *Collectio Vaticana* 170 (*Gregorii Thaumaturgi qui feruntur anathematismi*; FaFo § 118)).

153 Cf. Cyprian, *Epistula 73*, 5,2 (FaFo § 122d).

154 Cf. Ramelli, 'De recta in Deum fide', 2018.

155 Adamantius, *De recta in deum fide* (FaFo § 128).

As for the baptism which exists in the fullest sense, into which the Totalities will descend and in which they will be, there is no other baptism apart from this one alone, which is the redemption into God, Father, Son, and Holy Spirit, when confession is made through faith in those names, which are a single name of the gospel; when they have come to believe what has been said to them, namely that they exist. From this they have their salvation, those who have believed that they exist. This is attaining in an invisible way to the Father, Son, and Holy Spirit in an undoubting faith. And when they have borne witness to them, it is also with a firm hope that they attained them, so that the return to them might become the perfection of those who have believed in them and [so that] the Father might be one with them, the Father, the God whom they have confessed in faith and who gave [them] their union with him in knowledge.[156]

This text is opaque in many ways, but it does become clear that again faith in, and confession of, the Trinity precedes baptism which may have been performed in the name of the Father, the Son, and the Holy Spirit. Yet once more we are not told what this confession looked like in practice.

4.3.3 Christological summaries in the second and third centuries

Christological summaries are texts that condense the story of the incarnation, passion, and resurrection of Christ. A fragment from the *Preaching of Peter* contains such a christological summary, mentioning Christ's 'coming, death, cross, and all the other tortures which the Jews inflicted on him, his resurrection, and assumption into the heavens'.[157] Such summaries are also found elsewhere.[158] They occur several times in the writings attributed to Ignatius of Antioch (traditional date: 110–118 or slightly later). Ignatius is a particularly tricky case because the writings attributed to him survive in various recensions of differing length. In addition, their authenticity has been questioned in recent years.[159] Assuming, as had been the consensus, that the middle version of these letters is authentic (but which it need not be), the summary in the *Epistle to the Magnesians* deserves attention, not least because it mentions Pontius Pilate:

---

156 *Tractatus tripartitus* (NHC I,5), pp. 127, l. 25 – 128, l. 19 (FaFo § 130).
157 *Praedicatio (Kerygma) Petri* frg. 9 (Mara; FaFo § 94c).
158 Cf., e.g., *Ascension of Isaiah* 3,18 (FaFo § 95a): resurrection, cross, ascension (in this order); here combined with Mt 28:19.
159 Cf. recently Vinzent 2019, pp. 266–464; Vinzent 2023, pp. 248–324. Brent 2018 is more conservative.

These things [I address to you], my beloved, not because I know any of you to be in such a state, but [because], as less than you, I desire to protect you beforehand, that you might not fall upon the hooks of vain doctrine, but that you might rest assured in regard to the birth, passion, and resurrection which took place in the time of the government of Pontius Pilate (ἐν καιρῷ τῆς ἡγεμονίας Ποντίου Πιλάτου), being truly and firmly accomplished by Jesus Christ, who is our hope [1Tim 1:1]. May none of you ever be turned aside from him.[160]

A very similar summary of the incarnation is found in the *Epistle to the Trallians*:

Stop your ears, therefore, when anyone speaks to you at variance with Jesus Christ, who was descended from David and was also from Mary; who was truly born, and both ate and drank; he was truly persecuted under Pontius Pilate (ἐπὶ Ποντίου Πιλάτου); he was truly crucified and died in the sight of beings in heaven, on earth, and under the earth. He was also truly raised from the dead, his Father raising him up; whose Father will also after the same manner raise up in Jesus Christ us who believe him [cf. 2Cor 4:14], apart from whom we do not possess the true life.[161]

The third such text occurs in the *Epistle to the Smyrnaeans*:

I glorify Jesus Christ, the God who has given you such wisdom. For I have observed that you have been furnished with an immovable faith, as if you were nailed to the cross of our Lord Jesus Christ both in flesh and in spirit, and [that] you have been established in love through the blood of Christ, being fully persuaded about our Lord, that he was truly of the ancestry of 'David according to the flesh' [Rom 1:3] [and that he was] the Son of God according to the will and power of God; that he was truly born from a virgin, was baptized by John in order that all righteousness might be fulfilled [cf. Mt 3:15] by him; and that under Pontius Pilate and Herod the tetrarch (ἐπὶ Ποντίου Πιλάτου καὶ Ἡρώδου τετράρχου) he was truly nailed [to the cross] for us in his flesh. Of this fruit we [exist] by his divinely blessed passion so that through [his] resurrection he might forever raise up a standard [cf. Is 5:26; 49:22; 62:10] for all his holy and faithful [followers], whether among Jews or Gentiles, in the one body of his Church.[162]

Taking a stance against docetic views, (Pseudo-)Ignatius places the emphasis firmly on the factuality of these events by repeatedly using the adverb ἀληθῶς ('truly') and naming Pontius Pilate (and Herod) as historical guarantors of this factuality.[163] If genuine, this is the first mention of the crucifixion under Pontius Pilate in a credal context. (1Tim 6:13 refers to Christ's confession before Pilate.)

---

160 (Pseudo-)Ignatius of Antioch, *Ad Magnesios* (middle version) 11 (FaFo § 98b2a).
161 (Pseudo-)Ignatius of Antioch, *Ad Trallianos* (middle version) 9,1–2 (FaFo § 98c1).
162 (Pseudo-)Ignatius of Antioch, *Ad Smyrnaeos* (middle version) 1,1–2 (FaFo § 98e1).
163 Cf. Kelly 1972, p. 150.

However, it would then also be the *only* mention of Pilate in a christological summary from the *eastern* part of the empire before the fourth century – otherwise the mention of Pilate is typical of the *western* tradition[164] – which strongly suggests that this text was not written (or revised) before the fourth century, in which case Justin is the oldest witnesses for this clause in credal texts.[165]

We are on firmer ground with the *Letter to the Philippians* by Polycarp of Smyrna, written perhaps around the middle of the second century. Polycarp also offers us a christological summary which is seen as core Christian belief:

> 'Therefore, girding up your loins' [1Pet 1:13], 'serve the Lord in fear' [Ps 2:11] and truth, forsaking the vain, empty talk and error of the multitude, and believing in him who raised up our Lord Jesus Christ from the dead, and gave him glory [cf. 1Pet 1:21] and a throne at his right hand, to whom all things in heaven and on earth are subject [cf. 1Pet 3:22; Phil 2:10], to whom every spirit is subservient, who comes as the 'judge of the living and the dead' [Acts 10:42], whose blood God will require from those who do not believe in him [cf. Lk 11:50–51].[166]

Polycarp does not mention the passion here, but there are the well-known elements resurrection – ascension – sitting at the right hand – coming again – Last Judgement.

Justin also repeatedly quotes christological summaries. It may suffice here to cite one such example. In his *Dialogue with Trypho* Justin quotes his Jewish opponent as saying:

> It remains, then, to prove clearly that he submitted to be born through the Virgin as a human, according to the will of his Father, to be crucified, and to die. Prove also that after these things he rose again and ascended into heaven.[167]

Justin's summaries[168] mostly contain the following elements as a minimum: Son/ Word/Christ – virgin birth – crucifixion (under Pontius Pilate) – death – resurrection – ascension. The parousia is mentioned in only three passages, all from the *Dialogue*;[169] the Final Judgement only once.[170] In addition, Jesus is sometimes de-

---

164 Cf. Justin Martyr, *Apologia prima* 13,3 (FaFo § 104a2); 61,13 (§ 104a9); id., *Dialogus cum Tryphone* 85,2 (§ 104b3); Irenaeus, *Aduersus haereses* 3,4,2 (§ 109b7); Armenian frg. 2 (§ 109c1; authenticity uncertain); Tertullian, *De uirginibus uelandis* 1,4(3; § 111c). Possible exception: *Didascalia apostolorum* 26,8 (§ 121) for which cf. below in the text. In addition, cf. Staats 1987, p. 508.

165 Cf. the references in the previous footnote and above p. 92.

166 Polycarp, *Epistula ad Philippenses* 2,1 (FaFo § 102).

167 Justin, *Dialogus cum Tryphone* 63,1 (FaFo § 104b2).

168 Cf. also Justin, *Apologia prima* 21,1 (FaFo § 104a3); 31,7 (§ 104a5); 42,4 (§ 104a6); 46,5 (§ 104a7); id., *Dialogus cum Tryphone* 38,1 (§ 104b1); 85,1–2 (§ 104b3); 126,1 (§ 104b4); 132,1 (§ 104b5).

169 Cf. Justin, *Dialogus cum Tryphone* 38,1 (FaFo § 104b1); 126,1 (§ 104b4); 132,1 (§ 104b5).

170 Cf. Justin, *Dialogus cum Tryphone* 132,1 (FaFo § 104b5).

scribed as 'teacher'[171] and as a healer and miracle worker.[172] By contrast, Christ's sitting at the right hand is nowhere mentioned. In the end, however, Justin provides no information as to whether these summaries were used in catechesis or other contexts.

The aforementioned Heraclides first quotes Jn 1:1–3 in the credal statement which opens his debate with Origen. But he then expresses agreement with 'the faith', apparently a kind of summary of faith used in his congregation:

> Thus we agree with the faith (τῇ πίστει συμφερόμεθα) and accordingly we also believe that Christ took flesh, that he was born, that he ascended into the heavens in the flesh in which he rose again, that he sits at the right hand of the Father, whence he will come and 'judge the living and the dead' [2Tim 4:1; 1Pet 4:5], [as] God and man.[173]

Here we have, basically, another christological summary consisting of incarnation – birth – resurrection (in the flesh) – ascension (in the flesh) – sitting at the right hand of the Father – parousia and Last Judgement. The addition 'God and man' is perhaps not traditional because Christ's precise nature is the subject of the debate that ensued afterwards.

Although the body of the *Didascalia apostolorum* belongs to the third century, the framing chapters were probably written in the fourth century.[174] A later date would also fit the observation that the christological summary in the *Didascalia* mentions Pontius Pilate who does not appear in the eastern tradition until the fourth century.[175] (It is probably first attested in the Creed of Jerusalem which is of western origin.[176])

A summary very similar to that of Heraclides is found in a letter by Bishop Dionysius of Alexandria (*sedit* 247/248–264/265) to Bishop Stephen of Rome (*sedit* 254–257):

> Or if a man receive not all the mystery of Christ, or alter and distort – [saying] that he is not God, or that he did not become a man, or that he did not die, or that he did not rise, or that he will not come to judge the living and the dead [cf. 2Tim 4:1; 1Pet 4:5] – or preach anything else apart from what we preached, let him be a curse, says Paul [cf. Gal 1:8].[177]

---

171 Cf. Justin, *Apologia prima* 21,1 (FaFo § 104a3); 23,2 (§ 104a4).
172 Cf. Justin, *Apologia prima* 31,7 (FaFo § 104a5).
173 Origen, *Dialogus cum Heraclide* 1 (FaFo § 120a).
174 Cf. Stewart-Sykes, *Didascalia apostolorum*, 2009, pp. 49–55; Benga 2018.
175 Cf. *Didascalia apostolorum* 26,8 (FaFo § 121).
176 Cf. Kinzig, 'Origin', 2022, p. 196.
177 Dionysius of Alexandria, *Epistula V 1* (Feltoe; FaFo § 124a).

We again encounter the series: Christ's divinity – incarnation – death – resurrection – parousia – Last Judgement. It is, however, phrased in a negative manner and combined with the reference to Gal 1:8. This is the first instance in which disagreement with the christological summary incurs an anathema. However, the condemnation here is not directed against a specific person but against anyone who holds a particular doctrine (which slightly differs from the use in Gal 1:8–9 where Paul curses those who preach another 'gospel' – which must, of course, also have some doctrinal content). This indicates that the boundaries between orthodoxy and heterodoxy (heresy) were being drawn more sharply by the mid-third century and that those who were 'unorthodox' incurred some sort of curse (whose consequences are not specified). We will consider later what an anathema may have implied in legal and practical terms.[178]

We may leave aside the spurious creed against Paul of Samosata (bishop of Antioch 260/261–268/272) preserved among the acts of the Council of Ephesus (431).[179] Its concern with a two-nature Christology must belong to the fifth century. By contrast, Eusebius has preserved a christological summary contained in the *Legend of Abgar* from which he quotes. Here the Apostle Thaddaeus tells Abgar of Edessa that he would speak to the citizens of Edessa about Jesus on the following day:

> [. . .] I [sc. Thaddaeus] will preach before them and sow the word of life among them, concerning the coming of Jesus, how he came into existence; concerning his mission, for what purpose he was sent by the Father; concerning his power, his works, the mysteries which he proclaimed in the world, and by what sort of power he did these things; concerning his new preaching; and concerning his abasement and humiliation [cf. Phil 2:8], how he humbled himself, died, debased his divinity, was crucified, descended into the underworld, burst the bars which from eternity had not been broken, and raised the dead. He descended alone, but ascended to his Father with a great crowd.[180]

The summary is here extended to include Christ's preaching and miracles, his descent into the underworld, and the release of those imprisoned there.

We will see below in chapter 4.6 how a particular version of the western christological summary came to be inserted into the triadic rule of faith to form a 'full-blown' creed. But first we should take a look at what a 'rule of faith' actually is.

---

178 Cf. below ch. 6.4.6.
179 Cf. FaFo § 127.
180 Eusebius, *Historia ecclesiastica* 1,13,20 (FaFo § 129).

4.4 The rule of faith

4.4.1 Preliminary remarks

The 'rules of faith' constitute a rather elusive literary genre. Their content is nowhere clearly defined and even their name oscillates: they may be called 'rule of faith' (κανὼν τῆς πίστεως/regula fidei), but also 'rule of truth' (κανὼν τῆς ἀληθείας/regula ueritatis), 'rule of the Church' (κανὼν τῆς ἐκκλησίας or ἐκκλσιαστικός), or simply 'rule'.[181] Κανών/regula in these instances means 'standard', 'regulation', 'maxim', a κανών/regula originally being a long bar or rod used for measurement. In a wider sense the 'rule' comprises all that is normative within the Church. In Gal 6:16 Paul uses the term to designate the entirety of the Christian kerygma which the apostle draws on against those who demand circumcision.[182] Κανών thus serves as a rule by which to measure the truth of the Gospel in an apologetic context. Here, Paul refers to the rule's content in a summary fashion as the 'new creation' (cf. v. 15). Κανών later designates collections of basic theological tenets that are cited mostly in intra-Christian controversy as the norm by which the orthodoxy of controversial doctrines is judged. As we will see, their content often resembles creeds, although we are not yet dealing with fixed formulae but with – often elaborate – constructions made up of homological building blocks of various sizes and content. At the same time, it is important to keep in mind that κανών/regula may also be used in a wider sense to include standards of Church discipline and thus later comes to mean 'church law'. From the middle of the fourth century it is also used to designate the collection of biblical writings. Finally, rules of faith are presented as a doctrinal consensus about Christ's saving work which was handed down from generation to generation (and is, ultimately, apostolic). The idea behind this line of argument is that 'orthodoxy' goes back to the first-hand witnesses of Christ's earthly life, whereas 'heresy' crept in at a later stage as a distortion of the venerable truth.

---

181 Cf. Ohme 1998, esp. pp. 1–295; Ohme 2004; Markschies, 'Haupteinleitung', 2012, pp. 11–17; O'Donnell/Drecoll 2012–2018; Fogleman 2023; and the literature quoted in FaFo, vol. I, p. 165.
182 Cf. also 2Cor 10,13–16 (three times) which is irrelevant for us here. Phil 3:16 *v.l.* may be influenced by Gal 6:16.

4.4.2 *Third Letter to the Corinthians*

One of the earliest attestations of such a 'rule' which is often overlooked[183] already displays these features. It is found in the *Third Letter to the Corinthians*, a pseudo-Pauline epistle which forms part of the *Acts of Paul* and may date to the first half of the second century.[184] The author turns against Simon and Cleobius who, according to a (fictitious) letter sent from Corinth to Paul, make the following claims:

> They say that we must not use the prophets, and that God is not almighty, and that there will be no resurrection of the flesh, and that there was no formation (τὴν πλάσιν) of humankind by God, and that the Lord did not come into the flesh nor was born from Mary; and that there is no cosmos of God, but of angels.[185]

These opponents may, therefore, represent some kind of Christian gnostic group which cannot be clearly identified.[186]

In order to refute their claims the author first emphasizes that his preaching was handed down by the apostles 'who were at all times with the Lord Jesus Christ' (section 4). He then enumerates key points which are Jesus' birth, the redemption of all flesh, our resurrection in the flesh, and the creation of the universe and humankind by God Almighty. In the author's view God's redemption is rooted in his creative activity:

> Because man was formed by his Father, so was he sought when he was lost, that he might be quickened by adoption.[187]

This is followed by a quick run through the history of salvation: after the Fall, first the prophets were sent to the Jews, who, however, would not listen under the influence of 'the prince of iniquity'. Yet God did not stop there but sent Jesus into the world in order to overcome the enemy and to save all flesh 'whereby that wicked one had triumphed' (sections 9–18). The author then outlines the position of his opponents (sections 19–25) and goes on to give examples of a bodily

---

183 Cf., e.g., Kelly 1972 and, most recently, Ayres 2020, who both fail to mention Third Corinthians.

184 For what follows, cf. FaFo § 96. The date of composition of the correspondence is uncertain; cf. also Zwierlein 2013, pp. 214–18: after 180.

185 *Epistulae mutuae Corinthiorum et Pauli* (CANT-211.IV), *Epistula Corinthiorum* 10–15 (numbering according to Hennecke/Schneemelcher 1999, vol. II, p. 231). Cf. also the introduction to this letter where these claims are mentioned in somewhat divergent fashion.

186 Cf. Klijn 1963, pp. 22 f.; Luttikhuizen 1996, p. 91 *pace* Rordorf 1993, p. 42 who thinks that it is directed against the teachings of Saturninus.

187 *Epistulae mutuae Corinthiorum et Pauli* (CANT-211.IV), *Tertia Epistula ad Corinthios* 7–8 (FaFo § 96).

resurrection from nature and from the Bible (sections 26–32). The author himself bears Christ's wounds on his body in order to 'attain unto the resurrection of the dead' (section 35). He concludes his letter as follows:

> Whoever abides by the rule (καὶ εἴ τις ᾧ παρέλαβε κανόνι) which he has received by the blessed prophets and the holy gospel shall receive a recompense [cf. 1Cor 3:8. 14] from the Lord, <and when he rises from the dead shall obtain eternal life>. But whoever transgresses these things, fire is with him and with them that go before in the same way, who are men without God, a generation of vipers [cf. Mt 3:7; 12:34; 23:33; Lk 3:7]. Turn away from them in the power of the Lord, and peace, <grace, and love> shall be with you. Amen.[188]

The 'rule' here is not clearly defined – it appears to encompass the totality of the salvific content of the prophets and the gospel. However, the themes which are expressly mentioned include God's omnipotence and his creating the world, Christ being born from Mary (not yet called a virgin!) with the involvement of the Holy Spirit, the redemption of all flesh, the resurrection of Christ and of all humankind, and God's divine economy. Compliance with the 'rule' will be rewarded, non-compliance will be punished by fire. Thus the rule indeed serves as a boundary-marker separating orthodoxy from dissent.

4.4.3 Irenaeus

The rule of faith in Pseudo-Ignatius of Antioch, *Epistle to the Philippians* 1,1–3,3, will be omitted here as it probably belongs to the middle of the fourth century.[189] We are on firmer ground when we turn to Irenaeus of Lyons (d. *c.* 200). In his *Epideixis* (which is only preserved in Armenian; FaFo § 109a1) he mentions the 'rule of faith' (in Greek retroversion: κανὼν τῆς πίστεως) and calls upon his readers to hold to it 'without deviation'. He then goes on to explain the nature of faith:

> [. . .] and the truth brings about faith, for faith is established upon things truly real, that we may believe what really is, as it is, and <believing> what really is, as it is, we may always keep our conviction of it firm. Since, then, the conserver [. . .] of our salvation is faith, it is necessary to take great care of it, that we may have a true comprehension of what is.[190]

Irenaeus reiterates here the Pauline idea that faith is belief in the salvific nature of events that took place in the past. He goes on to emphasize that faith has been handed down by 'the elders, the disciples of the apostles'. These presbyters are also

---

188 *Tertia Epistula ad Corinthios* 36–39 (FaFo § 96).
189 Cf. Brent 2018. The date in FaFo § 98g is erroneous.
190 Irenaeus, *Epideixis* 3 (tr. Behr 1997, p. 41).

mentioned elsewhere in Irenaeus' œuvre and may designate an earlier source which is perhaps somehow related to Papias of Hierapolis (active *c.* 100), but which is now lost.[191] The presbyters vouchsafe the truth of the faith. Interestingly, Irenaeus does not mention that the apostles themselves wrote down and transmitted this faith, as the later legend claims.[192] These 'things that are', i.e. 'historical' facts, are then enumerated at the end of the section (my numbering):

> So, faith procures this for us, as the elders, the disciples of the apostles, have handed down to us:
> (I) firstly, it exhorts us to remember that we have received baptism for the remission of sins, in the name of God the Father, and in the name of Jesus Christ, the Son of God, [who was] incarnate, and died, and was raised, and in the Holy Spirit of God;
> (II) and that this baptism is the seal of eternal life and rebirth unto God that we may no longer be sons of mortal men, but of the eternal and everlasting God;
> (III) and that the eternally existing <God> <is> < . . . > above everything that has come into being and everything is subjected to him, and that which is subject to him is all made by him, so that God does not rule nor is Lord over what is another's, but over his own, and all things are God's: and therefore God is the Almighty and everything is from God.[193]

The structure of this text is threefold. Each section contains a series of elements:
(I)   baptism for remission of sins – trinitarian baptismal formula including divine origin, incarnation, death, and resurrection of Christ;
(II) baptism: seal of eternal life – rebirth – divine sonship;
(III) God: eternity – transcendence – rulership – creation – omnipotence.
Although this structure is clear, it is difficult to say whether the faith transmitted by the elders comprised all three sections or only the first one. Looking back from later developments the answer seems an obvious one: it is the section about the Trinity which is the object of faith. However, such a post hoc approach may actually skew our historical vision: we find what we want to find, because it has become an integral part of later tradition. On the basis of the text itself it appears impossible to give a definitive answer to this important question.

We may, however, note that in the tradition as reported by Irenaeus faith is again closely connected with baptism in the triune God. The christological propositions (divine origin, incarnation, death, resurrection) are inserted into what must be an allusion to the baptismal formula as it is preserved in Mt 28:19 and *Didache* 7,1. 3.[194] Whereas the second section was later no longer included in the

---

191 Cf. Körtner 2010, pp. 169 f.; Carlson 2021.
192 Cf. below ch. 5.4.
193 Irenaeus, *Epideixis* 3 (tr. Behr 1997, p. 42). In FaFo § 109a1 the extract stops after (I).
194 Cf. above pp. 75 and n. 78; 88.

creeds, the extensive insistence on God's omnipotence and creative activity, which is reminiscent of Third Corinthians, did – in an abbreviated form – become part and parcel of the creeds.

Irenaeus again recapitulates the principal tenets of the 'rule of faith' later in the *Epideixis*:

> This then is the order of the rule of our faith, the foundation of the building, and the stability of our conversation: God, the Father, unmade, immaterial, invisible; one God, the Creator of all things. This is the first point of our faith.
>
> The second point is: the Word of God, Son of God, Christ Jesus our Lord, who was revealed to the prophets according to the form of their prophesying and according to the method of the dispensation of the Father; 'through whom all things came into being' [Jn 1:3; 1Cor 8:6]; who also, in the last days, to complete and 'gather up all things' [Eph 1:10], became human among humans, visible and tangible, in order to abolish death, to display life, and to produce a community of union between God and humanity.
>
> And the third point is: the Holy Spirit, through whom the prophets prophesied, the fathers learned the things of God, and the righteous were led forth into the way of righteousness; and who in the end of the times was poured out in a new way upon humanity in all the earth, renewing humanity unto God.[195]

The passage contains elements corresponding to *Epideixis* 3: the trinitarian structure and a christological section which includes the divine origin ('Son of God') and the incarnation. However, some elements are missing (death and resurrection, baptism) whilst others have been added: God's immateriality, invisibility, and oneness; the christological titles Word of God and Lord; the revelation to the prophets; the cooperation in creation; the extensive description of the incarnation; the entire section following the mention of the Holy Spirit.

Clearly, neither section 3 nor section 6 contains a fixed formula. Therefore, Irenaeus' call in section 3 to 'hold to the rule of the faith without deviation' refers to a certain, more or less well-defined *content* rather than to a fixed *wording*. His enumerations point to a didactic *Sitz im Leben* which is no doubt pre-baptismal catechesis: bishops (or teachers) taught a list of the major tenets which the converts had to memorize without that these items were strictly fixed.

In his *opus magnum Against the Heresies* (written between 174 and 189) Irenaeus mentions the 'rule of truth' (κανὼν τῆς ἀληθείας/*regula ueritatis*) several times.[196] This one and immutable rule, which was handed down from the apostles, is proclaimed throughout the Church and guarantees its stability. Again the connection with pre-baptismal catechesis is obvious, but here readers are re-

---

195 Irenaeus, *Epideixis* 6 (FaFo § 109a2).
196 Cf. *Aduersus haereses* 1,9,4 (FaFo § 109b2); 1,22,1; 2,27,1; 3,2,1; 3,11,1; 3,12,6; 3,15,1; 4,35,4; cf. also 2,25,2; 2,28,1; 3,20,2.

minded of the rule they have received in order to combat heretics, because it enables them to distinguish right from wrong in gnostic exegesis.[197] It is opposed to the more recent, arbitrary, and fickle rules of the gnostics which have no apostolic authority, but are, in fact, depravations of the rule of truth.[198] A quick survey of the relevant passages reveals that *regula* here may not only mean 'rule' or 'ruler', but also 'system of doctrines' (if the Latin word is actually a translation of κανών[199]).

The content of this rule is expressly described as such in *Aduersus haereses* 1,22,1, but we find similar summaries in other places under different designations. It will be useful to place the individual propositions in a synopsis side by side:

1,10,1 (FaFo § 109b3)	1,22,1 (§ 109b4)	3,4,2 (§ 109b7)	4,33,7 (§ 109b13)	5,20,1 (§ 109b14)
Name of summary: πίστις ('faith')/ κήρυγμα ('proclamation')	Name of summary: *regula ueritatis* ('rule of faith')	Name of summary: *traditio uetus* ('ancient tradition')	Name of summary: πίστις ('faith')/ πεισμονὴ βεβαία ('firm conviction')/ γνῶσις ἀληθής ('true knowledge')/ ἡ τῶν ἀποστόλων διδαχὴ καὶ τὸ ἀρχαῖον τῆς ἐκκλησίας σύστημα ('the doctrine of the apostles and the ancient constitution of the Church')	Name of summary: *firma traditio* ('firm tradition')/ *fides* ('faith')
God one Father Almighty creation	God one Almighty creation from nothing (extensive description) cooperation in creation and government by Word and Spirit	God one creation	God one Almighty creation	God one and the same Father

---

197 Cf. *Aduersus haereses* 1,9,4 (FaFo § 109b2).
198 Cf. *Aduersus haereses* 1,31,3; 2, prol. 2; 2,7,2; 2,12,8; 2,18,4. 7; 2,19,8 (twice); 2,25,1; 2,35,1; 3,11,3; 3,16,1. 5; 4, prol. 2 (twice). 3; 4,35,2.
199 In *Aduersus haereses* 1,20,3 *regula* is a translation of ὑπόθεσις.

(continued)

1,10,1 (FaFo § 109b3)	1,22,1 (§ 109b4)	3,4,2 (§ 109b7)	4,33,7 (§ 109b13)	5,20,1 (§ 109b14)

Christ Jesus
  one
  Son of God
		Christ Jesus
		
		Son of God
			Jesus Christ
			
			Son of God
			Lord
			cooperation in
			creation
				
				Son of God

incarnation for our salvation		because of love towards his creation virgin birth uniting humanity to God through himself suffered under Pontius Pilate resurrection ascension coming in glory Judgement	incarnation	incarnation

Holy Spirit
  proclaimed
  through the
  prophets the
  dispensations;
  extensive
  description of
  virgin birth,
  passion,
  resurrection,
  ascension in the
  flesh,
  coming in glory,
  general
  resurrection of
  the flesh,
  Judgement
			Spirit of God	Spirit

			furnishes us with the knowledge of truth has set forth the dispensations of the Father and the Son	

(continued)

1,10,1 (FaFo § 109b3)	1,22,1 (§ 109b4)	3,4,2 (§ 109b7)	4,33,7 (§ 109b13)	5,20,1 (§ 109b14)
				commandments constitution of the Church advent of the Lord salvation of the complete man

In addition, there are some shorter summaries that are not given any particular name that are scattered throughout the work.[200]

Clearly, then, Irenaeus adapts the *regula* according to context. Thus in 1,22,1 he insists on God's oneness in order to fend off the gnostics' distinction between a transcendent God and a demiurge (cf. 1,21); there is no need in this context to include information about the Son or the Holy Spirit. By contrast, in 5,20,1 he focusses on the truth of the incarnation and the work of redemption against gnostic docetism (cf. 5,1,2) on account of which he omits the passion, resurrection, and ascension.

In sum, in Irenaeus the terms 'faith' and 'rule of truth' refer to brief summaries of basic doctrines about the Father, the Son, and the Holy Spirit which resemble each other without being identical. In fact, the differences are so considerable that we are prevented from assuming that a fixed formula forms the basis of these texts. Yet their similarities do point to a basic teaching used in baptismal catechesis which comprised lessons about the Father, the Son, and the Holy Spirit and covered God's oneness, omnipotence, and creative activity, Christ's divine origin, birth, passion, resurrection, and ascension, and probably some other biblical narratives. By contrast, no extensive doctrine of the Holy Spirit seems to exist as yet. Irenaeus himself indicates in 3,4,2 that the *regula* has an important function in the mission to the 'barbarians' because it can be learned by heart by converts who do not speak Greek (and are, therefore, unable to read the Scriptures).[201]

At the same time, we can also see that the rule of faith is not bound to one single *Sitz im Leben* in Irenaeus' work. The *Epideixis* is, as the author himself

---

200 Cf. *Aduersus haereses* 1,3,6 (FaFo § 109b1: 'faith in one God, the Father Almighty, and in one [Lord] Jesus Christ, the Son of God'); 3,1,2 (§ 109b6: 'one God, Creator of heaven and earth, announced by the Law and the Prophets, and one Christ the Son of God'). In addition, cf. 2,32,3 (§ 109b5); 3,16,5 (§ 109b8); 3,16,6 (§ 109b9); 3,18,3 (§ 109b10); 4,9,2 (§ 109b11); 4,20,4 (§ 109b12).
201 Cf. Irenaeus, *Aduersus haereses* 3,4,2 (FaFo § 109b7).

states at the beginning, a 'summary record' (κεφαλαιωδὴς ὑπόμνημα) which serves 'to demonstrate, by means of a summary, the preaching of the truth, so as to strengthen your faith'. The idea is to give its recipient Marcianus all that is necessary so that he may 'understand all the members of the body of the truth and through a summary receive the exposition of the things of God' in order to safeguard his salvation; that he 'may confound all those who hold false opinions'; and, finally, that he 'may deliver our sound and irreproachable word in all boldness' to those who are interested to hear it.[202]

So the work is described as a ὑπόμνημα, a loose collection of notes on a particular subject.[203] Its purpose is threefold: to provide a corpus of basic doctrinal tenets and to enable the recipient both to defend them against heresy and to spread this Christian teaching through catechetical or missionary activity. Irenaeus, therefore, goes beyond what the work's presumed title Ἐπίδειξις τοῦ ἀποστολικοῦ κηρύγματος ('Proof/Demonstration of the apostolic preaching/proclamation') suggests. The refutation of heretics is only one element of a broader endeavour which also contains catechetical elements. Yet the *Epideixis* is not, strictly speaking, in itself a catechetical work (there is no indication that Marcianus was a catechumen), but may well be addressed to a priest or even a bishop, or some kind of missionary, in order to provide a dogmatic basis (i.e. the 'rule of faith') for the instruction of others.[204]

By contrast the work *Against the Heresies* belongs to the philosophical-theological genre of ἔλεγχος ('proof', but also 'refutation') or ἀνατροπή ('refutation') which is generally well documented.[205] Its express purpose is to refute the arguments of the representative of a different school, in this case the gnostic doctrines of Valentinus and Ptolemy.[206] However, in this particular case the institutional setting is *not* a school. (Irenaeus does not seem to have had formal philosophical training.[207]) Instead he reacts to the request from a learned friend who, perhaps living in Asia Minor, seems to be the head of a circle of individuals interested in theology.[208]

In other words, we can distinguish three *Sitze im Leben* for the 'rule of truth' as regards Irenaeus: mission and pre-baptismal catechesis, theological instruction (perhaps of priests), and refutation and polemic. As a result, Irenaeus adapts the

---

202 Irenaeus, *Epideixis* 1 (tr. Behr 1997, p. 39).
203 On this literary genre cf. Eichele 1998; Montanari 2006.
204 Cf. Smith 1952, p. 14.
205 Cf. Eusebius, *Historia ecclesiastica* 5,7,1 (ἔλεγχος καὶ ἀνατροπή τῆς ψευδωνύμου γνώσεως; cf. 3,23,3) = Irenaeus, *Aduersus haereses* 4 prol. 1 (*detectio et euersio falsae cognitionis*). On this genre cf. Kinzig 2000, pp. 164–71.
206 Cf. Irenaeus, *Aduersus haereses* 1, prol. 2.
207 Cf. Wyrwa 2018, p. 883.
208 Cf. Irenaeus, *Aduersus haereses* 1, prol. 2–3.

rule according to these literary conventions and may even quote the rule in different configurations within one and the same work, according to the need of the respective argument. Returning to the image of building blocks, we can see different structures being assembled from basically the same blocks.

4.4.4 Tertullian

Tertullian (d. *c.* 220) was strongly influenced by Irenaeus in his anti-gnostic polemic. For him the one unalterable 'rule of faith' (*regula fidei*)[209] had been 'instituted' by Christ for the express purpose of refuting heretics and later propagated by the apostles to whom Christ had revealed its content.[210] It was made public by the 'catholic' churches, but Tertullian offers no details how this was done.[211] By contrast, the many doctrines of the heretics (which may also be called *regula*[212]) have sprung up later and threaten the one true rule.[213]

We find three extensive summaries of the faith in Tertullian's writings that are expressly called *regula fidei*.[214] Two of them occur in anti-heretical treatises, the other in a work of a practical nature. *De praescriptione haereticorum* (203) is directed against Marcion (*fl. c.* 150) and his pupil Apelles as well as against the gnostic Valentinus (*fl. c.* 150). *Aduersus Praxeam* (210/211) deals with the doctrines of the otherwise unknown and, perhaps, pseudonymous Praxeas whom Tertullian accuses of monarchianism and patripassianism: in his opponent's view Praxeas did not distinguish sufficiently between the divine persons of Father and Son which could lead to the idea that the Father had been crucified which was considered heretical.[215] In *De*

---

209 Cf. also the analysis of the term by Braun 1977, pp. 446–54, 716.

210 Cf., e.g., Tertullian, *De praescriptione haereticorum* 13,6 (FaFo § 111b1); 20,1–5 (§ 350b1); 21,1–7 (§ 111b3); 36,3 (§ 111b5); 37,1–7 (§ 111b6; here Tertullian may allude to Gal 6:16); *Apologeticum* 47,10 (§ 350a; *regula ueritatis*); id., *Aduersus Praxeam* 2,2 (§ 111e1); id., *Aduersus Marcionem* 4,2,5; 4,36,12; 5,3,1; 5,20,2; id., *De resurrectione mortuorum* 48,2 (*nostrae spei regula*); id., *De uirginibus uelandis* 1,4(3; § 111c); id., *De monogamia* 2,4; id., *De pudicitia* 12,3; 15,11.

211 Cf. Tertullian, *De praescriptione haereticorum* 26,9.

212 Cf., e.g., Tertullian, *Aduersus Marcionem* 1,1,7; 1,20,1 (where *regula* also seems to have been used by the Marcionites); 4,5,6; 4,17,11; id., *Aduersus Valentinianos* 4,3. 4; 30,1; id., *De anima* 2,5; id., *De carne Christi* 6,4.

213 Cf. Tertullian, *Aduersus Hermogenem* 1,1; id., *Aduersus Marcionem* 3,1,2; 5,19,1; id., *Aduersus Valentinianos* 4,1; id., *Aduersus Praxeam* 20,3; id., *De monogamia* 2,3. However, the Montanists destroy no 'rule of faith or truth' (*aliquam fidei aut spei regulam*); id., *De ieiunio* 1,3; id., *De pudicitia* 8,12.

214 There are other rule-like summaries or references in Tertullian's works: *Apologeticum* 17,1–3; 18,2–3 (FaFo § 111a); *De praescriptione haereticorum* 23,11 (§ 111b4); 36,5 (§ 111b5); *De carne Christi* 5,4. 7; 20,1 (§ 111d); *Aduersus Praxeam* 3,1; 4,1 (§ 111e2); 9,1; 14,1; 20,1; 30,5 (§ 111e3).

215 Cf. FaFo § 110 and below pp. 125, 139 f.

uirginibus uelandis (205–208?) Tertullian advocates the veiling of young unmarried women in his hometown Carthage. Here his rigorism betrays his sympathies with Montanism which had developed some years previously (*c.* 203). In all cases the content of the *regula* is introduced by some form of *credere*.

In order better to illustrate how flexible these texts are, I will once more present their content side by side:

De praescriptione haereticorum 13,1–5 (FaFo § 111b1)	*De uirginibus uelandis* 1,4(3) (§ 111c)	*Aduersus Praxeam* 2,1 (§ 111e1)
Name of summary: *regula fidei*	Name of summary: *regula fidei*	Name of summary: *regula*
God	God	God
one	one	one
	Almighty	
creator; creation out of nothing through his Word	creator	
Word = Son	Son Jesus Christ	Son/Word proceeded from him cooperation in creation
seen by the patriarchs; heard by the prophets		
virgin birth (through Spirit and power of God)	virgin birth	virgin birth
		being both man and God, the Son of Man and the Son of God
incarnation and birth as Jesus Christ preaching of the new law promise of the kingdom of heaven miracles		named Jesus Christ
		suffered died
crucifixion	crucifixion under Pontius Pilate	
		buried according to the Scriptures
resurrection on the third day ascension	resurrection on the third day ascension	resurrection ascension

(continued)

De praescriptione haereticorum 13,1–5 (FaFo § 111b1)	De uirginibus uelandis 1,4(3) (§ 111c)	Aduersus Praxeam 2,1 (§ 111e1)
sitting at the right hand of the Father sending of the power of the Holy Spirit coming with glory general resurrection of the flesh Last Judgement	sitting at the right hand of the Father coming general resurrection of the flesh Last Judgement	sitting at the right hand of the Father coming Last Judgement
		sends Holy Spirit Paraclete 'sanctifier of the faith of those who believe in the Father, the Son, and the Holy Spirit'

Similarly to Irenaeus, these three summaries share a number of common features: God – oneness – Son – virgin birth – passion (although expressed differently) – resurrection – ascension – sitting at the right hand of the Father – coming – Last Judgement. At the same time, it is obvious that the remaining differences would be hard to explain if a fixed formula had already existed. These differences are occasioned by the context and the rhetorical strategies of the individual treatises. Thus in *De praescriptione haereticorum* Tertullian insists on the oneness of God, the creation by this God,[216] and the revelation of the Word or Son in the Old Testament in order to argue against the separation of the gods of the Old and New Testament, and underlines the reality of the Son's incarnation (against docetism) in mentioning his preaching and miracles.[217]

By contrast, in *Aduersus Praxeas* the distinction between God and the Son/Word by 'procession' is emphasized (*qui ex ipso processerit*) in order to combat the idea that the Father himself suffered in the incarnation. In addition, in order to leave no doubt that God did not undergo earthly emotions of any kind, Tertullian adds 'being both man and God, the Son of Man and the Son of God' (*hominem*

---

216 Cf. also Tertullian, *Aduersus Marcionem* 1,21,5.
217 According to Tertullian, *Aduersus Marcionem* 3,17,5 and id., *Aduersus Iudaeos* 9,29 Christ's preaching and miracles can be seen from the *scripturarum regula*.

et deum, filium hominis et filium dei) in a way that sounds Chalcedonian *avant la lettre*. At the end of this rule Tertullian also mentions the Holy Spirit which was sent by Christ, without, however, being an explicit object of belief. Yet he then adds a trinitarian formula citing belief in the Father, the Son, and the Spirit, which is 'sanctified' by the Paraclete (*sanctificatorem fidei eorum, qui credunt in patrem et filium et spiritum sanctum*).

In many respects the *regula* in *De uirginibus uelandis* is the most significant of the three passages. Here Tertullian quotes the rule in order to explain that the doctrine in the Church is unalterable and thus to affirm his own orthodoxy. Consequently, he is likely to enumerate those tenets which he shares with his opponents and which constitute the basis of the teaching in his North African church. At the same time, Tertullian does advocate changes in the *disciplina* which regulates the life of the Church under the guidance of the Holy Spirit. Such changes will gradually lead to an improvement of customs:

> As this law of faith is abiding (*hac lege fidei manente*), the other [succeeding] points of discipline and conduct (*disciplinae et conuersationis*) now permit the newness of correction, as the grace of God is of course operating and advancing even to the end. [. . .] What, then, is the Paraclete's guidance but this: the direction of discipline, the revelation of the Scripture, the reformation of the intellect, the advancement towards the better things?[218]

Strikingly, although the role of the Spirit is thus paramount for Tertullian, he does not yet include it in his *regula*. In addition, its christological section displays such close similarities with the Roman Creed that we will have to consider these in a later chapter.[219] Finally, the relation of the *regula* to baptism is not emphasized in the same way as in Irenaeus' writings. Baptism is not mentioned in the context of the *regulae* just quoted nor is, conversely, any *regula* quoted or alluded to in Tertullian's treatise *De baptismo*. Nonetheless, it is likely that summaries such as those quoted above were regularly used in his church, because otherwise the recourse to them as a an agreed basis would lose its argumentative power.

4.4.5 Novatian

The presbyter Novatian (who was later one of the protagonists of a schism in the Roman church) refers to the *regula ueritatis* ('rule of truth'; he does not use the term *regula fidei*) in his book *On the Trinity* (written perhaps around 240). He ap-

---

218 Tertullian, *De uirginibus uelandis* 1,5(4). 8(5) (tr. ANF; altered). On the idea of progress in Tertullian, cf. Kinzig 1994, pp. 239–79, esp. 266–9.
219 Cf. below ch. 4.6.

pears to explain its content section by section:[220] He first mentions the belief in 'God, the Father and the Lord Almighty' and describes his creative activity.[221] This is later followed by a brief christological section:

> The same rule of truth teaches us to believe, in addition to the Father, also in the Son of God, Christ Jesus, the Lord our God, but the Son of God [. . .].[222]

Here Jesus is called Son of God, Christ, and 'the Lord our God' (*dominum deum nostrum*). The first two titles are already familiar to us. The final one may have been taken from Hos 6:1 and may rest on a christological exegesis of this biblical verse as found, for example, in Tertullian and Cyprian,[223] who both see it as prophesying the resurrection and ascension of Christ. This is the earliest evidence for *dominum deum nostrum* in a credal document. (The syntagma is, in any case, not very often attested.[224]) Nonetheless, it is obviously traditional in Novatian's context because the Roman theologian feels compelled to qualify it straight away, probably in order to prevent a modalist misinterpretation:

> but the Son of God – of that God who is both one and alone, indeed the Founder of all things (*conditor scilicet rerum omnium*) [. . .].[225]

In another passage Novatian again refers to the *regula* in a credal context:

> Therefore we must believe, according to the prescribed rule (*secundum praescriptam regulam*), in the Lord, the one true God (*in Dominum unum uerum Deum*), and in him whom he has fittingly (*consequenter*) sent, Jesus Christ, who would, as we have said, never have associated himself with the Father, unless he had also wanted to be understood as God.[226]

The *regula* is here, once more, dyadic. It is uncertain whether the expression *praescriptam regulam* actually refers to a written document of some kind – *praescribere* may also simply mean 'lay down', 'prescribe', or 'appoint' in a wider

---

220 Apart from the references discussed below the *regula ueritatis* is also mentioned in Novatian, *De trinitate* 11,10; 21,1; 29,19 (cf. also 16,4; 26,17); id., *Epistula de cibis Iudaicis* 7,3.

221 Novatian, *De trinitate* 1,1 (FaFo § 119a).

222 Novatian, *De trinitate* 9,1 (FaFo § 119b).

223 Cf. Tertullian, *Aduersus Iudaeos* 13,23; Cyprian, *De dominica oratione* 35 which give the text of Hos 6:1 as follows: 'Eamus et reuertamur ad dominum deum nostrum'. The same version in Jerome, *Commentarii in prophetas minores, In Osee 2, 6*.

224 For later western attestations cf. FaFo § 171 (Germinius of Sirmium); § 452 (*Constitutum Constantini*). For *dominum et deum nostrum* cf. § 154 (The Second Creed of Sirmium); § 186 (Wulfila); § 457 (Arian creed). For κύριον θεὸν ἡμῶν we have no reference in a credal text. For κύριον καὶ θεὸν ἡμῶν cf. § 174f (Basil of Caesarea).

225 Novatian, *De trinitate* 9,1 (FaFo § 119b).

226 Novatian, *De trinitate* 16,5.

sense; but it may be significant that Novatian replaces the appeal to tradition by a term which emphasizes the normative character of the rule. As regards content, it is not quite clear whether *in Dominum unum uerum Deum* (which is taken from Jn 17:3)[227] actually refers to the wording of a particular formula.[228]

In chapter 17 we find a reference to Christ's participation in creation, ostensibly as part of the *regula ueritatis*:

> What if Moses follows this same rule of truth (*regulam ueritatis*) and in the beginning of his writings has given us this: that we may learn that all things are created and founded through the Son of God (*omnia creata et condita esse per dei filium*), that is, through the Word of God?[229]

This may sound as if *omnia creata et condita esse per dei filium* (which alludes to Eph 3:9) somehow formed part of the *regula*, but there is no proof of that.

Later Novatian proceeds to a chapter on the Holy Spirit which he introduces as follows:

> But indeed, the order of reason and the authority of the faith in the disposition of the words and in the Scriptures of the Lord (*ordo rationis et fidei auctoritas digestis uocibus et litteris domini*) admonish us after these things to believe also in the Holy Spirit, [who was] once promised to the Church and given in the appointed occasions of times.[230]

Interestingly, here he fails to mention the *regula ueritatis* again, instead referring to the *ordo rationis* (whose exact meaning remains obscure) and the *fidei auctoritas*.

What then is the *regula ueritatis* in Novatian? Cyprian expressly says in a letter that Novatian baptizes 'with the same symbol' (*eodem symbolo*) which he himself uses.[231] In and by itself the *symbolum* is not necessarily identical with the *regula*, let alone a full-blown creed (*symbolum* could simply mean the baptismal formula). However, Dionysius of Alexandria claims in a letter to his namesake at Rome that Novatian 'rejects holy baptism, overturns the faith and confession which precede it (τήν τε πρὸ αὐτοῦ πίστιν καὶ ὁμολογίαν ἀνατρέποντι), and entirely banishes the

---

227 Cf. also Novatian, *De trinitate* 26,17.
228 It is later found in FaFo § 171 (Germinius of Sirmium) and § 486 (Creed of the First Council of Toledo (400) and its longer version by Pastor of Palencia). The expression *in unum solum uerum deum* occurs in § 453 (Auxentius); § 456 (Palladius of Ratiaria); its Greek equivalent ἕνα καὶ μόνον ἀληθινὸν θεόν formed part of various eastern creeds and credal formulae: the Synod of Niké (359; § 159); Eudoxius of Constantinople (§ 162); Eunomius (§ 163c2); Basil of Caesarea (§ 174f); *Apostolic Constitutions* (§ 182c); and Antioch (§§ 198 and 203).
229 Novatian, *De trinitate* 17,1.
230 Novatian, *De trinitate* 29,1 (FaFo § 119c).
231 Cyprian, *Epistula 69*, 7,1 (FaFo § 92a).

Holy Spirit from them'.[232] Taking all the aforementioned observations together, we must conclude that Novatian is referring to *some* kind of formula which had come to be used in Rome by the middle of the third century, probably in the context of pre-baptismal catechesis and, perhaps, during baptism. Just as the liturgy as a whole was not yet written down,[233] this formula may well have been transmitted only orally and may have formed part of a larger credal context which possibly still fluctuated to some extent. In particular, it did perhaps not yet include the Holy Spirit.

In any case, there is no indication that Novatian is referring here to 'the early Roman church's baptismal symbol of faith'[234] or 'the old Roman creed',[235] if that denotes a fixed single creed. Likewise, we are unable to tell from Novatian's evidence whether he is quoting the entire *regula* as used in Rome or just its beginning as a means of structuring his treatise. Themes like Christ's birth, passion, resurrection, ascension, and sitting at the right hand also occur later in the work, but without explicit reference to the *regula*. Finally, Novatian does not tell us whether the regula is interrogatory or declaratory. We will later see how one might best describe the situation in Rome on the basis of the available data.[236]

4.4.6 Later authors

In his exegesis of Revelation, written in *c.* 260, Victorinus of Poetovio (d. *c.* 304) explains the 'measuring rod' (κάλαμος = *arundo*) of Rev 11:1 in such a way that one is reminded of the 'rule of faith':[237] he adds *fidei* and calls for 'confessing' a number of propositions which he claims to have come from the Lord himself:

> The 'measure' of faith (*mensura fidei*) is the command of our Lord to confess (*confiteri*) the Father Almighty, as we have said,
>
> and that his Son, our Lord Jesus Christ, was begotten by the Father spiritually (*spiritaliter apud patrem genitum*) before the beginning of the world and became human; that, when he had overcome death and was received with his body into the heavens by the Father, he shed forth the Holy Spirit [cf. Acts 2:33], the gift and pledge of immortality [cf. Eph 1:14];
>
> that he (*hunc*) was announced through the prophets;

---

232 Dionysius of Alexandria, *Epistula V 4* (Feltoe = Eusebius, *Historia ecclesiastica* 7,8; FaFo § 87a).
233 Cf. below p. 131 and n. 303.
234 Dunn 2002, p. 390, referring to d'Alès 1922, p. 421.
235 Papandrea 2012, p. 57.
236 Cf. below chs. 4.5.1, 4.6, and 5.1.
237 For what follows cf. also Esterson 2015, pp. 51–4, 82 f., 325–41.

that he (*hunc*) was described by the Law;

that he (*hunc*) was God's hand [cf. Is 66:2: Acts 7:50], the Word of the Father Almighty, and founder (*conditorem*) of the whole world.

This is the 'reed' (*arundo*) and the 'measure' of faith (*mensura fidei*) such that no one worships at the holy altar except the one who confesses this: the Lord and his Christ [cf. Acts 4:26].[238]

The passage enumerates the following propositions:

Father: omnipotence; Son/our Lord Jesus Christ/God's hand/Word: preexistence – incarnation – death – bodily resurrection/ascension – sending of the Spirit – announcement in the Old Testament (prophets and Law) – founder of the world.

The commentary contains another credal statement comprising only christological tenets:

'Twenty-four elders and four animals, having harps and cups, and singing a new song' [cf. Rev 5:8–9]: <the proclamation of the Old Testament associated with the New shows the Christian people singing a new song>, that is, [the proclamation] of those who publicly recite their confession (*id est confessionem suam publice proferentium*).

It is new that the Son of God became human.

It is new that he was handed over to death by humans.

It is new that on the third day he rose again.

It is new that he ascended into the heavens bodily.

It is new that the remission of sins was granted to humankind.

It is new that humankind was sealed with the Holy Spirit.

It is new to receive the priesthood of intercession and to expect a kingdom of unbounded promise.

The harp with the chord stretched on its wooden [frame] signified the body of Christ, that is, the flesh of Christ linked with the passion whereas the cup signifies the confession (*confessionem*) and the lineage of the new priesthood.[239]

The first elements in this series are also found in the aforementioned triadic confession: incarnation – death – resurrection (here supplemented by the third day) – corporeal ascension. But in order to reach the number seven (which refers to the seven seals of the scroll mentioned in Rev 5:1. 5 that Victorinus identifies with the Old Testament) he adds three more items: remission of sins – seal of the Holy Spirit – priesthood and kingdom.[240]

---

238 Victorinus of Poetovio, *Explanatio in Apocalypsin* 3, ll. 110–19, on Rev 11:1 (CChr.SL 5, p. 204).

239 Victorinus of Poetovio, *Explanatio in Apocalypsin* 2, ll. 190–202, on Rev 5:8 f. (CChr.SL 5, pp. 170–2).

240 In his commentary on Revelation Caesarius of Arles, who clearly knew this exegetical tradition, only mentions the incarnation, death, resurrection, ascension, and remission of sins which

Taking both these passages together we may conclude that participation in worship presupposed some kind of confession and that this confession was recited in public. The divergences between both lists further suggest that this confession was not yet a fixed formula, which, in turn, probably means that the public confession was not one made by the entire congregation. Instead, Victorinus may either refer to the baptismal interrogations or to a separate liturgical act in which key tenets such as those enumerated above were expressed in public (as answers to credal questions? as a recitation of all or some of the tenets mentioned by Victorinus?). In any case, there is no indication that Victorinus knew a fixed formula.

∗

In a synodal letter supposedly sent by six bishops to Paul of Samosata prior to his deposition in *c.* 268, its authors begin by stating the character of their letter:

> When we conversed with each other we had already displayed our faith (τὴν ἑαυτῶν πίστιν). But in order that it may be clearer what each of us holds, and that we might have greater certainty about the disputed points (τὰ ἀμφισβητούμενα), it seemed good to us to set forth this written faith (ἔδοξεν ἡμῖν ἔγγραφον τὴν πίστιν), proclaimed from the Law, the Prophets, and the New Testament, which we received from the beginning and possess, handed down and preserved in the holy, catholic Church until the present day through the succession from the blessed apostles, who had become both 'eye-witnesses and servants of the Word' [Lk 1:2].[241]

One would, perhaps, expect a succinct rule of faith to follow this exposition. Yet the text itself is a lengthy binitarian treatise which insists on the divinity of the Son and on his existence distinct from the Father. Those who deny the Son's pre-existence and advocate an adoptionist theology are considered 'alien from the ecclesiastical rule' (ἀλλότριον τοῦ ἐκκλησιαστικοῦ κανόνος).[242] No explanation is given what this entailed in practice (excommunication?). There is no indication either that such censure would be identical with an anathema.

In its implicit opposition against theological doctrines as expressed by Neo-Arians and by Apolinarius of Laodicea, the bishops' letter better matches the theological debates of the second half of the fourth century.[243] In the end, the six ask Paul to confirm that he agreed by adding his signature. This too is a proce-

---

he found in his own creed. Cf. *Expositio de Apocalypsi Sancti Iohannis* 4,11, ll. 50–2 (CChr.SL 105, p. 119).

241 Pseudo-Hymenaeus of Jerusalem et al., *Epistula ad Paulum Samosatenum* (FaFo § 126[1]).

242 Pseudo-Hymenaeus of Jerusalem et al., *Epistula ad Paulum Samosatenum* (FaFo § 126[3]).

243 Cf. Uthemann 1994, cols. 78 f. and below p. 465 n. 1.

dure for which there is no precedent in the third century which is why I consider the authenticity of this letter spurious.

∗

In the fourth century the κανών/*regula* comes to be identified with N and C^2,[244] but it never remains tied to one particular text[245] and may indeed later refer to the teachings of popes and councils.[246] There is even one instance where *regula* denotes the Lord's Prayer.[247]

4.4.7 Conclusions

We do not find a single declaratory creed until the end of the third century. However, we do find triadic homologies and christological summaries that are assembled to form *regulae fidei* for missionary and teaching purposes and in order to combat various kinds of deviant doctrines. As such they are surprisingly homogeneous in that they always contain the same set of propositions: God the Father is termed almighty and is seen as the creator of the world, while Jesus Christ/the Son of God/the Word is often seen as cooperating in creation. In addition, the christolog-

---

244 Cf., e.g., FaFo § 154c (Phoebadius of Agen: N; *perfectam fidei catholicae regulam*); § 205[2] (Definition of Faith of the (eastern) Council of Ephesus (431): N; 'rule and norm', κανόνι καὶ γνώμονι); § 498 (Third Council of Braga (675): C^2); § 505 tit. (Seventeenth Council of Toledo (694): C^2); § 569b[944] (Second Council of Ephesus (449): N and C^2; 'rule of piety', τῷ κανόνι τῆς εὐσεβείας); § 570d[6] (Council of Chalcedon: N); § 586 (Synod of Soissons (744): N; *ecclesiastica regula*); § 688 (Isidore of Seville; N; *uerae fidei regula*); § 832a (*Opus Caroli regis contra synodum (Libri Carolini)*: C^2; *secundum uerissimam sanctae fidei regulam*).
245 Cf., e.g., FaFo § 232b (Cosmas Indicopleustes quoting Gal 6:16); § 255c (Leo the Great: Roman Creed); § 442[1] (Pope Hormisdas: *rectae fidei regulam*; Roman Creed); § 448[6] (Pope Agatho: *iuxta regulam sanctae catholicae atque apostolicae Christi*; Dyotheletism); § 449[6] (Pope Agatho: *pietatis regula*; Dyotheletism); § 451[1] (Pope Leo II: *regulis maiorum*; Dyotheletism); § 460[15] (Synod of Milan 680: *pietatis regula*; Dyotheletism); § 518 (Caelestius the Pelagian: *secundum regulam uniuersalis ecclesiae*); § 636c, g (Augustine: local creed; identification of *regula fidei* and *symbolum*); § 664[32. 33] (Ildefonsus of Toledo: local creed; *uerae fidei regulam, apostolicam regulam*); § 684c4[1], [8] (Mozarabic Liturgical Books: local creed; identification of *regula fidei* and *symbolum; sanctae fidei regulam*); § 790[1] (*Exhortatio ad plebem Christianam*; local creed).
246 Cf., e.g., FaFo § 479[4] (Deneboerht, bishop of Worcester); § 491 tit. (Isidore of Seville; here the *regula fidei*, i.e. the decisions of the councils, is seen as an addition to the *apostolicum symbolum*); § 496[2] (Eighth Council of Toledo (653)); § 497[1] (Council of Mérida (666): *priorum patrum regulam*); § 545 (Fourth Edict Confirming Chalcedon: *secundum patrum regulas*); § 710 (Arno of Salzburg: *certam et immutabilem catholicae fidei*).
247 Cf. FaFo § 659 (Ferrandus and Fulgentius: *piam regulam dominicae orationis*).

ical summaries usually enumerate Christ's incarnation, passion, resurrection, ascension, and sometimes his sitting at the right hand and his return. Finally, the Holy Spirit is often mentioned, but there are no consistent tenets attached to the Spirit yet. Many of these elements were later included in the Roman Creed and the eastern synodal creeds, whereas others were not adopted, such as the creation from nothing or references to Christ's preaching or miracles.

Furthermore, the christological summary and the triadic homologies are often quoted independently from one another and appear to have had distinct histories. Triadic homologies are often linked with baptism whereas christological summaries were used in an apologetic context: over against docetists who denied the reality of the incarnation in one way or another; over against pagans who were suspicious about the precise status Jesus had in Christian congregations (given that he had been executed as a criminal); and over against Jews who denied his messiahship. We will see below in chapter 4.6 where and at what point these two different traditions were first combined.

4.5 The emergence of credal interrogations

As demonstrated in the previous chapters, triadic homologies, although rare in the beginning, were quite common by the middle of the third century. In particular, it appears that the triadic baptismal formula preserved in Mt 28:19 and *Didache* 7,1. 3 was widely used, although we have no details of how it came to be so widespread.[248] In some places baptism may have even been practised without any particular formula.[249] In addition, baptisms that were performed 'into the name of Jesus' or 'upon the name of Jesus' only may also have taken place, but seem to have played no more than a marginal role.[250] We will see in this chapter that there is some evidence from the second half of the third century onwards that the baptismal formula was either combined with, or replaced by, questions about the faith which were posed to the convert either before or during baptism.

---

248 Cf. above p. 75 and n. 78.

249 Cf., e.g., Acts 8:38 and Campenhausen 1971(1979), pp. 202–5, who cites non-Christian parallels for similar ablution rites without accompanying formulae.

250 Cf. esp. 1Cor 1:13 where the 'baptism into the name of Paul' (εἰς τὸ ὄνομα Παύλου; rejected by Paul) may mirror baptism into the name of Jesus; Acts 2:38 (ἐπὶ τῷ ὀνόματι Ἰησοῦ Χριστοῦ); 8:16 (εἰς τὸ ὄνομα τοῦ κυρίου Ἰησοῦ); 10:48 (ἐν τῷ ὀνόματι Ἰησοῦ Χριστοῦ); 19:5 (εἰς τὸ ὄνομα τοῦ κυρίου Ἰησοῦ); cf. also 22:16. Furthermore Jas 2:7; *Pastor Hermae* 72 (= *Mandatum* VIII,6),4. This is not the place to deal with this intricate problem. Cf. esp. Campenhausen 1971(1979) who categorically denies that baptism 'into the name of Jesus' ever existed; by contrast, this is affirmed by Rouwhorst 2022, col. 986.

However, in some congregations the triadic baptismal formula may have sufficed. The motives for such a change are unknown. Perhaps the baptismal formula was transformed into questions in order to emphasize the binding character of the rite; at the same time, these changes may be related to the introduction of the renunciation of the devil which seems to have occurred around the middle of the second century.[251]

The earliest example for such a question about the convert's faith prior to baptism probably occurs in Acts 8:37 which in modern editions of the New Testament is relegated to the apparatus or to a footnote because it is an addition to the original text. In this addition the deacon Philip says to the Ethiopian eunuch when the latter asks whether he might be baptized (FaFo § 88):

'If you believe with all your heart, you may.' He replied (ἀποκριθείς), 'I believe that Jesus Christ is the Son of God.'

The earliest witness to this text is Irenaeus, *Aduersus haereses* 3,12,8 (written in 174/189) which perhaps suggests the middle of the second century as its date of composition.[252] Obviously, it was felt at some point in the transmission of Acts that some kind of 'faith statement' was missing. Strictly speaking, this is, of course, not a question, but, rather, a conditional permission. But the fact that the eunuch 'answers' (ἀποκριθείς) suggests the narration may well have been based on a preceding question: 'Do you believe that Jesus Christ is God?'

Be that as it may, from the late second century onwards, baptismal questions were widely used: there is clear evidence from Alexandria,[253] Palestine,[254] and Cappadocia;[255] but their development is best attested for Rome and North Africa.

4.5.1 Rome

As regards Rome, the best evidence comes from the *Old Gelasian Sacramentary* (OGS), a service book whose earliest preserved copy was written in *c.* 750. The

---

251 The first unequivocal testimony is found in Justin, *Apologia prima* 49,5 (cf. also 14,2; 25,2; 61,1). Cf. Kirsten 1960, esp. p. 35; Kretschmar 1970, pp. 42–5.
252 In 1Pet 3:21 (συνειδήσεως ἀγαθῆς ἐπερώτημα εἰς θεόν, δι' ἀναστάσεως Ἰησοῦ Χριστοῦ) ἐπερώτημα is probably not to be translated as 'question' but as 'appeal': 'an appeal to God for a good conscience, through the resurrection of Jesus Christ'. This is different in the Vulgate which reflects later practice: 'conscientiae bonae interrogatio in deum per resurrectionem Iesu Christi'. Cf. FaFo § 81.
253 Cf. Dionysius of Alexandria, *Epistula V 4* (Feltoe; FaFo § 87a); *V 5* (Feltoe; FaFo § 87b).
254 Cf. Origen, *In Numeros homilia 5*, 1 (FaFo § 83).
255 Cf. Firmilianus of Caesarea in Cyprian, *Epistula 75*, 10,5–11,1 (FaFo § 85).

attribution of this worship manual to Pope Gelasius (*sedit* 492–496), which was based on ambiguous evidence, is no longer upheld today. It was presumably compiled later, in the seventh century, on the basis of textual material that is much older.[256] The questions quoted in this sacramentary may even date from as early as the second half of the second century.[257] The Roman origin of the bulk of this sacramentary, already indicated by the title of the compilation (*Liber sacramentorum Romanae ecclesiae ordinis anni circuli*), cannot be further substantiated here, but is considered probable today by most liturgical historians. In it, the following questions were required to be asked during the baptismal act itself:

> Then, after the blessing of the font, you baptize everyone in turn, using these interrogations:
> 'Do you believe in God, the Father Almighty?'
> He answers, 'I believe.'
> 'Do you also believe in Jesus Christ, his only Son, our Lord, [who was] born and suffered (*natum et passum*)?'
> He answers, 'I believe.'
> 'Do you also believe in the Holy Spirit, the holy Church, the remission of sins, the resurrection of the flesh?'
> He answers, 'I believe.'
> Then each time you immerse him thrice in the water.[258]

In a recent article I have tried to show that, through a careful assessment of this text and other available evidence, we can reconstruct several versions of baptismal interrogations used in Rome in the second and third centuries. We may tentatively assign these to successive periods, and I call these versions OGS[G1], OGS*, OGS[G2], and TA[G].[259] Readers interested in the details of this process of reconstruction (which is very technical) may wish to consult this article.[260] In what follows I will not repeat this analysis, but limit myself to discussing these versions in turn. We have to keep in mind that they are nowhere directly attested and that the following paragraphs are, therefore, highly speculative. However, they may convey

---

256 Cf. Vogel 1986, pp. 64–70; Palazzo 1998, pp. 42–6. The sacramentary has come down to us in cod. Rome, Biblioteca Apostolica Vaticana, Reg. lat. 316, ff. 3–245 and cod. Paris, Bibliothèque Nationale, lat. 7193, ff. 41–56. Originally, they formed part of the same codex which was probably produced in the nunnery Notre-Dame-des-Chelles near Paris in the middle of the eighth century. The extant copies of the sacramentary and its original version must not, therefore, be confused. Cf. also below p. 503.
257 On their reconstruction and the details of dating, cf. Kinzig 1999(2017). For a criticism of this position (which I do not consider convincing) cf. Stewart-Sykes, 'Baptismal Creed', 2009.
258 *Sacramentarium Gelasianum Vetus* nos. 448–449 (FaFo § 675c). Similarly, § 675f.
259 In the article the abbreviations were slightly different: OGS[G1] = AGS[G1]; OGS* = AS*; OGS[G2] = AS[G2].
260 Cf. Kinzig, 'Ursprung', 2022.

a general idea of how the declaratory creeds at Rome (which I will discuss in chapter 5.1) gradually developed.

First version: OGS[G1]

The presumably earliest version of the baptismal questions used at Rome may have been even briefer and was probably in Greek (the language of the Roman Christian community at that time[261]):

Πιστεύεις εἰς θεὸν παντοκράτορα;	Do you believe in God Almighty?
Πιστεύεις εἰς Χριστὸν Ἰησοῦν [*or:* Ἰη-σοῦν Χριστόν], τὸν υἱὸν τοῦ θεοῦ [*or:* αὐτοῦ], (τὸν) γεννηθέντα καὶ παθόντα [*or:* γεν(ν)ητὸν καὶ παθητόν];	Do you believe in Christ Jesus [*or:* Jesus Christ], the Son of God [*or:* his Son], [who was] born and suffered?
Πιστεύεις εἰς τὸ ἅγιον πνεῦμα, ἁγίαν ἐκ-κλησίαν, σαρκὸς ἀνάστασιν;	Do you believe in the Holy Spirit, the holy Church, the resurrection of the flesh?

It seems that a simple triadic formula as preserved in Mt 28:19 and *Didache* 7,1. 3 was expanded by additional elements. The first addition παντοκράτορα is well-known from the Septuagint as translating Hebrew ṣᵉḇā'ôṯ and šadday and is used in combination with both κύριος and θεός.[262] In the New Testament it occurs once in 2Cor 6:18 as a quotation of Amos 3:13 and then exclusively in Revelation in the stereotypical formula ὁ θεὸς ὁ παντοκράτωρ.[263] In *First Clement* the phrase ὁ παντοκράτωρ θεός is also frequently used.[264] Here the dyadic formula

> Grace be to you, and peace from Almighty God through Jesus Christ (ἀπὸ παντοκράτορος θεοῦ διὰ Ἰησοῦ Χριστοῦ) be multiplied.[265]

is especially significant, because it shows that by the end of the first century the term had come to be used as God's attribute in greeting formulae in Rome. A similar greeting is found in the *Letter to the Philippians* by Polycarp.[266] The Jewish origin of the term is also visible in the writings of Justin Martyr who uses it only

---

261 Cf. below p. 153 and n. 35.
262 Cf. Michaelis 1965, p. 914.
263 Cf. 1:8; 4:8; 11:17; 15:3; 16:7. 14; 19:6. 15; 21:11.
264 Cf. *First Clement* praescr.; 2,3; 32,4; 62,2. Cf. also 8,5; 56,6; 60,4.
265 *First Clement* praescr. Similarly in 32,4.
266 Cf. Polycarp, *Epistula ad Philippenses*, praescr.: 'Mercy be upon you and peace from Almighty God (παρὰ θεοῦ παντοκράτορος) and Jesus Christ, our Saviour, be multiplied.'

in his *Dialogue with Trypho*, combining it repeatedly with ποιητὴς τῶν ὅλων ('creator of everything').[267]

In Justin we may even find an allusion to OGS[G1]:

> And his powerful word persuaded many to abandon the demons whom they used to serve, and to believe in [*or*: trust upon] Almighty God through him (καὶ ἐπὶ τὸν παντοκράτορα θεὸν δι' αὐτοῦ πιστεύειν).[268]

We have already seen above that God's omnipotence was by no means undisputed. The *Third Letter to the Corinthians* turned against Christian gnostic groups that seem to have rejected the idea, and Irenaeus also argued against such views.[269] This may have precipitated the insertion of the title into baptismal interrogations in order to make sure that the creator God was also identified as the Father of Jesus Christ and that there was no inferior demiurge with limited power who had created the (evil) world.

Incidentally, the English translation of παντοκράτωρ as 'almighty' or 'all-powerful' is not quite correct as κρατεῖν means primarily 'to rule', 'to conquer', 'to master', so that a translation as 'all-ruling' would probably be more accurate.[270] Instead, the English translation (like the German *allmächtig*) renders Latin *omnipotens*. It has often been said that its Greek equivalent is, strictly speaking, παντοδύναμος.[271] However, when παντοκράτωρ was translated into Latin there simply was no appropriate adjective available. We find *omnipotens* for παντοκράτωρ not only in early Latin versions of the Old Testament,[272] but also in Latin translations of 2Cor 6:18.[273]

The addition τὸν υἱὸν τοῦ θεοῦ/αὐτοῦ needs no further comment as dozens of examples are found in the New Testament. It was added in order better to define the relationship between Jesus Christ and God.

The syntagma (τὸν) γεννηθέντα καὶ παθόντα or, alternatively, γεν(ν)ητὸν καὶ παθητόν is more complex. Some time ago I argued that παθόντα/παθητόν is not a summary of the entire passion and resurrection of Christ, but that the emphasis is in fact solely on Christ's suffering in order to underline the connection between

---

267 Cf. Justin, *Dialogus cum Tryphone* 16,4; 38,2. Cf. also 22,4 (= Amos 3:13); 83,4; 96,3; 139,4; 142,2.
268 *Dialogus cum Tryphone* 83,4.
269 Cf. above chs. 4.4.2 and 4.4.3. As regards discussions about God's omnipotence in creation cf. the surveys in Koeckert 2012, col. 991; Koeckert 2019, cols. 1060–8.
270 Cf., however, Hommel 1956, p. 124 f. who translates παντοκράτωρ as 'all-preserving'.
271 Cf., e.g., Kelly 1972, pp. 136 f.
272 Cf. *Vetus Latina Database*. Cf., e.g., Amos 4:13 (κύριος ὁ θεὸς ὁ παντοκράτωρ ὄνομα αὐτῷ) which Ambrose translates as *dominus (deus) omnipotens nomen est ei*; cf. *De fide* 1,1; 2,4; *De spiritu sancto* 2,48; *De incarnationis dominicae sacramento* 10,115.
273 Cf., e.g., Lucifer of Cagliari, *De non conueniendo cum haereticis* 13 (twice); Ambrosiaster, *Commentarius in Pauli epistulas ad Corinthios*, ad Cor. II, 6,18.

baptism and the crucifixion as it is also found elsewhere.[274] Here it may suffice to mention Calixtus, later bishop of Rome (217–222), who is said to have persuaded his predecessor Zephyrinus (*sedit c.* 199 – *c.* 217) at the beginning of the century to declare 'publicly' (δημοσίᾳ):

> I know that there is one God, Christ Jesus, and aside from him [I know] none other who was begotten or subject to suffering (γενητὸν καὶ παθητόν).[275]

The creed-like formulation is so striking that one may assume a direct allusion to the interrogatory creed as preserved in the OGS.

A direct parallel to it is found in Tertullian's *Aduersus Praxeam*. In this treatise, Praxeas, who was active in Rome, is sharply attacked by the rhetor from Carthage because of his patripassianism. In the opening chapter, Tertullian claims that Praxeas, in his attempt to defend the oneness of the Lord, taught 'that the Father himself descended into the Virgin, was himself born from her, himself suffered (*ipsum ex ea natum, ipsum passum*), indeed was himself Jesus Christ'.[276] And a little later Tertullian reproduces the views of the Roman heretic in these words:

> In the course of time, then, the Father [was] born and the Father suffered (*pater natus et pater passus*), God himself, the Lord Almighty, whom they declare to be Jesus Christ.[277]

Possibly, Praxeas quoted the words *pater natus et pater passus* from baptismal questions in use in the Roman community, in such a way as to take the participles *natum et passum* from the second question whilst pointedly connecting them to the Father. Thus we have indications that at least the second of the baptismal questions was used in Rome in the form here called OGS[G1] already in the second half of the second century.

The addition of the holy Church and the resurrection of the flesh may both be connected to the struggle against Marcionitism and (gnostic) docetism. In the *Shepherd of Hermas* the angel of repentance makes the following announcement:

> I want to show you all things that the Holy Spirit, which spoke with you in the form of the Church, showed you. For that Spirit is the Son of God.[278]

Irenaeus repeatedly emphasizes that the proclamation of the truth of the Gospel is only found in the Church because it contains the Holy Spirit; those who do not

---

274 Cf. Kinzig 1999(2017), pp. 254–60. For wider background cf. also Kinzig 2013.
275 Quoted in Hippolytus, *Refutatio omnium haeresium* 9,11,3 (FaFo § 112).
276 Tertullian, *Aduersus Praxeam* 1,1 (FaFo § 110a). Cf. also below pp. 139 f.
277 Tertullian, *Aduersus Praxeam* 2,1 (FaFo § 110b).
278 *Pastor Hermae* 78 (= *Similitudo* IX,1),1.

participate in the Church but continue to teach their false doctrines and to behave in a depraved way have no part in the Spirit:

> For where the Church is, there is also the Spirit of God; and where the Spirit of God is, there is the Church, and every kind of grace; but the Spirit is truth.[279]

Irenaeus also calls the *regula fidei* 'the true knowledge, the doctrine of the apostles, and the ancient constitution of the Church throughout the whole world'.[280]

Tertullian offers clear evidence that the Church was mentioned in the version of the baptismal questions known to him:

> Moreover, after pledging both of the attestation of faith and the promise of salvation under the three [witnesses] (*sub tribus et testatio fidei et sponsio salutis*), there is of necessity added mention of the Church; inasmuch as, wherever there are three (that is, the Father, the Son, and the Holy Spirit), there is the Church, which is the body of the three [cf. Mt 18:20; 1Jn 5:7–8].[281]

In other authors of the second and third centuries we also find the attribute 'holy' attached to the Church.[282] In particular, Cyprian is propagating this attribute which is also found in the baptismal questions of North Africa.[283] North African texts add it to the 'Church', as do many other authors, in order to distinguish this particular kind of 'assembly' (which is the original meaning of ἐκκλησία) from that of all dissidents and schismatics.

Finally, the resurrection of the flesh was mentioned in order to reject all interpretations that saw the resurrection (both of Christ and of humankind) as solely a spiritual event or denied it altogether.[284] Jesus' fleshly resurrection was not only rejected by Marcion and the Valentinian gnostics but seems to have been disputed in many 'docetist' circles. Marcion saw matter as something dirty which should be shed rather than put on once more in the resurrection.[285] The Valentinians preferred to speak of the 'resurrection from the dead', instead 'of the flesh'.[286] This be-

---

279 Irenaeus, *Aduersus haereses* 3,24,1.

280 Irenaeus, *Aduersus haereses* 4,33,8 (FaFo § 109b13). Similarly, in 5,20,1 (FaFo § 109b14).

281 Tertullian, *De baptismo* 6,2 (FaFo § 82c). Cf. also 11,3.

282 Cf. already Eph 5:27. In addition, *Pastor Hermae* 1 (= *Visio* I,1),6; 3 (= *Visio* I,3),4; 22 (= *Visio* IV,1),3; *Martyrdom of Polycarp*, inscr.; Apollonius in Eusebius, *Historia ecclesiastica* 5,18,5; Theophilus of Alexandria, *Ad Autolycum* 2,14; 3,12; Tertullian, *Aduersus Marcionem* 5,4,8; 5,12,6; Hippolytus, *Contra Noetum* 18,10; Clement of Alexandria, *Stromata* 7,29,3; 7,87,4; Alexander of Jerusalem in Eusebius, *Historia ecclesiastica* 6,11,5; Cornelius of Rome in Eusebius, *Historia ecclesiastica* 6,43,6; Pseudo-Cyprian, *Sententiae episcoporum numero LXXXVII de haereticis baptizandis* 6. 13. 14.

283 Cf. Cyprian, *Epistula 69*, 7,2; 70, 1,2. 2,1 (FaFo § 92b); 71, 2,3; 73, 21,3; 75, 19,3 (Firmilianus). Cf. below pp. 132 f.

284 Cf. also Vinzent 2011, pp. 181–91.

285 Cf. Vinzent 2011, pp. 111–12.

286 Cf. Irenaeus, *Aduersus haereses* 2,31,2; Tertullian, *De resurrectione mortuorum* 18–19.

comes, for example, apparent from a passage, full of faith language, in the *Letter to the Philippians* by Polycarp of Smyra:

> For everyone who does not confess that Jesus Christ has come in the flesh is the antichrist [cf. 1Jn 4:2–3; 2Jn 7; cf. 1Jn 2:18. 22]; and [everyone] who does not confess the testimony of the cross, is from the devil [cf. 1Jn 3:8; Jn 8:44]; and [everyone] who perverts the words of the Lord to his own desires [cf. 2Tim 4:3; *First Clement* 3:4], and says that there is neither a resurrection nor a judgement, he is the first-born of Satan.[287]

(Pseudo-)Ignatius time and again emphasizes the 'truth' of the fleshly resurrection in his letters (if genuine).[288] Tertullian devoted two entire treatises (*De carne Christi* and *De resurrectione mortuorum*) to rebutting such views and to demonstrate the material 'reality' of the incarnation and of the general resurrection.[289]

Second version: OGS*

At a second stage, the oneness of God and the syntagma *mundi conditorem* were inserted into the first section, as well as *unicum, dominum nostrum* added in the second. We do not know what the third section looked like. (It was probably identical with OGS[G1].) In what follows I give a Latin version, but the language is uncertain – Greek and Latin versions probably coexisted side by side:

Credis in unum [*or:* unicum] deum omnipotentem, mundi conditorem?	Do you believe in the one God Almighty, the Creator of the world?
Credis (et) in Iesum Christum, filium eius unicum, dominum nostrum, natum et passum?	Do you (also) believe in Jesus Christ, his only Son, our Lord, [who was] born and suffered?
Credis in spiritum sanctum < . . . >?	Do you believe in the Holy Spirit < . . . >?[290]

The precise origin of the addition *mundi conditorem* in OGS*, which is found in Latin authors such as Noetus, Praxeas, and Tertullian, remains unclear.[291] Tertullian claims in his treatise *De praescriptione haereticorum* (written in Carthage in

---

287 Polycarp, *Epistula ad Philippenses* 7,1.

288 Cf. esp. (Pseudo-)Ignatius, *Ad Smyrnaeos* (middle version) 3,1–3; 12,2.

289 Treatises demonstrating the possibility of a bodily resurrection were written by many Christian authors in the first three centuries. For discussion cf. Bynum 1995, pp. 21–58; Lehtipuu 2015, esp. 109–57.

290 The precise wording of what followed is uncertain.

291 Cf. Tertullian, *Aduersus Praxeam* 1,1; (FaFo § 110a; for Praxeas); id., *De praescriptione haereticorum* 13,1 (§ 111b1); id., *De uirginibus uelandis* 1,4 (3; § 111c); Novatian, *De trinitate* 1,1 (§ 119a: *rerum omnium conditorem*); 9,1 (§ 119b: *conditor rerum omnium*).

203) that the Roman church 'knows one God the Lord, the Creator of the universe (*creatorem uniuersitatis*), and Christ Jesus [born] from the virgin Mary, the Son of God the Creator (*creatoris*), and the resurrection of the flesh'.[292] If we assume that *mundi conditorem* in OGS* and *creatorem uniuersitatis* in Tertullian[293] both render Greek τῶν (ἀ)πάντων/τῶν ὅλων κτίστην/δημιουργόν, Tertullian's rendering of the first section is actually quite close to OGS*.

The additions in the first section were necessary because the Marcionites and gnostics distinguished between an (inferior) creator God (demiurge) and a superior God Almighty which in the eyes of many proto-orthodox Christians threatened Christian monotheism[294] – perhaps, the addition of 'almighty' that had been made in OGS[G1] simply was not enough. By contrast, the addition to the second section emphasized the special relationship between God and Christ which excluded Christologies in which Jesus was seen as an angel who as such belonged to the created order. In early Latin versions *unicus* was used to translate μονογενής, whereas the neologism *unigenitus* is not attested before the time of Tertullian.[295]

Third version: OGS[G2]

The text of the christological summary τὸν γεννηθέντα – ζῶντας καὶ νεκρούς was inserted into OGS[G1] in one of the Roman congregations at the beginning of the third century, resulting in yet another version (OGS[G2]). This probably was an outcome of the controversy with both modalist monarchians, who advocated a strict monotheism,[296] and gnostics. It served to clarify, on the one hand, both the divine origin of Christ and the distinction between God Father and Son and, on the other hand, the historicity of the incarnation of the Son. We will look below at the origin of this passage.[297]

Πιστεύεις εἰς θεὸν παντοκράτορα;	Do you believe in God Almighty?
Πιστεύεις εἰς Χριστὸν Ἰησοῦν, τὸν υἱὸν τοῦ θεοῦ, τὸν γεννηθέντα ἐκ πνεύματος ἁγίου καὶ Μαρίας τῆς παρθένου, τὸν ἐπὶ	Do you believe in Christ Jesus, the Son of God, who was born from the Holy Spirit and the virgin Mary; who was

---

292 Tertullian, *De praescriptione haereticorum* 36,5 (FaFo § 111b5). On the 'confession' of or the 'belief' in the 'resurrection of the flesh' cf. also id., *De resurrectione mortuorum* 3,4; 48,13; id., *De uirginibus uelandis* 1,4(3; § 111c; cf. below p. 137).

293 On *creatorem uniuersitatis* cf. also Tertullian, *Aduersus Marcionem* 5,5,3.

294 Cf. Kelly 1972, pp. 141 f.; Kinzig 1999(2017), p. 263.

295 Cf. Braun 1977, pp. 247–51.

296 On the quasi-official monarchianism in Rome at around 200 cf. Hübner 1999; Vinzent 2013; Kinzig, 'Christus', 2017, pp. 281–7; Kinzig 2017(2022), pp. 148–54.

297 Cf. below ch. 4.6.

Ποντίου Πιλάτου σταυρωθέντα [*or:* τὸν σταυρωθέντα ἐπὶ Ποντίου Πιλάτου] καὶ ταφέντα καὶ τῇ τρίτῃ ἡμέρᾳ ἀναστάντα ἐκ (τῶν) νεκρῶν [*or:* ἀναστάντα τῇ τρίτῃ ἡμέρᾳ ἐκ (τῶν) νεκρῶν] καὶ ἀναβάντα εἰς τοὺς οὐρανοὺς καὶ καθήμενον ἐν δεξιᾷ τοῦ πατρός, ἐρχόμενον [*or:* ἐλευσό-μενον] κρίνειν [*or:* κρῖναι] ζῶντας καὶ νεκρούς;	crucified under Pontius Pilate, and was buried, and on the third day rose again from the dead, and ascended into the heavens, and is sitting at the right hand of the Father, coming to judge the living and the dead?
Πιστεύεις εἰς τὸ ἅγιον πνεῦμα καὶ ἁγίαν ἐκκλησίαν, σαρκὸς ἀνάστασιν;	Do you believe in the Holy Spirit and the holy Church, the resurrection of the flesh?

OGS[G2] in its original interrogatory or in a secondary declaratory version was later quoted by Marcellus of Ancyra. We will discuss this evidence when we come to the Roman Creed.[298]

Fourth version: TA[G]

So far we have been dealing with reconstructions. The first complete set of baptismal questions that has been preserved in actuality is found in the Ethiopic and Latin versions of the *Traditio Apostolica*, a Church order usually ascribed to Hippolytus.[299] They go back to a Greek original which may date from the early third century. TA[G] must have run like this:

Πιστεύεις εἰς ἕνα θεὸν παντοκράτορα;	Do you believe in one God Almighty?
Πιστεύεις εἰς Χριστὸν Ἰησοῦν, τὸν υἱὸν τοῦ θεοῦ, τὸν γεννηθέντα ἐκ πνεύματος ἁγίου καὶ Μαρίας τῆς παρθένου, τὸν ἐπὶ Ποντίου Πιλάτου σταυρωθέντα [*or:* τὸν σταυρωθέντα ἐπὶ Ποντίου Πιλάτου] καὶ ἀποθανόντα καὶ ταφέντα καὶ τῇ τρίτῃ ἡμέρᾳ ἀναστάντα ἐκ (τῶν) νεκ-ρῶν [*or:* ἀναστάντα τῇ τρίτῃ ἡμέρᾳ ἐκ (τῶν) νεκρῶν] ζῶντα[300] καὶ ἀναβάντα εἰς τοὺς οὐρανοὺς καὶ καθήμενον ἐν δεξιᾷ τοῦ πατρός, ἐρχόμενον [*or:* ἐλευ-	Do you believe in Christ Jesus, the Son of God, who was born from the Holy Spirit and the virgin Mary; who was crucified under Pontius Pilate, and died, and was buried, and on the third day rose again alive from the dead, and ascended into the heavens, and is sitting at the right hand of the Father, coming to judge the living and the dead?

---

298 Cf. below ch. 5.1.

299 The Latin and Ethiopic versions are found in FaFo § 89b and c and in Kinzig, 'Ursprung', 2022, p. 165. The ascription to Hippolytus is uncertain. Cf. below p. 148 and n. 11.

300 The origin of ζῶντα is unclear. Cf. Kinzig, 'Ursprung', 2022, pp. 175 f.

σόμενον] κρίνειν [*or:* κρῖναι] ζῶντας
καὶ νεκρούς;

Πιστεύεις εἰς τὸ ἅγιον πνεῦμα καὶ (εἰς) ἁγίαν ἐκκλησίαν καὶ (εἰς) σαρκὸς ἀνάστασιν;	Do you believe in the Holy Spirit and (in) the holy Church and (in) the resurrection of the flesh?

This version is basically identical with OGS[G2] but contains (like OGS*) the addition ἕνα in the first article and, furthermore, for the first time, the additions καὶ ἀποθανόντα and ζῶντα in the christological summary of the second article, which perhaps served to underline the reality of both Jesus' death and resurrection respectively. (These words may, of course, have been added at different times.) TA[G] served as the basis for the Latin and Ethiopic translations (TA[L] and TA[E] respectively) which we will discuss below in chapter 5.1.

*

All these considerations lead to the following stemma of the Roman credal questions:[301]

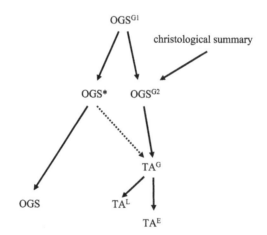

——————▶ = dependency with regard to both structure and content
············▶ = adoption of individual words/terms

---

301 This is an abbreviated version of the stemma printed in Kinzig, 'Ursprung', 2022, p. 174.

The aforementioned versions must not be conceived of as a series of successive revisions in strict chronological order but may have circulated in Rome (and beyond) simultaneously.[302] At the same time, we are probably not yet dealing with formulae that had been fixed once and for all (as in the case of the later synodal and baptismal creeds). Just as the liturgy as a whole had not yet been written down,[303] the baptismal questions in the various Roman (house) churches[304] will have been transmitted in an oral tradition in slightly different versions.[305] Even in the same community the questions may have varied from baptism to baptism, although their basic structure will have remained the same.

Cyprian also offers some testimony for the high degree of flexibility that still existed at the time. In his dispute with the Roman schismatic Novatian in 253 or 254, the bishop of Carthage denied his opponents the right to claim the same *symbolum* as the catholics. It is clear from the context that he is thinking of the baptismal questions here. We learn from Cyprian that the Roman *symbolum* was structured in a trinitarian fashion. He quotes one of the questions as follows:

> Credis in remissionem peccatorum et uitam aeternam per sanctam ecclesiam? / Do you believe in the remission of sins and eternal life through the holy Church?[306]

This formulation is similar to, but not identical with, the third question of the OGS. However, it is uncertain whether Cyprian is precisely reproducing the Roman version of the question or is following an African custom. This means that his testimony will probably not provide more than a general indication that Roman questions of faith existed around 250 and that they were identical with, or similar to, the version as transmitted by the OGS. We have no evidence of the increased fixation of the credal elements until the second half of the third century, and therefore no earlier evidence for the origin of the Old Roman Creed as such.

---

302 Cf. already Lietzmann 1922–1927(1962), pp. 270 f.; similarly, Holland 1965, p. 263 and others.

303 Cf., e.g., Vogel 1986, pp. 31 f. and n. 29; Kinzig 2011(2017), p. 338 and n. 44. In our context see also Kelly 1972, pp. 91 f.

304 On the structure of the Roman church in the second century cf. Brent 1995; Lampe 2003.

305 Similar questions have also been preserved in the *Martyrium Calixti* and the *Acta S. Stephani et martyris* (FaFo §§ 90, 91) which are probably also of Roman origin, but may date from a much later period. Pseudo-Cyprian, *De rebaptismate* 10 (FaFo § 86) also attests to the use of questions. However, it is not quite clear where this text originated (Italy? Africa?; cf. Antonie Wlosok in Sallmann 1997, pp. 579–81).

306 Cyprian, *Epistula 69*, 7,2 (FaFo § 92a). Cf. also next section.

4.5.2 North Africa

The second region from which clear evidence of baptismal interrogations has been preserved is North Africa. In Carthage Tertullian attests to the rite of renunciation or *Apótaxis*, that is, the abjuration of the devil and his pomp, as well as to the recitation of the faith in interrogatory form. This remained the 'normal' ritual sequence in the west where no corresponding formula of *Sýntaxis* ('allegiance' to Christ) was used.[307] The questions were posed individually before each of the three immersions into the baptismal font.[308] Tertullian calls these words *sacramenti uerba*, comparing them to a military oath,[309] and a *testatio fidei* (legal deposition).[310] We do not know what the questions and answers were, except that the latter seem not simply to have consisted in *credo*, because Tertullian says that the baptizands gave 'a somewhat ampler response than the Lord appointed in the Gospel' (*amplius aliquid respondentes quam dominus in euangelio determinauit*).[311]

The first direct evidence stems from around the middle of the third century. Cyprian mentions one baptismal question in two slightly different versions (see also previous section):

(I) 'Credis in remissionem peccatorum et uitam aeternam per sanctam ecclesiam?' / 'Do you believe in the remission of sins and eternal life through the holy Church?'[312]

(II) 'Credis in uitam aeternam et remissionem peccatorum per sanctam ecclesiam?' / 'Do you believe in eternal life and remission of sins through the holy Church?'[313]

The context of the writings in which these questions occur obviously influenced their wording. For in both letters, written during the controversy over the baptism of heretics, Cyprian stresses that faith in the remission of sins is only possible *through the (catholic) Church* and not through the heretics.[314] In this regard, the *sequence* of the first two objects of faith (remission of sins and eternal life) apparently did not really concern him. In this case, too, we can see that what mat-

---

307 Cf. Tertullian, *De spectaculis* 4,1 (FaFo § 82b). Cf. also Kinzig, "'I abjure Satan'", 2024 (*sub prelo*).

308 Cf. Tertullian, *De corona* 3,3 (FaFo § 82e). Cf. also id., *De resurrectione mortuorum* 48,11 (§ 82d).

309 Cf. Tertullian, *Ad martyras* 3,1 (FaFo § 82a).

310 Cf. Tertullian, *De baptismo* 6,2 (FaFo § 82c).

311 Tertullian, *De corona* 3,3 (FaFo § 82e). The biblical allusion is uncertain (Mt 28:19?). Cf. also Whitaker 1965, pp. 2 f.; Jílek 1979, p. 126 and n. 4.

312 Cyprian, *Epistula 69*, 7,2 (FaFo § 92a).

313 Cyprian, *Epistula 70*, 2,1 (FaFo § 92b).

314 Cf. Kinzig 1999(2017), p. 247.

tered was not the precise wording of these questions (which were obviously orally transmitted) but rather whether *specific elements* (in this case: *per sanctam ecclesiam*) were in fact included or omitted.

As mentioned in the previous section, Cyprian suggests that the same baptismal question was also asked at Rome. However, the striking phrase *per sanctam ecclesiam* is never attested for Rome, whereas we continue to find it in African versions of the creed.[315] The practice of asking questions about the faith at baptism was not restricted to Carthage. It is also attested for small country dioceses in the province of *Africa Proconsularis*.[316]

4.6 The emergence of the western christological summary

We saw above that at some point a christological summary was inserted into the baptismal questions (version OGS[G2]). Let us now take a closer look at this section.[317] Except for one small difference the version OGS[G2] is identical with the same section in the Roman creed as attested by Marcellus of Ancyra and Leo the Great.[318] Again, we have to bear in mind that minor differences between versions may be due to the purely oral transmission of these texts whose wording is not yet fully fixed. It was already suggested at the beginning of the last century that the tradition history of this summary is independent from that of the remainder of the confession and that the summary was secondarily inserted into a relatively brief trinitarian formula (similar to that of Mt 28:19).[319]

The brevity of the summary is striking. Important data concerning Jesus' activities on earth (miracles, proclamation etc.) are missing. The summary is also shorter than eastern summaries which are otherwise similar in structure (such as that of N) and which describe the relationship between Father and Son in some detail, thereby placing an emphasis on Christ's eternal birth and his participation in creation.[320] This suggests, first, that the western summary does not depend on

---

315 Cf. Augustine, *Sermo 215* (FaFo § 316g); Quodvultdeus, *Sermo 3*, 13,1 (§ 317c); Fulgentius of Ruspe, *Contra Fabianum*, frg. 36,14 (§ 319a2); Pseudo-Fulgentius, *Sermo de symbolo* (§ 320).

316 Caecilius of Biltha mentions it at the council held at Carthage on 1 September 256; cf. *Sententiae episcoporum numero LXXXVII de haereticis baptizandis* (FaFo § 84).

317 The following chapter is based on Kinzig, 'Christus', 2017.

318 The version above has ἐρχόμενον [*or:* ἐλευσόμενον] κρίνειν [*or:* κρῖναι] ζῶντας καὶ νεκρούς whereas Marcellus and Leo read: ὅθεν ἔρχεται κρίνειν ζῶντας καὶ νεκρούς // *unde uenturus est iudicare uiuos ac mortuos* (or: *ad iudicandos uiuos et mortuos*); cf. Marcellus, *Epistula ad Iulium papam* (Epiphanius, *Panarion* 72,3,1; FaFo § 253); Leo's creed as reconstructed in § 255g.

319 Cf. above pp. 19–21.

320 Cf. the synopses in Vinzent 1999, pp. 271–6.

them. Second, the brevity of the western summary may also point to an early date of composition. Is it possible to reconstruct how it came about?

The western christological summary contains the circumstances of Jesus' birth and passion (including the mention of Pontius Pilate), statements about his resurrection and ascension, his sitting at the right hand of the Father and his eschatological return including the Last Judgement. Thus it is made clear that the Son of God went through a period on earth, in the end ascended to his Father at whose right he is now sitting, and will eventually return to earth for the Last Judgement.

Above all, these statements are directed against gnosticism. They were inserted into the relevant baptismal question so as to safeguard the identity of the pre-existent Christ with the earthly Jesus.[321] It is further strengthened by a particular christological exegesis of Ps 109(110):1 which is found in the New Testament:[322] after his resurrection the same individual who was crucified under Pontius Pilate is accorded an eminent place of honour by being seated at God's right hand. This excludes any kind of docetic Christology. At the same time, the sitting at the right hand also excludes the Son's identification with the Father or a 'dissolution' of the Son into the Father – we will later return to this observation.[323]

The insertion of the christological statement concerning the 'sitting at the right hand' thus already indicates that the summary as a whole is *also*, but not *primarily* directed against docetism. This becomes even clearer when we compare it with the writings of Ignatius of Antioch (assuming the authenticity of the middle version of his letters). Throughout his letters Ignatius fights docetism and, therefore, supplements the individual stages of Jesus' earthly life by adding the adverb ἀληθῶς ('truly') in similar outlines.[324] By contrast, the summary under consideration here does not primarily argue against an incarnation 'by appearance' only (which, nonetheless, is clearly denied), but rather both for the *identification of the Son of God with the earthly Jesus* and thus against a dualist saviour figure and for *the persistent distinction between Father and Son* after the ascension.

---

321 Cf. also Kelly 1972, pp. 141–3.
322 In the version of the Septuagint: Εἶπεν ὁ κύριος τῷ κυρίῳ μου· Κάθου ἐκ δεξιῶν μου, ἕως ἂν θῶ τοὺς ἐχθρούς σου ὑποπόδιον τῶν ποδῶν σου. / 'The Lord said to my lord, "Sit at my right hand, until I make your enemies your footstool."' Reflexes in the New Testament include Mt 26:64; Mk 12:36 (quotation); 14:62; 16:19; Lk 20:42 (quotation); 22:69; Acts 2:34 (quotation); 7:55; Heb 1:13 (quotation). On the question as a whole cf. Markschies 1993(2000).
323 Cf. below p. 207 and n. 264; 282, 286, 352, 622.
324 (Pseudo-)Ignatius, *Ad Trallianos* 9,1–2 (middle version; FaFo § 98c1). Similarly id., *Ad Smyrnaeos* 1,1–2 (middle version, § 98e1).

This antignostic tendency is strengthened further by the insertion of Pontius Pilate. *Regulae fidei* and credal summaries of the first three centuries only rarely mention the governor of Judaea.[325] This is why passages where he is named take on a particular significance. Thus Irenaeus includes the mention of Pilate in an argument which is clearly directed against gnosticism:

> For how should it be if the apostles themselves had not left us writings? Would it not be necessary, [in that case,] to follow the order of the tradition which they handed down to those to whom they committed the churches?
>
> Many nations of those barbarians who believe in Christ do assent to this [order], having salvation written in their hearts by the Spirit without paper or ink [cf. 2Cor 3:3; 2Jn 12; 3Jn 13], carefully preserving the ancient tradition and believing in one God, the Creator of heaven, earth, and all things therein [cf. Ex 20:11; Ps 145(146):6, Acts 4:24; 14:15], and Christ Jesus, the Son of God; who, because of his surpassing love towards his creation [cf. Eph 3:19], endured a generation from a virgin, he himself uniting humanity to God through himself; [who] has suffered under Pontius Pilate, and rises again; and [who], having been received up in splendour [cf. 1Tim 3:16], will come in glory [cf. Mt 16:27; 24:30; 25:31] [as] the Saviour of those who are saved and the Judge of those who are judged, and sending into eternal fire [cf. Mt 25:41] those who transform the truth and despise his Father [and] his advent.[326]

Passages such as this make it clear that the mention of Pilate aims to historicize the crucifixion, yet not in such a way that it supplies a particular dating (in which case the insertion as is would have been incorrect, because it does not refer to the terms of office of emperors or consuls), but in order to emphasize the historical and geographical context in which the crucifixion took place: God incarnate was in fact (and not in appearance only) crucified.

Furthermore, another important observation can be made from a careful examination of the relevant passages in which Pilate appears within christological summaries. For the divine dignity of the historical Jesus, who was crucified under Pilate, is also emphasized (along with the historicity of his incarnation) over against both pagans and Jews. Such an anti-*pagan* tendency is particularly prominent in Justin's *First Apology*:

> Therefore, what sober-minded person will not acknowledge [. . .] that we are not atheists, since we worship the maker of this universe. We will make known Jesus Christ, our teacher of these things, who also was born for this purpose and was crucified under Pontius Pilate (who was procurator of Judaea in the times of Tiberius Caesar); we have learned that he is the Son of the true God himself, and we hold him in the second place and the prophetic Spirit in the third, because we honour him along with the Word [*or*: according to reason, μετὰ λόγου].[327]

---

325 Cf. above p. 98 n. 164.
326 Irenaeus, *Aduersus haereses* 3,4,1–2 (FaFo § 109b7).
327 Justin, *Apologia Prima* 13,1–3 (FaFo § 104a2).

This passage is particularly striking because here a trinitarian mode of speaking about God is linked to statements regarding the birth and passion of Jesus (which are, therefore, reminiscent of the early Roman baptismal interrogations such as OGS[G1]),[328] supplemented by a fairly precise date indicating Pilate and the Emperor Tiberius.

From another passage in the same *Apology* it also becomes apparent that we are dealing here with material taken from baptismal catechesis:

> [. . .] in the water the name of God the Father and Lord of the universe is pronounced over the one who chooses to be born again and has repented of his sins; the one who leads to the laver the person that is to be washed invokes [God] by this name alone. For no one has the right to give a name of the ineffable God; and if anyone might dare to say that there is a name, he raves with a hopeless madness. This washing is called 'illumination' because they who learn these things are illuminated in their understandings. He who is illuminated is also washed upon the name of Jesus Christ, who was crucified under Pontius Pilate, and upon the name of the Holy Spirit, who through the prophets foretold all things about Jesus.[329]

Finally, Justin uses a similar version of this christological summary (also mentioning Pontius Pilate) in the anti-Jewish polemics of his *Dialogue with Trypho*:

> For every demon, when exorcised in the name of this very Son of God – who is 'the first-born of all creation' [Col 1:15], was begotten through the Virgin, became a human who was subject to suffering, was crucified under Pontius Pilate by your nation, died, rose again from the dead, and ascended into heaven – is overcome and subdued [cf. Lk 10:17].[330]

From these texts it is evident, then, that in the time of Justin the link between trinitarian formula and christological summary was not yet fully forged. Its outlines are discernible in Irenaeus, but there are no hints of the existence of a fixed formula in the sense of a creed.

This situation changed at the beginning of the third century with Tertullian. In his treatise *Against Praxeas* from 210/211, he first quotes his opponent:

> In the course of time, then, the Father [was] born and the Father suffered, God himself, the Lord Almighty, whom they declare to be Jesus Christ.[331]

He then goes on to summarize his own rule of faith as follows:

> Nonetheless, as we always [have done] and now even more so, since we have been better instructed by the Paraclete [cf. Jn 16:13], who leads men indeed into all truth, we believe that there is one single God. But under the following dispensation, or *oikonomia*, as we call

---

328 Cf. above p. 123.
329 Justin, *Apologia Prima* 61,10–13 (FaFo § 104a9).
330 Justin, *Dialogus cum Tryphone* 85,2 (FaFo § 104b3).
331 Tertullian, *Aduersus Praxeam* 2,1 (FaFo § 110b).

it, [we believe] that there is also a Son of the single God, his very Word, who proceeded from himself, 'through whom all things were made, and without whom nothing was made' [Jn 1:3]. [We believe] him to have been sent by the Father into the Virgin and to have been born from her – being both man and God, the Son of Man and the Son of God, and named Jesus Christ. [We believe] him to have suffered, died, and been buried, according to the Scriptures [cf. 1Cor 15:3–4], and, after he had been raised up again by the Father and taken back into heaven, to be sitting at the right hand of the Father [cf. Mk 16:19]; that he will come to judge the living and the dead [cf. 2Tim 4:1; 1Pet 4:5]; who sent thence from the Father, according to his own promise, the Holy Spirit, the Paraclete, the sanctifier of the faith of those who believe in the Father, the Son, and the Holy Spirit [cf. Jn 16:7].[332]

Praxeas' view introduces this paragraph in the manner of a hypothesis.[333] It is followed by extended binitarian statements[334] which contain the elements death – burial – raising from the dead/resurrection – sitting at the right hand (for the first time![335]) – Last Judgement, and which resemble OGS^{G2},[336] although the wording still differs in detail.

Another version of the *regula fidei* which occurs in the treatise *On the Veiling of Virgins* is even closer to the summary in OGS^{G2}:

The rule of faith, indeed, is altogether one, alone immoveable and irreformable; [that is, the rule] of believing in one single God Almighty, the Creator of the universe, and his Son Jesus Christ, born from the virgin Mary, crucified under Pontius Pilate, on the third day raised again from the dead, received into the heavens, sitting now at the right hand of the Father, [who will] come to judge the living and the dead even through the resurrection of the flesh. As this law of faith is abiding, the other [succeeding] points of discipline and conversation now permit the newness of correction, as the grace of God is of course operating and advancing even to the end.[337]

For the sake of clarity I juxtapose the christological summaries found in Tertullian with that of the Roman version:

---

332 Tertullian, *Aduersus Praxeam* 2,1 (FaFo § 111e1).
333 Cf. above p. 125.
334 If the mission of the Paraclete is seen as an explication of faith in the Holy Spirit, we are in fact dealing here with an actual trinitarian formula.
335 But cf. also Melito, *De pascha* 104 (FaFo § 107) in a hymnic passage (quoted above p. 76).
336 Cf. above pp. 128 f.
337 *De uirginibus uelandis* 1,4–5 (3–4; FaFo § 111c).

Roman version (OGS^G2)[338]	Reconstruction of its presumed Latin text	Tertullian, *De uirginibus uelandis* 1,4 (FaFo § 111c)	Tertullian, *Aduersus Praxeam* 2,1 (FaFo § 111e1)
εἰς Χριστὸν Ἰησοῦν, τὸν υἱὸν τοῦ θεοῦ, τὸν γεννηθέντα ἐκ πνεύματος ἁγίου καὶ Μαρίας τῆς παρθένου,	et in Christum Iesum, filium dei, qui natus est [*or:* natum] de [*or:* ex] spiritu sancto et Maria uirgine,	et filium eius Iesum Christum, natum ex virgine Maria,	hunc missum a patre in uirginem et ex ea natum, hominem et deum, filium hominis et filium dei et cognominatum Iesum Christum;
τὸν ἐπὶ Ποντίου Πιλάτου σταυρωθέντα [*or:* τὸν σταυρωθέντα ἐπὶ Ποντίου Πιλάτου]	qui sub Pontio Pilato crucifixus est [*or:* crucifixum sub Pontio Pilato]	crucifixum sub Pontio Pilato,	hunc passum, hunc mortuum
καὶ ταφέντα	et sepultus [*or:* et sepultum]		et sepultum secundum scripturas
καὶ τῇ τρίτῃ ἡμέρᾳ ἀναστάντα ἐκ (τῶν) νεκρῶν [*or:* ἀναστάντα τῇ τρίτῃ ἡμέρᾳ ἐκ (τῶν) νεκρῶν],	et [*or:* qui] tertia die resurrexit a mortuis;	tertia die resuscitatum a mortuis,	et resuscitatum a patre
καὶ ἀναβάντα εἰς τοὺς οὐρανοὺς	ascendit [*or:* ascendentem] in caelos	receptum in caelis,	et in caelo resumptum
καὶ καθήμενον ἐν δεξιᾷ τοῦ πατρός,	et sedet [*or:* sedit *or* sedentem] ad dexteram patris [*or:* in dextera patris],	sedentem nunc ad dexteram patris,	sedere ad dexteram patris
ἐρχόμενον [*or:* ἐλευσόμενον] κρίνειν [*or:* κρῖναι] ζῶντας καὶ νεκρούς.	uenturum iudicare uiuos et mortuos.	uenturum iudicare uiuos et mortuos	uenturum iudicare uiuos et mortuos.
		per carnis etiam resurrectionem.	

---

338 A translation is found above on pp. 128 f.

This synopsis clearly shows that every single item of the Roman summary is found in the version which occurs in *De uirginibus uelandis*, which raises the possibility that Tertullian and the Roman summary may be based on a common *Vorlage*.

The treatise *Against Praxeas* may help us to explain these agreements as well as the *Sitz im Leben* of the christological summary found in Tertullian which, for the first time, included both Pontius Pilate and also the sitting at the right hand. Praxeas was a theologian from Asia Minor, who had come to Rome and reached a considerable degree of influence due to his status as confessor.[339] (His actual identity is unclear, 'Praxeas' perhaps being a pseudonym.) According to Tertullian Praxeas' influence (which had even extended to North Africa) had already passed its peak some time ago, but his doctrine had flared up again at least in Carthage, thus necessitating the composition of the treatise.[340] In order to preserve a strict monotheism[341] – which he may have called *monarchia*[342] – Praxeas claimed that the Father and the Son were identical, even going so far as to maintain that the Father had suffered in or with the Son. According to Tertullian he used the word *unicus* as the starting point for his argument:

> He [*sc. Praxeas*] maintains that there is a single (*unicum*) Lord, the Almighty, the Creator of the world (*omnipotentem, mundi conditorem*), in such a way that out of this [word] 'single' (*unico*) he may fabricate a heresy. He says that the Father himself descended into the Virgin, was himself born from her, himself suffered, indeed was himself Jesus Christ.[343]

Tertullian later repeats the charge of patripassianism in the passage quoted above: according to Praxeas the Father himself was born and had suffered.[344] In his treatise Tertullian repeats his claim that Praxeas affirmed the identity of Father, Son, and Spirit as if it were some kind of mantra.[345] Yet the position which his opponent allegedly maintained was probably much more nuanced than Tertullian allowed for. Praxeas used as his exegetical starting point the passages Is 45:5, Jn 10:30, and Jn 14:9–11 which for him, and the *monarchiani* (10,1), proved the strict identity of Father and Son.[346] They claimed that God had differentiated himself into Father

---

339 Cf. Tertullian, *Aduersus Praxeam* 1,4. On Praxeas cf. Handl 2022.

340 Cf. Tertullian, *De uirginibus uelandis* 1,9(6)–11(7).

341 Cf. esp. Tertullian, *Aduersus Praxeam* 19,7. Furthermore 31,1.

342 On the term 'monarchianism' and its meaning cf. Kinzig 2017(2022).

343 Tertullian, *Aduersus Praxeam* 1,1 (FaFo § 110a).

344 Cf. Tertullian, *Aduersus Praxeam* 2,1 (FaFo § 110b; quoted above p. 125). Likewise 10,9.

345 Cf. Tertullian, *Aduersus Praxeam* 2,3 (FaFo § 110c); 5,1; 9,1; 10,1; 11,1. Similarly 11,4; 25,4; 27,2; 31,3 etc.

346 Cf. Tertullian, *Aduersus Praxeam* 20,1.

and Son without in any way compromising his single identity.[347] According to Praxeas, the Scriptures spoke of two Gods on the one hand, and of one single God on the other hand – this contradiction could only be solved if the identity of the Father with the Son was presupposed.[348] Accordingly, the world had been created by *one* God only. Praxeas appears to have questioned the creative activity of the Son, but at the same time also denied the cooperation of other mediator figures such as had been introduced by the Marcionites and Valentinians.[349] Since this identity had never ceased, the biblical statements about Christ's lowliness must in actual fact refer to the Father.[350] Likewise, in the New Testament the Father acted 'in the name of the Son' (*in filii nomine*) and not vice versa.[351] The identity of Father and Son was even supported by Old Testament passages in which God was both visible and invisible at the same time (just as in the New Testament).[352]

Praxeas had not maintained a symmetry of the Son with the Father either, but had placed the Son as a mode of divine appearance beneath the Father. As the Father alone was almighty, there remained a clear difference between Father and Son which, however, must not be interpreted as some kind of subordinationism since the Son did not possess his own *hypóstasis* over against the Father.

Praxeas also drew conclusions from these insights with regard to the incarnation. He seems to have named Jesus incarnate as 'Son', whereas he called the 'Spirit' in the incarnate Jesus 'Father' whom he identified with 'Christ'.[353] Accordingly, the Father, too, had been crucified, but only the Son died because of his human 'substance'.[354] The Father, therefore, was a 'fellow-sufferer' (*conpassibilis*), but nevertheless ultimately 'impassible' (*inpassibilis*); only the Son suffered in the full sense of the term.[355] Thus apparently Praxeas thought a 'hard' patripassianism was to be avoided.

On the basis of the evidence quoted above it seems that he referred to the Roman baptismal interrogations. They were trinitarian in structure and con-

---

347 Cf. Tertullian, *Aduersus Praxeam* 10,7.

348 Cf. Tertullian, *Aduersus Praxeam* 18,1.

349 Cf. Tertullian, *Aduersus Praxeam* 19,1.

350 Cf. Tertullian, *Aduersus Praxeam* 16,6–7.

351 Tertullian, *Aduersus Praxeam* 17,1.

352 Cf. Tertullian, *Aduersus Praxeam* 14,5–6. By contrast, Tertullian denies that the Son was visible in Old Testament times; cf. 14,7.

353 Tertullian, *Aduersus Praxeam* 27,1. Cf. already 17,4. He based this claim on Lk 1:35. Cf. Tertullian, *Aduersus Praxeam* 26,2–3; 27,4.

354 Tertullian, *Aduersus Praxeam* 29,3. 5. It remains unclear to what extent we are dealing here with a docetic Christology – Tertullian does not polemicize against it.

355 Cf. Tertullian, *Aduersus Praxeam* 29,5.

tained in their first article the belief 'in one single God' (*in unicum deum*). In fact, in *De uirginibus uelandis* Tertullian himself uses such an expression when quoting the *regula fidei*: *in unicum deum omnipotentem, mundi conditorem* / 'believing in one single God Almighty, the Creator of the universe.'[356] When we compare this passage with *Aduersus Praxeam* 1,1 the first baptismal interrogation may be reconstructed with some degree of accuracy:

> Credis in unicum deum omnipotentem, mundi conditorem?
> Do you believe in the one God Almighty, the Creator of the world?

This is precisely the version of OGS*.[357] As we have seen above, Praxeas is quoted as saying that the Father was born and suffered (*itaque post tempus pater natus et pater passus*).[358] Similarly, Tertullian later claims that according to the twisted view of the heretics the Father was believed to have been born and to have suffered (*natus et passus*).[359]

In order to combat these views Tertullian enlarged the second article in *Aduersus Praxeam* 2,1 and, alluding to Jn 1:1–3, emphasized the *difference* between Father and Son. This difference also underlies the extended christological summary that leads up to the resurrection, assumption into heaven and the sitting at the right hand. Here Tertullian substantiated the difference between Father and Son by taking recourse to 1Cor 15:3–4 and Mk 16:19.[360]

Praxeas' position resembles the one Hippolytus attributed to Noetus, a theologian who originated from Smyrna, and to his followers who were active in Rome. Among the latter he mentions a certain Epigonus as well as his pupil Cleomenes.[361] Hippolytus creates the impression that the doctrine was being spread in Rome in particular by those attending the school of Cleomenes, including the Roman bishop Zephyrinus (*sedit c.* 199 – *c.* 217). According to Hippolytus' account these theologians, too, identified the creator of the universe with the Father alone. In addition, they maintained the identity of Father and Son in order to safeguard the divine monarchy and ascribed birth, passion, and death to the Father. Epiphanius quotes the following phrase by Noetus: 'I know one God and no other beside him [cf. Ex

---

356 Cf. *De uirginibus uelandis* 1,4 (3; FaFo § 111c); cf. also above p. 137.
357 Cf. above p. 127.
358 Cf. Tertullian, *Aduersus Praxeam* 2,1 (FaFo § 110b); cf. above p. 125.
359 Cf. Tertullian, *Aduersus Praxeam* 13,5.
360 On the christological summary and the soteriology which is linked to it cf. Viciano 1986, esp. 101–115.
361 For what follows cf. Hippolytus, *Refutatio omnium haeresium* 8,19,3; 9,7,1; 9,10,9–12; 10,26–27,2.

20:3; Is 45:5], who was born, suffered, and died'[362] – a clear allusion to the baptismal interrogation in OGS[G1] which resembles the above-mentioned sentence by Praxeas preserved by Tertullian (*itaque post tempus pater natus et pater passus*). Hippolytus ascribes the following statement to Bishop Zephyrinus:

> I know that there is one God, Christ Jesus, and aside from him [I know] none other who was begotten or subject to suffering (γενητὸν καὶ παθητόν).[363]

Once more the Roman baptismal interrogation is alluded to, just as in the case of Praxeas and Noetus, but the patripassian thrust of Praxeas (or, rather, of Tertullian's polemic, for Praxeas possibly only spoke of a 'fellow-suffering') and of Noetus is softened.

Finally, the Roman bishop Calixtus (*sedit* 217/218–222) held a similar view, again according to Hippolytus. He maintained the oneness of God and Father calling him the Demiurge of the universe (which may indicate that his doctrine, too, was directed against gnosticism). The same being was also the Son 'by name' (ὀνόματι), a claim which was made too by Praxeas.[364] Apparently the rest of his argument likewise was the result of his attempt to propound a coherent exegesis of the Gospel of John, in particular concerning the relationship of its prologue to Jn 4:24. As regards their spiritual nature, God and Logos did not differ from each other in any respect; rather, they were united by a single 'person' (πρόσωπον, the precise meaning of the term here is unclear). The distinction between Father and Son was to be understood 'by name' (ὀνόματι) only and was, therefore, not one of essence or substance (οὐσίᾳ). With regard to the incarnation Calixtus introduced a distinction which, once again, calls to mind Praxeas: the Son alone took on flesh and thus became tangible; the father 'dwelt' in him as a spirit and thus deified him. Consequently, the Father had 'suffered together' with the Son (συμπεπονθέναι). Like Praxeas, Calixtus may have wanted to avoid referring statements relating to suffering directly to the Father.

There are so many parallels between the doctrine of Calixtus as reported by Hippolytus and the views of Praxeas that scholars have time and again claimed their identity. However, serious objections have also been raised.[365] What matters for our purposes is not solving this problem but the fact that we are dealing here

---

362 Epiphanius, *Panarion* 57,1,8 (FaFo § 108b): Ἕνα θεὸν ἐπίσταμαι καὶ οὐκ ἄλλον πλὴν αὐτοῦ, γεννηθέντα, πεπονθότα, ἀποθανόντα.

363 Hippolytus, *Refutatio omnium haeresium* 9,11,3 (FaFo § 112).

364 Hippolytus, however, is not altogether clear in this respect. He claims in *Refutatio omnium haeresium* 9,12,16, as opposed to 10,27,3, that Calixtus had said the *Logos* was Son and Father 'by name only'.

365 Cf. Sieben 2001, pp. 31 f. and, most recently, Handl 2022, esp. pp. 266–70.

with a controversy between different theological schools over the relationship between Father and Son. Maintaining a strict monotheism (monarchianism) over against gnosticism, Noetus, Zephyrinus, Calixtus, and others (such as Sabellius, whose argumentation nevertheless was somewhat different) had underlined God's unity with regard both to the Old Testament (unity of creator and Father, refusal of intermediate powers such as a demiurge) and to the incarnation (unity of Father and Son). The latter was necessary to rebut the docetism which was popular in gnostic circles.[366] There are clear indications that the baptismal questions with their brief second article were referred to in this debate. As explained above, I suggest that, at the turn of the second and third centuries, these questions were those of OGS*.[367]

Finally, I return to the christological summaries in Tertullian. The summary in the version preserved in *Aduersus Praxeam* is clearly directed against monarchianism, but its kerygmatic thrust also becomes visible in other contexts such as in the version cited in *De uirginibus uelandis*. Christ's earthly actions are detailed to such an extent that both a docetic and a patripassian interpretation are rendered impossible. It was unnecessary to include information about Jesus' teaching and his miracles since only the exegesis of the gospel passages regarding Christ's lowliness were controversial (in particular birth and passion) – this is the reason why the summary could be kept brief, as I pointed out before.[368]

In my view, the great similarities between the christological summaries of Tertullian and of OGS[G2] can only be explained if we assume that Tertullian knew a summary such as that of OGS[G2]. This must have come into existence at the turn of the second and third centuries in order to combat modalist monarchianism and must have been used in baptismal instruction.

This does not mean, however, that the christological summary in R was composed in the form in which it is preserved for the purpose of inserting it into the creed. As has been shown above, such summaries were current in all kinds of variations from the early second century onwards. Yet it was a novelty to write down *one particular* version of this summary, as it was used in preaching and catechesis, and to combine it with the trinitarian formula.

It is difficult to imagine, however, that this summary in R – which is unattested in Rome at this time – could have been inserted there, if we consider the strictly monarchian stance of the major Roman theologians of the late second and

---

366 Details in Hainthaler 1995.
367 Cf. above p. 127.
368 Cf. above pp. 123 f.

early third centuries.[369] At the same time, contrasting trends such as that represented by Hippolytus will hardly have been responsible either, given that the christological summary plays no role in Hippolytus' writings. Instead one must allow for an influence from North Africa which already was considerable at the time of Tertullian and even more so at that of Cyprian.

The insertion of the christological summary into the baptismal questions may thus be considered to have been the result of a theological protest of a North African opposition against monarchianism, as is still clearly visible in Tertullian. Unfortunately, the present state of our knowledge leaves the question open when and how this happened, whether Tertullian himself used such a summary or whether it was composed by drawing on his own writings (or on the oral tradition recorded by him). This summary must have 'migrated' from North Africa to Rome at a time when opposition in the capital against strict monarchianism had grown.

Unfortunately, we know little about Roman theology of the mid-third century. As we saw above, Novatian based his book *On the Trinity* (*c.* 240) on the 'rule of truth' (*regula ueritatis*), but does not mention whether or not it was a fixed text nor what it may have looked like.[370] However, neither he nor Bishop Dionysius (*sedit* 259–268) who wrote a letter against both Sabellians and Marcionites[371] any longer represent a strictly monarchian position, but argue against both modalist and adoptionist views. One might, therefore, speculate that the christological summary was inserted into the baptismal questions in Rome around the middle of the third century. As we saw above,[372] the information from Novatian's book indicates indeed that *some* form of credal formula was used in Rome, and there is good reason to believe that it looked like OG[G2] or TA[G]. The baptismal questions may then have been transformed into propositions which were inculcated in the catechumens in order to establish an (anti-monarchian and anti-adoptionist) orthodoxy. This process may, in turn, have led to the development of the *Traditio* and *Redditio symboli* which we will consider below, a rite which was confined to Rome until the mid-fourth century.[373]

---

369 Cf. Haußleiter 1920, pp. 84–124. Cf. also Kelly 1972, p. 128 citing further scholars; Hübner 1999; Kinzig 2017(2022).
370 Cf. above ch. 4.4.5.
371 A fragment is preserved in Athanasius, *De decretis Nicaenae synodi* 26.
372 Cf. above ch. 4.4.5.
373 Cf. below ch. 11.1.1.

5 The Old Roman Creed and its Descendants

Our first unequivocal evidence for the existence of fixed declaratory creeds dates from the fourth century. As we will see, initially they were based on orally transmitted baptismal questions and/or rules of faith that differed from region to region and that were fluid in their wording. There are two exceptions: the formulae used at Rome and Jerusalem which were closely interlinked. Although the Old Roman Creed (R) was probably not the first declaratory creed, it was based on baptismal interrogations that were already largely fixed. In other words, the verbal 'coagulation' of credal content was more advanced in Rome than elsewhere. In Alexandria we discern this process no earlier than the first decades of the fourth century whereas such fixed formulae did not emerge in other parts of the Latin church until several decades later. Therefore, I will first turn to the situation in the western capital and describe the origin of the R and of cognate formulae as well as the transformation of R into the Apostles' Creed (T) in the Latin Church up to the time of Charlemagne. In this context I will also look at Jerusalem which, I suggest, is an eastern descendant of R.

5.1 The Creeds of Rome

The title of this chapter may mystify some knowledgeable readers, as previous scholarship claimed that only one Roman creed existed (which scholars called R). Meanwhile new evidence has come to light which suggests that a variety of credal texts may have co-existed in Rome in the second and third centuries and, perhaps, even beyond.[1]

(1) The Old Roman Creed (R), which is known to be the ancestor of our Apostles' Creed (T), is first attested in 340/341 by Marcellus of Ancyra in his *Letter to Pope Julius* (FaFo § 253) which has been preserved by Epiphanius of Salamis in his *Panarion* (72,2–3; creed: 72,3,1). The problem with this quotation (if indeed it is that) is that it is not easy to discern where it begins or finishes. Indeed, one could argue that the entire passage 72,2,6–3,3 is Marcellus' (personal) creed as it is introduced by the phrase πιστεύω δὲ ἑπόμενος ταῖς θείαις γραφαῖς ὅτι ('But following the divine Scriptures I believe that') and concludes with the following phrase:

---

1 The following chapter is partly based on Kinzig, 'Ursprung'. 2022. For further details cf. that article.

https://doi.org/10.1515/9783110318531-005

> Having received this faith from the divine Scriptures and having been taught by our fathers in God, I both preach it in the Church of God and have now written it to you [. . .].[2]

However, things are more complicated, because *within* this passage Marcellus begins a subsection once again with 'Therefore, I believe' (πιστεύω οὖν). He then quotes a brief text (R^M)[3] which is (with some minor variations) also attested a century later in the writings of Pope Leo the Great (FaFo § 255g; R^L) and which is usually considered to be the Old Roman Creed. In addition, fragments of it have been preserved in the *Explanation of the Creed* by Rufinus (FaFo § 254b; 404 or shortly thereafter; R^R) in which the author discusses deviations of the creed of Aquileia from that of Rome.

R^M (FaFo § 253)	R^R (§ 254b)	R^L (§ 255g)	
Πιστεύω [. . .] εἰς θεὸν	Credo in deo,	Credo [*or:* credimus] in deum,	I/We believe in God
παντοκράτορα	patre omnipotente,	patrem omnipotentem,	[the Father R^R, R^L] Almighty,
καὶ εἰς Χριστὸν Ἰησοῦν, τὸν υἱὸν αὐτοῦ τὸν μονογενῆ, τὸν κύριον ἡμῶν, τὸν γεννηθέντα ἐκ πνεύματος ἁγίου καὶ Μαρίας τῆς παρθένου,	< . . . >	et in Christum Iesum, filium eius unicum, dominum nostrum, qui natus est de spiritu sancto et Maria uirgine,	and in Christ Jesus, his only[-begotten] Son, our Lord, who was born from the Holy Spirit and the virgin Mary;
τὸν ἐπὶ Ποντίου Πιλάτου σταυρωθέντα	crucifixus sub Pontio Pilato	qui sub Pontio Pilato crucifixus est [et mortuus ?]	who was crucified under Pontius Pilate, [and dead R^L?]
καὶ ταφέντα καὶ τῇ τρίτῃ ἡμέρᾳ ἀναστάντα ἐκ τῶν νεκρῶν,	et sepultus < . . . >	et sepultus; tertia die resurrexit a mortuis;	and buried; [and] on the third day rose again from the dead;
ἀναβάντα εἰς τοὺς οὐρανοὺς		ascendit in caelos;	ascended into the heavens

---

2 Marcellus, *Epistula ad Iulium papam* (Epiphanius, *Panarion* 72,3,4; FaFo § 253): Ταύτην καὶ παρὰ τῶν θείων γραφῶν εἰληφὼς τὴν πίστιν καὶ παρὰ τῶν κατὰ θεὸν προγόνων διδαχθεὶς ἔν τε τῇ τοῦ θεοῦ ἐκκλησίᾳ κηρύττω καὶ πρὸς σὲ νῦν γέγραφα [. . .].

3 On a possible Latin reconstruction cf. below p. 159.

(continued)

R^M (FaFo § 253)	R^R (§ 254b)	R^L (§ 255g)	
καὶ καθήμενον ἐν δεξιᾷ τοῦ πατρός,		sedet ad dexteram patris,	and is sitting at the right hand of the Father,
ὅθεν ἔρχεται κρίνειν ζῶντας καὶ νεκρούς·		unde uenturus est iudicare uiuos ac mortuos [*or:* ad iudicandos uiuos et mortuos];	whence he is coming to judge the living and the dead;
καὶ εἰς τὸ ἅγιον πνεῦμα, ἁγίαν ἐκκλησίαν, ἄφεσιν ἁμαρτιῶν, σαρκὸς ἀνάστασιν, ζωὴν αἰώνιον.	< . . . >	credo/credimus [*or:* et] in spiritum sanctum, sanctam ecclesiam [catholicam *?*], remissionem peccatorum, carnis resurrectionem.	I/we believe [*or:* and] in the Holy Spirit, the holy [catholic R^L?] Church, the remission of sins, the resurrection of the flesh, [eternal life R^M].

The same creed (with slight variations) is also found in cod. Bodleian Library, MS Laud. Gr. 35 (Italy, Sardinia, or Rome, *c.* 600, f. 226^v; FaFo § 327[4]) and in the *Psalter of King Aethelstan* (British Library, Cotton MS Galba A XVIII; *s.* IX/2, f. 200v; FaFo § 295[5]). The creed in Laud. Gr. 35 was added later and is written in eighth-century uncial,[6] at a time when the manuscript must already have been in Britain, probably in the Abbey of Wearmouth and Jarrow. How it got there is a matter of scholarly debate.[7] In the *Psalter* the creed is written in Greek in Anglo-Saxon characters and forms part of a set of liturgical texts which (together with other material) was added to the codex by Israel the Grammarian in Winchester in the second quarter

---

4 Cf. URL: <https://digital.bodleian.ox.ac.uk/objects/55b2e494-4845-403e-9ba6-d812bda79329/> (08/11/2023). In the first section *patrem* is added as in R^L. Other differences to R^M and R^L only concern Latin style.

5 In the first section πατέρα is added as in R^R and R^L. Other differences to R^M and R^L only concern stylistic details.

6 Cf. *Codices Latini Antiquiores*, vol. II, no. 251 according to URL <https://elmss.nuigalway.ie/catalogue/570> (08/11/2023); Lai 2011, pp. 33 f.

7 For the early history of this codex see TM 61729; Walther 1980, vol. I, pp. 2–6; Parker 2008, pp. 289 f.; Lai 2011; and Houghton 2016, pp. 52, 167, 233.

of the tenth century. He, in turn, had taken it from 'a book or booklet of Greek prayers which very probably Archbishop Theodore brought with him when he arrived in England in 669'.[8] We know that Theodore had lived in Rome in a community of oriental monks, probably the monastery of Cilicians (St Athanasius *ad aquas Saluias*; today: Tre Fontane), before being appointed to the See of Canterbury.[9] There can, therefore, be no doubt that this is the (or: a) creed which was used in Rome from at least the 340s onwards until at least the seventh century.

(2) For a long time scholars had assumed that before R a creed in interrogatory form had been used in Rome which was contained in the so-called *Traditio Apostolica* (TA). However, the text of the TA, which had been attributed to Hippolytus of Rome (d. 235), has only been preserved in translations and heavily revised versions. This poses some serious difficulties which I cannot outline here in detail.[10] Suffice it to say that both the authorship of Hippolytus and the provenance of this text which is supposed to have been composed in Rome are very controversial; more recently, those scholars who doubt both these premises appear to be in a majority.[11]

In particular, this is true for the interrogatory baptismal creed which appears to have been contained in the TA. Earlier scholarship regarded it as the oldest preserved creed, dating it to the years before 200 or even earlier.[12] However, its exact wording was uncertain: the Sahidic translation and the related Arabic, Ethiopic and Bohairic versions as well as the various recensions differ considerably from each other.[13] Accordingly, the reconstructions of the supposedly 'original'

---

8 Gretsch 1999, p. 313 referring to Lapidge 1991, pp. 13–25 and Bischoff/Lapidge 1994, pp. 168–72. Cf. also Wood 1999, pp. 178–80; Gneuss/Lapidge 2014, pp. 256–8 (no. 334).

9 Cf. Lapidge 1995, pp. 19–26.

10 Further details on the complex transmission of the *Traditio Apostolica* (which only exists in reconstructed versions that differ from each other) are found in Steimer 1992, pp. 28–48; Markschies 1999; Bradshaw/Johnson/Phillips 2002, pp. 1–6, 11–15; Stewart(-Sykes) 2015, pp. 15–63; Bradshaw, 'Apostolic Tradition', 2018; and Bradshaw 2023, pp. 1–12.

11 Cf., e.g., the views collected in Kinzig 1999(2017), p. 251 n. 43; in addition, Markschies 1999; Bradshaw/Johnson/Phillips 2002, pp. 1–6; Westra 2002, p. 55; Stewart(-Sykes) 2015, pp. 28–38. See also the controversy between Bradshaw and Johnson on one side and Stewart-Sykes on the other: Bradshaw 2004; Stewart-Sykes 2004; Johnson 2005; Stewart-Sykes, 'Baptismal Creed', 2009; Bradshaw 2023, pp. 73 f.

12 Cf. below p. 153 and n. 36.

13 Cf. FaFo §§ 89d–f. The Arab version of the *Testamentum Domini* (as far as it has been published) contains no baptismal questions, but a declaratory creed. Cf. Baumstark 1901, p. 37: 'Confiteor te, Deus, Pater omnipotens, et Filium tuum unicum Iesum Christum et Spiritum tuum sanctum. Amen. Amen. Amen.' On the problem of textual transmission of the Arab version cf. Steimer 1992, p. 97; Bradshaw/Johnson/Phillips 2002, p. 11.

text which have been proposed by Gregory Dix, Bernard Botte, and (largely following Botte) Wilhelm Geerlings must be regarded with some caution[14] (and have, as we will see shortly, meanwhile become out of date). No common wording could be ascertained with any degree of probability for the second and the third article in particular. Consequently, editors of the TA no longer offer a reconstruction but present the textual evidence in synoptic form.[15]

Up until recent discoveries the earliest witness for the TA and its creed had been the so-called *Fragmentum Veronense* in cod. Verona, Biblioteca Capitolare, LV (53; North Italy, *s.* VIII/2).[16] The original Latin text of this palimpsest possibly dates from the late fifth century. It was probably translated from a Greek *Vorlage*. However, it is difficult to determine the date of this translation. Scholars tend to suggest the second half of the fourth century based on stylistic considerations and on the fact that the biblical quotations contained in the translation do not yet stem from the Vulgate; the translator is said to have come from an Arian congregation in Northern Italy.[17] Yet this place of origin for the translation is no more 'than an interesting guess';[18] likewise, the date is by no means certain. For, as Tidner has shown, the biblical quotations in the TA are not found in, or, rather, in a version of, the *Vetus Latina* translation of the Bible either but were produced by the translator himself.[19] In the same vein, I have serious doubts as to whether a date in the fourth century may be securely based on stylistic considerations. Some distinguished scholars have argued for a later date.[20] Moreover, the creed (abbrev. TA^L) is incomplete, owing to a *lacuna* in the manuscript.

(3) Meanwhile, the situation has changed completely since Alessandro Bausi published a new version of the TA which he took from a late Ethiopic codex (*s.* XIII). This manuscript which was restored in a complex process (Ms. Təgrāy, 'Urā Mas-

---

14 Dix/Chadwick 1992 (originally 1937), pp. 35–7 (= FaFo § 89a1); Botte 1989, pp. 49–51 (= FaFo § 89a2); Geerlings in Schöllgen/Geerlings 2000, pp. 261–3. Cf., in addition, Kelly 1972, p. 91 (= Botte); likewise Smulders 1970/1971/1980, p. 242.

15 Cf. Bradshaw/Johnson/Phillips 2002, pp. 114–7; synopsis 1 in Kinzig, 'Ursprung', 2022, pp. 179–85. But cf. again Stewart(-Sykes) in the second edition of his reconstruction of the TA (2015); Bradshaw 2023, p. 72.

16 Cf. CLA 507 (URL <https://elmss.nuigalway.ie/catalogue/857>); TM 66615.

17 Cf. Hauler 1896, pp. 4, 33–40; Hauler 1900, pp. VII–VIII; Steimer 1992, pp. 106–13; Bradshaw/Johnson/Phillips 2002, pp. 7 f.

18 Dix/Chadwick 1992, p. f.

19 Tidner 1963, pp. XIV–XX.

20 C.H. Turner apparently suggested the years 420–430 as date of origin; cf. Dix/Chadwick 1992, p. LIV. Jean Michel Hanssens even advocated a date as late as 500 (Hanssens 1965, pp. 19–30). In general, cf. Markschies 1999, pp. 58–60.

qal, Ethio-SPaRe UM-039 [*olim* C$_3$-IV-73][21]) contains a series of patristic, liturgical, canonical, and historical documents which Bausi calls the *Aksumite Collection*, as it stems from the Aksumite period (*s.* IV–VII). It also includes the new version of the TA.[22] Its credal interrogations (TA^E) are almost entirely identical with the Latin version TA^L. The following shows this version (in Bausi's Italian translation) side by side with the Latin version from the *Fragmentum Veronense*:

Fragmentum Veronense (TA^L; FaFo § 89b)	Ethiopic text in Italian translation (TA^E; FaFo § 89c[23])
[*lacuna*]	Credi in un unico Dio onnipotente?
Credis in Christum Iesum,	Credi in Cristo Gesù,
filium dei,	figlio di Dio,
qui natus est de spiritu sancto ex Maria uirgine	nato dallo Spirito Santo e da Maria vergine,
et crucifixus sub Pontio Pilato	crocifisso sotto Ponzio Pilato,
et mortuus est	morto
et sepultus	e sepolto,
et resurrexit die tertia uiuus a mortuis	risorse nel terzo giorno vivo dai morti,
et ascendit in caelis	e ascese ai cieli
et sedit ad dexteram patris	e siede alla destra del Padre,
uenturus iudicare uiuos et mortuos?	che verrà a giudicare i vivi e i morti?
Credis in spiritu sancto	Credi nello Spirito Santo
et sanctam ecclesiam	e nella santa chiesa
et carnis resurrectionem?	e nella resurrezione della carne?

There is a minimal variation in the second article: here TA^L reads *de spiritu sancto ex Maria uirgine* whereas TA^E does not appear to offer this differentiation (and may, therefore, have preserved an earlier version).[24] Likewise, in the third article the Ethiopic text has faith 'in' the Church and the resurrection, whereas a

---

21 A description of the manuscript and its content is found in Bausi/Camplani 2016, pp. 250 f. For a survey of the process of restoration of the manuscript cf. Bausi 2015.

22 A survey of the *status quaestionis* is found in Bausi/Camplani 2013 and Bausi 2014, pp. 60–4; Macé et al. 2015, pp. 367–70; Bausi 2016, pp. 134–8; Bausi 2020; Bradshaw 2023, pp. 5–8. Further parallels to texts contained in this manuscript are found in other manuscripts from Verona; cf. Bausi/Camplani 2013, pp. 222 f.

23 Bausi 2011, pp. 44 f.

24 However, my colleague Alessandro Bausi has kindly informed me that there is no clear difference in Ethiopic between *ex* and *de* anyway (email of 19 February 2019).

corresponding double *in* is missing in the Latin version. The basic identity of the Latin and Ethiopic version of the TA also extends to the remainder of the text (as far it has been preserved). This has led Bausi to the convincing conclusion that both versions go back to the same Greek *Vorlage* and that we are, therefore, dealing with *translations* in both cases. This should be stressed, because it was once argued that the creed in the TA as preserved in the fragment from Verona had been composed in Latin and was inserted into the *Traditio Apostolica* later, after the Church order had been translated from the Greek in order to adapt it to the changed circumstances.[25]

The text of the Greek *Vorlage* (TA[G]) may have run like this:[26]

Πιστεύεις εἰς ἕνα θεὸν παντοκράτορα;[27]	Do you believe in one God Almighty?
Πιστεύεις εἰς Χριστὸν Ἰησοῦν, τὸν υἱὸν τοῦ θεοῦ, τὸν γεννηθέντα ἐκ πνεύματος ἁγίου καὶ Μαρίας τῆς παρθένου, τὸν ἐπὶ Ποντίου Πιλάτου σταυρωθέντα [*or:* τὸν σταυρωθέντα ἐπὶ Ποντίου Πιλάτου]	Do you believe in Christ Jesus, the Son of God, who was born from the Holy Spirit and the virgin Mary; who was crucified under Pontius Pilate,
καὶ ἀποθανόντα	and died,
καὶ ταφέντα	and was buried,
καὶ τῇ τρίτῃ ἡμέρᾳ ἀναστάντα ἐκ [*add.* τῶν ?] νεκρῶν [*or:* ἀναστάντα τῇ τρίτῃ ἡμέρᾳ ἐκ [τῶν] νεκρῶν] ζῶντα	and on the third day rose again alive from the dead,
καὶ ἀναβάντα εἰς τοὺς οὐρανοὺς	and ascended into the heavens,
καὶ καθήμενον [*or:* καθεζόμενον] ἐν δεξιᾷ τοῦ πατρός,	and sits [*or:* sat down] at the right hand of the Father,
ἐρχόμενον [*or:* ἐλευσόμενον] κρίνειν [*or:* κρῖναι] ζῶντας καὶ νεκρούς;	coming to judge the living and the dead?

---

25 Cf. Bradshaw/Johnson/Phillips 2002, p. 126 referring to Kinzig 1999(2017), pp. 251 f. (= 93 f.); Vinzent 1999, p. 189, but giving an imprecise account of the argument set out in these publications. Furthermore Markschies 1999, p. 73; Westra 2002, p. 66; Stewart(-Sykes) 2015, pp. 24 f.; Bradshaw 2023, pp. 72–5.

26 Cf. also the English reconstruction in Stewart(-Sykes) 2015, p. 134 who has likewise used the Aksumite version, but draws slightly different conclusions with regard to the original text, as he also includes readings from the *Testamentum Domini* (cf. Stewart(-Sykes) 2015, p. 138). In my view, this complicates matters unnecessarily.

27 Stewart(-Sykes) 2015, p. 134: 'Do you believe in God the Father Almighty?'

Πιστεύεις εἰς τὸ ἅγιον πνεῦμα	Do you believe in the Holy Spirit
καὶ [εἰς] ἁγίαν ἐκκλησίαν	and [in] the holy Church
καὶ [εἰς] σαρκὸς ἀνάστασιν;[28]	and [in] the resurrection of the flesh?

The reconstruction contains some (minor) uncertainties:

- The wording of the first article is somewhat uncertain, because the Latin text is missing here.
- Likewise, it is uncertain whether in TA[G] τὸν σταυρωθέντα was placed after Pontius Pilate (as in R) or whether it anteceded him. There are parallels for the position of τὸν σταυρωθέντα before Pontius Pilate both in the east (Antioch) and in the west.[29]
- Furthermore, we do not know whether the text read τῇ τρίτῃ ἡμέρᾳ ἀναστάντα as in R or, conversely, ἀναστάντα τῇ τρίτῃ ἡμέρᾳ. A possible placement of ἀναστάντα before τῇ τρίτῃ ἡμέρᾳ is not found among the descendants of R,[30] but is widely attested in the east since Eusebius and could (if at all) have influenced the Greek text from there.
- *Sedit* may be translated as either καθήμενον or καθεζόμενον. Καθήμενον (cf. Mt 26:64) is also found in the *Psalter of King Aethelstan* whereas καθεζόμενον does not appear in creeds before 359.[31] Nota bene: In Latin versions *sedit* and *sedet* are often used indiscriminately. Therefore, the translations 'sits', 'is sitting', and 'sat down' are all accurate.
- Finally, it remains an open question whether the text contained ἐρχόμενον or ἐλευσόμενον. The Latin translation *uenturus* (which may also be translated: 'will come') may suggest the latter participle, but the former occurs much more frequently in other creeds.[32]

---

28 Stewart(-Sykes) 2015, p. 134: 'Do you believe in the Holy Spirit and the holy church and the resurrection of the flesh?'

29 In the east cf. esp. the Antiochene creeds in *Constitutiones apostolorum* 7,41,6 (*c.* 380; FaFo § 182c), in Eusebius of Dorylaeum (429–430; FaFo § 198), and in John Cassian (430/431; FaFo § 203). Regarding Aquileia (and, thus, perhaps also Rome), it is likewise attested by Rufinus (FaFo § 254b); later attestations include Quodvultdeus (437–453; FaFo § 317a) and Venantius Fortunatus (575–600; FaFo § 329).

30 Cf., however, the much younger text CPL 1762 (fifth c. or later; FaFo § 364).

31 'Dated Creed' of Sirmium: καθεζόμενον ἐκ δεξιῶν τοῦ πατρός (FaFo § 157[4]).

32 Ἐρχόμενον: cf., e.g., FaFo §§ 135c; 172b1 and b2; 184e, etc. ἐλευσόμενον: §§ 157[4] (translation from Latin); 160[3]; 427 (translation from Latin).

The latest date usually given for the text's translation into Ethiopic (TA^F) is the sixth century.[33] If the Latin manuscript was indeed written in the late fifth century, we might want to push back the *terminus ante quem* of the composition of the Greek original somewhat further.

As I have shown elsewhere, there is little doubt that TA^G is a western creed which, ultimately, originated in Rome.[34] It was not until the mid-fourth century that a Latin liturgy was introduced there,[35] which would point to a *terminus ante quem* of around 350 CE for this creed. This is, of course, no conclusive proof for a Roman origin of TA^G, but the similarities with R which I will deal with below may, I think, permit such an assumption. The hypothesis of a western and, indeed, Roman origin of the baptismal questions of the TA (although in versions such as those reconstructed by Dix and Botte) is not a new one – on the contrary: many scholars had defended precisely this assumption and had proposed the end of the second century as a date for the formula (as part of a Church order composed by Hippolytus, i.e. the *Traditio Apostolica*) – which as we will see, may be a little too early.[36]

When we place TA^G and R^M side by side, we can see how similar both creeds are to each other:

TA^G	R^M
	(FaFo § 253)
Πιστεύεις εἰς ἕνα θεὸν παντοκράτορα;[37]	Πιστεύω [. . .] εἰς θεὸν παντοκράτορα
Πιστεύεις εἰς Χριστὸν Ἰησοῦν,	καὶ εἰς Χριστὸν Ἰησοῦν,
τὸν υἱὸν τοῦ θεοῦ,	τὸν υἱὸν αὐτοῦ
	τὸν μονογενῆ,
	τὸν κύριον ἡμῶν,
τὸν γεννηθέντα ἐκ πνεύματος ἁγίου καὶ	τὸν γεννηθέντα ἐκ πνεύματος ἁγίου καὶ
Μαρίας τῆς παρθένου,	Μαρίας τῆς παρθένου,

---

33 Cf. Bausi 2009, p. 291; Bausi 2015; Bausi/Camplani 2016, p. 250; Bausi 2020, pp. 41 f.; cf. also Bausi 2010.

34 Cf. Kinzig, 'Ursprung', 2022, pp. 167–9.

35 On this complex question cf. Kelly 1972, pp. 111–13; Vogel 1986, pp. 293–7, citing earlier literature in n. 7; Kinzig 1999(2017), p. 250 n. 36.

36 Cf. Capelle 1927; Capelle 1930; Botte 1951; Holland 1965; Kelly 1972, pp. 126–30; Bradshaw/Johnson/Phillips 2002, p. 125. A survey is also found in Westra 2002, pp. 49, 54 f.; Vinzent 2006, pp. 219–66.

37 Stewart(-Sykes) 2015, p. 134: 'Do you believe in God the Father Almighty?'

τὸν ἐπὶ Ποντίου Πιλάτου σταυρωθέντα [or: τὸν σταυρωθέντα ἐπὶ Ποντίου Πιλάτου]	τὸν ἐπὶ Ποντίου Πιλάτου σταυρωθέντα
καὶ ἀποθανόντα	
καὶ ταφέντα	καὶ ταφέντα
καὶ τῇ τρίτῃ ἡμέρᾳ ἀναστάντα ἐκ [add. τῶν ?] νεκρῶν [or: ἀναστάντα τῇ τρίτῃ ἡμέρᾳ ἐκ [τῶν] νεκρῶν] ζῶντα	καὶ τῇ τρίτῃ ἡμέρᾳ ἀναστάντα ἐκ τῶν νεκρῶν,
καὶ ἀναβάντα εἰς τοὺς οὐρανοὺς	ἀναβάντα εἰς τοὺς οὐρανοὺς
καὶ καθήμενον ἐν δεξιᾷ τοῦ πατρός,	καὶ καθήμενον ἐν δεξιᾷ τοῦ πατρός,
ἐρχόμενον [or: ἐλευσόμενον] κρίνειν [or: κρῖναι] ζῶντας καὶ νεκρούς;	ὅθεν ἔρχεται κρίνειν ζῶντας καὶ νεκρούς·
Πιστεύεις εἰς τὸ ἅγιον πνεῦμα	καὶ εἰς τὸ ἅγιον πνεῦμα,
καὶ [εἰς] ἁγίαν ἐκκλησίαν	ἁγίαν ἐκκλησίαν,
	ἄφεσιν ἁμαρτιῶν,
καὶ [εἰς] σαρκὸς ἀνάστασιν;[38]	σαρκὸς ἀνάστασιν,
	ζωὴν αἰώνιον.

It is clear that neither creed can have been the *Vorlage* of the other, as both texts contain additional material. Instead, they must both go back to older versions of the baptismal questions which must be situated in Rome and which I have discussed above.[39]

However, this poses a serious problem for the thesis put forward by Markus Vinzent twenty-five years ago that R is ultimately the product of Marcellus and that the credal part of his letter was adopted by a Synod in Rome in 340/341, thus spreading throughout the western part of the empire.[40] At the time, I agreed with Vinzent.[41] However, even back then we allowed for the possibility that in formulating his creed Marcellus may have used 'some Roman baptismal interrogations'.[42] Yet this thesis must be reconsidered in the light of my present study of the christological section of R[43] and the emergence of the new witness of the baptismal interrogations in the TA. It now seems certain that Marcellus used an older set of baptismal questions in the central section of his letter (i.e. R^M), questions which he may simply have transformed from an interrogatory into a declaratory

---

38 Stewart(-Sykes) 2015, p. 134: 'Do you believe in the Holy Spirit and the holy church and the resurrection of the flesh?'
39 Cf. Kinzig, 'Ursprung', 2022 and above ch. 4.5.1.
40 Cf. Vinzent 1999. Cf. already above pp. 28 f.
41 Cf. Kinzig/Vinzent 1999, pp. 557–9.
42 Kinzig/Vinzent 1999, p. 558.
43 Cf. above ch. 4.6.

creed. R^M (in interrogatory form) must go back to the second half of the third century and have developed from earlier versions of the baptismal questions (chiefly OGS^{G2} and OGS^*).[44] TA^G is another descendant of these questions and probably existed simultaneously with R^M.

Likewise, given the evidence it can no longer be maintained that the Roman Synod of 340/341 actually transformed it into a creed by extracting this section from Marcellus' *pístis* (i.e. R^M). Rather, R^M in its *declaratory* (i.e. Marcellian) version may have been promulgated by the synod, precisely because it was recognized that its content was identical to one set of the older baptismal questions that was used in Rome.[45] Bishop Julius of Rome may actually be alluding to this fact in his letter to the Antiochene bishops:

> With respect to Marcellus, since you have charged him also with impiety towards Christ, I am anxious to inform you that when he was here, he positively declared that what you had written concerning him was not true; but when he was nevertheless requested by us to give an account of his faith (εἰπεῖν περὶ τῆς πίστεως), he answered in his own person with the utmost boldness, so that we recognized that he confesses (ὁμολογεῖ) nothing outside the truth. He confessed (ὡμολόγησε) his convictions concerning our Lord and Saviour Jesus Christ in an entirely godly fashion just like the catholic Church maintains as well; and he affirmed that he had held these convictions for a very long time, and had not recently [adopted them], as indeed our presbyters, who were at a former date present at the Council of Nicaea, testified to his orthodoxy [. . .].[46]

It seems that Marcellus was asked to produce a creed which was then examined and declared orthodox, because it agreed with the 'catholic Church' (i.e. the baptismal questions used at Rome) and was thus distributed together with the decisions of the synod.

TA^G, however, probably represents a fairly old sideline of this development; in any case, it is no immediate descendant of R, but also goes back to the Roman baptismal questions. Yet it does not yet contain the remission of sins although, according to Cyprian, by the middle of the third century the remission of sins did form part of the Roman credal questions.[47] It may, therefore, be reasonable to assume that it originated in the first half of the third century after the christological summary had been inserted into the trinitarian credal questions,[48] but before

---

44 Cf. Kinzig, 'Ursprung', 2022, pp. 169–78. Similarly, Smulders 1970/1971/1980, pp. 244 f.; Westra 2002, p. 67.

45 Cf. above pp. 128 f.

46 Julius, *Epistula ad Antiochenos episcopos* (Brennecke et al. 2007, *Dokument* 41.8) 48–49 (tr. NPNF; altered).

47 Cf. above p. 131.

48 Cf. above ch. 4.6.

the remission of sins had been added. By the middle of the fourth century it must have been translated into Latin. For the time being, it remains an open question whether or not TA^G originally belonged to the *Traditio Apostolica* and should, therefore, perhaps be considered the first 'official' record of an earlier, Roman baptismal creed only transmitted orally, or whether a younger creed was inserted into an existing order. Likewise, nothing is as yet decided with regard to authorship of the TA.

As we will see below, R influenced the western credal development down to the Apostles' Creed.[49] However, throughout much of the fourth century its use (and that of TA^G) remained confined to Rome. Elsewhere in the west no fixed baptismal creed was used until the late 350s, as is attested by Hilary of Poitiers. In the winter of 358/359, Hilary wrote a letter to his fellow bishops in Gaul, Germany, and Britain. He appears to have been living in exile in Asia Minor when he learned about the doctrinal controversies which shook the eastern churches to their core. Hilary's letter informed his western colleagues about these controversies relating to the creed. In fact, Hilary noted with some astonishment that these controversies had led to the *creation* of creeds as written documents, a literary genre which up to that point had been unknown in the west:

> But among these things, O you who are blessed and glorious in the Lord, who preserve the perfect and apostolic faith in the confession of your convictions, you have hitherto been ignorant of written creeds (*conscriptas fides*). For you, who abounded in the Spirit, have not needed the letter. You did not require the service of a hand to write what you believed in your heart [and] professed with [your] mouth unto salvation [cf. Rom 10:10]. You did not deem it necessary to read as bishops what you held when new-born converts. But necessity has introduced the custom of setting out creeds and signing what has been set out (*exponi fides et expositis subscribi*). Where the meaning of the convictions is in danger, there the letter is required. Of course, nothing prevents us from writing down that which is wholesome to confess.[50]

This testimony is remarkable for a number of reasons. (1) Hilary attests that no written creeds had previously existed in the dioceses of the west to which his missive is addressed (i.e. large parts of the western empire) at that time. (The plural *conscriptas fides* clearly refers not to a *particular* creed, but to written credal texts *tout court*.) (2) Hitherto western Christians had confessed their faith in a way which had not required a written text. This may mean that they had memorized the creed which had only been passed on to them orally or, as seems more plausible to me, that they had simply answered the baptismal interrogations

---

49 Cf. below ch. 5.2.
50 *De synodis* 63 (FaFo § 151d1).

(which in their wording may still have been fairly fluid). (3) The synods mandated that creeds be written down. (4) Bishops were thereafter required to sign those texts in order to publicly bear witness to their faith.

Therefore, we have here a first-hand account of the emergence of creeds as written texts in the west. Whereas in large parts of the western empire no such texts existed in written form prior to the late 350s, the doctrinal controversies of the fourth century required that the 'spirit' of the faith had to be written down as the 'letter'.

5.2 From the Creed of Rome to the Apostles' Creed

It has long been known that the first approximately datable attestation of T is found in the *Scarapsus* ('Excerpt'), a missionary handbook written by Pirmin between 725 and 750, perhaps at the Abbey of Hornbach in the Palatinate, a region in southwest Germany. The handbook cites T three times in basically identical versions, the third time in interrogatory form.[51] We have no direct information whether Pirmin cites a creed which was used locally (and if so, whether this was really the creed in circulation at Hornbach[52]), whether it is his baptismal creed (noting there is no unanimity among scholars where he came from), or whether he took it from some literary source. However, the evidence that we will review below strongly suggests that T originated in Gaul. In addition, the long list of witnesses to T assembled in FaFo § 344 attests to the popularity of this version of R from the time of the *Scarapsus*. (We will deal with the reasons for this standardization of the western creed in chapter 5.3.) This suggests that the final version of T had been in circulation for some time.

Unfortunately, we are unable to narrow down its date of origin any further. Two anonymous witnesses may belong to an earlier period. These texts are the *Sermo 242* (FaFo § 276c[53]) which is found among the works of Augustine and may have been written in the sixth or seventh century, and another explanation of the

---

51 Cf. Pirmin, *Scarapsus* 10 (FaFo § 376); 12 (§ 610); 28a (§ 298). The three versions are identical, except for the omission of *Amen* in 12 and 28a. There are small differences to T: Pirmin reads *sedit* instead of *sedet* and *est* after *uenturus*; *et* after *carnis resurrectionem*, and *Amen* are omitted. The confusion *sedit/sedet* is often found in late medieval manuscripts, the omissions of *est* and *et* are negligible. The final *Amen* was not always considered part of the creed.

52 Or, perhaps, Reichenau or Murbach, the abbeys in which Pirmin was active before coming to Hornbach. On Pirmin's life cf. Hauswald 2010, pp. IX–XIX.

53 The creed adds *huius* before *carnis* (as in the creed of Aquileia (cf. FaFo § 254b)) and omits *est* after *uenturus* and *et* after *resurrectionem*. Only the first variant may be relevant.

creed (CPL 1758; FaFo § 280[54]) which may be slightly younger. However, in both these cases there is no hard evidence when it comes to dates.[55] As regards *Sermo 242* there is also the additional problem that the initial citation of the creed and its later explanation do not entirely match. Furthermore, the text is not beyond any doubt either, given that no critical edition of this sermon has so far been produced. Given these uncertainties, I will leave both these texts aside.

In what follows we will investigate where and how T developed from R. Creeds that somehow belong to this intermediate period between R and T will summarily be called R/T. To describe this development is a tricky undertaking. Although it is fairly easy to point out all those creeds that derive from R, it is much more difficult to ascertain the contributions of specific regions, churches, or individuals to the creed. In many instances, we are unable to reconstruct the confession even of prominent theologians due to a dearth of evidence; for example, Ambrose's *symbolum* is only known to us in fragmentary form. In some cases a single bishop used not one, but several creeds, the most famous case being Augustine.[56] There even are explanations of the faith where the author initially quotes one creed, but then curiously goes on to explain another, because he has taken his explanation from a different source than the creed initially cited.[57] Creeds may have travelled owing to the bishops' mobility or for political reasons such as the relocation of the centre of the Visigothic Kingdom westwards to the Iberian Peninsula by the early sixth century. Finally, there may be variants in the textual transmission of individual creeds because copyists made mistakes or deliberately replaced the creeds in their exemplar with formulae of their own. We must, therefore, be aware that in many instances the creeds in our printed editions are artificial constructs, reflecting the evidence available at the time of publication. If an explanation of the creed was, for example, handed down in four manuscripts, that one text may in fact explain four slightly different versions of the creed. Conversely, if an ancient work has only survived in a single manuscript, we must be wary regarding the text of that creed as transmitted, as it could have been altered or corrupted in the process.

Given the sheer number of attested formulae deriving from R,[58] how can a student of the creeds decide what is important and what is not without getting lost in the thicket of texts that are, perhaps, irrelevant for the question at hand? I

---

54 The creed omits *est* after *uenturus*, *et* after *resurrectionem*, and the final *Amen*. This is not relevant.

55 Cf. Westra 2002, pp. 113 n. 45 (*Sermo 242*, citing further literature) and 371 (CPL 1758).

56 Cf. below pp. 184–7.

57 Cf., e.g., Caesarius of Arles, *Sermo 9* (FaFo § 271a1 in comparison with a2). Furthermore Westra 2002, p. 85 and n. 43.

58 Cf. FaFo, ch. 8.1.

suggest the following procedure. First, comparing R and T we trace significant changes between these two texts. For this purpose, we will have to decide, of course, what is significant and what is not. Once this is done, we will briefly look at additions and omissions that did not make it into T, but nonetheless seem significant for one reason or another.

First let us once more consider R as cited by Marcellus (FaFo § 253). When we look at the versions R/T in their entirety two Latin versions are possible (and attested) for the christological section which differ not in content but in grammar (abbreviated $R^{M/L1}$ and $R^{M/L2}$):

R^M	$R^{M/L1}$	$R^{M/L2}$	
Πιστεύω [. . .] εἰς θεὸν παντοκράτορα	Credo in deum omnipotentem,		I believe in God Almighty;
καὶ εἰς Χριστὸν Ἰησοῦν, τὸν υἱὸν αὐτοῦ τὸν μονογενῆ,	et in Christum Iesum, filium eius unicum [*or:* unigenitum],		and in Christ Jesus, his only [*or:* only-begotten] Son,
τὸν κύριον ἡμῶν,	dominum nostrum,		our Lord,
τὸν γεννηθέντα ἐκ πνεύματος ἁγίου καὶ Μαρίας τῆς παρθένου,	natum de [*or:* ex] spiritu sancto et Maria uirgine,	[qui] natus [est] de [*or:* ex] spiritu sancto et Maria uirgine,	who [*or:* he] was born [*or:* born] of [*or:* from] the Holy Spirit and the virgin Mary,
τὸν ἐπὶ Ποντίου Πιλάτου σταυρωθέντα	sub Pontio Pilato crucifixum [*or:* crucifixum sub Pontio Pilato]	[qui] sub Pontio Pilato crucifixus [est]	who [*or:* he] was crucified under Pontius Pilate [*or:* crucified under Pontius Pilate]
καὶ ταφέντα	et sepultum	et sepultus	and buried
καὶ τῇ τρίτῃ ἡμέρᾳ ἀναστάντα ἐκ τῶν νεκρῶν,	[qui] tertia die resurrexit a mortuis;		and [*or:* who] on the third day rose again from the dead;
ἀναβάντα εἰς τοὺς οὐρανοὺς	ascendit in caelos		ascended into the heavens;
καὶ καθήμενον ἐν δεξιᾷ τοῦ πατρός,	et sedet [*or:* sedit] ad dexteram patris,		sits [*or:* sat down] at the right hand of the Father
ὅθεν ἔρχεται κρίνειν ζῶντας καὶ νεκρούς·	unde [*or:* inde] uenturus [est] iudicare uiuos et mortuos;		whence [*or:* thence] he will come to judge the living and the dead;
καὶ εἰς τὸ ἅγιον πνεῦμα,	et in spiritum sanctum,		and in the Holy Spirit,
ἁγίαν ἐκκλησίαν, ἄφεσιν ἁμαρτιῶν, σαρκὸς ἀνάστασιν,	sanctam ecclesiam, remissionem peccatorum, carnis resurrectionem,		the holy Church, the remission of sins, the resurrection of the flesh,
ζωὴν αἰώνιον.	uitam aeternam.		eternal life.

As can easily be gleaned from the table, the sequence birth (γεννηθέντα) – crucifixion (σταυρωθέντα) – burial (ταφέντα) could be expressed in several ways:

(I) The sequence could be translated literally from Greek into Latin by perfect participle passive *natum – crucifixum – sepultum*.[59]

(II) The same sequence could be translated by relative clauses (*qui natus est – [qui] crucifixus est – et sepultus*).[60]

(III) Sometimes main clauses or mere participles in the nominative without *est* were used.[61] This version may have developed from (II) when the relative pronoun and/or *est* was simply dropped.

All three versions are attested in the history of the R/T. They seem to go back to two different translations, i.e. I and II/III. Version II is most often cited and is the one found in T.

For the following sequence resurrection (ἀναστάντα) – ascension (ἀναβάντα) – sitting at the right hand (καθήμενον) there is no direct equivalent in Latin because it has no active perfect participle. (The present participles *resurgentem – ascendentem – sedentem* which we do occasionally find in Latin translations of N and C^2 are inaccurate stopgap solutions.[62]) Therefore, the participles ἀναστάντα – ἀναβάντα – καθήμενον had to be translated either by relative clauses (or main clauses), in which case it would be much more harmonious to translate the preceding clauses in the same way. Alternatively, in the representatives of type I the participles were followed by main clauses after *sepultum* which looked less elegant.[63] In the course of time here, too, type II ousted all other versions.

---

59 Cf. FaFo §§ 265, 269, 273, 282 (here *passus* is in the nominative), 287, 316g, 375, 385, 676.

60 Cf. FaFo §§ 266a and b, 267 a and b2, 270, 271a1 and b1, 272, 274, 276c and d, 277d, 278, 280, 283, 285, 288, 290?, 293, 294, 298, 299, 306, 307, 314c, 326, 334, 336, 342, 343, 344 (= T), 345, 346, 347, 373, 376, 386, 387, 393, 400, 401, 404, 410, 418, 419, 421, 422, 423, 424, 428, 430, 527, 610, 676b, 678a1, 709, 763, 764, 765, 797d and e.

61 Cf. FaFo §§ 268, 271a2 and b2, 297, 316l, 324.

62 For N cf. FaFo § 135d, nos. 27.1, 42, 43. For C^2 § 184f type I and III. In the interrelated creeds §§ 265 (Gaul, *s.* V) and 273 (Gaul, *c.* 550 or later) the switch occurs after *resurgentem*: 'tertia die resurgentem ex mortuis [. . .] uictor ascendit ad caelos'.

63 Cf. in chronological order: FaFo §§ 316g (Augustine: *sepultum – resurrexit*), 375, and 676 (*Bobbio Missal*, Vienne, *s.* VII ex.: *sepultum – descendit*), 385 (St. Gallen? before 800: *sepultum – resurrexit*), 282 (Northern France, *s.* VIII or earlier: *sepultum – descendit*), 287 (Francia, 813–815: *sepultum – surrexit*). §§ 265 and 269 have only been preserved in a fragmentary version. – In two instances, the authors switch from participle to main clause after *natum*: § 317d (Quodvultdeus): '[. . .] natum de spiritu sancto ex uirgine Maria. Crucifixus sub Pontio Pilato [. . .]'; § 684d (*Liber misticus*, Toledo?, s. IX–X?): '[. . .] natum de spiritu sancto ex utero Mariae uirginis; passus sub Pontio Pilato [. . .]'. – There are a few cases where the accusative with perfect infinitive appears to have been used instead; cf. §§ 269, 308 (Priscillian), 609 (Eligius of Noyon). However, in none of

Let us take another look at R as cited by Marcellus (FaFo § 253) and at T in its standard version as it is firmly attested from the early eighth century onwards (§ 344).

R^M (Latin version reconstructed[64])		T	
Credo in deum	I believe in God	Credo in deum patrem	I believe in God, the Father
omnipotentem,	Almighty;	omnipotentem, creatorem caeli et terrae,	Almighty, Creator of heaven and earth;
et in Christum Iesum, filium eius unicum [*or:* unigenitum],	and in Christ Jesus, his only [*or:* only-begotten] Son,	et in Iesum Christum, filium eius unicum,	and in Jesus Christ, his only Son,
dominum nostrum,	our Lord,	dominum nostrum, qui conceptus est de spiritu sancto,	our Lord, who was conceived of the Holy Spirit,
qui natus est [*or:* natum] de [*or:* ex] spiritu sancto et Maria uirgine,	who was born [*or:* born] of [*or:* from] the Holy Spirit and the virgin Mary,	natus ex Maria uirgine,	born from the virgin Mary,
		passus sub Pontio Pilato,	suffered under Pontius Pilate,
qui sub Pontio Pilato crucifixus est [*or:* sub Pontio Pilato crucifixum // *or:* crucifixum sub Pontio Pilato]	who was crucified under Pontius Pilate [*or:* crucified under Pontius Pilate]	crucifixus,	was crucified,
		mortuus	dead,
et sepultus [*or:* et sepultum]	and buried	et sepultus;	and buried;
		descendit ad inferna;	descended to the underworld;

---

these cases can we be certain that the structure of the creed has not been adapted to its literary context. In one instance we find a switch from participle to infinitive; cf. § 297 (St. Gallen, *s.* VIII/1): '[. . .] sepultus; tertia die resurrexisse [. . .]'.

64 Cf. also above p. 159. Instead of the relative clauses *qui natus est – qui crucifixus est* simple participles may have ben used (*natus – crucifixus*).

(continued)

R^M (Latin version reconstructed)		T	
et [or: qui] tertia die resurrexit a mortuis;	and [or: who] on the third day rose again from the dead;	tertia die resurrexit a mortuis;	on the third day rose again from the dead;
ascendit in caelos	ascended into the heavens;	ascendit ad caelos;	ascended to the heavens;
et sedet [or: sedit] ad dexteram patris,	sits [or: sat down] at the right hand of the Father	sedet ad dexteram dei, patris omnipotentis;	sits at the right hand of God, the Father Almighty;
unde [or: inde] uenturus [est] iudicare uiuos et mortuos;	whence [or: thence] he will come to judge the living and the dead;	inde uenturus est iudicare uiuos et mortuos.	thence he will come to judge the living and the dead.
et in spiritum sanctum,	and in the Holy Spirit,	Credo in spiritum sanctum,	I believe in the Holy Spirit,
sanctam ecclesiam,	the holy Church,	sanctam ecclesiam catholicam, sanctorum communionem,	the holy catholic Church, the communion of saints,
remissionem peccatorum,	the remission of sins,	remissionem peccatorum,	the remission of sins,
carnis resurrectionem,	the resurrection of the flesh,	carnis resurrectionem	the resurrection of the flesh,
uitam aeternam.	eternal life.	et uitam aeternam. Amen.	and eternal life. Amen.

Let us first briefly look at changes that require no further investigation:

- the repetition or omission of *credo/credimus* at the beginning of the second and third section (this varies in the sources without any discernible difference in meaning);
- the sequence Christ Jesus or Jesus Christ: this has often been discussed,[65] but arguably without any results of consequence;
- *et* or *qui* before *tertia die* in R^M;

---

65 Cf., e.g., Kattenbusch 1900, pp. 541–62; Kelly 1972, pp. 139–41. The sequence *Christum Iesum* is neither unusual nor 'proof of the primitiveness of the core of the Old Roman Creed' (Kelly 1972, p. 139). Cf. in a credal context, e.g., Irenaeus, *Aduersus haereses* 3,4,2 (FaFo § 109b7); Tertullian, *De praescriptione haereticorum* 36,5 (§ 111b5); Novatian, *De trinitate* 9,1 (§ 119b); Peter Chrysolo-

-   *in* or *ad caelos*; likewise, there seems to be no difference between the singular and the plural of *caelum*;
-   *sedet/sedit*: these two are often confused in the manuscripts;
-   *dei* after *ad dexteram* (the Father was always considered divine);
-   *unde/inde*;
-   *est* after *uenturus*;
-   *Amen:* although this is sometimes discussed in explanations of the creed, there is no evidence that the mention or omission of *Amen* has any bearing on the history of R/T.

Additions and changes in T that do require further investigation:
-   *patrem*
-   *creatorem caeli et terrae*
-   *qui conceptus est de spiritu sancto, natus ex Maria uirgine*
-   *passus* and position of *sub Pontio Pilato*
-   *mortuus*
-   *descendit ad inferna*
-   *omnipotentis*
-   *catholicam*
-   *sanctorum communionem.*

There is one additional problem: Marcellus and T both conclude with *uitam aeternam*, but this phrase is found neither in Leo's version of R (R[L]; FaFo § 255g) nor in the long version of the baptismal interrogations in the *Old Gelasian Sacramentary* (§ 675c, f; Rufinus' version of R cannot be reconstructed here with sufficient certainty). We will also look into this problem below.[66]

In what follows I will try to outline the theological contexts and geographical areas within which these additions and changes were made. For this purpose, I will restrict myself to those texts and authors that can be clearly dated and localized, and disregard most explanations of the creed that are anonymous.

patrem

No doubt the earliest of the additions to R is *patrem*. R[M] and TA[G] only contained *deum omnipotentem*/θεὸν παντοκράτορα (in the case of TA[G] preserved only in its

---

gus, *Sermo 57* (§ 259a); id., *Sermo 58* (§ 259b); id., *Sermo 59* (§ 259c); id., *Sermo 61* (§ 259e); id., *Sermo 62* (§ 259f); anonymous explanations of the creed (§§ 263; 271b1; 330; 379); etc.

66 Cf. below pp. 182 f.

Ethiopic version)[67] which corresponds to the usage in the Septuagint and in the Book of Revelation.[68] By contrast, *patrem* does appear in the baptismal questions of the *Old Gelasian Sacramentary* (OGS) and in a brief creed by Marius Victorinus around 360,[69] that is, at about the time of the earliest Latin versions of N which also contain the syntagma *patrem omnipotentem* as a translation of πατέρα παντοκράτορα.[70] 'Father' may have been added by the middle of the fourth century to correspond to *filium eius* in the second section. The reason may have been a desire to ward off Arianism (as in Marius Victorinus who cites his creed in an anti-Arian treatise). In any case, Rufinus' version of R (R[R]; FaFo § 254b) and the version which can be reconstructed from the works of Leo the Great (R[L]; § 255g) clearly both contained *patrem*. The older version θεὸν παντοκράτορα/*deum omnipotentem* quickly vanished from versions of R/T.[71]

creatorem caeli et terrae

The Greek equivalent of *creatorem caeli et terrae* (ποιητὴν οὐρανοῦ καὶ γῆς, sometimes extended by further genitives such as ὁρατῶν τε καὶ ἀοράτων / 'of things visible and invisible') probably occurs for the first time in the creed of the Synod of Antioch in early 325 (FaFo § 133) and in J (§ 147); it later formed part of C[2] (§ 184e1). In Latin literature the syntagma *creator caeli/coeli et/atque terrae* does not seem to be attested before Hilary of Poitiers who uses it occasionally, referring to Gen 14:19 ('Benedictus Abraham deo summo, qui creauit caelum et terram.' / 'Blessed be Abraham by God Most High, who created heaven and earth.').[72] Whether or not the phrase was contained in the creed of Nicetas of Remesiana (modern Bela Palanka in Serbia; fl. *c.* 400) is uncertain.[73] In any case, it is widely attested in the Gaulish creeds of Caesarius of Arles, in the *Bobbio Missal* (*s.* VII *ex.*), and in Pirmin,[74]

---

67 Cf. also Tertullian, *De uirginibus uelandis* 1,4(3; FaFo § 111c).

68 Cf. below p. 254 n. 142.

69 Cf. *Sacramentarium Gelasianum Vetus* nos. 449 (FaFo § 675c), 608 (§ 675f), and p. 122; Marius Victorinus, *Aduersus Arium* 2,12 (§ 437).

70 Cf. FaFo § 135d1–6.

71 Cf., however, the baptismal questions in the so-called *Supplementum Anianense* to the *Gregorian Sacramentary* (FaFo § 806).

72 Cf. Hilary, *Tractatus super Psalmos* 134,18; id., *De trinitate* 12,4. Similarly, Jdt 13:24(Vg); Dan 14:4(Vg).

73 Cf. Nicetas, *Competentibus ad baptismum instructionis libelli* 5,2. Burn prints *creatorem caeli et terrae* as part of Nicetas' creed (Burn 1905, p. 39, ll. 13 f.), but a great number of codices do not cite the phrase. However, Nicetas says in his commentary, 'Deum bonum et iustum, caeli et terrae creatorem' (Burn 1905, p. 40, ll. 2 f.) Cf. also Westra 2002, pp. 212–13 and FaFo § 324.

74 Cf. Caesarius, *Sermo 9*, 1 (FaFo § 271a1, a2); *Sacramentarium Gallicanum* 184 (§ 676a); 245 (§ 676c); Pirmin, *Scarapsus* 10 (§ 376); 12 (§ 610); 28a (§ 298).

yet seems, for a long time, to have been confined to this region. Unlike the other additions, it migrated from Gaul to Spain at a very late stage.[75]

The reason for adding it to the creed may again have been the influence of the Greek creeds. At the same time, the threat of Manichaeism which taught that the universe had been created by a demiurge may also have played a certain role.[76] But we have no further information on this point.

qui conceptus est de spiritu sancto, natus ex Maria uirgine

The difference between Jesus' conception and birth (which was later also expressed by the prepositions *de* ('conceived *of* the Holy Spirit') and *ex* ('born *from* the virgin Mary')) is not usually found in Greek creeds, but typical of the western tradition. One of the earliest references to this difference occurs in the commentary on Matthew by Hilary of Poitiers (written in 353–356) where it is claimed that it was 'the content of all the prophets that he [sc. Christ] was conceived from the Holy Spirit and born from the virgin Mary (*conceptum ex spiritu sancto, natum ex Maria uirgine*)'.[77] However, Hilary does not refer to a creed.[78] Nonetheless, the context clearly shows that he made the distinction between conception and birth in order to ward off criticism of the allegedly illegitimate origin of Christ and to defend Mary's virginity.[79]

The Latin creed of the second session at Rimini (359) which Jerome included in his *Altercatio Luciferiani et Orthodoxi* (written in 378/379; FaFo § 159b) also contains the phrase. However, the difference between Jesus' conception and his birth is not found in the closely related Creed of Niké (§ 159a). Given the fact that all other references stem from a much later date, it is difficult to believe that it formed part of the original text.[80]

Otherwise all indications for the addition of this phrase point to Gaul where it is first clearly attested in a credal context by Faustus (d. *c.* 495) who was first monk and later (from 433) abbot of the abbey on the island of Lérins. In *c.* 458 he became bishop of Riez (Reji, Southern Gaul). In a letter of uncertain date he refers

---

75 Cf. the Mozarabic liturgy in the *Liber ordinum de ordinibus ecclesiasticis* (before 1052; FaFo § 684c4).

76 Cf. Hutter 2012, cols. 18 f.; Hutter 2023, pp. 96–113. On the spread of Manichaeism in the west cf. Hutter 2023, pp. 215–25.

77 Hilary, *Commentarius in Matthaeum* 1,3 (FaFo § 151a).

78 Hilary says that written creeds were unknown in the middle of the fourth century in much of the west (except Rome); cf. above pp. 156 f.

79 Cf. Ladaria 1977, pp. 112–16; Ladaria 1989, pp. 81–6. For general background cf. Cook 2002, pp. 28 f., 238 f., 330 and n. 353, 338.

80 Cf. also below pp. 317 f.

to Jesus' conception 'of' (*de*) the Holy Spirit and his birth 'from' (*ex*) the virgin Mary in precisely the same terms as T, and in this context lays claim to the 'authority of the creed' (*iuxta symboli auctoritatem*).[81] Moreover, he mentions the conception in his treatise on the Holy Spirit in *c.* 475.[82] The phrase is next attested in an anonymous *Expositio de fide catholica* (CPL 505; FaFo § 265) which may also stem from the fifth century, as well as in the *Collectio Eusebiana* (a collection of homilies ascribed to Eusebius of Emesa, though perhaps stemming from the pen of Faustus of Riez or from one or several of his pupils), Caesarius of Arles, Cyprian of Toulon (*sedit* 516–549), and Pirmin.[83] A slight variation between authors concerns the use of the prepositions: for example, Caesarius always writes *de Maria uirgine*.[84]

The reasons for this addition are not easily discernible. It appears that the phrase *natus est/natum de spiritu sancto et/ex Maria uirgine* is only attested in the west until the fourth century.[85] The Greek equivalent γεννηθέντα ἐκ πνεύματος ἁγίου καὶ Μαρίας τῆς παρθένου is first found in the Homoian creed of Constantinople (359/360; FaFo § 160) which in turn was based on the (western) creed of Niké (§ 159a).[86] However, it never made its way into either N^{Ant} (§§ 180a, 198/203, 208) or C^2 (§ 184e1), because it was open to misinterpretation. Instead, the less problematic phrase σαρκωθέντα ἐκ πνεύματος ἁγίου καὶ Μαρίας τῆς παρθένου was chosen in C^2.

The same concern was clearly also soon felt in the west. In addition, Lk 1:35 suggested that an exegetical distinction had to be made between Christ's conception and birth. As we saw above, Hilary used the phrase in an apologetic context. For Faustus the conception and birth in the creed are proof of the dual nature of Christ as God and man.[87] A theology of the two natures of Christ is also outlined by the author of the homily CPL 365 (FaFo § 274).[88] The authors of *Homily 10* of the *Collectio Eusebiana* (FaFo § 266b) and of the explanation of the creed included in the *Bobbio Missal* (FaFo § 676b) argue along similar lines as does Hilary of Poitiers, defending

---

81 Faustus, *Epistula 7*, 24 (FaFo § 267a).

82 Cf. Faustus, *De spiritu sancto* 1,3 (FaFo § 267b2).

83 Cf. *Collectio Eusebiana, Homilia 9* (FaFo § 266a); id., *Homilia 10* (§ 266b); Caesarius, *Sermo 9*, 1 (FaFo § 271a1); Cyprian of Toulon, *Epistula ad Maximum episcopum Genavensem* (§ 272); Pirmin, *Scarapsus* 10 (§ 376); 12 (§ 610); 28a (§ 298).

84 Cf. also the *Antiphonale Benchorense* 35 (680–691 or earlier; FaFo § 698b) and the creeds §§ 297 (*s.* VIII/1 or earlier; here the Spirit has no preposition), 307 (before *s.* XIII), 433 (England, before 1250).

85 Cf. FaFo §§ 89b (*Traditio Apostolica*), 159a (Niké 359).

86 Cf. also FaFo §§ 165 ((Pseudo-)Liberius, *Epistula ad Athanasium*, 362 or earlier), 177[4] (Vitalis of Antioch, 376, written in Rome!), 546 (Emperor Marcian, 454), 227 (Paul of Apameia, 536).

87 Cf. Faustus, *Epistula 7*, 24 (CSEL 21, p. 205, ll. 3–8).

88 Cf. Pseudo-Augustine, *Expositio super symbolum* 9 (Westra 2002, p. 429).

the miraculous conception and birth of Christ.[89] The author of a homily ascribed to Faustus of Riez emphasizes that Christ was 'not a portion of, but an operation of the Holy Spirit' (*non portio, sed operatio fuit spiritus sancti*).[90] Similarly, the author of an anonymous instruction on the baptismal liturgy which may date from the sixth century[91] edited by Keefe emphasizes that Christ was no son of the Spirit.[92] Nevertheless, the phrase was not introduced everywhere; for instance, it is missing in North Africa. Instead, there the creed ran: *natum de spiritu sancto ex uirgine Maria.*[93]

passus and position of *sub Pontio Pilato*

As we saw in a previous chapter, the statement that God/Christ 'suffered' was hotly debated in the controversy concerning patripassianism as advocated, for example, by Praxeas.[94] It is probably for this reason that *passum/passus* was not used in Rome – it is found neither in R nor in TA[G]. By contrast, Greek παθόντα occurs in both N (FaFo § 135c) and C[2] (§ 184e1), and *passus/passum* was widely cited in Latin credal texts from other regions, not least because it occurred in the New Testament.[95]

However, the first example of R/T with *passus* is not found until Nicetas of Remesiana. This is a particularly tricky case, since we do not really know whether Nicetas' creed included *crucifixus* and *mortuus*.[96] In any case, *sub Pontio Pilato*

---

89 Cf. *Collectio Eusebiana, Homilia 10*, 4; *Sacramentarium Gallicanum* 185.

90 *Collectio Eusebiana, Sermo extrauagans 2*, 4.

91 Cf. FaFo § 326.

92 Cf. text 50 (Keefe 2002, vol. II, p. 580, ll. 12–14).

93 Cf. Augustine, *Sermo 215*, 4 (FaFo § 316g – the reading *ex* instead of *et uirgine Maria* is attested in numerous manuscripts and my text in FaFo should be corrected accordingly); Quodvultdeus, *Sermo 1* (§ 317a); id., *Sermo 4* (§ 317d); id., *Sermo 10*, 6,7 (§ 317e); Fulgentius, *Contra Fabianum*, frg. 32,3 (§ 319a1: *qui natus est de spiritu sancto ex uirgine Maria*); Pseudo-Facundus of Hermiane, *Epistula fidei catholicae in defensione trium capitulorum* 13 (§ 322a: *natum ex spiritu sancto et Maria uirgine*).

94 Cf. above p. 125.

95 Cf. 1Pet 2:21 (Vulgate): '[. . .] quia et Christus passus est pro uobis [. . .]' / '[. . .] because Christ also suffered for you [. . .]'. 4:1: 'Christo igitur passo in carne [. . .]' / 'Since, therefore, Christ suffered in the flesh [. . .]'.

96 Perhaps my reconstruction in FaFo § 324, where I omitted *crucifixus* and *mortuus*, should be amended. In *Competentibus ad baptismum instructionis libelli* 5,5 (Burn 1905, p. 43, ll. 10–12) Nicetas says, 'Sequitur ut credas dominicae passioni, et passum confitearis Christum, crucifixum a Iudaeis, secundum praedicta prophetarum.' / 'It follows that you should believe the passion of the Lord and should confess that Christ suffered and was crucified by the Jews as the prophets predicted.' Id., *Competentibus ad baptismum instructionis libelli* 5,5 (Burn 1905, p. 44, l. 5): 'Svʙ Pontio ergo Pilato passvs est.' / 'Therefore, he suffered under Pontius Pilate.' *Competentibus ad baptismum instructionis libelli* 5,5 (Burn 1905, p. 44, ll. 13 f.): 'Mortuus est ergo, ut mortis iura dis-

was combined with *passus*.[97] This syntagma is nowhere found in Greek creeds where Pilate remains attached to the crucifixion, as, e.g., in N^Ant (FaFo §§ 180a, 198/203, 208) and C² (§ 184e1). The shift of Pilate from the crucifixion to the passion must have occurred because all that followed *passus* was understood as an explication of Christ's suffering which in its totality had occurred under Pilate.[98] Both the addition of *passus* and its combination with Pilate must already have taken place in the second half of the fourth century, because it is not only found in Dacia Mediterranea, but also in North Africa where Augustine quotes it occasionally.[99] As far as I can see, almost all later versions of R/T that contain *passus/passum* follow suit.[100]

However, *passus* was not universally received. In *c.* 400 Rufinus (FaFo § 254b) and Leo the Great (§ 255) do not yet mention it nor does Peter Chrysologus (§ 259). Although Augustine does cite it, it is omitted in other places (cf. § 316e, g, k) and later found in neither Quodvultdeus (§ 317a, d) nor Ferrandus of Carthage (§ 321).[101]

mortuus

The sequence (*crucifixus/passus*) – *mortuus* – *sepultus* is already found in Tertullian (*hunc mortuum et sepultum*)[102] and in TA^L/TA^G (*crucifixus* – *mortuus* – *sepultus* / σταυρωθέντα – ἀποθανόντα – ταφέντα). It was, therefore, included in one branch of the Roman credal tradition at a very early stage.[103] Hilary of Poitiers quotes it (*crucifixus* – *mortuus* – *sepultus*; *passus* – *mortuus* – *sepultus*)[104] as does the First Council of Toledo of 400 (*crucifixum* – *mortuum* – *sepultum*).[105] In R/T it is (perhaps) first attested by Nicetas.[106] Leo the Great may also have known it.[107]

---

solueret.' / 'Therefore, he died in order to abolish the rights of death.' This may suggest that *passus*, *crucifixus*, and *mortuus* formed part of the creed. However, Nicetas neither discusses Christ's crucifixion nor his death in any detail.

97 Cf. Burn 1905, p. 44, l. 5.

98 This is different in C² where the crucifixion was added before παθόντα which was taken over from N.

99 Cf. Augustine, *Sermo de symbolo ad catechumenos* 7 (cf. FaFo § 316l). The date of this sermon is unknown. Cf. also id., *Sermo 375B* (= *Sermo Denis 5*), 6 (FaFo § 316j).

100 An exception may be FaFo § 525 (Jacobi's Creed, Spain?, *s.* VII?).

101 It is uncertain whether one may conclude from Vigilius, *Contra Eutychetem* 2,8 (FaFo § 318a) that he read it in his creed. If so, it must have been inserted in Africa in the later fifth century.

102 Tertullian, *Aduersus Praxeam* 2,1 (FaFo § 111e1).

103 Cf. above ch. 4.5.1.

104 Cf. Hilary, *De trinitate* 7,6 (FaFo § 151c3); 10,65 (§ 151c5).

105 Cf. First Council of Toledo, *Regula fidei catholicae* 16 (FaFo § 486a).

106 Cf. above p. 167 n. 96.

107 Cf. Leo, *Tractatus 62*, 2 (FaFo § 255c).

In Gaul, however, we are on safe ground: the *Collectio Eusebiana*, Caesarius, and, of course, Pirmin all have it.[108] Its addition may have served to specify *passus/ passum* somewhat further. On the one hand, perhaps it served to emphasize the reality of Christ's death (over against docetic views), or possibly, on the other hand, was also connected to the development of the liturgical celebration of the Paschal Triduum (Good Friday – Holy Saturday – Easter Sunday) in the second half of the fourth century.[109]

descendit ad inferna

First a word on terminology and how the phrase is translated. The earlier sources usually offer *ad inferna*. Later this is often changed to *ad inferos*, which syntagma was then also accepted in the official Roman catechism and liturgy.[110] Occasionally, we also find *ad infernum*.[111] There is no difference in meaning between *infernum* and *inferna*. Both the singular and the plural refer to the underworld or netherworld. The translation as 'hell' is, by and large, erroneous, because an analysis of late-antique and early medieval explanations of the creed has made it clear that there was considerable confusion about the nature of the *inferna*, and not all authors equated it with hell. The *inferi* are the inhabitants of the *inferna*. Their precise identity, however, was also a matter of debate.[112]

The descent to the underworld had been discussed long before it came to be included in R/T. Hilary of Poitiers already mentions it in a sequence of *mortuus – sepultus – descendens ad inferna – ascendens*.[113] The first evidence for an inclusion in R/T comes from Rufinus whose creed contains *descendit in inferna*. His tes-

---

108 Cf. *Collectio Eusebiana*, *Homilia 9* (FaFo § 266a); Caesarius, *Sermo 9*, 1 (§ 271a1); Pirmin, *Scarapsus* 10 (§ 376); 12 (§ 610); 28a (§ 298).
109 Cf. Auf der Maur 1983, pp. 76 f.
110 Cf. FaFo §§ 282 (Northern France, *s.* VIII), 309 (CPL 1759, Spain (Ireland?), date unknown, cf. below p. 605 n. 50), 345 (*Catechismus Romanus*, 1566), 346 (*Rituale Sacramentorum Romanum*, 1584), 421 (Alexander of Hales), 422 (Bonaventura), 423 (Raimundus Martini), 424 (William Durand of Mende), 428 (Flanders, *s.* XIII), 430 (England, *s.* XI/1 or earlier), 493 (Toledo IV, 633), 698b (Antiphonary of Bangor), 711[8] (Haito of Basel, Basel/Reichenau?, 809?).
111 FaFo §§ 274 (CPL 365, Gaul, *s.* VI/2), 277 (CPL 1760 in the Sessorianus, Gaul, *s.* VI–VIII), 328 (CPL 915, *c.* 550), 329 (Venantius Fortunatus; Northern Italy or Poitiers, *c.* 575–600), 330 (before 780), 334 (Spain?, before *s.* IX *in.*), 339 (*s.* IX/1).
112 For details cf. Kinzig, 'Liberating the Dead', 2024 (*sub prelo*).
113 Cf. Hilary, *De trinitate* 10,65 (FaFo § 151c5). Cf. also id., *De trinitate* 2,24 (§ 151c1): 'Virgo, partus et corpus postque crux, mors, inferi salus nostra est.' / 'The Virgin, the birth, the body, then the cross, the death, the underworld; [these things] are our salvation.'

timony is particularly interesting, because he emphasizes that the phrase is not contained in the Roman creed nor in its eastern equivalents.[114] It is not yet mentioned either in the *Collectio Eusebiana* (FaFo § 266), but we find it in Caesarius, the *Bobbio Missal* (Vienne, *s.* VII *ex.*), and Pirmin.[115] It travelled from Gaul to Spain where it is found in Martin of Braga (574),[116] in witnesses of the seventh century (an inscription in Toledo: FaFo § 311), Ildefonsus of Toledo (*c.* 657–667),[117] and in later sources. Both Venantius Fortunatus (Northern Italy or Poitiers, *c.* 575–600) and the *Antiphonary of Bangor* (Bangor 680–691 or earlier) are further witnesses to the widespread popularity of the idea.[118]

The reasons for this addition are unknown. What the descent signified has been widely discussed in ancient and early medieval literature.[119] There is a wide consensus in explanations of the creed that the main purpose of Christ's descent was to overcome the devil and to release the deceased; by contrast Christ's preaching to the spirits in 1Pet 3:19–20 is only rarely mentioned. However, details remained controversial. Most authors insist that it is Christ's human soul that acts in the descent while his body remained in the tomb. One group of preachers argued that it was Christ's human soul only which descended to the underworld because Christ had promised the robber that 'today' they would be in paradise together (Lk 23:43) which must have referred to Christ's divine nature. Others, however, who were keen on safeguarding human salvation, which they thought presupposed Christ's acting as *God*, were convinced that Christ's divinity *and* his human soul had made this trip together. A few tried to tread some sort of middle path, arguing either that the soul of Christ had somehow been divinely empowered or that Christ's divinity was ubiquitous and hence present both in heaven *and* in the underworld.

Furthermore, the precise nature of the *infernum* was debated. It was generally seen as a sombre place and a kind of prison guarded by the devil. An alternative designation, taken from 2Pet 2:4, is the classical *Tartarus*. Some authors expressly mention tortures awaiting those inmates who have committed serious crimes or sins. Yet this caused some problems as those who had died before Christ included the patriarchs and prophets who were considered righteous, raising the

---

114 Cf. Rufinus, *Expositio symboli* 16.
115 Cf. Caesarius, *Sermo 9*, 1 (FaFo § 271a1); *Sacramentarium Gallicanum* 184 (§ 676); 591 (§ 375); Pirmin, *Scarapsus* 10 (§ 376); 12 (§ 610); 28a (§ 298).
116 Cf. Martin, *De correctione rusticorum* 15 (FaFo § 608).
117 Cf. Ildefonsus, *De cognitione baptismi* 37–95 (FaFo § 312).
118 Cf. Venantius, *Expositio symboli* (FaFo § 329); *Antiphonale Benchorense* 35 (§ 698b).
119 Cf. Gounelle 2000; Sarot/Van Wieringen 2018; and the survey in Kinzig, 'Liberating the Dead', 2024 (*sub prelo*) with numerous references.

question as to why they were held in the *infernum* at all. Some Latin fathers, therefore, pondered the possibility that the righteous elect stayed in the underworld after their deaths in a place of refreshment (*refrigerium*) or some kind of *locus amoenus*, but nonetheless had to concede that they were held behind lock and key. However, these reflections were only rarely taken up by later authors. If the problem was not simply ignored, it was often said that all the dead were kept imprisoned because of original sin.

The identity of those who were freed from this underworld likewise constituted a problem. Did Christ release only (part or all of) those who had died *before* his coming or did his action during his descent also include (all or some) humans who would die *in the future*? Opinions were divided on this issue. Moreover, there was disagreement as to whether or not the *infernum* was completely emptied by Christ (which might suggest the salvation of everyone, smacking of Origenism). Later authors usually included the patriarchs, the prophets, the saints, and sometimes also Adam as those released. By contrast, *infideles* and serious criminals were among those who were left behind. Finally, in the eyes of many later authors the liberation from the underworld became identical with the final resurrection. It is not easy to see how these authors reconciled the seemingly historical nature of the *descensus* (which had been completed at the time of Christ's resurrection) and the eschatological resurrection of all humankind. In fact, we find no detailed reflections on the problems involved in such an amalgamation. Instead the 'historical' account of the release of the pre-Christian prisoners in the underworld at the time of Christ's death quietly changed into a proclamation of the salvation of most or all Christians.

omnipotentis

The predicate 'almighty' was added to the Father in the christological section of R/T only at a fairly late stage, perhaps because it was not contained in N (FaFo § 135c) or C^2 (§ 184e1), but also because it formed a duplicate with *patrem omnipotentem* in the first section of R/T. It is later found in creeds from Gaul[120] and later[121] from Spain where it occurs in the second half of the seventh century in the writings of Ildefonsus of Toledo, Etherius of Osma and Beatus of Liébana, and

---

120 Cf. *Collectio Eusebiana, Homilia 9* (FaFo § 266a); id., *Homilia 10* (§ 266b); Caesarius, *Sermo 9* (§ 271a); *Sacramentarium Gallicanum* 184 (§ 676); 591 (§ 375); Pirmin, *Scarapsus* 10 (§ 376); 12 (§ 610); 28a (§ 298); *Missale Gallicanum Vetus* 26 (§ 678a1).
121 The only exception is Priscillian, if the text is genuine and uncorrupted (FaFo § 308).

in the Mozarabic (Hispanic) liturgy.[122] It is not found in North Africa nor in Italy (including Rome).[123] Later, the adjective seems to have intruded into Latin versions of both N and C².[124] The reason for this addition is unknown.

catholicam

The earliest Greek creed containing καθολικήν as predicate of the Church seems to be that set out by Alexander of Alexandria in his letter to Alexander of Byzantium (Constantinople) in *c.* 321/322.[125] The Synod of Antioch in early 325 followed suit, as did Arius and Euzoius in their creed submitted to the Emperor Constantine in 327.[126] N only mentioned καθολική in its anathemas (FaFo § 135c). However, in Jerusalem the word formed part of the creed in the 340s (§ 147). Later it is found in the so-called Dêr Balyzeh Papyrus (§ 146) and in the creed of Epiphanius of Salamis in 374,[127] in N^{Ant} (§§ 180a, 208), and in C² (§ 184e1). The first Latin witness may be Nicetas of Remesiana,[128] perhaps because he knew J.[129] In the fifth century *catholicam* may have formed part of Leo's version of R (§ 255g).[130] By that time it may already have been widespread as it is found in the same period in an inscription on the Croation island of Kres (*Symbolum Apsarense*, § 325). Later we find the adjective in most versions of R/T. The only region where it may not have been accepted is North Africa.[131]

---

122 Cf. Ildefonsus, *De cognitione baptismi* 37–95 (FaFo § 312); Etherius of Osma and Beatus of Liébana, *Aduersus Elipandum* 1,22 (§ 314a); for the Mozarabic liturgy cf. § 684c4, d.

123 Cf., however, *Antiphonale Benchorense* 35 (FaFo § 698b).

124 It is found in the Latin version of N in the *Collectio Vetus Gallica* (FaFo § 135d40), in a translation found in a codex dating from the middle of the ninth century (§ 135d45), and in Latin C² in the Spanish *Missale mixtum* (§ 184f30).

125 Cf. Alexander of Alexandria, *Epistula ad Alexandrum Thessalonicensem* (Byzantinum; Opitz 1934/1935, *Urkunde 14*; FaFo § 132) 53.

126 Cf. Synod of Antioch, *Epistula synodica* 12 (FaFo § 133); Arius and Euzoius, *Epistula ad Constantinum imperatorem* (Opitz 1934/1935, *Urkunde 30*; § 131c) 3–4.

127 Cf. Epiphanius, *Ancoratus* 119,11 (FaFo § 175).

128 Cf. Nicetas, *Competentibus ad baptismum instructionis libelli* 5 (FaFo § 324).

129 Cf. Cvetković 2017, pp. 109–15; Gemeinhardt, 'Vom Werden', 2020, pp. 50 f.

130 Leo often combines *catholica* with *fides*. It is combined with *ecclesia* in Leo, *Tractatus 75*, 5; *77*, 5; *79*, 2, and *91*; 2; id., *Epistula 15*, 2. 4. 11. 16. *Catholicam* is missing in my reconstruction in FaFo § 255g.

131 A possible exception is Augustine, *De fide et symbolo* 21 (FaFo § 316k): '[. . .] credimus et in sanctam ecclesiam, utique catholicam.' / '[. . .] we also believe in the holy Church, that is, the catholic Church.' The phrasing *utique catholicam* may indicate, however, that Augustine knew it, but did not find it in his creed.

The reason for its addition is obvious. The earliest predicate of the Church in the creeds is its holiness, found in both R and in TA[G].[132] However, in the course of the fourth century this came to be seen as no longer sufficient as various rivalling churches were competing over this claim, such as the North African 'catholic' Church and the Donatists. By the late fourth century *catholicus* had already taken on the double meaning of 'universal' and, therefore, 'orthodox' (since the congregations of the heretics and schismatics were considered to be dispersed and particular). It is not necessary to describe this development in greater detail here, as a number of useful accounts are available.[133] The trinitarian debates of the fourth century accelerated such an increasingly 'confessional' understanding during which various groups developed within the Church that all laid claim to universally valid orthodoxy. This fact becomes especially obvious looking at the anathemas appended to synodal creeds (beginning with N) in which 'the Church' condemns deviant theological tenets. Here 'catholic' is often combined with 'holy' (ἀγία), and sometimes with 'apostolic' (ἀποστολική), thus indicating the venerable age of the Church which derives its authority from the apostles themselves.[134] The belief in the 'holy catholic Church' in R/T, therefore, mirrors the self-designation of the Church in the eastern anathemas. It may suffice here first to quote the explanation of *ecclesia catholica* in the anonymous *Expositio de fide catholica* (CPL 505) which may belong to the fifth century:

> Believe the catholic Church, that is, the universal one on the whole world where the one God is worshipped, where the one baptism is observed, and the one faith is kept [cf. Eph 4:5–6].[135]

Furthermore, the opposition between the universal and orthodox Church and the particular churches of the heretics is explicitly addressed in the anonymous *Sermo de symbolo* (CPL 1759):

> It is not said 'in the holy catholic Church', but 'I believe the holy catholic Church', that is, the universal Church spread out over the entire world. When it is said: 'The Church [singular] is catholic', then the churches [plural] of the heretics are not catholic, because they are not universal, but belong to the remotest regions and places.[136]

---

132 Cf. also FaFo § 92a, b (Cyprian; baptismal interrogations: *per sanctam ecclesiam*).
133 Cf., e.g., Kelly 1972, pp. 384–6; Schindler 1986–1994, cols. 815–16 (with further literature).
134 From FaFo I reference only a few examples: §§ 135c (N: καθολικὴ καὶ ἀποστολική); 141 (Ant[4]: καθολική); 143 (Serdica 343, east: ἀγία καὶ καθολική); 145 (Macrostich Creed: καθολικὴ καὶ ἀγία and ἀγία καὶ καθολική); 148 (Sirmium 351, First Creed: ἀγία καὶ καθολική); 158 (Seleucia 359: καθολική) etc.
135 CPL 505, 8 (Westra 2002, p. 437).
136 CPL 1759, 22 (Westra 2002, p. 492).

There can be little doubt that the adjective *catholicus* was added precisely for this reason: to claim universality and hence orthodoxy for the Church of the believer who pronounced the creed.

This is, perhaps, the appropriate place to point out that it was by no means clear whether 'faith in' encompassed only the Holy Spirit or also the Church and the following cola. Liuwe Westra has given a detailed analysis of this discussion[137] so that I can be fairly brief. Faith 'in' the Church is found in many eastern creeds,[138] especially in J (FaFo § 147) and C² (§ 184e1), but also in the west.[139] Some authors explicitly state in their interpretations that we must (or may) also believe 'in' the Church, whereas others rigorously deny this.[140]

Ambrose (bishop of Milan 374–397) had an ingenious way of dealing with this problem. He writes in his *Explanatio symboli*:

> Now then, understand well the way in which we believe *in* the Creator [this was explained in the previous paragraph], lest perhaps you should say: But [the creed] has also '*in* the Church'; but it has also '*in* the remission of sins'; but it has also '*in* the resurrection'. What then? The reason is the same: we believe *in* Christ, we believe *in* the Father in just the same manner in which we believe *in* the Church and *in* the remission of sins and *in* the resurrection of the flesh. What is the reason? Because he who believes *in* the Creator believes also *in* the work of the Creator. And now, lest you imagine this to be a conceit of my own, take a testimony: 'If you believe not me, believe at least the works' [Jn 10:38].[141]

I have printed the crucial preposition *in* in italics here in order to underline Ambrose's point: the preposition *in* before the remission of sins and the resurrection indicates that we express faith in the Creator through faith in his creation (such as the Church).

---

137 Cf. Westra 2017.
138 Cf. FaFo §§ 89 (*Traditio Apostolica* in various eastern recensions), 103b (*Epistula Apostolorum*), 143a1 (Serdica 343, east, Latin version), 164a2[32] (Apolinarius), 175 (Epiphanius), 176[9] (*Didascalia CCCXVIII patrum Nicaenorum*), 182c[7] (*Apostolic Constitutions*), 185 (Pseudo-Athanasius), 204a (Charisius), 208 (Nestorians; cf. also below p. 353), 232c (Cosmas Indicopleustes).
139 Belief 'in the Church' is, for example, found in the following western creeds: FaFo §§ 256 (Ambrose), 257 (Pseudo-Athanasius, *Enarratio in symbolum apostolorum*), 259e, f (Peter Chrysologus), 260 (CPL 1751), 267b2 (Faustus of Riez), 308 (Priscillian), 316e, k (Augustine), 375 (*Sacramentarium Gallicanum*), 527 (Pseudo-Alcuin, *Disputatio puerorum*). Cf. also the German creeds and baptismal vows §§ 300, 766, 767.
140 Cf. above in the body of text the quotation from CPL 1759. Faustus of Riez even accuses his opponents of forging the creed; cf. *De spiritu sancto* 1,2 (FaFo § 267b2). Cf. also Pseudo-Alcuin, *Disputatio puerorum* 11 (§ 527[I,14. 18. 19]).
141 Ambrose, *Explanatio symboli* 6 (tr. Connolly 1952, pp. 23 f.; altered).

It seems that Rufinus argued precisely against such a position as expressed by the bishop of Milan. He is the first who explicitly rejects the inclusion of *in* before the cola that follow the Holy Spirit:

> It was not said 'in the holy Church', nor 'in the remission of sins', nor 'in the resurrection of the flesh'. For if the preposition 'in' had been added, it would have had the same meaning as in the preceding articles. Instead, however, in those clauses where faith as concerning the Godhead is declared, it is said, 'in God the Father', and 'in Jesus Christ, his Son', and 'in the Holy Spirit'; yet in the rest, where the text does not deal with the Godhead but with creatures and mysteries, the preposition 'in' is not added. And so it is not said 'we believe in the holy Church', but 'we believe the holy Church', not as God, but as the Church gathered together to God. So also that there is 'remission of sins'; [we do] not [say 'we believe] in the remission of sins'. And [so too we believe that there will be] a 'resurrection of the flesh'; [we do] not [say 'we believe] in the resurrection of the flesh'. Thus by means of this preposition of one syllable the creator is distinguished from the creatures, and things divine are separated from things human.[142]

There are indeed creeds where the remaining clauses are also prefixed by *in*. In fact, belief 'in the remission of sins and eternal life' already formed part of the African baptismal interrogations of the mid-third century.[143] In this argument it is rejected throughout because Rufinus, as opposed to Ambrose, made a distinction between the Trinity (which can only be referred to by the use of 'in') and the created world. Faustus of Riez added another aspect: he rejected faith 'in' the Church, because 'we believe the Church as the mother of our rebirth, we do not believe "in" the Church as if it were the author of our salvation'.[144]

In the middle ages Peter Abelard claimed that 'in the Church' was typical of Greek creeds and that it had been 'contained in that creed which Leo III produced in defence of the orthodox faith, had inscribed on a silver tablet, and attached to the altar of St Paul in Rome' – which was indeed correct, as this creed was C².[145]

---

142 Rufinus, *Expositio symboli* 34 (tr. Morison 1916, pp. 47 f.; altered).

143 Cf. FaFo § 92a (Cyprian: 'in remissionem peccatorum et uitam aeternam'); cf. above p. 132. In addition, cf. §§ 103b (*Epistula Apostolorum*: 'in the remission of sins'), 256 (Ambrose: '[et] in remissionem peccatorum [et] in carnis resurrectionem'), 259 (Peter Chrysologus: 'in remissionem peccatorum, carnis resurrectionem, uitam aeternam'), 260 ('in remissionem peccatorum, carnis resurrectionem et uitam aeternam'), 316e (Augustine: 'in remissionem peccatorum, carnis resurrectionem'), 317c (Quodvultdeus: ditto). Cf. also §§ 595b ('in paenitentiam et remissionem peccatorum'), 619 ('in remissionem peccatorum et carnis resurrectionem'). Cf. also the Old Franconian baptismal vows §§ 766 and 767 ('in the remission of sins').

144 Faustus, *De spiritu sancto* 1,2 (FaFo § 267b2).

145 Peter Abelard, *Expositio quod dicitur symboli apostolorum* (FaFo § 861c). On Leo's creed cf. below p. 569.

sanctorum communionem

In the case of *sanctorum communionem*, which occurs rarely outside credal literature,[146] we can safely say that the phrase is attested in Gaul in the fifth century,
the first datable examples coming from the *Collectio Eusebiana*, Faustus of Riez,
and Caesarius of Arles.[147] However, it may already have been added in the late
fourth century.[148] Nicetas of Remesiana possibly cites the phrase as *communionem sanctorum* though the authenticity of this passage is not entirely beyond
doubt.[149] In addition, it also appears in a creed ascribed to Jerome (*Fides Sancti
Hieronymi*, FaFo § 484), which André Wilmart located in Spain and attributed to
Gregory of Elvira (d. after 392/393). However, it is not a direct descendant of R,
but a curious mixture of N and R/T.

---

146 All early references stem from North Africa: Augustine, *Enarrationes in Psalmos* 36,2,20; id.,
Sermo 52, 3,6; id., *Sermo 149*, 10; id., *Contra epistulam Parmeniani* 1,10; *Gesta collationis Carthagi-
niensis* (411) 3,258, l. 50 (CSEL 104, p. 247). They do not provide further help in our context. Discussion in Kattenbusch 1900, pp. 931–3.
147 Cf. *Collectio Eusebiana*, *Homilia 10* (FaFo § 266b); Faustus, *De spiritu sancto* 1,2 (§ 267b2); Caesarius, *Sermo 9* (§ 271a1, a2); in addition, Westra 2002, pp. 251 f., 261, 263, 400.
148 Cf. below in the text on the Synod of Nîmes and the legislation by Emperor Theodosius
where the syntagma appears in the late fourth century in a non-credal context.
149 Cf. Nicetas, *Competentibus ad baptismum instructionis libelli* 5,10 (Burn 1905, p. 48, ll. 14 f.; cf.
FaFo § 324). It should be noted, however, that the whole passage Burn 1905, pp. 48, l. 11 – 52, l. 52 is
missing in the so-called 'Austrian recension' of the work (for details cf. Burn 1905, pp. LXVI–LXVII;
Keefe, *Catalogue*, 2012, pp. 151 f. (no. 262)). This affects the end of the creed in Nicetas' explanation:
communionem sanctorum – uitam aeternam. In addition, it has sometimes been doubted that *communionem sanctorum* could be extracted from this part of the explanation (e.g. by Westra 2002,
p. 215; Gemeinhardt 2012(2014), p. 83; Cvetković 2017, p. 113; Keller 2022, pp. 121–3). However, if the
end of the explanation as printed in Burn is genuine, I see no reason why it should not have been
included. In ch. 10 Nicetas says first that the 'holy catholic Church' is identical with the 'congregation
of all saints' (*sanctorum omnium congregatio*) who are then enumerated (cf. below in the text). The
decisive passage then runs like this (Burn 1905, p. 48, ll. 14–19): 'Ergo in hac una ecclesia credis te
COMMVNIONEM consecuturum esse SANCTORVM. Scito unam hanc esse ecclesiam catholicam in
omni orbe terrae constitutam; cuius communionem debes firmiter retinere. Sunt quidem et aliae
pseudo-ecclesiae, sed nihil tibi commune cum illis [. . .].' / 'Therefore you believe that in this one
church you will obtain the communion with the saints. Know that this one catholic Church is established throughout the entire world. You ought firmly to retain communion with it. However, there
are also other pseudo-churches, but you have nothing in common with them.' The expression *credis*
(which seems only to be transmitted in codex B and which Gemeinhardt, Cvetković, and Keller translate inaccurately as imperative) is baffling. Codex C reads *credere* instead of *credis te* which must be
erroneous. I suggest reading 'crede te' (in which case the modern translations would be correct). I
understand Nicetas as saying that the Church and the communion of saints are identical and that
we ought to strive for participation in this communion. If *communio sanctorum* did not form part of
the creed, it would be difficult to understand why this explanation was necessary.

The question what the addition actually meant has created a fair amount of scholarly discussion in the past.[150] Unfortunately, we have no information regarding the historical context in which the phrase was added. A brief survey of interpretations of this phrase in our earliest sources may show that the explanations of the creed are not very helpful on this point either.

Neither Faustus of Riez nor Caesarius offer us any such explanations. Where we do find them, they contradict each other. In the version offered by T it is unclear whether *sanctorum communionem* is (I) an attribute of the Holy Spirit or (II) of the Church or whether it is (III) an independent object of faith. In addition, it would require explanation whether *communio* means 'fellowship' in these contexts, in the sense of participation (*communicatio*) or 'assembly' (*congregatio*).

When we first look at (III), there is only one example of a Carolingian (interrogatory) creed where we find the phrase *in sanctorum communionem* which clearly indicates that it is an object of faith – a suggestion which is then immediately corrected:

Question: Do you believe in the holy catholic Church and in the communion of saints? Answer: [I believe] that there is indeed a holy Church, but I do not believe 'in' it because it is not God, but [it is] the assembly or congregation of Christians (*conuocatio seu congregatio Christianorum*) [. . .].[151]

It remains unclear whether the Church and the communion of saints are considered to be identical and whether the assembly of Christians is, in fact, the communion.

The above-mentioned *Fides Sancti Hieronymi* reads:

I believe the remission of sins[,] in the holy catholic Church, the communion of saints, the resurrection of the flesh unto eternal life.[152]

Here the sequence *sanctorum communio – resurrectionem* as objects of faith is separated from the Church (unless the communion of saints is understood as a result of the remission of sins *in* the Church); however, the repetition of *credo* before *remissionem* also makes clear that it is no attribute of the Holy Spirit either.

There is one instance where the communion of saints is described, above all, as a *work of the Spirit* (I). Thus the author of an explanation attributed to Augustine

---

150 Cf., e.g., Kattenbusch 1900, pp. 927–50; Kirsch 1910; Badcock 1920; Elert 1949; Benko 1964; Kelly 1972, pp. 388–97; Vokes 1978, p. 550; Gemeinhardt 2012(2014), esp. pp. 81–90; Keller 2022, esp. pp. 143–68.
151 Pseudo-Alcuin, *Disputatio puerorum* 11 (FaFo § 527).
152 *Fides sancti Hieronymi* (FaFo § 484): 'Credo remissionem peccatorum in sancta ecclesia catholica, sanctorum communionem, carnis resurrectionem ad uitam aeternam.'

says that all will be saints because all saints will 'in eternity' (*in aeternitate*) partake in equal measure of the gifts of the Holy Spirit that are now unevenly distibuted.[153]

Usually, however, the *sanctorum communio* is seen as an explanation of the *Church* (II). There are, roughly speaking, three different lines of argument. First, a *distinction* was made *between the saints and ordinary Christians*. In the (perhaps) earliest preserved explanation of the clause from around 400, Nicetas of Remesiana identifies the Church with the 'congregation of all saints' (*sanctorum omnium congregatio*) of heaven and earth. He counts not only the patriarchs, Prophets, apostles, martyrs, and all the righteous among the saints, but also the angels and the heavenly authorities and powers (*uirtutes et potestates*), referring to Col 1:20. In other words, the *communio* as *congregatio* is both cosmic and eschatological in that it encompasses the heavenly beings but also those righteous who have departed from this life. The individual Christian who makes the confession will in the end be included in this 'communion with the saints' (in the sense of an objective genitive).[154]

There are variations of this interpretation. Ordinary Christians could be considered as having already been received into the communion of saints. Thus the unknown author of another explanation ascribed to Augustine thought that we are bound together 'in the congregation <of faith> and the communion of hope with those saints who died in the same faith which we have accepted' ('cum illis sanctis qui in hac quam suscepimus fide defuncti sunt, societate <fidei> et spei communione teneamur').[155] Another anonymous exegete of the creed pursues the same line of argument. Its author thinks that we will join the communion of saints once we have fulfilled what we promised (probably at baptism).[156]

By contrast, the anonymous author of the *Collectio Eusebiana* limited the *communio* to the saints whom we are called upon to venerate because of their fear and love of God. At the same time, he warded off the idea that God himself could be venerated through the saints as if they were 'a part of God'.[157]

---

153 Pseudo-Augustine, *Sermo 240* (*s.* VIII?), 1 (FaFo § 383).
154 Nicetas, *Competentibus ad baptismum instructionis libelli* 5,10 (Burn 1905, p. 48).
155 Pseudo-Augustine, *Sermo 242* (*s.* VI–VII; cf. FaFo § 276c), 4. The same CPL 1758 (*s.* VII–VIII?; cf. FaFo § 280), 10 (Westra 2002, p. 478); *Traditio symboli* ed. Barbet/Lambot 1965, ll. 212–15 (p. 344; *s.* VIII or earlier; FaFo § 271b); Keefe 2002, vol. II, p. 591, ll. 8–10 (text 51; *s.* IX *in.?*; cf. FaFo § 338); Keefe 2002, vol. II, p. 601, ll. 7–9 (text 53; 813–15; cf. FaFo § 287); Keefe, *Explanationes*, 2012, text 8 (*s.* IX; cf. FaFo § 283), ll. 89–92 (p. 47); Keefe, *Explanationes*, 2012, text 32 (before 780?; cf. FaFo § 332), ll. 199–201 (p. 158); cf. also Keefe, *Explanationes*, 2012, text 30 (*s.* IX), ll. 288–90 (p. 143). Similarly, CPL 1761 (*s.* VII; cf. FaFo § 278), 15 (Westra 2002, p. 517).
156 Cf. CPL 1761 (*s.* VII?; cf. FaFo § 278), 15 (Westra 2002, p. 517): 'Et credo sanctorum communionem me habere, id est societatem sanctorum, si adimpleuero quae profiteor.'
157 Cf. *Collectio Eusebiana, Homilia 10*, 11 (*s.* V–VI).

Finally, yet another explanation is given by the anonymous author of a homily ascribed to Faustus of Riez (cf. FaFo § 268). He emphasizes that *sanctorum communionem* is contained in the creed in order to rebut those who argue against a veneration of the martyrs.[158] In all these cases, a difference is being made between the saints and ordinary believers.

In opposition to this particularistic view a universalistic interpretation considered all Christians to be *sancti* to a greater or lesser degree, depending on their faith and their way of life. An explanation from, perhaps, the eighth century argues that the 'saints' are those who have led a saintly life and will be rewarded in the hereafter:

> [We believe] that there is one [eternal] life for the saints, but that there will be diverse rewards for their labour [and] conversely that there will be punishments for the sinners according to the measure of their transgressions.[159]

An anonymous instruction on the baptismal liturgy states that the communion of saints is constituted 'here through faith and later in the kingdom'.[160]

By contrast, the author of yet another credal sermon preserved under Augustine's name is much more oriented towards the present: sainthood, he says, refers to all true Christians, because 'holy communion is where there is holy faith (*quia ubi est fides sancta, ibi est et sancta communio*)'.[161] Even more generally, Magnus, bishop of Sens (*fl.* 802–16), reads the 'communion of all (!) saints (*communionem omnium sanctorum*)' as an explication of the Church. According to him it is the 'assembly of all the faithful in Christ' (*congregationem omnium fidelium in Christo*).[162] This universalist view ultimately dates back to the fourth century. It is already found in a rescript by Theodosius I of 388 in which the Apolinarians are banned 'from all places, from the boundaries of the cities, from the assembly of the honourable persons, and from the communion of saints (*ab omnibus locis [. . .], a moenibus urbium, a congressu honestorum, a communione sanctorum*)'.[163] Likewise, canon

---

158 Cf. Pseudo-Faustus of Riez, *Sermo 2*, 10, ll. 123–6 (CChr.SL 101B, p. 833).

159 Kinzig, 'Glauben lernen', 2020(2022), p. 102, ll. 6–8 (III,3). Curiously, this description of the future judgement is adapted from the *Libellus fidei* of Pelagius (cf. Kinzig, 'Glauben lernen', 2020-(2022), p. 102 n. 113). The author may have thought that it was written by Augustine. Cf. FaFo § 517.

160 Keefe 2002, vol. II, p. 581, l. 15 (text 50; *s.* VI; cf. FaFo § 326) = Westra 2002, p. 472: 'Credo communionem sanctorum, id est hic per fidem et post in regno.'

161 Pseudo-Augustine, *Sermo 241* (*s.* IX *in.* or earlier; cf. FaFo § 386), 4.

162 Magnus of Sens, *Libellus de mysterio baptismatis* (FaFo § 783a[5]); cf. also the anonymous text § 783b[5].

163 *Codex Theodosianus* 16,5,14. Cf. Elert 1949, col. 584.

1 of the Synod of Nîmes of 394 or 396 deals with priests and deacons from the east who impose themselves 'on the communion of saints under the appearance of a pretended piety (*sanctorum communioni speciae simulatae religionis inpraemunt*)'.[164] Accordingly, in his explanation of baptism (812) Amalarius of Metz (*sedit* 810–14) calls for the 'communion of saints' to be 'preserved as a unity of spirit in the bond of peace (*in uinculo pacis unitatem spiritus seruare*)'.[165]

Finally, there is also a *sacramental interpretation* of the phrase in which *sanctorum communio* is equated with *sacramentorum communio*. Thus the anonymous *Expositio super symbolum* (CPL 1760) sees the communion of saints as the congregation of those who invoke the triune God and who celebrate the eucharist every Sunday.[166] This may possibly also be the interpretation which the author of the *Tractatus symboli* (CPL 1751; cf. FaFo § 260) has in mind.[167] Such a eucharistic interpretation is strengthened in an anonymous interrogation about the creed which may, however, not have been written before the tenth century:

> Question: In what way [do you believe] the communion of saints?

> Answer: That is the sharing (*communicatio*) of the body and blood of the Lord through the invocation of Father, Son, and Holy Spirit. By means of this sacrament all the faithful who are unanimous in the Church (*in aecclesia concordantes*) produce out of themselves (*ex se*) the one body of Christ.[168]

Here *sanctorum communio* is interpreted as a communion in the *sancta*, the eucharistic elements, an understanding which is also found in Greek interpretations of κοινωνία τῶν ἁγίων or τῶν μυστηρίων.[169] However, whereas κοινωνία τῶν μυστηρίων[170] clearly designates the communion in the eucharistic elements and occurs frequently in the writings of the fathers of the fourth and fifth centuries (above all,

---

164 Council of Nîmes (394/396), canon 1, ll. 10 f. (CChr.SL 148, p. 50). Cf. also Kelly 1972, p. 389.
165 Amalarius, *Epistula ad Carolum imperatorem de scrutinio et baptismo* 27.
166 Cf. CPL 1760 (s. VI–VIII; cf. FaFo § 277), 14 (Westra 2002, p. 507). The same in Keefe 2002, vol. II, p. 399, ll. 3–5 (text 28); Keefe, *Explanationes*, 2012, text 30, ll. 293–95 (p. 143).
167 Interestingly, he does not quote the *communio sanctorum* in his creed, but refers to it only in his interpretation of *in sanctam ecclesiam*. Cf. CPL 1751, 16 (Latin text: Westra 2002, p. 472): 'That holy Church is one and true in which the communion of saints for the remission of sins, the resurrection of this our flesh is preached.'
168 Latin text: Keefe 2002, vol. II, p. 597, ll. 1–5 (text 52; cf. FaFo § 773).
169 Cf. Elert 1949; Kelly 1972, pp. 389 f.
170 The Latin equivalent of κοινωνία τῶν μυστηρίων would be *communio mysteriorum*. This phrase is, in fact, already found in Ambrose, *De officiis* 1,170 in precisely this eucharistic sense.

John Chrysostom), the precise Greek equivalent of *communio sanctorum*, viz. κοινωνία τῶν ἁγίων, is fairly rare, never used in a technical sense, and may denote both the eucharist as well as the eschatological communion of saints.[171] In the west this sacramental interpretation also occurs elsewhere: a French translation of T in the *Eadwin (Cadbury) Psalter* from the mid-twelfth century offers *la communiun des seintes choses*.[172] Likewise Abelard writes in his exposition of T that *sanctorum* could be understood to refer to the sanctified bread and wine in the sacrament of the altar.[173]

This brief survey of the earliest interpretations of *sanctorum communio* shows that the late-antique and early medieval interpreters of this phrase were no more unanimous than modern commentators. Rebecca J. Keller has recently argued that there is a connection between the addition of the phrase and controversies over the veneration of saints in the Gallic church.[174] Protest against such veneration could indeed be heard at least since the times of Jerome who ascribed it to Vigilantius in particular.[175] This is, of course, possible judging by the evidence of the aforementioned Pseudo-Faustus, but it seems unlikely, not only because we find veneration of the saints perhaps already in Nicetas who lived in the province

---

171 Cf. Basil of Caesarea, *Asceticon magnum*, cap. 309 (PG 31, col. 1077D = 1301C, if genuine): possibly eucharist; id., *De baptismo* 1,17: eschatological 'communion of saints'; Amphilochius, *Contra haereticos* 17, ll. 652 f. (CChr.SG 3, p. 202; allusion to Heb 10:19): eschatological; Pseudo-John Chrysostom, *In ingressum sanctorum ieiuniorum* (PG 62, col. 727, l. 50): ditto; Cyril of Alexandria, *Epistula paschalis 6*, 12, ll. 108 f. (SC 372, p. 398): ditto; Cyril of Alexandria, *Epistula paschalis 25*, 3 (PG 77, col. 912, l. 56): ditto; Pseudo-Dionysius the Areopagite, *Epistula 9*, 5 (Heil/Ritter 2012, p. 205, ll. 11 f.): τῶν ἁγίων ἐπὶ τοῖς θείοις ἀγαθοῖς κοινωνίαν / 'the [eschatological] communion of saints with regard to God's gifts'. Cf. also the Latin translations in Origen, *In epistulam Pauli ad Romanos* 10,14, ll. 26 f. (Hammond Bammel 1998, p. 823): Paul speaks about the *sanctorum communio*; Theophilus of Alexandria, *Epistula ad Palaestinos et ad Cyprios episcopos missa* (= Jerome, *Epistula 92*) 3,2: excommunication of a heretic.
172 Cf. FaFo § 432 and below p. 587. For this and the following reference cf. also Peters 1991, pp. 216 f.
173 Cf. Peter Abelard, *Expositio symboli quod dicitur apostolorum* (PL 178, col. 630).
174 Cf. Keller 2022, pp. 166 f.: 'The seemingly innocuous phrase *sanctorum communio* is added to the Creed in some Gallic community as an affirmation of the belief in the saints and the efficacy of their relics, and spreads from there throughout Gaul. The phrase is unobjectionable, even to one such as Vigilantius, who protested the extravagancies of the relic veneration. Eventually, this Gallic form of the creed is propagated for the sake of liturgical uniformity.' This interpretation is already found in Kattenbusch 1900, p. 942.
175 Cf. Jerome, *Contra Vigilantium* 1; id., *Epistula 109*, 1; Gennadius of Marseille, *Liber siue definitio ecclesiasticorum dogmatum* 39; *Collectio Eusebiana*, *Homilia 11*, 5; Pseudo-Faustus of Riez, *Sermo 1*, 1, ll. 5 f. (CChr.SL 101B, p. 821). In addition, Hunter 1999.

of Dacia Mediterranea rather than Gaul, but also because it was not the *veneration* of the saints that was expressed, but *communion* of (or with) them. Unfortunately, the original reason for, and meaning of, the addition can no longer be ascertained. However, it may well be that *sanctorum communionem* was a gloss explaining *sanctam ecclesiam* which intruded in the text of R/T.[176]

uitam aeternam

I indicated above that *uitam aeternam* is included in R[M], but apparently neither in R[L] nor in OGS.[177] Yet when we look at the insertion of the phrase in other creeds, we notice that it already formed part of the baptismal questions attested by Cyprian in the mid-third century.[178] In the fourth century it occurs also in J (FaFo § 192), N[Ant] (§§ 180, 208), and elsewhere. (C[2] has ζωὴν τοῦ μέλλοντος αἰῶνος / 'life of the world to come'; cf. § 184e1.) If J indeed rests on (some version of) R,[179] then a version of R which contained the 'eternal life' must have circulated in Rome. In addition, *uitam aeternam* occurs in fifth-century authors from different regions such as Nicetas of Remesiana, Peter Chrysologus, Faustus of Riez, Augustine, Quodvultdeus,[180] etc. which makes it difficult to assume that the phrase had not been present in (some version of) R in Rome. Alternatively, one may speculate that a version of R without *uitam aeternam* had already been circulating in the western empire *before* the phrase was added to the creed (as quoted by Marcellus). This must then have happened before 340 – but we have no hard evidence for such an assumption.

Indeed we even have positive proof that the creed (or some version of it) *did* contain the phrase as well, at least in Aquileia, because Chromatius mentions in his

---

176 This suggestion was already made by Luther in his *Large Catechism* of 1529: 'a gloss or an explanation (*glose odder auslegung*)'; cf. WA 30, p. 189, ll. 24 f. Cf. also id., *Resolutio Lutheriana super propositione XIII. de potestate papae* (WA 2, p. 190, ll, 23–5): '[. . .] sed glossa aliqua forte ecclesiam sanctam Catholicam exposuit esse Communionem sanctorum, quod successu temporis in textum relatum nunc simul oratur' / '[. . .] but some gloss probably explained that the holy catholic Church is the communion of saints; in the course of time it was transferred into the text and is now also prayed.'
177 Cf. above p. 163.
178 Cf. Cyprian, *Epistula 69*, 7,2 (FaFo § 92a); id., *Epistula 70*, 2,1 (§ 92b); id., *Ad Demetrianum* 24,2 (§ 122b); and above p. 132.
179 Cf. below ch. 5.5.
180 Cf. Nicetas, *Competentibus ad baptismum instructionis libelli* 5 (FaFo § 324); Peter Chrysologus, *Sermo 57* (§ 259a); id., *Sermo 58* (§ 259b); id., *Sermo 59* (§ 259c); id., *Sermo 60* (§ 259d); id., *Sermo 62* (§ 259f); Faustus, *De spiritu sancto* 1,2 (FaFo § 267b2); Augustine, *Sermo 215* (§ 316g); id., *Sermo de symbolo ad catechumenos* (§ 316l); Quodvultdeus, *Sermo 1*, 12,1 (§ 317a).

Tractatus in Mathaeum (probably written between 397 and 407) that it ended like this: 'huius carnis resurrectionem, in uitam aeternam'.[181] Liuwe Westra tried to solve this conundrum by assuming that Rufinus quoted his baptismal creed whereas Chromatius was referring to the *actual* creed used in Aquileia and that, by consequence, *uitam aeternam* had been added sometime between 370 and 407, 'quite possibly by Chromatius himself'.[182] But this does not answer the question as to why *Marcellus* quotes eternal life as well; in addition, it is difficult to see why Chromatius would mention *uitam aeternam* whereas Rufinus did not when they were both preaching about the baptismal creed used in Aquileia at the turn of the fifth century. All in all, it is easier to assume that in Rome, Aquileia, and elsewhere there was a certain flexibility in the wording of R/T and that eternal life was not considered one of its 'core statements', since belief in the resurrection had already been expressed in the christological section.

Conclusions

When we look at the additions in chronological order we can see that *patrem* and *mortuus* may go back to the third century and may have been added to some version of R (not the one quoted by Marcellus), because they are attested in the Roman baptismal questions and in TA[G] respectively. However, we are unable to be more specific, because Rufinus apparently read *patrem* in the Roman creed (and that of Aquileia), but not *mortuus*. In around 400 Nicetas attests *passus* and *catholicam* as additions in Dacia Mediterranea. All remaining variants only appear in Gaulish creeds from the mid-fifth century onwards, although the creeds in the *Collectio Eusebiana* and in Caesarius also display certain variations compared to T. They seem to have travelled to Spain by way of Gaul. This may well have happened in the context of the conversion of Visigothic Spain to catholicism as a result of the Third Council of Toledo in 589, but, again, we have no details regarding this process.

---

[181] Chromatius, *Tractatus in Mathaeum 41*, 8, ll. 199 f. (CChr.SL 9A (Raymond Étaix/Joseph Lemarié), p. 396).

[182] Westra 2002, p. 91. As far as I can see, this problem was not discussed in research before Westra. Peter Gemeinhardt also notes the difference between the Latin R and Marcellus. However, he then comments that, given the wide attestation of the phrase in the west, 'the decisive question does not appear to be why this phrase is contained in the *Apostolicum*, but why it is missing in the *Romanum*' and speaks of a Roman *Sonderweg* (Gemeinhardt, 'Vom Werden', 2020, p. 53).

All in all, our analysis confirms the hypothesis of previous scholars that T in its present form is, by and large, a product of the Gaulish church where it was memorized and explained in catechesis,[183] but that it is not the product of a deliberate overall editing process as such. Instead the changes to R were made by different people at different times, and we must also allow for a certain variation in wording.

Liuwe H. Westra has pointed out that such a flexibility appears to have been generally accepted:

> None of our sources [. . .] betray any signs of discontent with this situation or condemn a certain variant as deviating from the 'original' Apostles' Creed. Therefore, the general assumption that in the early Church, the Apostles' Creed was considered essentially one seems to be correct and what we call differences between two forms of the Creed were considered variations and nothing more. Even additions like *Creatorem caeli et terrae*, *Descendit in inferna*, *Sanctorum communionem*, and *Vitam aeternam* were probably not always regarded as changes in the text of the Creed, so that there was no difficulty in the fact that, for example, two variants, one of which contained these additions while the other lacked them, both could claim to be the one and only 'Apostles' Creed'.[184]

Augustine offers no less than four versions of the creed in his works as the following synopsis illustrates:

Sermo 213 (= *Morin Guelf. 1*) (FaFo § 316e)	Sermo 215 (§ 316g)	De fide et symbolo (§ 316k)	Sermo de symbolo ad catechumenos (§ 316l)
Credo in deum,	[Credimus] in deum,	Credentes itaque in deum,	Credo/credimus in deum,
patrem omnipotentem,	patrem omnipotentem,	patrem omnipotentem [. . .].	patrem omnipotentem,
	uniuersorum creatorem, regem saeculorum, immortalem et inuisibilem.		
et in Iesum Christum,	[Credimus et] in filium eius Iesum Christum,	[. . .] credimus etiam in Iesum Christum,	et in Iesum Christum,

---

183 Cf., e.g., Kelly 1972, pp. 411–20; Vokes 1978, p. 536. More cautiously, Gemeinhardt, 'Vom Werden', pp. 20 f.

184 Westra 2002, pp. 84 f. Cf. also Vinzent 2006, p. 372.

(continued)

Sermo 213 (= Morin Guelf. 1) (FaFo § 316e)	Sermo 215 (§ 316g)	De fide et symbolo (§ 316k)	Sermo de symbolo ad catechumenos (§ 316l)
filium eius unicum, dominum nostrum, qui natus est de spiritu sancto et uirgine Maria,	dominum nostrum, natum de spiritu sancto et uirgine Maria,	filium dei patris unigenitum [. . .], dominum nostrum. [. . .] credentes in eum dei filium, qui natus est per spiritum sanctum ex uirgine Maria.	filium eius unicum, [dominum nostrum], natus de spiritu sancto et uirgine Maria,
sub Pontio Pilato		Credimus itaque in eum, qui sub Pontio Pilato	passus sub Pontio Pilato,
crucifixus	crucifixum sub Pontio Pilato	crucifixus est	crucifixus
et sepultus; tertia die resurrexit a mortuis;	et sepultum; tertia die a mortuis resurrexit;	et sepultus. Credimus etiam illum tertio die resurrexisse a mortuis [. . .].	et sepultus; [tertia die resurrexit a mortuis;]
ascendit in caelum; sedet ad dexteram patris;	ascendit in caelos; sedet ad dexteram patris;	Credimus in caelum ascendisse [. . .]. Credimus etiam, quod sedet ad dexteram patris;	ascendit in caelum; sedet ad dexteram patris;
inde uenturus iudicaturus uiuos et mortuos;	inde uenturus est iudicare uiuos et mortuos.	Credimus etiam inde uenturum conuenientissimo tempore et iudicaturum uiuos et mortuos.	inde uenturus iudicare uiuos et mortuos;
et in spiritum sanctum,	[Credimus] et in spiritum sanctum,	[Credimus in spiritum sanctum.]	et in spiritum sanctum,
in sanctam ecclesiam,		Credimus et in sanctam ecclesiam, utique catholicam.	sanctam ecclesiam,
in remissionem peccatorum,	remissionem peccatorum,	Itaque credimus et remissionem peccatorum.	remissionem peccatorum,

(continued)

Sermo 213 (= *Morin Guelf. 1*) (FaFo § 316e)	Sermo 215 (§ 316g)	De fide et symbolo (§ 316k)	Sermo de symbolo ad catechumenos (§ 316l)
carnis resurrectionem.[185]	resurrectionem carnis, uitam aeternam per sanctam ecclesiam.[186]	Et ideo credimus et in carnis resurrectionem. < . . . [?]>[187]	resurrectionem carnis, in uitam aeternam.[188]

Here we have not only variations in the number of cola, but also (in the christologi-cal section) in the syntactical construction.[189] In addition, Augustine apparently had no problem in sometimes adding *in* before the Church etc. and sometimes omitting it. The variations between the creeds point to the fact that in Augustine's church

---

185 'I believe in God, the Father Almighty, and in Jesus Christ, his only Son, our Lord, who was born of the Holy Spirit and the virgin Mary, was crucified and buried under Pontius Pilate; on the third day rose again from the dead; ascended into heaven; sits at the right hand of the Father; thence he will come to judge the living and the dead; and in the Holy Spirit; in the holy Church; in the remission of sins, the resurrection of the flesh.'
186 '[We believe] in God, the Father Almighty, Creator of the universe, king of the ages, immortal and invisible. [We also believe] in his Son Jesus Christ, our Lord, born of the Holy Spirit and the virgin Mary, crucified under Pontius Pilate, and buried; on the third day rose again from the dead; ascended into the heavens; sits at the right hand of the Father; thence he will come to judge the living and the dead. [We believe] also in the Holy Spirit, the remission of sins, the res-urrection of the flesh, eternal life through the holy Church.'
187 'Believing, therefore, in God, the Father Almighty [. . .]. [. . .] We also believe in Jesus Christ, the only-begotten Son of God the Father [. . .], our Lord. [. . .] Believing in this Son of God, who was born through the Holy Spirit from the virgin Mary. [. . .] We, therefore, believe in him who was crucified under Pontius Pilate and buried. [. . .] We also believe that on the third day he rose again from the dead [. . .]. We believe that he ascended into heaven [. . .]. We also believe that he sits at the right hand of the Father. [. . .] We also believe that thence he will come at the most proper time and judge the living and the dead. [We believe in the Holy Spirit.] [. . .] We also be-lieve in the holy Church, that is, the catholic Church. [. . .] We, therefore, also believe the remis-sion of sins. [. . .] And we, therefore, also believe in the resurrection of the flesh. < . . . [?]>'.
188 'I/we believe in God, the Father Almighty, and in Jesus Christ, his only Son, [our Lord,] born of the Holy Spirit and the virgin Mary, suffered under Pontius Pilate, was crucified and buried; [on the third day rose again from the dead;] ascended into heaven; sits at the right hand of the Father; thence he will come to judge the living and the dead; and in the Holy Spirit, the holy Church, the remission of sins, the resurrection of the flesh; in [*or:* for] eternal life.'
189 A fourth version (which cannot neatly be reconstructed) is found in *De fide et symbolo* (FaFo § 316k). The most extensive study of Augustine's creeds is still Eichenseer 1960.

the wording of the *symbolum* was not yet fixed, but that the creed could be subject to minor variations in the process of oral transmission in the *Traditio symboli*. Probably, Augustine did not insist on the recitation of a fixed formula in the *Redditio*, but on the enumeration of theological propositions (which could sometimes be extended).

Additions that have not stood the test of time

It is by no means all variants in R/T which had been added over the centuries that 'survived'. One might mention the addition of *per sanctam ecclesiam* to the pneumatological section in North Africa (this alteration was imported from the baptismal interrogations of the third century),[190] the addition of *uictor* after *ascendit* in Gaul,[191] the phrase *resurrexit uiuus a mortuis* which is first found in TA^G, Nicetas of Remesiana, and later especially in Spanish creeds,[192] or the addition of *deum et* before *dominum nostrum* which is first attested in Spain in the sixth century and clearly anti-Homoian.[193]

Sometimes peculiar syntagmata occur which cannot be assigned simply to one region and which later disappeared. The phrases *abremissa peccatorum*[194] and *abremissionem peccatorum*[195] which are first attested in the fifth century probably did not make it because of their highly unusual phrasing.[196] Caesarius of Arles and

---

190 Cf., e.g., Cyprian (FaFo § 92) and above p. 132. Furthermore Augustine (§ 316g); Quodvultdeus (§ 317b, c); Fulgentius of Ruspe (§ 319b2); Pseudo-Fulgentius (§ 320).

191 Cf. *Missale Gallicanum Vetus* (FaFo § 678a1); CPL 1760 (§ 277). Cf., however, CPL 1762 (§ 364 [2]) which according to Westra 2002, pp. 387–392, 561 f. is North Italian.

192 Cf. Nicetas of Remesiana (FaFo § 324). Spanish: Martin of Braga (§ 608); Ildefonsus of Toledo (§ 312); Etherius of Osma/Beatus of Liébana (§ 314a); *Formulae Hispanica in modum symboli* (§ 510 [16]); Mozarabic Liturgy (§§ 684c4, d). (Perhaps) not of Spanish origin: *Expositio symboli* (CPL 229a, Northern Italy, *s.* V–VIII; § 262); the anonymous explanation Keefe, *Explanationes*, 2012, text 9 (§ 334).

193 Cf. Martin of Braga (FaFo § 608); Ildefonsus of Toledo (§ 312); Etherius of Osma/Beatus of Liébana (§ 314a, b, d, e); Mozarabic liturgy (§ 684a, c2, c4). Not of Spanish origin: Quodvultdeus (§ 317e, but the context is unclear); *Bobbio Missal* (§ 375; clearly influenced by Etherius and Beatus).

194 Cf. *Collectio Eusebiana* (FaFo § 266b), Faustus of Riez (§ 267b2), *Antiphonary of Bangor* (§ 698b).

195 Cf. Pseudo-Faustus of Riez (FaFo § 268); creed § 297; *Missale Gallicanum Vetus* (§ 678a). Cf. also § 271b2 (Caesarius of Arles?).

196 *Abremissa* either stands for *abremissam* (from the noun *abremissa* = *remissa*) or is a neuter plural of *abremissus*. The relevant databanks offer no other form than *abremissa* which is always accompanied by *peccatorum*. The lexeme is confined to the authors mentioned in the previous footnotes. *Abremissio* is also found in Isidore, *Liber numerorum* 8 (PL 83, col. 1298B): *sanctorum abremissio pia*. Zeno of Verona, *Tractatus 1,2*, 24, ll. 218 f. (CChr.SL 22, p. 21) offers *remissa pecca-*

the *Bobbio Missal* read *filium eius unigenitum, sempiternum*.[197] *Sempiternum* is not attested elsewhere. Oddly, the more precise translation of μονογενῆ as *unigenitum* (instead of *unicum*) never made it into T either, although it is occasionally found in other authors.[198] In this context it is also worth mentioning that some expositors of the creed combine *unicum* with *dominum nostrum* (hence: 'our only Lord') which can be seen from the way they divide the cola.[199]

Some creeds emphasize that the Spirit had 'one substance with the Father and the Son' (*unam habentem substantiam cum patre et filio*).[200] This may have been influenced by Gregory the Great[201] in which case CPL 505 and 1763 must have been written later than is usually assumed.[202] Finally, it may be noted that the 'resurrection of the dead' (*resurrectionem mortuorum*), which is often found in modern versions of T, does not usually occur in R/T, but was taken over from C^2.[203] *Carnis resurrectionem* may not generally have been replaced because what mattered here was the resurrection of the *flesh* (and not just the soul) in order to emphasize a *full* (and not just spiritual) resurrection.[204]

The reasons why some variants of R/T survived and now form part of T while others simply vanished are manifold: some may have been considered superflu-

---

torum (cf. also *1,6* (p. 43, l. 9)). On discussion of the form *abremissa* cf. Bengt Löfstedt in CChr.SL 22, pp. 79–81.

197 These creeds are identical except for the fact that Caesarius uses relative clauses in the christological section while the Missal has participles; cf. Caesarius, *Sermo 9* (FaFo § 271a1, a2); *Sacramentarium Gallicanum* 184 (§ 676a).

198 Cf. FaFo §§ 272 (Cyprian of Toulon), 525 (Jacobi's Creed, Spain?, *s.* VII?).

199 Cf., e.g., Peter Chrysologus (FaFo § 259f), CPL 1761 (§ 278), CPL 1758 (§ 280), creed from Berne (§ 282), *Tractatus de symbolo apostolorum* (§ 283), the *Book of Deer* (§ 294), CPL 1759 (§ 309), *Apertio symboli* (§ 332), anonymous florilegium (§ 337), anonymous creed (§ 379a); Pseudo-Augustine, *Sermo 240* (§ 383); anonymous creed (§ 385). In *Sermo 58* of Peter Chrysologus *filium eius* is missing (§ 259b) – yet this must surely be a mistake by an early copyist, given that he quotes it on other occasions. It is also omitted in the creed § 379a and in the *Bobbio Missal* (§ 676b, c).

200 Cf. FaFo §§ 265 (CPL 505), 273 (CPL 1763), 698b (*Antiphonary of Bangor*).

201 Cf. Gregory, *Homilia in Euangelia 30*, 3: 'Qui unius substantiae cum Patre et Filio exorare pro delinquentibus perhibetur, quia eos quos repleuerit exorantes facit.' / The Spirit, 'who, being of one substance with Father and Son, is shown to pray for the sinners, because he makes those pray whom he has filled'.

202 CPL 505: fifth century, cf. Westra 2002, pp. 312–18; CPL 1763: 550 or later, cf. Westra 2002, pp. 393–5.

203 Exceptions: Peter Chrysologus (FaFo § 259c – but in one sermon only, otherwise always *carnis resurrectionem*); Alcuin (§ 702g3); furthermore the anonymous creed § 339.

204 It is difficult to say why CPL 505 (FaFo § 265) and 1763 (§ 273) read *ex mortuis* instead of *a mortuis* and whether this variant has any significance at all. Lk 20:35 (*resurrectione ex mortuis*) and Col 1:18 (*primogenitus ex mortuis*) may have played some role in this respect.

ous, others were omitted by negligence. Again others disappeared because the relevant region or the authors who used it did not have sufficient ecclesiastical or political influence. Not least, we should not discount the loss of manuscripts as having played a part. It is important to keep all these factors in mind: the final shape of T was not entirely the result of particular theological or liturgical developments but may also have come about by sheer happenstance.[205]

5.3 The general endorsement of T in the Carolingian Reform

When we look at the witnesses for T we can easily see that its general implementation was a result of the efforts during the reign of the Frankish king and emperor Charlemagne (king 768–814; emperor since 800) to achieve uniformity in the liturgy and to improve the religious knowledge of his subjects. We find T (with minor variations) in sacramentaries and baptismal liturgies from the late eighth century onwards.[206] Charlemagne insisted in his *Admonitio generalis* of 789 that 'the faith in the holy Trinity, and the incarnation of Christ, his passion, resurrection, and ascension into the heavens' be diligently (*diligenter*) preached to everybody.[207] For that purpose T was more helpful than C^2 which lay people had difficulties in understanding and memorizing. Alas, we have no direct testimony that the king and emperor promoted one particular version of T, but we do have a testimony that he considered R/T to be part of the basics that every believer ought to know. Sometime in the early 800s he wrote a letter to Bishop Gerbald (Garibaldus; Ghaerbald) of Liège (*sedit* 787–810). In it he mentions an incident that had happened at Epiphany at a baptismal ceremony in which the emperor took part and during which he found that none of the parents or sponsors were able to recite the creed and the Lord's Prayer. The emperor was indignant about the degree of sloppiness he found in the diocese of Liège, ordering the bishop to convene an assembly of priests for the matter to be investigated. In the same vein, he told the bishop to make sure that everybody knew at least the Lord's Prayer and 'the creed of the catholic faith, as the apostles have taught it' (*symbolum fidei catholicae, sicut apostoli docuerunt*) and that no infant was to be baptized before their parents and sponsors had recited both these texts in the presence of the officiating clergy.[208] The creed in question

---

205 Cf. also Gemeinhardt, 'Vom Werden', 2020, esp. p. 57.
206 Cf. the list in FaFo, vol. II, pp. 352 f.
207 Charlemagne, *Admonitio generalis* 32 (FaFo § 719a).
208 Cf. Charlemagne, *Epistula de oratione dominica et symbolo discendis* (FaFo § 731). Cf. also below p. 470.

must have been some version of R/T because only this creed was attributed apostolic origin, as we will see in the next chapter.

It may well be that Gerbald references this letter in another epistle in which he admonishes his clergy to be more diligent in teaching their flock the Lord's Prayer and 'the creed which the apostles have taught' (*symbolum, sicut docuerunt sancti apostoli*).[209] It may have been in the same context that he also addressed his congregation directly telling them no longer to neglect the Lord's Prayer and 'and the creed of the twelve apostles (*de symbolo duodecim apostolorum*), which begins like this, "I believe in God, the Father Almighty", and the remaining verses that follow'.[210] Gerbald's successor Waltcaud (*fl.* 811–381) continued this effort at improving religious education.[211]

In addition, a member of the king's court (perhaps Angilbert of Saint-Riquier, d. 814) issued an instruction in 802 or 803 to an ecclesiastical *missus dominicus* as to how to examine the religious knowledge of canons, monks, and lay people. Canons, he said, should be told 'to memorize the Apostles' Creed (*symbolum apostolorum*) and the faith of St Athanasius, the bishop [i.e. the *Symbolum Quicumque*]'.[212] The *symbolum apostolorum* is also mentioned in a number of ecclesiastical chapters of the same period from other dioceses as part of the minimum knowledge that both priests[213] and lay people ought to have.[214] In this respect, Haito of Basel (*sedit* 803–23) expressly mentions that the Lord's Prayer and the Apostles' Creed (*symbolum apostolorum*) are to be memorized 'both in Latin and in the vernacular' (*tam Latine quam barbarice*).[215] Indeed, the oldest German version of T in the so-called *Weissenburg Catechism* dates from precisely this period.[216] Two other examples that also call the creed used at baptism the *symbolum apostolicum* are a brief treatise on baptism by Alcuin (735–804) of *c.* 798 and the response by Leidrad of Lyons (*sedit* 798–814?) to Charlemagne's famous inquiry of 812 concerning baptismal practices in his realm (FaFo § 781).[217] However, we must allow for some varia-

---

209 Gerbald, *Ad dioeceseos suae presbyteros epistula* (*Epistula 2*; FaFo § 745c).
210 Gerbald, *Instructio pastoralis ad gregem suum* (*Epistula 3*) 1 (FaFo § 745d1). Cf. also id., *Instructio pastoralis ad gregem suum* (*Epistula 3*) 3 (§ 745d2).
211 Cf. Waltcaud of Liège, *Capitulary*, chs. 1–2 (FaFo § 749: *symbolum apostolicum*).
212 Angilbert (?), *Epistula* (FaFo § 727).
213 Cf. *Capitula Frisingensia Prima* 1–3 (FaFo § 756: *symbolum apostolicum*).
214 Cf. *Capitula Parisiensia* 2 (after 800; FaFo § 744: *symbolum apostolorum*); (Pseudo-)Gerbald of Liège, *Second Capitulary* 1 (§ 745b: *symbolum apostolorum*); Hrabanus Maurus, *De clericorum institutione* 1,27 (§ 769: *apostolicae fidei symbolum*).
215 Haito of Basel, *Capitulary*, ch. 2 (FaFo § 747a).
216 Cf. below pp. 584 f.
217 Cf. Alcuin, *De sacramento baptismatis* (FaFo § 775); Leidrad of Lyons, *Liber de sacramento baptismi ad Carolum Magnum imperatorem* 5 (§ 785).

tion because the exposition of the creed which Amalarius of Metz (*sedit* 810–814) included in his reply is very similar to, but by no means identical with, T.[218] Finally, we still possess an explanation of T from the pen of Hrabanus Maurus that was preached on the second Sunday of Lent.[219]

T is also the version of the *symbolum apostolicum* that was included (without title) in the magnificent *Dagulf Psalter* (cod. Vienna, Österreichische Nationalbibliothek, lat. 1861; FaFo § 299). This psalter was named after the scribe who wrote it in Aachen between 783 and 795 at the behest of Charlemagne to be gifted to Pope Hadrian. Kelly (who also mentions the *Psalter of Charles the Bald* (cod. Paris, Bibliothèque Nationale, lat. 1152), written in 842–869[220]) is, therefore, no doubt right when he says that 'T must have had something of the status and prestige of an official form if it was selected for inclusion in psalters prepared for the royal house'.[221]

In conclusion, although direct evidence is lacking, T was undoubtedly the version of the Apostles' Creed that was propagated by Charlemagne and the members of his court chapel in their effort to improve the general level of religious education and to curb the rank growth of the liturgy that had proliferated in the west over the previous centuries.[222] Why they chose Pirmin's version is not known. However, it may be significant as regards its spread in Francia that the oldest manuscript of the *Scarapsus* (cod. Paris, Bibliothèque Nationale, lat. 1603[223]) was written in the late eighth or early ninth century in a scriptorium close to the Frankish court. It also included, *inter alia*, Charlemagne's aforementioned *Admonitio generalis* which set out the king's ideas about reforming education and the Church. It is precisely through manuscripts such as these (which may have served the bishops 'for reference and instructing'[224]), and through its inclusion in the daily office, that T ultimately won the day as the definitive version of the creed attributed to the apostles.

---

218 Cf. Amalarius, *Epistula ad Carolum imperatorem de scrutinio et baptismo* 23–27 (FaFo § 782a1). However, he nowhere calls it the *symbolum apostolorum*.

219 Cf. Hrabanus, *Homilia 13* (PL 110, cols. 27–9; cf. FaFo § 306).

220 In this Latin Psalter T is called in Greek ΣΥΜΒΟΛΟΝ.

221 Kelly 1972, p. 426.

222 Cf. also Vogel 1986, pp. 147–50; Metzger 1997, pp. 114–19; Angenendt 2001, pp. 327–48; Ehrensperger 2006; Angenendt 2009, pp. 38–44; Klöckener 2013, pp. 66–9.

223 Cf. Hauswald 2010, pp. LXIV–LXVII; Keefe, *Catalogue*, 2012, pp. 304 f.; URL <http://www.mirabileweb.it/manuscript/paris-bibliothèque-nationale-de-france-lat-1603-manoscript/12069> (10/11/2023).

224 Keefe, *Catalogue*, 2012, p. 304.

5.4 The legend about the origin of the Apostles' Creed

Concomitantly to the spread of R/T in the west, the legend developed that this creed had its origins in a council of the apostles before they departed from Palestine in order to preach all over the world. The idea that the Church's teaching went back to the apostles and, ultimately, to Christ himself is, of course, very old and, for example, already found in *First Clement*, Irenaeus, and Tertullian.[225] Later on, however, it developed into a full-blown legend.

The *Apostolic Constitutions*, compiled in their present form in Antioch in c. 380, offer a summary of Christian teaching that allegedly derived from a council of the apostles, although the only details given is a list of names.[226] Two of the earliest accounts of this legend proved especially influential because they were quoted over and over again in later explanations of the creed; they are to be found in the writings of Ambrose and Rufinus. For Ambrose the major purpose of the council of the apostles was to establish a formula summarizing the main tenets of the Christian faith for religious instruction:

> Therefore, the holy apostles met together [and] made a brief summary of the faith (*breuiarium fidei*), so that we might express the sequence of the whole faith in a nutshell (*ut breuiter fidei totius seriem comprehendamus*). Brevity is needful so that it may be always remembered and recalled to mind.[227]

Ambrose insists on brevity so that the creed could be memorized and thus be protected from additions either by heretics or by overly cautious catholics concerned about the text's precise meaning. He concludes:

> Therefore, the holy apostles met together and briefly (*breuiter*) composed the creed.[228]

Whereas Ambrose's account is succinct and to the point, the presbyter Rufinus offered his congregation at Aquileia an embellished version of the legend in around 404 or shortly thereafter, adding a range of new elements:

---

225 Cf. *First Clement* 42,2–3 (FaFo § 348); Irenaeus, *Aduersus haereses* 3,4,1 (§ 349b); Tertullian, *De praescriptione haereticorum* 20,4–5 (§ 350b1).

226 Cf. *Constitutiones apostolorum* 6,14,1–15,2 (FaFo § 182b). The list in 6,14,1 is that of Mt 10:2–4 (see below), with Matthias replacing Judas Iscariot (Acts 1:26). The author also adds James, the brother of the Lord, and the Apostle Paul.

227 Ambrose, *Explanatio symboli* 2 (FaFo § 351a).

228 Ambrose, *Explanatio symboli* 3 (FaFo § 351a).

> Our fathers of old have related that, after the ascension of the Lord, when tongues of fire had
> rested upon each of the apostles at the coming of the Holy Spirit so that they might speak in
> manifold and diverse languages (through which no foreign people, no barbarous speech
> should appear inaccessible to them or beyond attainment) [cf. Acts 2:1–11], a commandment
> from the Lord was given to them to depart to each of the nations in order to preach the word
> of God [cf. Acts 1:8]. Thus, before separating from one another, they first agreed together
> upon a fixed standard for their future preaching (*normam prius futurae sibi praedicationis*) so
> that, when they had dispersed, they could not possibly vary when teaching those who were
> called to believe in Christ. When, therefore, they were all in one place and were filled with
> the Holy Spirit, they composed (as we have said) this brief token of their future preaching
> (*futurae praedicationis indicium*), each contributing his own decision to the one [decree]. They
> resolved that this rule (*regulam*) was to be given to believers. [. . .] When, therefore, as we
> have said, the apostles were about to depart to their preaching, they laid down this token of
> their unanimity and their faith (*unanimitatis et fidei suae indicium*).[229]

Here the event is linked to Pentecost and, therefore, located in Jerusalem. The
apostles were actually filled by the Holy Spirit when they laid down the creed.
Their aim was to demonstrate unanimity with regard to the contents of faith. This
version adds another new element which is not yet found in Ambrose: each apostle stated his own view and contributed it to the creed. As such the creed is invariable and cannot be changed.

Rufinus clearly emphasized the unanimity of the apostles in creating the
creed; later expositions ironically used this notion of its joint apostolic nature as
a means of discrimination: because of its venerable origin the creed serves to distinguish both faith from unbelief and orthodoxy from heresy. Leo the Great
pointed out in a letter to Empress Pulcheria that

> the brief and perfect confession of the catholic creed (*ipsa catholici symboli breuis et per-
> fecta confessio*) which was sealed by the twelve sentences of the twelve apostles is so well-
> furnished with heavenly fortification (*tam instructa sit munitione caelesti*) that all the opin-
> ions of heretics can be struck down by that one sword.[230]

The author of a sermon attributed to Maximus of Turin (*fl.* 408–423) which may
have been composed in *c.* 450 made a similar point:

> The blessed apostles [. . .] delivered the mystery of the creed (*mysterium symboli*) to the
> Church of God, which they armed against the troops of the furious devil so that the sign of
> the creed (*signaculum symboli*) would distinguish between believers and the infidels (be-
> cause there was to be a dissension between the believers under the one name of Christ),
> and the one who is an alien from the faith and an enemy of the Church would become ap-

---

229 Rufinus, *Expositio symboli* 2 (FaFo § 18).
230 Leo the Great, *Epistula 4b(31)*, 4 (FaFo § 360a). Cf. also *Tractatus 96*, 1 (§ 360b).

parent because, in spite of being baptized, he would not know it, or being a heretic he would have corrupted it.[231]

Later explanations of the creed attribute a clause of T to each apostle. It is difficult to say when this notion developed as the dates of the anonymous texts in which these attributions occur are mostly unknown. It may well be that it did not occur before the late seventh or early eighth century, the *Bobbio Missal* and Pirmin being among the earliest examples.[232]

There were, however, two problems with this assignation of individual clauses to each apostle. First, the various lists of apostles in the Latin translation of the New Testament, the Vulgate, differed from each other, and, second, the number of clauses did not quite fit the number of apostles so that certain adjustments had to be made which depended on the precise wording of the creed and, in the end, turned out not to be uniform. Thus, what was meant to lead to a 'stable' apostolic tradition resulted in considerable confusion. We do not need to rehearse the details of this phenomenon here. Rather, the following will outline some of the major trends and peculiarities that occur in manuscripts of the early and high middle ages when it comes to listing the apostles.

The New Testament contains four lists of apostles (Mt 10:2–4; Mk 3:16–19; Lk 6:14–16; Acts 1:13 and 26).[233] For the purpose of the creed these lists had, of necessity, to be modified, because Judas Iscariot had to be replaced by Mathias (Acts 1:26). The lists of apostles given in relation to T are only partly based on the New Testament as the following typology demonstrates.

Type Ia
It is hardly surprising that the most wide-spread sequence was that of Acts 1:13 (plus Mathias):

Peter – John – James – Andrew – Philip – Thomas – Bartholomew – Matthew – James – Simon – Jude – Mathias

It is found, for example, in
–   *Sacramentarium Gallicanum* (*Bobbio Missal*) 591 (FaFo § 375; Vienne, *s*. VII *ex*.?);
–   Pseudo-Augustine, *Sermo 241* (FaFo § 386; Gaul, *s*. IX *in*. or earlier);

---

231 Pseudo-Maximus, *Homilia 83* (FaFo § 23).
232 Cf. *Sacramentarium Gallicanum* 591 (FaFo § 375); Pirmin, *Scarapsus* 10 (§ 376).
233 For the New Testament evidence cf. Taylor 2009.

- creeds in cod. Paris, Bibliothèque Nationale, lat. 14085 (Corbie, *c.* 850), f. 230r and cod. Würzburg, Universitätsbibliothek, M.p.th.f. 109 (Germany, *s.* X), ff. 159r–v (FaFo § 404);
- cod. Troyes, Bibliothèque Municipale, 804 (France, *c.* 875–900), f. 69r (FaFo § 410);
- Alexander of Hales, *Summa theologica* III,3, inq. 2, tract. 2, q. 2, tit. 1, c. 1 (Paris, 1235–1245; FaFo § 421).[234]

The creeds contained in the Paris and Würzburg codices and in the Troyes manuscript respectively are largely identical and appear to be extended versions of that found in the *Bobbio Missal*. Alexander's creed is slightly different.

Type Ib

This is a small variant of the previous sequence, in which Mathias was not included in the list. As a result Thomas appears twice.
- *Collectio Vetus Gallica* (Lyons, *s.* VII/2; FaFo § 373);
- Pirmin, *Scarapsus* 10 (Abbey of Hornbach?, *c.* 725–750; FaFo § 376);
- cod. Karlsruhe, Badische Landesbibliothek, Augiensis perg. 18 (Abbey of Reichenau, *c.* 800–825), p. 26, col. 1 (FaFo § 393).

In these cases, all clauses are identical, as are their attributions to the apostles. Accordingly, it appears very likely that the three occurrences are related to each other: Pirmin was the founder of Reichenau where the Augiensis perg. 18 was later written. His version, in turn, may be related in some way to the *Collectio Vetus Gallica* (the relationship between these two texts is complicated).[235]

Type Ic

This list is also based on Acts 1:13+26, but on a distinctive western textual tradition which is represented by the so-called Codex E (08), also called E^a or E_2 or *Codex Laudianus* of the late sixth/early seventh century.[236]

Peter – Andrew – James – John – Philip – Thomas – Bartholomew – Matthew – James – Simon – Jude – Mathias

---

[234] Alexander mentions that sometimes Thomas is named as last apostle in this sequence. See below type Ib.

[235] Cf. FaFo § 373, introduction. Cf. also Hauswald 2010, p. XCIX.

[236] Cod. Oxford, Bodleian Library, Laud. gr. 35 (Italy, Sardinia, or Rome, *c.* 600), f. 4r; cf. above p. 147. Cf. also Wordsworth/White 1954, p. 39 app. ad loc.

Its only witness is the *Liber Floretus* (before 1200) that is preserved in cod. Utrecht, Universiteitsbibliotheek, 283 (Lübeck, 1454), ll. 29–37 (FaFo § 425; a hexametrical version).

Type IIa
This is the list found in Mt 10:2–4, except that Mathias is substituted for Judas Iscariot:

Peter – Andrew – James – John – Philip – Bartholomew – Thomas – Matthew – James – Thaddaeus – Simon – Mathias

- *De fide trinitatis quomodo exponitur* (CPL 1762; Northern Italy, s. V or later; FaFo § 364);
- cod. St. Gallen, Stiftsbibliothek, 40 (Switzerland, c. 780), pp. 322 f. (FaFo § 379a);
- cod. Paris, Bibliothèque Nationale, lat. 2796 (France, c. 813–815), f. 67v (FaFo § 379b).

CPL 1762 clearly differs from the creeds in the St. Gallen and Paris codices which are closely interrelated, although not identical.

Type IIb
This is a variant of the previous list, inverting Simon and Thaddaeus.
- Pseudo-Alcuin, *Disputatio puerorum* 11 (before 800; FaFo § 527);
- cod. Munich, Bayerische Staatsbibliothek, Clm 3909 (Augsburg, c. 1138–1143), f. 23r (FaFo § 418);
- William Durand of Mende, *Rationale diuinorum officiorum* 4,25,7 (Mende, 1292/1296); FaFo § 424).

Pseudo-Alcuin (which is slightly briefer than T) may be the ancestor of Clm 3909 (which is identical with T). William has a different distribution of clauses.

The following lists do not appear to be based on any biblical evidence.

Type IIIa
Peter – Andrew – James – John – Thomas – James – Philip – Bartholomew – Matthew – Simon – Thaddaeus – Mathias
- Pseudo-Augustine, *Sermo 240* (s. VIII?; FaFo § 383);

- cod. Karlsruhe, Badische Landesbibliothek, Augiensis perg. 229 (region of Chieti; 806–822 or 821), f. 222r–v (FaFo § 401; here Simon is missing – probably a scribal error – so that only eleven apostles are named);
- cod. Munich, Bayerische Staatsbibliothek, Clm 22053 (*olim* Cim. III.4.m.; diocese of Augsburg, *c.* 814), ff. 44r–45r (FaFo § 400);
- cod. Rome, Biblioteca Apostolica Vaticana, Reg. lat. 481 (*s.* XI/XII), f. 27r (cf. FaFo, vol. II, p. 406);
- cod. Vienna, Österreichische Nationalbibliothek, theol. gr. 190 (1475–1500), f. 302v (FaFo § 427; a Greek translation of T).

Due to differences in the distribution of clauses Pseudo-Augustine and Reg. lat. 481 appear to form one group, while Augiensis perg. 229, Clm 22053, and Vienna, theol. gr. 190 form another.

Type IIIb

This list is the same as IIIa except that John and *Iacobus maior* (James, son of Zebedee) are switched around.

- Bonaventura, *Commentaria in quattuor libros sententiarum* III, dist. XXV, art. I, quaest. I (Paris, 1250–1252; FaFo § 422).

Type IV

Peter – Andrew – John – James – Thomas – James – Philip – Bartholomew – Matthew – Simon – Jude – Mathias

- Raimundus Martini, *Explanatio symboli apostolorum ad institutionem fidelium* (Spain, 1258; FaFo § 423);
- cod. Uppsala, Universitetsbibliotek, C 194 (*s.* XIII?), f. 109v (cf. FaFo, vol. II, p. 407)
- Richard Rolle (cf. below p. 574 n. 19);
- cod. Wiesbaden, Hessische Landesbibliothek, 35 (*s.* XV), f. 52r (a hexametrical version; FaFo § 426).

Raimundus, C 194, and Richard Rolle are basically identical. In C 194 *nostrum* is missing after *dominum*, and *ad caelum* is replaced by *ad caelos*. Rolle reads *inferna* instead of *inferos* and *ad caelos* instead of *ad caelum*, also adding *est* after *uenturus* and *et* before *uitam aeternam*. He omits *Amen*. *Iudas Iacobi* (Raimundus) is called *Iudas Thadaeus*.

Type V
Peter – Andrew – John – James – Matthew – Philip – Bartholomew – Thomas – Barnabas – Simon – Jude – James – Mathias

- *Eadwin (Canterbury) Psalter* (cod. Cambridge, Trinity College, R.17.1 (Canterbury, *c.* 1155–1160)), ff. 281v–282r as part of the *Expositio super symbolum* (CPL 1760; FaFo § 419).

The existence of the Apostle Paul also caused some headaches. His name follows that of Peter in all lists that include him. As a result either the number of twelve apostles had to be expanded or one of the other apostles to be dropped. Both solutions are found.

Type VI
Peter – Paul – Andrew – James – John – Thomas – James – Philip – Bartholomew – Matthew – Simon – Thaddaeus
This is the same as type IIIa, with Paul added and Mathias omitted.

- *Expositio super symbolum* (CPL 1760; Gaul, *s.* VI–VIII; FaFo § 277).

Type VII
This list starts off in a similar vein but adds another sequence after Thomas which also includes Barnabas:[237]

Peter – Paul – Andrew – James – John – Thomas – Matthew – Philip – Bartholomew – James – Barnabas – Simon – Jude – Thomas – Mathias. In this case we end up with fifteen apostles!

- cod. Laon, Bibliothéque Municipale, 303 (*s.* XIII), ff. 9r–10r (FaFo § 420; part of a longer exposition of the creed).

---

[237] The inclusion of Paul and Barnabas is also found in the explanation of the creed by Albert of Padua (d. 1328), according to Voss 1701, p. 504.

Type VIII
Even more confusing is this final variant of the list in which Paul is inserted after Peter and the final apostle's name is omitted altogether (although twelve clauses are numbered):

Peter – Paul – Andrew – James – John – Bartholomew – Thomas – Matthew – James – Simon – Jude – ?

– cod. Cambrai, Bibliothèque municipale, 625 (576; Northern France or Brittany, *s.* IX/2), f. 67r–v (FaFo § 409).

There are further variations. A creed which is found in cod. Zurich, Zentralbibliothek, C.64 (286; St. Gallen?, *s.* VIII/IX), ff. 1r–v (FaFo § 385) identifies the apostles only by numbers, not by names ('The first said . . ., the second said . . .' etc.). The same is true of the creed found in cod. Montpellier, Bibliothèque Interuniversitaire, Section Médécine, H 141 (Flavigny, *s.* IX *in.*), f. 4r (FaFo § 387). However, the way it distributes the clauses differs considerably from that of the Zurich codex.

These lists are probably related to similar lists in medieval sacramentaries and prayer books (*libelli precum*) that contain prayers addressed to the individual apostles.[238] However, examination of this very complex evidence would lead us too far astray from our main line of investigation.

However, one peculiar feature must be mentioned. From the early fourteenth century onwards we find lists in which the names of the apostles are combined with quotations from the prophets. Examples of this type are given in FaFo § 428.[239]

Although it was generally acknowledged in the middle ages that T had been composed by the apostles, the authorship of the individual clauses and even their number remained a matter of dispute in learned circles.[240] A creed from Northern Italy has the list of apostles (type IIa) *follow* the actual creed, concluding with the remark: 'It is difficult to determine the sequence of those speaking, which of the apostles said this first'.[241] (A vague attempt is made to number the clauses instead

---

238 Cf., e.g., Dell'Omo 2008, p. 253 (litany) and Dell'Omo 2003, pp. 280 f. (no. 17), in both cases citing additional evidence and literature. Other early lists are found in Schermann, *Prophetarum*, 1907; cf. also Schermann, *Propheten- und Apostellegenden*, 1907.
239 For iconographic evidence cf. below pp. 592–4. For later written sources cf. Bühler 1953.
240 For details cf. Wiegand 1904, pp. 45–8; Vinzent 2006, pp. 29 f.
241 *Apertio symboli* (FaFo § 263; Northern Italy, 800 or earlier).

in the manuscripts attesting this creed but it is given up halfway through.) Likewise, Jocelin of Soissons (*sedit* 1126–1152), while claiming that the creed had been written by the Twelve (Matthias having replaced Judas), could not recall it being mentioned in the Scriptures who had written what.[242] Durandus of Saint-Pourçain (d. 1332/1334) remarked in his *Commentary on the Sentences* that the attribution of clauses of the creed to individual apostles was rather accidental and fairly artificial.[243] In the end, the learned English bishop Reginald Pecock (Pavo, 1393–1461) and the Italian humanist Laurentius Valla (1406–1457) went so far as to establish the pseudonymity of the Apostles' Creed; as a result both these scholars received an ecclesial condemnation leading them in turn to recant.[244]

5.5 A descendant of the Roman Creed: The Creed of Jerusalem

In[245] his chapter on 'eastern creeds' Kelly suggested that every major centre of Christianity in the east possessed its own declaratory creed by the first decades of the fourth century, 'and that some of them must go well back into the third century'.[246] This view reflected a consensus widely accepted in earlier scholarship, but a closer look shows there is no evidence for such a far-reaching claim. We will see that the alleged creed of Caesarea (which Kelly discusses in this chapter) probably did not exist as a fixed formula.[247] Of his remaining alleged examples some are not baptismal creeds, but theological declarations formulated ad-hoc (Alexander of Alexandria,[248] Arius and Euzoius[249]); all the others are revisions of N originating from the 370s (Antioch,[250] Mopsuestia,[251] and, perhaps also the

---

242 Cf. Jocelin, *Expositio in symbolum* 2 (PL 186, cols. 1480B–1481A): 'They prepared a spiritual banquet, that is, the creed (*symbolum*), in which they did not include all parts of the faith in detail, but only twelve sentences (*sententias*), as there were twelve (Judas having already been replaced by Matthias), such that each one contributed his own [sentence]. Who specifically (*quisquam*)? I do not remember having read this in the canonical Scripture.'
243 Cf. Durandus, *Scriptum super IV libros sententiarum*, lib. 3, dist. 25, qu. 3, n. 9 (Martimbos 1587, p. 581): '[. . .] sed quia talis assignatio per accidens est, et minus artificialis, ideo dimittatur.' Cf. also Wernicke 1887–1893, 1887, p. 126.
244 For details cf. Vinzent 2006, pp. 31–3.
245 This chapter is based on Kinzig, 'Origin', 2022.
246 Kelly 1972, pp. 181–193; quotation on p. 192.
247 Cf. below ch. 6.3.
248 Cf. FaFo § 132 and below pp. 217 f.
249 Cf. FaFo § 131c and below p. 217.
250 Cf. FaFo §§ 198, 203, and below pp. 346–9.
251 Cf. FaFo § 180a and below pp. 346–9.

creed in the *Apostolic Constitutions*[252]) or even later (the creed attributed to Macarius of Alexandria[253]). Only one creed remains that falls into Kelly's purported category: the Creed of Jerusalem (J). J is contained in homilies to those about to be 'illuminated', i.e. candidates for baptism (*Catecheses ad illuminandos*), which Cyril, bishop of Jerusalem (*sedit* 348–386/387), delivered during Lent 351.[254] In what follows, I wish to show that the singularity of J and its parallelism with R as a declaratory baptismal creed is not the result of a quirky turn of history – J must be a descendant of R.

In theological terms, J is non-distinct with regard to the debates of the fourth century. Above all, it displays no features which would allow us to classify it as Nicene or Arian (or whatever). N seems to have had no discernible theological influence on J, but this does not necessarily mean that Cyril was reticent over against Nicene theology.[255] (Cyril's explanations are clearly Nicene.[256]) Instead, he may have considered N in general and the *homooúsios* in particular unsuitable for catechesis.

Most strikingly, J differs from N in that it contains an extended pneumatological section, including – after the Spirit – baptism and forgiveness of sins, the Church, the resurrection of the flesh, and eternal life.[257] However, these elements (with some variations) are also found in R as preserved by Marcellus (R^M; FaFo § 253). A synopsis of both formulae is set out below, with identical wording and positioning underlined; similar wording underlined; identical wording in a divergent position underlined.

---

252 Cf. Kelly 1972, pp. 186 f.; FaFo § 182c.

253 Cf. Kelly 1972, pp. 190 f.; FaFo § 188a.

254 For Cyril cf. Jacobsen 2018. The role of the creed within the catechumenate in Jerusalem is described by Doval 2001, pp. 37–46 and Day 2007, pp. 57–65. On the date of the catecheses cf. the discussion in Doval 1997.

255 *Pace* Kelly 1972, p. 183.

256 Cf., e.g., Cyril, *Catechesis* 7, 4–5. His theology is discussed in Jacobsen 2018.

257 The same elements are also found in Hilary's version of the *Ecthesis* of Serdica (east) of 343 in the *Collectanea Antiariana Parisina (Fragmenta historica)* A IV 2,1–5; cf. FaFo § 143a1[3]: 'Credimus et in sanctam ecclesiam, in remissam peccatorum, in carnis resurrectionem, in uitam aeternam.' / 'We also believe in the holy Church, in the remission of sins, in the resurrection of the flesh, in eternal life.' This must be a later addition to the text, taken from R^M, as it is not contained in the parallel tradition in Hilary's *De synodis* 34 (FaFo § 143a2).

J[258]		R[M]	
Πιστεύομεν εἰς ἕνα θεόν, πατέρα, παντοκράτορα, ποιητὴν οὐρανοῦ καὶ γῆς ὁρατῶν τε πάντων καὶ ἀοράτων·	We believe in one God, the Father Almighty, Maker of heaven and earth, of all things both visible and invisible;	Πιστεύω [. . .] εἰς θεόν, παντοκράτορα,	[. . .] I believe in God Almighty,
καὶ εἰς ἕνα κύριον Ἰησοῦν Χριστόν, τὸν υἱὸν τοῦ θεοῦ τὸν μονογενῆ, τὸν ἐκ τοῦ πατρὸς γεννηθέντα θεὸν ἀληθινὸν πρὸ πάντων τῶν αἰώνων, δι᾽ οὗ τὰ πάντα ἐγένετο,	and in one Lord Jesus Christ, the only-begotten Son of God, who was born [begotten] from the Father as true God before all ages, through whom all things came into being,	καὶ εἰς Χριστὸν Ἰησοῦν, τὸν υἱὸν αὐτοῦ τὸν μονογενῆ, τὸν κύριον ἡμῶν,	and in Christ Jesus, his only-begotten Son, our Lord,
		τὸν γεννηθέντα ἐκ πνεύματος ἁγίου καὶ Μαρίας τῆς παρθένου, τὸν ἐπὶ Ποντίου Πιλάτου σταυρωθέντα καὶ ταφέντα	who was born from the Holy Spirit and the virgin Mary; who was crucified under Pontius Pilate, and buried,
< . . . >	< . . . >		
ἀναστάντα [ἐκ νεκρῶν] τῇ τρίτῃ ἡμέρᾳ καὶ ἀνελθόντα εἰς τοὺς οὐρανοὺς	and] rose again [from the dead] on the third day, and ascended into the heavens,	καὶ τῇ τρίτῃ ἡμέρᾳ ἀναστάντα ἐκ τῶν νεκρῶν, ἀναβάντα εἰς τοὺς οὐρανοὺς	and on the third day rose again from the dead; ascended into the heavens;

---

258 For the text of J cf. FaFo § 147, but I omit the passage indicated by < . . . >. See below in the text.

(continued)

J		R^M	
καὶ καθίσαντα ἐκ δεξιῶν τοῦ πατρὸς	and sat down to the right hand of the Father,	καὶ καθήμενον ἐν δεξιᾷ τοῦ πατρός,	and sits at the right hand of the Father,
καὶ ἐρχόμενον ἐν δόξῃ κρῖναι ζῶντας καὶ νεκρούς,	and will come in glory to judge the living and the dead;	ὅθεν ἔρχεται κρίνειν ζῶντας καὶ νεκρούς·	whence he is coming to judge the living and the dead;
οὗ τῆς βασιλείας οὐκ ἔσται τέλος·	of whose kingdom there will be no end;		
καὶ εἰς ἓν ἅγιον πνεῦμα,	and in one Holy Spirit,	καὶ εἰς τὸ ἅγιον πνεῦμα,	and in the Holy Spirit,
τὸν παράκλητον, τὸ λαλῆσαν ἐν τοῖς προφήταις·	the Paraclete, who spoke through the prophets;		
καὶ εἰς ἓν βάπτισμα μετανοίας εἰς ἄφεσιν ἁμαρτιῶν·	and in one baptism of repentance for the remission of sins;		
καὶ εἰς μίαν, ἁγίαν καθολικὴν ἐκκλησίαν·	and in one holy catholic Church;	ἁγίαν ἐκκλησίαν,	the holy Church,
		ἄφεσιν ἁμαρτιῶν,	remission of sins,
καὶ εἰς σαρκὸς ἀνάστασιν·	and in the resurrection of the flesh;	σαρκὸς ἀνάστασιν,	the resurrection of the flesh,
καὶ εἰς ζωὴν αἰώνιον.	and in eternal life.	ζωὴν αἰώνιον.	eternal life.

Given the high number of agreements between both creeds and considering that there is no other creed which displays such close similarities with either J or R^M, we may assume a close genealogical relationship between both texts. Furthermore, if we consider that R was composed before 340/341 (the date of Marcellus' letter) whereas J is first attested in 351 and that in the first decades of the fourth century Rome's ecclesial influence was far greater than that of Jerusalem, we are forced to conclude that either R^M must have had a direct impact on J (and not vice versa) or that both creeds are based on a common *Vorlage*. Several important differences notwithstanding, both R^M and J display the same basic pattern, which may have looked like this:

Πιστεύομεν/πιστεύω εἰς θεόν, παντοκράτορα·	We believe/I believe in God Almighty;
καὶ εἰς Ἰησοῦν Χριστόν [or: Χριστὸν Ἰησοῦν],	and in Jesus Christ [or: Christ Jesus],
τὸν υἱὸν τοῦ θεοῦ [or: αὐτοῦ] τὸν μονογενῆ	the only-begotten Son of God [or: his only-begotten Son],
< . . . >	< . . . >
ἀναστάντα ἐκ [τῶν] νεκρῶν τῇ τρίτῃ ἡμέρᾳ [or: τῇ τρίτῃ ἡμέρᾳ ἀναστάντα ἐκ [τῶν] νεκρῶν]	rose again from [the] dead on the third day [or: on the third day rose again from [the] dead],
καὶ ἀνελθόντα [or: ἀναβάντα] εἰς τοὺς οὐρανοὺς	ascended [or: went up] into the heavens,
καὶ καθίσαντα [or: καθήμενον] ἐκ δεξιῶν [or: ἐν δεξιᾷ] τοῦ πατρὸς	sat down [or: sits] to the right hand [or: at the right hand] of the Father,
καὶ ἐρχόμενον [or: ὅθεν ἔρχεται] κρῖναι [or: κρίνειν] ζῶντας καὶ νεκρούς·	and will come [or: whence he is coming] to judge the living and the dead;
καὶ εἰς ἅγιον πνεῦμα,	and in the Holy Spirit,
ἁγίαν ἐκκλησίαν,	the holy Church,
ἄφεσιν ἁμαρτιῶν,	the remission of sins,
σαρκὸς ἀνάστασιν,	the resurrection of the flesh;
ζωὴν αἰώνιον.	eternal life.

Alternatively, the order of the remission of sins and the holy Church may have been reversed (which I do not consider very likely; cf. below). This creed closely resembles R[M], but its wording is not entirely identical with it. All remaining variants are best explained if we posit two different translations from a *Latin* version which may have run like this:

Credimus/credo in deum omnipotentem

et in Iesum Christum/Christum Iesum, filium dei [or: *eius*] *unigenitum, < . . . > resurgentem[259] a* [or: *ex*] *mortuis tertia die* [or: *tertia die resurgentem a* [or: *ex*] *mortuis*] *et ascendentem in caelos et sedentem ad dexteram* [or: *in dextera*] *patris et uenturum* [or: *unde uenturus* [*est*]] *iudicare uiuos et mortuos;*

et in sanctum spiritum, sanctam ecclesiam, remissionem peccatorum, [or: *remissionem peccatorum, sanctam ecclesiam*], *carnis resurrectionem, uitam aeternam.*

---

259 It is, perhaps, more likely to assume that a Latin present participle *resurgentem* was rendered by the Greek aorist participle ἀναστάντα than that a Latin relative clause *qui* [. . .] *resurrexit* (as is usually found in Latin versions of R[M]) was rendered in Greek by a participle. See also below p. 205 n. 261.

If we accept this hypothesis of two translations, then this creed is identical with R^M as regards content (except perhaps for τὸν κύριον ἡμῶν[260]).[261]

One problem remains: the incarnation and passion which may have been expressed in a very different manner in J and R^M. Kelly, from whom the above-quoted reconstruction is taken,[262] supplies the clauses [τὸν σαρκωθέντα καὶ] ἐνανθρωπήσαντα, [τὸν σταυρωθέντα καὶ ταφέντα καί] / 'who [was incarnate and] became human, [who was crucified and buried and]' for the passage indicated by < . . . >. However, I have argued elsewhere that the missing part of J may have run like this:[263]

[τὸν σαρκωθέντα]	[who was incarnate]
καὶ ἐνανθρωπήσαντα	and became human,
τὸν ἐκ Μαρίας τῆς παρθένου [καὶ ἁγίου πνεύματος] γεννηθέντα	who was born from the virgin Mary [and the Holy Spirit],
τὸν [ἐπὶ Ποντίου Πιλάτου] σταυρωθέντα	who was crucified [under Pontius Pilate]
καὶ ταφέντα	and was buried

Whereas the crucifixion (under Pontius Pilate?) and the burial are also mentioned in R^M, the clauses τὸν σαρκωθέντα καὶ ἐνανθρωπήσαντα would have no equivalent. In fact, at least ἐνανθρωπήσαντα could not have been a translation from Latin, since there was no Latin equivalent. All of this is, of course, highly speculative and only serves to indicate that the clauses on Christ's incarnation and passion may have resembled each other more closely than Kelly's reconstruction suggests.

There are other elements that were added to the *Vorlage* of J. Again, these additions appear to have been made after this creed had 'travelled' to Palestine. In what follows, I provide a list of witnesses for all additions to the *Vorlage*:

1. ἕνα θεόν: God's uniqueness is inconspicuous – this is found in a vast array of witnesses.

2. πατέρα: Irenaeus, *Aduersus haereses* 1,3,6 (frg. 1; FaFo § 109b1); 1,10,1 (§ 109b3); Antioch 325 (§ 133[8]); Novatian, *De trinitate* 1,1 (§ 119a); Arius and Euzoius, *Epistula ad Constantinum imperatorem* (Opitz 1934/1935, *Urkunde 30*; FaFo § 131c) 2; Eus (§ 134a);

---

260 Cf. above pp. 146 f.

261 It is striking, however, that in the christological section apparently no relative clauses were used as we know them from the usual Latin versions of R (cf. above pp. 146 f.).

262 Cf. Kelly 1972, p. 183 f., reprinted in FaFo § 147.

263 Cf. Kinzig, 'Origin', 2022, pp. 194–6.

Eusebius, *De ecclesiastica theologia* 2,6 (§ 134b3); N (§ 135c); Asterius of Cappadocia, *Fragment* 9 (§ 137a); Ant³ (§ 141a[2]); Ant² (§ 141b[1]); Ant⁴ (§ 141d[1]); Pseudo-Dionysius of Rome, *Epistula ad Dionysium Alexandrinum* (§ 142); Serdica (east) 343 (§ 143a1[1], a2 [1], b[1], c[1]); Macrostich Creed (§ 145[1]); Dêr Balyzeh Papyrus (§ 146); cf. also Rᴸ (Roman creed as given by Leo the Great; § 255a, g).

3. ποιητὴν οὐρανοῦ καὶ γῆς: Irenaeus, *Aduersus haereses* 3,1,2 (FaFo § 109b6): *factorem caeli et terrae*; 3,4,2 (§ 109b7): *fabricatorem caeli et terrae*; Antioch 325 (§ 133[8]).

4. ὁρατῶν τε πάντων καὶ ἀοράτων: Eus (FaFo § 134a): τῶν ἁπάντων ὁρατῶν τε καὶ ἀοράτων; N (§ 135c): πάντων ὁρατῶν τε καὶ ἀοράτων.

5. ἕνα κύριον: Alexander of Alexandria, *Epistula ad Alexandrum Thessalonicensem* (*Byzantinum*; Opitz 1934/1935, *Urkunde 14*; FaFo § 132) 46; Antioch 325 (§ 133[9]); Eus (§ 134a); N (§ 135c); Ant² (§ 141b[2]).

6. τὸν ἐκ τοῦ πατρὸς γεννηθέντα θεὸν ἀληθινὸν πρὸ πάντων τῶν αἰώνων: creed against Paul of Samosata (FaFo § 127[1]): τὸν ἐκ τοῦ πατρὸς πρὸ αἰώνων κατὰ πνεῦμα γεννηθέντα; Eus (§ 134a): πρὸ πάντων τῶν αἰώνων ἐκ τοῦ πατρὸς γεγεννημένον; Eusebius, *De ecclesiastica theologia* 1,8 (§ 134b2): τὸν πρὸ πάντων αἰώνων ἐκ τοῦ πατρὸς γεγεννημένον; Ant³ (§ 141a[3]): τὸν γεννηθέντα ἐκ τοῦ πατρὸς πρὸ τῶν αἰώνων; Ant² (§ 141b[2]): τὸν γεννηθέντα πρὸ τῶν αἰώνων ἐκ τοῦ πατρός; Ant⁴ (§ 141d[2]): τὸν πρὸ πάντων τῶν αἰώνων ἐκ τοῦ πατρὸς γεννηθέντα = Serdica (east) 343 (§ 143a2[2]) = Macrostich Creed (§ 145[2]). Θεὸν ἀληθινόν: N (§ 135c): θεὸν ἀληθινὸν ἐκ θεοῦ ἀληθινοῦ. It appears that θεὸν ἀληθινόν was added (from N?) to τὸν ἐκ τοῦ πατρὸς γεννηθέντα πρὸ πάντων τῶν αἰώνων in order to emphasize the Son's divinity.

7. δι᾽ οὗ τὰ πάντα ἐγένετο: Jn 1:3 (πάντα δι᾽ αὐτοῦ ἐγένετο); 1Cor 8:6 and Heb 2:10 (δι᾽ οὗ τὰ πάντα); Irenaeus, *Epideixis* 6 (FaFo § 109a2); Tertullian, *Aduersus Praxeam* 2,1 (§ 111e1); Eus (§ 134a); Arius and Euzoius, *Epistula ad Constantinum imperatorem* (Opitz 1934/1935, *Urkunde 30*; FaFo § 131c) 2; N (§ 135c); Ant² (§ 141b[3]); Ant¹ (§ 141c[4]); Ant⁴ (§ 141d[2]); Serdica (east) 343 (§ 143a1[2], a2[2], b[2], c[2]); Macrostich Creed (§ 145[2]).

8. ἐν δόξῃ: Irenaeus, *Aduersus haereses* 3,4,2 (FaFo § 109b7); 3,16,6 (§ 109b9); Eus (§ 134a).

9. οὗ τῆς βασιλείας οὐκ ἔσται τέλος: no earlier references, but cf. Serdica (east) 343 (FaFo § 143a2): οὗ ἡ βασιλεία ἀκατάλυτος οὖσα διαμένει εἰς τοὺς ἀπείρους αἰῶνας.

10. ἓν ἅγιον πνεῦμα: Serdica (east) 343 (FaFo § 143b[3]).

11. τὸν παράκλητον: *Epistula Apostolorum* 5(16) (FaFo § 103b); Ant[3] (§ 141a[4]); Ant[4] (§ 141d[4]); Serdica (east) 343 (§ 143a1[3], a2[3], b[3], c[3]); Serdica (west) 343 (§ 144a2[9]); Macrostich Creed (§ 145[3]).

12. τὸ λαλῆσαν ἐν τοῖς προφήταις: no earlier references.

13. εἰς ἓν βάπτισμα μετανοίας εἰς ἄφεσιν ἁμαρτιῶν: no earlier references.

14. εἰς μίαν, *ἁγίαν καθολικὴν ἐκκλησίαν*: no earlier references, but cf. Arius and Euzoius, *Epistula ad Constantinum imperatorem* (Opitz 1934/1935, *Urkunde 30*; FaFo § 131c) 3: καὶ εἰς μίαν καθολικὴν ἐκκλησίαν τοῦ θεοῦ.

We can see from this list that almost none of the additions are found in western sources (not counting Irenaeus a western author). The only exceptions are no. 2: πατέρα which is also found in Novatian (but which is hardly significant) and no. 7: δι' οὗ τὰ πάντα ἐγένετο which is also found in Tertullian where, however, it forms part of an edited quotation of Jn 1:3.

Furthermore, we find a certain number of additions that are found nowhere else before J:

– It is clear from Cyril's own words that no. 9 οὗ τῆς βασιλείας οὐκ ἔσται τέλος is directed against Marcellus, who – as Cyril puts it – had recently taught that after the end of the world Christ would no longer be ruling and that the Logos would be resolved into the Father and cease existing.[264] It seems plausible to assume that Cyril himself made this addition to J (which was later taken over by the Second Ecumenical Council[265]) in order to combat Marcellus' doctrines.

– The reference to the prophets (no. 12: τὸ λαλῆσαν ἐν τοῖς προφήταις) was probably inserted in order to define the Spirit more precisely by tying it to the Old Testament: it is the Spirit of the *prophets* who is worshipped among Christians but

---

264 Cf. Cyril, *Catechesis ad illuminandos 15*, 27. Through his use of the present tense Cyril may even imply that Marcellus taught the end of the world had already come and Christ's reign had already ended. Cf. also Cyril, *Catechesis ad illuminandos 15*, 31–33. The eternity of the divine kingdom is also underlined in *Catecheses 4*, 15; *15*, 17; *18*, 20. On Marcellus' teaching on this point cf. frgs. 101–4, 106–7, 109, 111 (Vinzent) where an end to Christ's kingdom is envisaged after the Final Judgement. Cf. also Synod of Serdica (342), *Epistula synodalis* (east) (Brennecke et al. 2007, *Dokument 43.11*) 3: '[. . .] who [sc. Marcellus] with a sacrilegious mind, profane speech, and corrupt argument wishes to limit the everlasting, eternal, and timeless kingdom of Christ the Lord; he says that four hundred years ago the Lord had accepted the beginning of his reign and that the end for him would arrive together with the end of the world.' In addition, Seibt 1994, pp. 429–41; Vinzent 1997, pp. LXIV–LXVIII.
265 Cf. Kinzig, *Glaubensbekenntnis*, 2021, p. 45.

was already present and active at the time of the Old Testament.[266] The insistence on the Spirit's continuous activity across the history of salvation made it possible to ward off enthusiastic pneumatologies such as those held by the Montanists, who venerated Montanus as the Paraclete,[267] beliefs which certainly still existed in various forms in the fourth century, or those current among the Messalians and similar ascetic groups. Likewise, this reference rebutted any suggestion of a dualism between the God of the Old and New Testament and, as a result, of a duality of spirits. Such a doctrine was ascribed by Cyril himself to the Marcionites and the Manichaeans.[268] By contrast, Cyril seeks to demonstrate time and again in his sermons that the coming of Christ and the events in the New Testament were foretold by the prophets and that the Holy Spirit had spoken in both the Old and the New Testament.[269] He may, therefore, have added this clause himself.

– It is difficult to say why and by whom the belief 'in one baptism of repentance' (no. 13: εἰς ἓν βάπτισμα μετανοίας) was added, why it was combined with the remission of sins (εἰς ἄφεσιν ἁμαρτιῶν) and what it actually means.[270] Cyril himself discusses penitence at some length in *Catecheses 2* and *8,* but he does not discuss the syntagma βάπτισμα μετανοίας which occurs only in *18,* 22 in his sermons, in a quotation from J. It is even more puzzling when one remembers that in the New Testament, the phrase 'baptism of repentance' is associated with the baptism of John, which is superseded by the coming of Christ.[271] Most likely, the syntagma βάπτισμα μετανοίας is not technical here. The relation between penitence and baptism is discussed in *3,* 15, where Cyril quotes Acts 2:38 to show that penitence and baptism are intimately interconnected.

The emphasis on the singularity of baptism may be directed against its repetition. Cyril himself argues against a repetition of baptism, but it is difficult to see which groups he envisages in his polemics. They cannot have been those advocating rebaptism of heretics wishing to join the catholic Church, because Cyril himself sup-

---

266 This may, perhaps, be based on 2Pet 1:21; cf. Kelly 1972, p. 341; Staats 1999, p. 258 and pp. 261–4. Cf. also Rom 1:2 and Heb 1:1 and Kinzig, *Glaubensbekenntnis,* 2021, p. 48. Cf. also below pp. 372 f.

267 Cf. Cyril, *Catechesis ad illuminandos 18,* 8.

268 Cf. Cyril, *Catechesis ad illuminandos 16,* 6–7. The phrase was later transplanted into the creeds of Constantinople as τὸ λαλῆσαν διὰ τῶν προφητῶν. Cf. below pp. 372 f.

269 Cf., e.g., Cyril, *Catecheses ad illuminandos 4,* 16; *16,* 3–4. 24–32; *17,* 5. 18.

270 Cyril himself later quotes the phrase again in *Mystagogia 1,* 9 (FaFo § 631a; if authentic), but without the remission of sins. It is also given in Epiphanius, *Ancoratus* 119,11 (FaFo § 175) as well as in a closely related creed which is ascribed to Athanasius (*Interpretatio in symbolum* (§ 185)). In the first instance the remission of sins is not mentioned, in the Pseudo-Athanasian creed there is a characteristic variation: εἰς ἓν βάπτισμα μετανοίας καὶ ἀφέσεως ἁμαρτιῶν. Cf., furthermore, Proclus of Constantinople, *Homilia in theophania* 11,71 in a similar context.

271 Cf. Mk 1:4; Lk 3:3; Acts 13:24; 19:4.

ports this very practice.[272] He may instead have in mind Jewish-Christian groups such as the Hemerobaptists, which performed frequent cleansing rituals. The Elchasaites were credited with preaching the forgiveness of sins by means of a second baptism.[273] The Marcionites (who figure prominently in Cyril's catecheses[274]) were said to have repeated baptism to wash off post-baptismal sins.[275] There were also those who repeated baptism out of fear.[276]

Additionally, one may ponder whether J did not run like this: καὶ εἰς ἓν βάπτισμα μετανοίας καὶ εἰς ἄφεσιν ἁμαρτιῶν ('and in one baptism of repentance and in the remission of sins'). In this case, it would have contained two separate clauses explicating the work of the Spirit. Otherwise, the remission of sins may have been joined to the baptism of repentance in order to explain at what point it actually occurred.[277] Moreover, in J, baptism may precede the Church because the latter is thought to be constituted through that baptism. (However, Cyril does not comment on this.) By contrast, in R^M, baptism follows the Church because it is administered by the Church.[278]

– Finally, its oneness and catholicity were added to the holiness of the Church (no. 14: εἰς μίαν, ἁγίαν, καθολικήν ἐκκλησίαν). This oneness corresponds to that of the three persons of the Trinity and of baptism. Cyril emphasizes that there is only one true ἐκκλησία as opposed to the false churches of the heretics (18, 26). The Church is called 'holy' to distinguish the second Church in the history of salvation (i.e. of the Gentiles) from the first Church (of the Jews; 18, 25). Cyril also gives five reasons for its catholicity (i.e. universality): it has spread over the entire world; it teaches universally and unceasingly all that is necessary to know about the faith; it teaches the entire human race; it heals all sins that have been committed; lastly, it possesses every kind of Christian virtue (18, 23). The combination of the three attributes only occurs in J and may well stem from Cyril himself.

This list of additions not found before J also reveals a close proximity between J and Eus, which is hardly surprising, since J and the *regula fidei* on which Eus is

---

272 Cf. Cyril, *Procatechesis* 7.
273 Cf. Ferguson 2009, pp. 72–74. For the repetition of baptism to attain forgiveness of sins in the group of the Elchasaites cf. Hippolytus, *Refutatio omnium haeresium* 9,13,4.
274 Cf. Cyril, *Catecheses ad illuminandos 6*, 16; *16*, 4. 7; *18*, 26, but in a different context.
275 Cf. Epiphanius, *Panarion* 42,3,6–10 and Ferguson 2009, p. 278 and n. 9.
276 Cf. Leo the Great, *Epistula 159*, 7 and Ferguson 2009, p. 765.
277 The version in the Pseudo-Athanasian creed (cf. above p. 208 n. 270) makes it even clearer: εἰς ἓν βάπτισμα μετανοίας καὶ ἀφέσεως ἁμαρτιῶν.
278 Cf., e.g., Rufinus, *Expositio symboli* 37: 'Those therefore who have already been taught to believe in one God, under the mystery of the Trinity, must believe this also, that there is one holy Church, in which there is one faith and one baptism, [. . .]' (tr. Morison 1916, pp. 49 f.).

based[279] stem from the same region (nos. 2, 4, 5, 6, 7, 8). The most significant variant displayed only by Eus and J (excepting Irenaeus) is the addition of ἐν δόξῃ to the parousia. The almost identical overlaps found in N (nos. 2, 4, 5, 6, 7) are not particularly surprising either, given N's close relationship with Eus.[280] Thus, there is no conclusive evidence that N influenced J at all. However, earlier scholarship often assumed that J was the *Vorlage* for N.[281] This earlier hypothesis moreover appears to be difficult to continue supporting in view of those differences which are not easily explained as revisions.[282]

The remaining sources for J partly draw on N and are, therefore, bound to show the same similarities. This is true especially of Ant[2] (nos. 2, 5, 6, 7), Ant[4] (nos. 2, 6, 7, 11), of Serdica (east; nos. 2, 6, 7, 10, 12), and of the Macrostich Creed (nos. 2, 6, 7, 11).

The similarities of J to other sources are less significant:
- Irenaeus, *Aduersus haereses*: nos. 2, 3, 7, 8.
- Ant[3]: nos. 2, 6, 11.
- Antioch 325: nos. 2, 3, 5.
- Arius and Euzoius, *Epistula ad Constantinum*: nos. 2, 7, 14.

All other sources display only one parallel.

The complex case of Pontius Pilate notwithstanding, there may be a difference in wording, but J exhibits no discernible additions to the content in R[M] with possibly one exception. This concerns the positioning and precise formulation of belief in the 'Lord'. Whereas J places the 'one Lord' at the beginning of its christological section, R[M] places 'our Lord' after τὸν υἱὸν αὐτοῦ τὸν μονογενῆ. The reading in J seems to be certain and the word was probably moved to harmonize it with 'one God', 'one Holy Spirit', 'one baptism', and 'one Church'.[283] It appears, therefore, more likely that 'our Lord' in R[M] is the original reading.

---

279 Cf. below ch. 6.3.
280 Cf. ch. 6.4.2.
281 Cf., e.g., Lietzmann 1922–1927(1962), pp. 254–9; Staats 1999, pp. 162–5. Cf., however, Kelly 1972, pp. 227 f.
282 Cf., e.g., N's omission of οὐρανοῦ καὶ γῆς; πρὸ πάντων τῶν αἰώνων; καὶ καθίσαντα ἐκ δεξιῶν τοῦ πατρός, the position of μονογενῆ, and the brief third article.
283 Cf. Cyril, *Catecheses ad illuminandos* 7, 4; 10, title. Nevertheless, in *Catechesis 17*, 34 (Reischl/Rupp 1848/1860, vol. II, p. 292) Cyril sums up the content of the creed like this: [. . .] εἰς ἕνα θεὸν πατέρα παντοκράτορα, καὶ εἰς τὸν κύριον ἡμῶν Ἰησοῦν Χριστόν, τὸν υἱὸν αὐτοῦ τὸν μονογενῆ, καὶ εἰς τὸ πνεῦμα τὸ ἅγιον τὸν παράκλητον. / '[. . .] and in one God, the Father Almighty, and in our Lord Jesus Christ, his only-begotten Son, and in the Holy Spirit, the Paraclete.' It is somewhat surprising that Cyril here does not say εἰς ἕνα κύριον ('in one Lord') in relation to Jesus Christ, especially as the context does not warrant the mention of 'our' Lord. Could it be that here he remembers the old version of his creed?

In summary, J was probably based on a western creed that was closely related to, or even identical with, R[M] and which, therefore, likely originated in Rome.[284] Additions to this creed were made that might, in part or as a whole, stem from Cyril himself. That said, it is difficult to see how this creed would have made its way into the east, as relations between Rome and Jerusalem in the first half of the fourth century were infrequent if they existed at all.[285] I have suggested elsewhere that Cyril's predecessor Maximus (*sedit c.* 334–348/350) may have had a hand in its migration, in connection with the festivities which Emperor Constantine had convoked to mark the dedication of the Church of the Holy Sepulchre in mid-September 335.[286] It is also important to note that the dedication was not simply a festive gathering – it was also a proper synod that adopted and promulgated canonical decrees. We possess its encyclical in which the bishops in Alexandria and Egypt were asked to receive the Arians back into the Church. The synod had been prompted to reach this decision by Constantine who had examined the Arians' faith and had found no fault.[287] The emperor had a creed attached to his letter of invitation which documented this orthodoxy and to which the bishops assembled in Jerusalem had then agreed.[288] Unfortunately, this letter is no longer extant.[289] It is possible that the Arians, whose identity is unknown, had used the creed of the capital for this purpose because its theological indistinctness meant

---

284 Kelly's argument against such a hypothesis (cf. Kelly 1972, pp. 201 f.) rests on the unfounded assumption that the 'eastern creeds' which he enumerates (cf. above pp. 200 f.). were already in existence at the beginning of the fourth century (Kelly 1972, p. 181).

285 Cf. Drijvers 2004, pp. 1–31 mentions no such relations. Likewise there is no mention in Pietri 1976, vol. I, pp. 187–237. There is no convincing evidence that R[M] was adopted in Jerusalem (via Antioch or in whatever other way) before the fourth century, as Kattenbusch and (at least partly) Harnack assumed (cf. above pp. 17 f. and Kinzig, 'Origin', 2022, p. 190 n. 17). Several similar creeds appear to have co-existed in Rome at the beginning of the fourth century with R[M] ultimately winning the day. Cf. above ch. 5.1.

286 Cf. Kinzig, 'Origin', 2022, pp. 203–6.

287 Cf. Athanasius, *De synodis* 21,2–7.

288 Cf. Athanasius, *De synodis* 21,4: 'Our most-devout emperor has also in his letter testified to the correctness of [the men's] faith (πίστεως ὀρθοτομίαν). He has ascertained it from them, himself receiving the profession of it from them by word of mouth, and has made it manifest to us by subjoining to his own letters the men's orthodox opinion in writing (ὑποτάξας τοῖς ἑαυτοῦ γράμμασιν ἔγγραφον τὴν τῶν ἀνδρῶν ὀρθοδοξίαν), which we all confessed to be sound and ecclesiastical' (tr. NPNF; altered).

289 It is probably not the creed of Arius and Euzoius (cf. FaFo § 131c), as our sources claim (Rufinus, *Historia ecclesiastica* 10,12; Socrates, *Historia ecclesiastica* 1,33,1; cf. 1,25; Sozomen, *Historia ecclesiastica* 2,27), because by that time Arius himself appears no longer to have been alive. (Constantine only mentions the adherents of Arius and the presbyters around Arius in his lost letter to the council, but not the heresiarch himself; cf. Council of Jerusalem (335), *Epistula synodalis* (Brennecke et al. 2007, *Dokument* 39), 2. 5.) Cf. Brennecke et al. 2007, pp. XXXVI–XXXVIII, 129.

that it was entirely compatible with their doctrines (in which case their tactics would have been similar to that of Marcellus of Ancyra, who later also quoted the Roman credal interrogations in his letter to Julius of Rome for apologetic purposes). Alternatively, Constantine himself may have chosen R^M for the purpose of building theological bridges (perhaps on the suggestion of one of his advisers[290]), because it did not contain those very clauses in N that had offended the Arians.

This creed may well have been solemnly adopted by the bishops in the course of the celebrations that Eusebius mentions, so as to seal the Arians' reception back into the fold. In addition, the anniversary of the dedication was celebrated each year and new converts (or infants?) were baptized on the occasion, according to Sozomen.[291] A creed would have been necessary if baptisms were administered on a grander scale during the dedication festivities themselves. Cyril or one of his predecessors may have subsequently extended this confession.

This hypothesis regarding the transmission of the creed into the east is admittedly sheer speculation. The precise circumstances of the process remain shrouded in the darkness of time. Nevertheless, there can be little doubt that J is in its basic structure of western and that is, Roman, origin. As we shall see, it later influenced the production of the creeds of Constantinople (C^1/C^2).[292]

---

290 Unfortunately, we know nothing about personal encounters between Pope Silvester (*sedit* 314–335) and the emperor nor about the relations between Ossius of Córdoba and Constantine after Nicaea. For Ossius cf. Kreis 2017, esp. p. 425.

291 Cf. *Historia ecclesiastica* 2,26,4: 'Since that time the church of Jersualem has celebrated this anniversary of the consecration with great splendour in such a way that initiations [i.e. baptisms] are performed in it, Church assemblies are held over eight days in a row, and many people from more or less every region under the sun assemble [in Jerusalem] who gather from everywhere at the time of this festival, following the story of the sacred places.' Cf. also Egeria, *Peregrinatio* 48–49.

292 Cf. below ch. 7.

6 Eastern Synodal Creeds from Nicaea up to Constantinople

We only find solid ground in our search for creeds when we reach the fourth century. That is the earliest time that formulae are attested which we may call declaratory creeds whose wording had been fixed. Such declaratory creeds were, above all, the product of synods, the special cases of Rome and Jerusalem notwithstanding (and even in Rome the declaratory form of R may go back to the synod of 340/ 341[1]). As we will see these synodal creeds are not original products but act upon each other: the synods took doctrinal material from earlier creeds and reassembled it like building blocks, at times adding some new material in the process, in such a way that the previous creed is either confirmed or rebutted in specific sections.[2] The most famous, albeit probably not the first, synodal creed is the confession of the First Ecumenical Council convened in Nicaea in 325. We will deal with it in chapter 6.4. But where did N come from? Was it produced in Nicaea from scratch or was there a model that the council took up and modified? What was the context of its composition? In order to elucidate this context, we will first look for antecedents in the documents produced in the course of the so-called Arian controversy (which not only focussed on the teaching of Arius).[3]

6.1 Arius and Alexander of Alexandria

The controversy began with a dispute in Alexandria between the presbyter Arius and his bishop Alexander over the question of the relationship between God the Father and God the Son. Its details can be found in any textbook on the history of theology. I will discuss this controversy here only as far as its origin and early theological content of the creed are concerned. In the course of this dispute, a group of presbyters and deacons from Alexandria and bishops from the province of *Libya*

---

1 Cf. above ch. 5.1.
2 On this 'building-block model' cf. above pp. 80 f. and n. 101.
3 For the problems involved in defining 'Arianism' cf. Kinzig, 'Areios und der Arianismus', 2018, pp. 1478–81. Recent scholarship has underlined and widely discussed the theological differences among those whom their opponents have lumped together under this title, above all, Arius, Asterius the Sophist, Eusebius of Nicomedia, and (to a certain extent) Eusebius of Caesarea (cf. the literature quoted in Kinzig, 'Areios und der Arianismus', 2018). Nonetheless, it is clear from all our sources (both Nicene and anti-Nicene) that there was a serious clash both at Antioch (325) and Nicaea between the supporters and opponents of Arius which may justify the use of the term for our purposes.

https://doi.org/10.1515/9783110318531-006

superior (Pentapolis), led by Arius, produced a document in 321 in which they intended to present the 'faith' (πίστις) of their forefathers to their Bishop Alexander.[4] However, they introduced the body of the text with the phrase 'we acknowledge' (οἴδαμεν), not yet using the term πιστεύομεν (which was later indispensable for this purpose). What follows is also quite obviously not a traditional, fixed formula, but a brief theological treatise that gives a long-winded description of the relationship between God the Father and God the Son, endeavouring to ward off opposing theological views. The text is not yet structured by reference to the persons of the Trinity – in fact, it is difficult to discern any clear structure at all.

This is typical of Arius' thinking in general:[5] it is hardly possible to make out a consistent system in his views from the extant sources. He placed a great emphasis on the complete sovereignty and transcendence of God. God alone is 'unbegotten/unborn' (ἀγέν[ν]ητος) and without beginning or origin, immaterial and not subject to any form of change. He freely decided to create the Son, who is completely separate from and subordinate to him as a distinct *hypóstasis* ('ontological entity'). Although this happened 'before all time', it does not exclude a logical priority of the Father before the Son, since the Son does not subsist timelessly or before/beyond time in eternity like the Father (hence the famous phrase which was condemned in Nicaea 325: ἦν ποτε ὅτε οὐκ ἦν, 'there was [a time] when he was not'[6]). Rather, in being unoriginate, the Father is essentially dissimilar to the Son. Arius explicitly rejected the consubstantiality of Father and Son which was later proclaimed at Nicaea.[7] The Son is therefore unable to recognize the οὐσία ('being', 'essence', 'substance') of the Father. However, as a result of divine grace, he has received a special knowledge of the Father which is not accessible to other creatures (who nevertheless have *some* 'knowledge of God'). It is by virtue of God's will alone that the Son is unchangeable and a perfect creature, which secures him a unique position of dignity compared to the other creatures. Unlike these, the Son, exercising his free will, has served the Father from the beginning in every way. Although Arius speaks of three *hypostáseis*, his doctrine of the Spirit remains rudimentary.

The Alexandrian presbyter appears to have tried to find a balance between the biblical evidence and the Platonic notion of God. He sought to express the oneness of God, as revealed in the Old Testament and logically deduced in philosophy, in such a way that it would not be endangered by the existence of a Son of

---

4 Cf. Arius et al., *Epistula ad Alexandrum Alexandrinum* (Opitz 1934/1935, *Urkunde 6*; FaFo § 131a).
5 The following paragraph is based on Kinzig, 'Areios und der Arianismus', 2018, pp. 1483 f.
6 For the precise meaning of ποτε and the resulting problems in translating this phrase cf. Markschies 2022.
7 Cf. below ch. 6.4.5.

God. At the same time, however, the Son's pre-eminent position as revealed in the New Testament was to be maintained. It has become clear in recent decades that the dispute triggered by Arius was also about the principles of the right interpretation of Scripture in the service of a rational and consistent theological doctrine.

When we now turn to the creed that Arius and his supporters sent to Bishop Alexander, it is obvious that the authors underline the alleged ontological distance between the 'one God' and the 'Son' by repeating μόνον ('alone') no less than eight times.[8] The Son was begotten 'before eternal times' and is called 'only-begotten', but it appears from the continuation of the confession that other 'things' or 'beings begotten' may exist (which are unlike the Son). The Son is at one and the same time a 'creature' while differing from other creatures by virtue of being 'perfect'. The act of begetting is not described in further detail except that it was effected solely by the Father's will.[9]

Subsequently, the authors distance themselves from the views of earlier theologians before returning to their main point: the relation between the Father and the Son, and the Son's ontological status. They affirm three divine *hypostáseis*. God is called 'unbegun', whereas the Son – albeit timelessly begotten by the Father – by virtue of being created does not share the same being 'with the Father' as this would create a danger of introducing 'two unbegotten beginnings'. Rather, it is made clear that the God exists 'before the Son'.

Finally, the authors reject the idea of a consubstantiality of the Son with the Father (they use the term ὁμοουσίου / 'of like/identical substance'), because in that case the Father would be 'composite, divisible, alterable, and a body'.[10] The authors say nothing further about the third *hypóstasis*, the Spirit. It may be a minor detail, but it

---

8 Arius et al., *Epistula ad Alexandrum Alexandrinum* (Opitz 1934/1935, *Urkunde 6*; FaFo § 131a) 2: Οἴδαμεν ἕνα θεόν, μόνον ἀγέννητον, μόνον ἀίδιον, μόνον ἄναρχον, μόνον ἀληθινόν, μόνον ἀθανασίαν ἔχοντα, μόνον σοφόν, μόνον ἀγαθόν, μόνον δυνάστην [. . .]. / 'We acknowledge one God, alone unbegotten, alone everlasting, alone unbegun, alone true, alone possessing immortality, alone wise, alone good, alone sovereign [cf. 1Tim 6:15]; [. . .].'
9 Arius et al., *Epistula ad Alexandrum Alexandrinum* (Opitz 1934/1935, *Urkunde 6*; FaFo § 131a) 2: [. . .] πάντων κριτήν, διοικητήν, οἰκονόμον, ἄτρεπτον καὶ ἀναλλοίωτον, δίκαιον καὶ ἀγαθόν, νόμου καὶ προφητῶν καὶ καινῆς διαθήκης θεόν, γεννήσαντα υἱὸν μονογενῆ πρὸ χρόνων αἰωνίων, δι' οὗ καὶ τοὺς αἰῶνας καὶ τὰ ὅλα πεποίηκε, γεννήσαντα δὲ οὐ δοκήσει, ἀλλὰ ἀληθείᾳ, ὑποστήσαντα ἰδίῳ θελήματι, ἄτρεπτον καὶ ἀναλλοίωτον, κτίσμα τοῦ θεοῦ τέλειον, ἀλλ' οὐχ ὡς ἓν τῶν κτισμάτων, γέννημα, ἀλλ' οὐχ ὡς ἓν τῶν γεγεννημένων [. . .]. / 'Judge, Governor, and Overseer of all; unalterable and unchangeable, just and good, God of the Law, the Prophets, and the New Testament; who begot an only-begotten Son before eternal times, through whom he has made both the ages and the universe [cf. 1Cor 8:6]; begot him, not in appearance, but in truth; that he made him subsist by his own will, unalterable and unchangeable; perfect creature of God, but not as one of the creatures; offspring, but not as one of things begotten; [. . .].'
10 Cf. also below pp. 256 f.

is striking that they are careful to call the highest being 'God' when they describe his specific ontological status, his aseity (as medieval theologians would later say); yet 'Father' in his relation to the Son *and in this relation only*. What is implied here is the idea that 'Father' is a relational term and not a term describing God's essence. As God existed 'before' the generation of the Son he was not always 'Father'.[11]

Is this a creed? Yes and no. First of all, the text presents itself as an explication of the 'faith' held by a group of authors who express their personal commitment to the theological tenets it contains. But the authors are clearly struggling to formulate the content of their faith. This observation, however, is not irrelevant to the question of the origins of the creeds. For the authors do *not* refer to a 'rule of faith', let alone a fixed formula, that they have to hand and which might have been taken over from baptismal catechesis (and thus from the 'fathers'). Rather, their problem (and in the debate with Alexander also their vulnerable point) is precisely that they do *not* have such a formula at their disposition which they could then simply interpret. Instead, it seems as if Arius and his comrades-in-arms referred to a binitarian 'kerygma' that had not yet been firmly fixed, to the content of a baptismal catechesis which was still fluid and, therefore, open to very different and indeed even completely contradictory interpretations. The beginning of their credal statement mentions the 'faith from our forefathers' which the authors had allegedly learned

---

11 Arius et al., *Epistula ad Alexandrum Alexandrinum* (Opitz 1934/1935, *Urkunde* 6; FaFo § 131a) 3–5: '[. . .] but, as we say, by the will of God (θελήματι τοῦ θεοῦ), created before times and before ages, and receiving life, being, and glories from the Father since the *hypóstasis* of the Father existed together with him (συνυποστήσαντος αὐτῷ τοῦ πατρός). For the Father did not, in bestowing the inheritance of all things upon him, deprive himself of what he possesses ingenerately (ἀγεννήτως) in himself; for he is the fountain of all things. Thus there are three *hypostáseis*. And God, being the cause of all things, is unbegun, altogether singular (ἄναρχος μονώτατος); but the Son being timelessly begotten (ἀχρόνως γεννηθείς) by the Father, and being created and founded before the ages, did not exist before he was generated (οὐκ ἦν πρὸ τοῦ γεννηθῆναι); but being timelessly begotten before all things, he alone was caused to subsist by the Father (μόνος ὑπὸ τοῦ πατρὸς ὑπέστη). For he is not eternal or coeternal or co-unbegotten with the Father, nor does he have his being together with the Father, as some speak of relations, introducing two unbegotten beginnings (ὥς τινες λέγουσι τὰ πρός τι, δύο ἀγεννήτους ἀρχὰς εἰσηγούμενοι). But God exists before all things in this way as the Monad and beginning of all things (ὡς μονὰς καὶ ἀρχὴ πάντων). Wherefore also he exists before the Son, as we have learned also from your preaching in the midst of the Church. Therefore, insofar as he possesses [his] being from God, and glories, life, and all things are delivered unto him [from God], in such sense is God his origin. For he is superior to him, as he is his God and exists before him. But if the phrases "from him", and "from the womb" [Ps 109(110):3], and "I came forth from the Father, and I am come" [Jn 8:42], are understood by some people to be a part of him, consubstantial, or something issuing [from him] (ὡς μέρος αὐτοῦ ὁμοουσίου καὶ ὡς προβολὴ ὑπό τινων), then according to them the Father is composite, divisible, alterable, and a body, and, as far as they are concerned, the incorporeal God endures the attendant characteristics of a body.'

from Alexander; however, this surely does not refer to a fixed formula, because otherwise the authors would no doubt have quoted such a formula. Rather it is intended as a general reference to the sum of theological doctrines imparted in catechesis and preaching which is less clearly defined than even a 'rule of faith'. Even when Arius and Euzoius submitted a creed to the emperor long after the Council of Nicaea, in 327, in order to clear themselves from the charge of heresy, they referred neither to a creed passed down within the church of Alexandria nor to N, but to a 'faith' derived 'from the holy gospels'.[12] In view of this evidence there should be little doubt that no fixed declaratory creed existed in Alexandria, and its sphere of influence, in the first two decades of the fourth century.

In fact, when one browses through the documents of the early Arian controversy compiled by Hans-Georg Opitz none of the protagonists cite a 'faith' which could be interpreted as a fixed formula handed over in baptism. Instead they mention 'faith' in a vague sense or refer summarily to Scripture or the teaching of the 'Church'.[13] In this respect, it is interesting to take a look at the tome which Alexander of Alexandria sent to all bishops (preserved in Syriac fragments only). In this circular letter he states *inter alia*:

> [. . .] and with regard to the right faith concerning the Father and the Son: just as the Scriptures teach us, we confess the one Holy Spirit and the one catholic Church and the resurrection of the dead, of which our Lord and Saviour Jesus Christ became the first fruits [cf. ICor 15:20], who put on the body from Mary, the Mother of God, in order to dwell among the human race, died, rose from the dead, was taken up into the heavens, and sits at the right hand of the Majesty [cf. Heb 1:3].[14]

This *looks* like what we would consider a 'traditional' fixed creed, but the order of the theological statements does not correspond to any of the confessions that have come down to us. When we turn to the letter that this Alexander wrote to Alexander of Thessaloniki (or of Byzantium) we see that the above-quoted passage from his letter to the bishops probably formed part of a much larger treatment of the doctrine of the Trinity. The letter to Alexander is a rambling discourse against Arian doctrines. It too contains a passage which resembles a creed, since it is introduced by a solemn

---

12 Arius and Euzoius, *Epistula ad Constantinum imperatorem* (Opitz 1934/1935, *Urkunde 30*; FaFo § 131c) 2.

13 Cf., e.g., Alexander of Alexandria, *Arii depositio* (Opitz 1934/1935, *Urkunde 4a*) 1 (the 'sound and catholic faith'); id., *Epistula encyclica* (Opitz 1934/1935, *Urkunde 4b*) 19 ('catholic faith and catholic Church'); id., *Tomus ad omnes episcopos* (Opitz 1934/1935, *Urkunde 15*) 2 (the 'right faith'); Eusebius of Nicomedia, *Epistula ad Paulinum Tyrium* (Opitz 1934/1935, *Urkunde 8*) 4 ('Scripture').

14 Alexander of Alexandria, *Tomus ad omnes episcopos* (Opitz 1934/1935, *Urkunde 15*) 2. A very similar passage is found in id., *Epistula ad Alexandrum Thessalonicensem (Byzantinum*; Opitz 1934/1935, *Urkunde 14*; FaFo § 132) 53.

introduction: 'Concerning whom [i.e. the Father and the Son] we believe just as seems good to the apostolic Church'.[15] The solemn finite verb πιστεύομεν is used here for the first time in a credal text in order to emphasize the importance of what is to follow. Again, Alexander does not refer to a specific 'faith' transmitted to him in baptism or elsewhere. What follows is clearly no fixed formula. Rather, he offers an explanation of the ontological status of Father and Son and their mutual relation, emphasizing that the Son was 'begotten not from that which does not exist, but from the Father who exists'. Alexander then tries to describe the Son's relation to the Father with the term εἰκών ('image'; Col 1:15), also referring to Heb 1:3 where ἀπαύγασμα ('radiance') and χαρακτήρ ('express image') are used in this context. Alexander insists on the eternal generation of the Son, but he finds it difficult to reconcile it with the fact that generation is a specific *act* which as such can only happen in time. After a lengthy discussion of this matter Alexander returns to the Holy Spirit who had inspired both the 'holy men' of the Old Testament and the 'divine teachers' of the New Testament. The bishop then moves on to mentioning the 'one and only one catholic, apostolic Church' (μίαν καὶ μόνην καθολικὴν τὴν ἀποστολικὴν ἐκκλησίαν) and the resurrection of the dead. At this point Alexander once again appends a brief christological summary containing the same clauses as in his letter to the bishops.

Apparently, in the church of Alexandria as represented by Alexander certain clauses had started to 'coagulate' around Christ and the Spirit. As regards Christ these included the incarnation from Mary (here termed as *theotókos*), his death, resurrection, ascension (or rather: assumption), and the sitting at the right hand. The Spirit is followed by a mention of the Church and the resurrection of the dead. The attributes of the Church ('one', 'catholic', and 'apostolic') serve to ward off Arius' claim of following the fathers, just as the reference to the 'apostolic Church' in the introduction to the credal passage.[16] In other words, Alexander's discourse is interspersed with traditional theologumena like croutons in an onion soup.

At the same time, the fact that such doctrinal statements were personally signed by the participants of a synod (as in the case of Alexander's encyclical[17]) suggests that bishops were increasingly personally held accountable for the acceptance or refusal of certain doctrines. We will consider this development in further detail below.[18]

---

15 Alexander of Alexandria, *Epistula ad Alexandrum Thessalonicensem (Byzantinum*; Opitz 1934/1935, *Urkunde 14*; FaFo § 132) 46: Περὶ ὧν ἡμεῖς οὕτως πιστεύομεν, ὡς τῇ ἀποστολικῇ ἐκκλησίᾳ δοκεῖ· [. . .].
16 Cf. above pp. 216 f.
17 Cf. Alexander of Alexandria, *Tomus ad omnes episcopos* (Opitz 1934/1935, *Urkunde 15*).
18 Cf. below p. 467.

6.2 The Council of Antioch (Spring 325) and its context

The Council of Antioch belongs to a series of events ultimately culminating in the Council of Nicaea.[19] Considering the latter first, Constantine's letter of invitation to it is usually dated to spring 325.[20] In it the emperor mentions a previous invitation to Ancyra (see below). It is, therefore, possible that the council that was in the end held in Nicaea had already been in the making as a great council of ecclesial unity by late 324, briefly after Constantine's victory over Licinius at Chrysopolis on 18 September 324.[21] To achieve that purpose of unity, a number of issues had to be addressed, including the date of Easter which was observed at different times in the empire, the Melitian schism which threatened the Egyptian church, and a number of jurisdictional and disciplinary problems which had to be settled.[22] As regards the Arian controversy, the emperor considered this a nuisance to be removed ahead of the council by writing to Alexander of Alexandria and Arius and banging their heads together.[23]

At the same time, the Arian controversy posed probably not only a political, but also a religious problem for him. He feared that strife in the Church might anger the divinity who had granted him victory over Licinius – Constantine's army had been accompanied by Christian priests whose prayers had obviously been more effective than those of their pagan counterparts on whose support Licinius had relied.[24] An angry deity, however, threatened the *salus publica* ('public welfare'). Therefore, a speedy solution had to be sought in order to quell the disturbances. To this end the emperor sent Bishop Ossius of Córdoba in the autumn of 324 on

---

19 Reconstructions of the prehistory of Nicaea differ considerably between scholars. For an alternative view (the council was summoned as a council of appeal by Ossius when Antioch failed) cf. Fernández 2020; Fernández 2023. However, presupposing that Fernández' chronology is right, it would only have been after March/April 325 (Synod of Antioch) that Constantine, at Ossius' behest, would have invited the bishops first to Ancyra and to Nicaea, where the council was opened in June (cf. Fernández 2020, pp. 209 f.; Fernández 2023, pp. 102 f.). This period is too short.
20 Cf. Constantine, *Epistula ad episcopos* (Opitz 1934/1935, *Urkunde 20*).
21 Date according to Barnes 1982, p. 75.
22 Cf. Brennecke 1994, pp. 434–6. On the Easter question cf. also Gwynn 2021, pp. 102–4; McCarthy 2021; on the Melitian schism Gwynn 2021, pp. 104; on the disciplinary canons Gwynn 2021, pp. 105 f.; Weckwerth 2021.
23 In his letter to Alexander and Arius, Constantine emphasizes time and again that he considered the affair to be insignificant; cf. *Epistula ad Alexandrum Alexandrinum et Arium* (Opitz 1934/1935, *Urkunde 17*) 4–6. 9–10. 12–14. Stuart Hall, Paul Parvis, and Sophie Cartwright have suggested that this letter was directed to the Council of Antioch; cf. Hall 1998; Paul Parvis 2006; Cartwright 2015, pp. 15–16. The letter's address notwithstanding, I hesitate to concur in view of section 6 in which Alexander and Arius are explicitly addressed, although the argument of these scholars is admittedly powerful.
24 Cf. Eusebius, *Vita Constantini* 2,4.

a mission to reconcile Alexander and Arius, equipping his envoy with a letter addressed to both adversaries in which he ordered them to resolve their squabbles quietly among each other.[25] This mission was unsuccessful. Ossius then seems to have sought a settlement at a council held in Antioch, probably in March/April 325.[26]

*

The creed produced by this gathering is included in a letter of the synod which was, perhaps, addressed to Alexander of Byzantium (Constantinople).[27] The authenticity of this letter has often been questioned, not least because the synod is not mentioned anywhere else by the writers of the fourth and fifth centuries.[28] Eduard Schwartz edited it from a Syriac manuscript (cod. Paris, Bibliothèque Nationale, syr. 62, ff. 144r–147r; s. IX), together with an ancient editorial note (see below) and a Greek retroversion which was subsequently corrected by Luise Abramowski.[29] Meanwhile further manuscripts containing this letter have been discovered.[30] A new edition of all relevant documents, accompanied by an extensive commentary, was recently prepared by Matthias Simperl.[31]

There are problems concerning the identity of the synod. In most manuscripts the letter is appended to the twenty-five canons which appear to belong to

---

25 On Ossius cf. Kreis 2017 who points out how little we know about him, the precise nature of his mission, and his contacts with the court.

26 On the date of the council cf. the discussion in Burgess 1999, p. 189. Simperl now advocates a date between late autumn 324 and late winter 324/325 (Simperl 2022, p. 243).

27 Cf. Council of Antioch (325), *Epistula synodica*. The identity of the addressee is uncertain (Alexander of Thessaloniki?); cf. Simperl 2022, pp. 232–5.

28 Cf. the literature listed in FaFo § 133. The entire problem is now comprehensively discussed in Simperl 2022. There is a letter by Constantine which is quoted in the *Historia uniuersalis* by Agapius of Manbiǧ (Hierapolis; s. X) in which the emperor says (Vasiliev 1911, p. 546): 'With the first synod having met in the city of Antioch in a contentious manner, we have decided to convoke another meeting in the city of Nicaea' (tr. Galvão-Sobrinho 2013, p. 83). The problem with this citation is that the Council of Nicaea had first been summoned to Ancyra. This is also the emendation and translation by the editor of this text, Alexandre Vasiliev, who erroneously identifies it with the Synod in 314 (cf. also Galvão-Sobrinho 2013, p. 226 nn. 51 and 52). According to Simperl, the text of the passage is corrupt, and the translation suggested by Galvão-Sobrinho untenable (cf. Simperl 2022, p. 26 n. 167). The letter is largely identical with *Urkunde 20* and would urgently need further investigation.

29 Cf. Schwartz 1905(1959), pp. 136–143, reprinted (without the note) as *Urkunde 18* in Opitz 1934/1935, pp. 36–41. (Schwartz himself did not consider his Greek text, strictly speaking, a 'retroversion', cf. Schwartz 1905(1959), p. 135.) Cf. also Abramowski 1975(1992), pp. 1–4. An English translation of the letter (although without the beginning and without Abramowski's corrections) is found in Stevenson/Frend 1987, pp. 334–7. A complete English translation was made by Cross 1939, pp. 71–6. The credal part of this Greek version and an English translation is also found in FaFo § 133.

30 Cf. Simperl 2022, pp. 7 f., 34–81.

31 Cf. Simperl 2022.

the Dedication Council held in Antioch in 341.[32] In addition, it is followed by a rather confused note[33] from an unknown historical source saying that another letter on the same subject had been sent to the Italian bishops. They had replied and affirmed the creed and canons. In addition, they had sent another twenty-five canons to Antioch which had then been passed on to the eastern bishops and which the unknown author promises to include later in his book. (So he seems to assume that the series of twenty-five canons issued by the Antiochene Council of 341 (which are clearly eastern in origin) in fact originated from Italy.) The author finishes by expressing his astonishment regarding the fact that the fathers in Antioch had not used *homooúsios*, although their council had taken place after Nicaea where many of the Antioch synodals had also been present.

The origin of the letter is, therefore, slightly dubious. It is also peculiar that it begins in the first person singular, but later switches to the first person plural. The text opens with the salutation to Alexander and includes a long list of bishops who have sent the letter. Ossius of Córdoba and Eustathius, bishop of Antioch (who probably presided the synod[34]) headed the list. The following two sections (2–3) form a kind of cover letter, perhaps by Ossius,[35] that originally accompanied the synodal letter itself which begins not until section 4.[36] It is obvious from this cover letter that the synod took place as part of Ossius' mission of reconciliation between the quarrelling factions in the Arian dispute. The list of provinces included in section 3 (Palestine, Arabia, Phoenice, Coele Syria, Cilicia, and Cappadocia) demonstrates the extent of the problem in geographical terms.

The authors complain about the confusion that had arisen with regard to the 'law of the Church and its canon' (section 4).[37] They claim that bishops in these provinces had been prevented from holding synods. It is suggested (although not

---

32 Cf. below ch. 6.5.1. For the canons cf., e.g., Stephens 2015, pp. 60–80; Simperl 2022, pp. 63–76, 210–5. For the context cf. also Simperl 2022, pp. 52–5, 86–91.

33 Cf. Schwartz 1905(1959), p. 143; Simperl 2022, pp. 61–3.

34 Cf. Chadwick 1958(2017); Simperl 2022, pp. 279 f.

35 According to Simperl Eustathius authored the entire document; cf. Simperl 2022, pp. 251, 278–80.

36 There appears to be a brief return to the first person singular in Opitz 1934/1935, p. 37, l. 17 (Greek) text: λέγω δή. This may, however, either be a marginal gloss which was at some point inserted into the text, or, more likely, occurs because λέγω δή is used as a fixed formula regardless of the grammatical number (in the sense of 'that is'). Such carelessness is often found in papyri (cf. Mayser 1934(1970), p. 187).

37 Opitz 1934/1935 (who reproduces Schwartz' Greek retroversion), p. 37, l. 13 should, perhaps, read: ὁ ἐκκλησιαστικὸς νόμος καὶ ὁ κανών (instead of οἱ κανόνες). Cf. Hubert Kaufhold in Ohme 1998, p. 383. This has been overlooked in Brennecke et al. 2007, p. 102. Simperl 2022, p. 288 thinks that the Greek could have read θεσμός instead of κανών.

spelled out) that this is the reason why Ossius (as the emperor's envoy) convoked the synod in order to pacify the situation, together with the bishop of Antioch, the capital of the (political) Diocese of the East (in which most of the provinces named were situated). The most important item on the agenda was the 'mystery of our faith', 'concerning the Saviour of us all, the Son of the living God', as the erroneous Arian doctrines were spreading all over the place after Alexander of Alexandria had expelled the supporters of Arius. The letter explicitly states that the gathering at Antioch had dealt at length with the teachings of Alexander (section 7). Furthermore, a creed is included (sections 8–13) which we will discuss below. This in turn is followed by a brief (and not very clear) account of the dealings conducted at the council with three dissenting bishops (Theodotus of Laodicea, Narcissus of Neronias, and Eusebius of Caesarea). It seems that they had been accused of teaching false doctrines, had been interrogated by the bishops assembled at the synod, and, finally, been convicted of Arianism. As they refused to recant before the synod, they were excluded from the fellowship with the bishops present at the council and deposed (section 14). Finally, Alexander of Byzantium is asked neither to receive the deposed bishops nor to write to them or receive letters of communion from them. The end of the letter also makes it clear that by that time a 'great and holy' synod had been summoned to Ancyra. Here the suspended bishops would be given an opportunity to repent and learn the right doctrine (section 15).

The creed included in the letter is so important that we have to look at it in some more detail:[38]

Creed of Antioch (325)
(Opitz 1934/1935, *Urkunde 18*; FaFo § 133)

[8] Ἔστιν οὖν ἡ πίστις [. . .] πιστεύειν εἰς ἕνα θεόν, πατέρα, παντοκράτορα, ἀκατάληπτον, ἄτρεπτον καὶ ἀναλλοίωτον, διοικητὴν καὶ οἰκονόμον πάντων, δίκαιον, ἀγαθόν, ποιητὴν οὐρανοῦ καὶ γῆς καὶ πάντων τῶν ἐν αὐτοῖς, νόμου καὶ προφητῶν καὶ τῆς καινῆς διαθήκης κύριον·	[8] Therefore the faith is [. . .] to believe in one God, the Father Almighty, incomprehensible, immutable, and unchangeable, governor and administrator of all, just, good, Maker of heaven, earth, and of all the things in them [cf. Ex 20:11; Ps 145-(146):6; Acts 4:24; 14:15], Lord of the Law, of the Prophets, and of the New Testament;

---

38 Council of Antioch (325), *Epistula synodica*. Greek text as reconstructed by Schwartz (= Opitz 1934/35, *Urkunde 18*) with the corrections by Abramowski 1975(1992), pp. 1–4; cf. FaFo § 133; further emendations by Simperl 2022 are given in the following footnotes. Extensive commentaries are found in Vinzent 1999, pp. 240–382; Simperl 2022, pp. 305–74.

[9] καὶ εἰς ἕνα κύριον Ἰησοῦν Χριστόν, υἱὸν μονογενῆ, γεννηθέντα οὐκ ἐκ τοῦ μὴ ὄντος, ἀλλ᾽ ἐκ τοῦ πατρός, οὐχ ὡς ποιητόν,[39] ἀλλ᾽ ὡς γέννημα κυρίως, γεννηθέντα δὲ ἀρρήτως καὶ ἀλέκτως, διότι μόνος ὁ πατὴρ ὁ γεννήσας καὶ ὁ υἱὸς ὁ γεννηθεὶς[40] ἔγνω. *Οὐδεὶς γὰρ*[41] *ἔγνω τὸν πατέρα εἰ μὴ ὁ υἱός, ἢ τὸν υἱὸν εἰ μὴ ὁ πατήρ,* τὸν ἀεὶ ὄντα καὶ οὐ πρότερον οὐκ ὄντα.

[10] Χαρακτῆρα γὰρ αὐτὸν μόνον ἐκ τῶν ἁγίων γραφῶν μεμαθήκαμεν, οὐ ὡς τὸ ἐκ τοῦ πατρὸς σημάντεον ἀγέννητον ὄντα οὐ θέσει (ἀσεβὲς γὰρ καὶ βλάσφημον τοῦτο λέγειν)· ἀλλὰ κυρίως καὶ ἀληθῶς υἱὸν λέγουσιν αὐτὸν αἱ γραφαὶ τὸν γεννητὸν ὄντα,[42] ὥστε καὶ[43] πιστεύομεν ἄτρεπτον εἶναι καὶ ἀναλλοίωτον αὐτὸν οὐδὲ θελήσει ἢ θέσει γεννηθῆναι ἢ γενέσθαι, ὥστε ἐκ τοῦ μὴ ὄντος αὐτὸν εἶναι φαίνεσθαι, ἀλλὰ καθὸ γεννηθῆναι αὐτὸν εἰκός, οὐδ᾽ ὅπερ οὐ θέμις ἐννοεῖν καθ᾽ ὁμοιότητα τῆς φύσεως ἢ μῖξιν οὐδενὸς τῶν δι᾽ αὐτοῦ γενομένων, [11] ἀλλὰ διότι ὑπερβαίνει πᾶσαν ἔννοιαν ἢ διάνοιαν ἢ λόγον, ἐκ τοῦ πατρὸς τοῦ ἀγεννήτου γεννηθῆναι αὐτὸν ὁμολογοῦμεν, θεὸν λόγον, φῶς ἀληθινόν, δικαιοσύνην, Ἰησοῦν Χριστόν, πάντων κύριον καὶ σω-

[9] and in one Lord Jesus Christ, only-begotten Son, begotten not from that which does not exist, but from the Father, not as something made, but as properly an offspring, and begotten in an ineffable and indescribable manner, because only the Father who begot and the Son who was begotten know [it]. For 'no one knew the Father except the Son, and [no one knew] the Son except the Father' [Mt 11:27; Lk 10:22], [the Son] who exists eternally and did not previously not exist.

[10] For we have learned from the holy Scriptures that he alone is the express image [cf. Heb 1:3], not unbegotten (as 'from the Father' signifies), nor by adoption (for it is impious and blasphemous to say this). Rather, the Scriptures call him properly and truly Son, existing as begotten such that we believe also that he is immutable and unchangeable; but not that he was begotten or came into being by volition or by adoption (whereby it would be clear that he existed from that which does not exist), but as it befitted him that he was born; nor according to a similarity of nature or commixture with anything which came into existence through him (which it is not lawful to think), [11] but, since it transcends all reflection or understanding or reasoning, we confess him to have

---

39 Simperl: ποίημα.

40 Καὶ ὁ υἱὸς ὁ γεννηθείς. Simperl reads: τὸν υἱὸν τὸν γεννηθέντα. This would suggest: 'because only the Father who begot knew the Son who was begotten'. Cf. Simperl 2022, pp. 329 f.

41 Simperl: διότι.

42 Τὸν γεννητὸν ὄντα. Text according to Simperl. Schwartz/Abramowski: γεννηθέντα.

43 Simperl: καὶ ἡμεῖς.

τῆρα. Εἰκὼν γάρ ἐστιν οὐ θελήσεως οὐδ᾽ ἄλλου τινός, ἀλλ᾽ αὐτῆς τῆς πατρικῆς ὑποστάσεως.[44]

Οὗτος δ᾽ ὁ υἱὸς θεὸς λόγος καὶ ἐν σαρκὶ ἐκ τῆς θεοτόκου Μαρίας τεχθεὶς[45] καὶ σῶμα φορέσας, παθὼν καὶ ἀποθανὼν ἀνέστη ἐκ νεκρῶν καὶ ἀνελήφθη εἰς οὐρανόν, κάθηται δὲ ἐν δεξιᾷ τῆς μεγαλοσύνης τῆς ὑψίστης ἐρχόμενος κρῖναι ζῶντας καὶ νεκρούς.

[12] Ἔτι δὲ ὡς καὶ τὸν σωτῆρα ἡμῶν[46] αἱ ἱεραὶ γραφαὶ διδάσκουσιν καὶ ἐν πνεῦμα[47] πιστεῦσαι, μίαν καθολικὴν ἐκκλησίαν, τὴν νεκρῶν ἀνάστασιν, καὶ κρίσιν ἀνταποδόσεως καθὰ ἔπραξέν τις ἐν σώματι εἴτε ἀγαθὰ εἴτε κακά.

[13] Ἀναθεματίζοντες ἐκείνους, οἳ λέγουσιν ἢ πιστεύουσιν ἢ κηρύττουσιν τὸν υἱὸν τοῦ θεοῦ κτίσμα ἢ γενητὸν ἢ ποιητὸν[48] καὶ οὐκ ἀληθῶς γέννημα εἶναι ἢ ὅτι ἦν ὅτε οὐκ ἦν – ἡμεῖς γάρ, ὅτι ἦν καὶ ἔστιν καὶ ὅτι φῶς ἐστιν,[49] πιστεύομεν –, προσέτι δὲ κἀκείνους, οἳ τῇ αὐτεξουσίῳ θελήσει αὐτοῦ ἄτρεπτον εἶναι αὐτὸν ἡγοῦνται, ὥσπερ καὶ οἱ ἐκ τοῦ μὴ ὄντος παράγοντες τὴν γέννησιν καὶ μὴ φύσει ἄτρεπτον κατὰ τὸν πατέρα. Χαρακτὴρ γὰρ ὡς ἐν

been begotten from the unbegotten Father, the God Word, true light, righteousness, Jesus Christ, Lord and Saviour of all. He is the image, not of the will or of anything else, but of the paternal *hypóstasis* itself [cf. 2Cor 4:4; Col 1:15; Heb 1:3].

But this Son, God the Word, was also born in flesh from Mary the Theotokos, assumed a body, suffered, died, rose again from the dead, was taken up into heaven, sits 'at the right hand of the Majesty most high' [Heb 1:3], [and] will come to judge the living and the dead.

[12] Furthermore, as also [in the case of] our Saviour, the holy Scriptures teach us to believe also one Spirit, one catholic Church, the resurrection of the dead, and a judgement of retribution according to what someone has done in the body, whether good or bad [cf. 2Cor 5:10 *v.l.*].

[13] We anathematize those who say, believe, and preach God's Son to be a creature or originated or made, and not as truly begotten, or that there was when he was not; we believe, indeed, that he was and is and that he is light; but along with them [we anathematize] those who suppose he is immutable through his own act of will, just as [we anathematize] those who also derive his birth from that which does not exist and [say] that he is not immutable in

---

44 Αὐτῆς τῆς πατρικῆς ὑποστάσεως. Simperl reads: αὐτοῦ τοῦ πατρῴου προσώπου ('of the paternal person itself').

45 Simperl: γεννηθείς.

46 Simperl: τὸν σωτῆρα ἡμῶν αὐτόν ('our Saviour himself').

47 Simperl: εἰς ἓν πνεῦμα ('in one Spirit').

48 Simperl: ποίημα.

49 Καὶ ὅτι φῶς ἐστιν. Simperl: καὶ ὅτι ἔσται ('and will be'). Cf. Simperl 2022, p. 372.

πᾶσιν, οὕτως καὶ μάλιστα ἐν τῷδε τοῦ πατρὸς ἐκηρύχθη ὁ σωτὴρ ἡμῶν.

nature as is the Father. For as the express image of the Father [cf. Heb 1:3], just in all things, so in this respect particularly, is our Saviour proclaimed.

It is clear that the letter takes up expressions and phrases from the 'faith' of Arius and his followers which I discussed above. This can be clearly seen placing the two creeds side by side:

'Faith' of Arius et al.	Creed of Antioch (325)
(Opitz 1934/1935, *Urkunde 6*; FaFo § 131a)	
[2] Οἴδαμεν **ἕνα θεόν**, μόνον ἀγέννητον, μόνον ἀίδιον, μόνον ἄναρχον, μόνον ἀληθινόν, μόνον ἀθανασίαν ἔχοντα, μόνον σοφόν, μόνον ἀγαθόν, μόνον δυνάστην, **πάντων** κριτήν, **διοικητήν, οἰκονόμον, ἄτρεπτον καὶ ἀναλλοίωτον, δίκαιον καὶ ἀγαθόν, νόμου καὶ προφητῶν καὶ καινῆς διαθήκης** θεόν, [. . .].[50]	[8] Ἔστιν οὖν ἡ πίστις [. . .] πιστεύειν εἰς **ἕνα θεόν**, πατέρα, παντοκράτορα, ἀκατάληπτον, **ἄτρεπτον καὶ ἀναλλοίωτον, διοικητὴν** καὶ **οἰκονόμον πάντων, δίκαιον, ἀγαθόν**, ποιητὴν οὐρανοῦ καὶ γῆς καὶ πάντων τῶν ἐν αὐτοῖς, **νόμου καὶ προφητῶν καὶ τῆς καινῆς διαθήκης** κύριον· [. . .].

What is significant here is not the occurrence of the individual expressions (many of which are fairly conventional), but their accumulation in one brief paragraph. However, the synodal letter uses these terms to make a point which differs from Arius'. I will return to this problem below.

In its christological section the synodal letter clearly follows in the footsteps of Alexander of Alexandria's letter to Alexander of Thessaloniki (Byzantium):

Alexander of Alexandria, *Epistula ad Alexandrum Thessalonicensem (Byzantinum)*	Creed of Antioch (325)
(Opitz 1934/1935, *Urkunde 14*; FaFo § 132)	
[46] [. . .] **καὶ εἰς ἕνα κύριον Ἰησοῦν Χριστόν**, τὸν υἱὸν τοῦ θεοῦ **μονογενῆ, γεννηθέντα οὐκ ἐκ τοῦ μὴ ὄντος, ἀλλ'**	[9] [. . .] **καὶ εἰς ἕνα κύριον Ἰησοῦν Χριστόν**, υἱὸν μονογενῆ, γεννηθέντα **οὐκ ἐκ τοῦ μὴ ὄντος, ἀλλ'** ἐκ τοῦ πα-

---

50 'We acknowledge one God, alone unbegotten, alone everlasting, alone unbegun, alone true, alone possessing immortality, alone wise, alone good, alone sovereign; Judge, Governor, and Overseer of all; unalterable and unchangeable, just and good, God of the Law, the Prophets, and the New Testament; [. . .].'

ἐκ τοῦ ὄντος **πατρός**, οὐ κατὰ τὰς τῶν σωμάτων ὁμοιότητας ταῖς τομαῖς ἢ ταῖς ἐκ διαιρέσεων ἀπορροίαις, ὥσπερ Σαβελλίῳ καὶ Βαλεντίνῳ δοκεῖ, ἀλλ᾽ **ἀρρήτως** καὶ ἀνεκδιηγήτως [. . .].
[47] Ἅπερ οὐ παρ᾽ ἐμοῦ δεῖ μαθεῖν ἄνδρας τῷ τῆς ἀληθείας πνεύματι κινουμένους, ὑπηχούσης ἡμᾶς καὶ τῆς φθασάσης Χριστοῦ περὶ τούτου φωνῆς καὶ διδασκούσης· *Οὐδεὶς οἶδε τίς ἐστιν ὁ πατήρ, εἰ μὴ ὁ υἱός· καὶ οὐδεὶς οἶδε τίς ἐστιν ὁ υἱός, εἰ μὴ ὁ πατήρ.*

τρός, οὐχ ὡς ποιητόν, ἀλλ᾽ ὡς γέννημα κυρίως, γεννηθέντα δὲ **ἀρρήτως** καὶ ἀλέκτως,

διότι μόνος ὁ πατὴρ ὁ γεννήσας καὶ ὁ υἱὸς ὁ γεννηθεὶς ἔγνω. *Οὐδεὶς γὰρ ἔγνω τὸν πατέρα εἰ μὴ ὁ υἱός, ἢ τὸν υἱὸν εἰ μὴ ὁ πατήρ,* τὸν ἀεὶ ὄντα καὶ οὐ πρότερον οὐκ ὄντα.

[10] Χαρακτῆρα γὰρ αὐτὸν μόνον ἐκ τῶν ἁγίων γραφῶν μεμαθήκαμεν, οὐ ὡς τὸ ἐκ τοῦ πατρὸς σημάντεον ἀγέννητον ὄντα οὐ θέσει (ἀσεβὲς γὰρ καὶ βλάσφημον τοῦτο λέγειν)·

Ἄτρεπτον τοῦτον καὶ **ἀναλλοίωτον** ὡς τὸν πατέρα, ἀπροσδεῆ καὶ τέλειον υἱόν, ἐμφερῆ τῷ πατρὶ μεμαθήκαμεν, μόνῳ τῷ ἀγεννήτῳ λειπόμενον ἐκείνου.

ἀλλὰ κυρίως καὶ ἀληθῶς υἱὸν λέγουσιν αὐτὸν αἱ γραφαὶ τὸν γεννητὸν ὄντα, ὥστε καὶ πιστεύομεν **ἄτρεπτον** εἶναι καὶ **ἀναλλοίωτον** αὐτὸν οὐδὲ θελήσει ἢ θέσει γεννηθῆναι ἢ γενέσθαι, ὥστε ἐκ τοῦ μὴ ὄντος αὐτὸν εἶναι φαίνεσθαι, ἀλλὰ καθὸ γεννηθῆναι αὐτὸν εἰκός, οὐδ᾽ ὅπερ οὐ θέμις ἐννοεῖν καθ᾽ ὁμοιότητα τῆς φύσεως ἢ μῖξιν οὐδενὸς τῶν δι᾽ αὐτοῦ γενομένων, [11] ἀλλὰ διότι ὑπερβαίνει πᾶσαν ἔννοιαν ἢ διάνοιαν ἢ λόγον, ἐκ τοῦ πατρὸς τοῦ ἀγεννήτου γεννηθῆναι αὐτὸν ὁμολογοῦμεν, θεὸν λόγον, φῶς ἀληθινόν, δικαιοσύνην, Ἰησοῦν Χριστόν, πάντων κύριον καὶ σωτῆρα.

Εἰκὼν γάρ ἐστιν ἀπηκριβωμένη καὶ ἀπαράλλακτος τοῦ πατρός. [48] Πάντων γὰρ εἶναι τὴν εἰκόνα πλήρη δι᾽ ὧν ἡ μείζων ἐμφέρεια δῆλον, ὡς αὐτὸς ἐπαίδευσεν ὁ κύριος *ὁ πατήρ μου λέγων μείζων μού ἐστι.* Καὶ κατὰ τοῦτο καὶ τὸ ἀεὶ

Εἰκὼν γάρ ἐστιν οὐ θελήσεως οὐδ᾽ ἄλλου τινός, ἀλλ᾽ αὐτῆς **τῆς πατρικῆς ὑποστάσεως.**

εἶναι τὸν υἱὸν ἐκ τοῦ πατρὸς πιστεύο-
μεν· Ἀπαύγασμα γάρ ἐστι τῆς δόξης καὶ
χαρακτὴρ **τῆς πατρικῆς ὑποστάσεως**.
[. . .]
[54] Μετὰ τοῦτο τὴν ἐκ νεκρῶν ἀνάστασιν οἴδαμεν, ἧς ἀπαρχὴ γέγονεν ὁ κύριος
ἡμῶν Ἰησοῦς Χριστὸς **σῶμα φορέσας**
ἀληθῶς καὶ οὐ δοκήσει **ἐκ τῆς θεοτόκου**
Μαρίας ἐπὶ συντελείᾳ τῶν αἰώνων εἰς
ἀθέτησιν ἁμαρτίας, ἐπιδημήσας τῷ γένει
τῶν ἀνθρώπων, σταυρωθεὶς καὶ **ἀπο-**
θανών, ἀλλ᾽ οὐ διὰ ταῦτα τῆς ἑαυτοῦ
θεότητος ἥττων γεγενημένος, **ἀναστὰς**
ἐκ νεκρῶν, ἀναληφθεὶς ἐν οὐρανοῖς,
καθήμενος **ἐν δεξιᾷ τῆς μεγαλοσύνης**.[51]

Οὗτος δ᾽ ὁ υἱὸς θεὸς λόγος καὶ ἐν σαρκὶ
ἐκ τῆς θεοτόκου Μαρίας τεχθεὶς καὶ
σῶμα φορέσας, παθὼν καὶ **ἀποθανὼν**
ἀνέστη ἐκ νεκρῶν καὶ ἀνελήφθη **εἰς**
οὐρανόν, κάθηται δὲ **ἐν δεξιᾷ τῆς μεγ-**
αλοσύνης τῆς ὑψίστης ἐρχόμενος κρῖναι ζῶντας καὶ νεκρούς.

The syntagma κρίσιν ἀνταποδόσεως in section 12 (which is probably influenced by Is 34:8) – if original – is conspicuous as it occurs in no other creed that I know of (this is also true for its Latin equivalent *iudicium retributionis*). (We find it in a vaguely similar context in the *Regulae morales* by Basil of Caesarea.[52]) Further-

---

51 '[46] [. . .] and in one Lord Jesus Christ, the only-begotten Son of God, begotten not from that which does not exist, but from the Father who exists; yet not [begotten] after the likeness of bodies by severance or emanation [resulting] from divisions, as Sabellius and Valentinus think, but in an inexpressible and inexplicable manner, [. . .]. [47] But those men who are led by the Spirit of truth [cf. Jn 16:13] have no need to learn these things from me for the words long since spoken by the Saviour in his teaching yet sound in our ears: "No one knows who the Father is except the Son, and no one knows who the Son is but the Father" [cf. Mt 11:27; Jn 10:15]. We have learned that the Son is immutable and unchangeable, all-sufficient and perfect, just like the Father, lacking only his "unbegotten". He is the exact and precise image of his Father. [48] For it is clear that the image fully contains everything by which the greater likeness exists, as the Lord taught us, saying, "My Father is greater than I" [Jn 14:28]. In accordance with this we believe that the Son always existed from the Father; for he is "the radiance of [his] glory and the express image of his Father's *hypóstasis*" [Heb 1:3]. [. . .] [54] After this, we acknowledge the resurrection from the dead, of which our Lord Jesus Christ became the first fruits [cf. 1Cor 15:20]; [he] was truly and not in appearance clothed in a body derived from Mary the Theotokos "at the consummation of the ages for the destruction of sin" [Heb 9:26], who dwelt among the human race; was crucified and died, yet for all this suffered no diminution of his godhead; rose again from the dead, was taken up into the heavens, sits "at the right hand of the Majesty" [Heb 1:3].'
52 Cf. *Regulae morales* 1,2 (PG 31, col. 700C): Ὅτι τῆς μετανοίας καὶ τῆς ἀφέσεως τῶν ἁμαρτιῶν ὁ παρών ἐστι καιρός· ἐν δὲ τῷ μέλλοντι αἰῶνι ἡ δικαία κρίσις τῆς ἀνταποδόσεως. / 'That the present time is one of repentance and forgiveness of sins; but in the world to come [there is] the just

more, the expression ἐν σώματι in this context is found in no other creed. Likewise, phrases are used in the anathemas that occur nowhere else, e.g., κτίσμα ἢ γενητὸν ἢ ποιητόν and τῇ αὐτεξουσίῳ θελήσει αὐτοῦ ἄτρεπτον. This seems to point to the authenticity of the creed, as a forger would probably have chosen more common phrases.

Given the similarities to the writings of Arius and, in particular, Alexander, and the use of rare phrases it is difficult to maintain that the entire letter is a forgery unless one thinks that this was a deliberate ruse in order to give the letter an air of authenticity. However, the objections Holger Strutwolf and others have raised against the letter's theological stance and some other observations[53] are not entirely without foundation either, so that it appears that the original text may have undergone some editing. The bishops mentioned in the initial list of senders and its content suggest that it was written in early 325. It may, therefore, be wise to take the historical information contained in this letter seriously, but to be cautious with regard to its theological argument where it cannot be viewed as a *direct* response to the theologies of the period (especially Arius, Alexander of Alexandria, and, perhaps, Eusebius of Caesarea).

Against this backdrop, what is the main thrust of this letter? First of all, in setting out their doctrine the authors do not refer to a creed 'into which they were baptized', as the usual formula goes in the fifth century. Instead they refer to a 'faith which was set forth by spiritual men'. These men are briefly characterized as follows: they must 'not rightly be considered to have lived or thought in the flesh, but they meditated this in the Spirit together on the basis of the holy writings of the divinely inspired books' (section 8). Later, in sections 10 and 12 it is said that the basis for their argument is the Bible itself. After the end of the creed the letter continues:

> This is the faith set forth and the entire holy synod agreed to it and confessed that this was the apostolic and salvific doctrine. And all fellow ministers were unanimous about it.[54]

The procedure, then, seems to have been this: the creed which was included in sections 8–13 had been drafted by a committee of expert ascetics and was subsequently submitted to the entire council which agreed to it. This suggests that the creed itself as a whole did not go back to tradition, but was, in fact, a product of

---

judgement of retribution.' 18,4 (732B): Ὅτι ἀπὸ τῆς περὶ τὰ ἐλάττονα εὐγνωμοσύνης ἡ ἐπὶ τοῖς μείζοσι τῆς ἀνταποδόσεως κρίσις δικαιοῦται. / 'That the decision to retribute in more important matters is justified by the generosity in minor matters.' By contrast, the phrase κρίσις καὶ ἀνταπόδοσις is found very frequently.

53 Cf. Camplani 2013, pp. 69–72.

54 Council of Antioch, *Epistula synodica* (Opitz 1934/1935, *Urkunde 18*) 14.

the council itself. The rather peculiar reference to the holy lifestyle of its authors and the later reference to the Scriptures served to disguise precisely this fact.

The creed proper is trinitarian in character: section 8 deals with the Father, sections 9–11 with the Son, and section 12 with the Holy Spirit and a series of other items which may, perhaps, be regarded as the fruits of the Spirit. It concludes with a series of condemnations (section 13). The 'oneness' of the individual trinitarian 'persons' is emphasized at the beginning of each article.

The creed begins with a section on the Father which is fairly conventional and need not detain us here, except for one observation: the combination of διοικητής and οἰκονόμος ('governor and administrator') is *only* found in Arius' Letter to Alexander and was – together with some other expressions – clearly reproduced from there, as our synopsis above has shown.

In the christological section first the idea is refuted that the Son was begotten from nothing or that he was something 'made' (ποιητόν; or, perhaps, ποίημα). In positive terms, he is 'properly an offspring' (γέννημα κυρίως) and has existed from eternity. In order to avoid any anthropomorphic misunderstanding, the authors add that the manner of his begetting is 'ineffable and indescribable' (ἀρρήτως καὶ ἀλέκτως; section 9).

Subsequently (sections 10–11a) the manner of begetting is more closely defined. The authors refute the idea that the Son is 'unbegotten'. Likewise, generation 'by an act of will or by adoption' (θελήσει ἢ θέσει) is deemed unacceptable. Instead, the key terms to correctly describe the Son's relationship to the Father are 'express image' (χαρακτήρ) or 'image' (εἰκών) of the divine *hypóstasis* (a clear reference to Heb 1:3; cf. again section 13). By contrast, the Son possessed no 'similarity of nature' (ὁμοιότης τῆς φύσεως) with those things that came into being through him, let alone did he have a share in them through 'mixture' (μῖξις).

Finally, a summary of the Son's work of salvation is given which includes birth – suffering – death – resurrection – ascension – sitting at the right hand – Last Judgement (section 11b). This is followed in section 12 by a series of clauses including the 'one' Spirit, the 'one catholic Church', the resurrection of the dead, and, again, the Last Judgement.

The creed ends with a series of anathemas (section 13). Eight teachings are condemned here: (1) the Son as a 'creature'; (2) as 'originated'; (3) as 'made'; (4) as 'not truly begotten'; (5) as having some kind of temporal beginning; (6) that he is immutable as a result of his will (and not of his very nature); (7) that he was born from nothing; (8) and that he is 'not immutable in nature' (which could either mean that he is immutable by volition (= 6) or that he is not immutable at all).

Thus we see how the form of a three-fold creed (followed by the anathemas), as we know it from Nicaea and Constantinople, gradually takes shape. The length of each article is as yet unequal, the second article being the most extensive, as the controversy primarily focussed on the status of the Son. Unless the text was heavily expanded at a later stage, its rhetorical strategy oscillates: it discusses controversial points at some length in the christological section whereas it limits itself to an enumeration of important divine attributes and stages of salvation history in the first and third sections. It would be tempting to explain this unevenness by the later extension of a first draft which may have looked like this:

First draft	Extension
Ἔστιν οὖν ἡ πίστις [. . .]	
[8] πιστεύειν εἰς ἕνα θεόν, πατέρα, παντοκράτορα, ἀκατάληπτον, ἄτρεπτον καὶ ἀναλλοίωτον, διοικητὴν καὶ οἰκονόμον πάντων, δίκαιον, ἀγαθόν, ποιητὴν οὐρανοῦ καὶ γῆς καὶ πάντων τῶν ἐν αὐτοῖς, νόμου καὶ προφητῶν καὶ τῆς καινῆς διαθήκης κύριον· [9] καὶ εἰς ἕνα κύριον Ἰησοῦν Χριστόν, υἱὸν μονογενῆ, γεννηθέντα οὐκ ἐκ τοῦ μὴ ὄντος, ἀλλ᾽ ἐκ τοῦ πατρός, οὐχ ὡς ποιητόν, ἀλλ᾽ ὡς γέννημα κυρίως, γεννηθέντα δὲ ἀρρήτως καὶ ἀλέκτως,	
	διότι μόνος ὁ πατὴρ ὁ γεννήσας καὶ ὁ υἱὸς ὁ γεννηθεὶς ἔγνω. *Οὐδεὶς γὰρ ἔγνω τὸν πατέρα εἰ μὴ ὁ υἱός, ἢ τὸν υἱὸν εἰ μὴ ὁ πατήρ, τὸν ἀεὶ ὄντα καὶ οὐ πρότερον οὐκ ὄντα.* [10] Χαρακτῆρα γὰρ αὐτὸν μόνον ἐκ τῶν ἁγίων γραφῶν μεμαθήκαμεν, οὐ ὡς τὸ ἐκ τοῦ πατρὸς σημάντεον ἀγέννητον ὄντα οὐ θέσει (ἀσεβὲς γὰρ καὶ βλάσφημον τοῦτο λέγειν)· ἀλλὰ κυρίως καὶ ἀληθῶς υἱὸν λέγουσιν αὐτὸν αἱ γραφαὶ τὸν γεννητὸν ὄντα, ὥστε καὶ πιστεύομεν ἄτρεπτον εἶναι καὶ ἀναλλοίωτον αὐτὸν οὐδὲ

Οὗτος δ᾽ ὁ υἱὸς θεὸς λόγος καὶ ἐν σαρκὶ ἐκ τῆς θεοτόκου Μαρίας τεχθεὶς καὶ σῶμα φορέσας, παθὼν καὶ ἀποθανὼν ἀνέστη ἐκ νεκρῶν καὶ ἀνελήφθη εἰς οὐρανόν, κάθηται δὲ ἐν δεξιᾷ τῆς μεγα-λοσύνης τῆς ὑψίστης ἐρχόμενος κρῖναι ζῶντας καὶ νεκρούς.
[12] Ἔτι δὲ ὡς καὶ τὸν σωτῆρα ἡμῶν αἱ ἱεραὶ γραφαὶ διδάσκουσιν καὶ ἓν πνεῦμα πιστεῦσαι,
μίαν καθολικὴν ἐκκλησίαν,
τὴν νεκρῶν ἀνάστασιν,
καὶ κρίσιν ἀνταποδόσεως καθὰ ἔπραξέν τις ἐν σώματι εἴτε ἀγαθὰ εἴτε κακά.

θελήσει ἢ θέσει γεννηθῆναι ἢ γενέσθαι, ὥστε ἐκ τοῦ μὴ ὄντος αὐτὸν εἶναι φαίνεσθαι, ἀλλὰ καθὸ γεννηθῆναι αὐτὸν εἰκός, οὐδ᾽ ὅπερ οὐ θέμις ἐννοεῖν καθ᾽ ὁμοιότητα τῆς φύσεως ἢ μῖξιν οὐδενὸς τῶν δι᾽ αὐτοῦ γενομένων, [11] ἀλλὰ διότι ὑπερβαίνει πᾶσαν ἔννοιαν ἢ διάνοιαν ἢ λόγον, ἐκ τοῦ πατρὸς τοῦ ἀγεννήτου γεννηθῆναι αὐτὸν ὁμολογοῦμεν, θεὸν λόγον, φῶς ἀληθινόν, δικαιοσύνην, Ἰη-σοῦν Χριστόν, πάντων κύριον καὶ σω-τῆρα. Εἰκὼν γάρ ἐστιν οὐ θελήσεως οὐδ᾽ ἄλλου τινός, ἀλλ᾽ αὐτῆς τῆς πατρικῆς ὑποστάσεως.

[Anathemas]

Some material at the beginning of section 11 (such as ἐκ τοῦ πατρὸς τοῦ ἀγεννήτου γεννηθῆναι αὐτὸν ὁμολογοῦμεν, θεὸν λόγον, φῶς ἀληθινόν, δικαιοσύνην, Ἰησοῦν Χριστόν, πάντων κύριον καὶ σωτῆρα) may also have belonged to the *Vorlage*, but its extent can no longer be clearly identified.

It is difficult to say whether the extension (if indeed that is what happened) was added to the *Vorlage* (1) at the drafting stage by the committee or (2) during the full session of the council, or (3) whether it forms, in fact, part of a subsequent revision (which would then also explain why some of the theological tenets contained therein may reflect the trinitarian discussion of a later stage).[55] The fact that phrases from Alexander were also used in the added material seems to preclude the idea that the entire extension was added *after* the council (although *some* phrases may have been added).[56]

The text is clearly anti-Arian in tone, but its argument is more forceful in what it rejects than what it posits, because the precise nature neither of the generation of the Son, nor of his likeness to the Father are spelled out. The Son's generation from the Father involves the former's immutability. The term *hypóstasis* is introduced in relation to the Father, without clarifying what it means for the Son to be the image of this *hypóstasis* (section 11). In addition, there also appears to be a break halfway through section 11 where the argument gradually changes from an explanation of certain trinitarian tenets to a simple enumeration of the stages of incarnation. Moreover, new credal terms such as 'word' and 'true light' are introduced en passant (based on Jn 1:1–9) without further explanation. But when we compare Alexander's creed we can see that the letter from Antioch simply follows the structure of this earlier text – without, however, slavishly repeating its wording: thus the peculiar order Spirit – Christ in Alexander's text[57] is reversed. In addition, the pneumatological section was extended by including the Last Judgement which is missing in Alexander's text (or, perhaps, only hinted at).

What is new here, however, is the fact that the anathemas are collated at the end rather than appearing thoughout the argument. Interestingly, the creed itself does not name the opponents in contrast to Arius' creed and Alexander's statement.[58]

There is another difference: what exactly is meant when the creed says that the Arian doctrines are 'anathema' to the synod? It cannot mean excommunication because it is not directed against named *persons*, but against persons holding specific *views*. An excommunication of Arius and his adherents is nowhere mentioned, and Theodotus, Narcissus, and Eusebius of Caesarea who were found holding similar views were (provisionally) deposed, but not excluded from the Church either. We, therefore, have to ascertain whether ἀναθεματίζειν is a theo-

---

55 Strutwolf mentions, in particular, the condemnation of the Son's generation by the Father's will; the eikon-Christology; the anathema of the claim that the Son was 'a creature or originated or made'. Cf. Strutwolf 1999, pp. 40–3; Strutwolf 2011, pp. 313–20. *Pace* Strutwolf cf. now Simperl 2022, pp. 349–53, 369–71.

56 Such as οὐδὲ θελήσει ἢ θέσει and εἰκὼν γάρ – τῆς πατρικῆς ὑποστάσεως.

57 Cf. Alexander of Alexandria, *Tomus ad omnes episcopos* (Opitz 1934/1935, *Urkunde 15*) 2.

58 In Arius et al., *Epistula ad Alexandrum Alexandrinum* (Opitz 1934/1935, *Urkunde 6*; FaFo § 131a) 3 Valentinus, Mani, Sabellius, and Hieracas (of Leontopolis) are named, in Alexander of Alexandria, *Epistula ad Alexandrum Thessalonicensem (Byzantinum*; Opitz 1934/1935, *Urkunde 14*; FaFo § 132) 46 Sabellius and Valentinus. Cf. also Dionysius of Alexandria, *Epistula V 1* (Feltoe; FaFo § 124a) and above pp. 99 f.

logical or a legal term and what it implies. Strangely enough, this problem has received little discussion in previous scholarship – usually the condemnations are conflated with the system of excommunication.[59] However, it is important to draw certain distinctions.

In late antiquity excommunication was primarily a penalty which consisted in someone's temporary or total exclusion from the Christian congregation in general and the eucharist in particular, as a reaction to deviant behaviour or faith.[60] By contrast, an anathema was a certain type of curse against someone which was pronounced by an individual bishop or a synod.[61] In the period we are interested in this curse is found in an encyclical letter by Alexander of Alexandria that mentions a synod of 'almost one hundred bishops of Egypt and Libya' which had anathematized Arius and his followers.[62] However, Alexander did not primarily ask his fellow-bishops to bar the latter from participation in worship, rather, to refuse them fellowship and hospitality lest they spread their pernicious doctrines.[63] From another one of Alexander's letters, that to his namesake of Thessaloniki (or Byzantium), it also emerges that such an anathema was not primarily a canonical penalty involving exclusion from worship. Instead Alexander expelled Arius and his followers from his church, because they taught beliefs that were alien to the 'right' doctrine. In this context he quoted Gal 1:9[64] which obviously refers to their capacity as presbyters and ecclesiastical teachers that they were no longer allowed to exercise. But it remains obscure whether or not Alexander expected the other bishops to also exclude the Arians from the eucharist (although this may have been implied by asking them to refuse fellowship). In any case, when Arius wrote to Paulinus of Tyre, Eusebius of Caesarea, and Patrophilus of Scythopolis he did not ask to be granted communion, but to be reinstated as presbyter and to be allowed to celebrate mass.[65] Arius also reports in his

---

59 Cf., e.g., Hofmann 1950, p. 429; Doskocil 1969, col. 11; Jaser 2013, pp. 40–42.

60 Cf. the surveys in Doskocil 1969; Vodola 1986; Firey 2008; Konradt, 'Excommunication', 2014; Leppin 2014; Bührer-Thierry/Gioanni 2015; Uhalde 2018.

61 Cf. the surveys in Michel 1907; Hofmann 1950; Speyer 1969, esp. col. 1267; Aust/Müller 1977; Hunzinger 1980; May 1980; Zawadzki 2008–2010; Pennington 2009.

62 Cf. Alexander, *Epistula encyclica* (Opitz 1934/1935, *Urkunde 4b*) 11. Cf. also 16 and 19. The phrase in 16 (Opitz 1934/1935, p. 9, ll. 25 f.) διὸ καὶ ἀπεκηρύχθησαν καὶ ἀνεθεματίσθησαν ἀπὸ τῆς ἐκκλησίας is slightly awkward. Perhaps one has to read: διὸ καὶ ἀπεκηρύχθησαν ἀπὸ τῆς ἐκκλησίας καὶ ἀνεθεματίσθησαν (cf. the apparatus Opitz 1934/1935, p. 9, ll. 25 f.). Or ἀπό is a misspelling of ὑπό. In any case, this may also have meant that Arius et al. were simply stripped of their office.

63 Cf. Alexander, *Epistula encyclica* (Opitz 1934/1935, *Urkunde 4b*) 20.

64 Cf. Alexander of Alexandria, *Epistula ad Alexandrum Thessalonicensem (Byzantinum*; Opitz 1934/1935, *Urkunde 14*) 56. Cf. also id, *Tomus ad omnes episcopos* (Opitz 1934/1935, *Urkunde 15*) 2.

65 Cf. Sozomen, *Historia ecclesiastica* 1,15,11 (Opitz 1934/1935, *Urkunde 10*).

letter to Eusebius of Nicomedia that a series of bishops had been placed under anathema by Bishop Alexander.[66] This is obviously no excommunication in the sense of members of a congregation being excluded by their bishop for transgressions of disciplinary rules; rather it is the termination of ecclesial communion between bishops.

Furthermore, in synodal documents from the fourth century onwards anathemas were often not directed against the persons themselves, but against the *views* a person held (the model for this use of anathema is found in Gal 1:8–9 and 1Cor 16:22).[67] This is why excommunication was a possible, but not necessary sanction accompanying anathemas.[68] The creed of Antioch is one of the first texts in which this meaning becomes apparent:[69] it condemns unnamed persons holding heretical doctrines.[70] As no person was specifically named, clearly no canonical penalty (such as excommunication) could be pronounced. In general, there is no indication that the Arians were excommunicated. Their sympathizers lost their sees, but even this was, as we saw above, only a provisional measure. Likewise, we hear from Socrates that Arius and his followers were anathematized by the Council of Nicaea and were not to return to Alexandria – if this was contained in a synodal document it has not survived. Moreover, they were sent into exile by an edict of the emperor.[71] This means that they were excluded from communion with the Alexandrian church, but there is no indication that Arian theologians were no longer permitted to partake of the eucharist as such. We will see below how the use of anathemas contributed to the increasingly legal character of synodal creeds.[72]

---

66 Cf. Arius, *Epistula ad Eusebium Nicomediensem* (Opitz 1934/1935, *Urkunde 1*) 3.

67 Eusebius was even vaguer in his credal exposition, anathematizing 'every godless heresy' (πᾶσαν ἄθεον αἵρεσιν); cf. next chapter.

68 These reflections are partly inspired by Bührer-Thierry 2015, esp. pp. 7 f., 13; Graumann 2020, pp. 8–10. Cf. also Weckwerth 2010, pp. 20 f.

69 Cf. Hanson 1988, p. 150; Galvão-Sobrinho 2013, p. 82. The only earlier references may be Dionysius of Alexandria, *Epistula V 1* (Feltoe; FaFo § 124a), and canon 52 of the Synod of Elvira where someone putting up slanderous pamphlets in a church is anathematized. The date of this synod (314?) is highly controversial; cf. Weckwerth 2013, pp. 185 f. (no. 181).

70 There is a certain similarity here to the *cura morum* of the Roman censors who watched over the morals of the city's population. 'If the censors were not satisfied with giving a mere reproof, they entered their reprimands on the census list against the respective person's name (*nota*). The criticism was accompanied by an explanation' (Suolahti 1963, p. 50, listing numerous references). This was already noticed in antiquity, but Ambrose clearly states the difference in *De fide* 1,119 (FaFo § 455a2): the *notae* are secret, the anathemas are public.

71 Cf. Socrates, *Historia ecclesiastica* 1,8,33. The emperors seem to have seen in an anathema a parallel to the secular penalty of *infamia* and acted accordingly by meting out similar kinds of punishments. For *infamia* cf. esp. Kaser 1956; Scheibelreiter 2019, cols. 704–17.

72 Cf. below ch. 6.4.6.

6.3 A local creed in Caesarea? Eusebius' Letter to his Church

Eusebius of Caesarea's letter to his congregation which he wrote in June 325 in the wake of the Council of Nicaea plays a key role in the fixation of credal formulae. This document was perhaps meant to be read out during mass. The bishop was moved to composing his epistle, because he had signed N after some hesitation and wished to explain his signature to his congregation.[73] This document is the earliest witness for N which is why we will return to it further below.[74] Furthermore, Eusebius apparently says that N was a version of the creed of Caesarea which had been revised by the Council of Nicaea. It is, therefore, often claimed that N was directly based on the local creed of Caesarea or of wider Palestine.

However, this theory does not stand up to closer scrutiny.[75] First, it is striking that Eusebius does not actually mention a 'creed'; instead he calls the formula (which I will abbreviate as Eus) which he goes on to quote the 'text about the faith which we had submitted' (τὴν ὑφ' ἡμῶν προταθεῖσαν περὶ τῆς πίστεως γραφήν). He says that he read out this text in the presence of the emperor and received praise for it. He continues:

> As we have received from the bishops who preceded us, in our first catechesis, and when we received baptism; and as we have learned from the divine Scriptures; and as we constantly believed and taught as presbyter and now as bishop, so also believing at the time present, we report to you our faith, and it is this: [Here follows his 'creed'.][76]

We may draw the following conclusions from Eusebius' comment:

(1) Eusebius submitted a written document to the synod that was actually read out during one of its sessions.

(2) This document contained the 'faith' which Eusebius had received in his catechetical instruction and in baptism.[77]

(3) Its content corresponded to the Holy Scriptures.

(4) Eusebius held on to this 'faith' as a presbyter and bishop until the present day and taught it himself to others.

---

73 Cf. Socrates, *Historia ecclesiastica* 1,8,34.

74 Cf. Eusebius, *Epistula ad ecclesiam Caesariensem* (Opitz 1934/1935, *Urkunde 22*; FaFo §§ 134a, 135b); cf. also below ch. 6.4.2.

75 In what follows I come largely to the same conclusions as Hans von Campenhausen in his seminal article of 1976(1979).

76 Eusebius, *Epistula ad ecclesiam Caesariensem* (Opitz 1934/1935, *Urkunde 22*) 3 (FaFo § 134a).

77 This could be an indication that Eusebius was baptized as an adult (cf. Wallace-Hadrill 1960, p. 12). However, even in that case no conclusions may be drawn as regards his religious education, since baptism was often postponed until adulthood at this time.

This introductory passage provides astonishingly little information concerning our question about the emergence of fixed declaratory creeds. Eusebius does *not* say that he is going to recite a previously *fixed formula*. Indeed, he later says that he believed these things 'from as long as we have known ourselves'[78] – and this must certainly mean from earliest childhood which makes it quite unlikely that the credal text quoted is a traditional text 'handed over' before baptism in Caesarea. Instead, he possibly relates the *content* of the received faith which, before Nicaea, had not yet assumed a fixed form.[79] If this is the case, however, we have to examine whether, precisely *because* Eusebius' faith had been recorded in a particular structure for the council, it turned into a fixed formula exhibiting this very structure.

Why would Eusebius have done this? As we saw above, he and his two fellow-bishops had been deposed at Antioch, while being granted leave to appeal to the Council of Ancyra (later moved to Nicaea). He was, therefore, under considerable pressure to explain his theological position in order to regain his episcopal see. In such a situation it would not have been enough simply to fall back on a possibly pre-existent baptismal creed, rendering further explanations necessary. This is precisely what Eusebius provides in this text.

In what follows, I give the entire text of sections 4–6. The Greek sentence structure cannot be reproduced fully in English.

Exposition of faith ('creed') of Eusebius of Caesarea (Eus)
(Opitz 1934/1935, *Urkunde 22*; FaFo § 134a)

[4] Πιστεύομεν εἰς ἕνα θεόν, πατέρα, παντοκράτορα, τὸν τῶν ἁπάντων ὁρατῶν τε καὶ ἀοράτων ποιητήν·	[4] We believe in one God, the Father Almighty, the Maker of all things both visible and invisible [cf. Col 1:16];
καὶ εἰς ἕνα κύριον Ἰησοῦν Χριστόν, τὸν τοῦ θεοῦ λόγον, θεὸν ἐκ θεοῦ, φῶς ἐκ φωτός, ζωὴν ἐκ ζωῆς, υἱὸν μονογενῆ, *πρωτότοκον πάσης κτίσεως, πρὸ πάν-*	and in one Lord Jesus Christ, the Word of God, God from God, Light from Light, life from life, only-begotten Son [cf. Jn 1:18 *v.l.*], 'first-born of all creation' [Col

---

78 Cf. the quotation below p. 237.

79 I also remain unconvinced that Eusebius' credal text is based in some way on the writings of Arius and Alexander or on the creed of Antioch. *Pace* Vinzent 1999, pp. 257, 278–80, 312, 345–8; Simperl 2022, pp. 314–6, 323, 357. Thus the syntagma εἰς ἕνα θεόν, πατέρα, παντοκράτορα ('in one God, the Father Almighty') which is found both in Eus and the creed of Antioch is entirely traditional; cf., e.g., Irenaeus, *Aduersus haereses* 1,3,6 (FaFo § 109b1); 1,10,1 (§ 109b3). Likewise, εἰς ἕνα κύριον Ἰησοῦν Χριστόν ('in one Lord Jesus Christ') already occurs in Irenaeus, *Aduersus haereses* 1,1,6 (τὴν πίστιν εἰς ἕνα θεὸν πατέρα παντοκράτορα καὶ εἰς ἕνα κύριον Ἰησοῦν Χριστὸν τὸν υἱὸν τοῦ θεοῦ / 'the faith in one God, the Father Almighty, and in one Lord Jesus Christ, the Son of God').

των τῶν αἰώνων ἐκ τοῦ πατρὸς γεγεν-νημένον, δι' οὗ καὶ ἐγένετο τὰ πάντα· τὸν διὰ τὴν ἡμετέραν σωτηρίαν σαρκω-θέντα καὶ ἐν ἀνθρώποις πολιτευσάμε-νον καὶ παθόντα καὶ ἀναστάντα τῇ τρίτῃ ἡμέρᾳ καὶ ἀνελθόντα πρὸς τὸν πα-τέρα καὶ ἥξοντα πάλιν ἐν δόξῃ κρῖναι ζῶντας καὶ νεκρούς.

1:15], before all ages begotten from the Father, 'through whom' also 'all things came into being' [Jn 1:3; 1Cor 8:6]; who for our salvation became flesh, lived among men, suffered, on the third day rose again, and ascended to the Father, and will come again in glory to judge the living and the dead [cf. 2Tim 4:1; 1Pet 4:5].

Πιστεύομεν δὲ καὶ εἰς ἓν πνεῦμα ἅγιον.

And we believe also in one Holy Spirit.

[5] Τούτων ἕκαστον εἶναι καὶ ὑπάρχειν πιστεύοντες πατέρα ἀληθῶς πατέρα καὶ υἱὸν ἀληθῶς υἱὸν καὶ πνεῦμα ἅγιον ἀληθῶς ἅγιον πνεῦμα

[5] Believing each of these to be and to exist, the Father truly Father, the Son truly Son, and the Holy Spirit truly Holy Spirit

> (καθὼς καὶ ὁ κύριος ἡμῶν ἀπος-τέλλων εἰς τὸ κήρυγμα τοὺς ἑαυ-τοῦ μαθητὰς εἶπεν· *Πορευθέντες μαθητεύσατε πάντα τὰ ἔθνη βαπτί-ζοντες αὐτοὺς εἰς τὸ ὄνομα τοῦ πα-τρὸς καὶ τοῦ υἱοῦ καὶ τοῦ ἁγίου πνεύματος*),

> (just as our Lord, sending forth his disciples for the preaching, also said, 'Go and make disciples of all nations, baptizing them upon the name of the Father, the Son, and the Holy Spirit' [Mt 28:19]);

περὶ ὧν καὶ διαβεβαιούμεθα οὕτως ἔχειν καὶ οὕτως φρονεῖν καὶ πάλαι οὕτως ἐσχηκέναι καὶ μέχρι θανάτου ὑπὲρ ταύτης ἐνίστασθαι τῆς πίστεως ἀναθεματίζοντες πᾶσαν ἄθεον αἵρεσιν,

concerning whom we also confidently affirm that so we hold, so we think, and so we have held from long ago, and that we maintain this faith unto the death, anathematizing every godless heresy;

[6] ταῦτα ἀπὸ καρδίας καὶ ψυχῆς πάν-τοτε πεφρονηκέναι, ἐξ οὗπερ ἴσμεν ἑαυ-τούς, καὶ νῦν φρονεῖν τε καὶ λέγειν ἐξ ἀληθείας ἐπὶ τοῦ θεοῦ τοῦ παντοκρά-τορος καὶ τοῦ κυρίου ἡμῶν Ἰησοῦ Χριστοῦ **μαρτυρόμεθα**

[6] **we witness** before God Almighty and our Lord Jesus Christ that we have always held these things from our heart and soul, from as long as we have known ourselves, and now both truly think and say;

δεικνύναι ἔχοντες δι' ἀποδείξεων καὶ πείθειν ὑμᾶς, ὅτι καὶ τοὺς παρεληλυ-θότας χρόνους οὕτως ἐπιστεύομέν τε καὶ ἐκηρύσσομεν.

being able by proofs to show and to convince you that, in times past also, we have constantly believed and preached thus.

The creed itself seems at first glance to consist of three articles dealing with the Father, the Son, and the Spirit (section 4). But this is followed by a fourth 'article' (section 5–6) which is rather complex and requires some explanation. Here Opitz' punctuation in his edition (which I followed in my collection *Faith in Formulae*; i.e. inserting a full stop after the quotation from Mt 28:19) is misleading, because in that case the *participium coniunctum* πιστεύοντες lacks a corresponding finite verb. At a closer glance, however, it becomes clear that the sentence does not stop on p. 43 after the quotation in line 19 but runs all the way through to line 25.[80] It must, therefore, be punctuated as above (the main verb is printed in bold).

This minute detail is important in assessing the text because it is unclear where the creed ends. From the evidence of later creeds, especially N, one would have thought that it terminates after the mention of belief in the Holy Spirit (and this is precisely what has been suggested by most scholars until now[81]), but this is not the case. The *participium coniunctum* πιστεύοντες clearly indicated that Eusebius' credal statement continued right until the end of this rather cumbersome sentence, forming a kind of peroration summing up the previous sections and furnishing the exegetical basis for belief in the Trinity (Mt 28:19). This observation is strengthened by the fact that Eusebius explicitly emphasizes in the following sentence that *this* had been the exposition of his creed (section 7: ταύτης ὑφ' ἡμῶν ἐκτεθείσης τῆς πίστεως). Furthermore, he points out that his 'faith' was considered orthodox by each and every one, including the emperor.

Therefore, in my view we have to distinguish the trinitarian content in this exposition of faith from its actual literary manifestation as a creed. Eusebius, it is true, carefully describes the three persons of the Trinity one after the other, resulting in three distinct articles. However, he also expresses this faith in the *fourth* 'article' whose purpose is fivefold: (1) to give a kind of summary; (2) to furnish a biblical quotation underpinning belief in the Trinity (and thus implicitly justifying the trinitarian structure of the previous sections); (3) to emphasize the creed's venerability; (4) to condemn heresy; and (5) to underline the orthodoxy of its author.

This does not mean that Eusebius did not fall back on catechetical practice in Caesarea. In fact, he seems to indicate precisely this in the introduction to his text. But this reference makes it rather unlikely that he was using a *fixed* text, *because in that city no fixed formula existed as yet.* After all, why would the bishop have felt the need to communicate a traditional formula allegedly recited at each baptism to his own congregation? Instead he submitted a text to the council which conveyed the *content* of the catechetical teaching of Caesarea regarding

---

80 This is almost the same punctuation as in Parmentier's and Hansen's edition of the text as it is quoted in Theodoret's *Ecclesiastical History* 1,12,5–6; cf. Parmentier/Hansen 1998(2009), p. 49, l. 16 – 50, l. 4.

81 Cf., e.g., Vinzent 1999, pp. 346–8.

the faith. In other words, the 'creed' which Eusebius submitted was nothing but the *regula fidei* (or baptismal credal kerygma) that formed the basis for the baptismal catechesis in the coastal city of Palestine and which may also have formed the content of the questions to which the baptizands agreed, their precise wording differing from one baptism to the next. He took propositions about the first and second person of the Trinity from this 'rule of faith' which he considered useful for the present purpose. He did *not* use propositions about the fruits of the Holy Spirit such as we encountered in the creeds of Alexander and of Antioch, because they were irrelevant to Eusebius' situation. It is impossible, in my view, that such teaching about the Spirit did not exist in Caesarea as well; but there was as yet no *Traditio* and *Redditio symboli* in that city, rites which, as we will see below,[82] necessitated a fixed formula. Instead knowledge about the faith was imparted by preaching based on the *regula fidei*, without the memorization and rendition of a fixed formula. Incidentally, this also explains why the first person plural (πιστεύομεν, διαβεβαιούμεθα, μαρτυρόμεθα) is used throughout this declaration: the persons speaking are not the baptizands of Caesarea (in which case, given what we know about the preparation to baptism, it is most likely the singular would have been used), but the members of the council.

Eusebius begins the article on the Father with a conventional phrase, also found in the creed from Antioch (πιστεύομεν εἰς ἕνα θεόν, πατέρα, παντοκράτορα), but then adds a reference to Col 1:16 (τὸν τῶν ἁπάντων ὁρατῶν τε καὶ ἀοράτων ποιητήν). This no doubt serves to emphasize the transcendence of the Father vis-à-vis the rest of the universe (including the Son) and his creative activity. In his christological section, Eusebius clearly creates an intermediate position between the Arian defence of the Son's creation and his opponents' insistence on the Son's full divinity. Arian theology is reflected in the inclusion of Col 1:15 ('firstborn of all *creation*'), while the insistence that the Son is 'God from God' and that he was begotten from the Father may be an attempt to bridge the gap between Eusebius and his opponents. Yet once again, this apparent endorsement of the Son's 'full divinity' is not without qualifications, precisely because Jesus Christ is the 'Logos *of* God' (whereas in Antioch he was called 'God the Logos') and 'God *from* God, Light *from* Light, life *from* life' (as opposed to Antioch where 'God the Logos' was simply called 'true light').[83] Likewise, some ambiguity remains when it comes to the alternative between the Son's temporality and his coeternity with

---

82 Cf. below ch. 11.1.1.

83 As regards the history of the phrase 'Light from Light' cf. Munkholt Christensen 2023, esp. p. 255 n. 16. Eusebius describes its theological background in *Demonstratio euangelica* 4,3. Cf. esp. 4,3,7: 'For God wished to beget a Son, and established a second light, in everything made like himself (φῶς δεύτερον κατὰ πάντα ἑαυτῷ ἀφωμοιωμένον).'

the Father: the insistence on the Son's cooperation in the creation of 'all things' may suggest that he had been begotten 'beyond' or 'above' temporality (because time may be seen as part of the created order); at the same time the phrase 'before all ages' may point to the Son's being, as it were, the 'starting-point' of time (and as such part of temporality).

Eusebius does not mention the death of the Son nor his sitting at the right hand of the Father, as opposed to both Alexander and the Creed of Antioch. Markus Vinzent is probably right in pointing out that he omits any open confession of the Son's subordination and the description of the Son as a second lord, in view of his deposition in Antioch.[84]

Eusebius is the first to introduce the resurrection 'on the third day' in an eastern creed. The only earlier example is the creed in the so-called *Traditio Apostolica* which, however, must probably be attributed to Rome.[85] It is unclear whether Eusebius' insertion is in any way connected with the Creed from Jerusalem that is western in origin and also contained this addition[86] or whether this is a direct influence from 1Cor 15:4.

Eusebius also deviates from his predecessors in saying that the Son 'ascended' (ἀνελθόντα) to the Father[87] whereas both Alexander of Alexandria and the creed of Antioch retain the older expression that Christ was 'taken up' (ἀναληφθείς/ ἀνελήφθη) into heaven.[88] Furthermore in Eusebius' version the Son will return 'in glory' for the Final Judgement. This addition – which occurs frequently in earlier Christian literature[89] – is clearly influenced by Mt 16:27 and 24:30 (cf. also Phil 2:11) and is, as such, not particularly remarkable. However, it is worth mentioning that the earliest creed (other than that of Eusebius) that includes it, i.e. J, also comes from Palestine.[90]

Eusebius' final section insists on the 'true' existence of each of the persons of the Trinity, probably in order to ward off any ideas of trinitarian modalism.

---

84 Cf. Vinzent 1999, pp. 345 f.

85 Cf. TA^E/TA^L (FaFo § 89c) and above ch. 5.1. For earlier non-credal literature cf. the examples in Harnack 1897, pp. 380 f., esp. Irenaeus, *Aduersus haereses* 2,32,3 (§ 109b5); Tertullian, *De praescriptione haereticorum* 13,4 (§ 111b1); id., *De uirginibus uelandis* 1,4 (3; § 111c).

86 Cf. FaFo § 147 and above ch. 5.5.

87 It is not used in the New Testament. It is only rarely found before the fourth century: Justin, *Apologia prima* 42,4 (FaFo § 104a6); Melito of Sardes, *De pascha* 104 (l. 788; § 107). (Pseudo-)Ignatius, *Ad Magnesios* 11,3 (long version; § 98b2b) is probably later.

88 Cf. above pp. 217, 224. Further references in Harnack 1897, pp. 383 f.

89 Cf. Harnack 1897 pp. 385 f., esp. Irenaeus, *Aduersus haereses* 3,4,2 (FaFo § 109b7).

90 Cf. FaFo § 147 and above p. 203. Later in the fourth century it is found in the creed of the Synod of Seleucia (359; FaFo § 158a[4]); Epiphanius, *Ancoratus* 119,8 (§ 175); Pseudo-Athanasius, *Interpretatio in symbolum* (§ 185).

When we take all this into consideration and also look at the remainder of Eusebius' letter its purpose becomes clear. Its principal aim was not to justify a theological 'change of heart' on the part of Eusebius, as is often assumed in the literature on the subject.[91] Instead he wished, above all, to explain that his faith was considered orthodox by emperor and council and that, therefore, his deposition (about which there probably was considerable uncertainty in Caesarea) was null and void. To this end, Eusebius had drafted a statement of his faith. The emperor, obviously relieved that a text had been proposed which was flexible enough to encompass a variety of views on the Trinity ordered this text to be signed by the bishops present. However, objections that the creed was too close to Arius' views were raised. Constantine first tried to solve this problem by including *homoousios* in Eusebius' text. But the emperors' suggestion did not satisfy the opposition. Instead, 'on the pretext of the addition of the word *homoousios*' a text with further revisions was drafted which Eusebius then quotes: N.[92] Eusebius does not say here that the bishops added to *his* text, but that they actually wrote a *new* text.[93] However, this new text (N) must to a certain degree have been based on the previous creed drafted by Eusebius, because in the introduction to his letter he speaks of N as a text where 'supplements were appended to our expressions (ταῖς ἡμετέραις φωναῖς προσθήκας ἐπιβαλόντες)'.

Whatever the truth of the matter (and we will have to return to this point below), Eusebius himself concedes that N deviated in some important respects from his original text and that he found it difficult to accept these passages. He, therefore, had to explain why both his initial statement and that of Nicaea were, in fact, compatible with each other, which he does at some length in sections 9–16. The draft of N obviously proved controversial in a number of points and needed clarification which was then given at the council.[94] Eusebius followed a clear objective in this process which he in fact explicitly states: after the proper explanations had been given he did not reject the term *homoousios*, considering that the text was a compromise document which served to restore peace and he

---

91 Cf., e.g., Campenhausen 1976(1979), pp. 278 f.: 'Eusebius fears that adding his signature to the Nicene Creed could be interpreted as a betrayal of the theological convictions that he otherwise consistently held, and he wants to forestall such suspicions. His report thus aims at a preventive self-defence.'

92 Cf. Eusebius of Caesarea, *Epistula ad ecclesiam Caesariensem* (Opitz 1934/1935, *Urkunde 22*) 7 (FaFo § 135b1): Οἱ δὲ προφάσει τῆς τοῦ ὁμοουσίου προσθήκης τήνδε τὴν γραφὴν πεποιήκασιν [. . .]. / 'And the [bishops] composed this text on the pretext of the addition of the word *homoousios* [. . .]'.

93 Cf. Lietzmann 1922–1927(1962), p. 250; Kelly 1972, pp. 221–2.

94 Cf. below pp. 250 f.

no longer feared to be deviating 'from the correct meaning'.[95] After these difficulties in interpretation had been removed, Eusebius could agree to the compromise text as in his view N and his own declaration of faith agreed fundamentally.[96]

6.4 The Creed of Nicaea

It will have become clear in what was said above that the trinitarian declaratory creed gradually evolved in the early fourth century, the creeds of Antioch and of Eusebius approaching, while not yet quite achieving a conformity of literary structure and theological content.

Arguably,[97] the most important creed in ancient eastern Christianity was that of Nicaea. As we will see, it was the doctrinal standard by which all other theological declarations were measured until it was ultimately superseded by the Creed of Constantinople (which itself is a descendant from N). Given its enormous impact it is most regrettable that we have but scarce information about the circumstances of its composition. Most of it comes from Eusebius of Caesarea who clearly was no impartial observer, being, as we saw above, interested in clearing himself of the charge of heresy and thus may have exaggerated his role in the proceedings.

---

95 Eusebius, *Epistula ad ecclesiam Caesariensem* (*Urkunde 22*) 10 (Opitz 1934/1935, p. 45, ll. 12–14): Διόπερ τῇ διανοίᾳ καὶ ἡμεῖς συνετιθέμεθα οὐδὲ τὴν φωνὴν τοῦ ὁμοουσίου παραιτούμενοι τοῦ τῆς εἰρήνης σκοποῦ πρὸ ὀφθαλμῶν ἡμῖν κειμένου καὶ τοῦ μὴ τῆς ὀρθῆς ἐκπεσεῖν διανοίας. / 'On this account, we assented to the meaning ourselves, without declining the term "consubstantial", as peace lay within reach without deviation from the correct meaning' (tr. Stevenson/Frend 1987, pp. 345–6; altered).

96 Cf. Eusebius, *Epistula ad ecclesiam Caesariensem* (*Urkunde 22*) 17 (Opitz 1934/1935, p. 47, ll. 2–5): [. . .] τότε δὲ ἀφιλονείκως τὰ μὴ λυποῦντα κατεδεξάμεθα, ὅθ' ἡμῖν εὐγνωμόνως τῶν λόγων ἐξετάζουσι τὴν διάνοιαν ἐφάνη συντρέχειν τοῖς ὑφ' ἡμῶν αὐτῶν ἐν τῇ προεκτεθείσῃ πίστει ὡμολογημένοις. / '[. . .] but we received without contention what no longer pained us as soon as, on a candid examination of the sense of the words, they appeared to us to coincide with what we ourselves have confessed in the faith which we previously declared' (tr. Stevenson/Frend 1987, p. 347; altered).

97 This chapter is an extended version of Kinzig 2023.

6.4.1 The prehistory of the council

As we saw above,[98] Ossius' attempt to seek to establish peace between the war-ring factions at the Council of Antioch in the spring of 325 failed, because in the end the council suspended church communion with the Arian or 'Arianizing' bishops Eusebius of Caesarea, Theodotus of Laodicea, and Narcissus of Neronias, until they would – it was hoped – recant at the forthcoming council which the emperor had summoned to Ancyra. This must have angered Eusebius' powerful namesake at the imperial residence of Nicomedia, given that he himself sup-ported the Alexandrian presbyter.[99] Arius may even have stayed for a time in Nico-media in 319.[100] The emperor too spent some time in Nicomedia in the autumn and winter of 324/325.[101] The local bishop may, therefore, have been the driving force in urging the emperor to use the proposed council of unity to reinstate the deposed bishops and to settle the theological issues.[102]

When we look at the list of Arian supporters at Nicaea,[103] one particular group of powerful bishops stands out (Theognis of Nicaea, Maris of Chalcedon, Theodore of Heraclea, and, perhaps, Menophantus of Ephesus) whose sees were located not too far from Nicomedia, Theognis and Maris even coming from the same province (Bithynia). Theodore excepting, they were also related to each other in the sense that, together with other prelates and theologians, they had been 'Syllucianists' (συλ-λουκιανισταί[104]), pupils of the distinguished theological teacher Lucian of Antioch who had perished in 312 during the Diocletian persecution.[105] The bustling activity

---

98 Cf. above ch. 6.2.

99 On Eusebius of Nicomedia's relations with the court cf. Pohlsander 1993, pp. 156 f. and n. 27; Hillner 2023, p. 227. To what extent his sympathies actually make this Eusebius an 'Arian' is a matter of debate; cf. especially Luibhéid 1976; Gwynn 2007, pp. 116–20, 211–19.

100 This stay (which may be hinted at in Athanasius, *De synodis* 15,2 and is clearly, although un-reliably, attested by Epiphanius, *Panarion* 68,4,4; 69,5,2; 69,7,1) is disputed by some scholars; cf. Pohlsander 1993, p. 157 and n. 28.

101 Cf. Barnes 1982, p. 76.

102 Cf. also Constantine's letter to the church of Nicomedia (Opitz 1934/1935, *Urkunde 27*) 14, where he claims to have followed Eusebius' wishes in every respect.

103 The names are discussed in Bleckmann/Stein 2015, vol. II, pp. 85–6.

104 The term is only found in Arius, *Epistula ad Eusebium Nicomediensem (Urkunde 1)* 5 (Opitz 1934/1935, p. 3, l. 7).

105 Cf. Philostorgius, *Historia ecclesiastica* 2,14. He also adds to this group Leontius (later bishop of Antioch), Antony of Tarsus in Cilicia, Numenius, Eudoxius, Alexander, and Asterius of Cappa-docia (the Sophist). Later Athanasius of Anzarbus is mentioned (3,15). The identity of Numenius, Eudoxius, and Alexander is uncertain. Eudoxius may be identical with Eudocius (Eudoxius) of Germanicia who took part in the Dedication Council in Antioch in 341 (cf. below ch. 6.5.1) and in 360 became Bishop of Constantinople (360–after 366). The term 'pupil of Lucian' must, however,

of this network may have reinforced the impression at court that most bishops in the empire were seconding the presbyter from Alexandria.

Furthermore, Constantine himself may not have fully understood the gravity of the doctrinal problems involved.[106] He clearly thought that, after his victory over Licinius and prior to the twentieth anniversary of his reign (the *Vicennalia*) for which empire-wide festivities had been planned,[107] the council would be a splendid opportunity to demonstrate the doctrinal unity and peace within the Church, once the minor doctrinal squabbles had been settled.[108] So initially Constantine may have sympathized with the Arian cause under the influence of his local bishop. At the same time, the emperor may also have learned that the bishop of Ancyra, Marcellus (d. 374), was a fierce opponent of Arianism, whereas Theognis of Nicaea supported the Arian cause.[109] This may have been one of the reasons why the council was eventually moved from Ancyra to Nicaea (modern İznik in northwestern Turkey, some forty miles south of the imperial residence Nicomedia). However, there were other reasons for moving the venue: apart from practical considerations (Nicaea could be reached more easily from all regions of the empire[110]), the rationale behind this choice may also have been that Nicaea was close enough to the eastern capital Nicomedia for the emperor to be present at the council[111] and that it was far enough from the capital in order not to create the impression that the Arians were calling the shots.[112]

6.4.2 The creed of Eusebius and N

It is important to keep this background in mind because it helps us to understand what happened at the council with regard to its creed. It was to go down in history as the 'council of the 318' but was, in fact, attended by 250–300 bishops.[113] In some

---

be taken in the widest sense. As to the existence of a Lucianic 'school' cf. the description of the *status quaestionis* in Brennecke 1991, pp. 475–7; Bleckmann/Stein 2015, vol. II, pp. 157–9.

106 Cf. his remarks in his letter to Alexander and Arius (Opitz 1934/1935, *Urkunde 17*) 9–14.

107 Cf. Eusebius, *Vita Constantini* 3,15; Sozomen, *Historia ecclesiastica* 1,25,1.

108 Cf. his address to the council in Eusebius, *Vita Constantini* 3,12. Even if it is not quoted verbatim, Eusebius' version of it may well summarize the emperor's intentions.

109 Cf. also Drake 2006, p. 125.

110 Cf. Jacobs 2021, pp. 71 f.

111 Constantine mentions this reason himself in his letter of convocation; cf. above p. 219. Cf. also Drake 2021, pp. 122–3.

112 Cf. also Jacobs 2021, pp. 70–7.

113 Cf. Brennecke 1994, p. 431; Gwynn 2021, pp. 92–6: 220 participants. The number 318 which was later attached to the council is probably fictitious. It may go back to an allegorical interpreta-

sources, a Eusebius is named as the bishop who opened the council in June 325. There is good reason to think that this was the bishop of Nicomedia, given that he was 'the bishop of the current imperial residence and the local metropolitan'.[114] Constantine was in overall charge and even seems to have attended at least some of the council sessions.[115] Unfortunately, we do not really know the emperor's view on the proceedings, as with any of the later councils of the fourth century. Constantine famously considered himself a 'bishop of those outside' (τῶν ἐκτὸς ἐπίσκοπος),[116] but there is very little evidence as regards his take on things in Nicaea and, in particular, how he viewed the assembly of bishops and its decisions (including the creed) in institutional terms. He may possibly have considered them as some kind of consistory (the emperor's inner circle and advisory body) in matters spiritual, in which free speech was encouraged. Alas, not much is known about the consistory either, because its members were sworn to secrecy.[117] In any case, there can be no doubt that Constantine took a very active role in the proceedings, and his possible motives have to be taken into account also when it comes to the origin of N.[118]

It is most remarkable that he no longer imposed silence on the warring factions (as he had tried to do in his letter to Athanasius and Arius[119]), but actively sought a *theological* solution. The Arians were the first to provide a suggestion to this effect. Eustathius of Antioch reports that Eusebius of Nicomedia produced some sort of doctrinal statement (γράμμα). It may be identical with a letter which Ambrose of Milan claims was read at the council.[120] However, Theodoret writes that the supporters of Arius 'drew up' (or 'dictated' – the Greek is ambiguous) a

---

tion of the number of Abram's servants in Gen 14:14 and emphasized the liberation from the Arian heretics in analogy to the liberation of Lot. In this sense cf. Brennecke 1994, p. 431; Riedl 2004, pp. 32 f. (listing further literature). However, Ritter 1965, p. 40 n. 1 considers the number to be basically accurate. Cf. also CPG 8516 and the literature cited there. For the exegetical background cf. Aubineau 1966, pp. 10–13.

114 Gwynn 2021, p. 97. Cf. the heading of Eusebius, *Vita Constantini* 3,11 which only names 'the bishop Eusebius' (cf. Winkelmann 1991, p. 8, l. 29). In the text of the chapter the bishop remains unidentified. Sozomen, *Historia ecclesiastica* 1,19,2 identifies him with Eusebius of Caesarea, but this is wholly unlikely. Theodoret, *Historia ecclesiastica* 1,7,10 gives the bishop's name as Eustathius of Antioch, who had probably already been presiding over the Council of Antioch in 325 (cf. above p. 221).

115 Cf. Drake 2021, pp. 124–6.

116 Eusebius, *Vita Constantini* 4,24. Cf. also below pp. 473–5, 482.

117 Cf. Brown 1992, pp. 10, 66, 109; Harries 1999, pp. 38–42.

118 For further details cf. Girardet 1991(2015); Girardet 1993(2009); Girardet 2010, pp. 140–7.

119 Cf. Constantine, *Epistula ad Alexandrum Alexandrinum et Arium* (Opitz 1934/1935, *Urkunde 17*) 7–8. 11.

120 Cf. Ambrose, *De fide* 3,125 (cf. Opitz 1934/1935, *Urkunde 21*, in part).

text which he calls 'teaching of faith' (πίστεως διδασκαλία).[121] We do not know whether or not all these documents were one and the same.[122] Perhaps the Arians were asked to produce or draft a written statement of their theological views, or perhaps the council formed a committee from its midst and entrusted it with drafting such a statement which would settle the controversy. In the latter case, the committee must have been dominated by Arians. Be that as it may, the Arian statement, whatever it was, caused an uproar. It was completely unacceptable to the vast majority of the council so that it was ultimately torn to pieces.[123] However, as we will see, the creed drawn up at the Synod of Antioch in the previous spring (FaFo § 133) must also have been known and discussed in Nicaea and, because of its anti-Arian stance, was likewise deemed unacceptable as it was.

At this point Eusebius of Caesarea may have stepped in and may have produced his aforementioned exposition of faith.[124] After his suspension from office at Antioch, he may have been formally reinstated at Nicaea early in its proceedings.[125] He may then have suggested what he considered some sort of compromise, while at the same time trying to enhance his own status with the emperor. As we saw above, Eusebius maintains that N was based on this, his, statement.[126] Yet a synoptic comparison shows that the truth is more complicated:

Eus (Opitz 1934/1935, *Urkunde 22*; FaFo § 134a)		Creed of Nicaea (N) (FaFo § 135c)	
Πιστεύομεν εἰς ἕνα θεόν,	We believe in one God,	Πιστεύομεν εἰς ἕνα θεόν,	We believe in one God,
πατέρα,	the Father	πατέρα,	the Father
παντοκράτορα,	Almighty,	παντοκράτορα,	Almighty,

---

121 Eustathius of Antioch in Theodoret, *Historia ecclesiastica* 1,8,1–3 (FaFo § 135a2). Furthermore, Theodoret, *Historia ecclesiastica* 1,7,15 (FaFo § 135a1).

122 Cf. the long list of scholarly contributions in Tetz 1993.

123 Theodoret whose account in *Historia ecclesiastica* 1,7,14–15 depends on the fragment from Eustathius which he quotes in 1,8,1–3 (FaFo § 135a2) clearly understands Eustathius to say that the creed was 'torn up'. Martin Tetz, however, thinks that Theodoret misunderstood Eustathius who wished to say that the 'illegal writing had burst in the sight of all' (τοῦ παρανόμου γράμματος διαρραγέντος ὑπ' ὄψει πάντων ὁμοῦ; cf. Tetz 1993, pp. 230 f.). This ingenious interpretation allows him to identify the document mentioned by Eustathius and Theodoret with Eus. I remain unconvinced.

124 Cf. above ch. 6.3.

125 Cf. Gwynn 2021, p. 99.

126 Cf. above pp. 235, 241.

(continued)

Eus (Opitz 1934/1935, *Urkunde 22*; FaFo § 134a)		Creed of Nicaea (N) (FaFo § 135c)	
τὸν τῶν ἀπάντων ὁρατῶν τε καὶ ἀοράτων ποιητήν·	the Maker of all things both visible and invisible;	*πάντων ὁρατῶν τε καὶ ἀοράτων ποιητήν·*	Maker of all things both visible and invisible;
καὶ εἰς ἕνα κύριον Ἰησοῦν Χριστόν, τὸν τοῦ θεοῦ λόγον,	and in one Lord Jesus Christ, the *Word* of God,	*καὶ εἰς ἕνα κύριον Ἰησοῦν Χριστόν, τὸν υἱὸν τοῦ θεοῦ γεννηθέντα ἐκ τοῦ πατρός, μονογενῆ, τουτέστιν ἐκ τῆς οὐσίας τοῦ πατρός,*	and in one Lord Jesus Christ, the *Son* of God, *begotten from the Father, only-begotten, that is, from the substance of the Father;*
θεὸν ἐκ θεοῦ, φῶς ἐκ φωτός,	God from God, Light from Light,	*θεὸν ἐκ θεοῦ, φῶς ἐκ φωτός, θεὸν ἀληθινὸν ἐκ θεοῦ ἀληθινοῦ, γεννηθέντα οὐ ποιηθέντα, ὁμοούσιον τῷ πατρί,*	God from God, Light from Light, *true God from true God,* *begotten, not made,* *consubstantial with the Father;*
ζωὴν ἐκ ζωῆς, υἱὸν μονογενῆ, πρωτότοκον πάσης κτίσεως, πρὸ πάντων τῶν αἰώνων ἐκ τοῦ πατρὸς γεγεννημένον, δι᾽ οὗ καὶ ἐγένετο τὰ πάντα·	*life from life, only-begotten Son first-born of all creation* *before all ages begotten from the Father* through whom *also* all things came into being;	*δι᾽ οὗ τὰ πάντα ἐγένετο* *τά τε ἐν τῷ οὐρανῷ καὶ τὰ ἐν τῇ γῇ,*	through whom all things came into being, *both things in heaven and things on earth;*
τὸν	Who	*τὸν δι᾽ ἡμᾶς τοὺς ἀνθρώπους*	who *because of us humans*
διὰ τὴν ἡμετέραν σωτηρίαν σαρκωθέντα	because of our salvation became flesh,	*καὶ διὰ τὴν ἡμετέραν σωτηρίαν κατελθόντα καὶ σαρκωθέντα, ἐνανθρωπήσαντα,*	*and* because of our salvation *descended,* *and* became flesh, *became human,*
καὶ ἐν ἀνθρώποις πολιτευσάμενον καὶ παθόντα καὶ ἀναστάντα τῇ τρίτῃ ἡμέρᾳ	*and lived among humans,* *and* suffered, and on the third day rose again,	*παθόντα καὶ ἀναστάντα τῇ τρίτῃ ἡμέρᾳ,*	suffered, and on the third day rose again,

(continued)

Eus (Opitz 1934/1935, *Urkunde 22*; FaFo § 134a)		Creed of Nicaea (N) (FaFo § 135c)	
καὶ ἀνελθόντα πρὸς τὸν πατέρα	and ascended *to the Father,*	ἀνελθόντα εἰς τοὺς οὐρανούς,	ascended *into the heavens,*
καὶ ἥξοντα πάλιν ἐν δόξῃ	and will come again in glory	ἐρχόμενον	will come [*lit: coming*]
κρῖναι ζῶντας καὶ νεκρούς.	to judge the living and the dead	κρῖναι ζῶντας καὶ νεκρούς·	to judge the living and the dead
Πιστεύομεν δὲ καὶ εἰς ἓν πνεῦμα ἅγιον.	*And we believe also in one* Holy Spirit.	καὶ εἰς τὸ ἅγιον πνεῦμα.	and in the Holy Spirit.
		Τοὺς δὲ λέγοντας· Ἧν ποτε, ὅτε οὐκ ἦν, καί· Πρὶν γεννηθῆναι οὐκ ἦν, καὶ ὅτι ἐξ οὐκ ὄντων ἐγένετο ἢ ἐξ ἑτέρας ὑποστάσεως ἢ οὐσίας φάσκοντας εἶναι [ἢ κτιστὸν][127] ἢ τρεπτὸν ἢ ἀλλοιωτὸν τὸν υἱὸν τοῦ θεοῦ, τούτους ἀναθεματίζει ἡ καθολικὴ καὶ ἀποστολικὴ ἐκκλησία.	*The catholic and apostolic* Church anathematizes *those who say, 'There was when he was not', and, 'He was not before he was begotten', and that he came to be from nothing, or those who claim that* the Son of God *is from another hypóstasis or substance, (or created,) or alterable, or mutable.*
[. . .] ἀναθεματίζοντες πᾶσαν ἄθεον αἵρεσιν [. . .].	[. . .] anathematizing *every godless heresy* [. . .].		

As can easily be gleaned from this synopsis, although there are many similarities between the two texts, N is not simply an extended version of Eusebius' text.[128] Admittedly, the agreements between Eus and N are considerable: in both cases we have a three-part, trinitarian pattern whose third part is very brief. The first section of both texts is identical, minor editorial differences notwithstanding.

The christological section, however, exhibits considerable differences. Thus, instead of 'the Word of God', N contains an elaborate explanation of Christ's sonship und his origin from the substance of the Father (the title 'only-begotten Son' appears in Eus further below). Thus the 'sonship' (which in Eus is *added* to the

---

127 It is uncertain whether ἢ κτιστόν formed part of the original creed (as some good witnesses to the text attest) or whether it is a later addition by Athanasius (as argued by Wiles 1993). On the textual evidence cf. Dossetti 1967, p. 240. More recently, Edwards has suggested that the version of N quoted by Athanasius is 'the draft which was retained in Alexandria, and that this was not identical in all respects with the version that was finally promulgated' (Edwards 2012, p. 498; cf. also Edwards 2021, p. 151).

128 For what follows cf. also Lietzmann 1922–1927(1962), pp. 250–3; Kelly 1972, pp. 217–20.

'Word') *replaced* the 'Word' altogether in N. The divinity of the Son and his being light is again found in both creeds. Yet Eus contains surplus text after it ('life from life – from the Father'). In the continuation of the text until the end of the christological section both versions include the reference to Christ's collaboration in creation, to the incarnation 'for our salvation' and to the passion, resurrection, and the Last Judgement. At the same time, the details differ considerably: N adds a reference to the 'things in heaven and things on earth' and also extends the clause on salvation ('because of us humans') as well as the statement about the incarnation ('descended'). Whereas Eus refers to Christ's life among humans, N says that he 'became human' (ἐνανθρωπήσαντα).[129] In Eus the goal of ascension is the Father, in N the heavens. The clause on the resurrection differs, too. Finally, N makes no reference to the return 'in glory'.

The section on the Holy Spirit is characteristically brief in both versions, leaving aside the repetition of 'we believe' in Eus which is probably not very significant. In effect, this may be the most cogent argument why there must be *some* literary connection between Eus and N, because, as we saw above, both the creed of Alexander and of Antioch contain extended pneumatological articles. But again, the texts are not identical, and it is not easy to explain why Eus would have been changed in N, except if one assumes that 'in the Holy Spirit' in N is more succinct than 'and in one Holy Spirit' in Eus.

In N, however, the creed is followed by a series of condemnations that have no equivalent in Eus (which only contains a rather vague anathema) and to which we will return below.[130]

What conclusions can we draw from these peculiar findings? Supposing for a moment that Eusebius submitted a fixed formula in Nicaea which was then modified by additions, it cannot have been the formula which he quotes in his letter, for some modifications (such as the omission of 'and' between the participles in the second article) cannot really be explained as the result of an editorial process. Yet he insists that it was *this* text, i.e. Eus, which was read out at the council (section 2). The same differences also make it unlikely to suppose a joint *Vorlage*, quite apart from the fact that this would also be in direct contradiction to Eusebius' words.

---

129 Thomas Brüggemann has pointed out to me that it is difficult to understand why ἐνανθρωπήσαντα was added. It seems to clarify the preceding σαρκωθέντα (found in Eus) by underlining Christ's full humanity (including, probably, his human soul and intellect) – but why was this deemed necessary? Cf. Grillmeier 1975, p. 245 who thinks that 'there is no particular reason for suspecting here a retort against Arian teaching on the incarnation'.
130 Cf. below ch. 6.4.6.

Nevertheless, the structural resemblances are so striking that there must be *some* literary connection between both formulae. These resemblances are even more obvious when we compare them to the creeds by Arius, Alexander of Alexandria, and the Synod of Antioch, all of which look quite different.

Eusebius' statement according to which N was his revised creed is, therefore, hardly plausible, if we assume that he means the *exact wording* of the formula quoted by him. For the readers or hearers of his letter it must also have been obvious that N could not have been the revised version of a fixed formula from Caesarea. If this is so, how else should we interpret Eusebius' words?

As I mentioned before, after the Arian formula had failed to find general agreement, the council must have reached a dead end. A compromise formula was needed, and the emperor may have considered the learned bishop from Caesarea (who was not counted among the 'militant' Arians) to be a suitable mediator between both sides. Eusebius then submitted a text to the council which was initially approved of by the emperor who then referred it to a committee to add the *homoousios* at an appropriate place (section 7). Yet this committee (which Eusebius did not belong to and in which the Arians were by now outnumbered) was unable to agree on Eusebius' formula and drew up a 'new' text instead which was similar to that of Eusebius in some respects but not simply an extended version. This new text (N) was then discussed in plenary session, in particular the phrases τουτέστιν ἐκ τῆς οὐσίας τοῦ πατρός, γεννηθέντα οὐ ποιηθέντα, ὁμοούσιον τῷ πατρί (sections 9–13).

When we look at the way Eusebius introduces the quotation of N it becomes clear that he was himself aware of the fact that N was not simply an extended version of Eus. For he says that the bishops 'composed this text (τὴνδε τὴν γραφὴν πεποιήκασιν) on the pretext of the addition of the word *homoousios*'. In other words, according to Eusebius the 'identity' between his text and N was not a *verbal* identity, but an identity of *content*.[131]

This is confirmed by a look at his discussion of N. After his quotation of the creed he comments on what he saw as the differences between both texts. These were the additions that in his view had subsequently been made by the council:

- ἐκ τῆς οὐσίας τοῦ πατρός (sections 9–10);
- γεννηθέντα οὐ ποιηθέντα (section 11);
- ὁμοούσιον τῷ πατρί (sections 9–10, 12–13);
- and the anathemas, esp. ἦν ποτε, ὅτε οὐκ ἦν – ἐξ οὐκ ὄντων – πρὶν γεννηθῆναι οὐκ ἦν (sections 15–16).

---

131 Cf. Kelly 1972, p. 221; Behr 2004, vol. I, p. 155.

Eusebius obviously had no problems with these differences, considering both texts to be basically identical. In other words, while being based on the *content* of his text, N's *wording* was largely different from Eus which, in turn, was a written summary of the rule of faith at Caesarea.[132] The procedure for drawing up N was basically the same: the rule of faith on which the drafting committee agreed was written down. However, it was then supplemented by material from Eus and, probably, the creed of the Synod of Antioch. The latter creed was also deemed insufficient in itself: it insisted on the Son's being the 'express image' of the Father (cf. Heb 1:3) and tried to express the relationship between the Father and the Son in biblical terms, but this turned out not to be clear enough as Athanasius attests.[133] It was then stipulated, under imperial pressure, that N be signed by the assembled bishops. Thus, once and for all the *regula fidei* turned from oral kerygma into a creed whose wording was fixed and whose normativity was established by the bishops' signatures.[134]

6.4.3 The rule of faith underlying N

We may even be able to identify some of the elements which belonged to the *regula fidei* that lay at the heart of N. In this context it is, once again, important to remember that, N notwithstanding, the earliest declaratory creeds are R (in probably more than one version[135]) and J. It has been shown above that J is dependent on R.[136] But what about R and N? It is important to keep in mind that, given their overall similarity, R and N cannot have developed entirely independently from each other. When we compare the wording of both creeds we find a certain deal of overlap (identical words in italics; same words, but different word order underlined; similar wording broken underlined).

---

132 Cf. above pp. 238 f.
133 Cf. below p. 261.
134 In Antioch the creed had been implemented by means of a letter. There is no mention that it was separately signed by the bishops.
135 Cf. above ch. 5.1.
136 Cf. above ch. 5.5.

Roman creed as attested by Marcellus of Ancyra (R^M) (FaFo § 253)	N (FaFo § 135)
Πιστεύω [. . .] εἰς θεόν,	Πιστεύομεν εἰς ἕνα θεόν,
	πατέρα,
παντοκράτορα	παντοκράτορα,
	πάντων ὁρατῶν τε καὶ ἀοράτων ποιητήν·
καὶ εἰς Χριστὸν Ἰησοῦν,	καὶ εἰς ἕνα κύριον Ἰησοῦν Χριστόν,
τὸν υἱὸν αὐτοῦ	τὸν υἱὸν τοῦ θεοῦ
τὸν μονογενῆ,	
τὸν κύριον ἡμῶν,	
	γεννηθέντα ἐκ τοῦ πατρός,
	μονογενῆ,
	τουτέστιν ἐκ τῆς οὐσίας τοῦ πατρός,
	θεὸν ἐκ θεοῦ,
	φῶς ἐκ φωτός,
	θεὸν ἀληθινὸν ἐκ θεοῦ ἀληθινοῦ,
	γεννηθέντα οὐ ποιηθέντα,
	ὁμοούσιον τῷ πατρί,
	δι' οὗ τὰ πάντα ἐγένετο τά τε ἐν τῷ οὐρανῷ καὶ τὰ ἐν τῇ γῇ,
τὸν γεννηθέντα ἐκ πνεύματος ἁγίου καὶ Μαρίας τῆς παρθένου,	τὸν δι' ἡμᾶς τοὺς ἀνθρώπους καὶ διὰ τὴν ἡμετέραν σωτηρίαν κατελθόντα καὶ σαρκωθέντα, ἐνανθρωπήσαντα, παθόντα
τὸν ἐπὶ Ποντίου Πιλάτου σταυρωθέντα καὶ ταφέντα	
καὶ τῇ τρίτῃ ἡμέρᾳ ἀναστάντα	καὶ ἀναστάντα τῇ τρίτῃ ἡμέρᾳ,
ἐκ τῶν νεκρῶν,	
ἀναβάντα	ἀνελθόντα
εἰς τοὺς οὐρανοὺς	εἰς τοὺς οὐρανούς,
καὶ καθήμενον ἐν δεξιᾷ τοῦ πατρός,	
ὅθεν ἔρχεται κρίνειν ζῶντας καὶ νεκρούς	ἐρχόμενον κρῖναι ζῶντας καὶ νεκρούς·

καὶ εἰς τὸ ἅγιον πνεῦμα,
ἁγίαν ἐκκλησίαν,
ἄφεσιν ἁμαρτιῶν,
σαρκὸς ἀνάστασιν,
ζωὴν αἰώνιον.

καὶ εἰς τὸ ἅγιον πνεῦμα.
[condemnations]

As there is little evidence that earlier credal formulae existed (except for the credal interrogations which I discussed above[137]), these similarities may be considered as deriving from a *regula fidei* which provided the foundation for these creeds and which may explain these similarities. We may even be able to identify some of the elements which belonged to this *regula*. In this context, it is striking that N does not describe the passion story in the same detail as R does, instead simply using πα-θόντα which corresponds to *passum* in the early Roman interrogatory creeds.[138] Finally, N displays a number of additions which are clearly a result of the debates at the council: γεννηθέντα ἐκ τοῦ πατρός, and the passage τουτέστιν ἐκ τῆς οὐσίας – τὰ ἐν τῇ γῇ. The passage τὸν δι᾽ ἡμᾶς – ἐνανθρωπήσαντα may also belong into this context, though this is less certain.

When we omit the surplus text in both creeds we arrive at the following basic pattern:

Πιστεύω εἰς θεόν παντοκράτορα
καὶ εἰς Χριστὸν Ἰησοῦν/Ἰησοῦν Χριστόν,
τὸν υἱὸν αὐτοῦ/τοῦ θεοῦ [τὸν] μονογενῆ,
[γεννηθέντα
καὶ] παθόντα
καὶ τῇ τρίτῃ ἡμέρᾳ ἀναστάντα/ἀναστάντα τῇ τρίτῃ ἡμέρᾳ,
ἀναβάντα/ἀνελθόντα εἰς τοὺς οὐρανούς,
ὅθεν ἔρχεται κρίνειν ζῶντας καὶ νεκρούς/ἐρχόμενον κρῖναι ζῶντας καὶ νεκρούς·
καὶ εἰς τὸ ἅγιον πνεῦμα.

In my view, it is impossible to go any further than this. There is no evidence that this *regula* ever existed as such as a written formula. N does not seem to depend on R, whether directly or indirectly, in any meaningful sense or vice versa. This suggests that both these texts derive from a common oral tradition (as does Eus) which was the joint possession of the pre-Constantinian church and which we came across already when studying the *regulae fidei* of the second and third centuries.[139]

---

137 Cf. above ch. 4.5.
138 Cf. above ch. 4.5.1.
139 Cf. above ch 4.4.

6.4.4 The biblical basis of N

N is drenched in biblical language, although it contains only two actual quotations, i.e. the statement that 'through him [sc. the Son] all things came into being' (Jn 1:3, 1Cor 8:6) and that he will come 'to judge the living and the dead' (2Tim 4:1, 1Pet 4:5). With regard to the underlying biblical grammar, N largely follows Jn 1:1–14 down to the incarnation, without, however, using Logos terminology which was unsuitable for describing the intimate relationship between Father and Son and was, therefore, open to misinterpretations.[140] Interestingly, there are no clear allusions to Phil 2:6–11, although the internal dynamic of both biblical texts resembles each other.[141]

When we compare N with Eus we see that Mt 28:19 probably was the source for the basic trinitarian pattern, although the Great Commission is not quoted in N – though it is in Eus. Other important passages that have clearly influenced the text include Eph 4:5–6, 1Cor 8:6 (oneness of God the Father and of the Lord Jesus Christ); Rev 1:8 etc. (the Father's omnipotence);[142] 1Cor 8:6, Col 1:15–16, Heb 1:2 (Father as creator, Christ as intermediary/helper); Jn 1:14. 18, 3:16, 1Jn 4:9 (only-begotten); Jn 1:4. 9, 8:12 (light; cf. Heb 1:3); 3:33, 1Jn 5:20 (true God; cf. Jn 17:3); Jn 1:9, 3:13. 19, 11:27 (descent); 1Cor 15:3–4 (death, burial, and resurrection); Mk 16:19, Lk 24:51, Acts 1:11, 1Pet 3:22 (ascension); Mt 25:31, Acts 1:11 (return); Acts 10:42, 2Tim 4:1, 1Pet 4:5 (Last Judgement), and many others.[143] However, the creed's key term *homooúsios* is not found in the Bible and the underlying noun *ousía* occurs only in Lk 15:12–13 in quite a different context. This was one of the reasons why in the aftermath of the council N was by no means immediately accepted.

---

140 Cf. above p. 239.
141 On the reasons cf. Kinzig, "'Obedient unto death'", 2024 (*sub prelo*).
142 It must be noted, however, that, except for one reference in 2 Corinthians (6:18), the noun παντοκράτωρ is found in the New Testament *only* in Revelation, in most instances in combination with θεός (1:8; 4:8; 11:17; 15:3; 16:7. 14; 19:6. 15; 21:22). Revelation here deviates from the usage of the Septuagint where παντοκράτωρ is usually combined with κύριος. Furthermore, in the Greek Old Testament we do find a number of references of the extended type κύριος ὁ θεὸς ὁ παντοκράτωρ (Hos 12:6; Amos 3:13; 4:13; 5:8. 14. 15. 16. 27; 9:5. 6. 15; Nahum 3:5; Hag 1:14; Zech 10:3; Bar 3:1. 4; furthermore 2Sam(2Kings) 7:27: κύριε παντοκράτωρ θεὸς Ισραηλ; 1Chron 17:24: κύριε κύριε παντοκράτωρ θεὸς Ισραηλ; 2Macc 7:35: τοῦ παντοκράτορος ἐπόπτου θεοῦ; Jer 39:19: θεοῦ παντοκράτορος ἐθνῶν; Jer 39(32):19 ὁ θεὸς ὁ μέγας ὁ παντοκράτωρ καὶ μεγαλώνυμος κύριος; 3Macc 6:18: ὁ μεγαλόδοξος παντοκράτωρ καὶ ἀληθινὸς θεός; 6:28: τοῦ παντοκράτορος ἐπουρανίου θεοῦ ζῶντος). However, it never occurs together with πατήρ.
143 Cf. FaFo, ch. 3.

6.4.5 The theological cause of discontent: *homooúsios*

We must, therefore, take a closer look at this adjective *homooúsios*. How did the statement that the Son is 'consubstantial with the Father' come to be inserted into N, and what did it actually mean? Let us first recall the circumstances of its insertion. Eusebius (who skips the episode of the Arian creed submitted by his namesake of Nicomedia that I mentioned above in chapter 6.4.2) says that the council first discussed his own credal text in the presence of the emperor. The emperor then asked for *homooúsios* to be added and for the participants to sign the resultant creed, thus expressing their agreement (section 7).

As was outlined above, the council must have entrusted a committee with the necessary revisions because Eusebius indicates that N was 'dictated by them' in the general assembly (ταύτης τῆς γραφῆς ὑπ' αὐτῶν ὑπαγορευθείσης; section 9). Dictation was probably necessary, because the council fathers would not have been able to discuss this document unless they wrote it down first.[144] Eusebius is, however, coy about who was actually behind this draft.

Before the drafting committee began its work, the emperor seems to have addressed the council with a speech. At this point, Eusebius is quite explicit: Constantine 'added only the single word *homooúsios*' (ἑνὸς μόνου προσεγγραφέντος ῥήματος τοῦ ὁμοουσίου) himself providing the rationale behind this addition:

> \<The Son> was not called *homooúsios* with regard to corporeal affections; therefore, the Son did not subsist from the Father either by division or abscission, for a nature which was immaterial, noetic, and incorporeal could not possibly be subject to any corporeal affection, and it befitted [us] to contemplate such things with divine and ineffable expressions. Such was the philosophical view of the subject taken by our most-wise and most-pious emperor.[145]

One of the most frequently discussed areas of investigation regarding the Council of Nicaea concerns where the term *homooúsios* came from, why it was inserted into the creed, and what role Constantine actually played in this context. The painstaking research of the last fifty years, notably undertaken by Frauke Dinsen, Christopher G. Stead, and Martin von Ostheim, has cleared up the history of the term as much as possible.[146] By the beginning of the fourth century it could mean different things to different people. This was partly due to the fact that the underlying term

---

144 However, the verb ὑπαγορεύω is ambiguous and may also mean that N was 'drafted' by them.

145 Eusebius, *Epistula ad ecclesiam Caesariensem* (Opitz 1934/1935, *Urkunde 22*) 7 (FaFo § 135b1).

146 Cf. Dinsen 1976; Stead 1977, esp. pp. 190–222; Stead 1994; Ostheim 2008. In addition, Hanson 1988, pp. 190–202; Ulrich 1994, pp. 8–18; Beatrice 2002; Ayres 2004, pp. 92–8; Edwards 2012; Stępień 2018.

οὐσία might mean 'generic, shared being', while also referring to an individual 'being' (in that sense largely synonymous with ὑπόστασις[147]), just like the word 'car' could be used to refer to cars as such ('they drove by car') or to an individual specimen (such as a pink Mercedes identified by a certain licence plate). To add to the confusion, in second-century Valentinian gnosticism it could refer to 'belonging to the same order of being' within the gnostic three-tier hierarchy of being.[148]

The most influential theologian of the third century, Origen, may occasionally have used *homooúsios* to describe the Son's relation to the Father. However, on other occasions he insisted on a difference between the οὐσίαι and *hypostáseis* of Father and Son and distinguished between a first and second *hypóstasis*, the second clearly being subordinate to the first.[149]

Furthermore, *homooúsios* had also played a certain role in a controversy between Dionysius of Alexandria (*sedit* 247/248–264/265) and Dionysius of Rome (*sedit* 259–268) with the former declaring it unscriptural. Nevertheless, he reluctantly accepted its use, equating it both with ὁμογενής ('of the same descent/kind' as between parents and children) and ὁμοφυής ('of the same nature' as between seed and plant).[150] Much ink has been spilt over who introduced the term into the trinitarian debate of the third century and what role it played in this context. In addition, Paul of Samosata may have been censured for using the term which contributed to his condemnation and deposition in 268. However, details of Paul's use and understanding of *homooúsios* remain blurred and need not concern us here, because

> the one point which is quite clear in this obscure affair is that those who condemned Paul also condemned the use of the word *homooúsios* in a trinitarian context, thereby causing considerable embarrassment to those theologians who wanted to defend its inclusion in an official doctrinal statement in the next century.[151]

Arius and others very carefully distinguished between God/Father and Son, because – as Arius put it – the Son 'is neither part of God nor [does he exist] from any underlying being (ἐξ ὑποκειμένου τινός)'.[152] In his letter to Alexander Arius

---

147 For the history of this term cf. Hammerstaedt 1994.
148 Cf. Stead 1977, p. 209; Hanson 1988, p. 191. There has been an attempt in recent research to derive Constantine's interpretation of *homooúsios* from hermetic literature (cf. esp. Beatrice 2002; Digeser 2017; Chandler 2019, esp. 99–122). This has been refuted by O'Leary 2022.
149 For details cf. Stead 1977, pp. 209–14; Stead 1994, cols. 389–91; Hammerstaedt 1994, cols. 1005–8.
150 Cf. Athanasius, *De sententia Dionysii* 18,2–3.
151 Hanson 1988, p. 195.
152 Arius, *Epistula ad Eusebium Nicomediensem* (Opitz 1934/1935, *Urkunde 1*; FaFo § 131b) 5.

explicitly connected the use of *homooúsios* with the teaching of Mani.[153] He also rejected his opponents' exegesis of the preposition ἐκ in Psalm 109(110):3c ('From the womb (ἐκ γαστρός), before the morning-star I brought you forth') and Jn 8:42 ('I came forth from the Father (ἐκ τοῦ πατρός), and I am come'), because it suggested that the Son was a 'part' (μέρος) of the Father and therefore 'consubstantial' or some kind of emanation (προβολή).[154]

Eusebius of Nicomedia had expressed himself in a similar vein in a letter to Paulinus, bishop of Tyre:

> We have never heard that there are two unbegotten [beings] (δύο ἀγέννητα) nor that one has been divided into two, nor have we learned or believed that it has ever undergone any change of a corporeal nature, my lord; but [we affirm] that what is unbegotten is one and one also that which [exists] in truth by him, yet did not come into being from his substance (καὶ οὐκ ἐκ τῆς οὐσίας αὐτοῦ γεγονός), and does not at all participate in the nature of the unbegotten (τῆς φύσεως τῆς ἀγεννήτου) or exist from his substance (ἐκ τῆς οὐσίας αὐτοῦ), but came into being entirely distinct in his nature and in his power, and having become a perfect likeness both of disposition and power to the maker (ἀλλὰ γεγονὸς ὁλοσχερῶς ἕτερον τῇ φύσει καὶ τῇ δυνάμει, πρὸς τελείαν ὁμοιότητα διαθέσεώς τε καὶ δυνάμεως τοῦ πεποιηκότος γενόμενον). We believe that his beginning not only cannot be expressed by words but is also incomprehensible to the understanding not only of humans, but also of all beings superior to man.
>
> We advance these considerations not as our own, but we speak as we have learned from Holy Scripture. We have learned that the Son was created, established, and begotten in substance (γεννητὸν τῇ οὐσίᾳ) and in the same immutable and inexpressible nature and likeness as the Maker; and so the Lord himself says, 'God created (ἔκτισε) me in the beginning of his ways; I was set up from everlasting; before the hills he brings me forth' [Prov 8:22–23. 25b]. If he had been from him, that is, of him (ἐξ αὐτοῦ, τουτέστιν ἀπ' αὐτοῦ), as some portion of him or from an emanation of his substance, it could not be said that he was created or established (κτιστὸν οὐδὲ θεμελιωτόν); and of this you, my lord, are certainly not ignorant. For that which exists from the unbegotten could not be said to have been created or established, either by another or by him, since it exists as unbegotten from the beginning (τὸ γὰρ ἐκ τοῦ ἀγεννήτου ὑπάρχον κτιστὸν ἔτι ὑφ' ἑτέρου ἢ ὑπ' αὐτοῦ ἢ θεμελιωτὸν οὐκ ἂν εἴη, ἐξ ἀρχῆς ἀγέννητον ὑπάρχον). But if the fact of his being called the begotten gives any ground for the belief that, having come into being of the Father's substance (ἐκ τῆς οὐσίας τῆς πατρικῆς αὐτὸν γεγονότα), he also possesses from the Father the identity of nature (τὴν ταυτότητα τῆς φύσεως), we know that it is not of him alone that the Scriptures have spoken as begotten, but that they also thus speak of those who are entirely dissimilar to him by nature (ἐπὶ τῶν ἀνομοίων αὐτῷ κατὰ πάντα τῇ φύσει).[155]

---

153 For the background cf. Rose 1979, pp. 154–161, Heil 2002, and Hutter 2012, cols. 32 f. In addition, Hutter 2023, pp. 213–15.

154 Arius et al., *Epistula ad Alexandrum Alexandrinum* (Opitz 1934/1935, *Urkunde 6*; FaFo § 131a) 5.

155 Eusebius of Nicomedia, *Epistula ad Paulinum Tyrium* (Opitz 1934/1935, *Urkunde 8*), 3–6 (tr. NPNF; altered).

It appears that Eusebius tries to ward off a 'materialistic' interpretation of οὐσία in this passage: if something undergoes ('suffers', πεπονθός) change it must possess some form of material substratum which is actually able to change. Yet God's immutability would suffer if a being were to issue from God 'by some quasi-physical process of generation involving change or loss'.[156] Οὐσία and φύσις (he uses the terms synonymously) must not be understood to refer to some kind of material reality. If it did, the Son's coming into being would be like a 'cell division' (my term). Yet in its christological interpretation Proverbs 8 points to the 'creation' of the Son which, temporal factors notwithstanding, necessarily implies a substantial distinctness of that Son from the Father.

Here the rift which must have opened up between Constantine and his Arian advisers becomes especially palpable: both the emperor and Eusebius of Nicomedia denounced a 'material' interpretation of *homoousios*. Yet whereas Eusebius used this argument to *reject homoousios* entirely and to *deny* the full divinity of the Son, Constantine advocated the use of the adjective for *affirming* the Son's full divinity. Unfortunately, however, the emperor was unable to supply a positive definition of the term in the way he intended it to be understood, simply affirming that one should 'contemplate such things with divine and ineffable expressions'. He defined the Son's nature (φύσις), which he appeared to identify with οὐσία, as 'immaterial, noetic, and incorporeal' (ἄυλον καὶ νοερὰν καὶ ἀσώματον).[157] Whereas it was clear what φύσις was not (i.e. neither matter nor body), it was less clear what it actually was, except that it could only be perceived by the νοῦς (and not by the senses).[158]

As a result, the precise nature of the relationship between the Father and the Son remained hazy and open to misinterpretation which is why the insertion of the terms *ousía* and *homoousíos* caused a certain agitation among the council fathers. Eusebius reports:

> On their dictating this document, we did not let it pass without inquiry in what sense they used the expressions 'from the substance of the Father' (ἐκ τῆς οὐσίας τοῦ πατρός) and 'consubstantial with the Father (τῷ πατρὶ ὁμοούσιον)'. Accordingly, questions and explanations took place, and the meaning of the phrases was examined in rational argument. And they professed that the phrase 'from the substance' was indicative of the Son's being indeed from the Father, yet without being as if a portion of him (τοῦ ἐκ μὲν τοῦ πατρὸς εἶναι, οὐ μὴν ὡς μέρος ὑπάρχειν τοῦ πατρός).[159]

---

156 Stead 1977, p. 227.
157 Cf. Eusebius, *Epistula ad ecclesiam Caesariensem* (Opitz 1934/1935, *Urkunde 22*) 7 (FaFo § 135b1).
158 On φύσις cf. Zachhuber 2016, esp. cols. 763 f.
159 Eusebius, *Epistula ad ecclesiam Caesariensem* (Opitz 1934/1935, *Urkunde 22*) 9 (tr. NPNF; altered).

Eusebius stressed that the use of the phrases γεννηθέντα οὐ ποιηθέντα, ὁμοού-σιον τῷ πατρί ('begotten, not made, consubstantial with the Father') was used to ward off the (Arian) idea that the Son's *ousía* was in any way comparable or identical with earthly matter and that the Son, therefore, belonged to the created order. In this respect he also used the term *hypóstasis* synonymously with *ousía*: the Son was not of a different *hypóstasis* than the Father.[160] However, it remained obscure what *homooúsios* meant *exactly*: if Eusebius' account of the discussions is to be trusted, it did not necessarily mean 'of identical substance', but that the Son 'resembled in every respect the begetting Father alone'.[161]

This imprecision may have been introduced into the creed on purpose: the emperor or his advisers may have thought that *homooúsios* (although clearly not acceptable to the Arians) was a fuzzy enough description of the ontological proximity of Father and Son to be adopted by the council's majority. *Ousía* and *hypóstasis* were largely used synonymously in N as a whole (including the anathemas). Given the debates that took place at the council, οὐσία in N must, therefore, be translated as something like 'ontological manifestation'. *Homooúsios* then meant that the Son possessed the same 'ontological manifestation' as the Father which, in turn, implied that he, too, was immutable and did not belong to the created order. In other words, *ousía* filled the terminological gap which had opened up when one tried to preserve the distinction between Father and Son while, at the same time, emphasizing their unity in such a way that it was *more than* terminological, but existed on an ontological level, thus marking the categorical difference to the relationship between the creator and the created order. For this present purpose it was perfectly acceptable that *homooúsios* could mean the essential identity of Father and Son, as well as denoting a fundamental similarity in a wider sense between the two as long as it was clear that this similarity was due to *some* kind of common ontological substratum (their shared *ousía* or *hypóstasis*) which was neither merely conceptual nor material. Given this fuzziness, *homooúsios* served less as a definition of the Son's divinity, than to denote the ontological incomparability of the Son's *ousía* to that of the created order – an incomparability which excluded his origin from any other *hypóstasis* or *ousía* than that of the Father.[162]

Athanasius, who participated in the council as Alexander's secretary, says as much in his defence of Nicaea (*De decretis Nicaenae synodi*, written perhaps in 352/353):

---

160 Cf. Eusebius, *Epistula ad ecclesiam Caesariensem* (Opitz 1934/1935, *Urkunde 22*) 12.
161 Eusebius, *Epistula ad ecclesiam Caesariensem* (Opitz 1934/1935, *Urkunde 22*) 13.
162 Cf. Eusebius, *Epistula ad ecclesiam Caesariensem* (Opitz 1934/1935, *Urkunde 22*) 12–13.

> The fathers 'wrote "from God's substance" (ἐκ τῆς οὐσίας τοῦ θεοῦ), in order that "from God" (τὸ ἐκ τοῦ θεοῦ) might not be considered common and equal (κοινὸν καὶ ἴσον) in the Son and in things originate, but that everything else might be believed as a creature, and the Word alone as from the Father.'[163]

In this respect N went even further than Alexander of Alexandria who never used the term *homooúsios*, but tried to maintain the full divinity of the Son while attributing a different *hypóstasis* to him than that of the Father.[164] He merely insisted on some kind of 'likeness' between Father and Son which he derived *inter alia* from Col 1:15 ('image') and Heb 1:3 ('radiance'), without being more clearly defined.[165]

Incidentally, this is probably also the reason why the term Logos was not used in N, because according to traditional doctrine it could be understood either as the Father's λόγος ἐνδιάθετος ('inner mental', i.e. purely inwardly conceived, word or thought), in which case the distinction between Father and Son would not have been sufficiently clear), or as his λόγος προφορικός ('spoken/uttered word') which not only made it difficult to express the unity between Father and Son, but which could also be misunderstood to mean that the Word was some kind of (material) emanation from God, as the gnostics, Stoics, or Neo-Platonists supposedly held,[166] perhaps not possessing its own *hypóstasis*.[167]

Where did *homooúsios* come from all of a sudden? We have conflicting information in this regard. On the one hand, Basil of Caesarea repeatedly mentions that Hermogenes, bishop of Caesarea in Cappadocia, 'wrote' the creed.[168] But this

---

163 Athanasius, *De decretis Nicaenae synodi* 19,2 (tr. NPNF; altered).

164 Cf. Alexander of Alexandria, *Epistula ad Alexandrum Thessalonicensem* (*Byzantinum*; Opitz 1934/1935, *Urkunde 14*) 16. 19. 20–1. 38. 46. 48.

165 Cf. Alexander of Alexandria, *Epistula encyclica* (*Urkunde 4b*), 13 (Opitz 1934/1935, p. 9, ll. 3 f.): Ἢ πῶς ἀνόμοιος τῇ οὐσίᾳ τοῦ πατρὸς ὁ ὢν εἰκὼν τελεία καὶ ἀπαύγασμα τοῦ πατρὸς καὶ λέγων ὁ ἑωρακὼς ἐμὲ ἑώρακε τὸν πατέρα; 'Or how is he unlike the Father's substance, who is the perfect image and the radiance of the Father and says, "Whoever has seen me has seen the Father" [Jn 14:9]?' Cf. also Stead 1994, col. 405 f.

166 On this Logos doctrine cf. Mühl 1962; Kamesar 2004; Löhr 2010, cols. 337 f.; Becker 2016, pp. 372–4. Later in the fourth century those theologians who wished to retain the Logos terminology distanced themselves from the use of both the term λόγος ἐνδιάθετος and λόγος προφορικός. Cf., e.g., *Ecthesis macrostichos* (FaFo § 145) 9–10; Council of Sirmium (351), *Fidei confessio prima* (§ 148) 9(8); Pseudo-Athanasius (Marcellus?), *Expositio fidei* (§ 149), 1. On the idea of 'emanation' and its opponents cf. Ratzinger 1959; Dörrie 1965(1976) (who emphasizes that Plotinus used the term only sparingly).

167 Eusebius also refuted this distinction (cf. Löhr 2010, col. 407, listing references). Cf. also below pp. 292, 295, 297 f. and n. 330; 335, 351 n. 588.

168 Cf. Basil, *Epistula 81:* '[. . .] the offspring of the blessed Hermogenes who wrote the great and indestructible creed in the great synod (τοῦ τὴν μεγάλην καὶ ἄρρηκτον πίστιν γράψαντος ἐν τῇ μεγάλῃ συνόδῳ).' Id., *Epistula 244*, 9: Then the Arians 'went over to Hermogenes, who was diametrically

is rather unlikely, since his name does not appear on the lists of episcopal participants (instead, Leontius is shown as the city's bishop[169]). It is also unclear whether Basil regarded Hermogenes as the sole author, as head of the drafting committee, or as some kind of secretary to the council.

On the other hand, Philostorgius claims that Ossius and Alexander of Alexandria had schemed before the Council in Nicomedia to adopt *homooúsios* and to condemn Arius[170] – but how would the Church historian have known about this? Nevertheless, Philostorgius may not be entirely wrong, because Athanasius mentions in his *Historia Arianorum* written many years after the event (late 357) that Ossius 'had set out the faith in Nicaea (τὴν ἐν Νικαίᾳ πίστιν ἐξέθετο) and had everywhere proclaimed the Arians as heretics'.[171]

Whatever the authorship of N, in another context Athanasius reports that 'the council' first wanted to compose a creed entirely based on Scripture but was then forced to introduce *homooúsios* for greater precision, after the 'Eusebians' had given the original draft an Arian interpretation.[172]

Yet another version of what had happened is recorded in the writings of Ambrose of Milan. He says that *homooúsios* was included in the aforementioned letter by Eusebius of Nicomedia from which he then quotes one single sentence: 'If, however, we called the Son of God also uncreated, we would begin to confess him as *homooúsios* with the Father' – which to Eusebius is, of course, unacceptable.[173] Ambrose continues:

> When this letter had been read at the Council of Nicaea, the fathers inserted this word [i.e. *homooúsios*] into their treatise on the faith (*in tractatu fidei*), because they saw that it would shock their adversaries, in order that they, as it were, might take the sword, which their

---

opposed to the false teaching of Arius, as is declared by the creed originally published by that man at Nicaea (ὡς δηλοῖ αὐτὴ ἡ πίστις ἡ κατὰ Νίκαιαν παρ' ἐκείνου τοῦ ἀνδρὸς ἐκφωνηθεῖσα ἐξ ἀρχῆς).' Hermogenes is also mentioned in *Epistula 263*, 2 where Basil says that he ordained Eustathius of Sebaste.

169 Cf. Gelzer/Hilgenfeld/Cuntz 1898, p. LXII (no. 94). I consider it wholly unlikely that Hermogenes participated as priest and would have drafted N in that minor capacity.

170 Cf. Philostorgius, *Historia ecclesiastica* 1,7; 1,7a (anonymous *Life of Constantine*); 1,9a (*Life of Constantine*). The *Life* claims that Ossius and Alexander had even prepared N in advance to be signed by all bishops (Philostorgius, *Historia ecclesiastica* 1,9a), but then quotes the beginning of the Creed of *Constantinople* (1,9a,3: Πιστεύομεν εἰς ἕνα θεόν, πατέρα, παντοκράτορα, ποιητὴν οὐρανοῦ τε καὶ γῆς ὁρατῶν τε πάντων καὶ ἀοράτων) plus the anathemas of N as the creed prepared by Ossius and Alexander! This is possibly the creed in Epiphanius, *Ancoratus* 118,9–13 (FaFo § 184e5).

171 Athanasius, *Historia Arianorum* 42,3.

172 Cf. Athanasius, *De decretis Nicaenae synodi* 19–20; Behr 2004, vol. I, p. 157.

173 Cf. also Gwynn 2007, p. 213.

[opponents] had drawn, to sever the head of their own blasphemous heresy [cf. 1Sam (1Kings) 17:51].[174]

Although it is hardly likely that *homooúsios* was included in N in order to *provoke* the Arians, it could well be that it was the letter of Eusebius of Nicomedia which introduced the term into the debate, which was then inserted into N as 'an apotropaic formula for resisting Arianism'[175] precisely because it would have been rejected by cocksure Arians like Arius himself and Eusebius of Nicomedia. Conceivably, the staunch anti-Arian bishop of Antioch, Eustathius, and Ossius of Córdoba, who insisted on the one *hypóstasis* of Father and Son, may have been responsible for its inclusion, although the evidence remains inconclusive.[176] Be that as it may, it is difficult to believe that the emperor himself was behind this move; instead, he probably relied on the counsel of his theological advisers who by that time must have included anti-Arians such as Eustathius and Ossius.

It may be significant in that respect that Eusebius does not actually say that it was Constantine who *introduced homooúsios* into the debate, but only that he *added* it and also provided the key to interpreting the text (ἑρμήνευε).[177] Indeed, the bishop points out that he himself knew that 'even among the ancients some learned and illustrious bishops and writers' had used the term 'in their theological discourse about the Father and Son'[178] which may suggest a wider discussion among the council fathers in which traditional authorities such as Origen, Dionysius of Rome, or Dionysius of Alexandria were cited. It is even unclear whether the emperor *accepted* the addition and went on to provide a series of qualifications or whether he actually urged for it to be added, however with some explanations in order to make it palatable for those opposing the term, because *ousía* could be understood to refer to corporeal affections (τῶν σωμάτων πάθη) and to presuppose some kind of materiality of the Father and the Son, understandings that needed to be ruled out. The explanations given in the letter to the Church of Caesarea are found in other texts by Eusebius, almost word for word.[179] This may suggest that the bishop expresses what the emperor had actually said in his own

---

174 Ambrose, *De fide* 3,125 (cf. Opitz 1934/1935, *Urkunde 21*, in part).
175 Hanson 1988, p. 172.
176 On Eustathius' theology cf. Lorenz 1982, pp. 544 f.; Sara Parvis 2006, pp. 57–60; Cartwright 2015. Ossius also seems to have been sceptical with regard to the doctrine of two/three divine οὐσίαι. Cf. Narcissus of Neronias, *Epistula ad Chrestum, Euphronium et Eusebium* (Opitz 1934/1935, *Urkunde 19*) and Pietri/Markschies 1996(2010), p. 301.
177 Eusebius, *Epistula ad ecclesiam Caesariensem* (Opitz 1934/1935, *Urkunde 22*) 7 (FaFo § 135b1).
178 Eusebius, *Epistula ad ecclesiam Caesariensem* (Opitz 1934/1935, *Urkunde 22*) 13.
179 Cf. Eusebius, *Epistula ad ecclesiam Caesariensem* (Opitz 1934/1935, *Urkunde 22*) 7 (FaFo § 135b1) in comparison with the list in Stead 1977, p. 232.

words here.[180] Ultimately, it is impossible to give a conclusive answer as to who suggested *homooúsios* although Eustathius probably had a hand in it in some way, supported by Ossius.

6.4.6 The anathemas of N

The section on the Holy Spirit in N is very brief; but N does not end with it. It is followed by a series of condemnations which are clearly (although not explicitly) directed against Arius and his theology. In particular, the following doctrines are condemned:

(1) the temporal beginning of the Son;
(2) his creation from nothing;
(3) his origin from another *hypóstasis* or *ousía*;
(4) his mutability.

These are precisely the same tenets which had already been rejected in Antioch some months previously, although summarized in a more succinct fashion. It is, therefore, probable that either the authors of N had the creed of Antioch at their disposition or at least that those bishops who had drafted the earlier creed were also involved in the drafting of N.

Not only are N's anathemas clearly based on those of Antioch when it comes to their theological *content*: they also follow Antioch in not condemning specific *persons*. This was already remarked upon in antiquity and attributed to the council's 'moderation'.[181] However, there is also a characteristic difference between Antioch and Nicaea in this regard. In Antioch a synod condemned certain dissident doctrines (and communicated this decision to other churches), speaking in the first person plural: 'we condemn'. In N it was the 'catholic and apostolic Church' which performed this act. The weight of N's anathemas was increased even further by postponing this subject to the end of the sentence. In addition, it was not *a* church (or synod), but *the* Church whose eminence was underlined by the qualifying adjectives 'catholic' and 'apostolic'. Thus

---

180 The 'tenor' of Constantine's own interpretation of N (or of that of his advisers) may be gathered from his letter to the church of Nicomedia (Opitz 1934/1935, *Urkunde 27*) 1–5.

181 Cf. Rufinus, *Historia ecclesiastica* 10,12: '. . . since the moderation of the council [of Nicaea] was so great that they passed sentence not against [Arius'] person, but against his depraved doctrines [. . .].' Likewise Justinian, *Edictum rectae fidei* (Schwartz 1973, p. 160, ll. 29 f.): 'For the [synod] of Nicaea anonymously anathematized those who advocated the godless view of Arius [. . .].' Incidentally, in the *Edictum* this forms part of an entire paragraph on the practice of anathematizing: Schwartz 1973, pp. 160, l. 1 – 164, l. 33.

two claims were made: first, the Church pronouncing the anathema was 'universal' (καθολικός) as opposed to the particular minority view of the heretics; second, it stood in one unbroken and continuous line with the apostles (as opposed to the newfangled heresies). Clearly, these claims were not historical: it quickly turned out that many, if not most bishops did *not* accept N, because they held views similar to those which were being outlawed here; likewise, it was easy to prove that the real innovation consisted not in the subordinationism of the Arians, but in the introduction of the unbiblical *homooúsios*. Yet that was not the point: the phrasing chosen at Nicaea was intended to seize and defend a certain discursive space and to display the hegemony of one group of bishops, supported by the emperor, over dissenting views. The anathemas of Nicaea thus served to increase this creed's normativity even further. From then on the creeds were also used to test episcopal orthodoxy; dissent was sanctioned in the anathemas.[182]

Yet in the long term this discursive strategy was not altogether successful: the anathemas were not seen as forming a unified whole with the creed, but continued as a separate literary genre which might amalgamate with other genres. Thus, as we will see, in Constantinople the anathemas were no longer appended to the creed but included in canon 1 of the synod, here directed against certain groups which were each labelled with a collective term.[183]

Unfortunately, the evidence regarding how the creed might be 'enforced' and the nature of the sanctions expressed in the anathemas remains unclear, as the sources contradict each other about what happened after N had been produced at the council. There is some evidence to suggest that the document was ultimately forced upon the bishops as the emperor threatened them all with immediate exile should they refuse to sign it.[184] Apparently, this had the effect of Eusebius of Nicomedia, Theognis of Nicaea, and Maris of Chalcedon (hence three of the five aforementioned bishops from nearby the court) changing sides and adopting the synod's decrees, apparently persuaded by Constantine's sister Constantia. Philostorgius (who is sympathetic to the Arian cause) says that they changed *homooúsios* to *homoioúsios* ('of similar substance') when they signed the creed, but this is often doubted by modern scholars because it seems to exonerate Eusebius.[185] Be that as it may,

---

182 Cf. Turner, *History and Use*, 1910, pp. 28 f.

183 Cf. Council of Constantinople (381), canon 1 (FaFo § 565c): Eunomians/Anhomoians, Arians/Eudoxians, semi-Arians/Pneumatomachians, Sabellians, Marcionites, Photinians, Apolinarians. Cf. also below p. 357.

184 Cf. Philostorgius, *Historia ecclesiastica* 1,9a. It is unclear whether this information, provided by the aforementioned anonymous *Life of Constantine*, is accurate.

185 Cf. Philostorgius, *Historia ecclesiastica* 1,9; 1,9c and Bleckmann/Stein 2015, vol. II, p. 95.

these three did not subscribe to the anathemas which suggests that the creed and the anathemas were signed separately.[186]

The imperial *magister officiorum* Philumenus was charged with also collecting the signatures of Arius and his remaining adherents. (Arius himself may not have taken part in the council, although probably being nearby.[187]) They refused and suffered their fate and went into exile. Their exact number is unknown, but it appears that the Arian bishops Secundus of Ptolemais and Theonas or Marmarica belonged to this group, Arius and some of the priests in his retinue notwithstanding.[188] As regards Eusebius, Theognis, and Maris, it is not quite clear whether they were also exiled by the emperor straight away[189] or some months later.[190] Eusebius and Theognis later declared their willingness also to sign the anathemas in a joint letter to the emperor.[191]

Exile in any case involved a de facto deposition. However, as far as we can see, none of the bishops and priests in exile had to undergo a process of penance, which would have been required, had they been excommunicated. Instead they were required to recant their heretical doctrines; some of them (such as Arius and Euzoius[192]) did so and were then recalled and reinstated (which in Arius' case may not have happened due to his premature death[193]).

In other words, issuing the anathemas (which were pronounced by the synod and were, in this instance, not directed against persons) and enforcing the punishments (which were secular measures directed against specific individuals) were two distinct procedures and not necessarily interconnected. This becomes very clear from the letter which the council fathers sent to the Egyptian clergy. After first quoting the anathemas they added rather enigmatically:

---

186 Cf. Eusebius of Nicomedia and Theognis of Nicaea, *Libellus paenitentiae* (Opitz 1934/1935, *Urkunde 31*) 2; Socrates, *Historia ecclesiastica* 1,8,32.

187 Attendance is claimed by Rufinus, *Historia ecclesiastica* 10,1. However, the mention of Philumenus as being entrusted with collecting their signatures (if historical) only makes sense if Arius did *not* take part in the proceedings; but he 'may have been lurking in the wings' (Hanson 1988, p. 157).

188 Cf. Philostorgius, *Historia ecclesiastica* 1,9–10.

189 Cf. Socrates, *Historia ecclesiastica* 1,8,33.

190 Cf. Philostorgius, *Historia ecclesiastica* 1,10. Cf. also Constantine's letter to the church of Nicomedia (Opitz 1934/1935, *Urkunde 27*). Cf. also Sara Parvis 2006, p. 135.

191 Cf. Eusebius of Nicomedia and Theognis of Nicaea, *Libellus paenitentiae* (Opitz 1934/1935, *Urkunde 31*) 3; cf. Socrates, *Historia ecclesiastica* 1,8,34; 1,14,1.

192 Cf. Arius and Euzoius, *Epistula ad Constantinum imperatorem* (Opitz 1934/1935, *Urkunde 30*; FaFo § 131c).

193 Cf. below p. 268 n. 207. On the difference between anathema and excommunication cf. also above p. 233.

> But you have either learned already or will learn about the outcome the measures taken
> against him [sc. Arius] have had (καὶ τὰ μὲν κατ' ἐκεῖνον οἵου τέλους τετύχηκε πάντως ἢ
> ἀκηκόατε ἢ ἀκούσεσθε); for we would not seem to trample on a man who has received that
> which his peculiar sin deserved. Yet his impiety proved so powerful that it affected Theonas
> of Marmarica and Secundus of Ptolemais; for they have suffered the same things.[194]

The cautious phrasing of this significant passage (which is often mistranslated) can only mean that (a) the synod did not wish to preempt a message sent to Egypt by a third party, (b) that this message contained the punishment meted out to Arius, Theonas, and Secundus,[195] and (c) that the synod did not wish to impose further sanctions on the three heretics, because the message by the third party already contained punishments matching their offences. Hence the synod did *not* state that Arius 'was excommunicated and probably degraded from the presbyterate',[196] because the 'measures' (literally 'things') were not those taken by the synod, but by the third party. This third party must, of course, have been the emperor, and the imperial letter in question may be *Urkunde 25*.[197] Oddly, though, Constantine's epistle contains no information as to what happened to Arius but admonishes the church of Alexandria to restore ecclesial peace. Perhaps Arius' punishment was stipulated by a separate edict (which will also have been published in Alexandria but is no longer extant).

The creed had turned from an expression of faith into a legal document at the latest in Nicaea, given the protocol followed at the synod, the emperor's involvement in the proceedings, and the measures taken in its aftermath. Henceforth, dissent was – in principle (though not always in practice) – subject to secular punishment which could involve deposition and exile or other sanctions (see below). It is true, therefore, to say that 'Constantine's interference in the conflict and the establishment of an "official" doctrine "criminalized" theological dissent'.[198]

Nonetheless, developments had not yet reached a stage at which the Nicene Creed was made compulsory for *all* Christians – for the time being its binding force remained restricted to the bishops. As far as we can see, Constantine did not even make N compulsory for all clergy. He was content with, as he thought at the time, having established peace between the warring factions in the Arian controversy. In

---

194 Council of Nicaea (325), *Epistula ad ecclesiam Alexandrinam et episcopos Aegypti, Libyae et Pentapolis* (Opitz 1934/1935, *Urkunde 23*) 4–5.
195 The fact that in *Urkunde 23* only Arius, Theonas, and Secundus are mentioned does not mean that no other bishops were exiled, as this letter is directed to the Egyptian church and may, therefore, cite only those clerics that fell under its jurisdiction.
196 *Pace* Williams 2001, p. 70.
197 Cf. Constantine, *Epistula ad ecclesiam Alexandrinam* (Opitz 1934/1935, *Urkunde 25*).
198 Galvão-Sobrinho 2013, p. 91.

his letter to the church of Alexandria of June 325 he called the local clergy to settle their differences on the basis of the decisions of Nicaea where 'more than three hundred bishops' had 'confirmed one and the same faith' (μίαν καὶ τὴν αὐτὴν πίστιν) which remained unspecified.[199] In his encyclical letter to all the churches Constantine did not even consider it necessary to mention the doctrinal issues discussed at Nicaea.[200] Instead he imposed a poll tax on those bishops who followed Arius which was ten times higher than usual and withdrew certain privileges.[201] Finally, he ordered the heretic's writings to be burnt like those of the anti-Christian philosopher Porphyry had been.[202] But nowhere did he quote or paraphrase N. The emperor first paraphrased his own faith in a letter to the church of Nicomedia, going on to warn its clergy against sympathizing with Eusebius.[203] In a rather rambling and aggressive letter to Arius and his followers the emperor sought to refute Arius' theology, perhaps on the basis of N, but without explicit recourse to it.[204] Therefore, in the emperor's eyes the purpose of Nicaea was not to establish a specific creed but to achieve unity by whatever means necessary.

As regards the legal implications of the creed and its anathemas, we may, therefore, summarize our conclusions as follows: the bishops at Nicaea followed the precedent set by Antioch in defining the faith in writing by means of a three-part creed. In addition, they appended anathemas to the creed (as had also happened at Antioch). These anathemas were, as it were, the 'flip side' of defining the faith by means of a fixed formula. Yet they did not *necessarily* follow from this definition and, as a result, did not form an integral part of the creed; instead, they helped to delimit even more clearly the boundaries of what was permitted to be said about the Trinity and what was not. The emperor and/or the synod required the bishops to agree to N and to the anathemas by signing each of them separately. If this was refused, they were deposed and sent into exile. If they recanted, they were recalled and reinstated. In this respect, Constantine followed a

---

199 Constantine, *Epistula ad ecclesiam Alexandrinam* (Opitz 1934/1935, *Urkunde 25*) 5.
200 Cf. Constantine, *Epistula ad omnes ecclesias* (Opitz 1934/1935, *Urkunde 26*) 2 where he mentions only in passing that controversial matters regarding the veneration of God had been discussed and then concentrates on explaining the reasons for the date of Easter.
201 Cf. Constantine, *Epistula ad Arium et socios* (Opitz 1934/1935, *Urkunde 34*) 39 and 41 and *Codex Theodosianus* 16,5,1 (326).
202 Cf. Constantine, *Lex de Arii damnatione* (Opitz 1934/1935, *Urkunde 33*).
203 Cf. Constantine, *Epistula ad ecclesiam Nicomediensem* (Opitz 1934/1935, *Urkunde 27*), esp. 1–5 and 13.
204 Cf. Constantine, *Epistula ad Arium et socios* (Opitz 1934/1935, *Urkunde 34*; the date of this letter is controversial; cf., e.g., Williams 2001, p. 77: 333; Brennecke et al. 2007, p. XXXVIII: 325). Allusions to N are, perhaps, found in *Urkunde 34*, 14–15 and 26. Cf. Williams 2001, pp. 77 f.

procedure which he had already applied against the Donatists.[205] Nevertheless, in doing so he set an important precedent because theological dissent had so far not been considered a crime.[206]

6.5 Creeds between Nicaea and Constantinople

Nicaea was no success story. After the council Constantine once again changed tack: Arius was rehabilitated after he and his associates had submitted a creed, perhaps in early 328, which Constantine considered compatible with N.[207] The emperor may have thought that he had thus achieved ecclesial unity.[208] But the problem was not only one of politics. The formula adopted at Nicaea remained unacceptable to a large number of eastern bishops who in one way or another sympathized with Arius and Eusebius of Nicomedia and/or took exception to the use of a non-biblical term (*homooúsios*) to describe the relationship between God Father and the Son or Logos. Most bishops followed a view which Origen had already expressed a century previously: there was a clear hierarchy in heaven with the Father ranked at the top and the Son or Logos and the Holy Spirit being (in some way) subordinate to him. As Origen put it in his *Commentary on John*:

> But we are obedient to the Saviour who says, 'The Father who sent me is greater than I' [John 14:28 *v.l.*] and who, for this reason, did not permit himself to accept the title 'good' [cf. Mk 10:18] when it was applied to him, although it was perfectly legitimate and true. Instead, he graciously offered it up to the Father, and rebuked the one who wished to praise the Son excessively. This is why we say the Saviour and the Holy Spirit transcend all created beings, not by comparison, but by their exceeding pre-eminence (ὑπερβαλλούσῃ ὑπεροχῇ). The Father exceeds the Saviour as much (or even more) as the Saviour himself and the Holy Spirit exceed the rest (which are no ordinary beings). How great is the praise ascribed to him who transcends thrones, dominions, principalities, powers, and every name that is named not only in this world but also in that which is to come [cf. Eph 1:21]? And in addition to these <what must we> say also of holy angels, spirits, and just souls?

---

205 Cf. Lenski 2016, pp. 173 f. and 204 f. (nos. 39, 42).
206 On anti-heretical legislation cf. the discussion in Noethlichs 1971; Brox 1986, cols. 281–3; Riedlberger 2020, pp. 318–41, 495–810; in addition, Hillner 2015, pp. 198 f.
207 Cf. Arius and Euzoius, *Epistula ad Constantinum imperatorem* (Opitz 1934/1935, *Urkunde 30*; FaFo § 131c) 2 and Constantine, *Epistula ad Alexandrum* (Opitz 1934/1935, *Urkunde 32*). The details of Arius' readmission are controversial. Cf. Opitz 1934/1935, *Urkunde 23–34* and, e.g., Barnes 2009 *pace* Brennecke et al. 2007, pp. XXXVI–XXXVIII and Brennecke 2018. In addition, Galvão-Sobrinho 2013, pp. 165–71.
208 On Constantine's erratic ecclesial politics after Nicaea cf. Drake 2000, pp. 258–72; Barnes 2011 (2014), pp. 240–2.

But although the Saviour transcends in his substance, rank, power, divinity (for the Word is living), and wisdom, beings that are so great and of such antiquity, nevertheless, he is not comparable with the Father in any way.

For he is an image (εἰκών) [cf. 2Cor 4:4; Col 1:15] of the goodness and a radiance (ἀπαύγασμα; cf. Heb 1:3) not of God, but of God's glory and of his eternal light; and he is a vapour (ἀτμίς), not of the Father, but of his power; and he is a pure emanation (ἀπόρροια εἰλικρινής) of God's almighty glory, and an unspotted mirror of his activity [cf. Wis 7:25–26; Heb 1:3]. It is through this mirror that Paul and Peter and their contemporaries see God, because he says, 'He who has seen me has seen the Father who sent me' [cf. John 14:9; 12:45].[209]

Origen also made less explicit statements,[210] but there was little doubt that he saw the Son and the Spirit as subordinate to the Father, a notion which seemed entirely compatible with Scripture to many theologians of the first half of the fourth century.

Meanwhile, Eusebius of Nicomedia had been recalled from exile and been active in regaining his influence at court. He successfully propagated the fame of his teacher Lucian of Antioch: Constantine's mother Helena built a church dedicated to this martyr near her home town Drepanon/Helenopolis, in the vicinity of Nicomedia.[211] Here Constantine prayed briefly before his death on 22 May 337. The same Eusebius also baptized Constantine at around the same time.[212] By then, Nicene theologians such as Marcellus of Ancyra (d. 374) and Athanasius (d. 373), who had succeeded Alexander as bishop of Alexandria in 328, had come under pressure: Marcellus had been declared a heretic at a synod in Constantinople (perhaps in 336/337) because of what many considered an eccentric trinitarian doctrine. Likewise Athanasius had been stripped of his office at the Synod of Tyre (335) and sent into exile to Trier.

Things became even more complicated after Constantine's death, because now first three Augusti (Constantine II, Constans, and Constantius II) and then, from 340 onwards, two emperors (Constans for the west (d. 350) and Constantius II for the east (d. 361)) controlled religious policy in different ways. In addition, in the wake

---

209 Origen, *Commentarii in Iohannem* 13,151–153 (tr. FaCh 89, p. 100; altered). Cf. also id., *Commentarii in Iohannem* 32,363; id., *De principiis* 4,4,8; id., *Contra Celsum* 7,43; 8,14–15; id., *Homiliae in Psalmos*, hom. *4 in Ps 77* (Perrone et al. 2014, p. 404, ll. 20–5); id., *Commentarii in Matthaeum* 15,10.

210 Cf. Origen, *De principiis* 1 praef. 4 (FaFo § 116a); id., *Commentarii in Iohannem* 32,187–189 (§ 116b); id., *In Matthaeum commentariorum series* 33 (§ 116c); id., *Contra Celsum* 5,11.

211 Cf. Hillner 2023, pp. 19 f., 76–8, 259 f.

212 Eusebius of Caesarea, *Vita Constantini* 4,61–62; Jerome, *Chronicon*, a. 337. Cf. also Gelasius of Caesarea, *Historia ecclesiastica*, frg. 22a; Rufinus, *Historia ecclesiastica* 10,12; and Socrates, *Historia ecclesiastica* 1,39,3–4 with the story of how Constantine entrusted his testament to an Arian presbyter who is identified with Eusebius of Nicomedia in Philostorgius, *Historia ecclesiastica* 2,16. It is, perhaps, spurious.

of the growth of Christendom in the fourth century, the bishops of the metropolises of the empire (Rome, Nicomedia (which was later outstripped by Constantinople), Alexandria, Antioch, and, to a lesser extent, Jerusalem) attempted to extend their jurisdiction and power. Constans favoured the Nicenes and reinstated Athanasius, but the bishop was again expelled from Alexandria in 339. Pope Julius I of Rome (337–352) supported both Athanasius and Marcellus who had fled to the western capital. A Roman Synod of 340 or 341 rescinded the synodal decisions against these two bishops.[213]

6.5.1 The creeds associated with the Dedication Council in Antioch (341)

In the east Eusebius of Nicomedia and his circle of supporters led the opposition against Athanasius and Marcellus. They celebrated their greatest triumph at the Encaenia Synod (Dedication Council) in Antioch in the summer of 341, attended by ninety or ninety-seven eastern bishops,[214] among them Eusebius (who had meanwhile been promoted from Nicomedia to Constantinople), the local bishop Placetus (Flacillus), Acacius of Caesarea, Patrophilus of Scythopolis, Theodore of Heraclea, Eudocius of Germanicia, the designated bishop of Alexandria, Gregory, Dianius of Caesarea in Cappadocia (who was accompanied by Asterius the Sophist), George of Laodicea, Eusebius of Emesa, and Theophronius of Tyana.[215] It is unclear whether Julius of Rome, who was a defender of Nicaea and, therefore, critical of recent developments in the east, was represented by a delegation.[216] Maximus of Jerusalem stayed away, because, as Socrates says, he had been induced to subscribe the deposition of Athanasius which he regretted (and apparently feared being deposed himself at Antioch).[217] The emperor Constantius also attended as he was staying in the city on the occasion of the consecration of the 'Great Church' whose construction his father Constantine had commissioned.

---

213 Cf. Julius of Rome, *Epistula ad Antiochenos episcopos* (Brennecke et al. 2007, *Dokument* 41.8). Marcellus had previously appealed to Julius and the synod in the letter which was analyzed above; cf. ch.5.1.

214 For the number of participants cf. Durst 1993, vol. I, p. 24; Brennecke et al. 2007, p. 138.

215 Cf. Socrates, *Historia ecclesiastica* 2,8,5; Sozomen, *Historia ecclesiastica* 3,5,10–6,1; and Durst 1993, vol. I, pp. 24 f. The participation of Asterius is attested in the *Synodicon Vetus* 42, ll. 6–7 (Duffy/Parker 1979, p. 38 = *Libellus synodicus* (Mansi 2, col. 1350D)); cf. Kinzig 1990, p. 18 and n. 44; Vinzent 1993, p. 28. For Theophronius cf. below pp. 276–8.

216 It appears that Roman envoys were at that time staying in Antioch, but we do not know to what extent they took part in the proceedings of the synod. Cf. Socrates, *Historia ecclesiastica* 2,8,4; Sozomen, *Historia ecclesiastica* 3,6,8; and Durst 1993, vol. I, p. 25.

217 Cf. Socrates, *Historia ecclesiastica* 2,8,3; similarly, Sozomen, *Historia ecclesiastica* 3,6,8.

The precise agenda of this synod is unknown, but it appears that its purpose was first and foremost to draw up a reply to a letter by Julius of Rome who had demanded that an eastern delegation be sent to attend a synod in the western capital in order to confirm Nicaea and to support Athanasius. In this context, he seems to have accused the eastern bishops of Arianism. The assembled prelates refused Julius' request and rejected his suspicions with great indignation.[218] However, they also had to find a common platform vis-à-vis the followers of Arius, lest they lose their credibility; however, they wished to do so without expressly confirming N and its *homooúsios*, and also had to deal with the case of Theophronius of Tyana who had been accused of championing the teachings of Marcellus of Ancyra.

Oddly, four creeds are traditionally associated with this council (FaFo § 141a–d), which even confused ancient Church historians.[219] The second of these texts (abbrev. Ant²), which may chronologically have been the first,[220] was adopted by the council as its theological statement.[221] It is clear from the remark with which Athanasius introduces his quotation of the creed that it formed part of a letter (the remainder of which is missing).[222]

Second Creed of Antioch (341; Ant²)
(Brennecke et al. 2007, *Dokument* 41.4; FaFo § 141b)

Πιστεύομεν ἀκολούθως τῇ εὐαγγελικῇ καὶ ἀποστολικῇ παραδόσει εἰς ἕνα θεόν, πατέρα, παντοκράτορα, τὸν τῶν ὅλων δημιουργόν τε καὶ ποιητὴν καὶ προνοητήν, *ἐξ οὗ τὰ πάντα·*	We believe, following the evangelical and apostolic tradition, in one God, the Father Almighty, the Demiurge and Maker and Governor of the universe, 'from whom are all things' [1Cor 8:6];

---

218 Both Julius' letter and the synod's reply are lost. Summaries are given by Socrates, *Historia ecclesiastica* 2,15,5–6 and Sozomen, *Historia ecclesiastica* 3,8,3–8 (Brennecke et al. 2007, *Dokument* 41.1 and 41.6). Cf. also the beginning of the 'First Creed' (*Expositio fidei, Formula prima* (FaFo § 141c)); cf. below p. 278.

219 Socrates saw this as a tactic to undermine Nicaea; cf. *Historia ecclesiastica* 2,10,2: 'This being done, they altered the creed (μεταποιοῦσιν τὴν πίστιν); they did not criticize the events at Nicaea, but established a precedent by continuously holding councils and by publishing one definition of faith after the other, thus gradually moving towards the doctrine of the Arians.'

220 I follow the order suggested by Tetz 1989(1995), pp. 236–41.

221 Cf. Council of Antioch (341), *Expositio fidei/Formula altera* (FaFo § 141b).

222 Athanasius, *De synodis* 23,1: 'Here follows what they published in the second place at the same Dedication Council in another letter, changing their minds about the first [creed] and contriving something novel and more extensive: [. . .].' Similarly Socrates, *Historia ecclesiastica* 2,10,9 who may depend on Athanasius.

καὶ εἰς ἕνα κύριον Ἰησοῦν Χριστόν, τὸν υἱὸν αὐτοῦ, τὸν μονογενῆ θεόν, *δι' οὗ τὰ πάντα,*

and in one Lord Jesus Christ, his Son, the only-begotten God [cf. Jn 1:18], 'through whom are all things' [Jn 1:3; 1Cor 8:6; Col 1:16; Heb 1:2],

τὸν γεννηθέντα πρὸ τῶν αἰώνων ἐκ τοῦ πατρός, θεὸν ἐκ θεοῦ, ὅλον ἐξ ὅλου, μόνον ἐκ μόνου, τέλειον ἐκ τελείου, βασιλέα ἐκ βασιλέως, κύριον ἀπὸ κυρίου, λόγον ζῶντα, σοφίαν ζῶσαν, φῶς ἀληθινόν, ὁδόν, ἀλήθειαν, ἀνάστασιν, ποιμένα, θύραν, ἄτρεπτόν τε καὶ ἀναλλοίωτον, τῆς θεότητος οὐσίας τε καὶ βουλῆς καὶ δυνάμεως καὶ δόξης τοῦ πατρὸς ἀπαράλλακτον εἰκόνα, τὸν πρωτότοκον πάσης κτίσεως,

who was begotten before the ages from the Father, God from God, whole from whole, sole from sole, perfect from perfect, King from King, Lord from Lord, living Word [cf. Jn 1:4; 1Jn 1:1], living Wisdom, true Light [cf. Jn 1:9; 1Jn 2:8], Way, Truth, Resurrection, Shepherd, Door, both unalterable and unchangeable; precise image of the godhead, substance, will, power, and glory of the Father; the first-born of all creation [cf. Col 1:15],

τὸν ὄντα *ἐν ἀρχῇ πρὸς τὸν θεόν*, λόγον θεὸν κατὰ τὸ εἰρημένον ἐν τῷ εὐαγγελίῳ· *Καὶ θεὸς ἦν ὁ λόγος, δι' οὗ τὰ πάντα ἐγένετο, καὶ ἐν ᾧ τὰ πάντα συνέστηκε,*

who was 'in the beginning with God', God the Word, as it is written in the Gospel, 'And the Word was God' [Jn 1:1–2]; 'through whom all things came into being' [Jn 1:3; 1Cor 8:6], and 'in whom all things hold together' [Col 1:17];

τὸν *ἐπ' ἐσχάτων τῶν ἡμερῶν* κατελθόντα ἄνωθεν καὶ γεννηθέντα ἐκ παρθένου *κατὰ τὰς γραφὰς* καὶ *ἄνθρωπον γενόμενον, μεσίτην θεοῦ καὶ ἀνθρώπων* ἀπόστολόν τε τῆς πίστεως ἡμῶν καὶ *ἀρχηγὸν τῆς ζωῆς,* ὡς φησιν ὅτι· *Καταβέβηκα ἐκ τοῦ οὐρανοῦ, οὐχ ἵνα ποιῶ τὸ θέλημα τὸ ἐμόν, ἀλλὰ τὸ θέλημα τοῦ πέμψαντός με,* τὸν παθόντα ὑπὲρ ἡμῶν καὶ ἀναστάντα τῇ τρίτῃ ἡμέρᾳ καὶ ἀνελθόντα εἰς οὐρανοὺς καὶ καθεσθέντα ἐν δεξιᾷ τοῦ πατρὸς καὶ πάλιν ἐρχόμενον μετὰ δόξης καὶ δυνάμεως *κρῖναι ζῶντας καὶ νεκρούς·*

who 'in the last days' [Heb 1:2], descended from above, was born from a virgin according to the Scriptures [cf. Mt 1:23], and became human, mediator 'between God and humans' [1Tim 2:5], apostle of our faith [cf. Rom 1:5], and Prince of life [Acts 1:15], as he says, 'I have descended from heaven, not to do my own will, but the will of him who sent me' [Jn 6:38]; who suffered for us, on the third day rose again, ascended into the heavens, sat down at the right hand of the Father, and will come again with glory and power 'to judge the living and the dead' [2Tim 4:1];

καὶ εἰς τὸ πνεῦμα τὸ ἅγιον, τὸ εἰς παράκλησιν καὶ ἁγιασμὸν καὶ τελείωσιν τοῖς πιστεύουσι διδόμενον,

and in the Holy Spirit, who is given to those who believe for comfort, sanctification, and perfection,

καθὼς καὶ ὁ κύριος ἡμῶν Ἰησοῦς Χριστὸς διετάξατο τοῖς μαθηταῖς λέγων· *Πορευθέντες μαθητεύσατε πάντα τὰ ἔθνη βαπτίζοντες αὐτοὺς εἰς τὸ ὄνομα τοῦ πατρὸς καὶ τοῦ υἱοῦ καὶ τοῦ ἁγίου πνεύματος*, δηλονότι πατρός, ἀληθῶς πατρὸς ὄντος, υἱοῦ δὲ ἀληθῶς υἱοῦ ὄντος, τοῦ δὲ ἁγίου πνεύματος ἀληθῶς ἁγίου πνεύματος ὄντος, τῶν ὀνομάτων οὐχ ἁπλῶς οὐδὲ ἀργῶς [ἄργων *ed., sed cf. app. ad loc.*] κειμένων, ἀλλὰ σημαινόντων ἀκριβῶς τὴν οἰκείαν ἑκάστου τῶν ὀνομαζομένων ὑπόστασίν τε καὶ τάξιν καὶ δόξαν, ὡς εἶναι τῇ μὲν ὑποστάσει τρία, τῇ δὲ συμφωνίᾳ ἕν.	just as our Lord Jesus Christ also enjoined his disciples, 'Go and make disciples of all nations, baptizing them upon the name of the Father, the Son, and the Holy Spirit' [Mt 28:19], namely, of a Father who is truly Father, a Son who is truly Son, and of the Holy Spirit who is truly Holy Spirit, the names not being given without distinction or idly, but denoting accurately the respective subsistence (*hypóstasis*), rank, and glory of each one that is named, as they are three in subsistence, and one in harmony.
Ταύτην οὖν ἔχοντες τὴν πίστιν καὶ ἐξ ἀρχῆς καὶ μέχρι τέλους ἔχοντες ἐνώπιον τοῦ θεοῦ καὶ τοῦ Χριστοῦ πᾶσαν αἱρετικὴν κακοδοξίαν ἀναθεματίζομεν.	Therefore, holding to this faith, and holding to it from beginning to end in the sight of God and Christ, we anathematize every heretical false opinion.
Καὶ εἴ τις παρὰ τὴν ὑγιῆ τῶν γραφῶν ὀρθὴν πίστιν διδάσκει λέγων ἢ χρόνον ἢ καιρὸν ἢ αἰῶνα ἢ εἶναι ἢ γεγονέναι πρὸ τοῦ γεννηθῆναι τὸν υἱόν, ἀνάθεμα ἔστω.	If anyone teaches contrary to the sound faith of the Scriptures, saying that time, or season, or age, either is or has been before the Son was generated, let him be anathema.
Καὶ εἴ τις λέγει τὸν υἱὸν κτίσμα ὡς ἓν τῶν κτισμάτων ἢ γέννημα ὡς ἓν τῶν γεννημάτων ἢ ποίημα ὡς ἓν τῶν ποιημάτων καὶ μή, ὡς αἱ θεῖαι γραφαὶ παραδέδωκαν, τῶν προειρημένων ἕκαστον ἀφ᾽ ἑκάστου ἢ εἴ τις ἄλλο διδάσκει ἢ εὐαγγελίζεται παρ᾽ ὃ παρελάβομεν, ἀνάθεμα ἔστω.	If anyone says that the Son is a creature like one of the creatures, or an offspring like one of the offsprings, or a work like one of the works, and [does] not [affirm] each individual of the previously mentioned [articles] as the divine Scriptures have transmitted, or if anyone teaches or preaches [anything] beside what we received, let him be anathema.
Ἡμεῖς γὰρ πᾶσι τοῖς ἐκ τῶν θείων γραφῶν παραδεδομένοις ὑπό τε προφητῶν καὶ ἀποστόλων ἀληθινῶς τε καὶ ἐμφόβως καὶ πιστεύομεν καὶ ἀκολουθοῦμεν.	For we truly and reverentially both believe and follow all that has been transmitted in the divine Scriptures, whether by prophets or apostles.

At first glance, one is struck by the length of this text. Whereas N could be used in religious instruction, Ant[2] would have been less suited for this purpose. The creed is not only framed by appeals to Scripture – it is also interspersed with numerous biblical quotations and allusions, because its authors wished to buttress their doctrines, which deviated from N, by scriptural authority (something which the authors of N had largely neglected to do).

The first section emphasizes once more the omnipotence and creative power of God the Father who is the ultimate source of the universe. At first glance, it looks as if the christological section will follow in the footsteps of Nicaea. It first underlines the full divinity of the 'only-begotten God' who cooperates in creation – it does this seemingly even more forcefully than N, citing the preexistence, divinity, integrity, oneness, and perfection of the Son, all of which are followed by a host of biblical titles. However, *homoousios* is missing. The point of this section is concealed in the phrase concluding the descriptive part: 'precise image of the godhead, substance, will, power, and glory of the Father; the first-born of all creation'. The Son's divinity is almost imperceptibly lessened here: the text describes the relationship between Father and Son by using terms taken from Col 1:15 as 'image' and as 'first-born of all creation', the first term being supplemented by the unbiblical adjective ἀπαράλλακτον ('invariable', 'unchanged', hence 'precise'). The text continues with another declaration of the Word's divinity and his creative activity, quoting Jn 1:1–3. It then adds the christological summary, including the virgin birth – its first mention in an eastern synodal creed of the fourth century.

Its pneumatological section enumerates the functions of the Spirit (comfort (Jn 14:16 etc.), sanctification (2Thess 2:13; cf. 1Cor 6:11), perfection (Gal 3:3?)), a combination which is found nowhere else.

This is followed by a concluding section which, on the basis of Mt 28:19, outlines the three *hypostáseis* of Father, Son, and Spirit each possessing their respective rank and glory, but bound together by one 'harmony' (τῇ συμφωνίᾳ).[223] The perfect harmony of Father and Son was also emphasized by Asterius in his exegesis of Jn 10:30.[224] The Sophist had also maintained that Father and Son were hypostatically separate,[225] a terminology already found in Origen.[226]

---

223 This rare combination of ὑπόστασις and συμφωνία is also found in (Pseudo-)Didymus, *De trinitate* 1,36,9.

224 Cf. Asterius, frgs. 39 and 40 (Vinzent).

225 Cf. Vinzent 1993, pp. 229 f.

226 Cf. Origen, *Contra Celsum* 8,12, ll. 24–26 (SC 150, p. 200): Θρησκεύομεν οὖν τὸν πατέρα τῆς ἀληθείας καὶ τὸν υἱὸν τὴν ἀλήθειαν, ὄντα δύο τῇ ὑποστάσει πράγματα, ἐν δὲ τῇ ὁμονοίᾳ καὶ τῇ συμφωνίᾳ καὶ τῇ ταυτότητι τοῦ βουλήματος· [. . .] / 'Therefore we worship the Father of the truth and the Son who is the truth; they are two entities with regard to *hypóstasis*, but one in unanim-

Taken as a whole the creed emphasizes the divine nature of the Son, while apparently also drawing a clear ontological distinction between Father and Son (through the reintroduction of the term 'image'[227]) and allowing for the created and perhaps even temporal nature of the Son. Thus the precise relation between, on the one hand, the expressions 'God from God' and 'only-begotten' and, on the other hand, the claim that the Son was an 'image' and 'first-born of all creation' remains undefined. In addition, the three persons of the Trinity each appear to possess a *hypóstasis* specific to their individual rank and glory (which, by implication, must differ from each other, without this difference being spelled out).[228]

Sozomen mentions that the synod attributed the authorship of this creed to Lucian of Antioch (perhaps the teacher of Eusebius of Nicomedia, Asterius the Sophist, and Eudocius of Germanicia[229]) which he himself calls into doubt and which is not very likely.[230] Owing to a lack of evidence we do not know to what extent the creed represents the theology of a 'Lucianic school'. However, it has long been noticed that its christological section was influenced by the theology of Asterius.[231] We know that this Sophist (whose relationship with Arius is a matter of scholarly discussion[232]) championed a clearly subordinationist trinitarian doctrine.[233] However, whereas Asterius presented a rather elaborate theory for describing the relationship between Father and Son, in this text the tensions between, on the one hand, the repeated emphasis on the divinity of the Word and, on the other hand, the distinction between

---

ity, in harmony, and in identity of will.' Chadwick 1965(1980), p. 461 n. 1 gives further references from Origen. Cf. also Vinzent 1993, p. 230 and n. 10. Cf. also above p. 256 and n. 149.

227 On the 'image' terminology among the Eusebians cf. DelCogliano 2006. In addition, cf. above pp. 218, 229, 232, 251.

228 This was already noticed by Hilary of Poitiers, *De synodis* 31: 'Apparently this creed did not, perhaps, speak expressly enough about the undistinguished similarity of the Father and Son, [. . .].' Hilary then goes on to explain that the creed was primarily directed against trinitarian modalism (by which he probably means Marcellus of Ancyra) and gives a Nicene interpretation of the text; cf. *De synodis* 32–33.

229 Cf. above p. 243 and n. 105.

230 Cf. Sozomen, *Historia ecclesiastica* 3,5,9: 'They said that they had found this creed to have been entirely written by Lucian (ταύτην τὴν πίστιν ὁλόγραφον εὑρηκέναι Λουκιανοῦ), who was martyred in Nicomedia. In general, he was a man of high esteem who had investigated the Holy Scriptures very thoroughly. I cannot say whether this statement was really true, or whether they wished to give weight to their own document through the dignity of the martyr.' It is unclear whether ὁλόγραφον means that Lucian had composed the creed or that the synod had 'found' his creed in a manuscript which was written in his own hand.

231 Cf. Asterius, frgs. 9, 10, 57, 60 and Vinzent 1993, p. 28; Kinzig, 'Areios und der Arianismus', 2018, p. 1487.

232 Cf. Kinzig, 'Areios und der Arianismus', 2018, pp. 1486 f.

233 For details cf. Vinzent 1993, pp. 38–71 and Kinzig, 'Areios und der Arianismus', 2018, pp. 1488 f.

the three *hypostáseis* and, in particular, between Father and Son remains unresolved. Thus it is, for example, unclear to what extent the quotation of Col 1:15 implies *some* form of temporality of the 'first-born' and a form of created nature in the broadest sense which would put Christ ultimately on a par with the rest of creation.

The concluding anathemas do not offer any elucidation either. First all heresies are summarily condemned. This section is followed by three condemnations displaying a specific structure which is here found for the first time in a creed:[234] they consist of a conditional clause introduced by εἴ τις ('if anyone'), summarizing the opponent's position, and a main clause containing nothing but the formula ἀνά-θεμα ἔστω ('let him be anathema/accursed').[235] Here all forms of temporality before the generation of the Son appear to be condemned – but does this mean the Son is coeternal with the Father in every respect? Likewise, when the creed condemns those who speak of the Son as a 'creature like one of the other creatures', this may suggest that the Son is *some* kind of 'creature', albeit different from all others.

This vagueness as well as the omission of *homooúsios* may very well have been the result of an attempt to create an 'umbrella creed' which was acceptable to as many eastern bishops as possible while excluding both a 'hard' Nicene view (as defined by the *homooúsios*) and an unmitigated Arianism.[236]

*

We can be much briefer with regard to the other three creeds associated with the Synod of 341. The so-called 'third creed' (Ant[3]) was composed by the otherwise unknown Bishop Theophronius of Tyana who had apparently been accused of being a follower of Marcellus of Ancyra.[237] This may, in turn, have meant that he did not clearly distinguish between the *hypostáseis* of Father and Son, a charge which was also labelled Sabellianism (after the condemned theologian Sabellius who, in *c.* 220, had been accused by Calixtus of Rome of teaching patripassianism). In his defence, Theophronius submitted this text to the synod, similar to what Eusebius of Caesarea had done in Nicaea.[238] There is no reason to assume that he used an extant local baptismal creed as the basis of his text.[239]

His creed is fairly inconspicuous except for the omission of ἕνα in the first and second articles and for the corresponding claim that the Son was 'with God in *hypóstasis*' (πρὸς τὸν θεόν ἐν ὑποστάσει). Both these features may indicate that

---

234 That is, unless the creed of Theophronius antedates this text; cf. below in the text.
235 This structure was adapted from Gal 1:9 (cf. 1:8; 1Cor 16:22).
236 Cf. already Sozomen, *Historia ecclesiastica* 3,5,6–7.
237 Cf. Council of Antioch (341), *Expositio fidei. Formula tertia* (FaFo § 141a).
238 For a detailed analysis cf. Tetz 1989(1995); Sara Parvis 2006, pp. 173–7.
239 Cf. Tetz 1989(1995), p. 233 *pace* Kelly 1972, p. 267.

in Theophronius' view Father and Son were not ontologically distinct ('one' and 'one') but possessed a common *hypóstasis* (whatever this would mean). Such a meaning, in turn, would indeed point to certain sympathies with the theology of the bishop of Ancyra (or of Eustathius of Antioch).[240] The third article is much longer than that of Nicaea and underlines the operations of the Holy Spirit:

> And in the Holy Spirit, the Paraclete [cf. Jn 14:16 etc.], 'the Spirit of truth' [Jn 15:26], which God also promised by his prophet to pour out upon his servants [cf. Joel 3:1], and the Lord promised to send to his disciples; which he also sent, as the Acts of the Apostles witness [cf. Acts 2:3–4].

This expansion may indicate that there was discussion about the nature and precise identity of the Spirit (which had remained undefined in N).

The final anathemas (which display a similar structure to those of Ant²)[241] probably condemn Marcellus, Sabellius, and Paul of Samosata; however, the construction of the sentence as it stands does not make much sense.[242]

It is important to note, with regard to the procedure concerning the submission of personal creeds to councils, that Athanasius (who has preserved all creeds associated with Antioch 341) tells us in the introduction to this text that Theophronius submitted a statement which he had himself composed and that 'all subscribed it (πάντες ὑπέγραψαν), thus adopting the faith (πίστιν) of the man'.[243] Athanasius probably copied the creed from a codex in which the signatures were still extant.[244] Obviously, then, it no longer sufficed to confirm the orthodoxy of a bishop who had been charged with heresy by a simple raising of hands (as had apparently happened in Nicaea in the case of Eusebius[245]). Unfortunately, Athanasius does not tell us the reasons for this change of procedure. Was it because there were no official minutes in which such a vote could have been recorded?

---

240 Cf. Sara Parvis 2006, pp. 174–7.

241 Cf. above p. 273.

242 Cf. the discussion in Tetz 1989(1995), pp. 227–31; Sara Parvis 2006, pp. 176–7. The preserved text reads: Εἰ δέ τις παρὰ ταύτην τὴν πίστιν διδάσκει ἢ ἔχει ἐν ἑαυτῷ, ἀνάθεμα ἔστω. καὶ Μαρκέλλου τοῦ Ἀγκύρας ἢ Σαβελλίου ἢ Παύλου τοῦ Σαμοσατέως· ἀνάθεμα ἔστω καὶ αὐτὸς καὶ πάντες οἱ κοινωνοῦντες αὐτῷ. Following earlier scholarship in FaFo I added καὶ <εἴ τις διδάσκει τὰ> Μαρκέλλου which yields the following translation: 'But if anyone teaches, or holds in his mind, anything besides this faith, let him be anathema; <if anyone teaches the [doctrines]> of Marcellus of Ancyra, or Sabellius, or Paul of Samosata, let him be anathema both himself and those who communicate with him.'

243 Athanasius, *De synodis* 24,1.

244 I do not share Schneemelcher's scepticism with regard to Athanasius' statement; cf. Schneemelcher 1977(1991), p. 119. Cf. also Tetz 1989(1995), p. 235.

245 Cf. above p. 246.

Or was there a danger that too many bishops might in fact secretly sympathize with Theophronius (and Marcellus) and that pressure had to be increased?

*

The so-called First Creed of Antioch (Ant[1]) is an extract from the Tome in which the synod communicated its results to all bishops.[246] Those bishops assembled at Antioch claimed that they had examined the faith of Arius, but, at the same time, distanced themselves from him and, for that purpose, added a creed which is sometimes called an abbreviated version of the Second Formula.[247] It does, however, in fact display some interesting new features:

First Creed of Antioch (341; Ant[1])

(Brennecke et al. 2007, *Dokument* 41.5; FaFo § 141c)

Μεμαθήκαμεν γὰρ ἐξ ἀρχῆς εἰς ἕνα θεόν, τὸν τῶν ὅλων θεόν, πιστεύειν, τὸν πάντων νοητῶν τε καὶ αἰσθητῶν δημιουργόν τε καὶ προνοητήν,	We have learned from the beginning to believe in one God, the God of the universe, both the Demiurge and Governor of all things, both those intelligible and those perceptible;
καὶ εἰς ἕνα υἱὸν τοῦ θεοῦ μονογενῆ, πρὸ πάντων αἰώνων ὑπάρχοντα καὶ συνόντα τῷ γεγεννηκότι αὐτὸν πατρί, *δι' οὖ καὶ τὰ πάντα ἐγένετο, τά τε ὁρατὰ καὶ τὰ ἀόρατα*, τὸν καὶ ἐπ' ἐσχάτων ἡμερῶν κατ' εὐδοκίαν τοῦ πατρὸς κατελθόντα καὶ σάρκα ἐκ τῆς παρθένου ἀνειληφότα καὶ πᾶσαν τὴν πατρικὴν αὐτοῦ βούλησιν συνεκπεπληρωκότα, πεπονθέναι καὶ ἐγηγέρθαι καὶ εἰς οὐρανοὺς ἀνεληλυθέναι καὶ ἐν δεξιᾷ τοῦ πατρὸς καθέζεσθαι καὶ πάλιν ἐρχόμενον *κρῖναι ζῶντας καὶ νεκροὺς* καὶ διαμένοντα βασιλέα καὶ θεὸν εἰς τοὺς αἰῶνας.	and in one only-begotten Son of God, subsisting before all ages and co-existing with the Father who begot him, 'through whom' also 'all things' both visible and invisible 'came into being' [Jn 1:3; 1Cor 8:6; Col 1:16]; who 'in the last days' [Heb 1:2] according to the Father's good pleasure [cf. Mt 12:18; 17:5; Mk 1:11 parr.; 2Pet 2:17] descended and assumed flesh from the Virgin; and having fully accomplished all his Father's will [cf. Mk 14:36 parr.; Jn 4:34; 5:30; Heb 5:7], he suffered, was raised, ascended into the heavens, sits at the right hand of the Father, will come again 'to judge the living and the

---

246 Cf. Council of Antioch (341), *Expositio fidei. Formula prima* (FaFo § 141c). For the addressees cf. Socrates, *Historia ecclesiastica* 2,10,9.
247 Cf. Brennecke et al. 2007, p. 148.

	dead' [2Tim 4:1], and remains King and God forever.
Πιστεύομεν δὲ καὶ εἰς τὸ ἅγιον πνεῦμα.	And we also believe in the Holy Spirit.
Εἰ δὲ δεῖ προσθεῖναι, πιστεύομεν καὶ περὶ σαρκὸς ἀναστάσεως καὶ ζωῆς αἰωνίου.	If it is necessary to add this, we also believe about the resurrection of the flesh, and eternal life.

It is difficult to see why the synod produced another creed.[248] In particular, it remains a mystery why the 'good pleasure' and fulfillment of the 'will' of the Father were added here. Whereas the expression κατ᾽ εὐδοκίαν τοῦ πατρός in relation to the incarnation is traditional,[249] this appears to be the first time the Father's will is mentioned in a credal text.[250] The final additions of the resurrection of the flesh and of eternal life (which are identical with the final clauses in R[251]) may have been made in order to facilitate communication with Rome. Nevertheless, the precise sequence of events regarding this important synod and the reasons which led to the composition of its creeds remain unknown.

*

Finally, a fourth creed (Ant[4]) is also associated with the Dedication Council. However, it now seems clear that it must result from another synod which was also held in Antioch some months later.[252] It was handed to Emperor Constans at Trier by a delegation comprising Bishops Narcissus of Irenopolis (= Neronias in Cilicia), Maris of Chalcedon, Theodore of Heraclea, and Mark of Arethusa, who all appear to have belonged to the party of Eusebius of Nicomedia (Eusebius himself had died in 341). Socrates cites as the reason for their journey the western emperor's wish to be kept apprised of ecclesial developments in the east, especially with regard to the controversy involving Athanasius (who at that point was staying in Rome) and Paul of Constantinople (who had also been expelled from his see).[253] The creed itself had no immediate effect, but its long-term impact was considerable, as the (eastern)

---

248 Neither Athanasius nor Socrates nor Sozomen give any reasons for this; cf. Athanasius, *De synodis* 22; Socrates, *Historia ecclesiastica* 2,10,9; Sozomen, *Historia ecclesiastica* 3,5,8.

249 It is already found in Irenaeus, *Aduersus haereses* 1,1,20; 1,2,1; 3,4,2 (FaFo § 109b7).

250 Cf., however, already Tertullian, *Aduersus Praxeam* 4,1 (FaFo § 111e2).

251 Cf. above ch. 5.1.

252 Athanasius admits that this creed was produced 'after some months had passed' (μετὰ μῆνας ὀλίγους); cf. *De synodis* 25,1.

253 Cf. Socrates, *Historia ecclesiastica* 2,18,1. Kelly 1972, p. 273 is sceptical (cf. also Brennecke et al. 2007, p. 176). He thinks that in truth it was 'a manoeuvre on the part of the East to satisfy Constans that a general council (for which the Western emperor was pressing, but which they were anxious to avoid) was unnecessary'.

Council of Serdica (343) adopted it with some changes; it was also integrated into the Macrostich Creed of 344 and the First Creed of Sirmium (351).[254]

Ant[4] is a subtle mixture of phrases taken from N and from Theophronius, as the following table shows (single underlining = N; double underlining = Theophronius). By contrast, Ant[2] does not appear to have left any traces in this text.

Fourth Creed of Antioch (341; Ant[4])
(Brennecke et al. 2007, *Dokument* 42; FaFo § 141d)

Πιστεύομεν εἰς ἕνα θεόν, πατέρα, παντοκράτορα, κτίστην καὶ ποιητὴν τῶν πάντων, ἐξ οὗ πᾶσα πατριὰ ἐν οὐρανοῖς καὶ ἐπὶ γῆς ὀνομάζεται·	We believe in one God, the Father Almighty, Creator and Maker of all things, 'from whom all fatherhood in the heavens and on earth takes its name' [Eph 3:15];
καὶ εἰς τὸν μονογενῆ αὐτοῦ υἱόν, τὸν κύριον ἡμῶν Ἰησοῦν Χριστόν, τὸν πρὸ πάντων τῶν αἰώνων ἐκ τοῦ πατρὸς γεννηθέντα, θεὸν ἐκ θεοῦ, φῶς ἐκ φωτός, δι' οὗ ἐγένετο τὰ πάντα ἐν τοῖς οὐρανοῖς καὶ ἐπὶ τῆς γῆς, τὰ ὁρατὰ καὶ τὰ ἀόρατα, λόγον ὄντα καὶ σοφίαν καὶ δύναμιν καὶ ζωὴν καὶ φῶς ἀληθινόν, τὸν ἐπ' ἐσχάτων τῶν ἡμερῶν δι' ἡμᾶς ἐνανθρωπήσαντα καὶ γεννηθέντα ἐκ τῆς ἁγίας παρθένου, τὸν σταυρωθέντα καὶ ἀποθανόντα καὶ ταφέντα καὶ ἀναστάντα ἐκ νεκρῶν τῇ τρίτῃ ἡμέρᾳ καὶ ἀναληφθέντα εἰς οὐρανὸν καὶ καθεσθέντα ἐν δεξιᾷ τοῦ πατρὸς καὶ ἐρχόμενον ἐπὶ συντελείᾳ τοῦ αἰῶνος κρῖναι ζῶντας καὶ νεκροὺς καὶ ἀποδοῦναι ἑκάστῳ κατὰ τὰ ἔργα αὐτοῦ, οὗ ἡ βασιλεία ἀκατάπαυστος οὖσα διαμένει εἰς τοὺς ἀπείρους αἰῶνας· ἔσται γὰρ καθεζόμενος ἐν δεξιᾷ τοῦ πατρὸς οὐ μόνον ἐν τῷ αἰῶνι τούτῳ, ἀλλὰ καὶ ἐν τῷ μέλλοντι·	and in his only-begotten Son, our Lord Jesus Christ, who was begotten from the Father before all ages, God from God, Light from Light, 'through whom all things came into being' [Jn 1:3; 1Cor 8:6] in heaven and on earth, visible and invisible, being Word, Wisdom, Power [cf. 1Cor 1:24], Life, and true Light; who 'in the last days' [Heb 1:2] because of us became human and was born from the holy Virgin; was crucified, died, was buried, on the third day rose again from the dead, was taken up into heaven, sat down at the right hand of the Father, and will come 'at the consummation of the age' [Heb 9:26] 'to judge the living and the dead' and to render 'to everyone according to his works' [Prov 24:12; Ps61(62):13; Mt 16:27 *v. l.*; Rom 2:6; Rev 22:12]; whose kingdom endures unceasingly unto the infinite ages; for he will sit at the right hand of the Father 'not only in this age, but also in that which is to come' [Eph 1:21];

---

254 Cf. below pp. 287–91, 291–4, 294–7.

καὶ εἰς τὸ πνεῦμα τὸ ἅγιον, τουτέστι τὸν παράκλητον, ὅπερ ἐπαγγειλάμενος τοῖς ἀποστόλοις μετὰ τὴν εἰς οὐρανοὺς αὐτοῦ ἄνοδον ἀπέστειλε διδάξαι αὐτοὺς καὶ ὑπομνῆσαι πάντα, δι᾽ οὗ καὶ ἁγιασθήσονται αἱ τῶν εἰλικρινῶς εἰς αὐτὸν πεπιστευκότων ψυχαί.	and in the Holy Spirit, that is, <u>the Paraclete</u>, whom he sent forth after his ascension into the heavens, having promised [it] to the apostles, to teach them and to remind [them] of all things; through whom the souls of those who have sincerely believed in him will also be sanctified.
<u>Τοὺς δὲ λέγοντας ἐξ οὐκ ὄντων τὸν υἱὸν ἢ ἐξ ἑτέρας ὑποστάσεως</u> καὶ μὴ ἐκ τοῦ θεοῦ καί· Ἦν ποτε χρόνος, ὅτε οὐκ ἦν, ἀλλοτρίους οἶδεν <u>ἡ καθολικὴ ἐκκλησία.</u>	<u>But those who say that the Son is from nothing, or is from another</u> *hypóstasis* and is not from God, and that 'there was a time when he was not', the <u>catholic Church</u> regards as alien.

Whereas the influence of N cannot be pinpointed with absolute certainty in the first two articles (some of these elements also appear in the creeds of Antioch 325, Eusebius, Asterius, and Ant[2]),[255] the condemnations were almost literally taken from N. This is significant, in particular, with regard to the statement condemning the view that the Son is from another *hypóstasis*, because it excludes, in effect, a theology of two/three *hypostáseis*. Instead, *hypóstasis* and *ousía* continued to be seen as de facto identical. There is no indication either that the authors championed an explicitly subordinationist theology – on the contrary, it looks as if they had deliberately tried to phrase their creed as Nicene as possible while not using the *homooúsios*. It resembled N in its brevity, too.

Furthermore, there is a new element which is undoubtedly western. In what follows I place the clauses dealing with Christ's passion, resurrection, and ascension/assumption side by side with those of the Roman creed in the *Traditio Apostolica* (TA[G]; FaFo § 89c) and R as preserved by Marcellus (R[M]; § 253). The crucial terms here are σταυρωθέντα and ταφέντα which are not found in eastern creeds before Antioch.

Ant[4]	TA[G]	R[M]
τὸν σταυρωθέντα	τὸν ἐπὶ Ποντίου Πιλάτου σταυρωθέντα [*or:* τὸν σταυρωθέντα ἐπὶ Ποντίου Πιλάτου]	τὸν ἐπὶ Ποντίου Πιλάτου σταυρωθέντα

---

255 Cf. Vinzent 1999, pp. 266–7, 307.

(continued)

Ant⁴	TA^G	R^M
καὶ ἀποθανόντα	καὶ ἀποθανόντα	
καὶ ταφέντα	καὶ ταφέντα	καὶ ταφέντα
καὶ ἀναστάντα ἐκ νεκρῶν τῇ τρίτη ἡμέρα	καὶ τῇ τρίτη ἡμέρα ἀναστάντα ἐκ (τῶν) νεκρῶν [or: ἀναστάντα τῇ τρίτη ἡμέρα ἐκ (τῶν) νεκρῶν] ζῶντα	καὶ τῇ τρίτη ἡμέρα ἀναστάντα ἐκ τῶν νεκρῶν,
καὶ ἀναληφθέντα εἰς οὐρανὸν	καὶ ἀναβάντα εἰς τοὺς οὐρανοὺς	ἀναβάντα εἰς τοὺς οὐρανοὺς
καὶ καθεσθέντα ἐν δεξιᾷ τοῦ πατρός	καὶ καθήμενον ἐν δεξιᾷ τοῦ πατρός,	καὶ καθήμενον ἐν δεξιᾷ τοῦ πατρός,
καὶ ἐρχόμενον ἐπὶ συντελείᾳ τοῦ αἰῶνος κρῖναι ζῶντας καὶ νεκρούς²⁵⁶	ἐρχόμενον [or: ἐλευσόμενον] κρίνειν [or: κρῖναι] ζῶντας καὶ νεκρούς²⁵⁷	ὅθεν ἔρχεται κρίνειν ζῶντας καὶ νεκρούς²⁵⁸

Markus Vinzent has suggested that Ant⁴ refers and reacts directly to Marcellus, because in the months between the end of the Dedication Council and the composition of Ant⁴ the letter of the Roman synod backing Marcellus had arrived in Antioch which also contained Marcellus' letter to Julius which we have discussed above.[259] There can be no doubt that Ant⁴ contains an (indirect) condemnation of Marcellus in that it emphasizes in the strongest terms that Christ's kingdom 'endures unceasingly unto the infinite ages' and that he will sit at the Father's right hand also in the age to come which Marcellus rejected.[260] But a closer look at its christological section suggests that Ant⁴ does not refer to Marcellus (or R), but instead to the creed contained in the *Traditio Apostolica*, because the clause καὶ ἀποθανόντα is contained in TA^G, but not in R^M. Be that as it may, it is clear that Ant⁴ tries to accommodate western credal language as much as possible.

---

256 'Who was crucified, died, was buried, on the third day rose again from the dead, was taken up into heaven, sat down at the right hand of the Father, and will come at the consummation of the age to judge the living and the dead.'

257 'Who was crucified under Pontius Pilate, and died, and was buried, and on the third day rose again alive from the dead, and ascended into the heavens, and is sitting at the right hand of the Father, coming to judge the living and the dead.'

258 'Who was crucified under Pontius Pilate, and buried, and on the third day rose again from the dead; ascended into the heavens and is sitting at the right hand of the Father, whence he is coming to judge the living and the dead.'

259 Cf. Vinzent 1999, p. 373 and also pp. 227–35. For Julius' letter cf. above p. 155, 270 f.; for Marcellus' letter to Julius cf. above ch. 5.1.

260 Cf. above p. 207 and n. 264.

The differences with regard to N were subtle: on the one hand, in the anathemas the divinity of the Son was even further emphasized through the addition of καὶ μὴ ἐκ τοῦ θεοῦ than in the condemnations of N; on the other hand, the use of *ousía* had been dropped in this section (as it had in the entire creed) and the opponents' views were not 'anathematized' as in N, but only considered 'alien' – clearly the authors did not wish to burn all bridges with their Arian opponents (who were, therefore, not listed by name either). In any case, they wished to distance themselves from any kind of 'Arian' teaching which propagated a doctrine of two *hypostáseis* of Father and Son and some kind of temporality of the Son. Conversely, if this meant that the *hypóstasis* of Father and Son was identical (which was also suggested by the phrases ἐκ τοῦ πατρός γεννηθέντα / 'who was begotten from the Father' and θεὸν ἐκ θεοῦ / 'God from God'), then this creed could easily be considered Nicene, except for its omission of *homooúsios*. The term 'image' which had played such an important role in Ant^2 to describe the relation between Father and Son had been dropped. Indeed when one compares the only passage in the New Testament where *hypóstasis* is used in relation to the Son (Heb 1:3: the Son as 'the exact imprint' of God's *hypóstasis* – χαρακτὴρ τῆς ὑποστάσεως αὐτοῦ), it becomes clear how much the Eusebian party had, in fact, moved towards the Nicene position in order to allay western worries. At the same time, it remained unclear once more whether *hypóstasis* and *ousía* were considered de facto synonymous. But moving towards Nicaea was not the same as expressing support for Marcellus – on that point Antioch was crystal-clear. Nevertheless, Marcellus' doctrine was not expressly condemned either nor was his name named explicitly. On this point too the creed's language was conciliatory.

6.5.2 The Council of Serdica and its creeds (343)

The tensions between the eastern and western bishops came to a head at the council of Serdica (modern Sofia) in the autumn of 343.[261] It had been convened by the western Augustus Constans[262] who seems to have suggested to scrap N altogether and to start from scratch in defining the faith.[263] It actually disintegrated

---

[261] The date is controversial. The council is often dated to autumn 342; cf. Rist 2015, p. 70; DelCogliano 2017.

[262] On the council's preparation and development cf. Brennecke et al. 2007, pp. 179–85 and their introductions to each document; Rist 2015.

[263] Cf. Synod of Serdica (west), *Epistula ad Iulium papam* (Brennecke et al. 2007, *Dokument* 43.5) 3: 'The most religious emperors themselves gave leave for all points at issue to be discussed afresh and, principally, the issues relating to the holy faith (*de sancta fide*) and violations of the integrity of truth' (tr. Wickham 1997, p. 49).

into two separate assemblies whose participants excommunicated each other. Part of the problem was the position held by the bishops Athanasius and Marcellus who were both present at the western assembly which was headed by Ossius of Córdoba, Protogenes of Serdica, and Gaudentius of Naissus (together with delegates representing Julius of Rome). Athanasius, who had been deposed at the Synod of Tyre in 335 and had fled to Rome after a brief interval in his home diocese, hoped to be able to reverse his expulsion with the help of Pope Julius and the Council of Serdica; Marcellus, who had been charged with heresy and deposed by a synod held in Constantinople in 336 or 337, also sought support from the assembly. The eastern council ultimately confirmed and extended Ant[4] and banned Athanasius and Marcellus. By contrast, the western council attacked not only Arianism, but also, more generally, what they considered a subordinationist doctrine of the Trinity. At the same time, the western delegates defended Athanasius and Marcellus, supporting the actions of Bishop Julius in favour of the ousted bishop of Alexandria. In addition, the so-called canon 7 they issued affirmed the privileges of the Roman bishop with regard to a retrial in cases where a bishop had been deposed by the provincial synod, without any geographical restriction. Again, we need not discuss here the details of this process which showed the deep rift that had developed between the Latin and Greek churches in the meantime.[264]

Western synod
After the synod Ossius of Córdoba and Protogenes of Serdica wrote a letter to Julius of Rome, explaining what had been decided with regard to the creed.[265] All the bishops had agreed with N. Apparently, the condemnations of N were discussed at some length (the preserved Latin text is mutilated here). As a result of these discussions the council decided that further explanations were necessary in order to restrict the influence of the 'disciples of Arius' and to preserve the faith intact. Such explanations were intended for the use of teachers and catechists (*omnes docentes et catechizantes*) in order to rebut Arianism.

Athanasius' account of events (written twenty years after the council) paints a slightly different picture.[266] He also mentions a statement concerning the faith as associated with Serdica, but denies that the synod had in fact adopted a new definition. Athanasius intimates that there had been a heated discussion about

---

264 Cf., e.g., Hanson 1988, pp. 293–306; Sara Parvis 2006, pp. 210–45. Further literature is listed in FaFo §§ 143–144.
265 Cf. Ossius and Protogenes, *Epistula ad Iulium papam* (FaFo § 144b).
266 Cf. Athanasius, *Tomus ad Antiochenos* 5,1 (FaFo § 144c).

the sufficiency of N and that, in this context, a new creed had hastily been drawn up, but that, in the end, the synod had decided to leave N unaltered. We will return to his statement later.[267]

Hence the evidence provided by Ossius/Protogenes and Athanasius agrees in that the sufficiency of N had been discussed in Serdica and an additional document drawn up, but these two sources differ with regard to the status of this declaration. However, at that point Athanasius was strongly interested in confirming the continuous validity of N. By contrast, Ossius and Protogenes would probably not have sent the explanatory document to Julius, had it not been adopted by the council.[268]

The uneven structure of the lengthy credal statement which forms part of the even longer synodal letter differs considerably from the creeds which we have studied so far. A Greek and a Latin version have come down to us – we do not know which of these, if any, is the original.[269] There is no need here fully to reproduce and discuss this text. It begins with a condemnation of subordinationist theology and of the notion of a finite existence of the Son. Valens of Mursa (modern Osijek) and Ursacius of Singidunum (Belgrade) are explicitly mentioned as its proponents. (We will have to deal with details of their theology later.[270]) They were accused of claiming that 'the Logos and the Spirit were crucified and slaughtered, died and rose again'[271] and that Father, Son, and Holy Spirit each had their own *hypóstasis* (sections 1–2).

The authors of the western creed also rejected the idea of a relationship of Father and (incarnate) Son as defined by harmony and unanimity only (διὰ τὴν συμφωνίαν καὶ τὴν ὁμόνοιαν / *propter consensum et concordiam*). This seems to be directed against Origen,[272] but also against Ant[2] ('three in *hypóstasis*, and one in harmony').[273] By contrast, they identified *hypóstasis* (Latin *substantia*) with *ousía* and underlined

---

267 Cf. below pp. 326 f.

268 For further discussion cf. Sara Parvis 2006, pp. 236–9.

269 Cf. Council of Serdica (343, west), *Professio fidei ab episcopis occidentalibus promulgata* (FaFo § 144a). Sections are given according to Brennecke et al. The first two sections of the text, which I have omitted in FaFo, are found in Brennecke et al. 2007, pp. 206–7 (Greek). The Latin text is in Turner 1899–1939, vol. I 2/4, pp. 644–53.

270 Cf. below pp. 301 f., 305–11.

271 *Dokument* 43.2, 2 (Brennecke et al. 2007, p. 207, ll. 1–3): [. . .] καὶ ὅτι ὁ λόγος καὶ ὅτι τὸ πνεῦμα καὶ ἐσταυρώθη καὶ ἐσφάγη καὶ ἀπέθανεν καὶ ἀνέστη [. . .]. Latin text: Turner 1899–1939, vol. I 2/4, p. 651, ll. 15–17: '[. . .] et quod Verbum et Spiritus uulneratus est et occisus et mortuus et resurrexit [. . .].'The Greek text with its repetition of καὶ ὅτι is slightly odd. Likewise, the singular of the verbs requires an explanation. Sara Parvis 2006, p. 241 translates: '[. . .] and that the Word, even the Spirit [. . .]' (cf. Sara Parvis 2006, p. 241 n. 279) which does not do justice to the text as it stands: the Logos and the Spirit are clearly distinguished.

272 Cf. above p. 274 and n. 226.

273 Cf. above p. 273. This is also discussed elsewhere; cf. Vinzent 1993, p. 230 n. 11.

that there was only one joint *hypóstasis* of Father, Son, and Holy Spirit. The co-eternity of Father and Son was thus affirmed (sections 3–4, 7–8). The Son is begotten (γεγεννημένον / *natum*), without being 'in every respect a begotten creature (κτίσιν γεγεννημένον παντάπασιν – the Latin text is defective here)' (section 5). Obviously, some bishops made no clear terminological distinction between the Son's generation and his creation. The Son is called the Father's Logos, Wisdom, and Power. As Logos he is only-begotten, whilst with regard to his humanity he is first-born (section 6).[274] This distinction is particularly typical of Marcellus of Ancyra who makes this point in his writings against Asterius.[275] Nevertheless, although Marcellus was present at the council, the fathers affirmed the ever-lasting kingdom of the Son in the strongest possible terms, an idea which Marcellus clearly rejected.[276]

One of the issues which must have preoccupied the bishops was the role of the Spirit which they described in detail with some interesting reflections. The Spirit's designation as Paraclete is traditional. But what is new here is that the Spirit is the divine agent in Christ incarnate. This follows from the one-*hypóstasis* theology championed in this statement: if the Logos and the Spirit are of the same *hypóstasis* and the Logos is somehow present in Christ incarnate, then the same applies to the Spirit. (It would, of course, also apply to the Father, but the authors obviously did not wish to raise this problem here.) The bishops distinguished the Spirit from the man whom the Spirit had 'put on' (ἐνεδύσατο / *induit*) and 'taken' from the Virgin Mary. It was the man the Spirit had assumed who suffered, rose, and ascended to heaven. The Spirit brought this man whom he liberated (from death) 'as a gift to his Father' (section 9).[277]

This statement is not very concise, but it is clear that it was considered a kind of appendix to N. Nowadays it is usually assumed that its one-*hypóstasis* theology

---

274 Here the Greek text appears to be defective. The Latin text reads in section 6: 'Confitemur unicum et primogenitum, sed unicum uerbum, quod semper fuit <et> est in patre, primogenitum *sane a<d> hominem*.' The words in italics are missing from the Greek. But it is clear from the following reference to Col 1:18 that the Latin text must be correct.

275 Cf. Marcellus, frgs. 10, 12–16 where he argues against the Asterian identification of Jn 1:18 and Col 1:15. 18 (cf. also Vinzent 1993, pp. XXXVII–XXXVIII).

276 Cf. above p. 207 and n. 264.

277 [. . .] ἀλλ᾽ ὁ ἄνθρωπος ἐν τῷ θεῷ ἀνέστη, ὅντινα καὶ προσήνεγκε τῷ πατρὶ ἑαυτοῦ δῶρον, ὃν ἠλευθέρωσεν. / '[. . .] sed homo in deo surrexit, quem etiam obtulit patri suo munus, quem liberauit.' The subject of the relative clause must be the Spirit. There are two contemporary parallels, both in Latin authors; cf. Hilary of Poitiers, *Commentarius in Matthaeum* 3,2, ll. 16–17 (SC 254, p. 114): 'Quo in tempore exspectatum Deo patri munus hominem quem adsumpserat reportauit.' / 'At that time he brought back man, whom he had assumed, as a welcome gift to God the Father.' Pseudo-Hilary, *Epistula seu libellus* 6,129 (Blatt 1939, p. 78, l. 32): '[. . .] deo patri liberatum hominem afferens munus [. . .].' / '[. . .] offering the liberated man as a gift to God the Father [. . .].' In both these cases, however, the agent is the Son, not the Spirit.

is an expression of the influence which Marcellus had exerted on the synod and that, perhaps, the bishop of Ancyra even authored the document.[278] However, as we saw above, this text also has some anti-Marcellan features which are sometimes overlooked[279] or flatly denied.[280] Either Marcellus had revised his eschatology and no longer assumed that the Logos would, in the end, be reunited with the Father,[281] or the western bishops did not follow him on this point.

Eastern synod

By contrast, the eastern synod's encyclical letter condemned first and foremost Marcellus (because of his deviant doctrine) and Athanasius (because of his inacceptable conduct),[282] and – in a second step – also the leading figures of the western synod, Julius of Rome, Ossius, Protogenes, Gaudentius of Naissus, and Maximinus of Trier, because they did not follow the eastern example. At the end they demanded agreement with (their version of) the 'faith of the catholic Church' (*catholicae ecclesiae fidem*), once again mentioning the 'judaizing' Marcellus.[283] One might, therefore, ex-

---

278 Details in Sara Parvis 2006, pp. 239–40.

279 No discussion in Sara Parvis 2006.

280 Cf. Brennecke et. al. 2007, p. 210 n. b.

281 A testimony to this change of heart may be found in the *Epistula ad Iulium papam* (FaFo § 253) 2,6: 'But following the divine Scriptures I believe that [there is] one God and his only-begotten Son, the Word, who always exists with the Father and has never in any sense had a beginning of existence; truly existing from God; not created, not made, but always existing, always reigning with "God the Father" [1Cor 15:24]; "of whose kingdom", according to the testimony of the messenger [i.e. the angel Gabriel], "there will be no end" [Lk 1:33].' Cf. also the *Epistula synodalis* (west) (Brennecke et al. 2007, *Dokument* 43.1) 11; Pseudo-Athanasius (= Marcellus), *Epistula ad Liberium* 2 (FaFo § 150).

282 Cf. *Epistula synodalis* (east) (Brennecke et al. 2007, *Dokument* 43.11) 3–6 (Marcellus), 7–15 (Athanasius). The objections are summarized in 24: 'For we cannot reinstate Athanasius and Marcellus, who have at one time been deposed and condemned, in the office of bishop. For they have led a criminal life, impiously blaspheming against the Lord. They have also again crucified the Son of God and have him once more publicly fastened [to the cross] with heavy blows. For the one of them [Marcellus] has once and for all died an eternal death by blaspheming against the Son of God and his eternal kingdom; the other was deposed by the judgement of the bishops and condemned, because in his profane conduct he sins horribly against the body of the Lord <and> his mysteries and performs other terrible atrocities.'

283 Cf. *Epistula synodalis* (east) (Brennecke et al. 2007, *Dokument* 43.11) 29: 'And because Ossius' associates have intended to infringe the catholic and apostolic faith by introducing the novel doctrine of Marcellus who has united with Judaism (a novel doctrine which is a judaizing compound of Sabellius and Paul [of Samosata]), we have, of necessity, set down the faith of the Catholic Church denied by the aforesaid associates of Ossius who have introduced instead Marcellus', the heretic's. It follows that when you have received our letter you should each accord your agreement with this sentence and sign our decisions with your personal subscription' (tr. Wickham 1997, p. 37; slightly altered).

pect a creed with a series of anathemas (condemning the doctrines of Marcellus and, perhaps, Athanasius). But this is not the case.

This creed has a complex textual history which is difficult to unravel. For reasons which are discussed elsewhere[284] I consider the version which is preserved in *De synodis* 34 by Hilary of Poitiers closest to the Greek original.[285] It is basically identical with Ant⁴.[286] However, at the end six condemnations were added:[287]

(1) Ὁμοίως καὶ τοὺς λέγοντας τρεῖς εἶναι θεοὺς	(1) Likewise those who say that there are three Gods,
(2) ἢ τὸν Χριστὸν μὴ εἶναι θεὸν	(2) or that Christ is not God,
(3) ἢ πρὸ τῶν αἰώνων μήτε Χριστὸν μήτε υἱὸν αὐτὸν εἶναι θεοῦ	(3) or that before the ages neither the Christ nor the Son of God existed,
(4) ἢ τὸν αὐτὸν εἶναι πατέρα καὶ υἱὸν καὶ ἅγιον πνεῦμα	(4) or that Father, Son, and Holy Spirit are the same,
(5) ἢ ἀγέννητον τὸν υἱὸν	(5) or that the Son is unbegotten,
(6) ἢ ὅτι οὐ βουλήσει οὐδὲ θελήσει ἐγέννησεν ὁ πατὴρ τὸν υἱόν,	(6) or that the Father did not beget the Son by choice or will,
τούτους ἀναθεματίζει ἡ ἁγία καὶ καθολικὴ ἐκκλησία.	the holy catholic Church anathematizes.

The reasons for these additions are not obvious.[288] Nos. 1 and 2 are traditional condemnations of tritheism and of the outright denial of Christ's divinity (neither of which was seriously suggested by anyone in the present debate).[289] Interestingly, the first anathema does not explicitly condemn a theology of three *hypostáseis* – the term is not mentioned here. No. 3 is directed against those who deny the Son's coeternity with the Father, as did Arius, Marcellus, and his (possible[290]) pupil Photinus of Sirmium, although on the basis of fundamentally different presuppositions.[291] We will see below that this opposition against the bishops of Ancyra and Sirmium would

---

284 Cf. FaFo § 143 (introduction) and also Brennecke et al. 2007, pp. 272–3.

285 The versions in cod. Veronensis LX (FaFo § 143b) and the Syriac version (§ 143c), which are almost identical, clearly show signs of later pneumatological extensions.

286 The most important differences in the *Serdicense* are the omission of ἐπὶ συντελείᾳ τοῦ αἰῶνος (cf., however, FaFo § 143a1) and the addition of ἢ αἰών after ἦν ποτε χρόνος.

287 Council of Serdica (343, east), *Fides synodi* (FaFo § 143a2). Cf. Brennecke et al. 2007, *Dokument* 43.12.

288 A slightly different interpretation is found in Sara Parvis 2006, pp. 230–2.

289 The charge of tritheism had been raised by Dionysius of Rome against Dionysius of Alexandria; cf. Bienert 1978, pp. 211–17.

290 Cf., however, Williams 2006, esp. pp. 196–7.

291 On Marcellus cf. his claim that before the incarnation only the Logos existed; cf. Marcellus, frgs. 5–8 (Vinzent) and Vinzent 1997, p. XXXVI. Photinus, whose writings are lost, appears to have maintained that the Son existed only after his birth from the virgin. Cf. below p. 295.

lead to a remarkable theological shift.[292] The condemnations nos. 4 and 5 result from the aforementioned (implicit) one-*hypóstasis* theology which is contained in this creed, to try and prevent misinterpretations. It does not follow from presupposing one *hypóstasis* that Father, Son, and Spirit are identical (no. 4) nor that the Son is (like the Father) unbegotten (or unoriginated: ἀγέννητον = ἀγένητον; no. 5).

The position that the Father begot the Son 'neither by choice nor will' (οὐ βουλή-σει οὐδὲ θελήσει, no. 6) is, for example, found in the creed of Antioch 325,[293] but it is difficult to see why Serdica (east) should have turned against a creed that was, by now, outdated. Sara Parvis has suggested that nos. 5–6 were directed specifically against Athanasius,[294] and there are good reasons to follow her argument: there was indeed at the time a debate about the possibility of two ungenerate/unoriginate (ἀγέν-νητα/ἀγένητα) divine beings. According to Asterius this would have followed from the Nicene assumption of the Son's generation from God's essence, thus threatening monotheism.[295] By contrast, Athanasius had no problems conceding this conclusion, as long as the Son was no part of creation and indeed coeternal with the Father.[296]

As far as no. 6 was concerned, the discussion about whether God possessed some kind of 'will' through which he created the cosmos had been going on for some time. If one admitted this possibility, there was a danger that God was conceived of as being subject to human passions which the gnostic Basilides and his school may have rejected.[297] Later, Arius himself had insisted on the generation of the Son 'by the will of God'.[298] Likewise, Asterius had propagated the Son's genera-tion 'by choice and will' (βουλήσει καὶ θελήσει) of the Father (and hence intro-duced an ontological distinction between the two),[299] to which Athanasius had replied that the Son's existence as offspring was not subject to the Father's will,

---

292 Cf. below pp. 292 f.
293 Cf. FaFo § 133[10].
294 Cf. Sara Parvis 2006, pp. 231–2 and nn. 239–40.
295 Cf. Asterius, frgs. 2–4 (Vinzent).
296 Cf. Athanasius, *Contra Arianos* 1,31,2: 'But if they [believe], as it pleased Asterius, that what is not a work (ποίημα) but existed always is unoriginate (ἀγένητον), then they must be told ever so often that in this interpretation the Son must likewise be called unoriginate. For he belongs nei-ther to the things originated nor is he a work, but he has eternally existed together with the Fa-ther, as has already been shown, [. . .].' Cf. also Athanasius, *Contra Arianos* 3,16, esp. 3,16,4.
297 Cf., e.g., Hippolytus, *Refutatio omnium haeresium* 7,21,1. However, Winrich A. Löhr thinks that *Refutatio* 7,20–27 ought not to be used to reconstruct Basilidean gnosticism; cf. Löhr 1996, pp. 284–323.
298 Cf. Arius et al., *Epistula ad Alexandrum Alexandrinum* 3 (Opitz 1934/1935, *Urkunde 6*; FaFo § 131a).
299 Asterius, frg. 18 (Vinzent 1993, p. 90): [. . .] ἀλλὰ δεῖ λέγειν βουλήσει καὶ θελήσει γεγενῆσθαι τὸν υἱὸν ὑπὸ τοῦ πατρός. / '[. . .] but one has to say that the Son was generated by the choice and will of the Father.' Cf. also frg. 16 and Vinzent 1993, pp. 191–2.

but originated from the Father's substance.[300] It is easy to see why the eastern bishops would have wished to distance themselves from a doctrine of two ungenerate beings (which might have been construed as ditheism), but it is less obvious why they would have insisted on the Son's generation by the Father's will, given that the present creed's trinitarian doctrine was otherwise by no means Arian or Asterian. Perhaps there was a fear that, once again, the assumption of one divine *hypóstasis* might lead to some kind of 'merging' of the first and second person of the Trinity. Later, a different explanation was given in the Macrostich Creed: the Father ought not to be confined by any kind of necessity. It is unclear, however, to what extent the commentary in the Macrostich Creed actually reflects the considerations of Serdica.[301]

According to Hanson, with their six additional condemnations the easterners wished

> to allay Western fears that in maintaining the existence of three *hypostáseis* within the Godhead they are falling into tritheism, and to reject Arian doctrine equally with Sabellianism. The last clause may be aimed both at the Arian playing down the role of the Son as *Logos* and Wisdom and at pro-Nicene doctrine of the consubstantiality of the Father and the Son which appeared to rule out the moral union between the Father's being and that of the Son.[302]

But as we saw above the creed did not maintain a theology of three *hypostáseis* – on the contrary: it was as Nicene as possible without actually adopting its *homooúsios*. Furthermore, it does not necessarily follow from the Son being generated 'by choice and will' of the Father that he was not also consubstantial with the Father.

In any case, the interpretation presented above suggests that a considerable shift towards a quasi-Nicene position had taken place among many eastern bishops between the Dedication Council ('Second Creed') and Serdica. It is important to remember that there is little evidence in the many documents we have about what happened at Serdica that there was a fundamental doctrinal disagreement between east and west. As I said above, the controversial issues concerned the conduct of Athanasius (not his doctrine) which in the eyes of the eastern bishops

---

300 Cf. Athanasius, *Contra Arianos* 1,29,2, ll. 6–9 (Metzler/Savvidis 1998, p. 139): Τὸ ποίημα ἔξωθεν τοῦ ποιοῦντός ἐστιν, ὥσπερ εἴρηται, ὁ δὲ υἱὸς ἴδιον τῆς οὐσίας γέννημά ἐστι· διὸ καὶ τὸ μὲν ποίημα οὐκ ἀνάγκη ἀεὶ εἶναι· ὅτε γὰρ βούλεται ὁ δημιουργός, ἐργάζεται· τὸ δὲ γέννημα οὐ βουλήσει ὑπόκειται, ἀλλὰ τῆς οὐσίας ἐστὶν ἰδιότης. / 'A work is extraneous to its maker, as has been said before, but the Son is the proper offspring of the [Father's] substance. Therefore, also a work does not by necessity forever exist; for when the workman wills it [to exist] it is produced; but an offspring is not subject to will, but is proper to the substance.'
301 Cf. also the next chapter.
302 Hanson 1988, p. 298–9.

was utterly criminal and the refusal of the westerners to condemn Marcellus' theology. But the easterners did *not* indicate that they disagreed with the *doctrinal* position of the western council as expressed in its creed.

6.5.3 The Macrostich Creed (344)

This creed was issued at yet another synod held in Antioch of unknown size, in the summer of 344.[303] It was mockingly called the 'Macrostich Exposition' already in antiquity because of its inordinate length (μακρόστιχος ἔκθεσις = exposition with long lines, i.e. lengthy).[304] The synod sent a mission headed by Eudoxius of Germanicia (the future bishop of Antioch and of Constantinople),[305] Martyrius (his see is unknown), and Macedonius of Mopsuestia[306] to the west, to submit this text to the western bishops for approval. Obviously, it was an attempt to repair relations between east and west which had been further strained by the fact that a western delegation sent to Antioch had ended in utter disaster.[307] Unfortunately, we have no details about this mission nor its reception in Rome. According to Socrates the reason for the mission's failure was not so much theological, as caused by a breakdown in communication, as the western bishops, who for the most part did not read Greek, were unable to understand the text, but insisted on the continuing validity of N and wished to waste no more time over the composition of ever more credal texts.[308] Although it is hardly conceivable that the creed was not submitted in a Latin version, it may well be that the west looked on at the continuous doctrinal hagglings of the eastern bishops with growing incomprehension.

The text is an odd hybrid. Its first part is identical with the creed of Serdica (east), including its set of condemnations. This was by now the doctrinal platform for most eastern bishops who refused to adopt the *homoousios*. It is followed by a

---

303 Cf. Council of Antioch (344), *Ecthesis mascrostichos* (FaFo § 145). It is probably the same home synod which deposed Stephen of Antioch and replaced him with Leontius; cf. Theodoret, *Historia ecclesiastica* 2,10,2 and Hanson 1988, pp. 306–7. Socrates and Sozomen erroneously place it before Serdica; cf. Socrates, *Historia ecclesiastica* 2,19–20; Sozomen, *Historia ecclesiastica* 3,11.

304 The term occurs for the first time in Sozomen, *Historia ecclesiastica* 3,11,1. Cf. also Athanasius, *De synodis* 26,1; Socrates, *Historia ecclesiastica* 2,19,2.

305 Cf. below p. 294 and Löhr 1995; Vaggione 2018.

306 Little is known about Macedonius; Athanasius counts him among the Eusebians; cf. Gwynn 2007, pp. 110–1.

307 The salacious details of this episode which led to the deposition of Stephen of Antioch are found in Athanasius, *Historia Arianorum* 20 and Theodoret, *Historia ecclesiastica* 2,9,1–10,1.

308 Cf. Socrates, *Historia ecclesiastica* 2,20,1.

commentary (sections 5–16) explaining the two anathemas of Ant[4] and the six additional anathemas of Serdica[309] one by one. It is too lengthy to be printed here, but these additions make it much clearer where the group of bishops stood than either Ant[4] or the creed of Serdica (east) had done.

- The creed insists on the timeless generation from the Father's *hypóstasis* and thus (like Serdica) suggests that there was only *one* divine *hypóstasis* in which the Son participated through the generation, which indicates a remarkable proximity to N (section 5).
- It also argues that the Son 'has a beginning in the Father who begot him' (ἀρχὴν ἔχειν τὸν γεννήσαντα πατέρα) and is, therefore, not coeternal with the Father (although this is not explicitly stated; section 6).
- The creed affirms three divine πράγματα ('entities', 'realities'?) or πρόσωπα ('persons') of Father, Son, and Spirit, but insists on the oneness of the Father, thus trying to ward off any danger of tritheism. The precise meaning of both terms is left unexplained. It is striking that neither the term *ousía* nor *hypóstasis* is mentioned here; in particular, the creed does not explain whether *prágma* and *prósopon* are synonymous with *hypóstasis*, thus carefully avoiding a theology of three *hypostáseis* (section 7).
- The Son is subordinate to the Father by virtue of his generation, but shares the Father's 'nature' (φύσις) and is, therefore, also fully divine. The equation of *phýsis* with *hypóstasis* again points to a one-*hypóstasis* theology (section 8).
- The creed rejects any distinction between (pre-existent) Logos and incarnate Son, as well as the notion that before his incarnation the Son somehow did not fully subsist as Son and that his kingdom would come to an end after the Final Judgement. This is directed against those who call the Logos ψιλός ('mere', 'bare', or 'simple') and ἀνύπαρκτος ('non-existent'), having his subsistence from the Father. Some of them call the Logos 'a spoken utterance' (προφορικός), while others conceive of him as 'residing in the mind' (ἐνδιάθετος), ideas that are also condemned (section 9).[310] This section is followed by a digression directed specifically against the followers of Marcellus and Photinus of Sirmium (section 10). Oddly, the Logos is called ἐνυπόστατος here which can only mean that he had his own *hypóstasis* which is contradictory to what was said before. What is even more remarkable is that the authors claim that the Son is only 'similar to the Father in all things' (τῷ πατρὶ κατὰ πάντα ὅμοιον), in their attempt to ward off the theology of Marcellus and Photinus. Thus the new catch-

---

309 Cf. above pp. 281, 288.
310 On the opposition between the λόγος προφορικός and ἐνδιάθετος cf. above p. 260 and n. 166.

word ὅμοιος which would later have a remarkable career was introduced into the debate.

- After this digression the commentary returns to the next in the series of condemnations, explaining the rejection of all forms of patripassianism: the opponents trace the three names of Father, Son, and Spirit back to the same *prágma* and *prósopon*, an idea which had already been rejected in anathema 3. Once again, the text carefully avoids using the term *hypóstasis* (section 11).
- Strangely, the condemnation of the view that the Son is unbegotten is not commented upon. Here the commentary leaves a gap.
- The emphasis on the Son's generation by 'choice' (βουλήσει) and 'will' (θελήσει) is meant to avoid the danger of making the Father subject to any kind of necessity (section 12). This view had also been expressed in the sixth additional anathema of the creed of Serdica (east).[311]

Here the commentary on the condemnations of Serdica ends. What follows is another explanation of the Son's generation (section 13) and of the unique relation between Father and Son (section 14). The authors wish to distance themselves from a view which considers the Son a created being like any other. They quote Prov 8:22 to this purpose and clearly allude to Jn 1:3: the Son is creator and as such cannot himself belong to the created order. The Son alone was begotten by the Father. This generation then leads to a subsistence of the Son which is distinct from that of the Father without being separate from him. By contrast, the creed emphasizes the close proximity of Father and Son (which is even described as the Father 'embracing' (ἐνστερνισμένου) the Son). Again the question as to whether the Son possesses his own *hypóstasis* is touched upon, without mentioning the term itself.

The final section (section 15) resumes the subordinationist doctrine of the Trinity which had been developed throughout the commentary. The 'all-perfect' (παντέλειον) and 'most-holy' (ἁγιωτάτην) character of the Trinity is emphasized. The oneness of Father and Son is described with the help of the terms 'dignity' (ἀξίωμα) and 'harmony' (συμφωνία), but without using *ousía* or *hypóstasis*. Ant[2] (which had been influenced by Asterius) had used the term *symphonía* in this context, while in the same clause insisting on the hypostatic difference between Father, Son, and Spirit.[312] However, here the term *axíoma* is added, no explicit distinction is made between the *hypostáseis* of Father and Son, and the Spirit is not even mentioned in this context. Indeed, the Spirit is only referenced further

---

311 Cf. above p. 288.
312 Cf. above p. 273.

below: it is subordinate to the Son who bestows it (at Pentecost) upon the saints through the will of the Father (πατρικῷ βουλήματι).

As I have tried to make clear in my analysis there is a peculiar tension in this text: whereas sections 5–9 seem to lean towards a one-*hypóstasis* theology, the digression in 10 appears to presuppose a separate *hypóstasis* of the pre-existent Logos and even a relationship between Father and Son which is defined by similarity only, rather than (some kind of) identity. This correlates with the general impression that section 10 interrupts the carefully structured text and may, in turn, indicate that 10 was later inserted into the creed's commentary in 5–9, 11–12. The commentary without this digression may even have already been written in Serdica, but left unpublished for some reason (length?). Sections 13–15 may also have been appended later when 10 was inserted. Whatever the precise history of this text, it clearly shows traces of several stages of revision.

Be that as it may, we can detect a theology 'on the move' in this instance, gradually shifting from a position which may have been considered compatible with N towards a new theology which would later be called Homoian. This may well be connected with the fact that the chief delegate was Eudoxius who was to become one of the leaders of this ecclesial party. He had already taken part in the Dedication Council and in the Synod of Serdica, but appears to have not yet been one of the principal figures in these proceedings. The fact that he was heading the mission to the west suggests that by now he had obtained a leading role in the doctrinal negotiations. Perhaps it was he who had composed the digression which was then inserted into an already existing, earlier text at the Synod in Antioch in 344.

6.5.4 The First Creed of Sirmium (351)

The synod which was summoned in early 351 to Sirmium (modern Sremska Mitrovica in Serbia) by the Emperor Constantius II discussed the orthodoxy of Photinus.[313] He had been deposed as bishop of Sirmium at two Synods in Milan (345) and Sirmium (347), but the deposition had not come into effect. Finally, at the (second) Sirmian Synod of 351 Photinus was (again) deposed and sent into exile. On the same occasion a creed was adopted which is another extended version of Ant[4].[314] The dif-

---

313 Cf. above p. 288 and n. 291.
314 Cf. Council of Sirmium (351), *Fidei confessio prima* (Brennecke et al. 2014, *Dokument* 47.3; FaFo § 148). It is probably neither a revision of the *Ecthesis* of Serdica (east) nor of the Macrostich Creed, because in that case the additional condemnations in both these creeds (beginning with ὁμοίως, 'likewise') would have now been replaced by another set of anathemas which is less

ferences are minimal.[315] However, the anathema of Ant[4] is supplemented by a series of 26 new condemnations (altogether 27). They all display the same structure, consisting of a conditional clause introduced by εἴ τις ('if anyone') to summarize the opponent's position and a main clause containing nothing but the formula ἀνάθεμα ἔστω ('let him be anathema'). This structure already occurs in Ant[2],[316] but it is extended in such a way here that it almost functions like a litany or a responsory. Thus the emphasis is shifted from the credal text itself to the final condemnations. What do these additional anathemas reveal about their authors' theological tenets?

Father, Son, and Holy Spirit are not one *prósopon* (rejection of modalism, anathema 20(19)). The authors underline the pre-existence of Christ and his cooperation in the process of creation (anathemas 4(3), 6(5), 15(14)). The Logos is not in any way intrinsic to the Father (he is neither *endiáthetos* nor *prophorikós*)[317] nor is his generation the result of an 'expansion' or 'extension' (πλατυσμός) of the Father (anathemas 7(6)–9(8)). Here, once again, the text is directed against Marcellus of Ancyra and Photinus without their being named.[318] (Photinus had, according to the council's proceedings as reported by Epiphanius, distinguished the pre-existent Logos, who had subsisted in the Father but was no Son, from Christ, who had been named Son after the virgin birth.[319] Hence he probably championed a version of adoptionism.) The Son is subordinate to the Father who told the Son to sit at his right hand. The Father is the beginning of Christ who, in turn, is the beginning of all things. It is important to hold on to this notion of a hierarchy in the divinity, because otherwise there is the danger that two unbegun and unbegotten beings existed and thus, ultimately, two gods (anathemas 3(2), 19(18), 27(26)). At the same time, the Son has not come into

---

likely. It is easier to assume these Sirmian anathemas were added to an, at that stage, briefer text.

315 Differences which may be significant: καὶ δύναμιν καὶ ζωὴν καὶ φῶς ἀληθινόν was changed to καὶ φῶς ἀληθινόν καὶ ζωήν. In addition, ὅπερ ἐπαγγειλάμενος τοῖς ἀποστόλοις μετὰ τὴν εἰς οὐρανοὺς αὐτοῦ ἄνοδον ἀπέστειλε διδάξαι αὐτοὺς καὶ ὑπομνῆσαι πάντα was changed to ὅπερ ἐπαγγειλάμενος τοῖς ἀποστόλοις μετὰ τὴν εἰς οὐρανοὺς αὐτοῦ ἄνοδον ἀποστεῖλαι, διδάξαι καὶ ὑπομνῆσαι αὐτοὺς πάντα ἔπεμψε. – The additions ἦν χρόνος ἢ αἰών in the second anathema and ἡ ἁγία καὶ καθολικὴ ἐκκλησία are identical with those in Serdica and in the Macrostich Creed. Perhaps the present text of Ant[4] is defective in these places.

316 Cf. above p. 273.

317 For the distinction between the Logos *endiáthetos* and *prophorikós* cf. above pp. 260 and n. 167. Furthermore cf. Epiphanius, *Panarion* 71,9 (*Dokument* 47.2, 1,12 in Brennecke et al. 2014, p. 333).

318 For the theory of Christ's generation as a result of God's expansion cf. Marcellus, frgs. 48 and 73 (Vinzent). Cf., in addition, Vinzent 1997, pp. 262–77.

319 Cf. especially the report about the disputation at Sirmium in Epiphanius, *Panarion* 71,2,2–4 (*Dokument* 47.2, 1,8 in Brennecke et al. 2014, p. 331). In addition, Hübner 1989, pp. 187–8. On the teachings of Photinus in general cf. Uthemann 1999; Williams 2006; McCarthy Spoerl 2022.

being by the Father's will (βουλήσει), as this would indicate that he is a creature (which is clearly directed against Arius and Asterius, but also the creed of Serdica (east) and the Macrostich Creed;[320] anathema 25(24)). Conversely, the authors also reject the view that the Son has been generated *against* the Father's will, because this would render the Father subject to some kind of necessity or compulsion (anathema 26(25)). The Paraclete must be clearly distinguished from both Father and Son (anathemas 21(20)–23(22)), but this does not make Father, Son, and Spirit three gods (anathema 24(23)).

The synod insisted that in those passages of the Old Testament which had been used by Photinus to prove that the Son was not pre-existent it was precisely the Son and not the Father who had been active and had appeared to the patriarchs (anathemas 16(15)–19(18)). Christ incarnate is not unbegotten (anathemas 5(4), 11(10)), but he is no mere human either (anathema 10(9)). Interestingly, the authors also seem to turn against Jews who take Is 44:6 ('I, God, [am] the first and I [am] the last, and besides me there is no God') as proof that Christ could not have been divine (anathema 12(11)). However, the verse was also used by Marcellus in his polemic against Asterius where he argued that God's oneness excluded the pre-existence of another, younger divine figure.[321] God was not transformed or altered in the process of the incarnation, and did not suffer either (anathemas 13(12), 14(13)).

The final anathema (which was again directed against Photinus) sums up the doctrine of this creed:

> Once more giving a precise summary of the idea of Christianity, we say that if anyone might say not that Christ is God, Son of God, existing before the ages, and having assisted the Father in the framing of the universe, but that he was called Christ and Son and received the beginning of his existence as God [only] from the time when he was born from Mary, let him be anathema.[322]

There is nothing in this text which would have been offensive to defenders of Nicaea except for the omission of *homooúsios* and (perhaps for some) its rather distinctive subordinationism. The opponents against which this creed is directed (primarily Marcellus and Photinus and, to a lesser extent, Arians) remain unnamed. There is no indication that the authors championed a theology of three *hypostá-seis* – in fact, they seem to represent a one-*hypóstasis* theology, taking over the first condemnation from Ant⁴. In other words: the creed's condemnations explain the creed itself without adding any major new doctrinal reflections. They contain no

---

320 Cf. above pp. 288 f., 293.
321 Cf. Marcellus, frgs. 97–98 (Vinzent).
322 Council of Sirmium (351), *Fidei confessio prima* (FaFo § 148) 28(27).

inkling of a Homoian doctrine of the Trinity and thus take a step back from the Macrostich Creed. In fact, just like Ant[4] this creed represents a theology which is very close to Nicaea. Therefore, even the Roman bishop, by now Liberius (*sedit* 352–366), was ultimately able (although not without considerable political pressure[323]) to accept it as orthodox.[324]

6.5.5 The *Expositio fidei* attributed to Athanasius

We possess another *Expositio fidei* which the manuscript tradition attributed to Athanasius, but which – in the view of its most recent editors – was issued by an unknown Egyptian council in around 351.[325] Earlier scholars often attributed it to Marcellus, but this is now deemed unlikely.[326] Alas, we have no information about the context within which this creed was drafted. Nonetheless, it looks as if the authors knew and used the *Sermo maior de fide* (*Epistula ad Antiochenos*), which was perhaps written by the bishop of Ancyra,[327] and texts which are ascribed to Dionysius of Rome and his namesake of Alexandria by Athanasius.[328] The text is an extended creed which displays Nicene features. The authors reject certain descriptions of the Logos: he is 'neither a spoken nor a mental Word,'[329]

---

323 Cf. Barnes 1993, p. 138.
324 Cf. Liberius, *Epistula ad orientales episcopos* in Hilary, *Collectanea Antiariana Parisina (Fragmenta historica)* B VII 8,2(6): 'That you may know more truly that I express my true belief (*ueram fidem*) in this letter, let me say: because my lord and common brother Demofilus [bishop of Beroea where Liberius stayed in exile] kindly saw fit to set forth your creed, which is also the Catholic faith (*fidem uestram et catholicam*), as discussed and set forth by very many of our brothers and fellow bishops at Sirmium and accepted [. . .] by all present, I have accepted it gladly [. . .]. I have not contradicted it in any respect, I have concurred with it, follow it and hold to it' (Wickham 1997, pp. 77 f.; slightly altered). In my view, Liberius' letter fits better the First Sirmian Creed than the Second of 357 or Third of 358. However, problems remain; for a full discussion cf. Brennecke 1984, pp. 274–84 (who opts for the creed of 357; cf. also Brennecke et al. 2014, p. 376) and Hanson 1988, pp. 358–62 (p. 362: 'The matter must be left open.'). Cf. also Bleckmann/Stein 2015, vol. II, pp. 280 f. and Sághy 2018, citing further literature.
325 Cf. Pseudo-Athanasius, *Expositio fidei* (Brennecke et al. 2014, *Dokument* 48; FaFo § 149). Cf. also Brennecke et al. 2014, p. 346.
326 Cf. Seibt 1993; Brennecke et al. 2014, pp. 346 f.
327 Cf. Seibt 1993, pp. 285–90. Sara Parvis 2006, p. 246 rejects Marcellan authorship.
328 Detailed discussion in Seibt 1993, pp. 290–5. Seibt assumes that the texts by the two 'Dionysii' and the *Expositio fidei* were written by the same author; this is disputed by Heil 1999, pp. 41–3.
329 The idea that the Logos is *prophorikós* or *endiáthetos* was already rejected in the *Ecthesis macrostichos* 9–10 (cf. above p. 292). Cf. also the Council of Sirmium (351), *Fidei confessio prima* (FaFo § 148) 9(8) and above p. 295. In addition, cf. above p. 260 and n. 167.

nor an emanation of the Perfect, nor a division, nor an issue of the impassible nature; but an absolutely perfect Son, living and active [cf. Heb 4:12], the true image of the Father, equal in honour and glory'.[330] The Son is thus 'similar to the Father' (ὅμοιος τῷ πατρί; section 1). Yet this is no Homoian theology: the following quotation of Jn 14:9 ('Whoever has seen me has seen the Father') makes it clear that the authors do not wish to *distinguish* the Son from the Father; on the contrary: the Son's likeness is an expression of his *proximity* to the Father. Yet he is not identical with him either. There is, therefore, a certain similarity of this text with the aforementioned 'Homoian' passage in the Macrostich Creed,[331] but the divinity of the Son is emphasized in much stronger terms than in the earlier text.

The authors distance themselves from the 'Sabellians' who say that the Father-Son (υἱοπάτορα) is of a single substance, but not from the same (or, perhaps better, of a like) substance (μονοούσιον καὶ οὐχ ὁμοούσιον). Obviously they do not share the (later) Neo-Nicene position: for them *homoousios* does not (yet) mean identity of substance.[332] However, they also reject the division of Father, Son, and Spirit into three distinct *hypostáseis* (by which they mean something like 'entities' without a common ontological substratum), as this would lead to tritheism. The most appropriate metaphor is that of spring (Father) and river (Son): '[. . .] the godhead passes from the Father into the Son without flow[333] and without division (ἀρρεύστως καὶ ἀδιαιρέτως)' (section 3). This excludes the idea of the Son's being a creature. Every biblical text which is claimed to refer to the Son/Christ being a creature (e.g. Jer 38(31):22; Prov 8:22) in truth refers to the Lord's body (σῶμα; section 5).

Finally, the authors have little to say about the Holy Spirit, but what they do say is remarkable: the Spirit is an ἐκπόρευμα, something proceeding from the Father, and 'is ever in the hands of the Father who sends, and [is in the hands] of the Son who conveys him, through whom he filled all things [cf. Eph 4:10]' (section 6).

---

330 Pseudo-Athanasius, *Expositio fidei* 3 (FaFo § 149): [. . .] λόγον δὲ οὐ προφορικόν, οὐκ ἐνδιάθετον, οὐκ ἀπόρροιαν τοῦ τελείου, οὐ τμῆσιν τῆς ἀπαθοῦς φύσεως οὔτε προβολήν, ἀλλ᾽ υἱὸν αὐτοτελῆ, ζῶντά τε καὶ ἐνεργοῦντα, τὴν ἀληθινὴν εἰκόνα τοῦ πατρὸς ἰσότιμον καὶ ἰσόδοξον [. . .].

331 Cf. *Ecthesis macrostichos* (FaFo § 145[10]) and above pp. 292 f.

332 By contrast, cf., e.g., Pseudo-Athanasius (Marcellus?), *Epistula ad Liberium* (FaFo § 150) whose author identifies *ousía* with *hypóstasis*, advocates a theology of one divine *ousía*, and clearly assumes *homoousios* to express identity of substance.

333 The meaning of ἀρρεύστως here is difficult to ascertain. For how can a spring turn into a river without flow? I owe this observation to Kathrin Lüddecke.

All in all, the text is irenic in character: the opponents (mainly Arians) are nowhere named. The authors are struggling accurately to describe the relation between the persons of the Trinity, rejecting both a one-*ousía* and a three-*hypostáseis* theology. They affirm the *homooúsios*, but do not interpret it in the sense of an identity of substance: here it expresses that the Son most closely approximates the Father, while falling short of an actual identity.

6.5.6 The Second Creed of Sirmium (357)

It is uncertain whether new synodal creeds were produced in the period 351–357. Sulpicius Severus claims that Emperor Constantius II requested the western bishops to sign the condemnation of Athanasius at Synods in Arles (353) and Béziers (356). In turn, they told him that the *fides* first had to be debated before they were willing to do as he wished, but Bishop Valens (of Mursa) and his associates did not have the courage to take up the gauntlet (*de fide certare non ausi*).[334] After Arles Liberius of Rome sent a letter to Constantius II, calling for a new investigation into the case of Athanasius and the confirmation of the orthodoxy of N at a general council.[335] Similarly, according to Sulpicius Severus, the local bishop Dionysius said at the Synod of Milan (355) that he would not agree to Athanasius' condemnation, unless the bishops had considered the faith beforehand (*dummodo de fide inter episcopos quaeretur*).[336] Eusebius of Vercelli seems to have made the same request. He presented N and promised to do all that was expected of him if his opponents were to write down a 'profession of faith' (*fidei professionem scripsissent*). When Dionysius was on the point of actually doing so, bishop Valens tore quill and paper from his hand.[337] The bishops Valens and Ursacius (of Singidunum) then supposedly circulated a letter under the emperor's name. Had the letter met with resistance, then the emperor would have taken the blame. This would not have been a problem 'because also at that time a catechumen would have been excused for not knowing the mystery of the faith' (*quia etiam tum catechumenus sacramentum fidei merito uideretur potuisse nescire*; the em-

---

334 Sulpicius Severus, *Chronica* 2,39,3 (Brennecke et al. 2014, *Dokument* 50.2, 1). As regards Valens (and Ursacius) cf. already above p. 285.

335 Liberius, *Epistula ad Constantium imperatorem* (Brennecke et al. 2014, *Dokument* 50.1) 7. Cf. also Brennecke 1984, pp. 158–64 who expresses a certain scepticism and thinks that Liberius was referring to Serdica rather than to N.

336 Sulpicius Severus, *Chronica* 2,39,4 (Brennecke et al. 2014, *Dokument* 50.2, 2).

337 Cf. Hilary of Poitiers, *Collectanea antiariana Parisina (Fragmenta historica)*, app. II,3(8),2 (FaFo § 152).

peror had not yet been baptized).[338] Since our reports about events at Milan are incomplete and the imperial letter (if it ever existed) is lost, we do not know to what extent N was discussed at Milan. However, there can be little doubt that it did play some role. At that point a Latin translation must have existed which is no longer extant (the earliest surviving text stems from 356[339]). By contrast, it is controversial whether Constantius submitted a doctrinal formula to the Synods of Arles and Milan; in any case, there is no trace of it in our sources.[340]

There were clear signs, though, that Constantius was no longer willing to tolerate dissension in the Church.[341] Although the details remain blurred, it seems that he intended first to remove the trouble-maker Athanasius and his Nicene supporters from the scene through universal ecclesial condemnation, followed by exile, and subsequently to impose a credal formula which was wide enough to unite all bishops under its doctrinal umbrella. At first, however, his sympathies may not have lain with the opponents of Nicaea. An encyclical letter Athanasius sent to the bishops of Egypt and Libya, whose date is, unfortunately, uncertain (356 or 361), includes a report about a creed which 'Arians', followers of Eusebius of Nicomedia,[342] had drawn up to stir up public opinion against the Nicenes and to win the emperor over to their side.[343] Unfortunately, Athanasius fails to quote this document directly; but he concedes that its phrasing is scriptural and that its terminology is 'orthodox'[344] – and he goes on to give a long list of bishops whom he deems defenders of the right faith.[345] This description fits the First Sirmian Creed quite well – indeed, it seems that Athanasius does not deal with this (or a

---

338 Sulpicius Severus, *Chronica* 2,39,5 (Brennecke et al. 2014, *Dokument* 50.2).

339 Cf. Hilary of Poitiers, *Collectanea Antiariana Parisina (Fragmenta historica)* B II 10,1–3(27; FaFo § 135d1) and (perhaps somewhat later) Lucifer of Cagliari, *De non parcendo in deum delinquentibus* 18 (§ 135d2). The Synod of Milan is discussed in Brennecke 1984, pp. 147–95; Hanson 1988, pp. 332–4.

340 Cf. the discussion in Brennecke 1984, pp. 184–92 (listing earlier literature); Hanson 1988, pp. 329–34; Ulrich 1994, p. 219 n. 17.

341 Cf. Klein 1977, esp. pp. 86–93; Barnes 1993, pp. 138–41; Barceló 2004, pp. 148 f., 168–77; Crawford 2016, pp. 112 f.

342 Here and elsewhere Athanasius provides a long list of bishops supportive of 'Arian' views; cf. *Epistula ad episcopos Aegypti et Libyae* 7,2–6. For further lists cf. Metzler/Hansen/Savvidis 1996, p. 46, app. ad loc.

343 Cf. Athanasius, *Epistula ad episcopos Aegypti et Libyae*, esp. 5,1–4; 6,1; 7,2; 8,1–2; 18,3 (FaFo § 153).

344 Cf. Athanasius, *Epistula ad episcopos Aegypti et Libyae* 8,2: 'For even though they may write with phrases from the Scriptures, do not endure their writings; even though they may speak with the expressions of orthodoxy, do not pay attention to what they say in this way.' Cf. also 9,6; 11,1.

345 Cf. Athanasius, *Epistula ad episcopos Aegypti et Libyae* 8,4.

similar) creed in greater detail, precisely because he has some difficulties proving his opponents' heterodoxy. Instead he emphasizes time and again that they hide their true (Arian) views and avoid the contentious issues.[346] Had this letter been written after the Second Creed of Sirmium (357), it would have been easy for Athanasius to show its ante-Nicene character – which is why a date before 357 is perferable.[347]

However, with this Second Creed of 357 things began to shift significantly. It was drafted by the bishops Valens of Mursa, Ursacius of Singidunum, and Germinius of Sirmium[348] in Latin,[349] perhaps in the context of a small synod.[350] Strictly speaking, it is no creed (avoiding the formula *credo/credimus*[351]), but a kind of memorandum discussing contentious doctrinal issues. The text (which need not be cited here in full) first names those issues on which there was unanimity: the generation of the Son before the ages and God's oneness (section 2). It then addresses the points on which there was dissension, suggesting that the controversial terms *homoousios* and *homoiousios* (the latter as yet not having been used in a creed) ought to be avoided, because these terms were unscriptural and inappropriate for describing the Son's generation whose precise nature was unknown to us. Here the authors referred to Is 53:8 (cf. Acts 8:33): 'Who can describe his generation?' (section 3). The text then affirms the Son's subordination to the Father (sections 4–5), because

> the Father is greater in honour, dignity, glory, majesty (*honore, dignitate, claritate, maiestate*), and in the very name of Father [. . .]. No one is ignorant that it is catholic doctrine that there are two persons (*duas personas*) of Father and Son, and that the Father is greater,

---

346 Cf. esp. Athanasius, *Epistula ad episcopos Aegypti et Libyae* 3,5; 8,2; 9,6; 10–11; 19,7.

347 Cf. also Metzler/Hansen/Savvidis 1996, p. 39 app.

348 Phoebadius of Agen, *Contra Arianos* 8,2 names Potamius of Lisbon as the creed's third author (instead of Germinius). Hilary quotes the creed under the title *Exemplum blasphemiae apud Sirmium per Osium et Potamium conscriptae* / 'A copy of the blasphemy written by Ossius and Potamius in Sirmium' (*De synodis* 10 (PL 10, col. 487A)). Authorship by Ossius is, however, unlikely (cf. Hanson 1988, pp. 336 f., 345 f. and below in the text). According to Hanson, 'it is best to assign the authorship of this creed to Valens, Ursacius, Potamius and Germinius' (p. 346).

349 Cf. Council of Sirmium (357), *Fidei confessio altera* (Brennecke et al. 2014, *Dokument* 51; FaFo § 154a). We also possess a Greek translation (§ 154b) which differs from the Latin original in some respects.

350 Cf. Brennecke 1984, pp. 312–25; Hanson 1988, pp. 343–7; Barnes 1993, pp. 231 f.; Brennecke et al. 2014, p. 376. However, in the introductory section it is said that the text was discussed between the three bishops only. We do not know whether or not the Emperor Constantius was present.

351 In section 2 the expression *creditur* is used but no equivalent is found in the Greek translation which reads καταγγέλλεται / 'it is proclaimed' instead.

and the Son has been subordinated to the Father together with all things which the Father has subordinated to him [cf. 1Cor 15:28] [. . .].

Although this was no formal synodal creed, its implications were considerable, because if its agenda was to become official doctrine, then it was not only N that was rejected, but all attempts at bridging the terminological gaps between supporters and critics of N would be thwarted. In other words, it would no longer be possible simply to express the Nicene faith by quietly dropping its *homooúsios*. Now the claim was that it was theologically impossible as well as inappropriate to describe the Son's generation with *any* predicates. Furthermore, the text was so vague that it did not exclude the possibility that the Son ultimately belonged to the created order and might be posterior in some way to the Father. Incidentally, it is striking that the authors of these texts no longer focussed on the old enemies Marcellus and Photinus. (Marcellus was by that time rather isolated;[352] likewise, Photinus' sphere of activity had been temporarily reduced with his deposition in 351.[353])

It seems that the Second Creed of Sirmium was circulated across the empire to be signed by the bishops.[354] Among the signatories was Ossius, erstwhile defender of the Nicene faith; however, he refused to condemn Athanasius. The reasons for his change of heart are unknown.[355]

6.5.7 The formation of the Homoiousians in Ancyra (358)

In response to the Second Creed of Sirmium[356] a group of twelve bishops led by Basil of Ancyra and also including Macedonius of Constantinople and Eustathius of Sebaste met in early 358, issuing a lengthy statement in which a theological position was formulated that saw itself in continuity with the creed of the eastern council of Serdica.[357] This is usually seen as the founding document of the Homoi-

---

352 Cf. Vinzent 1997, pp. XXIV–XXV.

353 Cf. Williams 2006, pp. 191–2.

354 Cf. Hilary of Poitiers, *Liber (I) in Constantium imperatorem* 26; id., *De synodis* 2.

355 Athanasius claims that the reason for his turnabout was a one-year detention in Sirmium (*Historia Arianorum* 45,4; cf. also Socrates, *Historia ecclesiastica* 2,31 (who even claims that Ossius was tortured); Sozomen, *Historia ecclesiastica* 4,12,6). Cf. De Clercq 1954, pp. 474–525; Klein 1977, pp. 135 f.; Hanson 1988, pp. 336–7; Just 2003, pp. 88–93; Barceló 2004, p. 155.

356 The historical background which also involves the complicated situation at Antioch is described in Hanson 1988, pp. 348 f.

357 Cf. Council of Ancyra (358), *Epistula synodalis* (Brennecke et al. 2014, *Dokument* 55). Its first part also in FaFo § 155. An English translation is found in Steenson/DelCogliano 2017.

ousians, although the term ὁμοιούσιος ('of similar substance') is not used.[358] It consists of an introduction (sections 1–5), a theological treatise (sections 6–25), and nineteen anathemas (section 26) and was signed by Basil, Eustathius of Sebaste (d. after 377), and ten further bishops.

As this letter contains no creed, we will touch upon it only very briefly. Its authors do, however, present themselves as the torchbearers of the faith as set out in a series of earlier creeds which are enumerated twice (sections 2, 4): the Fourth Creed of Antioch[359] – Serdica (east) – Sirmium 351 – Macrostich Creed.[360] The Father is described in long biblical exegeses as the 'cause of a substance similar to his' (αἴτιον ὁμοίας αὐτοῦ οὐσίας) – which is, in effect, the same as *homoioúsios* (section 6; cf. also 8–9, 13–14, 16, 19, 21, 25). The reverse is, then, also true: that the Son's substance is similar to the Father's, although the text, interestingly, phrases it differently: 'When we hear the name of "Son" we understand him to be similar to the Father, whose Son he is.'[361] This change in terminology is no doubt influenced by the 'Homoian' passage in the Macrostich Creed which I discussed above, giving it, as it were, a Homoiousian twist.[362] The relationship between Father and Son can henceforth no longer (explicitly or by implication) be described as *homooúsios*, but neither is theirs 'only' some kind of (accidental) similarity; rather, it is something in between: the Son's substance derives from the Father's substance by way of generation which defines their similarity in substance as being like the way in which an image is similar to the original (Col 1:15) without actually sharing its substance (cf. sections 8–9, 19; anathemas 9–10). Here the authors, at first glance, seem to come close to the argument in Ant².[363] It must be borne in mind that the reason for the explicit rejection of *homooúsios* in anathema 19 is no longer its unbiblical provenance,[364] but fear that it may be confused with a complete identity of substance and mode of subsistence which leaves no more room to describe the different operations of Father and Son, leaving one

---

358 Cf. Hanson 1988, pp. 349 f. Kelly 1972, p. 288 is inaccurate on this point. *Homoioúsios* was never used in any creed in an affirmative sense. 'It certainly was not a slogan designed to unite a party, but a convenient way of referring to a theological group, used perhaps more by those who did not form part of the group than by those who did' (Hanson 1988, p. 350).

359 Cf., however, Hanson 1988, pp. 351 f.; Brennecke et al. 2014, p. 387 n. b: Ant².

360 The identification of the Macrostich Creed is not quite certain.

361 Cf. Council of Ancyra (358), *Epistula synodalis* (*Dokument* 55, 6 in Brennecke et al. 2014, p. 390, ll. 8–14): [. . .] ἵνα [. . .] καὶ τὸ ὄνομα τοῦ υἱοῦ ἀκούοντες ὅμοιον νοήσωμεν τὸν υἱὸν τοῦ πατρός, οὗ ἐστιν ὁ υἱός.

362 Cf. above pp. 292 f.

363 Cf. above p. 274 and Hanson 1988, p. 253.

364 Cf., however, above p. 301.

exposed to the danger of patripassianism.[365] This is also the reason why the Son is termed the Father's 'image' – the 'image' terminology rightly understood can no longer be used to downgrade the Son's ontological status. Here the text clearly distances itself from the Asterian theology expressed in Ant² (cf. esp. sections 19–20).[366]

On the basis of such theological considerations, then, the authors rejected all forms of Arianism, especially the new version as championed by Eunomius (to become bishop of Cyzicus in 360; d. 396/397).[367] Again and again they describe the Son's generation from the Father as fundamentally different to the relation between creator and creature. The Father's 'generative energy' (ἐνέργεια γεννητική) to which the Son owes his existence is distinct from his 'creative energy' (ἐνέργεια κτιστική):

> Instead he [sc. the apostle Paul in 1Cor 1:17] wants to proclaim – without the use of logic – the Father and the Son without [recourse to] passions: the Father had begotten the Son from himself without emission or passion, while the Son subsisted from the Father, being similar in substance, perfect from perfect [and] only-begotten. [These doctrines] are <either believed> by the believing or suspected <by the unbelieving>.[368]

The phrase ὅμοιον κατ' οὐσίαν ('similar in substance') indicated that a new position was emerging here whose proponents would soon be some of the key players in the further struggle for orthodoxy.

---

365 Cf. Council of Ancyra (358), *Epistula synodalis* (*Dokument* 55, 26(19.) in Brennecke et al. 2014, p. 408, ll. 3–6): Καὶ εἴ τις ἐξουσίᾳ καὶ οὐσίᾳ λέγων τὸν πατέρα πατέρα τοῦ υἱοῦ, ὁμοούσιον δὲ ἢ ταὐτοούσιον λέγοι τὸν υἱὸν τῷ πατρί, ἀνάθεμα ἔστω. / 'And if anyone says that the Father is the Father of the Son by authority and substance and then says that the Son is consubstantial or of identical substance with the Father, let him be anathema.' Cf. also section 25: the Son is God, but he is not 'the' God. This distinction does not serve to assign the Son to the created order as, e.g., in Asterius (cf. frg. 63 (Vinzent)), but to safeguard some kind of distinction between Father and Son while retaining the Son's full divinity (cf. also anathema 13).
366 Cf. above pp. 274 f.
367 Cf. the references to Eunomius' works in Brennecke et al. 2014, app. ad *Dokument* 55. Anhomoianism is explicitly rejected in anathemas 3, 5, 7, 9, 11–12, 14, 18.
368 Council of Ancyra (358), *Epistula synodalis* (*Dokument* 55, 15 in Brennecke et al. 2014, p. 396, ll. 24–32): [. . .] ἀλλ' ἀπαθῶς πατέρα καὶ υἱόν, πατέρα μὲν ἐξ ἑαυτοῦ γεγεννηκότα ἄνευ ἀπορροίας καὶ πάθους τὸν υἱόν, υἱὸν δὲ ὅμοιον καὶ κατ' οὐσίαν ἐκ τοῦ πατρός, τέλειον ἐκ τελείου, μονογενῆ ὑποστάντα, <πιστευόμενα> τοῖς πιστοῖς ἢ ὑποπτευόμενα <τοῖς ἀπίστοις> ἀσυλλογίστως κηρύξει. The conjecture <ἢ πιστευόμενα> suggested by Brennecke et al. seems unwarranted.

6.5.8 A union failed? The so-called Third Creed of Sirmium (358)

By the late 350s we see an increasing hardening of doctrinal frontlines: if the status of the Son as a creature and his temporal posteriority with regard to the Father are considered the hallmarks of Arianism, then the Anhomoians (Neo-Arians) led by Aetius (d. 365/366) and Eunomius who worked out the ontological implications with much greater precision were the true heirs of the first-generation Arians.[369] They taught a marked subordinationism: as God's creature the Son does not originate from the *ousía* or *hypóstasis* of the Father and is therefore not *homooúsios*. This applies in a similar way to the Spirit who is, in turn, subordinate to the Son. Although the Anhomoians (so called by their opponents) de facto posited the dissimilarity of the *ousía* of Father and Son, they probably did not qualify the relationship between Father and Son explicitly as 'dissimilar' (ἀνόμοιος), but preferred the predicate 'of a different substance' (ἑτεροούσιος). Right from the beginning they were largely isolated and rarely involved in synodal discussions which may be the reason why no Anhomoian creed seems to have been produced until the Council of Constantinople (381). According to Basil of Caesarea the only brief creed-like text which is found in Eunomius' writings stems from Arius himself who presented it to Alexander of Alexandria.[370] It displays no distinctive theological features.[371]

The Anhomoians notwithstanding, two groups were gradually starting to formulate their theological platforms: the Homoians led by the 'Illyrian trio'[372] of Valens of Mursa, Ursacius of Singidunum, and Germinius of Sirmium, and the Homoiousians led by Basil of Ancyra. They agreed in their rejection of the Neo-Arian positions: for both groups the Son was fully God, begotten from the Father before the ages. At the same time, there were considerable differences between them: the Homoians wished to leave the precise meaning of generation undefined (and might thus be suspected of clandestinely acknowledging the identity of generation and creation) and rejected, therefore, all talk of *homooúsios* and *homoíousios* (a terminology which they considered unbiblical), without suggesting a more appropriate term (such as ὅμοιος which had, at that point, not yet been introduced in the debate[373]). In sum, their trinitarian doctrine as outlined in the Second Creed

---

369 Cf. Kinzig, 'Neuarianismus', 2018, pp. 1491–6.
370 Cf. Eunomius, *Apologia* 5 (FaFo § 163a) and Basil of Caesarea, *Contra Eunomium* 1,4. In addition, a credal text is found in *Apologia* 28 (FaFo § 163b).
371 Eunomius only produced a *Confessio fidei* (which is, in fact, a brief theological treatise) in 383 after having been ordered by Emperor Theodosius I to outline his position (cf. FaFo § 163c).
372 Cf. Ritter 2011, p. 194.
373 Cf., however, Macrostich Creed 10 and above pp. 292 f.

of Sirmium was clearly subordinationist, strongly resembling Origen's description of the Trinity.[374]

By contrast, although the Homoiousians also rejected *homooúsios*, they did it not do so primarily because it was unbiblical (they knew full well that their own terminology of substance was not biblical either), but because for them it implied an insufficient distinction between Father and Son. Yet they held that the Son's *ousía* derived from the Father's and was, therefore, in every respect similar without being identical. Thus they insisted on the Son's full divinity in much stronger terms than the Homoians, leaving no doubt that the Son could in no way be considered created. However, their notion of *ousía* was still rather imprecise, because they lacked a clearly defined ontological category to describe the 'kinship' between Father and Son. The concept of an 'image' made it possible to explain this simultaneous distinction and similarity; above all, it was derived from Scripture, though it left the question unanswered as to what the Father's ontological substratum was that continued to exist in the Son and which constituted his essential similarity to the Father.

It appears that even at that point agreement between the parties would have been possible. Sozomen includes a report in his *Church History* about a meeting which had been called in Sirmium in 358 by Constantius II.[375] It consisted of the leaders of the Homoians who were associated with the court (Valens, Ursacius, and Germinius) and the Homoiousians led by Basil of Ancyra, Eustathius of Sebaste, and Eleusius of Cyzicus. Apparently, Constantius demanded that the bishop of Rome, Liberius – who had, for this meeting, been recalled from exile (into which he had meanwhile been sent) – condemn the *homooúsios* but was unsuccessful. The result of this meeting was the so-called 'Third Creed of Sirmium' (which is, unfortunately, lost). In fact, according to Sozomen's account it was no creed proper, but a collection of documents which included unspecified condemnations of Paul of Samosata and of Photinus and Ant[2] (unless Sozomen confuses it with Ant[4]).[376] Liberius was forced to sign this document, followed by four African priests in his retinue. However, he does not appear to have been entirely satisfied, because he submitted a personal 'confession' (ὁμολογία), denouncing 'those who affirm that the Son is not similar to the Father in substance nor in any other respect (ἀποκηρ-

---

374 Cf. above ch. 6.5.
375 Cf. Sozomen, *Historia ecclesiastica* 4,15,1–3 (FaFo § 156); cf. Brennecke et al. 2014, *Dokument* 56.1 (in part).
376 Sozomen's remark that the creed included *homooúsios* is incorrect.

ὑττουσαν τοὺς μὴ κατ' οὐσίαν καὶ κατὰ πάντα ὅμοιον τῷ πατρὶ τὸν υἱὸν ἀποφαίνοντα ς)'.[377] Probably, Liberius was by now espousing some form of Homoiousian position and may have thought that Ant^2 was not going far enough as it did not specifically exclude Anhomoian and Homoian views. Not all bishops present approved of Liberius' confession.

6.5.9 The victory of the Homoians: The Fourth Creed of Sirmium (359) and its successors

The attempts of 358 at a union failed. Although the Homoians, the Homoiousians, and even Liberius and Ossius had been brought into the fold then, something must have gone awry afterwards. Unfortunately, we have no details. Perhaps Constantius thought that the document produced at Sirmium in 358 was insufficient as a creed to be used throughout the empire. Be that as it may, on 22 May 359 yet another creed (the so-called 'Fourth Creed of Sirmium') was promulgated,[378] also mockingly called the 'Dated Creed' because of its precise date.[379] We know the background to its composition from a letter by Germinius of Sirmium.[380] According to Germinius Constantius assembled a group of bishops at his court in Sirmium. It consisted of Mark of Arethusa, George of Alexandria, Pancratius of Pelusium, Basil of Ancyra, Valens, Ursacius, Hypatian of Heraclea,[381] and Germinius himself. Here, the controversial doctrinal issues between Homoians and Homoiousians were discussed in the emperor's presence late into the night, until, finally, a compromise was found with Mark commissioned by all to write a creed summing up the results.[382] After Athanasius had also been condemned by the bishop of Rome and after the silencing of Marcellus and Photinus, the purpose of this meeting was to reach agreement between those bishops who all rejected the *homooúsios* (although for various reasons) but differed in how they described the relation between Father and Son. However,

---

377 Sozomen, *Historia ecclesiastica* 4,15,3 (FaFo § 156). Cf. also Liberius' letter to the oriental bishops in Hilary of Poitiers, *Collectanea Antiariana Parisina (Fragmenta historica)* B VII 8,2(6; quoted above p. 297 n. 324).

378 Council of Sirmium (359), *Fidei confessio quarta* (Brennecke et al. 2014, *Dokument* 57.2; FaFo § 157).

379 Cf. Athanasius, *De synodis* 3.

380 Cf. Hilary of Poitiers, *Collectanea Antiariana Parisina (Fragmenta historica)* B VI 3 (Brennecke et al. 2014, *Dokument* 57.1).

381 He is mentioned in Epiphanius, *Panarion* 73,22,8.

382 Cf. also Sozomen, *Historia ecclesiastica* 4,22,6 and 4,16,19–20; 4,17,3–5. 10; Socrates, *Historia ecclesiastica* 2,37,16–17. The original Latin text, if it ever existed (cf. Brennecke et al. 2014, p. 421), no longer survives.

rejecting the use of *ousía* and its cognates did not imply that there was any ontological dissimilarity between Father and Son as the Anhomoians had suggested. The resulting creed, therefore, attempts to steer a middle course between the Nicene and Neo-Arian positions which are both deemed unacceptable.

Fourth Creed ('Dated Creed') from Sirmium (359)
(Brennecke et al. 2014, *Dokument* 57.2; FaFo § 157)

[1] Πιστεύομεν εἰς ἕνα τὸν μόνον καὶ ἀληθινὸν θεὸν πατέρα, παντοκράτορα, κτίστην καὶ δημιουργὸν τῶν πάντων,	[1] We believe in one only and true God, the Father Almighty, the Creator and Demiurge of all things;
[2] καὶ εἰς ἕνα μονογενῆ υἱὸν τοῦ θεοῦ, τὸν πρὸ πάντων τῶν αἰώνων καὶ πρὸ πάσης ἀρχῆς καὶ πρὸ παντὸς ἐπινοουμένου χρόνου καὶ πρὸ πάσης καταληπτῆς ἐπινοίας γεγεννημένον ἀπαθῶς ἐκ τοῦ θεοῦ, *δι' οὗ* οἵ τε αἰῶνες κατηρτίσθησαν καὶ *τὰ πάντα ἐγένετο*, γεγεννημένον δὲ μονογενῆ, μόνον ἐκ μόνου τοῦ πατρός, θεὸν ἐκ θεοῦ, ὅμοιον τῷ γεννήσαντι αὐτὸν πατρὶ κατὰ τὰς γραφάς, οὗ τὴν γέννησιν οὐδεὶς ἐπίσταται εἰ μὴ μόνος ὁ γεννήσας αὐτὸν πατήρ.	[2] and in one only-begotten Son of God, before all ages, before every beginning, before all conceivable time, and before all comprehensible thought begotten from God without passion; 'through whom' the ages were framed and 'all things came into being' [Jn 1:3; 1Cor 8:6]; who was begotten as the only-begotten, the only one from the only Father, God from God, similar to the Father who begot him according to the Scriptures; whose birth no one knows except only the Father who begot him.
[3] Τοῦτον ἴσμεν τοῦ θεοῦ μονογενῆ υἱόν, νεύματι πατρικῷ παραγενόμενον ἐκ τῶν οὐρανῶν *εἰς ἀθέτησιν ἁμαρτίας* καὶ γεννηθέντα ἐκ Μαρίας τῆς παρθένου καὶ ἀναστραφέντα μετὰ τῶν μαθητῶν καὶ πᾶσαν τὴν οἰκονομίαν πληρώσαντα κατὰ τὴν πατρικὴν βούλησιν, σταυρωθέντα καὶ ἀποθανόντα καὶ εἰς τὰ καταχθόνια κατελθόντα καὶ τὰ ἐκεῖσε οἰκονομήσαντα, ὃν *πυλωροὶ ᾅδου ἰδόντες ἔφριξαν* καὶ ἀναστάντα ἐκ νεκρῶν τῇ τρίτῃ ἡμέρᾳ καὶ ἀναστραφέντα μετὰ τῶν μαθητῶν καὶ πᾶσαν τὴν οἰκονομίαν πληρώσαντα καὶ πεντήκοντα ἡμερῶν πληρουμένων ἀναληφθέντα εἰς τοὺς οὐρα-	[3] We know that this only-begotten Son of his descended from the heavens by his Father's command 'for the destruction of sin' [Heb 9:26], was born from the virgin Mary, dwelt with the disciples, and fulfilled every dispensation [cf. Eph 1:10] according to the Father's will; was crucified, died, descended into the lower parts of the earth, and disposed matters there; at the 'sight' of whom the 'door-keepers of the underworld trembled' [Job 38:17]; after rising from the dead on the third day, he again dwelt with the disciples; completed the whole dispensation [cf. Eph

νοῦς καὶ καθεζόμενον ἐκ δεξιῶν τοῦ πατρὸς καὶ ἐλευσόμενον ἐν τῇ ἐσχάτῃ
ἡμέρᾳ τῆς ἀναστάσεως τῇ δόξῃ τῇ πατρι-
κῇ ἀποδιδόντα *ἑκάστῳ κατὰ τὰ ἔργα
αὐτοῦ.*

1:10]; after fifty days were completed he ascended into the heavens; sits at the right hand of the Father; and at the last day of the resurrection he will come in his Father's glory to render 'to everyone according to his works' [Prov 24:12; Ps 61(62):13; Mt 16:27 *v.l.*; Rom 2:6; Rev 22:12].

---

[4] Καὶ εἰς τὸ ἅγιον πνεῦμα, ὃ αὐτὸς ὁ
μονογενὴς τοῦ θεοῦ υἱὸς Ἰησοῦς
Χριστὸς ἐπηγγείλατο πέμψαι τῷ γένει
τῶν ἀνθρώπων, τὸν παράκλητον, κατὰ
τὸ γεγραμμένον· *Ἀπέρχομαι πρὸς τὸν
πατέρα μου καὶ παρακαλέσω τὸν πατέρα
καὶ ἄλλον παράκλητον πέμψει ὑμῖν τὸ
πνεῦμα τῆς ἀληθείας, ἐκεῖνος ἐκ τοῦ
ἐμοῦ λήψεται καὶ διδάξει καὶ ὑπομνήσει
ὑμᾶς πάντα.*

[4] [We believe] also in the Holy Spirit, whom the only-begotten Son of God Jesus Christ himself promised to send to the human race as the Comforter, according to that which is written: 'I go away to my Father, and will ask him, and he will send you another Comforter, the Spirit of truth. He shall receive of mine, and shall teach you, and bring all things to your remembrance' [Jn 16:7, 13–14; 14:16–17; 15:26].

---

[5] Τὸ δὲ ὄνομα τῆς οὐσίας διὰ τὸ
ἁπλούστερον παρὰ τῶν πατέρων τε-
θεῖσθαι, ἀγνοούμενον δὲ ὑπὸ τῶν λαῶν
σκάνδαλον φέρειν διὰ τὸ μήτε τὰς
γραφὰς τοῦτο περιέχειν ἤρεσε τοῦτο
περιαιρεθῆναι καὶ παντελῶς μηδεμίαν
μνήμην οὐσίας ἐπὶ θεοῦ εἶναι τοῦ λοι-
ποῦ διὰ τὸ τὰς θείας γραφὰς μηδαμοῦ
περὶ πατρὸς καὶ υἱοῦ οὐσίας μεμνῆσθαι.
Ὅμοιον δὲ λέγομεν τὸν υἱὸν τῷ πατρὶ
κατὰ πάντα, ὡς καὶ αἱ ἅγιαι γραφαὶ λέ-
γουσί τε καὶ διδάσκουσι.

[5] As for the term 'substance' (which was used by our fathers for the sake of greater simplicity, but not being understood by the people has caused offense since the Scriptures do not contain it), it seemed desirable that it should be removed, and that henceforth no mention at all should be made of substance in reference to God, since the divine Scriptures have nowhere made mention of the substance of the Father and the Son. But we say that the Son is similar to the Father in all things, as the holy Scriptures also affirm and teach.

This creed is divided into five sections:
–   At first sight section 1 deals with the Father in a fairly traditional manner. However, the predicates 'one only and true God' were as yet unknown in the credal tradition and were added here to emphasize the oneness and full divinity of the Father. This implied, of course, that the Son was no 'true' God.

- The christological article is divided into two sections: section 2 deals with the pre-existent Son (the title of Logos is avoided). His pretemporal generation is emphasized in the strongest terms,[383] but the authors avoid affirmation of the Son's coeternity with the Father. The text is rather opaque in what follows: on the one hand, the Son is 'God from God', on the other, he is 'similar to the Father who begot him according to the Scriptures'.[384] The term 'similarity' is undefined, and it remains open what its precise implications are regarding the Son's ontological status: does he possess his own *ousía* and/or *hypóstasis*? Just as in the Second Creed of Sirmium, the mode of the Son's generation is said to be unknown.
- Section 3 deals with the incarnation. Oddly, it is introduced by ἴσμεν ('we know'). It is unclear whether or not this change of verb has any theological implications. The 'fulfilment of the dispensation' (which is mentioned twice) is already found in the Macrostich Creed 11. Other than that, this christological summary is fairly traditional, except for the reference to Job 38:17 and the descent to hell which occur here for the first time in a synodal creed.
- Section 4: The creed contains not much information regarding the Spirit. The composite quotation of passages from John is unique to this text.
- Section 5: Here the term *ousía* is rejected as unscriptural, but not as erroneous. It is even acknowledged that it was used in Nicaea 'for the sake of greater simplicity' (ἁπλούστερον).[385] Instead the Son is called 'similar to the Father in all things', an expression which, by contrast, is termed scriptural and which the authors may have found in the Macrostich Creed.[386]

This is the founding document of Homoianism. It now contained the rejection of *homooúsios* that Constantius had been demanding for some time. Yet its phrasing suggests that a compromise was sought at least with the Homoiousians. Nevertheless, the terminology proposed did not quite suffice to bridge the gulf between the parties. On the one hand, for staunch Homoians the creed went not far enough in its distinction between Father and Son; on the other hand, to a Homoiousian like Basil of Ancyra it left too much open to misinterpretation. He may have been right: in his signature Valens added that the Son was like the Father, but even

---

383 The addition δι' οὗ οἵ τε αἰῶνες κατηρτίσθησαν, that was later to become one of the hallmarks of the Antiochene creed (cf. below p. 351), occurs here for the first time.

384 The argument is obscure: ὅμοιος and cognate lexemes are not used in the New Testament in this context.

385 Much depends on the translation of ἁπλούστερον: Brennecke et al. 2014, p. 423, l. 21 translate it as 'allzu einfältig' ('too naively'), but the authors hardly wished to imply a low degree of intelligence among 'our fathers'.

386 Cf. Macrostich Creed 10 and above pp. 292 f.

wanted to go as far to drop 'in all things'. (He was forced by the emperor to re-insert the missing phrase.) By contrast, Basil added:

> I believe thus and I agree with what was written above, confessing that the Son is like the Father in all things. But in *all* things, not merely in [his] will, but, as the Divine Scriptures teach, in *hypóstasis*, subsistence, and being just like a son (κατὰ τὴν ὑπόστασιν καὶ κατὰ τὴν ὕπαρξιν καὶ κατὰ τὸ εἶναι ὡς υἱόν); spirit from spirit, life from life, Light from Light, God from God, true Son from true <Father>;[387] the Son, being Wisdom, from a wise God and Father; and in short, the Son similar to the Father in all things as a son is to [his] father (καὶ καθάπαξ κατὰ πάντα τὸν υἱὸν ὅμοιον τῷ πατρί, ὡς υἱὸν πατρί).
>
> And if someone says that [the Son] is similar [to the Father] in some [undefined] way (καὶ εἴ τις κατά τι λέγει ὅμοιον), as has been written above, he is alien to the Catholic Church, since he is not saying that the Son is similar to the Father in accordance with the Divine Scriptures.[388]

Basil then agreed to the use of *hómoios* but interpreted the adjective in a different manner from Valens – not as a term signifying distinction and difference, but parentage and proximity in the sense of the declaration of Ancyra 358.[389] He wanted to exclude an Anhomoian interpretation of the creed by explicitly rejecting the similarity in will only.[390]

On the one hand, then, the creed was very successful, because it could serve as an umbrella document allowing agreement by theologians from very different camps. On the other hand, the differences which continued to exist were only plastered over rather than settled. It was much easier for the Homoians to agree to this text than it was for the Homoiousians, let alone the Nicenes, because the points which mattered in their doctrinal controversies (the consubstantiality and coeternity of the Son with the Father) were not addressed. Therefore, once it had received imperial approbation, the document was subsequently seen as a victory of Homoianism.

∗

The Emperor Constantius II planned to enforce what he saw as a doctrinal settlement at two parallel synods in the western and eastern parts of the empire.[391] The western synod was to take place in Ariminum (Rimini), the eastern in Seleucia in

---

387 The phrasing resembles the theology of Eusebius of Caesarea; cf., e.g., *Epistula ad ecclesiam Caesariensem* 4 (FaFo § 134a; cf. above pp. 236 f.); id., *De ecclesiastica theologia* 1,8 (FaFo § 134b2).
388 Epiphanius, *Panarion* 73,21,5–8; the quotation at 7–8.
389 Cf. above ch. 6.5.7.
390 Cf., e.g., Eunomius, *Liber Apologeticus* 23–24. The book which was written in 360 (cf. Vaggione 1987, pp. 5–9) is almost contemporaneous.
391 On the emperor's strategy, cf. especially his letter to the Synod at Rimini: Constantius II, *Epistula ad synodum Ariminensem* (Brennecke et al. 2014, *Dokument* 59.1).

Isauria (Silifke). Obviously, he thought that the Dated Creed could serve as a platform for these deliberations 'on faith and unity' (*de fide atque unitate*). After agreement had been reached at each of the synods they were supposed to send a delegation to the court at Constantinople to negotiate a final settlement. The purpose of the emperor's involvement was also clearly stated: after all strife had been settled, 'the prosperity of all peoples would spread everywhere and firm concord would be safeguarded'.[392]

However, things did not quite work out as planned.[393] The Synod in Rimini, the largest clerical assembly so far,[394] met first (July 359). At its first session the Dated Creed was discussed. When it did not meet with the approval of the participants, alternative versions were drawn up but immediately dismissed.[395] In the end, a majority of the synod condemned all attempts at stepping back from the position reached at Nicaea.[396] N was declared sacrosanct and the use of *substantia* (= *ousía*) reaffirmed. The majority synod went so far as to say that the term had been 'suggested' by the Sacred Scriptures.[397] Ursacius, Valens, and Germinius (plus a Bishop Gaius whose identity is unclear), who had submitted the Dated Creed to the assembly, were solemnly declared heretics.[398] In order to make their position crystal-clear the western bishops also adopted a series of anathemas which explicitly condemned all forms of Arianism and the doctrine of two or three *substantiae* (= *ousíai/hypostáseis*).[399] Furthermore, the doctrines of Marcellus and Photinus were, once again, rejected. The synod then sent a delegation to the emperor, led by Bishop Restutus or Restitutus of Carthage. It carried a letter in which Constantius was apprised of the western synod's views on the contentious theological issues.[400]

---

392 Constantius II, *Epistula ad synodum Ariminensem* (Brennecke et al. 2014, *Dokument* 59.1) 1.

393 For what follows cf. also Brennecke 1984, pp. 352–9 (listing earlier literature); Hanson 1988, pp. 362–80; Williams 1995, pp. 11–37; Ayres 2004, pp. 160–6; Brennecke et al. 2014, pp. 445–6; Graumann 2016/2017, pp. 58–68.

394 On the number of participants (figures oscillate between 300 and 600 participants), cf. Brennecke et al. 2014, p. 445.

395 Cf. Council of Rimini (359), *Epistula synodalis episcoporum Catholicorum ad Constantium II imperatorem* (Brennecke et al. 2014, *Dokument* 59.5) 8.

396 Cf. Council of Rimini (359), *Definitio* (FaFo § 564a).

397 Cf. Council of Rimini (359), *Definitio* (FaFo § 564a): '[. . .] likewise, the term and the matter "substance", suggested to our minds by many sacred Scriptures, should be firmly maintained.'

398 Cf. Council of Rimini (359), *Fragmentum gestorum synodalium* (Brennecke et al. 2014, *Dokument* 59.4).

399 Cf. Council of Rimini (359), *Damnatio blasphemiae Arii* (Brennecke et al. 2014, *Dokument* 59.3; the text is mutilated).

400 Cf. Council of Rimini (359), *Epistula synodalis episcoporum Catholicorum ad Constantium II imperatorem* (Brennecke et al. 2014, *Dokument* 59.5; FaFo § 564b, in part).

As a result of the majority's defence of Nicaea, some eighty Homoian bishops, led by the bishops who had been condemned as heretics, walked out from the synod and met separately. They dispatched their own embassy to Constantinople to present their own exposition of the faith (probably the Dated Creed).[401]

In the end, the Homoians gained the upper hand: In October 359, the Nicene delegation abandoned their brief, after waiting first in Adrianople (Edirne) and then in Niké (a town in Thrace; perhaps modern Havsa in Turkey[402]; not to be confused with either Nicaea or modern Nice) and having been intimidated by long waits and imperial threats, and revoked the condemnations of the Homoians, also signing a creed to that effect.[403] Subsequently, this creed was endorsed by the Synod of Rimini (which had been ordered to stay put) at a second session in the same year.

It is often said that this creed was the Dated Creed with some minor alterations.[404] At first glance it seems obvious that the Dated Creed served as the basis for the creed of Niké. However, a closer look reveals that some considerable changes were introduced:

Creed of the Synod of Niké (359)
(Brennecke et al. 2014, *Dokument* 59.9; FaFo § 159a)

[1] Πιστεύομεν εἰς ἕνα καὶ μόνον ἀληθινὸν θεόν, πατέρα, παντοκράτορα, ἐξ *οὗ τὰ πάντα·*	[1] We believe in the one and only true God, the Father Almighty, 'from whom are all things';
[2] καὶ εἰς τὸν μονογενῆ υἱὸν τοῦ θεοῦ, τὸν πρὸ πάντων αἰώνων καὶ πρὸ πάσης ἀρχῆς γεννηθέντα ἐκ τοῦ θεοῦ, *δι' οὗ τὰ πάντα ἐγένετο, τά τε ὁρατὰ καὶ τὰ ἀόρατα,* γεννηθέντα δὲ μονογενῆ, μόνον ἐκ μόνου τοῦ πατρός, θεὸν ἐκ θεοῦ, ὅμοιον τῷ γεγεννηκότι αὐτὸν πατρὶ κατὰ τὰς γραφάς, οὗ τὴν γέννησιν οὐδεὶς οἶδεν εἰ μὴ μόνος ὁ γεννήσας αὐτὸν πατήρ.	[2] and in the only-begotten Son of God, who before all ages and before every beginning was begotten from God, 'through whom all things came into being' [Jn 1:3; 1Cor 8:6], 'things' both 'visible and invisible' [Col 1:16]; begotten as only-begotten, the unique one from the unique Father, God from God; similar to the Father who begot him, according to the Scriptures, whose generation no one knows, except only the Father who begot him.

---

401 Cf. Socrates, *Historia ecclesiastica* 2,37,52; 2,37,75; Sozomen, *Historia ecclesiastica* 4,17,11.
402 For discussion of its precise identity cf. Den Boeft et al. 2018, p. 186.
403 Cf. *Confessio fidei synodi Nicaeae Thraciae* (FaFo § 159a).
404 Cf., e.g., Brennecke et al. 2014, p. 446 ('die ursprünglich vorgesehene theologische Erklärung mit kleinen Modifikationen'); p. 471 ('eine nur in Details veränderte Fassung der vierten sirmischen Formel').

[3] Τοῦτον οἴδαμεν μονογενῆ θεοῦ υἱὸν πέμποντος τοῦ πατρὸς παραγεγενῆσθαι ἐκ τῶν οὐρανῶν, καθὼς γέγραπται, εἰς καθαίρεσιν ἁμαρτίας καὶ θανάτου καὶ γεννηθέντα ἐκ πνεύματος ἁγίου καὶ Μαρίας τῆς παρθένου, καθὼς γέγραπται, κατὰ σάρκα καὶ συναναστραφέντα μετὰ τῶν μαθητῶν καὶ πάσης τῆς οἰκονομίας πληρωθείσης κατὰ τὴν βούλησιν τοῦ πατρὸς σταυρῷ προσηλωθέντα, ἀποθανόντα καὶ ταφέντα καὶ εἰς τὰ καταχθόνια κατελθόντα, ὃν αὐτὸς ὁ ᾅδης ἐτρόμασε, καὶ ἀνελθόντα ἀπὸ τῶν νεκρῶν τῇ τρίτῃ ἡμέρᾳ, συναναστραφέντα μετὰ τῶν μαθητῶν τεσσαράκοντα ἡμερῶν πληρουμένων καὶ ἀναληφθέντα εἰς τοὺς οὐρανοὺς καὶ καθεζόμενον ἐκ δεξιῶν τοῦ πατρός, ἐρχόμενον δὲ τῇ ἐσχάτῃ ἡμέρᾳ τῆς ἀναστάσεως μετὰ δόξης πατρικῆς ἀποδοῦναι ἑκάστῳ κατὰ τὰ ἔργα αὐτοῦ·

[3] This only-begotten Son of God, sent by his Father, we know to have come down from the heavens, as it is written, for the destruction of sin and death; begotten from the Holy Spirit and the virgin Mary, as it is written, according to the flesh; dwelt together with his disciples, and, when all the dispensation was fulfilled [cf. Eph 1:10], according to the Father's will, was nailed to the cross, dead, and buried, and descended to the lower parts of the earth, at whom the underworld itself trembled [cf. Job 38:17]. On the third day he rose from the dead and dwelt together with his disciples for a period of forty days; was taken up into the heavens and sits at the right hand of his Father, but will come with his Father's glory on the last day of the resurrection, to render 'to everyone according to his works' [Prov 24:12; Ps 61(62):13; Mt 16:27 v.l.; Rom 2:6; Rev 22:12].

[4] καὶ εἰς πνεῦμα ἅγιον, ὅπερ αὐτὸς ὁ μονογενὴς τοῦ θεοῦ υἱὸς Ἰησοῦς Χριστὸς θεὸς καὶ κύριος ἐπηγγείλατο ἀποστεῖλαι τῷ γένει τῶν ἀνθρώπων, τὸν παράκλητον, καθὼς γέγραπται· τὸ πνεῦμα τῆς ἀληθείας, ὅπερ καὶ αὐτὸς ἀπέστειλεν ἀνελθὼν εἰς τοὺς οὐρανοὺς καὶ καθίσας ἐν δεξιᾷ τοῦ πατρός, ἐκεῖθεν δὲ ἐρχόμενος κρῖναι ζῶντας καὶ νεκρούς.

[4] And [we believe] in the Holy Spirit, whom the only-begotten Son of God himself, Jesus Christ, God and Lord, promised to send to the human race, the Paraclete [cf. Jn 14:26], as it is written, 'the Spirit of truth' [Jn 14:17; 15:26; 16:13; 1Jn 4:6], whom he himself sent after he had ascended into the heavens and sat at the right hand of the Father, thence to come to judge the living and the dead.

[5] Τὸ δὲ ὄνομα τῆς οὐσίας, ὅπερ ἁπλούστερον ἐνετέθη ὑπὸ τῶν πατέρων, ἀγνοούμενον δὲ τοῖς λαοῖς σκάνδαλον ἔφερε διὰ τὸ ἐν ταῖς γραφαῖς τοῦτο μὴ ἐμφέρεσθαι, ἤρεσε περιαιρεθῆναι καὶ παντελῶς μηδε-

[5] But the term 'substance', which was inserted by the fathers for the sake of greater simplicity, but not understood by the people, was a cause of scandal on account of the fact that it is not con-

μίαν μνήμην οὐσίας τοῦ λοιποῦ γίνεσθαι, διὰ τὸ μάλιστα τὰς θείας γραφὰς μηδαμοῦ περὶ τοῦ πατρὸς καὶ τοῦ υἱοῦ οὐσίας μεμνῆσθαι, μήτε μὴν δεῖν ἐπὶ προσώπου πατρὸς καὶ υἱοῦ καὶ ἁγίου πνεύματος μίαν ὑπόστασιν ὀνομάζεσθαι. Ὅμοιον δὲ λέγομεν τῷ πατρὶ τὸν υἱὸν καθὼς καὶ αἱ θεῖαι γραφαὶ λέγουσι καὶ διδάσκουσι.	tained in the Scriptures; it has seemed good to us to remove [it], and that there should no longer be any mention at all of 'substance', above all because the divine Scriptures nowhere make any mention of the 'substance' of the Father and the Son. Nor must one *hypóstasis* be predicated of the person of Father, Son, and Holy Spirit. But we say that the Son is similar to the Father, as the divine Scriptures also say and teach.
[6] Πάσας δὲ τὰς αἱρέσεις τὰς ἤδη πρότερον καθαιρεθείσας ἢ καὶ εἴ τινες νεωστὶ ἀνεφύησαν ὑπεναντίαι ταύτης τῆς γραφῆς τῆς ἐκτεθείσης, ἀνάθεμα ἔστωσαν.	But all the heresies, both those already previously condemned and any which have also recently arisen against this statement which is being set forth, let them be anathema.

In what follows I will indicate some of the major differences between the Dated Creed and the Creed of Niké:[405]

- Section 1: Κτίστην καὶ δημιουργὸν τῶν πάντων ('the Creator and Demiurge of all things') in the Dated Creed was dropped and the reference to 1Cor 8:6 added instead (cf. Ant[2]).
- Section 2:
  - The reference to the 'one' (ἕνα) only-begotten Son of God was dropped.
  - The repeated insistence on the preexistence of the Son (τὸν πρὸ πάντων τῶν αἰώνων καὶ πρὸ πάσης ἀρχῆς καὶ πρὸ παντὸς ἐπινοουμένου χρόνου καὶ πρὸ πάσης καταληπτῆς ἐπινοίας γεγεννημένον ἀπαθῶς ἐκ τοῦ θεοῦ / 'before all ages, before every beginning, before all conceivable time, and before all comprehensible thought begotten from God without passion') was replaced by the simpler πρὸ πάντων αἰώνων καὶ πρὸ πάσης ἀρχῆς γεννηθέντα ἐκ τοῦ θεοῦ ('before all ages and before every beginning was begotten from God').
  - The mention of the framing of the ages (αἰῶνες κατηρτίσθησαν) was excised.
  - By contrast, the reference to Col 1:16 was added.

---

405 For the Dated Creed cf. above pp. 308 f.

- Section 3:
  - The reference to the 'Father's command' (νεύματι πατρικῷ) was replaced by 'sent by his Father' (πέμποντος τοῦ πατρὸς; cf. Jn 20:21).
  - 'As it is written' (καθὼς γέγραπται) was added twice.
  - The reference to Heb 9:26 was altered (this may be due to translation from the original Latin) and extended by 'and death' (καὶ θανάτου).
  - The Holy Spirit was added to the virgin birth (ἐκ πνεύματος ἁγίου) – this is clearly a western addition as it is first found in the creeds from Rome.[406]
  - 'According to the flesh' (κατὰ σάρκα) was added.
  - Reference to Jesus' burial (ταφέντα) was added (cf. Ant[4] and the Roman creeds[407]).
  - The phrase καὶ τὰ ἐκεῖσε οἰκονομήσαντα ('and disposed matters there') was excised.
  - The reference to Job 38:17 was shortened and its wording altered.
  - The second reference to Eph 1:10 was dropped (καὶ πᾶσαν τὴν οἰκονομίαν πληρώσαντα / 'and fulfilled every dispensation').
  - The number of days for Christ's sojourn on earth was changed from fifty to forty (cf. Acts 1:3). This is particularly interesting, because it may reflect the introduction of the Feast of the Ascension (which was originally celebrated jointly with Pentecost) on the fortieth day after Easter. If so, this is the earliest (indirect) evidence for this feast.[408]
- Section 4:
  - After Ἰησοῦς Χριστός, 'God and Lord' (θεὸς καὶ κύριος) was added.
  - The composite quotation of passages taken from the Gospel of John was abbreviated.
  - Instead the phrase ὅπερ καὶ αὐτὸς ἀπέστειλεν ἀνελθὼν εἰς τοὺς οὐρανοὺς καὶ καθίσας ἐν δεξιᾷ τοῦ πατρός, ἐκεῖθεν δὲ ἐρχόμενος κρῖναι ζῶντας καὶ νεκρούς ('whom he himself sent after he had ascended into the heavens and sat at the right hand of the Father, thence to come to judge the living and the dead') was added, thus creating an odd repetition in relation to section 3: (καὶ ἀναληφθέντα εἰς τοὺς οὐρανοὺς καὶ καθεζόμενον ἐκ δεξιῶν τοῦ πατρός, ἐρχόμενον δὲ τῇ ἐσχάτῃ ἡμέρᾳ τῆς ἀναστάσεως μετὰ δόξης πατρικῆς ἀποδοῦναι ἑκάστῳ κατὰ τὰ ἔργα αὐτοῦ / 'was taken up into the heavens and sits at the right hand of his Father, but will come

---

406 Cf. above pp. 146, 151.
407 Cf. above pp. 146, 151.
408 For background cf. Cabié 1965, esp. pp. 185–97; Kinzig 2009, cols. 914 f.

with his Father's glory on the last day of the resurrection, to render to everyone according to his works').
- Section 5:
    - 'In reference to God' (ἐπὶ θεοῦ) was dropped.
    - The phrase μήτε μὴν δεῖν ἐπὶ προσώπου πατρὸς καὶ υἱοῦ καὶ ἁγίου πνεύματος μίαν ὑπόστασιν ὀνομάζεσθαι ('nor must one *hypóstasis* be predicated of the person of Father, Son, and Holy Spirit') was added.
    - The expression κατὰ πάντα ('in all things') was dropped.
- At the end a clause was added, thus creating a sixth section.

Other differences obviously result from different translations of the original (?) Latin text into Greek.

Not all changes are easily explicable – this need not detain us here. A certain western (Roman) influence becomes visible in section 3 through the additions of ἐκ πνεύματος ἁγίου and ταφέντα. The most important changes occurred in sections 5 and 6: the use of *ousía* was now forbidden not only with regard to God but altogether. Likewise, it was no longer permitted to speak of the one *hypóstasis* of the 'person' (πρόσωπον in the singular) of Father, Son, and Spirit. Here the creed's language was quite fuzzy: thus it remained unclear whether the authors intended their prohibition of the use of the term to be read as meant with regard to the Trinity as a whole (which is more likely given the fact that in Heb 1:3 *hypóstasis* was used for the Father) or to each 'person' (taken individually). In addition, the omission of κατὰ πάντα 'weakened' the similarity of Father and Son even further.

It looks as if some negotiations between the delegation of the majority council and the minority, supported by the court, may have taken place prior to the signing of this creed. The omission of κατὰ πάντα was clearly due to the influence of Valens who, in the negotiations at Sirmium, had already tried to get κατὰ πάντα excised from the document at the last minute.[409] In return, the addition of θεὸς καὶ κύριος in section 4 may have been pushed through by the Homoiousians. It is clear, however, that when all was said and done the Homoian position had carried a resounding victory.

Possibly, there were renewed negotiations after the return of the delegation to Rimini which led to further alterations to the creed. Jerome refers to the events at the second session of Rimini in his *Altercatio Luciferiani et Orthodoxi* (written in c. 378/379[410]), quoting sections of the creed allegedly signed at Rimini,[411] which he

---

409 Cf. above pp. 310 f.
410 Cf. Fürst 2016, p. 369.
411 Cf. Jerome, *Altercatio Luciferiani et Orthodoxi* (Brennecke et al. 2014, *Dokument* 59.11) 17–18. The creed is also found in FaFo § 159b.

perhaps took from the acts of that council. Whereas the beginning is largely identical with the creed of Niké, this formula is clearly an attempt, in its christological summary, at a harmonization with the Roman Creed (or one of its descendants):

> [. . .] qui de caelo descendit, conceptus est de spiritu sancto, natus ex Maria uirgine, crucifixus a Pontio Pilato, tertia die resurrexit, ascendit in caelum, sedet ad dexteram dei patris uenturus iudicare uiuos et mortuos.

> [. . .] who descended from heaven, was conceived of the Holy Spirit, born from the virgin Mary, crucified by Pontius Pilate, on the third day rose again, ascended into heaven, sits at the right hand of God the Father, will come to judge the living and the dead.

Brennecke et al. presume that Jerome correctly cites the version endorsed at Rimini and that this text is authentic, in which case the Homoian creeds of Rimini and of Niké (and later of Constantinople) would have differed considerably from each other, the western version being much closer to R.[412] However, the differentiation between the conception of the Holy Spirit and the birth from the Virgin Mary that occurs in Jerome's version is not found elsewhere until the fifth century when it first appears in Gaul.[413] It is, therefore, more likely that the text of the creed was altered at some stage during the transmission of the text of the *Altercatio*.[414]

Jerome goes on to quote a series of condemnations by which Valens of Mursa distanced himself from Arianism which was endorsed by the council. Sulpicius suggests that these anathemas were drawn up by Phoebadius of Agen and Servatius, bishop of the Tungri, and that only the fourth was added by Valens himself.[415]

The eastern Synod in Seleucia in September of 359 charted yet another course. We are fairly well informed about the proceedings at this assembly, because Socrates quotes extensive extracts from its acts which he had found in a collection of synodal documents by Sabinus of Heraclea.[416] The theological controversies were intertwined with charges brought against a number of bishops (Macedonius of Constantinople, Patrophilus of Scythopolis, Basil of Ancyra, Cyril of Jerusalem, and Eustathius of Sebaste) which need not detain us here. As regards the question concerning the faith, Hilary of Poitiers, who also took part in the proceedings, gives us some numbers con-

---

412 Cf. Brennecke et al. 2014, p. 477.

413 Cf. cf., e.g., FaFo §§ 265–7 etc. and above pp. 165–7.

414 Unfortunately, the account by Sulpicius Severus (*Chronica* 2,44) does not shed further light on the proceedings. The problem is also discussed in Simonetti 1975, p. 321–3 esp. n. 19.

415 The fourth anathema (Brennecke et al. 2014, p. 481, ll. 13–14): 'Si quis dixerit "creaturam filium dei ut sunt ceterae creaturae", anathema sit.' / 'If anyone calls "the Son a creature like any other creature", let him be anathema.' Cf. Sulpicius, *Chronica* 2,44,6–7.

416 Cf. Socrates, *Historia ecclesiastica* 2,39–40 (Brennecke et al. 2014, *Dokument* 60.1). On other sources cf. Brennecke et al. 2014, p. 484.

cerning the distribution of theological views:[417] the vast majority (105 bishops) were Homoiousians; but only some of them actually said that the Son was 'from God (*ex deo*)' in the sense that 'the Son was from God's substance' (*id est de substantia dei filius*). A minority of nineteen bishops were defenders of *anomoeusion* (which probably included both Homoians and, perhaps, some Anhomoians, although Hilary describes their views all as Anhomoian). Finally, there was an unspecified number of Egyptian bishops who championed *homooúsios* (except for the Homoian patriarch George of Alexandria (d. 361)). According to Socrates' account the synod fairly soon split into two parties. The smaller group consisted mainly of Homoian opponents to N. They were led by Acacius of Caesarea (*sedit* 341–364), George of Alexandria, Uranius of Tyre, and Eudoxius of Antioch. The majority group, headed by George of Laodicea, Sophronius of Pompeiopolis, and Eleusius of Cyzicus, were largely made up of Homoiousians. They were, in principle, ready to accept N, but rejected the *homooúsios*. They discussed Ant[4] instead and, in the end, subscribed to that.[418]

In the end, the two parties met again in the presence of Macedonius of Constantinople and Basil of Ancyra. Acacius proposed a different creed, perhaps with the intention to serve as a compromise between the parties.[419] In its introduction Ant[4] was accepted as an 'authentic faith' (αὐθεντικὴν πίστιν). Both *homooúsios* and *homoioúsios* were then rejected as being unscriptural, whereas *anhómoios* was even solemnly condemned. Instead the similarity of Father and Son was confirmed on the basis of Col 1:15. The creed itself was surprisingly simple (Hanson called it 'a wholly characterless, insignificant creed'[420]), affirming the divinity of the Son without further qualifications. However, in the end a sentence was added in which the identity of this creed's content with that of the Dated Creed was confirmed. Acacius' proposal met with fierce criticism by some of the council participants who defended N, while others took recourse to Ant[4]. In the end, his proposal was not accepted.

Much of the theological discussion then focussed on the term *hómoios* to describe the relationship between Father and Son. Was it a similarity by will only (κατὰ τὴν βούλησιν μόνον) or a similarity in substance (κατὰ τὴν οὐσίαν)?[421] The argument became so heated that the *comes* Leonas who presided over the proceedings in the end had to dissolve the synod, because it seemed impossible to

---

417 Cf. Hilary, *Liber (I) in Constantium imperatorem* 12.
418 Here and in the following proceedings it is not quite clear whether Ant[2] or Ant[4] is being referred to. Following Brennecke et al. I tend to assume that Ant[4] was under discussion, but cf., e.g., Hanson 1988, p. 373.
419 Cf. Acacius, *Expositio fidei* (FaFo § 158a).
420 Hanson 1988, p. 374.
421 Cf. Socrates, *Historia ecclesiastica* 2,40,31.

reach any kind of consensus. However, the Homoiousians assembled once again and, in the end, deposed Acacius, George of Alexandria, Uranius, Eudoxius, and other Homoian bishops.

Both the embassies of the deposed Acacians and of the Homoiousian majority group travelled to Constantinople where they met representatives from the Synod of Rimini in December 359. The leader of the Anhomoians Aetius was condemned and exiled. However, the further details of these negotiations are hazy.[422] In the end all attempts at reversing the decisions made at Niké failed. On New Year's Eve 359 almost all bishops signed a revised version of the creed of Niké, among them Wulfila, the bishop of the Goths, who transmitted his version of Homoianism to the Gothic Tervingi.[423] It marked the triumph of Homoian theology for almost two decades:[424]

Creed of the Synod of Constantinople (359/360)
Brennecke et al. 2014, *Dokument* 62.5; FaFo § 160

[1] Πιστεύομεν εἰς ἕνα θεόν, πατέρα, παντοκράτορα, *ἐξ οὗ τὰ πάντα·*	[1] We believe in one God, the Father Almighty, 'from whom are all things';
[2] καὶ εἰς τὸν μονογενῆ υἱὸν τοῦ θεοῦ, τὸν πρὸ πάντων αἰώνων καὶ πρὸ πάσης ἀρχῆς γεννηθέντα ἐκ τοῦ θεοῦ, *δι' οὗ τὰ πάντα ἐγένετο, τὰ ὁρατὰ καὶ τὰ ἀόρατα,* γεννηθέντα δὲ μονογενῆ, μόνον ἐκ μόνου τοῦ πατρός, θεὸν ἐκ θεοῦ, ὅμοιον τῷ γεννήσαντι αὐτὸν πατρὶ κατὰ τὰς γραφάς, οὗ τὴν γέννησιν οὐδεὶς οἶδεν εἰ μὴ μόνος ὁ γεννήσας αὐτὸν πατήρ.	[2] and in the only-begotten Son of God, who before all ages and before every beginning was begotten from God, 'through whom all things came into being' [Jn 1:3; 1Cor 8:6], 'things visible and invisible' [Col 1:16]; begotten as only-begotten, the unique one from the unique Father, God from God; similar to the Father who begot him, according to the Scriptures; whose generation no one knows, except only the Father who begot him.
[3] Τοῦτον οἴδαμεν μονογενῆ θεοῦ υἱὸν πέμποντος τοῦ πατρὸς παραγεγενῆσθαι ἐκ τῶν οὐρανῶν, ὡς γέγραπται, ἐπὶ καταλύσει τῆς ἁμαρτίας καὶ τοῦ θανάτου καὶ γεννηθέντα ἐκ πνεύματος ἁγίου καὶ Μαρίας τῆς παρθένου τὸ κατὰ σάρκα,	[3] This only-begotten Son of God, sent by his Father, we know to have come down from the heavens, as it is written, for the destruction of sin and death; begotten from the Holy Spirit and the virgin Mary according to the flesh, as it is

---

422 Cf. Brennecke et al. 2014, pp. 521–55, esp. 521 f.
423 Cf. Schäferdiek, 'Wulfila', 2004. On the spread of Homoianism in the west cf. also Heil 2011, pp. 117–22; Berndt/Steinacher 2014.
424 Council of Constantinople (359/360), *Confessio fidei* (Brennecke et al. 2014, *Dokument* 62.5; FaFo § 160).

ὡς γέγραπται, καὶ ἀναστραφέντα μετὰ τῶν μαθητῶν καὶ πάσης τῆς οἰκονομίας πληρωθείσης κατὰ τὴν πατρικὴν βούλησιν σταυρωθέντα καὶ ἀποθανόντα καὶ ταφέντα καὶ εἰς τὰ καταχθόνια κατεληλυθέναι, ὅντινα καὶ αὐτὸς ὁ ᾅδης ἔπτηξεν, ὅστις καὶ ἀνέστη ἀπὸ τῶν νεκρῶν τῇ τρίτῃ ἡμέρᾳ καὶ διέτριψε μετὰ τῶν μαθητῶν καὶ πληρωθεισῶν τεσσαράκοντα ἡμερῶν ἀνελήφθη εἰς τοὺς οὐρανοὺς καὶ καθέζεται ἐν δεξιᾷ τοῦ πατρὸς ἐλευσόμενος ἐν τῇ ἐσχάτῃ ἡμέρᾳ τῆς ἀναστάσεως ἐν τῇ πατρικῇ δόξῃ, ἵνα ἀποδῷ ἑκάστῳ κατὰ τὰ ἔργα αὐτοῦ·	written; dwelt with the disciples; and, when all the dispensation was fulfilled [cf. Eph 1:10], according to the Father's will, was crucified, dead, and buried, and descended to the lower parts of the earth; at whom the underworld itself trembled [cf. Job 38:17]; who also rose from the dead on the third day, dwelt with his disciples, and, forty days being fulfilled, was taken up into the heavens; and sits at the right hand of the Father, to come in his Father's glory on the last day of the resurrection, that he may render 'to everyone according to his works' [Prov 24:12; Ps 61(62):13; Mt 16:27 *v.l.*; Rom 2:6; Rev 22:12].
[4] καὶ εἰς τὸ ἅγιον πνεῦμα, ὅπερ αὐτὸς ὁ μονογενὴς τοῦ θεοῦ υἱὸς ὁ Χριστός, ὁ κύριος καὶ ὁ θεὸς ἡμῶν, ἐπηγγείλατο πέμπειν τῷ γένει τῶν ἀνθρώπων παράκλητον, καθάπερ γέγραπται· Τὸ πνεῦμα τῆς ἀληθείας, ὅπερ αὐτοῖς ἔπεμψεν, ὅτε ἀνῆλθεν εἰς τοὺς οὐρανούς.	[4] And [we believe] in the Holy Spirit, whom the only-begotten Son of God himself, Christ, our Lord and God, promised to send to the human race, the Paraclete [cf. Jn 14:26], as it is written, 'the Spirit of truth' [Jn 14:17; 15:26; 16:13; 1Jn 4:6], whom he sent to them when he had ascended into the heavens.
[5] Τὸ δὲ ὄνομα τῆς οὐσίας, ὅπερ ἁπλούστερον ὑπὸ τῶν πατέρων ἐνετέθη, ἀγνοούμενον δὲ τοῖς λαοῖς σκάνδαλον ἔφερε, διότι μηδὲ αἱ γραφαὶ τοῦτο περιέχουσιν, ἤρεσε περιαιρεθῆναι καὶ παντελῶς μηδεμίαν μνήμην τοῦ λοιποῦ τούτου γίνεσθαι, ἐπειδήπερ καὶ αἱ θεῖαι γραφαὶ οὐδαμῶς ἐμνημόνευσαν περὶ οὐσίας πατρὸς καὶ υἱοῦ. Καὶ γὰρ οὐδὲ ὀφείλει ὑπόστασις περὶ πατρὸς καὶ υἱοῦ καὶ ἁγίου πνεύματος ὀνομάζεσθαι. Ὅμοιον δὲ λέγομεν τῷ πατρὶ τὸν υἱόν, ὡς λέγουσιν αἱ θεῖαι γραφαὶ καὶ διδάσκουσι.	[5] But the term 'substance', which was inserted by the fathers for the sake of greater simplicity, but not understood by the people, was a cause of scandal because the Scriptures do not contain it. It has seemed good to us to remove [it], and that there should no longer be any mention at all of it since the divine Scriptures also have made no mention of the 'substance' of Father and Son. For neither ought *hypóstasis* be predicated of the Father, Son, and Holy Spirit. But we say that the Son is similar to the Father, as the divine Scriptures say and teach.

[6] Πᾶσαι δὲ αἱ αἱρέσεις, αἵ τε ἤδη πρότερον κατεκρίθησαν καὶ αἵτινες ἐὰν και-
νότεραι γένωνται, ἐναντίαι τυγχάνουσαι
τῆς ἐκτεθείσης ταύτης γραφῆς, ἀνάθεμα
ἔστωσαν.

[6] But all the heresies which are contrary to this statement which is being set forth, both those which were already previously condemned and whichever have come to be more recently, let them be anathema.

Alterations with regard to the creed of Niké were largely stylistic. Among the more important differences one might mention:

- Section 1: Omission of καὶ μόνον ἀληθινόν ('and only true').
- Section 4:
  - Reversal of ὁ κύριος καὶ ὁ θεὸς ἡμῶν.
  - Omission of καὶ καθίσας ἐν δεξιᾷ τοῦ πατρός, ἐκεῖθεν δὲ ἐρχόμενος κρῖναι ζῶντας καὶ νεκρούς ('and sat at the right hand of the Father, thence to come to judge the living and the dead'; a repetition from the christological summary).
- Section 5: The fuzzy phrase μήτε μὴν δεῖν ἐπὶ προσώπου πατρὸς καὶ υἱοῦ καὶ ἁγίου πνεύματος μίαν ὑπόστασιν ὀνομάζεσθαι ('nor must one *hypóstasis* be predicated of the person of Father, Son, and Holy Spirit') was replaced by the unequivocal expression καὶ γὰρ οὐδὲ ὀφείλει ὑπόστασις περὶ πατρὸς καὶ υἱοῦ καὶ ἁγίου πνεύματος ὀνομάζεσθαι ('for neither ought *hypóstasis* be predicated of the Father, Son, and Holy Spirit') which made it clear that the use of *hypóstasis* was not forbidden altogether (it could be used of the Father; cf. Heb 1:3), but that a one *hypóstasis*-theology was prohibited.

The creed marked the temporary victory of the Homoian party. Although synods continued to debate the faith, no further synodal creed was produced until the Council of Constantinople in 381. Leading bishops who were unsympathetic to the new faith were deposed and exiled, often on trumped-up charges of violating Church discipline. They were replaced by Homoians.[425] These harassments continued under Emperor Valens (r. 364–378).[426]

The damage that the emperor's religious policy, but also the bishops' theological bickerings, had done was enormous. Hilary of Poitiers, who had been an eyewitness to these developments, wrote a letter to Constantius in which he bitterly complained about the doctrinal chaos that had been created by changing the

---

425 Cf. Hanson 1988, pp. 381 f.; Barceló 2004, p. 172; Brennecke et al. 2014, pp. 552 f.
426 Cf., e.g., the descriptions in Basil of Caeasarea, *Epistula 243*, 2 and Theodoret, *Historia ecclesiastica* 4,13–19. Further details in Lenski 2002, pp. 255–61.

creed and thus unsettling simple believers. It is worth quoting some of his remarks to conclude this chapter:

> For after the meeting of the Council of Nicaea we are aware of nothing other than our tak-
> ing turns in writing the faith. While there is battle of words, dispute about novelties, occa-
> sion for ambiguities, complaint about the originators, struggle over aims, difficulty in
> agreement, while one anathema rises against another, almost nobody belongs to Christ. 'We
> wander in an uncertain wind of doctrines' [Eph 4:14], and either cause confusion when we
> teach or go astray when we are taught. Indeed, what change does last year's faith now con-
> tain? The first creed decrees to remain silent about *homousion*; the second, on the contrary,
> decrees and proclaims *homousion*; next, the third absolves [the use of] *ousía* as it had been
> previously used by the fathers in a simple fashion; finally, the fourth does not absolve but
> condemns [the term]. In the end where have we got to that nothing any more remains sa-
> cred and inviolable either to us or to anybody prior to us. But if the wretched faith of our
> time concerns the likeness of God the Son to God the Father, lest [the former] be unlike [the
> latter] either wholly or only partially, then we, the illustrious arbiters of heavenly mysteries,
> we inspectors of invisible mysteries, cheapen the faith in God through our professions. We
> determine 'faiths' about God yearly and monthly; we do penance for decrees; we defend the
> penitent; we anathematize those defended; we condemn either what is foreign in ours or
> ours in the foreign [creeds]; and as we bite one another we are already consumed by one
> another [cf. Gal 5:15].[427]

6.5.10 Debates about the sufficiency of N among Nicene theologians

When we consider the aforementioned events we must remember that even pro-
Nicene bishops did not use N in their catechesis, their preaching, or their liturgy
in the decades immediately following Nicaea. As Kelly put it:

> For as much as a whole generation after the council one hears singularly little, either from
> the 'orthodox' or from the 'Arianizing' camp, of the creed which bears its name. So far from
> occupying a position in the foreground of the controversy, the symbol and its characteristic
> key-word are rarely mentioned and practically never quoted in the literature of the period.
> Only in the 'fifties of the fourth century did they begin to emerge from their obscurity and
> play a prominent role as the rallying-point of the Athanasian party.[428]

This would be unusual only if the doctrinal developments between 325 and the
mid-350s had been considered a part of a victorious reception of N which they
clearly were not. The ongoing debate about the relationship between Father and
Son notwithstanding, N was deeply unpopular because of its use of the unbiblical
homooúsios. It was unpopular even among those who sympathized with the doc-

---

427 Hilary, *Liber (II) ad Constantium imperatorem* 5 (FaFo § 151e1).
428 Cf. discussion in Kelly 1972, pp. 254–62; quotation on p. 255.

trinal stance which the fathers had taken at Nicaea. Even Athanasius struggled with the *homoousios* and did not use it in his writings at all until the 350s.

However, this fact is even less astonishing than Kelly considered it to be when we remember that, in general, the use of declaratory creeds was not yet widespread in the Church. (We have dealt with the two exceptions of Rome and Jerusalem in earlier chapters.[429]) For this reason, the *Traditio* and *Redditio fidei* as formalized rites had not yet been introduced either. In their baptismal catechesis most bishops probably preached ad hoc about the rule of faith, and at baptism candidates were simply asked whether they agreed to a set of doctrinal propositions which may, to a certain extent, have varied in wording. It is, therefore, not surprising either that there is virtually no evidence for the use of *homoousios* in the literature of the first half of the fourth century. Even later on it is rarely N in its pure form that is used at baptism and/or in preaching, but rather some adaptation such as the creed of Antioch which is first found in the *Catechetical Homilies* by Theodore of Mopsuestia.[430] N 'was a conciliar and not a baptismal creed'[431] – it was at that time considered unsuitable for catechesis and preaching. However, this does not mean that it was not considered important – the reverse is true: as we will see the normativity of N increased over the fourth century. But its normativity was restricted to a clerical level – as far as we can see, it played – as yet – no role in the life of the laity.

However, in the mid-350s things began to change. Athanasius was the first to quote N (after Eusebius) in the appendix to his *De decretis Nicaenae synodi* which probably has to be dated to 352/353 and again in his letter to the Emperor Jovian (363/364).[432] He also presented N as the dogmatic rule against which all other creeds were to be measured in his letter to the bishops of Egypt and Libya (356).[433] Likewise, in his other works of the period such as the *De synodis Arimini in Italia et Seleuciae in Isauria* (361/362) he emphasized the importance of Nicaea and of N as point of reference in doctrinal questions.

This is precisely the time when the first Latin translation of N appeared in the writings of Hilary of Poitiers and Lucifer of Cagliari.[434] Hilary, who had 'never

---

429 Cf. above chs. 5.1 and 5.5.
430 Cf. below ch. 6.5.13.
431 Kelly 1972, p. 256.
432 Cf. Athanasius, *Epistula ad Iouianum imperatorem* 3.
433 Cf. Athanasius, *Epistula ad episcopos Aegypti et Libyae* 5,4 (FaFo § 153); 6,4–7,1; 8,1; 13; 18,3 (§ 153); 21,1. 5.
434 Cf. Hilary, *Collectanea Antiariana Parisina (Fragmenta historica)* B II 10,1–3(27; written in 356; FaFo § 135d1); id., *De synodis* 84 (358/359; § 135d3); Lucifer, *De non parcendo in deum delinquentibus* 18 (356/360; § 135d2). In his *Commentaria in euangelia*, ll. 2922–2928, 2935–2941 (CSEL 103, pp. 236 f.) Fortunatianus of Aquileia also seems to allude to N in which case the date of composition could be narrowed down from 330–360 to the last years of this period. Cf. Lukas

heard of the Nicene Faith' until he was about to be exiled in 353 (*fidem Nicaenam numquam nisi exulaturus audiui*),[435] now considered it 'full and perfect' (*plena atque perfecta*).[436] The participle future *exulaturus* here is important, because it points to an event that happened not long *before* his exile. Indeed, the event may well be the Synod of Milan in 355 at which N was no doubt discussed. The translation Hilary quotes may be that of Milan which is also referred to by Pope Liberius in his letter to Constantius II (written in 353/354).[437] This could point to Hilary's participation in this assembly, but this is uncertain,[438] whereas the participation of Lucifer is attested by Hilary himself.[439]

N appeared in Milan in particular circumstances. Eusebius of Vercelli was asked to sign the deposition and condemnation of Athanasius. However, he first demanded a debate about the creed. For this purpose he 'placed in [their] midst the faith set forth at Nicaea [. . .] pledging himself to do all they required, as soon as they had written a confession of faith'.[440] Dionysius of Milan was about to fulfil this request when Valens of Mursa wrestled the document out of his hand and shouted that such a procedure was unacceptable.

The story (if indeed it is historical[441]) is interesting for a number of reasons: first, because Eusebius of Vercelli (who was a staunch supporter of Nicaea) seems to have carried a copy of the creed with him to the synod which may suggest that a generation after Nicaea the text of N was no longer generally known and, in any case, was unfamiliar in the west. Eusebius' version of N must have been in Latin (which may well be the translation later quoted by Hilary and Lucifer[442]). Second, Eusebius did *not* demand that the bishops simply subscribe to N, but asked the council members to draft *their own creeds*. Third, Valens of Mursa in-

---

R. Dorfbauer in CSEL 103, pp. 1–105; Houghton 2017, pp. IX–XXIV. On the appearance of N in the west cf. Ulrich 1994, pp. 140–58.

435 Hilary, *De synodis* 91 (FaFo § 151d2).

436 Hilary, *Collectanea Antiariana Parisina (Fragmenta historica)* B II 11,1(28) (FaFo § 151b1).

437 Cf. Liberius, *Epistula ad Constantium imperatorem* (Brennecke et al. 2014, *Dokument* 50.1), 7. Brennecke thinks that this was, in fact, the creed of Serdica (west); cf. Brennecke 1984, pp. 158–64. On the Synod of Milan cf. also above ch. 6.5.6.

438 Cf. Brennecke 1984, p. 229.

439 Cf. Hilary of Poitiers, *Collectanea Antiariana Parisina (Fragmenta historica)*, app. II 3(8),1.

440 *Collectanea Antiariana Parisina (Fragmenta historica)*, app. II 3(8),2 (FaFo § 152): 'Expositam fidem apud Niceam [. . .] posuit in medio spondens omnia se, quae postularent, esse facturum, si fidei professionem scripsissent.'

441 Hanson 1988, p. 333; Williams 1995, pp. 57; and Ayres 2004, p. 136 consider the episode historical; by contrast, Brennecke 1984, p. 178–82; Brennecke 1986, p. 316; and Ulrich 1994, p. 320 think it is an invention by Hilary.

442 Cf. above 300 and n. 339.

tervened and rejected this demand, apparently on procedural grounds. Thus we can see that for Eusebius N apparently represented the doctrinal rule by which the faith of the bishops was to be measured. But he did not expect the other bishops simply to agree with the letter of N; instead he conceded each bishop some leeway to express their faith in personal statements.[443]

Three years later Phoebadius of Agen defended N over against the Second Creed of Sirmium.[444] He exclaimed:

> What did you accomplish, O men of blessed memory, who gathered from all parts of the world in Nicaea and, after having perused the sacred volumes, fixed the perfect rule of the catholic faith (*perfectam fidei catholicae regulam*) with circumspect wording, extending in common faith the right hand to those who believe aright, while [offering] the formula of belief (*formam credendi*) to those in error?[445]

∗

As time went by and new political and theological constellations emerged, discussions arose among the supporters of N as to whether the creed was sufficient as it stood or whether it had to be safeguarded against new 'heresies' through additions.[446] These discussions gained momentum when an opposition had formed against the official, Homoian creed, which intended to bring N to new prominence instead. Even if N's inclusion of *homooúsios*, together with the ensuing discussion, had made clear that N was immune to Homoiousian or Homoian misunderstandings, the question arose as to (1) whether, conversely, the christological article protected against views in which the *humanity* of Christ incarnate was insufficiently described, and (2) whether its short pneumatological article sufficed to ensure the consubstantiality of the Spirit.

I mentioned above that there had already been debates about the sufficiency of N at the (western) Council of Serdica (343) in the presence of Athanasius.[447] Among the then council members there seems to have been a view that more detailed explanations would make it possible to protect the Nicene faith against Arian misunderstandings and misinterpretations.[448] Serdica's declaration of faith aimed at leaving the text of N unchanged, while elucidating it with a small theo-

---

443 Cf. above p. 299.
444 Cf. above ch. 6.5.6.
445 Phoebadius, *Contra Arianos* 6,3 (FaFo § 154c).
446 This section is based on Kinzig, *Glaubensbekenntnis*, 2021, pp. 63–79.
447 Cf. above ch. 6.5.2.
448 Cf. the fragment of the letter of Ossius of Córdoba and of Protogenes of Serdica to Julius of Rome (FaFo § 144b) and the summary in Sozomen, *Historia ecclesiastica* 3,12,6 (Brennecke et al. 2007, *Dokument* 43.6). The creed is found in FaFo § 144a.

logical treatise, which, however, was not *stricto sensu* considered a *pístis*. Rather, as a letter of Ossius of Córdoba and Protogenes of Serdica to Julius of Rome testifies, the so-called canonization formula applied with regard to N itself; this formula was from then on repeated time and again, according to which one should 'add nothing to nor take anything away from' a given text.[449] It is attested in the Bible in Acts 22:18–19, where, in turn, Deut 4:2 and 13:1 is cited (cf. also Eccles 3:14), but it was also widely used elsewhere.[450] It was applied here for the first time to a credal text, namely N, thus contributing significantly to its sacralization and thus also its immutability. As a result of this procedure, Athanasius was able to claim two decades after the event that Serdica had not adopted a new *pístis*.[451] After the eventual victory of neo-Nicene theology, this principle of immutability was repeated for centuries like a mantra with reference to the formula of canonization,[452] although it was not always obvious what this meant in concrete terms, for instance, whether it excluded *any* clarifying additions and, if not, what form the latter might take (such as an amendment of the formula itself or perhaps an appendix).

In the west, the Council of Rimini attempted to solve the problem in July 359 by confirming the unshakeable validity of N and adopting the principle that nothing was to be changed or added to it.[453] Further developments in Rimini and the subsequent imposition of the Homoian creeds of Niké and Constantinople made it clear that such a position could not be maintained in view of the prevailing religio-political conditions.[454]

The sufficiency of N was also on the agenda, just a few years later, in the east, at the Synod of Alexandria, held in 362 after Athanasius' return to the Egyptian capital.[455] Here the divinity of the Holy Spirit and Christ's assumption of the

---

449 Cf. Ossius of Córdoba and Protogenes of Serdica, *Epistula ad Iulium papam* (FaFo § 144b[1]).

450 Cf. van Unnik 1949(1980); Meunier 2017.

451 Cf. Athanasius, *Tomus ad Antiochenos* 5,1 (FaFo § 144c).

452 Cf., e.g., the statement of the Council of Rimini 359 (FaFo § 564a); Ambrose, *Explanatio symboli* 7 (§ 15a2); Pseudo-Athanasius (Didymus?), *De sancta trinitate dialogus 3*, 1 (§ 183); Council of Ephesus (431), *Collectio Atheniensis 48*, 4 (*Relatio orientalium*; § 205); Council of Ephesus (431), *Collectio Vaticana 163/Orientalium relatio ad imperatores* (ACO I 1,5, p. 134, l. 38 – 135, l. 4); Cyril of Alexandria, *Epistula 33* (*Collectio Atheniensis 107*), 5 (to Acacius of Beroea); John of Antioch in Council of Ephesus, *Collectio Atheniensis 105*; Council of Chalcedon, *Actio IV*, 6 (§ 570d[6]). On the evidence from Ephesus II (449) cf. below p. 384. On Chalcedon and later evidence cf. below p. 388, 398 and n. 93; 399 and n. 96.

453 Cf. Council of Rimini (359), *Definitio* (FaFo § 564a). The Latin translation of N is found in § 135d4.

454 On events in Rimini cf. above pp. 311–13, 317 f.

455 On events in Alexandria cf. Brennecke et al. 2014, pp. 589 f; Graumann 2016/2017, pp. 55–8.

whole human being in the incarnation were debated. Again, the solution promoted by the synod was not to change N itself (it was even denied that Serdica
had adopted a new definition of faith[456]), but to add further anathemas condemning whoever claimed that the Holy Spirit was 'a creature and separate from the
substance of Christ (τοὺς λέγοντας κτίσμα εἶναι τὸ πνεῦμα τὸ ἅγιον καὶ διῃρημέ-
νον ἐκ τῆς οὐσίας τοῦ Χριστοῦ)'.[457] Accordingly, Eusebius of Vercelli and Paulinus
of Antioch also emphasized the sufficiency of N in their signatures to the tome.[458]
In addition, Paulinus specifically underlined that the Incarnate was 'begotten
from the holy virgin Mary and the Holy Spirit (ἐκ τῆς ἁγίας παρθένου Μαρίας καὶ
<τοῦ> ἁγίου πνεύματος γεννηθείς)'[459] and condemned those who deviated from
the right doctrine of the incarnation and of the Holy Spirit.[460] Furthermore, the
circular letter that was probably associated with this synod stated that it was the
intention of Nicaea that the Son be confessed as *homooúsios* with the Father and
the Spirit glorified together with Father and Son, whereupon the christological
statements of N were briefly recapitulated.[461] The reference to a trinitarian doxology is peculiar, given that one searches in vain for a corresponding formula in
N. However, we will see in a moment to what extent this remark has left its mark
on subsequent developments.

A Roman synod under Pope Damasus (*sedit* 366–384), which may have taken
place in 371,[462] took a different route in its synodal letter (*Confidimus quidem*),
which was widely circulated though addressed specifically to the Illyrian bishops.[463] Rejecting the Homoian position of Auxentius of Milan it succinctly explained the consubstantiality expressed in Nicaea; it was to be believed that

---

456 Cf. above pp. 284 f. and Tetz 1975(1995), pp. 115–17; De Halleux 1985(1990), pp. 37–9; De Halleux 1991, pp. 28 f.; Karmann 2009, pp. 214–8; Fairbairn 2015 (citing earlier scholarship); Smith
2018, pp. 22 f.
457 Athanasius, *Tomus ad Antiochenos* 3,1. On the sufficiency of N cf. also Athanasius, *Tomus ad
Antiochenos* 5,3; 6,4. In addition, Tetz 1975(1995), pp. 112–15.
458 Cf. Athanasius, *Tomus ad Antiochenos* 10,3; 11,2. In addition, Tetz 1975(1995), pp. 130–2.
459 Athanasius, *Tomus ad Antiochenos* 11,2.
460 On the subscription by Paulinus cf. also Amidon 2002.
461 Cf. Athanasius, *Epistula catholica* 8 (FaFo § 166b). In addition, Smith 2018, p. 23.
462 Cf. Reutter 2009, p. 307; Sieben 2014/2015, vol. I, pp. 194 n. 264, 195; Peter L. Schmidt/Michaela
Zelzer in Berger/Fontaine/Schmidt 2020, p. 24 f. Other suggestions concerning its date are listed
in Field 2004, p. 117 n. 2. Brennecke/Stockhausen 2020, pp. 735 f. date *Confidimus quidem* to 366/
367.
463 Athanasius and Basil seem to have known it. On the addressees cf. Reutter 2009, pp. 289–307;
Sieben 2014/2015, vol. I, p. 194 n. 263.

Father, Son, and Holy Spirit constituted 'one godhead (*deitas*), one power (*uirtus*), one likeness (*figura*), and one substance (*substantia*)'.[464]

Basil of Caesarea responded to this in a letter of 372 to the western bishops, praising their orthodoxy and bitterly lamenting the conditions in the east. For him, too, N was the orthodox reference document, the contents of which he summed up as follows: it had confessed the consubstantiality of the Son with the Father, and the Spirit had been 'ranked and worshipped as of equal honour (ὁμοτίμως συναρι- θμεῖταί τε καὶ συλλατρεύεται)'.[465] Basil thus essentially reverted to the aforementioned language that had already been adopted ten years earlier at the council in Alexandria under Athanasius.[466] Furthermore, Basil agreed with the decisions of the west.[467] Athanasius, too, in his letter to Epictetus of Corinth of *c.* 372, still held to the sufficiency of N, given it contained all that was necessary 'for the warding off of all ungodliness and for the strengthening of pious faith in Christ (πρὸς ἀνα- τροπὴν μὲν πάσης ἀσεβείας, πρὸς σύστασιν δὲ τῆς εὐσεβοῦς ἐν Χριστῷ πίστεως)'.[468]

In a synodal letter from Meletius of Antioch and a number of other bishops (including Basil) to the bishops in Italy and Gaul,[469] these eastern prelates asked their western colleagues for help both in the fight against the Homoians and in the resolution of the schism in Antioch, and for cooperation in a synod. The aim of this planned meeting was to confirm N, to ward off any heresy, and to bring about unity among the orthodox party. They expressly declared their agreement with the 'faith' and the synodal letter of Nicaea.[470] Still, there was no mention of any change of or addition to N.

The western bishops initially refused these advances because Rome did not support Meletius in the Antiochene schism, but rather his Nicene opponent Pauli- nus.[471] However, they also stipulated that the eastern bishops should first confirm

---

464 Damasus, *Epistula 1 (Confidimus quidem*; FaFo § 438). Cf. also Pietri 1976, vol. I, pp. 792 f., 797–800; Field 2004, pp. 117–22; Vinzent 2013, pp. 278 f.; Sieben 2014/2015, vol. I, p. 196 n. 274. On the following cf. also Hanson 1988, pp. 797 f.

465 Basil, *Epistula 90*, 2. Likewise, in *Epistula 91* (to Valerian of Aquileia) Basil repeats his allegiance to the 'sound doctrine' of Nicaea. Cf. also Kelly 1972, p. 342; Pietri 1976, vol. I, pp. 800 f.; Brennecke/Stockhausen 2020, pp. 760, 763.

466 On the reception of the *Tomus ad Antiochenos* in Basil's works cf. De Halleux 1991, pp. 30 f.; Drecoll, *Entwicklung*, 1996, pp. 270–6.

467 Cf. Reutter 2009, pp. 209 f.

468 Athanasius, *Epistula ad Epictetum 1*.

469 Cf. Basil, *Epistula 92* (written in 372). On the background of this letter cf. id., *Epistula 89* and Reutter 2009, p. 310; Brennecke/Stockhausen 2020, p. 765.

470 Cf. Council of Nicaea, *Epistula ad ecclesiam Alexandrinam et episcopos Aegypti, Libyae et Pentapolis* (Opitz 1934/1935, *Urkunde 23*).

471 Cf. Brennecke 2016, cols. 809 f.

verbatim an unspecified letter from Rome; in addition, an embassy should be sent to Rome to establish personal contact.[472] Unfortunately, we do not know whether the demand for literal agreement refers to a western creed (which would in that case have been lost) or to the letter *Confidimus quidem* already mentioned above.[473] The joint synod never took place – in retrospect, Theodore of Mopsuestia blamed the 'Arian persecution' in the east for this,[474] but the refusal of Basil to reach out by first sending an embassy to the west may also have played a role.[475] In addition, Basil also strictly opposed any change in the wording of N, as will be shown below, which could indicate that the contentious issue between west and east may also have been the approval of a revised version of N (which the easterners refused).

The problem soon intensified when it came to the pneumatological article of N, as can be seen from the confession which Basil presented to Eustathius of Sebaste to sign in the summer of 373.[476] After quoting N, the author stated that it defined sufficiently all points except for one. This one point concerned the doctrine of the Holy Spirit, which was only mentioned in passing in N, since his divinity had not been disputed at Nicaea. Basil then sketched out a concise Pneumatology and condemned those who denied the divinity of the Spirit without naming the proponents of this doctrine. Obviously, the bishop of Caesarea continued to try to fill the gap that had been identified in the meantime by supplementing the relevant doctrinal points and anathemas in the form of a commentary, rather than by adding to the wording of N.

He repeated this in a shorter form in the autumn of 373 in a letter to the church of Antioch:[477] here he rejected both a new creed written by others or adding explanations of his own regarding the Holy Spirit. N was the confession that had been in use in Caesarea 'since the fathers'. To his knowledge, this also applied in Antioch. Nevertheless, Basil again quoted N in full. He then stated that there had not yet been any need to condemn the Pneumatomachians at Nicaea, whence its teaching on the Holy Spirit remained 'indeterminate' (ἀδιόριστος).[478] Here,

---

472 Cf. Basil, *Epistula 138*, 2. Cf. also Pietri 1976, vol. I, pp. 803–6.

473 On *Confidimus quidem* cf. FaFo § 438 and above pp. 328 f. In addition, Reutter 2009, p. 313. Hanson 1988, p. 798 calls it a 'confession of faith'.

474 Theodore, *Homilia catechetica 9*, 1 (FaFo § 180b1), quoted below pp. 339 f.

475 Cf. Basil, *Epistula 156*, 3 and Hanson 1988, p. 798; Reutter 2009, p. 315.

476 Cf. Basil, *Epistula 125* (FaFo §§ 135c, 174a) and Dörries 1956, pp. 166 f.; De Halleux 1985(1990), pp. 40–2; De Halleux 1991, pp. 30 f.; Drecoll, *Entwicklung*, 1996, pp. 270–6; Reutter 2009, p. 314. On dating cf. Fedwick 1981, p. 16.

477 Cf. Basil, *Epistula 140*, 2 (373; FaFo §§ 135c, 174b) and Dörries 1956, p. 167; Pietri 1976, vol. I, p. 806; Reutter 2009, p. 313; Vinzent 2013, p. 281; Brennecke/Stockhausen 2020, p. 773. On dating cf. Fedwick 1981, p. 16.

478 Basil, *Epistula 140*, 2 (FaFo § 174b). On the Pneumatomachians cf. below p. 356.

too, Basil was apparently playing with the idea that one could compensate for the missing pneumatological precision in N with additional anathemas.

When the *comes* Magnenianus asked Basil for an exposition on the faith (374), Basil refused not only 'to leave behind a treatise on the faith (περὶ πίστεως σύνταγμα καταλιμπάνειν)' in his letter of reply, but also rejected the composition of new creeds on the grounds that it was sufficient to 'confess the names (ὀνόματα) which we have received from Holy Scripture'. One should 'avoid all innovation in this respect'. 'Our salvation', he continued, 'does not lie in the invention of forms of address, but in the sound confession of the Godhead in which we believe.'[479]

Similarly, Basil defended the normativity of N, briefly paraphrasing its content,[480] in the letter to an otherwise unknown Eupaterius and his daughter (*Epistula 159*, of uncertain date[481]). Again he stated that the pneumatological section at Nicaea did not answer certain questions that had recently arisen, and therefore briefly presented his own doctrine of the Holy Spirit, drawing a theological connection between baptism into the triune God, the trinitarian 'confession of faith (τὴν ὁμολογίαν τῆς πίστεως)', and the doxology used by Basil. That doxology is based on the creed which in itself is based on the baptismal formula. The Spirit is glorified together with the Father and the Son because he is not alien to the divine nature (συνδοξάζοντες πατρὶ καὶ υἱῷ τὸ ἅγιον πνεῦμα τῷ πεπεῖσθαι μὴ ἀλλότριον εἶναι τῆς θείας φύσεως).[482] Basil introduced corresponding doxological formulae in his own congregation, for which he was apparently severely criticized.[483]

The situation was further complicated by the fact that in the 370s, Rome and Antioch were apparently negotiating several creeds with each other. On the one hand, Damasus tried to establish church unity with Paulinus on the basis of a supplemented N; on the other hand, he produced his own confessions and doctrinal letters, which have only been preserved in fragments and are therefore difficult to place.

We know from a letter of Basil (*Epistula 216*, summer/autumn 376[484]) that a confession circulated in Antioch in the summer of 376 that played a role in the

---

479 Basil, *Epistula 175*. Cf. also Drecoll, *Entwicklung*, 1996, pp. 210 f. On dating cf. Fedwick 1981, p. 16.

480 Cf. also Dörries 1956, p. 166.

481 Written in 374/375? Cf. Fedwick 1981, p. 16.

482 Basil, *Epistula 159*, 2. The same connection between baptism and confession is also found in Basil, *De spiritu sancto* 12,28 (FaFo § 174c). Cf. also Kelly 1972, p. 342; Drecoll, *Entwicklung*, 1996, p. 210.

483 Cf. Basil, *De spiritu sancto* 1,3 and Hauschild 1967, pp. 50–2; Benoît Pruche in SC 17bis, pp. 41–52; De Halleux 1979(1990), p. 326; Drecoll, *Entwicklung*, 1996, pp. 196, 209–12.

484 On the date cf. Fedwick 1981, p. 17 (*pace* Pietri 1976, vol. I, p. 808 n. 3 and 821 n. 1, who dates the letters *214–218* to 375; Brennecke/Stockhausen 2020, p. 876: late 376). For background cf. also Reutter 2009, pp. 374–7; Brennecke/Stockhausen 2020, p. 876.

negotiations between the Paulinians and Meletians about church unity in the eastern metropolis.[485] Given the circumstances this confession must have been Nicene in character, since both Paulinus and Meletius represented the two Nicene camps in the dispute between the Antiochene bishops. However, this creed cannot simply have been identical with N, because N formed the credal basis in both camps from the outset, so no negotiations would have been necessary if it had simply been its original text.

If this formula was not identical with N, where did it come from? André de Halleux attributes authorship of this *pístis* to the Paulinians of Antioch,[486] whereas Ursula Reutter thinks that it was identical with the Roman *fides* mentioned in the letter *Per ipsum filium* (*Epistula 3*).[487] In this letter from Damasus to Paulinus (presumably written in 376[488]), the Roman bishop says that he had sent a *fides* to the east, which was to be signed by those who sought church unity with Paulinus.[489] Damasus writes further down:

> If, then, my aforesaid son Vitalis and those who are with him wish to join you, they must first sign the exposition of the faith (*expositione fidei*) which was established at Nicaea by the pious will of the fathers. Then, since no one can apply medicine to future wounds, this heresy must be eradicated, which is said to have arisen later in the east; i.e. it must be confessed that Wisdom itself, the Word, the Son of God assumed a human body, soul, and mind, i.e. the entire Adam, and, to put it more plainly, our whole old man without sin.[490]

In my view, these remarks only make sense if Damasus had sent a *fides* to Antioch which he regarded as essentially identical to N, though it did not correspond to the original version of N (knowledge of which he could assume in Antioch in any case) in all its formulations. His further explanations make clear that one of the heresies repelled here was Apolinarianism.[491] The fact that the teachings of Apolinarius were being discussed in Rome at that time is also evident from the letter fragment

---

485 Cf. also Basil, *Epistula 214*, 2 to the *comes* Terentius; however, Basil does not explicitly mention the creed, but speaks generally of 'writings' (γράμματα). On the confused situation in Antioch cf. Reutter 2009, pp. 358–61 who quotes further literature.

486 Cf. De Halleux 1984(1990), p. 119.

487 Cf. Reutter 2009, pp. 351 and nn. 352, 374–80. Furthermore, Sieben 2014/2015, vol. I, p. 211 n. 313.

488 Cf. Reutter 2009, pp. 372 and 517.

489 Cf. Damasus, *Epistula 3* (*Per ipsum filium*; Reutter 2009, pp. 350 f.).

490 Damasus, *Epistula 3* (*Per ipsum filium*; Reutter 2009, pp. 352 f.).

491 As regards the knowledge of Apolinarianism in Rome which was closely linked to the activities of the presbyter and later bishop of Antioch Vitalis, cf. Reutter 2009, pp. 362–74. Vitalis' creed is found in FaFo § 177 (where further literature is cited).

Illud sane miramur,[492] which can be dated to the year 377 or earlier (375).[493] In this case, the *fides* must have preceded the letter *Per ipsum filium*. However, this is not explicitly stated in Basil's *Letter 216* – Basil merely says in general that a *pístis* was 'presented' without explicitly naming its authors.

For reasons of textual history, it is probable that the *fides* mentioned in *Per ipsum filium* refers to the original version of the *Tomus Damasi* (Damasus, *Epistula 4*), which was issued by a Roman synod in around 375,[494] since *Per ipsum filium* and the *Tomus Damasi* were handed down together.[495] The *Tome of Damasus* is a doctrinal letter which, according to the title preserved in some manuscripts, Pope Damasus sent to Paulinus of Antioch and which in its present form consists of 24 anathemas.[496] They were indeed (also) directed against Apolinarianism and introduced by N. As I have shown elsewhere,[497] the *fides* (= N) in the *Tome* actually contained the addition *neque facturam neque creaturam sed de substantia deitatis* appended to the third article: 'and <in> the Holy Spirit which is neither a product nor a creature but of the deity's substance'.[498] The *Tome* appears to refer to this very addition in the introduction (or transition from N) to its anathemas[499] and in anathemas 3 and 18. It is quite clear that the addition is directed against those who deny the divinity of the spirit. According to anathema 3, these include Arius and Eunomius, who consider both Son and Spirit to be *creaturae*. It is not stated in anathema 18 which opponent speaks of the Spirit as *factura*. If Ursula Reutter's observation is correct, according to which anathemas 10–24 are intended 'as a kind of commentary on the Nicene Creed',[500] then anathema 18 clearly presupposes the addition *neque facturam* in the *Tomus*' version of N. The Greek syntagma corresponding to *facturam* and *creaturam*, i.e. κτίσμα καὶ

---

492 Cf. Damasus, *Epistula 2*, frg. 3 (*Illud sane miramur*; FaFo § 439b).

493 Cf. in detail Reutter 2009, pp. 367–74. On dating cf. Reutter 2009, p. 371 n. 456 and p. 517. In addition, Sieben 2014/2015, vol. I, p. 204 n. 301.

494 Cf. Reutter 2009, pp. 409 f. By contrast, Charles Pietri originally ascribed the entire *Tomus* to the Synod of 377 (cf. Pietri 1976, vol. I, pp. 834–40; 873–80). Yet cf. also Pietri 1996(2010), p. 442, where the two parts of the *Tomus* are seen as originating from the Roman Synods of 378 (!) and 382 respectively. Sieben 2014/2015, vol. I, p. 215: 377/378. In addition, Markschies 1995, pp. 144–64; Field 2004, pp. 139–43 (with a list of possible dates on p. 139 n. 10); Peter L. Schmidt and Michaela Zelzer in Berger/Fontaine/Schmidt 2020, pp. 27–9.

495 Cf. Reutter 2009, pp. 398 f., 410.

496 Edition: Reutter 2009, pp. 381–97.

497 Cf. Kinzig, *Glaubensbekenntnis*, 2021, pp. 71–5.

498 Cf. FaFo § 135d8. This addition to the earliest Latin version of the *Tomus Damasi* seems to be missing in the entire Greek tradition. Cf. Dossetti 1967, p. 236, app. ad loc.

499 The anathemas were formulated against those heretics who claim 'that the Holy Spirit was made through the Son (*spiritum sanctum factum esse per filium*)'.

500 Reutter 2009, p. 406.

ποίημα, is in any case well attested in the eastern debates in the second half of the fourth century.[501]

It is equally striking that the addition to N contains the consubstantiality of the Spirit with the Father. The anathemas display certain differences at this point: in anathema 1 the consubstantiality is clearly presupposed, as it is in the sentence that concludes the entire text.[502] However, in anathema 16 the formulation is less distinct.[503]

In any case, I see no compelling reason to regard the addition of *neque facturam neque creaturam sed de substantia deitatis* to N in the *Tomus Damasi* as a later interpolation.[504] If one assumes with Reutter that the original version of this text existed in N + sentence 1 + anathemas 10–24[505] and was issued around the year 375, then this would mean that an attempt to affirm the consubstantiality of the Spirit in N was already made in Rome before the Council of Constantinople, by adding an explanation to the text of N as well as corresponding condemnations (1 and 18).

Basil requested help from the bishops in Italy and Gaul in another letter (*Epistula 243*), probably in the same year 375.[506] They were also asked to inform the western emperor of the conditions in the east. Basil described the Homoian persecution of the eastern Church, especially in Anatolia, in drastic terms. The bishop added that not only Christology, but also the doctrine of the Spirit were in dispute. His opponents did not consider 'Son' to be a designation of divine nature but of rank, whereas the Holy Spirit was seen as no more than a creature.[507]

Rome probably reacted to this with the doctrinal letter *Ea gratia* (only fragments of which survive), which was presumably addressed to Basil.[508] In this let-

---

501 Cf. the references in Kinzig, *Glaubensbekenntnis*, 2021, p. 74 n. 293.

502 The same in Damasus, *Epistula 2*, frg. 2 (*Ea gratia*; FaFo § 439a), where the *una usia* is expressly named in section 1 and 2.

503 Cf. Reutter 2009, p. 391 (version 1): 'Si quis non dixerit Spiritum sanctum de Patre esse vere ac propriae, sicuut Filium, de divina substantia et Deum verum: hereticus est.' Depending on the translation of this syntactically opaque sentence, the Spirit is stated as coming from the Father as *vere ac propriae*, analogously to the Son, who comes from the Father's *substantia* and is therefore 'true God'; or else the Spirit, too, is seen as coming from the Father's substance and as, therefore, being truly divine.

504 *Pace* Ritter 1965, p. 163 n. 2; Abramowski 1992, p. 494.

505 Cf. Reutter 2009, p. 406. Similarly, Markschies 1995, pp. 155–60.

506 Cf. also Pietri 1976, vol. I, p. 822 and n. 1, 824; Hanson 1988, p. 798; Reutter 2009, pp. 329–31; Brennecke/Stockhausen 2020, p. 829.

507 Cf. Basil, *Epistula 243*, 4.

508 Cf. Damasus, *Epistula 2*, frg. 2 (*Ea gratia*; FaFo § 439a). In general, cf. Pietri 1976, vol. I, pp. 824 f., 828–31; Reutter 2009, pp. 317–49; Vinzent 2013, pp. 279–81; Sieben 2014/2015, vol. I, p. 200 n. 280; Brennecke/Stockhausen 2020, p. 837.

ter, the western bishops confirmed the divine union with words similar to those in *Confidimus quidem*.[509] The Son's divinity was described by recourse to Nicene terminology, while at the same time also emphasizing his full humanity. The Spirit was confessed as 'uncreated', being 'of one majesty, one substance, one power with God the Father and our Lord Jesus Christ'. The bishops expressly described this trinitarian confession as their *fides* and granted communion to those who followed this doctrinal view. It is possible that the fragment *Non nobis quidquam* also formed part of this letter.[510] The latter contained an explicit commitment to Nicaea, the wording of which was not to be altered, and to the divinity of the Spirit. One 'worships' the Spirit, 'perfect in all things, in power, in honour, in majesty, in godhead, together with the Father and the Son'. Photinus' idea, expressed rather casually in *Ea gratia*, that the Son is a 'spoken utterance' (*uerbum prolatiuum*), was rejected; rather, he must be seen as 'born' and 'not remaining in the Father'.[511]

The letter *Ea gratia* was not initially met with great enthusiasm by Basil, since the west evidently still did not recognize the Nicene sentiments of Meletius, whom the bishop of Caesarea had supported in the Antiochene schism, and rejected communion with him in favour of that with Paulinus. Later, however, he seems to have assented to a list of signatures which signalled approval of *Ea gratia*/*Non nobis quidquam* by the eastern bishops.[512] It may, possibly, have been this *Liber de fide* that Basil mentioned in a letter to three exiled Egyptian bishops in early 377.[513]

Further evidence concerning the debate as to whether N could be safeguarded against heresy by additions is found in a letter that Basil had addressed to pious women in Colonia in Cappadocia (*Epistula 52*; autumn 376[514]). The bishop first noted that N's *homooúsios* was not accepted by everyone, then offering a long explanation of its meaning. In addition, the women had apparently also inquired about the status of the Holy Spirit. In his reply, their correspondent dealt

---

509 Cf. Damasus, *Epistula 1* (*Confidimus quidem*; FaFo § 438) and above pp. 328 f.

510 Cf. Damasus, *Epistula 2*, frg. 4 (*Non nobis quidquam*; FaFo § 439c). For a different view cf. Brennecke/Stockhausen 2020, pp. 771 f.

511 Damasus, *Epistula 2*, frg. 4 (*Non nobis quidquam*; FaFo § 439c). On Photinus' doctrine on this point cf. Reutter 2009, p. 320 n. 235. Cf. also above nn. 292, 295.

512 Cf. Reutter 2009, pp. 335–44. I doubt, however, that this is the list of subscriptions preserved in the codex Veronensis LX (Reutter 2009, pp. 344–9). Cf. below pp. 345 f.

513 Cf. Basil, *Epistula 265* (to Eulogius, Alexander and Harpocration), 3. On dating cf. Fedwick 1981, p. 18. In addition, Reutter 2009, pp. 424 f.; Brennecke/Stockhausen 2020, p. 863 (autumn 376/377?).

514 On dating cf. Fedwick 1981, p. 17. On this letter cf. Drecoll, *Entwicklung*, 1996, pp. 276–81; in addition, Dörries 1956, pp. 114–6, 167 f.; Brennecke/Stockhausen 2020, p. 814 (giving as date 375/376).

inter alia with the view according to which the Spirit was older than the Son and therefore should be placed before him in the doxology, a view for which Basil himself seems to have been reproached.[515] In fact, he vehemently rejected this view – but there was no talk of changing N in this letter either.

By far the most important letter in our context is his *Epistula 258* to Epiphanius of Salamis from the end of 376.[516] A dispute had apparently broken out among the monks on the Mount of Olives in Jerusalem about the third section of N, the details of which we unfortunately do not know. However, it made great waves: both Epiphanius and Basil saw themselves compelled to intervene, with Epiphanius initially seeking a theological consensus with Basil. However, the latter had already written to the monks in his turn when the letter to this effect from the bishop of Salamis arrived. The fathers, Basil wrote, had treated the article rather casually because there had not yet been any dispute about the Spirit.[517] Nevertheless, he continued to remain sceptical about possible changes, saying that he could not make even the smallest addition to the third section, apart from a doxology of the Holy Spirit (πλὴν τῆς εἰς τὸ πνεῦμα τὸ ἅγιον δοξολογίας), which he had obviously added to the third article in some form after all. This trinitarian doxology represented, for him, a strong confession of the consubstantiality of the Spirit, and he therefore defended it vehemently in *De spiritu sancto* against the objections of Eustathius of Sebaste and others.[518]

However, the disputes were not only about the Pneumatomachians, but also about an effective defence against Apolinarianism.[519] In this context, Basil also mentioned additions to the christological article, especially concerning the incarnation. It is possible that he was referring here to the extended Nicene Creed of Epiphanius, which we will discuss below.[520] Basil rejected these additions too, as he felt they were too expansive. He warned against changes that would only lead to unnecessary discussion and confuse the minds of the simpler people.[521]

We do not know the details of the additions that were under discussion between the Jerusalem monks, Epiphanius, and Basil. If we follow *Epistula 159*,[522] Basil evidently allowed only one addition, which is then found later in $C^{1/2}$. His

---

515 Cf. Drecoll, *Entwicklung*, 1996, pp. 278–80.
516 Cf. Basil, *Epistula 258*, 2 (FaFo § 174e). On dating cf. Fedwick 1981, p. 17. In addition, Dörries 1956, pp. 116 f., 168 f.
517 Similarly also Epiphanius, *Panarion* 74,14,4–8; cf. also Kösters 2003, pp. 324 f.
518 Cf. Dörries 1956, pp. 154–6; Drecoll, *Entwicklung*, 1996, pp. 183–269.
519 Concerning the chronology of the controversy with Apolinarianism cf. Andrist 2005, pp. 65–8. A survey of the condemnations in the fourth century is found in Andrist 2015, pp. 286 f.
520 Cf. Smith 2018, p. 26.
521 Cf. Basil, *Epistula 258*, 2 (FaFo § 174e). Cf. also Smith 2018, p. 25.
522 Cf. above p. 331.

third section read: καὶ εἰς τὸ πνεῦμα τὸ ἅγιον, τὸ σὺν πατρὶ καὶ υἱῷ [συμπροσκυ-νούμενον καὶ?] συνδοξαζόμενον / 'and in the Holy Spirit who is [worshipped and?] jointly glorified with the Father and the Son'. The solution was elegant: Basil could thus conclude his confession with a doxology that did not earn him the reproach of falsifying the wording of N, while yet having – in his view – sufficiently expressed the divinity of the Spirit.

We have an expanded version of N from Epiphanius, which sheds light on the way in which other easterners were experimenting at this time:[523] in his *Ancoratus*, the bishop of Salamis first quoted the original version of N (which in later manuscripts was replaced by C², leading to considerable confusion[524]) and then appended an expanded version of the same creed.[525] The latter version is preceded by a protocol which contains a date (374) as well as an address to fellow bishops, suggesting that the text originated from a synodal letter. The extensions included here are directed against the Pneumatomachians, the Apolinarians, and against the deniers of the bodily resurrection (Origenists).[526]

Basil's unwavering view of the final doxology as a textual element which was distinct from N is also indirectly attested to by his *Epistula 251* to the Christians of Euaisa of early 377.[527] In it he affirmed that he had always adhered to the same *pístis* and subsequently developed his Neo-Nicene Pneumatology, which he linked with the creed once more via its concluding doxology.[528]

Similarly, Amphilochius of Iconium wrote around 377 that N was directed primarily against the Arians, but that the pneumatological question was not discussed because it had not yet been an issue. Therefore, it was necessary 'to glorify the Spirit together with the Father and the Son in the doxologies' (ἐν ταῖς δοξολο-γίαις τὸ πνεῦμα πατρὶ καὶ υἱῷ χρὴ συνδοξάζειν).[529]

The formation of Neo-Nicene theology thus led, from the 370s onwards, to broad discussions about possible additions to N, the content of which was aimed at emphasizing that Christ had assumed full humanity in the incarnation, the bodily resurrection, and the divinity of the Spirit.[530] The time was ripe to think

---

523 On the following cf. Kösters 2003, pp. 322–30.
524 Cf. FaFo § 175, introduction. In addition cf. above p. 32.
525 Cf. Epiphanius, *Ancoratus* 119,1–12 (FaFo § 175). The combination of N and the explanation in *Didascalia CCCXVIII patrum Nicaenorum* (FaFo § 176) may be a similar experiment.
526 Cf. Kösters 2003, p. 324; Kim 2017, pp. 16–20.
527 On its date cf. Fedwick 1981, p. 18.
528 Cf. Basil, *Epistula 251*, 4. Cf. also Drecoll, *Entwicklung*, 1996, p. 211; Brennecke/Stockhausen 2020, p. 809 (date: end 376).
529 Cf. Amphilochius, *Epistula synodalis* 2 (FaFo § 178) and 4.
530 Cf. also Smith 2018, pp. 24–8.

about whether the text of N sufficed for coping with the new challenges that had arisen in order to reach agreement among Neo-Nicene theologians.

6.5.11 The Roman Synod of 377/378

In 377/378,[531] yet another *fides* was negotiated between Rome and Antioch. The synod that was ultimately responsible for the Roman/Antiochene recension of N as preserved in N^Ant and the circumstances of its convocation are unfortunately shrouded in darkness.[532] Rufinus reports of a Roman assembly which was also attended by Peter of Alexandria, in his continuation of Eusebius' *Ecclesiastical History*, after summarizing the teaching of Apolinarius.[533] The patriarch of Alexandria had been expelled from his episcopal see and resided in Rome since 373.[534] It was probably not until 378 that he had been able to return, which is why the synod must be dated to the years 377/378.[535] The fact that the two leading patriarchs of Christendom were jointly responsible for this gathering must have given it a special weight. According to Rufinus, the synod had turned against Apolinarius, stating *inter alia* that whoever claimed that 'the Son of God, who was both true God and true man, lacked something of either his humanity or divinity' was to be condemned ('[. . .] ut decernerent, si quis filium dei, qui sicut vere deus, ita et vere homo fuit, vel humanitatis aliquid vel deitatis minus diceret habuisse, alienus ab ecclesia iudicaretur').[536]

Rufinus' wording is closely related to a synodal letter sent by Damasus to the eastern bishops. This letter is lost, although parts of it are quoted in another synodal letter from Rome that was again directed against the Apolinarians and preserved in Theodoret's *Church History*.[537] Here we learn that not only Apoli-

---

531 This chapter is based on Kinzig, *Glaubensbekenntnis*, 2021, pp. 80–8.
532 On the following cf. especially Schwartz 1935(1960), pp. 79–84; Pietri 1976, vol. I, pp. 811–18, 833–44; Abramowski 1992; Pietri 1996(2010), pp. 442–4; Field 2004, pp. 131 f. The reconstruction of events differs between these scholars.
533 This summary closely resembles that of Augustine, *Contra Iulianum opus perfectum* 4,47 and seems to come from the same source (Theodore of Mopsuestia, *De incarnatione?*). Cf. Lietzmann 1904, pp. 47 f.
534 Cf. Theodoret, *Historia ecclesiastica* 4,21,2; Basil, *Epistula 266*, 2; in addition, Griggs 2000, p. 182; Reutter 2009, p. 337 and n. 312; Brennecke/Stockhausen 2020, pp. 877 f.
535 Cf. Socrates, *Historia ecclesiastica* 4,37,1–2; Sozomen, *Historia ecclesiastica* 6,39,1; in addition, Reutter 2009, p. 436 n. 34.
536 Rufinus, *Historia ecclesiastica* 11,20. Cf. also Kelly 1972, p. 335.
537 Cf. Theodoret, *Historia ecclesiastica* 5,10,5. On this second letter cf. Lietzmann 1904, pp. 26 f.; Pietri 1976, vol. I, pp. 841–4; Reutter 2009, pp. 429–40; Sieben 2014/2015, vol. I, p. 222 n. 336.

narius but also his follower Timothy had previously been condemned.[538] Again, Peter of Alexandria's participation in the earlier synod is mentioned here.[539] Differences in wording[540] indicate that Rufinus did not take his information from the same letter that Theodoret quotes, but from the original synodal letter which contained anathemas (directed against Apolinarius or Timothy), which the (second) letter in Theodoret summarizes.

This (second) synodal letter, which may belong to the year 381,[541] is also of great interest in the present context because in it Damasus exhorts the eastern bishops to remember the 'apostolic faith' (τῆς ἀποστολικῆς πίστεως), 'and above all the (faith) which was set out in writing by the fathers in Nicaea (ταύτης μάλιστα ἥτις ἐν Νικαίᾳ παρὰ τῶν πατέρων ἐγγράφως ἐξετέθη)'.[542] He continues:

> For we have already given a formula (τύπον), such that anyone who professes himself a Christian may preserve what has been handed down by the apostles.[543]

Obviously such a τύπος (in the Latin original probably: *forma*) is a formula that was used in catechetical teaching. This formula cannot be the older *fides* mentioned by Basil in *Epistula 216*, because then one would have to assume that Damasus refers back, in the synodal letter of the year 381, to a formula that was by then four years old, if this formula did in fact at all originate from the west.[544] In addition, Basil does not mention the participation of Peter of Alexandria in its composition.

So it appears that, rather, the synod that elaborated the τύπος is probably identical with the western synod mentioned by Theodore of Mopsuestia in sermon 9 of his *Catechetical Homilies*:

> The question will deal now with the Holy Spirit, and our blessed fathers who assembled from all parts in the town of Nicaea for the sake of that wonderful council wrote about him simply and without amplification by saying, 'And in the Holy Spirit'. They thought that this would be sufficient for the ears of that period. Those who after them handed to us a complete doctrine concerning the Holy Spirit were the western bishops who by themselves assembled in a synod, as they were unable to come to the east on account of the persecution that the Arians inflicted on this region. And later, when divine grace put an end to the per-

---

538 Cf. Theodoret *Historia ecclesiastica* 5,10,2. Likewise, Leontius, *Aduersus fraudes Apollinaristarum* (Daley 2017, pp. 568–570). Cf. also Lietzmann 1904, p. 27.

539 Cf. Theodoret *Historia ecclesiastica* 5,10,5.

540 The relative clause quoted by Rufinus 'qui sicut uere deus, ita et uere homo fuit' is missing in Theodoret.

541 Cf. Reutter 2009, p. 437. Sieben 2014/2015, vol. I, p. 223: between 377 and 381.

542 Theodoret, *Historia ecclesiastica* 5,10,3.

543 Theodoret, *Historia ecclesiastica* 5,10,4.

544 Cf. above pp. 331–3.

secution, the eastern bishops gladly accepted the formula handed down by [the bishops of] that western synod, concurred in their decision, and, by subscribing to what they had said, showed their adhesion to them.

If one looks deeply into the matter, however, one will find that they derived their reason for the complementary addition that they made later in their teaching concerning the Holy Spirit from the blessed fathers who had assembled from the whole world in the first council held in the town of Nicaea.[545]

Theodore mentions an extension of the doctrine of the Holy Spirit. The 'complete doctrine' referenced was therefore obviously not a detailed synodal letter (or at any rate was not limited to that) but consisted in an expansion of the pneumatological section of N.

The western synod had met separately because no empire-wide assembly could be held due to the persecution by the 'Arians' in the east. It has been suggested on this evidence that this synod must have taken place in Rome before the end of the reign of Emperor Valens (378), who continued to harrass the Nicene bishops,[546] whereas the second (eastern) synod which Theodore mentions happened afterwards.[547]

In the same sermon Theodore then expends some energy (chapters 3–13) on demonstrating why Nicene Pneumatology was already laid out in nuce in the Holy Scripture, the Church's baptismal practice, and in N, and why, in principle, a more detailed pneumatological article would not have been necessary. Only then does he return to the later additions to N to explain them in more detail, stating, among other things:

It is with a sense of duty, therefore, that the doctors of the Church, who assembled from all parts of the world (οἰκουμένη) and who were the heirs of the first blessed fathers, proclaimed before all people the wish of their fathers and in accurate deliberations made manifest the truth of their faith and also interpreted what they had in mind. They wrote to us words which warn the children of faith and destroy the error of the heretics. As their fathers did in the profession of faith concerning the Son for the refutation of the ungodliness of Arius, so they did in their words concerning the Holy Spirit for the confutation of those who blasphemed against him.[548]

---

545 Theodore, *Homilia catechetica 9*, 1 (FaFo § 180b1). Here the relevant literature is quoted. In addition, cf. Witkamp 2018, pp. 10–18 on the basic information concerning the *Catechetical Homilies*. He thinks they originated in Antioch 'between the mid-380s and 392' (p. 13). However, Witkamp is not interested in the wording of the creed; cf. p. 10 n. 45.

546 Cf. above p. 322.

547 Cf. Bruns 1994, p. 203 n. 1; Gerber 2000, p. 128.

548 Theodore, *Homilia catechetica 9*, 14 (FaFo § 180b2).

Here, then, Theodore speaks of teachers of the Church having come together 'from all parts of the world' and, as it were, having spelled out the Pneumatology implicit in N. Adolf Martin Ritter, Luise Abramowski, and others have assumed that only the Council of Constantinople of 381 could have been meant, because of the ecumenicity claimed here. Both Ritter and Abramowski saw the synod held by the followers of Meletius in Antioch referenced in the eastern synod of chapter 1, but the council of 381 in that of chapter 14.[549] But this assumption suffers from the weakness that, if it were the case, a *new* assembly would have been introduced in chapter 14 – in passing, as it were – without in any way specifying a location or date, meaning that Theodore would therefore have had to assume prior knowledge of it among his (non-baptized) listeners. This actually contradicts the whole style of this homily. So if chapters 1 and 14 are about one and the same eastern synod, is it that of Constantinople, as Mingana tentatively suggested?[550] Of course, this cannot be completely ruled out, but the ecumenicity of Constantinople may not have been as famous at the time as chapter 14 claims.[551] Conversely, the Meletian synod was by no means inferior to that later synod in terms of 'ecumenicity', given the number of bishops attending.[552]

Furthermore, apart from a doctrinal letter, the most important result of the synod in Theodore's eyes was the following addition to the creed: 'and in *one* (ἓν) Holy Spirit'.[553] This insertion is, however, neither contained in N nor in C^2 nor does it occur in older western creeds. It is found for the first time in J (FaFo § 147), which is attested around the middle of the fourth century by Cyril of Jerusalem.[554] For this reason alone, Theodore cannot be referring to Constantinople.[555] Instead, it must be assumed that, for Theodore, ecumenicity resulted either from the fact

---

549 Cf. Ritter 1965, pp. 154 f., 201; Abramowski 1992, p. 496. Strangely, at a later point Abramowski calls the synod in ch. 16 once more that of the Meletians. Cf. also the criticism in Ritter 1993, p. 559. In addition, cf. above ch. 2.2.3.

550 Cf. Mingana 1932, p. 93 n. 1 (on ch. 1, considering the ascription to Antioch or Constantinople) and p. 100 n. 4 (on ch. 14; ascription to Constantinople).

551 Cf. Staats 1999, pp. 175 f.

552 Cf. below pp. 345 f. Likewise, Bruns 1994, vol. I, pp. 33–5 and 214 n. 15 compared with p. 203 and n.1. Reutter 2009, pp. 408 f. is undecided.

553 Theodore, *Homilia Catechetica 9*, 16 (FaFo § 180b2).

554 Cf. above ch. 5.5. The Latin translation of the creed of the eastern Synod of Serdica (343) in cod. Verona, Biblioteca Capitolare, LX (58; FaFo § 143b) also contains *in unum spiritum sanctum*, yet not the other witnesses to this text. Cf. also § 184f26 from the same codex (translation of C^2). The same in the Latin translation of N in Cyril of Alexandria, *Epistula 55* (§ 135d25). Abramowski 1992, pp. 497 f. assumes that the addition came from the Synod of Damasus. However, neither the Roman documents nor R offer any evidence for such an assumption.

555 Cf. Gerber 2000, pp. 146 f. and again Smith 2018, p. 31 and n. 150.

that the patriarch of Alexandria had been present at the Roman synod, in addition to the local patriarch, or from the fact that bishops of both west (Rome) and east (Antioch) had agreed to the additions that had been negotiated between them. In other words, chapter 14 refers to the *same* (separate) Synods of Rome and Antioch as chapter 1 does.

What is the 'formula' mentioned by Theodore (the *týpos* of the synodal letter preserved in Theodoret)? It is of course not simply N. R is also ruled out, because it had already been used as a creed earlier. However, I also consider it highly unlikely that Theodoret's remarks apply to the original version of the *Tomus Damasi* (N + anathema 1 concerning the Holy Spirit + detailed commentary on N with extended Pneumatology in anathemas 10–24), as some scholars have suggested.[556] It is true that 'there was a special emphasis on the doctrine about the Holy Spirit and the Nicene Creed was interpreted with an emphasis on the Holy Spirit' in the *Tomus Damasi*,[557] but in his own interpretation of the third article Theodore does not say a single word about the anathemas contained in the *Tomus*, although he considered the expansion to the creed made at the western and eastern councils, which he himself mentions, normative. Apart from that, none of the definitions and condemnations of Damasus in *Epistulae 1–4* were intended for catechesis.

But there is something else: after quoting Gal 1:9 the pope mentions, in the synodal letter that Theodoret has preserved, a major point of the *týpos*:

> For Christ, the Son of God, our Lord, by his own suffering, gave abundant salvation to the human race that he might free from all sin the whole human being (ὅλον τὸν ἄνθρωπον) entangled in sin.[558]

The phrase ὅλον τὸν ἄνθρωπον indicates that Christ saves the *whole* human being (and not, for instance, only the flesh). However, there is no mention of *homo totus* anywhere in the *Tomus Damasi*. In the synodal letter, however, Damasus refers to N to combat Apolinarianism, emphasizing Christ's suffering in this context. But this very passion is presented in greater detail in R, in N^{Ant}, and finally in C^1 and C^2 than it is in N, with N's simple παθόντα expounded as referring to crucifixion and burial. In other words, I still find Abramowski's thesis most plausible, according to which there was a 'Romano-Nicene Creed' which was largely identical with N^{Ant}, and that it is this creed in its final, i.e. Antiochene, recension that was preserved by

---

556 Cf. Reutter 2009, p. 409. Likewise, Bruns 1994, p. 203 n. 1; Gerber 2000, pp. 136–43. Cf. also above p. 334.
557 Reutter 2009, p. 409.
558 Theodoret, *Historia ecclesiastica* 5,10,4.

Theodore of Mopusestia.[559] The additions it included concerned (a) the full assumption of human nature (expressed by the insertion of the Mother of God, the crucifixion, and the burial) and (b) the third article.

Finally, there is another reference to the Roman Synod which has received too little attention in research so far in this context: the famous imperial edict *Cunctos populos* of 28 February 380. This edict, which I will discuss in a later chapter,[560] prescribes, as is well known, the trinitarian faith to the inhabitants of the empire as follows:

> We desire that all the nations which are governed by the moderate rule of Our Clemency shall abide by that religion which was handed over by the divine Peter the apostle to the Romans, as the religion which he introduced itself proclaims up to this day, and which is clearly followed by the Pontiff Damasus and by Peter, the bishop of Alexandria, a man of apostolic sanctity; that is, according to apostolic discipline and evangelical doctrine we should believe in the one godhead of the Father, the Son, and the Holy Spirit, as equal in majesty and as a pious Trinity (*secundum apostolicam disciplinam euangelicamque doctrinam patris et filii et spiritus sancti unam deitatem sub parili maiestate et sub pia trinitate credamus*).[561]

Sozomen writes that Theodosius had found out that in the west (extending as far as Macedonia) all churches were unanimous in their worship of the entire Trinity, but that the east was divided on this question. He therefore issued a law addressed to the inhabitants of the eastern capital in order to enforce his own (trinitarian) faith in the east without coercion.[562] This can probably only be explained by the fact that the Roman Synod of 377/378 had discussed this subject and that the result (in the form of a creed and a synodal letter) had been circulated in the eastern part of the empire. By contrast, it would not have been feasible to appeal to the bishop of the eastern capital, given that it was divided on religious issues. In other words, Theodosius' edict refers specifically to the Roman Synod at which – as we have seen – both Damasus and Peter had been present. Accordingly, it is quite conceivable that the final words quoted above derive from the synodal letter of this very synod. It is striking that the edict makes no mention of a unity of substance of the three persons of the Trinity. We will see in the next chapters that this is also missing in the 'Romano-Nicene Creed' (i.e. N^Ant).

---

559 Likewise, Bruns 1994, pp. 33 f. Typical 'Antiochene' traits include the reference to Col 1:15 ('first-born of all creation'). Similarly, Abramowski 1992, p. 498. Cf. also above p. 35. However, Abramowski's suggestion that the additions regarding the Holy Spirit were originally quoted in the introduction to the *Tomus Damasi* is less plausible; cf. Kinzig, *Glaubensbekenntnis*, 2021, p. 86.

560 Cf. below ch. 10.2.2.

561 *Codex Theodosianus* 16,1,2 (FaFo § 532a).

562 Cf. Sozomen, *Historia ecclesiastica* 7,4,4–5 (FaFo § 532b).

6.5.12 The Synod of the Meletians in Antioch (379)

As[563] I explained in the previous chapter the eastern council mentioned by Theodore in *Homilia catechetica 9*, 1 is probably not Constantinople 381 as has often been assumed in previous scholarship. In addition, it is unlikely that this council, which was not exactly Rome-friendly, would simply have adopted a western doctrinal letter or creed.[564] Furthermore, the creed Theodore mentions cannot be identical with C^2 because the pneumatological section he cites differs from C^2.[565] Nor does Theodore report anything about a (further) change of this section by the eastern synod, instead explicitly speaking of an 'adoption'.[566] Rather, he must be referring to the Synod of the Meletians in Antioch (379)[567] whose purpose it was to demonstrate 'who was in charge in Antioch and enjoyed the trust and recognition of the easterners'.[568]

Once again, only very scant information is available about this assembly too, though we do know it was convoked by Meletius after his return from exile. Gregory of Nyssa also took part – he was apparently still busy reconciling the adherents of Marcellus of Ancyra with the Nicenes.[569] We know from the synodal letter of the Synod of Constantinople of 382 that the assemblies of both Antioch and of Constantinople (381) published *Tomoi* in which their faith was confessed and specific heresies condemned.[570] In the so-called canon 5 of Constantinople 381 (which probably in fact belongs to the synod of the following year), we can see that the Antiochenes had 'confessed the one godhead of Father, Son, and Holy Spirit'.[571] In the collection of canons by Palladius of Amaseia (who lived at the time of the Council of Ephesus in 431), those who do not confess the 'consubstantial Trinity

---

563 This chapter is based on Kinzig, *Glaubensbekenntnis*, 2021, pp. 89–92.
564 Cf. Gerber 2000, p. 129.
565 Cf. above p. 341.
566 Cf. Bruns 1994, pp. 31 f. and 203 n. 1.
567 As regards this synod (which scholars have described in various ways) cf. Schwartz 1935 (1960), pp. 91–3; Ritter 1965, p. 76; Simonetti 1975, pp. 446–9; Pietri 1976, vol. I, pp. 844–9; De Halleux 1984(1990), pp. 180–6; Hanson 1988, pp. 802–4; Abramowski 1992; Pietri 1996(2010), p. 448; Staats 1999, pp. 175–9; Hausammann 2007, pp. 130–4; Karmann 2009, p. 458 and n. 19; Brennecke/ Stockhausen 2020, pp. 892 f., 895 f. On the dating cf. Gregory of Nyssa, *Vita Macrinae* 15: the council in which Gregory participated took place in the ninth month (or a little later) after the death of Basil of Caesarea. Basil died on 1 January 379; the council, therefore, took place in the early autumn of that year.
568 Gerber 2000, p. 130.
569 Cf. Gregory of Nyssa, *Epistula* 5,2; id., *Vita Macrinae* 15.
570 Cf. Theodoret, *Historia ecclesiastica* 5,9,13 (FaFo § 566a).
571 Council of Constantinople (381), canon 5 (FaFo § 566b).

according to the exposition of the tome of Antioch (τὴν ὁμοούσιον τριάδα κατὰ τὸν ἐν Ἀντιοχείᾳ ἐκτεθέντα τόμον)' are maligned as Pneumatomachians.[572]

Apart from this confession of the consubstantiality of the Spirit, the synod had agreed to a synodal letter from Rome and sent it back there, as can be seen from a note from the Roman archives, to be discussed below. The note states that the Antiochene synod had declared its 'unanimous faith' (*consona fide*) with the Romans and had agreed to the statement of faith by the signatures of all its participants. On this occasion, a creed had apparently also been sent from Rome to Antioch as part of the western tome, as we learn from the aforementioned *Ninth Catechetical Homily* of Theodore of Mopsuestia. According to Theodore, a more detailed doctrine of the Holy Spirit formed part of this 'formula'. Its teaching was then accepted by the eastern bishops after the persecution had ended. In this context, Theodore speaks of an addition that the fathers had made to their teaching on the Holy Spirit.[573]

Later he mentions that the doctors of the Church from all over the world had gathered to condemn the false doctrine concerning the Holy Spirit and to clarify the faith on this point. They had achieved this by adding the word 'one' to the Holy Spirit: 'and in *one* Holy Spirit'.[574] As I showed in the previous chapter Theodore did not refer to a separate assembly, for instance Constantinople 381, but rather to the combined western (Rome) and eastern (Antioch) synods.

Such a series of events is also suggested by the Roman note mentioned, which contains a list of signatures that probably stems from the Antiochene council and was sent back to Rome.[575] It survives as part five of a collection of Latin documents contained in cod. Verona, Biblioteca Capitolare, LX (58; Verona?, *c.* 700 or *s.* VIII *ex.*) which was edited by Schwartz. Its introduction states:

> Here ends this letter or exposition of the Roman Synod held under Pope Damasus. It was sent to the east, where, at a synod held at Antioch, the whole eastern Church unanimously expressed its faith and all who agreed in this way with the very faith set forth above individually confirmed [their consent] by their signatures.[576]

---

572 Cf. Palladius, *Kanonikon*, canon 18 (FaFo § 566b note).
573 Cf. Theodore, *Homilia catechetica 9*, 1 (FaFo § 180b1) and above pp. 339 f.
574 Theodore, *Homilia catechetica 9*, 16 (FaFo § 180b2).
575 Cf. Ritter 1965, p. 61; Peter L. Schmidt and Michaela Zelzer in Berger/Fontaine/Schmidt 2020, pp. 26 f. Reutter 2009, pp. 347–9 is more sceptical.
576 Schwartz 1936, p. 23 = Field 2004, p. 20 (ll. 114–7; *explicit* refers to what follows): 'Explicit haec epistula uel expositio synodi Romanae habitae sub Damaso papa et transmissa ad Orientem, in qua omnis Orientalis ecclesia facta synodo apud Antiochiam consona fide credentes et omnes ita consentientes eidem super expositae fidei singuli sua subscriptione confirmant.' Cf. already Schwartz 1926, pp. 42 f.

It is not necessary here to consider which of the preceding pieces *eidem super expositae fidei* references exactly, indeed whether it refers to *any* of the previous documents.[577] A total of 152 signatures are then mentioned, among which only the first six signatories, led by Meletius, are expressly named.

If one adds the presumed number of bishops assembled in Rome, as cited in the heading of the collection in the Veronensis LX (*Exemplum synodi habitae Romae ep<isco>por<um> XCIII*), to that of the bishops who had gathered in Antioch, one arrives at 245 bishops from west and east[578] – which could indeed be regarded as an ecumenical assembly in the sense that Theodore of Mopsuestia likely intended.

6.5.13 The text and theology of the 'Romano-Nicene Creed' (N^{Ant})

It[579] is easiest to understand what the revision of N in Rome and Antioch was about when we place it side by side with N^{Ant}. In this respect, it is important to note that two versions of this revision, N^{Ant1} and N^{Ant2}, are both reconstructions, derived from Theodore's *Catechetical Homilies* and from quotations by Eusebius of Dorylaeum and John Cassian respectively. N^{Ant3} is a creed contained in cod. Munich, Bayerische Staatsbibliothek, Syr. 4 (*olim* Or. 147), written in 1607, which was first edited by Caspari and later revised by Hort who used additional manuscripts. (Both recensions of N^{Ant3} can be found in FaFo § 208.) I quote Caspari's version in what follows. (There are slight differences in Hort's reconstruction.)

N (325) (FaFo § 135c)	Theodore of Mopsuestia (N^{Ant1}; 379–392) (FaFo § 180a)	Antioch (N^{Ant2}; *c.* 430)[580]	'Nestorian Creed' (N^{Ant3}) (FaFo § 208)
Πιστεύομεν εἰς ἕνα θεόν, πατέρα,	Πιστεύομεν εἰς ἕνα θεόν, πατέρα,	Πιστεύω εἰς ἕνα καὶ μόνον ἀληθινὸν θεόν, πατέρα,	Πιστεύομεν εἰς ἕνα θεόν

---

577 In principle, this could be a reference to either *Epistula 2*, frg. 2 (*Ea gratia*; FaFo § 439a) or to frg. 4 (*Non nobis quidquam*; FaFo § 439c) or to both (cf. Reutter 2009, pp. 344–9), but in that case the fragments could not be dated to 375/376. Cf. above pp. 334 f.

578 This presupposes, of course, that the title and the initial salutation refer to the Roman synodal letter in question. Cf. the reasons given in Reutter 2009, p. 318.

579 This chapter is based on Kinzig, *Glaubensbekenntnis*, 2021, pp. 33–7.

580 Eusebius of Dorylaeum, *Contestatio* (FaFo § 198) and John Cassian, *De incarnatione domini contra Nestorium* 6,3,2; 6,4,2; 6,9,1–2 (FaFo § 203).

(continued)

N (325) (FaFo § 135c)	Theodore of Mopsuestia (N[Ant1]; 379–392) (FaFo § 180a)	Antioch (N[Ant2]; c. 430)	'Nestorian Creed' (N[Ant3]) (FaFo § 208)
παντοκράτορα, πάντων ὁρατῶν τε καὶ ἀοράτων ποιητήν·	παντοκράτορα, πάντων ὁρατῶν τε καὶ ἀοράτων ποιητήν·	παντοκράτορα, πάντων ὁρατῶν τε καὶ ἀοράτων κτισμάτων ποιητήν [*or:* κτιστήν, *or:* δημιουργόν]·	παντοκράτορα, πάντων ὁρατῶν τε καὶ ἀοράτων ποιητήν·
καὶ εἰς ἕνα κύριον Ἰησοῦν Χριστόν,	καὶ εἰς ἕνα κύριον Ἰησοῦν Χριστόν,	καὶ εἰς τὸν κύριον [ἡμῶν] Ἰησοῦν Χριστόν,	καὶ εἰς ἕνα κύριον Ἰησοῦν Χριστόν,
τὸν υἱὸν τοῦ θεοῦ	τὸν υἱὸν τοῦ θεοῦ τὸν μονογενῆ, τὸν πρωτότοκον πάσης κτίσεως,	τὸν υἱὸν αὐτοῦ τὸν μονογενῆ, καὶ τὸν πρωτότοκον πάσης κτίσεως,	τὸν υἱὸν τοῦ θεοῦ μονογενῆ, τὸν πρωτότοκον πάσης κτίσεως,
γεννηθέντα ἐκ τοῦ πατρός, μονογενῆ, τουτέστιν ἐκ τῆς οὐσίας τοῦ πατρός,	τὸν ἐκ τοῦ πατρὸς γεννηθέντα	ἐξ αὐτοῦ γεννηθέντα	τὸν ἐκ τοῦ πατρὸς γεννηθέντα
	πρὸ πάντων τῶν αἰώνων καὶ οὐ ποιηθέντα,	πρὸ πάντων τῶν αἰώνων καὶ οὐ ποιηθέντα,	πρὸ πάντων τῶν αἰώνων καὶ οὐ ποιηθέντα,
θεὸν ἐκ θεοῦ, φῶς ἐκ φωτός, θεὸν ἀληθινὸν ἐκ θεοῦ ἀληθινοῦ, γεννηθέντα οὐ ποιηθέντα, ὁμοούσιον τῷ πατρί,	θεὸν ἀληθινὸν ἐκ θεοῦ ἀληθινοῦ, ὁμοούσιον τῷ πατρί,	θεὸν ἀληθινὸν ἐκ θεοῦ ἀληθινοῦ, ὁμοούσιον τῷ πατρί,	θεὸν ἀληθινὸν ἐκ θεοῦ ἀληθινοῦ, ὁμοούσιον τῷ πατρί,
δι' οὗ·	δι' οὗ οἱ αἰῶνες κατηρτίσθησαν	δι' οὗ οἱ αἰῶνες κατηρτίσθησαν	δι' οὗ οἱ αἰῶνες κατηρτίσθησαν
τὰ πάντα ἐγένετο τά τε ἐν τῷ οὐρανῷ καὶ τὰ ἐν τῇ γῇ, τὸν δι' ἡμᾶς τοὺς ἀνθρώπους καὶ διὰ τὴν ἡμετέραν σωτηρίαν κατελθόντα	καὶ τὰ πάντα ἐγένετο, τὸν δι' ἡμᾶς τοὺς ἀνθρώπους καὶ διὰ τὴν ἡμετέραν σωτηρίαν κατελθόντα ἐκ τῶν οὐρανῶν	καὶ τὰ πάντα ἐγένετο, τὸν δι' ἡμᾶς ἐλθόντα	καὶ τὰ πάντα ἐγένετο, τὸν δι' ἡμᾶς ἀνθρώπους καὶ διὰ τὴν ἡμετέραν σωτηρίαν κατελθόντα ἐκ τῶν οὐρανῶν

(continued)

N (325) (FaFo § 135c)	Theodore of Mopsuestia (N[Ant1]; 379–392) (FaFo § 180a)	Antioch (N[Ant2]; *c.* 430)	'Nestorian Creed' (N[Ant3]) (FaFo § 208)
καὶ σαρκωθέντα,	καὶ σαρκωθέντα		καὶ σαρκωθέντα ἐκ πνεύματος ἁγίου
ἐνανθρωπήσαντα,	καὶ ἐνανθρωπήσαντα,		καὶ ἄνθρωπον γενόμενον καὶ συλληφθέντα
	γεννηθέντα ἐκ Μαρίας τῆς παρθένου	καὶ γεννηθέντα ἐκ Μαρίας τῆς παρθένου	καὶ γεννηθέντα ἐκ Μαρίας τῆς παρθένου καὶ παθόντα
	καὶ σταυρωθέντα ἐπὶ Ποντίου Πιλάτου,	καὶ σταυρωθέντα ἐπὶ Ποντίου Πιλάτου	καὶ σταυρωθέντα ἐπὶ Ποντίου Πιλάτου
παθόντα	ταφέντα	καὶ ταφέντα	καὶ ταφέντα
καὶ ἀναστάντα τῇ τρίτῃ ἡμέρᾳ,	καὶ ἀναστάντα τῇ τρίτῃ ἡμέρᾳ κατὰ τὰς γραφὰς	καὶ ἀναστάντα τῇ τρίτῃ ἡμέρᾳ κατὰ τὰς γραφὰς	καὶ ἀναστάντα τῇ τρίτῃ ἡμέρᾳ κατὰ τὰς γραφάς,
ἀνελθόντα εἰς τοὺς οὐρανούς,	καὶ ἀνελθόντα εἰς τοὺς οὐρανοὺς καὶ καθεζόμενον ἐν δεξιᾷ τοῦ θεοῦ	καὶ ἀνελθόντα εἰς τοὺς οὐρανούς	ἀνελθόντα εἰς τοὺς οὐρανούς, καθεζόμενον ἐκ δεξιῶν τοῦ πατρὸς
ἐρχόμενον κρῖναι ζῶντας καὶ νεκρούς·	καὶ πάλιν ἐρχόμενον κρῖναι ζῶντας καὶ νεκρούς·	καὶ πάλιν ἐρχόμενον κρῖναι ζῶντας καὶ νεκρούς. < . . . >[581]	καὶ πάλιν ἐρχόμενον κρῖναι νεκροὺς καὶ ζῶντας·
καὶ εἰς τὸ ἅγιον πνεῦμα. [anathemas][582]	καὶ εἰς ἓν πνεῦμα ἅγιον, πνεῦμα τῆς ἀληθείας,		καὶ εἰς ἓν πνεῦμα ἅγιον, τὸ πνεῦμα τῆς ἀληθείας,

---

581 'I believe in the one and only true God, the Father Almighty, Creator of all visible and invisible creatures;

and in [our] Lord Jesus Christ, his only-begotten Son, first-born of all creation; born from him before all ages and not made; true God from true God; consubstantial with the Father; through whom also the ages were framed and all things came into being; who for us came and was born from the virgin Mary; was crucified under Pontius Pilate and was buried; on the third day rose again according to the Scriptures; ascended into the heavens; and will come again to judge the living and the dead < . . . >.'

582 English translation above pp. 246–8.

(continued)

N (325) (FaFo § 135c)	Theodore of Mopsuestia (N^Ant1; 379–392) (FaFo § 180a)	Antioch (N^Ant2; c. 430)	'Nestorian Creed' (N^Ant3) (FaFo § 208)
	τὸ ἐκ τοῦ πατρὸς ἐκπορευόμενον, πνεῦμα ζωοποιόν, μίαν ἐκκλησίαν καθολικήν, ἄφεσιν ἁμαρτιῶν, ἀνάστασιν σαρκὸς καὶ ζωὴν αἰώνιον.[583]		τὸ ἐκ τοῦ πατρὸς ἐκπορευόμενον, πνεῦμα ζωοποιόν, καὶ εἰς μίαν, ἁγίαν καὶ ἀποστολικὴν ἐκκλησίαν καθολικήν. Ὁμολογοῦμεν ἓν βάπτισμα εἰς ἄφεσιν ἁμαρτιῶν, ἀνάστασιν σαρκὸς καὶ ζωὴν αἰώνιον.[584]

---

583 'We believe in one God, the Father Almighty, Maker of all things both visible and invisible;
and in one Lord Jesus Christ, the only-begotten Son of God, the first-born of all creation [cf. Col 1:15], who was begotten from the Father before all ages and not made, true God from true God, consubstantial with the Father, through whom the ages were fashioned [cf. Heb 11:3] and all things came into being [cf. Jn 1:3; 1Cor 8:6]; who because of us humans and because of our salvation descended from the heavens, became incarnate and became human, being born from the virgin Mary; was crucified under Pontius Pilate; was buried and on the third day rose again according to the Scriptures; ascended into the heavens; sits at the right hand of God; and will come again "to judge the living and the dead" [2Tim 4:1; 1Pet 4:5];
and in one Holy Spirit, the Spirit of truth [cf. Jn 14:17; 15:26; 16:13; 1Jn 4:6], who proceeds from the Father, a life-giving Spirit; one catholic Church, the remission of sins, the resurrection of the flesh, and eternal life.'

584 'We believe in one God Almighty, Maker of all things both visible and invisible;
and in one Lord Jesus Christ, the only-begotten Son of God, the first-born of all creation, begotten from the Father before all ages and not made, true God from true God, consubstantial with the Father, through whom the ages were fashioned and all things came into being; who for us humans and for our salvation descended from the heavens, became incarnate from the Holy Spirit, became human, was conceived and born from the virgin Mary, suffered, was crucified under Pontius Pilate, was buried, on the third day rose again according to the Scriptures, ascended into the heavens, sits at the right hand of the Father, and will come again to judge the dead and the living;
and in one Holy Spirit, the Spirit of truth, who proceeds from the Father, the life-giving Spirit; and in one holy and apostolic catholic Church.
We confess one baptism for the remission of sins, the resurrection of the flesh, and eternal life.'

A detailed philological comparison which I have undertaken elsewhere shows that all versions of N^{Ant} are closely related to each other.[585] It is, therefore, legitimate to speak of one recension of N^{Ant}. It is this recension which was produced in Rome and adopted in Antioch that subsequently spread in the Dyophysite churches of the east.[586] N clearly served as its basis, but R and J also seem to have been used. This recension is likely to have been based on the following considerations:

In the first section the text of N remained largely unaltered. However, in the christological section there were major changes:

(1) (Τὸν) μονογενῆ was cited earlier (with R and J) in order to achieve an alignment with biblical (Johannine) language.

(2) The explanatory apposition τουτέστιν ἐκ τῆς οὐσίας τοῦ πατρός was dropped because it disturbed the context and had in fact become superfluous in the light of the other corrections and the state of theological discussion.

(3) In addition, the omission of the explanation τουτέστιν ἐκ τῆς οὐσίας τοῦ πατρός and the inclusion of the quotation from Col 1:15 may have been intended to accommodate the Homoiousians. If one looks through the other mentions of the syntagma 'first-born of all creation' in the creeds of the fourth century, it becomes clear that we are dealing with a specifically Antiochene tradition, which continued to be invoked especially in Homoiousian circles.[587] Its inclusion here could be explained by the fact that at some point attempts were made in Antioch to find a 'soft' Neo-Nicene compromise that would be acceptable to as many theologians as possible, including those from the Homoiousian camp.

(4) The word sequence τὸν ἐκ τοῦ πατρὸς γεννηθέντα (with J) instead of γεννηθέντα ἐκ τοῦ πατρός may again be a matter of style.

(5) The addition of οὐ ποιηθέντα, now moved forward, made it possible to delete γεννηθέντα οὐ ποιηθέντα which was mentioned in N further down. The addition of πρὸ πάντων τῶν αἰώνων (cf. J) also emphasized the pre-existence and uncreated nature of the Son and served primarily to ward off the Eunomians. The phrase may, therefore, have been added in Antioch. However, the emphasis on the (unique) generation and the eternity of the Son may also have

---

585 Cf. Kinzig, *Glaubensbekenntnis*, 2021, pp. 19–33.

586 Cf. below ch. 9.1.3.

587 Cf. Eus (FaFo § 134a); Council of Antioch (341), *Expositio fidei/Formula altera* (§ 141b[2]); Eunomius, *Confessio fidei* 3 (§ 163c2); *Constitutiones apostolorum* 7,41,5 (§ 182c). In addition, Sozomen, *Historia ecclesiastica* 6,12,4 and Ritter 1965, pp. 71, 75.

been a particular Roman concern as is evident from Damasus, who explicitly mentions both items in *Non nobis quidquam*.[588]

(6) Θεὸν ἐκ θεοῦ was (with R and J) probably omitted for stylistic reasons in order to erase the duplication with the following θεὸν ἀληθινὸν ἐκ θεοῦ ἀληθινοῦ.

(7) This deletion then had consequences for φῶς ἐκ φωτός: the phrase was also omitted (in line with R and J), because otherwise 'light from light' would have preceded 'true God from true God' which was ontologically 'stronger'. (This alteration was reversed in C².)

(8) The omission of γεννηθέντα οὐ ποιηθέντα resulted from moving οὐ ποιηθέντα forward (see above).

(9) The addition (δι' οὗ) οἱ αἰῶνες κατηρτίσθησαν alluded, on the one hand, to Heb 11:3 and emphasized once more the pre-existence of the Son, who was involved in the 'establishment' of the aeons (that is, of time itself) and whose existence therefore preceded the aeons (against the Eunomians).[589] Otherwise, it appears only in the Fourth Creed of Sirmium (359, so-called Dated Creed; FaFo § 157), written by Mark of Arethusa in Syria, which, however, has a different overall structure. It is unclear whether there is a direct connection here, in that a local Antiochene tradition was incorporated in both cases. Alternatively, we may be dealing once more with a western addition.[590]

(10) Conversely, since the entire universe had been designated by the phrase δι' οὗ οἱ αἰῶνες κατηρτίσθησαν καὶ τὰ πάντα ἐγένετο, one could dispense with the redundant addition of τά τε ἐν τῷ οὐρανῷ καὶ τὰ ἐν τῇ γῇ (in line with R and J).

(11) The addition ἐκ τῶν οὐρανῶν served to clarify κατελθόντα.

(12) The addition γεννηθέντα ἐκ Μαρίας τῆς παρθένου corresponded to Roman tradition. However, the mention of the Spirit (as in R) would perhaps have created misunderstandings and was therefore omitted here. At the same time, the addition served to ward off any docetism (as was attributed to the Apolinarians[591]) and also to oppose an interpretation as later advocated by

---

588 Cf. Damasus, *Epistula* 2, frg. 4 (*Non nobis quidquam*; FaFo § 439c): '[. . .] ita etiam plenitudinem dei verbi non prolatiui sed nati neque in patre remanentis, ut non sit, sed ex aeterno in aeternum subsistentis perfectum, id est, integrum transgressorem assumpsisse et saluasse confidimus.' / 'In like manner we are also convinced that the fullness of the Word of God (not uttered but born; not remaining in the Father, as if he did not exist, but subsisting from eternity [and] into eternity) assumed and saved the perfect, that is, the whole sinner.'

589 However, this rejection of Anhomoioan theology was rather cautiously worded. On the discussion about preexistence in this context cf. Vaggione 2000, pp. 141–3.

590 Cf., e.g., Hilary of Poitiers, *De trinitate* 7,6 (FaFo § 151c3): 'Credendus est filius, per quem saecula facta sunt [. . .].' / 'You ought to believe in a Son through whom the worlds were made [. . .].'

591 Cf. below p. 369.

Nestorius, according to which the incarnation in N was to be understood as an 'indwelling in man' (ἐνοίκησις εἰς ἄνθρωπον).[592] Finally, the emphasis on the virgin birth was probably also due to the growing devotion to Mary.

(13) The addition of the crucifixion under Pontius Pilate, which was also only attested in the west, again served anti-docetic purposes and, moreover, firmly established the passion as a fixed historical event. It most clearly shows the Roman influence.[593]

(14) By contrast, the participle παθόντα may have been seen as implying patripassianism.[594] In any case, it was now superfluous and could be deleted (as do R and possibly J). (The earlier position in N^Ant3 is probably secondary.)

(15) The addition (καὶ) ταφέντα again came from R or, perhaps, J and served once more to reject docetic ideas of whatever provenance.

(16) The addition κατὰ τὰς γραφάς, which is attested nowhere else, is not fully explicable. Possibly, it was yet again intended to be antidocetic. In any case, the resurrection was thereby authenticated by recourse to 1Cor 15:4.

(17) The 'sitting at the right hand' (only attested in N^Ant1 and N^Ant3) may again represent Roman tradition but is also attested for Jerusalem. Its inclusion strengthened the biblical connection (especially Col 3:1) and served to emphasize the permanent distinction between Father and Son and (against the Arians) their equal rank (against Marcellus of Ancyra).[595]

As regards the pneumatological section it is helpful also to take into account Theodore's explanations:

(1) The addition of the oneness of the Holy Spirit has been discussed above;[596] it may have come from J (*Homilia 9*, 16–18; *10*, 1–3).

(2) According to Jn 15:26 etc. the bishops added 'Spirit of truth' (πνεῦμα τῆς ἀληθείας) (*Homilia 10*, 3–7).

(3) The addition 'who proceeds from the Father' (τὸ ἐκ τοῦ πατρὸς ἐκπορευόμενον; *Homilia 10*, 7–10) also came from Jn 15:26, without, however, expressing strict consubstantiality.

(4) The addition 'life-giving Spirit' (πνεῦμα ζωοποιόν) alludes to Jn 6:63, 1Cor 15:45, and 2Cor 3:6 (*Homilia 10*, 11–12).[597]

---

592 Cf., e.g., Cyril of Alexandria, *Contra Nestorium* 1,7,3 (ACO I 1/6, p. 27, ll. 15–17).
593 Cf. Staats 1990, pp. 211 f.; Bruns 1994, pp. 29 f.; Staats 1999, pp. 168 f.
594 I owe this idea to Maria Munkholt Christensen.
595 Cf. Markschies 1993(2000), esp. pp. 47–59; Staats 1999, pp. 251 f.
596 Cf. above p. 341.
597 Cf. also De Halleux 1979(1990), pp. 325 f. (discussing C²), who thinks that this was directed against Pneumatomachians.

These are the additions to the third article that were presumably made in Rome (with, perhaps, the exception of no. 1) to clarify the divinity of the Spirit and which clearly served to strengthen its scriptural basis (cf. *Homilia 10*, 13).

However, further additions follow, which Theodore took from the same recension of N, but which are no longer explained by him. These are the fruits of baptism (which itself was presumably not mentioned in N^(Ant)),[598] all of which are also attested in R and J (*Homilia 10*, 14):

(1) faith '(in) the one (holy and apostolic) catholic Church' ([καὶ εἰς] μίαν [ἁγίαν καὶ ἀποστολικὴν] ἐκκλησίαν καθολικήν; *Homilia 10*, 15–19);

(2) '(for/in) the forgiveness of sins' ([εἰς] ἄφεσιν ἁμαρτιῶν; *Homilia 10*, 20);

(3) '(for/in) the resurrection of the flesh and eternal life' ([εἰς] ἀνάστασιν σαρκὸς καὶ ζωὴν αἰώνιον; *Homilia 10*, 21).

There are some uncertainties on minor points (bracketed here), but on the whole the text is clear. The elements Church – forgiveness of sins – resurrection of the flesh – eternal life even correspond exactly to R. The single change in the Church, i.e. its catholicity, may also go back to western influence, for it is also found in the version of R quoted by Leo (FaFo § 255g). However, like the oneness of the Church, it is also attested in J and elsewhere.[599]

It is thus clear that the revised version of N, as Antioch adopted it from Rome (and modified it in certain respects), was guided by the following principles:

(1) N was made more uniform in terms of style.

(2) The biblical references were strengthened (one can almost speak of a Johannine redaction), while unbiblical phrases were deleted.

(3) The consubstantiality of the Son was not phrased too 'strongly' in the sense of a complete equality of the two divine persons in order to build bridges with the Homoiousians (and possibly also 'mild' Homoians).

(4) Conversely, an Anhomoian Christology was rejected.

(5) All in all, the alignment with R built a bridge between east and west.

(6) The additions in the section on the Holy Spirit served to emphasize his divinity. In doing so, the council fathers dispensed with the unbiblical *homooúsios* and instead resorted to passages from the Gospel of John. The oneness of the

---

598 Cf. Gerber 2000, pp. 118 f. The mention of baptism in N^(Ant3) is probably secondary.

599 The oneness and catholicity of the Church are named in conjunction in Arius' and Euzoius' *Epistula ad Constantinum imperatorem* (Opitz 1934/1935, *Urkunde 30*; FaFo § 131c) 3; Alexander of Alexandria, *Epistula ad Alexandrum Thessalonicensem* (*Byzantinum*; Opitz 1934/1935, *Urkunde 14*; § 132) 53; Council of Antioch (325), *Epistula synodica* (Opitz 1934/1935, *Urkunde 18*; § 133) 12; Epiphanius, *Ancoratus* 119,11 (§ 175). Oneness: Apolinarius, *Fides secundum partem* 32 (§ 164a2); *Didascalia CCCXVIII patrum Nicaenorum* (§ 176[9]); catholicity: *Martyrium Calixti* 3 (FaFo § 90); Dêr Balyzeh Papyrus (§ 146); *Constitutiones apostolorum* 7,41,7 (§ 182c).

Spirit (like the inclusion of Col 1:15, the begetting from the Father before all time, and the inclusion of Heb 11:2 in the second section) is not a western but eastern heritage (namely, perhaps from Jerusalem), so that one may assume that the two versions of the creed were not completely identical, meaning that sent from Rome to Antioch and the revision that then was sent back from there, with the signatures of the Meletians.

(7) In addition, there were further explanations which Theodore obviously did not consider to be statements regarding the Spirit, but which were separated from the doctrinal part of the confession in *Homily 10*, 14.[600] Theodore tried to play down these additions, which apparently caused him difficulties, by detaching them from the (in the narrower sense) theological statements and discussing them in the context of baptism instead. We also find most of them in J.

In summary, N was expanded in the years 377–379 in Rome and Antioch in such a way that specifically 'Roman' propositions concerning the birth from the Virgin Mary and the crucifixion under Pontius Pilate were added, which were directed against Apolinarius and his followers. The statements about the Church and (depending on how one assesses the role of J) the forgiveness of sins, the resurrection of the flesh, and eternal life were probably also of Roman origin. In contrast, the allusion to Col 1:15, the generation from the Father before all ages (which was possibly lifted from J and expanded), and the emphasis on the Son's involvement in the creation of the aeons (allusion to Heb 11:3) were Antiochene. We may see concessions to Homoian or Homoiousian groups in the complicated ecclesiastical landscape of Antioch in for instance the inclusion of Col 1:15.[601] Likewise, the third section was supplemented in Antioch with statements that could be helpful in the controversy with the Pneumatomachians. However, there may still have been some room for compromise because the consubstantiality of the Spirit was not explicitly stated.

---

[600] Cf. the caesura in Theodore, *Homilia catechetica 10*, 14: 'This is the reason why our Lord caused baptism to follow the teaching so that baptism should be the completion of the teaching' (tr. Mingana 1932, p. 111; altered).
[601] Cf. Staats 1999, p. 173.

7 The Council of Constantinople (381) and its Creeds

7.1 The council's origin and history

The later so-called Second Ecumenical Council, the Council of Constantinople (381) was both a result and the expression of what modern scholarship called 'Neo-Nicene' theology.[1] The victory of the Neo-Nicene way of describing the mystery of the Trinity was ultimately due to two factors coming together: for one, the direction indicated by N was taken up and developed further by Church leaders in the eastern half of the empire, who had considerable political influence. In addition, the emperor adopted the stance set out by these theologians.

Oddly, the confusing situation in Antioch was the starting point for this process. The governance of its church was in complete disarray, with at times up to four bishops competing with each other as a result of complicated local schisms. Athanasius tried to intervene in 362, proposing a compromise in the aforementioned synodal letter (*Tomus ad Antiochenos*) by suggesting a clear distinction between *ousía* and *hypóstasis*.[2] The term *hypóstasis* was to be applied to the individual persons of the Trinity, which, strictly speaking, Nicaea had excluded in its anathemas and which had also been avoided in the confession of faith as worded by the western Synod of Serdica (343).[3] (Athanasius denied that the western Church had ever adopted such a confession.) *Homooúsios*, however, was an appropriate designation for the relationship between Father and Son. Moreover, the Spirit was now also to be described as 'indivisible' from the essence of Father and Son.

In addition, the most important protector of Homoiansm had left the stage when Constantius II died in 361. Now the moment had come for a counterattack by those who championed N in one way or another (which also included 'soft' Homoians). It was one of the Nicene bishops of Antioch, Meletius (*sedit* 360–381), who successfully brought together this initially relatively diffuse group. He recognized that Athanasius' explanations offered the chance for a compromise between those who grappled in their different ways with the problem of describing the relations between the persons of the Trinity. They did so while also avoiding

---

1 For what follows cf. Ritter 2011, pp. 201–12.
2 Cf. above p. 328.
3 Cf. Council of Serdica (343, east), *Professio fidei ab episcopis occidentalibus promulgata* (FaFo § 144a), 3: 'This we have received and have been taught; we hold this catholic and apostolic tradition, faith, and confession: that the *hypóstasis* (which the Greeks call *ousía*) of the Father, the Son, and the Holy Spirit is one.'

https://doi.org/10.1515/9783110318531-007

both a purely modalist ('Sabellian') view or the theology of Marcellus of Ancyra (which was seen as a kind of 'economic' modalism) and an Anhomoian (Neo-Arian) view in which Son and Spirit were relegated to the status of creatures.

Athanasius did not live to see the outcome of the controversy (he died in 373). But his cause found prominent supporters, albeit with some delay, namely the most important bishop of the west, Damasus of Rome, and the bishop of Caesarea in Cappadocia, Basil. Basil argued in his work *On the Holy Spirit* (*De spiritu sancto*, 374/375) that the doctrine of the divinity of the Holy Spirit was not an innovation, but in line with Scripture and the tradition of the fathers. In other writings he also adopted the differentiation between the Godhead's 'one substance' (μία οὐσία) and its 'three manifestations' (τρεῖς ὑποστάσεις), which Athanasius had introduced into the debate. Basil was supported in this theological work by his friend Gregory of Nazianzus (d. 390) as well as his own younger brother Gregory of Nyssa (d. *c.* 396). The theology of these so-called 'three Cappadocian Fathers' (sometimes Amphilochius of Iconium (d. before 403) is added as a fourth) is often referred to in research as 'Neo-Nicene theology', which on the one hand is intended to record the conscious link to Nicaea, and on the other hand to make clear that the work of the Cappadocians, introducing new conceptual differentiations, went beyond the mere reiteration of Nicaea.

However, the question of the consubstantiality of the Spirit led to divisions, especially among the Homoiousians who were not unsympathetic to Nicaea. This group, headed by Basil of Ancyra, had emerged at a synod in that city in 358.[4] Some of its members, who were labelled 'Spirit-fighters' (Pneumatomachians) by their opponents, rejected the consubstantiality of the Spirit, whereas its majority gradually moved towards a Neo-Nicene position.

At the same time, the political climate for the Nicene party continued to brighten: Emperor Theodosius I, ruler of the Eastern Empire since 379, was an ardent supporter of the Nicene party, determined to prescribe belief in the one Godhead of Father, Son, and Holy Spirit 'in like majesty and holy trinity' (*sub parili maiestate et sub pia trinitate*) as obligatory for all his subjects, which he did soon after coming to power in his famous edict *Cunctos populos* of 28 February 380.[5] Those who were not prepared to subscribe to this belief were threatened with both divine and secular punishments, which, however, remained unspecified.[6] In practice, Theodosius proceeded quite pragmatically, with his determination to strive for a synodal solution to the faith disputes evident in his convening

---

4 Cf. above ch. 6.5.7.
5 Cf. also above p. 343 and below p. 475–7.
6 Cf. the discussion in Riedlberger 2020, pp. 396–402.

a new empire-wide council for this purpose, which took place in Constantinople from May until July 381 (Second Ecumenical Council).

Although[7] it is not possible to be completely certain in view of the scanty evidence, it is most probable that the creed which modern scholars (not very elegantly) call the Nicene-Constantinopolitan Creed (C^2) was formulated in connection with the Council of 381. This follows from the fact that it was cited as the 'Creed of the 150 (fathers)' (the alleged number of those who assembled in Constantinople) since Chalcedon and was nowhere attributed to any other place of origin. Furthermore, this is also the conclusion from the synod's letter to Theodosius I, in which its dogmatic[8] agenda was succinctly summarized by stating that the fathers had 'ratified the faith of the Nicene fathers and condemned the heresies directed against it (τήν τε τῶν πατέρων πίστιν τῶν ἐν Νικαίᾳ κυρώσαντες καὶ τὰς κατ' αὐτῆς ἐπιφανείσας αἱρέσεις ἀναθεματίσαντες)'.[9] Finally, the same results of this Synod of 381 are found summed up in the tome of another synod, held in the same place the following year, according to which the Synod of Antioch of 379 and that of Constantinople of 381 had 'confessed the faith at greater length' in their respective tomes and had 'produced a written anathema against the heresies which had recently sprung up' (ἐν οἷς πλατύτερον τὴν πίστιν ὡμολογήσαμεν καὶ τῶν ἔναγχος καινοτομηθεισῶν αἱρέσεων ἀναθεματισμὸν ἔγγραφον πεποιήκαμεν).[10] The anathemas survive in canon 1 of Constantinople (381).[11] The 'more detailed' confession of faith could refer to a confession longer than N. But would this document, technically speaking, be a creed, and was it part of the tome of Antioch or the tome of Constantinople or both? And, finally, is this the same confession that Nestorius preserved as Creed of Constantinople (C^1) or is it rather the creed that has gone down in Church history as that of 'the 150 fathers' (of Constantinople) (C^2)?

In my opinion, the following picture emerges taking into account the few sources available as well as previous research on these questions: Theodosius convened the council of 381, among other things,[12] in order to clarify the question of faith through a 'reaffirmation' of Nicaea. The dogmatic issues had still not been settled, not least because the so-called 'Macedonians', a group of Pneumatomachian Homoiousians named after Macedonius of Constantinople (*sedit* 342–360), had not yet

---

7 The following sections are based on Kinzig, *Glaubensbekenntnis*, 2021, pp. 93–101.
8 There were other items which concerned matters of church order (canons 2–3).
9 Council of Constantinople (381), *Epistula synodalis ad Theodosium imperatorem* (FaFo § 565b).
10 Council of Constantinople (382), *Epistula synodalis* (FaFo § 566a[13]).
11 Cf. Council of Constantinople (381), canon 1 (FaFo § 565c).
12 On the other items on the agenda cf. Ritter 1990, p. 519.

been won over to the (Neo-)Nicene cause.[13] Among them was a relatively large group from the Hellespont that fell under the jurisdiction of the now Nicaea-oriented patriarchate of Constantinople. They were specifically invited by the emperor, who evidently took a lively part in the negotiations,[14] to persuade them to accept the *pístis* of Nicaea. On the side of the Neo-Nicenes, the synod was attended by Timothy I of Alexandria, Cyril of Jerusalem, Meletius of Antioch, Acholius of Thessalonica, Diodorus of Tarsus, Acacius of Beroea, Pelagius of Laodicea, Eulogius of Edessa, Isidore of Cyrus, Gelasius of Caesarea, and others, some of whom (like Timothy, Dorotheus of Oxyrhynchus, and Acholius) probably arrived late.[15] The Macedonian group included Eleusius of Cyzicus, the leader of the Pneumatomachian wing of the Homoiousians,[16] Marcian of Lampsacus, and thirty-four other bishops.

The exact dogmatic agenda of the negotiations is not entirely clear: Socrates and Sozomen intimate that the debates revolved around the consubstantiality of the Son.[17] In the process, according to Sozomen, the Macedonians formally withdrew the consent to N they had formerly given to Liberius of Rome. This refers to the embassy a synod at Lampsacus had sent to the capital in 364, 365, or 366, during the course of which leading Macedonians (Eustathius of Sebaste, Theophilus of Castabala, Silvanus of Tarsus) had indeed consented to a creed that was almost identical with N, at the request of the Roman bishop.[18] Adolf Martin Ritter and scholars that followed him, however, have suspected that this was not the only matter under negotiation in Constantinople. For

> the readiness of the Emperor, and certainly of the leading representatives of the council, to come to an understanding could not possibly have gone so far as to do the Pneumatomachians around Eleusius the great favour of passing over the main point of contention during the last years, namely the question of the nature and intra-trinitarian rank of the Holy Spirit.

---

13 As regards the following cf. Socrates, *Historia ecclesiastica* 5,8,1–10 (FaFo § 184b); Sozomen, *Historia ecclesiastica* 7,7,1–5 (§ 184c); and Ritter 1965, pp. 68–85.
14 Ritter 1965, p. 231 n. 2 is more sceptical concerning the emperor's participation. However, cf. Gregory of Nazianzus, *Carmen de uita sua* 1709, which Ritter 1965, pp. 260 f. sees as referring only to the negotiations with the Macedonians. Cf. also below p. 362.
15 On the extant lists of participants cf. CPG 8601 and the surveys in Ritter 1965, p. 38 n. 4; Ritter 1990, p. 522. As regards the 'Egyptians and Macedonians' who arrived late (or were invited at a later stage) cf. Gregory of Nazianzus, *Carmen de uita sua* 1800 and Ritter 1965, pp. 97 f.
16 Cf. Ritter 1965, pp. 73–6.
17 Cf. Socrates, *Historia ecclesiastica* 5,8,1–10 (FaFo § 184b); Sozomen, *Historia ecclesiastica* 7,7,1–5 (§ 184c).
18 Cf. Eustathius of Sebaste et al., *Epistula ad Liberium papam* (FaFo § 170).

Ritter continues: 'So there must have been more at stake in the negotiations with the Pneumatomachian embassy than Socrates and Sozomen were able to report.'[19]

This is, of course, not impossible, but we do not know for sure whether there was any room at all for discussions on the pneumatological questions, after the debates on the consubstantiality of the Son had failed. The bishops of the anti-Nicene party around Eleusius continued to reject *homooúsios* and left the synod.[20]

Since the Macedonians also sent letters to their followers all over the world, according to both Church historians, warning against agreeing with N,[21] and Socrates (and Sozomen?) possibly drew part of their information from these very letters,[22] it is striking to say the least that they apparently did not contain a single word about negotiations on the divinity of the Spirit. Furthermore, it is not quite understandable why, after the negotiations with the Pneumatomachians had collapsed, C^2 would not have simply been formally approved and solemnly proclaimed, when the way was now clear for recognizing the consubstantiality of the Spirit. Instead it is more likely that – perhaps as a result of the controversy with Apolinarianism – Christology was negotiated *first* and that the discussion moved on to the pneumatological questions only *later* (i.e. only after the departure of the Macedonians), questions which, as we will see below, then led to renewed debates among the council participants about the wording of the pneumatological section.

On the one hand, our sources state unanimously that N was 'confirmed' in Constantinople.[23] On the other hand, it does not seem that this confirmation was a simple ratification of N or N^{Ant}. Rather, as the synodal letter of 382 attests, a 'more detailed' confession of faith was developed, which seems to have been contained both in the tome of the council of Antioch and in that of Constantinople in 381.[24] This means, however, that both these confessions of faith must have been closely interrelated, although they were presumably not identical (otherwise Constantinople would only have 'confirmed' the confession of faith as elaborated at Antioch). In other words, the tome of 382 suggests, on closer inspection, that the creed of

---

19 Ritter 1965, p. 83. Similarly, for example, also Kelly 1972, pp. 326–9; Staats 1999, pp. 37 f.

20 According to Socrates, *Historia ecclesiastica* 5,8,10 (FaFo § 184b) and Sozomen, *Historia ecclesiastica* 7,7,5 (§ 184c) this happened at the beginning of the negotiations. Similarly, Hauschild 1994, p. 448; Staats 1999, p. 36. For a different view cf. Ritter 1965, p. 79 and n. 1.

21 Pseudo-Athanasius (Didymus the Blind?), *De sancta trinitate dialogus* 3, 1 (FaFo § 183) also suggests that the Macedonians rejected additions to N. Cf. also Ritter 1965, pp. 152 f.; Smith 2018, p. 27.

22 Cf. Socrates, *Historia ecclesiastica* 5,8,10 (FaFo § 184b); Sozomen, *Historia ecclesiastica* 7,7,5 (§ 184c).

23 Cf. Socrates, *Historia ecclesiastica* 5,10,14 (FaFo § 184b); Sozomen, *Historia ecclesiastica* 7,9,1 (§ 184c); Theodoret, *Historia ecclesiastica* 5,8,10 (§ 184d).

24 Note the plural of the relative pronoun: ἐν οἷς (FaFo § 566a[13]). Cf. above p. 357.

Antioch had not been adopted without changes in Constantinople in 381, but subjected to further revision, and that this *pístis* had been more 'detailed' than N.

One can only speculate about the reason for this: N^Ant had, after all, been established at a synod under Meletius, who was later also to preside the Council of Constantinople. After his premature death during this latter council, however, the assembly's new president, Gregory of Nazianzus, had expressed his sympathy for a solution according to which Meletius' episcopal throne in Antioch should remain unoccupied until his Nicene rival Paulinus had also died; yet he did not succeed with this proposal – the succession of Meletius remained unresolved, with the Meletians favouring the presbyter Flavian.[25] As a result, N^Ant was probably also drawn into these negotiations and was now branded by Meletius' opponents as being too accommodating towards the anti-Nicene party – for example, because of its inclusion of the quotation from Col 1:15.[26] One of these opponents may have been Timothy I of Alexandria (this patriarchate was to be the guardian of the 'pure' N in the fifth century[27]), about whom we, unfortunately, know very little.

The 'confirmation' of N by the council can also hardly mean C^2, which – as we will see in the next chapter – was a heavily revised and extended version of N and therefore later rightly called the (new) 'Creed of the 150 fathers'.[28] However, a much-discussed[29] passage in the autobiographical poem of Gregory of Nazianzus makes clear that the 'confirmed' N cannot simply have been the authentic creed of Nicaea either, but that something *was* actually changed in the text itself:

> I saw the sweet and beauteous spring of our ancient faith, which gathered in unity the venerable nature of the Trinity, which had once been conceived of in Nicaea, being wretchedly befouled with briny infusions poured into it by double-minded men sharing the beliefs favoured by the power [*or:* [His] Majesty], people who claim to be mediators – had they really been mediators and not blatantly [adherents] of the contrary cause, that would have been welcome![30]

---

25 Cf. Ritter 1965, pp. 62–8; Staats 1999, p. 43.

26 Cf. above p. 350.

27 Cf. below p. 399.

28 Cf. below pp. 382 f.

29 Cf. the various interpretations of these verses and the entire passage of Gregory of Nazianzus, *Carmen de uita sua* 1703–1759 in Ritter 1965, pp. 258–64; Jungck 1974, pp. 220 f., 223; Hauschild 1977; Ritter 1979(1993), pp. 171–173; Staats 1999, p. 36; Behr 2004, vol. II, pp. 374, 379.

30 *Carmen de uita sua* 1703–11 (FaFo § 184a2; Jungck 1974, p. 136):

> [. . .] τὴν γλυκεῖαν καὶ καλήν
> πηγὴν παλαιᾶς πίστεως, ἣ τριάδος
> εἰς ἓν συνῆγε τὴν σεβάσμιον φύσιν,
> ἧς ἦν ποθ' ἡ Νικαία φροντιστήριον,

At first it remains unclear in this fairly cryptic passage whether μέσοι ὄντες (literally 'those in the middle') in v. 1710 refers to an active mediating role assumed by certain bishops, possibly initiated by the emperor, or simply refers to their (in Gregory's view) fickleness and opportunism. Even if this must remain open, it cannot really be doubted that the 'briny infusions' actually refer to textual changes in the creed. It is also just as clear that what Gregory terms the 'sweet and beauteous spring' must be N and not N^Ant, since he still quoted N as the confession that was authoritative for him several years after Constantinople. It was necessary, he said, to 'add the words that had been missing to those about the Holy Spirit', since 'at that time [i.e. in Nicaea] this question had not yet been raised', such that the Father, Son, and Holy Spirit were confessed as one Godhead and thus the divinity of the Spirit was fully acknowledged.[31] This can hardly refer to the already quite broadly developed Pneumatology in N^Ant and certainly not to C², but must apply to N.

On the basis of all this evidence the conclusion is inescapable that there were *two* versions of C in Constantinople: namely, a version that was 'confirmed' as N (but according to Gregory contained changes: C¹) and a version that was later quoted as the 'Creed of the 150' whose third section had been expanded further. The version that was 'confirmed' as N survives in a recently discovered homily of Nestorius, who always speaks of his creed as that of Nicaea.[32] It may also be this creed of which Nicephorus Callistus (d. after 1328) says that Gregory of Nyssa supplemented it in Constantinople with regard to the Spirit's 'equality of honour and praise' (ἰσοτιμία and ὁμοδοξία) with Father and Son, in his *Church History* in a note based on an unknown source.[33] We do not know which addition he exactly refers to, but it is noteworthy that Nicephorus does not speak of a new creed either. Unfortunately, it is impossible to decide whether this information is correct.

As we saw above, it was assumed in earlier scholarship that the 'Creed of the 150' (C²) had been designed to negotiate with the Macedonians (Pneumatomachians).[34] This thesis was plausible based on the sources available at the time. In the meantime, however, the picture has changed considerably as a result of the dis-

---

ταύτην ἑώρων ἁλμυραῖς ἐπιρροαῖς
τῶν ἀμφιδόξων ἀθλίως θολουμένην,
οἳ ταῦτα δοξάζουσιν, οἷς χαίρει κράτος,
μέσοι μὲν ὄντες – ἀσμενιστὸν δ' εἰ μέσοι,
καὶ μὴ προδήλως κλήσεως ἐναντίας,
[. . .].

31 Gregory of Nazianzus, *Epistula 102*, 2 (FaFo § 184a1).
32 Edition, translation, and commentary in Kinzig, 'Zwei neuentdeckte Predigten', 2020(2022).
33 Cf. Nicephorus, *Historia ecclesiastica 12*, 13 (PG 146, col. 784A–B).
34 Cf. above pp. 358 f.

covery of C^1. Comparing the two creeds (as we will do in the next chapter), it is immediately clear that C^2 contains no additional phrases that are theologically significant with regard to the pneumatological question. In any case, had the situation been as assumed earlier, why did the Macedonians warn against the acceptance of N after the council's conclusion? It would certainly be difficult to imagine that C^2 could simply have been referred to without further explanation, as that would presuppose that N was named but C^2 was meant which is difficult for methodological reasons.[35]

So was C^1, which might well have been called 'N', the sole basis of the negotiations with the Macedonians? We do not know. But if one takes the sources seriously according to which these negotiations took place at the beginning of the council, the following scenario would be conceivable: first of all, the emperor (the 'power' in Gregory's *Carmen de uita sua* 1709) obviously exerted considerable pressure on the council participants, which led to negotiations with the Macedonians about drafts that seemed to Gregory to be theologically too ambiguous to exclude (malicious) misinterpretations. The details of these debates, which perhaps took place in a committee still under Gregory's presidency of the council, are unknown to us. Apparently, at the end, i.e. after the failure of the negotiations and Gregory's withdrawal, two drafts were on the table (under the chairmanship of Nectarius[36]), one of which, C^2, could not be agreed upon. The main reason is probably that it had moved too far away from N to pass as a simple supplement to it. Furthermore, C^2 may have been considered unsuitable for catechesis. Perhaps there were also discussions about the extent to which elements of J or also from the western tradition should be included in the third section. In this context, the confessional 'hierarchy' in this section[37] may also have been controversial. Be that as it may: C^2 was set aside.[38]

Such a scenario also solves the mystery of why N was – at times – named but C actually intended as the referent: in none of these (few[39]) cases is the pneumatological section quoted (as it is found in C^2) – reference was primarily made to the christological article, which was obviously quoted from the 'confirmed' version C^1. As will be shown in the next chapter the *Vorlage* for both versions was presumably N^{Ant}, which had been aligned with N and J in some formulations.

---

35 Cf. above ch. 2.4.
36 Cf. Sozomen, *Historia ecclesiastica* 7,9,1 (FaFo § 184c).
37 Cf. below p. 373.
38 However, on its inclusion in collections of canonical law cf. below pp. 386 f., 416, 468 f.
39 Cf. below pp. 376 and n. 106; 381 f.

It is quite doubtful whether minutes were taken in Constantinople as we know was the practice since Ephesus 431.[40] Rather, its outcomes were probably captured in four documents: the synodal letter to the emperor, the 'confirmed' but in actual fact extended text of N (= C[1]), the four authentic so-called[41] canons (including canon 1 with the confirmation of N [= C[1]] and the condemnation of heresies),[42] and the subscription list. (This is not the place to address the question as to whether the creed, canons, and list combined formed the tome of the council or whether there was another separate doctrinal letter which has been lost, as is widely assumed. However, assuming an additional epistle to have existed does not seem compelling to me). Furthermore, there was another creed (C[2]), which was expanded especially in its third section but which had probably not been generally accepted. Instead, 'N' was to apply unchanged, i.e. a confession that incorporated 'western' and Antiochene additions (N[Ant]), which had been partially reversed in accordance with N and J,[43] as well as given an expanded third section. It is this confession (C[1]) which was later quoted by Nestorius[44] and (in Chalcedon) by Diogenes of Cyzicus.[45] In this sense N had been both 'confirmed' *and* modified.

We will have to investigate below how it came about that in the end C[2] rather than C[1] came to be regarded as the 'Creed of the 150 fathers'.[46]

7.2 The text and theology of the creeds of Constantinople

Before[47] we do so, however, we will first look at the revisions that were made to N[Ant] in Constantinople. The following table places N, J, N[Ant1], C[1], and C[2] side by side. The other versions of N[Ant] (i.e. N[Ant2] and N[Ant3]) are found above on pp. 346–9.

---

40 Cf. below p. 386 n. 42.
41 Originally, the canons were not separate from each other; cf. Ohme 1998, pp. 523 f.
42 Cf. Socrates, *Historia ecclesiastica* 5,8 (FaFo § 184b; in part); Sozomen, *Historia ecclesiastica* 7,7–9 (§ 184c, in part); Theodoret, *Historia ecclesiastica* 5,8,10 (§ 184d); Council of Constantinople (381), canon 1 (FaFo § 565c). On the inauthenticity of canons 5–7 cf. Ritter 1965, p. 123 n. 1.
43 Cf. below p. 375.
44 Cf. below p. 376 and n. 106.
45 Cf. below p. 381.
46 Cf. below ch. 8.1.
47 This chapter is based on Kinzig, *Glaubensbekenntnis*, 2021, pp. 37–52.

N (325) (FaFo § 135c)[48]	J (FaFo § 147)[49]	Theodore of Mopsuestia (N^Ant1; 379–392) (FaFo § 180a)	c^1 (cf. Kinzig, 'Zwei neuentdeckte Predigten', 2020(2022), p. 43; furthermore, FaFo § 197a–g)[50]	c^2 (according to the Council of Chalcedon (451), *Actio* II(III) 14 (FaFo § 184e1))
Πιστεύομεν εἰς ἕνα θεόν,	Πιστεύομεν εἰς ἕνα θεόν,	Πιστεύομεν εἰς ἕνα θεόν,	Πιστεύω εἰς ἕνα [καὶ μόνον] θεὸν [ἀληθινόν],	Πιστεύομεν εἰς ἕνα θεόν,
πατέρα, παντοκράτορα,	πατέρα, παντοκράτορα, ποιητὴν οὐρανοῦ καὶ γῆς	πατέρα, παντοκράτορα,	πατέρα, παντοκράτορα, κτίστην	πατέρα, παντοκράτορα, ποιητὴν οὐρανοῦ καὶ γῆς
πάντων ὁρατῶν τε καὶ ἀοράτων ποιητήν·	ὁρατῶν τε πάντων καὶ ἀοράτων·	πάντων ὁρατῶν τε καὶ ἀοράτων ποιητήν·	πάντων ὁρατῶν τε καὶ ἀοράτων ποιημάτων.	ὁρατῶν τε πάντων καὶ ἀοράτων·
καὶ εἰς ἕνα κύριον Ἰησοῦν Χριστόν,	καὶ εἰς ἕνα κύριον Ἰησοῦν Χριστόν,	καὶ εἰς ἕνα κύριον Ἰησοῦν Χριστόν,	Πιστεύω εἰς ἕνα κύριον Ἰησοῦν Χριστόν,	καὶ εἰς ἕνα κύριον Ἰησοῦν Χριστόν,
τὸν υἱὸν τοῦ θεοῦ	τὸν υἱὸν τοῦ θεοῦ τὸν μονογενῆ,	τὸν υἱὸν τοῦ θεοῦ τὸν μονογενῆ, τὸν πρωτότοκον πάσης κτίσεως,	τὸν υἱὸν τοῦ θεοῦ τὸν μονογενῆ,	τὸν υἱὸν τοῦ θεοῦ τὸν μονογενῆ,
γεννηθέντα ἐκ τοῦ πατρός,	τὸν ἐκ τοῦ πατρὸς γεννηθέντα θεὸν ἀληθινὸν	τὸν ἐκ τοῦ πατρὸς γεννηθέντα	τὸν ἐκ τοῦ πατρὸς γεννηθέντα	τὸν ἐκ τοῦ πατρὸς γεννηθέντα
μονογενῆ, τουτέστιν ἐκ τῆς οὐσίας τοῦ πατρός,				
	πρὸ πάντων τῶν αἰώνων,	πρὸ πάντων τῶν αἰώνων καὶ οὐ ποιηθέντα,	πρὸ πάντων τῶν αἰώνων,	πρὸ πάντων τῶν αἰώνων,
θεὸν ἐκ θεοῦ, φῶς ἐκ φωτός, θεὸν ἀληθινὸν ἐκ θεοῦ ἀληθινοῦ, γεννηθέντα οὐ ποιηθέντα, ὁμοούσιον τῷ πατρί, δι᾽ οὗ	δι᾽ οὗ	θεὸν ἀληθινὸν ἐκ θεοῦ ἀληθινοῦ, ὁμοούσιον τῷ πατρί, δι᾽ οὗ	θεὸν ἀληθινὸν ἐκ θεοῦ ἀληθινοῦ, γεννηθέντα οὐ ποιηθέντα, ὁμοούσιον τῷ πατρί,	φῶς ἐκ φωτός, θεὸν ἀληθινὸν ἐκ θεοῦ ἀληθινοῦ, γεννηθέντα οὐ ποιηθέντα, ὁμοούσιον τῷ πατρί, δι᾽ οὗ

---

48 Cf. above ch. 6.4.
49 Cf. above ch. 5.5.
50 On the difference between versions cf. Kinzig, 'Zwei neuentdeckte Predigten', 2020(2022), pp. 43–52.

(continued)

N (325) (FaFo § 135c)	J (FaFo § 147)	Theodore of Mopsuestia (N^Ant1; 379–392) (FaFo § 180a)	C^1 (cf. Kinzig, 'Zwei neuentdeckte Predigten', 2020(2022), p. 43; furthermore, FaFo § 197a–g)	C^2 (according to the Council of Chalcedon (451), Actio II(III) 14 (FaFo § 184e1))
		οἱ αἰῶνες κατηρτίσθησαν		
τὰ πάντα ἐγένετο	τὰ πάντα ἐγένετο,	καὶ τὰ πάντα ἐγένετο,		τὰ πάντα ἐγένετο,
τά τε ἐν τῷ οὐρανῷ καὶ τὰ ἐν τῇ γῇ,				
τὸν δι᾽ ἡμᾶς τοὺς ἀνθρώπους καὶ διὰ τὴν ἡμετέραν σωτηρίαν κατελθόντα		τὸν δι᾽ ἡμᾶς τοὺς ἀνθρώπους καὶ διὰ τὴν ἡμετέραν σωτηρίαν κατελθόντα ἐκ τῶν οὐρανῶν	κατελθόντα	τὸν δι᾽ ἡμᾶς τοὺς ἀνθρώπους καὶ διὰ τὴν ἡμετέραν σωτηρίαν κατελθόντα ἐκ τῶν οὐρανῶν
καὶ σαρκωθέντα,	[τὸν σαρκωθέντα	καὶ σαρκωθέντα	καὶ σαρκωθέντα ἐκ πνεύματος ἁγίου καὶ Μαρίας τῆς παρθένου	καὶ σαρκωθέντα ἐκ πνεύματος ἁγίου καὶ Μαρίας τῆς παρθένου
ἐνανθρωπήσαντα,	καὶ] ἐνανθρωπήσαντα,	καὶ ἐνανθρωπήσαντα, γεννηθέντα ἐκ Μαρίας τῆς παρθένου	καὶ ἐνανθρωπήσαντα	καὶ ἐνανθρωπήσαντα
	[τὸν σταυρωθέντα	καὶ σταυρωθέντα ἐπὶ Ποντίου Πιλάτου,	καὶ σταυρωθέντα	σταυρωθέντα τε ὑπὲρ ἡμῶν ἐπὶ Ποντίου Πιλάτου
παθόντα				καὶ παθόντα
	καὶ ταφέντα	Ταφέντα	καὶ ταφέντα	καὶ ταφέντα
καὶ ἀναστάντα τῇ τρίτῃ ἡμέρᾳ,	καὶ] ἀναστάντα [ἐκ νεκρῶν] τῇ τρίτῃ ἡμέρᾳ	καὶ ἀναστάντα τῇ τρίτῃ ἡμέρᾳ	καὶ ἀναστάντα τῇ τρίτῃ ἡμέρᾳ	καὶ ἀναστάντα τῇ τρίτῃ ἡμέρᾳ
		κατὰ τὰς γραφὰς		κατὰ τὰς γραφὰς
ἀνελθόντα εἰς τοὺς οὐρανούς,	καὶ ἀνελθόντα εἰς τοὺς οὐρανοὺς καὶ καθίσαντα ἐκ δεξιῶν τοῦ πατρὸς	καὶ ἀνελθόντα εἰς τοὺς οὐρανοὺς καὶ καθεζόμενον ἐν δεξιᾷ τοῦ θεοῦ	καὶ ἀνελθόντα εἰς τοὺς οὐρανοὺς	καὶ ἀνελθόντα εἰς τοὺς οὐρανοὺς καὶ καθεζόμενον ἐν δεξιᾷ τοῦ πατρὸς
ἐρχόμενον	καὶ ἐρχόμενον ἐν δόξῃ	καὶ πάλιν ἐρχόμενον	καὶ πάλιν ἐρχόμενον	καὶ πάλιν ἐρχόμενον μετὰ δόξης
κρῖναι ζῶντας καὶ νεκρούς·	κρῖναι ζῶντας καὶ νεκρούς,	κρῖναι ζῶντας καὶ νεκρούς·	κρῖναι ζῶντας καὶ νεκρούς.	κρῖναι ζῶντας καὶ νεκρούς,

(continued)

N (325) (FaFo § 135c)	J (FaFo § 147)	Theodore of Mopsuestia (N^Ant1; 379–392) (FaFo § 180a)	c¹ (cf. Kinzig, 'Zwei neuentdeckte Predigten', 2020(2022), p. 43; furthermore, FaFo § 197a–g)	c² (according to the Council of Chalcedon (451), *Actio* II(III) 14 (FaFo § 184e1))
	οὗ τῆς βασιλείας οὐκ ἔσται τέλος·			οὗ τῆς βασιλείας οὐκ ἔσται τέλος·
καὶ εἰς τὸ ἅγιον πνεῦμα.	καὶ εἰς ἓν ἅγιον πνεῦμα, τὸν παράκλητον,	καὶ εἰς ἓν πνεῦμα ἅγιον,	Πιστεύω καὶ εἰς τὸ πνεῦμα τὸ ἅγιον,	καὶ εἰς τὸ πνεῦμα τὸ ἅγιον,
[anathemas][51]		πνεῦμα τῆς ἀληθείας,		
			τὸ κύριον καὶ ζωοποιόν,	τὸ κύριον καὶ ζωοποιόν,
		τὸ ἐκ τοῦ πατρὸς ἐκπορευόμενον, πνεῦμα ζωοποιόν,	τὸ ἐκ τοῦ πατρὸς ἐκπορευόμενον, τὸ σὺν πατρὶ καὶ υἱῷ συμβασιλεῦον καὶ συμπροσκυνούμενον καὶ συνδοξαζόμενον,	τὸ ἐκ τοῦ πατρὸς ἐκπορευόμενον, τὸ σὺν πατρὶ καὶ υἱῷ συμπροσκυνούμενον καὶ συνδοξαζόμενον,
	τὸ λαλῆσαν ἐν τοῖς προφήταις·		τὸ λαλῆσαν διὰ τῶν προφητῶν.	τὸ λαλῆσαν διὰ τῶν προφητῶν·
		μίαν ἐκκλησίαν καθολικήν,	Πιστεύω εἰς μίαν καθολικὴν καὶ ἀποστολικὴν ἐκκλησίαν.[52]	εἰς μίαν, ἁγίαν, καθολικὴν καὶ ἀποστολικὴν ἐκκλησίαν.
				Ὁμολογοῦμεν

---

51 English translation above pp. 246–8.

52 'I believe in the one [and only] [true] God, the Father Almighty, Creator of all creatures visible and invisible.

I believe in one Lord Jesus Christ, the only-begotten Son of God, begotten from the Father before all ages, true God from true God, begotten, not made, consubstantial with the Father; who descended; became flesh from the Holy Spirit and the virgin Mary; became human; was crucified and was buried; on the third day rose again; ascended into the heavens; and will come again to judge the living and dead.

I also believe in the Holy Spirit, the Lord and life-giver, who proceeds from the Father, who is jointly ruling, worshipped, and glorified with the Father and the Son, who spoke through the prophets.

I believe in one catholic and apostolic Church.'

(continued)

N (325) (FaFo § 135c)	J (FaFo § 147)	Theodore of Mopsuestia (N^Ant1; 379–392) (FaFo § 180a)	c¹ (cf. Kinzig, 'Zwei neuentdeckte Predigten', 2020(2022), p. 43; furthermore, FaFo § 197a–g)	c² (according to the Council of Chalcedon (451), *Actio* II(III) 14 (FaFo § 184e1))
	καὶ εἰς ἓν βάπτισμα μετανοίας εἰς ἄφεσιν ἁμαρτιῶν· καὶ εἰς μίαν, ἁγίαν καθολικήν ἐκκλησίαν·	ἄφεσιν ἁμαρτιῶν,		ἓν βάπτισμα εἰς ἄφεσιν ἁμαρτιῶν.
	καὶ εἰς σαρκὸς ἀνάστασιν·	ἀνάστασιν σαρκὸς		Προσδοκῶμεν ἀνάστασιν νεκρῶν
	καὶ εἰς ζωὴν αἰώνιον.[53]	καὶ ζωὴν αἰώνιον.[54]		καὶ ζωὴν τοῦ μέλλοντος αἰῶνος. Ἀμήν.[55]

I will first turn to C². Since Theodore, as explained, is not commenting on C² but on an older version of N in use in Antioch (namely the one agreed with Rome),[56] and since C² is closely linked to N^Ant in literary terms[57] and is presumably youn-

---

53 English translation above pp. 202 f.

54 English translation above p. 349 n. 583.

55 'We believe in one God, the Father Almighty, Maker of heaven and earth, of all things visible and invisible;

and in one Lord Jesus Christ, the only-begotten Son of God, begotten from the Father before all ages, Light from Light, true God from true God, begotten, not made, consubstantial with the Father; through whom all things came into being; who because of us humans and because of our salvation descended from the heavens; became flesh from the Holy Spirit and the virgin Mary; became human; was crucified for us under Pontius Pilate, suffered, and was buried; on the third day rose again according to the Scriptures; ascended into the heavens; sits at the right hand of the Father; and will come again with glory to judge the living and dead; of whose kingdom there will be no end;

and in the Holy Spirit, the Lord and life-giver, who proceeds from the Father, who is jointly worshipped and glorified with the Father and the Son, who spoke through the prophets;

in one holy catholic and apostolic Church.

We confess one baptism for the remission of sins.

We look forward to the resurrection of the dead and the life of the world to come. Amen.'

56 Cf. above ch. 6.5.12.

57 Cf. the detailed analysis in Kinzig, *Glaubensbekenntnis*, 2021, pp. 19–33.

ger, C² itself is probably a revision of N^Ant. In this revision, N and the creed of Cyril of Jerusalem (J) were also taken into account. (Cyril was also one of the participants in the Council of Constantinople).[58]

First section

(1) The rearrangement of ποιητήν leads to a smoother flow of words.

(2) The addition of οὐρανοῦ καὶ γῆς, which is also found in J,[59] further expands the reference to Col 1:16[60] (ὁρατῶν τε καὶ ἀοράτων; cf. also Gen 1:1; Acts 4:24; 14:15; Rev 14:7).

(3) Πάντων was transposed, thus achieving agreement with J.

Second section

(1) The omission of τὸν πρωτότοκον πάσης κτίσεως led to agreement with N. It may be that the quotation of Col 1:15 had been felt to be too strong a concession to the Homoiousians or Homoians.

(2) The reinsertion of φῶς ἐκ φωτός not only strengthened the reference to N, but at the same time also built a bridge to the non-Nicene confessional tradition.[61]

(3) Conversely, the reinsertion of γεννηθέντα οὐ ποιηθέντα, a phrase which is also found in N, drew a red line for the Anhomoians, signalling clearer opposition to their views than N^Ant had done.

(4) In the process, the now superfluous reference to the creation of the aeons was also excised again.

(5) The changes concerning the incarnation are striking. The authors of C² may have wished to reduce the inelegant triple designation of the incarnation in N^Ant (σαρκωθέντα – ἐνανθρωπήσαντα – γεννηθέντα). Thus, the Virgin was moved for-

---

58 Cf. also Gerber 2000, pp. 153–5. On Cyril's participation cf. Socrates, *Historia ecclesiastica* 5,8,3 (FaFo § 184b); Sozomen, *Historia ecclesiastica* 7,7,3 (§ 184c).

59 Cf. also Council of Antioch, *Epistula synodica* (325; Opitz 1934/1935, *Urkunde 18*), 8 (FaFo § 133); Acacius of Caesarea, *Expositio fidei* (FaFo § 158a[4]).

60 [. . .] ὅτι ἐν αὐτῷ ἐκτίσθη τὰ πάντα ἐν τοῖς οὐρανοῖς καὶ ἐπὶ τῆς γῆς, τὰ ὁρατὰ καὶ τὰ ἀόρατα, [. . .]. / '[. . .] for in him all things in the heavens and on earth were created, things visible and invisible, [. . .].'

61 Cf. Eus (FaFo § 134a); Council of Antioch (341), *Expositio fidei/Formula quarta* (§ 141d); Council of Serdica (343, east), *Fides synodi* (§ 143a2 and c); *Ecthesis macrostichos* (§ 145); Council of Sirmium (351), *Fidei confessio prima* (§ 148); Council of Sirmium (357), *Fidei confessio altera* (§ 154). On this formula cf. also Staats 1999, pp. 227, 231–4.

ward to the Son's becoming *flesh* (σαρκωθέντα). Furthermore, the Holy Spirit was added – one would like to attribute this to direct Roman influence, but this was minimal at the Constantinopolitan Synod.[62] Attributing the incarnation to both the Spirit and the Virgin also occurs elsewhere in the credal tradition of the fourth century.[63] However, this combination usually referred to Christ's *birth*, not his *incarnation*.[64] The moving forward of the Virgin and the addition of the Spirit to the incarnation have always been understood in the tradition as directed against Apolinarianism.[65] Ritter and Kelly have vehemently denied this interpretation,[66] However, I have shown elsewhere that Apolinarius and his followers were charged with advocating the idea that the incarnate Christ had been generated *before* he had been born from the virgin in such a way that the Logos had assumed the eternal flesh (without a human soul). In addition, they were accused of championing a double consubstantiality of Christ (with the divine Logos and with the flesh).[67] Both views could be understood as if the Apolinarians advocated docetism.[68] In addition, Athanasius accused his (Apolinarian?) opponents of introducing a divine quaternity.[69] The question as to whether or not Apolinarius and his followers advocated such ideas would require a detailed investigation of Apolinarius and his 'school'. It suffices here to say that the Apolinarians were accused of holding such views and that, therefore, his opponents sought to mitigate them by additions to N/N^{Ant}. It is probable that in this case, too, a phrase was chosen that was as broad as possible and thus acceptable to both Neo-Nicenes and (mild) Apolinarians such as Timothy of Berytus, a participant in the council,[70] and Vitalis, bishop of a schismatic congregation in Antioch,[71] while, at the same time, aiming at the greatest possible theological precision: the Spirit mentioned in Lk 1:35 is, on the one hand, linked to Christ's

---

62 Cf. Ritter 1965, p. 39 and n. 3.

63 Cf. TA^G (FaFo § 89c); Council of Niké (359), *Confessio fidei* (§ 159a[4]); Council of Constantinople (359/360), *Confessio fidei* (§ 160[3]); Epiphanius, *Ancoratus* 119,5 (§ 175). In addition, Ritter 1965, p. 194 n. 2.

64 Cf., however, Melito, *De pascha* 784 (FaFo § 107): ὁ ἐπὶ παρθένῳ σαρκωθείς / 'who became flesh upon the Virgin'. Council of Antioch (325), *Epistula synodica* (FaFo § 133[11]): καὶ ἐν σαρκὶ ἐκ τῆς θεοτόκου Μαρίας τεχθείς / 'was also born in flesh from Mary the Theotokos'.

65 Cf. Kelly 1972, p. 337 referring to Santer 1971; Grillmeier 1975, pp. 330 f.; Hübner 1989, pp. 209–29; Staats 1999, pp. 55, 109, 176, 239, 242.

66 Cf. Ritter 1965, pp. 192–195; Kelly 1972, pp. 332–7. In addition, Behr 2004, vol. II, p. 378.

67 Cf. Kinzig, *Glaubensbekenntnis*, 2021, pp. 39–45.

68 Cf. Apolinarius, *Ad Iouianum* 3 (FaFo § 164b). On the charge of docetism cf., e.g., Grillmeier 1975, pp. 330 f.; Andrist 2005, pp. 71 f.

69 Cf. Athanasius, *Epistula ad Epictetum* 2. Cf. especially Grelier 2011.

70 Apparently he was one of the signatories of the decrees of Constantinople. Cf. Lietzmann 1904, pp. 31, 153 f.; Raven 1923, p. 145.

71 On him cf. Mühlenberg 1969, pp. 45–63 and above p. 332 and n. 491.

(historical) *flesh*, which is named after the descent, thus ensuring the factuality of the incarnation in the sense of a material 'reification'. On the other hand, he is also connected with Christ's becoming *human* (καὶ ἐνανθρωπήσαντα), which means that in relation to Christ's humanity the incarnation is not reductive ('only the flesh') but involves the assumption of the *entire* human being.

This suggestion that Christ's becoming flesh and his becoming human must be considered one and the same is also confirmed by a look at the synodal letter of the Synod of Constantinople of 382. It does, in fact, make this connection explicit: the 'economy of the flesh' is understood in the sense of the perfect incarnation (that is, involving both soul and *noûs*).[72]

(6) The addition ὑπὲρ ἡμῶν in relation to the crucifixion is striking, strengthening the idea of redemption by recourse to Scripture (Rom 5:8; 8:32; 1Thess 5:10, etc.). It is also attested in the Antiochene tradition.[73]

(7) The sequence crucifixion – passion is probably the result of a conflation of καὶ σταυρωθέντα ἐπὶ Ποντίου Πιλάτου in N[Ant] and παθόντα in N.[74]

(8) The addition of the coming 'in glory' (μετὰ δόξης) is already found in J (ἐν δόξῃ).

(9) The addition οὗ τῆς βασιλείας οὐκ ἔσται τέλος after Lk 1:33 is commonly regarded as directed against Marcellus.[75] The phrase is also found in J. As regards Antioch, this expectation is also attested in the *Constitutiones apostolorum*.[76]

Third section

(1) Compared to N[Ant] (and J) C[2] lacks the oneness of the Spirit expressed by the addition of ἕν. For Ritter this was one of the reasons why he did not want to accept Gerber's thesis that N[Ant] was the *Vorlage* for C[2]. According to him, it was inexplicable why the (undisputed) oneness of the Spirit had been deleted.[77] It seems

---

72 Cf. Council of Constantinople, *Epistula synodalis* (FaFo § 566a[12]): 'We also preserve unperverted the doctrine of the incarnation of the Lord (τὸν τῆς ἐνανθρωπήσεως δὲ τοῦ κυρίου λόγον), affirming the tradition that the dispensation of the flesh was neither soulless nor mindless nor imperfect (οὔτε ἄψυχον οὔτε ἄνουν ἢ ἀτελῆ), and knowing full well that God the Word was both perfect before the ages, and became perfect man in the last days for our salvation.'

73 Cf. also (Pseudo-)Ignatius of Antioch, *Epistula ad Smyrnaeos* (middle and long recension) 1,2 (FaFo § 98e1 and e2); Council of Antioch (341), *Expositio fidei/Formula altera* (§ 141b); *Constitutiones apostolorum* 7,41,5 (§ 182c). In addition, Cyprian, *De mortalitate* 21 (§ 122c); Pseudo-Athanasius, *Expositio fidei* 1 (§ 149); Apolinarius, *Ad Iouianum* 2 (§ 164b).

74 Cf. also Gerber 2000, p. 153.

75 Cf., e.g., Molland 1970; Kelly 1972, pp. 338 f.; Behr 2004, vol. II, p. 378.

76 Cf. *Constitutiones apostolorum* 7,41,6 (FaFo § 182c).

77 Cf. above p. 37.

that the agreement between N^Ant and J on this point is indeed no coincidence.[78] But if one takes a closer look at the interpretation of Cyril as well as that of Theodore, it becomes clear that neither of them knew why the explicit 'oneness' had been added here. Cyril thought that it was a matter of warding off the Marcionites' idea that a different spirit spoke in the Old Testament than it did in the New.[79] But this was by now hardly a burning issue anymore. Theodore, however, explained the added 'one' with reference both to the one divine nature and to the oneness of Father and Son, hinting at the debate with the Pneumatomachians.[80] However, unless the third section in J and N^Ant was simply aligned with the first and the second, one might instead suppose that καὶ εἰς ἕν πνεῦμα ἅγιον, πνεῦμα τῆς ἀληθείας must be read together. There is *one* Holy Spirit, and *this* is the Spirit of *truth* (cf. Jn 16:13). At the same time, there exists also a 'spirit of error' (τὸ πνεῦμα τῆς πλάνης; 1Jn 4:6), but this is not the *Holy* Spirit. The Spirit of truth confesses 'that Jesus Christ has come in the flesh', whereas the spirit of the antichrist does not (1Jn 4:2 f.). We do not know what the context was that meant this issue may have played a role in Antioch, whereas it was obviously no longer ventilated in Constantinople. In Constantinople, however, the definite article τό was added.[81] Possibly, it was thought in the eastern capital that this article sufficed to describe the oneness of the Holy Spirit. Thus τό in the third section stood in for ἕνα in the two preceding sections. In those earlier sections ἕνα, which emphasizes his oneness even more strongly, had been inserted in allusion to 1Cor 8:6, in order to ward off the idea of a multiplicity of gods and lords. In 1Cor 8:6, however, the Holy Spirit was not mentioned, so that the phrasing in C² may be seen as an adaptation to this biblical usage. The oneness of the Spirit was seen as sufficiently determined by the definite article.

(2) Conspicuously, the doxological formula τὸ σὺν πατρὶ καὶ υἱῷ συμπροσκυνούμενον καὶ συνδοξαζόμενον appears in the middle of the passage on the Holy Spirit. In terms of form criticism, this may indicate an earlier stage of editing here: καὶ εἰς τὸ πνεῦμα ἅγιον had at first been concluded in the discussions at the council by the doxology τὸ σὺν πατρὶ καὶ υἱῷ συμπροσκυνούμενον καὶ συνδοξαζόμενον – this reflects the considerations by Basil and was also the solution favoured by

---

78 It is not correct to state that 'most eastern creeds' contained the oneness of God (*pace* Gerber 2000, p. 152).
79 Cf. Cyril, *Catechesis ad illuminandos 16*, 4.
80 Cf. Theodore, *Homilia catechetica 9*, 16–18; *10*, 1–3.
81 I am indebted to Thomas Brüggemann for the following idea.

Gregory of Nazianzus, because it concluded the creed in a liturgical fashion, thus elegantly emphasizing the consubstantiality of the Spirit without using *homooúsios* itself. It would have permitted an assertion that N had remained unaltered.[82]

(3) This position apparently did not prove sufficient in the discussions with the critics of the Spirit's full divinity. However, *homooúsios* was not inserted either to leave these critics room for manoeuvre on this point. At the same time, some characteristics of the Roman creed, which had already been adopted in N^{Ant}, were also given more prominence in C^2, albeit indirectly. Thus, further elements from N^{Ant} were copied:

- τὸ ἐκ τοῦ πατρὸς ἐκπορευόμενον,
- (πνεῦμα) ζωοποιόν,
- μίαν ἐκκλησίαν καθολικήν, now rephrased as εἰς μίαν, ἁγίαν, καθολικὴν καὶ ἀποστολικὴν ἐκκλησίαν (cf. R),
- (εἰς) ἄφεσιν ἁμαρτιῶν (cf. R),
- ἀνάστασιν (cf. R),
- ζωήν (cf. R).

(4) The problem of the strange duplication πνεῦμα τῆς ἀληθείας – πνεῦμα ζωοποιόν in N^{Ant} was solved by deleting the former syntagma and instead emphasizing the lordship and creative work of the Spirit through a new phrase. The deletion of the Johannine 'Spirit of truth' (rather than of πνεῦμα ζωοποιόν) could be due to the fact that the council wanted to distance itself from the Homoian or Anhomoian creeds, in which this predication often occurs.[83]

(5) Instead, the title of 'Lord'[84] – with recourse to biblical language (2Cor 3:17–18) – underlined the divinity of the Spirit and connected this with the biblical epithet ζωοποιόν from N^{Ant},[85] so that this epithet could then be moved further up in the text.

(6) The reference to the prophets (τὸ λαλῆσαν διὰ τῶν προφητῶν) was probably inserted in order to define the Spirit more precisely by connecting him with the Old Testament: it is the Spirit of the *prophets* who is worshipped here and whose identity can be ascertained from Scripture – this made it possible to ward off en-

---

82 Cf. above pp. 331, 336 f., 361. In addition, Kelly 1972, p. 337.
83 Cf. Council of Antioch (341), *Expositio fidei/Formula tertia* (FaFo § 141a[4]); Council of Niké (359), *Confessio fidei* (§ 159a[6]); Council of Constantinople (359/360), *Confessio fidei* (§ 160[4]); Auxentius, *Confessio fidei* (§ 453); Eunomius, *Confessio fidei* 4 (§ 163c2); Pseudo-John Chrysostom, *In illud: Simile est regnum caelorum patri familias* 3 (§ 196[7]); Charisius, *Confessio fidei* (§ 204a).
84 Cf. Kelly 1972, p. 341; De Halleux 1979(1990), p. 324; Abramowski 1992, p. 500; Staats 1999, pp. 24 f., 257 f.
85 Cf. above p. 352.

thusiastic pneumatologies as, for example, those of the Montanists, who worshipped Montanus as the Paraclete as Montanism still existed in various forms in the fourth century,[86] or of the Messalians and similar ascetic groups.[87] So the Trinitarian doxology could not be, as it were, 'undermined' by an 'enthusiastic' interpretation.[88] Conversely, it was thus emphasized that the *hypóstasis* of the Spirit had already been present and active in the Old Testament. The formula is attested in older creeds, above all again in J, which may also have had an influence here.[89]

(7) Discussions must have followed about whether the Church, baptism with forgiveness of sins, the resurrection of the flesh or of the dead, and eternal life in N^{Ant} were also objects of faith and to what extent they were to be assigned to the Holy Spirit and his activity. In the end, it must have been decided to include these items, but to assign them a lower 'pisteological' status.

(8) Therefore, a differentiated 'affirmation hierarchy' of the remaining credal clauses both in J and N^{Ant} (Church, baptism and forgiveness of sins, resurrection, and eternal life), was now introduced (possibly with recourse to a similar approach in N^{Ant}):[90] while the Church was demarcated from the Trinity by the doxological caesura it still remained an object of faith – indeed, it may even have been promoted to one in comparison to the *Vorlage* (a contention that remained controversial in the interpretation of R or its descendants, at least in the west[91]). Here, too, Cyril of Jerusalem could have been an influence.[92] It fits with this 'upgrading' of the Church (which was now actually added to the Trinity as a fourth article of faith) that its holi-

---

86 Cf. Markschies, 'Montanismus', 2012, cols. 1218 f. (however, the available evidence is scarce and unreliable).

87 Cf. Staats 1992, pp. 608 f.

88 On the fathers' understanding of the operation of the Holy Spirit in the Old Testament cf., e.g., Crouzel 1976, cols. 532 f. (Irenaeus), 535 (Origen).

89 Cf. also *Ecthesis macrostichos* (FaFo § 145[10]); Epiphanius, *Ancoratus* 119,9 (§ 175); *Didascalia CCCXVIII patrum Nicaenorum* (§ 176[4]); Amphilochius of Iconium, *De recta fide* (§ 181[2]); Pseudo-Athanasius, *Interpretatio in symbolum* (FaFo § 185). It is not altogether clear whether 2Pet 1:21 is alluded to, as Kelly and Staats have assumed (cf. Kelly 1972, p. 341; Staats 1999, p. 258 and Staats 1999, pp. 261–4) Cf. also Rom 1:2 and Heb 1:1.

90 However, the 'confession' of the one baptism in N^{Ant3} could also be due to a later influence from C^2 on N^{Ant3}.

91 Cf. Westra 2017 and above pp. 174 f.

92 Cf. also Arius and Euzoius, *Epistula ad Constantinum imperatorem* (Opitz 1934/1935, *Urkunde 30*; FaFo § 131c) 3; Apolinarius of Laodicea, *Fides secundum partem* 32 (§ 164a2); Epiphanius, *Ancoratus* 119,11 (§ 175); *Didascalia CCCXVIII patrum Nicaenorum* (§ 176[9]); Pseudo-Athanasius, *Interpretatio in symbolum* (§ 185).

ness and apostolicity were specifically emphasized, at least compared to N^{Ant1}. (The reference to its holiness is also found in J.)

(9) By contrast, the confession of one baptism 'for' the forgiveness of sins (whereby the reference to *one* baptism, which precludes further ablutions, seems to have been taken once more from J), as well as the expectation of the resurrection of the dead and of eternal life, were now no longer regarded as being part of the πίστις in the narrower sense (as it had been in J), but relegated to a lower tier of dogmatic normativity: single baptism 'for the remission of sins' was now merely 'confessed' (which is doctrinally less 'strong' than 'believed in'), while the resurrection of the dead and the life of the future aeon were no more than 'expected'. It is not entirely clear which of the following elements were drawn from N^{Ant}: τὸ ἐκ τοῦ πατρὸς ἐκπορευόμενον, μίαν ἐκκλησίαν καθολικήν, (εἰς) ἄφεσιν ἁμαρτιῶν, and ἀνάστασιν. The confession of baptism 'for the forgiveness of sins' may have been taken from J in which case it would, perhaps, be secondary in N^{Ant3} where it also occurs.

(10) The differences between N^{Ant1} and N^{Ant3} also mean that it remains unclear whether the 'holiness' and 'apostolicity' of the Church and the confession of baptism were already included in N^{Ant} or whether, which I consider more likely given the current state of the evidence, C^2 influenced N^{Ant3}.

(11) Replacing the term 'flesh' with the 'dead' certainly served to ward off a 'carnal' understanding of this process, which was current in the eschatology of Apolinarius and Jewish-Christian circles in the second half of the fourth century.[93]

(12) The mention of the 'world to come' (or, more literally, 'future aeon') was taken from Heb 6:5. Such a 'future aeon' is already combined with 'expectation' in the *Apology* of Aristides and in Origen,[94] but also corresponds to (Neo-)Nicene theology.[95]

*

---

93 Cf. Kinzig 2003.

94 Cf. Aristides, *Apologia*, frg. 15,3 (Vona 1950, p. 125); Origen, *Fragmenta in Lucam*, frg. 154 on Lk 9:58, ll. 3 f. (Rauer 1959, p. 288).

95 Cf. Athanasius, *Expositiones in Psalmos*, on Ps 111:1 (PG 27, col. 465B); on Ps 60:6 (col. 572C-D; ascribed to Eusebius and Athanasius). Cf. also Theodoret, *Interpretatio in Psalmos*, on Ps 60:6 (PG 80, col. 1325C); Basil of Caesarea, *Regulae morales* 68 (PG 31, col. 805C); Didymus, *Fragmenta in Psalmos*, frg. 22 (Mühlenberg 1975–1978, vol. I, p. 130, ll. 1 f.); frg. 624a on Ps 60:6b (vol. II, p. 35, ll. 17 f.).

By way of summary, it can be seen that:

(1) the third section in particular was further revised in Constantinople, resulting in a *new* creed (C^2), the 'Faith of the 150 fathers'. A comparison with its
Vorlage N^{Ant} shows that C^2 underlines the divinity of the Spirit even more
strongly than the *Vorlage*.[96]

(2) It is also clear that the Antiochene creeds offer little that is not found in C^2,
while conversely the text of C^2 is more detailed in some places. It is, therefore, reasonable to assume that C^2 represents a further revision.

(3) The similarities between N and C^2 and between J and C^2 indicate that the revision of C^2 was not carried out solely on the basis of the Antiochene creeds,
but that N and J were also available to the fathers at Constantinople.

(4) In the third section two stages of revision are discernible. At the first stage, the
creed concluded with a doxology, which may have run as follows: καὶ εἰς τὸ
πνεῦμα τὸ ἅγιον, τὸ σὺν πατρὶ καὶ υἱῷ συμπροσκυνούμενον καὶ συνδοξαζόμενον. It was certainly older than C^2. However, this version of the pneumatological section was discarded because the wider development of creeds suggested
that further phrases be included in (or appended to) the third article.

(5) The resulting revision C^2 presumably did not meet with approval because in
the end it had moved too far away from N and was therefore not accepted by
the council fathers.

∗

As regards C^1, I have shown elsewhere through philological analysis that this text,
which must be considered the council's official creed, also resulted from a revision of N^{Ant1} for which N and J were used.[97] Let us look more closely at the reasons for these revisions.

(1) In the first section the addition καὶ μόνον ἀληθινόν referring to Jn 17:3 was
adopted from N^{Ant2}. Furthermore, ποιημάτων was added to πάντων ὁράτων
τε καὶ ἀοράτων (perhaps for the sake of clarity) which, in turn, led to the
change of ποιητήν to κτίστην for stylistic reasons. In C^2 this was solved differently (and, in my view, better).[98]

(2) For the omission of τὸν πρωτότοκον πάσης κτίσεως see above on C^2.[99]

(3) For the omission of καὶ οὐ ποιηθέντα see above on C^2.[100]

---

96 Cf., however, Kelly 1972, p. 342: 'A feature of this article about the Spirit which is often thought
somewhat puzzling is the comparative mildness of its tone.'

97 Cf. Kinzig, *Glaubensbekenntnis*, 2021, pp. 51–60.

98 Cf. above p. 368.

99 Cf. above p. 368.

100 Cf. above p. 368.

(4) The insertion of γεννηθέντα οὐ ποιηθέντα corresponds to N (so also C²).[101]

(5) The omissions of a number of clauses from N^Ant1 (partly in agreement with J) in what follows were probably due to a concern that the creed be useful in catechesis.

(6) Conversely, the same reasons as suggested above for C² may have been responsible for the addition of Holy Spirit and Virgin.[102]

(7) The omission of Pontius Pilate and of κατὰ τὰς γραφάς corresponds to N and J.

(8) The omission of καὶ καθεζόμενον ἐν δεξιᾷ τοῦ θεοῦ corresponds to N.

(9) As regards the section on the Spirit, in so far as C¹ is identical with C², what has been said above on C² also applies.[103]

(10) I cannot explain the addition συμβασιλεῦον, which is unique in the credal tradition, though not uncommon in theological discussion of the time.[104]

(11) Significantly, in C¹, too, the pneumatological section did not conclude with the (certainly older) doxological formula τὸ σὺν πατρὶ καὶ υἱῷ (συμβασιλεῦον καὶ) συμπροσκυνούμενον καὶ συνδοξαζόμενον, although this must be the formula with which Basil ended his recitation of N.[105]

(12) The excision of the forgiveness of sins, the resurrection of the flesh, and eternal life (N^Ant1) can again be explained by an effort to be brief.

What can we conclude from this?

(1) C¹ and C² must have originated in close proximity to each other; however, they do not descend from each other.

(2) It is clear from the statements of Nestorius that he regarded his creed as a version of N.[106]

---

101 Cf. above p. 368.

102 Cf. above pp. 368–70.

103 Cf. above pp. 370–2.

104 Cf. also Kinzig, 'Zwei neuentdeckte Predigten', 2020(2022), pp. 35 f.

105 Cf. above pp. 331, 336 f.

106 Cf. Graumann 2002, p. 286 n. 30; Smith 2018, pp. 38–42. Particularly instructive in this regard is Cyril's confrontation with Nestorius in *Contra Nestorium* 1,7–8: both sides argue about the exact wording of N, with Cyril accusing Nestorius of altering the creed, even though Nestorius believed he was referring to the original text (especially ACO I 1/7, pp. 28, ll. 24–7; 29, ll. 11–13; cf. Schwartz 1926, pp. 82 f.; cf. also Gerber 2000, p. 277; Smith 2018, pp. 49 f.). This confrontation was repeated in a modified form during the first session of Chalcedon between Diogenes of Cyzicus and the Egyptian bishops, who certainly knew that N had been altered later (cf. below pp. 381 f.). Furthermore, Proclus of Constantinople, in his *Tomus ad Armenios* 33, refers to N (FaFo § 210b), although he probably had the same creed as Nestorius, i.e. C¹ (cf. below p. 498 and n. 93).

(3) It follows from the way that C^2 was presented in Chalcedon that this confession was no longer regarded as N, but as that of 'the 150 fathers'.[107]

(4) This cannot really mean anything other than that two versions of C were drafted in Constantinople in 381, C^1 being the version approved there and then, which continued to be considered as still being N.

Incidentally, this may also explain why C^2 played no role in the Council of Aquileia of September 381. As Daniel H. Williams observes, this synod

> produced no symbol nor is known to have formally reaffirmed an existing one. [. . .] It seems rather that the major purpose of Aquileia was to dispose of the leaders of western Homoianism and other local pockets of resistance, which *de facto* confirmed the state's recent wedding to Nicene Christianity.[108]

∗

The result of our investigations into the transformation of the creed from N first to N^{Ant} and, finally, to C^1 and C^2 can now be presented in the following stemma (regarding the reception of N and C^2 at Chalcedon see the next chapter):

---

107 Cf. below pp. 382 f.
108 Williams 1995, pp. 182 f.

italics = hypothetical because not preserved or directly attested
→ direct influence (adoption of basic structure and text)
----▸ indirect influence (adoption of individual phrases)

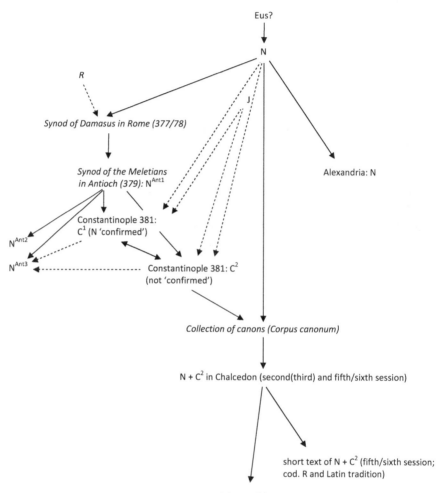

8 The Reception of N and C² in the Latin and Greek Churches until the Time of Charlemagne

8.1 The adoption of N and C² as normative creeds at the Council of Chalcedon (451)

There is not a single piece of evidence that C² was quoted between the Council of Constantinople and the Council of Chalcedon in 451, let alone that C² had the same status as N.[1] The first explicit mention of C² is not found until that later council. However, in order to understand what happened at Chalcedon, we first have to take a brief look at the Council of Ephesus of 431 which took place in sessions that were each separately attended by, on the one hand, the followers of Cyril of Alexandria (*sedit* 412–444) and, on the other hand, the 'eastern' bishops supporting John of Antioch (*sedit* 429–441). In its session of 22 June, which was attended by the supporters of Cyril of Alexandria, this council adopted N as the standard of faith. It was, therefore, read out in its original version, as it was current among the Alexandrians.[2] A letter, which was sent to the emperors after the session, mentioned the confession of the '318 most-holy fathers who were gathered to the city of Nicaea by Constantine', i.e. N, and went on to explain that letters of Cyril had been compared with this creed and found to be orthodox.[3]

At the next 'Cyrilline' meeting a month later on 22 July,[4] the synod issued a church law (*hóros*),[5] which has also been handed down as canon 7 of Ephesus. It confirmed the mandatory nature of N[6] and forbade the handing-over of a creed other than N to converts. If they did otherwise, bishops and other clerics were threatened with dismissal and lay people with excommunication.[7] In his famous letter to John of Antioch of 433, after the council, in which he agreed to a compro-

---

1 Cf. the detailed analysis in Kinzig, *Glaubensbekenntnis*, 2021, pp. 102–8. This chapter is based on Kinzig, *Glaubensbekenntnis*, 2021, pp. 105–27.
2 Cf. *Collectio Vaticana 43* (FaFo § 568a) and also *82*, 5 (ACO I 1,3, p. 6, ll. 30–5); *92*, 1 (ACO I 1,3, pp. 28, l. 24 – 29, l. 3); *94*, 3 (ACO I 1,3, p. 33, ll. 19–22).
3 *Collectio Vaticana 81*, 5 / *Synodi relatio ad imperatores* (FaFo § 568b). Cf. also the report to Pope Celestine in *Collectio Vaticana 82*, 5 / *Synodi relatio ad Caelestinum* (§ 568c).
4 On the problem of this session and its acts cf. Price/Graumann 2020, pp. 431–43. Further literature in FaFo § 204 and Kinzig, *Glaubensbekenntnis*, p. 105 n. 446.
5 The legally binding character is expressed in the introductory formula ὥρισεν ('it is decreed').
6 Cf. already *Collectio Atheniensis 74*, 2–4 / *Gesta Ephesena* (ACO I 1,7, p. 89, ll. 1–20).
7 Cf. *Collectio Atheniensis 77* (FaFo § 568e).

https://doi.org/10.1515/9783110318531-008

mise formula in the christological debate, the Formula of Union, Cyril of Alexandria invoked the authority of N by referring to this canon and emphasizing that no syllable of N must be changed.[8]

The synod of the 'eastern' bishops in Ephesus also confirmed the sufficiency of N, but without quoting the text of the creed in its Definition of Faith of August 431.[9] Instead, it presented its own confession, which later served as the basis of the Formula of Union (433).[10] Nevertheless, the easterners now presented the Twelve Chapters of Cyril[11] as a falsifying addition to the 'pure' text of N, meaning that the latter's 'authentic wording' now had to be officially reaffirmed. This was done, on the one hand, through their memorandum to the emperor of July 431, which was preceded by the text of N (no longer preserved),[12] and on the other hand by means of a letter carried by a delegation to Constantinople in which the text of N, quoted in its original form, was presented as absolutely authoritative.[13]

Therefore, it was clear to everyone, since Ephesus 431 at the latest, that – when N was invoked – a specific credal text was referred to, which had by now been officially authorized at least twice, namely the authentic creed of Nicaea. We shall see, however, that outside of Egypt C¹ continued to be quoted under the name of N, which led to new disputes about it at Chalcedon. At the same time, it was clear that any subsequent extensions of N, including C¹ and even more so C², could no longer be regarded as identical with the 'faith of Nicaea', in future negotiations at empire-wide councils, as soon as the acts of Ephesus were consulted, but at best as an interpretation of N.

*

We have to keep this development in mind when we now turn to the Council of Chalcedon. At its first session, an earlier letter by the staunchly Miaphysite Archimandrite Eutyches (d. 456), who was charged with heresy, was read out from the acts of the so-called Robber Synod (Ephesus 449), where, under dubious circum-

---

8 Cf. Cyril, *Epistula ad Iohannem Antiochenum* (*Epistula 39* (*Collectio Vaticana 127*); ACO I 1,4, p. 19, ll. 20–4; cf. ACO II 1,1, p. 110, ll. 25–9). Cf. also id., *Epistula 33* (*Collectio Atheniensis 107*), 5 (ACO I 1,7, p. 148, ll. 42–4).
9 Cf. *Collectio Atheniensis 48*, 2. 4–7 (FaFo § 205) and already *Collectio Vaticana 146* (§ 197g); *Collectio Vaticana 84*, 1 (ACO I 1,3, pp. 10, l. 29 – 11, l. 2); *151*, 10 (ACO I 1,5, p. 121, ll. 6–14). 12 (ACO I 1,5, p. 122, ll. 3–6). 15 (FaFo § 568g); *155* (ACO I 1,5, p. 127, ll. 16–23); *156* (ACO I 1,5, p. 128, ll. 16–21); *157*, 3 (ACO I 1,5, p. 129, ll. 20–5); *Collectio Casinensis II,96* (ACO I 4, p. 45, ll. 3–7).
10 Cf. FaFo § 207.
11 This document of Cyril's had condemned the theology of Nestorius in twelve short statements before the council.
12 Cf. *Collectio Vaticana 163* title and 3 (ACO I 1,5, p. 133, ll. 34–7; pp. 134, ll. 38 – 135, l. 4).
13 Cf. *Collectio Vaticana 96* (*Mandatum orientalium*; ACO I 1,3, p. 39, ll. 1–11) and FaFo § 205 (extract from the same document).

stances, the Alexandrians had confirmed Eutyches' Christology as orthodox. The reading created a disturbance: Eutyches had begun his epistle by confirming that his own faith accorded with that defined in Nicaea, while quoting, in this context, N in its original version as adopted in 325.[14] Subsequently he had pointed out that this confession had then been sanctioned in Ephesus in 431 under Cyril's presidency, referring to the so-called canon 7. When the reading had been completed Eusebius of Dorylaeum accused Eutyches of lying and said that there was no such *hóros* or canon.[15] This statement, in turn, drew heavy criticism from the Patriarch of Alexandria, Dioscurus (*sedit* 444–451). He said that he possessed a copy of the relevant conciliar documents which substantiated Eutyches' claim. In addition, Dioscurus emphasized that canon 7 was in fact a *hóros*, thus implying that the decision of the Council of Ephesus (431) was even more binding than a simple canon. This brusque statement makes it clear that both C^1 and C^2 were either unknown to the Alexandrian Miaphysites or were rejected by them.

Now it was the turn of Diogenes of Cyzicus to address the meeting. His diocese lay within the sphere of influence of the patriarch of Constantinople. While no friend of Eutyches, he did not advocate any punitive measures.[16] He pointed out that Eutyches' appeal to N had been erroneous, because, in order to refute the pernicious doctrines of Apolinarius (of Laodicea), Valentinus (a follower of Apolinarius), and of Macedonius,[17] the holy fathers had, after Nicaea, added the words ἐκ πνεύματος ἁγίου καὶ Μαρίας τῆς παρθένου ('from the Holy Spirit and the virgin Mary') to the phrase κατελθόντα καὶ σαρκωθέντα ('who descended and became flesh'). This addition to N had been omitted by Eutyches because he, too, was an Apolinarian. Apolinarius, Diogenes continued, had rejected 'from the Holy Spirit and the virgin Mary' in order not to have to express the unification (of God) with the flesh. Diogenes' statement almost certainly refers to the events in Constantinople, where Apolinarius and the Macedonians (Pneumatomachians) had actually been condemned in canon 1.[18] This also means that Diogenes was quoting C^1 here, which he regarded as an (extended) version of N.[19] Invariably, Diogenes did not speak of *another* confession, but of an *addition to N* – this fits perfectly with our assumption that C^1 was seen as a revision of N rather than as a new

---

14 Cf. Council of Chalcedon, *Actio I*, 157 (FaFo § 213b). The variants in the credal text are minimal.
15 Cf. Council of Chalcedon, *Actio I*, 159. Eusebius probably did not know the acts of the relevant session of 22 July 431; cf. Smith 2018, p. 187. Furthermore De Halleux 1985(1990), p. 60.
16 Cf. Council of Chalcedon, *Actio I*, 160.
17 Cf. above pp. 357 f.
18 Cf. above p. 264 n. 183.
19 Cf. above pp. 375–7.

confession.[20] Only if C^1 was a revision of N and was also seen as such, does the reaction of the Egyptian bishops make sense who cried out that nothing should be added to or taken away from the Nicene Creed, but that it ought to be confirmed in accordance with the emperor's orders (although in his letter of invitation Marcian (r. 450–457) had not specifically referred to N).[21] However, they also held that the reference to the Holy Spirit in relation to the incarnation belonged to the original wording of N.[22]

There was, therefore, considerable confusion among the council fathers at Chalcedon as to what was to be regarded as the authoritative text of the Nicene Creed. The presidents of the council, the *magister militum* Anatolius and a committee of imperial officials, decided at the end of this agitated session that the matters of faith would have to be postponed until the next session. After the imposition of disciplinary measures (a number of bishops, including the Patriarchs Dioscurus of Alexandria and Juvenal of Jerusalem, were suspended), the bishops were given a homework assignment: each of them was to produce a declaration of faith, with the presiding officials supplying the dogmatic standard they must employ: this was the Emperor Marcian's own faith which was described as agreeing with the 'exposition (ἔκθεσις) of the 318 holy fathers of Nicaea' and the 'exposition (ἔκθεσις) of the 150 after that', as well as with the Church Fathers Gregory of Nazianzus, Basil of Caesarea, Hilary of Poitiers, Athanasius, Ambrose, and Cyril of Alexandria, whose writings had been judged orthodox at the Council of Ephesus in 431. No agreement was required with the *Tomus Leonis* – which is the famous letter sent by Pope Leo the Great (*sedit* 440–461) to Patriarch Flavian of Constantinople (*sedit* 446–449) explaining his position in the christological controversy – which was only vaguely alluded to.[23] In other words, the *imperial* confession (in a broader sense) as defined by the aforementioned writings was to be established as the general *ecclesial* confession. Relevant normative writings now also included C^2 (which was understood as directed against the Miaphysites), but not Leo's Tome, because Rome's influence had to be curbed. Thus, a reference to both creeds, N and C^2, (and other writings) suddenly appeared in the negotiations, without it being made clear how they related to each other.

It is also noticeable that the exact place and date of origin of the 'exposition of the 150' is not mentioned – the council's presidents obviously assumed it to be

---

20 Cf. above p. 376 and n. 106, 380.
21 Cf. Council of Chalcedon, *Actio I*, 161. 163 and Smith 2018, pp. 189 f.
22 Cf. Council of Chalcedon, *Actio I*, 163. Interestingly, the Virgin is not mentioned – it may that they were referring to a version of N that merely read 'and became flesh from the Holy Spirit' (καὶ σαρκωθέντα ἐκ πνεύματος ἁγίου), as it is still preserved in in its later 'Nestorian' form, N^{Ant3}.
23 Cf. Council of Chalcedon, *Actio I*, 1072 (FaFo § 570b).

common knowledge that this confession of the '150 fathers' was that of Constanti-nople, or to be more precise, that everyone would take this to be C^2. It is clear from the account of the events at Constantinople by Socrates (writing in *c.* 439/440, so a decade before Chalcedon) that the '150 fathers' referred to the number of bishops who had gathered there.[24] It must therefore have been obvious to all those involved that Anatolius was referring to a creed adopted at Constantinople. Mentioning the comparatively large number of council fathers probably also served to emphasize the authority of this creed. By expressing themselves in the way they did the imperial commissioners suggested that C^2 had always been an authentic interpretation (or extension) of N, a fact which had been (implicitly) confirmed by the ecclesial authorities who were subsequently enumerated. It re-mains unclear, however, whether in fact all members of the council at Chalcedon actually knew C^2 (as its presidents did) or whether some may not rather have as-sumed that this confession of 'the 150' was, in fact, C^1!

Why did the imperial commissioners proceed in this manner? As I mentioned before, there were discussions about the question of the authentic wording of N and about what the council fathers had agreed in Constantinople, how C^1/C^2 was related to N, whether it was to be regarded as an *extended confirmation* or as a *change* and *innovation* (which would have been prohibited according to canon 7 of Ephesus I). The appeal of the council's presidents to the authentic text of N and, in addition, now clearly to C^2 was obviously initially intended to resolve this confu-sion, to restore the pure (but dogmatically incomplete) text of N, and to establish the authenticity of the credal texts N and C^2. However, another point was at least as important: by citing N and (as its extended confirmation) C^2, the imperial commis-sioners reaffirmed the normativity of the Nicene faith in Chalcedon also in terms of secular law, as it had been laid down in *Nullus haereticis* (*Codex Theodosianus* 16,5,6; FaFo § 533) and *Episcopis tradi* (16,1,3; FaFo § 534), where N had been pre-scribed throughout the Empire.[25] At the same time, they forced the council fathers to recognize this state of affairs as applying also to the entire Church. To put it suc-cinctly: the commissioners had made it clear, in unmistakable terms, that the *em-pire* defined the faith of the *Church* using traditional ecclesial formulae.[26] Thus, the imperial presidents of the council also sought to position themselves in theological terms against the Miaphysites, having already rehabilitated Flavian of Constantino-ple and Eusebius of Dorylaeum, who had both been deposed at the Robber Synod of 449.

---

24 Cf. Socrates, *Historia ecclesiastica* 5,8,4 (FaFo § 184b).
25 Cf. below pp. 477 f.
26 On the wider context cf. below ch. 10.2.

The presidents' suggested agenda, however, involved extensive consultation to ascertain the 'true faith' which was to be carried out at the council's second(third) session,[27] when council members were given the task of laying it down in an 'unadulterated' (καθαρῶς) fashion.[28] But whereas at the end of the first session it had seemed as if each father was to set out his own faith in writing, it now sounded more as if the debates were aimed at agreeing on one single creed.[29] To this end, the dogmatic rule for the subsequent discussions was reaffirmed once more, namely that of the 'orthodox faith transmitted by the 318 and the 150 [holy fathers] and likewise by the rest of the holy and glorious fathers (τὴν ὀρθόδοξον πίστιν τὴν παρὰ τῶν τιη′ καὶ παρὰ τῶν ρν′, ἔτι μὴν καὶ παρὰ τῶν λοιπῶν ἁγίων καὶ ἐπιδόξων πατέρων παραδοθεῖσαν)'. Marcian had thus altered the strategy of his predecessor Theodosius II: the latter had maintained in his opening letter to the Second Council of Ephesus in 449 (the 'Robber Synod') that the rule of the orthodox faith was to be found solely in N and its confirmation in Ephesus I.[30] In this context he had also quoted the canonization formula in a letter to Dioscurus of 6 August 449, which could be seen as referring to canon 7 of Ephesus I.[31] Ultimately, the Robber Synod had acted as Theodosius had suggested and had left N unchanged.[32]

The inclusion of C² in the series of witnesses for the orthodox faith was, therefore, by no means uncontroversial, but met with considerable resistance. Moreover, the bishops also refused to issue yet another confession. Faced with this situation, the presiding commissioners attempted to form a committee consisting of one or two bishops from each patriarchate who were entrusted with the task of drawing up a consensus paper, but this plan, too, met with protest: many bishops rejected it outright.

It also emerged as the debate progressed that not only was the composition of a new conciliar creed controversial, but so was the status of C². Cecropius of

---

27 The majority of scholars assume that the session which in the Greek acts (and in Schwartz' edition and FaFo) stands in third place should probably in fact be considered the second session. Cf. Kinzig, *Glaubensbekenntnis*, 2021, p. 113 n. 476. Another approach is found in Bevan 2017, who wants to change the dates of the second and third session in the sequence of the Greek acts. We may leave this matter unresolved here.

28 For what follows cf. Council of Chalcedon, *Actio II(III)*, 2–15 (FaFo § 570c).

29 Cf. Council of Chalcedon, *Actio II(III)*, 2 (FaFo § 570c).

30 The letter of invitation and the acts of Ephesus II are quoted in the acts of Chalcedon. Cf. here *Actio I*, 51 (ACO II 1, p. 73, ll. 28 f.).

31 Cf. Council of Chalcedon, *Actio I*, 52 (ACO II 1, p. 74, ll. 24–27). Later Theodosius added Ephesus II to the list of orthodox councils. Cf. his edict addressed to Dioscurus (FaFo § 540) and his letter to Juvenal of Jerusalem (§ 541); cf. Smith 2018, pp. 167 f.

32 For details cf. Kinzig, *Glaubensbekenntnis*, 2021, p. 108 and n. 459.

Sebastopol, for example, referred to N and a number of fathers as well as the *Tomus Leonis* as means to help determine the faith, but did not name C². Furthermore, he requested that N and the Tome be read out.[33]

But things turned out differently. The presiding officers first demanded that Eunomius of Nicomedia read out the Nicene Creed from an unspecified 'book' (βιβλίον), which the council fathers then acclaimed as the orthodox faith.[34] This was not followed, however, by the reading of the Tome; rather, the Archdeacon Aetius, who acted as the chief notary of the Patriarch of Constantinople, likewise read from a 'book' (βιβλίον), which was again not actually identified, 'the holy faith which the holy 150 fathers set forth, in harmony with the holy and great Council of Nicaea' (ἡ ἁγία πίστις, ἣν ἐξέθεντο οἱ ἅγιοι ρν΄ πατέρες, συμφωνοῦσα τῇ ἁγίᾳ καὶ μεγάλῃ συνόδῳ τῇ ἐν Νικαίᾳ).[35] The minutes then again record the unanimous consent of all the bishops.[36] Even at that stage, the reading of the Tome did not follow straight away, rather Cyril's *Second Letter to Nestorius* was read next, together with his *Letter to John of Antioch*, in which he had agreed to the union, before at long last Leo's letter was read out. This also led to overwhelming agreement, and so it was decided to have a committee draw up a consensus document, which was to be presented at a later meeting.[37]

The headings of the creeds as they appear in the acts of this session deserve a closer look. The text of N is preceded by a title, a precise date (19 June 325), and the place of composition:

> (1) Ἔκθεσις συνόδου γενομένης ἐν Νικαίᾳ (2) ἐν ὑπατείᾳ Παυλίνου καὶ Ἰουλιανοῦ τῶν λαμπροτάτων (3) ἔτους ἀπὸ Ἀλεξάνδρου χλς΄ ἐν μηνὶ Δαισίῳ (4) ιθ΄ τῇ πρὸ ιγ΄ Καλανδῶν Ἰουλίων (5) ἐν Νικαίᾳ τῇ μητροπόλει Βιθυνίας.

> (1) Exposition of the Council held at Nicaea (2) under the consulate of the most illustrious Paulinus and Julianus, (3) in the 636th year after Alexander, on the 19th of the month Daisius, (4) and on the 13th day before the Kalends of July, (5) at Nicaea, the capital of Bithynia.[38]

The title and authorship (1) are presented in a peculiar manner, for after ἔκθεσις (which simply means 'exposition') a specifying genitive is missing, e.g., τῆς (καθολικῆς καὶ ἀποστολικῆς) πίστεως, in order to make clear what is being interpreted here; instead we find a reference to the Council of Nicaea, so specifying the origin

---

33 Cf. Council of Chalcedon, *Actio II(III)*, 9 (FaFo § 570c).

34 Cf. Council of Chalcedon, *Actio II(III)*, 11 (FaFo § 570c).

35 Council of Chalcedon, *Actio II(III)*, 13–14 (FaFo § 570c).

36 Cf. Council of Chalcedon, *Actio II(III)*, 15 (FaFo § 570c).

37 Cf. Council of Chalcedon, *Actio II(III)*, 29–45.

38 Council of Chalcedon, *Actio II(III)*, 10–11 (ACO II 1, p. 79, ll. 12–15). The header should be added in FaFo § 570c.

rather than the object of the exposition. The dating consists of three elements: (2) date according to the consulate of Paulinus and Julianus, (3) date according to the Seleucid calendar,[39] and (4) date according to the Julian calendar. Finally (5) the place and province of origin are given.

The order of the elements in the dating of N is rather odd – one would have expected (4) before (3); in addition, the place of the synod is named twice. The latter is perhaps due to the fact that the date did not originally follow directly after the title, but is a secondary addition (originally, the title probably simply read: Ἔκθεσις [+ addition?, see above] συνόδου γενομένης ἐν Νικαίᾳ).

The heading of C² reads:

Ἡ ἁγία πίστις, ἣν ἐξέθεντο οἱ ἅγιοι ρν′ πατέρες, συμφωνοῦσα τῇ ἁγίᾳ καὶ μεγάλῃ συνόδῳ τῇ ἐν Νικαίᾳ.

The sacred faith which the holy 150 fathers set forth, in harmony with the holy and great Council of Nicaea.[40]

In this instance, place and date are absent from the heading. Instead, both the sheer size of the council and its agreement with Nicaea are emphasized. This is, as we will see, probably no coincidence.

Returning to the second(third) session of Chalcedon, it seems odd that there was a change of readers: N was recited by the Bishop of Nicomedia and Metropolitan of Bithynia (where the Council of Nicaea had taken place); C², however, was read out not by Patriarch Anatolius of Constantinople, but by one of his officials, Archdeacon Aetius, Anatolius' chief notary (*primicerius notariorum*)[41] – perhaps because there was as yet no agreement on the acceptance of C² and the patriarch who was a partisan of Cyril was sceptical about that confession.

The twice-mentioned βιβλίον is likely to have been a single codex, though hardly the actual minute book of the councils of Nicaea and/or Constantinople,[42] but rather a collection of council decisions. Such a collection featuring an (extended) date[43] – N – C² – list of signatures of Nicaea actually survives in Syriac translation in a *Corpus canonum* which was originally written in Greek and whose most important witness in our context is the cod. London, British Library,

---

39 Cf. Lietzmann 1984, p. 6.

40 Council of Chalcedon, *Actio II(III)*, 13 (FaFo § 570c).

41 Cf. Graumann 2021, p. 120.

42 'Official minutes' seem to have been taken neither in Nicaea nor in Constantinople. For details cf. Kinzig, *Glaubensbekenntnis*, 2021, p. 116 n. 496; Graumann 2021, pp. 17 f. On minute-taking at synods in general cf. Graumann 2021; Weckwerth 2023, cols. 601–3.

43 It was extended here by the Antiochene numbering of years (373 after Antiochus) which was widely used in Syria.

Add. 14528 (s. VI).[44] The model for this translation (which dates from 501/502) was, according to Schwartz, 'a copy of the Corpus canonum which had been slightly revised after 451 and which was in general use in the Greek east before Chalcedon'.[45] Schwartz had assumed, however, that C² had been inserted between N and the signature list in this collection only *after* Chalcedon. The finding in *Actio II(III)*, however, rather suggests the opposite. For the 'harmony' with N, as stated in the heading for C², only makes sense if N immediately preceded C² in the copy used by Archdeacon Aetius – it will, therefore, probably have been one and the same codex to which the readers Eunomius of Nicomedia and the chief notary Aetius lent their authority and which may have come from the patriarchal archives of the eastern capital. In this 'book' C² had obviously been appended to N, having thus been separated from the associated canons and the list of signatures of Constantinople, as in Add. 14528.[46]

In this way, the imperial commissioners established the authentic text of N and also safeguarded its 'correct' interpretation by, as it were, conjuring up C² from nothing as the authentic explanation of N. Before Chalcedon, C² had been a relatively insignificant synodal draft document,[47] which at an unknown point in time had been inserted, probably in Constantinople, into a collection of canons as the 'Faith of the 150 fathers'. As a result, it must have become known to a limited extent – though at least sufficiently well known that its authenticity was not questioned; *yet it was no longer regarded (as C¹ was) as a revision of N, but as an independent creed.* This enhancement of the status of C² (and, as it were, its belated 'approbation') only happened at Chalcedon.[48] But even here its exact status (new creed or explanatory 'appendix' to N?) had initially remained unclear.[49] The purpose of this move was to enhance the eastern capital's importance (also strength-

---

44 Cf. Schulthess 1908, pp. V–XIII; Schwartz 1904(1959), p. 80; Schwartz 1936(1960), pp. 161–9; Dossetti 1967, pp. 119–23, 158, 166 f.; Vööbus 1975/1976, vol. I (translation), p. 4. An older translation is found in Cowper 1861, pp. 5–21. For retroversions of the Syriac text into Greek cf. Dossetti 1967, pp. 122 f. (N: authentic text) and 192 f. (C²: the text is not quite identical with that of the second(third) session of Chalcedon). For the state of research cf. Selb 1989, vol. II, pp. 98–110; Mardirossian 2010; Kaufhold 2012, p. 244; Wagschal 2015, pp. 90 f.; Troianos 2017, pp. 53–7. Cf. also below p. 416.
45 Schwartz 1936(1960), p. 169. Cf. already Schwartz 1930, pp. 29–32.
46 For the content of Add. 14528 cf. the surveys in Schwartz 1936(1960), pp. 161–4; L'Huillier 1996, pp. 206–14.
47 Cf. above p. 362.
48 Cf. Ritter 1965, pp. 204 f.
49 At the fourth session even the terminology used for N and C² had become blurred. Some bishops used πίστις for the *one* faith as set out at Nicaea and Constantinople (and Ephesus), or spoke of two πίστεις. Likewise, the term 'exposition (of the faith)' could be used for both Nicaea and

ened by adopting canon 28 which accorded Constantinople second place in rank after Rome)[50] and to curb the influence of the *Tomus Leonis* as well as of the *urbs* in general. This may also be indicated by the number of '150 fathers', which perhaps does not refer to the actual number of participants, but could have symbolic meaning (just as the number 318, which is mentioned in relation to Nicaea and was probably taken from Gen 14:14[51]). If so, it may refer to the 150 Jews who sat around Nehemiah's table together with leaders of the Gentiles while the wall of Jerusalem was being built (2Ezra 15:17 LXX = Neh 5:17).[52]

C² was thus regarded as the creed of the imperial city and was therefore endowed with a special authority: it functioned, as it were, as a 'creed of government'. In this way, the influence of the capital of the east in ecclesial matters could be further increased.[53] At the same time, the mention of C² anticipated an anti-Miaphysite interpretation of N.[54] C² thus served as a precedent for the establishment of a new formula of faith in Chalcedon, bypassing canon 7.[55]

On 17 October, at the fourth session, the matter of doctrine was brought up again (the third session of 13 October having dealt with the case against Dioscurus).[56] Paschasinus of Lilybaeum, spokesman for the Roman delegation, now confirmed that the faith was defined by three sets of testimonies, first by N, as confirmed by C², second by the interpretation of N given at Ephesus, and third by the *Tomus Leonis*. Thus he tried to reverse the downgrading of Rome as expressed in the final declaration of the first session. To this end, Paschasinus also emphasized that the canonization formula (and thus canon 7 of Ephesus) would not be violated by what he proposed. His suggestion at first appeared to succeed, for shouts of approval could be heard from the council fathers: this, they said, was the consensus of faith. Some confirmed that they had been baptized in N and that it was the creed with which they themselves baptized. But this was not enough

---

Constantinople individually, or ἔκθεσις (singular) could also be taken to refer to the *one* 'exposition' of Nicaea *and* Constantinople jointly (and, perhaps, also Ephesus). In addition, other terms were used too. Cf. Kinzig, *Glaubensbekenntnis*, 2021, p. 119 n. 509.

50 Cf. Ritter 1965, p. 205. Henry Chadwick has suggested that in Chalcedon C² was probably also propagated, 'because it [sc. Constantinople] had enacted the famous canon according special dignity to Constantinople as New Rome. Anatolius had an interest in stressing the high dignity of this assembly' (Chadwick 1983(2017), p. 110). In general cf. also Pigott 2019, pp. 141–84.

51 Cf. above p. 244 n. 113.

52 Cf. Staats 1999, p. 36; Riedl 2004, pp. 32 f. Cf. also 1Chron 8:40. Furthermore, CPG 8601 and the literature cited there.

53 Cf. Kelly 1972, p. 317.

54 Cf. also Ritter 1965, pp. 205 f.

55 Cf. esp. Ritter 1965, pp. 206 f.

56 For what follows cf. Council of Chalcedon, *Actio IV*, 5–8 (FaFo § 570d).

for the council presidency. Instead, they demanded that the bishops individually signal their assent that the Tome was in agreement with N and with the confession of the imperial city (!), i.e. C², which they did. Furthermore, they also signed the Tome.[57]

However, a number of bishops continued to oppose this procedure. Some cited N alone in their statement.[58] In particular, a group of Egyptian prelates named only N, not C² – alongside a number of fathers – in a petition addressed to the emperors.[59] Later in the session, another petition was read out which had been composed by followers of Dioscurus, including the Constantinopolitan archimandrite Dorotheus, who insisted that Chalcedon should only have confirmed N and not dealt with any disciplinary measures (again, C² is not mentioned). They specifically appended the creed (N) and its confirmation in Ephesus I to their document.[60] Subsequently, they reaffirmed that they had been 'baptized in N' and therefore recognized no other confession, so consequently opposed the establishment of a new definition of faith, but also indirectly the promotion of C² and the *Tomus Leonis*.[61] In doing so, Archimandrite Dorotheus stated that he believed in the Saviour Christ 'who descended, became flesh from the holy Virgin, became human, and was crucified for us under Pontius Pilate (τὸν σωτῆρα ἡμῶν Χριστὸν τὸν κατελθόντα καὶ σαρκωθέντα ἐκ τῆς ἁγίας παρθένου καὶ ἐνανθρωπήσαντα σταυρωθέντα τε ὑπὲρ ἡμῶν ἐπὶ Ποντίου Πιλάτου)'.[62] While he too explicitly referred only to N as his baptismal confession,[63] he was in fact – similar to Diogenes of Cyzicus in the first session[64] – quoting C¹ (omitting the Spirit). Thus even Dorotheus was confused about the text of N. He seems to have noticed this himself, because he added: 'Bear with me and if anything escapes me, correct me.'[65]

This Miaphysite protest against the drafting of a new confession was, however, unsuccessful. At the beginning of the fifth session (22 October 451), the appointed committee presented a draft *hóros* dealing with the questions of faith, which was rejected not only by the Roman legates (because the *Tomus Leonis*

---

57 Cf. Council of Chalcedon, *Actio IV*, 9.
58 Cf. Council of Chalcedon, *Actio IV*, 9, no. 12: Seleucus of Amaseia; 14: Theodore of Damascus; 117: Polychronius of Epiphaneia; 131: Romanus of Myra. By contrast, Lucian of Ipsus (no. 139) probably omitted N by mistake.
59 Cf. Council of Chalcedon, *Actio IV*, 25.
60 Cf. Council of Chalcedon, *Actio IV*, 88 (FaFo § 570e).
61 Cf. Council of Chalcedon, *Actio IV*, 93–97, 108 (FaFo § 570f), 112, 115.
62 Council of Chalcedon, *Actio IV*, 108 (FaFo § 570f).
63 Cf. Council of Chalcedon, *Actio IV*, 94, 110, 112, 115 and already 88 in the petition to the council.
64 Cf. above p. 381.
65 Council of Chalcedon, *Actio IV*, 108 (FaFo § 570f).

had, once again, been omitted from the list of orthodox writings) but also by some eastern bishops and was not even included in the council records. It should be noted here that the term *creed* is nowhere used for this draft of the final definition[66] – rather, this definition was understood from the outset to be an explanation of N (and C²) which did not itself bear the character of a creed in a formal sense. In view of the lack of consensus on this draft, the council presidents proposed to appoint of another committee, consisting of Patriarch Anatolius of Constantinople, the Roman delegation, six eastern bishops, and three representatives each from the (secular) dioceses of Pontica, Asiana, Thracia, and Illyricum to revise the draft, referencing both the title of Theotokos (which had been omitted in the draft document) and the *Tomus Leonis*.[67] The latter was rejected by the majority of the council: the Definition of Faith had already confirmed the Tome in its content (apparently meaning: without explicitly mentioning it).

As it progressed, the fifth session had thus produced the ambivalent result that the omission of the Tome posed no problem for the majority of the synod, while it was rejected by the Roman delegation, as was to be expected: a serious rift between the western and the eastern churches threatened to derail the council. The session was, therefore, paused, and the council secretary hurried to the palace to report to the Emperor Marcian and await his instructions regarding further proceedings. The latter instructed the assembly 'to produce a correct and unimpeachable definition of the faith (τὰ περὶ τῆς πίστεως ὀρθῶς καὶ ἀνεπιλήπτως τυπῶσαι)' and to convene a committee for this purpose consisting of the aforementioned prelates. Alternatively, he said, each metropolitan might demonstrate the orthodoxy of his clergy by producing appropriate statements. (This was the procedure which had been announced at the end of the first session, but had then tacitly been changed in the second(third) session.[68]) If this were to prove unsuccessful, the synod would have to meet again in the west (and that meant in Rome).[69] Back at the council its presidents then stated that the decisive point of dissent, namely whether Christ existed 'in two natures' after the incarnation (as Leo had claimed) or whether Dioscurus' formula 'of two natures' should be chosen instead, still required clarification. The council majority was clearly in favour of Leo's view. When the presidents ordered that this should indeed be inserted into the draft, the committee, which had been enlarged by additional members, withdrew for deliberation. The result, which was subsequently read out at the

---

66 The only exception is found in Council of Chalcedon, *Actio V*, 8.
67 Cf. Council of Chalcedon, *Actio V*, 10.
68 Cf. above p. 382.
69 Council of Chalcedon, *Actio V*, 22 (FaFo § 542).

full council,[70] was the famous christological Definition of Faith, which was not intended to be a new creed (it was, not least, completely unsuitable for catechetical and liturgical use), but a 'learned' clarification of the disputed christological questions. It is, therefore, not necessary to consider its christological statements in more detail here. Rather, what matters here is the position and meaning of N and C² in this context.

According to the final Definition agreed at Chalcedon, the basis of the Christian faith was clearly the creed (σύμβολον) of the 318 fathers (N) in the form quoted in the Definition itself. The 150 fathers assembled in Constantinople had subsequently 'sealed' this faith of Nicaea (καὶ αὐτοὶ τὴν αὐτὴν ἐπισφραγισάμενοι πίστιν) in the face of new heresies. In order to avoid the accusation of violating canon 7 of Ephesus, the hierarchy of the confessions was then explicitly stated to be: the 'exposition of faith' (πίστεως τὴν ἔκθεσιν) of Nicaea was 'pre-eminent' (προλάμπειν); likewise, those things that had been decreed by the 150 holy fathers at Constantinople were also 'to prevail' (κρατεῖν δὲ καὶ τὰ παρὰ τῶν ρν' ἁγίων πατέρων ἐν Κωνσταντινουπόλει ὁρισθέντα), because they served to fend off heresies and because they confirmed the 'catholic and apostolic faith' (πρὸς ἀναίρεσιν μὲν τῶν τότε φυεισῶν αἱρέσεων, βεβαίωσιν δὲ τῆς αὐτῆς καθολικῆς καὶ ἀποστολικῆς ἡμῶν πίστεως). The implication clearly is that the wording of N was not affected by this in any way and thus canon 7 was not violated.

Subsequently, both creeds were successively quoted, with N again being called a 'symbol' in the heading, while it was merely stated of C² that it said 'the same thing' (καὶ τὸ αὐτὸ τῶν ρν' ἁγίων πατέρων τῶν ἐν Κωνσταντινουπόλει συναχθέντων). This was a remarkable demotion if compared with how C² had been described in the council presidents' statement made at the first session and in the canonical collection from which the confession had been recited during the second(third) session: there the text had still been termed an ἔκθεσις and a ἁγία πίστις, now it no longer bore any such generic designation.[71]

The subsequent explanation, which stated that 'this wise and salutary symbol of divine grace' (τὸ σοφὸν καὶ σωτήριον τοῦτο τῆς θείας χάριτος σύμβολον) was sufficient for the full knowledge and confirmation of godliness,[72] accordingly referred primarily to N, to which C² was an explanatory appendix, repeating N's theological statements while clarifying disputed points (which were expressly named: 'complete' doctrine of the Trinity and of the incarnation: περί τε γὰρ τοῦ πατρὸς καὶ τοῦ υἱοῦ καὶ τοῦ ἁγίου πνεύματος ἐκδιδάσκει τὸ τέλειον καὶ τοῦ κυρίου τὴν

---

70 Cf. Council of Chalcedon, *Actio V*, 30–34 (FaFo § 215).
71 Cf. above p. 382. For the complex problem of the headings of the creeds in the manuscript tradition of the Definition cf. Kinzig, *Glaubensbekenntnis*, 2021, p. 125 n. 540.
72 Cf. Council of Chalcedon, *Actio V*, 34 (FaFo § 215).

ἐνανθρώπησιν τοῖς πιστῶς δεχομένοις παρίστησιν / 'for it both teaches the perfect [doctrine] concerning Father, Son, and Holy Spirit, and presents the incarnation of the Lord to those that faithfully accept it'). Thus the divinity of Son and Spirit and the full incarnation of the Lord were emphasized both against Dyophysite and Pneumatomachian reductionism and against Miaphysite one-sidedness.

A further exposition followed, rehearsing the dogmatic controversies of the time: the council held to 'the faith of the 318 holy fathers' (τῶν τιη′ ἁγίων πατέρων τὴν πίστιν) both against the Nestorians and the Eutychians. By contrast, the fathers gathered in the 'imperial city' had explained 'the doctrine concerning the substance of the [Holy] Spirit' (περὶ τῆς τοῦ πνεύματος οὐσίας διδασκαλίαν) without adding anything that was substantially new. This statement is perplexing in that C², as we know, does not mention the consubstantiality of the Spirit at all. It indicates, therefore, how C² had come to be interpreted – probably rightly – by the middle of the fifth century. This was followed by a host of witnesses from the fathers against Nestorius and Eutyches, with the *Tomus Leonis* now being cited among them. Only then does the actual, now famous Definition of Faith follow.

This Definition was confirmed at the sixth session on 25 October 451 by Emperor Marcian and Empress Pulcheria. In his address,[73] the emperor referred only to the apostolic teachings as handed down by the 318 fathers and confirmed by the *Tomus Leonis*, obviously trying to heal the rift between Rome and the eastern churches.[74] C² (as well as the writings of the other fathers) was not mentioned. Finally, the Definition of Faith was solemnly read out and signed by the bishops present.

✳

Finally a word must be said about the Greek text of N and C² which was adopted at the fifth and sixth sessions. As can be easily seen from the following table, the credal text printed by Schwartz in his edition of *Actio V* of Chalcedon is not identical with that of the second(third) session (the Greek text of the Definition quoted at the sixth session no longer survives):

---

73 Cf. Council of Chalcedon, *Actio VI*, 4.
74 Cf. ACO II 1, p. 336, ll. 4–8; cf. also ll. 20 f. (Greek) = ACO II 2, p. 97, ll. 29–31 and 98, ll. 11 f. and II 3, p. 409, ll. 22–4 and 410, ll. 5 f. (Latin).

N *Actio II(III)* 11 (= version of 325; FaFo § 135c = ed. Schwartz[75])	C² *Actio II(III)* 14 (MB = ed. Schwartz)[76]	N *Actio V* 33 (ed. Schwartz)[77]	C² *Actio V* 33 (R = Vat. 1431, f. 351r–v[78] = ed. Schwartz)[79]
Πιστεύομεν εἰς ἕνα θεόν, πατέρα, παντοκράτορα, πάντων ὁρατῶν τε καὶ ἀοράτων ποιητήν·	Πιστεύομεν εἰς ἕνα θεόν, πατέρα, παντοκράτορα, ποιητὴν οὐρανοῦ καὶ γῆς ὁρατῶν τε πάντων καὶ ἀοράτων·	Πιστεύομεν εἰς ἕνα θεόν, πατέρα, παντοκράτορα, ποιητὴν οὐρανοῦ καὶ γῆς ὁρατῶν τε πάντων.καὶ ἀοράτων·	Πιστεύομεν εἰς ἕνα θεόν, πατέρα, παντοκράτορα, ποιητὴν οὐρανοῦ καὶ γῆς ὁρατῶν τε πάντων καὶ ἀοράτων·
καὶ εἰς ἕνα κύριον Ἰησοῦν Χριστόν, τὸν υἱὸν τοῦ θεοῦ γεννηθέντα ἐκ τοῦ πατρός, μονογενῆ, τουτέστιν ἐκ τῆς οὐσίας τοῦ πατρός, θεὸν ἐκ θεοῦ, φῶς ἐκ φωτός, θεὸν ἀληθινὸν ἐκ θεοῦ ἀληθινοῦ, γεννηθέντα οὐ ποιηθέντα, ὁμοούσιον τῷ πατρί, δι᾽ οὗ τὰ πάντα ἐγένετο τά τε ἐν τῷ οὐρανῷ καὶ τὰ ἐν τῇ γῇ,	καὶ εἰς ἕνα κύριον Ἰησοῦν Χριστόν, τὸν υἱὸν τοῦ θεοῦ τὸν μονογενῆ, τὸν ἐκ τοῦ πατρὸς γεννηθέντα πρὸ πάντων τῶν αἰώνων, φῶς ἐκ φωτός, θεὸν ἀληθινὸν ἐκ θεοῦ ἀληθινοῦ, γεννηθέντα οὐ ποιηθέντα, ὁμοούσιον τῷ πατρί,	καὶ εἰς ἕνα κύριον Ἰησοῦν Χριστόν, τὸν υἱὸν τοῦ θεοῦ τὸν μονογενῆ, τὸν ἐκ τοῦ πατρὸς γεννηθέντα πρὸ πάντων τῶν αἰώνων, θεὸν ἀληθινὸν ἐκ θεοῦ ἀληθινοῦ, γεννηθέντα οὐ ποιηθέντα, ὁμοούσιον τῷ πατρί,	καὶ εἰς ἕνα κύριον Ἰησοῦν Χριστόν, τὸν υἱὸν τοῦ θεοῦ τὸν μονογενῆ, τὸν ἐκ τοῦ πατρὸς γεννηθέντα πρὸ πάντων τῶν αἰώνων, θεὸν ἀληθινὸν ἐκ θεοῦ ἀληθινοῦ, γεννηθέντα οὐ ποιηθέντα, ὁμοούσιον τῷ πατρί,

---

75 ACO II 1, p. 275, ll. 16–26 and app.
76 ACO II 1, p. 276, ll. 3–16 and app.
77 ACO II 1, p. 323, ll. 10–19.
78 I checked the scans at URL <https://digi.vatlib.it/view/MSS_Vat.gr.1431> (16/11/2023).
79 ACO II 1, p. 324, ll. 2–14 and app.

(continued)

N *Actio II(III)* 11 (= version of 325; FaFo § 135c = ed. Schwartz)	C² *Actio II(III)* 14 (MB = ed. Schwartz)	N *Actio V* 33 (ed. Schwartz)	C² *Actio V* 33 (R = Vat. 1431, f. 351r–v = ed. Schwartz)
τὸν δι᾿ ἡμᾶς τοὺς ἀνθρώπους	τὸν δι᾿ ἡμᾶς τοὺς ἀνθρώπους	τὸν δι᾿ ἡμᾶς τοὺς ἀνθρώπους	τὸν δι᾿ ἡμᾶς τοὺς ἀνθρώπους
καὶ διὰ τὴν ἡμετέραν σωτηρίαν κατελθόντα	καὶ διὰ τὴν ἡμετέραν σωτηρίαν κατελθόντα ἐκ τῶν οὐρανῶν	καὶ διὰ τὴν ἡμετέραν σωτηρίαν κατελθόντα	καὶ διὰ τὴν ἡμετέραν σωτηρίαν κατελθόντα
καὶ σαρκωθέντα	καὶ σαρκωθέντα, ἐκ πνεύματος ἁγίου καὶ Μαρίας τῆς παρθένου	καὶ σαρκωθέντα	καὶ σαρκωθέντα ἐκ πνεύματος ἁγίου καὶ Μαρίας τῆς παρθένου
καὶ[80] ἐνανθρωπήσαντα,	καὶ ἐνανθρωπήσαντα σταυρωθέντα τε ὑπὲρ ἡμῶν ἐπὶ Ποντίου Πιλάτου	καὶ ἐνανθρωπήσαντα	καὶ ἐνανθρωπήσαντα σταυρωθέντα τε ὑπὲρ ἡμῶν ἐπὶ Ποντίου Πιλάτου
παθόντα	καὶ παθόντα καὶ ταφέντα	καὶ παθόντα	καὶ ταφέντα
καὶ ἀναστάντα τῇ τρίτῃ ἡμέρᾳ,	καὶ ἀναστάντα τῇ τρίτῃ ἡμέρᾳ κατὰ τὰς γραφὰς	καὶ ἀναστάντα τῇ τρίτῃ ἡμέρᾳ	καὶ ἀναστάντα τῇ τρίτῃ ἡμέρᾳ
ἀνελθόντα εἰς τοὺς οὐρανούς,	καὶ ἀνελθόντα εἰς τοὺς οὐρανοὺς καὶ καθεζόμενον ἐν δεξιᾷ [ἐκ δεξιῶν Μ] τοῦ πατρὸς	καὶ ἀνελθόντα εἰς τοὺς οὐρανοὺς	καὶ ἀνελθόντα εἰς τοὺς[81] οὐρανοὺς καὶ καθεζόμενον ἐν δεξιᾷ τοῦ πατρὸς
καὶ[82] ἐρχόμενον	καὶ πάλιν ἐρχόμενον μετὰ δόξης	καὶ ἐρχόμενον	καὶ πάλιν ἐρχόμενον μετὰ δόξης
κρῖναι ζῶντας καὶ νεκρούς·	κρῖναι ζῶντας καὶ νεκρούς, οὗ τῆς βασιλείας οὐκ ἔσται τέλος·	κρῖναι ζῶντας καὶ νεκρούς·	κρῖναι ζῶντας καὶ νεκρούς, οὗ τῆς βασιλείας οὐκ ἔσται τέλος·
καὶ εἰς τὸ ἅγιον πνεῦμα.	καὶ εἰς τὸ πνεῦμα τὸ ἅγιον,	καὶ εἰς τὸ ἅγιον πνεῦμα.	καὶ εἰς τὸ πνεῦμα τὸ ἅγιον,

---

80 Probably not contained in the authentic text of N.
81 Missing in R.
82 Probably not contained in the authentic text of N.

(continued)

N *Actio II(III)* 11 (= version of 325; FaFo § 135c = ed. Schwartz)	C² *Actio II(III)* 14 (MB = ed. Schwartz)	N *Actio V* 33 (ed. Schwartz)	C² *Actio V* 33 (R = Vat. 1431, f. 351r–v = ed. Schwartz)
[Anathemas]	τὸ κύριον καὶ ζωοποιόν, τὸ ἐκ τοῦ πατρὸς ἐκπορευόμενον, τὸ σὺν πατρὶ καὶ υἱῷ συμπροσκυνούμενον καὶ συνδοξαζόμενον, τὸ λαλῆσαν διὰ τῶν προφητῶν· εἰς μίαν, ἁγίαν, καθολικὴν καὶ ἀποστολικὴν ἐκκλησίαν. Ὁμολογοῦμεν ἓν βάπτισμα εἰς ἄφεσιν ἁμαρτιῶν. Προσδοκῶμεν ἀνάστασιν [ἐκ Bᵇ] νεκρῶν καὶ ζωὴν τοῦ μέλλοντος αἰῶνος. Ἀμήν.	[Anathemas]	τὸ κύριον καὶ ζωοποιόν, τὸ ἐκ τοῦ πατρὸς ἐκπορευόμενον, τὸ σὺν πατρὶ καὶ υἱῷ προσκυνούμενον καὶ συνδοξαζόμενον, τὸ λαλῆσαν διὰ τῶν προφητῶν· εἰς μίαν, καθολικὴν καὶ ἀποστολικὴν ἐκκλησίαν. Ὁμολογοῦμεν ἓν βάπτισμα εἰς ἄφεσιν ἁμαρτιῶν. Προσδοκῶμεν ἀνάστασιν νεκρῶν καὶ ζωὴν τοῦ μέλλοντος αἰῶνος. Ἀμήν.

From the comparison of these different versions it becomes clear that versions of N and C² have been aligned with each other in Schwartz' edition of the Definition of Faith. They are now identical in the first section and in the second section up to κατελθόντα; only then do various additions follow in C²:
(1) ἐκ πνεύματος ἁγίου καὶ Μαρίας τῆς παρθένου
(2) σταυρωθέντα τε ὑπὲρ ἡμῶν ἐπὶ Ποντίου Πιλάτου
(3) καὶ καθεζόμενον ἐν δεξιᾷ τοῦ πατρός
(4) the extension of καὶ ἐρχόμενον to καὶ πάλιν ἐρχόμενον μετὰ δόξης
(5) οὗ τῆς βασιλείας οὐκ ἔσται τέλος
(6) the entire pneumatological section.
In addition καὶ παθόντα was replaced by καὶ ταφέντα.

Since the original text of N is well known, it would be pointless to list the differences between the text of the fifth session and the original version. Matters are different with C², whose original text must first be determined. The text of the fifth session features five omissions and one variant reading compared to that of the second(third) session:

(1) φῶς ἐκ φωτός
(2) ἐκ τῶν οὐρανῶν
(3) καὶ παθόντα
(4) κατὰ τὰς γραφάς
(5) προσκυνούμενον instead of συμπροσκυνούμενον
(6) ἁγίαν.

None of these differences seems to be particularly significant theologically. Three of them (nos. 1, 2, and 4) align it more closely with the text (also revised) of N. However, the reason for the omission of nos. 3 and 6 and the change of no. 5 remains unclear.

In order to decide whether or not Schwartz' decision to print these versions as those of the fifth session is correct one must look at the complicated textual transmission of the Greek and Latin acts of the council. I have done this elsewhere and may, therefore, for the sake of brevity, refer the reader to these reflections.[83] They lead to the conclusion that it is more plausible that the original text of C² in the fifth/sixth session was the same as that in the second(third). It is so far unknown where the shortened text of C² in the Definition originated.[84]

Apart from these philological considerations, reasons connected to the reception history of the creeds make it very unlikely that the text of C² in the Definition was different from the one read in the second(third) session. In view of the facts that N and C² had already been authoritatively established in the second(third) session, that moreover its textual tradition is unproblematic, and that it was this text of the second(third) session that was received at the Third Council of Constantinople in 680/681 as part of the Chalcedonian Definition,[85] it is hardly conceivable that the text of the creeds at the fifth/sixth session should have been any different. On the contrary, precisely *because* the text of N had already been read out in an authoritative version, it is difficult to assume – in view of canon 7 of Ephesus – that *this* version, of all things, should have been changed. This would

83 Cf. Kinzig, *Glaubensbekenntnis*, 2021, pp. 128–63.
84 Cf. also Drecoll, 'Edition', 2015, pp. 122 f.
85 On N cf. *Actio XVIII* (ACO² II 2, p. 770, ll. 6–18); cf. FaFo, vol. I, p. 292 (no. 32; here the council followed the version contained in cod. B for Chalcedon which includes the addition of καὶ ἐν δεξιᾷ τοῦ πατρὸς καθήμενον in the christological section). On C² cf. *Actio XVIII* (ACO² II 2, p. 770, ll. 22–35; cf. FaFo, vol. I, p. 512).

have caused a storm of indignation, especially among the Egyptian participants in the council (as the debate at the first session and the Egyptian protest in response to Diogenes' remark had shown[86]).

It is indisputable that at a certain point in the tradition an alignment took place, but there is no compelling reason to assume that this should have happened at Chalcedon itself. It is much more plausible to assume that the credal texts of the two sessions were identical and corresponded to the text of the second(third) session. In other words, the version of C² read out at the second(third) session is the one that had first been discussed in Constantinople but not adopted there in the end.

8.2 Reception of C² after Chalcedon

The view traditionally held in classical credal research is that C² established itself relatively quickly as the 'standard' creed after Chalcedon.[87] According to Kelly, 'broadly speaking, C [= C²], to all intents and purposes in its original form, has enjoyed a monopoly of baptism since the sixth century'. At the same time, Kelly was quite aware that this did not apply to various oriental churches (he names 'the Jacobite church of Syria, and the Nestorian, Armenian and Abyssinian churches') and that 'the writings of Philoxenus of Hierapolis (Mabbug) and Severus of Antioch' showed 'that forms far from identical with C continued in use'. But after the Fifth Ecumenical Council of 553, the position of C² had been 'assured':

> As the creed of the metropolis of the patriarchate, it was, after all, only a matter of time before it was adopted wherever the writ of Constantinople ran.

In Kelly's view there was 'nothing surprising or out of the ordinary in this development: we should in any case have expected C eventually to oust all other creeds in the East.'[88] In truth, this process was clearly more complicated. In what follows, I will first look at the reception of C² within the Later Roman Empire and its western successor states. The credal developments in the oriental churches will be considered in chapter 9.

---

86 Cf. above pp. 381 f.
87 This chapter is based on Kinzig, *Glaubensbekenntnis*, 2021, pp. 164–84.
88 Kelly 1972, pp. 345 f.

8.2.1 Reception in the east

In the period after Chalcedon, there was resistance in Palestine and Egypt, directed not only against its christological Definition, but also against C², which formed an integral part of it. Subsequent emperors had to take this into account: the first imperial edict confirming Chalcedon mentioned, in addition to the Definition of Faith, the *expositiones et statuta* of the 318 and the 150 fathers, which obviously referred to N and C² as well as the canons of Nicaea and Constantinople.[89] Emperor Marcian proceeded similarly in his Second Edict of 13 March 452 and in his fourth edict of 18 July 452, wherein the results of the Council of Ephesus (431) were also mentioned.[90]

However, he then adopted a different tactic towards the Palestinian and Egyptian Miaphysites: he only mentioned N and the Council of Ephesus in a letter to the Palestinian monks (late 452/early 453).[91] Empress Pulcheria endorsed her husband's view in a letter to the same addressees.[92] And in a letter to a synod convened under Juvenal in Jerusalem from the end of 453, Marcian affirmed only N, now even alluding to the canonization formula and thus canon 7 of Ephesus.[93]

The emperor adopted the same approach as over against Juvenal in a letter to the abbot-bishop Macarius and the Sinaitic monks from about the same time.[94] In 454 he gave his *decurio silentiariorum* John a letter to deliver to the Alexandrian monks, which he hoped would bring about ecclesial peace.[95] Here, too, he referred twice to N alone, again alluding to canon 7, and even referred to the

---

89 Cf. Council of Chalcedon, *Collectio Vaticana 8* (FaFo § 543).

90 Cf. Council of Chalcedon, *Collectio Vaticana 9* (FaFo § 544); Council of Chalcedon, *Gestorum Chaledonensium Versio a Rustico Edita 108* (§ 545). Cf. also Smith 2018, p. 204.

91 Cf. ACO II 1, pp. 483–6 (Council of Chalcedon, *Gesta Chalcedone 26*), esp. 485, ll. 20 f., 34–7; 486, ll. 2–4 (Greek) = II 5, pp. 4–7 (Council of Chalcedon, *Collectio Sangermanensis 2*), esp. 6, ll. 11 f., 26–9, 30 f. (Latin).

92 Cf. ACO II 1, pp. 487 f. (Council of Chalcedon, *Gesta Chalcedone 27*), esp. 487, ll. 15–18 (where Constantinople is likewise omitted between mentions of Nicaea and Ephesus); 487, ll. 22–4 (Greek) = II 5, pp. 7 f. (Council of Chalcedon, *Collectio Sangermanensis 3*), esp. 7, ll. 39 – 8, l. 2; 8, ll. 6–8 (lat.).

93 Cf. ACO II 1, pp. 492 f. (*Marciani Imperatoris Epistula ad Synodum Palaestinam*), esp. 493, ll. 11 f., 22–4, 32–5 (canonization formula/canon 7). Likewise, Pulcheria's letter to Bassa of Jerusalem (Council of Chalcedon, *Gesta Chalcedone 31*; ACO II 1, pp. 494 f., esp. 494, ll. 10 f., 14–17, 31 f.; 495, ll. 2 f.: canonization formula/canon 7).

94 Cf. ACO II 1, pp. 490 f. (Council of Chalcedon, *Gesta Chalcedone 29*), esp. 490, ll. 13–15 (canonization formula/canon 7); 491, ll. 26–9.

95 It was related to unrest in Alexandria after Dioscurus' death in Gangra on 4 September 454. Cf. Pseudo-Zachariah Rhetor, *Historia ecclesiastica* 3,11; furthermore Grillmeier 1987, pp. 105 f.; Maraval 2001(2010), pp. 121 f.

creed as his baptismal confession at the second mention.[96] Subsequently, he seemed to quote the text of N,[97] although he used the form expanded by μονογενῆ after τὸν υἱὸν τοῦ θεοῦ and by the reference to the Holy Spirit and the Virgin, thus in fact in the version preserved in C¹ (and C²).

The omission of any reference to the Council of Constantinople cannot have been an oversight. Rather, Marcian refrained from explicitly mentioning C² in an attempt to accommodate the Miaphysite monks in the Egyptian capital, leading to the conclusion that C² remained controversial in Egypt, because the incarnation from the Virgin, as stated in C², was widely interpreted as being anti-Miaphysite. However, it is clear from Marcian's letter to the *praefectus praetorio Orientis* Palladius of 1 August 455, which declared the faith of Nicea *and* of Constantinople as mandatory, that this approach was only tactical.[98]

Even when Emperor Leo I (r. 457–474) issued his circular letter regarding the legitimacy of Timothy II Aelurus (Patriarch of Alexandria 454–460, 475–477) and the recognition of Chalcedon in October 457, the Egyptian bishops refused to recognize C² and Chalcedon, citing the canonization formula/canon 7. They even went so far as to claim that they had no knowledge at all of a 'synod of 150'.[99] Timothy Aelurus himself also quoted only N, not C²,[100] although he affirms in a letter to the city of Constantinople (*c.* 460/464) that he had learned 'the formulation of God's law [. . .] from the 318 and the 150 holy fathers'.[101]

It is uncertain which confession Peter Fuller (who intermittently served as Miaphysite patriarch of Antioch in the period 471–488) allegedly introduced in mass, as Theodore the Reader who reports this event is rather unreliable.[102] The

---

96 Cf. ACO II 1, pp. 488 f. (Council of Chalcedon, *Gesta Chalcedone 28*; FaFo § 546), esp. 489, ll. 1–3 (canonization formula/canon 7), 16–18 (Greek) = II 5, pp. 3 f. (Council of Chalcedon, *Collectio Sangermanensis 1*), esp. 3, ll. 17–19; 3, l. 32 – 4, l. 3 (Latin).

97 ACO II 1, p. 489, ll. 19–22 (FaFo § 546): [. . .] πιστεύουσα τὸν δεσπότην ἡμῶν καὶ σωτῆρα Χριστόν, τὸν υἱὸν τοῦ θεοῦ τὸν μονογενῆ, τὸν συναΐδιον καὶ ὁμοούσιον τῷ πατρὶ δι' ἡμᾶς καὶ διὰ τὴν ἡμετέραν σωτηρίαν ἐνηνθρωπηκέναι γεννηθέντα ἐκ πνεύματος ἁγίου καὶ Μαρίας τῆς θεοτόκου παρθένου [. . .]. The emperor believed 'that our Lord and Saviour Christ the only-begotten Son of God, coeternal and consubstantial with the Father, for us and for our salvation became human and was born from the Holy Spirit and the virgin, Theotokos Mary, [. . .]'.

98 Cf. ACO II 2, pp. 116, l. 29 – 117, l. 2 (Council of Chalcedon, *Collectio Vaticana 15*).

99 Cf. ACO II 5, pp. 21, l. 32 – 22, l. 10; 22, ll. 17–21 (partly in FaFo § 571). The text is apparently shortened. Cf. the paraphrases in ACO II 5, pp. 52, ll. 28–35; 68, ll. 6–15. In addition, Schwartz 1926, pp. 84 f.; Price 2009, pp. 308 f.; Siebigs 2010, vol. I, pp. 353–5 and n. 309; Smith 2018, pp. 205 f.; Leuenberger-Wenger 2019, pp. 408–11.

100 Cf. FaFo § 216.

101 Timothy, *Epistula ad Constantinopolitanos* (ed. Ebied/Wickham 1970, p. 333; tr. Ebied/Wickham 1970, p. 351).

102 Cf. Theodore the Reader, *Historia ecclesiastica*, epit. 429 (FaFo § 685a) and below pp. 508 f.

so-called *Liturgical Homily* (no. 35/17) attributed to Narsai of Edessa (d. *c.* 502) also offers no evidence for the reception of C² around the end of the fifth century, because it almost certainly dates from a later period. The creed found there is essentially N^Ant.[103]

Emperor Basiliscus (r. 475–476), leaning towards Miaphysitism, made no mention of C² either in his Encyclical but merely wrote in rather vague terms that the 150 fathers had 'affirmed' the council and opposed the Pneumatomachians. At the same time, he rejected not only the Definition of Faith of Chalcedon, but also the 'explanation of the creed' (ἔκθεσις συμβόλου), which probably referred to C².[104] Likewise, the *Henoticon* (482) of Emperor Zeno (r. 474–475, 476–491) only vaguely references the 'affirmation' of N by the 150 fathers.[105]

This evidence may shed new light on an incidental remark made by Theodore the Reader. In his *Church History*, he claims that the 'Creed of the 318 fathers' had originally been recited in the eastern capital during the bishop's Good Friday sermon (apparently as part of the *Traditio* or *Redditio symboli*). Subsequently, the Miaphysite Patriarch Timothy I (*sedit* 511–518) had introduced it into the ordinary of the mass in order to differentiate himself from his predecessor, the Chalcedonian-minded Macedonius II (*sedit* 496–511).[106] It may well be that Theodore is, in fact, referring to C¹, which was already established in Constantinople and which, as we have seen, was considered 'Nicene'. Even the Constantinopolitan Synod *endemousa* of 518 spoke of Constantinople, Ephesus, and Chalcedon as having merely 'reaf-

---

103 Cf. below p. 424.

104 Cf. Basiliscus, *Encyclion* (FaFo § 548).

105 Cf. Zeno, *Henoticon* 5 (FaFo § 550). However, he may, perhaps, allude to C² in the phrase: σαρκωθέντα ἐκ πνεύματος ἁγίου καὶ Μαρίας τῆς θεοτόκου ἀεὶ παρθένου ('having become incarnate from the Holy Spirit and the ever-virgin Mary'). Furthermore cf. Martyrius of Jerusalem (*sedit* 478–86) in his definition of faith (FaFo § 217), which may have served as the *Vorlage* of the *Henoticon*: 'Then everyone who holds, has held, or has taught an opinion contrary to the definition of the faith of our 318 holy fathers, the bishops [who assembled at] Nicaea, which the 150 believing and true bishops [who met] in the imperial city upheld and confirmed, as well as the Council of Ephesus, let him be condemned. [. . .] If any man teaches, innovates, maintains, or explains anything that is contrary to the tested and orthodox teaching of the faith of those 318 holy [bishops], of the 150 bishops, or of those [bishops] of [the Council of] Ephesus, or has a different definition or faith, he is alien to the holy Church.' There is no mention of a creed regarding to Constantinople. The 'orthodox teaching of the faith' could also refer to a synodal letter. A Miaphysite confession of Egyptian clergy also dates from the time of the *Henoticon*. Here the baptismal creed is N which had been 'confirmed' by the 150 holy fathers (FaFo § 219[1]). Cf. furthermore the letter of a number of Miaphysite bishops to Justinian of 532 (FaFo § 222[15c]). Sophronius of Jerusalem (*sedit* 634–8) in his *Epistula synodica ad Sergium Constantinopolitanum* 2,5,2 (FaFo § 235b) expresses himself in a similar vein.

106 Cf. also below p. 509.

firmed' the baptismal creed N (or C¹),[107] and Barsanuphius of Gaza (d. *c.* 545) calls 'the faith of the 318 fathers' the 'royal road' (τὴν βασιλικὴν ὁδόν; Num 21:22) to be kept to.[108] Given its close connection to the Council of Chalcedon this meant that C² remained fiercely contested.

However, it found its way into the already mentioned collection of canon law of the fifth century, the *Corpus canonum*, which has come down to us in Syriac translation.[109] Likewise, it is quoted by prominent Miaphysite theologians such as Philoxenus of Mabbug (d. 523) and Severus of Antioch (*sedit* 512–538).[110] In Coptic canon law sources, the tradition of C² also begins in the sixth century.[111]

The Emperor Justinian (r. 527–565) also seems to refer to C² when, in a letter to Epiphanius of Constantinople, he speaks of the 150 fathers having 'explained and interpreted' N. This document is also remarkable in that Justinian explicitly mentions the additions in C² compared to N which he considers of summary importance: the divinity of the Spirit and the incarnation 'from the holy ever-virgin and Theotokos Mary'.[112]

Justinian also uses a very similar wording in his *Edictum rectae fidei*: Constantinople had turned against the Pneumatomachian Macedonius and the 'Apolinarian Magnus' and had clarified the teaching on the Holy Spirit.[113] The reference to the Apolinarian Magnus is puzzling and shows how poorly informed even authorities in Constantinople were about this event.

In his instruction to the Fifth Ecumenical Council of 553, Justinian repeated these phrases, now saying that Apolinarius and Magnus had blasphemed against the incarnate Logos, claiming that the latter had not possessed a *sensus humanus*, but had been united with flesh, which had only possessed an *anima irrationabilis*. This had been rectified in Constantinople and thus the *recta fides* had been proclaimed.[114] In this instance, therefore, the 'right faith' of Constantinople was set alongside that of Nicaea, C² even surpassing N insofar as it had clarified the questions about the incarnation and the Holy Spirit that had been left unanswered in Nicaea.

---

107 Cf. *Collectio Sabbaitica* 5,27 / *Acclamationes et allocutiones* (FaFo § 574a1). Cf. also FaFo § 574a2 and b.
108 Cf. Barsanuphius, *Epistula 58*, ll. 28–32 (SC 426, p. 284). As regards context cf. Perrone 2019, pp. 195 f.
109 Cf. above p. 386 f. and below p. 416.
110 Cf. below pp. 416 f.
111 Cf. below p. 441.
112 Justinian, *Epistula ad Epiphanium Archiepiscopum Constantinopolitanum* 11 (FaFo § 554). Cf. also Kelly 1972, p. 334.
113 Justinian, *Edictum rectae fidei* (FaFo § 556[16]).
114 Cf. Justinian, *Actio I 7 / Iustiniani forma ante synodum lecta* 14 (FaFo § 557).

Justinian's authoritative intervention, however, by no means settled the matter. His successor Justin II (r. 565–578) even took a backwards step. At a meeting with the Miaphysites in the Monastery of Mar Zakai in Callinicum (around 568), he spoke again of the 'confirmation' of N by the fathers in Constantinople (and in Ephesus).[115] Later, he changed his policy, taking a consistently Chalcedonian position after all. Furthermore, according to John of Biclaro, he decided that the 'creed of the 150 fathers gathered in Constantinople' (i.e. C²) was now to be 'sung' in every mass before the Lord's Prayer.[116] This assertion, which scholars, including myself, have in the past always dismissed as unhistorical,[117] although it came from an eyewitness,[118] can now possibly be brought into connection with the testimony of Theodore the Reader in such a way that N (= C¹) was replaced by C² (although its position before the Lord's Prayer continues to be a problem).[119]

Nevertheless, the relationship of N to C² and the problem of the authority of the latter creed remained unresolved. John IV of Jerusalem (*sedit* 575–594) referred to the first four ecumenical councils in a letter to Abas, catholicos of the Albanians (*sedit* 552–596), in 575, in order to persuade Abas to accept the Chalcedonian Christology; in it he quoted a trinitarian and a christological creed as well as the central part of the Definition of Chalcedon but neither N nor C².[120] Maximus the Confessor (d. 662) deals with the question of the sufficiency of N in a debate with Miaphysites, in a – presumably early – work which only survives in fragments, rejecting the claim that Chalcedon had contradicted N and introduced a new faith. The fathers of Nicaea, Maximus argues, established the faith once and for all, whereas Constantinople (and later councils) only defended it 'in their own words and doctrinal statements' (διὰ τῶν οἰκείων φωνῶν καὶ δογμάτων) against heretics like Eunomius and Macedonius.[121] This seems to refer to the Tomus of Constantinople rather than the creed (even though he undoubtedly knew the latter).[122]

Furthermore, the Third Council of Constantinople (680/681) still referred to N as 'put forth by the 318 fathers' (τὸ παρὰ τῶν τριακοσίων δέκα καὶ ὀκτὼ πατέρων

---

115 Cf. Justin II., *Edictum primum de fide* (FaFo § 558).

116 John of Biclaro, *Chronicon* 2 (FaFo § 689). Cf. also below p. 510.

117 Cf. Kinzig, 'Das Glaubensbekenntnis', 2017, p. 319.

118 On John of Biclaro's stay in Constantinople cf. below p. 406.

119 Cf. below pp. 499, 508 f.

120 Cf. John IV of Jerusalem, *Epistula ad Abam* 9–10. 12 (Terian 2020, pp. 23 f., 26 f.).

121 Two fragments from an unknown writing, fragment 2 (CPG 7697[22]; Jankowiak/Booth 2015, p. 71; PG 91, cols. 260B–C). Cf. already 257D–260A. However, in Maximus' *Relatio motionis* (CPG 7736) 4 (Allen/Neil 2002, p. 56) his opponent clearly quotes the first section of C², which Maximus' response relates to Nicaea.

122 Cf. below p. 411.

ἐκτεθέν) and 'confirmed' (βεβαιωθέν) by the 150 fathers.[123] However, the Greek text of the council's Definition of Faith terms both N and C² an ἔκθεσις πίστεως,[124] continuing: 'This pious and orthodox σύμβολον of the divine grace sufficed for both the full knowledge and the confirmation of the orthodox faith.'[125] This sentence is taken almost verbatim from the Chalcedonian Definition – but the continuation, which indicated that 'symbol' primarily denoted N, commented on above, has been omitted here.[126] The present wording leaves open whether only N is to be seen as a 'symbol' or whether the term refers to *both* formulae. Likewise, it remains unclear whether 'knowledge' (N) and 'confirmation' (C²) applied to both formulae. Be that as it may, the conciliar upgrading of C² is already apparent in this instance.

By the time of the Seventh Ecumenical Council of 787 the situation is unambiguous. The creed cited in its *hóros* is now *exclusively* C².[127] Nonetheless, the council fathers also implicitly referred to canon 7 of Ephesus when they claimed that they had 'taken nothing away, added nothing', but preserved 'all (teachings) of the Catholic Church undiminished'.[128] However, N had by now in actual fact been dropped.

The use of C² in baptism is then also attested by the so-called *Barberini Euchologion*, a worship book which contains a Constantinopolitan baptismal service (composed before the second half of the eighth century).[129] Likewise, the confession used in the Liturgies of St James, St Basil, and St Chrysostom was now C².[130]

But even at that point the use of N persisted, in particular – as Kelly had correctly seen – in certain eastern churches.[131] In addition, a whole series of Greek

---

123 Third Council of Constantinople, *Actio XVIII* (FaFo § 242c).

124 Cf. ACO² II, p. 770, ll. 5–35 (Third Council of Constantinople, *Actio XVIII*). However, cf. the titles of the Latin translations of C² in *Actio XVII* and *XVIII*, ACO² II, pp. 716, l. 12 (*Actio XVII*, *Collectio Hispana*): *Item et CL sanctorum Patrum Constantinopoli congregatorum* and 717, l. 15 (*Actio XVII*) = 771, l. 20 (*Actio XVIII*): *Et centum quinquaginta sanctorum patrum Constantinopolim congregatorum*. In the latter passage Codex L offers for N: *Symbolum CL patrum in Constantinopolim congregatorum* and for C²: *Symbolum Constantinopolim CL sanctorum patrum*. Cf. also FaFo §§ 135d42 and 135d43. Here I cannot deal with the complex question of the textual transmission of the Greek and Latin acts; cf. Rudolf Riedinger in ACO² II, pp. XVIII–XXII.

125 Third Council of Constantinople, *Actio XVIII* (FaFo § 242c).

126 Cf. above p. 391.

127 Cf. ACO² III 3, p. 822, ll. 16–19 (Second Council of Nicaea, *Actio VII*).

128 ACO² III 3, p. 822, ll. 14–16 (Second Council of Nicaea, *Actio VII*).

129 Cf. FaFo § 677.

130 Cf. FaFo §§ 693 (Liturgy of St James); 694b (Liturgies of St Basil and St Chrysostom – unfortunately the text of the creed is omitted here, but cf. Brightman 1896(1965), p. 383, ll. 7–25 and FaFo, vol. I, p. 518).

131 Cf. Kelly 1972, p. 345 and below ch. 9.

and Coptic inscriptions, papyri, wooden tablets, and ostraca up to at least the seventh century survives, which all testify to a continuing use of N (as opposed to C²) especially in Egypt, above all in popular culture.[132] In one case, N also seems to have been used in a eucharistic liturgy.[133]

8.2.2 Reception in the west

The western reception of C² was different, but likewise greatly delayed. There is no evidence of the use of this creed in the writings of Leo the Great (*sedit* 440–461) – he almost always refers to the Roman one instead.[134] The *confessio* to which Leo refers in his famous *Tomus* is also clearly R.[135] This had already led to the accusation that Leo had not preserved the wording of N by the fifth century. An example from the end of the century, is Vigilius of Thapsus' book *Against Eutyches* in which he does not dispute this charge at all, but tries to parry it with the argument that the faith of Rome is apostolic and as such older than N.[136] This remark probably again refers to R, to which the dignity of N is subordinate.

We possess a *Fides* whose theology is rather unremarkable from Pope Hormisdas (*sedit* 514–523). He sent this document, in which neither Nicaea nor Constantinople are mentioned, to Constantinople in the summer of 515.[137]

Sometimes the letter *Dum in sanctae* (552) of Pope Vigilius (*sedit* 537–555) is cited as the first evidence of the reception of C² in the Latin Church.[138] But Vigilius attributes a creed as such only to Nicaea, noting summarily with regard to Constantinople, Ephesus, and Chalcedon that these councils 'declared and widely disseminated the same faith in one and the same opinion and spirit' (*eandem fidem uno eodemque sensu atque spiritu declarantes latissime ediderunt*).[139] Since nei-

---

132 Cf. below pp. 443, 538 f.

133 Cf. below pp. 507 f.

134 Cf. the references in FaFo §§ 255, 360, 441.

135 Cf. Leo, *Epistula 28*, 14 (FaFo § 255a): '[. . .] credere se in deum, patrem omnipotentem, et in Christum Iesum, filium eius unicum, dominum nostrum, qui natus est de spiritu sancto et Maria virgine [. . .]'. In addition, Smith 2018, p. 159.

136 Cf. Vigilius, *Contra Eutychetem* 4,1 (FaFo § 318a2).

137 Cf. the *Fides Hormisdae papae* (FaFo § 442).

138 Cf., e.g., Kelly 1972, p. 346; Riedl 2004, pp. 26 f. ('a slight allusion').

139 Vigilius, *Dum in sanctae* (*Epistula 15*; FaFo § 444[1]). Similarly, the phrase 'ex spiritu sancto et ex beata Maria semper uirgine humanitatis sumpsit initium' ('he took the beginning of humanity from the Holy Spirit and from the blessed, ever-virgin Mary') later in the text is not a direct quotation of C². Further down he says, 'Passus carne est pro nobis dei filius, crucifixus carne est, mortuus carne est et die tertio resurrexit' ('the Son of God suffered for us in the flesh, was cruci-

ther Ephesus nor Chalcedon adopted creeds, it is rather unlikely that in the case of Constantinople a creed is referred to, even though the word *fides* is used.[140] Vigilius merely cites C^2 as part of Chalcedon's Definition of Faith in his letter on the Three Chapters of early 554.[141]

Likewise, Pope Pelagius I (*sedit* 556–561), who expressed his orthodoxy on various occasions,[142] does not explicitly mention N or C^2 anywhere in his relevant letters 10 and 11, but states in the former epistle that he 'preserves the faith established by the sacred teaching of the apostles' and 'confirmed by the authority of the Synod of Nicaea, which had been expounded by the decisions of the holy Synods of Constantinople, Ephesus I, and Chalcedon'.[143] (Whether or not *sacra apostolorum doctrina* refers to R remains uncertain.) In *Epistula 11* he merely vows to faithfully observe what the first four ecumenical councils had decided 'in defence of the holy faith and in condemnation of heresies and heretics' (*in sanctae fidei defensione et damnationibus heresum atque hereticorum*).[144]

It is also instructive to note a statement of Pelagius II (*sedit* 579–590), whose first letter to the bishops of Histria (perhaps in fact authored by the later Pope Gregory) says the following:

> For with an entirely pure conscience we preach, hold, and defend to the last drop of our blood that faith which has been handed down by the apostles, was preserved inviolate by their successors, and was taken up and rendered into a creed by the reverend Nicene Council of the 318 fathers [. . .].[145]

Subsequently, Constantinople (along with Ephesus and Chalcedon) is indeed mentioned, but without reference to a creed. It is highly probable that Pelagius II is no longer referring to either R or T nor to C^2 when mentioning the *fides* handed down by the apostles, but most likely to N.[146]

Bishop Mansuetus of Milan mentions the composition of N in a brief outline about the councils included in a synodal letter (680) to the Byzantine Emperor

---

fied in the flesh, died in the flesh, and on the third day rose again') – here the sequence of the cola seems to follow T.

140 Similarly, Gemeinhardt 2002, p. 286 and n. 418.

141 Cf. Pope Vigilius, *Constitutum II* 6 (FaFo § 184f17.3).

142 An extensive confession from his pen is preserved in *Epistula 7* (FaFo § 445) which, however, offers no help as regards the question which interests us here.

143 Pope Pelagius I, *Epistula 10*, 4.

144 Pope Pelagius I, *Epistula 11* (D/H 444 = Gassó/Batlle 1956, p. 38, ll. 35–8).

145 Pope Pelagius II, *Epistula I ad episcopos Histriae* 8 (FaFo § 367).

146 Cf. also Pelagius, *Epistula I ad episcopos Histriae* 15 (ACO IV 2, p. 106, ll. 25–9).

Constantine IV (r. 668–685), but only references the condemnation of Macedonius with regard to Constantinople.[147]

Nonetheless, the reception of C² can be demonstrated in two ways, starting from the end of the sixth century: on the one hand, by means of synodal theological declarations; on the other hand, through the liturgy of baptism and of the mass. The earliest evidence of this reception is found not in Italy, but in Spain. Here, N and C² were cited as *sancta fides* in the confessions of Reccared and of the Visigoths at the Third Council of Toledo (589), in the course of their conversion from Homoianism to the Nicene faith (both creeds presumably taken from the Chalcedonian Definition of Faith).[148] At the same time, its canon 2 prescribed that C² (and not N) was to be recited by the congregation before the Lord's Prayer during mass in accordance with the eastern model.[149]

The adoption of N and C² by Reccared is thus linked to the reception of the Chalcedonian Definition in Spain. But how did this Definition reach Spain? Kelly suggested that the reception was linked to Justinian's conquests on the Iberian Peninsula from 554 onwards.[150] This may be so, but more recent research shows that the eastern Roman presence in Spain, which ended for good in 624, seems not to have had any lasting cultural impact.[151] Today the eastern influences in the Mozarabic rite, which Kelly also highlighted, are explained rather differently as well.[152] When it comes to these influences, Burns' earlier suggestion may be correct according to which Abbot John of Biclaro (d. *c.* 621) could have played an important role,[153] as he was influential at court, had spent seventeen years in Constantinople (*c.* 558–575),[154] and presumably also took part in the Third Council of Toledo (589).[155] It was he who brought the knowledge of the liturgical practice

---

147 Cf. Mansuetus, *Epistula ad Constantinum imperatorem* (CPL 1170; PL 87, cols. 1261C–1263A).

148 Cf. Third Council of Toledo (589), *Regis professio fidei* (FaFo § 135d26.1.4(3)) for N and *Regis professio fidei* (§ 184f24.3) and *Gothorum professio fidei* (§ 184f24.4) for C². However, the term *sancta fides* does not occur in the Chalcedonian definition, but only in the title of C² as quoted at the second(third) session. Cf. above p. 386 and ACO II 3, p. 265, l. 22.

149 Cf. Third Council of Toledo (589), canon 2 (FaFo § 687b = Heil/Scheerer 2022 (*Dokument* 120.2), p. 294, ll. 7–21); cf. also Third Council of Toledo (589), *Canones / Allocutio Reccaredi* (§ 687a = Heil/Scheerer 2022 (*Dokument* 120.2), pp. 291, l. 5 – 292, l. 13) and below pp. 510 f.

150 Cf. Kelly 1972, p. 352. Similarly, Heil/Scheerer 2022, p. 254.

151 Cf. Heather 2018, p. 298.

152 Cf. Spinks 2013, p. 192.

153 Cf. Burn 1899, p. 115; cf. also Heil/Scheerer 2022, p. 254.

154 Cf. Isidore of Seville, *De uiris illustribus* 31,44. In addition, Campos 1960, pp. 17–19; Kollautz 1983, p. 467.

155 Cf. Campos 1960, pp. 25 f.

of singing C² in mass first introduced by Justin II in Constantinople to Spain.[156] Only C² (which by now included the *filioque*) is regularly quoted at the synods of the capital and other places from the Eighth Council of Toledo (653) onwards.[157]

In Rome, the reception of C² can be traced to Gregory the Great (*sedit* 590–604). A 'private confession' is contained in an appendix to his letters and in his *Life* which has not yet been critically edited; it represents a skillful combination of C² and R.[158] But even a Pope as late as Theodore I (*sedit* 642–649) still speaks in traditional terms, referencing the confirmation of N at the Council of Constantinople.[159]

The confession of the Lateran Synod of 649[160] is also based on C² – this creed had in actual fact been read out at this gathering.[161] It is striking that the same terms are used to designate N and C² in this confession: both are called ἔκθεσις πίστεως or *symbolum*. We will have to examine below how this change to the status of C² came about.[162]

The next time C² is found in Rome is in the baptismal liturgy. A rite of the *Traditio symboli* has been preserved in the *Old Gelasian Sacramentary* (around 650), in which C² is 'handed over' as a baptismal confession, first in Greek and then in Latin.[163] This is also the case in a number of later sacramentaries that are closely related to this one,[164] while other service books that are also related to the OGS refer to R/T or even quote it.[165]

C², however, had by no means formed part of the *Traditio symboli* in Rome from the beginning. John the Deacon describes the scrutinies in his famous letter to Senarius from the early sixth century, and in this context clearly speaks of the

---

156 Cf. above p. 402.

157 Cf. FaFo § 184f24.5 until 24.14.

158 Cf. PL 77, cols. 1327D–29A (Appendix); PL 75, cols. 87B–8B (*Life*). The text is found in FaFo § 446.

159 Cf. his letter *Synodicas fraternitatis uestrae litteras* (CPL 1732) to the patriarch of Constantinople Paulus (PL 129, cols. 581B–582A).

160 Cf. FaFo § 447.

161 Cf. ACO² I, p. 218, ll. 19–34 (Greek) // p. 219, ll. 19–32 (Latin) = FaFo § 184f25.

162 Cf. below pp. 411–13.

163 Cf. FaFo §§ 675a and 184f2.2 and below pp. 503 f.

164 Cf. the Pontifical of Donaueschingen (uncertain; *s.* IX *ex.*; FaFo § 683a) and the sacramentaries of Angoulême (768–781; §§ 796a and 184f14), Gellone (*s.* VIII *ex.*; §§ 797a and 184f4), and Reims (uncertain; *c.* 800; § 799a) as well as the *Ordines Romani* XI (*s.* VII/2; §§ 808a, b and 184f4) and XV (uncertain; before 787; § 809a, b). In these sources the baptismal questions are based on R. On the *Ordo Romanus XI* cf. also below p. 409.

165 Cf. the baptismal questions in the Sacramentaries of Prague (*s.* VIII/2; FaFo § 679b) and Rheinau (795/796; § 798a). In addition, cf. the Spanish *Liber ordinum de ordinibus ecclesiasticis* (before 1052; § 684c4) and the *Liber misticus* (*s.* IX/X?; § 684d) and the medieval sources quoted in the note on § 684 where creeds are preserved which are similar to T.

creed 'handed down by the apostles' (*symboli ab apostolis traditi*), which was transmitted.[166] This is a strong indication that R or a descendant of it was still in use in Rome around 500. This older practice also becomes apparent when one looks at the exhortation handed down as part of the *Traditio* in the OGS, which is attributed to Pope Leo the Great and which, in its second part, also deals with the content of the creed.[167] This summary exhortation, in fact, does not, as one might expect, mention the important doctrinal features of C² (first and foremost the inclusion of *homooúsios*), but essentially deals with those points that are also mentioned in R. Only the references to the one, equal *potestas* of Father and Son and to the existence of the Holy Spirit in the same godhead as Father and Son could, perhaps, be seen as a dogmatically tempered expression of the consubstantiality established at Constantinople. This evidence can probably be explained by the fact that R initially stood in this place, but had later been replaced by C², without the exhortation framing the creed being adapted sufficiently. By contrast, Peter Gemeinhardt and Susan Keefe have assumed that C² was the original confession and that it was replaced by R/T in Gaul.[168] Yet the letter to Senarius notwithstanding, this does not explain why it was precisely R/T (and not C²) that was expounded in countless homilies during the celebration of the *Traditio symboli* in the west, and by no means just in Gaul, from the fourth century onwards.[169] This popularity can hardly be explained if the *Roman* creed had not also been the subject of the *Traditio symboli* in Rome, finding its way into the western provinces from there.

But there is also more concrete evidence. In the *Rituale Romanum* of 1584 the *Traditio symboli* forms part of the third scrutiny. It follows the OGS almost verbatim: at the beginning there is the first part of the aforementioned preface of Leo the Great. However, this is not followed by the recitation of C², but first by the *Traditio* of the *Symbolum apostolorum*, i.e. T, which is to be recited by the priest three times 'slowly in a loud voice' (*clara et lenta uoce*). This is to be done in such a way that the catechumens are able to learn and memorize the creed.[170] Then, in a short dialogue in Greek, an older candidate for baptism who speaks this language or – if no such candidate is present – the acolyte is asked by the priest in which language the confession is spoken, to which the candidate for baptism or

---

166 John the Deacon, *Epistula ad Senarium* 4 (FaFo § 655). Cf. Ferguson 2009, pp. 766–8.
167 Cf. Leo the Great, *Tractatus 98* (FaFo §§ 255g and 675a). Cf. also below pp. 527 f.
168 Cf. Gemeinhardt 2002, p. 50 n. 26; Keefe 2002, vol. I, p. 45 n. 8.
169 Cf. below ch. 13.
170 *Rituale Romanum* 1584, p. 41: 'Interim verò Catechumeni suscipientes symbolum, addiscant, & memoriae mandare studeant.' / 'Meanwhile, however, the catechumens who receive the creed should learn and seek to memorize it.'

the acolyte answers: Ἑλληνικῇ / 'in Greek'. The priest then calls for the confession to be recited. Only now does C² follow, both in Greek and in Latin. Apparently the *competentes* are expected to memorize this confession as well, for it is recorded afterwards: 'However, if the boys and the adults have already learned the creed, they recite it by themselves.'[171] The reading of C² is expressly adhered to even if there are no Greek-speaking baptismal candidates at all (neither children nor adults).[172]

If (with due caution) we may draw a conclusion from this later practice about what it may have looked like earlier, this may mean that C² had originally been *added* to R or its descendant T for the benefit of Greek-speaking baptismal candidates, thus doubling the creed. This duplication seems to have been eliminated in the OGS and in the sacramentaries dependent on the tradition it represents, to the effect that R was dropped at an unknown point in time. It is possible that this took place no longer in Rome, but at a later time in the Frankish-Gallic area, because otherwise R/T would have been first abolished in Rome but then later reintroduced – as the *Rituale Romanum* testifies.

Some early medieval witnesses even allow us to directly trace the original rite of the *Traditio* of R/T. A number of Carolingian manuscripts that contain a baptismal rite closely related to the OGS, which since Michel Andrieu's pioneering edition has been called *Ordo Romanus XI* and which may belong to the second half of the sixth century,[173] offer T instead of C² in both the *Traditio* and *Redditio symboli*. In these manuscripts, the presbyter asks the acolyte in which language the creed will be confessed. After the acolyte has answered that this should be in Latin, the priest asks him to recite the creed. However, this is not followed by C², but by a confession that is almost identical with T.[174] This practice can also be observed in the *Ordo Romanus XV* (before 787) and in the *Sacramentary of Gellone*

---

171 *Rituale Romanum* 1584, p. 42: 'Pueri verò & adulti, si iam didicerunt symbolum, etiam ipsi pronuntiant.'

172 Cf. also below pp. 504 f.

173 Cf. FaFo § 808. For the date cf. below p. 410 n. 179.

174 In the manuscripts of the so-called Collection B (FGKYZ) according to the apparatus in Andrieu the text reads (somewhat simplified) as follows (nos. 62–5 in Andrieu 1931–1961, vol. II, pp. 434, l. 3 – 435, l. 5): 'Qua lingua confitetur dominum nostrum Iesum Christum? Resp. <acolitus>: Latina. Et dicit ei presbiter: Adnuntia fidem ipsorum qualiter credent. Et ille cantat symbolum. [Here follows T.] Et dum hoc cantat semper manum super caput infantis tenet.' / 'In which language does he/she confess our Lord Jesus Christ? <The acolyte> answers: "In Latin." And the priest says to him: "Proclaim their faith as they believe." And he [i.e. the acolyte] chants the creed. [Here follows T.] And while chanting this he always places his hand upon the head of the infant.' Furthermore, cf. the note on FaFo § 344 and Angenendt 1977(2005), pp. 40–2, esp. 41 n. 26; Angenendt 1987, pp. 293 f. On Collection B cf. Andrieu 1931–1961, vol. I, pp. 471–3; II, pp. 365 f., 370–4; Vogel 1986, pp. 150–2.

(late eighth century), a Frankish descendant of the tradition represented in the *Old Gelasian Sacramentary*.[175] Unless there are any other reasons relating to the manuscript tradition of these texts not to do so,[176] one may cautiously conclude from the explicit question put to baptizands relating to the language to be used that this liturgy originates from a time when the congregation was still bilingual. Therefore, it first had to be established with regard to the baptized persons or their family, in which language the confession was to be recited (here, however, referring to R/T rather than to C²), and that R/T was then spoken in either Latin or Greek. In any case, Carolingian sources which I mentioned above clearly attest that R/T was handed over at baptism.

The question remains as to when and why C² came to be included in the liturgy of the *Traditio symboli* in the Roman sacramentaries, or those influenced by Rome to be precise. Assuming that the above-mentioned exhortation (*Tractatus 98*) still refers to R and that it was written by Leo the Great, the adoption of C² into the *Traditio* must have taken place after Leo. The time of the Acacian Schism (484–519) or the first half of the sixth century have been suggested,[177] but I believe this is very unlikely, in view of the fact that there is no evidence of a wider reception of N or C² in papal letters until at least the second half of the sixth century,[178] while the use of R continues to be attested. Michel Andrieu, on the other hand, has suggested that C² was adopted when Italy reverted to the control of the Byzantine Empire in the mid-sixth century and has narrowed the period down to from about 550 to the early seventh century.[179]

This is possible. However, it is also a possibility that Gregory the Great (*sedit* 590–604) was responsible, as he is known to have been a liturgical innovator and was indeed even accused of following the custom of Constantinople in this respect.[180] As shown above,[181] he is also the first person for whom the reception of C² in Rome

---

175 Cf. *Ordo Romanus XV*, nos. 106–8 (FaFo § 809a); *Sacramentarium Gellonense* nos. 2281–3 (FaFo 797d).

176 According to Andrieu, however, the text of the manuscript group A (with Greek and Latin C²) is superior to B. Cf. his stemma in Andrieu 1931–1961, vol. II, p. 374.

177 Cf., e.g., Willis 1994, p. 124; Ferguson 2009, p. 766 and n. 32: between 500 and 550, however, without any reasons being given.

178 Cf. above p. 405.

179 Cf. Andrieu 1931–1961, vol. II, p. 394. He gives as *terminus ante quem* the composition of *Ordo Romanus XI*, which, in the relevant section, is based on the OGS and dated by Andrieu to the period 550–700, 'perhaps even after the second half of the sixth [century]' (Andrieu 1931–1961, vol. II, p. 413); followed by Dossetti 1967, pp. 181–3. Cf. now also Romano 2019.

180 Cf. Gregory, *Epistula 9,26*. On his reform of the liturgy cf. Markus 1997, pp. 73–5; Mews/Renkin 2013, pp. 323 f.

181 Cf. above p. 407.

can be proven with certainty. But it remains unclear why he should have replaced the confession in this way.

We had seen above that the confession of the Lateran Synod of 649 already put C² on a par with N.[182] What was the reason for its reevaluation? We know from the letter of Maximus the Confessor to the priest Marinus in Cyprus (which was written in 645/646, but only survives in fragments) that at that time there were disputes in Rome about the *filioque*, which had above all been triggered by a (lost) synodal letter of Pope Theodore I (*sedit* 642–649). Theodore had claimed that the Spirit 'also' proceeds from the Son, a doctrine that had been objected to in Constantinople though subsequently defended by Maximus.[183] It is unclear whether Theodore explicitly referred to C². However, he was not able to prevail with his view: the letter of the Graeco-Sicilian Pope Agatho (*sedit* 678–681) and the Roman Synod of 125 Bishops of 680, presented at the Third Council of Constantinople, referred to C² and emphasized the procession of the Spirit from the Father alone.[184] Under the bilingual Pope Leo II (*sedit* 682–683) the liturgy was increasingly held in Greek, which was also due to the high proportion of Greek speakers in Rome. The details of this complex and controversial process cannot be examined here.[185] However, we should note that it is possible that the replacement of R/T by C² in the *Traditio symboli* in the preparation for baptism falls into this period, when the OGS, which does not contain the *filioque*,[186] also came into being.[187]

It was at that very time of the Greek-speaking popes Agatho, Leo II, and Sergius I (*sedit* 687–701) that the OGS also came to Francia.[188] It now already contained the bilingual C² in the *Traditio*, but without the *filioque* – in contrast to the Spanish tradition, where the *filioque* as a component of C² (as shown above[189]) had long been established not only at synods but also as part of the liturgy.[190] In Francia it now competed with the use of R/T.

---

182 Cf. above p. 407.
183 Cf. Maximus, *Ad Marinum Cypri presbyterum* (PG 91, col. 136A). Its authenticity is disputed; cf. Larchet in Larchet/Ponsoye 1998, pp. 76–84. On recent scholarship cf. Sode 2001, pp. 163–8; Gemeinhardt 2002, pp. 79 f. n. 22; Larchet 2003, pp. 129–31; Siecienski 2010, pp. 73–86; Jankowiak/ Booth 2015, p. 49; Blowers 2016, pp. 297–301.
184 Cf. FaFo § 449. In addition, Siecienski 2010, p. 88.
185 On the following cf. Atkinson 1982; Kaczynski 1988, pp. 99–113; Ekonomou 2007(2009), pp. 250–3; Wanek 2018; Romano 2019, p. 45; Westwell 2019, pp. 68 f.; Lang 2022, pp. 202–4.
186 Cf. FaFo § 184f2.
187 Cf. above p. 407.
188 Cf. Vogel 1986, p. 70.
189 Cf. above pp. 406 f. and also below 551–3.
190 Cf. also the quotation in the *Liber misticus* (FaFo § 184f13). Furthermore the Mozarabic *Missale Mixtum* (§ 184f30) and below p. 553 n. 27.

The fact that the Greek text of C² (still without the *filioque*[191]) was retained in Rome, even when it had become completely unintelligible to baptismal candidates, indicates that the retention of the Greek text was not primarily a matter of comprehensibility and also no longer a matter of accommodating Greek-speaking baptismal candidates,[192] but of *dogmatic authority* – which included the language: only the *Greek* text of C² was *dogmatically binding*.[193] Incidentally, this also explains why Pope Leo III (*sedit* 795–816) held so steadfastly to the authentic wording of C² in his discussions with the Carolingian envoys in 810 about the *filioque*, and even publicly displayed this confession in Rome on silver shields at the apostles' tombs. We will look at this evidence in the context of the controversy over the *filioque* below in chapter 16.

In the west, too, C² did not completely replace N until the Carolingian period and beyond.[194] Several synodal canons inculcate the authoritative nature of the creed of Nicaea or of the '318 bishops' – although it is not altogether clear whether they actually reference N.[195] However, an unknown author (Pseudo-Amalarius of Metz) claims in a letter to Charlemagne that he considered the 'faith of the Nicene Council of the 318 fathers' authoritative, whereupon he quotes N and not C².[196] Similarly, in a manual for missionaries or catechists written in Passau around 850 (cod. Munich, Bayerische Staatsbibliothek, Clm 19410, pp. 3–4), the faithful were to learn N and not C².[197] Finally, Meinhard of Bamberg (Bishop of Würzburg 1085–1088), mentions both N and C² as distinct confessions in his brief history of creeds, alongside the Apostles' Creed, calling N a 'most gentle and beneficial exposition of the faith' (*mitissima et saluberrima fidei expositio*) which was 'accepted and

---

191 This was different in the *Rituale Romanum* of 1584.

192 *Pace* Gemeinhardt 2002, p. 50. As regards the presence of Greek-speaking groups among Rome's inhabitants as late as the early middle ages cf. Romano 2014, p. 12.

193 Later it was said that the use of the Greek and Latin creed during the scrutinies signified the universality of the creed. Cf. Honorius Augustodunensis, *Gemma animae* 3,67 (PL 172, col. 661B): "'I believe in one God" is chanted over the males in Greek and over the females in Latin, because every tongue is denoted by these two languages. For the Greeks surpassed all nations in philosophy, whereas the Romans ruled over all nations. Hence the Greek language signifies the sages, the Latin the princes. Therefore, the faith is chanted in Greek and Latin, because all languages confess God.' Cf. Kaczynski 1988, pp. 111 f.

194 Cf. Keefe, *Catalogue*, 2012, no. 51 (= CPL 1746; *s.* V *in.*), 142 (= CPL 1745; 350–400), 201 (= CPL 551), 215 (= CPL 171; *s.* V/VI), 345 (*s.* VIII/IX). In addition, cf. the later Latin versions of N outside the translations of synodal acts or the writings of the Greek fathers: FaFo §§ 135d32, 38, 44, 45.

195 Cf. the Synod of Chalon-sur-Saône (*c.* 647–654), canon 1 (FaFo § 580); the Synod of Soissons (744; § 586); the so-called *Legatine Councils* in England (786), canon 1 (§ 588).

196 Cf. Pseudo-Amalarius, *Epistula ad Carolum imperatorem* 6 (Keefe 2002, vol. II, p. 544, ll. 15–16); for the quotation of N cf. FaFo § 135d38.

197 Cf. FaFo § 135d45.

preserved with the veneration due to it throughout Christendom'.[198] Although C² had by now also replaced N in the west at synods and in the Roman baptismal liturgy, the older creed continued to be used occasionally for some time.[199]

The fact that C² would come to replace R and N was therefore not a foregone conclusion in either east or west, but took place as part of a longer process. Initially, the introduction of the Chalcedonian Definition of Faith and its reception at subsequent councils played a central role in laying the foundations for rendering C² acceptable. Later, however, the decisive factor in C² eventually prevailing was its reception in the liturgy of both west and east.[200] At the end of that process, the Creed of Constantinople had replaced that of Nicea all across both the Latin and Greek churches, although originally it had only been intended to supplement N.

---

198 Meinhard, *De fide, uarietate symboli, ipso symbolo et pestibus haeresium* (Caspari 1883, p. 260). Cf. also FaFo § 135d46. The attribution to Meginhard of Fulda is no longer tenable; cf. URL <https://www.geschichtsquellen.de/repOpus_03385.html?pers_PND=PND118579924> and <https://www.geschichtsquellen.de/repPers_119063085.html> (29/11/2023).
199 Cf. also the other examples in FaFo, vol. I, p. 333 and below ch. 17.
200 Cf. below ch. 17.

9 The Reception of N and C² beyond the Latin and Greek Churches

A full account of the development of the creeds outside the Latin- and Greek-speaking areas would exceed the scope of this book and the expertise of its author. I will limit myself in what follows to some preliminary notes on the reception of N and C² within the period under investigation, with the addition of some information (no doubt incomplete) as regards other creeds, as far as they are accessible to me.[1] Much groundwork remains to be done in this area.

9.1 Syriac Christianity

9.1.1 Baptism and the creed

It has been said that the earliest signs indicating the existence of a baptismal creed in the Sasanian Empire are found in the *Demonstrations* of Aphrahat (*c.* 270 – *c.* 345).[2] Usually, the following passage from the first *Demonstration* 'On Faith' (which was written in 336/337[3]) is quoted in support of this view:

> Now this is faith: when a person believes in God, the Lord of all, who made heaven and earth, and the seas and all that is in them, and who made Adam in his image. He gave the Torah to Moses, sent [a portion] of his Spirit into the prophets, and sent his Anointed One into the world. Such a person also believes in the resurrection of the dead and the mystery of baptism. This is the faith of the Church of God.[4]

---

1 On the place of the creed in present-day baptismal and eucharistic liturgies of the eastern Churches the surveys by Bryan D. Spinks and Nikolaus Liesel are immensely useful. Cf. Spinks 2006(2016), pp. 71–108; Liesel/Makula 1963. In addition, Dalmais, 'Die nichtbyzantinischen orientalischen Liturgien', 1989; Dalmais, 'Die Mysterien', 1989; Suermann 2010.
2 On earlier research cf. Connolly 1906, pp. 203 f. On Aphrahat in general cf. Ramelli, 'Aphrahat', 2018. In the *Acts of Mari* (which describe Mari's mission to Syria in the first century) we also find credal formulae which may, however, not date to before the end of the sixth century; cf. Abramowski/Hainthaler 2022, pp. 15–18.
3 Cf. Lehto 2010, pp. 1 f.
4 Aphrahat, *Demonstratio 1*, 19. Edition: Parisot 1894, p. 44. Translation: Lehto 2010, p. 84. Cf. too the preceding letter to its author which also contains a creed-like statement which Pass assumed to be of Jewish origin (cf. Pass 1908, p. 270–80): Edition: Parisot 1894, p. 3; Lehto 2010, p. 65 f.

https://doi.org/10.1515/9783110318531-009

However, this passage has no parallel in any of the otherwise known creeds and must be regarded as a rule of faith rather than a fixed creed.[5] In addition, throughout the *Demonstrations* the ritual connection of faith with baptism remains unclear. R.H. Connolly once tried to cull credal clauses from the remainder of Aphrahat's writings, from the *Acts of Thomas*, and from the *Doctrine of Addai* in order to reconstruct their respective creeds,[6] but such a method presupposes that baptismal creeds were already used in Adiabene in the early fourth century and that their basic structure resembled that of N or R. We also possess a Syriac commentary on baptism from the first half of the fifth century in which the renunciation is followed by a confession, but we do not know what was confessed and whether it was even made using a fixed declaratory creed.[7]

In Syriac baptismal *ordines* the creed 'We believe in one God' (it is never quoted in full) is usually said after the renunciation, although the liturgical context varies:[8]

- In the Melkite *ordo* attributed to Basil the creed is repeated three times.[9]
- A Maronite baptismal liturgy ascribed to Jacob of Serugh contains, a confession which is found nowhere else after the renunciation, followed by the creed 'We believe in one God'.[10]
- In the various versions of the Syrian Orthodox *ordo* attributed to Severus the creed is usually said after the catechumens' dismissal following the *Sýntaxis* (formula of engagement to Christ).[11] In the version which is still in use in the

---

5 For discussion cf. Connolly 1906; Pass 1908.

6 Cf. Connolly 1906, esp. pp. 209 f., 218 f., 220.

7 Cf. Brock 1980, pp. 30–33. Cf. also the baptismal questions in the Syriac translation of the *Testamentum Domini* (FaFo § 615a) which resemble R as they probably derive from the *Traditio Apostolica* (cf. above pp. 129 f.). The translation dates from 686/687.

8 For what follows cf. the surveys and abbreviations in Brock 1970, p. 369; Brock 1972, pp. 16–21.

9 Edition and Latin translation: Assemani 1750, p. 211; Latin translation only: Denzinger 1863/1864, vol. I, p. 321.

10 Edition and Latin translation: Assemani, vol. II, 1749, p. 328; Latin translation only: Denzinger 1863/1864, vol. I, p. 340. French translation: Dib 1910, p. 76.

11 Cf., e.g., SA I (Assemani, vol. II, 1749, p. 282 // Denzinger 1863/1864, vol. I, p. 305); SA IV (Assemani, vol. I, 1749, p. 252 // Denzinger 1863/64, vol. I, p. 283); SA V (Assemani, vol. I, 1749, p. 271 // Denzinger 1863/1864, vol. I, p. 292); SA VI (Assemani, vol. II, 1749, p. 252 // Denzinger 1863/1864, vol. I, p. 298). No such dismissal: SA III (Assemani, vol. I, 1749, p. 238 // Denzinger 1863/1864, vol. I, p. 273). Cf. also Brock 1972, pp. 22, 40–4. Abbreviations are those of Brock.

Syrian Orthodox Church today, the creed is C^2 with some variants.[12] It is said by the godparents immediately after the renunciation.[13]

– Another *ordo* is ascribed to a Timothy of Alexandria who may be identical with Timothy Aelurus.[14] Here the creed (which begins 'I believe in one God' without being quoted in full) is said twice, once as part of a complex rite of renunciation and then after the dismissal of the catechumens before the baptismal water is consecrated.[15]

9.1.2 Miaphysites ('Jacobites')

We have little evidence as regards the Miaphysite tradition of N and C^2 up to the ninth century.[16] In the early sixth century both creeds made their way, as part of the Chalcedonian Definition, into the already mentioned collection of fifth-century canon law, the *Corpus canonum*, preserved in a Syriac translation in cod. British Library, Add. 14528, which was produced in 501/502 in Mabbug (Hierapolis).[17] Later C^2 is attested in a number of related codices, always together with (or as part of) the Definition of Chalcedon.[18] Philoxenus of Mabbug (d. 523) makes it clear that C^2 was also held in high esteem in Miaphysite circles *independently* of the Chalcedonian

---

12 Cf. *The Sacrament* 2011, p. 44 (English); Cf. also Çiçek 2010, p. 44 (German). Variants: 'in one *true* God' (not in German); 'before all worlds' instead of 'before all ages' (but German: 'vor allen Zeiten'); '*by* the Holy Spirit and *of* the Virgin Mary' // '*durch* den Heiligen Geist *aus* der *heiligen* Jungfrau Maria'; addition of 'Mother of God' and of 'died'; 'according to his will' instead of 'according to the Scriptures'; German: 'er wurde *sogar* für uns gekreuzigt' (not in English); 'with *great* glory'; German: 'an den *einen lebendigen* Heiligen Geist' (not in English); 'the giver of life *to all*'; 'who spoke through the prophets *and the apostles*'.

13 Cf. Spinks 2006(2016), p. 82. In an early baptismal *ordo* published by Sebastian Brock 'which stands directly between the Maronite rite and Severus' the creed is said after the formula of *Sýntaxis*. Cf. Brock 1971, pp. 368, 374; Spinks 2006(2016), p. 88 (quotation).

14 Cf. above p. 399.

15 Edition and translation: Brock 1970, pp. 380, 382; cf. also the commentary on pp. 411 and 415. In addition, Spinks 2006(2016), pp. 80 f.

16 The following texts are beyond the scope of this book: *Confession of the Syrian Orthodox Faith* by Dionysius Bar Ṣalibi (d. 1171), edited by Rabo 2015, and the unpublished explanations of the creed by the same author (Baumstark 1922, p. 296). For later creeds cf. Baumstark 1922, pp. 300 and 315. A curious Miaphysite creed attributed to the Council of Antioch (251) is found in cod. London, British Library, Add. 14528 (s. VI). English translation in Cowper 1861, pp. 40 f.

17 Cf. above pp. 386 f.

18 Cf. the list in Schulthess 1908, pp. VIII–IX and Dossetti 1967, pp. 191–5. On these codices cf. Dossetti 1967, pp. 119–23. Additional manuscripts are mentioned in Kaufhold 2012, p. 244, nn. 77, 79. Dossetti (loc. cit.) and Kaufhold 2012, pp. 244 f. also deal with the problem of translation.

Definition. Philoxenus clearly distinguishes C[2] from N by claiming that the fathers of Constantinople extended N in order to combat Macedonius and Apolinarius.[19] Oddly enough, Philoxenus' own text of C[2] displays some peculiarities which are not easily explainable.[20] In a very similar vein, Severus of Antioch (*sedit* 512–538), recognizing the authority of the Council of Constantinople, mentions the addition to the third article of C[2], associating it with the defence against Macedonius.[21] However, like Philoxenus, Severus was no stickler when it came to the text of the creed.[22] His prohibition to change the creed did not extend to its *text*, but to its *doctrines*, because otherwise the Council of Constantinople would also have to be blamed for violating N as Severus wrote in 509/511 in a letter to an otherwise unknown Isaac Scholasticus:

> For it is not saying what agrees with the 318 fathers that is prohibited to us, but adding anything to or detracting anything from the correctness of the doctrines. If not, the synod of the 150 also incurs blame, because it widened the theology relating to the Spirit, and, when the confession had been laid down with regard to the only Son who became incarnate for us, it added the words 'from the Holy Spirit and from Mary the Virgin', and 'he was crucified in the days of Pontius Pilate'; for these things were not stated by the 318.[23]

The codex London, British Library, Add. 12156 (written in 562)[24] contains a collection of credal texts which comprises N and C[2],[25] among letters and treatises of Timothy Aelurus (hence in a Miaphysite context).[26]

In both Miaphysite ('Jacobite') and Dyophysite ('Nestorian') churches psalters were used which also contained the canticles and the creed.[27] The Miaphysite version of the creed is C[2] (which in some manuscripts is ascribed to Nicaea), with minor variations.[28]

---

19 Cf. Lebon 1936, pp. 866 f. with 866 n. 4. Furthermore De Halleux, 'La philoxénienne', 1978.

20 Cf. Lebon 1936, p. 867. Cf. also Connolly 1906, p. 222. For further credal texts from Philoxenus' pen cf. De Halleux 1963, pp. 168–178 (information kindly supplied by Hubert Kaufhold).

21 Severus, *Liber contra impium Grammaticum* 3,11. Cf. Lebon 1936, p. 869 and n. 1.

22 Cf. Gribomont 1975/1976, esp. pp. 149 f.

23 Text and translation: Brooks 1919, pp. 291 f. Cf. also Gribomont 1975/1976, p. 150 n. 57.

24 On this manuscript cf. Abramowski 2021, pp. 21–85.

25 Edition and German translation: Caspari 1866–1875(1964), vol. I, pp. 101–3. Cf. also Schwartz 1926, pp. 71 f.; Dossetti 1967, p. 90. In N ποιητὴν οὐρανοῦ καὶ γῆς is added, in the anathemas ἢ κτιστόν is missing. In C[2] ἕνα is missing before κύριον. Further analysis in Caspari 1866–1875(1964), vol. I, pp. 103–12.

26 Cf. above p. 399.

27 A survey of Syriac psalters is found in Dickens 2013(2020).

28 Translation in Barnes 1906, pp. 442b–445b. Further examples in Mearns 1914, pp. 27 f., 43–9 (partly in Karshunic); Williams 2013, pp. 388 f. Sometimes 'and died' (ἀποθανόντα) is added in the christological section, and all manuscripts offer διὰ τῶν προφητῶν καὶ τῶν ἀποστόλων / 'through

A staunchly anti-Chalcedonian affirmation of the faith of Nicaea, Constantinople, and Ephesus is found in the *Profession of Faith* (written in *c.* 536/537) by John of Tella (482/483–538, bishop 519–521/522). He does not, however, cite the text of the respective creeds.[29]

In his *Commentary on the Liturgy*, Gabriel of Qatar (*s.* VII *in.*) mentions that the creed is said at the beginning of the eucharistic service:

> This indicates that everyone who does not correctly believe in the Holy Trinity and the Dispensation effected in Christ, is alien to the truth, and deprived of delight with our Lord Christ who was sacrificed for the salvation of the world.[30]

Here the creed clearly serves to confirm the orthodoxy of the worshippers.[31]

Likewise, a letter by Jacob of Edessa (d. 708) mentions the 'faith of the 318 fathers' as the introductory element of the Qurobo (eucharist) after the closing of the doors, which corresponds to its original place in the Byzantine liturgy.[32] Unfortunately, he does not quote it so that it is unclear whether he refers to N or C².[33] In addition, in a description of the baptismal rite he says that a three-fold creed followed the renunciation and the *Sýntaxis* when the catechumens registered for baptism and that, after entering the baptistry at the beginning of the baptismal rite itself, they recited the creed 'We believe in one God', but again he does not quote it in full.[34]

By contrast, Moses bar Kepha (d. 903) clearly refers to C² in his commentary on the liturgy. It is worth quoting his explanation in full:

---

the prophets and the apostles' in the pneumatological section. The holiness of the Church is not mentioned in all of them. Instead one sometimes finds 'and glorious'. In the end the text reads 'and for the new life (εἰς καινότητα ζωῆς? cf. Rom 6:4 and below p. 427) of/in the world to come'.

29 Cf. the edition, translation, and commentary in Menze/Akalin 2009.

30 Gabriel of Qatar, *Memra 5,* 2,52 (ed. Brock 2009, pp. 232 f.; tr. Brock 2009, p. 213). I owe this reference to Jibin Thomas Abraham. Gabriel's text was partly quoted by his contemporary (and perhaps relative) Abraham bar Lipeh in his commentary on the liturgy; cf. Brock 2009, pp. 199 f.

31 Cf. also below p. 515.

32 Cf. below pp. 509 f.

33 Cf. Jacob, *Epistula 35* (ed. Labourt 1903(1955), p. 7; Latin translation: Labourt 1903(1955), p. 37; English translation: Varghese 1998, p. 8 = Brightman 1896(1965), p. 491; cf. van Ginkel 2008, pp. 80 f.). In addition, Varghese 2008, pp. 248 f. (I owe this reference to Jibin Thomas Abraham.).

34 Cf. Mai 1838, app., p. 15; Whitaker/Johnson 2003, p. 62. The baptismal ordo for infant baptism which survives under Jacob's name (and that of Barhebraeus) confirms this practice. Here the first creed (which is pronounced by the sponsor) runs like this: 'I believe in you, Christ God, I, N.N., who is baptized, and all your doctrines which you have inspired through the prophets, the apostles, and the orthodox teachers. I confess and I believe and I am baptized in you and in your Father and in your living and holy Spirit.' The second creed begins: 'We believe in one God', but is not quoted in full; cf. Denzinger 1863/1864, vol. I, p. 283.

It is right to know that, from the holy apostles until (the time of) Constantine the believing king, after the thurible of incense nothing was said, but the priest used to begin the Offering (*Qurrābhā*). But after the same king had assembled the Synod of the 318, and it had set forth this orthodox faith which we both believe and confess, the Synod also commanded that the faithful should recite it first, before the *Qurrābhā*, and then the priest should begin the *Qurrābhā*. The faithful therefore recite it for these reasons. First: that they may let it be known that they believe and confess aright. Second: [to show] that their faith and their confession are one. Third: that by it minds and hearts and mouths may be hallowed. And it is right that he who offers should begin it, since he is the tongue of the whole body of the Church.

Again, it is right to know that the Synod set down 'I believe', and not 'We believe'. And it set down 'I believe', because it is not a prayer or a petition – for that we should pray and make petition each for other and each with other, [this] we are commanded, and this is fitting – but it is a faith and a confession; and that we should believe or confess for or with each other we are not commanded, nor is it becoming; but let each one confess by himself and for himself. Therefore it is right that each person should say 'I believe', as the holy Synod set down, and not 'We believe'.

Again, it is right to know that this faith is divided into five heads: the first, the theology; the second, the incarnation; the third, concerning baptism; the fourth, concerning the general resurrection; the fifth, concerning the future judgement and recompense.[35]

John (Iwannis) of Dara (s. IX/1) notes in his *Commentary on the Eucharist* that the creed should follow the second *Sedro* (opening prayer), because it symbolized 'the law of the Gospel, which demanded faith from all those who wished to be baptized'.[36] John then goes on to give a long (and fanciful) account of the origin of N and C^2, appending a long commentary on each individual clause of an unconventional version of C^2.[37]

---

35 Moses bar Kepha, *Commentarius in liturgiam*, ff. 152b–153a (ed. Connolly/Codrington 1913, pp. 236 f.; tr. Connolly/Codrington 1913, pp. 37 f.; slightly altered). I owe this reference to Jibin Thomas Abraham. On this commentary cf. also Gemayel 1965, pp. 157–160.

36 John, *De oblatione* 3,2 (ed. Sader 1970, p. 48; French translation: Sader 1970, p. 35; English translation: Varghese 1999, p. 60; slightly altered). Cf. also Gemayel 1965, pp. 154–6. A *Sedro* '(lit. a row, order, or series) [. . .] is a long prayer in the form of a series of expositions or meditations, usually preceded by a *Promiun* (introduction). Often, a *Sedro* summarises Syrian Orthodox theology' (Varghese 2019, p. 400). Dionysius Bar Ṣalibi (d. 1171) emphasizes that the recitation of the creed by the faithful denotes their consent to the *Sedro* of entrance (which is 'like an edict, written by the viceroy of the king, who is the priest'; *Expositio liturgiae* 6,12. 13 (ed. Labourt 1903(1955), pp. 28 f.; Latin translation: Labourt 1903(1955), pp. 52 f.; English translation: Varghese 1998, pp. 33, 35). I owe these references to Jibin Thomas Abraham.

37 He omits καὶ διὰ τὴν ἡμετέραν σωτηρίαν. Instead of καὶ Μαρίας τῆς παρθένου he reads ἐν τῇ Μαρίας τῆς παρθένου γαστρί ('in the womb of Mary the Virgin'). Ἀποθανόντα is added after παθόντα. The third section reads: 'life-giver of all' (= τὸ ζωοποιὸν τῶν πάντων?). It goes on: 'who spoke through the prophets and the apostles and through the one apostolic Church' (τὸ λαλῆσαν διὰ τῶν προφητῶν καὶ ἀποστόλων καὶ διὰ μιᾶς ἀποστολικῆς ἐκκλησίας). Finally, καινήν was added after ζωήν.

9.1.3 Dyophysites ('Nestorians')

In the Dyophysite Church of the East[38] N or C² (although well-known in the Syriac tradition[39]) were, by and large, not adopted in their 'pure' form. Nor did it immediately receive the creed that was later called that of the 'Nestorians' (N^Ant3; FaFo § 208) which is a version of the Antiochene creed (N^Ant2; §§ 198 and 203), although Theodore of Mopsuestia's *Catechetical Homilies* containing N^Ant1 were translated into Syriac in mid-fifth century Edessa.[40] We are informed about the synods this church held by the *Synodicon Orientale*, a collection of legal documents pertaining to them which was compiled in the eighth century.[41] Many of these synods published statements that included creeds or credal passages which I will briefly touch upon in what follows.

The canons of the Synod of Seleucia-Ctesiphon 410 which led to the establishment of a Persian church have been preserved in both a western and an eastern Syriac version.[42] The eastern version contains N in its 'pure' form with few variants.[43] The western version[44] is today generally regarded as the original version agreed by the synod. Here the creed (so-called *Persicum*), which is said to agree with N, runs as follows:

> We believe in one God, the Father Almighty, who in his Son made heaven and earth and in whom the worlds were established, the one above and the one below, and in whom he pro-

---

38 The creeds and credal texts of the synods of the Church of the East are conveniently collected in translation in Brock 1985(1992).

39 For Syriac witnesses cf. CPG 8521 (N) and Dossetti 1967, pp. 87 (N and C² as part of the Declaration of Chalcedon), 89 f. (N in Syriac translations of the works of the Miaphysite Patriarch Timothy Aelurus; cf. also Lebon 1936, pp. 864–866), 90, 119–23 (N), 191–5 (C²).

40 Cf. Bruns 1994, p. 22.

41 Edition and French translation: Chabot 1902; German translation: Braun 1898; Braun 1900(1975). There is no complete English translation. Cf. also Van Rompay 2011; Morgan Reed at URL <https://syri.ac/synodiconorientale> (17/11/2023).

42 For discussion of the background and the philological problems cf. Dossetti 1967, pp. 38–41 (who gives on p. 41 a Greek retroversion of the eastern text); Vööbus 1972; Gribomont 1977; De Halleux, 'Le symbole', 1978; Brock 1985(1992), p. 126; Gillman/Klimkeit 1999, pp. 112 f.; Bruns 2000; Winkler 2000, pp. 102 f.; Garsoïan 2001(2010), pp. 1169–71, 1174; Baum/Winkler 2003, pp. 14–17; Bruns 2005, pp. 48–50; Bruns 2008, pp. 47–9; Williams 2013, pp. 389 f.; Winkler 2013, pp. 624–7; Baumer 2016, pp. 74–8; Abramowski/Hainthaler 2022, p. 23.

43 Edition: Chabot 1902, pp. 22 f.; French translation: Chabot 1902, pp. 262 f.; English translation: Brock 1985(1992), p. 133; Greek retroversion: Dossetti 1967, p. 41. In the first section the text given by Dossetti reads: ποιητὴν οὐρανοῦ καὶ γῆς καὶ πάντων ὁρατῶν τε καὶ ἀοράτων. In the second section ἐκ τῶν οὐρανῶν is added after κατελθόντα. In the anathemas ἢ κτιστόν is omitted. All other differences are stylistic.

44 Edition: Vööbus 1972, p. 295.

duced an awakening and a renewal for the whole creation [*or:* in whom he produced consolation and joy for the whole creation[45]].

And in him, his only Son, who was born of him, that is, from the essence of his Father, God from God, Light from Light, true God from true God, begotten and not made, who is of one nature with his Father, who because of us humans, who are created by him, and for our salvation descended and put on body and became human, suffered and rose on the third day, and ascended to heaven and sits at the right hand of his Father, and will come to judge the dead and the living.

And we confess the living and holy Spirit, the living Paraclete who [is] from the Father and the Son, one Trinity, one essence, one will,

agreeing with the faith of the 318 bishops that took place in the town of Nicaea.[46]

It is not necessary here to provide a full analysis of this text.[47] It would show that the *Persicum* is dependent on N (not on N[Ant] nor on C[2]), but is not simply a translation, as the pneumatological section most clearly shows. Instead it displays certain theological features that are typically 'Syriac'.[48] Likewise, the reverse word order of 'to judge the dead and the living' is often found in Syriac versions of N as well as in Armenian translations from the Syriac.[49] Most importantly, the text may, perhaps, provide one of the earliest examples of the insertion of *filioque*.[50]

The canons which are ascribed to Mārūtā of Maipherqaṭ (d. 420/421), and which may also have played a certain role at the Synod of Seleucia-Ctesiphon 410,[51] contain two versions of the creed among their supplementary texts. The first is N with minor variations.[52] The second creed is basically C[2] which is, however, ascribed to Nicaea.[53] In addition, the recension of C[2] is rather idiosyncratic. For the sake of comparison with C[2] I give my Greek retroversion (which as such may never have existed); the translation is that of Vööbus (from the Syriac):

---

45 Cf. Bruns 2000, p. 10 n. 51.

46 The translation is that of Vööbus 1972, p. 294 with the corrections in De Halleux, 'Le symbole', 1978, pp. 162–4 and Bruns 2000, p. 10. A slightly different translation in Brock 1985(1992), p. 133.

47 Cf. De Halleux, 'Le symbole', 1978; Bruns 2000, pp. 11–16; Bruns 2005, pp. 48–50.

48 Cf. Bruns 2000, p. 16.

49 Cf. Winkler 2000, pp. 128 (18) = 131 (18), 130 (46) = 133 (46) and comm. on pp. 136, 551–4, 581–3; Winkler 2004, p. 116.

50 However, this is uncertain; cf. below p. 550 and n. 10.

51 The question of authenticity is unresolved; cf. Vööbus 1982, vol. II, pp. V–X. In addition, Drijvers 2001; Stutz 2019.

52 Edition: Vööbus 1982, vol. I, p. 116; English translation: Vööbus 1982, vol. II, pp. 96 f.; German translation: Braun 1898, p. 113. The text reads νεκροὺς καὶ ζῶντας. In the anathemas: ἔστι ποτε ὅτε (cf. Vööbus 1982, vol. II, p. 96 n. 10; in Greek retroversion); ἢ κτιστόν is omitted.

53 Vööbus 1982, vol. I, p. 141; English translation in Vööbus 1982, vol. II, pp. 117 f. The colophon reads: 'The symbol of the general synod of the 318 bishops who were gathered in the town of Nicaea through the care of Constantinus, the victorious kind, worthy of goof memory' (Vööbus 1982, vol. II, p. 117).

Πιστεύομεν εἰς ἕνα θεόν, πατέρα, παντοκράτορα, ποιητὴν οὐρανοῦ καὶ γῆς ὁρατῶν τε πάντων καὶ ἀοράτων·	We believe in one God, the Father Almighty, the Creator of heaven and earth, all that is visible and all that is invisible;
καὶ εἰς ἕνα κύριον Ἰησοῦν Χριστόν, τὸν υἱὸν τοῦ θεοῦ τὸν μονογενῆ, θεὸν ἀληθινὸν ἐκ θεοῦ ἀληθινοῦ, φῶς ἐκ φωτός, ποιητήν, οὐ ποιηθέντα, ὁμοούσιον τῷ πατρὶ αὐτοῦ, τὸν ἐκ τοῦ πατρὸς γεννηθέντα πρὸ πάντων τῶν αἰώνων καὶ δι' οὗ τὰ πάντα ἐγένετο τά τε ἐν τῷ οὐρανῷ καὶ τὰ ἐν τῇ γῇ, τὸν δι' ἡμᾶς τοὺς ἀνθρώπους καὶ διὰ τὴν ἡμετέραν σωτηρίαν κατελθόντα ἐκ τοῦ οὐρανοῦ καὶ σαρκωθέντα ἐκ πνεύματος ἁγίου [literally: ἁγιότητος] καὶ Μαρίας τῆς παρθένου καὶ ἐνανθρωπήσαντα κατὰ ἡμᾶς καὶ ὑπὲρ ἡμῶν καὶ σταυρωθέντα ἐπὶ Ποντίου Πιλάτου καὶ ἀποθανόντα καὶ ταφέντα καὶ ἀναστάντα τῇ τρίτῃ ἡμέρᾳ κατὰ τὰς γραφὰς καὶ ἀνελθόντα εἰς τὸν οὐρανὸν καὶ καθεζόμενον ἐν δεξιᾷ τοῦ πατρὸς αὐτοῦ καὶ πάλιν ἐρχόμενον κρῖναι ζῶντας καὶ νεκροὺς ἐν τῇ μεγάλῃ ἐπιφανείᾳ τῆς παρουσίας αὐτοῦ,[54] οὗ τῆς βασιλείας οὐκ ἔσται τέλος·	and in one Lord Jesus Christ,[55] the only Son of God, true God from true God, Light from Light, the Maker, and not made, of the same nature with his Father; who was born from the Father before all the worlds, and through whom everything has become that in heaven and that on earth; who because of us men and because of our salvation descended from heaven, and became incarnate from the Spirit of Holiness and from Mary the Virgin, and became human like we and because of us; and he was crucified in the days of Pontius Pilate and he died and was buried and rose on the third day as is written, and ascended into heaven and sits at the right [hand] of his Father, and he is about to come again to judge the living and the dead in the great revelation of his coming, whose kingdom has no end;
καὶ εἰς ἓν πνεῦμα τὸ ἅγιον [literally: ἁγιότητος], τὸ κύριον <καὶ> ζωοποιὸν πάντων, τὸ ἐκ τοῦ πατρὸς ἐκπορευόμενον, τὸ σὺν πατρὶ καὶ υἱῷ συμπροσκυνούμενον καὶ συνδοξαζόμενον καὶ συγγνωριζόμενον [?], τὸ λαλῆσαν διὰ τῶν προφητῶν καὶ ἀποστόλων·	and in one Spirit of Holiness who is the Lord <and>[56] the vivifier of all, who proceeds from the Father, is worshipped together with the Father and the Son, glorified and acknowledged; who has spoken in the prophets and the apostles;

---

54 Cf. 2Thess 2:8.

55 Vööbus translates 'and in our Lord Jesus Christ', but the Syriac text is identical with C². I am grateful to Hubert Kaufhold for pointing this out to me.

56 Hubert Kaufhold has kindly pointed out to me that 'and' is missing in the Syriac text.

καὶ εἰς μίαν, καθολικὴν, ἔνδοξον[57] καὶ ἀποστολικὴν ἐκκλησίαν·	and in one catholic, glorious, and apostolic Church,
καὶ εἰς ἓν βάπτισμα εἰς ἄφεσιν ἁμαρτιῶν·	and in one baptism for the remission of guilts;
καὶ εἰς ἀνάστασιν σωμάτων ἐκ τῆς οἰκίας τῶν νεκρῶν	and in the resurrection of bodies from the dwelling of the dead;[58]
καὶ εἰς τὴν κρίσιν κατὰ πάντων[59]	and in the judgement that is over all;
καὶ εἰς ζωὴν αἰώνιον.	and in the life that is for ever and ever.

The differences with C² are considerable: in the second section Mārūtā omitted τὸν ἐκ τοῦ πατρὸς γεννηθέντα πρὸ πάντων τῶν αἰώνων, reversed φῶς ἐκ φωτός and θεὸν ἀληθινὸν ἐκ θεοῦ ἀληθινοῦ, and read ποιητήν instead of γεννηθέντα.[60] Furthermore, his creed reads τῷ πατρὶ αὐτοῦ, followed by τὸν ἐκ τοῦ πατρὸς γεννηθέντα πρὸ πάντων τῶν αἰώνων καί (which had been omitted before). Τά τε ἐν τῷ οὐρανῷ καὶ τὰ ἐν τῇ γῇ was added. Ἐνανθρωπήσαντα was followed by κατὰ ἡμᾶς; ὑπὲρ ἡμῶν refers to ἐνανθρωπήσαντα instead of σταυρωθέντα; καὶ παθόντα was replaced by καὶ ἀποθανόντα. Αὐτοῦ was added after τοῦ πατρὸς; μετὰ δόξης was omitted, whereas ἐν τῇ μεγάλῃ ἐπιφανείᾳ τῆς αὐτοῦ παρουσίας was added. The third section reads εἰς ἓν πνεῦμα τὸ ἅγιον; πάντων is added after ζωοποιόν; καὶ συγγνωριζόμενον and καὶ ἀποστόλων were also added, as was ἔνδοξον. The resurrection is expressed like this: εἰς ἀνάστασιν σωμάτων ἐκ τῆς οἰκίας τῶν νεκρῶν; this refers to the realm of the dead, which is their graves. The phase καὶ εἰς τὴν κρίσιν κατὰ πάντων was added. The creed probably concluded with καὶ εἰς ζωὴν αἰώνιον instead of καὶ εἰς ζωὴν τοῦ μέλλοντος αἰῶνος. The omission of ὁμολογοῦμεν and προσδοκῶμεν in the fourth and fifth section makes this, in fact, a seven-part creed.

It is obvious that the biblical character of C² was strengthened by the addition of certain phrases: ἐν τῇ μεγάλῃ ἐπιφανείᾳ τῆς παρουσίας αὐτοῦ (2Thess 2:8); ἔνδοξον (Eph 5:27); καὶ εἰς τὴν κρίσιν κατὰ πάντων (Jude 15). However, not all variant readings can be explained that way. Some we will find again in creeds discussed below.

Mārūtā's canons (whether or not authentic) gained wide recognition by their inclusion with other canonical texts in manuscripts of the Church of the East.[61]

---

57 Cf. Eph 5:27.
58 Vööbus: 'from the dead' which is not a precise translation of the Syriac (note by Hubert Kaufhold).
59 Cf. Jude 15.
60 According to the apparatus in Vööbus two manuscripts read (like C²) 'begotten' instead of 'Maker'. Cf. also Braun 1898, p. 113.
61 Cf. Vööbus 1982, vol. I, pp. VI–XVIII.

They were then also translated into Arabic, although the creed may not have been included.[62]

The creed of the Synod of 486 under Catholicos Aqaq (*sedit* 485–495/496) contains in its first part a trinitarian and its second part a Dyophysite christological declaration, but no creed proper.[63]

The Syriac translation of Theodore of Mopsuestia's *Catechetical Homilies* notwithstanding,[64] the Antiochene version of N is not attested in the Syriac Church until the sixth century. The reasons for this change are unknown and do not seem to be based on Antiochene jurisdiction over the Persian church which did not exist.[65] A creed in the so-called *Liturgical Homily* (no. 35/17), attributed to Narsai (d. *c.* 502)[66] but probably written in the sixth century,[67] is a Dyophysite paraphrase of the creed of the Church of the East ('Nestorians'; N^Ant3; FaFo § 208).[68] It runs like this (words identical with N^Ant3 in italics):[69]

> And as soon as the priests and the deacons together have taken their stand, they begin to recite the faith of the Fathers:
>
> Now we *believe in one God* the Father who is from eternity, who *holds all* by the hidden nod of his divinity; *who made* and fashioned *all things visible and invisible*; and he brought the creation of the height and depth out of nothing.
>
> *And in one Lord Jesus Christ, the Son of God* – one person, double in natures and their *hypostáseis*. He is the *Only-begotten* in his godhead and *first-born* in his body, who became *first-born unto all creatures* from the dead: *he who of his Father is begotten* and is without beginning, and he in no wise became *nor was made* with creatures; for he is *God* who is *from God*, Son who is of the Father, and *of the nature of his Father*, and equal with him in all his proper things; and *by him the worlds were shown forth and everything was created* that was [made]; and in authority and worship and glory he is equal with his Father; *who for our sake came down from heaven* without change (of place), that he might redeem our race from the slavery of the evil one and death, and fashioned (as a body) a temple by the

---

62 Cf. Vööbus 1982, vol. I, pp. XXII–XXIII. In addition, Stutz 2019.

63 Edition: Chabot 1902, pp. 54 f.; French translation: Chabot 1902, p. 302; English translation: Brock 1985(1992), pp. 133–4. Cf. also Baum/Winkler 2003, pp. 29 f.; Abramowski/Hainthaler 2022, pp. 224–8.

64 Cf. above pp. 346–9.

65 Cf. Baum/Winkler 2003, pp. 17, 20 f.

66 Cf. Kitchen 2019.

67 On the pseudonymity of this text cf. Abramowski 1996; Witkamp 2018, p. 22 n. 131; Abramowski/Hainthaler 2022, p. 66. On the date cf. Abramowski 1996, p. 88. Kitchen appears to regard it as genuine; cf. Kitchen 2019. This creed may also be alluded to by John of Dalyatha (*fl.* 600–670), *Homilia 25*, 4 (cf. Abramowski/Hainthaler 2022, p. 689 and n. 161) and by the Catholicos Timothy I (*sedit* 780–823), *Epistula 41* (edition: Bidawid 1956, p. 639 f. (of the codex); Latin translation: Bidawid 1956, p. 122; cf. Abramowski/Hainthaler 2022, p. 750 and nn. 410 and 411).

68 Cf. Bruns 2005, pp. 51–3.

69 Edition: Mingana 1905, vol. I, p. 274–5; translation: Connolly 1909, pp. 5 f. (slightly adapted); cf. also Connolly 1909, pp. LXXII–LXXV.

power of the Holy Spirit from a daughter of David; *and he became human*, and he deified his temple by the union. And his body was *conceived* in the temple *of Mary* without wedlock, and he was *born* above the manner of men. And *he suffered and was crucified* and received death through his humanity, while *Pilate* held the governorship. And *he was in the grave* three days like any dead [man]; *and he rose* and was resuscitated according *as it is written* in the prophecy; *and he ascended* to the height, *to the heaven* of heavens, that he might accomplish everything; and *he sat* in glory *at the right hand of the Father* that sent him. *And he is ready to come* at the end of the times for the renewal of all things, and *to judge the living and the dead* also who have died in sin.

And we confess also *the Holy Spirit*, an eternal being, equal in *ousía* and in godhead to the Father and the Son, *who proceeds from the Father* in a manner unsearchable, and *gives life* to all reasonable beings that by him were created.

And we confess again *one Church, catholic*, patristic, and *apostolic*, sanctified by the Spirit.

And again, *we confess one* bath and *baptism*, wherein we are baptized *unto pardon of debts* and the adoption of sons [cf. Rom 8:15; Gal 4:5].

And we confess again the *resurrection* which is *from the dead*;[70] and that we shall be in new *life for ever and ever*.

This did the 318 priests seal; and they proscribed and anathematized everyone that confesses not according to their confession. The Church confesses according to the confession of the Fathers, and she employs their confession also at the time of the mysteries. At the time of the mysteries her children thunder forth with their faith, reciting it with mouth and heart, without doubting.

The Synod of 544 produced a long trinitarian creed followed by a brief section on the Trinity which is contained in an encyclical letter of Catholicos Mar Aba (*sedit* 540–552).[71] It is obviously an attempt not only to fill in the 'gaps' in N (for example, with regard to Jesus' teaching and miracles), but also to reinterpret the creed in biblical language and referencing texts from Scripture. This renders it ultimately impossible to discern whether N, N[Ant], or C[2] served as the basis of this text. However, canon 40 of the canons attributed to Mar Aba in the *Synodicon Orientale* explicitly refers to N in the interpretation of Theodore of Mopsuestia which may point to N[Ant].[72]

---

70 Here the text in FaFo § 208 corresponds only to the reconstruction by Hort. The creed by Caspari/Bruns/Lietzmann reads: σαρκός.

71 Edition: Chabot 1902, pp. 541–3; French translation: Chabot 1902, pp. 551–3; English translation: Brock 1985(1992), pp. 134 f. Cf. also Baum/Winkler 2003, pp. 33 f.; Bruns 2008, pp. 50 f.; Abramowski/Hainthaler 2022, pp. 243–50. ʿAbdīšōʿ bar Brīḵā (Ebedjesus of Nisibis) cites the first part of Mar Aba's creed in his *Ordo iudiciorum ecclesiasticorum* 1,1; cf. Kaufhold 2019, pp. 22–7 (edition and German translation; information kindly supplied by Hubert Kaufhold).

72 Edition: Chabot 1902, p. 550; French translation: Chabot 1902, p. 561; German translation: Abramowski/Hainthaler 2022, p. 253. Cf. Abramowski/Hainthaler 2022, pp. 253 f.

In a brief statement the Synod of 554 under the Catholicos Joseph (*sedit* 552–567), while summarily confirming the canons of Nicaea and Constantinople, again concentrated on christological questions.[73]

The confession of the Synod of 576 under the Catholicos Ezekiel (*sedit* 570–581) is a theological declaration on the Father (interpreted in a trinitarian fashion) and the Son rather than a creed.[74]

The Synod of 585 (Catholicos Išoʻyahb I, *sedit* 582–595) claimed that the creed had been preached by the Lord, transmitted by the apostles, and laid down by the councils of Nicaea and Constantinople. It then quoted a text[75] which (after an explanation of the Trinity) offers a running commentary on the creed, from which the following creed can be reconstructed (in Greek retroversion; translation by Brock from the Syriac text):

[Πιστεύομεν εἰς ἕνα θεόν, πατέρα, παντοκράτορα, καὶ εἰς ἕνα κύριον Ἰησοῦν Χριστόν, τὸν υἱὸν τοῦ θεοῦ, καὶ εἰς ἓν πνεῦμα ἅγιον τὸ ἐκ τοῦ πατρὸς ἐκπορευόμενον.][76]	[We believe in one God, the Father Almighty, and in one Lord Jesus Christ, the Son of God, and in one Holy Spirit who proceeds from the Father.]
< . . . > ἕνα θεόν, πατέρα, παντοκράτορα, πάντων ὁρατῶν τε καὶ ἀοράτων ποιητήν·	< . . . > one God, the Father Almighty, Maker of all things visible and invisible;
καὶ εἰς ἕνα κύριον Ἰησοῦν Χριστόν, < . . . ?>, μονογενῆ καὶ τὸν πρωτότοκον πάσης κτίσεως, δι᾽ οὗ οἱ αἰῶνες κατηρτίσθησαν καὶ τὰ πάντα ἐγένετο [?], τὸν ἐκ τοῦ πατρὸς αὐτοῦ γεννηθέντα πρὸ πάντων τῶν αἰώνων καὶ οὐ ποιηθέντα, φῶς ἐκ φωτός, θεὸν ἀληθινὸν ἐκ θεοῦ ἀληθινοῦ, ὁμοούσιον τῷ πατρί, δι᾽ οὗ τὰ πάντα ἐγένετο, τὸν δι᾽ ἡμᾶς ἀνθρώπους	and in one Lord Jesus Christ, < . . . ?>, the only-begotten and the first-born of all created things, through whom the worlds were established and everything was created; who was born from his Father before all worlds and who was not made, Light from Light, true God from true God, *homoousios* with the Father; through whom everything came into

---

73 Edition: Chabot 1902, pp. 97 f.; French translation: Chabot 1902, p. 355; English translation: Brock 1985(1992), p. 135. Cf. also Baum/Winkler 2003, p. 34; Bruns 2008, pp. 51 f.; Winkler 2013, p. 628; Abramowski/Hainthaler 2022, pp. 308–11.

74 Edition: Chabot 1902, pp. 113 f.; French translation: Chabot 1902, pp. 371–3; English translation (shortened): Brock 1985(1992), pp. 135 f. Cf. also Baum/Winkler 2003, p. 34; Abramowski/Hainthaler 2022, pp. 311–5.

75 Edition: Chabot 1902, pp. 133–6; French translation: Chabot 1902, pp. 394–7; English translation: Brock 1985(1992), pp. 136–8. Cf. also Abramowski 1996, pp. 95–8; Baum/Winkler 2003, p. 35; Bruns 2005, pp. 53–5; Bruns 2008, pp. 52–4; Winkler 2013, pp. 628 f.; Abramowski/Hainthaler 2022, pp. 320–6.

76 This initial quotation may be a summary and may not actually have formed part of the creed.

καὶ διὰ τὴν ἡμετέραν σωτηρίαν κατελθόντα ἐκ τοῦ οὐρανοῦ καὶ σαρκωθέντα ἐκ πνεύματος ἁγίου καὶ Μαρίας τῆς παρθένου καὶ ἄνθρωπον γενόμενον [or: ἐνανθρωπήσαντα] καὶ σταυρωθέντα ὑπὲρ ἡμῶν ἐπὶ Ποντίου Πιλάτου καὶ παθόντα καὶ ἀποθανόντα καὶ ταφέντα καὶ ἀναστάντα τῇ τρίτῃ ἡμέρᾳ κατὰ τὰς γραφὰς καὶ ἀνελθόντα εἰς τὸν οὐρανὸν καὶ καθεζόμενον ἐκ δεξιῶν/ἐν δεξιᾷ τοῦ πατρὸς αὐτοῦ καὶ ἐρχόμενον ἐν δόξῃ κρῖναι ζῶντας καὶ νεκρούς, οὗ τῆς βασιλείας οὐκ ἔσται τέλος·

being; who for the sake of us human beings and for the sake of our salvation came down from heaven; and was embodied of the Holy Spirit and of Mary the virgin and became human; and he was crucified for us in the days of Pontius Pilate, and he suffered and died and was buried and rose after three days as the holy Scriptures say; and he ascended to heaven and sat at the right hand of his Father; and he will come in glory to judge the living and the dead; whose kingdom has no end;

καὶ εἰς ἓν πνεῦμα ἅγιον, τὸ κύριον, ζωοποιόν, τὸ ἐκ τοῦ πατρὸς ἐκπορευόμενον, τὸ σὺν πατρὶ καὶ υἱῷ συμ[?]προσκυνούμενον, τὸ λαλῆσαν διὰ τῶν προφητῶν καὶ τῶν ἀποστόλων·

and in one Holy Spirit, Lord, life-giving, who proceeds from the Father and is worshipped with the Father and the Son, who spoke in the prophets and apostles;

καὶ εἰς μίαν, ἁγίαν, καθολικὴν καὶ ἀποστολικὴν ἐκκλησίαν·

and in one holy, catholic and apostolic Church;

καὶ εἰς ἓν βάπτισμα εἰς ἄφεσιν ἁμαρτιῶν·

and in one baptism for the forgiveness of sins;

καὶ εἰς ἀνάστασιν νεκρῶν·
καὶ εἰς καινότητα ζωῆς·[77]
καὶ εἰς τὸν μέλλοντα αἰῶνα.[78]

and in the resurrection of the dead;
and in the new life;
and in the world to come.

Τοὺς δὲ λέγοντας· Ἦν [or: ἔστι[79]] ποτε, ὅτε οὐκ ἦν, καί· Πρὶν γεννηθῆναι οὐκ ἦν, καὶ ὅτι ἐξ οὐκ ὄντων ἐγένετο ἢ ἐξ ἑτέρας ὑποστάσεως ἢ οὐσίας φάσκοντας εἶναι τρεπτὸν ἢ ἀλλοιωτὸν τὸν υἱὸν τοῦ θεοῦ, τούτους ἀναθεματίζει ἡ καθολικὴ καὶ ἀποστολικὴ ἐκκλησία.

Those who say, 'There is a time when he was not', and, 'Before he was begotten he was not', and that he came into being out of nothing, or who say that he is from (another) *qnoma* or another essence, or who consider the Son of God to be subject to change and alteration: (all) these the catholic and apostolic Church anathematizes.

---

77 Cf. Rom 6:4.

78 Here I follow Brock. Chabot: 'et en la vie nouvelle dans le siècle futur' which would presuppose in Greek: εἰς καινότητα ζωῆς ἐν τῷ μέλλοντι αἰῶνι or ἐν τῷ αἰῶνι τῷ ἐρχομένῳ (cf. Mk 10:30 par. Lk 18:39). However, there is no parallel for this in the Greek credal tradition.

79 Cf. above p. 421 n. 52.

The underlying creed is an odd mixture of N, N^Ant3, and C²: the anathemas are those of N, the clauses καὶ τὸν πρωτότοκον πάσης κτίσεως and καὶ οὐ ποιηθέντα are typical of the Antiochene creeds whereas the Virgin is added to σαρκωθέντα ἐκ πνεύματος ἁγίου as she is in C². Other additions from C² include ἐν δόξῃ[80] and οὗ τῆς βασιλείας οὐκ ἔσται τέλος. There are other particularities: the clause δι' οὗ – ἐγένετο follows straight after τὸν πρωτότοκον πάσης κτίσεως; δι' οὗ τὰ πάντα ἐγένετο is later repeated; καὶ ἀποθανόντα was again added as in Mārūtā's creed. The pneumatological section follows C², on the whole, but omits ὁμολογοῦμεν and προσδοκῶμεν. Finally, the phrase εἰς καινότητα ζωῆς which clearly alludes to Rom 6:4 was added in the psalters of the Miaphysite version.[81]

Luise Abramowski has suggested that N^Ant3 served as this creed's basis, supplemented by clauses from C² (and the Nicene anathemas). She thought that this was the work of the catholicos.[82] By contrast, Peter Bruns saw the Syriac translation of C² as the basis which Išoʻyahb I 'extended by some traditional Syriac-Antiochene phrases'.[83]

The *Synodicon Orientale* also contains an exposition of the creed composed, it claims, by the councils of Nicaea and Constantinople. This exposition, a brief treatise on the Trinity and on Christology which does not quote the creed at all, is ascribed to Išoʻyahb I.[84] Brock thought that this text, that displays certain similarities to the letter of Mar Aba and the creed of 585,[85] 'evidently belongs to the occasion of Ishoʻyahb's diplomatic mission to the emperor Maurice'.[86] However, the chronicler ʻAmr (s. XIV) quotes another creed in his history of the patriarchs of the Church of the East which is explicitly attributed to this mission that seems to have taken place in 587.[87]

In 596, a synod was held during the reign of the Catholicos Sabrīšōʻ (*sedit* 596–604), which adopted an interpretation of the Nicene faith that was explicitly based

80 For ἐν δόξῃ instead of μετὰ δόξης in the received text of C² cf. Dossetti 1967, p. 248 app. ad loc.
81 Cf. above p. 418 n. 28.
82 Cf. Abramowski 1996, p. 98; Abramowski/Hainthaler 2022, p. 321.
83 Bruns 2005, p. 55.
84 Edition: Chabot 1902, pp. 193–5; French translation: Chabot 1902, pp. 452–5; German translation: Braun 1900(1975), pp. 273–77; English translation: Brock 1985(1992), pp. 138 f.
85 Cf. Brock 1985(1992), p. 138 n. 68.
86 Brock 1985(1992), p. 127. Cf. also Baum/Winkler 2003, p. 36.
87 Edition: Gismondi 1897, vol. II/1, pp. 45–7; Latin translation: Gismondi 1897, vol. II/2, pp. 26 f.; French translation: Sako 1986, pp. 166–8 (appendix III). Cf. also the analysis in Abramowski/Hainthaler 2022, pp. 333–38.

on the explanation of Theodore of Mopsuestia.[88] If this refers to Theodore's *Catechetical Homilies* (as suggested by Sebastian Brock[89]), then the underlying creed was probably N^{Ant} (in whatever version). This would fit the observation that the Council of Constantinople is nowhere mentioned. The synod's version contains a series of anathemas, followed by a christological section.

By contrast, the Synod of 605 under the Catholicos Gregory (*sedit* 605–609) does mention both Nicaea and Constantinople and then offers a brief treatise on the Trinity.[90] It also seems that Babai the Great (d. 628) refers to C^2 in his *Liber de unione*.[91]

In addition, the assembly of bishops held in 612 produced a lengthy document on the Father and the Son which nowhere betrays its credal basis.[92]

Finally, the creed presented by Išoʻyahb II (*sedit* 628–646) to Emperor Heraclius in 630 also seems to be based on C^2.[93] By contrast, the creed quoted by the same catholicos in his *Christological Letter* presupposes N^{Ant}.[94]

Ultimately, N^{Ant3} carried the day in the Church of the East: it was included in the baptismal liturgy of the Catholicos Išoʻyahb III (*sedit* 649–659).[95] It is likewise

---

88 Edition: Chabot 1902, pp. 197 f.; French translation: Chabot 1902, pp. 457–9; German translation: Braun 1900(1975), pp. 283–5; English translation: Brock 1985(1992), pp. 139 f. Cf. also Baum/Winkler 2003, pp. 36 f.; Abramowski/Hainthaler 2022, pp. 340–2.

89 Cf. Brock 1985(1992), p. 139 n. 74.

90 Edition: Chabot 1902, pp. 209 f.; French translation: Chabot 1902, pp. 473 f.; German translation: Braun 1900(1975), pp. 300 f.; English translation: Brock 1985(1992), p. 140. Cf. also Bruns 2008, pp. 55 f.; Abramowski/Hainthaler 2022, pp. 347–50.

91 Babai, *Liber de unione* 2,8 (edition: Vaschalde 1915, vol. I, p. 58; Latin translation: Vaschalde 1915, vol. II, p. 47). Cf. Abramowski/Hainthaler 2022, pp. 448 f. The creed that is partly quoted here cannot be N^{Ant} where the phrase *incarnatus est et inhumanatus per Spiritum sanctum et ex Maria virgine* is not found (C^2: καὶ σαρκωθέντα ἐκ πνεύματος ἁγίου καὶ Μαρίας τῆς παρθένου καὶ ἐνανθρωπήσαντα). *Pace* Abramowski/Hainthaler 2022, p. 448. In 6,21 Babai claims that the creed used *assumpsit* to describe God's becoming human. This is not found in any of the major creeds. Abramowski/Hainthaler 2022, p. 509 think that it refers to Pseudo-Athanasius, *Expositio fidei* 1 (FaFo § 149). Cf. also Abramowski/Hainthaler 2022, p. 540 and n. 878.

92 Edition: Chabot 1902, pp. 564–7; French translation: Chabot 1902, pp. 582–4; German translation: Braun 1900(1975), pp. 309–14; English translation: Brock 1985(1992), pp. 140–2. Another edition: Abramowski/Goodman 1971, vol. I, pp. 150–7; English translation: Abramowski/Goodman 1971, vol. II, pp. 88–93. On the historical background cf. Brock 1985(1992), pp. 127 f.; Baum/Winkler 2003, p. 39; Bruns 2005, p. 55; Abramowski/Hainthaler 2022, pp. 383–411.

93 Edition: Gismondi 1897, vol. II/1, pp. 53 f.; Latin translation: Gismondi 1897, vol. II/2, p. 31 (*incarnatus et homo factus est ex Spiritu Sancto et ex Maria Virgine sanctissima*); French translation: Sako 1986, pp. 169 f. (Appendix IV). Cf. Abramowski/Hainthaler 2022, pp. 577 f.

94 Edition of the letter in Sako 1983, pp. 165–92, esp. 192–206; French translation: Sako 1983, pp. 141–64, esp. 160–2. Cf. Abramowski/Hainthaler 2022, pp. 590–2.

95 German translation: Diettrich 1903, pp. 31–2. There seems to be no satisfactory edition of this liturgy (whose authenticity would need further investigation). Cf. also Brock 1977 (I owe this ref-

found in medieval and modern Syriac manuscripts of the psalter;[96] it is also said in modern versions of the Liturgy of Addai and Mari and of baptism[97] and in the Holy Qurbana, the Eastern Syriac eucharistic liturgy.[98] In addition, it forms part of the daily office as contained in the *Qdām w-Bāthar* (*Book of before and after*) on certain given dates.[99] There is even a Sogdian version of this creed at the end of a psalter found at the Turfan oasis (East Turkestan; Xinjiang).[100] All along, the Church of the East remained aware of the fact that versions of N^Ant differed from each other: in the legal collection ascribed to Gabriel of Baṣra (compiled between 884 and 891) it is discussed whether the position of the creed is spoken before or after the anaphora. The author affirms that it was decided at both Nicaea and Constantinople that the creed was to be recited after the 'antiphon of secrets'. At the same time he affirms that variations of the creed do not alter its meaning.[101]

In what follows I offer an overview of some further information concerning other creeds in Syriac:

- The creed forms part of the pre-anaphoral rites, concluding the entrance of the bishop and clergy in a Syriac codex from the Library of Ignatius Ephrem II Raḥmani (1848–1929, patriarch of the Syriac Catholic Church 1898–1929).[102] This codex is a modern copy of a manuscript written in *'Esṭrangēlā* which dates from the eighth or ninth century; the liturgy itself is considered to belong to the sixth century.[103] Unfortunately, it cannot be located within a clear denomi-

---

erence to Jibin Thomas Abraham); Baum/Winkler 2003, pp. 43 f.; Spinks 2006(2016), pp. 73–5; Abramowski/Hainthaler 2022, pp. 597–619, esp. 604 f., citing further literature.

96 Cf. Barnes 1906, pp. 442–5 (in a late manuscript *filioque* is included; in another supplied in the margin; cf. Barnes 1906, p. 448). This is Caspari's text (without *filioque*) which is found in FaFo § 208. Cf. also Bruns 2005, pp. 45–8. – A list of five manuscripts which contain N^Ant (with minor variants) in an appendix to the psalter is given by Baumstark and Bruns (cf. Baumstark 1922, p. 112 n. 4; Bruns 2005, p. 46 n. 17). The oldest seems to date from the thirteenth century.

97 Cf. *The Liturgy of the Holy Apostles* 1893(2000), pp. 15 (anaphora = Brightman 1896(1965), pp. 270 f. (different translation)), 72 (recitation by the congregation at baptism).

98 Cf. Yousif 2000, p. 27; Bruns 2005, p. 62.

99 Cf. MacLean 1894(1969), pp. 22 f.; cf. also pp. 84, 109, 253. On the *Qdām w-Bāthar* cf. Coakley 2011.

100 Edition and translation: Martin Schwartz and Nicholas Sims-Williams in Sims-Williams/Schwartz/Pittard 2014, pp. 30–3. Cf. also Gillman/Klimkeit 1999, pp. 252 f.

101 Cf. Kaufhold 1976, p. 232 (information kindly supplied by Hubert Kaufhold).

102 The manuscript is cod. Charfet, Bibliothèque patriarchale syro-catholique, Fonds Raḥmani 87; cf. Binggeli et al. 2021, p. 265 (information kindly supplied by Hubert Kaufhold). Latin translation of the relevant text in Raḥmani 1908, p. 22. French translation and commentary in Khouri-Sarkis 1957, p. 162. English translation in Taft 1978, pp. 40 f.

103 Cf. Taft 1978, pp. 40–2, also giving an English translation of the liturgy; furthermore Taft 2006, pp. 40 f., 64–7 (*non uidi*).

national tradition.[104] Here the entrance of the clergy is accompanied by the deacons shouting: 'All those who have not received the seal, depart!' This is, then, the point in the liturgy when the catechumens must leave the church. The doors are closed, the bishop enters and approaches the altar. The eucharistic elements are placed upon the altar, the bishop offers incense, and all say the creed (which is not quoted).[105] This corresponds to the placement of the creed (which is not N) in the *Liturgical Homily* attributed to Narsai (perhaps *s.* VI).[106]

– A creed displaying the key features of Antiochene theology was translated from a Greek original (written in *c.* 433) and included in a Dyophysite collection of christological texts.[107]

– Explanations of the creed appear to have been written by Cyriacus of Nisibis and Henana of Adiabene (d. 610).[108]

– A Syriac translation of the creed against Paul of Samosata preserved in the acts of the Council of Ephesus (431; FaFo § 127) is found in cod. London, British Library, Add. 14533 (syr. 859; *s.* VIII/IX), p. 42.[109]

– John of Maron (d. 707), first patriarch of the Maronite Church, composed a treatise which contained long credal passages, testimonies from Scripture, and a florilegium from the Fathers.[110]

– A lengthy *Apology Concerning the Faith* is contained in the upper writing of the palimpsest codex in the Monastery of St Catherine on Mount Sinai (ff. 163v–165v) which contains (in the lower writing) the Gospels in Old Syriac (so-called *Syrus Sinaiticus* (Sin. Syr. 30), *s.* IV/V).[111] The upper text was written in 778.[112] It was edited and translated by Agnes Smith Lewis.[113] The text begins with a creed (translation slightly modernized):

I believe in one holy Trinity, of the Father, and of the Son, and of the Holy Spirit, a glorious essence, and an exalted godhead. The Son, who is not younger than his Father; and the Fa-

---

104 Cf. Taft 1978, p. 41 n. 99 who thinks that the ordo of the liturgy is closer to that of the Greek *Liturgy of St James* 'than to that of the actual Jacobite or Nestorian liturgies,.' Cf., however, Gemayel 1965, p. 152.

105 Cf. Taft 1978, pp. 40 f.

106 Cf. above p. 424.

107 Edition: Abramowski/Goodman 1971, vol. I, pp. 146 f.; English translation: Abramowski/Goodman 1971, vol. II, p. 88. Cf. also Abramowski/Goodman 1971, vol. II, pp. XXXVIII–XLII.

108 Cf. Baumstark 1922, pp. 127, 196.

109 Edition in Flemming/Lietzmann 1904, pp. 42 f.

110 Cf. John of Maron, *Expositio fidei*, ed. Breydy 1988. On John's life cf. Breydy 1992.

111 Cf. Metzger 1977(2001), pp. 37 f. and URL <http://sinaipalimpsests.org/> (17/11/2023).

112 Cf. Vööbus 1951, p. 108.

113 Edition: Smith Lewis in Bensly/Harris/Burkitt 1894, pp. VIII–XII; English translation: Bensly/Harris/Burkitt 1894, pp. XII–XIV. Cf. also Connolly 1906, pp. 222 f.

ther, who is not older than his offspring; and the Holy Spirit, proceeding, of the same substance as the Father and the Son.

We confess one Trinity with distinction of persons, but one God with equality of nature. For there is one power, and one authority, one worship, one lordship, one government, one godhead, in which there is neither greater nor lesser, nor commanding, nor commanded, nor weaker, nor more powerful.[114]

This initial creed is followed by a long christological summary, a series of anathemas, and a brief conclusion. The anathemas confirm the faith of the first four Ecumenical Councils which reveals the Chalcedonian disposition of the text's author.

- A special case is the creed submitted by a monk Nestorius who had been accused of Messalianism to a synod held under Patriarch Timothy I (*sedit* 780–823). It contains a fairly brief credal part, followed by a long series of anathemas.[115]

9.2 Armenia

The credal development of Armenia has been comprehensively studied by Gabriele Winkler.[116] Again, in what follows I concentrate on the reception of N. (C² is not attested.) In Winkler's view the creeds of Antioch 341 strongly influenced the language of the prayers in the Armenian version of the Liturgy of St Basil. A declaratory creed (probably N) was introduced into the liturgy at a later stage.[117] Likewise, a western Syriac influence (creeds of Antioch 325 and Antioch 341 (Ant² and Ant⁴)[118]) is discernible in the *Teaching of Saint Gregory* (a kind of catechism),[119] in a creed ascribed to Gregory the Illuminator,[120] in the histories of Łazar Pʻarpecʻi (*s. V ex.*) and of Ełišē (*s. VI*),[121] in the *Buzandaran Patmutʻiwnkʻ* ('Epic Histories', *c.* 470),[122] in

---

114 Smith Lewis in Bensly/Harris/Burkitt 1894, p. XII. On this text cf. also Winkler 2000, pp. 317; Winkler 2004, p. 147.

115 Edition and German translation: Braun 1902, pp. 302–11 and Heimgartner 2012, vol. I (edition), pp. 107–13 and vol. II, pp. 89–95 (German translation and commentary). A confession of faith ascribed to Jacob of Edessa (d. 708) is contained in cod. London, British Library, Or. 2307 (*s. XVII*). Cf. Margoliouth 1899, p. 7 and Baumstark 1922, p. 254.

116 Cf. Winkler 1997; Winkler 2000. On the earlier history of scholarship cf. Catergian 1893.

117 Cf. Winkler 2015, pp. 241–7, 254.

118 Cf. Winkler 2004, pp. 154 f.

119 Cf. Winkler 2000, pp. 11–32, Winkler 2004, p. 137.

120 Cf. Winkler 2000, pp. 33–6.

121 Cf. Winkler 2000, pp. 37–64.

122 Cf. Winkler 2000, pp. 65–89; Winkler 2004, pp. 118, 141–54.

the creed at the end of the *History* of Pseudo-Agathangelos,[123] and in a creed and a letter by Eznik of Kolb (d. *c.* 455).[124]

9.2.1 N and cognate creeds

The earliest translation of N forms part of the textual tradition of the Armenian version of the *Didascalia CCCXVIII patrum Nicaenorum.*[125] In this context, an Armenian *Fides quae in Nicaea*, preserved among the works of Evagrius Ponticus, consists of the creed proper and an explanatory section. This appears to be the oldest version of N in Armenian.[126] A Greek retroversion (which may as such never have existed, but which facilitates comparison) is given below (ignoring the philological particularities of the Armenian translation):

Πιστεύομεν εἰς ἕνα θεόν, παντοκρά-τορα, ποιητὴν οὐρανοῦ καὶ γῆς, ὁρατῶν τε καὶ ἀοράτων κτισμάτων·	We believe in one God, the Almighty, Maker of heaven and earth, of visible and invisible creatures;
καὶ εἰς ἕνα κύριον Ἰησοῦν Χριστόν, τὸν υἱὸν τοῦ θεοῦ, μονογενῆ, τουτέστιν ἐκ τῆς οὐσίας τοῦ πατρός, δι' οὗ τὰ πάντα ἐγένετο, θεὸν ἐκ θεοῦ, φῶς ἐκ φωτός, γεννηθέντα οὐ ποιηθέντα, ὁμοούσιον τῷ πατρί, τὸν δι' τοὺς ἀνθρώπους κα-τελθόντα καὶ σαρκωθέντα, παθόντα, ἀναστάντα τῇ τρίτῃ ἡμέρᾳ καὶ ἀνελθόντα εἰς τοὺς οὐρανούς καὶ πάλιν ἐρχόμενον κρῖναι νεκρούς καὶ ζῶντας·	and in one Lord Jesus Christ, the Son of God, only-begotten, that is, from the power of the Father; through whom all things came into being, God who is from God, Light that is from Light, begotten, not made, of equal power with the Father; who for the sake of humankind descended and put on a body,[127] suffered, on the third day rose again, and ascended into the heavens, and will come again to judge the dead and the living;

---

123 Cf. Winkler 2000, pp. 90–100.
124 Cf. Winkler 2000, pp. 120–4; Winkler 2004, pp. 136 f. For the letter cf. also Frivold 1981, pp. 169–72.
125 For background cf. FaFo § 176; Winkler 2000, pp. 104–7; Winkler 2013, pp. 629–33; Avagyan 2014, pp. 84 f.; Blumell 2017. A list of the translations is found in Kohlbacher, 'Rabbula', 2004, p. 250 n. 76.
126 Edition and German translation in Winkler 2000, pp. 128b–133b, 575b–80b; extensive commentary in Winkler 2000, pp. 581–91. Cf. also Dossetti 1967, pp. 55 f.; Winkler 2004, pp. 115–18, 138–40. This text is not identical with the *Faith of Mar Evagrius* (*Professio fidei*, CPG 2478) preserved in Syriac and edited by Muyldermans 1952, pp. 139 f. (text); pp. 167–9 (French translation); cf. also Muyldermans 1952, p. 93.
127 Winkler: 'und einen Leib anzog'. On the translation cf. Winkler 2000, pp. 390–8; 587–9.

καὶ εἰς τὸ ἅγιον πνεῦμα, τὸ ζωοποιόν.	and in the Spirit, the holy, the life-giver.[128]
Τοὺς[129] δὲ λέγοντας· Ἦν ποτε, ὅτε οὐκ ἦν, καί· Πρὶν γεννηθῆναι οὐκ ἦν, καὶ ὅτι ἐξ οὐκ ὄντων ἐγένετο καὶ ἐξ ἑτέρας ὑποστάσεως ἢ οὐσίας ἢ εἶναι τρεπτὸν ἢ ἀλλοιωτόν, τούτους ἀναθεματίζομεν.	We anathematize those who say, 'There was when he was not', and, 'He was not before [his] birth', and that he came to be from nothing, and from another power or substance, or that he is through what is perishable, or that he is through what is decaying.[130]

This creed is basically N with some variants: in the first section the title of Father is missing, whereas οὐρανοῦ καὶ γῆς and, perhaps, κτισμάτων was added. In the second section the phrases γεννηθέντα ἐκ πατρός, θεὸν ἀληθινὸν ἐκ θεοῦ ἀληθινοῦ, τά τε ἐν τῷ οὐρανῷ καὶ τὰ ἐν τῇ γῇ, ἡμᾶς, καὶ διὰ τὴν ἡμετέραν σωτηρίαν, and ἐνανθρωπήσαντα are omitted.[131] Δι' οὗ τὰ πάντα ἐγένετο is mentioned earlier than in N. Πάλιν before ἐρχόμενον may have been added. The final phrase reads in the order νεκρούς καὶ ζῶντας. In the third article τὸ ζωοποιόν is added. In the anathemas neither ἢ κτιστόν, τὸν υἱὸν τοῦ θεοῦ, nor the Church are mentioned. Perhaps, φάσκοντας was also omitted and ἢ and εἶναι reversed. In addition, the translation of οὐσία and ὁμοούσιος as 'power' is striking.[132]

A similar version of the creed and explanation is contained in a synodal letter preserved under the name of Patriarch Sahak the Great (enthroned 387; deposed 428; d. 438/439) in which the Armenian bishops assembled at a Synod in Aštišat in 435 acknowledged receipt of the tome of Proclus of Constantinople.[133] They declared it to be N, while it is, in fact, an abbreviated version of N which also displays some additions such as οὐρανοῦ καὶ γῆς and, perhaps, κτισμάτων. In the second article γεννηθέντα ἐκ τοῦ πατρός, δι' οὗ τὰ πάντα ἐγένετο τά τε ἐν τῷ οὐρανοῦ καὶ τὰ ἐν τῇ γῇ, θεὸν ἀλη-

---

128 On the translation cf. Winkler 2000, pp. 583 f.

129 The reconstruction of the anathemas is uncertain.

130 Winkler: 'oder: "durch das Vergängliche sei er", oder: "durch Verwesendes sei er"'. This is, of course, not a precise rendering of the presumed Greek text.

131 On the omission of ἐνανθρωπήσαντα which is omitted in the *Didascalia* as well cf. Winkler 2004, pp. 114 f.

132 Cf. Winkler 2000, pp. 134, 585–7.

133 Edition: Winkler 2000, p. 128a, 575a–80a. The text of the creed in Greek retroversion and English translation is found in FaFo § 210c. Extensive commentary in Winkler 2000, pp. 581–91. The authorship of Sahak is controversial. On the problem of dates cf. Winkler 2000, pp. 109–11. On the historical background cf. Dossetti 1967, pp. 56 f.; Winkler 2000, pp. 114–7; Kohlbacher, 'Rabbula', 2004, pp. 251 f.; Stopka 2016, pp. 59 f.

θινὸν ἐκ θεοῦ ἀληθινοῦ, καὶ διὰ τὴν ἡμετέραν σωτηρίαν, and ἐνανθρωπήσαντα are omitted. After ἐξ οὐσίας the creed reads οὐσία γεννηθεῖσα, δι' οὗ τὰ πάντα ἐγένετο. In the anathemas ἢ κτιστόν and τὸν υἱὸν τοῦ θεοῦ, εἶναι, and the Church are missing.

N is found again in the creed which Catholicos Babgēn I (d. 515/516) inserted into a letter the Armenian Synod of Duin (506) sent to Miaphysite bishops in Persia and which was 'the official creed of the Armenians from the first half of the fifth until the beginning of the sixth century'.[134] In a Greek retroversion it reads like this:

Πιστεύομεν εἰς ἕνα θεόν, πατέρα, παντοκράτορα, πάντων ὁρατῶν τε καὶ ἀοράτων ποιητήν·	We believe in one God, the Father Almighty, Maker of all things both visible and invisible;
καὶ ἕνα κύριον Ἰησοῦν Χριστόν, εἰς τὸν υἱὸν τοῦ θεοῦ γεννηθέντα ἐκ τοῦ πατρός, μονογενῆ, τουτέστιν ἐκ τῆς οὐσίας τοῦ πατρός, θεὸν ἐκ θεοῦ, φῶς ἐκ φωτός, θεὸν ἀληθινὸν ἐκ θεοῦ ἀληθινοῦ, γεννηθέντα οὐ ποιηθέντα, ὁμοούσιον τῷ πατρί, δι' οὗ τὰ πάντα ἐγένετο ἐν τοῖς οὐρανοῖς καὶ ἐν τῇ γῇ, τὸν δι' ἡμᾶς τοὺς ἀνθρώπους καὶ διὰ τὴν ἡμετέραν σωτηρίαν κατελθόντα, σαρκωθέντα ἐκ τῆς ἁγίας παρθένου Μαρίας, παθόντα ὑπὲρ τῶν ἁμαρτιῶν ἡμῶν, ἀποθανόντα καὶ ἀναστάντα τῇ τρίτῃ ἡμέρᾳ, ἀνελθόντα εἰς τοὺς οὐρανούς, καθεζόμενον ἐν δεξιᾷ τοῦ πατρός, ἐρχόμενον κρῖναι ζῶντας καὶ νεκρούς·	and one Lord Jesus Christ, in the Son of God, begotten from the Father, only-begotten, that is, from the substance of the Father; God from God, Light from Light, true God from true God, begotten, not made, consubstantial with the Father; through whom all things came into being in the heavens and on earth; who because of us humans and because of our salvation descended, became flesh[135] from the holy virgin Mary, suffered for our sins, died, and on the third day rose again, ascended into the heavens; sat down at the right hand of the Father; comes to judge the living and dead;
καὶ πιστεύομεν εἰς τὸ πνεῦμα τὸ ἅγιον, τὸ ἄκτιστον, τὸ τέλειον.	and we believe in the Holy Spirit, the uncreated one, the perfect one.
Τοὺς δὲ λέγοντας· Ἦν ποτε, ὅτε οὐκ ἦν, καί· Πρὶν γεννηθῆναι οὐκ ἦν, καί· Ἐξ οὐκ ὄντων ἐγένετο ἢ ἐξ ἑτέρας ὑποστάσεως ἢ οὐσίας εἶναι ἢ τρεπτὸν ἢ ἀλλοιωτὸν [? or: ἐφήμερον?[136]] τὸν υἱὸν τοῦ	The catholic and apostolic Church anathematizes those who say, 'There was when he was not', and, 'He was not before he was born', and, 'He came to be from nothing', or that he is allegedly

---

134 Winkler 2000, p. 622. Text and German translation Winkler 2000, pp. 176–8. English translation: Frivold 1981, p. 176 (incomplete); French translation Garsoïan 1999, pp. 442 f. For background cf. Winkler 2013, pp. 632 f.; Winkler 2000, pp. 167–72; Stopka 2016, pp. 67–9.
135 Winkler: 'sich verleiblichte'.
136 Winkler: 'vergänglich'.

θεοῦ, τούτους ἀναθεματίζει ἡ καθολικὴ καὶ ἀποστολικὴ ἐκκλησία.	from another essence or substance, [who say] that the Son of God is alterable or mutable [*or:* perishable].

Again, there are some variations. In the second section ἐνανθρωπήσαντα is missing, whereas ἐκ τῆς ἁγίας παρθένου Μαρίας, ὑπὲρ τῶν ἁμαρτιῶν ἡμων, ἀποθανόντα, and καθεζόμενον ἐν δεξιᾷ τοῦ πατρός are added. In the third section τὸ ἄκτιστον, τὸ τέλειον is added. In the anathemas ἢ κτιστόν and, perhaps, φάσκοντας is missing.

Further fragments of N are found in a second letter which Babgēn sent to the Miaphysite Syrians of Persia between 505 and 515/516.[137] According to Winkler all these versions were taken from (different recensions of) the *Didascalia CCCXVIII patrum Nicaenorum*.

Yet another version of N forms part of an Armenian translation of the *Third Letter to Nestorius* by Cyril of Alexandria contained in the *Girkʻ Tʻłtʻocʻ* (*Book of Letters*).[138] This translation is the most accurate although it also displays some peculiarities with regard to the text of N.[139] Versions of N in Cyril's letter (and elsewhere) in the Armenian acts of the Council of Ephesus are as yet unedited.[140]

The Georgian Catholicos Kiwrion had written to the Catholicos Abraham (*sedit* 607–611/615);[141] in response, the latter issued an encyclical in 608/609 in which he broke off relations with the Iberians (Georgians). Here he quoted a creed which he claimed was that of Nicaea, Constantinople, and Ephesus.[142]

An extended version of N (*Armeniacum*) which was called the 'Creed of the Nicene Council' and which is still used at baptism and during the celebration of the eucharist today, is first attested in the first half of the seventh century. It is, in fact, a translation of an 'Exposition of the Creed' ascribed to Athanasius (FaFo § 185)

---

137 Cf. Winkler 2000, pp. 170 f.

138 Text: Winkler 2000, pp. 193 f. There seems to be no modern translation. Cf. also Rucker 1930, pp. 29 f.; Dossetti 1967, p. 46.

139 They are listed in Winkler 2000, p. 192.

140 Cf. Rucker 1930, pp. 29 f.

141 Cf. below p. 462.

142 Unfortunately, it is not entirely clear where it ends. French translation in Garsoïan 1999, p. 579:

‘Je crois en un seul Dieu, Père tout-puissant, créateur du ciel et de la terre, des choses visibles et invisibles.

Et en un Seigneur, Jésus-Christ, au Fils de Dieu engendré de Dieu le Père, Monogène, mais ni créé ni confirmé, consubstantiel au Père et non pas du néant, créateur de toutes les choses visibles et invisibles.

Et au Saint-Esprit, créateur et vivificateur et régénérateur, non né mais procédant.

Dieu, est dit le Père, Dieu, le Fils, Dieu, le Saint-Esprit, non pas trois dieux, mais une seule Trinité glorifiée par sa divinité, volonté et puissance [. . .]’.

with some minor changes.[143] Winkler published an edition, German translation, and detailed study of this creed.[144] In what follows I give Brightman's translation of the Armenian text,[145] modernized and revised according to Winkler's translation.[146] Additions to the Greek critical text (FaFo § 185) are indicated in italics. Words omitted from the Greek are enclosed in {}:

> We believe in one God, the Father Almighty, *in the* Maker *of heaven and earth,* of {all} things visible and invisible;
>
> and in one Lord Jesus Christ, *in* the Son of God, born from *God* the Father as only-begotten, that is, from the substance of the Father, God from God, Light from Light, true God from true God, an offspring and not a creature, the same substance from *the nature of* the Father, through whom all things were made in *the* heavens and on earth, both visible and invisible; who for us humans and for our salvation came down *from the heavens* and was incarnate, became human,[147] {that is,} was born perfectly from the *holy* {ever-}virgin Mary through the Holy Spirit, *by whom he took* body, soul, and mind and everything that is in humans, {yet without sin}, in truth and not in semblance; after he had suffered, {that is,} crucified, was buried, rose again on the third day, ascended into the heavens in the same body, he sat down {gloriously} at the right hand of the Father; he will come in the same body *and* in the glory *of the Father* to judge the living and the dead; whose kingdom will have no end.
>
> We also believe in the Holy Spirit {who is not alien to the Father and the Son, but consubstantial with the Father and the Son,} *in the* uncreated one *and in the* perfect one, {the Paraclete,} who spoke in the Law and in the Prophets and in the Gospels, who came down upon the Jordan, preached in the apostles [*v.l.:* preached the Messenger], and dwelt in the saints.
>
> We also believe in one [and] only [one] catholic and apostolic Church, in one baptism, in repentance, in *propitiation and* remission of sins [*Greek:* in one baptism of repentance and of the remission of sins,] in the resurrection of the dead, in the everlasting judgements of souls and bodies, in the kingdom of {the} heaven{s} and in the life ever-lasting.
>
> But those who say there was when the Son was not, or that there was when there was no Holy Spirit, or that they [*Greek:* he] came into being out of nothing, or who say that the Son of God or the Holy Spirit be of a different {*hypóstasis* or} substance and that they be changeable

---

143 Cf. Kohlbacher, 'Rabbula', 2004, p. 252. Winkler 2000, p. 225 sees in FaFo § 185 only one *Vorlage* among others.

144 Cf. Winkler 2000, pp. 223–34. Cf. already Winkler 1979. An even further elaborated version of the *Armeniacum*, interspersed with anti-heretical comments based on Epiphanius, is found in cod. Vienna, Library of the Mekhitarists, 324 (s. XIV), f. 159r–v. Text and translation in Akinian/Casey 1931, pp. 147–51. The age of the text is unknown, but 'none of the heretics mentioned are later than the fifth century' (Akinian/Casey 1931, p. 147). It is largely identical with a creed found in the *Knik' Hawatoy* ('Seal of Faith'; for which see below in the text); cf. Winkler 2000, pp. 235–7.

145 Cf. Brightman 1896(1965), pp. 426 f.

146 Cf. Winkler 2000, pp. 230 f. A Greek retroversion taken from Ter-Mikelian 1892, pp. 22–4 is found in Hahn/Hahn 1897, pp. 151–4 (§ 137). However, as can be seen from the footnotes in Hahn/Hahn, there are considerable differences in the various attempts at retranslating this creed into Greek. Therefore, in what follows I give the English version.

147 Winkler: 'sich "verleiblichte", "inhominisierte"'.

or alterable, such does the catholic and apostolic Church anathematize [*Greek:* these we anathematize because these the catholic and apostolic Church, our mother, anathematizes].

{And we anathematize all those who do not confess the resurrection of the flesh, and
all the heresies, that is, those who are not of this faith of the holy and only catholic Church.}

The most important difference to FaFo § 185 is the omission of the consubstantiality
of the Holy Spirit and the final anathema. Michael Kohlbacher has suggested that
the Greek version of this creed was written by Epiphanius of Salamis and was used
by the congregation of Paulinus in Antioch.[148]

From the second half of the sixth century onwards we have creeds which were
issued by individual catholicoi. In all instances, N was extended, depending on the
doctrinal situation at the time.[149]

9.2.2 Liturgical use of the creeds

Originally, credal questions and brief declaratory creeds were used at baptism
which seem to be unrelated to N.[150] The use of 'the creed of Nicaea' (N?) at baptism
is only attested in a rubric in a baptismal liturgy contained in cod. Venice, San Laz-
zaro, 320 (*olim* 457; *s.* IX–X).[151] The baptismal questions themselves are much simpler,
merely expressing belief in the Trinity.[152] They were later extended and adapted to
the declaratory creed.[153]

It appears that by the end of the seventh century the creed had come to be recited in the anaphora after the Gospel. This creed may well be the *Armeniacum*.[154]
(The entire text of N is not attested in any Armenian liturgy.[155])

---

148 Cf. Kohlbacher, 'Rabbula', 2004, pp. 252–5. Kohlbacher here clearly (and in my view correctly) deviates from Winkler who suggested that the *Armeniacum* is a 'fusion of sections from
the so-called *Hierosolymitanum* [= J], the Nicene Creed, the *Hermeneia* [= Pseudo-Athanasius],
and the Creed of Babgēn' (Winkler 2015, p. 251; cf. Winkler 2000, pp. 225–9).
149 Cf. Yovhannēs II Gabełean (*sedit* 557–574): Winkler 2000, pp. 251–7 (text, German translation,
and commentary); Terian 2020, pp. 35–7 (text and English translation); Frivold 1981, pp. 179 f.
(partial English translation). – Abraham (*sedit* 607–610/611): Winkler 2000, pp. 259–61 (text, German translation, and commentary). – Komitas (*sedit* 610/611–628): Winkler 2000, pp. 261–7 (text,
German translation, and commentary). Cf. also the credal statement by the monk theologian
Yovhannēs Mayragomec'i (d. *c.* 652; Winkler 2000, pp. 267–70).
150 Cf. Winkler 2000, pp. 149–57.
151 Cf. Winkler 2000, p. 150. Cf. also Winkler 2015, p. 251.
152 Edition and German translation: Winkler 1982, pp. 196–9; Winkler 2000, pp. 150 f.
153 Cf. Winkler 2000, pp. 152–4.
154 Cf. Winkler 2001, pp. 412–14.
155 Cf. Winkler 2015, p. 251.

Likewise, the lengthy creed which opens the night office in the present Armenian Horologion may have originated at baptism.[156] Remarkably, it is the only eastern creed to include the 'communion of saints'. The relevant passage is as follows: 'In the holy Church we believe in the remission of sins, with the communion of saints.'[157] However, Winkler adds a footnote explaining that instead of 'the communion of saints' one could also translate: 'through the communion with the sacred [things]',[158] which would suggest the eucharistic communion. There are some similarities with the pneumatological section in R/T which has led to considerable scholarly discussion. Winkler leaves the question open as to whether the Armenian creed was influenced by Latin practice (which she considers possible).[159]

9.2.3 Creeds other than N

In a letter which the Syrian church sent to the Armenian one and their Catholicos Nersēs II (*sedit* 548–557) before the second Synod of Duin (555), asking them to consecrate the monk Abdiso(y) as bishop, it referred to the first three ecumenical councils, adding a creed which consisted only of a christological section.[160] Nersēs consecrated Abdiso(y) as requested and sent another creed in reply which closely followed that of the Syrians.[161] Abdiso(y) himself also produced a lengthy creed in his second letter to Nersēs.[162]

The *Knik' Hawatoy*, a florilegium compiled during the reign of the Catholicos Komitas (*sedit* 610/611–628), contains an Armenian translation of the creed against Paul of Samosata, preserved in the acts of the Council of Ephesus (431; FaFo § 127).[163]

---

156 Cf. Winkler 2000, pp. 203–22, 593–620; Winkler 2004, pp. 155–9.

157 Edition: Winkler 2000, p. 205. My translation follows Winkler's German translation (Winkler 2000, p. 207): 'Wir glauben in der heiligen Kirche an die Vergebung der Sünden, mit der Gemeinschaft der Heiligen.'

158 Winkler 2000, p. 207 n. 9 (cf. pp. 209, 571): 'durch die Gemeinschaft mit den heiligen [Dingen]'.

159 Cf. Winkler 2000, p. 571.

160 Edition and German translation: Winkler 2000, pp. 214 f.; French translation: Garsoïan 1999, pp. 458. Background: Garsoïan 1999, pp. 207–15; Winkler 2000, pp. 213 f.

161 Edition and German translation: Winkler 2000, pp. 216–18; English translation: Frivold 1981, pp. 177 f.; French translation: Garsoïan 1999, pp. 461 f.

162 Edition and German translation: Winkler 2000, pp. 219–22; French translation: Garsoïan 1999, pp. 467–9.

163 Cf. Lebon 1929, p. 31.

A creed which is attributed to Athanasius is found in cod. Vienna, Library of the Mekhitarists, 324 (*s.* XIV), f. 159v which its editors date to the sixth century.[164] Here I give their translation (slightly altered):

Creed of St. Athanasius:

[I] Eternal Father, omnipotent and everlasting, maker of heaven and earth and the creatures which are upon it;

and the Son, begotten of the Father and coeternal [with him], having come into being timelessly and immaterially from the same substance and not from elsewhere, and all things were made by him;

and the Holy Spirit, appearing from their essence as light from light, who illumines all creatures by the light of knowledge and, like a spring, distributes gifts by grace, and he did not come into being from elsewhere but came from the Father and appears from the Son,

one Godhead appearing in three <persons> and preserving unchanged its individuality, a perfect Trinity and one glorious Godhead.

[II] And concerning the incarnation of God we thus confess that he who was indescribably and immaterially begotten of the Father, the same was incarnate of the Holy Virgin and mixed the unmixable in her womb indescribably and incomprehensibly.

God made him by combinations, and one Son is confessed, worshipped, and glorified with one worship; who passed through all human sufferings without blemish, voluntarily and not by necessity, so that he will renew for us the way to fulfil all righteousness.

And we do not divide the Son according to an economy, because Jesus Christ, yesterday and today the same and forever, is praised with the Father and the Holy Spirit by things in heaven and things on earth with a Trisagion, being summed up in the one Lordship and Godhead of the all-holy Trinity.

And now we thus confess; and he who does not so confess we anathematize as the holy Fathers anathematized Arius and all the heretics with him.

Winkler divides this text in [I] a creed and [II] an 'Ekthesis'. She thinks the creed was not composed before the sixth century, whereas the Ekthesis has to be dated to 'the fifth and sixth centuries'.[165]

The *Expositio fidei* (FaFo § 149) and the *Epistula ad Liberium* (FaFo § 150), ascribed to Athanasius, were also translated into Armenian. In each case the earliest manuscript dates from the twelfth century.[166]

An unpublished treatise on baptism preserved in two manuscripts from, perhaps, the fourteenth and from the nineteenth centuries respectively, contains a brief baptismal creed:

---

164 Edition: Akinian/Casey 1931, pp. 145 f.; English translation: Akinian/Casey 1931, pp. 146 f.; German translation: Winkler 2000, pp. 189–91. The same text with some variants is found in the so-called Armenian 'Socrates Minor'. Cf. Akinian/Casey 1931, pp. 143–4; Avagyan 2014, p. 139.

165 Winkler 2000, pp. 188 f.

166 Cf. CPG 2804, 2805, and Avagyan 2014, pp. 86 f. For later Armenian creeds cf. Terian 2011.

I believe in the Father Almighty and his only-begotten Son and the Holy Spirit, and the resurrection of the flesh and the holy catholic Church.[167]

9.3 Coptic Egypt

The Greek *Corpus canonum*[168] appears to have been translated into Coptic in the fifth or early sixth century. This version has not survived in its entirety but has been reconstructed in a process spanning more than 150 years. N seems to have been included twice in this collection, namely at the beginning (mutilated) and as part of the *Didascalia CCCXVIII patrum Nicaenorum* (cf. FaFo § 176). Dossetti reconstructed the Greek text of the first of these versions of N.[169] Apart from some stylistic variants the text differs from N, both in its original version and in the Greek version of the *Didascalia*,[170] in that it omits κατελθόντα καί and παθόντα, adding ἀποθανόντα instead. In the anathemas ὁ υἱός is added after the first οὐκ ἦν. Finally, it reads κτιστὸν ἢ τρεπτόν, omitting εἶναι and ἢ ἀλλοιωτόν. The version of N included in the *Didascalia*[171] is different: here πάντων is missing in the first section and ἐνανθρωπήσαντα in the second section (ἐνανθρωπήσαντα is also missing in the version of N in the Greek *Didascalia*) whereas ἀποθανόντα after παθόντα is added. In the anathemas ἢ κτιστὸν is missing (as it is in the Greek *Didascalia*).

The Coptic *Corpus canonum* also contained C². It is preserved only in mutilated form (the beginning is missing) in cod. Paris, Bibliothèque Nationale, coptus 129/14 (originally part of a larger papyrus manuscript which was written in the Monastery Mar Severus in Rifeh/Asyut in 1003). A Greek retroversion of what remains was, again, published by Dossetti.[172] Major differences to C² include the addition of ἀποθανόντα and of αὐτοῦ ἐν ὑψίστοις after ἐν δεξιᾷ τοῦ πατρός, and the change of μετὰ δόξης to ἐν δόξῃ αὐτοῦ. It omits ἁγίαν as attribute of the Church and adds αἰώνιον after ζωήν.[173]

167 Avagyan 2014, pp. 134–6. I translate from her German translation on p. 136.
168 Cf. above pp. 386 f. For what follows cf. also Dossetti 1967, pp. 53 f. and n. 51, 123–9.
169 Cf. Dossetti 1967, pp. 128 f.
170 Cf. Riedinger/Thurn 1985, p. 84, ll. 1–15.
171 Edition: Rossi 1885, pp. 147 f.; Italian translation: Rossi 1885, p. 178; German translation: Haase 1920, pp. 28 f.
172 Cf. Dossetti 1967, pp. 195 f.; cf. also p. 126.
173 Cf. also the later evidence from manuscripts in Quecke 1970, pp. 476 f. Αὐτοῦ ἐν ὑψίστοις is missing again from the wooden tablet discussed below.

N was also included in a collection of documents of the Council of Ephesus inserted into a kind of novel about the Egyptian monk Victor of unknown date which was translated from Greek.[174] Its text in Greek must have run like this:[175]

Πιστεύομεν εἰς ἕνα θεόν, πατέρα, παντοκράτορα, ὁρατῶν τε καὶ ἀοράτων ποιητήν·[176]	We believe in one God, the Father Almighty, Maker of things both visible and invisible;
καὶ εἰς ἕνα κύριον Ἰησοῦν Χριστόν, τὸν υἱὸν τοῦ θεοῦ, γεννηθέντα ἐκ τοῦ πατρός, μονογενῆ, τουτέστιν ἐκ τῆς οὐσίας τοῦ πατρός, θεὸν ἐκ θεοῦ, φῶς ἐκ φωτός, θεὸν ἀληθινὸν ἐκ θεοῦ ἀληθινοῦ, γεννηθέντα οὐ ποιηθέντα, ἀλλ᾽ ὁμοούσιον τῷ πατρί, δι᾽ οὗ τὰ πάντα ἐγένετο εἴτε ἐν τῷ οὐρανῷ εἴτε ἐν τῇ γῇ, τὸν δι᾽ ἡμᾶς τοὺς ἀνθρώπους σαρκωθέντα, ἐνανθρωπήσαντα, ἀποθανόντα καὶ ἀναστάντα τῇ τρίτῃ ἡμέρᾳ, ἀνελθόντα εἰς τὸν οὐρανὸν καὶ καθεζόμενον ἐν δεξιᾷ τοῦ πατρός, πάλιν ἐρχόμενον κρῖναι ζῶντας καὶ νεκρούς·	and in one Lord Jesus Christ, the Son of God, begotten from the Father, only-begotten, that is, from the substance of the Father; God from God, Light from Light, true God from true God, begotten, not made, but consubstantial with the Father; through whom all things came into being, be it in heaven or on earth; who because of us humans became flesh, became human, died, and on the third day rose again, ascended into the heaven and sat down at the right hand of the Father; will come again to judge the living and dead;
καὶ πιστεύομεν εἰς τὸ πνεῦμα τὸ ἅγιον, τὸν παράκλητον.	and we believe in the Holy Spirit, the Paraclete.
Τοὺς δὲ λέγοντας· Ἦν ποτε, ὅτε οὐκ ἦν, καί· Πρὶν γεννηθῆναι οὐκ ἦν, καὶ ὅτι ἐξ οὐκ ὄντων ἐγένετο ἢ ἐξ ἑτέρας ὑποστάσεως ἢ οὐσίας ἢ εἶναι τρεπτὸν ἢ ἀλλοιωτὸν τὸν υἱὸν τοῦ θεοῦ, τούτους ἀναθεματίζει ἡ καθολικὴ ἐκκλησία.	The catholic Church anathematizes those who say, 'There was when he was not', and, 'He was not before he was begotten', and that he came to be from nothing or from another *hypóstasis* or substance, or that the Son of God is alterable or mutable.

There are some differences compared to N: apart from stylistic minutiae it is worth noting that in the first section πάντων and in the second section καὶ διὰ ἡμετέραν

---

174 There is no full critical edition of the Coptic text. A German translation on the basis of a collation of the Coptic manuscripts is found in Kraatz 1904, pp. 85 f. On the historical background cf. Schwartz 1928.

175 Cf. also Dossetti 1967, p. 48.

176 Cf. Winkler 2000, pp. 300–3.

σωτηρίαν κατελθόντα καί are missing. Instead of παθόντα we read ἀποθανόντα. Καὶ καθεζόμενον ἐν δεξιᾷ τοῦ πατρός and (perhaps) πάλιν was added as was the reference to the Paraclete in the third section. In the anathemas φάσκοντας and ἢ κτιστόν are missing.

At some point, C² was inserted into the monastic daily office. The earliest manuscript attesting to this practice is cod. New York, Pierpoint Morgan Library, M 574 (Faiyum, s. IX ex.).[177] Here the creed is entitled 'Faith of Nicaea', although the text is almost 'pure' C².[178]

From Egypt and Nubia we also possess non-literary evidence for the use of N and C². A monk named Theophilus painted N onto the whitewashed walls of an anchorite's grotto in Faras, Nubia (now destroyed), in the first half of the eighth century. The formula was probably taken from the *Didascalia*[179] and occupied 'a conspicuous place as the first text on the west end of the north wall'. It marked the monk's cell 'as a space dedicated to orthodoxy'.[180]

Ostraca (which were a cheap writing material) were probably used by catechumens, or in other types of religious educations settings, to memorize the creed.[181] Perhaps the earliest example, containing probably C², is found on British Museum, O. Sarga 14 (TM 108458; s. IV–VI) from Wadi Sarga in Upper Egypt.[182] It reads as follows:

> We believe in [God, the Al]mighty, He that created the things we see and those we see [not.]
> And in one Lord, Jesus, the Christ, the only Son [?] he [?] whom the Father begat before [all ages.] Light of [light] [. . .].[183]

Fragmentary versions of N are attested on O.Berol.Inv.P. 20892 (TM 140550; Thebes?, s. VI–VII)[184] and, perhaps, on O.Crum ST 15 (TM 111154; Thebes?, s. VI–VIII).[185]

---

177 Edition and German translation: Quecke 1970, pp. 436–9.

178 In the first section the text omits πάντων and in the second section adds ἀποθανόντα and ἐκ τῶν νεκρῶν as well as (after πατρός) αὐτοῦ ἐν ὑψίστοις. Μετὰ δόξης was changed to ἐν δόξῃ αὐτοῦ. In the section on baptism the text adds ἡμῶν after ἁμαρτιῶν. This partly corresponds to the aforementioned Coptic version of the *Corpus canonum*. Versions of the creed in later manuscripts are edited in Quecke 1970, pp. 468–73 and 506–8.

179 Edition: Griffith 1927, pp. 84–6. Cf. also Sanzo 2014, pp. 77 f. (no. 1); Van der Vliet 2017, pp. 160 f.

180 Van der Vliet 2017, p. 161.

181 Cf. below pp. 538 f.

182 Edition: Crum/Bell 1922, p. 45. Cf. also Quecke 1970, p. 321; URL <https://www.britishmuseum.org/collection/object/Y_EA55764_1> (18/11/2023).

183 Crum/Bell 1922, p. 46.

184 Edition: Delattre 2011, p. 114. Translation: Delattre 2011, pp. 114 f. Cf. also Mihálykó 2019, p. 143 n. 235.

185 Edition: Crum 1921, p. 5 (no. 15). Cf. also Quecke 1970, p. 321; Mihálykó 2019, p. 143 n. 235.

C² is almost fully attested on the verso of a papyrus of unknown provenance which is preserved in two fragments (P.Stras. Inv. Kopt. 221+224 (s. IX/1)).[186] The text of the recto is written in Arabic (an official protocol which served as a mark of authenticity). The papyrus was reused to write the creed (rather carelessly) on its blank verso. Its purpose is unknown. In Greek it may have looked like this:

Πιστεύομεν εἰς ἕνα θεόν, πατέρα, παντοκράτορα, ποιητὴν οὐρανοῦ καὶ γῆς ὁρατῶν τε καὶ ἀοράτων·	We believe in one God, the Father Almighty, Maker of heaven and earth, of things visible and invisible;
καὶ εἰς ἕνα κύριον Ἰησοῦν Χριστόν, τὸν υἱὸν τοῦ θεοῦ, τὸν μονογενῆ υἱὸν τοῦ πατρός, τὸν ἐκ τοῦ πατρὸς γεννηθέντα πρὸ πάντων τῶν αἰώνων, φῶς ἐκ φωτὸς καὶ θεὸν ἀληθινὸν ἐκ θεοῦ ἀληθινοῦ, γεννηθέντα καὶ οὐ ποιηθέντα, ὁμοούσιον τῷ πατρὶ αὐτοῦ, δι' οὗ τὰ πάντα ἐγένετο, τὸν δι' ἡμᾶς τοὺς ἀνθρώπους καὶ διὰ τὴν ἡμετέραν σωτηρίαν κατελθόντα εἰς τὴν γῆν καὶ σαρκωθέντα ἐν πνεύματι ἁγίῳ καὶ τῇ παρθένῳ Μαρίᾳ καὶ ἐνανθρωπήσαντα, σταυρωθέντα ὑπὲρ ἡμῶν ἐπὶ Ποντίου Πιλάτου, παθόντα, ἀποθανόντα, ταφέντα καὶ ἀναστάντα ἐκ τῶν νεκρῶν τῇ τρίτῃ ἡμέρᾳ κατὰ τὰς γραφάς, ἀνελθόντα εἰς τὸν οὐρανόν, καθεζόμενον ἐκ δεξιῶν τοῦ πατρὸς αὐτοῦ ἐν ὑψίστοις[187] < . . . >	and in one Lord Jesus Christ, the Son of God, the only Son of the Father, begotten from the Father before all ages, Light from Light and true God from true God, begotten and not made, consubstantial with the Father; through whom all things came into being; who because of us humans and because of our salvation descended to earth and became flesh in the Holy Spirit and the virgin Mary and became human; was crucified for us under Pontius Pilate, suffered, died, was buried, and on the third day rose again from the dead according to the Scriptures; ascended into the heaven; sat down at the right hand of his Father in the heavens; < . . . >
<Ὁμολογοῦμεν> ἐν <βάπτισμα> εἰς ἄφεσιν ἁμαρτιῶν ἡμῶν·	<We confess>[188] one <baptism> for the remission of our sins;
καὶ προσδοκῶμεν ἀνάστασιν νεκρῶν καὶ ζωὴν μέλλουσαν εἰς τοὺς αἰῶνας τῶν αἰώνων.[189] Ἀμήν.	and we look forward to the resurrection of the dead and the future life forever and ever. Amen.

---

186 Edition and French translation: Delattre/Vanthieghem 2013, pp. 245 f.

187 On the reconstruction cf. above pp. 441, 443 n. 178.

188 Delattre/Vanthieghem supply 'Nous croyons en'.

189 Cf., however, also the bilingual text in Quecke 1970, pp. 510 f. where the Greek reads καὶ ζωὴν τοῦ μέλλοντος αἰῶνος whereas the Coptic text reads in translation: 'and the life that remains/lasts into the eternities of eternities'.

In the first section πάντων is missing.[190] In the second section υἱὸν τοῦ πατρός and αὐτοῦ after τῷ πατρί are added. Instead of ἐκ τῶν οὐρανῶν we read εἰς τὴν γῆν, and instead of ἐκ πνεύματος ἁγίου καὶ Μαρίας τῆς παρθένου we read ἐν πνεύματι ἁγίῳ καὶ τῇ παρθένῳ Μαρίᾳ. Ἀποθανόντα and ἐκ τῶν νεκρῶν are also added as is αὐτοῦ ἐν ὑψίστοις after πατρός. In the section on baptism the text adds ἡμῶν. At the end the text reads εἰς τοὺς αἰῶνας τῶν αἰώνων instead of τοῦ μέλλοντος αἰῶνος.

A possible attestation of C² on a papyrus is found on P.Mon.Epiph. 43 (Memnoneia-Djerne (Thebes west), Sheikh Abd el-Gurna, Monastery of Epiphanios, s. VII; TM 112546).[191] However, due to the fragmentary state of the papyrus it is unclear whether the text is actually the Creed of Constantinople.[192]

Finally a wooden tablet from Egypt of unknown date (London, British Museum, EA 54037; TM 131618) also contains C².[193]

The *Synodus Alexandrinus*[194] was also translated from Greek into Coptic (first into Sahidic, then into Bohairic). Its version of the *Traditio Apostolica* contains baptismal interrogations that run like this:

> And (δέ) likewise (ὁμοίως) let the deacon (διάκονος) go with him down into the water and let (the deacon) speak to him, enjoining him to say,
>
> 'I believe (πιστεύειν) in the only true God, the Father Almighty (παντοκράτωρ), and his only-begotten (μονογενής) Son Jesus Christ (Χριστός), our Lord and Saviour (σωτήρ), with his Holy Spirit (πνεῦμα), the one who gives life to everything: three (τρίας) in one substance (ὁμοούσιος), one divinity, one Lordship, one kingdom, one faith (πίστις), one baptism (βάπτισμα); in the holy catholic (καθολική), apostolic (ἀποστολική) Church (ἐκκλησία), which lives forever. Amen (Ἀμήν).'
>
> And (δέ) the one who receives [baptism] let him say this to (κατά) all: 'I believe (πιστεύειν) thus.'
>
> The one who confers (baptism) will put his hand on the head of the one who receives [it] and immerse him three times, confessing (ὁμολογεῖν) these things each time (κατά –).
>
> Afterward, let him say,
>
> '[Do] you believe (πιστεύειν) in our Lord Jesus Christ (Χριστός), the only Son of God the Father, that he became human wondrously for us in an incomprehensible unity, in his Holy Spirit (πνεῦμα) from the holy virgin Mary, without human seed (σπέρμα); he was crucified (σταυροῦν) for us under Pontius Pilate; he died willingly for our salvation; he rose on the

---

190 Cf. Winkler 2000, pp. 301 f.
191 Edition: Crum/Evelyn-White 1926, p. 8. Translation: Crum/Evelyn-White 1926, p. 160.
192 Cf. also Quecke 1970, pp. 320 f.; Mihálykó 2019, pp. 118 and n. 108, 143 n. 235.
193 Edition and translation: Quecke 1970, pp. 514 f. The text omits πάντων in the first section and adds ἀποθανόντα and ἐκ τῶν νεκρῶν in the second section. Μετὰ δόξης is changed to ἐν δόξῃ αὐτοῦ. In the section on baptism the text adds ἡμῶν. At the end the text reads εἰς τοὺς αἰῶνας τῶν αἰώνων.
194 Cf. FaFo § 89d–f.

third day; he released those who were bound; he ascended to heaven; he sat in the heights at the right hand of his good (ἀγαθός) Father; and he comes to judge (κρίνειν) the living and the dead by (κατά) his appearance with his kingdom;

and [do] you believe (πιστεύειν) in the good (ἀγαθός) and life-giving Holy Spirit, who purifies the universe in the holy Church (ἐκκλησία)?'

[*Lacuna in the Sahidic manuscript; the Bohairic text continues:*]

Again (πάλιν) let him say, 'I believe.'[195]

Finally, Coptic psalters containing N (or C²) are described by Mearns.[196]

9.4 Ethiopia

N was known in Ethiopia from the early sixth century onwards,[197] however, not in its original form but in an extended version taken from the *Ancoratus* of Epiphanius of Salamis (FaFo § 175) which was translated from Greek and included in the *Qērellos*, a collection of patristic writings attributed to Cyril of Alexandria.[198] The *Qērellos* also contains homilies on the faith by Epiphanius,[199] Proclus of Constantinople,[200] and Severian of Gabala.[201] It was not until the fifteenth century that the entire *Ancoratus* was translated into Ethiopic from an Arabic *Vorlage*. This included N in its original version.[202] Likewise, the *Didascalia CCCXVIII patrum Nicaenorum* (FaFo § 176), which in its original Greek version also contains N, was translated into Ethiopic several times.[203] However, the version included in the *Sinodos* does not contain N.[204]

---

195 Edition: Till/Leipoldt 1954, pp. 18–20. Translation based on Bradshaw/Johnson/Phillips 2002, pp. 114–18 (= FaFo § 89d).

196 Cf. Mearns 1914, pp. 29 f., 33.

197 On the baptismal questions in Ethiopic versions of the *Traditio Apostolica* cf. FaFo § 89c and f and above p. 150.

198 Edition of the extended version and German translation: Weischer 1977, pp. 26–31; Weischer 1979, pp. 52–7. Cf. Weischer 1977, p. 24; Weischer 1978, p. 411.

199 This is a version of Epiphanius, *De fide* 14–18 which forms part of the *Anacephalaeosis* (cf. CPG 3765).

200 Cf. Proclus, *Homilia 23 De dogmate incarnationis* (CPG 5822).

201 Cf. Severian, *De fide* (CPG 4206).

202 Edition and German translation: Weischer 1979, pp. 96–101. By contrast, in the Greek text of *Ancoratus* 118,9–12 as we have it at some point C² was interpolated instead of N, yet is followed by the anathemas of N in 118,13. Cf. Weischer 1978; Weischer 1979, pp. 49, 90–3; Kösters 2003, p. 322 n. 940 and FaFo § 175.

203 For details cf. Bausi 2004, pp. 225 f.

204 Cf. Bausi 2004, p. 239 n. 1.

But a liturgical use of N (or C²) is not attested until fairly late. The creed used at baptism was not N. Instead, a variety of different formulae have been preserved. The earliest versions occur in the so-called *Aksumite Collection* (s. IV–VII). It contains a baptismal ritual where the following creed is cited (after the renunciation):

> Faith in the Trinity:
> And I believe in you, Father of Jesus Christ, and in your only Son Jesus Christ, our Lord, and in the Holy Spirit, and in the resurrection of the flesh, and in the holy, one, catholic, apostolic Church.[205]

This creed closely resembles that of the so-called Dêr Balyzeh Papyrus (FaFo § 146) which may date to the second half of the fourth century. A slightly different version is found in the Ethiopic *Synodus Alexandrinus* (FaFo § 89f2).[206]

A creed closely resembling R (because it derives from the *Traditio Apostolica*[207]) which was used at baptism is found in the Ethiopic version of the *Testamentum Domini* (FaFo § 615b).

A longer baptismal creed occurs in the Ethiopic version of the *Traditio apostolica* in the *Aksumite Collection* (FaFo § 89c) which is, in fact, a version of the Roman creed.[208]

A related formula, again from a baptismal ritual was printed in translation by Rodwell 'from the Aethiopic MS. (probably of the fourteenth century) in the library of the British and Foreign Bible Society, marked MS. F':[209]

> And again he shall be turned towards the east, and [the priest] shall bid him say, 'I believe in you, Father, Son, and Holy Spirit, whom every soul fears, implores, and supplicates. Grant me, O Lord, to do your will, without blame.'
> Then after this, he shall turn towards the priest who is to baptize him, and they shall stand in the water naked. A deacon also shall go down with the person who is to be baptized into the water and shall say to him who is still turned (eastward), with his hand upon his head, 'Do you believe in God the Father Almighty?' and he who is to be baptized shall affirm it, and the priest shall dip him once.
> And he shall say again, 'Do you believe in Jesus Christ, the Son of God, of the same godhead with the Father, who was before the world with his Father, who was born of the virgin Mary by the Holy Spirit, who was crucified by Pontius Pilate, who died, and rose again on the third day alive from the dead, and ascended into heaven, and will come to judge the living and the dead?' And he shall say, 'I believe in Him.' [*And he shall dip him a second time.*]

---

205 Edition: Bausi 2020, p. 66. German translation: Bausi 2020, p. 67.
206 Cf. Bausi 2020, app. ad loc.
207 Cf. above pp. 129 f.
208 Cf. Kinzig, 'Ursprung' and above pp. 149–54.
209 Rodwell 1867, p. 69.

And the priest shall say to him again, the third time, 'Do you believe in the Holy Spirit and in the holy Christian Church?' and he shall say, 'I believe.' And so he shall dip him the third time.[210]

Other versions are contained in a baptismal ritual in cod. Rome, Biblioteca Apostolica Vaticana, et. 4 (s. XIV?)[211] and, again, in the *Synodus Alexandrinus* (FaFo § 89f1; translation from Arabic).

A creed from a *Confessio fidei Claudii Regis Aethiopiae* (i.e. King Galawdewos, *sedit* 1540–1559) was edited in 1661 by Johann Michael Wansleben (1635–1679) with a Latin translation by Hiob Ludolf (1642–1704). It is an extended version of C².[212]

---

210 Rodwell 1867, p. 70 (translation modernized).

211 Ethiopic text and Latin translation in Grébaut 1927/1928. The creed runs like this (Grébaut 1927/1928, pp. 162 f.): 'Credimus in unum Deum, Dominum, Patrem omnipotentem, et in unicum Filium ejus Jesum Christum Dominum nostrum, et in Spiritum Sanctum vivificantem, et in resurrectionem carnis, et in unicam sanctam, quae super omnes est, Ecclesiam apostolicam, et credimus in unum baptismum, in remissionem peccatorum in saecula saeculorum. Amen.' / 'We believe in one God, the Lord, the Father Almighty, and in his one Son Jesus Christ, our Lord, and in the life-giving Holy Spirit, and in the resurrection of the flesh, and in one holy, apostolic Church which is above everybody, and we believe in one baptism, in the remission of sins forever and ever. Amen.'

212 Cf. Wansleben/Ludolf 1661 (no pagination; emphasis original):

'Nos credimus in unum Deum,

et in Filium ejus unicum Jesum Christum, qui est Verbum ejus, et Potentia ejus; Consilium ejus et Sapientia ejus [.] Qui fuit cum eo antequam crearetur mundus. In ultimis verò diebus venit ad nos, non tamen ut decederet throno divinitatis suae; et Homo factus est ex Spiritu sancto, et ex Mariâ sanctâ Virgine; Et baptizatus fuit in Jordane trigesimô annô; Et factus est Homo perfectus, et suspensus est in ligno crucis in diebus Pontii Pilati; passus, mortuus, et sepultus est, et resurrexit tertiâ die. Et deinde quadragesimâ die ascendit cum gloriâ in caelos, Et sedet ad dextram patris sui. Et iterum veniet cum gloria judicaturus vivos et mortuos, et non erit finis regno ejus.

Et credimus in Spiritum Sanctum, Dominum vivificantem, qui processit à Patre.

Et credimus in unum Baptismum ad remissionem peccatorum.

Et speramus resurrectionem mortuorum ad vitam venturam in aeternum. *Amen.*'

'We believe in one God,

and in his only Son Jesus Christ, who is his Word and his Power, his Counsel and his Wisdom; who was with him before the world was created; who in the last days came to us, yet not as if he would leave the throne of his divinity; and became human from the Holy Spirit and from Mary, the holy Virgin; and was baptized in the Jordan in his thirtieth year; and became a perfect human and was hung up on the wood of the cross in the days of Pontius Pilate; who suffered, died, was buried, and rose again on the third day; and thereafter on the fortieth day ascended into the heavens with glory and sits at the right hand of his Father; and will come again with glory to judge the living and the dead; and his kingdom will have no end.

And we believe in the Holy Spirit, the life-giving Lord who proceeded from the Father.

And we believe in one baptism for the remission of sins.

Variants of C^2 used in the anaphora are also attested. A curious version was published by Johann Georg Nissel in 1654:

> We believe in one God, the Father Almighty, Creator of heaven and earth, who sees and is not seen;
>
> and we believe in one Lord Jesus Christ, the only Son of the Father, who was together with him in substance before the world was established, Light from Light, God from true God; who was begotten and not made, equal with the Father in divinity; through whom all things came into being; without whom nothing exists which came into being [Jn 1:3], neither in heaven nor on earth; who because of us humans and because of our salvation descended from the heavens; became human of the Holy Spirit and became human from the holy virgin Mary; and was crucified for us in the days of Pontius Pilate, suffered, died, and was buried; and on the third day rose again as is written in the Holy Scripture; ascended through glory into the heaven and sits at the right hand of his Father; thence he will come in glory to judge the living and dead; of whose kingdom there will be no end;
>
> and we believe in the Holy Spirit, the life-giver, who proceeds from the Father and the Son; let us worship and glorify him with the Father and the Son, who spoke through the prophets;
>
> and we believe in one holy house of the Christians which is built upon the universal and apostolic congregation;
>
> and we believe in one baptism for the remission of sins;
>
> and we expect resurrection of the dead and the life which is to come forever and ever.[213]

And we expect the resurrection of the dead for the future life in eternity. Amen.'

Cf. also Winkler 2000, pp. 282 f.

213 Nissel 1654, pp. 30–1 (*ex Liturgiis Aethiopum depromptum*; emphasis original):

'Credimus in unum Deum, Patrem omnipotentem, creatorem Caeli et terrae, qui videt et non videtur.

Et credimus in unum Dominum Jesum Christum Filium Patris unicum, qui *una* cum ipso substantia antequam conderetur mundus, lumen de lumine, Deum de Deo vero. Qui genitus est, et non factus, qui aequalis cum Patre in divinitate, per quem omnia facta sunt, sine ipso autem non est quod factum est, neque in coelo, neque in terra. Qui propter nos homines et propter nostram salutem descendit de caelis, et homo factus est de Spiritu Sancto, et ex Maria sancta virgine factus est homo, et crucifixus est propter nos in diebus Pontii Pilati, passus mortuus, et sepultus est, et resurrexit a mortuis tertio dei, sicut scriptum est in Scriptura Sacra. Ascendit per gloriam in coelum, et sedit ad dextram Patris sui, inde veniet in gloria judicaturus vivos et mortuos, et non erit finis regni ejus.

Et credimus in Spiritum Sanctum, vivificatorem, qui procedit a Patre et Filio, adoremus et glorificemus eum cum Patre et Filio, qui locutus est per Prophetas.

Et credimus in unam sanctam domum Christianorum, quae super universa congregatione Apostolica *aedificata* est.

Et credimus in unum Baptisma, ad remissionem peccatorum, et expectamus resurrectionem mortuorum, et vitam quae ventura est in secula seculorum.'

The same version (with some minor variants such as the omission of *filioque*) is found in Rodwell 1864, pp. 15 f. ('The ordinary canon of the Abyssinian Church').

C² is also printed at the head of the *Anaphora of the Three Hundred and Eighteen Orthodox* which is still today celebrated in the Ethiopian Church on special feast days.[214] Ethiopic liturgies contain a variety of other credal texts that cannot be discussed here.[215]

9.5 N and C² in Arabic

By and large, credal traditions continued without major changes in the aforementioned churches after the Arab conquest. Nonetheless, the reception of N and C² in Arabic requires further investigation.[216] From the ninth century onwards the Bible, patristic literature, but also collections of canon law were translated into Arabic, because over time Greek, Syriac, and Coptic came to be no longer spoken in the regions under Arab rule. In the process, N and the extended version which Epiphanius produced, both of which are included in his *Ancoratus* (FaFo § 175), were translated from Greek into Arabic between the eighth and tenth centuries.[217] In the fourteenth century the *Didascalia CCCXVIII Patrum* which contained N was also translated from Coptic into Arabic by Abu'l-Barakāt (d. 1325). From the eleventh century onwards the creed and canons of Nicaea were included in canonical collections in Arabic, some of which are translations from Greek. It would exceed the scope of this book to study these developments in detail.[218] Suffice it to say that as a result N and C² were amalgamated with each other, although always seen as the creed of the 318 fathers of Nicaea.[219]

N is quoted in the *Universal History* of Agapius (Maḥbūb, d. *c.* 945), the Melkite Bishop of Manbiǧ (Mabbūg, Hierapolis) in Northern Syria,[220] as part of an account of the events at Nicaea.[221] In what follows I give a reconstructed Greek

---

214 Cf. Daoud/Hazen 1959, pp. 153 f.

215 Cf. also Winkler 2000, pp. 282–7.

216 On the baptismal questions in the Arabic *Traditio Apostolica* cf. FaFo § 89e. The credal questions in the *Canons of Hippolytus* (only preserved in Arabic) exhibit a close resemblance to R, because they probably derive from the *Traditio Apostolica*; cf. FaFo § 606 and Stewart-(Sykes) 2021, pp. 51–3. For the baptismal declaratory creed in the Arabic *Testamentum Domini* cf. above p. 148 n. 13.

217 Cf. Guidi 1932, p. 69; Graf 1944–1953, vol. I, p. 356; Weischer 1977, p. 24; Weischer 1978, p. 411.

218 Cf. in general Graf 1944–1953, vol. I, pp. 556–621. On the creed cf. Dossetti 1967, p. 54 and n. 53, 197–200.

219 Cf. the creed given in Dossetti 1967, pp. 199 f.

220 Cf. Graf 1944–1953, vol. II, pp. 39–41; Breydy 1989; Hoyland 1997(2001), pp. 440–2; Stutz 2017, pp. 77–113; Hoyland 2021.

221 Edition and French translation: Vasiliev 1911, pp. 548 f. Cf. also Dossetti 1967, pp. 210 f.

version, though omitting the Greek text of the anathemas, because it would be too hypothetical.

Πιστεύομεν εἰς ἕνα θεόν, πατέρα, παν-τοκράτορα, ποιητὴν οὐρανοῦ καὶ γῆς, [πάντων] ὁρατῶν τε καὶ ἀοράτων·	We believe in one God, the Father Almighty, Maker of heaven and earth, [of all things] visible and invisible;
καὶ εἰς ἕνα κύριον Ἰησοῦν Χριστόν, τὸν υἱὸν τοῦ θεοῦ, μονογενῆ, γεννηθέντα ἐκ τοῦ πατρὸς πρὸ πάντων τῶν αἰώνων, φῶς ἐκ φωτός, θεὸν ἀληθινὸν ἐκ θεοῦ ἀληθινοῦ, γεννηθέντα οὐ ποιηθέντα, ὁμοούσιον τῷ πατρί, δι' οὗ τὰ πάντα ἐγέ-νετο, τὸν δι' ἡμᾶς τοὺς ἀνθρώπους καὶ διὰ τὴν ἡμετέραν σωτηρίαν κατελθόντα ἐκ τοῦ οὐρανοῦ, σαρκωθέντα ἐκ πνεύμα-τος ἁγίου καὶ Μαρίας τῆς παρθένου, ἐνανθρωπήσαντα, σταυρωθέντα ὑπὲρ ἡμῶν ἐπὶ Ποντίου Πιλάτου, παθόντα, ἀποθανόντα, ταφέντα καὶ ἀναστάντα τῇ τρίτῃ ἡμέρᾳ κατὰ τὰς γράφας, ἀνελθόντα εἰς τὸν οὐρανόν, καθεζόμενον ἐν δεξιᾷ τοῦ πατρός, πάλιν ἐρχόμενον μετὰ δόξης κρῖναι ζῶντας καὶ νεκρούς, οὗ τῆς βασι-λείας οὐκ ἔσται τέλος·	and in one Lord Jesus Christ, the Son of God, only-begotten, begotten from the Father before all ages, Light from Light, true God from true God, begotten, not made, consubstantial with the Father; through whom all things were made; who because of us humans and because of our salvation descended from heaven, became flesh from the Holy Spirit and the virgin Mary, became human; was crucified for us at the time of Pontius Pilate, suffered, died, was buried; and on the third day rose again as it is written; ascended into the heaven; sits at the right hand of the Father; will come again with glory to judge the living and dead; and his kingdom will have no end;
καὶ εἰς τὸ πνεῦμα τὸ ἅγιον, τὸ κύριον, τὸ ζωοποιόν, τὸ ἐκ τοῦ πατρὸς ἐκπορευόμενον.	and in the Holy Spirit, the Lord, the life-giver, who proceeds from the Father.
<?>	As regards those who say, 'He was and he is dead'; 'he did not exist before he was begotten'; 'he was made from nothing or from another substance or essence or from another *ousía*'; 'he is alterable or mutable'; or he who describes the Son of God by one of these qualities, this [person] is anathematized, excommunicated, and cursed.

At first glance it is obvious that this is not pure N, but a mixture of N and C². The anathemas are not those of N either but have been altered (and, perhaps, partly corrupted).

When dealing with the Council of Constantinople Agapius does not quote C² but says that the council fathers completed and confirmed the creed (i.e. that of Nicaea) and added 'that the Son is from the substance of the Father and that the Holy Spirit is God and Lord, life-giver, proceeding from the substance of the Father and the Son'.[222] The final phrase, in particular, deviates from C² in that it includes the terms *ousía* and *filioque*.[223]

Further versions of N are contained in the two books of the *History of the Councils* by the Coptic bishop Severus ibn al-Muqaffaʻ (bishop of al-Ašmūnain sometime between 953 and 975, d. after 1000) who is said to be the first Coptic theologian to have written in Arabic.[224] The second book was completed in 955 and later also translated into Ethiopic.[225] In the first volume Severus quotes C² (which in his view derives from the creed of the apostles) when dealing with Nicaea.[226] However, it stops after the christological section. Severus claims that the fathers prescribed it to be recited during every mass and as part of all prayers, and to be taught to everybody. Lay people were expected to memorize it and to recite it as part of their prayers, be it day or night. Subsequently, the 150 fathers at Constantinople had added a pneumatological section (which is precisely that of C²) to the creed of the 318.[227]

In the second book of his work which was written at a later stage Severus returned to the history of the early councils. Here he gave the following version of the Nicene Creed:[228]

---

222 Vasiliev 1912, p. 401.

223 Cf. also below ch. 16.

224 Regarding what follows cf. also Dossetti 1967, pp. 200–10; Bruns 2005, pp. 55–8. Cf. already Renaudot 1847, p. 198; Caspari 1866–1875(1964), vol. I, pp. 114 f. On Severus cf. Graf 1944–1953, vol. II, pp. 300–17, esp. 306–8.

225 Cf. Graf 1944–1953, vol. II, p. 309.

226 Cf. Severus, *Historia Conciliorum* 1,3. Edition and French translation: Chébli 1909, pp. 162 f.

227 Cf. Severus, *Historia Conciliorum* 1,3. Edition and French translation: Chébli 1909, p. 164.

228 Severus, *Historia Conciliorum* 2,5. Edition and French translation: Leroy/Grébaut 1911, pp. 494 f. The book was epitomized by Abu'l-Barakāt (d. 1325) in his *Lamp of Darkness* 2 where the creed is quoted again; cf. the edition and French translation in Villecourt/Tisserant/Wiet 1928(1974), pp. 712–28. Cf. also Dossetti 1967, pp. 209 f.

Πιστεύομεν εἰς ἕνα θεόν, πατέρα, παν-τοκράτορα, πάντων ὁρατῶν τε καὶ ἀ-οράτων ποιητήν [?].

We believe in one God, the Father Almighty, by whom all things have existed, the things visible and invisible.

Πιστεύομεν εἰς ἕνα κύριον Ἰησοῦν Χριστόν, τὸν υἱὸν τοῦ θεοῦ μονογενῆ, γεννηθέντα ἐκ τοῦ πατρὸς πρὸ πάντων τῶν αἰώνων, τουτέστιν ἐκ τῆς οὐσίας τοῦ πατρός, φῶς ἐκ φωτός, θεὸν ἀλη-θινὸν ἐκ θεοῦ ἀληθινοῦ, γεννηθέντα οὐ ποιηθέντα, ὁμοούσιον τῷ πατρί, δι' οὗ τὰ πάντα ἐγένετο [?], τὸν δι' ἡμᾶς τοὺς ἀνθρώπους καὶ διὰ τὴν ἡμετέραν σωτηρ-ίαν κατελθόντα ἐκ τοῦ οὐρανοῦ, σαρκω-θέντα τῇ τοῦ ἁγίου πνεύματος δυνάμει ἐν τῇ Μαρίας τῆς παρθένου γαστρὶ [cf. Is 7:14; Lk 1:31][229] καὶ ἐνανθρωπήσαντα, σταυρωθέντα ὑπὲρ ἡμῶν ἐπὶ Ποντίου Πι-λάτου, παθόντα, ἀποθανόντα, ταφέντα, ἀναστάντα τῇ τρίτῃ ἡμέρᾳ, ἀνελθόντα εἰς τὸν οὐρανὸν καὶ καθεζόμενον ἐν δεξιᾷ τοῦ θεοῦ, πάλιν ἐρχόμενον ἐν δόξῃ αὐτοῦ κρῖναι ζῶντας καὶ νεκρούς, οὗ τῆς βασιλείας οὐκ ἔσται τέλος.

We believe in one Lord Jesus Christ, the only Son of God, born from the Father before all ages, that is, from the substance of the Father, Light from Light, true God from true God, begotten, not created, consubstantial with the Father; through whom all things have existed; who because of us humans and because of our salvation descended from heaven; became flesh by the power of the Holy Spirit in the womb of the virgin Mary and became human; was crucified for us under Pontius Pilate, suffered, died, was buried; on the third day rose again; ascended into the heaven and sits at the right hand of God; he will come again in his glory to judge the living and dead and his kingdom will have no end.

Πιστεύομεν εἰς τὸ ἅγιον πνεῦμα.

We believe in the Holy Spirit.

Τοὺς δὲ λέγοντας· Ἦν ποτε, ὅτε οὐκ ἦν, καί· Πρὶν γεννηθῆναι οὐκ ἦν, καὶ ὅτι ἐξ οὐκ ὄντων ἐγένετο ἢ ἐξ ἑτέρας ὑποστά-σεως ἢ οὐσίας εἶναι, ὡσεὶ ὁ υἱὸς τοῦ θεοῦ ἐκτισθῇ, ἢ τρεπτὸν ἢ ἀλλοιωτὸν [?], τούτους ἀναθεματίζει ἡ καθολικὴ ἐκκλησία.

The catholic Church excommunicates those who say, 'There was a time when he was not', and, 'He was not before he was begotten', that he came to be from nothing, or he is from another person or from another substance, as if the Son had been created, that he has changed and undergone alterations.

---

229 Cf. also Justinian, *Epistula contra tria capitula* 21 (Schwartz 1973, p. 96, ll. 5 f.): [. . .] ἀλλ' ὁ ἐν ὑστέροις καιροῖς ἐν τῇ μητρῴᾳ γαστρὶ τῇ τοῦ ἁγίου πνεύματος δυνάμει διαπλασθείς [. . .]. / '[. . .] but in the last days he was fashioned in his mother's womb by the power of the Holy Spirit [. . .].'

This creed is a mixture of N and C² with some peculiarities especially with regard to the incarnation.[230] In addition, Severus claims that the 318 fathers had added another set of anathemas condemning all forms of tritheism and adoptionism (Paul of Samosata being explicitly mentioned).[231]

Later in his second book, Severus mentions the Council of Constantinople and compares the creed of the 'orthodox' (i.e. 'the Copts, the Greeks, and their followers'[232]) to that of the Nestorians (2,9 – he has in mind foremost the bishop of Damascus, Elias 'Alī ibn 'Ubaid[233]). In what follows, I extract the credal fragments from his wider discussion.[234]

C² (according to Severus)	Nestorian creed (according to Severus)[235]
Πιστεύω[236] εἰς ἕνα θεόν, πατέρα, παντοκράτορα, ποιητὴν οὐρανοῦ καὶ γῆς ὁρατῶν τε[237] καὶ ἀοράτων.	Πιστεύω εἰς ἕνα θεόν, πατέρα,[238] παντοκράτορα, πάντων ὁρατῶν τε καὶ ἀοράτων ποιητήν·
Πιστεύομεν καὶ εἰς ἕνα κύριον Ἰησοῦν Χριστόν, τὸν υἱὸν τοῦ θεοῦ τὸν μονογενῆ,	καὶ εἰς ἕνα κύριον Ἰησοῦν Χριστόν, τὸν υἱὸν τοῦ θεοῦ μονογενῆ, τὸν πρωτότοκον τῆς[239] κτίσεως,
τὸν ἐκ τοῦ πατρὸς γεννηθέντα πρὸ πάντων τῶν αἰώνων,	τὸν ἐκ τοῦ πατρὸς γεννηθέντα πρὸ[240] τῶν αἰώνων καὶ οὐ ποιηθέντα

---

230 I have tried to render the phrase 'became flesh by the power of the Holy Spirit in the womb of the virgin Mary' in the Greek version of the creed above. It is also attested in the creed of the Quartodecimans discussed at the Council of Ephesus 431 (FaFo § 204b[8]).

231 Cf. Severus, *Historia Conciliorum* 2,5 (Leroy/Grébaut 1911, p. 496): 'Nous condamnons quiconque dit qu'il y a trois dieux et renie le Fils de Dieu; quiconque dit qu'il n'existait pas avant d'etre enfanté par la Vierge Marie. Nous excommunions encore ceux qui pretendent, avec Paul de Samosate, que le Fils de Dieu n'existait pas avant que la Vierge Marie l'eût mis au monde, tandis qu'elle ne lui a donne que la génération corporelle; nous condamnons ceux qui disent que le Fils de Dieu est différent du Verbe de Dieu. Pour ces raisons nous anathématisons toutes les hérésies dont nous avons parlé en même temps que la folie d'Arius rempli d'impiété.'

232 Cf. Severus, *Historia Conciliorum* 2,9 (Leroy/Grébaut 1911, p. 522).

233 On Elias cf. Graf 1944–1953, vol. II, pp. 132–5.; Bruns 2005, p. 56 n. 62.

234 Cf. Severus, *Historia Conciliorum* 2,9 (Leroy/Grébaut 1911, pp. 519–23). For the reconstructed Arabic text cf. Bruns 2005, p. 57.

235 Cf. also the Latin reconstruction in Dossetti 1967, p. 203 n. 13.

236 In what follows Severus changes from the singular to the plural.

237 Πάντων is missing.

238 Πατέρα is missing in N^Ant3, but present in N^Ant1 and N^Ant2.

239 Severus seems to omit πάσης.

240 N^Ant reads: πρὸ πάντων.

φῶς ἐκ φωτός, θεὸν ἀληθινὸν ἐκ θεοῦ
ἀληθινοῦ, γεννηθέντα οὐ ποιηθέντα,
ὁμοούσιον τῷ πατρί, δι᾽ οὗ τὰ πάντα
ἐγένετο,

καὶ τὸν δι᾽ ἡμᾶς τοὺς ἀνθρώπους καὶ διὰ
τὴν ἡμετέραν σωτηρίαν κατελθόντα ἐκ
τοῦ οὐρανοῦ καὶ σαρκωθέντα ἐκ πνεύματος ἁγίου ἐν τῇ Μαρίας τῆς παρθένου
γαστρὶ [cf. Is 7:14; Lk 1:31][243] καὶ
ἐνανθρωπήσαντα

σταυρωθέντα τε ὑπὲρ ἡμῶν ἐπὶ Ποντίου
Πιλάτου, παθόντα, [ἀποθανόντα[247]] καὶ
ταφέντα

καὶ ἀναστάντα ἐκ νεκρῶν[248] τῇ τρίτῃ
ἡμέρᾳ κατὰ τὰς γραφάς, ἀνελθόντα εἰς
τὸν οὐρανὸν καὶ καθεζόμενον ἐν δεξιᾷ
τοῦ πατρὸς αὐτοῦ[249]

καὶ[252] ἐρχόμενον ἐν δόξῃ αὐτοῦ[253] κρῖναι ζῶντας καὶ νεκρούς, οὗ τῆς βασιλείας οὐκ ἔσται τέλος·

θεὸν ἀληθινὸν ἐκ θεοῦ ἀληθινοῦ, υἱὸν
ἐκ τῆς οὐσίας τοῦ πατρὸς αὐτοῦ,[241] δι᾽
οὗ οἱ πάντες αἰῶνες καὶ τὰ πάντα
κατηρτίσθησαν,[242]

καὶ τὸν δι᾽ ἡμᾶς ἀνθρώπους καὶ διὰ τὴν
ἡμετέραν σωτηρίαν κατελθόντα ἐκ τοῦ
οὐρανοῦ, σαρκωθέντα δυνάμει[244] πνεύματος ἁγίου ἐν τῇ Μαρίας τῆς παρθένου
γαστρὶ[245] καὶ ἄνθρωπον γενόμενον,
συλληφθέντα καὶ γεννηθέντα ἐκ τῆς
παρθένου,[246]

παθόντα καὶ σταυρωθέντα ἐπὶ Ποντίου
Πιλάτου καὶ ταφέντα

καὶ ἀναστάντα ἐκ νεκρῶν[250] τῇ τρίτῃ
ἡμέρᾳ κατὰ τὰς γραφάς, ἀνελθόντα εἰς
τὸν οὐρανὸν καὶ καθεζόμενον ἐκ δεξιῶν
τοῦ πατρὸς αὐτοῦ[251]

καὶ ἐρχόμενον ἐν δόξῃ αὐτοῦ[254] κρῖναι
ζῶντας καὶ νεκρούς,[255] οὗ τῆς βασιλείας
οὐκ ἔσται τέλος·[256]

---

241 N[Ant] reads: ὁμοούσιον τῷ πατρί.

242 N[Ant] reads: δι᾽ οὗ οἱ αἰῶνες κατηρτίσθησαν καὶ τὰ πάντα ἐγένετο.

243 Cf. above p. 419 n. 37.

244 Δυνάμει is missing in N[Ant]. Cf. also below p. 457 and n. 269.

245 Ἐν τῇ Μαρίας τῆς παρθένου γαστρὶ is added here.

246 Μαρίας is missing.

247 According to Severus only 'the inhabitants of Saïd and the Syrians' add ἀποθανόντα whereas this is omitted by 'the inhabitants of Lower Egypt and the Greeks'. Cf. also Dossetti 1967, p. 204 n. 13 and p. 246 app. ad loc.

248 Ἐκ νεκρῶν is added.

249 Αὐτοῦ is added.

250 Ἐκ νεκρῶν is added.

251 Αὐτοῦ is added.

252 C² adds πάλιν.

253 C²: μετὰ δόξης.

254 N[Ant]: καὶ πάλιν ἐρχόμενον κρῖναι.

255 N[Ant3]: νεκροὺς καὶ ζῶντας.

256 The phrase οὗ τῆς βασιλείας οὐκ ἔσται τέλος is missing in N[Ant].

Πιστεύομεν²⁵⁷ εἰς ἕν πνεῦμα ἅγιον,²⁵⁸ τὸ πνεῦμα τῆς ἀληθείας, τὸ ἐκ τοῦ πατρὸς ἐκπορευόμενον, τὸ πνεῦμα τὸ ζωο-ποιόν,²⁵⁹ τὸ σὺν πατρὶ καὶ υἱῷ συμ[?]-προσκυνούμενον καὶ συν[?]δοξαζόμε-νον, τὸ λαλῆσαν διὰ τῶν προφητῶν·	< . . . ?>²⁶⁰
καὶ εἰς μίαν,²⁶¹ καθολικὴν καὶ ἀποστο-λικὴν ἐκκλησίαν.	εἰς μίαν,²⁶² καθολικὴν καὶ ἀποστολικὴν ἐκκλησίαν.
Ὁμολογοῦμεν ἓν βάπτισμα εἰς ἄφεσιν ἁμαρτιῶν	Ὁμολογοῦμεν ἓν βάπτισμα εἰς ἄφεσιν ἁμαρτιῶν
καὶ προσδοκῶμεν ἀνάστασιν νεκρῶν καὶ ζωὴν αἰώνιον²⁶³ τοῦ μέλλοντος αἰῶ-νος. Ἀμήν.²⁶⁴	καὶ τὴν τῶν σωμάτων ἡμῶν ἀνάστα-σιν²⁶⁵ καὶ ζωὴν αἰώνιον. Ἀμήν.²⁶⁶

---

257 The pneumatological article is not that of C² (which Severus later quotes correctly, except that there he reads τὸ ἐκ τῆς οὐσίας τοῦ πατρὸς ἐκπορευόμενον; cf. 2,10 (Leroy/Grébaut 1911, p. 579)).

258 C²: εἰς τὸ πνεῦμα τὸ ἅγιον.

259 Τὸ πνεῦμα τῆς ἀληθείας, τὸ ἐκ τοῦ πατρὸς ἐκπορευόμενον, τὸ πνεῦμα τὸ ζωοποιόν] C² reads τὸ κύριον καὶ ζωοποιόν, τὸ ἐκ τοῦ πατρὸς ἐκπορευόμενον.

260 Severus: 'Les Nestoriens ne disent pas cela.' Bruns thinks that this refers only to τὸ σὺν πατρὶ καὶ υἱῷ συμπροσκυνούμενον καὶ συνδοξαζόμενον, τὸ λαλῆσαν διὰ τῶν προφητῶν in its Coptic version; cf. Bruns 2005, p. 58.

261 Ἁγίαν is missing.

262 Ἁγίαν is missing.

263 Αἰώνιον is added.

264 'I believe in one God, the Father Almighty, Maker of heaven and earth, of things visible and invisible.

We also believe in one Lord Jesus Christ, the only-begotten Son of God, begotten from the Father before all ages, Light from Light, true God from true God, begotten, not made, consubstan-tial with the Father; through whom all things came into being; who because of us humans and because of our salvation descended from heaven; and became flesh by the Holy Spirit in the womb of the virgin Mary and became man; and was crucified for us under Pontius Pilate, suf-fered, and was buried; and on the third day rose again from the dead according to the Scriptures; ascended into the heaven and sits at the right hand of his Father; and will come in his glory to judge the living and dead; and his kingdom will have no end;

We believe in one Holy Spirit, the Spirit of truth, who proceeds from the Father, the life-giving Spirit whom we worship and glorify with the Father and the Son, who spoke through the prophets;

and in one catholic and apostolic Church.

We confess one baptism for the remission of sins;

and we look forward to the resurrection of the dead and the eternal life that will come. Amen.'

265 Nᴬⁿᵗ: ἀνάστασιν σαρκός.

266 'I believe in one God, the Father Almighty, Maker of all things visible and invisible;

He later says that the creed of the Maronites agrees with that of the Nestorians except that the Maronites omit τὸν πρωτότοκον τῆς κτίσεως. In the next chapter (which concludes the book) he offers a long explanation and defence of C² in which he once more quotes it phrase by phrase:[267]

Πιστεύω εἰς ἕνα θεόν, πατέρα, παντο-κράτορα,	I believe in one God, the Father Almighty,
ποιητὴν οὐρανοῦ καὶ γῆς, ὁρατῶν τε[268] καὶ ἀοράτων·	Maker of heaven and earth, of things visible and invisible;
καὶ εἰς ἕνα κύριον Ἰησοῦν Χριστόν, τὸν υἱὸν τοῦ θεοῦ τὸν μονογενῆ,	and in one Lord Jesus Christ, the only-begotten Son of God,
τὸν ἐκ τοῦ πατρὸς γεννηθέντα πρὸ πάντων τῶν αἰώνων,	begotten from the Father before all ages,
φῶς ἐκ φωτός, θεὸν ἀληθινὸν ἐκ θεοῦ ἀληθινοῦ,	Light from Light, true God from true God,
γεννηθέντα οὐ ποιηθέντα, ὁμοούσιον τῷ πατρί, δι' οὗ τὰ πάντα ἐγένετο,	begotten, not made, consubstantial with the Father; through whom all things came into being;
τὸν δι' ἡμᾶς τοὺς ἀνθρώπους καὶ διὰ τὴν ἡμετέραν σωτηρίαν κατελθόντα ἐκ τοῦ οὐρανοῦ καὶ σαρκωθέντα τῇ τοῦ ἁγίου πνεύματος δυνάμει[269] ἐν τῇ Μαρίας τῆς παρθένου γαστρὶ [cf. Is 7:14; Lk 1:31][270] καὶ ἐνανθρωπήσαντα,	who because of us humans and because of our salvation descended from the heavens; became flesh by the power of the Holy Spirit in the womb of the virgin Mary and became human;

and in one Lord Jesus Christ, the only-begotten Son of God, first-born of the creatures, begotten from the Father before the worlds and not created, true God from true God, a Son from the substance of the Father; through whose hand all worlds and all things were created; and because of us humans and because of our salvation he descended from heaven; became flesh by the power of the Holy Spirit in the womb of the virgin Mary and became man; he was conceived and born by the Virgin; suffered and was crucified under Pontius Pilate and was buried; and on the third day rose again from the dead according to the Scriptures; ascended into the heaven and sits at the right hand of his Father; and will come in his glory to judge the living and dead; and his kingdom will be have end;

and in one catholic and apostolic Church.

We confess one baptism for the remission of sins and the resurrection of our bodies and eternal life. Amen.'

267 Cf. Severus, *Historia Conciliorum* 2,10 (Leroy/Grébaut 1911, pp. 523–90).

268 Πάντων is missing. Cf. Winkler 2000, pp. 301 f.

269 C²: ἐκ πνεύματος ἁγίου. Cf. also above p. 455 and n. 244.

270 Cf. above p. 419 n. 37. C²: καὶ Μαρίας τῆς παρθένου.

σταυρωθέντα ὑπὲρ ἡμῶν ἐπὶ Ποντίου Πιλάτου, παθόντα, ταφέντα καὶ ἀναστάντα τῇ τρίτῃ ἡμέρᾳ κατὰ τὰς γραφάς,	was crucified for us under Pontius Pilate, suffered, was buried, and on the third day rose again according to the Scriptures;
ἀνελθόντα εἰς τὸν οὐρανὸν καὶ καθεζόμενον ἐν δεξιᾷ τοῦ πατρὸς αὐτοῦ,	ascended into the heaven and sits at the right hand of his Father;
πάλιν ἐρχόμενον ἐν δόξῃ αὐτοῦ²⁷¹ κρῖναι ζῶντας καὶ νεκρούς, οὗ τῆς βασιλείας οὐκ ἔσται τέλος·	will come again in his glory to judge the living and dead; of whose kingdom there will be no end;
καὶ εἰς ἓν πνεῦμα ἅγιον, τὸ κύριον, τὸ ζωοποιόν, τὸ ἐκ τῆς οὐσίας²⁷² τοῦ πατρὸς ἐκπορευόμενον, τὸ σὺν πατρὶ καὶ υἱῷ συμπροσκυνούμενον καὶ συνδοξαζόμενον,	and in one Holy Spirit, the Lord, the life-giver, who proceeds from the substance of the Father, who is jointly worshipped and glorified with the Father and the Son,
τὸ λαλῆσαν διὰ τῶν προφητῶν καὶ εἰς μίαν,²⁷³ καθολικὴν καὶ ἀποστολικὴν ἐκκλησίαν.	who spoke through the prophets, and in one catholic and apostolic Church.
Ὁμολογοῦμεν ἓν βάπτισμα εἰς ἄφεσιν ἁμαρτιῶν	We confess one baptism for the remission of sins
καὶ προσδοκῶμεν ἀνάστασιν νεκρῶν καὶ ζωὴν βεβαίαν [?]²⁷⁴ καὶ αἰώνιον. Ἀμήν.	and we look forward to the resurrection of the dead and a firm and eternal life. Amen.

It is unclear why these versions differ from each other.[275]

Yet another version of Nᴬⁿᵗ is attested by the Persian theologian Al-Shahrastānī (d. 1153) who quotes it in his *Book of Religious and Philosophical Sects* as the creed of the Melkites, attributing it to the Council of the 313 (*sic*) fathers which had assembled near Constantinople.[276]

---

271 C²: μετὰ δόξης.

272 Τῆς οὐσίας added.

273 Ἁγίαν is missing.

274 Βεβαίαν missing in C².

275 Cf. Dossetti 1967, pp. 209 f. who thinks that the variations in the sources used by Severus account for these differences.

276 For what follows cf. Bruns 2005, pp. 58–61. On Al-Shahrastānī cf. Monnot 2012. Edition: Cureton 1842/1846(2002), vol. I, pp. 174 f. German translation (which I have used for my Greek retroversion): Haarbrücker 1850, p. 264. For other editions and translations cf. Bruns 2005, p. 58 n. 70; Monnot 2012.

Πιστεύομεν εἰς ἕνα θεὸν, πατέρα, παν- | We believe in one God, the Father, Ruler
τοκράτορα [*or:* τὸν τῶν ὅλων κύριον ;²⁷⁷], | of all things and Creator of all things vis-
πάντων ὁρατῶν τε καὶ ἀοράτων ποιητήν· | ible and invisible;

καὶ εἰς ἕνα υἱὸν²⁷⁸ Ἰησοῦν Χριστόν, τὸν | and in one Son Jesus Christ ['Ishu, the
υἱὸν τοῦ θεοῦ μόνου,²⁷⁹ τὸν πρωτότοκον | Messiah'], the Son of the only God, the
πάσης κτίσεως,²⁸⁰ οὐ ποιηθέντα, θεὸν | first-born of all creation, who was not
ἀληθινὸν ἐκ θεοῦ ἀληθινοῦ, ὁμοούσιον | created, true God from true God, con-
τῷ πατρί, δι' οὗ οἱ αἰῶνες καὶ τὰ πάντα | substantial with the Father, through
κατηρτίσθησαν·²⁸¹ τὸν δι' ἡμᾶς²⁸² καὶ διὰ | whom the worlds and all things were
τὴν ἡμετέραν σωτηρίαν κατελθόντα ἐκ | fashioned; who for us and for our salva-
τοῦ οὐρανοῦ, σαρκωθέντα ἐκ πνεύματος | tion descended from heaven, became
ἁγίου,²⁸³ γεννηθέντα ἐκ Μαρίας τῆς | flesh from the Holy Spirit, was born
παρθένου,²⁸⁴ σταυρωθέντα ἐπὶ Πιλάτου | from the virgin Mary, was crucified in
καὶ ταφέντα καὶ ἀναστάντα τῇ τρίτῃ | the days of Pilate, and was buried; and
ἡμέρᾳ²⁸⁵ καὶ ἀνελθόντα εἰς τὸν οὐρανὸν | on the third day rose again, and as-
καὶ καθεζόμενον ἐκ δεξιῶν τοῦ πατρὸς | cended into heaven, and sits at the right
αὐτοῦ²⁸⁶ καὶ πάλιν ἐρχόμενον κρῖναι | hand of his Father, and will come again
νεκροὺς καὶ ζῶντας.²⁸⁷ | to judge the dead and the living;

καὶ πιστεύομεν εἰς ἓν πνεῦμα ἅγιον, τὸ | and we believe in one Holy Spirit, the
πνεῦμα τῆς ἀληθείας, τὸ ἐκ τοῦ πατρὸς | Spirit of truth, who proceeds from the
ἐκπορευόμενον²⁸⁸ καὶ εἰς²⁸⁹ ἓν βάπ- | Father; and in one baptism for the remis-
τισμα εἰς ἄφεσιν ἁμαρτιῶν καὶ εἰς μίαν, | sion of sins; and in one holy, Christian,

---

277 Missing in Nᴬⁿᵗ. Cf. Winkler 2000, pp. 295–300.
278 Nᴬⁿᵗ: κύριον.
279 Nᴬⁿᵗ: μονογενῆ.
280 Here τὸν ἐκ τοῦ πατρὸς γεννηθέντα πρὸ τῶν πάντων τῶν αἰώνων καί is missing.
281 Nᴬⁿᵗ reads: δι' οὗ οἱ αἰῶνες κατηρτίσθησαν καὶ τὰ πάντα ἐγένετο.
282 Ἀνθρώπους is missing.
283 Here the creed follows Nᴬⁿᵗ¹ and Nᴬⁿᵗ². Nᴬⁿᵗ³ adds: καὶ ἄνθρωπον γενόμενον καὶ συλληφθέντα καί.
284 Here again the creed follows Nᴬⁿᵗ¹ and Nᴬⁿᵗ². Nᴬⁿᵗ³ adds: καὶ παθόντα καί.
285 Κατὰ τὰς γράφας is missing.
286 Αὐτοῦ is added.
287 Here the creed follows Nᴬⁿᵗ³. Nᴬⁿᵗ¹ and Nᴬⁿᵗ² read ζῶντας καὶ νεκρούς.
288 Πνεῦμα ζωοποιόν is missing. Baptism and the Church are in reversed order.
289 Nᴬⁿᵗ³: ὁμολογοῦμεν.

ἁγίαν Χριστιανῶν [?] ἐκκλησίαν κα-   catholic community; in the resurrection
θολικήν· εἰς τὴν τῶν σωμάτων ἡμῶν   of our bodies; and in eternal life.
ἀνάστασιν καὶ εἰς ζωὴν αἰώνιον.[290]

Peter Bruns has analyzed this creed, demonstrating its Nestorian character (although, as can be seen from my footnotes, it is not identical with N^Ant).

The *Synodus Alexandrinus*[291] which contained a baptismal rite was translated into Arabic from Sahidic only in the thirteenth century.[292] Its baptismal questions (FaFo § 89e) are largely identical with its Coptic *Vorlage*.[293]

I was unable to obtain an exposition of the creed ascribed to Elijah of Nisibis (d. *c.* 1049) and edited by Emmanuel-Karim Delly.[294] An anonymous exposition of N of unknown provenance is found in cod. Rome, Biblioteca Apostolica Vaticana, ar. 148 (*s.* XVI *ex.*), ff. 38v–40r.[295] Some manuscripts feature confessions ascribed to Hierotheus (the legendary first bishop of Athens) and his pupil Dionysius the Areopagite.[296]

Further unedited creeds, some accompanied by explanations, are listed by Graf.[297]

9.6 Georgia

The fragments of creeds from ancient Georgia have been collected by Gabriele Winkler.[298] She cites no full versions of either N or C². All credal fragments are associated, directly or indirectly, with accounts of the conversion of the Georgian King Mirean (Mirian) by the female Apostle Nino in *c.* 330. They are contained in two

---

290 N^Ant: ἀνάστασιν σαρκὸς καὶ ζωὴν αἰώνιον.
291 Cf. above p. 445.
292 Cf. Bradshaw/Johnson/Phillips 2002, pp. 8 f.; Mühlsteiger 2006, pp. 233–5.
293 Cf. above pp. 445 f.
294 Cf. Samir 1977(1996), pp. 282 f.; Lange-Sonntag 2007, col. 372.
295 Cf. Graf 1944–1953, vol. I, p. 485.
296 Cf. Riedel 1900, pp. 66, 115, 139, 141–3, 184–7; Graf 1944–1953, vol. I, p. 371. Translation of Hierotheus: Riedel 1900, pp. 184–6.
297 Cf. Graf 1944–1953, vol. I, p. 593.
298 Cf. Winkler 2000, pp. 271–81.

legendary accounts of this conversion, the *Mok'c'evay K'art'lisay* ('The Conversion of K'art'lis')[299] and the *K'art'lis C'xovreba* ('Georgian Chronicles').[300]

The fragments in Winkler's collection display certain unusual characteristics. In Nino's prayer in *Mok'c'evay K'art'lisay* 1,7 (Šatberdi version; frg. 1)[301] we find the sequence crucifixion (no mention of Pilate) – burial – resurrection – ascension to the Father – return 'in glory'. This is precisely the same sequence as in J (yet which occurs in neither N nor C²). In the *K'art'lis C'xovreba* (frg. 1) Nino utters the following formula:

> By the power of Christ, Son of the God of eternities, who is enthroned with the Father and the Holy Spirit, and became human for our salvation, was crucified, was buried, and rose on the third day, ascended to heaven, is seated at the right hand of the Father, and will come again with glory to judge the living and the dead – he will give you your desire.[302]

This is once more paralleled by J, except that 'for our salvation' (διὰ τὴν ἡμετέραν σωτηρίαν) is added to 'became human' (ἐνανθρωπήσαντα).

Another credal text in the same work (frg. 4),[303] again attributed to St Nino, is virtually identical with frg. 1 from the *Mok'c'evay K'art'lisay* except that here the third day is added to the ascension.

All this evidence, scant as it is, fits with the overall picture of the early history of Georgian Christianity whose worship and liturgy were strongly influenced by Palestine traditions.[304]

By contrast, in *Mok'c'evay K'art'lisay* 14 (Šatberdi version; frg. 3)[305] a prayer is attributed to King Mirean which may show an influence of N^Ant3: crucifixion under Pontius Pilate – burial – resurrection on the third day (fulfillment of the prophecies ≙ κατὰ τὰς γράφας) – ascension to heaven – sitting at the right hand of the Father – return 'to judge the living and dead'.

---

299 Cf. Tarchnišvili 1955, pp. 406–10; URL <https://www.late-antique-historiography.ugent.be/database/works/421/>; <https://www.late-antique-historiography.ugent.be/database/works/737/> (20/11/2023).
300 Cf. Rapp Jr. 2017.
301 Cf. Winkler 2000, pp. 272 f.
302 Thomson 1996, p. 102; cf. Winkler 2000, pp. 275 f.
303 Cf. Thomson 1996, p. 132 f.; Winkler 2000, pp. 278 f.
304 Cf. Martin-Hisard 2001(2010), pp. 1249, 1283 f.; Rapp Jr. 2007, p. 141; Grdzelidze 2011, p. 267; Khoperia 2018.
305 Cf. Winkler 2000, pp. 274.

N and C² are attested in a letter which the Georgian Catholicos Kiwrion (*sedit* 595/599–610) sent to his Armenian counterpart Abraham in 608.[306] His version of N runs like this (in Greek retroversion):

Πιστεύομεν εἰς ἕνα θεόν, πατέρα, παντοκράτορα, ποιητὴν οὐρανοῦ καὶ γῆς ὁρατῶν τε πάντων·[307]	We believe in one God, the Father Almighty, Creator of heaven and earth and all things visible;
καὶ εἰς ἕνα κύριον Ἰησοῦν Χριστόν, τὸν υἱὸν τοῦ θεοῦ, τὸν μονογενῆ ἐκ τοῦ πατρὸς πρὸ τῶν αἰώνων,[308] ἐκ θεοῦ ἀληθινοῦ γεννηθέντα καὶ οὐ ποιηθέντα, ὁμοούσιον [*or:* ὅμοιον?] τῷ πατρί, δι' οὗ τὰ πάντα ἐγένετο,[309] τὸν διὰ τῶν ἀνθρώπων σωτηρίαν κατελθόντα ἐκ τῶν οὐρανῶν,[310] σαρκωθέντα καὶ ἐνανθρωπήσαντα, παθόντα καὶ ἀποθανόντα,[311] ἀναστάντα τῇ τρίτῃ ἡμέρᾳ καὶ ἀνελθόντα εἰς τὸν οὐρανὸν καὶ ἐρχόμενον κρῖναι ζῶντας καὶ νεκρούς·	and in one Lord Jesus Christ, the Son of God, the only-begotten from the Father before the ages, begotten from the true God and not created, similar to the Father; through whom all things came into being, who for the salvation of humankind descended from the heavens, became flesh and made himself human, suffered and died; on the third day he rose again and ascended into the heaven; and he will come to judge the living and dead;
καὶ εἰς τὸ ἅγιον πνεῦμα.	and in the Holy Spirit.
Τοὺς δὲ λέγοντας· Ἦν ποτε, ὅτε οὐκ ἦν, καί· Πρὶν γεννηθῆναι οὐκ ἦν, καὶ ὅτι ἐξ οὐκ ὄντων ἐγένετο ἢ ἐξ ἑτέρας ὑποστάσεως ἢ οὐσίας ἢ φάσκοντας εἶναι[312] τρεπτὸν[313] τὸν υἱὸν τοῦ θεοῦ, τούτους ἀναθεματίζει ἡ καθολικὴ καὶ ἀποστολικὴ ἐκκλησία.	The catholic and apostolic Church anathematizes those who say, 'There was a time when he was not', and, 'Before his birth he was not', and that he came to be from nothing or from another *hypóstasis* or essence, or who say that the Son of God is alterable.

---

[306] The letter is printed in French translation in Garsoïan 1999, pp. 570–6; creeds on pp. 572 f. Cf. also Kohlbacher, 'Rabbula', 2004, p. 250 and n. 80.

[307] N: πάντων ὁρατῶν τε καὶ ἀοράτων ποιητήν.

[308] Τὸν μονογενῆ – αἰώνων] N: γεννηθέντα ἐκ τοῦ πατρός, μονογενῆ, τουτέστιν ἐκ τῆς οὐσίας τοῦ πατρός, θεὸν ἐκ θεοῦ, φῶς ἐκ φωτός, θεὸν ἀληθινόν.

[309] N adds: τά τε ἐν τῷ οὐρανῷ καὶ τὰ ἐν τῇ γῇ.

[310] Τὸν διὰ – οὐρανῶν] N: τά τε ἐν τῷ οὐρανῷ καὶ τὰ ἐν τῇ γῇ, τὸν δι' ἡμᾶς τοὺς ἀνθρώπους καὶ διὰ τὴν ἡμετέραν σωτηρίαν κατελθόντα καί.

[311] Ἀποθανόντα is missing in N.

[312] Ἢ κτιστὸν ἢ is omitted.

[313] Ἢ ἀλλοιωτόν is omitted.

As regards C² the letter offers the following version:

Πιστεύομεν εἰς ἕνα θεόν, πατέρα, παντοκράτορα, ποιητὴν οὐρανοῦ καὶ γῆς ὁρατῶν τε πάντων καὶ ἀοράτων·	We believe in one God, the Father Almighty, Creator of heaven and earth, of all things visible and invisible;
καὶ εἰς ἕνα κύριον Ἰησοῦν Χριστόν, τὸν υἱὸν τοῦ θεοῦ, τὸν μονογενῆ ἐκ τοῦ πατρὸς πρὸ τῶν αἰώνων,[314] θεὸν ἀληθινὸν ἐκ θεοῦ ἀληθινοῦ, γεννηθέντα οὐ ποιηθέντα, ὁμοούσιον [or: ὅμοιον?] τῷ πατρί, δι᾽ οὗ τὰ πάντα ἐγένετο, τὸν δι᾽ ἡμᾶς τοὺς ἀνθρώπους[315] κατελθόντα ἐκ τῶν οὐρανῶν καὶ σαρκωθέντα ἐκ πνεύματος ἁγίου καὶ ἐνανθρωπήσαντα ἐκ Μαρίας τῆς παρθένου,[316] σταυρωθέντα ὑπὲρ ἡμῶν ἐπὶ Ποντίου Πιλάτου[317] καὶ ταφέντα, ἀναστάντα τῇ τρίτῃ ἡμέρᾳ,[318] ἀνελθόντα εἰς τὸν οὐρανὸν καὶ καθεζόμενον ἐν δεξιᾷ τοῦ πατρὸς καὶ πάλιν ἐρχόμενον[319] κρῖναι ζῶντας καὶ νεκρούς, οὗ τῆς βασιλείας οὐκ ἔσται τέλος·	and in one Lord Jesus Christ, the Son of God, the only-begotten from the Father before the ages, true God from true God, begotten, not made, similar to the Father; through whom all things came into being; who because of us humans descended from the heavens and became flesh from the Holy Spirit and made himself human from the virgin Mary; he was crucified for us by Pontius Pilate and was buried; on the third day he rose again; he ascended into the heaven and sits at the right hand of the Father; and he will come again to judge the living and dead; of whose kingdom there will be no end;
καὶ εἰς τὸ πνεῦμα τὸ ἅγιον,[320] τὸ ἐκ τοῦ πατρὸς ἐκπορευόμενον, τὸ σὺν πατρὶ καὶ υἱῷ συμ[?]προσκυνούμενον καὶ συν[?]δοξαζόμενον, τὸ λαλῆσαν διὰ τῶν προφητῶν·	and in the Holy Spirit, who proceeds from the Father and who is worshipped and glorified with the Father and the Son, who spoke through the prophets;
καὶ εἰς μίαν, καθολικὴν καὶ ἀποστολικὴν ἐκκλησίαν.	and in one catholic and apostolic Church.

---

314 C²: τὸν μονογενῆ, τὸν ἐκ τοῦ πατρὸς γεννηθέντα πρὸ πάντων τῶν αἰώνων, φῶς ἐκ φωτός.
315 Καὶ διὰ τὴν ἡμετέραν σωτηρίαν is omitted.
316 Καὶ ἐνανθρωπήσαντα ἐκ Μαρίας τῆς παρθένου] C²: καὶ Μαρίας τῆς παρθένου καὶ ἐνανθρωπήσαντα.
317 Καὶ παθόντα is omitted.
318 Κατὰ τὰς γραφάς is omitted.
319 Μετὰ δόξης is omitted.
320 Τὸ κύριον καὶ ζωοποιόν is omitted.

Ὁμολογοῦμεν ἓν βάπτισμα, μίαν μετά- νοιαν[321] εἰς ἄφεσιν ἁμαρτιῶν·	We confess one baptism, one penitence for the remission of sins;
καὶ προσδοκῶμεν ἀνάστασιν νεκρῶν καὶ ζωὴν αἰώνιον.[322] Ἀμήν.	and we look forward to the resurrection of the dead and eternal life. Amen.

Both creeds display significant variants from the received texts of the creeds. What is unique here is the addition of one penance after baptism.

The acts of the Council of Ephesus of 431 (including Cyril's *Third Letter to Nestorius*) were translated from Armenian into Georgian in modern times. They also contain versions of N and C².[323]

Finally, the Georgian treatise *De fide*, ascribed to Hippolytus,[324] is mostly a cento from the Armenian *History of the Armenians* by Pseudo-Agathangelos (*s.* V/2). However, it contains credal fragments from another source in 12,1–2 and 13,1–2. 12,1 is a quotation from the anathemas of N whereas 12,2 and 13,1–2 seems to be influenced by a variety of creeds.[325]

---

321 Μίαν μετάνοιαν is added.
322 C²: ζωὴν τοῦ μέλλοντος αἰῶνος.
323 Cf. Rucker 1930, pp. 30–32; 100 f.; Dossetti 1967, pp. 46, 48.
324 Text and translation: Garitte 1965.
325 Cf. Bonwetsch 1907, pp. 7–8, 25–27; Garitte 1965, p. 120.

10 Creeds as Means of Control in Synodal and Imperial Legislation

10.1 The bishops, the synods, and the creeds

Creeds served to summarize the Christian faith and settle dogmatic conflicts, but they were also a means of controlling the clergy and of keeping them in line. Clerics who held doctrinal views that differed from the prevailing orthodoxy were forced to justify themselves by means of creeds – a process which probably begins with Arius.[1] An important function of synodal confessions was to establish this orthodoxy in any given case, with N and C[2] being by far the most important documents in this context. Synodal creeds were no longer simple aide-mémoires which helped to recapitulate the basics of the Christian faith, rather, from the synod of Antioch of early 325 onwards they were also *legal documents which defined that faith*. Thus they became instrumental in establishing doctrinal orthodoxy in that they offered a legal tool by which deviation could be measured and sanctioned, if necessary. Such sanctions included anathemas (whose precise consequences remained vague), but also depositions and, perhaps, excommunication which, in turn, often entailed the clerics concerned being sent into exile by the emperor.[2]

I suggest that at least six factors contributed to this process of creating doctrinal dependency:

(1) As far as we can see, the first time a creed was recorded in writing was in Alexandria in, perhaps, 321 by a group of fifteen clerics, including the bishops of Pentapolis, of Libya, and of an unnamed see, a group led by the presbyter Arius.[3] The local bishop Alexander seems to have reacted with the encyclical Ἑνὸς σώματος which

---

1 The authenticity of both the letter of the six bishops to Paul of Samosata (FaFo § 126) and of the creed against Paul, allegedly issued by a 'synod of 318 fathers', which is preserved among the acts of the Council of Ephesus (431; § 127), is spurious. Cf. also above p. 118.
2 Cf. above ch. 6.4.6 and Hillner 2015, p. 198: 'In both the Donatist and the Trinitarian controversies, the emperor endorsed the decision of a church council as the orthodox position (Arles in 314 and Nicaea in 325, respectively) and imposed a public penalty, exile, on those who did not subscribe to it. From then on, emperors regularly followed up church councils' depositions of bishops, or other high-ranking clerics deemed heretical, with a public penalty of exile.' More generally on bishops being exiled Barry 2019 and the database *The Migration of Faith: Clerical Exile in Late Antiquity 325–600* URL <https://www.clericalexile.org/> (20/11/2023).
3 Cf. Arius et al., *Epistula ad Alexandrum Alexandrinum* (Opitz 1934/1935, *Urkunde 6*; FaFo § 131a). Cf. also above ch. 6.1.

https://doi.org/10.1515/9783110318531-010

was signed by the clergy of Alexandria and of Mareotis.[4] Although it was theological in nature, this letter did not yet contain a creed in any meaningful sense of the term. As we saw above, the first document to record a credal statement that had been issued as a result of the deliberations of a synod was another encyclical sent out by Alexander. According to its (secondary) introduction this encyclical was signed (Schwartz' Greek retroversion of the Syriac: ὑπογράψαντες) by around two hundred bishops.[5] Unfortunately, this credal statement has only come down to us in mutilated form. (The sections on the Father and the Son are lost, only the section on the Holy Spirit has been preserved.) The first fully preserved synodal creed is, therefore, that of the synod of Antioch of early 325 which was, perhaps, sent to Alexander of Byzantium (Constantinople) in the name of over fifty clerics.[6] The composition of synodal creeds, to formulate (some kind of) compromise and settle doctrinal controversy, was in effect the first step in the creation of doctrinal dependency, because, ultimately, bishops throughout the empire were expected to accept these formulae.

(2) As we saw above, orthodoxy was defined not only in positive terms. Creeds were sometimes accompanied by anathemas which could involve the deposition of clergy or the severance of communion between dioceses.[7] Anathemas did not necessarily take the shape of appendices to creeds as in Nicaea, but, where they did, they reinforced the normativity of the creeds themselves by threatening unspecified spiritual punishments (and, by implication, legal measures) against dissidents. However, this emerging process of doctrinal discipline concerned, above all, the clergy. We are less well informed about the consequences it had for lay people. There is scant evidence that 'regular' worshippers were actually punished for holding deviant trinitarian tenets;[8] they were only held accountable if they

---

4 Cf. Alexander of Alexandria, *Epistula encyclica* (Opitz 1934/1935, *Urkunde 4b*); the letter drumming up support for his initiative is preserved as *Urkunde 4a* (*Arii depositio*). Other synods whose tomes are lost seem not to have made pronouncements on theological matters; cf. Alexander, *Epistula encyclica* (*Urkunde 4b*) 11 and Synod of Bithynia (*c.* 320), *Epistula synodica* (*Urkunde 5*) and Palestinian Synod (*c.* 321/322), *Epistula synodica* (*Urkunde 10*).
5 Cf. Alexander, *Tomus ad omnes episcopos* (Opitz 1934/1935, *Urkunde 15*); also above p. 217.
6 Cf. Council of Antioch (325), *Epistula synodica* (Opitz 1934/1935, *Urkunde 18*; FaFo § 133); on which above ch. 6.2.
7 Cf. also above ch. 6.4.6.
8 Cf., e.g., canon 7 of Ephesus (cf. below in the text) and the *Paenitentiale Bigotianum* VII 2: 'He who dares to follow another doctrine beside the Scriptures, or a heresy (*heressim*), is a stranger from the Church; if he repents he shall publicly condemn his opinion and shall convert to the faith those whom he has deceived and shall fast according to the judgment of a priest' (tr. Bieler/ Binchy 1963, p. 237). However, this penitential, which may have been written between the late seventh and the late eighth century, was probably used in a monastic context; cf. Meens 2014, pp. 61 f. As regards the beginnings of ecclesial measures against heresy in general cf. Maison-

had illicit dealings with heretics (for example, through marriage), if they converted to heretical congregations that were prohibited, or if they held public assemblies or openly practiced rituals that were considered 'heretical'.[9] In these cases it was the *public* association with heretics that was liable to punishment, not one's private views as such. Extravagant theological claims made by lay people were usually ascribed to ignorance and dealt with by instruction through sermons, rather than by harsh disciplinary measures.[10] This may have changed with the Third Council of Toledo 589 whose first anathema condemned everybody who remained steadfast in their Arian views.[11]

(3) From the fourth century onwards each individual bishop was required to indicate his agreement to canons, synodal letters, and also creeds, either by signing them directly or by subscribing the entire synodal acts into which these documents were inserted. Alexander's aforementioned credal encyclical, reportedly subscribed by approximately two hundred bishops, may be the first such example. A similar procedure is then also attested for Nicaea and may be assumed for the creeds of later councils, even where such lists are either not preserved or their inclusion in the acts cannot be safely determined. The purpose of these signatures was not only to confirm approval and ratification; they also obliged the signatories *ad intra* to conform to the disciplinary (canons) and doctrinal (creeds) standards set out in these documents and *ad extra* to demonstrate this conformity and thus to lend additional authority to these synodal texts also among bishops who had not participated in the synods. The fact that in Nicaea a refusal to subscribe so would result in exile makes clear that the purpose of such subscription was to enforce orthodoxy among the signatories.[12] We possess long lists of the episcopal signatures from many councils in late antiquity.[13]

---

neuve 1960, pp. 29–51. On the normative character of the creeds as defined by the emperor for all subjects in the Byzantine Empire cf. the next chapter.
9 Cf., e.g., Brox 1986, cols. 277–81; Noethlichs 2006, pp. 120–5; Humfress 2007, pp. 243–68; Riedlberger 2020, pp. 319 f.
10 Cf. Humfress 2007, pp. 229–32.
11 Cf. Third Council of Toledo, *Gothorum professio fidei*, ll. 344–6 (Martínez Díez/Rodríguez 1966–2002, vol. V, pp. 78 f. = Heil/Scheerer 2022 (*Dokument* 120.2), p. 279, ll. 15–19).
12 Cf. above ch. 6.4.6.
13 Cf., e.g., the list of bishops in CPG 8502 (Ancyra 314), 8505 (Neocaesarea 314/320?), 2000 = 8506 (Alexander of Alexandria, *Epistula encyclica* (Opitz 1934/1935, *Urkunde 4b*) 21), 8516 and BHG 1431n (Nicaea 325), 8571 (Serdica 343), 8601 (Constantinople 381), 8940 (Ephesus 449), 9023 (Chalcedon), 9445 (Quinisext 691), 9481.3 (Nicaea 787, *Actio II*), 9482.4 (Nicaea 787, *Actio III*), 9483.4 (Nicaea 787, *Actio IV*). For signatures at western councils cf. Weckwerth 2010, pp. 7 and n. 28, 8, 53, 56 f., 58 f., 69, 95, 107–9, 117 f., 143 f., 188 n. 148; Weckwerth 2013, esp. pp. 38, 40, 43;

(4) In this respect, the size of a synod was important. The fact that the Council of Nicaea was called the 'council of the 318' and that of Constantinople the 'council of the 150' is not only a matter of biblical symbolism,[14] but also of authority. Most importantly, Chalcedon was said to have been attended by 630 fathers which lent its Definition of Faith (and by implication also N and C^2 contained therein) the highest degree of authority.[15] A maximum number of bishops (possibly from all over the empire) signified an ecclesial consensus (brought about by the Holy Spirit), thus calling for a high degree of compliance from lower clergy and those who had not participated in the event.

(5) After any given synod the creed it had adopted had to be disseminated. The primary means of doing so were encyclical letters sent out to the *oikuméne*, letters which communicated the *Tomus* (i.e. the body of decisions including the creeds) to a wider public.[16] However, such letters could be forgotten, suppressed, or even simply lost. (Thus, famously we no longer possess the *Tomus* of Constantinople 381.) An alternative way of ensuring the enduring normativity of council decisions was to include them in collections of canons made available to every bishop which were treated as ecclesiastical law. Although creeds, above all N, were never considered canons in themselves, they assumed a quasi-legal function by being included in collections of ecclesial law, often being placed prominently at the beginning.[17] I cannot trace this development in its entirety here as it would involve an investigation into the textual tradition of the various canonical collections.[18] It may suffice to mention a highly influential collection, usually simply called *Corpus canonum*, which originally comprised the canons of the Synods of Ancyra (314), Neocaesarea (319?), Antioch (341), Gangra (c. 340), and Laodicea (unknown date) and, according to Eduard Schwartz, was compiled at Antioch between 361 and 378.[19] N, the list of subscriptions, and the Nicene canons were placed at the beginning of this collection, in the context of the rise of the Neo-Nicenes, perhaps in 379.[20] C^2 was inserted

---

Weckwerth 2023, cols. 633 f. On signatures in classical antiquity in general cf. Steinacker 1927, pp. 112–16; Wolff 1978, vol. II, pp. 164–6.

14 Cf. above p. 244 n. 113 and p. 388.

15 On the number of participants cf. Wickham 1981, p. 669; Price/Gaddis 2005, vol. I, p. 43.

16 Cf. Weckwerth 2010, pp. 22 f., 26–33; Weckwerth 2013, p. 40; Weckwerth 2023, cols. 634 f.

17 Cf. Schwartz 1936(1960), pp. 193 f.; Wagschal 2015, pp. 90–2.

18 An early example is found in the (fictitious) *Canons of Hippolytus* (336–340 or later) which open in canon 1 with a credal formula (FaFo § 138).

19 Cf. Schwartz 1936(1960), pp. 194–200. The original collection may have been compiled by Euzoius, Homoian bishop of Antioch 360–376. Cf. the extensive study in Mardirossian 2010 and above pp. 386 f., 416.

20 Cf. Schwartz 1936(1960), pp. 200–2.

between N and the list of subscriptions sometime before Chalcedon, thus assigning both N and C² pride of place.[21] This collection was translated into Latin in the early fifth century (the so-called *Collectio Frisingensis prima*[22]) and in 501/502 into Syriac[23] and more or less simultaneously into Coptic.[24] There are other western collections such as the *Collectio Quesnelliana* (s. V ex/VI in.,[25] FaFo § 135d31) that are also opened by N (in the *Quesnelliana* N is followed by the list of subscriptions).[26] Ath, N, and T (in this order) were added to the influential *Collectio Vetus Gallica* in the eighth century in some of the manuscript tradition.[27] These are just a few examples which demonstrate the increasingly juridical status of the creeds, a process in which N was accorded the highest degree of normativity whereas C², Ath, and T trailed behind.

(6) As regards N, the so-called canon 7 of Ephesus 431 (FaFo § 568e) threatened clerics who dared to alter it with deposition and placed lay people under an anathema (whose details remained once again unspecified).

This process of 'juridification' (German: *Verrechtlichung*)[28] in the establishment of trinitarian orthodoxy primarily concerned the eastern synodal creeds, above all N and (later) C², even at western synods.[29] Thus the creeds which were prescribed by the Third Council of Toledo in 589 were N, C², and the Chalcedonian Definition of Faith, but not R/T. R and R/T were initially much less affected by this process (and were, therefore, also handled with greater freedom). Only rarely do we find an explicit episcopal or synodal obligation from the fourth to the sixth century directed towards priests to instruct converts in R/T and the Lord's Prayer.[30] In a sermon ascribed to Caesarius of Arles the clergy are told to learn Ath and to instruct their flock accordingly.[31]

In the west this gradually changed in the seventh century. The Synod of Autun of *c.* 670 appears to have been the first to have stipulated that all clergy

---

21 Cf. Schwartz 1936(1960); Kinzig, *Glaubensbekenntnis*, 2021, pp. 116 f. (addition of C² before Chalcedon).
22 Cf. Kéry 1999, pp. 2 f.
23 Cf. Kaufhold 2012, pp. 244 f.
24 Cf. above p. 441.
25 Cf. Van der Speeten 1985; Kéry 1999, pp. 27–9.
26 Cf. Turner 1899–1939, vol. I 1/2, pp. 36–91 (column IV).
27 Cf. Mordek 1975, pp. 356–358 and FaFo §§ 135d40, 373.
28 On the term cf. Hensel/Klippel 2015.
29 Cf. above ch. 8.
30 Cf. Nicetas of Remesiana (FaFo § 625a) who adds the sign of the cross.
31 Cf. (Pseudo-)Caesarius, *Sermo 2* (FaFo § 656a).

should know 'the creed which the apostles handed down under the inspiration of the Holy Spirit and the confession of the holy Patriarch Athanasius', i.e. R/T and Ath. Failure to do so resulted in 'condemnation' by the bishop. This sanction (whatever it meant in practice) indicated the increasingly juridical character that R/T, too, took on.[32] Shortly before his death Beda Venerabilis (672/673–735) wrote a letter to Bishop Egberht of York (*sedit* 732–766) admonishing him 'to implant deeply in the memory' of all his flock knowledge of the 'Apostles' Creed' (which he does not quote) and of the Lord's Prayer.[33]

During the reign of Charlemagne doctrinal control was further tightened by a concerted effort of both the emperor and his bishops.[34] Charlemagne relates the following story in his *Epistula de oratione dominica et symbolo discendis* to Bishop Gerbald of Liège (*sedit* 787–809):

> As we have recently learned, on the day of the appearance of our Lord [i.e. Epiphany] many people were found among us who wanted to receive infants from the sacred font of baptism; we ordered them to examine them individually and carefully and to find out whether they knew and kept by heart the Lord's Prayer and the creed, as we have said above. There were several who at that time knew neither by heart. We told them to keep away, as they should not take the liberty of receiving anyone from the sacred font of baptism before they are able to understand and recite the Prayer and the creed. They blushed strongly because of this, and wanted to promise that, if they were given permission, they would be able to remove this disgrace from themselves at the right time. At that moment we understood that there was no convention for them, and, as you can find in our capitulary [*this capitulary is lost*], we made the decision that each of them should abstain from this task until a proper guarantor might be at hand for these proceedings; that is: either they had to find someone else straight away who knew [the texts], or, unless infirmity did not prevent [a delay], to wait from Easter until Pentecost, until he himself had learned what we have said above.[35]

In the same letter the emperor instructed Gerbald of Liège to convene an assembly of his clergy and to carefully ascertain the size of the problem.

Synods, bishops, and Charlemagne himself prescribed knowledge of T and of the Lord's Prayer for all Christians under their rule – something that went beyond just having these texts recited at baptism by the infant's parents or sponsors.[36] However, as far as we can see, the reason for this tightening of 'credal

---

32 Synod of Autun (*c.* 670; FaFo § 581).
33 Beda, *Epistula ad Egbertum* 5–6 (FaFo § 584).
34 Cf. also above ch. 5.3.
35 Charlemagne, *Epistula de oratione dominica et symbolo discendis* (FaFo § 731).
36 Ecclesial: *Capitula Rotomagensia* (s. VIII–X; FaFo § 737: T and Lord's Prayer are obligatory for everybody); Riculf of Mainz? (787–800?; § 738: T and Lord's Prayer for everybody); *Capitula Parisiensia* (after 800?; § 744: Ath and T for all (?) clergy); Gerbald of Liège (various pronouncements of *c.* 800; FaFo § 745: T and Lord's Prayer for everybody); *Interrogationes examinationis* (after 803?;

control' in Francia was not primarily to establish a particular type of trinitarian orthodoxy or the threat of competing heterodoxies in a narrow sense (like Arianism, Homoianism, or adoptionism), but rather religious ignorance and the persistence of pagan beliefs and cultic practices. The fact that even priests had to be told to memorize these texts points to a high degree of illiteracy among the clergy. In a letter to Boniface (747/748) Pope Zachary (*sedit* 741–752) mentioned priests who did not teach their flock about the creed and baptismal rites, because they did not know them themselves.[37] The *Collectio Heroualliana*, a capitulary from *c.* 770–800, deals *inter alia* with a priest (or several priests?) who performed baptism without knowing either the creed, the Lord's Prayer, or the Psalms. He was defrocked and imprisoned in a monastery.[38] In a report on an episcopal synod held near the river Danube in the territory of the Avars in the summer of 796, written by Paulinus II of Aquileia, it is discussed whether or not baptisms are valid where neither did the baptizand know the creed nor the priest the baptismal formula. (They were not.)[39]

In other words, knowledge of T as summarizing the basics of the Christian faith remained paramount. Yet at the same time, it often seems to have been deemed insufficient correctly to understand the Trinity which is why Ath assumed

---

§ 730: *symbolum* and Lord's Prayer for priests); Haito of Basel (806–813?; § 747a: T and Lord's Prayer for everybody in both Latin and the vernacular; b: Ath for all priests); Waltcaud of Liège (811/812–814; § 749: Ath, T, and Lord's Prayer for all clergy); Théodulf of Orléans? (before 813; § 750b: Ath, T, and Lord's Prayer for all clergy); *Capitula Frisingensia Prima* (before 814; § 756: Ath, T, and Lord's Prayer for all clergy); *Capitula de presbyteris admonendis (Capitula Cordesiana)* (875–900?; § 736: T and Lord's Prayer for everybody). – Secular: Charlemagne (802–803?; § 727: Ath and T for all canons); id. (803–811; § 731: T and Lord's Prayer for everybody). – Many other documents only mention the *fides* or the *symbolum* which is to be preached – given the other evidence this must be T. Ecclesial: *Capitulare Francofurtense* (794; § 740: *symbolum* and Lord's Prayer for everybody); Synod of Friuli (796/797; § 741: ditto); *Capitula Vesulensia* (*c.* 800?; § 742a: ditto); Théodulf of Orléans (before 813; § 750: ditto); *Capitula Moguntiacensia* (before 813; § 751: *symbolum* and Lord's Prayer for priests); Synod of Mainz (813; § 754: *symbolum* and Lord's Prayer for everybody); Herard of Tours, *Capitulary* (858), cap. 16: ditto. – Secular: Charlemagne (802?; § 725: *fides catholica* and Lord's Prayer for everybody); id. (802?; § 726: *symbolum* and Lord's Prayer for all priestes); id. (802–813; § 729: *symbolum* and Lord's Prayer for everybody); id. (805–813; § 732: ditto); id. (813; § 734: ditto); id.? (813 or later; § 735: ditto). – A similar development can be observed in England: Second Synod of Clofesho (747; § 587b: *symbolum fidei* and Lord's Prayer for all clergy); English synods of the Papal Legates George of Ostia and Theophylact of Todi ('legatine councils'; 786; § 588: *symbolum* and Lord's Prayer for everybody). – Cf. also Mitalaité 2013.

37 Cf. Boniface, *Epistula 80* (MGH Epp. sel. I, pp. 175, l. 23 – 176, l. 5).

38 Cf. *Collectio Heroualliana*, cap. 13 (Ubl 2007, p. 444).

39 Cf. Paulinus, *Conuentus episcorporum ad ripas Danubii* (MGH Conc. II 1, p. 186, ll. 7–11). Cf. also Lotter 2003, pp. 185 f. On the ignorance of priests in later times cf. also below pp. 533 f.

ever greater importance as a supplement, outlining the details of this understanding. A number of decrees (both ecclesial and secular) prescribed knowledge of both these texts at least for the clergy.[40] Finally, in particular as regards T we may also link its importance to the fact of its legendary, 'apostolic' origin and the iconographic tradition which this legend gave rise to, which I will explain below.[41] To hear and see that the apostles themselves had composed the creed lent it an enormous authority which could never be called into doubt.

By way of summary, creeds not only created a *doctrinal* dependence but, combined with sanctions in the case of proven deviance, led to *institutional* dependence on the Church thus playing an integral part in establishing both doctrinal uniformity and institutional loyalty. Dissent was sanctioned by threatening both unspecified spiritual punishment (anathemas) and quite specific secular penalties, imposed by the Church (through expulsion of clergy and subsequently also excommunication) and the emperors (through exile) which would, at a later stage, come to affect not only clergy but also lay people. The quasi-legal character of the creeds made it immensely difficult to develop alternative models of describing God's salvific work in Christ.

10.2 The emperors and creeds

Charlemagne already moved into focus in my previous section. He signals a development which involved ancient and early medieval rulers, above all the emperors of the Roman Empire, in enforcing a trinitarian orthodoxy based on the creeds.[42]

As far as we can see from the evidence available, this process of imperial involvement took place in three stages. In the *first* phase, which lasted from 325 to 380 and in a sense represents its prehistory, we find imperial statements concerning the creed, which on the whole are of a rather formal nature and addressed to the higher clergy. As regards doctrinal issues, they only referred to tenets which synods had already pronounced on and even this primarily for the purpose of promoting ecclesial peace. In a *second* phase (380–482), the emperors themselves appear in a normative role: they attempt to resolve ecclesial conflict by increasingly specifying a certain doctrinal content. However, the emperor's personal beliefs are not yet in any way related to this content. The question remained unresolved whether the prescribed faith should only apply to clergy or to all inhabitants of the empire, as did the related problem of whether it was a matter of

---

40 Cf. above p. 470 n. 36 and below p. 573.
41 Cf. above ch. 5.4 and below ch. 18.
42 This section is based on Kinzig 2016(2022).

public order or private religious loyalty. This only changed with the *Henoticon* (482), which presented itself as a confession of the emperor *himself*, which was henceforth mandatory – at least in theory – for the entire population of the empire. This third phase reached its climax in the great confessions of Justinian.

The emperors used a variety of legal resources in order to express their theological views and to implement the religious policies resulting from these tenets: imperial laws and law-like documents dealing with matters of faith[43] began to flourish in late antiquity under Theodosius the Great – after a prehistory from Constantine onwards – and, in the end, took on the form of full-blown, indeed one might almost say: excessive, confessions with Justinian. In their final form, these legal texts constituted a peculiar mixture of discourse on law and faith.

In line with the three phases identified, I will describe this development in more detail in three sections and then turn to enquire into the reasons behind such imperial activity.

10.2.1 First Phase: Appeal to the creed as a means of Church discipline

Beginning with Constantine, the emperors repeatedly considered the possibility of fixing the basic doctrines of the Christian faith in writing – reluctantly at first, but later with increasing interest in terms of the doctrinal content and with a growing desire to intervene in dogmatic questions not only out of considerations of religious policy, but also for theological reasons.

As we saw above,[44] Constantine himself is said to have introduced the adjective *homooúsios* into the discussion at the Council of Nicea in 325. This intervention (if it took place at all) certainly owed less to an interest in trinitarian questions than to the ruler's endeavour to find a universally acceptable term for describing the relationship between God the Father and God the Son. Constantine wished to settle the dogmatic disputes that had arisen in the Church as quickly as possible in order to safeguard the *salus publica* ('public welfare'). In terms of legislation, the emperor intervened only insofar as in several letters he described and confirmed the consensus reached at Nicaea, imposed punishments on Arius and his supporters, called for unity on the basis of the true faith that had been

---

43 On the vague nomenclature in Roman law-making cf. Honoré 1998, pp. 37 f., 127–32, 136, 161, 209 f., 249 f., 264 f.; Harries 1999, pp. 20 f., 24 f., 36 f.; Wieacker 2006, pp. 192 f.; Riedlberger 2020, esp. pp. 26–77.
44 Cf. above ch. 6.4.5.

affirmed,[45] and, finally, instructed his provincial governors in documents that have not been preserved to ensure they implemented the councils' decisions.[46] (To what extent the letters to the governors referred to the creed is unclear.) As far as we know, however, Constantine did not prescribe N throughout the empire – unlike, for example, the uniform date of Easter, which he solemnly proclaimed in a circular letter.[47]

Constantine did not comment on the content of the disputed theological questions as such in his pronouncements after the council with the exception of a letter to the Church of Nicomedia, which is difficult to interpret and contains an idiosyncratic description of the relationship between Father and Son.[48] The formulations chosen with regard to the creed aim less at its empire-wide acceptance than at the preservation of the new-found unity.[49] Conversely, the punishments imposed on dissenters are justified not by heresy on their part, but by 'error' or 'folly'.[50] The emperor's own person moves into focus solely as a legislator, and not yet as a confessor himself.

The same applies, in broad terms, to the emperors that followed him, up to Theodosius. They sometimes interfered forcefully in the theological disputes within the Church, to the point that Constantius II (r. 337–361) attempted to impose the Homoian confession on the Church against much opposition.[51] But even in these doctrinal disputes what mattered was the *bishops'* agreement by way of signing creeds, not the consent of the population as a whole. When Constantius emphasized in his letter against the Antiochene bishop Eudoxius, a representative of the Anhomoians, in 358 that the Saviour was the Son of God and 'similar to the Father in substance (κατ' οὐσίαν ὅμοιος τῷ πατρί)',[52] he did not formulate a new

---

45 Cf., above all, Constantine, *Epistula ad ecclesiam Alexandrinam* (Opitz 1934/1935, *Urkunde 25*); id., *Epistula ad omnes ecclesias* (*Urkunde 26*); id., *Epistula ad ecclesiam Nicomediensem* (*Urkunde 27*); id., *Lex de Arii damnatione* (*Urkunde 33*).

46 Cf. Eusebius, *Vita Constantini* 4,27,2; here, Nicaea is not specifically mentioned.

47 Cf. Constantine, *Epistula ad omnes ecclesias* (Opitz 1934/1935, *Urkunde 26*).

48 Cf. Constantine, *Epistula ad ecclesiam Nicomediensem* (Opitz 1934/1935, *Urkunde 27*).

49 Cf. esp. Constantine, *Epistula ad ecclesiam Alexandrinam* (Opitz 1934/1935, *Urkunde 25*) 6–9.

50 Constantine, *Epistula ad ecclesiam Nicomediensem* (Opitz 1934/1935, *Urkunde 27*), esp. 8–17; id., *Epistula ad Theodotum Laodicenum* (*Urkunde 28*), esp. 1.

51 Cf. above ch. 6.5.9.

52 Cf. Sozomen, *Historia ecclesiastica* 4,14,4 (Brennecke et al. 2014, *Dokument* 56.4; FaFo § 531). In addition, Diefenbach 2012, p. 86 n. 78.

confession, but rather recalled the formulae of the previous Synods of Ancyra[53] and Sirmium,[54] at which precisely this tenet had been established.[55]

10.2.2 Second phase: The confession as part of imperial legislation

This situation changed with the famous edict *Cunctos populos* (28 February 380) of Theodosius I (r. 379–395).[56] Constantine may have seen himself as performing the role of a Christian bishop[57] – but at the same time he was and remained *pontifex maximus* of the old Roman cults. By contrast, Gratian and Theodosius renounced their supervision of traditional religion[58] – a development accompanied, on the one hand, by an increased persecution of pagans (since Theodosius),[59] but, on the other hand, also by increasing intervention in the internal affairs of the church. This development shows that the understanding of the status of a particular religious cult within the empire had changed completely. While Constantine pursued a religious policy of *inclusion*, propagating the cult of the sun as part of this endeavour, a cult which many of his subjects could relate to in one way or another,[60] the emperors from Gratian and Theodosius I onwards increasingly thought *exclusively* about religion in relation to the state. Apart from Christianity, all other cults were now declared illegitimate (with the exception of Judaism, which was more or less tolerated).

With Christianity's claim to exclusivity, however, the density of norms associated with it also increased. Up to Gratian and Theodosius, the emperors' ecclesial

---

53 Cf. Epiphanius, *Panarion* 73,2 (FaFo § 155).

54 Cf. Sozomen, *Historia ecclesiastica* 4,15,3 (FaFo § 156).

55 The ecclesiastical opponents of Constantius' Homoian policy also insisted, according to a saying handed down by Theodoret, that only the decision relating to punishment lay in the emperor's power, whereas distinguishing true from false faith lay in that of the bishops. Cf. Theodoret, *Historia ecclesiastica* 2,27,20; in addition, Leppin 1996, p. 196.

56 *Codex Theodosianus* 16,1,2 (= *Codex Iustinianus* 1,1,1; FaFo § 532a). The literature on this law is extensive; cf., e.g., Errington, 'Church', 1997, esp. pp. 31, 36 f., 39; Errington, 'Christian Accounts', 1997, esp. pp. 411–6; Leppin 2003, pp. 71–3; Hebblewhite 2020, pp. 52–5; Riedlberger 2020, pp. 396–402. In this context we may leave the question open as to whether *Codex Theodosianus* 16,2,25 originally also belonged to this law.

57 Cf. Girardet 2010, p. 147–63. Cf. also below above pp. 245, 473 f., and below 482.

58 According to the much-discussed evidence by Zosimus (*Historia noua* 4,36,3–5) Gratian explicitly rejected the title. Cf. Rösch 1978, pp. 85–8; Ridley 1982, pp. 195 f. n. 106; Stepper 2002. Cameron 2011, pp. 51–6 is critical.

59 Cf. Noethlichs 1971, pp. 166–82; Noethlichs 1986, esp. cols. 1160–3; Leppin 2004; Noethlichs 2006, pp. 122 f.; Leppin 2012, pp. 271 f.

60 Cf. Wallraff 2013, pp. 165–79.

policy had essentially tried to unify the different Christian groupings based on the lowest common denominator. This was true of Constantine, but also of Constantius II and his failed Homoian policy of uniting the various ecclesial parties. In Roman religion, detailed notions and definitions of the divine played only a subordinate role in comparison to a cult practice where rites had to be performed with the greatest accuracy.[61] In this context Jörg Rüpke speaks of a 'primacy of action' as regards ancient religions in general. Such focus on action did not exclude reflection upon what was done nor reflection about the gods for whom or with whom something was done, but ancient interpretation of these religious actions remained 'amorphous, indeed desultory'.[62] Within the framework of such a tradition, initially there was no need to agree on the details of the trinitarian questions as part of any religious policy.

This policy of the lowest common denominator, however, failed to address the genuine *theological* problems behind the trinitarian disputes over an adequate description of the divinity that would both do justice to the biblical evidence and be acceptable to the pagan educated elite. This prominence of theological reflection within the Christian religion therefore sooner or later posed a particular challenge to the emperors. In the course of the fourth century, they began to realize that in Christianity ortho*doxy* was at least as important for the practice of its cult as ortho*praxy*. In other words, not only did ritual or cultic negligence endanger the practice of the cult and thus the *salus publica* ('public welfare'), but at the same time theological differences undermined the unity of the Church and thus weakened the efficiency of Christianity for official cult purposes.[63]

In the absence of a formula describing the divine able to command consensus, Theodosius first tried to solve this problem in *Cunctos populos* by assigning the power to decide a definition to two bishops, namely Damasus of Rome and Peter of Alexandria. The choice of the bishop of the *urbs* was obvious. However, the choice of Peter instead of the patriarch of the New Rome was certainly primarily due to the ecclesiastical-political situation in Constantinople at the time. There were disputes between different factions (Homoiousians, Homoians, Neo-Arians, Novatians, and Apolinarians), and even the Nicene minority had fallen out with each other.[64] Interestingly, Theodosius addressed this law specifically to the inhabitants of his capital. Sozomen tells us what his reasoning behind this

---

61 On Roman views on this point cf., e.g., Girardet 2010, pp. 150 f.
62 Rüpke 2007, p. 87.
63 On the concept of *salus publica* cf. esp. Kinzig 1994, pp. 441–67, 541–66 (citing earlier scholarship); Winkler 1995. On the emperor's interest in ecclesial unity cf. Kötter 2014, p. 18.
64 Details are found, e.g., in McGuckin 2001, pp. 229–369; Daley 2006, pp. 14–19; Kinzig, *Glaubensbekenntnis*, 2021, pp. 86–8.

may have been: Theodosius wanted to avoid the appearance of coercion in matters of faith (which, as we know, had led to further ecclesial in-fighting under his predecessors), so he expressed 'the doctrine which he held concerning the Godhead' in very general terms and initially addressed his instructions only to the population of Constantinople; their pacification would set an example for the empire as a whole.[65] It is unclear whether Sozomen's claim is based on his personal assessment of the situation or on other sources that have not been preserved.[66] It should be noted, however, that a *personal* commitment of the emperor to the Neo-Nicene confession is not yet specifically expressed – in contrast to later laws.

Less than one year on, another law was passed (*Nullus haereticis* of 10 January 381[67]) in which Theodosius specified what in his view (or of that of his advisers) a homogeneous empire-wide faith should encompass; in addition, he now also sanctioned non-compliance with specific punishments. In this law Theodosius first prescribed the *Nicaena fides* as the imperial creed. He then solemnly rejected deviating confessions as heretical (Photinus, Arius, and Eunomius are named, in wrong chronological order) and paraphrased the doctrine of the Trinity, incorporating terms from N. In this regard, the law was marked by an increasingly personal note. The emperor himself approved of the faith thus defined and hoped to be inspired by the Holy Spirit himself. However, a confessional formula of the kind 'I/We believe' was not yet used. Finally, deviations from this faith were now punishable: heretics were to be banned from assembling and threatened with expulsion if public order was disturbed. However, the threat of sanctions remained limited to these measures. It was thus aimed exclusively at the practice of deviant beliefs in the *public* sphere. Moreover, this law was not addressed to all 'nations', but only to the pretorian prefect Eutropius, who was in charge of Illyricum, and its content obviously referred only to (orthodox or heterodox) church officials. *Nullus haereticis* thus even fell short of *Cunctos populos*, since there was no explicit mention of all the inhabitants of the empire subscribing to a uniform creed. Instead, the emperor reduced the scope of his religious strategy compared to that evident in *Cunctos populos*. He wanted to enforce Neo-Nicene orthodoxy throughout the empire via the *bishops*, not by means of a diktat to all citizens. Conversely, he limited himself to trying to prevent the *spread* of deviant opinions, rather than to prohibit them as such.

---

65 Sozomen, *Historia ecclesiastica* 7,4,4–6 (FaFo § 532b). Cf. esp. Errington, 'Christian Accounts', 1997, p. 415. By contrast, Riedlberger 2020, pp. 401 f. thinks that Theodosius' law was promulgated in the empire as a whole.

66 Riedlberger 2020, pp. 398 f. argues that Sozomen had no information other than the law itself.

67 *Codex Theodosianus* 16,5,6 (= *Codex Iustinianus* 1,1,2; FaFo § 533).

Theodosius continued to pursue this policy, which was restrained in comparison with *Cunctos populos*, with the law *Episcopis tradi* of 30 July 381 (addressed to Asia).[68] Following the Second Ecumenical Council (May to July 381) in Constantinople, he felt entitled to further extend the doctrinal norms of the imperial church, given the newly reached agreement between east and west. In *Episcopis tradi* the content of the faith is again described, with a de facto reference to the Neo-Nicene doctrine of the Trinity, but in terms of its form without any explicit reference to a creed or to the Council of Constantinople and without using the term *homooúsios*. This description is followed by an enumeration of orthodox bishops, beginning with the Patriarchs Nectarius of Constantinople and Timothy of Alexandria, followed by bishops of the (secular) dioceses of Oriens, Asia, and Pontus.[69] (According to Sozomen, these bishops were chosen on the basis of Theodosius' personal knowledge of the persons concerned, after he had convinced himself of their orthodoxy.[70]) The sanctions were further tightened insofar as any heretics had to give up their churches not only if the peace was disturbed, but regardless; any heresy which was manifested in public now also entailed consequences in terms of property law. Nonetheless, once again only or at least primarily ecclesial functionaries are in its purview. The population of the empire as a whole is not mentioned.

10.2.3 Third phase: The emperor's personal confession

Things changed once more with Emperor Zeno (r. 474–491) and his famous *Henoticon* of 482 (FaFo § 550). In 454, Marcian (r. 450–457) had already named and paraphrased N as his own baptismal confession in a letter to unspecified Alexandrian monks and had even declared anathema those who 'affirm or assert two sons or two persons'.[71] In addition, in Chalcedon the bishops had been instructed by the imperial commissioners to define their faith on the basis of N and of C[2] (which was ultimately seen as explaining N).[72] Basiliscus (r. 475–476) had massively interfered with the traditional rights of the synod in matters of faith in 475 with his *Encyclical* (FaFo § 548), when he condemned the Chalcedonian Definition on his own authority

---

68 *Codex Theodosianus* 16,1,3 (FaFo § 534).
69 The governors of the other dioceses named in the law will have received the same ordinances. An alternative interpretation is found in Errington, 'Christian Accounts', 1997, pp. 440–2; Errington, 'Church', 1997.
70 Cf. Sozomen, *Historia ecclesiastica* 7,9,7. Cf. esp. Errington, 'Christian Accounts', 1997, p. 421.
71 Marcian, *Epistula ad monachos Alexandrinos* (FaFo § 546).
72 Cf. above pp. 391 f.

without a prior council decision.[73] But Zeno (r. 474/475, 476–491) was the first emperor to prescribe a *new* version of the faith to his fellow Christians and also *personally* to profess its content in the text of that document.[74] Scholars have argued that this process must not be overestimated because the *Henoticon* is not a law, but a letter.[75] Nevertheless, the normative power of this letter should not be underestimated: de facto Zeno made N (or C^2 – his wording is deliberately vague[76]) compulsory for all the inhabitants of the empire, yet ostensibly not by means of a diktat, but, for irenic reasons, by referring back to the creed's general liturgical use at baptism.

A full-blown christological formula was part of the definition of faith believers were expected to follow; this was formulated as the emperor's personal confession and was intended to bring about doctrinal agreement between the adherents of the Chalcedonian Definition of Faith and its opponents. Ultimately it did not achieve its intended purpose and was finally revoked in 519 by Emperor Justin (r. 518–527). Its text was concluded by an anathema against anybody disagreeing with this faith, naming Nestorius and Eutyches in particular. For our context, the question of how far the text departs from the actual Definition of Chalcedon is not important. Here, my concern is rather that Zeno assumed the function of the councils themselves, insofar as he sought to replace the confessional formula of Chalcedon with a new one. This step, which amounted to a theological disempowerment of the councils, was new and previously unheard of; it may have contributed to the fact that the new formula was in the end not generally accepted.

However, the emperor exercised restraint in another respect: he did not attempt to replace the trinitarian confession of N (or C^2), instead explicitly stressing its normativity. He, therefore, did not comment on the content of the doctrine of the Trinity, but limited himself – as Chalcedon had done – to the disputed *christological* questions, although treating them differently from Chalcedon for the sake of concord with the Miaphysites and without even mentioning this council.[77] By doing so the prohibition earlier church assemblies, especially the Council of Ephe-

---

73 As regards details cf. Dovere 1985(2011); Kolditz 2013, pp. 27–38; Trostyanskiy 2013. *Pace* Kolditz who says that Basiliscus 'based his rejection of the Definition of Chalcedon not on his imperial position, but on the consensus of the imperial Church as expressed in earlier synodal statements' (p. 32).

74 On the background cf. also Ullmann 1977(1978), pp. 36 f.; Ullmann, 'Grundsatz', 1978, pp. 46 f.

75 Cf. Dovere 1988(2011). On the problem of the juridical genre of the *Epistulae* and their normative force cf. Wieacker 2006, pp. 73–5, 192 f.; Riedlberger 2020, pp. 48–61.

76 Cf. above p. 400 and n. 105, and below p. 501 and n. 111.

77 Aloys Grillmeier recognized 'a weighting in favour of the Alexandrian monophysite christology' (Grillmeier 1987, p. 255).

sus of 431 (canon 7), had issued against changing the creed in any form was not formally violated. Again following the example of Chalcedon Zeno did not start his christological definition with the solemn πιστεύομεν ('we believe'), but the dogmatically less solemn ὁμολογοῦμεν ('we confess').

Justinian finally abandoned any such caution.[78] Five texts preserved under his name must be regarded as both laws and confessions:
- CI 1,1,5 (c. 527; FaFo § 552);
- CI 1,1,6 (= *Chronicon paschale*, Dindorf 1832, pp. 630–3: *Epistula ad Constantinopolitanos (Contra Nestorianos)*; 15 March 533; § 553);
- CI 1,1,7 (*Epistula ad Epiphanium Archiepiscopum Constantinopolitanum*; 26 March 533; § 554);
- CI 1,1,8 (= *Collectio Auellana, Epistula 84: Epistula ad Iohannem II papam*; 6 June 533; § 555);
- the *Edictum rectae fidei* (551; § 556).[79]

The first four laws were also included in the *Codex Iustinianus*, as published in its second version (*Codex repetitae praelectionis*) in 534, in fact placed at the beginning of the first book devoted to matters of religion. This gave them an authority beyond the specific religious situation which had led to their original creation. That is, these texts were, on the one hand, geared towards a specific political situation: they constituted an attempt to establish a union between powerful patriarchs, in this case the Chalcedonians and the anti-Chalcedonian Severians, the followers of Severus of Antioch (d. 538), one of the most eloquent advocates of Miaphysitism.[80] On the other hand, their inclusion in the *Codex* established the confession to be adopted by all inhabitants of the empire once and for all, accompanied by clear penal provisions in the event of dissidence.[81]

But Justinian also went far beyond his predecessors in terms of theological substance. At first, he followed Zeno's line in expressing his personal commitment to the Christian faith as expressed in N and C[2]. But later he no longer shrank from supplementing these sacrosanct creeds and the Definition of Faith of Chalcedon,

---

78 After Zeno's policy of union had failed and the Silentiary Anastasius was about to ascend the throne, the patriarch of Constantinople Euphemius expressed doubts about the orthodoxy of the pretender. They could only be dispelled once Anastasius had produced a confession (ὁμολογία); cf. Evagrius Scholasticus, *Historia ecclesiastica* 3,32; Theodore the Reader, *Historia ecclesiastica*, Epitome 446 (Hansen 1995(2009), pp. 125, l. 25 – 126, l. 15) and frg. 39 (Hansen 1995(2009), p. 126, ll. 2–8; from Victor Tunnunensis); cf. also FaFo § 551. Unfortunately it has not survived and, in any case, may not have been a legal text *stricto sensu*.

79 Cf. Noethlichs 2001, cols. 733 f., 752–5. In addition, Uthemann 1999(2005).

80 Cf. Grillmeier/Hainthaler 1995, pp. 345 f.; Lange 2012, pp. 311–22.

81 This is emphasized by Noethlichs 2001, cols. 733 f.

the latter having in the meantime regained its reputation, with his own theological tenets. He, thereby, de facto violated the principle that had been established by Ephesus in the aforementioned canon 7 and reaffirmed by Chalcedon, according to which the creed must neither be extended nor abridged.

I have explained the normative process by which Justinian extended the content of the creed in a Neo-Chalcedonian direction in detail elsewhere.[82] Here it may suffice to point out that these laws show a close resemblance to synodal decrees, including in their condemnation of theologians who, in the emperor's view, deviated in one direction or another (Nestorius, Eutyches, Apolinarius).

With Justinian, the apex of the formation of imperial confessions had been reached. No other emperor made such extensive use of the formulae contained in the great creeds in order to proclaim his personal faith as a universal norm, although the hybrid form of creed and law remained in use among Justinian's successors. In this context, one could mention the two edicts *De fide* by Justin II (r. 565–578; FaFo § 558), the *Ecthesis* of Emperor Heraclius (r. 610–641) of autumn 638, which was authored by Sergius of Constantinople (*sedit* 610–638) and declared Monotheletism, the doctrine of the one will in the incarnate Christ, to be authoritative (§ 560), and finally the edict by which Emperor Constantine IV Pogonatos (r. 668–685), conversely confirmed Dyotheletism, the two-will doctrine of the Third Council of Constantinople (the Sixth Ecumenical Council; § 561).

10.2.4 Reasons for the emperors' new confessional focus

In conclusion, it seems difficult to explain the new imperial approach on the basis of pre-Christian practice. For a process such as the writing down of a 'faith', as we have it in N, and its standardization by the solemn signature of the bishops present at Nicaea had not existed anywhere before in pagan cults, and thus could not have fallen within the emperor's remit as *pontifex maximus*.[83] Rather, in pagan times, his role was exclusively concerned with questions of cult execution or cult personnel.[84]

What we are dealing with here, therefore, is a fundamentally new self-definition by the emperor of his religious function, the outlines of which – as we have seen – first emerged with Theodosius I[85] and which was then continuously

---

82 Cf. Kinzig 2016(2022), pp. 218–22.

83 Cf. Noethlichs 2006, pp. 116 f.

84 Details are discussed in a controversial interpretation in Draper 1988; Stepper 2003, esp. pp. 228–38; Rüpke 2005, pp. 1601–16; Cameron 2007; Hamlyn 2011; Cameron 2016.

85 Cf. Noethlichs 2006, p. 122.

developed, universalized, and personalized up to Justinian. This extended role was able to tie in with older law insofar as the famous Roman jurist Ulpian (d. 223/224) had already formulated that the area of public law (*ius publicum*) also included the *sacra* and *sacerdotes*. The fact that the law continued to be understood in this way under the Christian emperors can be seen from the fact that Ulpian's definition was included in a prominent place in Justinian's *Digest*.[86] In this respect, the emperor always remained responsible for the cult. Nevertheless, the new self-image did not result from the ancient pontifical definition, but from the episcopal redefinition of the emperor's role in religious matters, which had emerged under Constantine.[87] As is well known, Constantine had already called himself 'bishop of those outside'.[88] In concrete terms this meant that the emperors increasingly saw it as their episcopal duty to ensure the implementation of a creed for all the inhabitants of the empire, with the emperor himself at its head. This was a paradoxical process in that an act of confession was thereby imposed, although the confession as an expression of an inner faith by its very nature could not be prescribed. The emperors, especially Justinian, tried to mitigate this paradox by integrating their own act of confession into the corresponding laws, thus adding sacred overtones. In other words, in the third phase outlined above, the laws not only aimed to enforce acts of confession, but also presented themselves as such acts. The substance of the law and the act of its promulgation thus de facto coincided: the confession demanded was already carried out by the emperor in the process of publication.

One might call this process a confessionalization of the emperor's office. The creed became the basis of imperial self-understanding, culminating in the collection of relevant laws in the *Codex Iustinianus* which were headed by *Cunctos populos* in a programmatic fashion. In the process, deviant beliefs were gradually declared intolerable and illegal. Not only were they targeted by the authorities when they disturbed the peace, but even declared illegal in the private sphere, when held as personal beliefs. In this respect, they formed an indispensable part

---

86 Cf. *Digesta* 1,1,1,2: 'Publicum ius in sacris, in sacerdotibus, in magistratibus constitit.' / 'Public law covers sacred matters and [the duties of] priests and magistrates.' Cf. also Ullmann 1976(1978), p. 5; Ullmann 1977(1978), p. 28; Ullmann, 'Grundsatz', 1978, pp. 43 f., 64–6.

87 On the altered religious role of the emperor cf. Dvornik 1966, vol. II, pp. 635–8, 724–850; Leppin 2013. Bréhier 1948(1975) is in my view too critical. Kötter 2014 offers stimulating reflections as regards the relationship between 'empire' and 'Church'.

88 Eusebius, *Vita Constantini* 4,24; cf. also Kinzig 1994, p. 565 and n. 305 and p. 572 n. 8 (citing earlier literature); Noethlichs 2006, p. 117.

of what Hartmut Leppin has called the period of totalization (*Totalisierung*) connected with the Christianization of the Roman Empire.[89]

The question of whether or not the promulgated confessional texts actually reflected the emperor's personal faith is ultimately irrelevant when it comes to explaining his new political role. (In the case of the *Henoticon*, formulated as an imperial confession, we even know that it had been composed not by the emperor but the patriarch.) The aforementioned law texts are thus an indication of an increased personal involvement, but they must not be misunderstood in an individualizing or psychologizing manner. Rather, as we have seen, they arose from the emperors' episcopal self-definition, which had become ever more important since the fifth century and which was also widely accepted by the Church. Valentinian I (r. 364–375) is said to have described himself as a layman and therefore refused to interfere in ecclesiastical matters.[90] But Theodosius II (r. 402–450) was acclaimed ἀρχιερεύς ('chief priest') by participants of the Council of Constantinople in 448.[91] Marcian was also considered a priest-emperor by the council fathers assembled at Chalcedon[92] and he – like Anastasius (r. 491–518) – used the designation *pontifex inclitus* ('august Pontifex') in his titulature.[93] In 449, Leo the Great observed a *sacerdotalis animus* ('a priestly mind') in Theodosius II,[94] and thirty years later Pope Simplicius likewise praised the *animus fidelissimus sacerdotis et principis* ('the most faithful mind of a priest and emperor') of Emperor Zeno.[95] In particular, the task of protecting the faith and acting as *defensor fidei* ('Defender

---

89 Cf. Leppin 2012, pp. 265–76.

90 Cf. Sozomen, *Historia ecclesiastica* 6,7,2; Philostorgius, *Historia ecclesiastica* 8,8a. On the discussion concerning the reliability of this evidence cf., e.g., Leppin 1996, pp. 195 f., 203; Dovere 1999, pp. 195 f.; Hunt 2007, pp. 80 f. Valentinian is also said to have refused to nominate a bishop for Milan because he felt it fell outside his jurisdiction; cf. Theodoret, *Historia ecclesiastica* 4,7,1 and Leppin 1996, p. 197. Furthermore, cf. Sozomen, *Historia ecclesiastica* 6,21,7.

91 Cf. ACO II 1 1, p. 138, l. 28. On the quasi-priestly image of the emperor in Socrates cf. Leppin 1996, pp. 194 f.

92 Cf. ACO II 1 2, p. 157, l. 29.

93 Cf. ACO II 3, p. 346, l. 38 (Rösch 1978, p. 165, no. 34); *Collectio Auellana, Epistula 113* (Anastasius I, *Epistula ad senatum urbis Romae*; CSEL 35/2, p. 506, l. 20; Rösch 1978, p. 167, no. 42). In addition, Lippold 1972, p. 163; Rösch 1978, pp. 30 f., 86; Ullmann 1977(1978), pp. 25 f.; Ullmann 1981, pp. 84 f.; Nicol 1988(2003), p. 70; Stepper 2003, p. 224; Meier 2009, pp. 113–15, 317 f. and n. 428; Cameron 2007, pp. 363–6, 370–7; Cameron 2011, pp. 53–5. As regards *pontifex inclitus* as an episcopal title cf. Jerome, *Apologia aduersus libros Rufini* 2,2; Fulgentius of Ruspe, *De ueritate praedestinationis et gratiae dei* 2,31; Gregory of Tours, *Historiae* 2,34.

94 Cf. Leo, *Epistula 24* (449; ACO II 4, p. 3, l. 15). In addition, Ullmann 1977(1978), pp. 24 f.

95 Cf. Simplicius, *Epistula 15* (479) = *Collectio Auellana, Epistula 66*, 1 (CSEL 35/1, p. 147, ll. 7 f.).

of the faith') was now widely attributed to the emperor.[96] Under Justinian, this process culminated in the fact that the emperor, by now endowed with quasi-papal authority, charged the bishops with enforcing the Neo-Chalcedonian confession by way of catechesis and preaching.[97] In the west, the Visigoth king Reccared (r. 586–601) seems to have followed Justinian's example when he converted to Catholicism at the Third Council of Toledo (589): he made a trinitarian confession, based on the eastern creeds, and then prescribed this to his subjects.[98]

The empire-wide implementation of creeds, backed by the Church, remained a powerful tool for the emperors to suppress dissent not only theologically, but also politically, as political dissent was often expressed in a theological guise. But it was also a precarious one: Constantius II failed in implementing a Homoian creed; Chalcedon met with considerable opposition and, ultimately, led to serious rifts in the Church of the empire. Finally, Justinian was unable to contain the christological debates – his own 'credal laws' remained no more than an episode. N and (later) C^2 were not widely accepted because of the say-so of an emperor, but because their theology had stood the test of time.

---

96 Cf. Leo the Great, *Epistula 24* (449; ACO II 4, p. 3, l. 16); Valentinian III to Theodosius II (450): ACO II 3, p. 14, ll. 5 f.; Leo the Great, *Epistula 169* (460) = *Collectio Auellana, Epistula 51*, 1 (CSEL 35/1, p. 117, ll. 5 f.); Simplicius, *Epistula 15* (479) = *Collectio Auellana, Epistula 66*, 1 (p. 147, l. 5). In addition, Ullmann 1977(1978), pp. 30 f.
97 On sacralization under Justinian cf. also Dvornik 1966, vol. II, pp. 815–39; Uthemann 1999(2005); Meier 2004, pp. 608–41; Leppin 2011, pp. 286–8. On the later period cf. Treitinger 1938(1956), esp. pp. 124–57 and the critique of Bréhier 1948(1975).
98 Cf. Third Council of Toledo (589), *Regis professio fidei* (FaFo § 490) = Heil/Scheerer 2022 (*Dokument* 120.2), pp. 259, l. 21 – 261, l. 15 and below pp. 551–3.

11 Creeds and the Liturgy

11.1 The creed at baptism

11.1.1 The development of the *Traditio* and *Redditio symboli*

The Church had grown in number since the toleration and promotion of Christianity under Constantine.[1] A credible estimate suggests that close to one thousand catechumens were seeking baptism each year in the Antioch of the late fourth century.[2] This increased influx of converts needed to be organized, channelled, and controlled by procedures and rituals of admission. People interested in Christianity had to be taught the basics of the faith during their catechumenate. In addition, infant baptism became more widespread.[3] This created a certain pressure for efficiency and uniformity in dealing with converts. But it cannot have been the only factor that prompted the introduction of fixed declaratory creeds in catechesis more generally.

Other developments pushed in the same direction. By the end of the fourth century it had become clear that a *specific* version of Christianity as it had been laid down by the great patriarchates (which were in the process of consolidating their power and jurisdiction) was the normative version which was to be followed from now on by all (Christian) inhabitants of the empire. The edict *Cunctos populos* of Theodosius I defined this version in broad outline. Other laws to the same effect were introduced in due course.[4] In other words, creeds were no longer only a means of teaching converts the basics of their new faith (and thus a distinguishing feature of Christians over against pagans), but they were now also used to separate 'orthodox' Christians from dissenters. This problem was more acutely felt in the east than in the west, although in some western regions additions were made to R which served the same purpose.[5]

---

1 This chapter is partly based on Kinzig, 'Formation des Glaubens', 2019(2022), pp. 229–40. On the growth of Christianity cf., e.g., MacMullen 1984; Thrams 1992; Stark 1996(1997); Salamito 1996 (2010), pp. 770–9; Brown 2013, pp. 62–5. For the problems of methodology cf. especially Hopkins 1998(2018); Leppin 2012. In addition, Gemeinhardt 2022, pp. 184–6.
2 Cf. Auguste Piédnagel in SC 366, p. 43. Palladius mentions 'about three thousand' newly baptized Christians in Constantinople in 404 in his *Dialogus de uita Ioannis Chrysostomi* 9, l. 221 f. (SC 341, p. 200). The number may be exaggerated (cf. Acts 2:41).
3 For the development of the catechumenate in the fourth and fifth centuries cf. Metzger/Drews/ Brakmann 2004, esp. cols. 518–44; Pignot 2020.
4 Cf. above ch. 10.2.
5 Cf. above ch. 5.2.

https://doi.org/10.1515/9783110318531-011

Nonetheless, fixed creeds at baptism were only introduced gradually over the course of the fourth century. They were unknown in many western regions with the exception of Rome where the creed had turned into a stable formula by the early fourth century.[6] It is not surprising, therefore, that rituals involving the creed first developed in the capital. As we saw above, the baptismal questions that had been in use since the late second century were at some point transformed into a declaratory formula which may have been more or less fixed. Vigilius of Thapsus claimed in the late fifth century that, 'The creed has been handed over to the believers in Rome [. . .] even before the Council of Nicaea assembled, from the times of the apostles until now [. . .].'[7] But this was fiction. It was not until Christianity came to be tolerated and gradually promoted in the fourth century that the step of joining the new religion was turned into a lengthy and detailed initiation rite into the Christian mysteries which extended over several weeks. During this process, as part of their catechumenate the bishop 'handed' the creed 'over' to the candidates in a solemn act, explaining its clauses in the process (*Traditio symboli*). The candidates for baptism (often called *competentes*) were given the task of memorizing it. At a later stage they 'handed it back', i.e. they recited it in the presence of the bishop or were interrogated about it (*Redditio symboli* – no comparative fixed terms for both these rites exist in Greek). This 'handing back' could happen at some point before the baptism (for example on one of the preceding Sundays) or as part of the baptismal service itself.

The first example of such a *Redditio* in the west is found in Augustine's *Confessions* (*c.* 397). Here the bishop of Hippo describes how Marius Victorinus recited the creed in Rome in 356 or 357.[8] Augustine did not witness the event with his own eyes, but had been told about it by his friend Simplicianus who was himself involved in the conversion of the famous rhetorician and philosopher. We learn from Augustine's second-hand report[9] that Victorinus had memorized a fixed credal formula which he then recited from a kind of dais in front of the assembled congregation. Augustine also tells us that this was by no means always the case. Candidates who were shy could perform the *Redditio* in front of the priest alone. The way this famous Roman orator and philosopher made his public confession attracted admiration from his audience.

Rufinus provides further details about Roman practice in his *Expositio symboli* (*c.* 404). He mentions the creed's brevity and adds that it was customary in

---

6 Cf. above ch. 5.1.

7 Vigilius of Thapsus, *Contra Eutychetem* 4,1 (FaFo § 318a2).

8 The exact date is controversial. Cf., e.g., Cooper 2005, pp. 20–2. For what follows cf. also Saxer 1988, pp. 568 f.

9 Cf. Augustine, *Confessiones* 8,5 (FaFo § 636a).

the capital to recite it in public so that the congregation could assure itself of its unadulterated rendition.[10] In return, this may imply that around 400 the *Redditio symboli* was practised in the presence of just the bishop or a presbyter in Aquileia, Rufinus' home town. Moreover, at the time of Marius Victorinus, the *Redditio* was something that each believer had to perform individually. It is not entirely clear from the information Rufinus provides whether this was still the case at the turn of the century or whether baptismal candidates recited the confession jointly.

In any case, these two testimonies attest that a fixed confession formed the catechetical basis for preparing to be baptized in Rome around the middle of the fourth century. Moreover, this creed seems to have been declaratory. This is also corroborated in the 370s by Nicetas of Remesiana:

> Therefore the person who is setting himself free from these evil deeds, casting these chains behind his back, as if in the face of the enemy, proclaims now with a sincere voice, 'I believe in God, the Father Almighty', and the rest.[11]

Nicetas thus confirms the sequence renunciation – *Redditio* for his church in Dacia Mediterranea.

The evidence so far covers – strictly speaking – only the practice of the *Redditio symboli*. The first example of the corresponding rite of *Traditio* in the west is, as far as we know, attested for Milan in a letter of Ambrose written in 385. Here the bishop reports on disputes with the Homoian imperial court over who owned the churches in Milan. He mentions rather casually that he handed over the creed to the candidates for baptism (*competentes*) in the baptistery on an unspecified Sunday after the readings, the sermon, and the dismissal of the catechumens.[12] The practice may therefore have been in use for some time. Later in the same letter he writes that this was followed by the celebration of mass.[13] This means that in Milan the *Traditio symboli* was inserted between the Liturgy of the Word and the celebration of the eucharist, and that for that purpose participants moved from the church to the baptistery (and presumably back to the church for

---

10 Cf. Rufinus, *Expositio symboli* 3 (FaFo § 638). Similarly, Leo the Great, *Tractatus 24*, 6 (FaFo § 643a).

11 Nicetas, *Competentibus ad baptismum instructionis libelli* 2, frg. 4 (FaFo § 625).

12 Cf. Ambrose, *Epistula 76(20)*, 4 (FaFo § 632a). Cf. also Schmitz 1975, pp. 69–75.

13 Cf. Ambrose, *Epistula 76(20)*, 4 (not in FaFo).

mass).[14] The act of *Traditio* was accompanied by a sermon by the bishop, a version of which has survived.[15]

In the late fourth and in the fifth century, the practice of *Traditio* and *Redditio symboli* spread throughout large parts of the Latin Church. Interposed between, or linked to them, were – at least in Rome – the so-called scrutinies (*scrutinia* / 'examinations'): John the Deacon mentions in his letter to Senarius sometime in the first half of the sixth century that the creed was handed over to the *competentes* or *electi* after the *exsufflatio*[16] and renunciation. At some unspecified point in the proceedings they were also examined about their faith. This, in turn, was followed by them being anointed with the oil of sanctification.[17] The scrutinies (which in other churches were also linked to exorcism) seem to have lost their function of verifying the knowledge of the candidates at a certain point in time, perhaps as a result of the spread of infant baptism.[18] In addition, there were local variations in how these rites were performed, which do not need to be discussed here in detail. However, there was widespread agreement that the creed, once memorized, was not to be recited aloud or written down outside of worship, so that it would not be overheard by the uninitiated or indeed fall into their hands. Rather, the faithful were to keep it within their hearts. If a negligent priest had forgotten the *Redditio*, according to Pope Gregory II (*sedit* 715–731) this did not make baptism invalid.[19]

As regards North Africa, we can get a fairly good picture of the liturgical setting there from the writings of Augustine.[20] In Hippo Regius the *Traditio* took place on the fourth Sunday of Lent or on the previous Saturday. (The dates and precise sequence of events are controversial.) Here the creed was handed over to the candidates (*competentes*) after the bishop had explained the formula. The *Red-*

---

14 For the complex archaeological evidence regarding the baptisteries at Milan cf. Schmitz 1975, pp. 6–14; Ristow 1998, pp. 183 f. (no. 376) and tables 13 f.; pp. 317 f. (nos. 993–5).
15 Cf. Ambrose, *Explanatio symboli* and Schmitz 1975, pp. 70–5.
16 Here the priest blows air into the face of candidate in order to expel the devil and to make room for Christ.
17 Cf. John the Deacon, *Epistula ad Senarium* 4 (FaFo § 655).
18 Cf. briefly Kretschmar in Kretschmar/Hauschildt 1989, p. 4; Edward J. Yarnold in Gerlitz et al. 2001, p. 681. As regards the problem of the scrutinies in general (whose precise function and place in the western liturgy remains unclear), cf. Dondeyne 1932; Kretschmar 1970, pp. 253 f.; Rubellin 1982, pp. 40–2; Saxer 1988, pp. 592 f., 603 f.; Cramer 1993(1994), pp. 142 f.; Keefe 2002, vol. I, pp. 44 f; Pasquato/Brakmann 2004, cols. 475, 481; Metzger/Drews/Brakmann 2004, cols. 537, 543 f.; 565–7. In general cf. also Stenzel 1958, pp. 199–240.
19 Boniface, *Epistula 26* (FaFo § 666; written in 726).
20 The following section is based on Kinzig, 'Symbolum', *AugL*, 2021. Cf. now also Pignot 2020, pp. 210–28.

ditio took place on the following Saturday or Sunday[21] and seems to have followed upon the renunciation.[22] On this occasion the creed was either explained again,[23] or the *Redditio* was followed straight away by an explanation of the Lord's Prayer.[24] The *Redditio* may have taken the form of interrogations whose details are, unfortunately, unknown. (However, it is also possible that these interrogations were separate from the *Redditio* of the declaratory creed and held during the baptismal service itself.[25]) Those who were unable to recite the creed were given another opportunity during the Easter vigil. In this context, Augustine tries to reassure his listeners that no one ought to be afraid of mispronouncing the formula.[26] At the baptism of an infant its parents (or sponsor) had to answer the questions.[27] They were told to teach their children the creed and the Lord's Prayer once they were old enough.[28] If, at the time of baptism, the candidates were seven years of age or older they had to recite the creed and to answer the questions themselves.[29] Again, their parents were entrusted with the necessary instruction in the lead-up to the rite.[30] Dying catechumens who were no longer able to speak were baptized without interrogations.[31]

---

21 Cf. Augustine, *Sermo 213* (= *Morin Guelf. 1*), 1. 11 (FaFo § 636d).
22 Cf. Augustine, *Sermo 215*, 1; cf. also id., *Sermo 216*, 2. 6 and (for Carthage) Quodvultdeus, *Sermo 2*, 2,1 (FaFo § 317b); id., *Sermo 3*, 1,21; and Pignot 2020, pp. 252–9. There is no evidence that there were two renunciations in Hippo as scholars have claimed (cf., e.g., Kretschmar 1970, p. 242 and n. 330). This may have been different for infant baptism where the child's sponsor seems to have renounced the devil and recited the creed a second time immediately prior to baptism. Cf. Augustine, *De peccatorum meritis et remissione* 1,63: 'The person who held the infant would certainly have had to answer me for him, for he could not answer for himself. How would it be possible then for him to declare that he renounced the devil, if there was no devil in him? that he was converted to God, if he had never been averted from him? that he believed, besides other things, in the forgiveness of sins, if no sins were attributable to him?' (tr. NPNF; altered).
23 Cf. Augustine, *Sermo 215* (cf. FaFo § 636f).
24 Cf. Augustine, *Sermo 59*, 1; *58*, 1 (cf. FaFo § 636b1, c).
25 Cf. Augustine, *De fide et operibus* 1,14 (FaFo § 599c); id., *De baptismo* 1,21 (§ 599a1); 4,31 (§ 599a2); id., *Contra litteras Petiliani* 3,9 (§ 599b); id., *Epistula 98*, 7 (§ 618); id., *De natura et origine animae* 1,12 (§ 599d1); 3,12 (§ 599d2); id., *Epistula 5**, 2,2–3. Cf. also below as regards the practice in Carthage described by Ferrandus.
26 Cf. Augustine, *Sermo 58*, 1. 13 (FaFo § 636b); cf. also id., *Sermo 213* (= *Morin Guelf. 1*), 11 (§ 636d).
27 Cf. Augustine, *Epistula 98*, 7 (FaFo § 618) and above n. 22.
28 Cf. Augustine, fragment of a sermon in *Decretum Gratiani* 3,4,105 (FaFo § 636h).
29 Cf. Augustine, *De natura et origine animae* 3,12 (FaFo § 599d2).
30 Cf. Augustine, *Sermo 213* (= *Morin Guelf. 1*), 11 (FaFo § 636d).
31 Cf. Augustine, *De adulterinis coniugiis* 1,33 (FaFo § 599e).

Here it might be worth looking at a story which serves to further illustrate how a Christian mind conceived of the *Redditio* in late antiquity.[32] Ferrandus of Carthage wrote to his mentor Bishop Fulgentius of Ruspe (*sedit* 507/508–527/533) sometime before 527–533, so a century after Augustine, asking him for advice in relation to a particular case. An adolescent Ethiopian slave whom his Christian owners wished to have baptized had gone through the exorcisms, pronounced the renunciation, and then been given the creed. At a later stage (the text is unclear at what stage in the process this happened) he recited the creed in front of the entire congregation and was taught the Lord's Prayer. However, he fell seriously ill before his actual baptism and, on the point of death, became unconscious. Therefore, here was a rush to have him baptized there and then. Deacon Ferrandus himself answered the credal questions for him just as he did in the case of an infant baptism. The slave died soon after without having regained consciousness. Ferrandus was greatly worried that the slave's eternal happiness could have been impaired by the fact that he had not answered the questions himself and that God had, therefore, judged him unworthy of baptism.[33]

For the modern reader the story is interesting for a number of reasons. First of all, Ferrandus mentions that the slave was black, gives an explanation for his skin colour common at the time (it has been blackened by the sun), and then points out that he had not yet been 'whitened by the glittering grace of Christ' (*micante Christi gratia dealbatus*).[34] Ferrandus is interested in emphasizing the effect of baptism which consists in washing away human sin and thus restores humanity to its original whiteness.

Second, the slave's own wishes appear to be irrelevant. We do not know whether or not he actually wanted to be baptized. What matters here are the aspirations of his Christian owners. Ultimately, his faith is ascertained not by scrutinizing his conscience, but by his knowledge of the creed and the Lord's Prayer and his ability to answer the baptismal questions.

Third, once he is enrolled as a catechumen, although a slave, he is treated like any other catechumen and has to follow exactly the same procedures.

Fourth, at that time there was no *Sýntaxis* (formula of engagement to Christ) in Carthage. Instead the *Traditio symboli* followed upon the renunciation (which took place some days or weeks before baptism). Ferrandus was aware that this

---

32 The correspondence is also discussed in Pignot 2020, pp. 290–307.

33 Cf. Ferrandus, *Epistula 11*, 2–3 (FaFo § 659a).

34 Ferrandus, *Epistula 11*, 2 (FaFo § 659a). In other contemporary texts the devil takes on the form of an Ethiopian or a black boy – this is not the case here. Cf., e.g., Athanasius, *Vita Antonii* 6,1 and Gerard J.M. Bartelink in SC 400, p. 147 n. 2; Vivian/Athanassakis 2003, p. 71 n. 49, both citing further literature.

might be unusual, because he adds that 'custom here required this (*sicut hic consuetudo poscebat*)'.[35]

Fifth, at infant baptism in sixth-century Carthage the baptismal questions were not answered by the parents or the godparents, but by the deacon.

Finally, the precise execution of the rite required candidates who were 'capable of reason' (*rationis capax*) to answer for themselves. If they were prevented by illness from doing this their eternal happiness was endangered. Again, the candidate's actual faith which had, in principle, already been proven in the *Redditio symboli* only played a secondary role. Rather, in Ferrandus' mind the slave's salvation was safeguarded by his correct reply to the baptismal questions.

Fulgentius reacted to Ferrandus' queries with a lengthy treaty. Interestingly, his view on the importance of faith differed from that of Ferrandus. Fulgentius distinguishes between the candidate's own 'work' (*opus*) which consists in the confession and the 'reward' (*merx*) it earns, i.e. baptism. He goes on to point out that the credal questions at baptism only serve to confirm what the candidate had, in this case, already demonstrated himself by the *Redditio symboli*. Therefore, his eternal happiness was not impaired by the fact that he had fallen unconscious before being able to answer these questions. Loss of consciousness did not entail loss of faith. Fulgentius concludes, 'What the illuminated will began in him through belief and confession, fraternal charity completed on his behalf.'[36] This illustrates in a nutshell how two different understandings of faith and baptism clashed with each other: Ferrandus was a representative of a ritualistic interpretation of faith which placed the main emphasis upon the rite's correct execution. This involved reciting the creed at the *Traditio* and then answering the baptismal questions. If the second element was missing, this might be a sign that God judged the baptizand unworthy of a second birth. By contrast, Fulgentius represented the Augustinian view of the faith and the sacraments where, ultimately, what mattered was whether the candidates had demonstrated that they actually believed – this was the decisive salvific event. The baptism itself was only the outward sign and confirmation of this inner faith.

There is some further information concerning the *Traditio/Redditio*, this time from Spain. The Spanish bishop Martin of Braga reports in his treatise *De correctione rusticorum* (574) that either the baptizands or their parents and sponsors first renounced the devil and then answered the credal questions (which was R/T) with 'yes'.[37] Isidore of Seville (d. 636) tells us that the *Traditio* took place on Palm

---

35 Ferrandus, *Epistula 11*, 2 (FaFo § 659a).
36 Fulgentius, *Epistula 12*, 6,14–16 (FaFo § 659b). The quotation is found in 16: '[. . .] et quod in illo uoluntas illuminata credendo et confitendo coepit, hoc pro illo caritas fraterna perfecit.'
37 Cf. Martin, *De correctione rusticorum* 15 (FaFo § 608).

Sunday after a preceding period of instruction.[38] The *Redditio* also followed upon the renunciation without any words of *Sýntaxis*.[39] (A similar procedure seems to have been followed in (parts of) England[40] and Ireland.[41]) Ildefonsus of Toledo (*sedit* 657–667) gives us the following sequence of liturgical actions: on the 'day of anointing' (*in die unctionis*): exorcism – anointment – acceptance as candidate for baptism (*competens*) – *Traditio*; on Maundy Thursday: *Redditio*.[42]

As regards Gaul, in Arles the creed was handed over at the time of Bishop Caesarius (*sedit* 503–542) as part of a homily which commenced with the bishop reciting the creed thrice.[43] The *Traditio symboli* took place on Palm Sunday,[44] probably in the church dedicated to St Stephen, where the Cathedral of St Trophime stands today.[45] Unfortunately, Caesarius says little about the rites for Lent and the catechumenate associated with it. The *Expositio breuis antiquae liturgiae Gallicanae*, an explanation of the Gallic liturgy, provides more information. This work was ascribed to Germanus of Paris (*sedit* 555–576), but probably stems from the early seventh century.[46] Unfortunately, the text is mutilated, but it does give us a glimpse of what happened at the *Traditio*. Apparently the creed was written on a sheet and then laid out on a bed of feathers or on a white towel on top of the rails separating the nave from the choir. The vials containing chrism and oil were placed next to it, as was a Gospel codex covered with a red cloth. The author appends an allegorical (and rather forced) explanation of these rites. It should be noted, however, that here the gospel and the creed were placed side by side and thus took on the same ritual significance. The creed was no longer 'just' a text to be memorized and a summary of the faith to be learned, but a sacred text on a par with the gospel.[47]

The introduction of the *Redditio* and *Traditio* did not mean that the older baptismal questions were simply abolished.[48] Some of the earliest sacramentaries

---

38 Cf. Isidore, *De origine officiorum (De ecclesiasticis officiis)* 2,22(21),2 (FaFo § 39a); id., *Etymologiarum siue originum libri XX* 6,8,15 (§ 661b). The contents of this instruction are found in id., *De origine officiorum (De ecclesiasticis officiis)* 2,24(23),1–7 (§ 491).

39 Cf. Isidore, *De origine officiorum (De ecclesiasticis officiis)* 2,25(24),5 (FaFo § 661a).

40 Cf. Second Synod of Clofesho (747), canon 11 (FaFo 587b).

41 Cf. the *Stowe Missal* (FaFo § 680a).

42 Cf. Ildefonsus of Toledo, *De cognitione baptismi* 30–35 (FaFo § 664).

43 Cf. Caesarius of Arles, *Sermo 9*, 1 (FaFo § 271a1).

44 On the date cf. canon 13 of the Synod of Agde (506; FaFo § 573).

45 Cf. Klingshirn 1994(1995), pp. 61 f.

46 Cf. Pseudo-Germanus of Paris, *Expositio breuis antiquae liturgiae Gallicanae, Epistula secunda de communi officio* 6–9 (FaFo § 662).

47 Cf. below ch. 15.

48 For what follows cf. the source texts in FaFo, chs. 10.1.1, 10.1.3 and 11.3.1.1., 11.3.1.3.

contain both a rite of *Redditio*, usually on the morning of Holy Saturday, and credal interrogations used as baptismal formulae during the baptism in the evening
of that same day.[49] The extent of these questions may have varied: some could be
very brief as are those in the OGS and cognate sacramentaries;[50] others could be
T in interrogatory form.[51] Once more, it must be emphasized that the short questions in the OGS are, in fact, the earlier version, perhaps dating back to the
late second century.[52] However, there was great variation.

Finally, the *Professio Iudeorum* is a special case of *Redditio* which was prescribed for anyone converting from Judaism to Christianity in the Visigothic Kingdom under King Erwig (r. 680–687). Here C^2 was included in a formulary to be
signed by the convert.[53] The ritual took the form of a solemn renunciation of Judaism, followed by the creed and a promise never to return 'to the vomit of Jewish superstition' (*ad uomitum superstitionis Iudaicae*; cf. Prov 26:11; 2Pet 2:22).[54]
This law is followed by another one containing a lengthy oath which included the
following clause:

> [. . .] I shall keep with all purity of faith anything that has been verified as having been
> included in this declaration (*in eadem professione*) that I have drawn up concerning the ob-
> servation of the holy faith, so that I shall be obliged to live henceforth according to the apos-
> tolic tradition or the rule of the sacred creed (*iuxta apostolicam traditionem uel sacri
> symboli regulam*).[55]

∗

Likewise, the baptismal interrogations (to which the baptizand answered with a
simple 'yes') also seem to have persisted for a long time in the east.[56] Cyril of Jerusalem offers the first evidence of the *Traditio*'s existence. In his *Catecheses ad
illuminandos* (351) he admonishes the baptizands (whom he calls φωτιζόμενοι /

---

49 Cf. FaFo, chs. 10.1.3., 11.3.1.3.
50 Cf. FaFo, chs. 10.1.1.2.1; 11.3.1.1.2.1.
51 Cf. FaFo, chs., 10.1.1.2.2; 11.3.1.1.2.2.
52 Cf. *Sacramentarium Gelasianum Vetus* nos. 449 (FaFo § 675c), 608 (§ 675f). Cf. above ch. 4.5.
53 Cf. FaFo 184f24.8.
54 *Lex Visigothorum* 12,3,14. Cf. also *Lex Visigothorum* 12,3,13 where the *symbolum* is also
mentioned.
55 *Lex Visigothorum* 12,3,15 (tr. Linder 1997, p. 317; altered). Cf. also Kinzig, 'Die Verpflichtungser-
klärungen', 2019(2022) and below p. 587.
56 Cf., e.g., canon 19 of the *Canons of Hippolytus* (Northern Egypt?, 336–340 or later; FaFo § 606;
sequence: *Apótaxis* – anointing with the oil of exorcism – *Sýntaxis* – credal questions and immersions); *Testamentum Domini* 2,18 (Syria, *s.* IV *ex.*/V *in.*; cf. § 615; sequence: *Apótaxis* – anointing
with the oil of exorcism and final exorcism – *Sýntaxis* – credal questions and immersions).

'the illuminated', distinguishing them from catechumens[57]) to memorize the creed and to rehearse it quietly lest it be overheard by the catechumens. Here the *Traditio* opened a series of homilies on the content of the creed delivered during Lent.[58] Given what I said above about the spread of the declaratory creed this may well be an isolated case – we should by no means assume that this custom was already well established throughout the eastern part of the empire. We do not know either whether, in Jerusalem, the creed was, at any point, recited by the baptizands themselves.

The picture becomes clearer when we look at Egeria's *Peregrinatio* (written in 381–384).[59] She reports that the bishop of Jerusalem teaches the baptizands and their parents three hours a day for forty days (five weeks[60]) about Scripture, a process which Egeria explicitly calls *catechesis*. This is followed by the *Traditio symboli* and another series of sermons on the faith which continues for another two weeks.[61] The *Redditio symboli* itself is a fairly informal affair: during Holy Week

> the bishop comes in the morning into the Great Church at the martyrium, and the chair is set out for him in the apse behind the altar, to which they come one by one, men with their fathers and women with their mothers, and recite the creed to the bishop.[62]

Unfortunately, Egeria fails to tell us which creed was used.

According to the *Mystagogical Catecheses* (which were probably also delivered by Cyril) the renunciation (*Apótaxis*) was not followed (as everywhere else in the east) by the formula of engagement (*Sýntaxis*), but by the *Redditio*.[63] The same as in some western churches this led to an odd doubling of the confession of faith, because the baptizands were then led into the baptistery[64] and asked whether they believed in the name of the Father, Son, and Holy Spirit, once more

---

57 For the catechumenate in Jerusalem cf. Metzger/Drews/Brakmann 2004, cols. 520–523.

58 Cf. Cyril, *Catechesis ad illuminandos 5*, 12 (FaFo § 624a). Cf. also *18*, 21 (§ 624b) and 32.

59 Cf. Egeria, *Peregrinatio* 46,1–5 (FaFo § 630).

60 The numbers do not add quite up.

61 However, Cyril delivered only eighteen lectures; the *Traditio* took place at the end of the fifth. According to Maxwell Johnson, Cyril may have known only a Lent that extended over three weeks. Cf. Johnson 1988 and Spinks 2006(2016), p. 39.

62 Egeria, *Peregrinatio* 46,5 (FaFo § 630).

63 Cf. (Pseudo-)Cyril of Jerusalem, *Mystagogia 1*, 9 (FaFo § 631a): Πιστεύω εἰς τὸν πατέρα καὶ εἰς τὸν υἱὸν καὶ εἰς τὸ ἅγιον πνεῦμα καὶ εἰς ἓν βάπτισμα μετανοίας. / 'I believe in the Father, in the Son, and in the Holy Spirit, and in one baptism of repentance.' – probably abbreviating the full version of the creed (Day 2007, p. 59 *pace*, e.g., Kelly 1972, p. 33).

64 This must have been the baptistery of the Church of the Holy Sepulchre; cf. Wharton 1992 and Ristow 1998, p. 168 (no. 309) who discuss the scant archaeological and literary evidence.

making the 'saving confession' (τὴν σωτήριον ὁμολογίαν) before being immersed in the water.[65]

The evidence for Jerusalem notwithstanding, we have relatively little proof of the *Traditio* and/or *Redditio symboli* as established rites from the eastern part of the empire. Instead, the more ancient practice continued which was to instruct converts in the basics of the Christian faith employing some kind of *regula fidei*. As shown above, the congregation of Caesarea is a useful case in point: Eusebius felt compelled to lay down this (as yet unfixed) *regula* in the letter he sent to his congregation.[66]

As regards Asia Minor, the earliest evidence for the use of N in catechesis is found in a letter by Basil of Caesarea (written in 373) – although he refers only to converts from another, non-Nicene church who are instructed in the contents of N which is thus used as a test for orthodoxy.[67] The same procedure is prescribed in canon 7 of the Council of Laodicea in Phrygia Pacatiana (probably convened in the second half of the fourth century) which was also widely applied in the Latin church; but in this canon no specific creed is named.[68] In the same letter Basil refuses to speak of the Holy Spirit as begotten, 'for by the handing over of the faith we have been taught a single Only-begotten'.[69] It is unclear whether the author refers to the ceremonial act of *Traditio* or to the 'tradition of the faith' in a wider sense. In another letter from the early autumn of the same year he writes that N had been in use in Caesarea 'since the fathers' without, however, providing any further context.[70] Gregory of Nyssa uses the term παράδοσις πίστεως in his *Refutation of the Confession of Eunomius* (383) in saying that 'we have learned about the Father, the Son, and the Holy Spirit from the truth in the "handing over" of the faith'.[71] But it is again uncertain what exactly he means by that.

---

65 Cf. (Pseudo-)Cyril, *Mystagogia 2*, 4 (FaFo § 631b).

66 Cf. above ch. 6.4.2.

67 Cf. Basil, *Epistula 125*, 1 (FaFo § 174a): 'Those who previously held to some other confession of faith and now wish to change over to the congregation of the orthodox and also those who now desire to be instructed in the teaching of the doctrine of truth [cf. Eph 1:13; Col 1:5] for the first time, must be taught the creed written by the blessed fathers in the council which was previously assembled at Nicaea.'

68 Cf. FaFo § 562a. The date of this council is uncertain.

69 Basil of Caesarea, *Epistula 125*, 3 (FaFo § 174a): [. . .] οὔτε γεννητόν· ἕνα γὰρ μονογενῆ ἐν τῇ παραδόσει τῆς πίστεως δεδιδάγμεθα.

70 Cf. Basil of Caesarea, *Epistula 140*, 2 (FaFo § 174b).

71 Gregory of Nyssa, *Refutatio confessionis Eunomii* (= *Contra Eunomium* II) 108 (Jaeger 1960, p. 357, ll. 14–16): Πατέρα καὶ υἱὸν καὶ πνεῦμα ἅγιον ἐν τῇ παραδόσει τῆς πίστεως παρὰ τῆς ἀληθείας ἐμάθομεν.

By contrast, the aforementioned Council of Laodicea clearly states that 'those to be enlightened [i.e. baptized] must learn the creed by heart and recite it to the bishop or to the presbyters on the fifth day of the week.'[72] Evidently a formula was memorized and recited on a Friday (either on the Friday after the creed had been 'handed over', if baptism was performed more than once a year, or, perhaps, on Good Friday, if it was performed at Easter[73]), but again we hear nothing about the liturgical setting, if any. Those who receive baptism during a serious illness are exhorted to memorize the creed once they have recovered.[74]

Our earliest evidence relating to Antioch dates from the late 370s, but it is rather confusing. Catechumens were taught about the faith in sermons delivered by a presbyter or the bishop, apparently during the regular Liturgy of the Word with both initiated and non-initiated Christians present.[75] The *Catechetical Homilies 1–10* by Theodore of Mopsuestia (even if they clearly were located in Mopsuestia not Antioch) give us a clear idea what this instruction looked like; they also contain the text of the creed.[76]

There is no firm evidence that the *Traditio* or *Redditio symboli* followed a formalized rite. Theodore tells his listeners that after the *Traditio* (which is not described in any detail) they should learn the creed by heart so that they could then recite it at the *Redditio*.[77] It has been suggested that this recitation may have taken place, in some form, after the *Sýntaxis* and again during baptism itself,[78] but we have no positive proof of this.[79] On the contrary, according to Theodore the *Redditio* seems to have *preceded* the *Sýntaxis* rite.[80] By contrast, the baptismal

---

72 Council of Laodicea, canon 46 (FaFo § 562b).

73 The Latin translations of canon 46 in the *Collectio Dionysiana* and the *Collectio Hispana* (FaFo § 562b) are more specific: they explicitly place the *Redditio* on Good Friday.

74 Cf. Council of Laodicea, canon 47 (FaFo § 562c).

75 Cf. John Chrysostom, *Catechesis baptismalis 2/3*, 4, ll. 1–6 (SC 366, p. 226) and Knupp 1995, pp. 98–100; Metzger/Drews/Brakmann 2004, col. 525.

76 Cf. also the summary of catecheses of this type in *Constitutiones apostolorum* 7,39,1–4. For the text of the creed cf. above pp. 346–9.

77 Cf. Theodore, *Homilia catechetica 12*, 25.

78 Cf. Auguste Piédnagel in SC 366, pp. 61–4.

79 It is possible that John Chrysostom alludes to some form of *Traditio* in his *Catechesis baptismalis 2/3* (CPG 4462), 3 (FaFo § 597). This catechesis may have been delivered in 388; cf. CPG 4462.

80 Cf. Theodore of Mopsuestia, *Homilia catechetica 12*, 27 (FaFo § 635b): 'We approach, therefore, the majordomo of this house, that is to say, of the Church – and this majordomo is the priest, who has been found worthy to preside over the Church – and after we have recited our profession of faith before him, we make with God, through him, our contract and our engagements concerning the faith'. Cf. also id., *Homilia catechetica 13*, 13–16; Knupp 1995, pp. 98–116, 130–3; and Witkamp 2018, pp. 78, 187.

liturgy of the *Apostolic Constitutions* (whose precise origin is unknown[81]) has the *Redditio* immediately *following* upon the *Sýntaxis*. It uses a creed which is otherwise unknown.[82] John Chrysostom seems to suggest in one of his homilies on First Corinthians (392/393) that the creed was recited right before baptism, but wishes to keep its content secret, because his audience encompasses unbaptized listeners. Nevertheless, the following credal fragments can be extracted from his words:

[. . .] ἁμαρτιῶν ἄφεσιν.
Πιστεύω εἰς νεκρῶν ἀνάστασιν
καὶ εἰς ζωὴν αἰώνιον.

[. . .] the remission of sins.
I believe in the resurrection of the dead
and in eternal life.[83]

Unfortunately, this fits neither N, N^{Ant}, nor C^1 or C^2. However, one must beware of taking Chrysostom at his word, because he mentions in a sermon on the Gospel of John, belief 'in the resurrection of the bodies' (εἰς ἀνάστασιν σωμάτων) instead of 'the dead' as part of a brief creed.[84] In addition, Chrysostom gives an explanation of the creed in one of his baptismal catecheses (delivered in 391), but its wording cannot be identified.[85] Finally, John Cassian also attests to the use of N^{Ant} at baptism for Antioch in his work against Nestorius (written in *c.* 430).[86] Again, from

---

81 Cf. Bradshaw, '*Apostolic Constitutions*', 2018. Most scholars assume that it was written in Antioch between 375 and 380.

82 Cf. *Constitutiones apostolorum* 7,41,3–8 (FaFo § 182c). The creeds in the *Constitutiones* have always baffled scholars (cf. the literature quoted in § 182). In his edition of the text Marcel Metzger considered the baptismal creed in book 7 a 'cento' of Ant^4, N, C^2, and J (cf. Metzger in SC 320, p. 29). However, things are more complicated. For example, the final clause εἰς ζωὴν τοῦ μέλλοντος αἰῶνος / 'and into the life of the coming age' is otherwise only attested in Arius and Euzoius, *Epistula ad Constantinum imperatorem* 3 (§ 131c). Markus Vinzent emphasized the creed's anti-Marcellan character because of the addition οὖ τῆς βασιλείας οὐκ ἔσται τέλος / 'of whose kingdom there will be no end' (Vinzent 1999, p. 244). However, this may well be an indirect inheritance, because the clause is already found in J. Cf. also Epiphanius, *Ancoratus* 119,8 (§ 175). Later it also forms part of C^2. Cf. above p. 370.

83 Cf. John Chrysostom, *In epistulam I ad Corinthios homilia 40*, 1–2 (FaFo § 189c). Cf. also id., *In Iohannem homilia 17*, 4 (§ 189d); id., *In epistulam ad Colossenses homilia 6*, 4 (§ 189e).

84 John Chrysostom, *In Iohannem homilia 17*, 4 (FaFo § 189d).

85 Cf. John Chrysostom, *Catechesis baptismalis 3/1*, 19 (FaFo § 189a).

86 Cf. John Cassian, *De incarnatione domini contra Nestorium* 6,6: 'The creed then, O you heretic, of which we gave the text above, though it is that of all the churches (for the faith of all is but one) is yet especially that of the city and church of Antioch, i.e. of that Church in which you were brought up, instructed, and regenerated. The faith of this creed, therefore, led you to the fountain

one of John Chrysostom's homilies it appears that the form of the creed was interrogatory and that the candidates were expected to answer, 'I believe'.[87]

In Constantinople, Gregory of Nazianzus writes in a homily on baptism from around 380 that he wants to teach his listeners about the faith and adds that he had kept that faith 'from the beginning until this greyness of hair'. One expects a quotation from N or some other creed to follow, but instead Gregory continues with a 'new decalogue' outlining important tenets of Neo-Nicene trinitarian thought (which are probably meant to be counted on the fingers of both hands).[88] Therefore, it is unlikely that N or any other fixed formula was used in this process at this point. Likewise, Chrysostom's homilies which may be dated to the time when he was patriarch of the eastern capital include no hint as to the role of the creed in preparing for baptism.[89]

By the time of Nestorius (*sedit* 428–431) and Proclus (*sedit* 434–446) things had changed. In a recently discovered homily which may be attributed to the former and which was probably delivered during Lent in 428 or 429 a version of the creed is explained which can be identified as the shorter creed of the Council of Constantinople (381; C[1]).[90] According to his own words Nestorius' audience was made up of baptized and non-baptized Christians. He mentions that a mystagogy would follow in due course which will be addressed to believers only.[91] This sermon on the creed may have been preceded by another on the Trinity.[92] As regards Proclus, he does not give us the full text of the creed but rather quotes only the beginning of each section which is basically identical with that of Nestorius (C[1]).[93] However, from the sequence of the rituals which he explains in his *Mystagogy on Baptism*[94] we may assume that the creed followed the *Apótaxis* and *Sýntaxis*.[95]

---

of life, to saving regeneration, to the grace of the eucharist, to the communion of the Lord – and what more!' (tr. NPNF; altered).

87 Cf. John Chrysostom, *Catechesis baptismalis 2/3* (CPG 4462), 3 (FaFo § 597).

88 Gregory of Nazianzus, *Oratio 40*, 11. 41. 44–45 (FaFo §§ 628, 179).

89 Cf. Day 2005, p. 34.

90 Cf. above p. 361.

91 Cf. Nestorius, *In symbolum fidei* 4 (Kinzig, 'Zwei neuentdeckte Predigten', 2020(2022), pp. 21 f.).

92 Cf. Nestorius, *Aduersus haereticos de diuina trinitate* (Kinzig, 'Zwei neuentdeckte Predigten', 2020(2022), pp. 5–10).

93 Cf. Proclus, *Homilia 27*, 4,16. 19. 20. 21. 23; 9,55. 56: Πιστεύω εἰς ἕνα καὶ μόνον ἀληθινὸν θεὸν παντοκράτορα < . . . > Πιστεύω εἰς τὸν κύριον Ἰησοῦν Χριστόν, τὸν υἱὸν τοῦ θεοῦ < . . . >. Πιστεύω εἰς τὸ πνεῦμα τὸ ἅγιον < . . . >. / 'I believe in the one and only true God, the Almighty < . . . > I believe in the Lord Jesus Christ, the Son of God < . . . > I believe in the Holy Spirit.' In the first section πατέρα is missing, in the second section ἕνα. Cf. also below p. 525.

94 Text in Leroy 1967, pp. 96–9; English translation and commentary in Day 2005.

95 Cf. Day 2005, pp. 37 f.

We have already seen that the revision N^Ant was the basis for Theodore's preaching on the creed. An indication that the authentic version of N was more widely used at the *Traditio* in the east is found in a remark by Rufinus in his exposition of the creed in *c.* 404. Here Rufinus explains the differences between the creed used in Aquileia and that used in the eastern churches in these terms:

> The eastern churches almost all hand over (*tradunt*) [the creed] thus: 'I believe in one God, the Father Almighty (*credo in uno deo patre omnipotente*)'; and again in the next phrase, where we say, 'And in Jesus Christ, his only Son, our Lord (*et in Iesu Christo, unico filio eius domino nostro*)' they hand it over (*tradunt*): 'And in one Lord, our [Lord] Jesus Christ, his only Son (*et in uno domino nostro Iesu Christo unico filio eius*)'. Hence they confess 'one God' and 'one Lord,' in accordance with the authority of the Apostle Paul [cf. 1Cor 8:6].[96]

Later Rufinus adds that this eastern creed does not include the descent to hell.[97]

Although Rufinus' quotations are admittedly very brief, it is reasonable to assume that they refer to N which he clearly knew.[98] All his quotations from the creed are identical with N – except for one interesting exception: he cites *domino nostro* (the ablative instead of the accusative is unremarkable) which is not found in the Greek version, but in early *Latin* versions of N.[99] Moreover, his phrasing (*tradunt*) suggests that by the end of the fourth century the *Traditio symboli* had come, more widely, to play a role in preparing for baptism.

In an incidental remark Theodore the Reader mentions that the creed was 'only recited once a year, on the Holy Friday of God's passion, during the bishop's catechesis' until the time of Timothy I of Constantinople (*sedit* 511–518).[100] Theodore identifies this creed with N, but it may well have been N's revised version C^1.[101] This fits exactly the evidence from the *Barberini Euchologion* (*s.* VIII or earlier) which contains an order of baptism and its preparations for the eastern capital. Here the candidates are asked to recite the creed (which is now definitely C^2) straight after the *Sýntaxis*.[102] So in Constantinople the *Traditio* took place during the bishop's catechesis from the time of Nestorius onwards (or perhaps earlier) whereas the *Redditio* followed upon the *Sýntaxis*.

---

96 Rufinus, *Expositio symboli* 4. Cf. also 5.
97 Cf. Rufinus, *Expositio symboli* 16.
98 Rufinus' version of N is found in *Historia ecclesiastica* 10,6 (FaFo § 135d12).
99 Cf., e.g., FaFo § 135d3–6, 8, 10.2 and Dossetti 1967, p. 227 (apparatus).
100 Theodore the Reader, *Historia ecclesiastica*, epit. 501 (FaFo § 685a).
101 Cf. above p. 400.
102 Cf. *Barberini Euchologion* 119,8–12; 143,16–22 (FaFo § 677a and b). Cf. also Spinks 2006(2016), p. 96.

N was used at baptism in Cyrrhus in the province Euphratensis from the 430s onwards. In 431/432 the local bishop Theodoret explicitly states that he instructs candidates for baptism 'in the faith set out in Nicaea', repeating this almost verbatim twenty years later.[103] We can reconstruct part of his version of N from his *Eranistes* (447/448, reissued after 451) which is very similar, but not quite identical with the original, perhaps showing an influence from the creed of Antioch.[104] This is no surprise as Theodoret originated from that city and alludes to the faith in which he had been baptized in *Epistula 151*.[105]

As regards Alexandria evidence is scant for the first half of the fifth century.[106] However, Egypt is an area where N enjoyed considerable popularity already in the 350s – after all, the Egyptian bishops (except their Homoian Patriarch George of Cappadocia (*sedit* 356–361)) defended its *homooúsios* at the Synod of Seleucia in 359.[107] Cyril of Alexandria (who was born in *c.* 380) mentioned N as his baptismal creed in 433, without offering any detail.[108]

By the middle of the fifth century many bishops attest that they had been baptized in the faith (N or some version of it). Many participants of the Council of Chalcedon (451) expressed themselves in this manner.[109] N was also the baptismal creed of the Emperors Marcian (born in *c.* 392 in Thrace) and Basiliscus (origin

---

103 Theodoret, *Quod et post humanitatis assumptionem unicus filius sit dominus noster Iesus Christus* (FaFo § 642b). Cf. also id., *Epistula 146(145*; § 642a).

104 Cf. Theodoret, *Eranistes* (FaFo § 202c). Theodoret reads καὶ εἰς τόν κύριον ἡμῶν instead of καὶ εἰς ἕνα κύριον (cf. N^Ant2); adds σταυρωθέντα (cf. N^Ant); and in the anathemas adds τινὸς before ὑποστάσεως; omits ἢ κτιστόν; adds ἁγία before καθολική. In addition, in *Epistula 151* (FaFo § 202b) he asserts that 'our Lord Jesus Christ is the only-begotten and first-born Son of God'. (Φαμὲν τοίνυν τὸν κύριον ἡμῶν Ἰησοῦν Χριστὸν υἱὸν εἶναι μονογενῆ τοῦ θεοῦ καὶ πρωτότοκον· [. . .]). This may be an allusion to N^Ant.

105 Cf. Theodoret, *Epistula 151* (FaFo § 202b): Ἡμεῖς δὲ τὸν πατρῷον κλῆρον ἄσυλον φυλάττειν σπουδάζομεν καί, ἣν παρελάβομεν, πίστιν, μεθ' ἧς καὶ ἐβαπτίσθημεν καὶ βαπτίζομεν, ἀνέπαφον καὶ ἀκήρατον διατηροῦμεν [. . .]. / 'We however, are zealous to keep our heritage unsullied, and we preserve unharmed and undefiled the faith which we have received, and in which we have been ourselves baptized and baptize [others] [. . .].'

106 The first witness to the use of N at baptism in Egypt may be Mark the Monk (cf. FaFo § 200). However, his biographical data are as controversial (did he live in *c.* 430–500 or before?) as the creed which he alludes to, since it is not entirely congruent with N.

107 Cf. above ch. 6.5.9.

108 Cf. Cyril, *Epistula 93* (*Collectio Atheniensis 126*; ACO I 1,7, p. 163, l. 8).

109 Cf. FaFo § 645 and further references in Kinzig, *Glaubensbekenntnis*, 2021, pp. 121–3 and nn. 523, 529. For later references to N as a baptismal creed cf., e.g., §§ 574a1 (John II of Constantinople, 518); 574b2 (Chalcedonian monks, 518); 574b3 (Synod *endemousa* of Constantinople 518); 647 (Epiphanius of Perge and other bishops from Pamphylia in their response to the *Codex encyclius* of Emperor Leo I, written in 457/458; *Traditio*).

unknown).[110] This suggests that N was widely used at baptism in the east in the first half of the fifth century. Emperor Zeno even claimed in his *Henoticon* of 482 that 'the holy symbol of the 318 holy fathers' which the '150 holy fathers' had confirmed was the universal baptismal creed – which, however, leaves open the question as to whether he was referring to N or C^2 or to both.[111] By that time, Jerusalem, too, seems to have given up its local creed J and to have replaced it with either N or C^2, as Martyrius of Jerusalem expresses himself in *c.* 480 in terms very similar to the emperor.[112]

Taken together this evidence suggests that no local creeds existed in the east (except for Jerusalem). Instead N or some variant of it came to be used from the late 370s onwards, first, in Antioch and, almost simultaneously, in Constantinople and (perhaps) in Alexandria whence it spread to other regions. This is, of course, no coincidence as it was precisely at this time that the (neo-Nicene) version of the faith became prevalent in the eastern part of the empire. Yet, in contrast to the west, there seems to have been a great variety of ways in which the baptizands' faith was ascertained: by declaration or by answering credal questions either simply affirming a given set of doctrinal propositions or themselves expressing their faith in their own words.[113]

✳

During the Carolingian period it seems that in the areas under Frankish influence the bishops paid greater attention to the quality of catechesis and candidates' knowledge of the faith, fuelled by Charlemagne's zeal for an improved religious education,[114] but also because mission received an increased significance as his empire expanded: Alcuin (d. 804) urged missionaries to teach the faith to converts with 'peaceful and wise words' (*pacificis uerbis et prudentibus*) before baptizing them.[115] Furthermore, the priest is told to conduct intensive interrogations into their faith prior to baptizing converted pagans in instructions contained in two manuscripts from the beginning and the middle of the ninth century respectively.[116]

---

110 Cf. Marcian, *Epistula ad monachos Alexandrinos* (FaFo § 546; written in 454); Basiliscus, *Encyclion* (§ 548); id., *Antiencyclion* (§ 549).

111 Zeno, *Henoticon* 5 (FaFo § 550): [. . .] πίστιν πλὴν τοῦ προειρημένου ἁγίου συμβόλου τῶν τιη´ ἁγίων πατέρων, ὅπερ καὶ ἐβεβαίωσαν οἱ μνημονευθέντες ρν´ ἅγιοι πατέρες, [. . .]. Cf. also above p. 400 and n. 105.

112 Cf. Pseudo-Zachariah Rhetor, *Historia ecclesiastica* 5,6c–d (FaFo § 217).

113 On the oriental churches cf. above ch. 9.

114 Cf. above ch. 5.3 and pp. 470 f.

115 Alcuin, *Epistula 111* (MGH Epp. IV, p. 160, ll. 25 f.).

116 Cf. Keefe 2002, vol. II, pp. 534–7 (text 38; FaFo § 779) and Keefe 2002, vol. II, pp. 234–8 (text 8.1; § 759). The manuscripts are cod. Munich, Bayerische Staatsbibliothek, Clm 14410 (cf. Keefe,

We also read in various commentaries on the baptismal liturgy and on credal interrogations that scrutinies were carried out with converts, after the *Traditio* and immediately following the renunciation, in order to determine the extent to which the words of the creed were anchored in the hearts of the catechumens.[117] However, the liturgy was never quite uniform: in a report about an episcopal synod near the river Danube (796) the order of renunciation and *Redditio* is inversed.[118] Two years later, Alcuin gives the following order of rites: renunciation – *exsufflatio* (the priest blows into the candidate's face in order to make room for Christ) – exorcism – *Traditio* – scrutinies etc.[119] There are other variations, sometimes with more than one renunciation.[120] A number of interrogations about the faith have come down to us which may have been used during the scrutinies or separately.[121] They were then quickly translated from Latin into the vernacular.[122] In the case of infants their parents or godparents answered in their stead.[123] The *Traditio* sometimes took place on the Wednesday of the fourth week of Lent and the *Redditio* on Maundy Thursday or Holy Saturday.[124]

There were thus efforts under the Carolingians to restore the scrutinies to their original meaning in pagan mission.[125] However, the extent to which these instructions were implemented or could be implemented at all, given the sometimes high numbers of converts, is beyond our knowledge. In any case, the surviving sacramentaries no longer offer a liturgical place for such scrutinies.

11.1.2 The creed at the baptism of infants

The widespread implementation of infant baptism inevitably had serious consequences for the rites of *Traditio* and *Redditio symboli*, because the baptizands were as yet unable to recite the creed. Unfortunately, our sources flow rather

---

Catalogue, 2012, pp. 282 f. (a 'missionary catechism')) and cod. St. Gallen, Stiftsbibliothek, 40 (cf. Keefe, *Catalogue*, 2012, pp. 336 f. (a 'clerical instruction reader')).
117 Cf. FaFo §§ 63, 75, 760, 779, 782a2, 783a, 784b, 791, 792, 793, 794. Cf. also Phelan 2014, pp. 177, 183 f., 187.
118 Cf. Paulinus II of Aquileia, *Conuentus episcoporum ad ripas Danubii* (FaFo § 774).
119 Cf. Alcuin, *De sacramento baptismatis* (FaFo § 775). Similarly, Theodulf of Orléans, *Liber de ordine baptismi* 5 (§ 787a).
120 Cf., e.g., Keefe 2002, vol. I, pp. 46–50.
121 Cf. FaFo §§ 757–773. Cf. also the questions on faith in § 776.
122 Cf. FaFo §§ 766–768, 771.
123 Cf. Theodulf of Orléans, *Liber de ordine baptismi* 8 (FaFo § 787b). Cf. also §§ 788[1], 789, 790.
124 Cf. Amalarius of Metz, *Liber officialis* 1,8,2; 1,12,1 (FaFo § 782b1 and b2).
125 Cf. Wiegand 1899, pp. 315, 327; Keefe 2002, vol. I, index s.v. 'scrutinies'.

sparsely over the centuries. Caesarius of Arles admonishes his listeners that at the *Traditio*

> those who are older may return it [the creed] on their own, but in the case of infants those who are to receive them [from the font, i.e. the parents or godparents] should have it returned either by themselves or by someone else.[126]

However, our best evidence comes from the *Old Gelasian Sacramentary* (OGS) which reflects, at least in parts, a much older liturgical practice as it was cultivated in the western capital.[127] It is reasonable to assume that the practice of *Traditio* and *Redditio symboli* set down in the OGS in the form in which it survives may actually date from the fifth century, with elements probably being even older. Here[128] the *Traditio* refers to the baptism of babies or infants.[129] To better understand the relevant rubrics of the OGS one must first bear in mind a peculiarity of the Roman liturgy: John the Deacon wrote in his famous *Letter to Senarius* in the first decades of the sixth century that in Rome infants were baptized in the same way as adults, even if they did not understand the process. In this case the confession of the parents or others took the place of that by the baptizands themselves.[130] In other words, certain liturgical tensions, which will be considered in more detail below, are explained by the fact that the old rites of *Traditio* and *Redditio* which had been developed for the baptism of adults were not adapted to the new circumstances of christening infants; instead, the latter were treated as if they were adults: they were addressed in the second person, and the parents or godparents apparently responded in their place, in the first person.

According to the OGS the *Traditio* took place on the Saturday before Palm Sunday and began with a preface that was probably written by Leo the Great, which will also be considered in greater detail in a later chapter.[131] In reality, this

---

126 Caesarius of Arles, *Sermo 130*, 5 (FaFo § 656f).

127 Cf. above pp. 121 f. and n. 256.

128 For what follows cf. *Sacramentarium Gelasianum Vetus* nos. 310–315 (FaFo §§ 675a and 255g). Cf. also Stenzel 1958, pp. 207–19; Kretschmar 1970, pp. 253–7; Angenendt 1987, pp. 289–94; Saxer 1988, pp. 597–624; Keefe 2002, vol. I, pp. 43–6; Johnson 2007, pp. 222–9.

129 Distinctions remain blurred. Since the preferred date of baptism was Easter, children brought to the font could be a year old. Carolingian legal sources mention an age of between one day and three years at most. Easter notwithstanding, Epiphany and Pentecost were also popular days for baptism. Finally, in a situation of danger, an emergency baptism could be performed at any time. Cf. Rubellin 1982, pp. 34–42; Cramer 1993(1994), pp. 137–9; Georg Kretschmar in Gerlitz et al. 2001, pp. 688 f.

130 Cf. John the Deacon, *Epistula ad Senarium* 7. Cf. Didier 1965, pp. 86 f.; Saxer 1988, pp. 589–95; Johnson 2007, pp. 164–9; Ferguson 2009, pp. 767 f.

131 Cf. below pp. 527 f.

address was unnecessary as the godparents had already been baptized and thus already 'owned' the creed. Obviously, the preface had originated in adult baptism, which by then was no longer the rule. However, a separate exhortation of the parents or godparents as such is missing.

The bishop then left it to the clergy assisting him to direct the following rites. One of the acolytes (altar boys) took a boy from the crowd of children to be baptized on his left arm and placed his hand on the baptizand's head. The priest asked the acolyte, 'In what language do [the baptizands] confess our Lord Jesus Christ?' to which the acolyte replied, 'In Greek'. The priest then invited the acolyte to recite the creed. The acolyte responded accordingly, the recitation being performed *decantando*, that is, presumably by chanting.[132] The creed chanted, however, was not R (as one might have expected in a Roman sacramentary) but C².[133] In the manuscript we have it is not reproduced in Greek script, but in a Latin transliteration, immediately followed by a Latin translation.[134] This indicates that at least at the time when the manuscript was copied (*c.* 750) Greek was no longer understood.

This was followed by a very brief exposition of the creed, which again probably goes back to Leo the Great and whose reading is expressly entrusted to the priest. The brevity of this interpretation could be due to the fact that a detailed explanation was no longer considered necessary, as the godparents had already been baptized.

Like all divine services in antiquity, the rite of the *Traditio* on Palm Sunday will probably have been a lively and perhaps noisy ceremony. Thus we know from John Cassian that at the beginning of the fifth century the people of Marseille applauded at the *Traditio* or at any rate clearly expressed their approval.[135] Snippets like this put into perspective the impression of serious solemnity that one might gain from reading the sacramentaries alone.

The *Redditio* followed a week later, i.e. on Holy Saturday, early in the morning immediately after the renunciation.[136] The rubric begins with the puzzling remark: 'Mane reddunt infantes symbolum.' / 'In the morning the infants (*infantes*)

---

132 Cf. below ch. 19.

133 It is the version from the third session of Chalcedon; cf. FaFo § 184e1 in comparison with § 184f2.1.

134 Cf. FaFo §§ 184f2.2 and 675a. Other sacramentaries also contain a Greek version of C² in Latin script. Cf., e.g., Angoulême (§§ 184f14 and 796a), Gellone (§§ 184f6 and 797a); *Ordo Romanus XI* (§§ 184f4 and 808a), Saint-Amand (§ 184f16); *Pontificale Parisiense (of Poitiers;* cod. Paris, Bibliothèque Nationale, Arsenal 227, ff. 54v–56r; scan: URL <https://gallica.bnf.fr/ark:/12148/btv1b55005681f/f120.item.r=pontifical%20poitiers> (21/11/2023); ed. Martini 1979, pp. 63–6 (no. 128); cf. also Westwell 2019, pp. 73 f.); *Pontificale Romano-Germanicum* (§ 184f12.1). Cf. also Reims (§ 799a) where the creed itself is not quoted.

135 Cf. John Cassian, *De incarnatione domini contra Nestorium* 6,11,1 (FaFo § 641b).

136 Cf. *Sacramentarium Gelasianum Vetus* nos. 418–424 (FaFo § 675b).

recite the creed.' This presupposes that the baptizands were actually capable of doing so. By that time, however, they were hardly more than a year old. Here, therefore, the aforementioned tension becomes apparent once more: the *Redditio symboli* as such presupposed the active participation of the *competentes* themselves, which, however, in this case they were not yet capable of. In fact, the ceremony took a different course: first, the bishop invoked Satan and warned him of imminent expulsion. This was followed by the rite of *effata* (by which the nose and ears of the baptizands were 'opened') and the renunciation. Here the *competentes* or, more precisely, their parents or godparents were asked whether they would renounce Satan, his works, and his pomp which they were to answer by saying, 'I renounce'. Then the creed was recited by the bishop, with the laying on of hands on the candidates. Of course, since the baptizands were babies, they were not expected to recite the creed themselves, yet neither are their parents or godparents explicitly told to do this in their stead.[137] The creed itself is not quoted, but it must also have been C^2. This means, however, that already in the late fifth century the *Redditio* had become a purely ceremonial act, at least in Rome, that, perhaps, no longer required the active participation of parents or godparents in the recitation of the entire confession. The ceremony was concluded with a prayer.

The creed appears a third time in the OGS, namely in interrogatory form during baptism itself. The questions were addressed to the baptizand, but answered by their parents/godparents or, again, a member of the clergy. These baptismal questions, which in their wording go back neither to C^2 nor to R/T, represent a strange duplication of the *Traditio/Redditio* in this sacramentary, which can presumably be explained by the fact that they are in actual fact older than the rite of *Traditio/Redditio*.[138]

The rites of *Traditio* and *Redditio symboli* outlined so far are also found, with modifications, in the *Ordo Romanus XI*, a Roman order of baptismal service perhaps dating to the second half of the sixth century, as well as in sacramentaries dependent on the OGS or its *Vorlage*. There are, however, characteristic deviations which need not concern us here, except that in the *Ordo* it is said that it is the priest (not the bishop) who chants the creed.[139]

The situation is different in the so-called non-Roman western liturgies[140] since, for example, the *Stowe Missal* mentions no *Traditio* or *Redditio symboli* at all,[141] whereas in the Mozarabic liturgy the candidates (or their parents or god-

---

137 Cf. also Lynch 1986, pp. 293 f. with regard to the closely related *Ordo Romanus XI*.
138 Cf. above ch. 4.5.1.
139 Cf. *Ordo Romanus XI*, 86 (FaFo § 808b); on which, e.g., Lynch 1986, pp. 294–7; Spinks 2006 (2016), pp. 114 f. In addition, Romano 2019.
140 Cf. Vogel 1986, pp. 273–89.
141 Cf. FaFo § 680.

parents) answer the credal questions with a simple 'yes', no longer having to demonstrate that they have memorized the creed.[142] By contrast, in England the Second Council of Clofesho (747)[143] and the so-called Legatine Councils of 786[144] impressed upon priests that they had to employ suitable means to ensure the candidates, or their godparents, could recite the renunciation and the creed.

As regards the significance of the *Redditio* for the individual believer, faith (*fides*) was generally seen as the trustworthiness displayed towards the divine overlord, expressed by reciting the sacred and legally binding creed. As I have explained elsewhere in greater detail, this allegiance to God, which was mediated through the Church, was first and foremost encapsulated in the dual rite of renunciation and *Redditio* (or credal questions). In the west the creed served as the *Sýntaxis* (engagement with Christ) which was done through a separate formula in eastern baptismal liturgies. In any case, the *Apótaxis* and *Sýntaxis/Redditio* indicated the baptizand's change of allegiance from Satan to Christ whose legal implications Theodore of Mopsuestia, John Chrysostom, and others have described in great detail.[145] The legal character of this change of allegiance was underlined by the presence of a guarantor (who was called ἀνάδοχος, *fideiussor, sponsor, patrinus/matrina*, or *conpater/conmater*).[146] Both *sponsor* and *fideiussor* were originally guarantors in the Roman law of obligations: 'Suretyship guaranteed a debt in that an accessory debtor undertook to make the same performance which the principal debtor owed.'[147] When infant baptism became the norm the guarantor also gave their assurance that the infant would believe according to what he or she had promised at baptism in lieu of the child. From this perspective, the recitation of the creed was seen as a binding contractual obligation over against Christ which was made possible through the Church.[148]

One western example of this kind of quasi-legal faith discourse may suffice. In a homily Gerbald of Liège (*sedit* 787–809) pointed out in no uncertain terms:

142 Cf. FaFo § 684 and also Saxer 1988, p. 553. However, Ildefonsus of Toledo clearly mentions a full *Redditio symboli* on Maundy Thursday in front of the priest (*De cognitione baptismi* 35; FaFo § 664). Likewise, the *Traditio symboli* in the *Liber ordinum de ordinibus ecclesiasticis* (FaFo § 684c4) may also point to a *Redditio* of the confession.
143 Cf. canon 11 (FaFo § 587b).
144 Cf. canon 2 (FaFo § 588).
145 Cf. Kinzig, "'I abjure Satan'", 2024 (*sub prelo*).
146 Cf. Dick 1939; Dujarier 1962; Hornung 2015.
147 Kaser 1984, p. 277. Cf. also Kaser 1971/1975, vol. I, pp. 660–7; vol. II, pp. 457–61.
148 This increasingly legalistic interpretation of the godparents' role is no doubt secondary and partly eclipsed the original reasons for introducing this office, i.e. to assure the bishop of the integrity of the baptismal candidates and to oversee their progress in the Christian faith during the catechumenate. Cf. the literature quoted above n. 146 and Kinzig/Wallraff 2002, pp. 343 f.

As each Christian must hold, believe, and profess, and should believe what their guarantor promised (*fideiussor eius promisit*) at their baptism [this] is contained in these twelve verses in which our salvation can be confessed in such a way that one might believe with the heart and profess with the mouth. For this is what the Apostle says, 'One believes with the heart unto justification, and one confesses with the mouth unto salvation' [Rom 10:10]. So also each Christian who professes that he believes [in] God should confess with the mouth what he believes with the heart such that others may hear how he believes and how he is faithful to God. For when he says that he believes with the heart [in] God, but does not profess with the mouth, who knows whether he is faithful or an infidel? This is what we speak in public, and every one of you who possesses a serf (*seruum*) can take him as an example: if someone has a serf and he asks [the serf] if he is faithful (*fidelis*) to him, if [the serf] is silent and does not respond whether he is faithful to him, his lord will not quite believe him until he has professed that he is faithful to his lord. And, after the profession of his fidelity (*post professionem fidelitatis*), if he does not demonstrate it in deed, his lord will not be pleased that he has professed his fidelity in words only (unless a [corresponding] deed follows and it is demonstrated in deed to what degree the serf proves to be faithful to his lord).[149]

Here *fides* is not just 'faith' in the sense of belief in credal content – it is the unconditional loyalty (*fidelitas*) of the believers over against God such as that of clients over against their *patronus* or slaves over against their master.[150]

11.2 The creed in the mass

Although[151] one must be cautious with *argumenta e silentio*, the evidence suggests that the creed was not introduced into the liturgy of the eucharist in the eastern part of the empire until the fifth or sixth century. Although it is always notoriously difficult to determine the 'meaning' of any given liturgical rite, the creed's position in the early eastern liturgies is so prominent that at least *one* of its functions can be determined more clearly.[152]

Curiously, an Egyptian source may offer the earliest liturgical evidence in Greek.[153] It comes from two pieces of parchment from Upper Egypt which have

---

149 Gerbald, *Instructio pastoralis ad gregem suum (Epistula 3)* 1 (FaFo § 745d1).
150 Cf. Schneider 1969, cols. 807 f.; Busch/Nicols/Zanella 2015, col. 1112; Morgan 2015, pp. 50–5, 60–5.
151 This chapter is based on Kinzig, 'Creed', 2007.
152 Here I will confine myself to the Byzantine and Latin churches. On the evidence for eastern Christianity cf. above ch. 9.
153 For a possible reference to the creed in Pseudo-Dionysius the Areopagite, *De ecclesiastica hierarchia* 3 (Heil/Ritter 2012, p. 80, ll. 20 f.; 87, l. 20 – 88, l. 9) cf. Capelle 1951(1967), p. 60 note 2; Taft 1978, pp. 49 f. and also Heil 1986, p. 117 and n. 40. The description of the rite in Pseudo-Dionysius does not, however, really fit in with the recitation of a creed, but more with it being a prayer

been dated to the fifth or sixth centuries and are today preserved in the library of Brigham Young University.[154] Here Greek N 'is preceded by the end of a prayer whose phraseology marks it rather clearly as belonging to a eucharistic liturgy'.[155] Alas, the provenance of the parchment and its wider liturgical context are unknown.

Otherwise, our oldest Byzantine source, Maximus the Confessor's *Mystagogy* (628–630), in which the creed appears as an element of the preanaphoral rites of Constantinople, is not much more recent.[156] In it the recitation of the creed is preceded by the exclusion of the catechumens and closing of the doors.[157] Likewise, in the Byzantine recensions of both the Liturgies of St Basil and of St John Chrysostom – indeed, virtually throughout the entire eastern liturgical tradition – the creed immediately follows the order to close the doors,[158] thereby marking the beginning of the Divine Liturgy, from which all unbaptized persons were excluded. This suggests that the recitation of the creed (by the entire congregation) was meant to ensure that only baptized Christians – i.e. full members of the congregation – took part in the eucharist, thereby preventing the sacred liturgy from being profaned by the non-initiated. In this context, therefore, the creed fulfilled the traditional function of the *symbolum* in mystery cults, i.e. that of a 'password' or 'watchword' or 'distinctive mark' known only to the initiated.[159]

We have some external evidence as to when and where the creed was inserted into the Divine Liturgy.[160] Theodore the Reader references it twice in his *Church History* (*c.* 520–530). The first reference based on an unknown source reports that the Miaphysite patriarch of Antioch, Peter Fuller (*sedit* 471, 475–477 and 485–488), introduced the creed into the celebration of the eucharist (συνάξεις) for the first time.[161] If this was indeed the case, he must have done so at some point after his election as Patriarch of Antioch in 471. Nothing is known about the circumstances surrounding these liturgical changes which, in view of the many

---

commemorating God's saving works. On the *Liturgical Homily* 35/17, which is attributed to Narsai (d. 502), cf. above p. 424.

154 Brigham Young University Collection of Coptic Fragments, no. 90 (Upper Egypt; *s.* V/VI), ed. Macomber 1993. Cf. also Mihálykó 2019, pp. 59, 143 n. 235, 221 and TM 108862.

155 Macomber 1993, p. 99.

156 Cf. Maximus the Confessor, *Mystagogia* 18 (FaFo § 690); cf. Taft 1978, 43–5.

157 Cf. Maximus the Confessor, *Mystagogia* 15.

158 Cf. FaFo § 694b. For detailed treatment cf. Jungmann 1951, vol. I, pp. 474–80; Jungmann 1962, vol. I, pp. 606–14; Taft 1978, pp. 405–16. On the stational character of the Byzantine Rite cf., e.g., Taft 1992, pp. 28–41.

159 Cf. above ch. 3.

160 For what follows cf. Jungmann 1951, vol. I, pp. 467–74; Jungmann 1962, vol. I, pp. 598–606; Kelly 1972, pp. 348–57; Taft 1978, pp. 396–425; Krueger 2014, pp. 123–6; Lumma/Vonach 2015, pp. 74 f.

161 Cf. Theodore the Reader, *Historia ecclesiastica*, epit. 429 (FaFo § 685a).

amendments to the liturgy made by Peter Fuller, are not necessarily *a priori* implausible. It is, however, not very likely that this was the origin of the subsequent Byzantine custom.[162]

It is much more probable that its origin lies in a liturgical amendment that Theodore the Reader ascribes to the Miaphysite Patriarch Timothy I of Constantinople (*sedit* 511–518).[163] According to Theodore, Timothy decreed that the 'Symbol of faith of the 318 Fathers' (τὸ τῶν τιη΄ πατέρων τῆς πίστεως σύμβολον) be recited during each mass (σύναξις) in order to defame his Chalcedonian predecessor Macedonius II (*sedit* 496–511) by creating the impression that Macedonius had never accepted this creed. Theodore says that previously it had only been recited once a year, namely during the bishop's catechism on Good Friday.[164] According to this source, therefore, Timothy inserted the creed into the Divine Liturgy in order to draw a clear distinction between Miaphysitism and the Chalcedonian beliefs of Patriarch Macedonius II. If this is true, the use of the creed in mass had a dual function: to make sure that all unbaptized persons had left the service (because they would have been unable to recite the creed) and to emphasize the Miaphysite character of that service. How the use of N or, more likely, C^1 would have served this second purpose is not altogether clear.[165]

By 518 at any rate, reciting the creed during mass had already become customary in Constantinople. On 16 July of that year, the population of Constantinople succeeded in wresting a proclamation of the canons of Chalcedon from Patriarch John II (*sedit* 518–520) during mass in the Great Church after the deaths of Patriarch Timothy and Emperor Anastasius I (r. 491–518; who was succeeded by the orthodox Christian Justin I, r. 518–527). This proclamation took place after the Liturgy of the Word as part of the eucharist; the canons of the four Ecumenical Councils were read out 'after the doors had been closed and the holy doctrine (ἅγιον μάθημα = the creed) had been said as usual'.[166] The point at which the creed (precisely which version is unclear) is included in the liturgy in this case therefore corresponds to the practice in the Liturgies of St Basil and of St John Chrysostom, i.e. after the doors had been closed.

It seems certain that – whatever the precise date of its insertion – by the early sixth century the creed formed part of the Great Entrance (a procession during which the bishop and other clergy enter into the church) in the Divine Liturgy

---

162 Cf. Capelle 1951(1967), pp. 61–3.
163 Cf. also above p. 400.
164 Cf. Theodore the Reader, *Historia ecclesiastica,* epit. 501 (FaFo § 685b). For the use of the creed in the *Traditio symboli* at Constantinople cf. also above pp. 498 f.
165 For the use of C^1 cf. above p. 400.
166 *Collectio Sabbaitica* 5,27 (FaFo § 686).

not only in the Greek church, but also in Syriac-speaking congregations, subsequently spreading to other churches.[167]

∗

However, John of Biclaro (d. *c.* 621) makes a confusing reference,[168] claiming in his *Chronicle* (written in 601/602) that Emperor Justin II (r. 565–578) decreed that 'the creed of the assembly of the 150 fathers at Constantinople, which had been laudably accepted at the Council of Chalcedon (*symbolumque sanctorum CL patrum Constantinopolim congregatorum et in synodo Calcidonense laudabiliter receptum*, i.e. C^2)' be 'sung together by the congregation (*a populo concinendum*)' in all churches prior to the Lord's Prayer.[169] Perhaps John means to say not that Justin was the first to insert the creed into the Divine Liturgy (which would have been mistaken), but that he actually introduced the use of C^2 (instead of N/C^1) in this context.[170] However, he also claims that C^2 was recited before the Lord's Prayer (i.e. apparently after the canon), which does not correspond to eastern practice at all and would instead appear to reflect a western practice.

There may be a simple reason: John of Biclaro originated from, and later lived and worked in the Visigothic Kingdom. There is evidence to suggest that it was the Visigoth king Reccared I (r. 586–601) who introduced C^2 'according to the convention of the eastern churches' into the Sunday liturgy at the Third Council of Toledo in 589 'so that, before the Lord's Prayer is said, the creed (*symbolum fidei*) shall be proclaimed (*praedicetur*; alternative reading: *decantetur* = chanted[171]) aloud by the congregation. By this', he continued, 'let the true faith bear clear testimony and also, the people's hearts having been cleansed by the faith, let them draw near to partake of the body and blood of Christ'.[172] This was phrased from an anti-Arian or, to be more accurate, from an anti-Homoian point of view, because Reccared had renounced the Homoian ('Arian') faith at the very same council.[173] It is striking that here, too, the creed and the Lord's Prayer are recited immediately prior to the eucharist, and in that order. The creed is to be said 'according to the version of the

---

167 Cf. above ch. 9.
168 Cf. Capelle 1951(1967), p. 63: 'La notice est passablement fantaisiste'.
169 John of Biclaro, *Chronicon* 2 (FaFo § 689).
170 Cf. above p. 402.
171 Cf. below p. 599.
172 Third Council of Toledo, canon 2 (FaFo § 687b). Cf. also above p. 406.
173 For details of the differences between Arianism and the Homoian faith of the Visigoths cf. the relevant essays in Schäferdiek 1996, and Schäferdiek 2001; Schäferdiek, 'Der gotische Arianismus', 2004.

eastern churches' (*secundum formam orientalium ecclesiarum*)[174] i.e., in effect, the Latin version of C^2 (and not R/T).[175] The purpose of reciting C^2 is to avow the *uera fides*, i.e. the trinitarian doctrine of the Council of Constantinople in 381. It is used in conjunction with the Lord's Prayer to prepare for receiving the eucharist. It must, therefore, have followed the canon, and thus come at a different point than it did in the eastern liturgies. The information provided by John of Biclaro is, therefore, directly linked to the decree of the Third Council of Toledo and does not correspond to eastern custom, but instead to western or, to be more precise, Visigothic practice.[176]

The object of moving the creed to a different part of the liturgy is not difficult to comprehend. Once it was no longer necessary to determine whether or not a member of the congregation had been baptized, the primary purpose of the creed shifted to verifying and confirming the faithful's orthodoxy by its joint recitation. This was particularly effective in those cases where the creed was positioned at a crucial and, as it were, especially 'sacred' part of the eucharistic celebration, namely before the Lord's Prayer, as obviously was the case in Toledo. Nevertheless, this change in the Mozarabic liturgy was not generally adopted in the western development of the mass.

By contrast, in the Celtic rite the creed was placed between the reading of the Gospel and the offertory – as illustrated by the *Stowe Missal* (*s.* VIII *ex.*).[177] By now, the distinction between the Liturgy of the Word and the eucharist, marked by the exit of the catechumens, had disappeared so that the creed no longer functioned as a proof of baptism, but, as we will see below, took on a new meaning as a joint response by the congregation to the gospel. Soon after this development in the Celtic world, the creed also appeared at this point in the liturgy of the Carolingians. The first testimony to this development is found in the history of the translations of the relics and of the miracles of St Marcellinus and St Peter by Einhard (d. 840), scholar and biographer of Charlemagne. He describes events which allegedly occurred in Maastricht, in the monastery of St-Servais the Confessor, on

---

174 The translation given in Kelly 1972, p. 351 'according to the use of the Eastern churches' is imprecise.

175 Incidentally, this Latin version of C^2, which then became customary in Spain (cf. FaFo § 184f24), is not identical with the creed's authentic Greek text, but displays a number of variants.

176 Cf. Taft 1978, pp. 402 f. Cf. also the Eighth Council of Toledo (653), canon 1 (FaFo § 496): '[. . .] as finally we profess and we say with a united voice in the solemn celebrations of the mass: [here follows C^2].' That the creed had this position is also confirmed by manuscripts of the old Spanish/ Mozarabic liturgy of the mass; cf. Capelle 1951(1967), p. 64 and, for a general treatment, Meyer 1989, pp. 157–9; Gemeinhardt 2002, p. 52. Not much later Isidore of Seville also provides testimony to the recitation of the creed in mass. Cf. *De origine officiorum (De ecclesiasticis officiis)* 1,16 (FaFo § 688).

177 Cf. Capelle 1951(1967), pp. 66 f. and, in general, Meyer 1989, pp. 160 f. The text of the creed is found in FaFo § 184f8. For its context cf. Warner 1906/1915, vol. II, pp. 8 f.

14 June 828, when a man suffering from some kind of tremor entered the church during mass on Sunday:

> After the Gospel reading was over and the creed of the Christian faith was being chanted (*cumque post recitatam euangelii lectionem Christianae credulitatis symbolum caneretur*), that trembling man suddenly fell to the ground and while the divine service was being brought to a close he lay there almost completely still more like a dead man than a living one.[178]

Here the creed once again follows upon the Gospel reading. This sequence is basically confirmed by Florus of Lyons (d. *c*. 860), who enumerates the following liturgical elements in his explanation of mass (written in 833/834): reading 'from the apostles and the gospels' – (sometimes) 'sermon and address of the teachers' – 'confession of the creed' – offertory.[179]

Another witness to this order is Walahfrid Strabo's book on the origin and development of certain ecclesiastical customs (*Libellus de exordiis et incrementis quarundam in obseruationibus ecclesiasticis rerum*, written in 840/842). The future abbot of Reichenau (807–849, abbot from 842) even provided some additional information:

(1) In the celebration of mass, the creed follows the Gospel, because the Gospel awakens faith in man's heart, thus leading to justification, whereas the creed proclaims the faith, thus leading to salvation (cf. Rom 10:10).

(2) The inclusion of the creed in the liturgy was modelled on Greek custom.

(3) The Greeks chanted C^2 instead of N during the liturgy, even though N was the older of the two creeds. Walahfrid explained this, on the one hand, by the fact that C^2 was more suited to being sung than N and, on the other, by C^2's greater anti-heretical effect; C^2 had, after all, been composed in the city where the emperors resided (and, therefore, possessed greater authority).

(4) The custom had travelled to Rome from Byzantium.

---

[178] Einhard, *Translatio et miracula sanctorum Marcellini et Petri* 4,14 (tr. Dutton 1998(2006), p. 124; altered).

[179] Florus of Lyons, *De expositione missae* 11–12,1 (Duc 1937, pp. 98 f.): 'First of all, therefore, when all the faithful have come together in one place and stand in the house of God, after the divine praise has been chanted, after the apostles and gospels have been read, after also sometimes a sermon and address of the teachers has taken place, also followed by the confession of the creed (*subiuncta quoque symboli confessione*) and the offering of the congregation, after the consecration of the sacraments has begun in which the mind of all participants is prepared to consider and to covet things divine and celestial, the priest stands at the altar and, at the beginning of the celebration of the divine mysteries, prays in greeting the church and greets in prayer (*ecclesiam salutando orat et orando salutat*), saying, "The Lord be with you."'

(5) In Gaul and Germany the recitation of C^2 only entered into widespread use after the heretic Felix of Urgel (condemned 798, d. 818), the major theologian of Spanish adoptionism, had been deposed.

(6) Finally, Walahfrid quoted the already cited provision from the documents of the Third Council of Toledo, albeit altered in such a way 'that every Sunday [!] that creed be recited according to the custom (*secundum morem orientalium*, not *formam*; cf. above pp. 406, 510) of the eastern churches'.[180]

Walahfrid's statements must be treated with a degree of caution. The custom did not, for example, travel to Rome where, as we will see below, the creed did not come to be introduced into the eucharistic liturgy until the early eleventh century. There are, however, good reasons to assume that the use of C^2 in the liturgy of mass really did catch on in the Frankish Empire as a reaction to the condemnation of Felix of Urgel, which is in line with the fundamentally anti-heretical function of this creed. Alcuin may have fallen back on the liturgical practice (and indeed on the Latin version of C^2) contained in the Irish *Stowe Missal* in his struggle against Spanish adoptionism.[181] In any case, there are numerous examples of the use of C^2 in the mass in the Carolingian empire in the ninth century.[182]

---

180 Walahfrid Strabo, *Libellus de exordiis et incrementis quarundam in obseruationibus ecclesiasticis rerum* 23 (FaFo § 851): 'The creed of the catholic faith (*symbolum fidei catholicae*) is also correctly recited after the [reading of the] Gospel in the celebration of mass, so that by means of the holy Gospel "[a person] believes with the heart unto justice", but by means of the creed "[a person] makes a confession with [their] mouth unto salvation" [Rom 10:10]. As for the creed which we have adopted into the mass in imitation of the Greeks, it should be noted that they converted this one rather than others into the sweetness of chant (*in cantilenae dulcedinem [. . .] transtulisse*) because it is the particular creed of the Council of Constantinople (and perhaps it seemed more suited to musical rhythms (*fortasse aptius uidebatur modulis sonorum*) than the Nicene Creed, which is from an earlier period). [They also chose it] so that the piety of the faithful should, even in their celebration of the sacraments, counter the poison of heretics with medicine concocted at the imperial capital. That practice, therefore, is believed to have come to the Romans from them [i.e. the Greeks]; but among the Gauls and Germans that creed (*idem symbolum*) came to be repeated in the liturgy of the mass more widely and frequently after the deposition of Felix [of Urgel] the heretic, [who was] condemned under the most-glorious Charles, ruler of the Franks. At the Council of Toledo it was also established that every Sunday that creed (*idem symbolum*) "be recited according to the custom of the eastern churches so that, before the Lord's Prayer is recited, the true faith might bear clear testimony, and, after the people's hearts have been cleansed, they might draw near to partake of the body and blood of Christ" [cf. FaFo § 687b].'

181 Cf. FaFo §§ 184f8 (type II), 702g. For a detailed treatment cf. Capelle 1929(1967); Capelle 1934 (1962); Capelle 1951(1967), pp. 66–75; Kelly 1972, pp. 355 f.; Gemeinhardt 2002, pp. 90–107.

182 Cf. the references below pp. 566, 568 f., 601 f.

This corresponds to the situation described in the minutes of an interview between envoys of Emperor Charlemagne and Pope Leo III (*sedit* 795–816) in the year 810.[183] This colloquium took place at the behest of the Synod of Aachen (809), which had remitted the problem of the inclusion of *filioque* to the pope. The minutes show that while Leo had in principle approved the creed's liturgical use in the Frankish Empire in accordance with the Roman model, it was only *read* in Rome (by the bishop), for catechetical purposes, and not – as was the case with the Franks – *sung* (by the congregation during mass). Leo III now demanded that Charlemagne's palace chapel also conform to the Roman rite in order to lessen the creed's normative force and to find a diplomatic solution to the problem of removing *filioque* from liturgical use.[184]

However, Walahfrid's testimony is more important for another reason: the creed was now no longer considered to be opening the Liturgy of the Eucharist, but rather as concluding that of the Word. In terms of the theology of liturgy, the creed's position *after the Gospel* instead of *before the preparations of the offerings* is the decisive factor. Here, too, the changed situation of the Church is evident: as I mentioned above, in the middle ages the entire population was (at least nominally) Christian, so there was no longer any need to verify whether members of the congregation belonged to the Church or not. This 'freed' the creed 'up' for other liturgical functions.

Eventually, the Order of the Mass of the Rhineland, which originated in St. Gallen, replaced all its predecessors in most parts of the western church at the turn of the millennium. It became the archetype of that order and, as regards the ordinary parts of the mass, remained in general use until the reforms of Vatican II. It was adopted not only in the countries north of the Alps but spread to Italy and Rome. It thus contributed to a harmonization of the western liturgy of the mass, promoted both by the Benedictine monks of Cluny and by the Ottonian emperors.[185]

Originally, this order of the mass contained no creed at all. In fact, as regards Rome, the creed was apparently inserted into the mass at the behest of the last Ottonian emperor, Henry II, who travelled to the city in 1014 for his coronation. Berno, abbot of Reichenau (d. 1048), witnessed this event, reporting that the Romans, when asked why it was not customary for them to recite the creed, replied that their church had never been sullied by the dregs of heresy, but had instead remained stalwart in the purity of the catholic faith according to Peter's doctrine.

---

183 For detailed treatment cf. below pp. 566–8.

184 Cf. *Ratio Romana de symbolo fidei*, esp. 6–8, 12, 25–26, 31–32 (FaFo § 848).

185 Cf. Meyer 1989, p. 204. The Ordo of the Rhineland was described in Luykx 1946/1947; Luykx 1961; Meyer 1989, pp. 204–8; Odenthal 2007(2011); Lang 2022, pp. 262–8.

This is why, they continued, those who had allowed themselves to become stained by heresy needed 'to practise that creed through frequent chanting (*illud symbolum saepius cantando frequentare*)'. In other words, here, too, the creed was primarily considered to be a test of orthodoxy. Henry then persuaded the pope that the creed also be chanted in the mass of Rome. However, Berno remained unsure as to whether the Romans had in fact retained this custom. In this context, Berno also mentioned that the Germans recited the creed after the Gospel.[186]

This corresponds with the observation that in the Ordo of the Rhineland, too, the creed was now placed after the gospel or after the homily (which was inserted after the gospel) and before the preparation of the offerings. In this order it was therefore also seen as being closely connected with the gospel, which explains why the General Prayer of the Church, public confession, and other elements were inserted into the liturgy only *after* the creed but before the offertory.[187]

Even though the exact details of how C^2 came to be introduced into the Liturgy of the Eucharist are only partially known, the overall picture is relatively consistent. The evidence suggests that:

(1) the creed used to instruct the catechumens and prepare them for baptism (probably C^1) 'immigrated' into the Divine Liturgy in the early sixth century, perhaps initially in Constantinople (where it was, in any case, quickly replaced by C^2);

(2) the recitation of the creed originally preceded the eucharist and constituted the opening of the Liturgy of the Eucharist;

(3) the creed was originally used to verify that the person attending the eucharist had been baptized and that their faith was orthodox;

(4) the creed was later considered the (orthodox) response of the congregation to the gospel and, therefore, concluded the Liturgy of the Word of God.

This meant that the creed's purpose in the liturgy changed significantly over the centuries: it no longer served only to verify the Christian beliefs of candidates for baptism, as had mostly been the case in the first centuries; rather, it was also used to control access to the eucharist and, increasingly, to demonstrate the orthodoxy of the faithful. The creed's significance changed once again when the creed linked back to the gospel reading that preceded it, viewed as the congregation's answer to

---

186 Cf. Berno, *Libellus de quibusdam rebus ad missae officium pertinentibus* 2 (FaFo § 854). Cf. Capelle 1951(1967), p. 78; Gemeinhardt 2002, pp. 313–16; Lang 2022, pp. 269–71.
187 For details cf. Jungmann 1951, vol. I, pp. 474–94; Jungmann 1962, vol. I, pp. 606–33. Cf. also Lumma/Vonach 2015, pp. 74 f. For more information on the various uses of the creed in the middle ages cf. below ch. 17.

this gospel. With this shift, the creed's function as a demonstration of orthodoxy faded. We will look at the liturgical use of the creeds in later periods in chapter 17.

11.3 The creed in the liturgy of hours

In eastern monasticism there is little evidence for the creed being part of the liturgy of hours. It is mentioned in the account of Abbots John and Sophronius visiting Abbot Nilus of Sinai, from the late sixth or early seventh century.[188] According to this report the creed was recited in Palestine on a Saturday night during an all-night vigil (ἀγρυπνία) between the *Gloria in excelsis* and the Lord's Prayer.[189] However, this practice was discontinued in the Byzantine church.[190] In the Coptic church the creed was and is recited at Morning prayer, at the Offering of Incense, and at the Psalmodia;[191] in the Ethiopic rite the creed appears in the cathedral office at the Solemn Vespers (Wāzēmā) and at matins (Sebehāta nagh), at the night office of the Sa'ātāt za-Gebs ('Horologion of the Copts'), and at the vespers of a Sa'ā-tāt found in cod. Rome, Biblioteca Apostolica Vaticana, et. 21 (s. XV–XVI).[192]

As regards Latin Christianity, in the period under discussion here,[193] only sparse information has come down to us: in the first half of the seventh century Fructuosus of Braga (d. c. 665) prescribes the creed's recitation (*Christianae fidei symbolum* – he does not specify which one) for compline. That means that, if a monk were to die at night, he would be able to lay before the Lord his 'pure (*puram*)' faith as he had just confessed it prior to going to sleep. This may point to the creed's anti-heretical function.[194] The *Antiphonary of Bangor* (s. VII *ex.*) contains the credal hymn *Spiritus diuinae lucis gloriae*, to be sung at Sunday matins, as well as a version of T which was to be recited at the office of nightfall (*ad initium noctis*, i.e. compline) together with the Lord's Prayer.[195] Likewise the *Book of*

---

188 Cf. Longo 1965/1966; Taft 1986, pp. 198–200, 274 f.

189 Cf. Longo 1965/1966, p. 252 (l. 25).

190 Cf. Taft 1986, pp. 277–83.

191 Cf. Taft 1986, pp. 253 f., 256. Cf. also above p. 443.

192 Cf. Taft 1986, pp. 263, 265, 267, 271; further details in Kidane 1998, esp. pp. 308–58. On the Syriac and Armenian tradition cf. also above pp. 430, 439.

193 On the development in the high middle ages cf. also below p. 572 and n. 14.

194 Cf. Fructuosus of Braga, *Regula complutensis* 1 (FaFo § 697). Dr Julia Winnebeck (Bonn) has kindly drawn my attention to Jonas of Bobbio, *Vita Columbani* 2,15, describing the death of the moribund nun Deurechilda. She recites the Lord's Prayer and the creed with the help of her abbess on her final evening and is then taken up to heaven.

195 Cf. *Antiphonale Benchorense* 12 and 35 (FaFo § 698).

Mulling (s. VIII/2) prescribes T together with the Lord's Prayer as part of the office.[196] Both texts are also found in medieval psalters.[197] In *c.* 820/823 Amalarius of Metz mentions them as part of the office of prime.[198] Benedict of Aniane (d. 821) ordered his monks to walk around the altar three times every day and, the first time, to recite the Lord's Prayer and the creed.[199] Haito of Basel (*sedit* 803–823) prescribed that T was to be replaced (or supplemented) by Ath on Sundays.[200]

196 Cf. *Book of Mulling* (cod. Dublin, Trinity Library, 60 (A. I. 15)), f. 94v; online: URL <https://digitalcollections.tcd.ie/concern/works/9019s695d?locale=en> (21/11/2023); cf. FaFo § 699.
197 Cf. below p. 572 and n. 14.
198 Cf. Amalarius of Metz, *Liber officialis* 4,2,22 (FaFo § 855).
199 Cf. Ardo Smaragdus, *Vita Benedicti Anianensis* 38.
200 Cf. Haito of Basel, *Capitulary*, ch. 4 (FaFo § 747b).

12 The Creed and the Liturgical Year

I have shown elsewhere that the earlier liturgical diversity in the Roman Empire came to be reduced, from approximately 380, to a standardized sequence of dominical feasts (Lord's feasts, devoted to Christ's life: Christmas/Epiphany, Easter, Ascension, and Pentecost), which were considered to be the liturgical core of the Church year and incorporated into a narrative structure.[1] They were accompanied by catecheses or sermons that spelled out the significance of each individual feast. This development occurred in the context of a broader trend towards the standardization of the liturgy, which likewise started around the turn from the fourth to the fifth centuries. The question that arises, then, is whether there is any connection between the increasingly standardized wording of the creed (and thus the establishment of orthodoxy by means of credal texts), and the introduction of a fully-fledged Church calendar.

In fact, there are both catechetical and liturgical indications of just such a connection. First, the creed, formulated to express a dogmatic consensus, was used in a liturgical context to instruct the community of Christians assembled there. This often happened on the dominical feasts as baptism was celebrated on these most solemn occasions (Easter being the principal, but not the only feast for such rites[2]). As we will see in the next chapter, baptism was accompanied by special catecheses which expounded upon repentance, baptism, and, of course, the creed. In this respect it is particularly significant that these rites were carried out, at least to a certain extent, in the presence of the entire congregation and that the concomitant catecheses were also addressed to that congregation as a whole.[3] This means that each year the tenets of the faith were recapitulated and expounded anew in the services leading up to baptism.

However, the relation between the creed and liturgy was not only a formal one; the interpretation of the dominical feasts itself was based on the creed. In this context it is interesting to take a closer look at the encyclical letter on baptism which Macarius, Bishop of Jerusalem (*sedit* 314–333), sent to the Armenian bishops. It is preserved only in Armenian fragments (cited by Ananias of Shirak, *fl. s.* VII).[4] In this letter Macarius commends Epiphany, Easter, and Pentecost as occasions for baptism, because the birth of the Lord was celebrated on Epiphany,

---

1 Cf. Kinzig 2011(2017), esp. pp. 332–9. This chapter is based on Kinzig 2011(2017), pp. 339–52. Cf. now also Edwards 2024.

2 Cf. Bradshaw 1993(1995); Rouwhorst 2022, col. 1001. Cf. also above p. 503 n. 129.

3 Cf. Kretschmar 1970, pp. 157, 240.

4 Cf. on this point Förster 2000, pp. 109–14; Förster 2007, pp. 148–52.

https://doi.org/10.1515/9783110318531-012

the Passion of Christ on Easter, and the descent of the Holy Spirit on Pentecost.[5] (Macarius does not yet appear to recognize either Christmas or Ascension as holy days.) This early document may already point to a close interrelation between the creed and major Christian feasts.

The *Apostolic Constitutions* is a vast collection of legal and liturgical documents which in its present form was compiled in Antioch in *c.* 380. It refers to the following days as days of rest for slaves: Sabbath, Sunday, Holy Week, Easter Octave, Ascension, Pentecost, Christmas, Epiphany (the Baptism of Christ), the feasts of the apostles, and the feasts of the martyrs. The rationales given for identifying these as the dominical feasts are clearly informed by the propositions of the creed:

> Let slaves rest [from their work] all the great week, and that which follows it – for the one is that of the Passion, and the other that of the Resurrection; and there is need they should be instructed who it is that died and rose again, or who it is permitted him [to suffer], and raised him again. Let them rest on the Ascension, because it was the conclusion of the dispensation by Christ. Let them rest at Pentecost, because of the coming of the Holy Spirit which was granted to those that believed in Christ. Let them rest on the festival of his birth, because on it the unexpected favour was granted to humankind, that Jesus Christ, the Word of God, should be born from the virgin Mary, for the salvation of the world.[6]

This interdependence between the creed and the Church calendar becomes ever more marked when we look at the festal sermons delivered after 381, so in close chronological proximity to the Council of Constantinople, and its western counterpart, the Synod of Aquileia (381). It is significant in this respect that the festal homily actually only developed in its entire baroque splendour at this juncture; the new liturgical structure demanded a corresponding development of the homily's rhetoric.[7] John Chrysostom is an especially interesting case in point. We encounter two lists of Christian holidays in his work, which differ from one another. They appear in two sermons that probably date to the year 386. The first list occurs in Chrysostom's first *Homily on Pentecost* in which he looks to clarify why it is incum-

---

5 Cf. Terian 2008, p. 83: 'Hence the ordinance of baptism of the holy font and the earnest observance of the three feasts during which those who are dedicated to God desire most eagerly to bring unto baptism those in darkness and to carry out the great form of the salutary mystery, which is carried out on these holy and prominent days. And this (form of mystery) they hasten to carry out with great eagerness in the holy places of Christ; which all Christians, those who fear Christ, must also carry out in the baptismal service on these (days): on the holy Epiphany of the Nativity of the Lord, and <on> the saving Easter of the life-giving passion of Christ, and on Pentecost full of grace – when the Divine descent of the life-giving Spirit overflowed among us.'

6 *Constitutiones apostolorum* 8,33,3–6 (tr. NPNF; altered).

7 On the wider context cf. Sachot 1994, cols. 160 f.; Kinzig 1997; Stewart-Sykes 2001; Boodts/ Schmidt 2022 (listing further literature).

bent upon the Christians, in contrast to the Jews (cf. Ex 23:17), to celebrate at all times; he uses the three main Christian feasts to justify this perpetual celebration. Epiphany is mentioned because 'God appeared on earth and dwelt among men, because God, the only-begotten child of God, was with us'. We proclaim the death of the Lord at Pascha, while we observe Pentecost 'because the Spirit came to us.'[8] In each case Chrystostom offers christological or pneumatological reasons for his argument.

Surprisingly, Chrysostom mentions neither Christmas nor the Ascension here. I concur with the argument often made that the reason lies in the fact that – in the very year in which Chrysostom wrote – the celebration of Christmas started in Antioch in the congregation of bishop Flavian where Chrysostom preached[9] as the latter does refer to all five dominical feasts in another festal homily he delivered that year. Here Christmas even serves as the source and grounds for all the other holidays:

> For a celebration is approaching, a feast which is the most august and awe-inspiring of all feasts and which one can no doubt call the 'capital' of all feasts (μητρόπολιν πασῶν τῶν ἑορτῶν). Which do I mean? The birth of Christ in the flesh. In it the Theophany, the Holy Pascha, the Ascension, and Pentecost have their origin and their foundation. For if Christ had not been born in the flesh, he would not have been baptized, which is Theophany; he would not have been crucified, which is the Pascha; and he would not have sent the Spirit, which is Pentecost. Just as different rivers flow from one source, so these feasts have been born for us.[10]

Christmas, Theophany/Epiphany (which Chrysostom now interprets as a celebration of the baptism of Christ), Pascha, Ascension, and Pentecost are named here and justified in christological or pneumatological terms in a way which approximates the creed.[11]

Turning to the west, we come across Filastrius who was the bishop of Brescia from the late 370s onwards. Sometime before 397 he composed an anti-heretical treatise (*Diuersarum haereseon liber*) in which he inveighed against liturgical heresies, among other things. According to Filastrius, the celebration of Epiphany on

---

8 John Chrysostom, *De sancta pentecoste 1*, 1 (PG 50, col. 454).

9 Cf. also Kelly 1995, p. 70.

10 John Chrysostom, *De beato Philogonio 3–4* (PG 48, cols. 752 f.). On the designation of Christmas as a μητρόπολις cf. also John Chrysostom, *De sancta pentecoste 2*, 1, where this title is accorded to Pentecost. In addition, Cabié 1965, pp. 185 f.

11 If one may draw conclusions from the mention of the feast of Ascension here, is it possible that this feast also was first introduced in Antioch in 386? Cf. Kinzig 2009, cols. 914 f. listing the earliest clear references for this feast's liturgical celebration.

6 January is in no way to be superseded by the celebration of Christmas on 25 December, as many *haeretici* suggest it should be. In this context he asserts:

> As is proper, for the sake of our salvation the following four days of the year have been established for the great feasts: first, [the day] on which he was born; then, [the day] on which he appeared, that is, twelve days later; thereafter, [the day] on which he suffered on Pascha; and finally, [the day] near Pentecost when he ascended into heaven, for this is his victorious consummation. But whoever ignores [or] overlooks one of these days might then also doubt the other days. Such a person does not have the entire truth at their disposal. For different joys from the Lord Christ have thus sprouted for us at the four seasons of each year, that is, when he was born, then, when he appeared, the third time, when he suffered and rose again and was seen, and the fourth time, when he ascended into heaven, such that we can celebrate this throughout the year without interruption, rejoicing at all times. Let us adhere to and preserve these [feasts] completely and without abbreviation.[12]

Filastrius clearly refers to the christological section of R/T. The liturgical year is modelled upon the stages of the earthly sojourn of Christ. We should also observe that, just as in R/T, Filastrius' comments on the major feasts make no mention of Jesus' teachings or miracles.

Finally, one may observe the same rhetorical strategy in a famous passage from a letter Augustine wrote to Januarius in 400. In this epistle Augustine grapples with the problem of defining which of the customs and ceremonies of the catholic Church are the most important and whence the justification for their existence is derived (*Epistula 54*). He argues that the sacraments of baptism and the eucharist were already established in the New Testament. Nonetheless, there is a whole array of customs which are not set forth in the Holy Scripture, but which still ought to be observed, on the grounds of tradition:

> As to those other things which we hold on the authority, not of Scripture, but of tradition, and which are observed throughout the whole world, it may be understood that they are held as approved and instituted either by the apostles themselves, or by plenary councils, whose authority in the Church is most useful, e.g., the annual celebration, by special solemnities, of the Lord's passion, resurrection, and ascension into heaven, and of the arrival of the Holy Spirit from heaven, and whatever else is in like manner observed by the whole Church wherever it has been established.[13]

Here once again a sequence of four dominical feasts is given, namely, Good Friday, Easter Sunday, Ascension, and Pentecost. Augustine goes on to say that the feasts in question either possess apostolic origins or go back to the general coun-

---

12 Filastrius, *Diuersarum haereseon liber* 140,2–4.
13 Augustine, *Epistula 54*, 1 (tr. NPNF; altered).

cils. This is remarkable insofar as – at the First Ecumenical Council – Constantine merely set Sunday as the day for celebrating the already much older feast of Easter (Pascha).[14] Yet as far as we can ascertain, no provisions were made to celebrate officially either Good Friday, Ascension, or Pentecost at that time or in Constantinople in 381. Whatever Augustine may have meant by those remarks, they proved to be highly consequential since they were incorporated into the *Decretum Gratiani* in the high middle ages and thus passed into canon law.[15]

So in this passage we once again witness that explicit connection between the content of Christian feasts and the creed; the Passion (Good Friday), Resurrection (Easter Sunday), Ascension, and the arrival of the Spirit on Pentecost recall the second and third articles of the creed. In Augustine we see what Hansjörg Auf der Maur called the 'isolating, historicizing view' of the Easter events which he considered typical of the development of the Easter cycle in the fourth and fifth centuries.[16]

In conclusion, the Church calendar played a key role in the use of the trinitarian creed being implemented across the Church. The newly unified faith as it was expressed in the creed was mapped onto the Church calendar so that it might be experienced by the worshippers in both the liturgy and mass. The Church year, based as it was on the principal christological feasts (Christmas/Epiphany, Easter, Ascension, and Pentecost), thus served to commemorate as well as to recapitulate the contents of that creed and consequently contributed to it becoming an instrument of dogmatic normalization. We will later see how the connection between the creed and the annual cycle of Christian feasts was spelled out at some length by medieval theologians in the west.[17]

---

14 For further discussion of this question cf. Kinzig 2006, pp. 366 f.; Kinzig, 'Sunday Observance', 2022, p. 322.

15 Cf. *Decretum Gratiani* 12,1,11.

16 Auf der Maur 1983, p. 82; cf. also Rexer 2003, p. 285 n. 26.

17 Cf. below pp. 576–80.

13 Preaching the Creed

During their catechumenate the converts were instructed in the basics of the Christian faith. It would be a worthwhile endeavour to analyze in detail the catechetical and rhetorical techniques which the bishops were using to introduce these catechumens to their new faith, to examine the content of their sermons, and to ask what they discussed and what they omitted and why. No such comprehensive analysis exists as yet. Within the framework of this book, a few summary remarks, illustrated by some examples, must suffice. In doing so, I will concentrate on sermons in Greek and Latin.[1]

Interestingly, the number of extant catecheses dealing with the creed differs considerably between east and west. In the east, although a great many baptismal homilies have come down to us, those explaining the creed (as opposed to Christian life or the rites of initiation) are surprisingly few in number. The first preserved examples are the eighteen *Catecheses ad illuminandos* of Cyril of Jerusalem, probably delivered during Lent 351. According to a scribal note in one codex they may have been taken down in writing by some listeners as they were being delivered.[2] They are based on the local creed J,[3] but do not strictly follow its sequence. Instead, the bishop begins with three discourses on the pernicious power of sin, on repentance, and on the purpose and nature of baptism. *Catechesis 4* which is entitled 'On the Ten Doctrines' contains a summary exposition of the creed, followed by remarks on the soul, the body, dress, the general resurrection (left out before), and Holy Scripture. Starting from a reading of Hebrews 11 *Catechesis 5* contains a general discourse on faith whereupon the creed was 'handed over'. *Catecheses 6–18* explain every clause of the creed in detail. A number of attempts have been made by scholars to explain Cyril's peculiar syllabus which need not detain us here.[4] If a scribal note at the end of the *Procatechesis*, which serves as an introduction to the whole series, is accurate, the discourses were delivered not to all catechumens, but only to those already baptized and the φωτιζόμενοι, the 'illuminated', i.e. those catechumens that had actually been accepted and registered for baptism in that year. It was explicitly forbidden to circulate copies of the sermons among ordinary catechumens and non-Christians.[5]

---

1 Expositions of the creed in languages other than Greek and Latin have been mentioned above in ch. 9.
2 Cf. Reischl/Rupp 1848/1860, vol. II, pp. 342 f. app. Cf. Anthony A. Stephenson in FaCh 61, pp. 1 f.
3 Cf. above ch. 5.5.
4 Cf. the literature quoted in FaFo § 147.
5 Cf. Reischl/Rupp 1848/1860, vol. I, p. 26.

https://doi.org/10.1515/9783110318531-013

Although there is further evidence attesting to the practice of preaching on the creed in the Greek church,[6] only one further set of discourses has come down to us:[7] the famous *Catechetical Homilies 1–10* by Theodore of Mopsuestia which were delivered in Antioch during Lent at some point before 392 and, like those of Cyril, seem to have been taken down in writing by one or more members of Theodore's audience.[8] Theodore opens his series with explanations of the nature of faith and of belief in the one Christian God which he sets in opposition to the Jews' refusal to believe in Jesus as the only-begotten Son of God and to the polytheism of the pagans (*Homilia Catechetica 1*). Like Cyril he then goes through the clauses of the creed (in his case N^{Ant1}) one by one. His second homily deals with the nature of the relationship between God the Father and his Son. Theodore then turns to the christological section of the creed which he discusses at some length in *Homilies 3–8*. His final two homilies focus on the Holy Spirit, ecclesiology, and eschatology. In terms of theology, Theodore expects much more from his audience than Cyril – certainly a result of the trinitarian debates that had taken place in the fourth century, but which may also indicate a much higher level of theological curiosity on the part of his listeners which Theodore felt compelled to satisfy.[9] He explains the basic trinitarian tenets in surprising detail, desirous to ensure they cannot be misinterpreted in the way of heretics like Arius.

Except for these two series we only possess individual sermons. Gregory of Nazianzus' *Homily 40* on baptism was preached in Constantinople before the *Traditio symboli* sometime between 379 and 381. This very lengthy sermon also includes a general introduction into the contents of the Christian faith, but Gregory does not cite the creed since he is delivering his discourse in front of an audience including those who are not yet entitled to hear it (be it because they have just entered the catechumenate or because they are non-Christians):

> This is all that may be divulged of the sacrament to you and that is not [kept] secret from the ears of the many. The rest you will learn within [the Church] by the grace of the holy Trinity; and those matters you should also hide within yourself, being secured with a seal.[10]

---

6 Cf., e.g., Egeria, *Peregrinatio* 46,3 (FaFo § 630).

7 John Chrysostom does not offer a detailed explanation of the creed in his *Baptismal Catecheses*, just an (incomplete) paraphrase and occasional comments on a few clauses. Cf. FaFo §§ 189, 597 and above pp. 497 f.

8 Cf. the literature cited in FaFo § 180. In addition, Toom 2021.

9 On these expectations cf. Olivar 1991, pp. 776–9.

10 Gregory, *Homilia 40*, 45 (FaFo § 179); cf. also § 628. On the commandment to keep the creed secret cf. below pp. 536 f.

By contrast, Nestorius (bishop of Constantinople 428–431) gives a full (albeit brief) explanation of the creed in a recently discovered sermon, which was delivered in 429 or 430.[11] After an introduction he turns to the creed itself and describes God's oneness in contrast to Greek polytheism. He then opens his exposition on the Trinity by explaining the title of 'Father'. This is followed by a christological section in which the author discusses, above all, the relationship of the uncreated and created nature in the incarnate Christ, whereas he only briefly touches on Christ's Second Coming. Rather, he goes on to discuss in detail the credal statements about the Holy Spirit and the Church, wanting above all to prove the equality of the Spirit with the Father and the Son and thus that of the three divine *hypostáseis*, to ward off any misunderstandings about the Spirit's origin. Belief in the one Church is read by the author as further evidence of the oneness of God, in contrast to the many temples of the pagans, which is thus integrated into the doctrine of the Trinity that is set out here. In the end, Nestorius turns his audience's attention back to the Trinity and the trinitarian status of the Spirit. Unfortunately, we have no information as to precisely when or on what occasion this homily was delivered.

By contrast, we know that another sermon from the same city was delivered during the baptismal service after the renunciation, the *Redditio*, and the recitation of the Lord's Prayer. Its author Proclus of Constantinople (*sedit* 434–446) explains the rites associated with baptism, but devotes the most important part of his sermon to a brief commentary on the creed (*Homilia 27*, 4–7). However, he only cites its first section while paraphrasing the remainder which unfortunately does not allow us to reconstruct the creed he uses.[12] Finally, a lengthy exposition of N by Theodotus of Ancyra (d. before 446), one of Nestorius' opponents at Ephesus 431, has so far received little attention. He quotes N in full in chapter 8 and continues to explain its individual clauses, defending it against a Nestorian interpretation.[13]

∗

Far more explanations of R/T have been preserved in Latin, whereas expositions of N or C^2 are rare: a commentary on N which may have been written in Northern Italy in the fourth century has been published by Turner.[14] Another commentary,

---

[11] Cf. Kinzig, 'Zwei neuentdeckte Predigten', 2020(2022), pp. 21–52.

[12] Cf. also Leroy 1967, pp. 184–7. The creed is probably C^1. Cf. above p. 498 and n. 93.

[13] Cf. Theodotus, *Expositio symboli Nicaeni* (PG 77, cols. 1313–48).

[14] Cf. *Commentarius in Symbolum Nicaenum* (Turner 1899–1939, vol. I 2/1, pp. 330–47, cf. FaFo § 135d5).

written after 400, focuses on N too, while also including the *Tomus Damasi*.[15] However, these are not sermons but learned theological treatises. There are no commentaries on N or C[2] at all from the period between the sixth and the early ninth century,[16] though we do find a few commentaries on Ath.[17]

As regards T a number of expositions in the form of question and answer survive, some of which were used to train priests.[18] By contrast, the laity was instructed by means of homilies (and some longer treatises which, like Rufinus' *Expositio*, may have nominally been addressed to a single individual, but aimed at a wider educated readership). However, in the Latin church we do not encounter any examples of a series of credal homilies spanning the entire period of Lent;[19] instead the creed is, by and large, explained only once on the occasion of the *Traditio symboli* and, sometimes, at the *Redditio*.[20]

The earliest example is probably that of Ambrose (*Explanatio symboli*, 374–397; cf. Fafo §§ 15, 256, 351), followed by treatises and sermons by Nicetas of Remesiana,[21] Rufinus,[22] Augustine,[23] Peter Chrysologus,[24] Quodvultdeus,[25] and Caesarius of Arles.[26] In addition, a number of anonymous texts attributed to Church fathers

---

15 Cf. *Commentarius alter in Symbolum Nicaenum siue potius in Tomum Damasi papae* = Pseudo-Jerome, *Epistula 17*, 1 (Turner 1899–1939, vol. I 2/1, pp. 355–63; cf. FaFo § 135d11).

16 Cf. Kinzig, 'Formation des Glaubens', 2019(2022), p. 244 n. 67.

17 Cf. Keefe, *Catalogue*, 2012, nos. 265, 267–71, 273, 275, 276, 277, 279. Some are, perhaps, post-Carolingian. Cf. also (Pseudo-)Caesarius of Arles, *Sermo 2* (FaFo § 656a).

18 Cf., e.g., FaFo §§ 31, 75, 76, 510, 526, 527, 528, 708, 714, 716, 730, 793, 794. They are to be distinguished from baptismal interrogations.

19 The Second Council of Braga (572) stated in canon 1 that during the twenty days prior to baptism 'the catechumens should be specifically taught the creed' (FaFo § 578). No such extended series of homilies survives.

20 A helpful survey of *explanationes* from Italy and Gaul is now found in Wheaton 2022, pp. 17–36.

21 Cf. Nicetas, *Competentibus ad baptismum instructionis libelli*, book V: *De symbolo* (c. 370–375?; cf. FaFo §§ 14, 324).

22 Cf. Rufinus, *Expositio symboli* (c. 404; cf. FaFo §§ 18, 254b, 638).

23 Cf. Augustine, esp. *Sermones 212–215*, the *De fide et symbolo*, and the *Sermo de symbolo ad catechumenos* (395–430; cf. FaFo §§ 19, 316e–g, k, l; 636d–g).

24 Cf. Peter Chrysologus, *Sermones 56–62* (431–458; cf. FaFo §§ 22, 259a–f).

25 Cf. Quodvultdeus, *Sermones 1–3* (437–453; cf. FaFo § 317a–c).

26 Cf. Caesarius of Arles, esp. *Sermones 9, 10* (perhaps inauthentic), *130* (503–542; cf. FaFo §§ 269, 271, 656f).

were also often copied, like, e.g., sermons said to be by Augustine or by Eusebius of Emesa.[27] There are many more homilies from the early middle ages.[28]

In such expositions baptismal candidates were regularly exhorted to memorize the creed and by no means to forget it,[29] and they were cautioned against making any changes to its wording. Thus Rufinus warns not to add even a single word to the creed, the Roman version of which was unsoiled by heresy and therefore authoritative.[30] Ambrose, too, maintains that the creed's wording was irrevocably fixed. In addition, he appeals expressly to the so-called 'canonization-formula' of the Book of Revelation (Rev 22:18–19)[31] and also invokes the creed's Petrine (that is, Roman) origin.[32] Finally, the legend of its apostolic origin, which had been systematically promulgated throughout the west since the time of Rufinus, served not only to authorize the creed, but also to safeguard its text.[33]

Augustine often began his expositions with an introduction to the meaning of the term *symbolum*, then quoted the full text of the creed, and finally repeated and commented on it, clause by clause (*Sermones 214; 213; De symbolo ad catechumenos*). On other occasions, after introductory words explaining *symbolum*, he succinctly interpreted the entire creed before it was 'handed over' to the baptizands (*Sermo 212*). At the *Redditio*, the creed was sometimes explained again (*Sermo 215*).

However, the sermon that was probably the most influential is a one usually ascribed to Leo the Great (*Tractatus 98*; cf. FaFo § 255g). It owes it prominence to the fact that it was included in the Roman *Old Gelasian Sacramentary* (FaFo

---

27 Cf. Pseudo-Augustine, *Sermones 237–239* (before 600; cf. FaFo § 275); Pseudo-Augustine, *Sermo 242* (s. VI–VII; cf. §§ 32, 276c); Pseudo-Eusebius of Emesa (*Collectio Eusebiana*), *Homiliae 9* and *10* (s. V–VI?; cf. §§ 30, 266).

28 Cf., e.g., the editions in Keefe 2002, vol. II; Westra 2002, pp. 409–538; Keefe, *Explanationes*, 2012; Kinzig, *Neue Texte I*, 2017, pp. 3–159; Kinzig, 'Glauben lernen', 2020(2022). A helpful survey of the relevant Carolingian manuscripts is found in Keefe, *Catalogue*, 2012.

29 Cf. Ambrose, *Explanatio symboli* 2 (FaFo § 351a). 9 (§ 15a3); Rufinus, *Expositio symboli* 2 (§ 18); Augustine, *Sermones 58*, 13 (§ 636b2); *212*, 2 (§ 19a); *214*, 1 (§ 636e); *215*, 1 (§ 636f); id., *Sermo de symbolo ad catechumenos* 1,1–2 (§ 636g); Nicetas of Remesiana, *Competentibus ad baptismum instructionis libelli* 2, frg. 4 (§ 625); Peter Chrysologus, *Sermones 56*, 3. 5 (§ 22a1 and 3); *57*, 16 (§ 22b); *58*, 2 (§ 22c); *59*, 1. 18 (§ 22d); *60*, 18 (§ 22e2); *61*, 2. 15 (§ 22f); *62*, 3 (§ 22g). Furthermore, Leo the Great, *Tractatus 98* (§ 255g) and the *Missale Gallicanum Vetus*, no. 27 (§ 678a1). For the east, cf., e.g., the Council of Laodicea, canons 46 and 47 (§ 562b and c) and Cyril, *Catechesis ad illuminandos 5*, 12 (FaFo § 624a); *18*, 21 (§ 624b). Cf. also Berzon 2021.

30 Cf. Rufinus, *Expositio symboli* 3 (FaFo § 638).

31 On this formula cf. also above p. 327.

32 Cf. Ambrose, *Explanatio symboli* 7 (FaFo § 15a2). Similarly, Pseudo-Facundus of Hermiane, *Epistula fidei catholicae in defensione trium capitulorum* 12 (§ 37).

33 Cf. above ch. 5.4.

§ 675a)[34] and consequently also incorporated in later sacramentaries.[35] Leo first exhorted the baptizands to embrace the faith with all their heart, because this is how justification is received. He then invited them to come and receive the creed as inspired by the Lord and written by the apostles under the guidance of the Holy Spirit. Finally, they were admonished to learn the confession by heart, but not to write it down. In the second part Leo emphasized once again that the creed was inspired by God and that it could be understood and learned by everyone. Then the content of the confession was briefly recapitulated. At the end came an admonition to learn the creed 'without changing its wording' (*nullo mutato sermone*). *Tractatus 98* is quite brief, and, concerning its place in the above-mentioned sacramentaries, it is not quite clear whether it is to be regarded as a regular component of the liturgy (to which a longer explanation may have been added) or only as a kind of placeholder or perhaps simply a cue for a longer explanation. Given that this particular order was intended for the baptism of infants and that their parents and godparents had already been instructed in the faith, a more detailed explanation may also have been deemed superfluous.

Later western explanations of the faith are rather schematic. Although a great number of them have been published in recent years, they have not yet received the attention they deserve.[36] They invariably begin with an explanation of the term *symbolum*, before turning to expound the individual clauses of R/T. By and large, these later explanations do not contain much 'high' theology. However, as they reflect catechesis, as it were, 'on the ground', as it may have happened in chapels across the countryside in late antiquity and the early middle ages, they may have been at least as influential as the discourses given by bishops in the city cathedrals. Again, the surviving representatives of the genre of explanations of the faith, especially from the early middle ages, are often astonishingly short, indeed in parts they consist of nothing more than barely comprehensible key words. This indicates that the preacher extemporized during his explanation. Therefore it is impossible to draw any conclusions solely from the length of the surviving texts about the actual duration of these sermons.

In the context of this book, it may suffice to introduce two examples of the western genre of *Explanatio symboli*, one from the sixth century, the other from the ninth century; the first from a famous preacher, the second from an anonymous author.

∗

---

34 Cf. also *Ordo Romanus XI* (s. VI/2; FaFo § 808a).

35 Cf. *Sacramentaries of Angoulême* (768–781; FaFo § 796a), *Gellone* (790–800; § 797a, d), and *Reims* (c. 800; § 799a). In addition, Jesse of Amiens, *Epistula de baptismo* (802; § 780a); *Pontifical of Donaueschingen* (s. IX ex.; § 683a).

36 Cf. above p. 527 n. 28 and Kinzig, 'Formation des Glaubens', 2019(2022); Van Rhijn 2022, pp. 73–7.

A sermon by Bishop Caesarius was so influential that it eventually came to be adopted as a model catechesis in the baptismal liturgy of the Gallican rite, continuing to be used at least into the ninth century (*Sermo 9*; cf. FaFo § 271a).[37] Caesarius began his catechesis by inculcating the importance of faith in his listeners. Only those who held fast to faith in this life would attain eternal life. Caesarius then warned against trying to explore the divine secrets, since our limited intellect is incapable of grasping the heavenly mystery. Subsequently, he solemnly recited the entire creed three times (corresponding to the number of persons of the Trinity) and reminded his listeners that it should not be written down but learned by heart.

After this had been completed, Caesarius set out to explain what his audience had just heard. First, he spoke briefly about the relationship between God the Father and God the Son. The Son's generation seems to have been a matter of discussion in his congregation, for Caesarius emphasizes that one should not speculate about the way in which the Father had begotten the Son. Rather, such generation was clearly proven in the Bible and therefore to be believed, not discussed.

The bishop then immediately turned to the christological section, explaining the name of Jesus Christ and why he was called 'only-begotten' (*unigenitum*). The words 'who was conceived of the Holy Spirit' (*qui conceptus est de spiritu sancto*) then gave rise to a short digression on that very Spirit, who is the creator of the flesh and temple of the Lord. Caesarius succinctly explained why the Spirit had to be regarded as one person of the Trinity.

The preacher postponed further interpretation until the following day. It appears that on that second day he no longer preached the sermon himself, but entrusted it to one of his priests, who seems to have read out what his bishop had written down. Caesarius answered the famous question as to why Pontius Pilate was named in the creed by saying that this clearly established the historicity of the one Christ as opposed to false saviours. Furthermore, he emphasized the factuality of the death and resurrection of the Son of God. The resurrection had taken place not until the third day, thus proving that Christ had in actual fact died. Explaining Christ's 'sitting at the right', he rejected the idea that it might be a physical sitting beside God. Instead, sitting at his right signified that there was no 'leftness' (i.e. 'wrongness' – *sinisteritas*, a rare word) in Christ.

---

[37] It formed part of the *Missale Gallicanum Vetus*; cf. Mohlberg/Eizenhöfer/Siffrin 1958, pp. 17, l. 31 – 21, l. 4 (nos. 62–65). The following remarks are based on Kinzig, 'Das Apostolische Glaubensbekenntnis', 2018(2022), pp. 290–2.

The bishop then turned to the pneumatological section, underlining the Spirit's full divinity. Here, too, he dispensed with more detailed trinitarian considerations and merely stated with great emphasis that all divine persons were of equal power and dignity. Furthermore, the other clauses of this section were mentioned, but Caesarius only commented on eternal life. This had its place at the end of the creed because faith was rewarded by the eternity of this new life. Thus the order of the creed leads the believer up to the summit where eternal salvation awaits.

The brevity and incompleteness of Caesarius' exposition is striking. Numerous clauses are not commented on: he says nothing about the Father's omnipotence or creative activity. The virgin birth, crucifixion, and burial do not seem, in his view, to require explanation. The coming of Christ to judgement is mentioned, but remains unexplained, too. Nor does he have anything to say about the holy catholic Church, the communion of saints, or the resurrection of the flesh although these clauses were all contained in his creed.

This is different in other credal explanations: the fleshly resurrection of Christ and of the faithful in particular was the subject of much comment, as was the question of whether one had to also believe 'in' the Church or whether the mention of the Church was to be understood merely as an explanation of the wider work of the Holy Spirit, an interpretation found in the majority, but by no means the entirety, of credal sermons.[38]

Incidentally, Caesarius does not always seem to have interpreted the creed at the *Traditio symboli*. Thus, according to its title, *Sermo 130* was also intended to be read on this occasion. This sermon, however, is about the prophet Elisha who is depicted as a prototype of Christ. Caesarius then exhorts the faithful to preserve 'sweetness of love, purity of heart, and chastity of body (*dulcedinem caritatis, puritatem cordis et castitatem corporis*)' and also to teach their own children to do so.[39] Likewise, *Sermo 201* served as a model sermon for the *Traditio*: it instructs the faithful to lead a chaste life in preparation for the upcoming feast of Easter and warns against drinking too much alcohol during the festivities. In a brief discourse entitled *Ad competentes post traditum symbolum* ('To the candidates after the handing over of the creed'; cf. FaFo § 654) the ten Egyptian plagues are compared to the struggle against demons at the Christian initiation; it was probably written in North Africa in *c.* 500 and attributed to Fulgentius of Ruspe. The *Traditio* therefore not necessarily had to be accompanied by teaching the creed's contents. Possibly, the bishop did not consider it necessary to instruct the parents

---

38 Cf. above pp. 174 f.
39 Caesarius, *Sermo 130*, 3. Cf. also id., *Sermo 130*, 5 (FaFo § 656f).

and godparents, who had already been baptized, at infant baptisms, especially since they, as members of the congregation, frequently witnessed such paraenesis in any case.

∗

The second western exposition which is presented here by way of illustration is preserved, more or less complete, in six manuscripts in two slightly different recensions.[40] Its titles as preserved in that tradition (*Apertio symboli* // *Sermo antequam symbolum traditur*) make it clear that the sermon was delivered in the context of the *Traditio symboli*.

It begins with an explanation of the term *symbolum* that differs in the two recensions. According to the more detailed version of cod. I, *symbolum* means 'token' (*indicium*) or 'collection (or pooling) of money' (*conlatio pecuniae*): 'token', since it indicates the 'truth, through which we can attain eternal life'; 'collection/ pooling of money', however, as in payment for a ticket for a ship's passage. The required sum would be pooled on the ship and jealously guarded by the passengers until arrival, then handed over to the ship's owner. This explanation is followed by a concise allegorical interpretation, which amounts to the apostles having, as it were, 'pooled' the creed in order to preserve the church on its journey.

The second part of the text is the creed itself, whose clauses one manuscript assigns to the individual apostles. A concluding sentence extant in four manuscripts, however, also indicates a certain confusion with regard to the exact sequence of the apostles, for the author confesses that he cannot be certain about assigning the creed's clauses to the individual apostles.[41]

In the third part, the interpretation of the individual clauses begins, each of which comprises only a few lines. First, the problem of the Godhead's simultaneous unity and Trinity is explained, yet not by recourse to the relevant dogmatic terms, but by two analogies. The sun consists of three parts: the sun itself, its light, and its heat – and yet everything forms a single whole. The same is true of the three parts of the soul: memory (*memoria*), talent (*ingenium*), and intellect (*intellectus*). In the Bible, when a divine person is mentioned, the whole Godhead is always meant. Furthermore, God is omnipotent because he cannot err, die, or sin.

---

40 The text, a German translation, and a commentary are found in Kinzig, *Neue Texte I*, 2017, pp. 18–65; cf. also FaFo §§ 44, 47, 263, 332, 387, 418. The following remarks are based on Kinzig, 'Formation des Glaubens', 2019(2022), pp. 241–6.

41 Cf. *Apertio symboli* 2,13 (codd. M Z Q V): 'Ordo dicentium, quis primus de apostolis hoc dixit, difficile inuenitur.'

Next, the name of Jesus Christ is briefly explained. 'Jesus' is a proper name, whereas Christ means the 'anointed one'. He is to be regarded as both man and God. The author expends a little more effort on the explanation of the word *unicus*. Although Adam, according to Lk 3:38, and John, according to Jn 19:26–28, were also called the Son of God and of Mary respectively, only Christ was the 'natural' Son, whereas the others were adopted. The designation 'Lord' (*dominum*) refers to the divinity of the Son; the addition *nostrum* on the other hand to his humanity.

As regards his birth through the Holy Spirit and the Virgin Mary (the author obviously does not yet know conception through the Spirit), the idea that Christ could have had two fathers, namely God the Father and the Spirit, is first rejected. Instead, the Spirit is relegated to the position of a helper and cooperator in the birth (*per administrationem spiritus sancti et ipso cooperante*). Mary's virginity was the reason why she was chosen to give birth to the Saviour. Her faith is particularly emphasized. The flesh of Christ was sinless. Pontius Pilate is mentioned in order clearly to pinpoint the date of Christ's passion (i.e. 'at the time of this king' (*sic*)) and to exclude confusion with the antichrist. The author mentions the crucifixion, death, and burial only briefly; the descent into the underworld was obviously not part of the creed interpreted and is not mentioned. According to Hos 6:3, the resurrection of Jesus serves as a model for the eschatological resurrection of the faithful. At the request of the patriarchs and prophets, Christ took on the 'humanity of the flesh' (*humanitatem carnis*) and thus ascended to heaven. There he sits in his human flesh at the right hand of the Father, that is, in the state of eternal life. The Second Coming and the Last Judgement are explained in relative detail: Christ will preside over the court of the apostles and judge sinful humanity.

This is followed by explanations about the Holy Spirit. Again, these are kept very brief. The function of the Holy Spirit within the Trinity is to give life, the author says, referring to Rom 11:36 and the beginning of Genesis (1:1–2). The Spirit precedes the Church because the Church is enlightened by the Spirit. It is very important to the preacher that one should not believe 'in' the Church, but instead confess that it exists as a 'holy' Church. The catholic Church is the place where sins are forgiven, whereas this is impossible in the church of the heretics. The author expects the resurrection of the flesh, which he understands to be the bodily resurrection of all people. The conclusion is again unclear – apparently, the preacher assumes that the deceased already receive rewards and punishments now, but that these only affect their *souls*. After the resurrection, however, the soul *and body* will both receive their due reward. How this idea relates to that of the Last Judgement, as it was confessed in the christological section, is not explained further.

Taken as a whole this explanation is no more than a collection of cues (and, what is more, written in a Latin style that is faulty by classical standards). Its unevenness may result from the piecing together of different sources. It is also possible that the brevity of many such credal expositions can be explained by the fact that they were originally glosses in the margin of the credal text written in the centre of a page.[42] Overall, it is very noticeable that the theological debates of the fourth and fifth centuries have left hardly any traces in this text. The doctrine of the Trinity is only hinted at, and the christological statements make no discernible reference, for example, to the Definition of Faith at Chalcedon, let alone to the decisions of later councils.

Such theological scarcity is not necessarily typical. Other *Expositiones* contain longer explanations of the doctrine of the Trinity or more extensive theological reflections on individual articles of the creed. However, they are rarely original, but usually taken from patristic authors. While the quality of instruction certainly varied, the contents of the faith were consistently understood as fixed and unquestionable.

A *lingua catechetica* developed as a result of referring back to a narrow canon of reference texts, which were cited in ever new variations, a language which was mainly derived from a limited fund of theological formulae – as in the example cited – and only in exceptional cases showed traits of kerygmatic originality. The ubiquity of this formulaic *lingua catechetica* also makes the dating and localization of the sermons, most of which have survived anonymously or pseudonymously, difficult.

*

All in all, preachers (both western and eastern) by and large attempted to speak in a plain style that was easy to understand for their audiences, while using all the rhetorical devices at their disposal (metaphors, analogies, word play, alliterations, anaphoras, epiphoras, etc.).[43] Their theological reasoning, however, spans a wide range of complexity, from the aforementioned brief anonymous address to the doctrinally very elaborate sermons by Theodore and Nestorius. Later we have evidence that Ath was also used in catechesis: for example, an anonymous explanation of baptism from Mainz, written before *c.* 850, cites clauses from Ath.[44]

However, the theological quality of credal sermons in the west should not be overestimated. Their theology is often rudimentary and the sloppiness of many

---

42 An example is found in cod. St. Gallen, Stiftsbibliothek, 27, pp. 690–2; cf. Westra 2002, pp. 474–9; Keefe, *Catalogue*, 2012, no. 75 and FaFo § 280. In addition, cf. already Wiegand 1904, p. 12 n. 2.
43 Cf. also Auksi 1995; Kinzig 1997.
44 Cf. FaFo § 791.

notes (which are hardly intelligible) suggests that their authors did not fully understand what they were supposed to talk about. After all, not all priests were able to write sermons,[45] and they often also lacked the necessary tools like access to Bibles or theological literature. This is even true for the Carolingian period when attempts were made to improve the theological education of priests, attempts which have in recent years been described as a success.[46] By contrast, it may be useful to recall the preface of an anonymous author to his commentary on Ath (the so-called 'Oratorian Commentary'[47]), probably from the beginning of the ninth century, which was written in a much more sombre mood:

> You have charged me to explain in a kind of commentary that little work on the faith which is recited everywhere in our churches and on which our priests reflect more frequently than on the other works, by means of sentences from the holy fathers. For you are concerned about the priests of our diocese, who in no way have sufficient books, but rarely and only with difficulty acquire psalters, lectionaries, and missals, with the help of which they can celebrate holy mass and the offices. But because, owing to the lack of books, neither the zeal to read nor to learn is fostered in most, it is your desire that they should be induced at least to reflect on this interpretation of the faith, so as to know and understand a little more of God. For the greatest ruin for all is that the priests, who should have been instructing the people of God, have themselves proved not to know God.[48]

We do not know whether its author succeeded.

---

45 On the religious knowledge of priests in late antiquity and the early middle ages cf. the sceptical view in Kinzig, 'Formation des Glaubens', 2019(2022), pp. 246–59.

46 Cf. esp. Mitalaité 2013; Patzold 2020, pp. 305–88; and, more generally, Van Rhijn 2022.

47 Edited by Ommanney 1880, pp. 327–55.

48 Codex Vaticanus Reg. lat. 231 (*c.* 820–30), f. 152v, ed. Keefe, *Explanationes*, 2012, p. VI n. 2: 'Iniunxisti mihi illud fidei opusculum, quod passim in ecclesiis recitatur, quodque a presbyteris nostris usitatius quam caetera opuscula meditatur, sanctorum Patrum sententiis quasi exponendo dilatarem, consulentes parochiae nostrae presbyteris, qui sufficienter habere libros nullo modo possunt, sed uix et cum labore sibi psalterium, lectionarium uel missalem acquirunt, per quos diuina sacramenta uel officia agere queant; et quia cum inopia librorum plerisque neque studium legendi aut discendi suffragatur, idcirco uultis ut saltem hanc fidei expositionem meditari cogantur, ut aliquanto amplius de Deo possint sapere et intelligere. Quia maxima omnium ista pernicies est, quod sacerdotes, qui plebes Dei docere debuerant, ipsi Deum ignorare inueniuntur.' Cf. also Burn 1896, p. LIV. Furthermore, Keefe, *Catalogue*, 2012, no. 275, where she suggests Theodulf of Orléans as author (cf. also Burn 1896, pp. LII–LIII).

14 Creeds in Daily Life

Where did a Christian encounter the creed and what did he or she 'do' with it?[1] Let us look for the answer in Arles in southern Gaul in the first few decades after the year 500, because here the evidence is particularly rich. Bishop Caesarius ascended the episcopal throne in 502 and in fact dominated ecclesiastical life across Gaul in what were politically uncertain times for four decades until his death in 542. We should not assume that infant baptism was the norm at that time; instead a mixture of infant baptism and that of adult converts is more likely, as paganism was by no means extinct in the Gaul of the early sixth century.[2] In addition, it was quite common to postpone baptism because of the significance of this event in the life of every Christian.

As we saw in the chapter on the creed and baptism the creed's primary *Sitz im Leben* was pre-baptismal catechesis.[3] The profession of faith was 'handed over' to the candidates in a solemn ceremony at the end of their catechumenate. This *Traditio symboli* was accompanied by a credal instruction by the local bishop. The candidates then had to learn it by heart and solemnly 'return' it, i.e. recite it, during the ceremony of *Redditio symboli* on one of the following weekends. In Arles, the *Traditio symboli* took place on Palm Sunday.[4] Either Christian parents would have brought their children to be baptized, or another adult might have taken responsibility for the child of a relative as sponsor. In the latter case, the task of holding the infant over the baptismal font would have fallen to the sponsors, who would have been admonished to instruct their charge in the creed and the Lord's Prayer.[5] If it had been their own child, the bishop would have charged them in the *Traditio symboli* with teaching their son or daughter, indeed their whole *familia* (which included any servants), these two key texts.[6]

On the evidence of the sermons of the Bishop of Arles, the creed was a daily companion in all situations of life. After it had been first 'handed over' the new converts were to carry it home in their minds and recite it several times a day in order to memorize it fully.[7] Nicetas of Remesiana asked his listeners to recite the confession twice a day, in the morning after getting up and in the evening before

---

1 For what follows cf. also Kinzig 2018(2022), pp. 289–96.
2 Cf., e.g., Caesarius, *Sermo 84*, 6; *225*, 6. Survival of Gallo-Roman religion: Klingshirn 1994(1995), pp. 47–51, 213–15, 218–26.
3 Cf. above ch. 11.1. On baptismal practice in Arles cf. Saxer 1988, pp. 512–25.
4 On the date cf. Synod of Agde (506), canon 13 (FaFo § 573).
5 Cf. Caesarius, *Sermo 229*, 6 (FaFo § 656h).
6 Cf. Caesarius, *Sermo 13*, 2 (FaFo § 656d); *130*, 5 (§ 656f).
7 Cf. the references in FaFo § 656.

https://doi.org/10.1515/9783110318531-014

going to bed;[8] for Ambrose, a morning recitation was sufficient.[9] Augustine could sometimes follow Nicetas' practice,[10] but he could also be more rigorous in his demands:

> So you have received and recited that which you always ought to retain in mind and heart, which you should recite in your beds, which you should think about in the streets, and which you should not forget during your meals; in which your hearts should be awake, even when your bodies are asleep.[11]

Curiously, when it comes to Arles, we learn next to nothing about the *Redditio symboli*, the traditional recitation of the creed. Even the Synod of Agde (506), convened by Caesarius himself, which furnishes us with the obligatory date of the *Traditio* in the church year (Palm Sunday), does not mention the *Redditio*.[12] Caesarius notes more or less in passing that those baptized who were old enough should recite the creed on their own, while with younger children someone else might have to step in.[13]

Many church fathers strongly warned against ever writing down the creed, lest it fell into the hands of the uninitiated and enemies of Christianity, who might then use it for sinister purposes.[14] Ambrose even admonished his listeners to recite it silently in church, because when they revisited it aloud in the presence of believers, they might later also revisit it 'among the catechumens or heretics'.[15] It was to be kept confidential because it was a text which explained Christian understanding of their divinity, and there was a certain fear that non-Christians (whether Jews or pagans) might use it for polemical purposes,[16] such as accusing Christians of venerating three gods or poking fun at the virgin birth, the crucifixion, and the resurrection.[17] But other reasons are also mentioned. Ambrose says in this regard:

---

8 Cf. Nicetas, *Competentibus ad baptismum instructionis libelli* 2, frg. 4 (FaFo § 625).
9 Cf. Ambrose, *De uirginibus* 3,20 (FaFo § 15b).
10 Cf. Augustine, *Sermo 58*, 13 (FaFo § 636b2); id., *Sermo de symbolo ad catechumenos* 1,1 (§ 636g).
11 Augustine, *Sermo 215*, 1 (FaFo § 636f).
12 Cf. Synod of Agde (506), canon 13 (FaFo § 573).
13 Cf. Caesarius, *Sermo 130*, 5 (FaFo § 656f).
14 Cf. above p. 527 n. 29.
15 Ambrose, *Explanatio symboli* 9 (FaFo § 15a3).
16 Cf., e.g., Cyril of Jerusalem, *Catechesis ad illuminandos 6*, 29; Peter Chrysologus, *Sermo 56* (*De symbolo I*), 5 (FaFo § 22a3); *58* (*De symbolo III*), 2 (§ 22c); *60* (*De symbolo V*), 18 (§ 22e2); *61* (*De symbolo VI*), 15 (§ 22f2).
17 Cf. Cook 2002, pp. 337–9 who uses T as a helpful template to organize the pagan objections.

You are able to memorize it better if it is not written down. For what reason? Listen to me! For what you write down is safe insofar as you [can] re-read it; as a result you do not undertake to review it by daily meditation. But what you do not write down, you daily begin to review out of fear that you might lose it.[18]

Rufinus says that the reason not to write it down was 'that it may be certain that no one has learned [these words] by reading (as is sometimes the custom even with unbelievers) but has learned them from the tradition of the apostles'.[19] Augustine supplies a rather refined exegetical reasoning:

> But the fact that it was thus collected and edited in a certain form and is not permitted to be written down recalls God's promise when he announced the New Testament through the prophet, saying, 'This is the testament that I will establish for them after those days, says the Lord, through putting my laws in their mind. And I will write them on their hearts' [Jer 31:33]. In order to signify this, the creed is learned by ear; it is not written on tablets or any other material, but on the hearts [cf. 2Cor 3:3]. He 'who has called you to his kingdom and glory' [1Thess 2:12] will make sure that, once you are reborn, his grace is also written upon your hearts through the Holy Spirit so that you may love what you believe, and that the faith may 'operate through the love' [Gal 5:6] in you, and that you may thus please the Lord God, the dispenser of all good things, yet not [pleasing him] because you fear his punishment like a slave, but because you love his justice like a free-born.[20]

Peter Chrysologus thought that 'paper and letter indicate debt obligations (*cauta*) rather than grace':

> But where that divine gift, the grace of God, exists, faith suffices to serve as a contract (*pactum*).[21]

However, the creed was not deliberately kept secret. As far as we can see, there was no *Disciplina arcani* which obliged believers to keep the rites of a cult from the uninitiated, as is the case in many mystery cults (of whose rites we are, as a consequence, poorly informed).[22] Creeds were the subject of sermons addressed to converts *before* their initiation through baptism and they *were* written down for that purpose. Still, in the west the copies of creeds preserved in the early medieval codices are presumably all – apart from liturgical books – from textbooks to train the clergy or from manuals for priests, but not for or by lay people.[23] One

---

18 Ambrose, *Explanatio symboli* 9 (FaFo § 15a3).
19 Rufinus, *Expositio symboli* 2 (FaFo § 18).
20 Augustine, *Sermo 212*, 2 (FaFo § 19a).
21 Peter Chrysologus, *Sermon 57* (*De symbolo II*), 16 (FaFo § 22b). Cf. also *62* (*De symbolo VII*), 3–4 (§ 22g) where this idea is elaborated at some length.
22 Cf., e.g., esp. Auffarth 2013, cols. 453 f.; Metzger 2010(2018).
23 On these types of codices, which in recent years have received much scholarly attention, cf. Keefe 2002, vol I, pp. 23–6, 28–35; Patzold 2016; Kinzig, 'Formation des Glaubens', 2019(2022), p. 246;

example where the creed may have been written down by a lay person in North Africa will be considered in the next chapter. I have mentioned previously the unusual rite described in the *Expositio breuis antiquae liturgiae Gallicanae* in which the creed was written down on a sheet of paper which was then laid out on a bed of feathers in the church.[24]

By the early middle ages creeds were also used and recited in public, outside worship. A telling and rather sinister example is found in an anti-Jewish law by the Visigoth king Egica (r. 687–702) who persisted in attempts to suppress Judaism by forced conversion. He enacted a law prescribing how to proceed if there was any doubt whether anyone a Christian did business with had truly converted from Judaism to Christianity:

> [. . .] if any Christian, unaware of their conversion, should wish to buy anything from them, he shall not be allowed to do this until [the converted Jew] says that he is entirely Christian, and recite to him before witnesses the Lord's Prayer or the Apostles' Creed, and eat the food of Christians or accept it willingly like all true worshippers of Christ.[25]

If this law was followed at all, this recitation seems to have taken place in public, rather than in a church.[26]

*

In the east, the rules were even more lax: the Council of Laodicea prescribed that those who came to be baptized had to memorize the creed, but did not forbid to write it down.[27] Indeed, here creeds were recorded in writing to facilitate religious education – whether only in a monastic setting or also outside (for example, as an aide-mémoire for catechumens) is unknown. We possess several copies of N and C^2 on papyrus (at least some of which seem to have formed part of codices),[28]

Kinzig, 'Ethik', 2019(2022), pp. 282 f.; Kinzig, 'Glauben lernen', 2020(2022); Patzold 2020, pp. 305–88; many articles by Carine van Rhijn and her synthesis in van Rhijn 2022, esp. pp. 52–83; Stein 2023. A seventh-century slate tablet originating from the Province of Salamanca and containing fragments of C^2 in awkward Latin may also belong in the context of theological training; cf. Ruiz Asencio 2004.

24 Cf. above p. 492.

25 *Lex Visigothorum* 12,2,18 (tr. Linder 1997, p. 283; slightly altered).

26 For wider background cf. Kinzig, 'Die Verpflichtungserklärungen', 2019(2022).

27 Cf. Council of Laodicea, canons 46 and 47 (FaFo § 562b, c).

28 N: P.Oxy. XVII 2067 (TM 64762; Oxyrhynchos, *s.* V); C^2: P.Colon. inv. 684 (TM 64739; *s.* V); P.Oxy. XV 1784 (TM 64771; Oxyrhynchos, *s.* V); P.Naqlun inv. 20/87 = P.Naqlun 2 18 (TM 65097; *s.* VI); P. Cairo JE 65738 (TM 65175; *s.* VII *in.*). Other creeds: FaFo § 146 (Dêr Balyzeh Papyrus); § 168 (P.

ostraca,[29] a parchment leaf,[30] and wooden tablets[31] which may have been used for that purpose.[32] In Byzantine times both N and C^2 were even present in inscriptions as can be seen from two mutilated examples from Ephesus.[33] Monks also wrote the creed on the wall in or near their cells or monasteries.[34]

There may be another reason why in the west, in contrast, the warning against recording the creed seems to have been largely heeded. Indeed, it is perhaps no coincidence that no amulets with verses from the creed have survived from the west. As we will see in the next chapter, instead, the creed was widely treated as a magic spell that initiates could only access through oral tradition.

Palau Rib inv. 68; TM 61458; IV *ex./*V *in.*). In some cases a use as amulet or phylactery may also be possible.

29 C^2 (in Greek; for ostraca in Coptic cf. above p. 443): Jerusalem, Israel Museum no. 69 74 312 (TM 65186; *s.* VI); O.Heid. Inv. 419 (= O.Heid. 437; TM 65232; *s.* VI–VII); Jerusalem, Israel Museum no. 87 56 560 (TM 65317; *s.* VII *in.*?); P.Gen. IV 154 (TM 128550; Thebes, Deir el-Bahari, *s.* VIII/1; ed. Paul Schubert in Gaffino-Mœri et al. 2010, pp. 63 f.).

30 Cf. P.Lond. Copt. 155 Fr. 2 (TM 65445; Asyut, *s.* VII–VIII; the creed is C^2 in Greek). Another attestation of C^2 on parchment which is as yet unpublished is mentioned in Łajtar 2018, p. 42.

31 N: O.Deir el-Bahari 16 (TM 68649; Thebes, Deir el-Bahari, *s.* VI–VII; ed. Delattre, 'Symbole', 2001); C^2: T.Med. Inv. 71.00 A (TM 65065; *s.* VI). For editions of all texts where no reference is given cf. FaFo, vol. I, p. 517.

32 On the use of ostraca in religious education cf. Ullmann 1996, p. 194; Römer 2003, p. 190; Lougovaya 2020, p. 121. For non-literary evidence in Coptic cf. above pp. 443–5.

33 I.Eph. V.1675 (Byzantine?): N; I.Eph. IV.1278 (date: 938): C^2. For editions and further literature cf. FaFo, vol. I, pp. 292, 517.

34 C^2: Graffiti de la Montagne Thébaine, no. 3122 (Valley of the Queens; date unknown, ed. Delattre, 'Graffitis', 2001, pp. 333–6); Old Dongola (*s.* XI/XII; ed. Łajtar 2018, p. 46); Łajtar 2018, p. 42, mentions another example for the attestation of Greek C^2 in yet another inscription from Old Dongola that is so far unpublished. Unknown versions: FaFo § 252 (Old Dongola; *s.* XII *in.*); cf. also Łajtar 2018, pp. 43, 46 (text and translation), who calls it *Symbolum Dongolanum*. Another version of this creed on a parchment leaf is as yet unpublished (cf. Łajtar 2018, p. 43).

15 From Summary to Sacred Formula: Creeds, Magic, and Miracles

One of the areas in which the changes in the creed's *Sitz im Leben* is most obvious to see is late antique and early medieval magic.[1] The creed always had tended to assume a function comparable to the baptismal formula itself, through its use in the context of the baptismal liturgy (especially where it was combined in some way with the rite of *Apótaxis*[2]) and in the act of baptism itself. As a result, it also easily mutated into a kind of sacrament of the word: it might be understood as conveying the baptismal grace simply by means of being recited. Such an understanding of the creed was strengthened by the fact that, as we saw in previous chapters, Christians were always told not to write it down and – especially with regard to N – not to alter it in any way, lest one would risk being anathematized.[3] This miraculous character of the creed later took on a life of its own: the creed virtually morphed into a magical formula with an apotropaic character.

The view that the credal formula possessed such miraculous powers is well documented in our sources. For Ambrose revisiting the creed helped against 'stupefactions of the soul and body', 'the temptation of the adversary who is never silent', and even 'some trembling of the body, [or] weakness of the stomach' – an admonition which was later alluded to by Bede.[4] Caesarius of Arles told his flock to use the creed as substitute for the vulgar love songs that were popular among the peasant population. Instead of those songs, Christians were supposed to recite the creed, the Lord's Prayer, some antiphons, and Psalm 50 or 90 (51 and 91 in the Hebrew Bible) in order to protect one's soul from the devil.[5] The confession thus protected against evil of various kinds, especially the machinations of the devil. It could also provide succour in other life situations: for example, it was a widespread bad omen to sneeze after getting up in the morning.[6] Many then went

---

1 I use the term 'magic' in a wide sense. On the problems of definition cf. Frenschkowski 2010, pp. 873–6 and Frenschkowski 2016, ch. 1. Magical rites of late antiquity and the early middle ages in the west are described in McKenna 1938, esp. pp. 227–54; Flint 1991; Klingshirn 1994(1995), pp. 209–26; Lavarra 1994, esp. pp. 15–36; Neri 1998, pp. 258–86, esp. 277 f., 284–6; Frenschkowski 2010, cols. 935–41; Marrone 2015, esp. pp. 32–81; Frenschkowski 2016, pp. 243–59.

2 Cf. above pp. 132, 415 f., 418, 490, 492 f. and n. 56; 494, 496–9, 506.

3 Cf. above pp. 379, 536 f.

4 Ambrose, *Explanatio symboli* 9 (FaFo § 15a3); Bede, *Epistula ad Egbertum* 5 (§ 584).

5 Cf. Caesarius, *Sermo 6*, 3 (FaFo § 656b). On the apotropaic function of Psalm 50(51) cf. Kinzig 2018(2022), p. 293 n. 25.

6 Cf. Harmening 1979, pp. 81 f. and Filotas 2005, p. 240, citing further evidence. More generally, Sartori 1934/1935.

https://doi.org/10.1515/9783110318531-015

back to bed for fear of the consequences, a practice that Augustine had already ridiculed.[7] Caesarius found this superstition more sacrilegious than amusing and urged his listeners to cross themselves instead, to recite the creed and the Lord's Prayer, and then to set out on their daily business – this would protect them sufficiently.[8]

Others also cautioned against attaching any ominous significance to a sneeze, but recommended reciting the creed and the Lord's Prayer in any case before setting out, among them Eligius, Bishop of Noyon in northern France, in the middle of the seventh century, an unknown preacher in the same region less than a century later, and finally none other than Hrabanus Maurus, archbishop of Mainz (847–856) and follower of Emperor Lothair I, in the mid-ninth century.[9]

That the creed and Lord's Prayer were not simply regarded as texts to comfort and strengthen before any arduous journey, but indeed as magical formulae, is also evidenced by the writings of Martin of Braga in the second half of the sixth century. In a missionary sermon, Martin chided his listeners for abandoning the 'sacred incantation' (*incantationem sanctam*), namely the creed and the Lord's Prayer, and using 'diabolical incantations and charms' (*diabolicas incantationes et carmina*) instead.[10] An example of the practice Martin condemns is preserved for us on a slate tablet from Asturias from the eighth or ninth century, which contains an elaborate spell against hailstorms with a peculiar mixture of pagan and Christian elements.[11] The use of such spells was unacceptable to Martin. For whosoever used formulae invented by sorcerers had abandoned the 'sacred incantation of the creed and the Lord's Prayer (*incantationem sanctam symboli et orationis dominicae*)' which he had received in faith in Christ, and had trampled on the faith, 'for one could not serve God and the devil at the same time'.[12] Such formulae could refer specifically to those pronounced while gathering medicinal herbs in order to increase their potency, as a Spanish collection of canons from the same period which was quoted time and again attests.[13] In the high middle ages, this practice

---

7 Cf. Augustine, *De doctrina Christiana* 2,31.

8 Cf. Caesarius, *Sermo 54*, 1 (FaFo § 656e).

9 Cf. *Vita Eligii* 2,16 (FaFo § 668); Pseudo-Augustine, *Homilia de sacrilegiis* 8 (27; § 669b); and Hrabanus Maurus, *Homilia 43* (PL 110, col. 81B). Similarly, Ælfric, *Sermo in laetania maiore (De auguriis)*, ll. 96–9 (Skeat 1881–1900, vol. I, pp. 370 f.) and Foxhall Forbes 2013, p. 82; Calhoun 2020, p. 449 and n. 141.

10 Martin of Braga, *De correctione rusticorum* 16,6 (FaFo § 660). Cf. also Filotas 2005, p. 257.

11 Cf. Abascal/Gimeno 2000, pp. 337–9 (no. 547); Velázquez Soriano 2004, pp. 368–84 (no. 104). On the context cf. also Fernández Nieto 2010; Velázquez Soriano 2010.

12 Martin of Braga, *De correctione rusticorum* 16,7.

13 Cf. *Capitula Martini episcopi Bracarensis*, cap. 74 (FaFo § 576b). The prescription was often repeated by medieval theologians. Cf. the references in Kinzig 2018(2022), p. 295 n. 35. Further-

was punishable by a church penance of ten days of fasting on bread and water.[14] Similarly, the creed and the Lord's Prayer were used to fight fever[15] and heart disease (or heartache?),[16] in preparing concoctions against against 'elf disease' or 'elfish magic',[17] as well as in blessings of bees.[18] Even Ath was used against fever.[19]

A sermon, probably from northern France in the early ninth century, states that anyone using pagan spells instead of the creed and the Lord's Prayer is not a Christian but pagan.[20] In penitentials the use of spells other than the creed or (Christian) prayers is said to be punishable by 120 days of fasting.[21] It should be noted that the contrast here is not between a magic formula and a sacred creed, but between a pagan and a Christian spell! In this text, too, the medical effects of the formulae are paramount.[22]

Finally, the creed and the Lord's Prayer were also recited when looking to capture snakes as can be seen from glosses at the bottom of the page in a codex from Tegernsee Abbey in Bavaria.[23]

*

The creed's magical function was not limited to the west. We have non-literary evidence from the eastern part of the Byzantine Empire (and beyond) which attests this use of the creed. A number of papyrus fragments from the fifth and sixth centuries survive from Egypt that combine credal-like formulations with requests for

---

more, McKenna 1938, pp. 102 f.; Harmening 1979, p. 227; Salisbury 1985, p. 242; Flint 1991, pp. 240–53, 301–28; Klingshirn 1994(1995), pp. 221 f.; Jolly 1996, pp. 93, 161; Filotas 2005, p. 96; Marrone 2015, p. 51.

14 Burchard of Worms 10,20 (= 19,5,6, Friedberg 1868, p. 85 = Wasserschleben 1851, p. 644 (Corrector, cap. 56; with minor variants) = Hansen 1901, p. 42 (§ 65[56])). In addition, Harmening 1979, pp. 224 f., citing further evidence. – If someone began an 'assembly' (*congregatio*) with an *incantatio* instead of with the Lord's Prayer and the creed, he or she even had to fast for forty days; cf. *Paenitentiale Pseudo-Egberti* 2,23 (PL 89, col. 419D). In addition, Filotas 2005, p. 284.

15 Cf. *Leechbook* 1,62.

16 Cf. *Leechbook* 3,68; *Lacnunga* 176. Cf. Storms 1948, pp. 82, 262; Pettit 2001, vol. II, p. 349.

17 Cf. *Leechbook* 3,62; *Lacnunga* 29; cf. Storms 1948, p. 223; Jolly 1996, pp. 140 f., 160, 164; Pettit 2001, vol. II, pp. 36–42. In addition, Thomas 2020, pp. 204, 208. Cf. also the exorcism in the *Leofric Missal* (Jolly 1996, p. 164).

18 Cf. Schönbach 1893, pp. 29 f. (no. 2; s. XIV); English tr. in Storms 1948, p. 139.

19 Cf. Storms 1948, pp. 295 f. (no. 64; s. XII). In general, Thomas 2020, pp. 177–226.

20 Cf. Pseudo-Augustine, *Homilia de sacrilegiis* 4 (14; FaFo § 669a).

21 Cf., e.g., *Paenitentiale Floriacense* (s. IX) 42.

22 This also applies in a similar way to the healing power of the eucharist. On Arles cf. Klingshirn 1994(1995), pp. 162 f., 222.

23 Cf. cod. Munich, Bayerische Staatsbibliothek, Clm 19417 (Tegernsee, 800–830), ff. 25v–27r and Franz 1909, pp. 172 f. and n. 6. On the manuscript cf. Kinzig, *Neue Texte I*, 2017, p. 111 and URL <https://glossen.germ-ling.uni-bamberg.de/manuscripts/12815> (22/11/2023).

the healing of fevers.[24] Possibly they were carried in small vials around the neck. A tenth-century paper leaf from the vicinity of the monastery of Apa Apollo at Deir el-Bala'izah in Upper Egypt contains C^2 followed by some drawings that have been interpreted as a magical charm (perhaps against snakes?).[25] The faulty Greek may suggest that the scribe no longer understood the content of this text, but treated it as a spell (which needed not to be comprehensible to do its job).[26]

But the confession may even have served to influence the fertility of the earth. Contrary to its designation as a papyrus,[27] P.Lond.Lit. 239 (TM 62209), perhaps from Faiyum (s. VI/VII), is actually a small parchment codex measuring only 6.8 × 4.5 cm and consisting of 9 folia.[28] It contains a prayer for the annual flooding of the Nile, followed by C^2 and Psalm 132(133) at the end.[29] But how was this combination of pagan and Christian texts, which were written in the same hand, used? Is it an amulet, as its first editor H.J.M. Milne assumed?[30] Or is it, rather, a portable prayer book, combining an older, pagan prayer with Christian texts that were recited together on a regular basis?[31]

Whereas these charms and invocations served to effect a better life in the here and now, the (mutilated) papyrus P.Ryl. I 6 (TM 65060) from the sixth century inscribed with N may have had an eschatological purpose. If the reconstruction of the missing text by its editor Arthur S. Hunt is correct, the owner intended to use it, as they put it, to approach 'the terrible judgment-seat of the Lord Christ on that dreadful [day when he will come again in] his own glory to judge the living and the dead'.[32] This may mean that they expected to fare better at the Last Judgement if they had the text of the creed with them.

✳

Closely related to the use of creeds as charms is their power as recounted in miracle stories.[33] The sacred power with which the creed had come to be invested by

---

24 Cf. the examples in FaFo § 653.

25 Cf. P.Laur.Inv. III/960 (TM 382538; ed. Pintaudi 2001, pp. 48–53; cf. Horak 2001).

26 The same seems to be true for the as yet unpublished papyrus P.Berlin 11631 which also contains C^2, perhaps followed by a magic spell. I owe this information to Sebastian Buck who posted a photograph on his blog www.antike-christentum.de. A publication is currently being prepared by Fabian Reiter, Bologna.

27 Here the information given in FaFo, Bd. I, p. 518 (§ 184) needs to be corrected.

28 Cf. Bonneau 1964, pp. 410–3; Bonneau 1987; Contino 2020/2021, vol. I, pp. 97–100, citing further literature.

29 On the use of Psalms as amulets in Egypt cf. Sanzo 2014, pp. 40–7.

30 Cf. Milne 1927, pp. 200–4.

31 Thus De Bruyn 2010, p. 161, following Bonneau.

32 Hunt 1911, p. 12. The supplement is that of the editor.

33 On the following story cf. also Kinzig, "'I abjure Satan'", 2024 (*sub prelo*).

the time of Augustine can be illustrated by some ecclesial gossip which the bishop of Hippo Regius shared with his ageing friend Alypius in a letter (perhaps 428/429[34]). The protagonist of this story, which Augustine heard from the otherwise unknown *comes* Peregrinus, was the chief physician (*archiater*) of an unknown town, Dioscorus.[35] While a kind man, Dioscorus seems to have been a fierce critic of Christianity. Nonetheless, when his daughter fell seriously ill, he prayed to Christ and vowed to become a Christian, should his daughter be saved. Yet although his prayer was answered, the good doctor reneged on his vow. Subsequently, he experienced temporary sight loss which he interpreted as a divine punishment for breaching his promise. Here is the central section of the story in Augustine's own words:

> He cried out and confessed and vowed again that he would fulfill what he had vowed if light be returned to him. It returned; he fulfilled [his vow], and still the hand [of the Lord] was raised. He had not committed the creed to memory, or perhaps had refused to commit it, and made the excuse that he was unable. God saw. Immediately after all the ceremonies of his reception he was undone by a paralysis in many, indeed almost all, his members. Then, being warned by a dream, he confessed in writing that he had been told that this had happened because he had not recited the creed. After that confession the use of all his members was restored to him, excepting only the tongue; nevertheless he, being still under the same affliction, disclosed in writing that he had nonetheless learned the creed and still retained it in his memory; and so that frivolity which, as you know, blemished his natural kindness and made him exceedingly profane when he mocked Christians, was altogether destroyed in him.

The story is interesting on various levels: first of all, we are not told why Dioscorus decided to pray to Christ at all. Was his daughter a Christian? It is not impossible, but not very likely since she appears to have been unmarried and therefore probably still was in his *potestas*. It appears more probable that Dioscorus first tried several cures which were all unsuccessful and then turned to praying, perhaps, first to some local deity and, finally, when no help was forthcoming, to Christ. His prayer basically consisted in a vow. Or, we might say nowadays, Dioscorus struck a deal: he promised to become a Christian and, in return, expected

---

34 Cf. Augustine, *Epistula 227* (FaFo § 636i). The date is uncertain. In the title and the explicit of the letter Alypius is called a *senex*. This may, however, be a honorific title; cf. *PCBE*, vol. I, s.v. 'Alypius', pp. 53 and 64. Cf. also Pignot 2020, p. 226. On this story cf. now also Berzon 2021, pp. 593–6.

35 Cf. *PLRE*, vol. II, s.v. 'Dioscurus 3', p. 367 (cf. also *PLRE*, vol. I, s.v. 'Dioscorus 2', p. 261); *PCBE*, vol. I, s.v. 'DIOSCORVS 1', p. 279. It is not very likely that Dioscorus was *archiater* in Hippo, because in this case Augustine would no doubt have known the story first-hand. On public physicians in antiquity cf. Nutton 1977(1988).

his daughter to be cured. Dioscorus' behaviour is by no means eccentric: he continued to move within the parameters of Roman religion which were based on the principle *do ut des*: I promise to venerate you, if you do something in return for me.[36] Having made this vow, he was now obliged to honour the promise he had made.[37] When he tried to withdraw, he was struck by illness. Augustine does not tell us whether Dioscorus first put this down to natural causes. At some point he clearly realized that any cures he had tried had failed and, therefore, once more attributed this failure to divine intervention. He must then have realized that the God responsible could be none else than that of the Christians. In other words, Dioscorus understood that his fate was no longer determined by the traditional gods, but that this god had taken over, prompted by his vow and prayer to Christ.

According to Augustine Dioscorus then fulfilled his vow. Apparently, he was baptized. If so, then the whole sequence of events must have taken place over an extended period which included Dioscorus' catechumenate and baptism. However, there appears to have been a problem with his *Redditio symboli*. Augustine does not seem to know exactly what went wrong when Dioscorus was asked to recite the creed – the physician may either have excused himself on some ground or other, or he may have cheated in some way. This shows that by now the creed had become the central element in someone's conversion. It was by means of the *Redditio* after the *Apótaxis* that allegiance to the new deity was formally pledged. By comparison, the baptismal act itself recedes into the background. After his baptism Dioscorus was struck by paralysis. Unable to speak, but obviously still able to hold a stylus he wrote down a dream experience: in it, he had been told that his illness was caused by his failure to perform the *Redditio*. His health partly restored, he was still unable to speak. Dioscorus then acted as any other Roman would have acted: he produced a votive tablet as proof that he had honoured his obligations. However, this tablet no longer contained the name of some pagan deity to whom he attributed his (partial) cure,[38] but the content of the creed, perhaps with Christ's name at the top and his own name at the bottom. Thus he killed two birds with one stone: according to the parameters of Roman religion he had fulfilled his vow and had produced the tablet as his testimony; at the same time he had inscribed this tablet with a new sacred text which attested to his having internalized the requirements of his new religion. He had demonstrated that he had accepted his new divine overlord and had publicly acknowledged that he

---

36 Cf. Hoheisel 1990; Latte 1992, pp. 46 f.; Rüpke 2007, p. 149.
37 Cf. Kötting/Kaiser 1976, cols. 1078–1080; Rüpke 2016, pp. 121–4.
38 For dedicatory inscriptions in Roman religion cf. Haensch 2013, pp. 180–5.

owed his cure to him. Incidentally, this is one of the few western examples of the creed having been written down by a lay person (which may have been due to the person's disability). Unfortunately, we do not hear whether Dioscorus eventually regained his speech.

As regards Augustine, he interprets the story entirely within the framework of the Christian religion. The fact that the doctor's daughter was cured is seen as an act of Christ's mercy (*Christi misericordiam*). Augustine thus indicates that the ancient system of reciprocity in dealing with a divinity had become shaky. Christ did not heal the daughter because her father's vow obliged him to, but because he felt compassion towards the suffering doctor for whom his daughter was 'his only comfort' (*in qua unica acquiescebat*).

Another story in which the creed figured prominently relates to the remains of the first Christian martyr Stephen.[39] In a way that is no longer entirely clear, the small town of Uzalis in the province of Africa Proconsularis (today's El Alia in northern Tunisia) came into possession of Stephen's bones in the summer of 416 after they had recently been discovered in Jerusalem. The following incident was recorded by an unknown author a few years later:[40] A dilapidated house had collapsed in Uzalis and killed a certain Dativus. His body was dug out from the rubble and moved into a neighbouring building. The inconsolable widow immediately ran to the shrine of St Stephen, where that saint's bones had been stored, and tearfully implored him to return her husband to her, upon which the dead man suddenly stirred and opened his eyes. When he had regained full consciousness, he reported that he had met a young man dressed in the bright white robe of a deacon. The man ordered him: 'Give me back what you have received.' ('Redde quod accepisti.') But Dativus did not understand what the man was talking about. The latter repeated his demand. When Dativus still did not understand, the man asked him a third time to return what he had received. Only then did it dawn on Dativus that the stranger possibly meant the confession of faith, which had been given to him at the *Traditio symboli* and which he had 'returned' at the *Redditio*. So Dativus muttered: 'Are you directing me to return the creed?' 'Give it back (*redde*)!' was the gruff reply. So Dativus recited the creed and, when he had finished, continued: 'If you wish, I will also recite the Lord's Prayer.' When the man agreed, he duly said the Lord's Prayer. Thereupon the stranger made the sign of the cross on the head of Dativus, who was stretched out before him, and said to him: 'Rise, you are now healed.' And so it happened.[41] In this thoroughly entertaining legend about the ap-

---

39 On the following two stories cf. also Kinzig 2018(2022), pp. 286–8.

40 Apparently after the summer of 424; cf. Saxer 1980, p. 270.

41 Cf. *De miraculis sancti Stephani* 1,6 (FaFo § 637).

parition of the deacon Stephen, a special power is attributed to the creed: Dativus is cured of mortal injuries by reciting the *symbolum* (and the Lord's Prayer).

These miracle stories surrounding the creed start to be told at the turn of the fourth to the fifth century. They are then projected back into earlier times. Thus Rufinus, in his continuation of the *Ecclesiastical History* of Eusebius (c. 401), reports how pagan philosophers and dialecticians were attracted to the Council of Nicaea in 325. One of them engaged the bishops in daily discussions on matters of faith. Although the clergy were themselves expert in rhetoric, the philosopher proved superior to them in his knowledge. Finally, an old *confessor* appeared who had suffered for his faith during persecution and who, as Rufinus says, was 'of a very simple mind (*simplicissimae naturae*)' and 'knew nothing but Christ Jesus and his crucifixion'. This manifestly non-expert theologian finally succeeded in converting the philosopher to the Christian faith and persuading him to be baptized simply by reciting a creed.[42] Rufinus says in introducing the anecdote that the power of simple Christian faith was thus revealed – there can be no doubt that he means a specific *miraculous* power that emanated from the Christian creed. The story proved so popular that later Church historians such as Sozomen and Pseudo-Gelasius of Cyzicus (475/476) repeated and further embellished it in their historical works.[43]

Finally, the acts of the Sixth Ecumenical Council in Constantinople contain a bizarre story that can even be dated precisely: it took place on 26 April 681.[44] A certain Polychronius, a monk-priest, had been charged with heresy. He believed that there had only been one will and one operation (ἐνέργεια) at work during Christ's earthly stay, namely that of God – he was a Monothelete. Believing that, however, endangered certainty in the full incarnation of God and thus the salvation of humankind. For in order to save humanity, God had to take on the whole human being in Christ, including body, heart, senses, and mind, the majority of theologians at that time believed, and that meant that in the earthly Christ there had to be, in addition to the divine will, a human will together with its corresponding human mode of operation. Because Polychronius had denied this, he had been imprisoned. When he was brought into the council chamber and interrogated, he refused to recant, instead producing a copy of a letter he had sent to Emperor Constantine IV (r. 668–685), writing down his faith. The acts of the coun-

---

42 Rufinus, *Historia ecclesiastica* 10,3 (cf. FaFo § 136a).

43 Cf. Sozomen, *Historia ecclesiastica* 1,18 (cf. FaFo § 136b); Pseudo-Gelasius of Cyzicus, *Historia ecclesiastica* 2,13 (cf. FaFo § 136c).

44 Cf. ACO² II 2 (Rudolf Riedinger), pp. 672, l. 18 – 682, l. 8 (FaFo § 582a). For further details cf. Kinzig 2021(2022), pp. 119–21.

cil only contain an extract from this document which makes it clear that Polychronius had been stimulated to send his missive to the emperor by a vision:

> I saw a crowd of men clad in white and in their midst a man whose virtue I cannot describe, telling me, 'He [sc. the emperor] is preparing a new faith; hurry and speak to the Emperor Constantine: Do not make or introduce a new faith!' After I came from Heraclea to Chrysopolis and stood in the midday heat (for it was around the seventh hour of the day), I saw a terrifying man clad all in white. He stood before me and said, 'He who does not confess one will and operation of the God-man is no Christian'; and I said, 'The most-wise Emperor Constantine has decreed precisely this, one will and operation of the God-man.' And he said, 'This is very good and pleasing to God.'

In order to prove the truth of his heretical convictions he proposed to bring a dead man back to life with the help of his Monothelete creed as contained in the letter. The council fathers took him at his word. A corpse was fetched and placed on a silver bier in a public place outside the palace. Polychronius deposited his written confession on the dead man and muttered unintelligible words for several hours. When nothing happened Polychronius had to admit his failure. However, brought back into the assembly hall he continued to refuse to recant. In the end, he was solemnly condemned as an impostor and heretic and deposed from his office.

One wonders why the council fathers took Polychronius so seriously that they were willing to test his claim. Perhaps, the emperor had been so impressed by Polychronius' vision contained in the letter to him that he had asked the council to look into the truth of the matter. In any case, it is striking that the only extracts from his epistle inserted into the acts are the passages narrating the vision. At the same time, the ineffectual attempted resuscitation may have demonstrated to the public at large that Monotheletism was erroneous. Whatever the background to this story, it may suffice to note here that Polychronius ascribed magical powers to his faith as outlined in his written document, and that the council fathers considered this to be a possibility (at least to a certain extent).

16 The Controversy over *Filioque*

After the trinitarian conflict of the fourth century, the controversy over the question whether the Holy Spirit proceeded solely from the Father (as the Greeks claimed) or from the Father and the Son (which the Latin church maintained) was the most serious quarrel relating to the creed. It contributed substantially to the Great Schism of 1054 – although other factors also played a role in the mutual condemnation of Patriarch Michael I Cerularius and Pope Leo IX (or, rather, his western legate Cardinal Humbert of Silva Candida).

In the context of this book I cannot unravel the entire story of, or the complex historical background to, this historical rift. It has admirably been described by Peter Gemeinhardt.[1] Instead I wish to concentrate on those aspects that relate to the development of the credal genre.[2]

The earliest testimony for the origin (though not yet the procession) of the Spirit from the Father and the Son[3] is found in a panegyrical sermon on the saints by Victricius of Rouen (*sedit* 380/386–before 409) which was perhaps written in 396/397. The sermon is suddenly interrupted in the middle by a credal passage which begins as follows:

> We confess God the Father; we confess God the Son; we confess God the Holy Spirit. We confess that 'the three are one' [1Jn 5:8]. I said one because [the three exist] from one. As the Son exists of the Father, so the Father is in the Son [cf. Jn 17:21]; moreover, as the Holy Spirit is of the Father and the Son (*spiritus sanctus* [. . .] *de patre et filio*), so the Father and the Son are in the Holy Spirit.[4]

Gemeinhardt does not mention this text, although Burn and De Aldama had already drawn attention to the *et filio* contained therein.[5] Its significance lies in the fact that – in view of its date – it cannot depend on Augustine, although, no doubt, 'the categories and the terminology of the early medieval Latin doctrine of the Trinity with which the *filioque* was justified internally and defended externally, are largely based on the writings of Augustine of Hippo'.[6] Augustine did,

---

1 Cf. Gemeinhardt 2002. In addition, cf. Oberdorfer 2001; Kolbaba 2008; Siecienski 2010; Alexopoulos 2023. Further literature is listed in FaFo, vol. IV, p. 295.

2 The relevant sources are conveniently listed in ch. 11.3.2.1 of FaFo.

3 There seems to be no discernible difference between *et filio* and *filioque*. As far as I can see *atque filio* is never used. The *Fides catholica* (*Fides Damasi*, FaFo § 522b1) did not originally contain the *filioque* phrase; *pace* Kelly 1972, p. 360.

4 Victricius, *De laude sanctorum* 4 (FaFo § 462).

5 Cf. Burn 1899, p. 116; De Aldama, *Símbolo*, 1934, pp. 126–9.

6 Gemeinhardt 2002, p. 56.

https://doi.org/10.1515/9783110318531-016

then, serve as a point of reference, but probably mainly from Fulgentius of Ruspe (462/468–527/533) onwards.[7] Unfortunately, Victricius (like so many other theologians quoting the *filioque* in credal formulae) does not elaborate on his understanding of the procession of the Spirit.

Another puzzle relating to this credal passage is the fact that the next part of that passage seems to allude to the actual creed, but we do not know which one.[8] The key passages are here: *uerus deus de deo uero – lumen de lumine* / 'true God from true God – Light from Light' and, above all:

> Qui pro salute generis humani de sublimi descendens, de Maria uirgine incarnatus et hominem induit, passus est, crucifixus, sepultus. Tertia die resurrexit a mortuis, ascendit in caelum, sedet ad dexteram dei patris; inde uenturus est iudicare uiuos et mortuos.

> Coming down from on high for the salvation of the human race, he was incarnate of the virgin Mary and put on man, suffered, was crucified, was buried. On the third day he rose again from the dead, ascended into heaven, sits at the right hand of God the Father; thence he will come to judge the living and the dead.[9]

'True God from true God – Light from Light' may allude to N, but the phrase *hominem induit* (= ἄνθρωπον συλληφθέντα?) fits much better with (some version of) N^{Ant}. Perhaps Victricius did not yet know a fixed creed, but rather continued to refer to a *regula fidei*.

Even more puzzling is the fact that the so-called *Persicum*, i.e. the extended version of N which was adopted by the Dyophysite Church of the East at the Synod of Seleucia-Ctesiphon in 410, also contained the *filioque* – a fact which has so far remained unexplained, because this specific version of N is not attested anywhere else.[10]

Later quotations clearly point to Spain as the place where *filioque* was inserted into C^2. The principal reason for this addition was no doubt the struggle against Homoianism which also involved denying the Spirit's divine substance. It was thought that adding the phrase *filioque* would enhance the Spirit's status, given the fact that the pneumatological section of C^2 did not contain *homooúsios*.

---

7 Cf. Gemeinhardt 2002, p. 67.

8 Cf. also Mulders 1956/1957, pp. 284–7; Jacques Mulders/Roland Demeulenaere in CChr.SL 64, pp. 55–65.

9 Victricius, *De laude sanctorum* 4 (FaFo § 462).

10 Cf. above p. 421. Cf. also Grohe 2015, pp. 15–18. However, Hubert Kaufhold has suggested to me (email 13 October 2023) that it is, strictly speaking, the Paraclete who is from the Father and the Son in the *Persicum*. This may refer to Jn 14:16, 15:26, and 16:7. Kaufhold asks, 'Could it not be that what is meant is: "the Paraclete who is (i.e., is sent) from the Father and the Son"? This would then have nothing to do with any intra-trinitarian process or the *filioque*.'

As regards later authors we can probably disregard Bachiarius (*fl. c.* 400) who was accused of Priscillianism and wrote a *Libellus de fide* to vindicate his orthodoxy. In this work *filioque* must be a secondary addition, because it is missing in one manuscript and because its author repeatedly mentions the Spirit's procession from the Father only in the wider context of the quotation of *filioque*.[11]

If Bachiarius is omitted, then our first Spanish witness is the *Libellus in modum symboli* which was written by Pastor, bishop of Palencia in Galicia (consecrated in 433), possibly for a synod which took place in 447. The creed is an extended version of a creed which, perhaps, originated from the First Council of Toledo (400; the attribution is controversial) but was, in any case, included in its acts.[12] The crucial passage runs as follows:

> We believe in one true God, Father, Son, and Holy Spirit, Maker of things visible and invisible, through whom all things were created in heaven and on earth; that he is one God, and that this is one Trinity of divine substance, but that the Father is not the Son himself, but holds the Son who is not the Father; that the Son is not the Father, but that the Son of God is of the Father's nature; that the Spirit also is the Paraclete, who is neither the Father nor the Son, but proceeding from the Father and the Son (*sed a patre filioque procedens*). The Father, then, is unbegotten, the Son begotten; the Paraclete is not begotten, but proceeding from the Father and the Son (*sed a patre filioque procedens*).[13]

It has been claimed that Pastor may have been influenced by a letter of Pope Leo I to Bishop Turribius of Astorga (dated 21 July 447), directed against Priscillianism,[14] but the passage in question is so formulaic that it is difficult to prove such a hypothesis.[15]

In any case, the event which was to prove crucial for the further history of *filioque* in Spain was the decision by Visigoth king Reccared (r. 586–601), implemented at the Third Council of Toledo in 587, to abandon the Homoian faith of his father and predecessor Leovigild (r. 568–586) and to convert to catholicism. If the information Gregory of Tours received is correct, Leovigild had acknowledged

---

11 Cf. Bachiarius, *Libellus de fide* 5 (FaFo § 487).

12 For further details cf. Weckwerth 2004, pp. 59–67.

13 Pastor, *Libellus in modum symboli* (FaFo § 486b).

14 Cf. Leo, *Epistula 15*, 1 (PL 54, cols. 680C–681A): 'And so in the first chapter it is shown what unholy views they hold about the divine Trinity: they affirm that the person of the Father, the Son, and the Holy Spirit is one and the same, as if the same God were named now Father, now Son, and now Holy Spirit, and as if he who begot were not one, he who was begotten, another, and he who proceeded from both (*qui de utroque processit*), yet another; but an undivided unity must indeed be understood under three names, but not in three persons' (tr. NPNF; altered).

15 Cf. Kelly 1964, p. 90; cf. also Gemeinhardt 2002, p. 55 n. 46. In addition, Künstle argued that Leo's letter is a Spanish forgery from the late sixth century (cf. Künstle 1905, pp. 117–26).

the coeternity of Father and Son at a council in Toledo assembled in 580,[16] but denied 'that the Holy Spirit was essentially God, because his divinity was not mentioned in any codices'.[17] This is confirmed by John of Biclaro (Bishop of Girona 591–*c.* 631) who remarks in his *Chronicle*:

> King Leovigild gathered a synod of bishops of the Arian sect into the city of Toledo, and he amended the old heresy with a novel error: he said that converts from the Roman religion to our Catholic [i.e. Homoian] faith (*ad nostram catholicam fidem*) need not be baptized, but [should] only be cleansed by imposition of the hand and the order of communion, and give glory to the Father through the Son in the Holy Spirit (*et gloriam patri per filium in spiritu sancto dare*).[18]

The final doxology as quoted (which was apparently taken from the acts of the synod[19]) clearly indicated the king's Homoian (or, perhaps, even Arian) views.[20]

By contrast, at the council of 589 Reccared published a creed in which he confessed that the Holy Spirit 'proceeds from the Father and the Son and is of one substance with the Father and the Son (*a patre et filio procedere et cum patre et filio unius esse substantiae*).'[21] Although the version of C^2 quoted at this council did not yet contain the *filioque*,[22] the condemnations adopted by the assembly made it crystal-clear how it was to be interpreted:

> If anyone will not believe or has not believed that the Spirit proceeds from the Father and the Son (*a Patre et Filio procedere*) and [if anyone] has not said that he is coeternal and co-essential with the Father and the Son, let him be anathema.[23]

---

16 Cf. Collins 2004, p. 57. The council is not mentioned in Weckwerth 2013.

17 Gregory of Tours, *Historiae* 6,18 (MGH.SS rer. Merov. I/1, p. 287, ll. 15 f. = Heil/Scheerer 2022 (*Dokument* 119.4), p. 236, ll. 8–12): 'Manifeste cognoui, esse Christum filium dei aequalem patri; sed spiritum sanctum deum penitus esse non credo, eo quod in nullis legatur codicibus deus esse.' Cf. Gemeinhardt 2002, p. 54 f.

18 John of Biclaro, *Chronicon* 57 (= Heil/Scheerer 2022 (*Dokument* 119.3), p. 234, ll. 4–12).

19 This is indicated by *ad nostram catholicam fidem* which must form part of a quotation.

20 Cf. also Theodore of Mopsuestia, *Contra Eunomium*, frg. 2 (Vaggione 1980, p. 413); Theodoret, *Historia ecclesiastica* 2,24,3 (= Cassiodorus, *Historia ecclesiastica tripartita* 5,32,1); and Philostorgius, *Historia ecclesiastica* 3,13 (with the commentary in Bleckmann/Stein 2015, vol. II, pp. 229–31).

21 Third Council of Toledo (589), *Regis professio fidei* (FaFo § 490) = Heil/Scheerer 2022 (*Dokument* 120.2), p. 261, ll. 12–14.

22 It was later inserted in a sizeable number of codices containing the acts of the council. Cf. Martínez Díez/Rodríguez 1966–2002, vol. V, p. 67, app. ad l. 198; Heil/Scheerer 2022 (*Dokument* 120.2), p. 270, app. ad l. 24.

23 Third Council of Toledo, *Gothorum professio fidei* (Martínez Díez/Rodríguez 1966–2002, vol. V, p. 79, ll. 350–2) = Heil/Scheerer 2022 (*Dokument* 120.2), p. 280, ll. 1–5 (anathema 3).

In a later anathema the council even explicitly condemned the aforementioned doxology of the previous council.[24]

From 587 onwards *filioque* formed part of the Visigothic confessional tradition, was explicitly mentioned in the credal texts produced by Toledo councils,[25] and was finally inserted as *et filio* into C[2] at the Eighth Council of Toledo (653).[26] The Spanish translations of C[2] that contain *et filio* are mostly of type III ('mixed translations').[27] At the same time, we also find a great number of credal texts independent from C[2], written by highly influential Spanish theologians, that contain the assertion that the Spirit proceeded from both Father and Son.[28]

When we look at other regions we see that in North Africa *filioque* was also defended against the Homoianism of its Vandal rulers. This anti-Homoian background clearly emerges from a fragment of a treatise against the otherwise unknown 'Arian' Fabius by Fulgentius of Ruspe (*sedit* 507/508–527/533), written in c. 523. Fulgentius may refer to C[2] in this passage (although he usually quotes the African version of R/T[29]):

> But after the complete confession of the true divinity and true humanity of the only Son of God, we confess that we believe in the Holy Spirit, who is the one Spirit of the Father and the Son, proceeding from the Father and the Son (*de patre filioque procedens*), remaining by nature (*naturaliter*) in the Father and the Son, having the origin of [his] divinity from the

---

24 Cf. Third Council of Toledo, *Gothorum professio fidei* (Martínez Díez/Rodríguez 1966–2002, vol. V, pp. 82 f., ll. 382–6) = Heil/Scheerer 2022 (*Dokument* 120.2), p. 282, ll. 7–14 (anathema 16).
25 Cf. Fourth Council (633; FaFo § 493[2]); Sixth Council (638; § 495[2]); Eleventh Council (675; § 499[5]); Sixteenth Council (693; § 504[2], [7], [8], [14], [30]). Cf. also the creed of the converted Jews of Toledo submitted to the Sixth Council (637/638, § 494 and Kinzig, 'Die Verpflichtungser-klärungen', 2019(2022), p. 56, ll. 15 f.).
26 Cf. FaFo §§ 184f24, 823 (the Latin version from 653 onwards). I am not convinced by the argument put forward by Shawn C. Smith that Isidore's *Epistula 6* (which contains the *filioque*, cf. *6, 4* (PL 83, col. 903C)) is genuine (cf. Smith 2014), because it reflects a discussion which belongs to the ninth century at the earliest. In addition, the letter's claim that Rome had accepted *filioque* in its creed is erroneous. If I am mistaken, the letter must have been written before 636 (Isidore's death).
27 The different types of translation are explained in FaFo, vol. I, p. 519. It is a mixture of the version of C[2] quoted in *Actio II(III)* 14 and of the version in *Actio V* 33. Cf. also FaFo §§ 184f30 (*Missale mixtum*, before 1500); 184f31 (*Breuiarium secundum regulam beati Isidori*; before 1502). This version has *et filio*. The version in the *Liber misticus* (s. X or later; § 184f13) is of type I/ii (version of *Actio II(III)* 14 using relative clauses in the christological section) and has *et filioque* [sic].
28 Cf. Isidore of Seville, *De origine officiorum (De ecclesiasticis officiis)* 2,24(23),1 (598–615; FaFo § 491); Beatus of Liébana, *Tractatus de Apocalipsin* II, prologus 10,2 (c. 776; § 506b). Furthermore cf. the so-called Jacobi's Creed (s. VII?; § 525[3], [17]) and the *Formulae Hispanicae in modum symboli* (s. VIII ex.; § 510[3]).
29 Cf. FaFo § 319b2.

Father and the Son, possessing by nature the reality (*naturaliter ueritatem*) of one godhead with the Father and the Son.[30]

Likewise, Fulgentius' pupil Ferrandus included the *et filio* in his letter addressed to the *scholasticus* Severus of Constantinople in a credal passage directed *inter alia* against 'Arians'.[31]

Furthermore by the middle of the eighth century we find examples of credal texts from Gaul, Germany, Rome, Britain, and even Ireland in which the Spirit's procession from the Father and the Son is explicitly mentioned.[32] Here the growing popularity of Ath (which originated in Gaul or Spain and which also contained the Spirit's procession from the Father and the Son; FaFo § 434[23]) may have contributed to the spread of *filioque*.[33] But although in these areas, in contrast to Spain, *filioque* was employed in anti-Homoian treatises and in other contexts it was never quoted as part of C².

It was not until the mid-seventh century that the addition of *filioque* became a matter of serious concern among Nicene theologians from both east and west.[34] The first inklings of such debates are found in sources dealing with the Synod of Gentilly, held in 767 by Charlemagne's father Pepin the Short (r. 751–768). The circumstances leading up to the synod (whose acts are lost) are as unclear as is its agenda.[35] We do know that it was attended by both western and Byzantine bishops and that trinitarian questions as well as the problem of the veneration of icons were discussed. This suggests some connection with the first phase of the

---

30 Fulgentius, *Contra Fabianum*, frg. 36,13 (FaFo § 319a2). Fulgentius quotes the *filioque* in many places.

31 Ferrandus, *Epistula 5*, 2 (FaFo § 321b1). Cf. also id., *Epistula 4*, 1 where Ferrandus argues against an 'Arian' subordinationist doctrine of the Trinity.

32 Gaul: Pseudo-Augustine, *Sermo 244* (CPL 368) = (Pseudo-)Caesarius of Arles, *Sermo 10* (CPL 1008; s. VI; FaFo § 269); Gregory of Tours (591–594; § 469[7]). The provenance of a creed attributed to Gennadius of Marseille (FaFo § 523) is extremely controversial. The dates suggested range from the late fifth to the eighth century. Its author is also anxious to underline the Spirit's co-equality and coeternity with the Father and the Son (yet without affirming his consubstantiality). – Germany: (Pseudo-)Boniface (s. VIII/1?; § 483a). – Rome: (Pseudo-)Gregory the Great (c. 600; § 446); *Liber diurnus Romanorum pontificum* (after 680/681; § 450[1]); lost letter by Pope Theodore I (cf. above p. 411). – Britain: Synod of Hatfield (679–680; § 474[4]); later testimony: Denebeorht of Worcester (798–800; § 479[3]). – Ireland: Pseudo-Isidore, *Liber de ordine creaturarum* (655–680; § 472[4]; cf. Smyth 2011, p. 165 n. 10). – Unknown provenance: *Florilegium Frisingense* (§ 467b[4]; s. VII–VIII).

33 This is clearly the case for Denebeorht of Worcester (798–800; § 479[3]); the *Fides catholica* (before 800–830; § 707[6]); and the Interrogations on the creed of unknown origin (§ 708[2]).

34 Cf., however, the debates mentioned by Maximus the Confessor. Although triggered by a papal letter they seem mainly to have been confined to Constantinople (cf. above p. 411).

35 For details cf. Sode 2001, pp. 168–71; Gemeinhardt 2002, pp. 76–81.

Iconoclastic Controversy and the situation after the council of Hiereia (754) which had adopted a (moderate) iconoclastic position. But, of course, political issues may also have played a role. Ado of Vienne (d. 874) reports that at this synod

> the topic of the Trinity was discussed between the Greeks and the Romans, ([specifically,]) whether the Holy Spirit proceeds from the Son as he proceeds from the Father), as well as [the topic] of the images of the saints ([specifically,] whether they might be sculpted or painted in churches).[36]

However, Gemeinhardt points out that Ado wrote his *Chronicle* at the time of the Photinian Schism when *filioque* was indeed controversial, that we have no other sources making such a claim, and that later Carolingian theologians never refer to Gentilly when discussing the problem. These observations taken together make it unlikely that Ado's information is correct. Instead, in Gentilly *filioque* was probably not yet seen as a problem between east and west and the debate about the Trinity likely formed part of the wider debate about images.[37]

However, there are clear indications that the doctrine of the double procession of the Spirit had reached the Frankish Kingdom by the 770s (at the latest).[38] To give just one example: Lullus, first archbishop of Mainz (bishop 754–86, archbishop since 780/782), included it in the personal creed he composed in the context of his receiving the *pallium*:[39]

> I believe in the Holy Spirit, true God, proceeding from the Father and the Son, neither made nor begotten but proceeding; equal in all things with the Father and the Son; through whom the Father and the Son are recognized to be the only God over all things and in all things.[40]

---

36 Ado, *Chronicon* 6 (FaFo § 829).

37 Cf. Gemeinhardt 2002, pp. 78–81. By contrast, Harald Willjung cautiously maintains the authenticity of Ado's information. Cf. Willjung in MGH Conc. 2, Suppl. 2, pp. 12–15.

38 Cf., in addition, the supplement to the *Fides Catholica* in cod. St. Gallen, Stiftsbibliothek, 125 (770–780; FaFo § 522b2); the creed § 705 (*c.* 800 or earlier); the questions on faith from a Carolingian schoolbook (*c.* 800; § 776[3]); anonymous explanation of the creed (*s.* IX *in.*; § 336). Cf. also below p. 556 n. 44.

39 Cf. Levison 1946(1973), pp. 233–5.

40 FaFo § 700[4]: 'Credo in spiritum sanctum, deum uerum, ex patre procedentem et filio, non factum nec genitum sed procedentem, aequalem per omnia patri et filio, per quem pater et filius deus solus super omnia et in omnibus cognoscitur.'

This section is essentially a pastiche of the creed of Pelagius[41] and Rufinus' Latin translation of the creed of Gregory Thaumaturgus.[42] However, the words 'and the Son, neither made nor begotten but proceeding' (*et filio, non factum nec genitum sed procedentem*) are found in neither. It would be, therefore, tempting to assume that Lullus himself had added *et filio*. However, things are more complicated because by the ninth century versions of Pelagius' creed were circulating in Francia which included *et filio*. This is proven by an anonymous Carolingian treatise *De baptismo* which quotes the same passage in the version given by Lullus, including *et filio*.[43] In addition, we find a passage in the creed of the Fourth Council of Toledo of 633 which bears a striking resemblance to the passage quoted above and also has *et filio*.[44] In other words, the *filioque* was, as it were, already floating around by the time Lullus composed his creed. Incidentally, his rephrasing of Gregory/Rufinus is particularly interesting, as he uses the double procession to underpin an order of the Trinity in which the Spirit is clearly *subordinate* to the Father and the Son.

It seems, then, that *filioque* only became a problem in the aftermath of the Second Council of Nicaea (787) which sanctioned the veneration of images.[45] At this assembly a letter by the patriarch of Constantinople Tarasius (*sedit* 784–806) had been read out in which he professed the Holy Spirit to have proceeded 'from the Father through the Son (τὸ ἐκ τοῦ πατρὸς δι' υἱοῦ ἐκπορευόμενον / *ex patre*

---

41 Cf. Pelagius, *Libellus fidei* 4 (FaFo § 517): 'Credimus et in spiritum sanctum, deum uerum ex patre procedentem, aequalem per omnia patri et filio [. . .]'. 'We also believe in the Holy Spirit, true God, proceeding from the Father, equal in all things with the Father and the Son [. . .].'

42 Schwartz/Mommsen 1908(1999), p. 956, ll. 6–7: '[. . .] per quem deus super omnia et in omnibus cognoscitur et filius per omnes.' '[. . .] through whom God is recognized to be over all things and in all things and the Son to be through everyone [?].' For the Greek original cf. FaFo § 117[3].

43 Cf. the edition by Van Egmond 2012, p. 186, ll. 15 f. On this treatise cf. Van Egmond 2012, pp. 127–31.

44 Cf. Fourth Council of Toledo, canon 1 (FaFo § 493[2]): '[. . .] spiritum uero sanctum nec creatum nec genitum sed procedentem ex patre et filio profitemur; [. . .]' / '[. . .] the Holy Spirit, however, neither created nor begotten, but proceeding from the Father and the Son'. Cf. also the anonymous Carolingian *Expositio de credulitate* in Keefe, *Explanations*, 2012, p. 66 (ll. 23 f.; text 11): '[. . .] Spiritum Sanctum nec creatum nec genitum, sed procedentem ex Patre et Filio.' / '[. . .] that the Holy Spirit is neither created nor begotten, but proceeding from the Father and the Son.' Similarly, the Carolingian *Interrogationes* of Etty (§ 526[3]): '[. . .] spiritum uero sanctum non genitum, non creatum neque factum, sed de patre et filio procedentem, patri et filio coaeternum et coaequalem et cooperatorem [. . .].' / '[. . .] the Holy Spirit, however, neither begotten nor created nor made, but proceeding from the Father and the Son, coeternal, coequal, and cooperating with Father and Son [. . .].' There may also be a connection with the *Symbolum Quicumque* which reads in § 434[23]: 'Spiritus sanctus a patre et filio, non factus nec creatus nec genitus sed procedens.' / 'The Holy Spirit [exists] from the Father and from the Son, being neither made, nor created, nor begotten, but proceeding.'

45 For what follows cf. also Sode 2001, pp. 171–6; Gemeinhardt 2002, pp. 81–107.

per filium procedentem)'.[46] In 792 Charlemagne sent Bishop Angilbert of Saint-Riquier to Pope Hadrian I (*sedit* 772–795), carrying a capitulary which was critical of the council. It is known as the *Capitulare aduersus synodum* and later served as a *Vorlage* for the *Opus Caroli regis* to which I will return below. We are interested here neither in the political background of Charlemagne's action nor in his position with regard to the veneration of the images.[47] What is of import here is that the capitulary also criticized Tarasius for his description of the origin of the Holy Spirit. The 'faith of the Creed of Nicaea' (= C^2) had stated his procession 'from the Father and the Son' (*ex patre et filio*); Tarasius, therefore, 'held an erroneous view' (*non recte sentiat*).[48] Clearly, the version of C^2 then used at court must have included the *filioque*. The origin of this version can probably be traced to Theodulf of Orléans (798 bishop of Orléans, 800–821 archbishop) who authored the *Opus Caroli regis* (and hence probably also the *Capitulary*).[49] Hadrian replied that Tarasius had not invented a novel doctrine but followed the teaching of the holy fathers. He did not discuss the original version of C^2, but went on to quote an array of extracts from the writings of Athanasius, Eusebius, Hilary of Poitiers, Basil the Great, Ambrose, Gregory of Nazianzus, Augustine, Cyril of Alexandria, Leo the Great, Gregory the Great, and Sophronius intended to prove his point. However, at least the quotations from Augustine and Gregory the Great proved exactly the opposite, insisting as they did on the Spirit's double procession.[50]

The theses of the *Capitulare* were included in revised form, and indeed extended, in the *Opus Caroli regis contra synodum* (formerly called: *Libri Carolini*), a comprehensive memorandum completed in 793 which was critical of the decisions of Nicaea 787. However, by that time Theodulf must have realized that it was by no means certain that *filioque* had formed part of the original version of C^2, because the corresponding rubric in the *Opus Caroli* is phrased much more cautiously:

> Does Tarasius hold the correct view when he professes in his version of the creed (*in suae credulitatis lectione*) that the Holy Spirit does not proceed from the Father and the Son, as the truest rule of the holy faith [affirms] (*secundum uerissimam sanctae fidei regulam*), but from the Father through the Son (*ex patre per filium*)?[51]

---

46 Tarasius, *Epistula ad episcopos Antiochiae, Alexandriae et Hierosolymae* (FaFo § 245c).
47 Cf., e.g., Ann Freeman in MGH Conc. 2, Suppl. 1, pp. 4–8.
48 Charlemagne, *Capitulare aduersus synodum* 1 (FaFo § 831a).
49 Cf. the detailed analysis by Ann Freeman in MGH Conc. 2, Suppl. 1, pp. 12–23.
50 Cf. Augustine, *De trinitate* 15,45; Gregory, *Homilia in euangelia 26*, 2. Cf. Gemeinhardt 2002, p. 111.
51 *Opus Caroli regis contra synodum* (*Libri Carolini*) 3,3 (FaFo § 832a).

Here the 'Nicene' creed is no longer mentioned, but only the much vaguer 'rule of faith'. As the text of the chapter reveals, Theodulf saw this 'rule' as the norm by which the creed was to be interpreted (i.e. in the sense of the double procession). He now accused Tarasius of actually wanting to alter the creed's text by adding *per filium*. Theodulf agreed that the Spirit had indeed been given to believers through the Son, but to assert a *procession* from the Father through the Son was 'quite unusual for a synodical confession' (*synodicae confessioni inusitatum est*).[52]

Theodulf no doubt referred to C^2 – this can clearly be seen from his complaint that in the creed of Nicaea II 'there are some novel and unusual expressions (*noua uerba quaeque et inusitata*) which have not in any way been recorded in the creed by the holy Council of Nicaea'. These, Theodulf asserts, had been discussed 'in the beginning of the third book' of the *Opus*[53] – hence in the aforementioned passages dealing with the Holy Spirit. In other words, Theodulf mainly accused Tarasius of having de facto altered C^2 by adding *per filium* in his own statement of faith, which in turn may suggest that Theodulf had himself silently corrected his own version of C^2, realizing that originally it did not include *filioque*.

Oddly, in its final revision the third book of the *Opus* opened with the creed of Pelagius (FaFo § 517). This creed is ascribed to the 'holy fathers', indicating that it replaced a number of different creeds that had been recorded there originally.[54] This demonstrates the work's unfinished character: apparently the *Opus Caroli regis* was approved by Charlemagne,[55] but never published because it became clear that its basis, the Latin translation of the acts of Nicaea, was faulty.[56] In any case, the polemic against Tarasius regarding *filioque* was only one of many issues the Franks had with Nicaea II.

However, the fact that by the end of the eighth century *filioque* was widely used at Charlemagne's court is not only evident from the *Libellus sacrosyllabus episcoporum Italiae*, which Patriarch Paulinus II of Aquileia (*sedit* 776–802) wrote at the Synod of Frankfurt in 794 against Spanish adoptionism as championed by Felix of Urgel (d. 818; FaFo § 701a),[57] or from a lengthy creed which probably stemmed from the pen of Alcuin (FaFo § 702k[1], [2]), but also from Charlemagne's own writings. After the Synod of Frankfurt he sent a letter, drafted by Alcuin, to

---

52 *Opus Caroli regis contra synodum* (*Libri Carolini*) 3,3 (FaFo § 832a).

53 *Opus Caroli regis contra synodum* (*Libri Carolini*) 4,13 (FaFo § 832h).

54 Cf. *Opus Caroli regis contra synodum* (*Libri Carolini*) 3,1 (MGH Conc. 2, Suppl. 1, pp. 336–40) and pp. 44, 336 n. 1, 353 apparatus (Ann Freeman).

55 Cf. Ann Freeman in MGH Conc. 2, Suppl. 1, pp. 48–50.

56 Cf. Ann Freeman in MGH Conc. 2, Suppl. 1, pp. 9 f.

57 Cf. Knecht 2022, pp. 2, 73–7.

the Spanish bishops who supported adoptionism. Here we find a clear (albeit not explicit) reference to C^2 which includes the *filioque*:

> We also believe in the Holy Spirit, the true God, life-giver to all, who proceeds from the Father and the Son, who with the Father and the Son is jointly worshipped and jointly glorified.[58]

In what follows the text is also keen to emphasize the *et filio*, yet always within passages that deal with belief in the Trinity in general rather than specifically with the Holy Spirit.

The first explicit quotation of *filioque* as part of C^2 occurs in the acts of the provincial Synod of Friuli (796–797), presided over by Paulinus. In his opening address Paulinus gave a lengthy explanation of the Trinity, the ecumenical councils, and the creeds. With regard to the Holy Spirit, he realized that N and C^2 were by no means identical: N had very briefly expressed belief in the Spirit, but the 150 holy fathers of Constantinople had not been content with that:

> But in order to explain their own understanding [of that phrase] they have made an addition and confess that they believe 'in the Holy Spirit, the Lord and life-giver, who proceeds from the Father, who is worshipped and glorified with the Father and the Son'. For this and the other things that follow are not contained in the sacred doctrine of the Nicene Creed (*in Nicaeni symboli sacro dogmate non habentur*). Yet even later, that is, on account of those heretics who are hissing that the Holy Spirit only belongs to the Father and proceeds only from the Father, it was added, 'who proceeds from the Father and the Son'. And yet these holy fathers are not to be blamed as if they had added anything to or taken anything from the faith of the 318 fathers, because they gave no interpretation which differed from the latters' understanding, but strove to supplement their immaculate understanding in a sound manner (*sed immaculatum eorum intellectum sanis moribus supplere studuerunt*).[59]

Paulinus, then, realizes that the *filioque* was not contained in the original extension of the pneumatological article added at Constantinople, but was 'added' later. However, he leaves it open who actually made this addition and which heretics he has in mind as being targeted by it. Instead he goes on to say that these supplements had been made on the basis of new exegetical insights. The first related to Jn 15:26 (*qui a patre procedit*), the second to Jn 14:9–10: if the Father and the Son were one, the Spirit must have proceeded from both. Paulinus goes on to spill some ink on elaborating this argument further using other passages from

---

58 Charlemagne, *Epistula ad Elipandum et episcopos Hispaniae* (FaFo § 722[3]): 'Credimus et in spiritum sanctum, deum uerum, uiuificatorem omnium, a patre et filio procedentem, cum patre et filio coadorandum et conglorificandum.'
59 Synod of Friuli, *Gesta synodalia* 7 (FaFo § 703a).

John and drawing on his own maxim and that of his ancestors (*nostrisque maior-ibus*) that the works of the Trinity are inseparable.[60] He concludes with some enthusiasm:

> In what an orthodox manner (*catholice*) have also the holy fathers, standing firmly on this foundation of the faith, professed that the Holy Spirit proceeds from the Father (*a patre sanctum Spiritum procedere*)? How gloriously have also those [expressed themselves] who confess that he proceeds from the Father and the Son (*ex patre filioque procedere*)?[61]

Paulinus does not defend *filioque* against specific objections, but rather seeks to show that it is actually derived from Scripture in order to underline the unity of the Trinity against what he sees as adoptionist misinterpretations which were primarily directed against divine equality of the Son with the Father.[62] In other words, in Paulinus' ecclesial context there was no theological controversy about the *filioque* as such, but about the *Son*.

Why does he then raise the problem at all? Perhaps the reason why Paulinus felt he had to justify *filioque* may have been the use of a Greek version of C^2 in the baptismal liturgy which did not contain the phrase.[63] If that is correct, Paulinus means to say that *filioque* was added to the *Latin* version. In the acts of the Synod of Friuli the aforementioned Latin version of C^2 is then quoted which indeed includes the *filioque* (FaFo § 184f7). It is this translation which later became the standard Latin version.[64] It runs like this:

> Credo in unum deum, patrem omnipotentem, factorem caeli et terrae, uisibilium omnium et inuisibilium;
>
> et in unum dominum Iesum Christum, filium dei unigenitum, ex patre natum ante omnia saecula, deum de deo, lumen de lumine, deum uerum de deo uero, genitum, non factum, consubstantialem patri; per quem omnia facta sunt; qui propter nos homines et prop-

---

60 This was indeed often affirmed. Cf. Augustine, *Epistula 164*, 17; id., *In Iohannis euangelium tractatus 95*, 1; id., *Sermo 213 auctus* (= *Guelferbytanus* 1) 7 (Morin 1930, p. 446, ll. 29 f.); id., *De adulterinis coniugiis* 1,21; id., *De praedestinatione sanctorum* 8,13; id., *Contra sermonem Arianorum* 4,4; 11,9; and later authors.

61 Synod of Friuli, *Gesta synodalia* 8 (MGH Conc. II 1, p. 184, ll. 15–17).

62 Cf. esp. Synod of Friuli, *Gesta synodalia* 11 (MGH Conc. II 1, p. 187, ll. 1–4). In addition, cf. the contemporary *Dicta Leonis episcopi* that are also directed against adoptionism (FaFo § 706[14]). *Filioque* is only mentioned in passing.

63 On the use of Greek versions of C^2 at baptism cf. above p. 504 and n. 134.

64 Cf., e.g., FaFo §§ 184f9 (*Catholica Fides, s.* VIII ex. – IX in.), 184f10 (*Phillipps Sacramentary/Sacramentary of Autun, c.* 800; here *qui ex patre filioque procedit* is missing altogether!), 184f11 (Anastasius Bibliothecarius, *c.* 767–778: here *filioque* is missing), 184f12.2 (*Pontificale Romano-Germanicum*, 950–962), and the codices mentioned in 184f7 (these creeds represent type I/ii and all contain *filioque*). In addition § 184f29 (manuscript from Albi, s. XI or earlier; type III: *et filio*).

ter nostram salutem descendit de caelis et incarnatus est de spiritu sancto et Maria uirgine et homo factus est; crucifixus etiam pro nobis sub Pontio Pilato, passus et sepultus est et resurrexit tertia die secundum scripturas; ascendit in caelum; sedet ad dexteram patris et iterum uenturus est cum gloria iudicare uiuos et mortuos; cuius regni non erit finis;

    et in spiritum sanctum, dominum et uiuificantem, qui ex patre filioque procedit, qui cum patre et filio simul adoratur et conglorificatur, qui locutus est per prophetas; et unam sanctam catholicam et apostolicam ecclesiam.

Confiteor unum baptisma in remissionem peccatorum
et exspecto resurrectionem mortuorum et uitam futuri saeculi.

The *filioque* notwithstanding, it differs from the Greek version of C² in that it reads *adoratur* instead of *coadoratur*/συμπροσκυνούμενον and *et unam . . . ecclesiam* instead of *in unam*/εἰς μίαν. Comparing it to the *textus receptus* of Latin C² there are four minor variants:[65] *et* before *ex patre* and before *ascendit* is missing; the *textus receptus* has *ex Maria* instead of *et Maria*; *futuri saeculi* was changed to *uenturi saeculi*. This was the version of C² which is later also found in manuscripts with musical notation.[66]

Alcuin congratulated Paulinus for his felicitous revision in the warmest terms:

You have completed a work which will be most useful and very necessary for a great many people for the examination of the catholic faith and which I have desired for a long time. For I have frequently urged the lord king that the creed of the catholic faith should be compiled on one sheet in the plainest meanings and the most splendid words (*ut symbolum catholicae fidei planissimis sensibus et sermonibus luculentissimis in unam congereretur cartulam*) in order that it might be distributed to all the priests in every parish of the episcopal dioceses for them to read and to commit to memory such that, although various languages might be spoken, nonetheless one faith would resound everywhere.[67]

Paulinus had obviously done what Alcuin had in mind. In particular, the phrase *et homo factus est* was not only more elegant than the clumsy *et humanatum* of the earlier translation (which, as we will see, was still used in Rome[68]) – it was also much better suited to the fight against adoptionism: Christ had not only been 'humanized', he had actually become *man* (in the sense of a human person), as Paulinus repeats over and over again in his book against the adoptionist Felix of

---

65 Cf. Capelle 1951(1967), p. 71.
66 Cf. Capelle 1951(1967), pp. 71 f. and below p. 603 f.
67 Alcuin, *Epistula 139* (7 Cuscito; FaFo § 703c).
68 Cf. below p. 569.

Urgel.[69] In addition, Bernard Capelle has pointed out that Paulinus' translation was worded even more precisely than the Greek original which had used the same word γεννηθέντα twice: τὸν ἐκ τοῦ πατρὸς γεννηθέντα – γεννηθέντα οὐ ποιηθέντα. Perhaps prompted by the Athanasian creed,[70] Paulinus introduced a terminological difference between *ex patre natum* and *genitum, non factum* in order to underline the opposition between the Son's *generation* and the world's *creation*, an opposition which he also expressed in his polemic against Felix.[71]

By the beginning of the ninth century two archetypes of the pneumatological section of C^2 existed: the *Greek* text never contained the *filioque* whereas in the west at least two *Latin* translations were current that included the Spirit's procession from the Father and the Son (FaFo § 184, type I and II). In theory, this situation could have continued without causing any friction, much as since Chalcedon C^2 had been in use in various forms that differed from each other in minor details. Yet, for reasons unknown, this difference led to a controversy in the Holy Land, between monks resident in Jerusalem and its surroundings. We hear about this affair in a letter which six monks from the Frankish congregation of the Mount of Olives sent to Pope Leo III (*sedit* 795–816), probably in 807.[72] A John, monk at the famous Monastery of St Sabas, some seven and a half miles east of Bethlehem, had accused the Frankish monks who lived on the Mount of Olives of heresy because of their use of *filioque*. According to the letter, he was even driven to shout: 'All the Franks are heretics.' Some of John's followers caused a scandal at the holy manger in Bethlehem at Christmas trying in vain to throw out the Franks among shouts of heresy. The Frankish monks brought their grievances against John and his party to the bishop of Jerusalem who set a hearing which was to be held in the Church of the Holy Sepulchre. On that occasion the Franks affirmed that their faith was that of the Roman church, but that there were differences between the liturgy of the Greeks and that of the Franks which concerned the *Gloria patri*, the *Gloria in excelsis*, and the Lord's Prayer. As far as the creed proper was concerned, theirs was indeed longer than that used in Jerusalem on account of the *filioque*. They asked the Jerusalem clergy to not condone John's

---

69 Cf. Paulinus, *Contra Felicem* 1,14. 16. 30. 34; 2,1; 3,27. Cf. Capelle 1951(1967), p. 74.

70 Cf. FaFo § 434[21]–[23], [31].

71 Cf. Paulinus, *Contra Felicem* 1,17; 2,1. In addition, Capelle 1951(1967), pp. 74 f.

72 For what follows cf. *Epistulae selectae pontificum Romanorum 8* (MGH Epp. V, pp. 64–6). Extracts and further literature in FaFo § 844a. In addition, Harald Willjung in MGH Conc. II Suppl. 2, pp. 20–9; Sode 2001, pp. 176–94; Gemeinhardt 2002, pp. 141–6. Callahan 1992 has argued that this letter as well as Pope Leo's letter to Charlemagne (for which see below in the main text) are forgeries by Ademar of Chabanne (d. 1034). *Pace* Callahan cf. Gemeinhardt 2002, p. 142 n. 223. I follow Gemeinhardt in assuming their authenticity.

machinations, because this would mean that 'the throne of the blessed Peter' itself would be called heretical. The priests of Jerusalem then wrote down a summary of their faith, asking the Franks whether they agreed with this statement.
The latter replied that this was indeed the creed of 'the holy resurrection of the
Lord', i.e. the Church of Jerusalem, and the 'holy apostolic See of Rome' whereupon the archdeacon of Jerusalem together with the Frankish monks read out
this creed in the church to his congregation. In addition, the Franks condemned
'every heresy' and those who had called the Apostolic See of Rome heretical.

Yet although the Franks had gained the upper hand in this controversy it
seems that they had become uncertain about what they ought to believe and
wanted not only to apprise the pope of the situation, but also to be reassured that
filioque was indeed part of the creed. One of the letter's authors, a monk named
Leo, affirmed that he had heard the phrase *qui ex patre filioque procedit* both in
Rome and at Charlemagne's court. In addition, the emperor himself had given
Leo a copy of an Easter Homily by Gregory the Great in which this tenet was expressed.[73] It was also contained in the Rule of St Benedict which he had also received from the king,[74] in a *dialogus* which the pope had given Leo[75] and, finally,
in the 'faith of St Athanasius', i.e. in the *Symbolum Quicumque*.[76] By contrast, John
had not only caused an uproar in the holy city and in the surrounding monasteries by denying the double procession, but had also asked the Franks to surrender
their creed and their books. Worst of all, he was saying that it was prohibited to
read Pope Gregory's writings.[77]

Nonetheless, the Frankish monks had noticed that *filioque* was missing in the
Greek version of the creed so were now imploring the pope to search for the
phrase in both the Greek and the Latin fathers, because the Greeks were taking
offence at this addition (*et uident istum sermonem grauem*). They also asked the
pope to notify Charlemagne, because they had heard the *filioque* in his chapel.

The pope forwarded a copy of the monks' letter to Charlemagne in order to
keep him up to date adding that he had sent the monks an 'orthodox' version of
the creed 'so that all might keep the right and inviolate faith according to this our

---

73 Cf. Gregory, *Homilia in Euangelia 26*, 2. Cf. above p. 557 and n. 50.
74 To my knowledge, no copy of the rule containing a creed survives. However, the quotation
which the letter contains (*Epistulae selectae pontificum Romanorum 8* (MGH Epp. V, p. 65, ll.
38 f.): 'Credo Spiritum sanctum deum verum, ex Patre procedentem et Filio') is found in the
aforementioned creed of Archbishop Lullus of Mainz (FaFo § 700). Cf. Harald Willjung in MGH
Conc. II Suppl. 2, pp. 23–5.
75 No author is given, but it must again be Gregory; cf. Gregory, *Dialogus* 2,38,4.
76 Cf. FaFo § 434[23].
77 Cf. *Epistulae selectae pontificum Romanorum 8* (MGH Epp. V, p. 66, ll. 5 f.).

holy, catholic, and apostolic Church'.[78] Unfortunately, both this version of C^2 and of the covering letter are lost.[79] But given Leo's further actions there can be no doubt that Leo's creed did *not* contain the *filioque*. This is also confirmed by the *Life of Michael the Synkellos* according to which the pope 'refused to add anything that had not been jointly expressed by the divine fathers in the divine creed'.[80] Therefore, it was not actually necessary to search in the writings of the fathers for confirmation of the term. However, it is important to note here that by the beginning of the ninth century the *filioque* did indeed already form part of the creed used in the liturgy at Charlemagne's court and that in this respect a rift had opened up between the pope and the emperor. We will return to this problem below.

According to the *Life* the pope also wrote to Patriarch Thomas of Jerusalem (*sedit* 807–821) asking him for help in suppressing the use of *filioque* by the Franks. Thomas is said to have held a synod as a result and to have sent an embassy to Rome (via Constantinople) in order to outline the position of the church of Jerusalem, and to ask the pope in return to resist the use of *filioque* offering him support in this struggle. This delegation (which was also charged with other tasks) never seems to have reached its final destination. It is difficult to say to what extent the account of the *Life* conforms to the historical facts.[81] If accurate, the Jerusalem clergy would have changed its view with regard to the heretical nature of *filioque*.

Be that as it may, Leo probably did not take the whole affair very seriously and may, at that point, also have assumed that Charlemagne did not use an adulterated version of C^2 in his liturgy at court. However, not only was he mistaken in this assumption, but Charlemagne in fact took the whole matter so seriously that he placed it high on the agenda of a synod which he held at Aachen in 809. In the scholarly literature there has been much speculation about the reasons for the emperor's nervous reaction. One of them may have been the struggle against Spanish adoptionism: in this context, the *filioque* served as an argument to underline the one *substantia*, *potentia*, and *essentia* of the Trinity and thus to reject the idea of the Son's adoption, as Charlemagne had made clear in his letter to Elipandus and the Spanish bishops in September 794.[82] Perhaps the emperor was also

---

78 *Epistulae selectae pontificum Romanorum 8* (FaFo § 844b).

79 It was not the creed handed down under Leo's name (FaFo § 702k) which includes *filioque*. Cf. also Gemeinhardt 2002, pp. 145 f.

80 *Vita Michaelis Syncelli 6* (FaFo § 846).

81 Sode argues that the account is ficticious; cf. Sode 2001, pp. 186–94.

82 Cf. Charlemagne, *Epistula ad Elipandum et episcopos Hispaniae* (FaFo § 722[4]). Cf. also above pp. 558 f. and Gemeinhardt 2002, pp. 123–7.

afraid that the affair could further strain relations with Byzantium which were tense as a result of Charlemagne's claiming of the title of 'Most-Christian Emperor' (*Imperator christianissimus*).[83]

The Aachen Synod seems not to have reached a final decision about the *filioque*, but sent Bishops Bernhar of Worms (d. 826) and Jesse of Amiens (*sedit c. 799–836*), together with Abbot Adalhard of Corbie (abbot 781–814, 821–826), to Rome to seek approval from the pope for a decree, the so-called *Decretum Aquisgranense de processione spiritus sancti a patre et filio*.[84] It opened with the following statement:

> These things regarding the basis of the catholic faith and the procession of the Holy Spirit from the Father and the Son (*de ratione catholicae fidei et de processione spiritus sancti a patre et filio*) must be firmly believed by all those who are orthodox and faithful. They must confess with a pure and sincere heart without any doubt those things which have formerly been handed down and decreed by the holy fathers and the irreproachable teachers of the Church who participated in the four eminent and universal councils, that is, those of Nicaea, Ephesus, Chalcedon, and Constantinople.[85]

The remainder of the text was an extensive collection of testimonies from Scripture, the fathers, and the councils underpinning this doctrine.

---

83 Cf., e.g., Harald Willjung in MGH Conc. 2 Suppl. 2, p. 27.

84 Cf. *Annales Regni Francorum*, a. 809 (MGH SS rer. Germ. VI, p. 129); letter of Leo III to Riculf of Mainz, *Epistulae selectae pontificum Romanorum 9* (MGH Epp. 5, pp. 67 f.). For the participation of Jesse, not mentioned by either the *Annals* or Leo, cf. Harald Willjung in MGH Conc. 2 Suppl. 2, p. 88. Ado of Vienne does not mention this embassy in his *Chronicle*. Instead he writes (PL 123, cols. 132D–133A): 'The monk John from Jerusalem had raised this question, because the ecclesiastical rule and faith affirms that the Holy Spirit proceeds from the Father and the Son (*a patre et filio*), not created, not begotten, but coeternal and consubstantial with the Father and the Son. The term "procession from the Father and the Son" is clearly indicated in the Apocalypse as follows: "Then the angel (no doubt this is the angel) showed me the river of the water of life, bright as crystal, flowing from the throne of God and of the Lamb (*procedens de sede dei et agni*)" [Rev 22:1].' It seems that in his exegesis of Rev 22:1 Ado is referring to the *Libellus de processione spiritus sancti* 16 by Theodulf of Orléans who, in turn, quotes Ambrose, *De spiritu sancto* 3,152–153 as testimony for the double procession (MGH Conc. 2 Suppl. 2, p. 344, ll. 1–3: 'Item idem in eodem libro quod fluuius de sede dei et agni procedens spiritus sanctus sit, ubi intelligitur eius a patre et filio processio.' 'Likewise the same [says] in the same book that the river that is flowing from the throne of God and of the Lamb is the Holy Spirit which refers to his procession from the Father and the Son.' However, Ambrose never explicitly mentions the double procession. Theodulf's treatise had been written specifically for the Synod of Aachen (cf. Gemeinhardt 2002, pp. 152–7). The same quotation from Ambrose is found in the *Testimonia de aequalitate spiritus sancti cum patre et filio* by Adalwin of Regensburg (no. 28; MGH Conc. 2 Suppl. 2, p. 410, ll. 14–23).

85 *Decretum Aquisgranense* (FaFo § 748).

A couple of months after this synod, the decree and the collection of excerpts were taken by the envoys (*missi*) to Rome and submitted to the pope for approval in an audience with him. We still possess an anonymous eyewitness report of the proceedings that took place 'in the sacristy of St Peter' (*in secretario beati Petri apostoli*),[86] the so-called *Ratio Romana de symbolo fidei*.[87] Unfortunately, it was written down from memory, and its author, who belonged to the papal party,[88] confesses no longer to remember all the details. However, it becomes clear that, although Leo first fully agreed with the testimonies presented, later some disagreement seems to have arisen which led to a heated discussion. The notes of the eyewitness are in some ways enigmatic. It seems that the pope agreed with the *missi* that the clause *filioque* was de facto part of the faith, but he refused to alter the text of the creed (C^2) itself accordingly, because this had been forbidden by the councils (section 8).[89] The *missi* then asked the pope whether those ignorant on this point of doctrine (*nescientes*) were to be instructed in the double procession and whether, if that did not happen or if they did not understand what they were taught, their salvation was at risk. The pope answered that the faithful should indeed be instructed about the *filioque* and that the salvation of those who knew of, but refused to accept it was indeed in danger (sections 2–5). In addition, there seems to have been some misunderstanding about the way the faithful were taught the words of the creed. Clearly, at Charlemagne's court C^2 was not simply spoken, but was in some way chanted in mass. (There is other evidence pointing to this practice which we will discuss below.[90]) The envoys seem to have assumed that the pope rejected chanting the creed on principle, but the further course of the conversation shows that Leo did not mind either way, as long as no words were added to the creed whether spoken or chanted (sections 6–7).

The debate then turned to the question why the council fathers had not actually added the 'four syllables' (*quattuor syllabas*) and thus made 'the most-necessary sacrament of the faith' (*pernecessarium fidei sacramentum*) easily comprehensible (section 10). Leo refused to be drawn into a debate whether the creed was in actual fact incomplete, because he did not wish to question the wisdom of the fathers (section 11). The *missi* hurriedly denied that they wished to correct the fathers but expressed their desire to be useful to their brethren, as the end of the world (*finis*

---

86 On the venue cf. Harald Willjung in MGH Conc. 2 Suppl. 2, p. 108.

87 For what follows cf. MGH Conc. 2 Suppl. 2, pp. 287–94. Extracts in FaFo § 848. A complete German translation (with some inaccuracies) by Harald Willjung is found in MGH Conc. 2 Suppl. 2, pp. 295–300.

88 Harald Willjung in MGH Conc. 2 Suppl. 2, pp. 108–10.

89 Cf. above p. 379.

90 Cf. below ch. 19.

mundi) was drawing near. Given the fact that some were chanting the creed including *filioque* anyway and very many people had successfully learned the creed that way, the Franks had granted general permission for the extended creed to be chanted and thus to instruct many people about this great mystery (*de tanto mysterio*; section 12). The pope provisionally agreed, but continued to query whether in this case other doctrinal details concerning the creed should also be added to the actual text which the *missi* denied, 'because not everything was equally important' (*quia non aeque omnia necessaria sunt*; sections 13–14). The pope expressed doubts: many doctrines not contained in the creed were crucially important for true catholics. When asked to give an example he was unable to do so and adjourned the meeting to the next day in order 'to leave space for reflection' (*detur considerandi locus*; sections 15–19).

After a night's sleep the pope cited divine wisdom and truth (which belonged to both the Father's and the Son's common essence while also being predicated of either individually) as examples for the fact that not all important theological givens were contained in the creed (section 20). He also intimated that the envoys should not create such a fuss as regards this question (section 22). The *missi* replied that they could not let the matter rest, because there was the danger of losing 'the prize of the pious endeavour' (*pii laboris praemium*) and by implication thus of jeopardizing the salvation of the faithful, if *filioque* was omitted (section 23). Leo again urged his interlocutors not to press the matter any further lest they expose themselves to the charge of stubborn presumption, if the hallowed creed was altered. In his rather meandering statement the pope also seemed to indicate that, after all, he was not happy about the creed being chanted (section 24). At this point the Frankish envoys asked with some concern whether the custom of chanting the creed had not actually come from Rome and had received papal approval (section 25). The pope confirmed that he had given permission to chant the creed, but denied that this practice was Roman in origin, where it was read out instead, and repeated that the creed had to remain unaltered. All doctrines not contained in the creed were to be supplied 'in the appropriate places and at the appropriate times' (*locis temporibusue opportunis*; section 26).

The envoys then tried to summarize the provisional results of their audience so far: the *filioque* was to be removed from the creed which could then be either recited or chanted. Leo confirmed this summary and asked, in turn, for confirmation from the emperor (sections 27–28). However, the legates were still uneasy about chanting the creed and repeated their question whether it was right to do so. The pope made clear that he had not ordered but rather tolerated this practice (sections 29–30). But, the envoys continued, 'if an entire word [i.e. the *filioque*] be removed from the central part of the true faith, will then not precisely this word be condemned by all as if it were contrary to the faith' ('[. . .], numquid non, si sermo plenus recta fide e medio tollatur, idem sermo ab omnibus, ac si contra fidem sit, condemnabitur'; section 31)?[91] In other words, the envoys were anxious that eliding the *filioque* from the creed itself might in fact be understood as if implying that it was henceforth to be considered heretical. Leo advised simply to drop the custom of chanting the creed in the palace chapel which would then be imitated in the other Frankish churches. As part of this process *filioque* might then also be removed without anyone's faith be harmed (section 32).

My paraphrase hopefully has made clear that what was at stake here was not primarily a matter of politics, but of liturgical custom which, if altered, might have repercussions on orthodoxy and the salvation of the individual believers. In early ninth-century Francia, the custom of chanting the creed including the *filioque* had existed for some time.[92] By contrast, in Rome the creed was read out in baptismal catechesis. (Here the creed was not yet recited in mass.[93]) Faced with this situation the pope allowed the chanting of the creed, but refused to enjoin it as obligatory, while strictly rejecting *filioque* to be either chanted or recited (although he nonetheless considered it doctrinally correct). In turn, Charlemagne's *missi* feared that omitting the *filioque* so familiar to the ears of believers in their homeland (including its ruler) might lead to misunderstandings that might actually jeopardize their salvation.

The double solution suggested by Leo, i.e. to seize chanting the creed and, at the same time, no longer to recite the *filioque*, was not heeded in the Carolingian Empire. *Filioque* continued to be used,[94] and we will see below that there is ample evidence to suggest that C[2] continued to be chanted.[95] Here it may suffice to cite one example from the *Liber aduersus Graecos* by Aeneas of Paris (*sedit* 857–870):

> Likewise as regards the catholic faith, which the entire church of Gaul chants (*decantat*) on Sundays during mass, among other things we chant as follows: 'I also believe in the Holy Spirit, the

---

91 I have slightly changed my translation from FaFo § 848d.
92 For the insertion of *filioque* cf. above p. 554. For the custom of chanting cf. below ch. 19.
93 Cf. above p. 514.
94 Some further examples from credal texts (not C[2]) in later Carolingian and post-Carolingian sources include: Haito of Basel (809?; FaFo § 711[1], [3]); Theodulf of Orléans, *Liber de ordine baptismi* 7 (812; § 787b – this text, which is a paraphrase of T, is also quoted by Hrabanus Maurus and Smaragdus of Saint-Mihiel; cf. § 787b, introduction); Magnus of Sens (812; § 783[4]); Leidrad of Lyons (812; § 785[1]); 'Troyes Anonymous' (*c.* 812; § 788[6]); anonymous Carolingian *Expositio de credulitate* (813–815; § 713); anonymous credal statement (before 850; § 714); anonymous explanation of the ceremonies of baptism (before 850; § 63[7]); anonymous explanation of baptism (850–875 or earlier; § 783b[3]); Pseudo-Alcuin, *De diuinis officiis* 41 (*c.* 900?; § 70); interrogation on the creed (before 1000; § 716); Pseudo-Eleutherius, *Sermo 1* (§ 529a[5]; *s.* XII/1). Cf. also above p. 560 n. 64.
95 Cf. below ch. 19.

Lord and life-giver, who proceeds from the Father and the Son (*ex patre filioque*), who is jointly worshipped and glorified with the Father and the Son, who spoke through the prophets.'[96]

By contrast, Leo resorted to an unusual measure in order to inculcate the creed's original text in the mind of his congregation (and in the minds of all passers-by, whether from Francia or elsewhere): he had three silver shields inscribed with C^2 without the *filioque*. Two – each bearing the text in Greek and Latin – were placed over the entrance to the tomb of St Peter, the third stood over the entrance to the tomb of St Paul.[97]

The Latin text was later cited by Peter Abelard (FaFo § 184f5) as running as follows:

Credo in unum deum, patrem omnipotentem, factorem caeli et terrae, uisibilium omnium et inuisibilium;

    et in unum dominum Iesum Christum, filium dei unigenitum, qui ex patre natus est ante omnia saecula, lumen de lumine, deum uerum de deo uero, natum, non factum, consubstantialem patri; per quem omnia facta sunt; propter nos homines et propter nostram salutem descendentem de caelo et incarnatum de spiritu sancto et Maria uirgine et humanatum crucifixumque pro nobis sub Pontio Pilato et passum et sepultum et resurgentem tertia die secundum scripturas et ascendentem in caelis et sedentem ad dexteram patris et iterum uenturum cum gloria iudicare uiuos et mortuos; cuius regni non erit finis;

    et in spiritum sanctum, dominum et uiuificatorem, ex patre procedentem, cum patre et filio coadorandum et conglorificandum, qui locutus est per prophetas;

    in unam sanctam, catholicam et apostolicam ecclesiam.

    Confiteor unum baptisma in remissionem peccatorum.

    Spero resurrectionem mortuorum et uitam futuri saeculi. Amen.

This is basically a translation of the acts of the Third Council of Constantinople (FaFo § 184f1) which is also cited (with some minor variations) in the *Old Gelasian Sacramentary* (FaFo § 184f2), i.e. type I.[98] It differs from that current among the Carolingians in that participles are used instead of relative clauses. Given this, it seems difficult to assume that the Franks had followed the Romans in chanting the creed, as the *missi* had claimed,[99] or if they did, they must have altered it considerably on the basis of the revision of the Latin C^2 probably carried out by Paulinus of Aquileia: here the participles were replaced by the more elegant relative clauses which may also have lent themselves better to chanting.[100]

---

96 Aeneas, *Liber aduersus Graecos* 93 (FaFo § 852).
97 Cf. *Liber pontificalis* 98,84–85 (FaFo § 856).
98 Cf. above p. 411.
99 Cf. above p. 567.
100 Cf. above pp. 560 f.

Leo's silver shields with the creeds were still in place at the time of John XI Beccus (patriarch of Constantinople 1275–1282).[101] They had survived although by that time *filioque* had long come to be accepted in Rome too.[102] Emperor John V Palaeologus (r. 1341–1391) may have been the known last witness to the existence of these tablets when he visited Rome in October 1369. By then they had been removed from their original positions and stored away from public view. The version of the creed recorded on them served John in his defence of the original text of C^2.[103]

The earliest liturgical book that includes *filioque* in its creed is not found until the mid-tenth century: it is the *Pontificale Romano-Germanicum* which was written in Mainz in *c.* 950–962. It contains a baptismal liturgy which despite its traditional name (*Ordo Romanus L*) in fact seems to have been produced in Mainz.[104]

I cannot discuss the controversy over the *filioque* any further in the context of this book. The affair had started in the Holy Land and had kept the emperor, his ecclesiastical entourage, and the pope busy. In the end, the emperor ignored the papal wishes – he may have considered it too risky to abandon the *filioque*, because doing so would have caused unnecessary agitation among his subjects and because he was seriously afraid that it could also have eschatological consequences of unknown proportions. In the end 'nothing was resolved between Rome and Aachen, but only a dissent established'.[105]

---

101 Cf. John XI Beccus, *Refutatio libri Photii de processione spiritus* 32,89 (FaFo § 862). In addition, cf. the references FaFo §§ 857–61.

102 Cf. Gemeinhardt 2002, pp. 313–16.

103 Cf. FaFo § 863a. The story may, however, be apocryphal.

104 Cf. FaFo § 184f12 and Vogel 1986, pp. 187, 232 f. In addition, cf. § 184f13 (*Liber misticus* from Spain).

105 Gemeinhardt 2002, p. 163.

17 The Apostles' Creed, the Creed of Constantinople, and the Athanasian Creed as Standard Creeds in the Middle Ages and Beyond

The history of the creeds in the Byzantine and Latin churches in the period between the Carolingians and the Reformation urgently calls for further investigation.[1] The following summary remarks can, therefore, only be preliminary ones. In order not unduly to inflate the size of this book I will not deal further with the *filioque* controversy (on which some excellent recent monographs already exist[2]), but will instead focus on the liturgical and practical uses of C^2, T, and Ath.

∗

The role of C^2 in the Byzantine liturgy has been discussed in previous chapters.[3] As regards its use beyond worship much work remains to be done. Expositions of this creed are rare, one example being a small treatise by Euthymius Zigabenus (or Zigadenus, *fl. c.* 1100) whose precise purpose is unknown.[4] An as yet unedited exposition of C^2 is contained in cod. Venice, Biblioteca Nazionale Marciana, gr. Z. 502 (coll. 0804; *s.* XIV *in.*), ff. 275v–276v.[5] T and Ath were not entirely unknown in the Greek church[6] and were also commented upon,[7] but their influence in Byzantium remained, by and large, insignificant (not least because Ath contained the controversial *filioque*).

By contrast, in the west C^2 (mostly called the 'Nicene' creed), T, and Ath were not only regularly recited in worship, but were also subject to theological discus-

---

1 For the time being cf. Kattenbusch 1900, pp. 867–70; Wiegand 1904; Weidenhiller 1965, esp. pp. 17 f.; Vokes 1978, pp. 543–4; Foreville 1984; Blanchet/Gabriel 2016.
2 Cf. above p. 549 n. 1.
3 Cf. above chs. 11.2 and 11.3.
4 Cf. Euthymius, *Expositio symboli* (PG 131, cols. 9–20).
5 Cf. Kattenbusch 1900, p. 741 and URL <https://www.internetculturale.it/jmms/iccuviewer/iccu. jsp?id=oai%3A193.206.197.121%3A18%3AVE0049%3ACSTOR.240.10230> (23/11/2023).
6 Greek versions of both creeds usually sit in the context of the controversies and negotiations between east and west. Cf. for T: FaFo § 427 (1475–1500) and further examples in Caspari 1866–1875(1964), vol. III, pp. 25–8; Hahn/Hahn 1897, §§ 24β, 26–28, 30; Blanchet 2022, pp. 408–11; for Ath: FaFo § 434b and Laurent 1936; Grumel 1938; Kelly 1964, pp. 44–8. For translations of Ath into Coptic and Arabic cf. also Kohlbacher, 'Das *Symbolum Athanasianum*', 2004, p. 108; for a creed in Ethiopic that is influenced by Ath cf. Guerrier 1915–1917.
7 Two brief expositions of T were edited in Blanchet 2022.

https://doi.org/10.1515/9783110318531-017

sion and controversy. Sometimes the different creeds were distinguished by their initial words: *Credo in deum (patrem)* referred to T, whereas *Credo in unum deum (patrem)* usually denoted C^2.[8] (However, N and C^2 were rarely distinguished from each other, and, as we will see below, there was much confusion with regard to their origin and history.) The *Sitze im Leben* of the creeds differed from each other: T continued to be the creed of baptismal catechesis; it was, as it were, the creed of the people. C^2 was seen as a solemn declaration of faith to be chanted in mass on Sundays and major festivals where it usually functioned as 'the conclusion of the reading service, the joyous "yes" of the faithful to the message they have received'.[9] By contrast, Ath was a 'summary of orthodox theological teaching',[10] seemingly authorized by one of the greatest Fathers of the Church, and was primarily recited on Sundays at prime. However, there was great variation. In the psalters we sometimes find just T,[11] sometimes both T and Ath,[12] and sometimes only Ath,[13] usually placed at the end, often together with C^2, the canticles, and the Lord's Prayer, which reflects the practice of the daily office.[14]

---

8 Cf. Haring, 'Two Redactions', 1974, p. 40.

9 Jungmann 1951, vol. I, p. 471; cf. Jungmann 1962, vol. I, p. 602. Cf. also above ch. 11.2.

10 Kelly 1964, p. 42.

11 Cf. cod. Paris, Bibliothèque Nationale, lat. 1152 (*Psalter of Charles the Bald*; 842–869), ff. 167r–v; cf. also FaFo II, p. 352.

12 Cf., e.g., the *Dagulf Psalter* (Aachen, 783–795; cf. FaFo § 299), ff. 156v–157r (T), 157r–158v (Ath) and the *Utrecht Psalter* (Abbey of Hautvillers, 816–835 or 850; cf. § 288), ff. 90r–v (T; *symbolum apostolorum*), 90v–91r (Ath).

13 Cf., e.g., cod. Paris, Bibliothèque Nationale, lat. 13159 (*Paris Psalter*; Rhine/Meuse?, 795–800), ff. 161v–163r.

14 Cf. also Mearns 1914, pp. 5, 21–4, 53, 55, 66, 70, 78, 81; Leroquais 1940, p. LV; Hughes 1982(2004), pp. 76, 234, 236; Christopher P. Evans in CChr.CM 226, p. 101 n. 1; Gneuss/Lapidge 2014, p. 937. There are also bilingual psalters that contain T, C^2, and/or Ath in both Latin and Greek; cf. FaFo § 433 and further examples in Mearns 1914, pp. 19 f., 23 f. From his list, I have inspected:

- Paris, Bibliothèque Nationale, Arsenal 8407 (written in Liège by Sedulius Scottus, *c.* 850), ff. 63v–64r: C^2 in Latin and Greek on facing pages; cf. URL <http://archivesetmanuscrits.bnf.fr/ ark:/12148/cc87359n> (23/11/2023).
- Berlin, Staatsbibliothek, Ms. Ham. 552 (Milan, S. Ambrogio, *s.* IX/2), f. 191v: Latin C^2 with interlinear Greek in transliteration; cf. URL <https://digital.staatsbibliothek-berlin.de/werkan sicht/?PPN=PPN736607951> (23/11/2023).
- Rome, Biblioteca Apostolica Vaticana, lat. 81 (*s.* XII), f. 163r–v: Ath (*Fides catholica*) in two columns in Latin and Greek (incomplete); cf. URL <https://digi.vatlib.it/view/MSS_Vat.lat.81> (23/11/2023).

The practice of chanting Ath as part of the office is described in the sources quoted by Christopher P. Evans in CChr.CM 226, p. 101 n. 3.

By and large, clergy were expected to know T, C^2, and Ath in Latin and to instruct their flocks accordingly.[15] However, as in earlier times[16] the reality was very often different: Ratherius of Verona (887–974, bishop of Verona 931–934, 946–948, 961–968; bishop of Liège 953–955/956) found to his dismay that most of his clergy 'did not even know that creed which is thought to stem from the apostles'[17] and, in a synodical letter addressed to his priests in 966, prescribed knowledge of T, which they could find in the psalters, C^2, which was sung in mass, and Ath. He announced that they would soon be called up to give proof of their knowledge.[18] Similar episcopal and synodal admonitions were regularly repeated in successive centuries.

*

T was the standard version of the western (Roman) creed in the high middle ages throughout Europe as attested to by numerous sermons and expositions that were mostly used in baptismal catechesis or to instruct priests with regard to such catechesis.[19] Such catechetical instructions were later expanded to cover other parts of the liturgy like the Lord's Prayer or the *Ave Maria*, forming the

---

15 Cf., e.g., Hincmar of Reims, *First Capitulary* (852) 1 (he only mentions an *expositio symboli*, without specifying which creed he refers to, and Ath). In the apparatus to the edition in MGH.CE 2, pp. 34 f. numerous other testimonies are listed which need not be repeated here. Cf. also McKitterick 1977, p. 63; Longère 1991; Reeves 2010; Mériaux 2016; Van Rhijn 2022, pp. 122–6; and above p. 470 n. 36.
16 Cf. above pp. 533 f.
17 Ratherius, *Epistula 26* (MGH.B 1, p. 145, ll. 5 f.).
18 Cf. Ratherius, *Epistula 25* (MGH.B 1, p. 125, ll. 5–18), cf. id., *Epistula 26* (MGH.B 1, p. 145, ll. 4–21). Cf. also above p. 45 and n. 188.
19 Cf. the expositions mentioned in what follows. In addition there are:
– Pseudo-Alcuin, *De diuinis officiis* 41 (*c.* 900; cf. FaFo § 342).
– John of Fécamp (d. 1078), *Confessio fidei* (*c.* 1050; PL 101, cols. 1027–98 (under the name of Alcuin); cf. Leclercq/Bonnes 1946, pp. 41–4).
– Peter Abelard (d. 1142), *Expositio symboli quod dicitur apostolorum* (PL 178, cols. 617–30). This exposition is also sometimes attributed to Bernard of Clairvaux.
– Hugh of Amiens (Hughe de Boves; archbishop of Rouen 1130–1164), *De fide catholica et oratione dominica* (1155–1159; PL 192, cols. 1323–46): a treatise addressed to his nephew, Archdeacon Egidius (Giles), later (1170–1179) bishop of Évreux. In cod. Geneva, Bibliothèque de Genève, Ms. lat. 41 (1150–1175) the treatise is divided into two. The first part on the creed ends at col. 1328B ('et potest, et habet'). Cf. URL <https://www.e-codices.unifr.ch/de/searchresult/list/one/bge/lat0041> (23/11/2023). In addition, Van den Eynde 1953, pp. 80–2.
– Theobaldus Brito, Canon of Tours, *Abbreuiati symboli apostolorum expositio* (s. XIII; ed. Caspari 1883, pp. 292–300), which is full of literary allusions also to pagan authors like Horace, Ovid, and Lucan.
– Anonymous pupil of Alan of Lille, *Tractatus magistri Alani: quid sit fides, et quid articulus fidei, et quid coarticulus, et quot sint articuli* (ed. Raynaud de Lage 1943–1945): this treatise is

basis for the catechisms of the late middle ages.[20] However, not every priest had access to such explanations; sometimes glosses written on the margin of the folio which contained the creed had to do.[21] We also possess medieval credal interrogations that are based on T such as the influential *Disputatio puerorum* which was attributed to both Alcuin and Bruno of Würzburg (d. 1045).[22]

By and large, only minor variants occur in the text of T, such as *inferna/inferos*, differences in the use of *et*, or a missing *est* or final *Amen*. Yet sometimes it was treated with a degree of laxity even by eminent theologians. Thus, for exam-

---

strongly influenced by Alan and may be a work of one of his students; cf. d'Alverny 1965, pp. 69 f.

–   Raimundus Martini (1220–1285), *Explanatio symboli apostolorum ad institutionem fidelium* (ed. March 1908; cf. FaFo § 423), a lengthy exposition containing strong anti-Jewish polemic, which also shows signs of the struggle with Islam.

–   Thomas Aquinas (d. 1274), *De articulis fidei et ecclesiae sacramentis* (ed. Verardo 1954, pp. 141–51; written in 1261–1270).

–   (Pseudo-)Thomas Aquinas, *In symbolum apostolorum scilicet 'Credo in Deum' expositio* (ed. Spiazzi/Calcaterra 1954, pp. 193–217). This work, which also survives under other titles (*Deuotissima expositio super Symbolum apostolorum* or *Collationes de Credo in Deum*), goes back to a report of homilies which may have been delivered by Aquinas in Naples during Lent 1273. Cf. Torrell 1996, p. 358.

–   Anonymous, *Tractatus super simbolo*, in cod. Paris, Bibliothèque Nationale, lat. 3640 (*s.* XIV), ff. 131r–v; cf. URL <https://gallica.bnf.fr/ark:/12148/btv1b9067642j/f2.item> (23/11/2023).

–   Richard Rolle (d. 1349), *Symboli apostolici clarissima et admodum catholica enarratio*, in Rolle 1535, ff. 31r–41v: here the individual clauses are attributed to the apostles according to the sequence type IV (above p. 197).

–   *Catechismus Romanus* of 1566 (cf. FaFo § 345).

I have not seen the unedited commentary on T contained in cod. Munich, Bayerische Staatsbibliothek, Clm 16086 (*s.* XII/XIII); cf. Caspari 1866–1875(1964), vol. I, p. 233 n. 22; Kattenbusch 1900, p. 764 n. 7. – There are many more such expositions from the late middle ages including by Albert of Diessen ('Teuto', *s.* XIV/2), Henry of Langenstein (d. 1397), Johannes Marienwerder (1343–1417), Henry of Hesse (d. 1427), Nikolaus of Dinkelsbühl (d. 1433), Johannes Geuss (d. 1440), Nicholas of Graz (d. 1441), Narcissus Herz of Berching (d. 1442), Thomas Ebendorfer (d. 1464), and others that are partly unedited. Cf. Wiegand 1904, pp. 35–48. They increasingly formed part of catechisms (cf. below p. 589 n. 129). For the use of the creed in anti-heretical polemics cf. the unedited example in Wiegand 1904, pp. 24 f. The *Credo* of Jean de Joinville (d. 1317), which is a French commentary on T, is found in Friedman 1958 with extensive commentary (cf. also below p. 596). As regards late medieval works in French for lay people cf., e.g., Hasenohr 1994. Further works are found in RBMA; cf. URL <https://repbib.uni-trier.de/cgi-bin/rebihome.tcl> (23/11/2023).

20 Cf., e.g., the unedited examples by a pupil of William de Leicester (d. 1213) and by John of Waldby (d. 1372) mentioned in Wiegand 1904, pp. 26–7. In addition, Wiegand 1904, pp. 32–5.

21 Cf. above p. 533 and n. 42.

22 Cf. FaFo § 527 (new edition by Rabin/Felsen 2017). Cf. also §§ 763–765.

ple, Ivo of Chartres (*sedit* 1090–1115) fails to mention the phrase *descensus ad inferos* in his *Sermo 23*.[23] The same is true for Martin of Leon (d. 1203) who depends on Ivo. In addition, he omits the ascension.[24] Similarly, Jocelin of Soissons (*sedit* 1126–1152), opponent of Peter Abelard, omits *crucifixus*, the third day, and the final *Amen* in his *Expositio in symbolum*, in the initial list of the *twelve sententiae* which make up the creed, yet comments on all these clauses in his commentary proper.[25] Simon of Tournai (d. 1201) failed to mention *omnipotentis* after *sedet ad dexteram dei patrem*.[26] By contrast, the *Catechismus Romanus* of 1566 reads *credo sanctam ecclesiam* (FaFo § 345) – a significant addition given what has been said above![27] Honorius Augustodunensis (of Autun? origin uncertain; *s.* XII/1) included an extended T followed by a brief catechesis in his *Speculum ecclesiae*. His christological section begins: 'Et credo in suum unigenitum Filium.'[28] In some cases such omissions may, of course, also be due to scribal error.

As we saw before, T developed in Gaul and then came to be widely employed across the Frankish Empire.[29] From there it seems to have migrated to the place of origin of its ancestor R: Rome. It looks, as if the earlier practice of reciting R/T instead of C^2 at baptism had persisted in Francia and may then have ousted C^2 at baptism in Rome again.[30] With the Ottonian emperors Frankish influence may have extended to Rome. So, perhaps, that version of R most widely used in the Frankish Empire (i.e. T) came to be adopted there, too, in the tenth or eleventh century as part of 'a drastic Gallicanization of the Roman rite'.[31]

*

---

23 Cf. PL 162, cols. 604–7. He only says in col. 606B that Christ's 'soul triumphed over the underworld' (*anima illa de inferis triumphauit*).

24 Cf. Martin of Leon, *Sermo 34* (*In festiuitate sanctae trinitatis*; PL 208, cols. 1269–1350), a very long homily which can hardly have been delivered on a single occasion; it also comments upon the clauses of T (cols. 1326B–1329A).

25 Cf. Jocelin, *Expositio in symbolum* (PL 186, cols. 1479–88).

26 Simon, *Expositio super symbolum* (ed. Haring, 'Two Redactions', 1974); preserved in two recensions. *Omnipotentis* is only missing in the first recension.

27 Cf. above pp. 174 f.

28 Honorius Augustodunensis, *Speculum ecclesiae* (PL 172, cols. 823 f.; cf. Hahn/Hahn 1897, § 107). On an unedited explanation by the same author cf. Wiegand 1904, pp. 21 f.

29 Cf. above chs. 5.2 and 5.3 and the list of witnesses in FaFo § 344. For what follows cf. also Kelly 1972, pp. 426–34.

30 Cf. above pp. 408 f. The cod. Rome, Biblioteca Nazionale Vittorio-Emanuele, 2096 (Sessorianus 52; Nonantola?, *s.* XI *ex.*), discussed by Kelly 1972, pp. 428–30, is one of these witnesses.

31 Kelly 1972, p. 433.

In liturgical terms little changed until the eleventh century when renewed reflection about the order and nature of mass also extended to the creed's role in worship.[32] This may, in part, have been sparked by the introduction of C^2 in the celebration of mass in Rome at that time.[33]

The front flyleaf of cod. Reims, Bibliothèque Carnegie, 213 (320; *s.* IX) shows an eleventh-century list of all feasts during which the creed was chanted in mass.[34] These include Christmas, Epiphany, Presentation of Jesus (*ypapanti* [= ὑπαπαντή] *domini*), Annunciation, Easter, Pentecost, feasts of Saints Peter and Paul, Assumption of Mary, Nativity of Mary, All Saints, the Dedication Festival, as well as every Sunday.

John of Avranches (bishop of Avranches 1060–1067; archbishop of Rouen 1067–1079) says that the priest should begin intoning C^2 (*a sacerdote inceptum*) every Sunday, during the octaves of Easter, Pentecost, and Christmas, on Epiphany, and Ascension, and on all Marian feast days except Annunciation, on the Nativity of John the Baptist, on the feasts of all the apostles, that of the Holy Cross, St Michael, All Saints, and on the Dedication Festival. C^2 is not sung on Holy Saturday, on the Saturday before Pentecost, or any other festivals.[35]

In 1086–1090 Bernold of Constance (d. 1100) wrote a treatise about the liturgy entitled *Micrologus de ecclesiasticis obseruationibus*.[36] In it he states that 'according to the canons' (*iuxta canones*) the *Credo in unum* (i.e. C^2) was to be sung 'on all Sundays and all feasts of the Lord, likewise on the feasts of Holy Mary, the apostles, the Holy Cross, All Saints, and the Dedication', because they are mentioned in the creed.[37] No such canons survive.

Rupert of Deutz (d. 1129) called the creed (which he did not clearly identify) a *fidei tripudium* ('celebration of faith'), to be sung on Sundays and similarly solemn feast days by the choir after the gospel reading, during which a subdeacon carried the book containing the gospel to be kissed by the faithful.[38]

---

32 For what follows cf. also Capelle 1951(1967), pp. 78–81.

33 Cf. above pp. 514 f.

34 Scan: URL <https://gallica.bnf.fr/ark:/12148/btv1b84489883/f1.item> (23/11/2023).

35 Cf. John of Avranches, *De officiis ecclesiasticis* (Delamare 1923, p. 17).

36 Cf. URL <https://www.geschichtsquellen.de/werk/630>; <https://www.mirabileweb.it/title/micrologus-de-ecclesiasticis-observationibus-berno-title/668> (23/11/2023).

37 Bernold, *Micrologus de ecclesiasticis obseruationibus* 46 (PL 151, col. 1011D). Cf. Capelle 1951 (1967), p. 78–81; Gemeinhardt 2002, p. 315; Grohe 2015, p. 38.

38 Rupert, *De diuinis officiis* 2,1. He also mentions Easter and Pentecost as occasions for the *Redditio*. Honorius Augustodunensis, *Gemma animae* 3,119 also says that the gospel book is to be kissed during the recitation of the creed. His list of feasts is identical with that of Bernold. Cardinal Bernard of Porto (d. 1176) wrote an *Ordo officiorum ecclesiae Lateranensis* (*c.* 1153) which reflects Roman practice; the following feasts on which C^2 is to be sung are mentioned: every

Pope Innocent III (*sedit* 1198–1216) wrote an explanation of the church and of mass when he was still a cardinal (*Mysteriorum euangelicae legis et sacramenti eucharistiae libri VI*, 1195–97). In traditional fashion Innocent divides T into twelve *particulae*. However, he fails to indicate when and where it was recited. T is followed by C^2 which is used in mass and which in the future pope's view was also made up of twelve *clausulae* (2,50).[39] Innocent erroneously claims that Pope Damasus had decreed that the *symbolum* (he obviously refers to C^2) be chanted in mass, based on a decision by the Council of Constantinople (2,49).[40] Furthermore, he also offers a long list of feasts at which the catholic faith is to be confessed 'in solemn celebration' (*solemni tripudio*), viz. at those feasts that (in his view) were mentioned in the creed: every Sunday, Christmas, Epiphany, Maundy Thursday, Easter, Ascension, Pentecost, all Marian feast days, and all feasts of the Cross, the angels, and the apostles, the Dedication Festival, and All Saints. In addition, it was to be chanted during the octaves of Christmas (except on the Feast of the Holy Innocents), Epiphany, Easter, Ascension, Pentecost, of the Feast of Saints Peter and Paul, and of the Assumption of Mary. Special regulations applied to the Feast of the Birth of John the Baptist, of St Laurentius, and of St Agnes. Innocent had to admit that it was not in all cases obvious if a given feast was mentioned in the creed and offered detailed justificatory explanations for his choices. He also conceded that, in the view of some, the feasts of the angels were to be excluded because the angels had no need of faith, possessing, as they did, a full vision of God. Likewise, he mentions that some chanted the creed every day between Easter Sunday and Ascension, and also at the Feast of St Mary Magdalene. Good Friday and Easter Saturday were specifically excluded because the liturgy was different on these occasions anyhow, although the passion and crucifixion were mentioned in the creed (2,51). If the pope himself celebrated mass, the creed was to be chanted not by the choir but by the subdeacons at the altar (2,52). Since T is no longer mentioned, it seems that it was not used as part of mass.

Similar precepts with regard to the feasts at which C^2 was to be chanted are also found in other liturgical handbooks of the period, albeit with some modifications.[41]

Sunday, all Feasts of the Lord, of Holy Mary, of St Michael, and of all the apostles, also on All Saints, and the Festival of the Dedication. Cf. Bernard, *Ordo officiorum ecclesiae Lateranensis* 65 (Fischer 1916, p. 24, ll. 24–8). Throughout his work Bernard gives detailed instructions as to when T and C^2 are to be sung (or omitted).

39 In the 1575 edition of Innocent's works published by Cholinus at Cologne the names of the apostles were added to both creeds in the margins. Cf. Innocent 1575, pp. 354–5 and Kattenbusch 1900, p. 868.

40 Similarly, Honorius Augustodunensis, *Gemma animae* 1,78. This may be a confused reminiscence of John of Biclaro, *Chronicon* 2 (FaFo § 689) for which cf. above p. 510.

41 In his largely unpublished *Expositio super symbolum apostolicum et Nicenum*, Alan of Lille (d. 1203) mentions (d'Alverny 1965, pp. 84 f.) that T is recited quietly (*submissa uoce*) in church

Like Bernold and Innocent, Jean Beleth (*fl.* 1135–1182), who supposedly taught in Paris, holds that the creed was to be chanted at those feasts directly mentioned in the creed. His list is shorter than that of the pope as he omits Maundy Thursday, the feasts of the angels, and the Dedication Festival. Instead he adds the Feasts of the Trinity, Circumcision, and the Transfiguration of the Lord.[42] His list was repeated by Sicard of Cremona (*sedit* 1185–1215) although he added the Dedication Festival back in. In his church the creed was sung by the clergy, after the gospel reading by the deacon and the sermon by the bishop, with the voices of that clergy taking the place of that of the lay people.[43] Both authors note, however, that there was considerable discussion whether further feasts should not be added. Jean then goes on to enumerate four creeds, i.e. T (which should be said by everyone in daily prayer), Ath (which Athanasius, erroneously equated by most (!) with Anastasius, wrote against the Arians[44]), C^2 (which is sung during mass), and N (whose authorship he seems to ascribe to Hilary of Poitiers[45]).[46] Like Innocent Sicard adds that Damasus instructed C^2 to be sung during mass and mentions that when the words *et homo factus est* were spoken knees were bent.[47] The recitation of the creed concluded in both Jean and Sicard with the congregation making the sign of the cross.

The allegorical explanation of the creed's place in mass given by William Durand the Elder (bishop of Mende 1286–1296) largely depends on older interpretations.[48] At some point he seems to place the creed between the gospel reading and the sermon (4,26,1); yet he adds a little later: 'Nonetheless, in general (*commu-*

---

whereas C^2 'which is equivalent (*equipollet*) to the Apostles' Creed' is chanted 'in a loud and joyous voice (*eleuata uoce et celebriter*)' 'on the feasts of the apostles, of the blessed Virgin, and of others who were present at the publication of the Apostles' Creed' (such as Mary Magdalene, mentioned before). It is omitted on the feasts of the angels who did not need to have faith because they possessed knowledge (*scientia*) instead. This is precisely the position rejected by Innocent (cf. above in the main text). Likewise, Thomas Aquinas says (*Summa theologiae* III q83 a4c) that C^2 should be chanted on the feasts mentioned in the creed: the feasts of Christ and of the blessed Virgin, of the apostles and on similar (unspecified) occasions.

42 Cf. Jean Beleth, *Summa de ecclesiasticis officiis* 40.
43 Cf. Sicard of Cremona, *Mitralis de officiis* 3,4.
44 For the erroneous identification of the author as Pope Anastasius II (*sedit* 496–498) cf. Haring 1972, p. 208 and n. 1.
45 Jean probably refers to Hilary, *De synodis* 84 (FaFo 135d3); cf. Haring, 'Two Redactions', 1974, p. 40 n. 7.
46 Cf. Jean Beleth, *Summa de ecclesiasticis officiis* 40. Likewise, Honorius Augustodunensis distinguishes four creeds: T (*Credo in deum*), N (*Credo in deum patrem*), C^2 (*Credo in unum* – this is chanted at mass), and Ath (*Quicunque uult*). Ath was written by Athanasius 'at the behest of the Emperor Theodosius' and is recited at prime (id., *Gemma animae* 2,59).
47 Similarly, a liturgical manuscript from Florence quoted in Thompson 2005, p. 251.
48 Cf. William Durand, *Rationale diuinorum officiorum* 4,25–26.

niter tamen) the creed is chanted after the sermon, because the Church professes that it holds the faith preached."[49] He says that C^2 was to be said out aloud during mass so that it could be memorized by everyone, except for prime and compline where it should be recited silently.[50] The priest should begin chanting while standing right in front of the altar with outstretched hands first raised up high, then joining them together once he has begun. The congregation listens and makes the sign of the cross when the priest has ended his chant.[51]

Durand then goes on to enumerate the creeds: first, he calls T the 'minor creed' (*symbolum minus*). By order of Pope Damasus, he says, this is silently said on feast days during each office.[52] He goes on to quote T, ascribing each article to an apostle.[53] *Amen* is missing.[54] Second, he mentions Ath which was written by Athanasius when in Trier,[55] followed, third, by the 'major creed' (*symbolum maius*), the 'Nicene' one, which Pope Damasus instructed to be sung as part of mass, on the basis of the decrees of the Council of Constantinople, although Pope Marcus I is also said to have decreed that it be chanted aloud (*alta uoce cantari*; Marcus must be the pope who reigned for only a brief period in 336).[56] The practice of chanting the creed had come to Rome from the Greeks. Like Innocent, Durand divides C^2 into twelve clauses (*clausulae*) and, like Sicard, references the practice of genuflecting at the phrase *et homo factus est*.[57] He claims that the words *secundum scripturas* and the *filioque* had not been contained in N and C^2 (which he does not clearly distinguish from each other). At the end of the creed (*in fine ipsius symboli*) the Greeks had expressly forbidden *sub anathemate* to alter the creed which is why they consider the Roman church anathematized. But they err, because they do not acknowledge the superiority of the Roman church over the councils. Durand points out that *secundum scripturas* had been added at Constantinople, gives theological reasons for the addition of *filioque*, and refers to the Second Council of Lyons 1274.[58] The creed is to be chanted at the feasts of the twelve apostles and at the same feasts that Innocent

---

49 William Durand, *Rationale diuinorum officiorum* 4,26,1. Cf. also Morard 2008, pp. 110–11; Lang 2022, p. 304.
50 Cf. William Durand, *Rationale diuinorum officiorum* 4,25,1–2.
51 Cf. William Durand, *Rationale diuinorum officiorum* 4,25,3–4.
52 Cf. William Durand, *Rationale diuinorum officiorum* 4,25,5.
53 For the sequence (IIb) cf. above p. 196.
54 Cf. William Durand, *Rationale diuinorum officiorum* 4,25,7 (FaFo § 424).
55 Cf. William Durand, *Rationale diuinorum officiorum* 4,25,8.
56 Cf. also Radulph of Rivo (d. 1403), *De canonum obseruantia liber, propositio* 23 (Mohlberg 1911/1915, vol. II, p. 141).
57 Cf. William Durand, *Rationale diuinorum officiorum* 4,25,9–10.
58 Cf. William Durand, *Rationale diuinorum officiorum* 4,25,11–12.

had mentioned as well as the Feasts of the Trinity and of the Transfiguration of the Lord.[59] Durand gives the same instructions as to how the creed is to be chanted as Innocent does.[60] This is followed by an explanation of the individual clauses of T.[61]

Johann Burchard (d. 1506) gives an even longer lists of feast days on which C[2] is to be recited.[62] He strongly influenced the Roman Missal of 1570 by Pope Pius V (*sedit* 1566–1572).[63]

∗

We have some commentaries on Ath,[64] whereas western expositions of C[2] are much rarer. A long treatise ascribed to Albertus Magnus (d. 1280) appears to be as yet unedited.[65] A very interesting, but hitherto only partly edited *Expositio super symbolum apostolicum et Nicenum* stems from the pen of Alan of Lille (d. 1203).[66] Alan compares T and C[2] in order to demonstrate their fundamental agreement. According to him, they are similar in structure as they both contain twelve 'parts of the Christian faith' (*partes fidei christiane*) or 'articles' (*articuli*), though C[2] is more explicit than T and is also directed against the heretics wherefore Alan chooses it to serve as the basis for his detailed exposition.

Alan's mention of the *partes* or *articuli fidei* points to a debate which had arisen in the middle of the twelfth century. The creed's twelve individual 'articles' were widely discussed by canonists and theologians with regard to both their nature and hierarchy. In particular, it was asked how the individual articles were to be distributed among the apostles, whether their content was adequately phrased, whether it was in fact necessary for an individual's salvation to believe in every single article,

---

59 Cf. William Durand, *Rationale diuinorum officiorum* 4,25,13.

60 Cf. William Durand, *Rationale diuinorum officiorum* 4,25,14.

61 Cf. William Durand, *Rationale diuinorum officiorum* 4,25,15–30.

62 Cf. Johann, *Ordo Missae*, in Legg 1904, p. 148.

63 Cf. *Missale Romanum* 1570, f. b2 and Capelle 1951(1967), p. 80.

64 For earlier commentaries cf. above p. 526 and n. 17. Further commentaries (often anonymous) are listed in Burn 1896, pp. 43–5; Haring 1972 (cf. also the additions in Haring, 'Poem', 1974, pp. 225–9). For Hildegard of Bingen (1098–1179), *Explanatio symboli Sancti Athanasii* (Burn 1896, p. 44 no. 15; Haring 1972, p. 239 no, 4) cf. the edition by Christopher P. Evans in CChr.CM 226, pp. 99–133 (tr. Izbicki 2001). Simon of Tournai (d. 1201), *Expositio symboli* (Burn 1896, p. 44 no. 18; Haring 1972, pp. 240 f. no. 7) has been edited in Haring 1976. A poem about Ath was probably written by Alan of Lille (d. 1203; ed. Haring, 'Poem', 1974).

65 Cf. (Pseudo-)Albertus Magnus, *Expositio symboli*, in cod. St. Gallen, Stiftsbibliothek, 974 (*s.* XIV), pp. 558–615; cf. Caspari 1866–1875(1964), vol. I, p. 233 n. 22 (he claims that this is an exposition of N); Scherrer 1875, p. 369; Kattenbusch 1900, p. 764 n. 7, 868 n. 119. Further manuscript: Kühne/Tönnies/Haucap 1993, p. 89: cod. Osnabrück, Gymnasium Carolinum, Hs. 2 (Abbey of Iburg, *s.* XII/XIII), ff. 2r–138v. In addition, RBMA, no. 1049 (and suppl.).

66 Cf. d'Alverny 1965, pp. 79–85.

and, conversely and even more importantly, why certain dogmas such as the transubstantiation were not mentioned at all. This discussion, which has repeatedly attracted the attention of modern scholars,[67] was partly caused by the fact that the creeds used in worship did not cover altogether identical ground. The debate also deeply influenced the way in which theological subject matter was structured in academic teaching. As a result, discussion of the creed and its contents also came to be included in commentaries on the *Sentences* (beginning with Peter Lombard himself[68]) and the Summas such as that of Alexander of Hales (d. 1245)[69] or of Thomas Aquinas (d. 1274).[70] Thus the gap between what ordinary people were expected to believe and what was debated in academia widened ever further as can be seen from Lombard's section entitled 'On the faith of the simple-minded' (*De fide simplicium*).[71] He thought that the simple-minded should believe the entire content of the creed, even if they did not understand it, and he compared them (and the simple-minded of the times before the coming of Christ) to the donkeys feeding beside the oxen in Job 1:14 (which represented the patriarchs and, at least by implication, teachers of theology like Lombard himself).

∗

As regards the use of the creed in the life of the Church outside worship, there were attempts to popularize it by way of poems. For example, T formed part of a didactic poem entitled *Liber Floretus*, erroneously attributed to Bernard of Clairvaux, which was very popular in the late middle ages because it was used in schools.[72] A similar poem is contained in cod. Wiesbaden, Hessische Landesbibliothek, 35 (*s.* XV), f. 52r (FaFo § 426).[73] It probably served the same purpose as the *Liber Floretus*. We also have other credal poems.[74]

The creed could also be included in religious plays. A German play which was performed in Innsbruck on Corpus Christi 1391 (or in the following week)

---

67 Cf. Wiegand 1904, pp. 35–40; Hödl 1962; Becker 1973 citing on pp. 517–19 earlier literature; Evans 1979; Gössmann 1985; Longère 1991, esp. pp. 319–29; Frank 2017, pp. 112–33. For the early modern period Joest 1983.

68 Cf. Peter, *Sententiae* 3,25. Cf. also, e.g., Bonaventura, *Commentaria in quattuor libros sententiarum* III, dist. XXV, art. 1, quaest. 1 (cf. FaFo § 422).

69 Cf. Alexander, *Summa theologica* III,3, inq. 2, tract. 2, q. 2.

70 Cf. Thomas, *Summa theologiae* II-II q1, esp. a9 and a10. Thomas discussed this problem repeatedly; cf. above p. 574 n. 19, 578 n. 41.

71 Peter Lombard, *Sententiae* 3,25,2.

72 Cf. Bernard, *Liber Floretus*, ll. 29–37 (FaFo § 425).

73 A variation of this poem is found in cod. Cologne, Historisches Archiv der Stadt Köln, GB 8⁰ 96 (*s.* XV in.), f. 147v. Scan available at URL <https://historischesarchivkoeln.de/> (29/11/2023).

74 Cf. FaFo, vol. II, p. 405.

contained an introduction in which the apostles entered the scene, following Adam and Eve. Each apostle was preceded by a prophet who briefly announced what his successor would explain at greater length.[75] The *communio sanctorum* was, in accordance with the feast's purpose, given a eucharistic interpretation as the partaking of Christ's body 'without which no one can be saved neither in heaven nor on earth'.[76] A similar creed play, which is lost, was performed at York every tenth year at Lammastide (Lammas = 1 August).[77] We have already encountered this technique of pairing prophets and apostles when we discussed the legend of T.[78] Its representation in medieval art, which we will discuss in the next chapter, may well have influenced the authors of these plays and, conversely, may also have served to illustrate what was happening on stage.[79]

Other evidence suggests that credal questions were used as an introduction to penance. A fairly brief version of such questions occurs in the manual *De diui-*

---

[75] The play is contained in cod. Innsbruck, Universitätsbibliothek, 960 (written in 1391), ff. 50v–59r. Scan URL <https://diglib.uibk.ac.at/urn:nbn:at:at-ubi:5-815> (23/11/2023). The text is edited in Mone 1841, pp. 145–64. Cf. Woolf 1972, p. 72; Tydeman 1978, p. 101; Neumann 1982; URL <https://www.handschriftencensus.de/2318> (23/11/2023). The pairs that can be reconstructed from the Innsbruck play are as follows (Old Testament verses sometimes tentative):

Jeremiah 3:19 – Peter: Credo in deum, patrem omnipotentem, creatorem caeli et terrae.
David: Ps 2:7– Andrew: Et in Iesum Christum, filium eius unicum, dominum nostrum.
Isaiah 7:14 – James: Qui conceptus est de spiritu sancto, natus ex Maria uirgine.
Daniel: Is 53:7 – John: Passus sub Pontio Pilato, crucifixus, mortuus et sepultus.
Hosea 13:14 – Thomas: Descendit ad inferna; tertia die resurrexit a mortuis.
Amos 9:6 – James: Ascendit ad caelos; sedet ad dexteram dei, patris omnipotentis.
Joel 3:8 – Philip: Inde uenturus est iudicare uiuos et mortuos.
Haggai: Joel 2:28 – Bartholomew: Credo in spiritum sanctum.
Zephaniah 3:20 – Matthew: Sanctam ecclesiam catholicam, sanctorum communionem.
Malachi: Mic 7:19 – Simon: Remissionem peccatorum.
Zechariah: Ezek 37:12 – Jude: Carnis resurrectionem.
Obadiah 21 – Mathias: Et uitam aeternam.

The sequence of the apostles follows type IIIa (cf. above p. 196). Most prophets also sing a Latin antiphon before their speech. As regards these pairs cf. FaFo § 428 and above p. 199.

[76] Mone 1841, p. 156: '[. . .] ich gloube ouch in dyᵉ meynschaft der heilgen, // alzo wil ich uch daz bezeygen, // ich meyn den fronlichnam, // den got mit willen an sich nam // von Maria der reynen mayt, // alz Yzaias hat gesayt [cf. Is 7:14]; // an en mag nymant selig werden // wedir in hymmel noch uf der erden.' Cf. also above pp. 180 f.

[77] Cf. Anderson 1963, p. 38; Woolf 1972, pp. 59–61; Tydeman 1978, pp. 116 f., 207, 241. In addition, cf. Woolf 1972, pp. 156 f.

[78] Cf. above ch. 5.4.

[79] Cf. below pp. 592–5.

nis officiis, ascribed to Alcuin, but probably dating to around 900.[80] A longer, but closely related version survives in the *Ordo ad penitentiam agendam et confessionem faciendam* as part of an interpolated Rule of Chrodegang (compiled in England in *c.* 900–920), contained in cod. Cambridge, Corpus Christi College, Ms. 191 (Exeter, 1050–1075), p. 59.[81] Here the following interrogation can be found:

> Servant of God, do you believe in God, the Father Almighty, creator of heaven and earth? I believe.
>
> Again: Do you believe in the Father, the Son, and the Holy Spirit? I believe.
>
> Again: Do you believe that these three persons whom we named [*or:* as we said, *quomodo diximus*], Father, Son, and Holy Spirit, are three persons and one God? I believe.
>
> Again: Do you believe that you will receive in this same flesh in which you now exist [according to] what you have done and what you will do, either good or ill [cf. 2Cor 5:10]? I believe.
>
> Again: Do you believe that there is a resurrection and life after death? I believe.
>
> Again: Do you wish to forgive all those how have sinned against you all evil deeds in order that God will forgive you all sins, as the same Lord says in the Gospel: 'If you forgive others their sins, your sins are forgiven' [cf. Mt 6:14]? I wish.[82]

The Latin is accompanied by a translation into Old English.[83] Other handbooks for priests contain introductions detailing for what purpose such interrogations were to be conducted.[84] Similar questions and liturgical instructions regarding the creed are also included in orders for the visitation of the sick.[85]

In addition, the practice of bishops and archbishops publishing personal creeds, typical of the English church, continued into the mid-tenth century.[86]

Finally, creeds continued to be used as incantations in medicine and magic.[87] As such they did not necessarily have to be translated into the vernacular, since a magical formula did not have to be comprehensible to be effective.

*

---

80 Cf. Pseudo-Alcuin, *De diuinis officiis* 13 (FaFo § 761b). The same interrogation is found with minor variants in the *Paenitentiale Cantabrigiense* (*s.* X; ed. Delen et al. 2002, p. 356 (ll. 37–42)) and in numerous other sources; cf. Meens 1994, pp. 206 f. and Delen et al. 2002, p. 346 n. 24.

81 Cf. description and scan: URL <https://parker.stanford.edu/parker/catalog/rs890dd0432> (23/11/2023). As regards this version of the Rule cf. Bertram 2005, pp. 175–83.

82 Pseudo-Chrodegang, *Regula Longior Canonicorum seu Regula S. Chrodegangi Interpolata* 32. My translation from the manuscript. Cf. also Napier 1916, p. 39, ll. 1–12; PL 89, col. 1072B–D; Bertram 2005, p. 202. An English translation was made in *c.* 1000 (cf. Bertram 2005, pp. 178 f.).

83 Cf. (Pseudo-)Chrodegang of Metz, *Regula canonicorum* 30 (Napier 1916, p. 40, ll. 11–24). Cf. also Wulfstan's *English Handbook for the Use of a Confessor* below p. 586.

84 Cf. Schmitz 1898, pp. 57 f., 405, 430, 680; McNeill/Gamer 1938(1990), pp. 281, 315 f., 324; Frantzen 1983, pp. 165–7 and below p. 585.

85 Cf. Dinkler-von Schubert 1964, pp. 77–81.

86 Cf. FaFo §§ 477–480 and 482; in addition, Wilcox 2014, pp. 330–5.

87 Cf. above ch. 15.

However, in catechesis this was a different matter.[88] As C[2] was not used for this purpose, we do not find many vernacular versions of this creed in the western Church as opposed to the oriental churches where N, C[2], and related creeds were widely translated.[89] The first evidence that T was memorized in the vernacular stems from the first half of the eighth century. Bede writes that he had translated the creed and Lord's Prayer into the *lingua Anglorum* for priests who did not speak Latin.[90] The Second Synod of Clofesho (747) decreed that those priests

> who are [as yet] ignorant should learn to interpret and set out in their own tongue (*propria lingua*) the creed, the Lord's Prayer, and also the most-sacred words that are solemnly recited during the celebration of the mass and the office of baptism.[91]

In England as elsewhere the believers were expected to know both texts by heart and were threatened with excommunication if they did not.[92] The *Capitulary* of Haito of Basel (*sedit c.* 806–813) demanded that everyone know the Lord's Prayer and T by heart in both Latin and the vernacular (*barbarice*).[93] The bishops of the Synod of Mainz in 813 were sufficiently realistic to assume that the Lord's Prayer and the creed would be learned in the vernacular, even if Latin was preferable.[94] Later bishops left the problem which version of the creed (Latin or vernacular) was to be memorized to the baptizand's parents or sponsors. As Jocelin of Soissons (*sedit* 1126–1152) put it:

> It does not matter in which language the creed is being taught or learned, as long as [the baptized children when they have reached an appropriate age] firmly believe it.[95]

*

The first examples of the creed in Old High German date from the Carolingian period. A German translation of T (together with the Lord's Prayer) which displays some peculiarities is found in a codex from St. Gallen from the late eighth century; its context is unclear (FaFo § 300). By contrast the so-called Weissenburg Catechism (*s.* IX/1) which contains T and Ath in German primarily served to in-

---

88 For what follows, cf. also Kinzig, 'Formation des Glaubens', 2019(2022), pp. 259–61.
89 Cf. above ch. 9.
90 Cf. Bede, *Epistula ad Egbertum* 5 (FaFo § 584). In addition, Angenendt 1987, pp. 292 f.; Blair 2005, pp. 109, 161.
91 Synod of Clofesho (747), canon 10 (FaFo § 587b).
92 Cf. Jolly 1996, p. 69; Raw 1997, pp. 29 f.; Wilcox 2014, pp. 318 f.
93 Cf. Haito of Basel, *Capitulary*, ch. 2 (FaFo § 747a) and Diesenberger 2016, p. 176.
94 Cf. Synod of Mainz (813), canon 45 (FaFo § 754). In addition, Geuenich 1983, pp. 120 f.; Diesenberger 2016, p. 176.
95 Jocelin, *Expositio in symbolum* 2 (PL 186, col. 1431A–B).

struct priests, though it may also have been used for catechetical purposes (§§ 303, 434c; cf. also § 302).[96] Likewise, a number of brief Carolingian baptismal interrogations survive which show that the baptizands were expected to affirm their faith in the Trinity at baptism (§§ 766–8, 771).[97]

We can get an idea of what teaching about the creed may have looked like in German from the explanation by Notker Labeo (d. 1022), a monk and teacher at St. Gallen, which is appended to the psalter and the canticles. Each of the Latin clauses of T is accompanied by a translation and some notes explaining, for example, the name of Pontius Pilate or *filioque*.[98] It is followed by a German explanation of the Latin text of Ath.[99] A further brief exposition is found in another version of this German psalter in cod. Vienna, Österreichische Nationalbibliothek, 2681 (the so-called 'Vienna Notker'; Wessobrunn?, *c.* 1100), ff. 227r–v.[100]

∗

Bede's aforementioned remark notwithstanding, the first formulae of T and Ath in Old English (Anglo-Saxon) date from the tenth century and are, from that point onwards, fairly frequently attested, often as part of a psalter, subsequent to the canticles.[101] Ælfric of Eynsham (*c.* 955 – *c.* 1010) translated the Lord's Prayer, T (which he called 'the minor creed') and C² ('the mass creed') into English.[102] In T he omitted *catholicam*. In C² he read 'God of God' (*Gode of Gode*) before 'light of light' (*Leoht of Leohte*) and *passus est, crucifixus est pro nobis* (Pilate's name is omitted). 'The life-giving God' (*ðone Lif-fæstendan God*) seems to presuppose *deum uiuificantem*. Instead of *catholicam* we read *geleaffullan* ('believing').[103] He also

---

96 Cf. also Haubrichs 1995, p. 238; Masser 2013.
97 As regards later creeds cf. Hahn/Hahn 1897, §§ 100–21; Stammler 1960(1978), col. 760; Barbian 1964; Steer 2004; Hellgardt 2013. In addition, Geuenich 1983, p. 121. For Ath cf. also Ommanney 1897, pp. 320–2.
98 Cf. Sehrt 1955, pp. 1101 f.//Tax 1983, pp. 565 f. Text also in Hahn/Hahn 1897, § 101. In addition, Tax 1972, pp. XLIII–XLIV.
99 Cf. Sehrt 1955, pp. 1107–17//Tax 1983, pp. 568–75. In addition, Tax 1968; Tax 1972, pp. XLIV–XLV.
100 Cf. Hahn/Hahn 1897, § 103 and URL <https://www.handschriftencensus.de/9386> (23/11/2023). As regards the different versions cf. Glauch 2013, pp. 298 f.
101 Cf. the list in Wilcox 2014, pp. 314 f. and the texts in Hahn/Hahn 1897, §§ 78–89. In addition, Förster 1942/1943. For Ath cf. also Ommanney 1897, pp. 304–20; Holthausen 1942/1943; Gretsch 1999, pp. 273–80, 430 f.
102 Cf. Thorpe 1846, pp. 596–9. Cf. also Gatch 1977, p. 52.
103 Another version of C² is found in cod. Oxford, Bodleian Library, MS Junius 121, f. VIr (secondary gloss, *s.* XIII; ed. Crawford 1928, p. 5). Cf. also Bethurum 1957, pp. 104–6; Pope 1967, pp. 185–8.

wrote two consecutive homilies on the Lord's Prayer and the creed.[104] In the second homily, which was delivered on a Wednesday in Rogationtide, he offered an introduction to the creed based on C^2 and Ath.[105] In the words of Malcolm Godden, 'no other Anglo-Saxon homily provides any sort of parallel for this detailed discussion of trinitarian doctrine [. . .].'[106]

Wulfstan (bishop of London 996–1002, of Worcester and York 1002–1016/1023) told his priests that each lay person was to learn the Lord's Prayer and the creed.[107] For that purpose he again translated both texts into English in his *Homily VIIa* which is appended to a homily on the creed (*Homily VII*) and in which he introduced each clause by the words 'we believe' (*we gelyfað*) as well as making some additions.[108] Wulfstan may also be the author of the *English Handbook for the Use of a Confessor*.[109] This is introduced by a brief Latin *Ordo confessionis* ascribed to Jerome which contains instructions for private confession. Here the penitent is told to recite the creed *Credo in unum Deum* (hence probably C^2) before confession.[110] However, the English text that follows offers a different creed:

> Ic gelife on Drihten heahfæder, ealra þinga wealdend, *and* on þone sunu, *and* on þone halgan gast; *and* ic gelife to life æfter deaðe; and ic gelife to arisenne on domes dæge. *And* eal þis ic gelife þurh Godes mægen *and* his miltse to weorðone.

> I believe in the Lord, the heavenly Father, ruler of all things; and in the Son; and in the Holy Ghost; and I believe in life after death; and I believe to arise on doomsday; and all this I believe to take place through God's power and mercy.[111]

Wulfstan also gave extensive explanations of the baptismal rite of his time in his sermons.[112]

---

104 Cf. Ælfric, *Catholic Homilies I*, 19–20.

105 Edition: Clemoes 1997, pp. 335–44. Commentary: Godden 2000, pp. 159–66. Translation: Thorpe 1844, pp. 275–95. Cf. also Raw 1997, pp. 31–5.

106 Godden 2000, p. 159.

107 Cf. Wulfstan, *Canons of Edgar*, canons 17 and 22 (Rabin 2015, pp. 90 f.); cf. Frantzen 1983, p. 175.

108 Ed. Bethurum 1957, pp. 157–65 and 166–8 respectively. Cf. also Raw 1997, pp. 30 f.; Lionarons 2010, pp. 82, 85–92.

109 Edited by Fowler 1965. As regards the problem of Wulfstan's authorship cf. Heyworth 2007.

110 Cf. *Handbook*, ll. 17–19 (Fowler 1965, p. 16).

111 Text: *Handbook*, ll. 27–31 (Fowler 1965, p. 17; emphasis original). Translation: Thorpe 1840, p. 403.

112 Cf. *Sermones VIIIa–c* (Bethurum 1957, pp. 169–184); in addition, Spinks 2006(2016), pp. 132 f.

A versified Old English rendition of T (where the verses follow the individual original Latin articles) is found in cod. Oxford, Bodleian Library, MS Junius 121 (s. XI), ff. 46r–47r as part of the Benedictine office.[113]

Sometimes the Old English text was added as an interlinear gloss to the creed's Latin text.[114] This practice is continued into the late middle ages, as can be seen from the *Middle English Glossed Prose Psalter* (s. XIV) which contains an interlinear translation of Ath.[115] As regards the position of the creed in medieval Anglo-Saxon baptismal rites it may suffice here to refer to the learned account by Bryan D. Spinks.[116]

∗

The earliest version of T in (Anglo-Norman) French seems to date from the mid-twelfth century and is contained in the *Eadwin (Canterbury) Psalter* (cod. Cambridge, Trinity College, R.17.1 (Canterbury, 1155–1160)), where it is written in between the lines of the Latin version (FaFo § 432, cf. § 419). French translations of Ath also emerge at about the same time.[117]

∗

So far little research has been carried out about the role of the creeds in the medieval history of Jewish-Christian relations. The trinitarian doctrine as defined in T and C^2 served to define Christian orthodoxy both over against dissent from within Christianity, but also over against other religions. In that process, the early Christian creeds no doubt contributed to widening the gulf between Judaism and Christianity. Christian dissenters (such as the Arians) who saw monotheism endangered by this doctrine were often accused of 'Judaizing' in intra-Christian polemic. In addition, specially adapted creeds and credal texts played an important role in converting Jews to Christianity, be it voluntarily or by force. A famous example is the so-called *Placitum* of 637 which was signed by the Jewish Christians of Toledo and which contains a lengthy credal passage.[118] The Twelfth Council of Toledo (681) decreed in canon 9 that Jews had to set out their new Christian faith in writing. However, there was great variety: no similar passage is found in the *Placitum* of 654

---

113 Cf. Dobbie 1942, pp. 78–80; Ure 1957, pp. 87, l. 16 – 88, l. 14 and URL <https://digital.bodleian. ox.ac.uk/objects/44360db1-f67e-47c3-8136-6515a090d968/> (23/11/2023).
114 Cf. Wilcox 2014, p. 314. Cf. also FaFo §§ 430, 432.
115 Edition: Black/St-Jacques 2012, vol. I, pp. 102–4.
116 Cf. Spinks 2006(2016), pp. 127 f.
117 Cf. Ommanney 1897, pp. 322–30 and Black/St-Jacques 2012, vol. II, pp. 179 f. For further Anglo-Norman literature from the thirteenth century cf. Reeves 2010, pp. 65–71.
118 Cf. *Placitum* (637) 2–3 (FaFo § 494; Kinzig, 'Die Verpflichtungserklärungen', 2019(2022), pp. 55–7).

which was included in the *Visigothic Code* (*Liber Iudiciorum*), thus serving as a model formula across Spain. Often it sufficed that the new converts confessed their allegiance to Christ.

Furthermore, there are narratives describing conversions of Jews in which credal texts were being used. One such example is the account of a spontaneous conversion after Jews had perceived the healing miracles performed by an image of Christ in Berytus. This conversion was allegedly accompanied by a 'spontaneous' recitation of a credal text that forms part of a homily preserved under the name of Athanasius which was very popular in the middle ages.[119]

The creeds also figured to a certain extent in Jewish–Christian polemic. They formed, of course, the backdrop to Jewish–Christian debates on the Trinity.[120] However, sometimes we also find explicit quotations. Thus the *Niẓẓaḥon Vetus*, an anti-Christian polemic compiled in the late thirteenth or early fourteenth century first quotes the creed in Latin, Hebrew, and Yiddish (all in Hebrew transliteration) and then goes on to comment:

> Now, one may ask that since they say that they believe in God and in Jesus, it follows that Jesus is not God. Moreover, they say that he sits at the right hand of God; this indicates that he himself is not God. Otherwise, they should have said, 'He who sits on a lofty and exalted throne' [Isa. 6:1]; only that would indicate that he himself is divine.[121]

A Hebrew translation of T in Latin script was contained in a (now lost) codex from Essen (*c.* 950?).[122] In some cases, these translations were used in mission to the Jews. For example, Fabiano Fioghi, himself a convert who was active in late-sixteenth century Rome in the *House of the Catechumens* (an establishment for instructing converts), translated Christian prayers as well as T into Hebrew for this purpose.[123] Furthermore, a Hebrew version of T in Latin script is found in the religious play *Le mystère de la Résurrection*, performed in Angers in May 1456 and perhaps written by Jean du Prier.[124]

The use of the creeds in Jewish-Christian debates and polemics, in modern Christian catechisms in Hebrew, and in other Christian literature addressed to Jews requires further investigation.

∗

---

119 Cf. Pseudo-Athanasius, *Sermo de miraculo Beryti* 6 (FaFo § 192).
120 Cf. Lasker 2007, esp. pp. 45–104.
121 *Niẓẓaḥon Vetus* 231 (Berger 1979, p. 155 (Hebrew), 220 (English)).
122 Text and translation in FaFo § 429.
123 Cf. Stow 1976, pp. 221, 225.
124 Text in Schwab 1902; cf. also URL <https://www.arlima.net/mp/mystere_de_la_resurrection.html> (23/11/2023).

These are only some highlights of what clearly was a complex process. We may conclude our account here, because a new era dawned in the late middle ages which would lead to the development of catechetical tables and textbooks that were used in instructing lay people in the creed, the Lord's Prayer, and the Ten Commandments, the seven principal sins, and the seven sacraments; the subsequent eras of Humanism and the Reformation would then commence critical investigation into the history of the creeds and their contents. As yet, no one study exists that fully covers these developments in sufficient detail. A useful collection of sources compiled by Jaroslav Pelikan and Valerie Hotchkiss also includes modern creeds;[125] Pelikan provides a helpful survey of the genre's development over the centuries, written from the point of view of systematic theology.[126] The relevant sections in the article 'Glaubensbekenntnis(se)' in the *Theologische Realenzyklopädie* and the history by Fairbairn and Reeves also cover the later developments, but are primarily interested in 'confessions' (in their definition) rather than creeds.[127] The creed's development in Byzantium up to the seventeenth century is described in the contributions to a volume edited by Marie-Hélène Blanchet and Frédéric Gabriel that also contains a number of editions of later credal texts.[128] A number of studies considers the development of catechetical literature.[129] An excellent overview of research into the history of T has been published by Markus Vinzent.[130] Supplementary material is found in the relevant sections of the present book.[131] The controversies surrounding T in the later nineteenth and early twentieth centuries in Switzerland, Germany, and (to a certain extent) England have been described by Rudolf Gebhard, Hanna Kasparick, and Julia Winnebeck.[132] However, much work remains to be done.

---

125 Cf. Pelikan/Hotchkiss 2003.
126 Cf. Pelikan 2003.
127 Cf. Schwarz, 'Glaubensbekenntnis(se) VII.', 1984; Schwarz, "Glaubensbekenntnis(se) VIII.', 1984; Fairbairn/Reeves 2019. Cf. also above p. 2 n. 7.
128 Cf. Blanchet/Gabriel 2016.
129 Cf., e.g., Göbl 1880; Reu 1904–1935; Jungmann 1959, pp. 1–64; Weidenhiller 1965; and Fraas et al. 1988. Catholic scholarship is summarized in Burkard 2020, pp. 22 f.
130 Cf. Vinzent 2006.
131 Cf. above ch. 2.
132 Cf. above p. 14 n. 5.

18 The Creeds in Medieval Art

Interestingly T and C^2 have fared quite differently when it comes to visual representations and musical settings. By and large, one may say that T was the creed which was painted and C^2 the creed which was sung. In what follows I will first take a look at art, confining myself to the period up to the fourteenth century.[1]

As far as I can see, Ath was rarely painted in western medieval art although general representations of the Trinity may, of course, have been influenced by it.[2] Similarly, representations of N or C^2 (either with regard to their text or their content) are only rarely found in the Latin Church. By contrast, scenic representations of the content of C^2 became popular in Russian icon painting in the seventeenth century though that is outside our purview here.[3] The text of C^2 also frequently appears on icons depicting the Council of Nicaea or of St Paraskeva Pyatnitsa (Paraskevi of Iconium) who holds a scroll inscribed with this creed as a sign of her faith.[4]

*

As soon as T no longer had to be kept a secret known only to the baptized, because (at least nominally) all of the populace in Francia and its successor states had been converted to Christianity and there no longer was, therefore, any danger of its falling into the hands of 'heathens',[5] its text and content were frequently depicted in western Christian art: in inscriptions, in manuscripts, in paintings, in wooden carvings on choir stalls, and in mural frescoes. The creed thus no longer was just a matter of catechism and of liturgy, but also became a part of religious imagery.

Medieval inscriptions containing the entire creed (other than the clauses attributed to the individual apostles in images discussed below) are fairly rare. I have already described the earliest examples above.[6] T was, for example, inscribed on a lead panel attached to the tomb of Archbishop Adalbert I of Mainz (d. 1137) which is preserved in the Dom- und Diözesanmuseum in Mainz.[7] It begins as follows: 'I, the sinner Adalbert, Archbishop and Legate of the Apostolic See, died on 23 June, believing in God [. . .].' Subsequently the full creed seems to have been quoted. (The panel

---

1 For secondary literature cf. the list in FaFo, vol. II, p. 408. In addition, cf. Boespflug 1990; Wochnik 2010; Backes 2011; Kendrick 2016.
2 Cf. the catalogue of relevant representations in Iacobone 1997.
3 Cf. van Os 1968, col. 463, offers an example which is kept in the Ikonen-Museum Recklinghausen.
4 Cf. Knoben 1976(1994); Grossman 1980, p. 39.
5 Cf. above p. 536.
6 Cf. above pp. 170, 172, 539.
7 Description, transcription, and image: URL <https://nbn-resolving.de/urn:nbn:de:0238-di002mz00k0001306> (Rüdiger Fuchs/Britta Hedtke/Susanne Kern; 29/11/2023).

https://doi.org/10.1515/9783110318531-018

is, unfortunately, highly damaged.) It may be that T here serves not only to demonstrate the archbishop's orthodoxy, but also to protect him from evil's harm just as in the cases we discussed above in chapter 15. In a famous early-fourteenth century mural by Giotto di Bondone (d. 1337) as part of a series of painted sculptures featuring virtues and vices in the Cappella degli Scrovegni (Arena Chapel) in Padua, the personification of Fides is depicted largely in white and black, holding a staff with a red cross in one hand and a scroll inscribed with the creed in the other.[8]

✳

Otherwise, the legend of T's apostolic origin and the distribution of individual clauses to each apostle is central to medieval representations of T. Copies of the *Somme le Roi* (*A Survey for a King*, a guide to virtue), which was written by Laurent d'Orléans in the late thirteenth century, contain colourful miniatures of the fictitious council of the Apostles where they allegedly composed this creed.[9]

Most frequent, however, are representations of the apostles holding scrolls showing parts of the creed. Their figures may appear individually or in combination with other imagery. Unfortunately, the unique frescoes of the apostles in the church of St George on the Isle of Reichenau (late ninth century), who appear to have held scrolls with credal text, were largely destroyed and later largely supplemented by modern copies by Carl Philipp Schilling (1855–1924) during his work on the site undertaken between 1889 and 1892.[10]

Perhaps the earliest preserved examples are found on the splendid shrine of St Heribertus in Cologne-Deutz, completed in *c.* 1175.[11] Here each apostle sits on a stool, some holding a scroll with the relevant section of T. In between them we see the prophets standing, accompanied by banners with quotes from the Old Testament.

Another magnificent example, again from the Rhineland, is found on the lid of the Portable Altar of Eilbertus (part of the Guelph Treasure) which was made in Cologne in the middle of the thirteenth century and is today kept in the Kunstgewerbemuseum in Berlin.[12] The central square of its lid shows Christ in Majesty, surrounded

---

8 Image: URL <https://de.m.wikipedia.org/wiki/Kardinaltugend#/media/Datei%3AFides_-_Capella_dei_Scrovegni_-_Padua_2016.jpg> (23/11/2023).

9 See a list of manuscripts and further literature in Kinzig 2018(2022), p. 304 n. 69.

10 Cf. Jakobs 1998, p. 186 n. 53.

11 For details cf. Wernicke 1887–1893, 1889, pp. 43–5; Seidler 2016, pp. 14, 80–97 and plates 33–51; pp. 103–10 and plates 159–77. This is a unique sequence, because the apostles, led by Peter and Paul, are distributed across the long sides of the shrine: Peter – Andrew – James – John – Bartholomew – Thomas // Paul – James – Philip – Matthew – Simon – Jude (= Thaddaeus).

12 Description and transcription: URL <https://nbn-resolving.de/urn:nbn:de:0238-di035g005k0001108> (Andrea Boockmann; 23/11/2023). Cf. also URL <https://id.smb.museum/object/1830347> (23/11/2023). A stimulating interpretation of the imagery of this altar is found in Lipton 2011, pp. 53–63.

by the symbols of the evangelists. This square is surrounded by twelve other squares, each depicting an apostle holding a scroll containing the creed.[13] On both the left and the right there are four additional scenes, depicting the Annunciation, Mary with Elizabeth, the nativity, Jesus' Presentation at the Temple, his crucifixion, resurrection, descent to hell (in this order!), and ascension. An inscription along the altar's upper edge runs as follows: 'Doctrina pleni fidei patres duodeni testantur ficta non esse prophetica dicta.' ('Filled with the doctrine of faith, the twelve fathers bear witness that the words of the prophets are not made up.') On the lower edge another inscription refers to the prophets, reading, 'Celitus afflati de Cristo vaticinati hi predixerunt que post ventura fuerunt.' ('Inspired by heaven, they prophesied about Christ; they foretold those things which were to come after.') On the side panels are representations of sixteen prophets holding scrolls with their principal prophecies. Old and New Testament, prophets and apostles, prophecy and creed are thus closely linked.

The apostles are also portrayed on the shrine of St Elizabeth (*c.* 1235–1249) in the church erected in her memory in Marburg, Germany. Here the clauses of the creed are written in the pointed arches above their heads. The sequence of the apostles and the attribution of the credal clauses are unique.[14] In Brunswick Cathedral the apostles are depicted on the vault of its crossing where they are inserted into the walls of the heavenly Jerusalem (1230–1250).[15] They are again complemented by prophets with some of their sayings, although there are only eight.

✳

Whereas the relationship between individual prophets and apostles is not clearly defined on the shrine of St Heribertus, the Altar of Eilbertus, and in Brunswick, in other places we find portrayals in which individual apostles are paired with a prophet each, something which we had already encountered in the literary evidence.[16] Unfortunately, a very early example of a mural painting of this type in the Abbey Church of Bad Gandersheim (Lower Saxony) no longer exists. It probably dated to the early eleventh century.[17] These combinations became particularly pop-

---

13 The text is identical with T; the sequence corresponds to type IIIa as represented by Clm 22053 and others (cf. above pp. 196 f.).
14 Details in Dinkler-von Schubert 1964, pp. 69–84, 173 and plates 1, 22 f.
15 Description and transcription: URL <https://nbn-resolving.de/urn:nbn:de:0238-di035g005k0002308> (Andrea Boockmann; 23/11/2023); image: URL <https://commons.wikimedia.org/wiki/File:BraunschweigerDom_Vierung_WB2485_DSC00065_PtrQs.jpg> (23/11/2023). The text is identical with T (abbreviated); the sequence corresponds to type IIa (cf. above p. 196).
16 Cf. above p. 199.
17 Description and (fragmentary) transcription: URL <https://nbn-resolving.de/urn:nbn:de:0238-di096g017g1000802> (Jörg H. Lampe/Christine Wulf; 23/11/2023). The sequence of the apostles probably corresponded to type IIIa.

ular from the early fourteenth century onwards. In the *Queen Mary Psalter* (cod. London, British Library, Royal MS 2 B VII; *c.* 1310–1320), ff. 69v–70r[18] miniatures of this kind are executed in beautiful colours with red, blue, gold, and white dominating.[19] A contemporary representation of both prophetic sayings and clauses from T, accompanied by the names of the prophets and apostles respectively, is found in cod. British Library, Arundel MS 83 II (from the so-called *De Lisle Psalter*; *c.* 1310, f. 128r[20]). The words form the shape of a tree with Christ as its head. The prophets and the apostles are shown, grouped together, in the top left- and right-hand corners respectively.[21]

Even more sophisticated is a representation of the prophets and the apostles in the first part of the same manuscript (the so-called *Howard Psalter*, written in *c.* 1310/1320, f. 12r): it shows the prophets on the far left and apostles on the far right, arranged in rows, each with a banner carrying prophetic sayings (on the left) and credal clauses (on the right), and connecting each pair with a scene in the middle representing the credal content from top to bottom.[22]

A representation of the creed which closely resembles that in the *De Lisle Psalter* is found in cod. Yale University Library, Beinecke MS 416, f. 2r which was probably produced at the Cistercian monastery of Kempen near Düsseldorf in *c.* 1300.[23] However, there are no images depicting the prophets and apostles. Instead a second hand added C^2 (in twelve numbered clauses) beneath the diagram and, further below, a brief explanation of the creeds. There are other manuscripts with similar

---

18 Description cf. URL <https://www.bl.uk/manuscripts/FullDisplay.aspx?ref=Royal_MS_2_b_vii>; scan of the codex: URL <https://www.bl.uk/manuscripts/Viewer.aspx?ref=royal_ms_2_b_vii_f001r> (22/01/2021).

19 The text is identical with T (abbreviated); the sequence corresponds to type IIIa as represented by Pseudo-Augustine and Reg. lat. 481 (cf. above pp. 196 f.).

20 As regards the complex history of this codex which consists of two parts (the *Howard Psalter* and the *De Lisle Psalter*) cf. Sandler 1983, pp. 11–13 and the descriptions: URL <https://www.bl.uk/manuscripts/FullDisplay.aspx?ref=Arundel_MS_83> (11/05/2013); <https://www.bl.uk/catalogues/illuminatedmanuscripts/record.asp?MSID=6458&CollID=20&NStart=83> (12/05/2023). A reproduction of the miniature is found in Sandler 1983, plate 7 and online: URL <https://www.bl.uk/manuscripts/Viewer.aspx?ref=arundel_ms_83_f001r> (20/10/2023).

21 Cf. URL <http://www.bl.uk/manuscripts/Viewer.aspx?ref=arundel_ms_83_f128r> (11/05/2023). This is type IIIa in the version also found in Pseudo-Augustine and Reg. lat. 481 (cf. above pp. 196 f.).

22 Cf. URL <http://www.bl.uk/manuscripts/Viewer.aspx?ref=arundel_ms_83_f012r> (11/05/2023). This is again type IIIa, but with another distribution of clauses than on f. 128r.

23 Cf. the description: URL <https://pre1600ms.beinecke.library.yale.edu/docs/pre1600.ms416.htm> (23/11/2023). Scan: URL <https://brbl-archive.library.yale.edu/exhibitions/speculum/pages/2r.jpg> (23/11/2023).

diagrams (which also contain other catechetical content). It has been suggested that they may go back to John of Metz (Johannes Metensis; *fl. c.* 1270–1280).[24]

Much less spectacular are ink drawings in cod. Pommersfelden, Schloss Weissenstein, 215 (2837; Abbey of Kastl, *c.* 1322–1356, f. 160r–v)[25] where prophets and apostles are shown not accompanied by any other imagery.

By contrast, in a series of French illuminated manuscripts they consistently appear at the bottom of a page, combined with architectural representations.[26] It is unclear whether or not they meant to relate in any way to the images at the top of each page above the text:

- the *Book of Hours* of Joan of Navarre (cod. Paris, Bibliothèque Nationale, NAL 3145; *c.* 1330–1340), ff. 4r–9v;[27]
- the *Breviary of Belleville* (cod. Paris, Bibliothèque Nationale, lat. 10483–10484; 1323–1326), ff. 6r–v (incomplete);[28]
- the *Petites heures de Jean de Berry* (cod. Paris, Bibliothèque Nationale, lat. 18014; 1375–1410), ff. 1r–6v.[29]

Prophets and apostles are also paired in frescoes and stained-glass windows of the same period found in simple parish churches in various regions.[30] These representations served both esthetic and didactic purposes.

---

24 Cf. Sandler 1983, p. 23 and n. 52. For a list of similar manuscripts cf. Sandler 1983, pp. 134–9. In addition, cf. Castelberg 2013, pp. 81 f.

25 Description: URL <http://www.handschriftencensus.de/9431> (23/11/2023). This is in many ways a unique series, because not only the sequence of apostles differs from all that are known so far, but also because it has been supplemented by Paul and Athanasius: Peter – John – James – Andrew – Thomas – Bartholomew – Philip – Matthew – James – Simon – Thaddaeus – Mathias – Paul (+ Heb 11:6) – Athanasius (+ Athanasian Creed 42).

The creed reads *qui uenturus est* (which is clearly influenced by C^2).

26 Cf. Mâle 1949, pp. 246–53.

27 Description: URL <https://archivesetmanuscrits.bnf.fr/ark:/12148/cc71029k>; scan: URL <https://gallica.bnf.fr/ark:/12148/btv1b10025448r> (23/11/2023). The sequence of the apostles corresponds to type Ia (cf. above p. 194).

28 Description: URL <https://archivesetmanuscrits.bnf.fr/ark:/12148/cc785374>; scan: URL <https://gallica.bnf.fr/ark:/12148/btv1b8451634m> (23/11/2023).

29 Description: URL <https://archivesetmanuscrits.bnf.fr/ark:/12148/cc784809>; scan: URL <https://gallica.bnf.fr/ark:/12148/btv1b8449684q> (23/11/2023). The sequence of apostles corresponds to type IIIa in the version also found in Pseudo-Augustine and Reg. lat. 481 (cf. above p. 196).

30 For frescoes cf. the following examples:

- Church of St Peter and Paul in Dollnstein in Upper Bavaria from 1320–1330 (images: URL <https://de.wikipedia.org/wiki/Dollnstein#/media/File:Kirche_von_Dollnstein_im_Landkreis_Eichst%C3%A4tt,_Fresko_im_Chorraum.jpg>; 23/11/2023)
- Church of St Pancras in Hamm-Mark (North Rhine-Westphalia) from *c.* 1350 (image: URL <https://www.deutsche-digitale-bibliothek.de/item/NEJ2MSVN5JPQ6IW5VBYGA2ZCGE NUSHOZ>; 23/11/2023)

A very unusual panel, which was produced in *c.* 1380 for the Abbey of Wormeln (North Rhine-Westphalia), and is today preserved in the Gemäldegalerie der Staatlichen Museen zu Berlin, shows the Virgin and Child representing the throne of Solomon with twelve lions standing on the steps to the right and left which represent the apostles, accompanied by floating scrolls containing the creed.[31]

✳

It is difficult to identify depictions illustrating the content of the creed without any explicit reference to the apostles or to the creed's text, as the biblical scenes which the creed evokes were, of course, painted over and over again. By way of example, I have mentioned the *Howard Psalter* above. Perhaps the earliest scenic representation of credal content is found in the *Utrecht Psalter* (cod. Utrecht, Universiteitsbibliotheek, 32) from the time of Louis the Pious.[32] On f. 90r–v T is quoted in between the Lord's Prayer and Ath, preceded by a drawing which combines a number of scenes that include Christ's birth, the trial before Pontius Pilate, the crucifixion, the resurrection of Christ, the ascension, Pentecost, the general resurrection of the dead, and the Final Judgement. The text of T is followed by an image which may represent the fictitious council of the apostles convened to compose this creed – however, the number of apostles is much greater than a dozen. The fact that very similar images are found in the *Eadwin Psalter* from the middle of the thirteenth century (cod. Cambridge, Trinity College, R.17.1; Canterbury, *c.* 1155–1160;

– Church of St Martin in Billigheim (Southern Palatinate) from *c.* 1400 (images: URL <http://www.ingenheim.evpfalz.de/index.php?id=4976#c11355>; 23/11/2023)
– Church of St Andrew in Oberacker (near Karlsruhe) from *c.* 1400; cf. Backes 2011, p. 151 and plate 145 (images: URL <http://kirchenwandmalereien.de/html/o.html#Oberacker>; 23/11/2023).
For later examples cf. Backes 2011. – Further examples from stained glass windows are found, e.g., in the Church Divi Blasii in Mühlhausen (Thuringia; 1310/30). Cf. URL <https://de.wikipedia.org/wiki/Divi-Blasii-Kirche#/media/Datei:M%C3%BChlhausen_Divi-Blasii_Fenster_228.JPG>; <https://de.wikipedia.org/wiki/Divi-Blasii-Kirche#/media/Datei:M%C3%BChlhausen_Divi-Blasii_Fenster_229.JPG>; <https://de.wikipedia.org/wiki/Divi-Blasii-Kirche#/media/Datei:M%C3%BChlhausen_Divi-Blasii_Fenster_231.JPG> (23/11/2023). Cf. Wernicke 1887–1893, 1889, p. 61.

31 Image and description: URL <https://id.smb.museum/object/867143> (23/11/2023). The text of the creed is incomplete and faulty; the sequence of the apostles corresponds to type IV (cf. above p. 197). Cf. also van Os 1968, col. 463.

32 The secondary literature is found in FaFo § 288. For a scan of the codex cf. URL <https://psalter.library.uu.nl/> (23/11/2023).

cf. FaFo § 432) on f. 279r–v may suggest that these illuminations (like others in these manuscripts) go back to a common ancestor.

The *codex unicus* of the commentary on the creed by Jean de Joinville (d. 1317), cod. Paris, Bibliothèque Nationale, NAF 4509 (*s.* XIII/XIV) contains a series of illuminations depicting the content of the creed.[33] A mystifying series of related drawings also illustrating Joineville's *Credo* is contained in cod. Paris, Bibliothèque Nationale, lat. 11907 (late 1280s), ff. 231r–232v.[34] These sketches may have been intended as a model for church paintings, possibly in Acre in the Holy Land. Here the text of T is written above scenes taken from both the Old and New Testament.

A later example is a series of nine panels illustrating the second article of C^2 by Benedetto di Bindo (d. 1417) which is kept in the Museo dell'Opera del Duomo in Siena.[35]

In the early twentieth century D.T.B. Wood published an inventory of tapestries dating from the fifteenth to the sixteenth centuries which contained the clauses of the creed (or parts thereof) accompanied by appropriate imagery.[36] According to written sources such tapestries were already produced in the fourteenth century, but no early examples seem to have survived.[37]

*

In the fifteenth century the use of credal imagery exploded. This cannot be described here in any greater detail. It may suffice to highlight the fact that we now also find pictorial instructions to help memorize the creed. One fine example is found in an early print of the German treatise *Schatzbehalter der wahren Reichtümer des Heils* (*Treasury of the True Riches of Salvation*) written by the Franciscan monk Stephan Fridolin (d. 1498) and published by Anton Koberger in Nuremberg (1491).[38] On f. UIIIv it contains a representation of the twelve apostles on the fingers of a left hand depicted, each finger numbered and labeled, showing three apostles on each. (The phalanges of the thumb are covered by Christ and the Virgin.) The

---

33 Description: Friedman 1958; URL <https://archivesetmanuscrits.bnf.fr/ark:/12148/cc403993> (23/11/2023); for a scan of the codex cf. URL <https://gallica.bnf.fr/ark:/12148/btv1b52511232w> (23/11/2023).

34 Description: URL <https://archivesetmanuscrits.bnf.fr/ark:/12148/cc73300s/cd0e180>; for a scan of the codex cf. URL <https://gallica.bnf.fr/ark:/12148/btv1b10507275b> (23/11/2023). Discussion of purpose and date in Folda 2005, pp. 500–502.

35 Image: URL <https://commons.wikimedia.org/wiki/File:Bindo_Credo.JPG> (23/11/2023).

36 Cf. Wood 1913/1914.

37 Cf. Wood 1913/1914, p. 248.

38 I am grateful to Maria Munkholt Christensen for drawing my attention to this book. Cf. Bartl 2010, esp. pp. 238–40; Bartl/Gepp-Labusiak 2012, plates pp. 148 f.

text of T with the twelve numbered articles is printed next to this hand.[39] On the opposite page we once more encounter Christ and the Virgin as well as another twelve figures, including the evangelists, John the Baptist, and Joseph who are 'written' into the right hand. The corresponding text makes it clear that the association of the apostles/the creed and the remaining figures with the phalanges of the fingers not only served as a mnemonic device, but also had an apotropaic function. It shows 'how to arm the hands against the temptation of the evil enemy'.[40] The remainder of the text gives *inter alia* clear instructions how to use one's left hand at encounters with a heretic. Once more the creed is used here as a sacred formula which protects both the mind and the body of the person who has duly memorized it.[41]

---

39 Cf., e.g., the copy in the Badische Landesbibliothek in Karlsruhe which can be viewed at URL <https://digital.blb-karlsruhe.de/blbihd/content/pageview/5953392> (23/11/2023).

40 Fridolin 1491, f. T IIIIr: '[. . .] dass ist, wie man die hend wider die anfechtung des bösen veindes woppenen soll.'

41 Cf. above ch. 15.

19 The Creeds in Medieval Music

When was the creed first sung?[1] It is not easy to answer this question, because we know very little about late antique and early medieval Church music. In addition, the terminology is ambiguous, because both the Latin verb *canere/cantare* and Greek ᾄδειν and ὑμνεῖν cover a wide semantic field, from reciting a poetic text, to some kind of chanting, or to full-out singing.[2] Finally, one has to take into account considerable regional differences in music making.

However, given that neither C^2 nor T were ever regarded as poetic texts as such and given that we have unambiguous evidence from a later period of the creeds being sung, the use of *canere* in relation to C^2 or T may indicate that at least *some* kind of singing, similar to plainchant, was taking place from a fairly early stage. As I am no musicologist, I will not delve into the details of this development. Instead, it may suffice to present some of the evidence we have that the creed was sung in what follows.

*

Let us first look at the Byzantine tradition. Unfortunately, we know very little about the way the creeds were recited in Greek worship.[3] Very often our liturgical sources say that it was 'said' by the people or by both the clergy and the people. Earlier scholars, therefore, surmised that the creed was never sung in Byzantine worship.[4] But λέγειν in this context may actually refer to some kind of chanting. In some instances, ψάλλειν is used instead of λέγειν; the archdeacon begins and the congregation chimes in. In some manuscripts there are indications that the creed was sung by a choir.[5] As we saw in an earlier chapter, John of Biclaro

---

1 Good introductions to vocal music in late antiquity and the early middle ages include Levy 1998; Page 2010(2012); Eberhardt/Franz 2013; Everist/Kelly 2018; Oefele 2022. On the creed in music cf. Stäblein 1952; Miazga 1976; Huebner 1986; Hiley 1993, pp. 168–71; Probst 1994; Schlager 1995; Crocker/Hiley 2001; Petersen 2012; Russin 2021.

2 Cf. Krebs/Schmalz 1905, 254–7; Schlier 1964, pp. 163 f.; Delling 1972, p. 490; Thraede 1994, cols. 916–17.

3 Cf. Taft 1978, pp. 416–18; Kritikou 2011, pp. 167 f.; Russin 2021, pp. 94–6.

4 Cf. Baumstark 1921, p. 174; Jungmann 1951, vol. I, p. 468; Jungmann 1962, vol. I, pp. 599 f.

5 Cf. Goar 1730, p. 155 from the now lost *Codex Isidori Pyromali*: Ὁ διάκονος· Πρόσχωμεν καὶ τὸ σύμβολον ψάλλωμεν. Καὶ τοῦ Ἀρχιδιακόνου ἀρχομένου πάντες τὸ σύμβολον ψάλλουσιν. / 'The deacon: Let us pay attention and let us sing the creed. And after the archdeacon has begun all sing the creed.' The same in Cochlaeus 1549, p. 125 (from a now lost codex once kept in the monastery of Johannisberg near Mainz) which may go back 'at least to the tenth century' (Taft 1978, p. XXVII; cf. also Taft 1998, pp. 68–71). Similarly, the liturgy from cod. London, British Library, Add. 34060 (*s.* XV), 7,4–5 (ed. Taft 1979(1995), p. 298; emphasis original): Λέγει ὁ ἀρχιδιάκονος· Ἐν

https://doi.org/10.1515/9783110318531-019

claimed in 601/602 that the creed had been sung by the congregation (*a populo con-cinendum*) in the Byzantine Empire since the times of Emperor Justin II (r. 565–578), but this may be a reflection of western practice.[6] In 840–842 Walahfrid Strabo claims that the Greeks had begun to chant C^2 as a means of fighting heresy.[7]

Nonetheless, there seems to be only one relatively early manuscript which gives us some indication as regards the eastern practice of chanting the creed: cod. Oxford, Bodleian Library, Holkham gr. 6, written in Antioch in 1050–1055. It contains the texts for the six feasts dedicated to the ecumenical councils during which N and C^2 (with certain variants) are sung, accompanied by ecphonetic nota-tion.[8] Other than that, there is no evidence in our eastern liturgical sources for musical settings of C^2 until the fifteenth century.[9] It is, therefore, also difficult to say whether there is any connection between Byzantine chanting of the creed and that of the western tradition (or traditions).

✳

As we saw in a previous chapter, C^2 is the confession of faith which initially served as the primary creed in the western mass.[10] We get the first inklings that the creed was chanted at the Third Council of Toledo (589) where it was ordained that C^2 'be recited (*recitetur*) according to the convention of the eastern churches so that, before the Lord's Prayer is said, the creed shall be proclaimed (*praedice-tur*) aloud by the congregation'.[11] A variant reads *decantetur* which may be trans-lated as 'shall be chanted'.[12] The manuscript tradition thus indicates that at a certain point liturgical practice had changed and the creed was no longer spoken aloud, but chanted by the congregation. However, as the earliest codex containing

---

σοφία πρόσχωμεν. Καὶ οὕτως ψάλλει τὸ ἱερατεῖον μετὰ τοῦ λαοῦ τὸ *Πιστεύω εἰς ἕνα θεόν*. / 'The archdeacon says, "Let us wisely pay attention." And thus the clergy sing with the laity, "I believe in one God."' (The folia containing the liturgy date from the twelfth century.) In addition, Goar 1730, pp. 60, 140 f. Cf. also Taft 1978, pp. 378 f.; Russin 2021, p. 95.

6 Cf. above p. 510.

7 Cf. Walahfrid, *Libellus de exordiis et incrementis quarundam in obseruationibus ecclesiasticis rerum* 23 (FaFo § 851), quoted above 513 n. 180.

8 Cf. Engberg 1962 and URL <https://medieval.bodleian.ox.ac.uk/catalog/manuscript_6185>; <https://www.doaks.org/resources/mmdb/manuscripts/1830> (29/11/2023).

9 Cf. FaFo §§ 692 (*Liturgy of St Mark*); 693a (*Liturgy of St James*); 694b (Liturgies of St Basil, St Gregory, and St Chrysostom). In addition, Engberg 1962, p. 300; Kritikou 2011, pp. 168 f.

10 Cf. above ch. 11.2. For what follows cf. Wagner 1901, p. 91; Wagner 1911, pp. 102–5; Wagner 1921, pp. 458–61; Jungmann 1951, vol. I, pp. 468 f., 472–4; Jungmann 1962, vol. I, pp. 599 f., 604–6.

11 Third Council of Toledo (589), canon 2 (FaFo § 687b = Heil/Scheerer 2022 (*Dokument* 120.2), p. 2794, ll. 7–21). Cf. already above pp. 406, 510.

12 Cf. Martínez Díez/Rodríguez 1966–2002, vol. V, p. 110, app. ad l. 743; Heil/Scheerer 2022 (*Dokument* 120.2), p. 294, app. ad l. 17.

this variant dates from the second half of the eighth century,[13] it is possible that this development occurred at a later stage than the council. This suggestion is strengthened by the fact that the earliest additional evidence which mentions 'chanting' of the creed is not found until a century after Toledo.

This evidence is contained in the baptismal liturgy at Rome.[14] The *Old Gelasian Sacramentary* (OGS), whose final redaction may date to the seventh century, records in the context of the *Traditio symboli* that an acolyte first 'says the creed in Greek by chanting' (*decantando*) and then does the same in Latin.[15] (By contrast, during the *Redditio* the creed is recited only by the bishop.[16]) This may indicate that the custom of chanting the creed was adopted when R/T was replaced in the Roman baptismal liturgy by Greek and Latin C^2 under the influence of the Greek popes of the later seventh century.[17]

A variation is found in the *Ordo Romanus XI*, a Roman order for the preparation and celebration of infant baptism which is probably based on the OGS and may stem from the second half of the sixth century. Its *Traditio* resembles that of the OGS.[18] However, at the *Redditio* the priest lays his hand on the heads of the baptizands and chants the creed 'in a high voice' (*decantando excelsa uoce*)[19] which indicates that by that time the liturgy had further evolved and the chanting of the creed by a member of the clergy had become standard in both the *Redditio* and *Traditio*.

The creed was also sometimes sung in Greek (transliterated in Latin letters) as part of a Greek mass (*Missa Graeca*) which perhaps also originated in Rome in the later seventh century.[20] However, it is difficult to say whether this 'Hellenization' of baptism and of the mass in Rome happened simultaneously and to what extent they may have influenced each other. In addition, this does not mean that the creed was chanted (or even said) during the Latin mass at Rome, because

---

13 The codex Φ listed in the apparatus of Martínez Díez/Rodríguez 1966–2002, vol. V, p. 110 is cod. Den Haag, Het huis van het boek (Museum Meermanno-Westreenianum), 10.B.4 (*s*. VIII/2; on this codex and the collection it represents cf. Martínez Díez/Rodríguez 1966–2002, vol. I, p. 339; vol. V, p. 21; Kéry 1999, p. 45).

14 In the Irish *Book of Mulling* (*s*. VIII/2) chanting of the creed may also be attested (cf. FaFo § 695); but the evidence is thin.

15 Cf. *Sacramentarium Gelasianum Vetus* nos. 311, 314 (FaFo § 675a). Cf. also above p. 504.

16 Cf. *Sacramentarium Gelasianum Vetus* no. 422 (FaFo § 675b).

17 Cf. above p. 411.

18 Cf. *Ordo Romanus XI*, nos. 62, 64 (FaFo § 808a).

19 Cf. *Ordo Romanus XI*, no. 86 (FaFo § 808b).

20 Cf. FaFo § 184g. For a list of western liturgical manuscripts containing chanted versions of C^2 in Greek cf. Atkinson 1982, pp. 120–125, 136. However, the *Missa Graeca*'s place of origin and the date are extremely controversial. Cf. the survey of different scholarly opinions in Wanek 2018; in addition, Atkinson 1989; Atkinson 1993 and above p. 411 and n. 185.

Pope Leo III denied in his conversation with the Frankish envoys that the Franks had inherited the custom of chanting the creed from Rome.[21]

The custom of chanting the creed *at baptism* migrated from Rome to Francia as we can see when we look at Frankish (eighth-century) sacramentaries that are based on the OGS. Perhaps the earliest example comes from the so-called *Ordo Romanus XV* which was compiled a little before 787, probably by a Burgundian or Austrasian monk. Here the creed is chanted in Latin by an acolyte at the *Traditio* and by the priest at the *Redditio*.[22] In the *Sacramentary of Gellone* of the late eighth century both the Greek and Latin versions of C^2 are chanted at the *Traditio* by two acolytes.[23] By contrast, at the *Redditio* the creed is not recited or chanted by the clergy at all, but replaced by baptismal interrogations.[24] The Sacramentary of Reims (*c.* 800) follows the same procedure.[25] Jesse of Amiens (*sedit c.* 799–836) only mentions the Latin creed in his explanation of the order of baptism where it is chanted at the *Traditio*, whereas the renunciation is followed by baptismal questions.[26] The *Pontifical of Donaueschingen* (*s.* IX *ex.*) contains further modifications: here the creed is chanted at the *Traditio* in both Greek and Latin by the acolytes, but at the *Redditio* the creed and the Lord's Prayer are recited only by the priest, and then followed by brief baptismal questions.[27] The introduction of baptismal questions may well be a result of the reform of the liturgy and chant that was undertaken during the reign of Pepin III (*sedit* 751–768), although its extent remains a matter of controversy.[28]

In any case, by the end of the eighth century, C^2 had also come to be chanted during mass in the territories under Frankish rule. In a letter to Beatus of Liébana, one of the leaders of Spanish adoptionism, Alcuin reminded his addressee of there being two natures and one person in Christ, 'as we are accustomed to chant in the creed of the catholic peace' (*sicut in symbolo catholicae pacis cantare solemus*). He went on to quote C^2.[29] A set of interrogations in the *Collectio duorum librorum* of unknown provenance edited by Keefe (*s.* IX *in.*) confirms that C^2 was

---

21 Cf. above p. 567.

22 Cf. *Ordo Romanus XV* (FaFo § 809a, b).

23 Cf. *Sacramentarium Gellonense*, nos. 545, 547 (FaFo § 797a).

24 Cf. *Sacramentarium Gellonense*, no. 671 (FaFo § 797b). Cf. also above pp. 409 f.

25 Cf. *Sacramentarium Remense* (FaFo § 799a, b).

26 Cf. Jesse, *Epistula de baptismo* (FaFo §§ 757, 780a[2]).

27 Cf. *Pontifical of Donaueschingen*, nos. 324, 342 (FaFo § 683a, b).

28 Cf. Hen 2001, pp. 42–64; Page 2010(2012), pp. 281–328; Pfisterer 2018, pp. 84 f.; Dyer 2018; Fassler 2018, pp. 180 f.; Haug 2018, pp. 286, 290; Planchart 2018, pp. 638 f.

29 Alcuin, *Epistula ad Beatum Liebanensem abbatem* (FaFo § 702f). As regards the phrase *catholicae pacis* cf. Levison 1946(1973), p. 320 n. 1. Alcuin repeatedly mentions the creed being chanted in his writings against Felix of Urgel: *Epistula 23* (§ 702c); *Aduersus Felicem Urgellitanum episcopum* 1,9 (§ 702g1); 1,16 (§ 702g2). 17 (PL 101, col. 143A); 3,6 (col. 274C); 4,4 (col. 288D). Cf. also Alcuin,

the creed 'which we now chant during mass' (*quod ad missam canitur*).[30] In the later eighth century Angilbert of Saint-Riquier prescribed the singing of all three creeds by the *scola puerorum* (which included girls) and, as far as possible, by all of the laity in his Rogations liturgy.[31] This practice was also attested to by the Frankish envoys during their aforementioned visit to Leo III.[32]

Walahfrid Strabo also comments on the custom of chanting in his important testimony concerning the introduction of the creed into mass (840–842). I have quoted his explanation above.[33] He mentions not only that the creed was inserted into mass 'in imitation of the Greeks', but, in addition, claims that the Greeks had also begun to chant C^2. This practice (*ille usus*) then migrated to Rome in the first instance; later the creed 'came to be repeated' (*coepit [. . .] iterari*) 'among the Gauls and Germans' (*apud Gallos et Germanos*) during mass in the struggle against adoptionism. Above I suggested that the Roman church accepting the practice of chanting the creed may be connected with the aforementioned appearance of the *Missa Graeca*. However, from Walahfrid's testimony it is not quite clear whether the same practice was also found among the 'Gauls and the Germans' or whether Walahfrid simply wishes to say that they, too, were using the creed during mass. Whatever he may have meant it is clear that in Francia the creed had at that point been chanted for some time, and (as we saw above) there is some evidence to suggest that the Franks did inherit this custom from Rome, at least with regard to baptism. In Frankish churches the creed was chanted during mass as a response to the Gospel reading.[34]

De trinitate ad Fredegisum quaestiones XXVIII, *quaestio* 25 (§ 702l) and Capelle 1934(1962), pp. 215 f.; Levison 1946(1973), p. 320 n. 2.

30 *Collectio duorum librorum, De symbolo* (Keefe, *Explanationes*, 2012, p. 48, ll. 14–15 (text 31); FaFo § 528[2]).

31 Cf. Angilbert, *Institutio de diuersitate officiorum* 9 and Rabe 1995, pp. 130 f.

32 Cf. also Amalarius of Metz, *Ordinis missae expositio I*, 9 (812/813–852/853; FaFo § 850a; cf. below n. 34); Herard of Tours, *Capitulary* (written in 858), cap. 16: All should know the Lord's Prayer and the creed (*simbolo*) by heart. The Gloria patri, Sanctus, creed (*credulitas* – this must be C^2), and Kyrie are 'to be sung reverently by all (*a cunctis reuerentur canatur*)'. The same in Walter of Orléans, *Capitulary* (869–870), cap. 1. As regards additional evidence from the late ninth and tenth centuries cf. *Ordo Romanus V* (s. IX ex.), no. 40 (Andrieu 1931–1961, vol. II, p. 218, l. 2); *Ordo Romanus IX* (s. IX ex.), no. 21 (Andrieu 1931–1961, vol. II, p. 332, l. 19); *Ordo Romanus X* (s. X/1), no. 32 (Andrieu 1931–1961, vol. II, p. 357, ll. 13 f.). However, provenance from Francia is not always certain. Cf. Vogel 1986, pp. 161 f., 164.

33 Cf. Walahfrid, *Libellus de exordiis et incrementis quarundam in obseruationibus ecclesiasticis rerum* 23 (FaFo § 851); cf. above p. 513 n. 180.

34 Cf. Amalarius of Metz, *Ordinis missae expositio I*, 9 (812/813–852/853; FaFo § 850a). Strangely, in *Missae expositionis codex I*, 8,2 (812–816; § 850b) he only says that, after the Gospel reading,

Whether or not C² was chanted as part of the Roman (Latin) mass in the ninth century is unclear. In June 880 Pope John VIII (*sedit* 872–882) wrote a letter to the Moravian ruler Svatopluk in which he mentions a conversation with Archbishop Methodius of Moravia, asking him 'whether he believed the creed of the orthodox faith and sang it (*caneret*) during the holy celebration of mass' in the same way as was Roman custom and as it had been handed down by the six Ecumenical Councils.[35] As no such synodal instruction to sing the creed during mass exists, John may simply have wanted to make certain that the creed used in Moravia did not include *filioque*.[36] Nonetheless, it is remarkable that the chanting of the creed during mass is specifically mentioned.

Be that as it may, the practice of chanting C² may not have been introduced into the (Latin) mass at Rome until the early eleventh century. As mentioned above,[37] in 1014 Abbot Berno of Reichenau travelled to the Eternal City in the retinue of the German King Henry who was to be crowned emperor (Henry II) by Pope Benedict VIII (*sedit* 1012–1024). Berno says that at Henry's behest the creed was chanted during mass in Rome from then on.[38] Indeed, in 1054 Humbert of Silva Candida defended the council of Nicaea against the charge of not mentioning the *filioque* 'which the Roman Church now sings' (*quod romana mater nunc canit ecclesia*).[39] The *nunc* may indicate that this custom had been introduced not that long ago.[40]

We find the first examples of C² accompanied by neumes in the tenth century,[41] and there have been attempts at reconstructing the 'authentic' melodies

---

the congregation professes the creed 'with a loud voice' (*praeclara uoce*). Furthermore, cf. Aeneas of Paris, *Liber aduersus Graecos* 93 (868; § 852).

35 Pope John VIII, *Epistula 255* (MGH Epp. 7, p. 223, ll. 6–10). For general background cf. Betti 2014, pp. 87, 152 f., 162–8, 182.

36 Cf. also Capelle 1951(1967), p. 77. As regards the *filioque* controversy in 879/880 cf. Gemeinhardt 2002, pp. 244–65.

37 Cf. above pp. 514 f.

38 Cf. Berno, *Libellus de quibusdam rebus ad missae officium pertinentibus* 2 (FaFo § 854). Cf. Gemeinhardt 2002, pp. 314 f.

39 Humbert, *Rationes de sancti spiritus processione a patre et filio* 4,1 (Michel 1924/1930, vol. I, p. 100, ll. 14–16); cf. Gemeinhardt 2002, p. 313.

40 Cf. also Grohe 2015, pp. 35–8.

41 Cf. Capelle 1951(1967), pp. 71 f. and the literature quoted above pp. 598 n. 1, 599 n. 10. In addition, Miazga 1976, p. 18; Russin 2021, pp. 80 f. The earliest manuscripts seem to be:
- cod. Chartres, Bibliothèque Municipale, Ms. 47 (Bretagne, *s*. X), f. 69r–v (mutilated). The codex was destroyed in 1944, but had already been heavily damaged before. URL <https://bvmm.irht.cnrs.fr/resultRecherche/resultRecherche.php?COMPOSITION_ID=17376> (23/11/2023)
- cod. Bamberg, Staatsbibliothek, Msc. Lit. 6 (Regensburg (St Emmeram), *c*. 1000), f. 95v; URL <https://zendsbb.digitale-sammlungen.de/db/0000/sbb00000128/images/index.html> (23/11/2023)

used then.[42] Almost all these Latin versions of C^2 follow the translation attributed to Paulinus.[43] Although initially the chant of the *Credo* 'remained in the simplest form of a syllabic recitation',[44] once it had been set to polyphony in the fourteenth century,[45] it often 'became the show-piece amongst the chants of the Ordinary'.[46] As Jungmann notes:

> In fact, because of its broad presentation and because of the musical unfolding of its inexhaustible contents, it has attained such an importance in the full course of the mass that it leaves the eucharistic prayer (which, in its design, is much akin to it) quite in the shadow.[47]

However, this fascinating development lies outside the scope of the present book.

✳

As regards T, there is evidence that it was sung at least occasionally in some places. However, 'no source with diastematic notation is known'.[48] Around 475 Faustus of Riez describes it as a 'salutary poem/song' (*symboli salutare carmen*).[49] The unknown author of a *Sermo de symbolo* from around the same time speaks of the

---

- cod. St. Gallen, Stiftsbibliothek, 381 (*s*. XI), pp. 18–22 (called *Symbolum apostolorum*); URL <https://www.e-codices.unifr.ch/en/list/one/csg/0381> (23/11/2023)
- cod. Paris, Bibliothèque Nationale, lat. 776 (Albi, *s*. XI), f. 92v–93r (FaFo § 184f29); cf. also Hiley 1993, pp. 169 f.
- cod. Paris, Bibliothèque Nationale, lat. 887 (Saint-Martial Abbey, Limoges, *s*. XI), f. 59v–60v (a second Latin version on ff. 60v–61v is different); URL <https://gallica.bnf.fr/ark:/12148/btv1b84322963> (23/11/2023); cf. also Hiley 1993, p. 169
- cod. Berlin, Staatsbibliothek, theol. qu. 11 (today in Cracow, Jagiellonian Library; St Gallen, 1024–7), ff. 100r–101r (*Symbolum apostolorum*); 101r–103v (*Symbolum apostolorum Grece et Latine*; Greek transcribed) 103v–104r (*Aliter*; Greek transcribed/Latin); URL <https://www.e-codices.unifr.ch/en/searchresult/list/one/bj/Berol-Theol-Lat-Qu-0011> (23/11/2023)
- cod. Colmar, Bibliothèque Municipale, 443 (cat. 218; *s*. XI/1), f. 4v; URL <https://bvmm.irht.cnrs.fr/iiif/1960/canvas/canvas-539894/view> (23/11/2023).

42 Cf., e.g., Mocquereau 1909; Huglo 1951(2005); Schlager 1984. On the earliest musical versions cf. also Wagner 1911, 102–5; Wagner 1921, pp. 458–61; Russin 2021, pp. 77–110.
43 Cf. above pp. 560 f.
44 Cf. also *Graduale Triplex* 1979, pp. 769–84 which ascribes the oldest musical settings of the creed (*Credo I* and *Credo VI*) to the eleventh centuries; cf., however, Russin 2021, pp. 79–87.
45 An earlier example in a manuscript from Sens (*s*. XIII) is mentioned by Charles Burney (1726–1814); cf. Burney 1789(1935), p. 504; Schlager 1995, col. 1039.
46 Jungmann 1951, vol. I, p. 473; cf. Jungmann 1962, vol. I, p. 605.
47 Jungmann 1951, vol. I, p. 473; cf. Jungmann 1962, vol. I, p. 605.
48 Hiley 1993, p. 168. He adds, 'Likewise unknown in any notated source is the Athanasian Creed ("Quicumque vult salvus esse"), said at Prime.'
49 Faustus, *De spiritu sancto* 1,1 (FaFo § 363).

Apostles as having 'sung' (*cantare*) the verses of the confession.[50] Beda Venerabilis, writing to Bishop Egberht of York in 734, exhorts the faithful to sing (*decantare*) the creed in their own language every morning as a spiritual antidote to the devil's poison.[51] Here chanting evidently enhances the creed's magical effect, which is now also attributed to its vernacular versions![52] In the Frankish Empire, T and the Lord's Prayer were also chanted, as can be seen from the writings of Alcuin[53] and the Bishop of Metz, Amalarius.[54] What this looked like in detail, whether it was actually sung at full voice, rendered as a recitative-like chant, or simply a half-voiced murmuring or humming, eludes us. St. Gallen codices from the late ninth century onwards also contain T in Greek, written in Latin letters and provided with neumes.[55]

---

50 Anon., *Sermo de symbolo* 4 (CPL 1759; FaFo § 357). The date suggested in FaFo § 357 (*s.* V) cannot be correct since the text depends on Gregory the Great; cf. Kinzig, 'Liberating the Dead', 2024 (*sub prelo*).

51 Bede, *Epistula ad Egbertum* 5 (FaFo § 584).

52 Cf. above ch. 15.

53 Cf., e.g., Alcuin, *Epistula 23* (to Felix of Urgel; FaFo § 702c). Further references in Levison 1946-(1973), p. 320 n. 2.

54 Cf. Amalarius, *Epistula ad Carolum imperatorem de scrutinio et baptismo* 40 (FaFo § 782a2).

55 Early examples:

- cod. St. Gallen, Stiftsbibliothek, 17 (St. Gallen, AD 880–900), pp. 334–6; URL <https://www.e-codices.unifr.ch/en/csg/0017/> (24/11/2023). T is bilingual. Only the Greek text is accompanied by neumes.
- cod. Berlin, Staatsbibliothek, theol. qu. 11 (today in Cracow, Jagiellonian Library; St Gallen, 1024–1027), ff. 103v–104r; URL <https://www.e-codices.unifr.ch/en/bj/Berol-Theol-Lat-Qu-0011/> (24/11/2023). T is bilingual. Only the Greek text is accompanied by neumes.
- cod. St. Gallen, Stiftsbibliothek, 338 (St. Gallen, *c.* 1050–1060), pp. 308 f. (FaFo § 431); URL <https://www.e-codices.unifr.ch/en/csg/0338/> (24/11/2023). Greek only.
- cod. St. Gallen, Stiftsbibliothek, 381 (St. Gallen, *s.* XI), pp. 14 f. (cf. Atkinson 1982, p. 124); URL <https://www.e-codices.unifr.ch/en/csg/0381> (24/11/2023). Greek only.
- cod. Zurich, Zentralbibliothek, Rh. 97 (St. Gallen?; *s.* XI), p. 36 (*non uidi*, cf. Mohlberg 1951, p. 206; Atkinson 1982, p. 125).

Cf. also Wagner 1911, p. 102 n. 5 (citing the text from Rh. 97; the reference to the Tropary of Winchester seems to be erroneous); Hiley 1993, pp. 168–71, 235 f. (referring to cod. Laon, Bibliothèque Municipale, 263 (Laon; *s.* XII/XIII; Tropary), f. 139r–v: an extended ('farsed') Latin T with neumes), 528. I could not verify the reference in: Atkinson 1982, p. 122 to cod. Oxford, Bodleian Library, Selden Supra 27 (*s.* XI *in.*). The codex seems to contain no Greek; cf. URL <https://medieval.bodleian.ox.ac.uk/catalog/manuscript_8900> (24/11/2023).

20 By Way of Summary: A Very Brief History of the Early Christian Creeds

We have come to the end of a long journey tracing more than eight centuries of credal development. It is time to sum up some of our most significant insights into this development. In doing so, I will not summarize the previous chapters one by one, but, for the sake of clarity, will try to give a synthetic account of the results of this study.

In the writings of the New Testament 'faith' predominantly signifies an inward trust in and conviction of the veracity of the salvific divine actions, whereas a 'confession' involves publicly admitting to or proclaiming such a faith. By the end of the first century a set of certain theological propositions had emerged in Christian communities that included the confession of Jesus' lordship and the affirmation of his Sonship, death, and resurrection, and other statements relating to the incarnation. Such confession took place in a variety of *Sitze im Leben* including worship, mission and conversion, paraenesis and praise, and martyrdom.

These christological statements gradually came to be assembled to form homological 'building blocks', which in turn were combined with traditional divine attributes relating to God the Father, such as his omnipotence and his activity as creator. Thus slowly dyadic and triadic homologies developed as evidenced in Christian writings from the first three centuries. They were extended to form loose summaries of the Christian faith, called either a 'rule of faith' (κανὼν τῆς πίστεως/*regula fidei*) or 'rule of truth' (κανὼν τῆς ἀληθείας/*regula ueritatis*), to be used in mission and catechesis, but also to define normative Christian belief over against dissenting views which were considered heretical. In addition, there is evidence from the end of the second century onwards that in many places candidates for baptism were asked a series of credal questions prior to or during the act of baptism; they were to reply to these interrogations with 'I believe'.

Written creeds were unknown in large parts of the Roman Empire until well into the fourth century. Most Christians confessed their faith in a way which did not require a written text. They memorized the creed which had been handed over to them only orally, or they simply answered the baptismal interrogations in the positive.

＊

The doctrinal controversies, but also the expansion of the Church and the concomitant mass conversions of Christians in the fourth century required that the faith be laid down in standardized written formulae. Perhaps the first such formula is the Roman Creed (R). We have no direct evidence as to when R was actu-

https://doi.org/10.1515/9783110318531-020

ally composed. It is first attested in a letter Marcellus sent to Pope Julius of Rome in 340/341, but it is unclear to what extent Marcellus should in fact be regarded as R's author. There is a view that this is indeed the case; if so, R may then have been extracted from this letter and adopted by a Roman synod, with subsequent dissemination in the west. Yet we also have some, and I think stronger, evidence to suggest that R was in some way modelled in the third century on even earlier credal interrogations used at baptism in order to combat not only 'docetic' gnostic views on the relation between the Father and the Son, which were being propagated in Rome at around 150, but also a monarchian theology which tended to consider the Father and Son to be identical, popular in Rome some fifty years later. Still, the precise process through which this happened is as unclear as is the exact text of R, which may not even have been fully fixed in its wording, let alone written down. In addition, it is now considered to be likely that several creeds (in either interrogatory or declaratory form) circulated in the capital.

Yet there is no doubt that by the end of the fourth century most of the Latin west considered R normative. In the wake of the Church being promoted by the emperors the numbers of converts had steadily increased, which necessitated the development of a uniform procedure in transmitting the creed to these converts. As a result, a ceremony prior to baptism had been introduced in which, at a certain point during Lent, the bishop solemnly explained the creed's text and 'handed it over' to the catechumens (that is, he recited it three times or more; *Traditio symboli*). Catechumens were then expected to learn the creed by heart and, some days later, to 'hand it back' by reciting it solemnly in the presence of the bishop, their sponsors, and, at least in some places, of the entire congregation (*Redditio symboli*).

The creed now had to be standardized to facilitate its memorizing and to avoid doctrinal confusion. Nonetheless, at that time R was not considered primarily a dogmatic creed, but, owing to its brevity, it was well-suited for mission and for the catechesis of adults prior to their baptism, precisely because it could easily be memorized. In that respect, R's function approximated that of the earlier credal interrogations (which were not, however, jettisoned; therefore, in the early sacramentaries we find a strange duplication of credal texts at baptism, i.e., baptismal rites include both interrogatory and declaratory creeds). The legend of R's apostolic origins that took hold from the late fourth century onwards, culminating in the idea that the apostles had each contributed a clause to the creed, should perhaps also be seen against this backdrop, since the legend, mainly spread through explanations of the creed, served to increase that creed's authority.

The rites of *Traditio* and *Redditio symboli* thus came to be inserted into baptismal preparations in the mid-fourth century. This apparently first happened in Rome, whence it spread elsewhere. However, these rites only made sense as long as the catechumens were old enough to do so. But, as infant baptism started to become the norm, these rites lost their original function. Nonetheless, both *Traditio* and *Redditio* persisted for centuries, although from that point on the parents or godparents had to recite the creed on behalf of the infants entrusted to them.

Owing to the old capital's influence, by the end of antiquity R or some form thereof had spread throughout the west. All the creeds used in the west in preparing for baptism from the second half of the fourth century onwards were either R or one of its descendants. Still, until the ninth century no unified western text existed. Minor variations appeared in the various western regions of the empire. As a result of the ongoing liturgical standardization in the early middle ages and, in particular, at Charlemagne's instigation, one particular descendant of R became so popular that it superseded all other versions and is still used in the worship of both Catholics and Protestants today: the Apostles' Creed (T).

∗

There is no evidence that declaratory creeds existed in the Greek-speaking east of the Roman Empire in the first three centuries. It is widely assumed, therefore, that the emergence of such creeds is closely related to the doctrinal debates of the fourth century. (The only exception is the Creed of Jerusalem which seems to be closely related to R.) The Arian controversy sparked the production of a whole string of creeds, the earliest example probably being the one Arius sent to Alexander of Alexandria in *c.* 321. The fourth century also saw an important institutional innovation, introduced by the emperor himself, which was to play a pivotal role in the production of creeds: synods which drew together as many bishops as possible from across the empire in order to resolve doctrinal conflict. In fact, the composition of creeds and credal texts by these episcopal assemblies was a means to this very end. Subsequently, each confession came to build upon the previous one, taking up material from the earlier creed while adding some new phrases, thus turning the existing material against whichever opponent the newer creed was targeting ('building-block model').

The first synod to use this compositional technique was probably held in Antioch in the spring of 325. However, much more influential was the creed that originated at the first ecumenical council held in Nicaea in 325. The council condemned Arius' views and signed a creed (N) whose origins are unclear. In a letter that Bishop Eusebius of Caesarea sent to his congregation sometime after the council he claimed that N was based on a creed which he himself had submitted to the council and which he quotes in his letter. According to Eusebius, his creed had been revised by the council to include certain additions, in particular the adjective *homooúsios* ('of like/identical substance'), which had allegedly been suggested by the emperor himself in order to describe the relation between God the Father and the Son.

It has, therefore, often been assumed that the *Vorlage* quoted by Eusebius was the local creed used in Palestine. However, for various reasons it now seems more likely that the bishop himself had drafted this creed on the basis of the 'rule of faith' in use in his local church. Furthermore, N seems to be the product of a committee which probably used other *Vorlagen* besides Eusebius' text. In this context the information that Constantine himself was responsible for the addition of *homooúsios* is not altogether implausible, given the emperor's own interest in Christianity and the fact that he had theological advisers at his disposal. The bishops present at the council were asked to indicate their agreement with the draft creed by adding their signatures (which a small number refused). Therefore, from Nicaea onwards synodal creeds were considered not only theological, but also legal documents (both ecclesial and secular) which later synods referred to as definitions of orthodoxy and which emperors also enacted as law.

N failed to settle the trinitarian debates of the fourth century. Rather, a whole string of creeds was produced at synods over the following decades: Antioch 341 (esp. Ant^2; Ant^4), Serdica 343 (east and west), the Macrostich Creed of 344, the First Creed of Sirmium 351, the Second Creed of Sirmium 357. The so-called 'Dated Creed', promulgated in Sirmium on 22 May 359, rejected the use of the term *ousía* as unscriptural, instead propagating the formula that the Son was 'similar to the Father in all things' (ὅμοιος τῷ πατρὶ κατὰ πάντα). This formula became the hallmark of Homoianism. Emperor Constantius II used it to impose doctrinal unity across both parts of the empire (Synods of Rimini 359; Niké 359; Constantinople 359/360).

Constantius' religious policy did, however, fail to produce the desired results. It was only the Second Ecumenical Council summoned by Emperor Theodosius I to Constantinople in 381 which largely settled the controversy over the precise nature of the Trinity. Later tradition associated a creed with this council (C^2, in previous research referred to as C or NC) which was, however, not officially named the 'Creed of Constantinople' or adopted as such until the much later Council of Chalcedon (451). It is a matter of controversy whether C^2 was in fact a result of the council of 381, as there are no unequivocal attestations of its existence until 451.

In my view, N was revised at a Synod in Rome under Pope Damasus in the years 377/378. This was done as a defence against Apolinarianism, but also because the synod sought to harmonize N with R. This revision is lost. It was then sent to the east, where it was again revised and approved in Antioch in 379 by a large number of bishops led by Meletius of Antioch (N^{Ant}). This creed is essentially identical with that of Theodore of Mopsuestia (N^{Ant1}). Its 'Roman' features include Christ's virgin birth and his crucifixion under Pontius Pilate. Finally, N^{Ant} was revised twice at Constantinople: C^1 and C^2.

N^{Ant} was not adopted at Constantinople without alterations because this confession had been approved at a synod presided over by Meletius, one of the parties in the Antiochene schism. During the presidency of Gregory of Nazianzus at Constantinople, however, the party supporting Paulinus, Meletius' rival, had been strengthened, which is why N^{Ant} was possibly rejected as 'Meletian'. Instead, a new compromise was worked out (C^1), which continued to be considered N. It represents a revision of N^{Ant} with additions from N itself and from the Creed of Jerusalem (J). It emphasized the Son's divinity more strongly than N^{Ant} did, by excising N^{Ant}'s quotation from Col 1:15 ('first-born of all creation'). This shorter redaction of N, C^1, which Nestorius later quoted, was adopted at Constantinople and henceforth functioned as a baptismal creed in the capital of the east, but was not received throughout the Empire.

That meant that, in the period up to 451, at least three variants of N were in use in the east, namely N, N^{Ant}, and C^1, all of which were (rightly) understood as Nicene both in literary and theological terms:

- The authentic text of N was mainly used in Alexandria.
- The version of N revised in Rome and Antioch (N^{Ant}) in 379 was subsequently used especially in Antioch and later in the 'Nestorian' Syriac Church of the East (see below).
- The version actually agreed in Constantinople (C^1) in 381 continued to be regarded as N, although in reality it was N^{Ant} with deletions and additions, drawing on both N and J, in order to refute any form of subordinationism and (possibly) to achieve an anti-Apolinarian consensus. It was in use especially in Constantinople and is attested by Nestorius.

By contrast, C^2 contains further changes to N and an expansion of the third article to include statements on baptism, the resurrection of the dead, and eternal life. This creed was not adopted in Constantinople, probably because of massive opposition from those for whom C^2 was too far removed from N (e.g., Gregory of Nazianzus), although it was included in a local collection of canons underneath N. (The reason for its failure to gain acceptance was therefore not, as has been widely assumed, non-acceptance by the Pneumatomachians.)

It was not until Chalcedon that C^2 was reintroduced into the ecumenical discussion as the confession of 'the 150 Fathers' by the imperial officials presiding over this council, in order to clear up confusion over the 'true' text of N and to resolve the multiplication of creeds in N, N^{Ant}, and C^1. In addition, they were interested in presenting a confession of the eastern capital, henceforth to be regarded as an authoritative explication of N. Thus, not only was the authentic text of N reaffirmed, but C^2 filled the theological 'gaps' in N with regard to the incarnation and the doctrine of the Holy Spirit. However, more than one version of C^2

can be found in the printed edition *Acta Conciliorum Oecumenicorum*. Recent re-search suggests that the text of C^2 officially adopted at the council is not that of the fifth session as printed in the *Acta* as part of the Definition of Faith, but prob-ably that of the second (or third) session. It is this version of C^2 which may reason-ably be linked to the Council of 381.

Like N, both C^1 and C^2 are marked by the theological debates of their time. They emphasized the full humanity of the incarnate Christ over against Apolinar-ius of Laodicea and his followers (who claimed that Christ possessed some kind of celestial body) by referring to the virgin birth and (only in C^2) his suffering under Pontius Pilate. Furthermore, the Son's sitting at the right hand of the Father (the former, therefore, remaining a distinct hypostasis from the Father even after his ascension) and, again only in C^2, the endless nature of his kingdom were added to the formula (against Marcellus of Ancyra).

The reason for extending the article on the Holy Spirit in C^1 and C^2 is that from *c.* 360 theologians such as Athanasius of Alexandria and Basil of Caesarea argued that the Spirit, too, was of divine origin and status and as such was to be accorded the same veneration as the Father and the Son. This led to considerable controversy at Constantinople and may be the reason why the term *homooúsios* was not included in this section in order to find a compromise with theologians who were more cautious when it came to the divinity of the Spirit (they need not necessarily have been militant 'Spirit-fighters'). A dogmatic decree of this synod, however, stated in no uncertain terms that there was one God, subsisting in three consubstantial persons or hypostases; the original is lost, but its contents are sum-marized in a synodal letter of another Synod held at Constantinople a year later in 382.

Rather, in C^2 the Holy Spirit is described as 'Lord and life-giver who proceeds from the Father, who is jointly worshipped and glorified with the Father and the Son' (in C^1 this section is extended even further) which was no doubt meant to paraphrase *homooúsios* and indeed amounted to the same thing. In the middle ages the idea that the Spirit proceeds from the Father 'and the Son' (Latin *filio-que*), which was only expressed in Latin versions of C^2, provoked a long-lasting and tortuous controversy between western and eastern theologians and partly contributed to the ultimate split between the Latin and the Orthodox churches.

In subsequent centuries C^2 gradually came to supersede N in both east and west. N and/or C^2 were seen as standard creeds by which all later confessions and definitions of faith were to be measured. It may, therefore, be more than just a co-incidence that in the period under consideration no further eastern synod pro-duced a text which was solemnly introduced by πιστεύομεν εἰς ('we believe in') which had been the standard formula introducing a creed. In addition, alterations to the liturgical calendar in the late fourth century suggest that attempts were made to illustrate the christological content of the creeds ritually through celebrating the Feasts of the Lord such as Christmas, Easter, Ascension, and Pentecost.

However, notwithstanding the existence and authority of N and C^2, the production of credal formulae for various purposes continued unabated into the sixth and subsequent centuries. The authors of later declarations, whether individuals or synods, all acknowledged the importance of the 'Nicene faith', but went on to set out their own theological views, depending on the doctrinal controversy in which they were involved at the time.

∗

In the sixth century C^2, which like N had by then come to be used in catechesis, may also have been introduced into the Greek mass. Perhaps this liturgical innovation goes back to the Miaphysite patriarch of Constantinople, Timothy I, but details are unclear. Nonetheless, C^2's function in the great Byzantine liturgies of St Basil and of St John Chrysostom may be determined with relative certainty: in both the recital of C^2 follows the liturgical imperative to close the church doors, an instruction which marked the beginning of the eucharistic liturgy. The reason for its prominent placement probably was to make sure that catechumens and other unbaptized persons would stand out as unable to recite the creed; in that case they could then be excluded from the most sacred part of the service. Thus, C^2 was, at least in this context, indeed used as a 'password' or 'watchword' (which is one of the original meanings of *symbolum*, the Latin term for the creed borrowed from the Greek).

As indicated above, for a long time C^2 does not appear to have been widely used in the west. Setting aside Latin translations of the acts of the Council of Chalcedon in 451, it does not appear to be quoted in any Latin source for two centuries after it had first been composed. From the end of the sixth century onwards it came to be cited by synods when some doctrinal issue or other was at stake. We find it quoted as a matter of course in introducing the decrees of the various Councils of Toledo in the Visigothic Kingdom, beginning with the Third Council of 589. At the Eighth Council of Toledo in 653 *filioque* was finally and firmly inserted into the credal tradition, although the doctrine had *de facto* already been defended at the Third Council of 589 and even earlier. It had been in 589 that the Visigoth king Reccared had decided to convert from Homoian Christianity to Catholicism, a move which also led him to abandon the beliefs of his father and predecessor Leovigild regarding the Holy Spirit, insofar as his father had denied the Spirit's divinity.

Whereas in Spain people did not shy away from altering C^2 when they felt it necessary to combat heresy, the Roman Church was much more conservative in handling the creed's text. In one of the earliest extant sacramentaries, the *Old Ge-*

lasian Sacramentary (*c.* 650; OGS), we find that the creed used for the *Traditio symboli* is C^2 – without the addition of *filioque*. It seems to have replaced R which had originally been used in Rome. C^2 is first recited in Greek and then in Latin, the Greek having been transcribed in Latin letters. This may indicate that the OGS retains evidence of an earlier period when the Roman community was still bilingual (the sixth century), as has sometimes been suggested. Nonetheless, on the basis of the sources available it seems more likely that R was replaced by the more elaborate C^2 in the second half of the seventh century under the Greek-speaking popes Agatho or Leo II. When the Roman liturgy of baptism spread to the Frankish empire in the later eighth century, it appears that either C^2 or (some form of) T were used at baptism. We have no evidence of *filioque* being quoted in the baptismal rite in any liturgical book before the mid-tenth century.

In Spain the Visigoth king Reccared appears to have made an attempt to introduce C^2 into the Sunday liturgy at the Third Council of Toledo in 589, locating it just before the recital of the Lord's Prayer. This practice appears to have been generally adopted in Spain. Elsewhere in the west, however, the creed does not appear to have been introduced into the liturgy of the mass before the late eighth century. Charlemagne insisted that C^2 be chanted during mass and that *filioque* be included, perhaps in order to combat Spanish adoptionism. In his sphere of influence C^2 appears to have been placed after the Gospel reading. Pope Leo III firmly resisted this order, apparently continuing to recite C^2 for catechetical purposes only. Oddly, none of the preserved Frankish Gelasian Sacramentaries of the eighth and ninth centuries contain the creed in the liturgy of the mass. It appears that C^2 was perhaps not introduced into the celebration of the eucharist in the Holy Roman Empire at large until the eleventh century, even then remaining largely restricted to Sundays and certain feast days. On those occasions the creed was chanted after the Gospel or after the homily, and preceded the preparation of the offerings. Thus, it did not introduce the Liturgy of the Eucharist as in the east, but instead concluded the Liturgy of the Word of God, thus serving as the congregation's (orthodox) answer to the Gospel.

The creed's ritualistic handling and the widespread prohibition to write it down led to an increased sacralization of its text. As a result the creed, like the Lord's Prayer, played a major role in the everyday lives of believers as charms, recited, for example, to protect from the danger of travelling and to enhance the efficacy of medicinal herbs.

However, the creed never lost its didactic purpose nor its character as a summary of the faith which could be imparted to converts by way of preaching. In this respect, the number of pertinent sermons is much greater from the Latin than it is from the Greek church. It appears that in the west such credal instruction was much more formalized in that each individual clause of R or one of its descendants was explained in turn. In addition, the creed's contents were displayed in paintings and on murals, and its text was later also chanted and sung. Finally, the creeds also played a role in academic teaching. For instance, in scholasticism the creed's articles were included in theological textbooks and in the great summae.

*

Whereas in the Byzantine Empire N and later C^2 remained the only normative creeds, the situation was more complex in those eastern churches that lay beyond the boundaries of the Roman Empire. In particular, from 410 onwards we find a particular recension of N in the Syriac Church of the East that is often called *Persicum*. From the sixth century onwards the creed used in its baptismal liturgy was the Roman-Antiochene recension of N (i.e. N^{Ant}). In Armenia what is referred to as the Nicene Creed is often not N in its pure form but some recension, the most important being the so-called *Armeniacum* from the first half of the seventh century which continues to be used to this day at baptism and during the celebration of the eucharist. In Coptic Egypt, by and large, N and later C^2 prevailed (with some variations), just as they did in the Arabic-speaking regions of the Middle East and in Georgia. Initially, in Ethiopia a variety of different creeds were used until, from the sixteenth century onwards, we find predominantly variants of C^2 attested in the anaphora.

21 A Theology of the Creeds? Some Concluding Thoughts

I hope the preceding pages have made clear what enormous importance the creeds had in regulating theological discourse in antiquity and the middle ages. For the average worshipper who did not know the Bible very well they may have even surpassed Scripture in importance in their everyday religious lives and, therefore, played a role in the formation of Christendom that can hardly be overestimated. On the one hand, this development was a positive one for Christianity because the creed, in its evolution and use, was an important tool of elementary instruction in the Christian faith and contributed to the new religion's comparatively rapid spread. On the other hand, it also represented a loss because this confession developed from a (necessarily reductionist) memory aid and orientation marker into a foundational formula that suggested theological sufficiency and was even regarded as having magical powers. Such a one-sided appreciation entailed a loss of the richness, and a reduction, of the many different ways in which the faith is expressed in the Bible. In this final chapter I would like to address these aspects in a little more detail by taking a summary look at the four most important representatives of the genre as a group. What do the creeds offer in doctrinal terms? Is it possible to speak of a 'theology' of the creeds? What do the creeds cover and what is missing? And finally, why have creeds at all? Could we do without them?

It is difficult to speak of 'a' theology of the creeds if by 'theology' one understands a uniform and coherent system of religious thought. No such system lies at the base of R, T, N, or C^2 because, as I have tried to show in this book, these are texts that have developed over a long period of time and been altered and added to according to the circumstances and challenges of each era. Moreover, we are only able to reconstruct the rationale for certain expressions and the clauses included in the creeds to a limited extent. And even where we are able to do so, this rationale may have altered over time as later theologians may have interpreted the same clause or clauses differently. Above all, due to a lack of evidence we do not know how 'regular' believers (whoever that may have been) 'heard' the creeds, what they associated with them, and what value they attached to them, except for the fact that later on they used them as magical formulae. Any 'understanding' of the creed that individual believers may have had must have been closely linked to the degree of biblical knowledge which the 'average' churchgoer possessed. As Bibles were not readily available, much depended on how regularly they attended church and on the quality of catechesis and preaching they encountered (which in village churches may have been very low, if homilies were preached at all).

https://doi.org/10.1515/9783110318531-021

However, this is not to say that creeds are an incoherent assemblage of theological propositions which could be interpreted in whatever way one wanted. In what follows, I will try to show and explain which traits all creeds have in common and then point out some of their respective differences. For the sake of convenience, I will place the above-named four creeds side by side, in English – first R with T, then N with C^2.

	R	T	N	C^2
I	I/We believe in God [the Father R^R, R^L] Almighty,	I believe in God the Father Almighty, Creator of heaven and earth;	We believe in one God, the Father Almighty, Maker of all things both visible and invisible;	We believe in one God, the Father Almighty, Maker of heaven and earth, of all things visible and invisible;
II	and in Christ Jesus, his only[-begotten] Son,	and in Jesus Christ, his only Son,	and in one Lord Jesus Christ, the Son of God, begotten from the Father, only-begotten, that is, from the substance of the Father; God from God, Light from Light, true God from true God, begotten, not made, consubstantial with the Father; through whom all things came into being, both things in heaven and things on earth; who for (*or:* because of) us humans and for our salvation descended,	and in one Lord Jesus Christ, the only-begotten Son of God, begotten from the Father before all ages, Light from Light, true God from true God, begotten, not made, consubstantial with the Father; through whom all things came into being; who for (*or:* because of) us humans and for our salvation descended, from the heavens;

(continued)

R	T	N	C²
		became flesh,	became flesh from the Holy Spirit and the virgin Mary;
		became human,	became human,
our Lord, who was born from the Holy Spirit and the virgin Mary;	our Lord, who was conceived of the Holy Spirit, born from the virgin Mary, suffered under Pontius Pilate,	suffered,	
who was crucified under Pontius Pilate,	was crucified,		was crucified for us under Pontius Pilate, suffered,
[and dead *R*.*?*] and buried;	dead, and buried; descended to the underworld;		and was buried;
[and] on the third day rose again from the dead;	on the third day rose again from the dead;	on the third day rose again,	on the third day rose again according to the Scriptures;
ascended into the heavens and is sitting at the right hand of the Father,	ascended to the heavens; sits at the right hand of God, the Father Almighty;	ascended into the heavens,	ascended into the heavens; sits at the right hand of the Father;
whence he is coming to judge the living and the dead;	thence he will come to judge the living and the dead.	will come to judge the living and dead;	and will come again with glory to judge the living and dead; of whose kingdom there will be no end;
III I/we believe [*or:* and] in the Holy Spirit,	I believe in the Holy Spirit,	and in the Holy Spirit.	and in the Holy Spirit,
			the Lord and life-giver, who proceeds from the Father, who is jointly worshipped and glorified with the Father and the Son, who spoke through the prophets;

(continued)

R	T	N	C²
the holy [catholic R^{L}?] Church,	the holy catholic Church, the communion of saints,		in one holy catholic and apostolic Church.
			We confess one baptism for
the remission of sins,	the remission of sins,		the remission of sins.
			We look forward to
the resurrection of the flesh, [eternal life R^{M}].	the resurrection of the flesh, and eternal life.		the resurrection of the dead and the life of the world to come.
	Amen.		Amen.

As may easily be seen, all four creeds share a basic structure which derives from their common predecessors, the *regulae fidei* and baptismal interrogations. The trinitarian pattern is probably a result of the triadic baptismal formula or of triadic questions used at baptism which, in turn, are closely linked to Mt 28:19 (although the details of this relationship remain unknown).

All four creeds are primarily concerned with God's activity as it appertains to humankind and to the universe (although N and C² do add terms describing intratrinitarian relations as a result of the fourth-century controversies). The three sections relate to the three persons of the Trinity and are introduced by 'I/we believe in' or simply 'and in', thus indicating a personal relationship between the speaker – be it as an individual or as member of a group – and the 'object' of their faith. The choice of the singular or plural depends on the situation, e.g., whether the creed is said individually or in a liturgical setting jointly by the congregation. The explicit mention of 'belief' suggests more than simple affirmation of a set of theological propositions: the creed is not only an 'intellectual possession' but expresses a personal relationship between the speaker and the triune God, one based on trust, as well as fellowship among Christians (whenever the phrase '*we* believe' is said).

The first section emphasizes the belief that God is the Father of Jesus Christ, but also of humankind (as also expressed in the Lord's Prayer). It is also stressed that the Father is 'almighty'. In R the Father's omnipotence remains unspecified; in T, N, and C² it is further explained by the mention of his creative activity: he has simply created everything, that is the entire universe.

Christ is confessed as God's Son and our Lord. No further explanations of the precise nature of his lordship are given. In particular, it is not specified how

Christ's lordship relates to that of secular powers such as the emperor. One might call this a 'sleeping' proposition which only came to be 'activated' if and when these two lordships happened to clash (in which case Christ's was clearly seen as superior to that of the emperor). The creeds also agree in Christ being God's only Son. I will return to this point below. This is followed by the christological summary which in all creeds consists of the generation (in R by implication) and birth in which, according to R, T, and C^2, both the Holy Spirit and Mary were involved. R, T, and C^2 also stress the *virgin* birth, but do not specify what its implications might be. In particular, nothing further is added about the precise nature of this event. Nor is anything said about Christ's activities during his sojourn on earth, in particular his proclamation and miracles. By contrast, all creeds mention the passion (although the details differ). R, T, and C^2 place this passion in the time of Pontius Pilate, thus emphasizing the factuality of the event itself: Christ's death occurred at a particular point in history, and it did happen in actual fact (rather than just *seeming* to happen). All creeds also agree on Christ's resurrection on the third day, on his ascension into the heavens, and on his eventual return to act as judge over all of humankind. R, T, and C^2 also add his sitting at the right hand of God/the Father: after his ascension Christ does not 'dissolve' into the Godhead, he remains distinct from the Father and is assigned a particular dignity resembling that granted to the son of an emperor. By implication, his 'sitting' also indicates that the risen Christ is not just a spiritual, incorporeal being but continues to possess some kind of body.

Finally, all creeds mention belief in the Holy Spirit, but they differ in what follows. Interestingly, they fail to spell out the details of Christ's saving action. In fact, the western creeds do not specify at all *why* the incarnation happened, whereas N and C^2 only briefly indicate that it was 'for us humans and for our salvation'. It may, therefore, be fair to say that the creeds contain no (elaborate) soteriology. In this they leave an 'opening' that would later to be filled by a very diverse range of concepts of human salvation.

*

Let us now look at the specifics of R/T and N/C^2 in turn. The earliest creeds, R and T, are much blander than the eastern creeds. In fact, R offers nothing more than the basic tenets I outlined in the previous section except for the pneumatological article. In this the holy (catholic) Church, the remission of sins, the resurrection of the flesh, and eternal life were added, all of which were later repeated in T. It is not explained how these elements relate to the Spirit, if at all. The fact that they are not preceded by 'in' may indicate that they are attributes or operations of the Spirit: they detail what we should think of when imagining the 'nature' and work of the Spirit. The Church is a product of the Spirit which he fills with his presence and thus sanctifies. However, the notion of 'Church' remains strangely ill-defined: is it the invisible body of Christ which is filled with the Spirit (in the sense of 1Cor 12:1–13) or is it also seen as an institution? Does it include only the Church hierarchy (as opposed to the laity)? Are, by implication, all bishops and priests holy? All these questions were posed in expositions of the creed, but they remain unanswered in the text of the creed itself.

In addition, the Church is seen as 'catholic' which in the beginning simply meant that it was 'universal'. This could be understood as a claim to Christendom's world-wide presence and importance (which, perhaps, even included the angels), but it also quickly came to be used to distinguish certain forms of Christianity from others considered 'particular' and as such heretical. Furthermore, the remission of sins takes place through the work of the Holy Spirit, first at baptism and then in penance. As regards the resurrection, the Spirit is the life-giving force in the description of the raising from the dead in Ezek 37:1–14. One may, perhaps, also cite the contrast drawn between the 'spiritual' and the 'physical' body in 1Cor 15:44–46. Finally, the endings of R and T provide no answer as to what the Spirit's role, if any, might be in relation to eternal life.

However, the clauses following the Spirit were not always interpreted in this manner, that is as further defining his activity: sometimes 'in' was added to them – with 'believe' implied, and explanations were given according to which all or some of the clauses were themselves objects of faith. If truth be told we do not really know precisely why these clauses were added, while others such as about baptism and the eucharist or any kind of ethical commandment were not. (Baptism was later introduced in C^2.)

Furthermore, there are some clauses which were inserted only in T: in the first section God's creative activity (a manifestation of his omnipotence) is specifically highlighted. Moreover, the Spirit's involvement in Christ's conception is referred to in order to prevent certain misinterpretations of the virgin birth. Christ's suffering was also added, probably in order to emphasize the reality of his passion. We also find his descent to the underworld mentioned though it was interpreted in a range of different ways; in any case it signified Christ's participation in this aspect of human existence after death (as it was envisaged in antiquity) too, as well as the universality of Christ's saving action which included those who had died before his coming. The addition of the 'Father Almighty' to the sitting at the right hand is, perhaps, less significant. Finally, the 'communion of saints' in the third section might, again, be interpreted in different ways: it could refer to all Christians, dead and alive, or to the assembly of saintly Christians (martyrs and miracle-workers) past and present, or to every believer's participation in the 'holy elements' of the eucharist. The final 'Amen' (though not always spoken) concluded the recitation of the creed and once more marked the speaker's agreement with its content.

*

N is also divided into three sections (to which anathemas were appended which were mostly not considered an integral part of N). N focusses on the relation between Father and Son and summarizes their respective actions in salvation history. In the first section God's creative activity is emphasized even more strongly by including the realm of invisible beings (such as angels and spirits). As a result of the Arian controversy the relationship between the Father and the Son is further defined by emphasizing generation 'from the Father' (ἐκ τοῦ πατρός) and the Son's full divinity. The verb 'to beget' (γεννᾶν) is used to describe this particular relationship which is in every respect unique: the Son is the only being to whom this status is accorded (μονογενῆ / 'only-begotten'). He participates in the 'substance' of the Father (ἐκ τῆς οὐσίας τοῦ πατρός / 'from the substance of the Father'), he is 'God from God' and differs from all creatures which have been 'made' and came into being not from God but out of nothing (although the creation *ex nihilo* ('out of nothing') is not explicitly mentioned). This status is then summarized in two clauses: 'begotten, not made' (γεννηθέντα οὐ ποιηθέντα), and 'consubstantial with the Father' (ὁμοούσιον τῷ πατρί). The adjective *homooúsios* serves to underline this particular relationship, which nonetheless remains somewhat fuzzy because it is not said what 'from the substance of the Father' means precisely: is the substance of the Father and the Son completely identical or simply, in one way or another, of the same nature? Moreover, the Son's cooperation in creation (Jn 1:10) is added which strengthens the underlying Johannine dynamic of this creed (Jn 1:1–14).

The process of the incarnation is also set out in further detail with the terms 'descended' (κατελθόντα), 'became incarnate' (σαρκωθέντα), and 'became human' (ἐνανθρωπήσαντα). The descended Son does not only take on human flesh but becomes a full human being. The verb ἐνανθρωπεῖν and cognate noun ἐνανθρώπησις are typical Christian neologisms[1] which literally mean 'inhumanization', i.e. 'to become' or 'to be an ἄνθρωπος', i.e. a human being.[2] Incarnation and 'inhumanization' are obviously considered identical (which was later denied by Apolinarians and Anhomoians alike, although for different reasons).

Christ's birth (including the Spirit and the Virgin) is not explicitly listed – nor is the sitting on the right mentioned either; the passion is summarized by the word 'suffered'. The third section is limited to naming the Holy Spirit, without any further details as to its nature or operation being given.

---

1 The only exception may be Heliodorus (s. III/IV), *Aethiopica* 2,31,1.
2 Later Latin translations of N use *inhumanatus* here (cf. FaFo § 135d23.1.3 etc.). The translation 'to become/be incarnate' (suggested in Lampe 1961(1984), s.v.) is imprecise because it may imply that Christ only became *caro*, i.e. flesh.

This section is expanded in C^2. By contrast, in its first two sections C^2 does not differ much from N in terms of theological content. Its first section concerning the Father's creative activity is the most ponderous of all the four creeds, combining as it does the creation of 'heaven and earth' and of 'all things visible and invisible'. The second section emphasizes that the Son was begotten before time (and is, therefore, coeternal with the Father). This served to underline the consubstantiality of Father and Son which by then had come to be understood as an identity of substance rather than simply as some kind of 'likeness' (although this 'identity' posed new conceptual problems which, interestingly, were not often addressed). The birth as such is not mentioned in this creed either, but the Holy Spirit and the Virgin Mary are added to 'became flesh' without any further elaboration. The supplement 'according to the Scriptures' was added to the resurrection; it was probably taken from 1Cor 15:3–4 to lend authority to this extraordinary event. Furthermore, C^2 adds the sitting at the right hand. It also contains the additions 'with glory' and 'of whose kingdom there will be no end'. 'With glory' may allude to 2Tim 2:10. The second addition is a quotation from Lk 1:33 and is directed against the theology of Marcellus of Ancyra. But even if someone was not aware of this particular controversy, the references to the sitting at the right hand and of the endless nature of his kingdom served as a hermeneutical guide to the interpretation of 1Cor 15:28 ('When all things are subjected to him, then the Son himself will also be subjected to the one who put all things in subjection under him, so that God may be all in all.'): this sentence is not to be understood in such a way that the Son and the Father will disappear as distinct *hypostáseis*, but rather that they will forever remain own separate persons.

C^2's section on the Holy Spirit is the most elaborate of the creeds under consideration. I have discussed these expansions at some length above.[3] It may suffice in the present context to point out once again that the Holy Spirit is described as 'Lord and life-giver who proceeds from the Father, who is jointly worshipped and glorified with the Father and the Son' which was no doubt meant to paraphrase *homoousios* and indeed amounts to the same thing. But even worshippers who did not know the finer details of the controversies behind these terms would realize that the Spirit was 'Lord', that as 'life-giver' he also had a role in creation and in even in their daily lives, and that he was to be worshipped just like the Father and the Son (which meant that he had some kind of divine status). After the doxology C^2 added that the Spirit 'spoke through the prophets', thus defining his nature more precisely by tying him with the Old Testament: it is the Spirit of the prophets who is venerated here, who is only found within the Judeo-Christian

---

3 Cf. above pp. 370–4.

tradition. One, therefore, ought to be wary of anyone who wished to ban the Old Testament as outdated, as the Marcionites and some gnostic groups did, or of those who claimed to possess the Spirit, without knowing its nature as evident from the sayings of the prophets. Likewise, C^2 thus implied that the divine *hypóstasis* of the Spirit had already been active in the Old Testament.

The clauses added after the section on the Spirit are introduced by 'in' the Church (with 'believe' implied), followed by 'we confess' baptism and 'we expect' the resurrection. Thus a clear hierarchy of doctrinal propositions is indicated: 'belief statements' are restricted to the persons of the Trinity and, perhaps, to the Church (unless its mention is, as – perhaps – in R/T, seen as an extension of the article on the Holy Spirit). At the same time the abrupt changes in confessional 'intensity' (from belief in to confessing and expectation) give this section a somewhat uneven structure. In the statement on the Church 'one' and 'apostolic' were added as further attributes. Salvation could only be obtained within the fold of the episcopal churches in apostolic succession which held 'orthodox' trinitarian beliefs and were part of the official diocesan structure of the Roman Empire, as such forming one orthodox Church that extended all over the world (as opposed to the many congregations of the heretics that were only present in small areas). It is much less clear why the oneness of baptism was affirmed and why baptism was mentioned at all, whereas the eucharist, for example, was not. In terms of sacramental theology, there seems to be a distinct gap here. This may have been caused by C^2 being intended for use in catechesis during which it was important to impress on the catechumens that baptism could only be received once and that its purpose was the forgiveness of sin.

*

I have already indicated in the previous sections what is missing from the creeds. Harnack phrased it like this, in a small treatise on the history of the Apostles' Creed:

> What gives [the creed] its greatest and lasting value is – apart from the confession of God as the almighty Father – the confession of Jesus Christ, the only-begotten Son of God our Lord, and the testimony that through him the holy Christendom, the forgiveness of sins, and eternal life have come about. But one misses references to his preaching, to his characteristics as Saviour of the poor and sick, of tax-collectors and sinners, to his personality as it shines in the Gospels. In actual fact, the creed contains nothing more than headings. In this sense it is imperfect; for no confession is perfect that does not paint the Saviour before one's eyes and impresses him upon one's heart.[4]

---

4 Harnack 1892(1904), p. 254.

The accusation that the creeds lack any reference to Jesus' preaching and the ethical instructions contained therein, which enable the Christian to follow Christ, was not new. Indeed, it is repeated to the present day: there is no reference to how Christians are to live their lives and relate to other human beings, although the Bible contains ethical summaries such as the Ten Commandments (Ex 20:1–17; Deut 5:6–21), the double commandment of love (Mk 12:29–31 par.), or the Golden Rule (Lev 19:18; Mt 7:12; Lk 6:31), which would have been suitable for inserting into a creed or could at least have been referred to (in the case of the Decalogue). Instead, right from the beginning the creed was understood to offer a summary of *dogmatic* but not ethical teachings.

Of course, this does not have to remain the case going forward, but it would be unfortunate to try to fill this gap in the creeds today by changing their texts, because they are ecumenically acknowledged as they are, and thus are part of the common heritage of Christendom and as such also of the wider world.[5] Having said that, I think it would be helpful if many churches could agree to supplement the confession with the double commandment of love in both their preaching and liturgy. This could address the justified concern of many Christians who see their religion as not exclusively a religion of salvation but also as one of active love.

The theological reflection that the creeds encapsulate helped to establish a wide consensus on how we describe the Christian God and his saving work in Christ and in the Holy Spirit.[6] This consensus continues to influence Christian theology all over the world 1700 years later. However, with the rise of evangelicalism and Pentecostalism, trinitarian theology has come under heavy criticism, some of it justified. But we should not be too quick to belittle the achievements of the Church Fathers. The trinitarian debates of the fourth century have shown that the biblical evidence is not unequivocal, but that patient conceptual work is needed to ensure we have a coherent and communicable narrative about God.

Nevertheless, these debates also had problematic consequences that have left, and continue to leave, their mark on the theology of later centuries. On the one hand, as I hope to have shown, they promoted the exclusion of those who maintained that the 'orthodox' theology as expressed in the creeds did not do justice to the biblical evidence in its entirety. This was done for good reasons and with honourable motives, either because they sought to protect the sovereignty of the one God or because they feared that the Nicene way of speaking about Jesus unduly overshadowed other aspects of his ministry and teaching. On the other hand, the Nicenes contributed significantly to the formation of an 'elitist' theol-

---

5 This does not, of course, mean that new creeds *supplementary* to T or C² could not be used.
6 The following reflections are based on Kinzig 2023, pp. 233 f.

ogy, which was thenceforth discussed in learned institutions and could no longer be easily communicated to ordinary Christians.

Both these troublesome legacies are, in my opinion, clearly evident in the Protestant tradition to which I belong. In our churches there is both an inability and an unwillingness to explain the achievements of fourth-century trinitarian theology in a way that resonates with today's congregation. The doctrine of the Trinity is considered by some to be incomprehensible and removed from the simple truth contained in the Bible. Others argue that normative creeds deprive the individual believer of their intellectual independence and do not sufficiently take into account the diversity of human spirituality.

There are two common reactions to these criticisms both of which I consider fallacious: some retreat to insisting time and again on the creed's venerable authority which expresses truths contained in the Bible in a timeless manner, while others choose to ignore the theological insights contained in the creeds, resorting to simple biblical paraphrases or to problematic moralizing in their catechesis or preaching. The problem with the first reaction is that a truth which ever more Christians regard as outlandish will hardly be acknowledged by them as relevant to their religion. By contrast, the second reaction's plain paraphrases of biblical stories or moralizing discourses about sin and Christian virtues seriously underrate the intellectual energy embodied in the New Testament: the ancient trinitarian debates developed for a reason. That reason is the intellectual challenge the biblical message posed as it claimed that God had come down to earth, together with the clues it contained as to how he did so, which later generations used to work out solutions that would – to a certain extent – satisfy the desire for conceptual consistency.

There is no easy solution to this dilemma. In order to come to terms with the biblical evidence, most Church Fathers in fact took recourse to a Platonist ontology that gave the divine substance pride of place, whereas the environment in which we live, which is characterized by manifold and often conflicting ideas, experiences, and emotions, was accorded a lesser degree of reality in this hierarchy of being. In an age abounding with scientific explanations of the world and with technologies that go a long way towards improving people's daily lives, such an ontology is no longer plausible. It is to be hoped that the present book, in studying the history of the creeds, may contribute to developing new ways to communicate the significance of Christ's incarnation, passion, and resurrection for our salvation to a wider public.

Bibliography

Abascal, Juan M./Gimeno, *Helena, Epigrafía hispánica. Catálogo del Gabinete de Antigüedades*, Madrid 2000 (Publicaciones del Gabinete de Antigüedades de la Real Academia de la Historia 1/ Antigüedades 1)

Abramowski, Luise, 'Die Synode von Antiochien 324/25 und ihr Symbol', *ZKG* 86 (1975), pp. 356–66; English version under the title 'The Synod of Antioch 324/25 and Its Creed', in: id., *Formula and Context: Studies in Early Christian Thought*, Hampshire/Brookfield, VT 1992 (CStS), no. III (page numbers according to English version)

Abramowski, Luise, 'Was hat das Nicaeno-Constantinopolitanum (C) mit dem Konzil von Konstantinopel 381 zu tun?', *ThPh* 67 (1992), pp. 481–513

Abramowski, Luise, 'Die liturgische Homilie des Ps. Narses mit dem Messbekenntnis und einem Theodor-Zitat', *BJRL* 78/3 (1996), pp. 87–100

Abramowski, Luise, *Neue christologische Untersuchungen*, ed. by Volker H. Drecoll, Hanns C. Brennecke, Christoph Markschies, Berlin/Boston 2021 (TU 187)

Abramowski, Luise/Goodman, Alan E., *A Nestorian Collection of Christological Texts*, 2 vols., Cambridge 1971 (UCOP 18–19)

Abramowski, Luise/Hainthaler, Theresia, *Jesus der Christus im Glauben der Kirche*, vol. II/5: Die Kirche in Persien, Freiburg etc. 2022

Akinian, Nerses/Casey, Robert P., 'Two Armenian Creeds', *HTR* 24 (1931), pp. 143–51

Alexopoulos, Theodoros, *Photios' von Konstantinopel - 'Mystagogie des Heiligen Geistes': Übersetzung und theologischer Kommentar*, Berlin/Boston 2023 (AKG 153)

Alikin, Valeriy A., *The Earliest History of the Christian Gathering: Origin, Development and Content of the Christian Gathering in the First to Third Centuries*, Leiden/Boston 2010 (SVigChr 2010)

Allen, Pauline/Neil, Bronwen, *Maximus the Confessor and his Companions: Documents from Exile*, edited and translated, Oxford 2002 (OECT)

Amidon, Philip R., 'Paulinus' Subscription to the *Tomus ad Antiochenos*', *JThS* 53 (2002), pp. 53–74

Anderson, Mary D., *Drama and Imagery in English Medieval Churches*, Cambridge 1963

Andrieu, Michel, *Les Ordines Romani du Haut Moyen Age*, 5 vols., Leuven 1931–1961 (SSL 11, 23, 24, 28, 29)

Andrist, Patrick, 'Les protagonistes égyptiens du débat apollinariste', *RechAug* 34 (2005), pp. 63–141

Andrist, Patrick, 'The Two Faces of Apollinarius: A Glimpse into the Complex Reception of an Uncommon Heretic in Byzantium', in: Bergjan/Gleede/Heimgartner 2015, pp. 285–306

Angenendt, Arnold, 'Bonifatius und das Sacramentum initiationis: Zugleich ein Beitrag zur Geschichte der Firmung' [1977], in: id., *Liturgie im Mittelalter: Ausgewählte Aufsätze zum 70. Geburtstag*, ed. by Thomas Flammer/Daniel Meyer, second ed., Münster 2005 (Ästhetik – Theologie – Liturgik 35), pp. 35–87

Angenendt, Arnold, 'Der Taufritus im frühen Mittelalter', in: *Segni e riti nella chiesa altomedievale occidentale*, vol. I, Spoleto 1987 (SSAM 33), pp. 275–336

Angenendt, Arnold, *Das Frühmittelalter: Die abendländische Christenheit von 400 bis 900*, third ed., Stuttgart etc. 2001

Angenendt, Arnold, *Geschichte der Religiosität im Mittelalter*, fourth ed., Darmstadt 2009

Articles. wherevpon it was agreed by the archbysshops and Bisshops of both the prouinces, and the whole Clergye, in the Conuocation holden at London in the yere of our Lord God .M.D.lxii. accordyng to the computation of the Churche of England, for thauoydyng of the diuersities of opinions, and for the stablyshyng of consent touchyng true religion. Put foorth by the Quenes aucthoritie, London 1563

https://doi.org/10.1515/9783110318531-022

Ashwin-Siejkowski, Piotr, *The Apostles' Creed: The Apostles' Creed and Its Early Christian Context*, London/New York 2009

Assemani, Giuseppe L., *Codex Liturgicus Ecclesiae Universae*, vol. I, Rome 1749

Assemani, Giuseppe L., *Codex Liturgicus Ecclesiae Universae*, vol. II: De baptismo, Rome 1749

Assemani, Giuseppe L., *Codex Liturgicus Ecclesiae Universae*, vol. III: De confirmatione, Rome 1750

Atkinson, Charles M., 'Zur Entstehung und Überlieferung der "Missa graeca"', *AfMW* 39 (1982), pp. 113–45

Atkinson, Charles M., 'The *Doxa*, the *Pisteuo* and the *ellinici fratres*: Some Anomalies in the Transmission of the Chants of the "Missa Graeca"', *Journal of Musicology* 7 (1989), pp. 81–106

Atkinson, Charles M., 'Further Thoughts on the Origin of the Missa Graeca', in: Peter Cahn/Ann-Katrin Heimer (eds.), *De Musica et cantu: Studien zur Geschichte der Kirchenmusik und der Oper. Helmut Hucke zum 60. Geburtstag*, Hildesheim 1993 (Musikwissenschaftliche Publikationen/ Hochschule für Musik und Darstellende Kunst Frankfurt/Main 2), pp. 75–93

Aubineau, Michel, 'Les 318 serviteurs d'Abraham (Gen., XIV, 14) et le nombre des pères au concile de Nicée (325)', *RHE* 61 (1966), pp. 5–43

Auf der Maur, Hansjörg, *Feiern im Rhythmus der Zeit I: Herrenfeste in Woche und Jahr*, Regensburg 1983 (GDK 5)

Auffarth, Christoph, art. 'Mysterien (Mysterienkulte)', in: *RAC*, vol. XXV, 2013, cols. 422–71

Auksi, Peter, *Christian Plain Style: The Evolution of a Spiritual Idea*, Montreal etc. 1995

Aust, Hugo/Müller, Dieter, 'art. ἀνάθεμα', in: *TBLNT*, vol. I, Studien-Ausgabe, 1977, pp. 348 f.

Avagyan, Anahit, *Die armenische Athanasius-Überlieferung: Das auf Armenisch unter dem Namen des Athanasius von Alexandrien tradierte Schrifttum*, Berlin/Boston 2014 (PTS 69)

Ayres, Lewis, *Nicaea and Its Legacy: An Approach to Fourth-century Trinitarian Theology*, Oxford 2004

Ayres, Lewis, 'Irenaeus and the "Rule of Truth": A Reconsideration', in: Lewis Ayres/H. Clifton Ward (eds.), *The Rise of the Early Christian Intellectual*, Berlin/Boston 2020 (AKG 139), pp. 145–63

Backes, Katharina, 'Zur Ikonographie der *Credo*-Apostel und ihren Beispielen in der Wandmalerei zwischen Rhein, Neckar und Enz', in: Beuckers Klaus G(ed.), *Die mittelalterlichen Wandmalereien zwischen Rhein, Neckar und Enz*, Ubstadt-Weiher etc. 2011 (Heimatverein Kraichgau/ Sonderveröffentlichung 35), pp. 147–62

Badcock, Francis J., 'The Council of Constantinople and the Nicene Creed', *JThS* 16 (1915), pp. 205–25

Badcock, Francis J., '*Sanctorum communio* as an Article of the Creed', *JThS* 21 (1920), pp. 106–26

Badcock, Francis J., 'The Old Roman Creed,' *JThS* 23 (1922), pp. 362–89

Badcock, Francis J., *The History of the Creeds*, second ed., New York 1938

Barbet, Jeanne/Lambot, Cyrille, 'Nouvelle tradition du symbole de rite gallican', *RBen* 75 (1965), pp. 335–45

Barbian, Karl-Josef, *Die altdeutschen Symbola: Beiträge zur Quellenfrage*, Sankt Augustin 1964 (VMStA 14)

Barceló, Pedro, *Constantius II. und seine Zeit: Die Anfänge des Staatskirchentums*, Stuttgart 2004

Barnes, Timothy D., *The New Empire of Diocletian and Constantine*, Cambridge, Mass./London 1982

Barnes, Timothy D., *Athanasius and Constantius: Theology and Politics in the Constantinian Empire*, Cambridge, Massachusetts/London 1993

Barnes, Timothy D., 'The Exile and Recalls of Asterius', *JThS* 60 (2009), pp. 109–29

Barnes, Timothy D., *Constantine: Dynasty, Religion and Power in the Later Roman Empire*, Chichester, West Sussex 2011 (paperback 2014; Blackwell Ancient Lives)

Barnes, W. Emery, 'The "Nicene" Creed in the Syriac Psalter', *JThS* 7 (1906), pp. 441–9

Barry, Jennifer, *Bishops in Flight: Exile and Displacement in Late Antiquity*, Oakland, California 2019 (The Joan Palevsky Imprint in Classical Literature)

Barth, Gerhard, art. 'πίστις κτλ.', in: *EDNT*, vol. III, 1993, pp. 91–7

Bartl, Dominik, *Der Schatzbehalter: Optionen der Bildrezeption*, unpublished PhD diss., Heidelberg 2010; download: URL <http://www.ub.uni-heidelberg.de/archiv/10735> (27/11/2023)

Bartl, Dominik/Gepp-Labusiak, Miriam, *Der Mainzer Schatzbehalter: Ein koloriertes Andachtsbuch von 1491*, Darmstadt 2012

Bauckham, Richard J., *Jude – 2 Peter*, Dallas etc. 1990 (Word Biblical Themes)

Baum, Wilhelm/Winkler, Dietmar W., *The Church in the East: A Concise History*, London/New York 2003

Baumer, Christoph, *The Church of the East: An Illustrated History of Assyrian Christianity*, new edition, London/New York 2016

Baumstark, Anton, 'Eine aegyptische Mess- und Taufliturgie vermutlich des 6. Jahrhunderts', *OrChr* 1 (1901), pp. 1–45

Baumstark, Anton, *Die Messe im Morgenland*, 4. Tausend, Kempten etc. n.d. (1921; Sammlung Kösel 8)

Baumstark, Anton, *Geschichte der syrischen Literatur mit Ausschluss der christlich-palästinensischen Texte*, Bonn 1922

Bausi, Alessandro, 'La versione etiopica della *Didascalia dei 318 niceni* sulla retta fede e la vita monastica', in: Ugo Zanetti/Enzo Lucchesi (eds.), *Aegyptus Christiana: Mélanges d'hagiographie égyptienne et orientale dédiés à la mémoire du P. Paul Devos Bollandiste*, Geneva 2004, pp. 225–48

Bausi, Alessandro, 'The "so-called *Traditio apostolica*": Preliminary Observations on the New Ethiopic Evidence', in: Heike Grieser/Andreas Merkt (eds.), *Volksglaube im antiken Christentum*, Darmstadt 2009, pp. 291–321

Bausi, Alessandro, art. 'Traditio Apostolica', in: *Encyclopaedia Aethiopica*, vol. IV, 2010, pp. 980–1

Bausi, Alessandro, 'La "nuova" versione etiopica della Traditio apostolica. Edizione e traduzione preliminare', in: Paola Buzi/Alberto Camplani (eds.), *Christianity in Egypt: Literary Production and Intellectual Trends. Studies in Honor of Tito Orlandi*, Rome 2011, pp. 19–69 (SEAug 125)

Bausi, Alessandro/Camplani, Alberto, 'New Ethiopic Documents for the History of Christian Egypt', ZAC 17 (2013), pp. 195–227

Bausi, Alessandro, 'Writing, Copying, Translating: Ethiopia as a Manuscript Culture', in: Jörg B. Quenzer/Dmitry Bondarev/Jan-Ulrich Sobisch (eds.), *Manuscript Cultures: Mapping the Field*, Berlin etc. 2014, pp. 37–77

Bausi, Alessandro, 'Zufallsfund in den Tigray-Bergen: Wenn ein Wissenschaftler unter einen Kirchenschrank schaut . . .', in: Centre for the Study of Manuscript Cultures (CSMC), *manuskript des monats* 08/2015; download: URL <https://www.manuscript-cultures.uni-hamburg.de/mom/2015_08_mom.html> (25/10/2018)

Bausi, Alessandro, 'Composite and Multiple-Text Manuscripts: The Ethiopian Evidence', in: Michael Friedrich/Cosima Schwarke (eds.), *One-Volume Libraries: Composite and Multiple-Text Manuscripts*, Berlin/Boston 2016 (Studies in Manuscript Cultures 9), pp. 111–53

Bausi, Alessandro/Camplani, Alberto, 'The *History of the Episcopate of Alexandria* (HEpA): Editio minor of the fragments preserved in the *Aksumite Collection* and in the *Codex Veronensis* LX (58)', *Adam.* 22 (2016), pp. 249–302

Bausi, Alessandro, 'The *Baptismal Ritual* in the Earliest Ethiopic Canonical Liturgical Collection', in: Heinzgerd Brakmann et al. (eds.), *'Neugeboren aus Wasser und Heiligem Geist': Kölner Kolloquium zur Initiatio Christiana*, Münster 2020 (JThF 37), pp. 31–83

Beatrice, Pier F., 'The Word "Homoousios" from Hellenism to Christianity', *ChH* 74 (2002), pp. 243–72

Becker, Carl, art. 'Fides', in: *RAC*, vol. VII, 1969, cols. 801–39

Becker, Karl J., 'Articulus fidei (1150–1230): Von der Einführung des Wortes bis zu den drei Definitionen Philipps des Kanzlers', *Gr.* 54 (1973), pp. 517–69

Becker, Matthias, *Porphyrius*, Contra Christianos: *Neue Sammlung der Fragmente, Testimonien und Dubia mit Einleitung, Übersetzung und Anmerkungen*, Berlin/Boston 2016 (TK 52)

Becker, Oswald/Michel, Otto, art. 'Faith, Persuade, Belief, Unbelief', in: *NIDNTT*, vol. I, 1975, pp. 587–606

Behr, John, *St Irenaeus of Lyons: On the Apostolic Preaching*. Translated and with an Introduction, Crestwood, New York 1997

Behr, John, *The Nicene Faith*, 2 vols., Crestwood, NY 2004 (The Formation of Christian Theology 2)

Belsheim, Johannes, art. 'Caspari, Carl Paul', in: *RE*, third ed., vol. III, 1897, pp. 737–42

Benga, Daniel, art. 'Didascalia Apostolorum', in: *Brill Encyclopedia of Early Christianity Online*, 2018; URL <http://dx.doi.org/10.1163/2589-7993_EECO_SIM_00000927> (27/11/2023)

Benko, Stephen, *The Meaning of Sanctorum Communio*, London 1964 (Studies in Historical Theology 3)

Bensly, Robert L./Harris, J. Rendel/Burkitt, F. Crawford, *The Four Gospels in Syriac Transcribed from the Sinaitic Palimpsest*, Cambridge 1894

Berger, David, *The Jewish-Christian Debate in the High Middle Ages: A Critical Edition of the Niẓẓaḥon Vetus with an Introduction, Translation, and Commentary*, Philadelphia 1979

Berger, Jean-Denis/Fontaine, Jacques/Schmidt, Peter L. (eds.), *Die Literatur im Zeitalter des Theodosius (374–430 n. Chr.)*, part II: Christliche Prosa, München 2020 (HLLA VI/2)

Berger, Klaus, 'Hellenistische Gattungen im Neuen Testament', in: *ANRW*, vol. II 25/2, 1984, pp. 1031–432, 1831–85

Berger, Klaus, *Einführung in die Formgeschichte*, Tübingen 1987 (UTB 1444)

Berger, Klaus, *Formen und Gattungen im Neuen Testament*, Tübingen 2005 (UTB 2532)

Bergjan, Silke-Petra/Gleede, Benjamin/Heimgartner, Martin (eds.), *Apollinarius und seine Folgen*, Tübingen 2015 (STAC 93)

Bergmann, Rolf (ed.), *Althochdeutsche und altsächsische Literatur*, Berlin/Boston 2013, pp. 293–315

Berndt, Guido M./Steinacher, Roland (eds.), *Arianism: Roman Heresy and Barbarian Creed*, Farnham, Surrey/Burlington, VT 2014

Bertram, Jerome, *The Chrodegang Rules: The Rules of the Common Life of the Secular Clergy from the Eigth and Ninth Centuries. Critical Texts with Translations and Commentary*, Abingdon/New York 2005 (Church, Faith and Culture in the Medieval West)

Berzon, Todd S., 'Between Presence and Perfection: The Protean Creed of Early Christianity', *JECS* 29 (2021), pp. 579–606

Bethurum, Dorothy, *The Homilies of Wulfstan*, Oxford 1957

Betti, Maddalena, *The Making of Christian Moravia (858–882): Papal Power and Political Reality*, Leiden/Boston 2014 (East Central and Eastern Europe in the Middle Ages, 450–1450 24)

Bevan, George A., 'The Sequence of the First Four Sessions of the Council of Chalcedon', in: *StPatr*, vol. XCII, 2017, pp. 91–102

Bidawid, Raphaël J., *Les lettres du patriarche Nestorien Timothée I: Étude critique avec en appendice La lettre de Timothée I aux moines du Couvent de Mār Mārōn (traduction latine et texte chaldéen*, Vatican City 1956 (StT 187)

Bieler, Ludwig/Binchy, Daniel A. (eds.), *The Irish Penitentials*, Dublin 1963 (SLH 5)

Bienert, Wolfgang A., *Dionysius von Alexandrien: Zur Frage des Origenismus im dritten Jahrhundert*, Berlin/New York 1978 (PTS 21)

Binggeli, André et al., *Catalogue des manuscrits syriaques et* garshuni *du patriarcat syriaque-catholique de Charfet (Liban)*, vol. I: Fonds patriarcal (Raḥmani) 1–125, Dar'un-Harissa 2021

Bischoff, Bernhard/Lapidge, Michael, *Biblical Commentaries from the Canterbury School of Theodore and Hadrian*, Cambridge 1994 (CSASE 10)

Black, Robert R./St-Jacques, Raymond (eds.), *The Middle English Glossed Prose Psalter: Edited from Cambridge, Magdalene College, MS Pepys 2498*, 2 vols., Heidelberg 2012 (Middle English Texts 45/46)

Blair, John, *The Church in Anglo-Saxon Society*, Oxford 2005

Blanchet, Marie-Hélène/Gabriel, Frédéric (eds.), *L'Union à l'épreuve du formulaire: Professions de foi entre Églises d'Orient et d'Occident (XIIIᵉ-XVIIIᵉ siècle)*, Leuven etc. 2016 (Collège de France – CNRS – Centre de Recherche d'Histoire et Civilisation de Byzance, Monographies 51)

Blanchet, Marie-Hélène, 'Deux commentaires byzantins au Symbole des apôtres (fin XIVᵉ-début XVᵉ siècle) et leurs modèles latins', in: Panagiotis Ch. Athanasopoulos (ed.), *Translation Activity in the Late Byzantine World*, Berlin/Boston 2022 (Byzantinisches Archiv – Series Philosophica 4), pp. 407–40

Blatt, Franz, 'Un nouveau texte d'une apologie anonyme', in: ΔΡΑΓΜΑ *Martino P. Nilsson A. D. IV ID. IUL. ANNO MCMXXXIX dedicatum*, Lund 1939 (Acta Instituti Romani Regni Sueciae, series altera 1), pp. 67–95

Bleckmann, Bruno/Stein, Markus, *Philostorgios – Kirchengeschichte: Ediert, übersetzt und kommentiert*, 2 vols., Paderborn 2015 (Kleine und Fragmentarische Historiker der Spätantike E7)

Blowers, Paul M., *Maximus the Confessor: Jesus Christ and the Transfiguration of the World*, Oxford 2016 (Christian Theology in Context)

Blumell, Lincoln H., 'P.Mich. inv. 4461kr: The Earliest Fragment of the *Didascalia CCCXVIII Patrum Nicaenorum*', *JThS* 68 (2017), pp. 607–20

Bochinger, Christoph et al., art. 'Bekenntnis', in: *RGG*, fourth ed., vol. I, 1998, cols. 1246–69

Boespflug, François, 'Autour de la traduction picturale du Credo au Moyen Âge (XIIᵉ-XVᵉ siècle)', in: Paul De Clerck/Éric Palazzo (eds.), *Rituels. Mélanges offerts à Pierre-Marie Gy, o.p.*, Paris 1990, pp. 55–84

Böttrich, Christfried, '"Sorgt euch nicht, was ihr sagen sollt . . .": Bekenntnisbildung im frühen Christentum', in: Thomas K. Kuhn (ed.), *Bekennen – Bekenntnis – Bekenntnisse: Interdisziplinäre Zugänge*, Leipzig 2014 (GTF 22), pp. 61–102

Bonneau, Danielle, *La crue du Nil: Divinité égyptienne à travers mille ans d'histoire (332 av. – 641 ap. J.-C.) d'après les auteurs grecs et latins, et les documents des époques ptolémaïque, romaine et byzantine*, Paris 1964 (EeC 52)

Bonneau, Danielle, 'Les courants d'eau d'Isis (P. Lond. lit. 239)', in: Sebastià Janeras (ed.), *Miscel·lània Papirològica Ramón Roca-Puig*, Barcelona 1987, pp. 89–96

Bonwetsch, G. Nathanael, *Die unter Hippolyts Namen überlieferte Schrift über den Glauben nach einer Übersetzung der georgischen Version*, Leipzig 1907 (TU 31/2, pp. 1–36)

Boodts, Shari/Schmidt, Gleb, art. 'Sermon/Homiletics', in: *Brill Encyclopedia of Early Christianity Online*, 2022; URL<http://dx.doi.org/10.1163/2589-7993_EECO_SIM_00003126> (27/11/2023)

Botte, Bernard, 'Note sur la symbole baptismal de S. Hippolyte', in: *Mélanges Joseph de Ghellinck*, vol. I: Antiquité, Gembloux 1951 (ML.H 13), pp. 189–200

Botte, Bernard, *La Tradition apostolique des Saint Hippolyte: Éssai de reconstitution*, fifth ed., Münster, Westfalen 1989 (LQF 39)

Bradshaw, Paul F., '"Diem baptismo sollemniorem": Initiation and Easter in Christian Antiquity' [1993], in: Maxwell E. Johnson (ed.), *Living Water, Sealing Spirit: Readings on Christian Initiation*, Collegeville, Minnesota 1995, pp. 137–47

Bradshaw, Paul F./Johnson, Maxwell E./Phillips, Edward, *The Apostolic Tradition: A Commentary*, ed. by Harold W. Attridge, Minneapolis 2002 (Hermeneia)

Bradshaw, Paul F., 'Who Wrote the *Apostolic Tradition*? A Response to Alistair Stewart-Sykes', *SVTQ* 48 (2004), 195–206

Bradshaw, Paul F., art. '*Apostolic Constitutions*', in: *Brill Encyclopedia of Early Christianity Online*, 2018; URL <http://dx.doi.org/10.1163/2589-7993_EECO_SIM_00000246> (27/11/2023)

Bradshaw, Paul F., art. '*Apostolic Tradition (Traditio Apostolica)*', in: *Brill Encyclopedia of Early Christianity Online*, 2018; URL <http://dx.doi.org/10.1163/2589-7993_EECO_SIM_00000250> (27/11/2023)

Bradshaw, Paul F., Apostolic Tradition*: A New Commentary*, Collegeville, Minnesota 2023

Brandscheidt, Renate, art. 'Glauben (AT)' [2013], in: *Das wissenschaftliche Bibellexikon im Internet (WiBiLex)*; URL <http://www.bibelwissenschaft.de/stichwort/19652 > (27/11/2023)

Braun, Oskar, *De sancta Nicaena synodo: Syrische Texte von Maruta von Maipherkat nach einer Handschrift der Propaganda zu Rom übersetzt*, Münster i.W. 1898 (KGS 4/3)

Braun, Oskar, *Das Buch der Synhados oder Synodicon Orientale: Die Sammlung der nestorianischen Konzilien, zusammengestellt im neunten Jahrhundert nach der syrischen Handschrift, Museo Borgiano 82, der Vatikanischen Bibliothek*, übersetzt und erläutert, mit kritischen und historischen Anmerkungen, Namen- und Sachregistern, Stuttgart/Wien 1900 (repr. Amsterdam 1975)

Braun, Oskar, 'Zwei Synoden des Katholikos Timotheos I.', *OrChr* 2 (1902), pp. 283–311

Braun, René, *Deus Christianorum: Recherches sur le vocabulaire doctrinal de Tertullien*, second ed., Paris 1977

Bréhier, Louis, ΊΕΡΕΥΣ ΚΑΙ ΒΑΣΙΛΕΥΣ [1948], in: Herbert Hunger (ed.), *Das byzantinische Herrscherbild*, Darmstadt 1975 (WdF 341), pp. 86–93

Bremmer, Jan N., *Maidens, Magic and Martyrs in Early Christianity: Collected Essays I*, Tübingen 2017 (WUNT 379)

Bremmer, Jan N., 'God and Christ in the Earlier Martyr Acts', in: Matthew V. Novenson (ed.), *Monotheism and Christology in Greco-Roman Antiquity*, Leiden/Boston 2020 (NT.S 180), pp. 222–48

Brennecke, Hanns C., *Hilarius von Poitiers und die Bischofsopposition gegen Konstantius II.: Untersuchungen zur 3. Phase des Arianischen Streites (337 – 361)*, Berlin/New York 1984 (PTS 26)

Brennecke, Hanns C., art. 'Hilarius von Poitiers *(gest. 367 oder 368)*', in: *TRE*, vol. XV, 1986, pp. 315–22

Brennecke, Hanns C., art. 'Lucian von Antiochien *(Martyrium 7.1.312)*', in: *TRE*, vol. XXI, 1991, pp. 474–9

Brennecke, Hanns C., art. 'Nicäa, Ökumenische Synoden, I. Ökumenische Synode von 325', in: *TRE*, vol. XXIV, 1994, pp. 429–41

Brennecke, Hanns C., art. 'Paulinus von Antiochien', in: *BBKL*, vol. XXXVII, 2016, cols. 803–13

Brennecke, Hanns Christof, Das *Athanasianum* – ein Text aus dem Westgotenreich? Uberlegungen zur Herkunft des *Symbolum quicumque*, in: Uta Heil (ed.), *Das Christentum im frühen Europa: Diskurse – Tendenzen – Entscheiungen*, Berlin/Boston 2019 (Millennium Studies 75), pp. 317–38

Brennecke, Hanns C. et al., *Dokumente zur Geschichte des Arianischen Streites*, 3. Lieferung: Bis zur Ekthesis makrostichos, Berlin etc. 2007 (Athanasius Werke 3/1,3)

Brennecke, Hanns C. et al., *Dokumente zur Geschichte des Arianischen Streites*, 4. Lieferung: Bis zur Synode von Alexandrien 362, Berlin/Boston 2014 (Athanasius Werke 3/1,4)

Brennecke, Hanns C., art. 'Arianism', in: *Brill Encyclopedia of Early Christianity Online*, 2018; URL <http://dx.doi.org/10.1163/2589-7993_EECO_SIM_00000280> (27/11/2023)

Brennecke, Hanns C./Stockhausen, Annette von, *Dokumente zur Geschichte des Arianischen Streites*, 5. Lieferung: Bis zum Vorabend der Synode von Konstantinopel (381), Berlin/Boston 2020 (Athanasius Werke 3/1,5)

Brennecke, Hanns C./Grasmück, Ernst Ludwig/Markschies, Christoph (eds.), *Logos: Festschrift für Luise Abramowski zum 8. Juli 1993*, Berlin/New York 1993 (BZNW 67)

Brent, Allen, *Hippolytus and the Roman Church in the Third Century: Communities in Tension before the Emergence of a Monarch-Bishop*, Leiden 1995 (SVigChr 31)

Brent, Allen, art. 'Ignatians, Pseudo-', in: *Brill Encyclopedia of Early Christianity Online*, 2018; URL <http://dx.doi.org/10.1163/2589-7993_EECO_SIM_00001666> (27/11/2023)

Brewer, Heinrich, *Das sogenannte Athanasianische Glaubensbekenntnis ein Werk des heiligen Ambrosius*, Paderborn 1909 (FChLDG 9/2)

Breydy, Michael, Jean Maron – Exposé de la foi et autres opuscules, 2 Bände, Löwen 1988 (CSCO 497–498/Scriptores Syri 209–210)

Breydy, Michael, 'Richtigstellungen über Agapius von Manbiğ und sein historisches Werk', *Oriens Christianus* 73 (1989), pp. 90–6

Breydy, Michael, art. 'Johannes Maron', in: *BBKL*, vol. III, 1992, cols. 480–2

Brightman, Frank E., *Liturgies Eastern and Western Being the Texts Original or Translated of the Principal Liturgies of the Church: Edited with Introductions and Appendices*, vol. I: Eastern Liturgies, Oxford 1896 (repr. 1965)

Brinktrine, Johannes, 'Die trinitarischen Bekenntnisformeln und Taufsymbole: Beiträge zu ihrer Entstehung und Entwicklung', *ThQ* 102 (1921), pp. 156–90

Brock, Sebastian, 'A New Syriac Baptismal *Ordo* Attributed to Timothy of Alexandria', *Muséon* 83 (1970), pp. 367–431

Brock, Sebastian, 'A Remarkable Syriac Baptismal Ordo (BM Add. 14518)', *ParOr* 2 (1971), pp. 365–78

Brock, Sebastian, 'Studies in the Early History of the Syrian Orthodox Baptismal Liturgy', *JThS* 23 (1972), pp. 16–64

Brock, Sebastian, 'The Syrian Baptismal Ordines (With Special Reference to the Anointings)', *STLi* 12 (1977), 177–83

Brock, Sebastian, 'Some Early Syriac Baptismal Commentaries', *OCP* 46 (1980), pp. 20–61

Brock, Sebastian, 'The Christology of the Church of the East in the Synods of the Fifth to Early Seventh Centuries: Preliminary Considerations and Materials', in: George Dragas (ed.), *Aksum-Thyateira: A Festschrift for Archbishop Methodios of Thyteira and Great Britain*, London 1985, pp. 125–42; also in: Sebastian Brock, *Studies in Syriac Christianity: History, Literature and Theology*, Aldershot/Brookfield Vermont 1992 (CStS CS357), no. XII

Brock, Sebastian, 'Gabriel of Qatar's Commentary on the Liturgy', *Hugoye* 6 (2009), pp. 197–248

Brooks, Ernest W., *A Collection of Letters of Severus of Antioch from Numerous Syriac Manuscripts Edited and Translated*, Paris 1919 (PO 12/2)

Brown, Peter, *Power and Persuasion in Late Antiquity: Towards a Christian Empire*, Madison, Wisconsin/London 1992

Brown, Peter, *The Rise of Western Christendom: Triumph and Diversity, A.D. 200–1000*, Tenth Anniversary Revised Edition, Chichester, West Sussex 2013

Brox, Norbert, art. 'Häresie', in: *RAC*, vol. XIII, 1986, cols. 248–97

Bruns, Peter, *Theodor von Mopsuestia – Katechetische Homilien*, vol. I, übersetzt und eingeleitet, Freiburg etc. 1994 (FC 17/1)

Bruns, Peter, 'Bemerkungen zur Rezeption des Nicaenums in der ostsyrischen Kirche', *AHC* 32 (2000), pp. 1–22

Bruns, Peter, 'Das sogenannte "Nestorianum" und verwandte Symbole', *OrChr* 89 (2005), pp. 43–62

Bruns, Peter, 'Die Haltung der "Kirche des Ostens" zum Nicaenum', *AHC* 40 (2008), pp. 47–60

Buber, Martin, *Two Types of Faith*, New York 1951

Bühler, Curt F., 'The Apostles and the Creed', *Spec.* 28 (1953), pp. 336–9

Bührer-Thierry, Geneviève, 'Introduction', in: Bührer-Thierry/Gioanni 2015, pp. 1–18

Bührer-Thierry, Geneviève/Gioanni, Stéphane (eds.), *Exclure de la communauté chrétienne: Sens et pratiques sociales de l'anathème et de l'excommunication (IVᵉ–XIIᵉ siècle)*, Turnhout 2015

Bultmann, Rudolf/Weiser, Artur, art. 'πιστεύω κτλ.', in: *TDNT*, vol. VI, 1968, pp. 174–228

Burgess, Richard W., *Studies in Eusebian and post-Eusebian Chronography*, Stuttgart 1999 (Hist.E 135)

Burkard, Dominik, 'Katechismen als Gegenstand kirchenhistorischer Forschung – Eine Einführung, *RoJKG* 39 (2020), pp. 15–24

Burn, Andrew E., *The Athanasian Creed and Its Early Commentaries*, Cambridge 1896 (TaS 4/1)

Burn, Andrew E., *An Introduction to the Creeds and to the Te Deum*, London 1899

Burn, Andrew E., *Niceta of Remesiana: His Life and Works*, Cambridge 1905

Burn, Andrew E., *The Apostles' Creed*, New York 1906 (Oxford Church Text Books)

Burn, Andrew E., *Facsimiles of the Creeds from Early Manuscripts*, London 1909 (HBS 36)

Burn, Andrew E., *The Nicene Creed*, London 1909

Burn, Andrew E., *The Athanasian Creed*, second ed., London 1918 (Oxford Church Text Books)

Burn, Andrew E., *The Council of Nicaea: A Memorial for its Sixteenth Centenary*, London 1925

Burney, Charles, *A General History of Music from the Earliest Ages to the Present Period (1789)*, ed. by Frank Mercer, vol. I, New York, n.d. (1935)

Busch, Anja/Nicols, John/Zanella, Francesco, art. 'Patronage (Patronus, Patronat)', in: *RAC*, vol. XXVI, 2015, cols. 1109–38

Bynum, Caroline Walker, *The Resurrection of the Body in Western Christianity, 200–1336*, New York 1995

Cabié, Robert, *La Pentecôte: L'évolution de la Cinquantaine pascale au cours des cinq premiers siècles*, Paris 1965 (Bibliothèque de Liturgie)

Calhoun, Robert M., 'The Lord's Prayer in Christian Amulets', *Early Christianity* 11 (2020), pp. 415–50

Callahan, Daniel F., 'The Problem of the "Filioque" and the Letter from the Pilgrim Monks of the Mount of Olives to Pope Leo III and Charlemagne', *RBen* 102 (1992), pp. 75–134

Cameron, Alan, 'The Imperial Pontifex', *HSCP* 103 (2007), pp. 341–84

Cameron, Alan, *The Last Pagans of Rome*, Oxford 2011

Cameron, Alan, '*Pontifex Maximus*: From Augustus to Gratian – and beyond', in: Maijastina Kahlos (ed.), *Emperors and the Divine – Rome and its Influence*, Helsinki 2016 (Collegium 20), pp. 139–59

Campenhausen, Hans von, 'Taufen auf den Namen Jesu' [1971], in: Campenhausen 1989, pp. 197–216

Campenhausen, Hans von, 'Das Bekenntnis im Urchristentum' [1972], in: Campenhausen 1979, pp. 217–72

Campenhausen, Hans von, 'Der Herrentitel Jesu und das urchristliche Bekenntnis' [1975], in: Campenhausen 1979, pp. 273–77

Campenhausen, Hans von, 'Das Bekenntnis Eusebs von Caesarea (Nicaea 325)' [1976], in: Campenhausen 1979, pp. 278–99

Campenhausen, Hans von, *Urchristliches und Altkirchliches: Vorträge und Aufsätze*, Tübingen 1979

Camplani, Alberto, 'Fourth-Century Synods in Latin and Syriac Canonical Collections and their Preservation in the Antiochene Archives (Serdica 343 CE – Antioch 325 CE)', in: Sofía Torallas Tovar/Juan P. Monferrer-Sala (eds.), *Cultures in Contact: Transfer of Knowledge in the Mediterranean Context. Selected Papers*, Córdoba/Beyrouth 2013 (CNERU – CEDRAC Series Syro-Arabica 1), pp. 61–72

Campos, Julio, *Juan de Bíclaro, obispo de Gerona: Su vida y su obra. Introducción, texto crítico y comentarios*, Madrid 1960 (Consejo Superior de Investigaciones Científicas/Estudios 32)

Capelle, Bernard, 'Le symbole romain au second siècle', *RBen* 39 (1927), pp. 33–45

Capelle, Bernard, 'L'origine antiadoptianiste de notre texte du symbole de la messe' [1929], in: Capelle 1967, pp. 47–59

Capelle, Bernard, 'Les origines du symbole romain', *RThAM* 2 (1930), pp. 5–20

Capelle, Bernard, 'Alcuin et l'histoire du symbole de la messe' [1934], in: id., *Travaux liturgiques de doctrine et d'histoire*, vol. II: Histoire. La messe, Leuven 1962, pp. 211–21

Capelle, Bernard, 'L'introduction du symbole à la messe' [1951], in: id. 1967, pp. 60–81

Capelle, Bernard, *Travaux liturgiques de doctrine et d'histoire*, vol. III: Histoire. Varia – L'assomption, Leuven 1967

Carlson, Stephen C., 'The Fragments of Papias', in: Michael F. Bird/Scott D. Harrower (eds.), *The Cambridge Companion to the Apostolic Fathers*, Cambridge 2021, pp. 332–50

Cartwright, Sophie, *The Theological Anthropology of Eustathius of Antioch*, New York/Oxford 2015 (Oxford Early Christian Studies)

Caspari, Carl P., *Ungedruckte, unbeachtete und wenig beachtete Quellen zur Geschichte des Taufsymbols und der Glaubensregel herausgegeben und in Abhandlungen erläutert*, 3 vols, Christiania 1866–1875 (repr. Brussels 1964)

Caspari, Carl P., *Kirchenhistorische Anecdota nebst neuen Ausgaben patristischer und kirchlich-mittelalterlicher Schriften*, vol I.: Lateinische Schriften. Die Texte und die Anmerkungen, Christiania 1883

Castelberg, Marcus, *Wissen und Weisheit: Untersuchungen zur spätmittelalterlichen 'Süddeutschen Tafelsammlung' (Washington, D.C., Library of Congress, Lessing J. Rosenwald Collection, ms. no. 4)*, Berlin/Boston 2013 (ScFr 35)

Catergian, Joseph, *De fidei symbolo quo Armenii utuntur observationes*, Vienna 1893

Chabot, Jean-Baptiste, *Synodicon Orientale ou recueil des synodes nestoriens: Publié, traduit et annoté*, Paris 1902

Chadwick, Henry, 'Ossius of Cordova and the Presidency of the Council of Antioch, 325 ' [1958], in: id., *Selected Writings*, Grand Rapids, Mich. 2017, pp. 87–100

Chadwick, Henry, *Origen – Contra Celsum*, repr. with corrections Cambridge 1965 (Pb 1980)

Chadwick, Henry, 'The Chalcedonian Definition' [1983], in: id., *Selected Writings*, ed. by William G. Rusch, Grand Rapids, Michigan 2017, pp. 101–14

Chandler, Kegan A., *Constantine and the Divine Mind: The Imperial Quest for Primitive Monotheism*, Eugene, Oregon 2019

Chébli, P., *Sévère Ibn-al-Moqaffaʾ, évêque d'Aschmounain: Réfutation de Saʿîd Ibn-Batriq (Eutychius) (Le livre des conciles)*, texte arabe publié et traduit, Paris 1909 (PO 3/2)

Çiçek, Julius Y. (ed.), *The Sacraments of Holy Baptism, Marriage, and Burial of the Dead According to the Ancient Rite of the Syrian Orthodox Church of Antioch*, Piscataway, NJ 2010 (Bar Ebroyo Kloster Publications 17)

Clemoes, Peter, *Ælfric's Catholic Homilies: The First Series. Text*, Oxford etc. 1997

Coakley, James F., art. 'Qdām w-Bāthar (Book of before and after)', in: *Gorgias Encyclopedic Dictionary of the Syriac Heritage* 2011, p. 345

Cochlaeus, Johannes, *Speculum antiquae devotionis circa missam, et omnem alium cultum dei: ex antiquis, et antea nunquam evulgatis per Typographos Autoribus*, Mainz 1549

Collins, Roger J.H., art. 'Athanasianisches Symbol', in: *TRE*, vol. IV, 1979, pp. 328–33

Collins, Roger J.H., *Visigothic Spain 409–711*, Malden, MA/Oxford 2004

Connolly, R. Hugh, 'The Early Syriac Creed', *ZNW* 7 (1906), pp. 202–23

Connolly, R. Hugh, *The Liturgical Homilies of Narsai: Translated into English with an Introduction*, Cambridge 1909 (TaS 8/1)

Connolly, R. Hugh, *The* Explanatio symboli ad initiandos*: A Work of Saint Ambrose*, Cambridge 1952 (TaS 10)

Connolly, R. Hugh/Codrington, Humphrey W., *Two Commentaries on the Jacobite Liturgy by George Bishop of the Arab Tribes and Moses Bār Kēphā: Together with the Syriac Anaphora of St James and a Document Entitled* The Book of Life, text and English translation, London/Oxford 1913 (Text and Translation Society)

Contino, Carlo, *La célébration du Nil dans les papyrus littéraires grecs*, vol. I: Présentation des témoignages papyrologiques, unpublished MA thesis, 2 vols. plus Liège 2020/2021; download: URL <http://hdl.handle.net/2268.2/12888> (27/11/2023)

Cook, John G., *The Interpretation of the New Testament in Greco-Roman Paganism*, Peabody, Massachusetts 2002

Cooper, Stephen A., *Marius Victorinus' Commentary on Galatians. Introduction, Translation, and Notes*, Oxford 2005 (OECS)

Cowdrey, Herbert E.J., 'John Norman Davidson Kelly, 1909–1997', in: *PBA* 101 (1999), pp. 419–37

Cowper, Benjamin H., *Syriac Miscellanies; or Extracts Relating to the First and Second General Councils, and Various Other Quotations, Theological, Historical, & Classical: Translated into English from Mss. in the British Museum and Imperial Library of Paris with Notes*, London/Edinburgh 1861

Cramer, Peter, *Baptism and Change in the Early Middle Ages, c. 200–c. 1150*, Cambridge etc. 1993 (repr. 1994)

Crawford, Peter, *Constantius II: Usurpers, Eunuchs and the Antichrist*, Barnsley, South Yorkshire 2016

Crawford, Samuel J., 'The Worcester Marks and Glosses of the Old English Manuscripts in the Bodleian, Together with the Worcester Version of the Nicene Creed', *Anglia* 52 (1928), pp. 1–25

Crocker, Richard L./Hiley, David, art. 'Credo', in: *Grove Music Online*, 2001; URL <https://doi.org/10.1093/gmo/9781561592630.article.06803> (27/11/2023)

Cross, Frank L., 'The Council of Antioch in 325 A.D.', *CQR* 128 (1939), pp. 49–76

Crouzel, Henri, art. 'Geist (Heiliger Geist)', in: *RAC*, vol. IX, 1976, cols. 490–545

Crum, Walter E., *Short Texts from Coptic Ostraca and Papyri*, London etc. 1921

Crum, Walter E./Bell, Harold I., *Wadi Sarga: Coptic and Greek Texts from the Escavations Undertaken by the Byzantine Research Account*, Copenhagen 1922 (Coptica 3)

Crum, Walter E./Evelyn-White, Hugh G., *The Monatery of Epiphanius at Thebes*, Part II: Coptic Ostraca and Papyri/Greek Ostraca and Papyri, New York 1926 (The Metropolitan Museum of Art Egyptian Expedition)

Cullmann, Oscar, *The Earliest Christian Confessions*, London 1949

Cureton, William, *Book of Religious and Philosophical Sects by Muhammad Al-Shahrastani: Now First Edited from the Collation of Several Mss.*, 2 vols. London 1842/1846 (repr. Piscataway, NJ 2002)

Cvetković, Carmen A., 'Greek Thought in Latin Language: Niceta of Remesiana's View of the Church', in: Peter Gemeinhardt (ed.), *Was ist Kirche in der Spätantike? Publikaton der Tagung der Patristischen Arbeitsgemeinschaft in Duderstadt und Göttingen (02.–05.01.2015)*, Leuven etc. 2017 (Studien der Patristischen Arbeitsgemeinschaft 14), pp. 101–16

d'Alès, Adhémar, 'Novatien et la doctrine de la Trinité à Rome au milieu du troisième siècle', *Gr.* 3 (1922) pp. 420–46, 497–523

d'Alverny, Marie-Thérèse, *Alain de Lille: Textes inédits. Avec une introduction sur sa vie et ses œuvres*, Paris 1965 (EPhM 52)

Daley, Brian E., *Gregory of Nazianzus*, London/New York 2006 (The Early Church Fathers)

Daley, Brian E., *Leontius of Byzantium – Complete Works: Edited and Translated, with an Introduction*, Oxford 2017 (OECT)

Dalmais, Irénée-Henry, 'Die Mysterien (Sakramente) im orthodoxen und altorientalischen Christentum', in: Nyssen et al. 1989, pp. 141–81

Dalmais, Irénée-Henry, 'Die nichtbyzantinischen orientalischen Liturgien: Entwicklung und Eigenart der einzelnen Riten, besonders der Eucharistiefeier und des Stundengebets', in: Nyssen et al. 1989, pp. 101–40

Daoud, Marcos/Hazen, Marsie, *The Liturgy of the Ethiopian Church*, n.p., n.d. (Cairo 1959)

Day, Juliette, Proclus on Baptism in Constantinople, Norwich 2005 (Joint Liturgical Study 59)

Day, Juliette, *The Baptismal Liturgy of Jerusalem: Fourth- and Fifth-Century Evidence from Palestine, Syria and Egypt*, Aldershot, Hampshire/Burlington, VT 2007 (Liturgy, Worship and Society)

De Aldama, José A., *El Símbolo Toledano I: Su texto, su origen, su posición en la historia de los símbolos*, Rome 1934 (AnGr 7)

De Boer, Martinus C., *Galatians: A Commentary*, Louisville, Kentucky 2011 (The New Testament Library)

De Bruyn, Theodore, 'Papyri, Parchments, Ostraca, and Tablets Written with Biblical Texts in Greek and Used as Amulets', in: Thomas J. Kraus/Tobias Nicklas (eds.), *Early Christian Manuscripts: Examples of Applied Method and Approach*, Leiden/Boston 2010 (Texts and Editions for New Testament Study 5), pp. 145–89

De Clercq, Victor C., *Ossius of Cordova: A Contribution to the History of the Constantinian Period*, Washington 1954 (SCA 13)

De Halleux, André, *Philoxène de Mabbog: Sa vie, ses écrits, sa théologie*, Louvain 1963 (DGMFT III/8)

De Halleux, André, 'La philoxénienne du symbole', in: *Symposium Syriacum: Célébré du 13 au 17 septembre 1976 au Centre culturel Les Fontaines de Chantilly, France: Communications*, Rome 1978 (OCA 205), pp. 295–315

De Halleux, André, 'Le symbole des évêques perses au synode de Séleucie-Ctésiphon (410)', in: Gernot Wiessner (ed.), *Erkenntnisse und Meinungen II*, Wiesbaden 1978 (GOF I/17), pp. 161–90

De Halleux, André, 'La profession de l'Esprit Saint dans le symbole de Constantinople' [1979], in: id. 1990, pp. 303–37

De Halleux, André, '"Hypostase" et "personne" dans la formation du dogme trinitaire' [1984], in: id. 1990, pp. 113–214

De Halleux, André, 'La réception du symbole œcuménique, de Nicée à Chalcédoine' [1985], in: id. 1990, pp. 25–67

De Halleux, André, *Patrologie et Œcuménisme: Recueil d'études*, Leuven 1990 (BEThL 93)

De Halleux, André, 'Toward a Common Confession of Faith according to the Spirit of the Fathers', in: S. Mark Heim (ed.), *Faith to Creed: Ecumenical Perspectives on the Affirmation of the Apostolic Faith in the Fourth Century. Papers of the Faith to Creed Consultation Commission on Faith and Order NCCCUSA, October 25–27, 1989 – Waltham, Massachusetts*, Grand Rapids, Michigan 1991 (Faith & Order USA/Faith and Order Series), pp. 20–44

Delamare, René, *Le De Officiis ecclesiasticis de Jean d'Avranches, Archevêque de Rouen (1067–1079): Étude liturgique et publication du texte inédit du Manuscrit H. 304 de la Bibliothèque de la Faculté de Montpellier*, Paris 1923

Delattre, Alain, 'Graffitis de la montagne thébaine. I', *ChrEg* 76 (2001), pp. 333–9

Delattre, Alain, 'Un symbole de Nicée à Deir el-Bahari', *JJP* 31 (2001), pp. 7 f.

Delattre, Alain, 'Un symbole de Nicée en copte sur ostracon: Édition de O. Berol. Inv. 20892', *Journal of Coptic Studies* 13 (2011), pp. 113–15

Delattre, Alain/Vanthieghem, Naïm, 'Un symbole de Nicée-Constantinople en copte au verso d'un protocole arabe: Édition de P. Stras. Inv. Kopt. 221+224', *Journal of Coptic Studies* 15 (2013), pp. 239–52

DelCogliano, Mark, 'Eusebian Theologies of the Son as the Image of God before 341', *JECS* 14 (2006), pp. 459–84

DelCogliano, Mark, 'The Date for the Council of Serdica: A Reassessment of the Case for 343', *Studies in Late Antiquity* 1 (2017), pp. 282–310

Delen, Karijn M. et al., 'The *Paenitentiale Cantabrigiense*: A Witness of the Cariolingian Contribution to the Tenth-century Reforms in England', *SE* 41 (2002), pp. 341–73

Dell'Omo, Mariano, 'Il più antico *libellus precum* in scrittura beneventana (cod. Casin. 575, già Misc. T. XLV): Un testimone di rapporti tra Nonantola e Montecassino nel secolo IX', *RBen* 113 (2003), pp. 235–84

Dell'Omo, Mariano, 'Nel raggio di Montecassino: Il *libellus precum* di s. Domenico di Sora (Vat. Reg. Lat. 334)', in: Frank T. Coulson/Anna A. Grotans, *Classica et Beneventana: Essays Presented to Virginia Brown on the Occasion of her 65th Birthday*, Turnhout 2008 (Textes et Études du Moyen Âge 36), pp. 235–91

Delling, Gerhard, art. 'ὕμνος κτλ.', in: *TDNT*, vol. VIII, 1972, pp. 489–503

Den Boeft, Jan, et al., *Philological and Historical Commentary on Ammianus Marcellinus XXXI*, Leiden/Boston 2018

Denzinger, Heinrich, *Ritus Orientalium, Coptorum, Syrorum et Armenorum, in Administrandis Sacramentis*, 2 vols., Würzburg 1863/1864

Dib, Pierre, 'L'initiation chrétienne dans le rite maronite', *ROC* 15 (1910), pp. 73–84

Dick, Ernst, 'Das Pateninstitut im altchristlichen Katechumenat', *ZKTh* 63 (1939), pp. 1–49

Dickens, Mark, 'The Importance of the Psalter at Turfan' (2013), in: id., *Echoes of a Forgotten Presence: Reconstructing the History of the Church of the East in Central Asia*, Vienna 2020 (OPOe 15), pp. 149–72

Didier, Jean-Charles, 'Une adaptation de la liturgie baptismale au baptême des enfants dans l'Église ancienne', *MSR* 22 (1965), pp. 79–90

Diefenbach, Steffen, 'Constantius II. und die "Reichskirche" – ein Beitrag zum Verhältnis von kaiserlicher Kirchenpolitik und politischer Integration im 4. Jh.', *Millennium* 9 (2012), pp. 59–122

Diesenberger, Maximilian, *Predigt und Politik im frühmittelalterlichen Bayern: Karl der Große, Arn von Salzburg und die Salzburger Sermones-Sammlung*, Berlin/Boston 2016 (Millennium-Studien 58)

Diettrich, Gustav, *Die nestorianische Taufliturgie ins Deutsche übersetzt und unter Verwertung der neusten handschriftlichen Funde historisch-kritisch erforscht*, Gießen 1903

Digeser, Elizabeth D., 'Platonism in the Palace: The Character of Constantine's Theology', in: M. Shane Bjornlie (ed.), *The Life and Legacy of Constantine: Traditions through the Ages*, London/New York 2017, pp. 49–61

Dindorf, Ludwig, *Chronicon Paschale*, vol. I, Bonn 1832 (CSHB)

Dingel, Irene (ed.), *Die Bekenntnisschriften der Evangelisch-Lutherischen Kirche: Vollständige Neuedition*, Göttingen 2014

Dinkler-von Schubert, Erika, *Der Schrein der hl. Elisabeth zu Marburg: Studien zur Schrein-Ikonographie*, Marburg an der Lahn 1964 (Veröffentlichungen des Forschungsinstitutes für Kunstgeschichte Marburg/Lahn)

Dinsen, Frauke, *Homousios: Die Geschichte des Begriffs bis zum Konzil von Konstantinopel*, diss. theol., Kiel 1976

Dix, Gregory, *The Treatise on the Apostolic Tradition of St. Hippolytus of Rome, Bishop and Martyr*, ed. by G.D.; reissued with corrections, preface and bibliography by Henry Chadwick, London 1992

Dobbie, Elliott V.K. (ed.), *The Anglo-Saxon Minor Poems*, New York 1942

Dörrie, Heinrich, 'Emanation: Ein unphilosophisches Wort im spätantiken Denken [1965]', in: id., *Platonica Minora*, Munich 1976 (Studia et Testimonia Antiqua 8), pp. 70–86

Dörries, Hermann, *De spiritu sancto: Der Beitrag des Basilius zum Abschluß des trinitarischen Dogmas*, Göttingen 1956 (AAWG.PH 3/39)

Dondeyne, Albert, 'La discipline des scrutins dans l'église avant Charlemagne', *RHE* 28 (1932), pp. 5–33, 751–87

Doskocil, Walter, art. 'Exkommunikation', in: *RAC*, vol. VII, 1969, cols. 1–22

Dossetti, Giuseppe L., *Il simbolo di Nicea e di Costantinopoli: Edizione critica*, Rome etc. 1967 (TRSR 2)

Doval, Alexis J., 'The Fourth Century Jerusalem Catechesis and the Development of the Creed', in: *StPatr*, vol. XXX, 1997, pp. 296–305

Doval, Alexis J., *Cyril of Jerusalem, Mystagogue: The Authorship of the Mystagogic Catecheses*, Washington, D.C. 2001 (North American Patristic Society/Patristic Monograph Series 17)

Dovere, Elio, 'Normazione e Credo: Enciclica e Antienciclica di Basilisco' [1985], in: id. 2011, pp. 1–40

Dovere, Elio, 'L'Enotico di Zenone Isaurico, un preteso editto dogmatico' [1988], in: id. 2011, pp. 41–70

Dovere, Elio, *Ius principale e catholica lex (secolo V)*, second ed., Naples 1999 (Collezione di opere giuridiche e storiche 4)

Dovere, Elio, *Medicina legum*, vol. II: *Formula fidei* e normazione tardoantica, Bari 2011

Drake, Harold A., *Constantine and the Bishops: The Politics of Intolerance*, Baltimore/London 2000

Drake, Harold A., 'The Impact of Constantine on Christianity', in: Noel Lenski (ed.), *The Cambridge Companion to the Age of Constantine*, Cambridge 2006, pp. 111–36

Drake, Harold A., 'The Elephant in the Room: Constantine at the Council', in: Kim 2021, pp. 111–32

Draper, Richard D., *The Role of the Pontifex Maximus and Its Influence in Roman Religion and Politics*, diss., Ann Arbor 1988

Drecoll, Volker H., *Die Entwicklung der Trinitätslehre des Basilius von Cäsarea: Sein Weg vom Homöusianer zum Neonizäner*, Göttingen 1996 (FKDG 66)

Drecoll, Volker H., 'Wie nizänisch ist das Nicaeno-Constantinopolitanum? Zur Diskussion der Herkunft von NC durch Staats, Abramowski, Hauschild und Ritter', *ZKG* 107 (1996), pp. 1–18

Drecoll, Volker H., review of Gerber 2000, *ThLZ* 127 (2002), cols. 62–4

Drecoll, Volker H., 'Das Symbolum Quicumque als Kompilation augustinischer Tradition', *ZAC* 11 (2007), pp. 30–56

Drecoll, Volker H., 'Das Symbolum Athanasianum', in: Gemeinhardt 2011, pp. 386–90

Drecoll, Volker H., 'Apollinarius, *Ad Iovianum*: Analyse und Bedeutung für die Apollinariuschronologie', in: Bergjan/Gleede/Heimgartner 2015, pp. 35–57

Drecoll, Volker H., 'Die Edition des Textes des Nicaeno-Constantinopolitanums in den Konzilsakten von Chalkedon durch Schwartz', in: Uta Heil/Annette von Stockhausen (eds.), *Crux interpretum: Ein kritischer Rückblick auf das Werk von Eduard Schwartz*, Berlin/Boston 2015 (TU 176), pp. 111–27

Drijvers, Jan W., 'Marutha of Maipherqat on Helena Augusta, Jerusalem and the Council of Nicaea', in: *StPatr*, vol. XXXIV, 2001, pp. 51–64

Drijvers, Jan W., *Cyril of Jerusalem: Bishop and City*, Leiden 2004 (SVigChr 72)

Duc, Paul, *Étude sur l'"Expositio Missae' de Florus de Lyon suivie d'une édition critique du texte*, Belley 1937

Duffy, John/Parker, John, *The Synodicon vetus: Text, Translation, and Notes*, Washington, DC 1979 (CFHB Series Washingtonensis 15)

Dujarier, Michel, *Le parrainage des adultes aux trois premiers siècles de l'église: Recherche historique sur l'évolution des garanties et des étapes catéchuménales avant 313*, Paris 1962 (ParMiss)

Dunn, Geoffrey D., 'The Diversity and Unity of God in Novatian's *De Trinitate*', *ETL* 78 (2002), pp. 385–409

Dunn, James D.G., *Romans 9–16*, Dallas, Texas 1988 (WBC 38B)

Dunn, James D.G., *Unity and Diversity in the New Testament: An Enquiry into the Character of Earliest Christianity*, second ed., London 2006

Durst, Michael, *Studien zum 'Liber de synodis' des Hilarius von Poitiers*, 3 vols., Habilitationsschrift, Bonn 1993

Dutton, Paul E., *Charlemagne's Courtier: The Complete Einhard*, edited and translated, Peterborough, Ontario 1998 (repr. 2006; Readings in Medieval Civilizations and Cultures 3)

Dvornik, Francis, *Early Christian and Byzantine Political Philosophy. Origins and Background*, 2 vols., Washington, D.C. 1966 (DOS 9)

Dyer, Joseph, 'Sources of Romano-Frankish Liturgy and Music', in: Everist/Kelly 2018, pp. 92–122

Eberhardt, Johannes/Franz, Ansgar, art. 'Musik II (Vokalmusik)', in: RAC, vol. XXV, 2013, cols. 247–83

Ebied, Rifaat Y./Wickham, Lionel R., 'A Collection of Unpublished Syriac Letters of Timothy Aelurus', *JThS* 21 (1970), pp. 321–69

Edwards, Mark, 'Alexander of Alexandria and the *Homoousion*', *VigChr* 66 (2012), pp. 482–502

Edwards, Mark, 'The Creed', in: Kim 2021, pp. 135–57

Edwards, Robert G.T., 'Travelling Festivals in Late Antiquity: How Christians Came to the Greek East', *JEH* 75 (2024; forthcoming)

Ehrensperger, Alfred, *Karolingische Liturgiereformen*, 2006; download: URL <https://www.gottesdienst-ref.ch/liturgie/gottesdienst-geschichte/mittelalter> (27/11/2023)

Eichele, Hermann, art. 'Hypomnema', in: HWRh, vol. IV, 1998, cols. 122–8

Eichenseer, Caelestin, *Das Symbolum Apostolicum beim heiligen Augustin mit Berücksichtigung des dogmengeschichtlichen Zusammenhangs*, St. Ottilien 1960 (KGQS 4)

Ekonomou, Andrew J., *Byzantine Rome and the Greek Popes: Eastern Influences on Rome and the Papacy from Gregory the Great to Zacharias, A.D. 590–752*, Lanham, Md. etc. 2007 (Pb 2009)

Elert, Werner, 'Die Herkunft der Formel Sanctorum communio', *ThLZ* 74 (1949), pp. 577–86

Elliott, John H., *1 Peter: A New Translation with Introduction and Commentary*, New York etc. 2000 (AncB 37B)

Engberg, Gudrun, 'Les credos du synodicon', *CM* 23 (1962), pp. 293–301

Errington, R. Malcolm, 'Christian Accounts of the Religious Legislation of Theodosius I', *Klio* 79 (1997), pp. 398–443

Errington, R. Malcolm, 'Church and State in the First Years of Theodosius I', *Chiron* 27 (1997), pp. 21–72

Esterson, Zachary C., *A Translation of and Select Commentary on Victorinus of Pettau's Commentary on the Apocalypse*, PhD diss., Cardiff University 2015; download: URL <https://orca.cardiff.ac.uk/id/eprint/97767/> (27/11/2023)

Evans, Gillian R., 'The Academic Study of the Creeds in Twelfth-Century Schools', *JThS* 30 (1979), pp. 463–80

Everist, Mark/Kelly, Thomas F. (eds.), *The Cambridge History of Medieval Music*, vol. I, Cambridge etc. 2018

Fairbairn, Donald, 'The Sardican Paper, Antiochene Politics and the Council of Alexandria (362): Developing the "Faith of Nicaea",' *JThS* 66 (2015), pp. 651–78

Fairbairn, Donald/Reeves, Ryan M., *The Story of Creeds and Confessions: Tracing the Development of the Christian Faith*, Grand Rapids, Michigan 2019

Fassler, Margot, 'Music and Prosopography', in: Everist/Kelly 2018, pp. 176–209

Fedwick, Paul J. (ed.), *Basil of Caesarea: Christian, Humanist, Ascetic. A Sixteen-Hundredth Anniversary Symposium*, Parte One, Toronto, Ontario 1981

Feeney, Denis, *Literature and Religion at Rome: Cultures, Contexts, and Beliefs*, Cambridge 2001 (Roman Literature and its Contexts)

Feldmeier, Reinhard, *The First Letter of Peter: A Commentary on the Greek Text*, Waco, Texas 2008

Ferguson, Everett, *Baptism in the Early Church: History, Theology, and Liturgy in the First Five Centuries*, Grand Rapids, MI/Cambridge 2009

Fernández, Samuel, 'Who Convened the First Council of Nicaea: Constantine or Ossius?', *JThS* 71 (2020), pp. 196–211

Fernández, Samuel, 'Eusebio de Cesarea y desarrollo del sínodo de Nicea', *Anuario de Historia de la Iglesia* 32 (2023), pp. 97–122

Fernández Nieto, Francisco J., 'A Visigothic Charm from Asturias and the Classical Tradition of Phylacteries Against Hail', in: Richard L. Gordon/Francisco M. Simón (eds), *Magical Practice in the Latin West: Papers from the International Conference held at the University of Zaragoza, 30 Sept. – 1 Oct. 2005*, Leiden/Boston 2010 (Religions in the Greco-Roman World 168), pp. 551–99

Ffoulkes, Edmund S., *The Athanasian Creed: By whom Written and by whom Published; with Other Enquiries on Creeds in General*, London n.d. (1871)

Field, Lester L., *On the Communion of Damasus and Meletius: Fourth-Century Synodal Formulae in the Codex Veronensis LX. Edited and translated*, Toronto 2004 (STPIMS 145)

Filotas, Bernadette, *Pagan Survivals, Superstitions and Popular Cultures in Early Medieval Pastoral Literature*, Toronto 2005 (STPIMS 151)

Firey, Abigail (ed.), *A New History of Penance*, Leiden/Boston 2008 (Brill's Companions to the Christian Tradition 14)

Fischer, Ludwig (ed.), *Bernhardi Cardinalis et Lateranensis ecclesiae prioris Ordo officiorum ecclesiae Lateranensis*, Munich/Freising 1916 (Historische Forschungen und Quellen 2–3)

Flemming, Johannes/Lietzmann, Hans, *Apollinarische Schriften Syrisch: Mit den griechischen Texten und einem syrisch-griechischen Wortregister*, Berlin 1904 (AGWG, NF VII/4)

Flint, Valerie I.J., *The Rise of Magic in Early Medieval Europe*, Oxford 1991

Fogleman, Alex, *Knowledge, Faith, and Early Christian Initiation*, Cambridge etc. 2023

Förster, Hans, Die Feier der Geburt Christi in der Alten Kirche. Beiträge zur Erforschung der Anfänge des Epiphanie- und des Weihnachtsfests, Tübingen 2000 (STAC 4)

Förster, Hans, Die Anfänge von Weihnachten und Epiphanias, Tübingen 2007 (STAC 46)

Förster, Max, 'Die altenglischen Bekenntnisformeln', *Englische Studien* 75 (1942/1943), pp. 159–69

Folda, Jaroslav, *Crusader Art in the Holy Land, from the Third Crusade to the Fall of Acre, 1187–1291*, Cambridge etc. 2005

Foreville, Raymonde, art. 'Glaubensbekenntnis(se), VI. Mittelalter', in: *TRE*, vol. XIII, 1984, pp. 412–14

Fowler, Roger, 'A Late Old English Handbook for the Use of a Confessor', *Anglia* 83 (1965), pp. 1–34

Foxhall Forbes, Helen, *Heaven and Earth in Anglo-Saxon England: Theology and Society in an Age of Faith*, Farnham, Surrey/Burlington, VT 2013 (Studies in Early Medieval Britain)

Fraas, Hans-Jürgen et al., art. 'Katechismus', in: *TRE*, vol. XVII, 1988, pp. 710–44

Frank, Günter, *Topik als Methode der Dogmatik: Antike – Mittelalter – Frühe Neuzeit*, Berlin/Boston 2017 (TBT 179)

Frantzen, Allen J., *The Literature of Penance in Anglo-Saxon England*, New Brunswick, New Jersey 1983

Franz, Adolph, *Die kirchlichen Benediktionen im Mittelalter*, vol. II, Freiburg im Breisgau 1909

Frenschkowski, Marco, art. 'Magie', in: *RAC*, vol. XXIII, 2010, cols. 857–957

Frenschkowski, Marco, *Magie im antiken Christentum: Eine Studie zur Alten Kirche und ihrem Umfeld*, Stuttgart 2016 (Standorte in Antike und Christentum 7)

Fridolin, Stephan, *Schatzbehalter der wahren Reichtümer des Heils*, Nuremberg 1491 (cf. URL <https://digital.blb-karlsruhe.de/urn/urn:nbn:de:bsz:31-130913> (27/11/2023)

Friedberg, Emil, *Aus Deutschen Bussbüchern: Ein Beitrag zur deutschen Culturgeschichte*, Halle 1868

Friedman, Lionel J., *Text and Iconography for Joinville's Credo*, Cambridge, Massachusetts 1958 (MAAP 68)

Frivold, Leif, *The Incarnation: A Study of the Doctrine of the Incarnation in the Armenian Church in the 5th and 6th Centuries according to the Book of Letters*, Oslo etc. 1981

Fürst, Alfons, *Die Liturgie der Alten Kirche: Geschichte und Theologie*, Münster 2008

Fürst, Alfons, *Hieronymus: Askese und Wissenschaft in der Spätantike*, Freiburg etc. 2016

Fürst, Dieter, art. 'Confess', in: *NIDNTT*, vol. I, 1975, pp. 344–8

Gabriel, Frédéric, 'Des professions de foi à l'Église, une communauté de parole mise à l'épreuve', in: Blanchet/Gabriel 2016, pp. 1–27

Gaffino-Mœri, Sarah et al. (eds.), *Les papyrus de Genève: Textes littéraires et documentaires. Bibliothèque Publique et Universitaire 4, nos 147–205.* Textes littéraires, semi-littéraires et documentaires, Geneva 2010

Galvão-Sobrinho, Carlos R., *Doctrine and Power: Theological Controversy and Christian Leadership in Later Roman Empire*, Berkeley etc. 2013 (Transformation of the Classical Heritage 51)

Garitte, Gérard, 'Le traité géorgien "Sur la Foi" attribué à Hippolyte', *Le Muséon* 78 (1965), pp. 119–72

Garsoïan, Nina, *L'église arménienne et le grand schisme d'Orient*, Leuven 1999 (CSCO.Sub 100)

Garsoïan, Nina, 'Persien: Die Kirche des Ostens', in: Pietri 2001(2010), pp. 1161–86

Gassó, Pius M./Batlle, Columba M., *Pelagii I papae epistulae quae supersunt collexit, notulis historicis adornavit P.M.G.: Ad fidem codicum recensuit, praefatione et indicibus instruxit C.M.B.*, Abadía de Montserrat 1956 (SDM 8)

Gatch, Milton McC., *Preaching and Theology in Anglo-Saxon England: Ælfric and Wulfstand*, Toronto/ Buffalo 1977

Gebhard, Rudolf, *Umstrittene Bekenntnisfreiheit: Der Apostolikumsstreit in den reformierten Kirchen der Deutschschweiz im 19. Jahrhundert*, Zurich 2003

Gelzer, Heinrich/Hilgenfeld, Heinrich/Cuntz, Otto, *Patrum Nicaenorum Nomina Latine Graece Coptice Syriace Arabice Armeniace*, Leipzig 1898 (BSGRT/Scriptores Sacri et Profani 2)

Gemayel, Pierre-Edmond, *Avant-messe maronite: Histoire et structure*, Rome 1965 (OCA 174)

Gemeinhardt, Peter, *Die Filioque-Kontroverse zwischen Ost- und Westkirche im Frühmittelalter*, Berlin/ New York 2002 (AKG 82)

Gemeinhardt, Peter (ed.), *Athanasius Handbuch*, Tübingen 2011

Gemeinhardt, Peter, review of Siecienski 2010, *ThLZ* 137 (2012), cols. 69–71

Gemeinhardt, Peter, 'Die Heiligen der Kirche – die Gemeinschaft der Heiligen' [2012], in: id., *Die Kirche und ihre Heiligen: Studien zu Ekklesiologie und Hagiographie in der Spätantike*, Tübingen 2014, pp. 71–98 (STAC 90)

Gemeinhardt, Peter, 'Sphärenwechsel im Christusmythos: Höllen- und Himmelfahrt Christi als mythische Strukturmomente in spätantiken christlichen Glaubensbekenntnissen und ihren Kontexten', in: Annette Zgoll/Christian Zgoll (eds.), *Mythische Sphärenwechsel: Methodisch neue Zugänge zu antike Mythen in Orient und Okzident*, Berlin/Boston 2020, pp. 539–622 (Mythological Studies 2)

Gemeinhardt, Peter, 'Vom Werden des Apostolikums', in: Anne Käfer/Jörg Frey/Jens Herzer (eds.), *Die Reden von Gott Vater und Gott Heiligem Geist als Glaubensaussage: Der erste und dritte Artikel des Apostolischen Glaubensbekenntnisses im Gespräch zwischen Bibelwissenschaft und Dogmatik*, Tübingen 2020 (UTB 5268), pp. 15–58

Gemeinhardt, Peter, *Geschichte des Christentums in der Spätantike*, Tübingen 2022 (Neue Theologische Grundrisse)

Gerber, Simon, *Theodor von Mopsuestia und das Nicänum. Studien zu den katechetischen Homilien*, Leiden etc. 2000 (SVigChr 51)

Gerlitz, Peter et al., art. 'Taufe', in: *TRE*, vol. XXXII, 2001, pp. 659–741

Geuenich, Dieter, 'Die volkssprachige Überlieferung der Karolingerzeit aus der Sicht des Historikers', *DA* 39 (1983), pp. 104–30

Gillman, Ian/Klimkeit, Hans-Joachim, *Christians in Asia before 1500*, Richmond, Surrey 1999

Girardet, Klaus M., 'Kaiser Konstantin d. Gr. als Vorsitzender von Konzilien: Die historischen Tatsachen und ihre Deutung' [1991], in: id., *Studien zur Alten Geschichte der Europäer*, Bonn 2015, pp. 435–47

Girardet, Klaus M., 'Der Vorsitzende des Konzils von Nicaea (325) – Kaiser Konstantin d. Gr.' [1993], in: id., *Kaisertum, Religionspolitik und das Recht von Staat und Kirche in der Spätantike*, Bonn 2009 (Ant. 56)

Girardet, Klaus M., *Der Kaiser und sein Gott: Das Christentum im Denken und in der Religionspolitik Konstantins des Großen*, Berlin/New York 2010 (Millennium-Studien 27)

Gismondi, Henry, *Maris Amri et Slibae De Patriarchis Nestorianorum Commentaria ex Codicibus Vaticanis Eddidit ac Latine Reddidit*, 2 vols. in 4 parts, Paris 1897

Glauch, Sonja, 'Notker III. von St. Gallen', in: Bergmann 2013, pp. 293–315

Gneuss, Helmut/Lapidge, Michael, *Anglo-Saxon Manuscripts: A Bibliographical Handlist of Manuscripts and Manuscripts Fragments Written or Owned in England up to 1100*, Toronto etc. 2014

Goar, Jacques, *ΕΥΧΟΛΟΓΙΟΝ sive Rituale Graecorum completes ritus et ordines divinae liturgiae, officiorum, sacramentorum, consecrationum, benedictionum, funerum, orationum, etc. cuilibet personae, statui, vel tempori congruos, juxta usum orientalis ecclesiae*, second ed., Venice 1730

Godden, Malcolm, *Ælfric's Catholic Homilies: Introduction, Commentary and Glossary*, Oxford etc. 2000 (EETS S.S. 18)

Göbl, Peter, *Geschichte der Katechese im Abendlande vom Verfalle des Katechumenats bis zum Ende des Mittelalters*, Kempten 1880

Gössmann, Elisabeth, art. 'Glaube, V. Mittelalter', in: *TRE*, vol. XIII, 1985, pp. 308–18

Gounelle, Rémi, *La descente du Christ aux enfers: Institutionnalisation d'une croyance*, Paris 2000 (CEAug/Série Antiquités 162)

Graduale Triplex seu Graduale Romanum Pauli PP.VI cura recognitum & rhythmicis signis a Solesmensibus monachis ornatum neumis Laudunensibus (cod. 239) et Sangallensibus (codicum San Gallensis 359 et Einsidlensis 121) nunc auctum, Solesmes 1979

Gräßer, Erich, *An die Hebräer*, 1. Teilband: Hebr 1–6, Zurich etc. 1990 (EKK XVII/1)

Gräßer, Erich, *An die Hebräer*, 3. Teilband: Hebr 10,19–13,25, Zurich etc. 1997 (EKK XVII/3)

Graf, Georg, *Geschichte der christlichen arabischen Literatur*, 5 vols., Vatican City 1944–1953 (StT 118, 133, 146, 147, 172)

Graumann, Thomas, *Die Kirche der Väter: Vätertheologie und Väterbeweis in den Kirchen des Ostens bis zum Konzil von Ephesus (431)*, Tübingen 2002 (BHTh 118)

Graumann, Thomas, 'Frieden schließen auf Konzilien? Zwei Beispiele aus dem vierten Jahrhundert', *AHC* 48 (2016/2017), pp. 53–69

Graumann, Thomas, 'Die Verschriftlichung synodaler Entscheidungen: Beobachtungen von den Synoden des östlichen Reichsteils', in: Wolfram Brandes et al. (eds.), *Konzilien und kanonisches Recht in Spätantike und frühem Mittelalter: Aspekte konziliarer Entscheidungsfindung*, Berlin/Boston 2020 (FBRG Neue Folge 2), pp. 1–24

Graumann, Thomas, *The Acts of the Early Church Councils: Production and Character*, Oxford 2021 (OECS)

Grdzelidze, Tamara, art. 'Georgia, Patriarchal Orthodox Church of', in: John A. McGuckin (ed.), The Encyclopedia of Eastern Orthodox Christianity, 2 vols., Malden, MA 2011, vol. I, pp. 264–75

Grébaut, Sylvain, 'Ordre du baptême et de la confirmation dans l'église éthiopienne', *ROC* 26 (1927/1928), pp. 105–89

Grelier, Hélène, 'Comment décrire l'humanité du Christ sans introduire une quarternité de Dieu? La controverse de Grégoire de Nysse contre Apolinaire de Laodicée', in: Volker H. Drecoll/Margitta Berghaus (eds.), *Gregory of Nyssa: The Minor Treatises on Trinitarian Theology and Apollinarism.*

Proceedings of the 11th International Colloquium on Gregory of Nyssa (Tübingen, 17–20 September 2008), Leiden 2011 (SVigChr 106), pp. 541–56

Gretsch, Mechthild, *The Intellectual Foundations of the English Benedictine Reform*, Cambridge 1999 (CSASE 25)

Gribomont, Jean, 'La catéchèse de Sévère d'Antioche et le *Credo*', *Parole de l'Orient* 6/7 (1975/1976), pp. 125–58

Gribomont, Jean, 'Le symbole de la foi de Séleucie-Ctesiphon (410)', in Robert H. Fischer (ed.) *A Tribute to Arthur Vööbus: Studies in Early Christian Literature and its Environment*, Chicago 1977, pp. 283–94

Griffith, Francis L., 'Oxford Excavations in Nubia', *AAA* 14 (1927), pp. 57–116

Griggs, C. Wilfred, *Early Egyptian Christianity from its Origins to 451 CE*, Leiden etc., n.d. [2000] (Brill's Scholars' List)

Grillmeier, Aloys, *Christ in Christian Tradition*, vol. I: From the Apostolic Age to Chalcedon (451), second ed., 1975

Grillmeier, Aloys, *Christ in Christian Tradition*, vol. II: From the Council of Chalcedon (451) to Gregory the Great (590–604), Part One: Reception and Contradiction: The development of the discussion about Chalcedon from 451 to the beginning of the reign of Justinian, Atlanta, Georgia 1987

Grillmeier, Aloys/Hainthaler, Theresia, *Christ in Christian Tradition*, vol. II: From the Council of Chalcedon (451) to Gregory the Great (590–604), Part Two: The Church of Constantinople in the sixth century, London/Louisville, Kentucky 1995

Grohe, Johannes, 'Storia del *Filioque* prima del 1014 e il suo inserimento nel Credo', in: Mauro Gagliardi (ed.), *Il Filioque: A mille anni dal suo inserimento nel Credo a Roma (1014–2014): Atti del Convegno di Studi Ateneo Pontificio "Regina Apostolorum", Roma (27–28 novembre 2014)*, Vatican City 2015, pp. 15–38

Grossman, Joan D., 'Feminine Images in Old Russian Literature and Art', *California Slavic Studies* 11 (1980), pp. 33–70

Grumel, Venance, 'Le symbole "Quicumque" et Jean Italos', *EOr* 37 (1938), pp. 136–140

Guerrier, Louis, 'Un texte éthiopien du symbole de saint Athanase', *ROC* 20 (1915–1917), pp. 68–76, 133–41

Guidi, Ignazio, *Storia della letteratura etiopica*, Rome 1932 (Pubblicazioni dell'Istituto per l'Oriente)

Gwynn, David M., *The Eusebians: The Polemic of Athanasius of Alexandria and the Construction of the 'Arian Controversy'*, Oxford etc. 2007 (OTM)

Gwynn, David M., 'Reconstructing the Council of Nicaea', in: Kim 2021, pp. 90–110

Haacker, Klaus, art. 'Glaube, II/. Neues Testament', in: *TRE*, vol. XIII, 1985, pp. 289–304

Haarbrücker, Theodor, *Abu-'l-Fath· Muhammad asch-Scharastâni's Religionspartheien und Philosophen-Schulen: Zum ersten Male vollständig aus dem Arabischen übersetzt und mit erklärenden Anmerkungen versehen*, vol. I, Halle 1850

Haase, Felix, *Die koptischen Quellen zum Konzil von Nicäa: Übersetzt und untersucht*, Paderborn 1920 (SGKA 10/4)

Haensch, Rudolf, 'Inscriptions as Sources of Knowledge for Religions and Cults in the Roman World of Imperial Times', in: Jörg Rüpke (ed.), *A Companion to Roman Religion*, Malden, MA etc. 2013, pp. 176–87

Hahn, August, *Bibliothek der Symbole und Glaubensregeln der Apostolisch-katholischen Kirche*, Breslau 1842

Hahn, August/Hahn, G. Ludwig, *Bibliothek der Symbole und Glaubensregeln der alten Kirche*, second rev. ed., Breslau 1877

Hahn, August/Hahn, G. Ludwig, *Bibliothek der Symbole und Glaubensregeln der Alten Kirche*, third rev. ed., Breslau 1897

Hahn, Ferdinand, *Theologie des Neuen Testaments*, 2 vols., third ed., Tübingen 2011 (UTB 3500)

Hainthaler, Theresia, art. 'Doketismus', in: *LThK*, third ed., vol. III, 1995, cols. 301 f.

Hall, Stuart G., 'Some Constantinian Documents in the *Vita Constantini*', in: Samuel N.C. Lieu/Dominic Montserrat (eds.), *Constantine: History, Historiography and Legend*, London 1998, pp. 86–103

Hamlyn, Timothy, *Pontifex Optimus Maximus: The Office of Pontifex Maximus from the Middle Republic to Caesar*, Saarbrücken 2011

Hammerstaedt, Jürgen, art. 'Hypostasis', in: *RAC*, vol. XVI, 1994, cols. 986–1035

Hammerstaedt, Jürgen/Terbuyken, Peri, art. 'Improvisation', in: *RAC*, vol. XVII, 1996, cols. 1212–84

Hammond Bammel, Caroline P., *Der Römerbriefkommentar des Origenes*, vol. III: Buch 7–10. Kritische Ausgabe der Übersetzung Rufins, Freiburg 1998 (VL/AGLB 34)

Handl, András, 'Praxeas und die Ausbreitung des "Monarchianismus" in Rom zwischen Migration, innerchristlichen Konflikten und der Entstehung der "Orthodoxie"', in: Carl J. Berglund et al. (eds.), *Why We Sing: Music, Word, and Liturgy in Early Christianity. Essays in Honour of Anders Ekenberg's 75th Birthday*, Leiden 2022 (SVigChr 177), pp. 250–82

Hansen, Günther C. (ed.), *Theodoros Anagnostes – Kirchengeschichte*, second ed., Berlin/New York 1995 (repr. 2009; GCS NF 3)

Hansen, Joseph, *Quellen und Untersuchungen zur Geschichte des Hexenwahns und der Hexenverfolgung im Mittelalter*, Bonn 1901

Hanson, Richard P.C., *The Search for the Christian Doctrine of God: The Arian Controversy 318–381*, Edinburgh 1988

Hanssens, Jean M., *La liturgie d'Hippolyte: Ses documents, son titulaire, ses origines et son caractère*, second ed., Rome 1965 (OCA 155)

Haring, Nicholas M., 'Commentaries on the Pseudo-Athanasian Creed', *MS* 34 (1972), pp. 208–52

Haring, Nicholas M., 'A Poem by Alan of Lille on the Pseudo-Athanasian Creed', *RHT* 4 (1974), pp. 225–38

Haring, Nicholas M., 'Two Redactions of a Commentary on a Gallican Creed by Simon of Tournai', *AHDL* 41 (1974), pp. 39–112

Haring, Nicholas M., 'Simon of Tournai's Commentary on the So-called Athanasian Creed', *AHDL* 43 (1976), pp. 135–99

Harmening, Dieter, *Superstitio: Überlieferungs- und theoriegeschichtliche Untersuchungen zur kirchlich-theologischen Aberglaubensliteratur des Mittelalters*, Berlin 1979

Harnack, Adolf, 'Das apostolische Glaubensbekenntnis, ein geschichtlicher Bericht nebst einer Einleitung und einem Nachwort (1892)', in: id., *Reden und Aufsätze*, vol. I, Gießen 1904, pp. 219–64

Harnack, Adolf (von), art. 'Apostolisches Symbolum', in: *RE*, third ed., vol. I, 1896, pp. 741–55

Harnack, Adolf (von), 'Anhang: Materialien zur Geschichte und Erklärung des alten römischen Symbols aus der christlichen Litteratur der zwei ersten Jahrhunderte', in: Hahn/Hahn 1897, pp. 364–90

Harnack, Adolf (von), art. 'Konstantinopolitanisches Symbol', in: *RE*, third ed., vol. XI, 1902, pp. 12–28

Harnack, Adolf (von), 'Zur Abhandlung des Hrn. Holl: "Zur Auslegung des 2. Artikels des sog. apostolischen Glaubensbekenntnisses"', in: *SPAW* 1919, pp. 112–16

Harries, Jill, *Law and Empire in Late Antiquity*, Cambridge etc. 1999

Harrisson, Juliette, *Dreams and Dreaming in the Roman Empire: Cultural Memory and Imagination*, London etc. 2013

Hartman, Lars, 'Usages – Some Notes on the Baptismal Name-Formulae', in: Hellholm et al. 2011, vol. I, pp. 397–413

Hasenohr, Geneviève, 'Religious Reading amongst the Laity in France in the Fifteenth Century', in: Peter Biller/Anne Hudson (eds.), *Heresy and Literacy, 1000*–1530, Cambridge 1994, pp. 205–21

Haubrichs, Wolfgang, *Geschichte der deutschen Literatur von den Anfängen bis zum Beginn der Neuzeit*, vol. I: Von den Anfängen zum hohen Mittelalter, Teil 1: Die Anfänge: Versuche volkssprachiger Schriftlichkeit im frühen Mittelalter (ca. 700–1050/60), second ed., Tübingen 1995

Haug, Andreas, 'Tropes', in: Everist/Kelly 2018, pp. 263–99

Hauler, Edmund, 'Eine lateinische Palimpsestübersetzung der *Didascalia apostolorum*', *SAWW.PH* 134 (1896), pp. 1–54

Hauler, Edmund, *Didascaliae Apostolorum – Fragmenta Veronensia Latina. Accedunt Canonum Qui Dicuntur Apostolorum et Aegyptiorum Reliquiae*, vol. I, Leipzig 1900

Hausammann, Susanne, *Alte Kirche*, vol. III: Gottes Dreiheit – des Menschen Freiheit, second ed., Neukirchen-Vluyn 2007

Hauschild, Wolf-Dieter, *Die Pneumatomachen: Eine Untersuchung zur Dogmengeschichte des vierten Jahrhunderts*, Diss. theol., Hamburg 1967

Hauschild, Wolf-Dieter, review of Jungck 1974, *AHC* 9 (1977), pp. 213–16

Hauschild, Wolf-Dieter, art. 'Nicäno-Konstantinopolitanisches Glaubensbekenntnis', in: *TRE*, vol. XXIV, 1994, pp. 444–56

Haußleiter, Johannes, *Trinitarischer Glaube und Christusbekenntnis in der alten Kirche*, Gütersloh 1920 (BFChTh 25/4)

Hauswald, Eckhard, *Pirmin – Scarapsus*, Hannover 2010 (MGH.QG 25)

Heather, Peter, *Rome Resurgent: War and Empire in the Age of Justinian*, Oxford 2018

Hebblewhite, Mark, *Theodosius and the Limits of Empire*, London/New York 2020

Heil, Günter, *Pseudo-Dionysius Areopagita – Über die himmlische Hierarchie: Eingeleitet, übersetzt und mit Anmerkungen versehen*, Stuttgart 1986 (BGrL Abteilung Patristik 22)

Heil, Günter/Ritter, Adolf Martin (eds.), *Corpus Dionysiacum*, vol. II: Pseudo-Dionysius Areopagita, *De coelesti hierarchia, De ecclesiastica hierarchia, De mystica theologia, Epistulae*, second ed., Berlin/Boston 2012 (PTS 67)

Heil, Uta, *Athanasius von Alexandrien: De Sententia Dionysii*. Einleitung Übersetzung und Kommentar, Berlin/New York 1999 (PTS 52)

Heil, Uta, '". . . bloß nicht wie die Manichäer!" Ein Vorschlag zu den Hintergründen des arianischen Streits', *ZAC* 6 (2002), pp. 299–319

Heil, Uta, 'Markell von Ancyra und das Romanum', in: Stockhausen/Brennecke 2010, pp. 85–104

Heil, Uta, *Avitus von Vienne und die homöische Kirche der Burgunder*, Berlin/Boston 2011 (PTS 66)

Heil, Uta, 'Kontingenz und Varianz: Zur Verbindlichkeit der altkirchlichen Christologie', in: Christian Danz/Michael Hackl (eds.), *Transformationen der Christologie: Herausforderungen, Krisen und Umformungen*, Göttingen 2019 (Wiener Forum für Theologie und Religionswissenschaft/Vienna Forum for Theology and the Study of Religions 17), pp. 15–39

Heil, Uta/Scheerer, Christoph, *Dokumente zur Geschichte des Arianischen Streites: Die Entwicklungen in den Nachfolgestaaten des Römischen Reiches bis zum Symbolum Quicumque*, Berlin/Boston 2022 (Athanasius Werke 3/2)

Heimgartner, Martin, *Die Briefe 42–58 des ostsyrischen Patriarchen Timotheos I.: Einleitung, Übersetzung und Anmerkungen*, 2 vols., Louvain 2012 (CSCO 644/Scriptores Syri 248–249)

Hellgardt, Ernst, '"Altsächsisches/frühmittelniederdeutsches Glaubensbekenntnis", auch "Niederdeutscher Glaube"', in: Bergmann 2013, pp. 18–20

Hellholm, David et al. (eds.), *Ablution, Initiation, and Baptism: Late Antiquity, Early Judaism, and Early Christianity/Waschungen, Initiation und Taufe: Spätantike, Frühes Judentum und Frühes Christentum*, 2 vols., Berlin/Boston 2011 (BZNW 176/2)

Hen, Yitzhak, *The Royal Patronage of Liturgy in Frankish Gaul: To the Death of Charles the Bald (877)*, London 2001 (HBS)

[Hennecke, Edgar]/Schneemelcher, Wilhelm, *Neutestamentliche Apokryphen in deutscher Übersetzung*, sixth ed., 2 vols., Tübingen 1999

Hensel, Roman/Klippel, Diethelm, art. 'Juridification' in: *Encyclopedia of Early Modern History Online*, 2015; URL <http://dx.doi.org/10.1163/2352-0272_emho_COM_029645> (27/11/2023)

Hermansen, Marcia, 'The *shahāda*: faith', in: Zafar I. Ansari/Ismacil I. Nawwab (eds.), *The Different Aspects of Islamic Culture*, vol. I: Foundations of Islam, Paris 2016, pp. 627–52

Heyworth, Melanie, 'The "Late Old English Handbook for the Use of a Confessor": Authorship and Connections', *NQRW* 54 (2007), pp. 218–22

Hiley, David, *Western Plainchant*, Oxford 1993

Hillner, Julia, *Prison, Punishment and Penance in Late Antiquity*, Cambridge 2015

Hillner, Julia, *Helena Augusta: Mother of the Empire*, New York 2023 (Women in Antiquity)

Hills, Julian, *Tradition and Composition in the* Epistula Apostolorum, Minneapolis 1990 (HDR 24)

Hödl, Ludwig, 'Articulus fidei: Eine begriffsgeschichtliche Arbeit', in: Joseph Ratzinger/Heinrich Fries (eds.), Einsicht und Glaube, Freiburg etc. 1962, pp. 358–76

Hoffmann, Thomas, art. 'Nicene Creed, II. Islam', in: *EBR*, vol. XXI, 2023, cols. 399 f.

Hofius, Otfried, art. 'ὁμολογέω κτλ.', in: *EDNT*, vol. II, 1991, cols. pp. 514–17

Hofmann, Karl, art. 'Anathema', in: *RAC*, vol. I, 1950, cols. 427–30

Hoheisel, Karl, art. 'Do ut des', in: *HRWG*, vol. II, 1990, p. 229

Holl, Karl, 'Zur Auslegung des 2. Artikels des sog. apostolischen Glaubensbekenntnisses' [1919], in: id., *Gesammelte Aufsätze zur Kirchengeschichte*, vol. II: Der Osten, Tübingen 1928, pp. 115–22

Holland, David L., 'The Earliest Text of the Old Roman Symbol. A Debate with Hans Lietzmann and J.N.D. Kelly', *ChH* 34 (1965), pp. 262–81

Holland, David L., 'Die Synode von Antiochien (324/25) und ihre Bedeutung für Eusebius von Caesarea und das Konzil von Nizäa', *ZKG* 81 (1970), pp. 163–81

Holthausen, Ferdinand, 'Eine altenglische Interlinearversion des athanasianischen Glaubensbekenntnisses', *Englische Studien* 75 (1942/1943), pp. 6–8

Hommel, Hildebrecht, *Schöpfer und Erhalter: Studien zum Problem Christentum und Antike*, Berlin 1956

Honoré, Tony, *Law in the Crisis of Empire 379–455 AD: The Theodosian Dynasty and Its Quaestors*, Oxford 1998

Hopkins, Keith, 'Christian Number and its Implications' [1998], in: id., *Sociological Studies in Roman History*, ed. by Christopher Kelly, Cambridge 2018 (Cambridge Classical Studies), pp. 432–80

Horak, Ulrike, 'Credo mit magischen Zeichnungen', *Analecta Papyrologica* 13 (2001), pp. 55–61

Horn, Friedrich W., 'Glaube – Nicht Weisheit der Menschen, sondern Kraft Gottes', in: id., *Glaube*, 2018, pp. 33–63

Horn, Friedrich W. (ed.), *Glaube*, Tübingen 2018 (utb 5034/Themen der Theologie 13)

Hornung, Christoph, art. 'Pate', in: *RAC*, vol. XXVI, 2015, cols. 1077–91

Hornung, Christian, *Apostasie im antiken Christentum: Studien zum Glaubensabfall in altkirchlicher Theologie, Disziplin und Pastoral (4.–7. Jahrhundert n. Chr.)*, Leiden/Boston 2016 (SVigChr 138)

Hort, Fenton J.A., *Two Dissertations: I. On ΜΟΝΟΓΕΝΗΣ ΘΕΟΣ in Scripture and Tradition, II. On the 'Constantinopolitan' Creed and Other Eastern Creeds of the Fourth Century*, Cambridge 1876

Houghton, Hugh A.G., *The Latin New Testament: A Guide to its Early History, Text, and Manuscripts*, Oxford 2016

Houghton, Hugh A.G., *Fortunatianus of Aquileia – Commentary on the Gospels*, Berlin/Boston 2017 (CSEL Extra Seriem)

Hoyland, Robert G., *Seeing Islam as Others Saw It: A Survey and Evaluation of Christian, Jewish and Zoroastrian Writings on Early Islam*, Princeton, New Jersey 1997 (repr. 2001; SLAEL 13)

Hoyland, Robert G., 'Agapius of Manbiğ, Qusṭā ibn Lūqā and the Graeco-Roman Past: The Beginnings of Christian Arabic and Muslim Historiography', *Quaderni di Studi Arabi* 16 (2021), pp. 7–41

Huebner, Dietmar von, art. 'Credo, 2. Liturgisch-musikalische Entwicklung', in: *LMA*, vol. III, 1986, cols. 338 f.

Hübner, Reinhard M., *Die Schrift des Apolinarius von Laodicea gegen Photin (Pseudo-Athanasius, Contra Sabellianos) und Basilius von Caesarea*, Berlin/New York 1989 (PTS 30)

Hübner, Reinhard M., *Der paradox Eine: Antignostischer Monarchianismus im zweiten Jahrhundert.* Mit einem Beitrag von Markus Vinzent, Leiden etc. 1999 (SVigChr 50)

Hughes, Andrew, *Medieval Manuscripts for Mass and Office: A Guide to their Organization and Terminology*, Toronto etc. 1982 (repr. 2004)

Huglo, Michel, 'Origine de la mélodie du Credo "authentique" de la Vaticane', *Revue Grégorienne* 30 (1951), pp. 68–78; also in: id., *Les anciens répertoire de plain-chant*, Aldershot, Hampshire/Burlington VT 2005 (CStS 804), no. XVII and p. 22 (Addenda et Corigenda)

Humfress, Caroline, *Orthodoxy and the Courts in Late Antiquity*, Oxford 2007

Hunt, Arthur S., *Catalogue of the Greek Papyri in the John Rylands Library, Manchester*, vol. I: Literary Texts (Nos. 1–61), Manchester 1911

Hunt, David, 'Valentinian and the Bishops: Ammianus 30.9.5 in Context', in: Jan den Boeft et al. (eds.), *Ammianus after Julian: The Reign of Valentinian and Valens in Books 26–31 of the* Res Gestae, Leiden 2007 (Mnemosyne Supplementum 289), pp. 71–93

Hunter, David G., 'Vigilantius of Calagurris and Victricius of Rouen: Ascetics, Relics, and Clerics in Late Roman Gaul', *JECS* 7 (1999), pp. 401–30

Hunzinger, Claus-Hunno, art. 'Bann, II. Frühjudentum und Neues Testament', in: *TRE*, vol. V, 1980, pp. 161–7

Hutter, Manfred, art. 'Manichäismus', in: *RAC*, vol. XXIV, 2012, cols. 6–48

Hutter, Manfred, *Der Manichäismus: Vom Iran in den Mittelmeerraum und über die Seidenstraße nach Südchina*, Stuttgart 2023 (Standorte in Antike und Christentum 11)

Iacobone, Pasquale, *Mysterium Trinitatis: Dogma e Iconografia nell'Italia medievale*, Rome 1997 (TG.T 28)

Ingram, Robert G., *Reformation Without End: Religion, Politics and the Past in Post-revolutionary England*, Manchester 2018

Innocent III (pope), *D. Innocentii Pontificis Maximi Eius Nominis III. Viri Eruditissimi Simul Atque Grauissimi Opera* [. . .], Cologne 1575

Izbicki, Thomas M., *Hildegard of Bingen – An Explanation of the Athanasian Creed: Translated, with Introduction and Notes*, Toronto 2001 (Peregrina Translation Series; not accessible to me)

Jacobs, Ine, 'Hosting the Council in Nicaea: Material Needs and Solutions', in: Kim 2021, pp. 65–89

Jacobsen, Anders-Christian, art. 'Cyril of Jerusalem', in: *Brill Encyclopedia of Early Christianity Online*, 2018; URL <http://dx.doi.org/10.1163/2589-7993_EECO_SIM_00000832> (27/11/2023)

Jaeger, Werner (ed.), *Contra Eunomium Libri*, vol. II: Liber III (uulgo III–XII). Refutatio confessionis Eunomii (uulgo lib. II), Leiden 1960 (GNO 2)

Jakobs, Dörthe, 'Die Wandmalereien von St. Georg in Reichenau-Oberzell. Untersuchung – Dokumentation – Kontroversen', in: Matthias Exner (ed.), *Wandmalerei des frühen Mittelalters: Bestand, Maltechnik, Konservierung*, Munich 1998, pp. 161–90 (ICOMOS 23)

Jankowiak, Marek/Booth, Phil, 'A New Date-List of the Works of Maximus the Confessor', in: Pauline Allen, Pauline/Bronwen Neil (eds.), *The Oxford Handbook of Maximus the Confessor*, Oxford 2015, pp. 19–83

Jaser, Christian, *Ecclesia maledicens: Rituelle und zeremonielle Exkommunikationsformen im Mittelalter*, Tübingen 2013 (SMHR 75)

Jilek, August, *Initiationsfeier und Amt: Ein Beitrag zur Struktur und Theologie der Ämter und des Taufgottesdienstes in der frühen Kirche (Traditio Apostolica, Tertullian, Cyprian)*, Frankfurt am Main etc. 1979 (EHS.T 130)

Joest, Wilfried, art. 'Fundamentalartikel', in: *TRE*, vol. XI, 1983, pp. 727–32

Johnson, Maxwell E., 'Reconciling Cyril and Egeria on the Catechetical Process in Fourth-Century Jerusalem', in: Paul F. Bradshaw (ed.), *Essays in Early Eastern Initiation*, Bramcote, Nottingham 1988 (Alcuin/Grow Liturgical Study 8/GLS 56), pp. 18–30

Johnson, Maxwell E., 'The Problem of Creedal Formulae in *Traditio Apostolica* 21:12–18', *EO* 22 (2005), pp. 159–75

Johnson, Maxwell E., *The Rites of Christian Initiation: Their Evolution and Interpretation*, second ed., Collegeville, Minnesota 2007

Jolly, Karen L., *Popular Religion in Late Saxon England: Elf Charms in Context*, Chapel Hill/London 1996

Jungck, Christoph, *Gregor von Nazianz – De vita sua: Einleitung, Text, Übersetzung Kommentar. Herausgegeben, eingeleitet und erklärt*, Heidelberg 1974 (WKLGS)

Jungmann, Josef A., *The Mass of the Roman Rite: Its Origins and Development (Missarum Sollemnia)*, 2 vols., New York etc. 1951

Jungmann, Josef A., *Handing on the Faith: A Manual of Catechetics*, Freiburg 1959

Jungmann, Josef A., *Missarum Sollemnia: Eine genetische Erklärung der römischen Messe*, 2 vols., fifth ed., Vienna etc. 1962

Just, Patricia, *Imperator et Episcopus: Zum Verhältnis von Staatsgewalt und christlicher Kirche zwischen dem 1. Konzil von Nicaea (325) und dem 1. Konzil von Konstantinopel (381)*, Stuttgart 2003 (Potsdamer Altertumswissenschaftliche Beiträge 8)

Kaczynski, Bernice M., *Greek in the Carolingian Age: The St. Gall Manuscripts*, Cambridge, Mass. 1988 (Spec.AM 13)

Kamesar, Adam, 'The *Logos Endiathetos* and the *Logos Prophorikos* in Allegorical Interpretation: Philo and the D-Scholia to the *Iliad*,' *GRBS* 44 (2004), pp. 163–81

Karmann, Thomas R., *Meletius von Antiochien: Studien zur Geschichte des trinitätstheologischen Streits in den Jahren 360–364 n.Chr.*, Frankfurt am Main 2009 (RSTh 68)

Kaser, Max, 'Infamia und ignominia in den römischen Rechtsquellen', *ZSRG.R* 73 (1956), pp. 220–78

Kaser, Max, *Das römische Privatrecht*, second ed., 2 vols., Munich 1971/1975 (HAW 10,3,3,1–2; Rechtsgeschichte des Altertums 3,3,1–2)

Kaser, Max, *Roman Private Law*, fourth ed., Muckleneuk, Pretoria 1984

Kasparick, Hanna, *Lehrgesetz oder Glaubenszeugnis? Der Kampf um das Apostolikum und seine Auswirkungen auf die Revision der preußischen Agende (1892–1895)*, Bielefeld 1996 (UnCo 19)

Kattenbusch, Ferdinand, *Beiträge zur Geschichte des altkirchlichen Taufsymbols*, Gießen 1892 (Programm Sr. Königlichen Hoheit dem Grossherzoge von Hessen und bei Rhein Ernst Ludwig Ihrem Rector Magnificentissimus zum 25. August gewidmet von Rector und Senat der Landesuniversität)

Kattenbusch, Ferdinand, *Das Apostolische Symbol: Seine Entstehung, sein geschichtlicher Sinn, seine ursprüngliche Stellung im Kultus und in der Theologie der Kirche: Ein Beitrag zur Symbolik und Dogmengeschichte*, vol. I: Die Grundgestalt des Taufsymbols, Leipzig 1894

Kattenbusch, Ferdinand, review of Burn 1896, *ThLZ* 22 (1897), cols. 138–46

Kattenbusch, Ferdinand, review of Hahn/Hahn 1897, *ThLZ* 22 (1897), cols. 561–5

Kattenbusch, Ferdinand, *Das Apostolische Symbol: Seine Entstehung, sein geschichtlicher Sinn, seine ursprüngliche Stellung im Kultus und in der Theologie der Kirche: Ein Beitrag zur Symbolik und Dogmengeschichte*, vol. II: Verbreitung und Bedeutung des Taufsymbols, Leipzig 1900

Kaufhold, Hubert, *Die Rechtssammlung des Gabriel von Baṣra und ihr Verhältnis zu den anderen juristischen Sammelwerken der Nestorianer*, Berlin 1976 (MUS/Juristische Fakultät/Abhandlungen zur rechtswissenschaftlichen Grundlagenforschung 21)

Kaufhold, Hubert, 'Sources of Canon Law in the Eastern Churches', in: Wilfried Hartmann/Kenneth Pennington (eds.), *The History of Byzantine and Eastern Canon Law to 1500*, Washington, D.C. 2012 (History of Medieval Canon Law), pp. 215–342

Kaufhold, Hubert, *Ebedjesus von Nisibis: "Ordo iudiciorum ecclesiasticorum": Eine Zusammenstellung der kirchlichen Rechtsbestimmungen der ostsyrischen Kirche im 14. Jahrhundert*, herausgegeben, übersetzt und eingeleitet, Wiesbaden 2019 (Eichstätter Beiträge zum christlichen Orient 7)

Keefe, Susan A., *Water and the Word: Baptism and the Education of the Clergy in the Carolingian Empire*, 2 vols., Notre Dame, Ind. 2002 (PMS)

Keefe, Susan A., *A Catalogue of Works Pertaining to the Explanation of the Creed in Carolingian Manuscripts*, Turnhout 2012 (IPM 63)

Keefe, Susan A., *Explanationes Symboli Aevi Carolini*, Turnhout 2012 (CChr.CM 254)

Keener, Craig S., *The Gospel of John: A Commentary*, Peabody, Mass. 2003 (repr. Grand Rapids, Michigan 2012)

Keller, Rebecca J., *His Hands are Laden with the Relics of the Saints*: Sanctorum Communio, *the Apostles' Creed, and the Cult of the Saints*, PhD diss., The Catholic University of America 2022

Kelly, John N.D., *The Athanasian Creed: The Paddock Lectures for 1962–3*, London 1964

Kelly, John N.D., *Early Christian Creeds*, third ed., London 1972

Kelly, John N.D., *Golden Mouth: The Story of John Chrysostom. Ascetic, Preacher, Bishop*, London 1995

Kendrick, Laura, *Medieval Remediations of the Apostles' Creed (NCS working paper)*, 2016; URL: <http://dhmedievalist.com/scalar/medievaldigital-multimodalities/medieval-remediations-of-the-apostles-creed> (03/10/2017; this page is no longer available)

Kéry, Lotte, *Canonical Collections of the Early Middle Ages (ca. 400–1140): A Bibliographical Guide to the Manuscripts and Literature*, Washington, DC 1999 (History of Medieval Canon Law 1)

Khoperia, Lela, art. 'Georgia', in: *Brill Encyclopedia of Early Christianity Online*, 2018; URL <http://dx.doi.org/10.1163/2589-7993_EECO_SIM_00000435> (27/11/2023)

Khouri-Sarkis, Gabriel, 'Réception d'un évêque syrien au VIe siècle', *OrSyr* 2 (1957), pp. 137–84

Kidane, Habtemichael, *L'ufficio divino della Chiesa etiopica: Studio storico-critico con particolare riferimento alle ore cattedrali*, Rome 1998 (OCA 257)

Kim, Young R., 'Nicaea is Not Enough: The Second Creed of Epiphanius' *Ancoratus*, in: *StPatr*, vol. XCVI, 2017, pp. 11–20

Kim, Young R. (ed.), *The Cambridge Companion to the Council of Nicaea*, Cambridge etc. 2021

Kinzig, Wolfram, *In Search of Asterius: Studies on the Authorship of the Homilies on the Psalms*, Göttingen 1990 (FKDG 47)

Kinzig, Wolfram, *Novitas Christiana: Die Idee des Fortschritts in der Alten Kirche bis Eusebius*, Göttingen 1994 (FKDG 58)

Kinzig, Wolfram, 'The Greek Christian Writers', in: Stanley E. Porter (ed.), *Handbook of Classical Rhetoric in the Hellenistic Period 330 B.C.-A.D. 400*, Leiden 1997, pp. 633–70

Kinzig, Wolfram, '". . . natum et passum etc." Zur Geschichte der Tauffragen in der lateinischen Kirche bis zu Luther' [1999], in: id., *Neue Texte I*, 2017, pp. 237–67

Kinzig, Wolfram, 'Überlegungen zum Sitz im Leben der Gattung Πρὸς Ἕλληνας/*Ad nationes*', in:
  Raban von Haehling (ed.), *Rom und das himmlische Jerusalem: Die frühen Christen zwischen*
  Anpassung und Ablehnung, Darmstadt 2000, pp. 152–83

Kinzig, Wolfram, review of Westra 2002, *JEH* 56 (2005), pp. 548–9

Kinzig, Wolfram, 'Jewish and "Judaizing" Eschatologies in Jerome', in: Richard Kalmin/Seth Schwartz
  (eds.), *Jewish Culture and Society under the Christian Roman Empire*, Leuven 2003 (Interdisciplinary
  Studies in Ancient Culture and Religion 3), pp. 409–29

Kinzig, Wolfram, '"Auszeit": Anmerkungen zu Ursprung und Sinn von Sonn- und Feiertagen aus
  kirchenhistorischer Sicht', *ThZ* 62 (2006), pp. 357–75

Kinzig, Wolfram, 'The Creed in the Liturgy: Prayer or Hymn?' in: Albert Gerhards/Clemens Leonhard
  (eds.), *Jewish and Christian Liturgy and Worship: New Insights into its History and Interaction*, Leiden
  etc. 2007 (JCPS 15), pp. 229–46

Kinzig, Wolfram, 'The Nazoraeans', in: Oskar Skarsaune/Reidar Hvalvik (eds.), *Jewish Believers in Jesus*,
  vol. I: The Early Centuries, Peabody, Mass. 2007, pp. 463–87

Kinzig, Wolfram, 'Eigenart und Aussprache des Tetragramms bei den Kirchenvätern', in: Heinrich
  Assel/Hans-Christoph Askani (eds.), *Sprachgewinn: Festschrift für Günter Bader*, Berlin 2008 (AHST
  11), pp. 202–33

Kinzig, Wolfram, art. 'Ascension of Christ, II. Christianity', in: *EBR*, vol. II, 2009, cols. 913–17

Kinzig, Wolfram, 'The Creed and the Development of the Liturgical Year in the Early Church' [2011],
  in: id., *Neue Texte I*, 2017, pp. 329–64

Kinzig, Wolfram, 'From the Letter to the Spirit to the Letter: The Faith as Written Creed' [2013], in: id.,
  Neue Texte I, 2017, pp. 293–310

Kinzig, Wolfram, '"Gründungswunder" des Christentums? Die Auferstehung Christi in der
  altkirchlichen Diskussion', in: id./Jochen Schmidt (eds.), *Glaublich – aber unwahr? (Un-)*
  Wissenschaft im Christentum, Würzburg 2013 (Studien des Bonner Zentrums für Religion und
  Gesellschaft 10), pp. 41–59

Kinzig, Wolfram, 'Herrschaft und Bekenntnis: Überlegungen zur imperialen Normierung des
  christlichen Glaubens in der Spätantike' [2016], in: id., *Neue Texte III*, 2022, pp. 208–26

Kinzig, Wolfram, 'Christus im Credo: Überlegungen zur Herkunft und Alter des Christussummariums
  im Apostolikum', in: id., *Neue Texte I*, 2017, pp. 269–91

Kinzig, Wolfram, 'Das Glaubensbekenntnis im Gottesdienst – Gebet oder Hymnus?', in: id., *Neue Texte*
  I, 2017, pp. 311–27

Kinzig, Wolfram, *Faith in Formulae: A Collection of Early Christian Creeds and Credal Formulae*, 4 vols.,
  Oxford 2017 (OECT)

Kinzig, Wolfram, 'Ist das Christentum monotheistisch? Bemerkungen aus kirchenhistorischer Sicht',
  in: id., *Neue Texte I*, 2017, pp. 217–35

Kinzig, Wolfram, 'Monarchianismus und Monarchie: Überlegungen zum Zusammenhang zwischen
  Theologie und Politik im 2. und 3. Jahrhundert' [2017], in: id., *Neue Texte III*, 2022, pp. 137–60

Kinzig, Wolfram, *Neue Texte und Studien zu den antiken und frühmittelalterlichen Glaubensbekenntnissen*
  [Neue Texte I], Berlin 2017 (AKG 132)

Kinzig, Wolfram, '§ 122. Areios und der Arianismus', in: Christoph Riedweg/Christoph Horn/Dietmar
  Wyrwa (eds.), *Grundriss der Geschichte der Philosophie: Die Philosophie der Antike*, vol.
  V: Philosophie der Kaiserzeit und der Spätantike, part 2, Basel 2018, pp. 1478–90

Kinzig, Wolfram, '§ 123. Neuarianismus', in: Christoph Riedweg/Christoph Horn/Dietmar Wyrwa
  (eds.), *Grundriss der Geschichte der Philosophie: Die Philosophie der Antike*, vol. V: Philosophie der
  Kaiserzeit und der Spätantike, part 2, Basel 2018, pp. 1491–6

Kinzig, Wolfram, 'Das Apostolische Glaubensbekenntnis – Leistung und Grenzen eines christlichen Fundamentaltextes' [2018], in: id., *Neue Texte III*, 2022, pp. 286–307

Kinzig, Wolfram, 'Die Verpflichtungserklärung der getauften Juden von Toledo aus den Jahren 637 und 654' [2019], in: id., *Neue Texte III*, 2022, pp. 53–90

Kinzig, Wolfram, 'Formation des Glaubens: Didaktische und liturgische Aspekte der Rezeption altkirchlicher Symbole in der lateinischen Kirche der Spätantike und des Frühmittelalters' [2019], in: id., *Neue Texte III*, 2022, pp. 227–62

Kinzig, Wolfram, 'Warum es im Glaubensbekenntnis keine Ethik gibt: Überlegungen aus kirchenhistorischer Perspektive' [2019], in: id., *Neue Texte III*, 2022, pp. 263–85

Kinzig, Wolfram, 'Glauben lernen im Mittelalter: Eine Predigt über das Apostolicum in cod. Paris, Bibliothèque Nationale, lat. 18104' [2020], in: id., *Neue Texte III*, 2022, pp. 91–116

Kinzig, Wolfram, 'Zwei neuentdeckte Predigten des Nestorios: *Adversus haereticos de divina trinitate* (CPG 5691) und *In symbolum fidei*: Edition, Übersetzung und Kommentar' [2020], in: id., *Neue Texte III*, 2022, pp. 3–52

Kinzig, Wolfram, *Christian Persecution in Antiquity*, Waco, Texas 2021

Kinzig, Wolfram, *Das Glaubensbekenntnis von Konstantinopel (381): Herkunft, Geltung und Rezeption. Neue Texte und Studien zu den antiken und frühmittelalterlichen Glaubensbekenntnissen II*, Berlin/Boston 2021 (AKG 147)

Kinzig, Wolfram, art. 'Symbolum', in: *AugL*, vol. V, fasc. 3/4, 2021, cols. 621–6

Kinzig, Wolfram, art. 'Symbolum', in: *RAC*, vol. XXXI, Lieferung 244, 2021, cols. 381–93

Kinzig, Wolfram, 'What's in a Creed? A New Perspective on Old Texts' [2021], in: id., *Neue Texte III*, 2022, pp. 119–36

Kinzig, Wolfram, 'Der Ursprung des römischen Glaubensbekenntnisses', in: id., *Neue Texte III*, 2022, pp. 161–88

Kinzig, Wolfram, *Neue Texte und Studien zu den antiken und frühmittelalterlichen Glaubensbekenntnissen III*, Berlin/Boston 2022 (AKG 151)

Kinzig, Wolfram, 'Sunday Observance – Norms and Norm Deviation in Late Antiquity', in: Uta Heil (ed.), *From Sun-Day to the Lord's Day: The Cultural History of Sunday in Late Antiquity and the Early Middle Ages*, Turnhout 2022 (Cultural Encounters in Late Antiquity and the Middle Ages 39), pp. 319–72

Kinzig, Wolfram, 'The Origin of the Creed of Jerusalem', in: id., *Neue Texte III*, 2022, pp. 189–207

Kinzig, Wolfram, 'The Creed of Nicaea: Old Questions, New Answers', *ER* 75 (2023), pp. 172–84

Kinzig, Wolfram, '"I abjure Satan, his Pomp, and his Service": Exchanging Religious Dependencies in the Early Church', in: id./Barbara Loose (eds.), *Control, Coercion, and Constraint: The Role of Religion in Overcoming and Creating Structures of Dependency*, Berlin/Boston 2024 (*sub prelo*)

Kinzig, Wolfram, 'Liberating the Dead – The Descent to the Underworld as Redemptive Event in Late-antique and Early Medieval Explanations of the Creed', in: Hermut Löhr (ed.), *Freedom and Liberation in Mediterranean Antiquity*, Berlin/Boston 2024 (Dependency and Slavery Studies; *sub prelo*)

Kinzig, Wolfram, '"Obedient unto death". Christ as Slave in Late Antique Commentaries on the Epistle to the Philippians', in: Julia Winnebeck/Maria Munkholt Christensen (eds.), *In the Grip of the Supernatural: Dependencies Above, Within, and Before Us*, Berlin/Boston 2024 (*sub prelo*)

Kinzig, Wolfram/Markschies, Christoph/Vinzent, Markus, *Tauffragen und Bekenntnis: Studien zur sogenannten 'Traditio Apostolica', zu den 'Interrogationes de fide' und zum 'Römischen Glaubensbekenntnis'*, Berlin/New York 1999 (AKG 74)

Kinzig, Wolfram/Vinzent, Markus, 'Recent Research on the Origin of the Creed', *JThS* 50 (1999), pp. 535–59

Kinzig, Wolfram/Wallraff, Martin, 'Das Christentum des dritten Jahrhunderts zwischen Anspruch und Wirklichkeit', in: Dieter Zeller (ed.), *Das Christentum I: Von den Anfängen bis zur Konstantinischen Wende*, Stuttgart 2002 (RM I), pp. 331–88

Kirsch, Johann P., *The Doctrine of the Communion of Saints in the Ancient Church: A Study in the History of Dogma*, Edinburgh/London n.d. (1910)

Kirsten, Hans, *Die Taufabsage: Eine Untersuchung zu Gestalt und Geschichte der Taufe nach den altkirchlichen Taufliturgien*, Berlin 1960

Kitchen, Robert A., art. 'Narsai', in: *Brill Encyclopedia of Early Christianity Online*, 2019; URL <http://dx.doi.org/10.1163/2589-7993_EECO_SIM_040689> (27/11/2023)

Klauck, Hans-Josef, *Der erste Johannesbrief*, Zurich etc. 1991 (EKK XXIII/1)

Klauck, Hans-Josef, *Der zweite und der dritte Johannesbrief*, Zurich etc. 1992 (EKK XIII/2)

Klein, Anja et al., art. 'Faith', in: *EBR*, vol. VIII, 2014, cols. 690–732

Klein, Richard, *Constantius II. und die christliche Kirche*, Darmstadt 1977 (IdF 26)

Klijn, Albertus F.J., 'The Apocryphal Correspondence between Paul and the Corinthians', *VigChr* 17 (1963), pp. 2–23

Klingshirn, William E., *Caesarius of Arles: The Making of a Christian Community in Late Antique Gaul*, Cambridge 1994 (repr. 1995; CSMLT IV/22)

Klöckener, Martin, 'Liturgiereformen in der Geschichte', in: Gordon Lathrop/Martin Stuflesser (eds.), *Liturgiereformen in den Kirchen: 50 Jahre nach Sacrosanctum Concilium*, Regensburg 2013 (Theologie der Liturgie 5), pp. 57–79

Knecht, Johannes J., Verus filius Dei incarnatus: The Christologies of Paulinus II of Aquileia, Benedict of Aniane, and Agobard of Lyon in the Context of the Felician Controversy, Münster 2022 (ArVe.S 20)

Knoben, Ursula, art. 'Paraskeve (Pjatnika)', in: *LCI*, vol. VIII, 1976 (repr. 1994), cols. 118–20

Knupp, Josef, *Das Mystagogieverständnis des Johannes Chrysostomus*, ed. by Anton Bodem and Alois Kothgasser, Munich 1995 (BBSt 4)

Koch, Klaus, *The Growth of the Biblical Tradition: The Form-Critical Method*, New York n.d. (1969)

Koeckert, Charlotte, art. 'Creation and Cosmogony, VI. Christianity, A. Patristics, Orthodox Churches, and Early Medieval Times', in: *EBR*, vol. V, 2012, cols. 989–92

Koeckert, Charlotte, art. 'Schöpfung', in: *RAC*, vol. XXIX, 2019, cols. 1006–113

Körting, Corinna et al., art. 'Doxology', in: *EBB*, vol VI, 2013, cols. 1135–42

Körtner, Ulrich H.J., 'The Papias Fragments', in: Wilhelm Pratscher (ed.), *The Apostolic Fathers: An Introduction*, Waco, Texas 2010. pp. 159–79

Koester, Craig R., *Hebrews: A New Translation with Introduction and Commentary*, New Haven etc. 2001 (AB 36)

Köster, Helmut, art. ὑπόστασις, in: *TDNT*, vol. VIII, 1972 (repr. 1995), pp. 572–89

Kösters, Oliver, *Die Trinitätslehre des Epiphanius von Salamis: Ein Kommentar zum 'Ancoratus'*, Göttingen 2003 (FKDG 86)

Kötter, Jan-Markus, 'Die Suche nach der kirchlichen Ordnung: Gedanken zu grundlegenden Funktionsweisen der spätantiken Reichskirche', *HZ* 298 (2014), pp. 1–28

Kötting, Bernhard/Kaiser, B., art. 'Gelübde', in: *RAC*, vol. IX, 1976, cols. 1055–99

Kohlbacher, Michael, 'Das *Symbolum Athanasianum* und die orientalische Bekenntnistradition: Formgeschichtliche Anmerkungen', in: Martin Tamcke (ed.), *Syriaca II: Beiträge zum 3. deutschen Syrologen-Symposium in Vierzehnheiligen 2002*, Münster 2004 (SOKG 33), pp. 105–64

Kohlbacher, Michael, 'Rabbula *in* Edessa: Das Weiterwirken eines Schismas in der armenischen Bekenntnistradition', in: Martin Tamcke (ed.), *Blicke gen Osten: Festschrift für Friedrich Heyer zum 95. Geburtstag*, Münster 2004, pp. 233–73

Kolbaba, Tia M., *Inventing Latin Heretics: Byzantines and the Filioque in the Ninth Century*, Kalamazoo 2008

Kolditz, Sebastian, 'Ein umstrittener Kaiser und patriarchale Kirchen im späteren fünften Jahrhundert: Weltliche und geistliche Macht unter Basiliskos', in: Michael Grünbart/Lutz Rickelt/Martin Marko Vučetić (eds.), *Zwei Sonnen am Goldenen Horn? Kaiserliche und patriarchale Macht im byzantinischen Mittelalter*, vol. II, Berlin 2013, pp. 19–53

Kollautz, Arnulf, 'Orient und Okzident am Ausgang des 6. Jh. Johannes, Abt von Biclarum, Bischof von Gerona, der Chronist des westgotischen Spaniens', *Byzantina* 12 (1983), pp. 464–506

Konradt, Matthias, art. 'Excommunication, II. New Testament', in: *EBR*, vol. VIII, 2014, cols. 367–9

Konradt, Matthias, art. 'Faith, II. New Testament', in: *EBR*, vol. VIII, 2014, cols. 691–701

Kraatz, Wilhelm, *Koptische Akten zum ephesinischen Konzil vom Jahre 431: Übersetzung und Untersuchungen*, Leipzig 1904 (TU 26/2)

Krebs, Johann Ph./Schmalz, Joseph H., *Antibarbarus der lateinischen Sprache: Nebst einem kurzen Abriss der Geschichte der lateinischen Sprache und Vorbemerkungen über reine Latinität*, eventh ed., Basel 1905

Kreis, Oliver, 'Ein hispanischer Bischof am Hof des römischen Kaisers. Welchen Einfluss hatte Ossius von Corduba auf die Kirchenpolitik Konstantins des Großen?', in: Sabine Panzram (ed.), *Oppidum – Civitas – Urbs: Städteforschung auf der Iberischen Halbinsel zwischen Rom und al-Andalus*, Berlin 2017 (Geschichte und Kultur der Iberischen Welt 13), pp. 401–27

Kretschmar, Georg, 'Die Geschichte des Taufgottesdienstes in der alten Kirche', in: *Leit.*, vol. V, 1970, pp. 1–348

Kretschmar, Georg/Hauschildt, Karl, art. 'Katechumenat/Katechumenen', in: *TRE*, vol. XVIII, 1989, pp. 1–14

Kritikou, Flora, 'The Byzantine Compositions of the "Symbolon of Faith"', in: Nina-Maria Wanek (ed.), *Psaltike: Neue Studien zur Byzantinischen Musik: Festschrift für Gerda Wolfram*, Vienna 2011, pp. 167–86

Kropp, Manfred, 'Tripartite, but ant-Trinitarian formulas in the Qur'ānic Corpus, Possibly pre-Qur'ānic, in: Gabriel S. Reynolds (ed.), *New Perspectives on the Qur'ān: The Qur'ān in its Historical Context 2*, London/New York 2011 (Routledge Studies in the Qur'ān), pp. 247–64

Krueger, Derek, *Liturgical Subjects: Christian Ritual, Biblical Narrative, and the Formation of the Self in Byzantium*, Philadelphia 2014 (Divinations: Rereading Late Ancient Religion)

Kühne, Udo/Tönnies, Bernhard/Haucap, Anette, *Handschriften in Osnabrück: Bischöfliches Archiv, Gymnasium Carolinum, Bischöfliches Generalvikariat, Kulturgeschichtliches Museum, Niedersächsisches Staatsarchiv, Diözesanmuseum, Pfarrarchiv St. Johann*, Wiesbaden 1993 (Mittelalterliche Handschriften in Niedersachsen; Kurzkatalog 2)

Künstle, Karl, *Antipriscilliana: Dogmengeschichtliche Untersuchungen und Texte aus dem Streite gegen Priscillians Irrlehre*, Freiburg 1905

Kunze, Johannes, *Das nicänisch-konstantinopolitanische Symbol*, Leipzig 1898 (SGTK III/3)

Kunze, Johannes, 'Die Entstehung des sogenannten apostolischen Glaubensbekenntnisses unter dogmengeschichtl[ichem] Gesichtspunkt', *IMW* 8 (1914), cols. 1311–30

Labahn, Michael, 'Kreative Erinnerung als nachösterliche Nachschöpfung: Der Ursprung der christlichen Taufe', in: Hellholm et al. 2011, vol. I, pp. 337–76

Labourt, Jérôme, *Dionysius bar Ṣalībī: Expositio Liturgiae*, Paris 1903 (repr. Leuven 1955; CSCO 13–14/Scriptores Syri 13–14)

Ladaria, Luis F., *El Espíritu Santo en San Hilario de Poitiers*, Madrid 1977

Ladaria, Luis F., *La cristología de Hilario de Poitiers*, Rome 1989 (AnGr 255/SFT A 32)

Lai, Andrea, *Il codice Laudiano greco 35: L'identità missionaria di un libro nell'Europa altomedievale*, Cargeghe 2011

Łajtar, Adam, 'The Constantinopolitan Creed in an Inscription from the Monastery Church on Kom H in Dongola,' in: Włodzimierz Godlewski/Dorota Dzierzbicka/Adam Łajtar (eds.), *Dongola 2015-2016: Fieldwork, Conservation and Site* Management, Warsaw 2018 (PCMA Excavation Series 5), pp. 37–46

Lampe, Geoffrey W.H., *A Patristic Greek Lexicon*, Oxford 1961 (seventh impression 1984)

Lampe, Peter, *From Paulus to Valentinus: Christians at Rome in the First Two Centuries*, ed. by Marshall D. Johnson, Minneapolis 2003

Lang, Uwe M., *The Roman Mass: From Early Christian Origins to Tridentine Reform*, Cambridge 2022

Lange, Christian, *Mia Energeia: Untersuchungen zur Einigungspolitik des Kaisers Heraclius und des Patriarchen Sergius von Constantinopel*, Tübingen 2012 (STAC 66)

Lange-Sonntag, Ralf, art, 'Elias von Nisibis', in: *BBKL*, vol. XXVII, 2007, cols. 369–74

Lapidge, Michael (ed.), *Anglo-Saxon Litanies of the Saints*, London 1991 (HBS 106)

Lapidge, Michael, 'The Career of Archbishop Theodore', in: id. (ed.), *Archbishop Theodore: Commemorative Studies on his Life and Influences*, Cambridge 1995 (CSASE 11), pp. 1–29

Larchet, Jean-Claude/Ponsoye, Emmanuel, *Saint Maxime le Confesseur: Opuscules théologiques et polémiques*, introduction par J.-C- L., traduction et notes par E.P., Paris 1998 (Sagesses Chrétiennes)

Larchet, Jean-Claude, *Saint Maxime le Confesseur (580-662)*, Paris 2003 (Initiations aux Pères de l'Église)

Lasker, Daniel J., *Jewish Philosophical Polemics Against Christianity in the Middle Ages*, Liverpool 2007 (The Littman Library of Jewish Civilization)

Latte, Kurt, *Römische Religionsgeschichte*, second ed. (second repr.), Munich 1992 (Handbuch der Altertumswissenschaft V/4)

Lattke, Michael, *Hymnus: Materialien zur Geschichte der antiken Hymnologie*, Freiburg, Schweiz/ Göttingen 1991 (NTOA 19)

Lattke, Michael, *Odes of Solomon: A Commentary*, Minneapolis 2009 (Hermeneia)

Laurent, Vitalien, 'Le Symbole "Quicumque" et l'Église byzantine', *EOr* 39 (1936), pp. 385–404

Lavarra, Caterina, *Maghi, santi e medici: Interazioni culturali nella Gallia merovingia*, Galatina 1994

Lebon, Joseph, 'Les citations patristiques grecques du "Sceau de la foi"', *RHE* 25 (1929), pp. 5–32

Lebon, Joseph, 'Les anciens symboles dans la définition de Chalcédoine', *RHE* 32 (1936), pp. 809–76

Leclercq, Jean/Bonnes, Jean-Paul, *Jean de Fécamp: Un maître de la vie spirituelle au XIe siècle*, Paris 1946 (ETHS 9)

Legg, John W. (ed.), *Tracts on the Mass*, London 1904 (HBS)

Lehtipuu, Outi, *Debates over the Resurrection of the Dead: Constructing Early Christian Identity*, Oxford 2015 (OECS)

Lehto, Adam, *The Demonstrations of Aphrahat, the Persian Sage*, Piscataway, NJ 2010 (Gorgias Eastern Christian Studies 27)

Lenski, Noel, *Failure of Empire: Valens and the Roman State in the Fourth Century A.D.*, Berkeley etc. 2002 (The Joan Palevsky Imprint in Classical Literature)

Lenski, Noel, 'Imperial Legislation and the Donatist Controversy: From Constantine to Honorius', in: Richard Miles (ed.), *The Donatist Schism: Controversy and Contexts*, Liverpool 2016 (Translated Texts for Historians, Contexts 2), pp. 166–219

Leppin, Hartmut, *Von Constantin dem Großen zu Theodosius II: Das christliche Kaisertum bei den Kirchenhistorikern Socrates, Sozomenus und Theodoret*, Göttingen 1996 (Hyp. 110)

Leppin, Hartmut, *Theodosius der Große*, Darmstadt 2003 (Gestalten der Antike).

Leppin, Hartmut, 'Zum Wandel des spätantiken Heidentums', *Millennium-Jahrbuch* 1 (2004), pp. 59–82

Leppin, Hartmut, *Justinian: Das christliche Experiment*, Stuttgart 2011

Leppin, Hartmut, 'Christianisierungen im Römischen Reich: Überlegungen zum Begriff und zur Phasenbildung', *ZAC* 16 (2012), pp. 247–78

Leppin, Hartmut, 'Kaisertum und Christentum in der Spätantike: Überlegungen zu einer unwahrscheinlichen Synthese', in: Andreas Fahrmeir/Annette Imhausen (eds.), *Die Vielfalt normativer Ordnungen: Konflikte und Dynamik in historischer und ethnologischer Perspektive*, Frankfurt am Main 2013, pp. 197–223

Leppin, Volker, art. 'Excommunication, III. Christianity', in: *EBR*, vol. VIII, 2014, cols. 369 f.

Leroquais, Victor, *Les psautiers manuscrits latins des bibliothèques publiques de France*, vol. I, Paris 1940

Leroy, François J., *L'homilétique de Proclus de Constantinople: Tradition manuscrite, inédits, études connexes*, Città del Vaticano 1967 (StT 247)

Leroy, Lucien/Grébaut, Sylvain, Sévère ibn al-Muqaffaʻ, évêque d'Aschmounaïn: Histoire des conciles (second livre), édition et traduction du texte arabe par L.L., étude de la version éthiopienne par S.G., Paris 1911 (PO 6/4)

Leuenberger-Wenger, Sandra, *Das Konzil von Chalcedon und die Kirche: Konflikte und Normierungsprozesse im 5. und 6. Jahrhundert*, Leiden/Boston 2019 (SVigChr153)

Levin, Christoph, 'Glaube im Alten Testament', in: Horn, *Glaube*, 2018, pp. 9–31

Levison, Wilhelm, *England and the Continent in the Eighth Century: The Ford Lectures Delivered in the University of Oxford in the Hilary Term, 1943*, Oxford 1946 (repr. 1973)

Levy, Kenneth, *Gregorian Chant and the Carolingians*, Princeton, New Jersey 1998

L'Huillier, Peter, *The Church of the Ancient Councils: The Disciplinary Work of the First Four Councils*, Crestwood NY 1996

Liesel, Nikolaus/Makula, Tibor, *The Eucharistic Liturgies of the Eastern Churches*, Collegeville, Minnesota 1963

Lietzmann, Hans, *Apollinaris von Laodicea und seine Schule: Texte und Untersuchungen*, Tübingen 1904

Lietzmann, Hans, 'Die Urform des apostolischen Glaubensbekenntnisses' [1919], in: id. 1962, pp. 182–8

Lietzmann, Hans, 'Symbolstudien I–XIV', *ZNW* 21 (1922), pp. 1–34; 22 (1923), pp. 257–279; 24 (1925), pp. 193–202; 26 (1927), pp. 75–95; also separately: Darmstadt 1966; also in: id. 1962, pp. 189–281 (quoted thereafter)

Lietzmann, Hans, *Kleine Schriften*, vol. III: Studien zur Liturgie- und Symbolgeschichte: Zur Wissenschaftsgeschichte, Berlin 1962 (TU 74)

Lietzmann, Hans, *Zeitrechnung der römischen Kaiserzeit und der Neuzeit für die Jahre 1–2000 n.Chr.*, fourth ed., Berlin/New York 1984

Lindemann, Andreas, 'Zur frühchristlichen Taufpraxis: Die Taufe in der Didache, bei Justin und in der Didaskalia', in: Hellholm et al. 2011, vol. II, pp. 767–815

Linder, Amon, *The Jews in the Legal Sources of the Early Middle Ages: Edited with Introductions, Translations, and Annotations*, Detroit/Jerusalem 1997

Lionarons, Joyce T., *The Homiletic Writings of Archbishop Wulfstan: A Critical Study*, Woodbridge, Suffolk 2010 (Anglo-Saxon Studies 14)

Lippold, Adolf, *Die Kaiser Theodosius der Große und Theodosius II*, Stuttgart 1972

Lipton, Sara, 'Unfeigned Witness: Jews, Matter, and Vision in Twelfth-Century Christian Art', in: Herbert L. Kessler/David Nirenberg, *Judaism and Christian Art: Aesthetic Anxieties from the Catacombs to Colonialism*, Philadelphia/Oxford 2011, pp. 45–73

Löhr, Hermut, *Studien zum frühchristlichen und frühjüdischen Gebet: Untersuchungen zu 1 Clem 59 bis 61 in seinem literarischen, historischen und theologischen Kontext*, Tübingen 2003 (WUNT 160)

Löhr, Hermut, 'Der Messias als Richter: Zur Entstehung und Bedeutung einer Aussage im zweiten Artikel des Credos in den Anfängen des christlichen Glaubens', in: Jens Herzer/Anne Käfer/Jörg

Frey (eds.), *Die Rede von Jesus Christus als Glaubensaussage: Der zweite Artikel des Apostolischen Glaubensbekenntnisses im Gespräch zwischen Bibelwissenschaft und Dogmatik*, Tübingen 2018, pp. 457–77

Löhr, Winrich A., art. Eudoxios, in: *LThK*, third ed., vol. III, 1995, cols. 978 f.

Löhr, Winrich A., *Basilides und seine Schule: Eine Studie zur Theologie- und Kirchengeschichte des zweiten Jahrhunderts*, Tübingen 1996 (WUNT 83)

Löhr, Winrich A., art. 'Logos', in: *RAC*, vol. XXIII, 2010, cols. 327–435

Longère, Jean, 'L'enseignement du *Credo*: conciles, synodes et canonistes médiévaux jusqu'au XIIIe siècle', *SacEr* 32 (1991), pp. 309–41

Longo, Augusta, 'Il testo integrale della "Narrazione degli abati Giovanni e Sofronio" attraverso le "Ἑρμηνεῖαι" di Nicone', *RSBN* 12/13 (1965/1966), pp. 223–50

Loofs, Friedrich, art. 'Athanasianum', in: *RE*, third ed., 1897, vol. II, 177–94

Lorenz, Rudolf, art. 'Eustathius von Antiochien', in: *TRE* vol. X, 1982, pp. 543–6

Lotter, Friedrich, *Völkerverschiebungen im Ostalpen-Mitteldonau-Raum zwischen Antike und Mittelalter (375–600)*, Berlin/New York 2003 (RGA.E 39)

Lougovaya, Julia, 'Greek Literary Ostraca Revisited', in: Clementina Caputo/Julia Lougovaya (eds.), *Using Ostraca in the Ancient World: New Discoveries and Methodologies*, Berlin/Noston 2020 (Materiale Textkulturen 32), pp. 109–41

Lührmann, Dieter, art. 'Glaube', in: *RAC*, vol. XI, 1979, cols. 48–122

Luibhéid, Colm, 'The Arianism of Eusebius of Nicomedia', *IThQ* 43 (1976), pp. 3–23

Lumby, J. Rawson, *The History of the Creeds*, Cambridge 1873 (second ed. 1880)

Lumma, Liborius O./Vonach, Andreas, 'Glaubensbekenntnis', in: Birgit Jeggle-Merz/Walter Kirchschläger/Jörg Müller (eds.), *Das Wort Gottes hören und den Tisch bereiten: Die Liturgie mit biblischen Augen betrachten*, Stuttgart 2015 (Luzerner biblisch-liturgischer Kommentar zum Ordo Missae II), pp. 67–78

Luttikhuizen, Gerard, 'The Apocryphal Correspondence with the Corinthians and the Acts of Paul', in: Jan N. Bremmer (ed.), *The Apocryphal Acts of Paul and Thecla*, Kampen 1996 (Studies on the Apocryphal Acts of the Apostles 2), pp. 75–91

Luykx, Bonifaas, 'Essai sur les sources de l'"Ordo missae" Prémontré', *APraem* 22/23 (1946/1947), pp. 35–90

Luykx, Bonifaas, 'Der Ursprung der gleichbleibenden Teile der Heiligen Messe', LuM 29 (1961), pp. 72–119

Luz, Ulrich, *Matthew 21–28: A Commentary*, Minneapolis 2005 (Hermeneia)

Luz, Ulrich, *Matthew 1–7: A Commentary*, Minneapolis 2007 (Hermeineia)

Lynch, Joseph H., *Godparents and Kinship in Early Medieval Europe*, Princeton, N.J., 1986

Macé, Caroline et al., 'Chapter 3. Textual Critsicism and Text Editing', in: Alessandro Bausi (ed.), *Comparative Oriental Manuscript Studies: An Introduction*, n.p. (Hamburg) 2015, pp. 321–465

MacLean, Arthur J., *East Syrian Daily Offices: Translated from the Syriac with Introduction, Notes, and Indices and an Appendix Containing the Lectionary and Glossary*, London 1894 (repr. Westmead, Farnborough 1969)

MacMullen, Ramsay, *Christianizing the Roman Empire (A.D. 200–400)*, New Haven, Conn. 1984

Macomber, William F., 'The Nicene Creed in a Liturgical Fragment of the 5th or 6th Century from Upper Egypt', *OrChr* 77 (1993), pp. 98–103

Madoz, José, *Excerpta Vincentii Lirinensis según el códice de Ripoll, n. 151 con un estudio crítico introductorio*, Madrid 1940

Madoz, José, Un tratado desconocido de San Vicente de Lerins: "Excerpta sancte memorie Vincentii Lirinensis insule presbiteri ex uniuerso beate recordacionis Agustini in unum collecta", *Gr.* 21 (1940), pp. 75–94

Mai, Angelo, *Scriptorum Veterum Nova Collectio e Vaticanis Codicibus Edita*, vol. X, Rome 1838

Maisonneuve, Henri, *Études sur les origines de l'inquisition*, second ed., Paris 1960 (EEMA 7)

Mâle, Émile, *L'art religieux de la fin du moyen âge en France: Étude sur l'iconographie du moyen age et sur ses sources d'inspiration*, fifth ed., Paris 1949

Maraval, Pierre, 'Die Rezeption des Chalcedonense im Osten des Reiches', in: Luce Pietri (ed.), *Der lateinische Westen und der byzantinische Osten*, Freiburg etc. 2001(2010; GeChr 3), pp. 120–57

March, Joseph M., 'En Ramón Martí y la seva "Explanatio simboli apostolorum"', *Anuari de l'Institut d'Estudis Catalans* 2 (1908), pp. 443–96

Mardirossian, Aram, *La Collection canonique d'Antioche. Droit et hérésie à travers le premier recueil de législation ecclésiastique (IVe siècle)*, Paris 2010 (Collège de France – CNRS/Centre de Recherche d'Histoire et Civilisation de Byzance/Monographies 34)

Margoliouth, George, *Descriptive List of Syriac and Karshuni Mss. in the British Museum Acquired since 1873*, London 1899

Markschies, Christoph, '"Sessio ad dexteram": Bemerkungen zu einem altchristlichen Bekenntnismotiv in der Diskussion der altkirchlichen Theologen' [1993], in: id., *Alta Trinità Beata: Gesammelte Studien zur altkirchlichen Trinitätstheologie*, Tübingen 2000, pp. 1–69

Markschies, Christoph, *Ambrosius von Mailand und die Trinitätstheologie: Kirchen- und theologiegeschichtliche Studien zu Antiarianismus und Neunizänismus bei Ambrosius und im lateinischen Westen (364–381 n.Chr.)*, Tübingen 1995 (BHTh 90)

Markschies, Christoph, 'Wer schrieb die sogenannte *Traditio Apostolica*? Neue Beobachtungen und Hypothesen zu einer kaum lösbaren Frage aus der altkirchlichen Literaturgeschichte', in: Kinzig/Markschies/Vinzent 1999, pp. 1–74

Markschies, Christoph, 'Haupteinleitung', in: id./Jens Schröter/Andreas Heiser (eds.), *Antike christliche Apokryphen in deutscher Übersetzung*, seventh edition, vol. I: Evangelien und Verwandtes, fasc. 1, Tübingen 2012, pp. 1–180

Markschies, Christoph, art. 'Montanismus', in: *RAC*, vol. XXIV, 2012, cols. 1197–220

Markschies, Christoph, 'On Classifying Creeds the Classical German Way: "Privat-Bekenntnisse" ("Private Creeds")', in: *StPatr*, vol. LXIII, 2013, pp. 259–71

Markschies, Christoph, ἦν ποτε ὅτε οὐκ ἦν oder: Schwierigkeiten bei der Beschreibung dessen, was vor aller Zeit war', in: Eve-Marie Becker/Holger Strutwolf (eds.), *Platonismus und Christentum: Ihre Beziehungen und deren Grenzen*, Tübingen 2022, pp. 11–40

Markus, Robert A., *Gregory the Great and His World*, Cambridge 1997

Marrone, Steven P., *A History of Science, Magic and Belief: From Medieval to Early Modern Europe*, London etc. 2015

Martimbos, Nicolas, *D.D. Durandi a Sancto Porciano in Sententias Theologicas Petri Lombardi Commentariorum Libri Quatuor*, Lyons 1587

Martin-Hisard, Bernadette, 'Das Christentum und die Kirche in der georgischen Welt', in: Pietri 2001(2010), pp. 1231–305

Martínez Díez, Gonzalo/Rodríguez, Félix, *La colección canónica Hispana*, 6 vols., Madrid/Barcelona 1966–2002 (MHS.C 1–6)

Martini, Aldo (ed.), *Il cosidetto Pontificale di Poitiers (Paris, Bibliothèque de l'Arsenal, cod. 227)*, Rome 1979 (RED.F 14)

Masser, Achim, '"Weißenburger Katechismus"', in: Bergmann 2013, pp. 506–8

May, Gerhard, art. 'Bann, IV. Alte Kirche und Mittelalter', in: *TRE*, vol. V, 1980, pp. 170–82

Mayser, Edwin, *Grammatik der griechischen Papyri aus der Ptolemäerzeit mit Einschluss der gleichzeitigen Ostraka und der in Ägypten verfassten Inschriften*, vol. II/3: Satzlehre. Synthetischer Teil, Berlin/Leipzig 1934 (repr. 1970)

McCarthy, Daniel P., 'The Council of Nicaea and the Celebration of the Christian Pasch', in: Kim 2021, pp. 177–201

McGowan, Andrew B., *Ancient Christian Worship: Early Church Practices in Social, Historical, and Theological Perspective*, Grand Rapids, Michigan 2014

McGuckin, John, *Saint Gregory of Nazianzus: An Intellectual Biography*, Crestwood, New York 2001

McKenna, Stephen, *Paganism and Pagan Survivals in Spain up to the Fall of the Visigothic Kingdom*, Washington 1938 (SMH.NS 1)

McKitterick, Rosamond, *The Frankish Church and the Carolingian Reforms, 789–895*, London 1977

McNeill, John T./Gamer, Helena M., *Medieval Handbooks of Penance: A Translation of the principal* libri poenitentiales *and Selections from Related Documents*, New York/Chichester 1938 (repr. 1990)

Mearns, James, *The Canticles of the Christian Church Eastern and Western in Early and Medieval Times*, Cambridge 1914

Meens, Rob, *Het tripartite boeteboek: Overlevering en betekenis van vroegmiddeleeuwse biechtvoorschriften (met editie en vertaling van vier tripartita)*, Hilversum 1994 (Middeleeuwse Studies en Bronnen 41)

Meens, Rob, *Penance in Medieval Europe, 600–1200*, Cambridge 2014

Meier, Mischa, *Das andere Zeitalter Justinians: Kontingenzerfahrung und Kontingenzbewältigung im 6. Jahrhundert n. Chr.*, Göttingen 2004 (Hyp. 147)

Meier, Mischa, *Anastasios I. Die Entstehung des Byzantinischen Reiches*, Stuttgart 2009

Menze, Volker/Akalin, Kutlu, *John of Tella's Profession of Faith*, Piscataway, NJ 2009 (Texts from Christian Late Antiquity 25)

Mériaux, Charles, 'Ideal and Reality: Carolingian Priests in Northern Francie', in: Patzold/Van Rhijn 2016, pp. 78–97

Metzger, Bruce M., *The Early Versions of the New Testament: Their Origin, Transmission, and Limitations*, Oxford 1977 (repr. 2001)

Metzger, Marcel, *History of the Liturgy: The Major Stages*, Collegeville, Minnesota 1997

Metzger, Marcel/Drews, Wolfram/Brakmann, Heinzgerd, art. 'Katechumenat', in: *RAC*, vol. XX, 2004, cols. 497–574

Metzger, Paul, 'Arkandisziplin', in: *WiBiLex* 2010 (version 2018); URL <https://www.bibelwissenschaft.de/stichwort/49934> (27/11/2023)

Metzler, Karin/Hansen, Dirk U./Savvidis, Kyriakos, *Die dogmatischen Schriften*, 1. Lieferung: Epistula ad Episcopos Aegypti et Libyae. Edition, Berlin/New York 1996 (Athanasius Werke 1/1,1)

Metzler, Karin/Savvidis, Kyriakos (eds.), *Die dogmatischen Schriften*, 2. Lieferung: Orationes I et II Contra Arianos. Edition, Berlin/New York 1998 (Athanasius Werke 1/1,2)

Meunier, Bernard, 'Ni ajouter ni retrancher: une qualification du texte inspiré?', *REAugP* 63 (2017), pp. 311–26

Mews, Constant J./Renkin, Claire, 'The Legacy of Gregory the Great in the Latin West', in: Bronwen Neil/Matthew Dal Santo (eds.), *A Companion to Gregory the Great*, Leiden/Boston 2013 (Brill's Companions to the Christian Tradition 47), pp. 315–42

Meyer, Hans B., *Eucharistie: Geschichte, Theologie, Pastoral*, Regensburg 1989 (GDK 4)

Miazga, Tadeusz, *Die Melodien des einstimmigen Credo der römisch-katholischen lateinischen Kirche*, Graz 1976

Michaelis, Wilhelm, art. κράτος κτλ., in: *TDNT*, vol. III, 1965, pp. 905–15

Michel, Anton, *Humbert und Kerullarios: Quellen und Studien zum Schisma des XI. Jahrhunderts*, 2 vols., Paderborn 1924/1930 (QFG 21, 23)

Michel, Charles, art. 'Anathème', in: *DACL*, vol. II, 1907, cols. 1926–40

Michel, Otto, art. 'ὁμολογέω κτλ.', in: *TDNT*, vol. V, 1967, pp. 199–220

Mihálykó, Ágnes T., *The Christian Liturgical Papyri: An Introduction*, Tübingen 2019 (STAC 114)

Milne, Herbert J.M., *Catalogue of the Literary Papyri in the British Museum*, London 1927

Mingana, Alphonse, *Narsai doctoris Syri Homiliae et Carmina*, 2 vols., Mossul 1905

Mingana, Alphonse, *Commentary of Theodore of Mopsestia on the Nicene Creed*, Cambridge 1932 (WoodSt 5)

Missale Romanum ex Decreto Sacrosanctio Concilii Tridentini Restitutum Pii V. Pont. Max. Iussu Editum, Venice n.d. (1570)

Mitalaité, Kristina, 'La transmission de la doctrine dans la prédication carolingienne', *RSPhTh* 97 (2013), pp. 243–76

Mocquereau, André, 'Le chant "authentique" du Credo selon l'édition vaticane', in: *PalMus*, vol. X, 1909, pp. 90–176

Mohlberg, Leo C., *Radulph de Rivo, der letzte Vertreter der altrömischen Liturgie*, 2 vols., Münster 1911/ 1915 (RTCHP 29)

Mohlberg, Leo C., *Mittelalterliche Handschriften*, Zurich 1951 (Katalog der Handschriften der Zentralbibliothek Zürich 1)

Mohlberg, Leo C./Eizenhöfer, Leo/Siffrin, Petrus, *Missale Gallicanum Vetus (Cod. Vat. Palat. lat. 493)*, Rome 1958 (RED.F 3)

Molland, Einar, '"Des Reich kein Ende haben wird": Hintergrund und Bedeutung einer dogmatischen Aussage im nicäno-constantinopolitanischen Glaubensbekenntnis', in: id., *Opuscula Patristica*, Oslo etc. 1970 (BTN 2), pp. 235–253

Mone, Franz Joseph (ed.), *Altteutsche Schauspiele*, Quedlinburg/Leipzig 1841 (BDNL 21)

Monnot, Guy, art. 'al-Shahrastānī', in: *Encyclopaedia of Islam*, second ed., 2012; URL <http://dx.doi. org/10.1163/1573-3912_islam_SIM_6769> (27/11/2023)

Montanari, Franco, art. 'Hypomnema', in: *Brill's New Pauly* online, 2006; <http://dx.doi.org/10.1163/ 1574-9347_bnp_e519990> (27/11/2023)

Morard, Martin, 'Quand liturgie épousa predication: Note sur la place de la prédication dans la liturgie romaine au moyen âge (VIIIe – XIVe siècle)', in: Nicole Bériou/Franco Morenzoni (eds.), *Prédication et liturgie au Moyen Âge: Études réunies*, Turnhout 2008 (Bibliothèque d'histoire culturelle du Moyen Âge 5), pp. 79–126

Mordek, Hubert, *Kirchenrecht und Reform im Frankenreich: Die Collectio Vetus Gallica, die älteste systematische Kanonessammlung des fränkischen Gallien. Studien und Edition*, Berlin/New York 1975 (BGQMA 1)

Morgan, Teresa, *Roman Faith and Christian Faith: Pistis and Fides in the Early Roman Empire and Early Churches*, Oxford 2015

Morin, Germain, 'Le Symbole d'Athanase et son premier témoin: Saint Césaire d'Arles', *RBen* 18 (1901), pp. 337–62

Morin, Germain, 'L'origine du symbole d'Athanase', *JThS* 12 (1911), pp. 160–90, 337–59

Morin, Germain, 'L'origine du symbole d'Athanase: Témoignage inédit de S. Césaire d'Arles', *RBen* 44 (1932), pp. 207–19

Morin, Germain, *Sancti Augustini Sermones post Maurinos reperti*, Rome 1930 (Miscellanea Agostiniana 1)

Morison, Ernest F., *A Commentary on the Apostles' Creed by Tyrannius Rufinus, Presbyter of Aquileia*, London 1916

Mühl, Max, 'Der λόγος ἐνδιάθετος und προφορικοός von der älteren Stoa bis zur Synode von Sirmium 351', *ABG* 7 (1962), pp. 7–56

Mühlenberg, Ekkehard, *Apollinaris von Laodicea*, Göttingen 1969 (FKDG 23)

Mühlenberg, Ekkehard, *Psalmenkommentare aus der Katenenüberlieferung*, 3 vols., Berlin/New York 1975–1978 (PTS 15, 16, 19)

Mühlsteiger, Johannes, *Kirchenordnungen: Anfänge kirchlicher Rechtsbildung*, Berlin 2006 (KStT 50)

Müller, Christian, 'Das Phänomen des "lateinischen Athanasius"', in: Stockhausen/Brennecke 2010, pp. 3–42

Müller, Christian, 'From Athanasius to "Athanasius": Usurping a "Nicene Hero" or: The Making-of of the *"Athanasian Creed"*', in: Jörg Ulrich/Anders-Christian Jacobsen/David Brakke (eds.), *Invention, Rewriting, Usurpation: Discursive Fights over Religious Traditions in Antiquity*, Frankfurt am Main etc. 2012 (Early Christianity in the Context of Antiquity 11), pp. 19–40

Müller, Christian 'Revisiting an Authority's Secret(s) of Success: The Rise and Decline of the Latin Athanasius', in: Shari Boodts/Johan Leemans/Brigitte Meijns (eds.), *Shaping Authority: How Did a Person Become an Authority in Antiquity, the Middle Ages and the Renaissance?*, Turnhout 2016 (Lectio-E 4), pp. 197–22

Mulders, Jacques, 'Victricius van Rouaan: Leven en leer', *Bijdr.* 17 (1956), pp. 1–25; 18 (1957), pp. 19–40, 270–89

Munkholt Christensen, Maria, '"Light from Light": A Nicene Phrase and Its Use in the Early Church', *ER* 75 (2023), pp. 249–62

Muyldermans, Joseph, *Evagriana Syriaca: Textes inédits du British Museum et de la Vaticane édités et traduits*, Louvain 1952 (BMus 31)

Napier, Arthur S., *The Old English Version of the Enlarged Rule of Chrodegang together with the Latin Original: An Old English Version of the Capitula of Theodulf together with the Latin Original: An Interlinear Old English Rendering of the Epitome of Benedict of Aniane*, London 1916

Neri, Valerio, *I marginali nell'occidente tardoantico: Poveri, 'infames' e criminali nella nascente società cristiana*, Bari 1998 (Munera 12)

Neumann, Bernd, art. 'Innsbrucker (thüringisches) Fronleichnamsspiel', in: *VerLex*, second ed., vol. IV, 1982, cols. 398–400

Nicol, Donald M., 'Byzantine Political Thought', in: James H. Burns (ed.), *Medieval Political Thought c. 350–c. 1450*, Cambridge 1988 (repr. 2003)

Nissel, Johann G., *S. Jacobi Apostoli Epistolae Catholicae Versio Arabica et Aethiopica*, Leiden 1654

Noethlichs, Karl L., *Die gesetzgeberischen Maßnahmen der christlichen Kaiser des vierten Jahrhunderts gegen Häretiker, Heiden und Juden*, Diss., Köln 1971

Noethlichs, Karl L., art. 'Heidenverfolgung', in: *RAC*, vol. XIII, 1986, cols. 1149–90

Noethlichs, Karl L., art. 'Iustinianus (Kaiser)', in: *RAC*, vol. XIX, 2001, cols. 668–763

Noethlichs, Karl L., 'Revolution from the Top? "Orthodoxy" and the Persecution of Heretics in Imperial Legislation from Constantine to Justinian, in: Clifford Ando/Jörg Rüpke (eds.), *Religion and Law in Classical and Christian Rome*, Stuttgart 2006 (Potsdamer Altertumswissenschaftliche Beiträge 15), pp. 115–25

Nutton, Vivian, 'Archiatri and the Medical Profession in Antiqity', *PBSR* 45 (1977), pp. 191–226 and plates XXXI–XXXII; also in: id., *From Democedes to Harvey: Studies in the History of Medicine*, London 1988 (CStS CS 277), no. V (and *Addenda et Corrigenda*)

Nyssen, Wilhelm et al. (eds.), *Handbuch der Ostkirchenkunde*, vol. II, [second ed.], Düsseldorf 1989

Oberdorfer, Bernd, *Filioque: Geschichte und Theologie eines ökumenischen Problems*, Göttingen 2001 (FSÖTh 96)

Odenthal, Andreas, '"Ante conspectum diuinae maiestatis tuae reus assisto": Liturgie- und frömmigkeitsgeschichtliche Untersuchungen zum "Rheinischen Messordo" und dessen Beziehungen zur Fuldaer Sakramentartradition' [2007]', in: id., *Liturgie vom Frühen Mittelalter zum Zeitalter der Konfessionalisierung: Studien zur Geschichte des Gottesdienstes*, Tübingen 2011 (SMHR 61), pp. 16–49

O'Donnell, James J./Drecoll, Volker H., art. 'Regula, regula fidei', in: *AugL*, vol. IV, 2012–2018, cols. 1128–34

Oefele, Christine, art. 'Music', in: *Brill Encyclopedia of Early Christianity Online*, 2022; URL <http://dx.doi.org/10.1163/2589-7993_EECO_SIM_00002315> (27/11/2023)

Ohme, Heinz, *Kanon ekklesiastikos: Die Bedeutung des altkirchlichen Kanonbegriffs*, Berlin/New York 1998 (AKG 67)

Ohme, Heinz, art. 'Kanon I (Begriff)', in: *RAC*, vol. XX, 2004, cols. 1–28

O'Leary, Joseph S., 'The Homoousion as Shield of the Son's Divinity', *Eastern Theological Journal* 8 (2022), pp. 145–64

Olivar, Alexandre, *La predicación cristiana antigua*, Barcelona 1991 (BHer.TF 189)

Ommanney, George D.W., *Early History of the Athanasian Creed: The Results of Some Original Research upon the Subject*, London etc. 1880

Ommanney, George D.W., *A Critical Dissertation on the Athanasian Creed: Its Original Language, Date, Authorship, Titles, Text, Reception, and Use*, Oxford 1897

Opitz, Hans-Georg (ed.), *Athanasius – Werke*, vol. III, 1–2: Urkunden zur Geschichte des Arianischen Streites, Berlin 1934/1935

Ostheim, Martin von, *Ousia und Substantia: Untersuchungen zum Substanzbegriff bei den vornizänischen Kirchenvätern*, Basel 2008

Packer, James I., *Affirming the Apostles' Creed*, Wheaton, Illinois 2008

Padwick, Constance E., *Muslim Devotions: A Study of Prayer-Manuals in Common Use*, London 1961 (repr. 1969)

Page, Christopher, *The Christian West and its Singers: The First Thousand Years*, New Haven/London 2010 (second printing 2012)

Palazzo, Éric, *A History of Liturgical Books from the Beginning to the Thirteenth Century*, Collegeville, MN 1998

Papandrea, James L., *Novatian of Rome and the Culmination of Pre-Nicene Orthodoxy*, Eugene, Oregon 2012 (PTMS 175)

Parisot, Jean, *Patrologia Syriaca*, pars I: Ab initiis usque ad annum 350, vol. I, Paris 1894

Parker, David C., *An Introduction to the New Testament Manuscripts and their Texts*, Cambridge 2008

Parmentier, Leon/Hansen, Günther Christian (eds.), *Theodoret – Kirchengeschichte*, third ed., Berlin/New York 1998 (repr. 2009; GCS NF 5)

Parmentier, Martien/Rouwhorst, Gerard, 'Early Christian Baptismal Questions and Creeds', *Bijdr.* 62 (2001), pp. 455–66

Parvis, Paul, 'Constantine's Letter to Arius and Alexander', in: *StPatr*, vol. XXXIX, 2006, pp. 89–95

Parvis, Sara, *Marcellus of Ancyra and the Lost Years of the Arian Controversy 325–345*, Oxford etc. 2006 (OECS)

Pasquato, Ottorino/Brakmann, Heinzgerd, art. 'Katechese (Katechismus)', in: *RAC*, vol. XX, 2004, cols. 422–96

Pass, H. Leonard, 'The Creed of Aphraates', *JThS* 9 (1908), pp. 267–84

Patzold, Steffen, '*Pater noster*: Priests and the Religious Instruction of the Laity in the Carolingian *populus christianus*', in: id./Van Rhijn 2016, pp. 199–221

Patzold, Steffen, *Presbyter: Moral, Mobilität und die Kirchenorganisation im Karolingerreich*, Stuttgart 2020 (MGMA 68)

Patzold, Steffen/Van Rhijn, Carine (eds.), *Men in the Middle: Local Priests in Early Medieval Europe*, Berlin/Boston 2016 (RGA.E 93)

Peitz, Wilhelm M., 'Das Glaubensbekenntnis der Apostel', *Stimmen der Zeit* 94 (1918), pp. 553–66

Pelikan, Jaroslav, *Credo: Historical and Theological Guide to Creeds and Confessions of Faith in the Christian Tradition*, New Haven/London 2003

Pelikan, Jaroslav/Hotchkiss, Valerie, *Creeds and Confessions of Faith in the Christian Tradition*, 4 vols. and CD-ROM, New Haven/London 2003

Pennington, Kenneth, art. 'Anathema', in: *EBR*, vol. I, 2009, cols. 1097–9

Perrone, Lorenzo, 'Christus-Frömmigkeit im Zeitalter der christologischen Auseinandersetzungen: Das Zeugnis des Mönchtums von Gaza', in: Theresia Hainthaler/Dirk Ansorge/Ansgar Wucherpfennig (eds.), *Jesus der Christus im Glauben der einen Kirche: Christologie – Kirchen des Ostens – Ökumenische Dialoge*, Freiburg etc. 2019, pp. 187–216

Perrone, Lorenzo et al. (eds.), *Origenes Werke, Dreizehnter Band: Die neuen Psalmenhomilien. Eine kritische Edition des Codex Monacensis Graecus 314*, Berlin/Munich/Boston 2015 (GCS NF 19)

Peters, Albrecht, *Kommentar zu Luthers Katechismen*, vol. II: Der Glaube – *Das Apostolikum*, ed. by Gottfried Seebaß, Göttingen 1991

Petersen, Nils H., art. 'Credo', in: *EBR*, vol. V, 2012, cols. 1015–18

Pettit, Edward, *Anglo-Saxon Remedies, Charms, and Prayers from British Library MS Harley 585*: The Lacnunga, 2 vols., Lewiston/Lampeter 2001 (Mellen Critical Editions and Translations 6)

Pfisterer, Andreas, 'Origins and Transmission of Franco-Roman Chant', in: Everist/Kelly 2018, pp. 69–91

Phelan, Owen M., *The Formation of Christian Europe: The Carolingians, Baptism, and the* Imperium Christianum, Oxford 2014

Phrantzolas, Konstantinos G., ΟΣΙΟΥ ΕΦΡΑΙΜ ΤΟΥ ΣΥΡΟΥ ΕΡΓΑ, vol. VII, Thessaloniki 1998

Pietras, Henryk, *Council of Nicaea (325): Religious and Political Context, Documents, Commentaries*, Rome 2016

Pietri, Charles, *Roma Christiana: Recherches sur l'Église de Rome, son organisation, sa politique, son idéologie de Miltiade à Sixte III (311–440)*, 2 vols., Paris 1976 (BEFAR 224)

Pietri, Charles/Markschies, Christoph, 'Theologische Diskussionen zur Zeit Konstantins: Arius, der "arianische Streit" und das Konzil von Nizäa, die nachnizänischen Auseinandersetzungen bis 337', in: Pietri/Pietri 1996(2010), pp. 271–344

Pietri, Charles, 'Vom homöischen Arianismus zur neunizänischen Orthodoxie (361–385)', in: Charles Pietri/Luce Pietri (eds.), *Das Entstehen der einen Christenheit (250–430)*, Freiburg etc. 1996 (repr. 2010; GCh 2), pp. 417–61

Pietri, Charles/Pietri, Luce (eds.), *Das Entstehen der einen Christenheit (250–430)*, Freiburg etc. 1996 (repr. 2010; GCh 2)

Pietri, Luce (ed.), *Der lateinische Westen und der byzantinische Osten*, Freiburg etc. 2001 (repr. 2010; GCh 3)

Pignot, Matthieu, *The Catechumenate in Late Antique Africa (4th-6th Centuries)*, Leiden/Boston 2020 (SVigChr 162)

Pigott, Justin, *New Rome Wasn't Built in a Day: Rethinking Councils and Controversy at Early Constantinople 381–451*, Turnhout 2019 (Studia Antiqua Australiensia 9)

Pintaudi, Rosario, 'Filatterio su carta araba originale: Il simbolo Niceno-Costantinopolitano (*PL* III/ 960)', *Analecta Papyrologica* 13 (2001), pp. 47–53

Planchart, Alejandro E., 'Institutions and Foundations', in: Everist/Kelly 2018, pp. 627–73

Pogatscher, Alois, *Zur Lautlehre der griechischen, lateinischen und romanischen Lehnworte im Altenglischen*, Strassburg/London 1888 (QFSKG 64)

Pohlsander, Hans A., 'Constantia', *Ancient Society* 24 (1993), pp. 151–67

Pope, John C., *Homilies of Ælfric: A Supplementary Collection Being Twenty-one Full Homilies of his Middle and later Career for the Most Part not Previously Edited with Some Shorter Pieces Mainly Passages*

Added to the Second and Third Series: Edited from all the Known Manuscripts with Introduction, Notes, Latin Sources and a Glossary, London etc. 1967 (EETS 259)

Price, Richard, 'The Development of a Chalcedonian Identity in Byzantium (451–553)', *CHRC* 89 (2009), pp. 307–25

Price, Richard/Gaddis, Michael, *The Acts of the Council of Chalcedon: Translated with an Introduction and Notes*, 3 vols. Liverpool 2005 (Translated Texts for Historians 45)

Price, Richard/Graumann, Thomas, *The Council of Ephesus: Documents and Proceedings*. Translated by R.P. with introduction and notes by Th.G., Liverpool 2020 (Translated Texts for Historians 72)

Probst, Manfred, art. 'Credo', in: *LThK*, third ed., vol. II, 1994, cols. 1340 f.

Quecke, Hans, *Untersuchungen zum koptischen Stundengebet*, Leuven 1970 (PIOL 3)

Rabe, Susan A., *Faith, Art, and Politics at Saint-Riquier: The Symbolic Vision of Angilbert*, Philadelphia 1995 (University of Pennsylvania Press Middle Ages Series)

Rabin, Andrew, *The Political Writings of Archbishop Wulfstan of York: Selected Sources Edited and Translated*, Manchester 2015

Rabin, Andrew/Felsen, Liam, *The* Disputatio Puerorum: *A Ninth-Century Monastic Instructional Text.* Edited from Vienna, Österreichische Nationalbibliothek, 458, Toronto 2017 (TMLT 34)

Rabo, Gabriel, 'Dionysius Jacob Bar Ṣalibi's Confession of the Syrian Orthodox Faith', *Hekamtho* 1 (2015), pp. 20–39

Rad, Gerhard von, 'The Form-Critical Problem of the Hexateuch' [1938], in: id., *The Problem of the Hexateuch and Other Essays*, New York 1966, pp. 1–78

Rad, Gerhard von, *Old Testament Theology*, 2 vols., Edinburgh 1962/1965

Rad, Gerhard von, *Genesis: A Commentary*, revised ed., Philadelphia 1973 (OTL)

Rahmani, Ignatius Ephrem II, *Vetusta Documenta Liturgica Primo Edidit, Latine Vertit, Notis Illustravit*, Charfeh 1908 (Studia Syriaca 3)

Ramelli, Ilaria L.E., art. 'Aphrahat', in: *Brill Encyclopedia of Early Christianity online*, 2018; URL <http://dx.doi.org/10.1163/2589-7993_EECO_SIM_00000212> (29/11/2023)

Ramelli, Ilaria L.E., art. 'De recta in Deum fide', in: *Brill Encyclopedia of Early Christianity online*, 2018; URL <http://dx.doi.org/10.1163/2589-7993_EECO_SIM_036558> (29/11/2023)

Rapp Jr., Stephen H., 'Georgian Christianity', in: Parry 2007, pp. 137–55

Rapp Jr., Stephen H., 'The Making of *K'art'lis c'xovreba*, the So-Called Georgian Chronicles', *SE* 56 (2017), pp. 465–88

Ratzinger, Joseph, art. 'Emanation', in: *RAC*, vol. IV, 1959, cols. 1219–28

Rauer, Max,*Origenes Werke*, vol. IX: Die Homilien zu Lukas in der Übersetzung des Hieronymus und die griechischen Reste der Homilien und des Lukas-Kommentars, second ed., Berlin 1959 (GCS)

Raven, Charles E., *Apollinarianism: An Essay on the Christology of the Early Church*, Cambridge 1923

Raw, Barbara C., *Trinity and Incarnation in Anglo-Saxon Art and Thought*, Cambridge 1997 (CSASE 21)

Raynaud de Lage, Guy, 'Deux questions sur la foi inspirées d'Alain de Lille: Bibliothèque Nationale, manuscrit latin 2504', *AHDL* 14 (1943–1945), pp. 323–36, 609

Reeves, Andrew, 'Teaching the Creed and Articles of Faith in England: 1215–1281', in: Ronald J. Stansbury (ed.), *A Companion to Pastoral Care in the Late Middle Ages (1200–1500)*, Leiden/Boston 2010 (Brill's Companions to the Christian Tradition 22), pp. 41–72

Reischl, Wilhelm K./Rupp, Joseph, *S. Patris Nostri Cyrilli Hierosolymorum Archiepiscopi Opera Quae Supersunt Omnia*, 2 vols., Munich 1848/1860

Renaudot, Eusèbe, *Liturgiarum Orientalium Collectio*, vol. I, Frankfurt a.M./London 1847

Reu, Johann M., *Quellen zur Geschichte des kirchlichen Unterrichts in der evangelischen Kirche Deutschlands zwischen 1530 und 1600*, 10 vols., Gütersloh 1904–1935

Reutter, Ursula, *Damasus, Bischof von Rom (366–384): Leben und Werk*, Tübingen 2009 (STAC 55)

Rexer, Jochen, 'Die Entwicklung des liturgischen Jahres in altkirchlicher Zeit', *JBTh* 18 (2003), pp. 279–305

Reynolds, Gabriel S., *The Qur'ān and the Bible: Text and Commentary*, New Haven/London 2018

Ridley, Ronald T., *Zosimus – New History: A Translation with Commentary*, Canberra 1982 (Australian Association for Byzantine Studies/Byzantina Australiensia 2)

Riedel, Wilhelm, *Die Kirchenrechtsquellen des Patriarchats Alexandrien: Zusammengestellt und zum Teil übersetzt*, Leipzig 1900

Riedinger, Rudolf/Thurn, Hans, 'Die Didascalia CCCVIII Patrum Nicaenorum und das Syntagma ad monachos im Codex Parisinus graecus 1115 (a. 1276)', *JÖB* 35 (1985), pp. 75–92

Riedl, Gerda, *Hermeneutische Grundstrukturen frühchristlicher Bekenntnisbildung*, Berlin/New York 2004 (TBT 123)

Riedlberger, Peter, *Prolegomena zu den spätantiken Konstitutionen: Nebst einer Analyse der erbrechtlichen und verwandten Sanktionen gegen Heterodoxe*, Stuttgart 2020

Rist, Josef, 'Die Synode von Serdika 343: Das Scheitern eines ökumenischen Konzils und seine Folgen für die Einheit der Reichskirche', in: Roald Dijkstra/Sanne van Poppel/Daniëlle Slootjes (eds.), *East and Weist in the Roman Empire of the Fourth Century*, Leiden/Boston 2015, pp. 63–81

Ristow, Sebastian, *Frühchristliche Baptisterien*, Münster, Westfalen 1998 (JbAC.E 27)

Ritter, Adolf Martin, *Das Konzil von Konstantinopel und sein Symbol: Studien zur Geschichte und Theologie des II. Ökumenischen Konzils*, Göttingen 1965 (FKDG 15)

Ritter, Adolf Martin, 'Zum Homousios von Nizäa und Konstantinopel: Kritische Nachlese zu einigen neueren Diskussionen' [1979], in: id., *Chrisma und Caritas: Aufsätze zur Geschichte der Alten Kirche*, Göttingen 1993, pp. 161–79

Ritter, Adolf Martin, art. 'Glaubensbekenntnis(se), V. Alte Kirche', in: *TRE*, vol. XIII, 1984, pp. 399–412

Ritter, Adolf Martin, art. 'Konstantinopel (Ökumenische Synoden I)', in: *TRE*, vol. XIX, 1990, pp. 518–24

Ritter, Adolf Martin, 'Creeds', in: Ian Hazlett (ed.), *Early Christianity: Origins and Evolution to AD 600. In Honour of W H C Frend*, London 1991, pp. 92–100

Ritter, Adolf Martin, 'Noch einmal: "Was hat das Nicaeno-Constantinopolitanum (C) mit dem Konzil von Konstantinopel zu tun?"', *ThPh* 68 (1993), pp. 553–60

Ritter, Adolf Martin, review of Gerber 2000, *ZAC* 8 (2004), pp. 137–40

Ritter, Adolf Martin, 'Dogma und Lehre in der Alten Kirche', in: Carl Andresen et al., *Die christlichen Lehrentwicklungen bis zum Ende des Spätmittelalters*, bearbeitet von Adolf Martin Ritter, new ed., Göttingen 2011, pp. 99–288

Ritter, Adolf Martin, 'The "Three Main Creeds" of the Lutheran Reformation and their Specific Contexts: Testimonies and Commentaries', in: *StPatr*, vol. LXIII, 2013, pp. 287–311

Ritter, Adolf Martin, 'Die altkirchlichen Symbole', in: Dingel 2014, pp. 35–60

Rituale Romanum Ex veteri Ecclesiae usu restitutum. Gregorii XIII. Pont. Max. Iussu Editum, Rome: Ex typographia Dominici Basae 1584

Rodwell, John M., *Aethiopic Liturgies and Prayers: Translated from MSS. in the Library of the British Museum and of the British and Foreign Bible Society, and from the Edition Printed at Rome in 1548*, London 1864

Rodwell, John M., *Aethiopic Prayers and Baptismal Offices, and Selections from the Degua or Hymnal of Jared; Including Hymns of the Abyssinian Church, and Prayers: Translated from MSS. in the Library of the British Museum and of the British and Foreign Bible Society, and from the Edition Printed at Rome in 1548*, London 1867

Römer, Cornelia E., 'Ostraka mit christlichen Texten aus der Sammlung Flinders Petrie', *ZPE* 145 (2003), pp. 183–2001

Rösch, Gerhard, *ONOMA BAΣIΛEIAΣ: Studien zum offiziellen Gebrauch der Kaisertitel in spätantiker und frühbyzantinischer Zeit*, Vienna 1978 (ByV 10)

Roldanus, Johannes, *The Church in the Age of Constantine: The Theological Challenges*, Abingdon/ New York 2006

[Rolle, Richard,] *D. Richardi Pampolitani eremitae, scriptoris perquam vetusti ac eruditi, de Emendatione peccatoris opusculum, nunc primum typis excusum, cum alijs aliquot appendicibus, quas versa indicabit pagella*, Cologne 1535

Romano, John F., *Liturgy and Society in Early Medieval Rome*, Farnham/Burlington 2014

Romano, John F., 'Baptizing the Romans', *AAAHP* 31 (2019), pp. 43–62

Rordorf, Willy, 'Hérésie et orthodoxie selon la Correspondance apocryphe entre les Corinthiens et l'apôtre Paul', in: *Hérésie et orthodoxie dans l'Église ancienne* (Cahier de la RThPh 17), 1993, pp. 21–63 (quoted thereafter); also in: id. *Lex orandi, lex credendi: Gesammelte Aufsätze zum 60. Geburtstag*, Freiburg, Schweiz 1993 (Par. 36), pp. 389–431 (no. XXV)

Rose, Eugen, *Die manichäische Christologie*, Wiesbaden 1979 (StOR 5)

Rossi, Francesco, 'Trascrizione di alcuni testi copti tratti dai papiri del Museo Egizio di Torino con traduzione italiana e note', in: *MAST.M*, vol. XXXVI, Turin 1885, pp. 89–182

Rouwhorst, Gerard A.M., art. 'Taufe I (Liturgie, Theologie)', in: RAC, vol. XXXI, 2022, cols. 976–1016

Rubellin, Michel, 'Entrée dans la vie, entrée dans la chrétienté, entrée dans la société: Autour du baptême à l'époque carolingienne', in: *Les entrées dans la vie: Initiations et apprentissages. XIIe Congrès de la Société des historiens médiévistes de l'enseignement supérieur public, Nancy 1981*, Nancy 1982, pp. 31–51 (AEst, série 5, no. 1/2; numéro spécial)

Rucker, Ignaz, *Ephesinische Konzilsakten in armenisch-georgischer Überlieferung*, Munich 1930 (SBAW.PH 1930, Heft 3)

Rüpke, Jörg, *Fasti sacerdotum. Die Mitglieder der Priesterschaften und das sakrale Funktionspersonal römischer, griechischer, orientalischer und jüdisch-christlicher Kulte in der Stadt Rom von 300 v. Chr. bis 499 n. Chr., Teil 3: Beiträge zur Quellenkunde und Organisationsgeschichte. Bibliographie. Register*, Wiesbaden 2005 (Potsdamer Altertumswissenschaftliche Beiträge 12/3)

Rüpke, Jörg, *Religion of the Romans*, Cambridge 2007

Rüpke, Jörg, *On Roman Religion: Lived Religion and the Individual in Ancient Rome*, Ithaca/London 2016 (Townsend Lectures/CSCP)

Ruiz Asencio, José M., 'Pizarra visigoda con Credo', in: Manuel C. Díaz y Díaz/Manuela Domínguez García/Mercedes Díaz de Bustamante (eds.), *Escritos dedicados a José María Fernández Catón*, vol. II, León 2004, pp. 1317–28

Russin, Harrison B., *'I believe': The Credo in Music, 1300 to 1500*, PhD diss., Duke University 2021

Sachot, Maurice, art. 'Homilie', in: *RAC*, vol. XVI, 1994, cols. 148–75

Sader, Jean, *Le De oblatione de Jean de Dara*, Leuven 1970 (CSCO 308/Scriptores Syri 1970)

Sághy, Marianne, art. 'Liberius (Bishop of Rome)', in: *Brill Encyclopedia of Early Christianity Online*, 2018; URL <http://dx.doi.org/10.1163/2589-7993_EECO_SIM_036561> (29/11/2023)

Sako, Louis R., *Lettre christologique du patriarche syro-oriental Īšōʿyahb II de Gḏālā (628–646): Étude, traduction et édition critique*, Rome 1983

Sako, Louis R., *Le rôle de la hierarchie syriaque orientale dans les rapports diplomatiques entre la Perse et Byzance aux Ve – VIIe siècles*, Paris 1986

Salamito, Jean-Marie, 'Christianisierung und Neuordnung des gesellschaftlichen Lebens', in: Pietri/ Pietri 1996(2010), pp. 768–815

Salisbury, Joyce E., *Iberian Popular Religion 600 B.C. to 700 A.D.: Celts, Romans and Visigoths*, New York/ Toronto 1985 (TSR 20)

Sallmann, Klaus (ed.), *Die Literatur des Umbruchs von der römischen zur christlichen Literatur*, 117 bis 284 n. Chr., Munich 1997 (HLLA IV)

Salzmann, Jorg C., *Lehren und Ermahnen: Zur Geschichte des christlichen Wortgottesdienstes in den ersten drei Jahrhunderten*, Tübingen 1994 (WUNT II/59)

Samir, Samir K., 'Bibliographie du dialogue islamo-chrétien: Élie de Nisibe (Iliyyâ al-Naṣîbî) (975– 1046)', *IslChr* 3 (1977), pp. 257–86; also in: id., Foi et culture en Irak au XIe siècle: Elie de Nisibe et l'Islam, Aldershot, Hampshire/Brookfield, Vermont 1996 (CSS 544), no. I

Sandler, Lucy F., *The Psalter of Robert de Lisle in the British Library*, London etc. 1983

Santer, Mark, 'ΕΚ ΠΝΕΥΜΑΤΟΣ ἉΓΙΟΥ ΚΑΙ ΜΑΡΙΑΣ ΤΗΣ ΠΑΡΘΕΝΟΥ', *JThS* 22 (1971), pp. 162–7

Sanzo, Joseph E., *Scriptural* Incipits on Amulets from Late Antique Egypt: Text, Typology, and Theory, Tübingen 2014 (STAC 84)

Sarot, Marcel/Van Wieringen, Archibald L.H.M. (eds.), *The Apostles' Creed*: 'He Descended Into Hell', Leiden 2018 (STAR 24)

Sartori, Paul, art. 'Niesen', in: *HWDA*, vol. VI, 1934/1935, cols. 1072–83

Saxer, Victor, *Morts, martyrs, reliques en Afrique chrétienne aux premiers siècles: Les témoignages de Tertullien, Cyprien et Augustin à la lumière de l'archéologie africaine*, Paris 1980 (ThH 55)

Saxer, Victor, *Les rites de l'initiation chrétienne du IIe au VIe siècle: Esquisse historique et signification d'après leurs principaux témoins*, Spoleto 1988 (Centro Italiano di Studi sull'Alto Medioevo 7)

Schäferdiek, Knut, *Schwellenzeit: Beiträge zur Geschichte des Christentums in Spätantike und Frühmittelalter*, ed. by Winrich A. Löhr/Hanns C. Brennecke, Berlin/New York 1996 (AKG 64)

Schäferdiek, Knut, 'Die Anfänge des Christentums bei den Goten und der sog. gotische Arianismus', *ZKG* 112 (2001), pp. 295–310

Schäferdiek, Knut, 'Der gotische Arianismus', *ThLZ* 129 (2004), cols. 587–94

Schäferdiek, Knut, art. 'Wulfila (Ulfila) *(gest. 383)*', in: *TRE*, vol. XXXVI, 2004, pp. 374–8

Schaff, Philip, *The Creeds of Christendom with a History and Critical Notes*, 3 vols., New York 1877 (Bibliotheca Symbolica Ecclesiae Universalis); sixth ed., revised and enlarged [by David S. Schaff] 1931

Scheibelreiter, Philipp, art. 'Schande', in: *RAC*, vol. XXIX, 2019, cols. 699–726

Schermann, Theodor (ed.), *Prophetarum Vitae Fabulosae Indices Apostolorum Discipulorumque Domini Dorotheo Epiphanio Hippolyto Aliisque Vindicata inter quae nonnulla primum edidit recensuit schedis vir. cl. Henr. Gelzer usus prolegomenis indicibus testimoniis appparatu critico instruxit*, Leipzig 1907 (BSGRT)

Schermann, Theodor, *Propheten- und Apostellegenden nebst Jüngerkatalogen des Dorotheus und verwandter Texte*, Leipzig 1907 (TU 31)

Scherrer, Gustav, *Verzeichniß der Handschriften der Stiftsbibliothek von St. Gallen*, Halle 1875

Schindler, Alfred, art. 'Catholicus, -a', in: *AugL*, vol. I, 1986–1994, cols 815–19

Schlager, Karlheinz, 'Eine Melodie zum griechischen Credo', *AMl* 56 (1984), pp. 221–34

Schlager, Karlheinz, Art. Credo, in: *MGG*, second ed., Sachteil, vol. II, 1995, cols. 1036–40

Schlier, Heinrich, 'art. ᾄδω, ᾠδή', in: *TDNT*, vol. I, 1964, pp. 163–5

Schmitz, Hermann J., *Die Bußbücher und die Bußdisciplin der Kirche*, vol. II: Die Bußbücher und das kanonische Bußverfahren nach handschriftlichen Quellen dargestellt, Düsseldorf 1898

Schmitz, Josef, *Gottesdienst im altchristlichen Mailand: Eine liturgiewissenschaftliche Untersuchung über Initiation und Meßfeier während des Jahres zur Zeit des Bischofs Ambrosius († 397)*, Cologne/Bonn 1975 (Theoph. 25)

Schneemelcher, Wilhelm, 'Die Kirchweihsynode von Antiochien 341' [1977], in: id., *Reden und Aufsätze: Beiträge zur Kirchengeschichte und zum ökumenischen Gespräch*, Tübingen 1991, pp. 94–125

Schneider, Carl, art. 'Fides', in: *RAC*, vol. VII, 1969, cols. 801–39

Schöllgen, Georg/Geerlings, Wilhelm, *Didache – Zwölf-Apostel-Lehre/Traditio Apostolica – Apostolische Überlieferung*, third ed., Freiburg etc. 2000 (FC 1)

Schönbach, Anton E., 'Eine Auslese altdeutscher Segensformeln', in: *Analecta Graeciensia: Festschrift zur 42. Versammlung deutscher Philologen und Schulmänner in Wien 1893*, Graz 1893, pp. 25–50

Schulthess, Friedrich, *Die syrischen Kanones der Synoden von Nicaea bis Chalcedon nebst einigen zugehörigen Dokumenten*, Berlin 1908 (AGWG.PH N.F. 10/2)

Schwab, Moïse, 'Le Credo traduit en hébreu et transcrit en caractères latins', *REJ* 45 (1902), pp. 296–8

Schwartz, Eduard, 'Die Aktenbeilagen in den Athanasiushandschriften' [1904], in: id. 1959, pp. 73–85

Schwartz, Eduard, 'Die Dokumente des arianischen Streits bis 325' [1905], in: id. 1959, pp. 117–68

Schwartz, Eduard, 'Das Nicaenum und das Constantinopolitanum auf der Synode von Chalkedon', *ZNW* 25 (1926), pp. 38–88

Schwartz, Eduard, *Cyrill und der Mönch Viktor*, Wien/Leipzig 1928 (SAWW.PH 208/4)

Schwartz, Eduard, *Der sechste nicaenische Kanon auf der Synode von Chalkedon*, Berlin 1930 (= SPAW.PH 27, 1930, pp. 611–40)

Schwartz, Eduard, 'Über die Sammlung des Cod. Veronensis LX', *ZNW* 35 (1936), pp. 1–23

Schwartz, Eduard, 'Zur Kirchengeschichte des 4. Jahrhunderts' [1935], in: id. 1960, pp. 1–110

Schwartz, Eduard, 'Die Kanonessammlungen der alten Reichskirche' [1936], in: id. 1960, pp. 159–275

Schwartz, Eduard., *Gesammelte Schriften*, vol. III: Zur Geschichte des Athanasius, ed. by Walther Eltester und Hans-Dietrich Altendorf, Berlin 1959

Schwartz, Eduard, *Gesammelte Schriften*, vol. IV: Zur Geschichte der Alten Kirche und ihres Rechts, ed. by Walther Eltester und Hans-Dietrich Altendorf, Berlin 1960

Schwartz, Eduard, *Drei dogmatische Schriften Iustinians*, second ed. by Mario Amelotti/Rosangela Albertella/Livia Migliardi, Milan 1973 (Legum Iustiniani Imperatoris Vocabularium. Subsidia 2)

Schwartz, Eduard/Mommsen, Theodor, *Eusebius – Werke*, vol. II Die Kirchengeschichte, Zweiter Teil: Die Bücher VI bis X/Über die Märtyrer in Palästina, Leipzig 1908 (GCS 9/2 = repr. 1999, GCS N.F. 6/2)

Schwarz, Hans, art. 'Glaubensbekenntnis(se), VII. Reformationszeit bis 17. Jh.', in: *TRE*, vol. XIII, 1984, pp. 416–29

Schwarz, Hans, art. 'Glaubensbekenntnis(se), VIII. 18. Jahrhundert bis Neuzeit', in: *TRE*, vol. XIII, 1984, pp. 430–7

Schwertner, Siegfried M., *IATG³ – Internationales Abkürzungsverzeichnis für Theologie und Grenzgebiete: Zeitschriften, Serien, Lexika, Quellenwerke mit bibliographischen Angaben*, third ed., Berlin/Boston 2014

Seeberg, Reinhold, 'Zur Geschichte der Entstehung des apostolischen Symbols', *ZKG* 40 (1922), pp. 1–41

Sehrt, Edward H. (ed.), *Notkers des Deutschen Werke: Nach den Handschriften neu herausgegeben*, vol. II/3: Der Psalter. Psalmus CI–CL. nebst Cantica und katechetischen Stücken, Halle, Saale 1955

Seibt, Klaus, 'Beobachtungen zur Verfasserfrage der pseudoathanasianischen "Expositio fidei"', in: Brennecke/Grasmück/Markschies 1993, pp. 281–96

Seibt, Klaus, *Die Theologie des Markell von Ankyra*, Berlin/New York 1994 (AKG 59)

Seidler, Martin, *Der Schrein des Heiligen Heribert in Köln-Deutz*, Regensburg 2016

Selb, Walter, *Orientalisches Kirchenrecht*, vol. II: Die Geschichte des Kirchenrechts der Westsyrer (von den Anfängen bis zur Mongolenzeit), Wien 1989 (SÖAW.PH 543/Veröffentlichungen der Kommission für Antike Rechtsgeschichte 6)

Sieben, Hermann-Josef, *Tertullian – Adversus Praxeas: Im Anhang: Hippolyt – Contra Noëtum/Gegen Noët, übersetzt und eingeleitet*, Freiburg 2001 (FC 34)

Sieben, Hermann-Josef, *Vetustissimae Epistulae Romanorum Pontificum: Die ältesten Papstbriefe, eingeleitet und herausgegeben von H.-J. S.*, 3 vols., Freiburg im Breisgau 2014/2015 (FC 58)

Siebigs, Gereon, *Kaiser Leo I.: Das oströmische Reich in den ersten drei Jahren seiner Regierung (457–460 n. Chr.)*, 2 vols., Berlin 2010

Siecienski, A. Edward, *The Filioque: History of a Doctrinal Controversy*, Oxford etc. 2010

Simonetti, Manlio, *La crisi ariana nel IV secolo*, Rome 1975 (SEAug 11)

Simperl, Matthias, *Das Schreiben der Synode von Antiochia 324/325 (Urk. 18): Überlieferungsgeschichtliche Einordnung, Edition, Übersetzung und Kommentar*, unpublished diss., Augsburg 2022 (forthcoming in *TU*, Berlin/Boston 2024)

Sims-Williams, Nicholas/Schwartz, Martin/Pittard, William J. (eds.), *Biblical and other Christian Sogdian Texts from the Turfan Collection*, Turnhout 2014 (Berliner Turfantexte 32)

Skeat, Walter W. (ed.), *Aelfric's Lives of Saints: A Set of Sermons on Saints' Days formerly observed by the English Church*, 2 vols., London 1881–1900 (EETS 76, 82, 94, 114)

Smith, Joseph P., *St. Irenaeus: Proof of the Apostolic Preaching. Translated and Annotated*, Westminster, Maryland/London 1952 (ACW 16)

Smith, Mark S., *The Idea of Nicaea in the Early Church Councils, AD 431–451*, Oxford 2018 (OECS)

Smith, Shawn C., 'The Insertion of the *Filioque* into the Nicene Creed and a Letter of Isidore of Seville', *JECS* 22 (2014), pp. 261–86

Smulders, Pieter, 'Some Riddles in the Apostles' Creed', *Bijdr.* 31 (1970), pp. 234–60; 32 (1971), pp. 350–66; 41 (1980), pp. 3–15

Smulders, Pieter, 'The *Sitz im Leben* of the Old Roman Creed: New Conclusions from Neglected Data', in: *StPatr*, vol. XIII/2, 1975 (TU 116), pp. 409–21

Smyth, Marina, 'The Seventh-Century Hiberno-Latin Treatise *Liber de ordine creaturarum*: A Translation', *Journal of Medieval Latin* 21 (2011), pp. 137–222

Sode, Claudia, *Jerusalem – Konstantinopel – Rom: Die Viten des Michael Synkellos und der Brüder Theodoros und Theophanes Graptoi*, Stuttgart 2001 (Altertumswissenschaftliches Kolloquium 4)

Speyer, Wolfgang, art. 'Fluch', in: *RAC*, vol. VII, 1969, cols. 1160–288

Spiazzi, Raimondo M./Calcaterra, Mannes, *S. Thomae Aquinatis Doctoris Angelici Opuscula Theologica*, vol. II: *De re spirituali cura et studio R.M.S., accedit Expositio super Boetium De Trinitate et De Hebdomadibus cura et studio M.C.*, Turin/Rome 1954

Spinks, Bryan D., *Early and Medieval Rituals and Theologies of Baptism: From the New Testament to the Council of Trent*, Farnham, Surrey/Burlington, VT 2006 (repr. 2016; Liturgy, Worship and Society)

Spinks, Bryan D., *Do This in Remembrance of Me: The Eucharist from the Early Church to the Present Day*, London 2013 (SCM Studies in Worship and Liturgy)

Spoerl, Kelly McC., 'Photinus of Sirmium', in: *Brill Encyclopedia of Early Christianity online*, 2022; URL <http://dx.doi.org/10.1163/2589-7993_EECO_SIM_00002752> (27/11/2023)

Staats, Reinhart, 'Die römische Tradition im Symbol von 381 (NC) und seine Entstehung auf der Synode von Antiochien 379', *VigChr* 44 (1990), pp. 209–21

Staats, Reinhart, art. 'Messalianer', in: *TRE*, vol. XXII, 1992, pp. 607–13

Staats, Reinhart, *Das Glaubensbekenntnis von Nizäa-Konstantinopel: Historische und theologische Grundlagen*, second ed., Darmstadt 1999

Staats, Reinhart, 'Das Taufbekenntnis in der frühen Kirche', in: Hellholm et al. 2011, vol. II, pp. 1553–83

Stäblein, Bruno, art. 'Credo', in: *MGG*, vol. II, 1952, 1769–73

Stammler, Wolfgang, 'Mittelalterliche Prosa in deutscher Sprache', in: id. (ed.) *Deutsche Philologie im Aufriß*, vol. II, second ed., Berlin 1960 (repr. 1978), cols. 749–1102

Stark, Rodney, *The Rise of Christianity: How the Obscure, Marginal Jesus Movement Became the Dominant Religious Force in the Western World in a Few Centuries*, Princeton, N.J. 1996 (PB n.p. 1997)

Stead, Christopher, *Divine Substance*, Oxford 1977

Stead, Christopher, art. 'Homousios (ὁμοούσιος)', in: *RAC*, vol. XVI, 1994, cols. 364–433

Steenson, Jeffrey/DelCogliano, Mark, 'Basil of Ancyra, *The Synodal Letter of the Council of Ancyra*', in: Andrew Radde-Gallwitz (ed.), *The Cambridge Edition of Early Christian Writings*, Cambridge 2017, pp. 134–49

Steer, Georg, art. 'Glaubensbekenntnisse (Deutsche Übersetzungen und Auslegungen)', in: *VerLex*, second ed., vol. XI, 2004, cols. 529–42

Steimer, Bruno, *Vertex Traditionis: Die Gattung der altchristlichen Kirchenordnungen*, Berlin/New York 1992 (BZNW 63)

Stein, Evina, 'Early Medieval Catechetic Collections Containig Material from the *Etymologiae* and the Place of Isidore of Seville in Carolingian *Correctio*', in: Sinéad O'Sullivan/Arthur Ciaran (eds.), *Crafting Knowledge in the Early Medieval Book: Practices of Collecting and Concealing in the Latin West*, Turnhout 2023 (Publications of the Journal of Medieval Latin 16), pp. 315–56

Steinacker, Harold, *Die antiken Grundlagen der frühmittelalterlichen Privaturkunde*, Leipzig/Berlin 1927 (GdG Ergänzungsband 1)

Stenzel, Alois, *Die Taufe: Eine genetische Erklärung der Taufliturgie*, Innsbruck 1958 (FGTh 7/8)

Stephens, Christopher, *Canon Law and Episcopal Authority: The Canons of Antioch and Serdica*, Oxford 2015 (Oxford Theology and Religion Monographs)

Stępień, Tomasz, art. 'Ousia', in: *Brill Encyclopedia of Early Christianity Online*, 2018; URL <http://dx.doi.org/10.1163/2589-7993_EECO_SIM_00002497> (29/11/2023)

Stepper, Ruth, 'Zum Verzicht Kaiser Gratians auf den Oberpontifikat', in: Carles Rabassa/Ruth Stepper (eds.), *Imperios sacros, monarquías divinas/Heilige Herrscher, göttliche Monarchien*, Castelló de la Plana 2002 (Collecció Humanitats 10), pp. 39–55

Stepper, Ruth, *Augustus et sacerdos: Untersuchungen zum römischen Kaiser als Priester*, Stuttgart 2003 (Potsdamer Altertumswissenschaftliche Beiträge 9).

Stevenson, James/Frend, William H.C., *A New Eusebius: Documents Illustrating the History of the Church to AD 337*, London 1987

Stewart-Sykes, Alistair C., *From Prophecy to Preaching: A Search for the Origins of the Christian Homily*, Leiden 2001 (SVigChr 59)

Stewart-Sykes, Alistair C., '*Traditio Apostolica*: The Liturgy of Third-century Rome and the Hippolytan School or *Quomodo historia liturgica conscribenda sit*', *SVTQ* 48 (2004), pp. 233–48

Stewart-Sykes, Alistair C., 'The Baptismal Creed in *Traditio Apostolica*: Original or Expanded?, *QuLi* 90 (2009), pp. 199–213

Stewart-Sykes, Alistair C., *The Didascalia apostolorum: An English Version Edited, Introduced and Annotated*, Turnhout 2009 (StTT 1)

Stewart(-Sykes), Alistair C., *Hippolytus – On the Apostolic Tradition: An English Version with Introduction and Commentary*, second ed.,Yonkers, New York 2015 (SVPPS 54)

Stewart(-Sykes), Alistair C., *The Canons of Hippolytus: An English Version, with Introduction and Annotation and an Accompanying Arabic Text*, Sydney 2021 (Early Christian Studies 22)

Stiglmayr, Josef, 'Das "Quicunque" und Fulgentius von Ruspe', *ZKTh* 49 (1925), pp. 341–57

Stiglmayr, Josef, Der im sog. Symbolum Athanasianum verwendete Vergleich der Einheit von Leib und Seele mit der Einheit der zwei Naturen in Christus, *ZKTh* 49 (1925), pp. 628–32

Stiglmayr, Josef, art. 'Athanase (Le prétendu symbole d')', in: *DHGE*, vol. IV, 1930, cols. 1341–8

Stockhausen, Annette von/Brennecke, Hanns C. (eds.), *Von Arius zum Athanasianum: Studien zur Edition der 'Athanasius Werke'*, Berlin/New York 2010 (TU 164)

Stopka, Krysztof, *Armenia Christiana: Armenian Religious Identity and the Churches of Constantinoplr and Rome (4ᵗʰ–15ᵗʰ Century)*, Cracow 2016

Storms, Godfrid, *Anglo-Saxon Magic*, The Hague 1948

Stow, Kenneth R., 'Conversion, Christian Hebraism, and Hebrew Prayer in the Sixteenth Century', *HUCA* 47 (1976), pp. 217–36

Strutwolf, Holger, *Die Trinitätstheologie und Christogie des Euseb von Caesarea: Eine dogmengeschichtliche Untersuchung seiner Platonismusrezeption und Wirkungsgeschichte*, Göttingen 1999 (FKDG 72)

Strutwolf, Holger, 'Das Konzil von Antiochien 324/5 und sein vermeintliches Symbol – einige metakritische Bemerkungen', *ZKG* 122 (2011), pp. 301–23

Stuiber, Alfred, art. 'Doxologie', in: *RAC*, vol. IV, 1959, cols. 210–26

Stutz, Jonathan, *Constantinus Arabicus: Die arabische Geschichtsschreibung und das christliche Rom*, Piscataway, NJ 2017 (Islamic History and Thought 4)

Stutz, Jonathan, 'The Writings of Mārūtā of Maipherqat and the Making of Nicaea in Arabic', *JEastCS* 71 (2019), pp. 1–28

Suermann, Harald, 'Die syrische Liturgie im syrisch-palästinensischen Raum in vor- und frühislamischer Zeit', in: Tilmann Nagel/Elisabeth Müller-Luckner (eds.), *Der Koran und sein religiöses und kulturelles Umfeld*, Munich 2010 (Schriften des Historischen Kollegs/Kolloquien 72), pp. 157–72

Suolahti, Jaakko, *The Roman Censors: A Study on Social Structure*, Helsinki 1963 (STAT.H 117)

Swainson, Charles A., *The Nicene and Apostles' Creeds: Their Literary History; Together with an Account of the Growth and Reception of the Sermon on the Faith Commonly Called 'The Creed of St Athanasius'*, London 1875

Swanson, Dwight D./Satlow, Michael, art. 'Faith, III. Judaism', in: *EBR*, vol. VIII, 2014, cols. 701–4

Sweeney, Marvin A./Dormeyer, Detlev, art. 'Form Criticism', in: *EBR*, vol. IX, 2014, cols. 468–74

Taft, Robert F., *The Great Entrance: A History of the Transfer of Gifts and other Pre-anaphoral Rites of the Liturgy of St. John Chrysostom*, second ed., Rome 1978 (OCA 200)

Taft, Robert F., *The Liturgy of the Hours in East and West: The Origins of the Divine Office and Its Meaning for Today*, Collegeville, Minnesota 1986

Taft, Robert F., *The Byzantine Rite: A Short History*, Collegeville, Minnesota 1992 (American Essays in Liturgy Series)

Taft, Robert F., 'The Pontifical Liturgy of the Great Church according to a Twelfth-Century Diataxis in Codex *British Museum Add. 34060*, *Orientalia Christiana Periodica* 45 (1979), pp. 279–307; 46 (1980), pp. 89–124; also in: id., *Liturgy in Byzantium and Beyond*, Aldershot, Hampshire/Brookfield, Vermont 1995 (CStS CS 493), no. II (additional notes and comments on pp. 1–2)

Taft, Robert F., '*Quaestiones disputatae*: The Skeuophylakion of Hagia Sophia and the Entrances of the Liturgy Revisited', *OrChr* 82 (1998), pp. 53–87

Taft, Robert F., *Through their Own Eyes: Liturgy as the Byzantines Saw it*, Berkeley Calif. 2006 (The Paul G. Manolis Distinguished Lectures 2005; *non uidi*)

Tarchnišvili, Michael, *Geschichte der kirchlichen georgischen Literatur*, Vatican City 1955 (StT 185)

Tax, Petrus W., 'Notkers Erklärung des Athanasianischen Glaubensbekenntnisses und seine angebliche Schrift *De sancta trinitate*', in: Frithjof A. Raven/Wolfram K. Legner/James C. King (eds.), *Germanic Studies in Honor of Edward Henry Sehrt, Presented by his Colleagues, Students, and Friends on the Occasion of His Eightieth Birthday, March 3, 1968*, Coral Gables, Florida 1968 (Miami Linguistic Series 1), pp. 219–28

Tax, Petrus W., *Notker latinus: Die Quellen zu den Psalmen. Psalm 1–50*, Tübingen 1972 (ADTB 74)

Tax, Petrus W. (ed.), *Notker der Deutsche: Der Psalter., Psalm 101–150, die Cantica und die katechetischen Texte*, Tübingen 1983

Taylor, Justin, art. 'Apostles, The Twelve', in: *EBR*, vol. II, 2009, cols. 493–8

ter Haar Romeny, Bas (ed.), *Jacob of Edessa and the Syriac Culture of His Day*, Leiden/Boston 2008 (MPIL 18)

Terian, Abraham, *Macarius of Jerusalem – Letter to the Armenians, A.D. 335: Introduction, Text, Translation and Commentary*, Crestwood, NY 2008 (AVANT Series)

Terian, Abraham, 'The Early Creeds of the Armenian Church', *Warszawskie Studia Teologiczne* 24 (2011), pp. 299–312

Terian, Abraham, 'Monastic Turmoil in Sixth-Century Jerusalem and the South Caucasus: The Letter of Patriarch John IV to Catholicos Abbas of the Caucasian Albanians', *DOP* 74 (2020), pp. 9–40

Ter-Mikelian, Aršak, *Die armenische Kirche in ihren Beziehungen zur byzantinischen (vom IV. bis zum XIII. Jahrhundert)*, Leipzig 1892

TeSelle, Eugene, art. 'Credere', in: *AugL*, vol. II (1996–2002), cols. 119–31

Tetz, Martin, 'Über nikäische Orthodoxie: Der sog. Tomus ad Antiochenos des Athanasius von Alexandrien' [1975], in: id. 1995, pp. 107–34

Tetz, Martin, 'Die Kirchweihsynode von Antiochien (341) und Marcellus von Ancyra: Zu der Glaubenserklärung des Theophronius von Tyana und ihren Folgen [1989]', in: id. 1995, pp. 227–48

Tetz, Martin, 'Zur strittigen Frage arianischer Glaubenserklärung auf dem Konzil von Nicaea (325)', in: Brennecke/Grasmück/Markschies 1993, pp. 220–38

Tetz, Martin, *Athanasiana: Zu Leben und Lehre des Athanasius*, ed. by Wilhelm Geerlings/Dietmar Wyrwa, Berlin/New York 1995 (BZAW 78)

The Liturgy of the Holy Apostles Adai and Mari Together with Two Additional Liturgies to be said on Certain Feasts and Other Days: and the Order of Baptism, Urmi 1893 (repr. Piscataway, NJ 2002)

Thomas, Kate, *Late Anglo-Saxon Prayer in Practice: Before the Book of Hours*, Berlin/Boston 2020 (Richard Rawlinson Center Series for Anglo-Saxon Studies)

Thompson, Augustine, *Cities of God: The Religion of the Italian Communes 1125–1325*, University Park 2005

Thomson, Robert W., *Rewriting Caucasian History: The Medieval Armenian Adaptation of the Georgian Chronicles: The Original Georgian Texts and the Armenian Adaptation*, Oxford 1996 (OOM)

[Thorpe, Benjamin], *Ancient Laws and Institutes of England*, [vol. I], London 1840

Thorpe, Benjamin, *The Homilies of the Anglo-Saxon Church: The First Part, Containing the Sermones Catholici or Homilies of Ælfric. In the Original Anglo-Saxon, with an English Version*, vol. I, London 1844

Thorpe, Benjamin, *The Homilies of the Anglo-Saxon Church: The First Part, Containing the Sermones Catholici or Homilies of Ælfric. In the Original Anglo-Saxon, with an English Version*, vol. II, London 1846

Thraede, Klaus, art. 'Hymnus I', in: *RAC*, vol. XVI, 1994, cols. 915–46

Thrams, Peter, *Christianisierung des Römerreiches und heidnischer Widerstand*, Heidelberg 1992

Tidner, Erik, *Didascaliae Apostolorum, Canonum Ecclesiasticorum, Traditionis Apostolicae Versiones Latinae*, Berlin 1963 (TU 75)

Till, Walter/Leipoldt, Walter, *Der koptische Text der Kirchenordnung Hippolyts*, Berlin 1954 (TU 58)

Tixeront, Joseph, art. '2. Athanase (Symbole de saint)', in: *DThC*, vol. I, 1903, cols. 2178–87

Toom, Tarmo, 'Appealing to Creed: Theodore of Mopsuestia and Cyril of Alexandria', *HeyJ* 62 (2021), pp. 290–301

Toom, Tarmo, 'Creed as *Verbum Breviatum*', *JEBS* 22 (2022), pp. 143–67

Torrell, Jean-Piere, *Saint Thomas Aquinas* vol. I: The Person and his Work, Washington, D.C. 1996

Treitinger, Otto, *Die oströmische Kaiser- und Reichsidee nach ihrer Gestaltung im höfischen Zeremoniell*, Jena 1938 (repr. Darmstadt 1956)

Troianos, Spyros, *Die Quellen des byzantinischen Rechts*, Berlin/Boston 2017

Trostyanskiy, Sergey, 'The *Encyclical* of Basiliscus (475) and its Theological Significance: Some Interpretational Issues', in: *StPatr* LXII, 2013, pp. 383–94

Turner, Cuthbert H., *Ecclesiae Occidentalis Monumenta Iuris Antiquissima*, 2 vols (9 fascicles; incomplete), Oxford 1899–1939

Turner, Cuthbert H., 'A Critical Text of the *Quicumque vult*', *JThS* 11 (1910), pp. 401–411

Turner, Cuthbert H., *The History and Use of Creeds and Anathemas in the Early Centuries of the Church*, second ed., London/Brighton 1910 (CHS 6)

Tydeman, William, *The Theatre in the Middle Ages: Western European Stage Conditions*, c. 800–1576, Cambridge etc. 1978

Ubl, Karl, 'Der lange Schatten des Bonifatius: Die Responsa Stephans II. aus dem Jahr 754 und das fränkische Kirchenrecht', *DA* 63 (2007), pp. 403–50

Uhalde, Kevin, art. 'Excommunication', in: *Brill Encyclopedia of Early Christianity Online*, 2018; URL <http://dx.doi.org/10.1163/2589-7993_EECO_SIM_00001223> (29/11/2023)

Ullmann, Lisa, 'Two Ostraca with the Niceno-Constantinopolitan Creed in the Israel Museum', *ZPE* 113 (1996), pp. 191–96

Ullmann, Walter, 'The Constitutional Significance of Constantine the Great's Settlement', *JEH* 27 (1976), pp. 1–16; also in: id., *Scholarship*, 1978, no. 1

Ullmann, Walter, 'Über die rechtliche Bedeutung der spätrömischen Kaisertitulatur für das Papsttum', in: Peter Leisching et al. (eds.), *Ex aequo et bono: Willibald M. Plöchl zum 70. Geburtstag*, Innsbruck 1977 (FRKG 10), pp. 23–43; also in: Ullmann, *Scholarship*, 1978, no. 2

Ullmann, Walter, 'Der Grundsatz der Arbeitsteilung bei Gelasius I.', *HJ* 97/98 (1978), pp. 41–70

Ullmann, Walter, *Scholarship and Politics in the Middle Ages: Collected Studies*, London 1978 (CStS 72)

Ullmann, Walter, *Gelasius I. (492–496): Das Papsttum an der Wende der Spätantike zum Mittelalter*, Stuttgart 1981 (PuP 18)

Ulrich, Jörg, *Die Anfänge der abendländischen Rezeption des Nizänums*, Berlin/New York 1994 (PTS 39)

Ure, James M. (ed.), *The Benedictine Office: An Old English Text*, Edinburgh 1957 (Edinburgh University Publications/Language and Literature 11)

Uthemann, Karl-Heinz, art. 'Paulus von Samosata', in: *BBKL*, vol. VII, 1994, cols. 66–89

Uthemann, Karl-Heinz, art. 'Photeinos', in: *LThK*, third ed., vol. VIII, 1999, col. 267

Uthemann, Karl-Heinz, 'Kaiser Justinian als Kirchenpolitiker und Theologe' [1999], in: id., *Christus, Kosmos, Diatribe: Themen der frühen Kirche als Beiträge zu einer historischen Theologie*, Berlin/ New York 2005 (AKG 93), pp. 257–331

Vaggione, Richard P., 'Some Neglected Fragments of Theodore of Mopsuestia's *Contra Eunomium*', *JThS* 31 (1980), pp. 403–70

Vaggione, Richard P., *Eunomius – The Extant Works: Text and Translation*, Oxford 1987 (OECT)

Vaggione, Richard P., *Eunomius of Cyzicus and the Nicene Revolution*, Oxford 2000

Vaggione, Richard P., art. 'Eudoxius of Antioch', in: *Brill Encyclopedia of Early Christianity online*, 2018; URL <http://dx.doi.org/10.1163/2589-7993_EECO_SIM_036680> (29/11/2023)

Van den Eynde, Damien, 'Nouvelles précisions chronologiques sur quelques œuvres théologiques du XIIe siècle', *FrS* 13 (1953), pp. 71–118

Van der Speeten, Joseph, 'Le dossier de Nicée dans la Quesnelliana', *SE* 28 (1985), pp. 383–450

Van der Vliet, Jacques, 'The Wisdom of the Wall: Innovation in Monastic Epigraphy', in: Malcolm Choat/Maria C. Giorda (eds.), *Writing and Communication in Early Egyptian Monasticism*, Leiden/Boston 2017 (Texts and Studies in Eastern Christianity 9), pp. 151–64

Van Egmond, Peter J., *"A Confession Without Pretense": Text and Context of Pelagius' Defence of 417 AD*, diss. theol., no place 2012

Van Ginkel, Jan J., 'Greetings to a Virtuous Man: The Correspondence of Jacob of Edessa', in: ter Haar Romeny 2008, pp. 67–81

Van Os, Hendrik W., art. 'Credo', in: *LCI*, vol. I, 1968, cols. 461–4

Van Rhijn, Carine, *Leading the Way to Heaven: Pastoral Care and Salvation in the Carolingian Period*, London/New York 2022 (The Medieval World)

Van Rompay, Lucas, art. 'Synodicon Orientale', in: *Gorgias Encyclopedic Dictionary of the Syriac Heritage* 2011, pp. 387–9

Van Unnik, Willem C., 'De la règle Μήτε προσθεῖναι μήτε ἀφελεῖν dans l'histoire du Canon' [1949]; in: id., *Sparsa Collecta: The Collected Essays of W.C. van Unnik*, vol. II, Leiden 1980 (NT.S. 30), pp. 123–56

Varghese, Baby, *Dionysius bar Salibi: Commentary on the Eucharist*, translated from Syriac, Kottayam 1998 (Mōrān 'Eth'ō 10)

Varghese, Baby, *John of Dara – Commentary on the Eucharist*, translated from the Syriac, Kottayam 1999 (Mōrān 'Eth'ō 12)

Varghese, Baby, 'The Anaphora of Saint James and Jacob of Edesse', in: ter Haar Romeny 2008, pp. 239–64

Varghese, Baby, 'The Liturgy of the Syriac Churches', in: Daniel King (ed.), *The Syriac World*, London/New York 2019 (The Routledge Worlds), pp. 391–404

Vaschalde, Arthur, *Babai Magni Liber de Unione*, 2 vols., Paris 1915 (CSCO 79–80/Scriptores Syri 34–35)

Vasiliev, Alexandre, *Kitab al-'Unvan: Histoire Universelle Écrite par Agapius de Menbidj*, éditée et traduite en français, seconde partie, fasc. 1, Paris 1911 (PO 7/4)

Vasiliev, Alexandre, *Kitab al-'Unvan: Histoire Universelle Écrite par Agapius de Menbidj*, éditée et traduite en français, seconde partie, fasc. 2, Paris 1912 (PO 8/3)

Velázquez Soriano, Isabel, *Las pizarras visigodas (Entre el latín y su disgregación. La lengua hablada en Hispania, siglos VI–VIII)*, n.p. [Burgos] 2004 (Colección Beltenebros 8).

Velázquez Soriano, Isabel, 'Between Orthodox Belief and ,Superstition' in Visigothic Hispania', in: Richard L. Gordon/Francisco M. Simón (eds.), *Magical Practice in the Latin West: Papers from the International Conference Held at the University of Zaragoza 30 Sept.–1 Oct. 2005*, Leiden/Boston 2010 (RGRW 168), pp. 601–27

Verardo, Raimondo A. (ed.), *S. Thomae Aquinatis Doctoris Angelici Opuscula Theologica*, vol. I: De re dogmatica et morali, Turin/Rome 1954

Veyne, Paul, *Did the Greeks Believe in their Myths: An Essay on the Constitutive Imagination*, Chicago/London 1988

Viciano, Alberto, *Cristo salvador y liberador del hombre: Estudio sobre la soteriología de Tertuliano*, Pamplona 1986

Vielhauer, Philipp, *Geschichte der urchristlichen Literatur: Einleitung in das Neue Testament, die Apokryphen und die Apostolischen Väter*, Berlin/New York 1975 (fourth print-run 1985; GLB)

Villecourt, Louis/Tisserant, Eugène/Wiet, Gaston, *Livre de la Lampe des Ténèbres et de l'Exposition (Lumineuse) du Service (de l'Église) par Abû'l-Barakât Connu sous le Nom d'Ibn Kabar: Texte Arabe Édité et Traduit*, Turnhout 1928 (repr. 1974; PO 20/4, no. 99)

Vinzent, Markus, *Asterius von Kappadokien, Die Theologischen Fragmente: Einleitung, kritischer Text, Übersetzung und Kommentar*, Leiden 1993 (SVigChr 20)

Vinzent, Markus, *Markell von Ankyra – Die Fragmente/Der Brief an Julius von Rom*, herausgegeben, eingeleitet und übersetzt, Leiden etc. 1997 (SVigChr 39)

Vinzent, Markus, 'Die Entstehung des "Römischen Glaubensbekenntnisses"', in: Kinzig/Markschies/Vinzent 1999, pp. 185–409

Vinzent, Markus, *Der Ursprung des Apostolikums im Urteil der kritischen Forschung*, Göttingen 2006 (FKDG 89)

Vinzent, Markus, *Christ's Resurrection in Early Christianity and the Making of the New Testament*, Farnham, Surrey/Burlington, VT 2011

Vinzent, Markus, 'From Zephyrinus to Damasus – What Did Roman Bishops Believe?', in: *StPatr*, vol. LXIII, 2013, pp. 273–86

Vinzent, Markus, *Writing the History of Early Christianity: From Reception to Retrospection*, Cambridge 2019

Vinzent, Markus, *Resetting the Origins of Christianity: A New Theory of Sources and Beginnings*, Cambridge 2023

Vivian, Tim/Athanassakis, Apostolos N., Athanasius of Alexandria – The Life of Antony, Kalamazoo, Michigan 2003 (CistSS 202)

Vodola, Elizabeth, *Excommunication in the Middle Ages*, Berkeley etc. 1986

Vööbus, Arthur, *Studies in the History of the Gospel Text in Syriac*, Leuven 1951 (CSCO.Sub 3)

Vööbus, Arthur, 'New Sources for the Symbol in Early Syrian Christianity', *VigChr* 26 (1972), pp. 291–6

Vööbus, Arthur, *The Synodicon in the West Syrian Tradition*, 4 vols., Leuven 1975/1976 (CSCO 367, 368, 375, 376/Scriptores Syri 161, 162, 163, 164)

Vööbus, Arthur, *The Canons Ascribed to Mārūtā of Maipherqaṭ and Related Sources*, 2 vols., Leuven 1982 (CSCO 439, 440/Scriptores Syri 191, 192)

Vogel, Cyrille, *Medieval Liturgy: An Introduction to the Sources*, Washington, DC 1986

Vokes, Frederick E., art. 'Apostolisches Glaubensbekenntnis, I. Alte Kirche und Mittelalter', in: *TRE*, vol. III, 1978, pp. 528–54

Vollenweider, Samuel, 'III. Frühe Glaubensbekenntnisse', in: Jens Schröter/Christine Jacobi (eds.), *Jesus Handbuch*, Tübingen 2017, pp. 504–15

Vona, Costantino, *L'Apologia di Aristide: Introduzione, versione dal Siriaco e commento*, Rome 1950 (Lat. NS 16,1–4)

Voss, Gerhard J., *Opera*, vol. VI: Tractatus theologici, Amsterdam 1701

Wagner, Peter, *Introduction to the Gregorian Melodies: A Handbook of Plainsong*, part I: Origin and Development of the Forms of the Liturgical Chant up to the End of the Middle Ages, second ed., London 1901

Wagner, Peter, *Einführung in die gregorianischen Melodien: Ein Handbuch der Choralwissenschaft*, Erster Teil: Ursprung und Entwicklung der liturgischen Gesangsformen bis zum Ausgange des Mittelalters, third ed., Leipzig 1911

Wagner, Peter, *Gregorianische Formenlehre: Eine choralische Stilkunde*, Leipzig 1921

Wagschal, David, *Law and Legality in the Greek East: The Byzantine Canonical Tradition, 381–883*, Oxford 2015 (OECS)

Wallace-Hadrill, David S., *Eusebius of Caesarea*, London 1960

Wallraff, Martin, *Sonnenkönig der Spätantike: Die Religionspolitik Konstantins des Großen*, Freiburg im Breisgau 2013

Walther, Otto K., *Codex Laudianus G35 – a Re-Examination of the Manuscript: A Reproduction of the Text and an Accompanying Commentary*, 3 vols., PhD Thesis, University of St. Andrews 1980; download: URL <http://hdl.handle.net/10023/2670> (29/11/2023)

Wanek, Nina-Maria, '*Missa graeca*: Mythen und Fakten um griechische Gesänge in westlichen Handschriften', in: Falko Dain et al. (eds.), *Menschen, Bilder, Sprache, Dinge: Wege der Kommunikation zwischen Byzanz und dem Westen*, vol. II: Menschen und Worte, Mainz 2018 (Byzanz zwischen Orient und Okzident 9/2), pp. 113–26

Wansleben, Johann M./Ludolf, Hiob, *Confessio fidei Claudii regis Aethiopiae* [. . .], London 1661

Warner, George F., *The Stowe Missal*, 2 vols., London 1906/1915 (HBS 31, 32)

Wasserschleben, Friedrich W., *Die Bussordnungen der abendländischen Kirche nebst einer rechtsgeschichtlichen Einleitung*, Halle 1851

Waterland, Daniel, *A Critical History of the Athanasian Creed*, Cambridge 1724

Waterland, Daniel, *A Critical History of the Athanasian Creed*, second ed., Cambridge 1728

Waterland, Daniel, *A Critical History of the Athanasian Creed*, a new edition revised and corrected by John R. King, Cambridge 1870

Weckwerth, Andreas, *Das erste Konzil von Toledo: Ein philologischer und historischer Kommentar zur Constitutio concilii*, Münster, Westfalen 2004 (JbAC.KR 1)

Weckwerth, Andreas, *Ablauf, Organisation und Selbstverständnis westlicher antiker Synoden im Spiegel ihrer Akten*, Münster, Westfalen 2010 (JbAC.KR 5)

Weckwerth, Andreas, *Clavis Conciliorum Occidentalium Septem Prioribus Saeculis Celebratorum*, Turnhout 2013 (CChr/Claves – Subsidia 3)

Weckwerth, Andreas, 'The Twenty Canons of the Council of Nicaea', in: Kim 2021, pp. 158–76

Weckwerth, Andreas, art. 'Synode (synodos, concilium)', in: *RAC*, vol. XXXI, 2023, cols. 592–638

Weidenhiller, Egino, *Untersuchungen zur deutschsprachigen katechetischen Literatur des späten Mittelalters: Nach den Handschriften der Bayerischen Staatsbibliothek*, Munich 1965 (Münchener Texte und Untersuchungen zur deutschen Literatur des Mittelalters 10)

Weischer, Bernd M., 'Die Glaubenssymbole des Epiphanios von Salamis und des Gregorios Thaumaturgos im Qērellos', *OrChr* 61 (1977), pp. 20–40

Weischer, Bernd M., 'Die ursprüngliche nikänische Form des ersten Glaubenssymbols im Ankyrōtos des Epiphanios von Salamis: Ein Beitrag zur Diskussion um die Entstehung des konstantinopolitanischen Glaubenssymbols im Lichte neuester äthiopistischer Forschungen', *ThPh* 53 (1978), pp. 407–14

Weischer, Bernd M., *Quērellos IV 2: Traktate des Epiphanios von Zypern und des Proklos von Kyzikos*, Wiesbaden 1979 (ÄthF 6)

Wengst, Klaus, art. 'Glaubensbekenntnis(se), IV. Neues Testament', in: *TRE*, vol. XIII, 1984, pp. 392–9

Wensinck, Arent J., *The Muslim Creed: Its Genesis and Historical Development*, second impression, London 1965

Wernicke, Ernst, 'Die bildliche Darstellung des apostolischen Glaubensbekenntnisses in der deutschen Kunst des Mittelalters', *CKBK* 29 (1887), pp. 102–5, 123–6, 135–9, 155–60, 171–5; 30 (1888), pp. 10–15; 31 (1889), pp. 42–6, 59–64; 35 (1893), pp. 20–7, 41–6, 72–9

Westra, Liuwe H., *The Apostles' Creed: Origin, History, and Some Early Commentaries*, Turnhout 2002 (IPM 43)

Westra, Liuwe H., 'Creating a Theological Difference: The Myth of Two Grammatical Constructions with Latin *Credo*', in: *StPatr* vol. XCII, 2017, pp. 3–14

Westwell, Arthur, 'The *Ordines Romani* and the Carolingian Choreography of a Liturgical Route to Rome', *AAAHP* 31 (2019), pp. 63–79

Wharton, Annabel J., 'The Baptistery of the Holy Sepulcher in Jerusalem and the Politics of Sacred Landscape', *DOP* 46 (1992), pp. 313–25

Wheaton, Benjamin, *Venantius Fortunatus and Gallic Christianity: Theology in the Writings of an Italian Émigré in Merovingian Gaul*, Leiden 2022 (BSEMA 29)

Whitaker, Edward C., 'The History of the Baptismal Formula', *JEH* 16 (1965), pp. 1–12

Whitaker, Edward C./Johnson, Maxwell E., *Documents of the Baptismal Liturgy*, third ed., Collegeville, Minnesota 2003

Wickham, Lionel R., art. 'Chalkedon. ökumenische Synode (451)', in: *TRE*, vol. VII, 1981, pp. 668–75

Wickham, Lionel R., *Hilary of Poitiers: Conflicts of Conscience and Law in the Fourth-century Church*. Translated with Introduction and Notes, Liverpool 1997 (Translated Texts for Historians 25)

Wieacker, Franz, *Römische Rechtsgeschichte, Zweiter Abschnitt: Die Jurisprudenz vom frühen Prinzipat bis zum Ausgang der Antike im Weströmischen Reich und die oströmische Rechtswissenschaft bis zur justinianischen Gesetzgebung*, ed. by Joseph Georg Wolf, Munich 2006 (HAW X 3,1; Rechtsgeschichte des Altertums 3,1)

Wiegand, Friedrich, *Die Stellung des apostolischen Symbols im kirchlichen Leben des Mittelalters*, vol. I: Symbol und Katechumenat, Leipzig 1899 (SGTK 4/2)

Wiegand, Friedrich, *Das apostolische Symbol im Mittelalter*, Gießen 1904 (VTKG 21)

Wilcox, Miranda, 'Confessing the Faith in Anglo-Saxon England', *JEGP* 113 (2014), pp. 308–41

Wiles, Maurice F., 'A Textual Variant in the Creed of the Council of Nicaea', *StPatr*, vol. XXVI, 1993, pp. 428–33

Wiles, Maurice F., *Archetypal Heresy: Arianism through the Centuries*, Oxford 1996 (repr. 2004)

Williams, Daniel H., *Ambrose of Milan and the End of the Nicene-Arian Conflicts*, Oxford 1995 (OECS)

Williams, Daniel H., 'Monarchianism and Photinus of Sirmium as the Persistent Heretical Face of the Fourth Century', *HTR* 99 (2006), pp. 187–206

Williams, Daniel H., 'The Evolution of Pro-Nicene Theology in the Church of the East', in: Li Tang/ Dietmar W. Winkler (eds.), *From the Oxus River to the Chinese Shores: Studies on East Syriac Christianity in China and Central Asia*, Vienna/Berlin 2013 (OPOe 5), pp. 387–95

Williams, Rowan, *Arius: Heresy and Tradition*, revised ed., Grand Rapids, MI/Cambridge 2001

Willis, Geoffrey G., *A History of Early Roman Liturgy to the Death of Pope Gregory the Great*, London 1994 (HBS Subsidia 1)

Winkelmann, Friedhelm, *Eusebius Werke, Erster Band, Erster Teil: Über das Leben des Kaisers Konstantin*, second ed., Berlin/New York 1991 (GCS)

Winkler, Dietmar W., 'Zur Rezeptiuon "Ökumenischer Konzilien" am Beispiel der persischen und armenischen Kirche', in: Peter Bruns/Hein O. Luthe (eds.), *Orientalia Christiana: Festschrift für Hubert Kaufhold zum 70. Geburtstag*, Wiesbaden 2013, pp. 615–36

Winkler, Gabriele, 'Eine bemerkenswerte Stelle im armenischen Glaubensbekenntnis: *Credimus et in Sanctum Spiritum qui descendit in Jordanem proclamavit missum*', *Oriens Christianus* 63 (1979), pp. 130–62

Winkler, Gabriele, *Das armenische Initiationsrituale: Entwicklungsgeschichtliche und liturgievergleichende Untersuchung der Quellen des 3. bis 10. Jahrhunderts*, Rome 1982 (OCA 217)

Winkler, Gabriele, 'Armenian Anaphoras and Creeds: A Brief Overview of Work in Progress', in: Robert F. Taft (ed.), *The Armenian Christian Tradition; Scholarly Symposium in Honor of the Visit to the Pontifical Oriental Institute, Rome of His Holiness Karekin I, Supreme Patriarch and Catholicos of all Armenians, December 12, 1996*, Rome 1997 (OCA 254), pp. 41–55

Winkler, Gabriele, *Über die Entwicklungsgeschichte des armenischen Symbolums: Ein Vergleich mit dem syrischen und griechischen Formelgut unter Einbezug der relevanten georgischen und äthiopischen Quellen*, Rome 2000 (OCA 262)

Winkler, Gabriele, 'Zur Erforschung orientalischer Anaphoren in liturgievergleichender Sicht II: Das Formelgut der Oratio post Sanctus und Anamnese sowie Interzessionen und die Taufbekenntnisse', in: Robert F. Taft/Gabriele Winkler (eds.), *Comparative Liturgy Fifty Years after Anton Baumstark (1872–1948): Acts of the International Congress*, Rome 2001 (OCA 265), pp. 403–97

Winkler, Gabriele, 'Anhang zur Untersuchung "Über die Entwicklungsgeschichte des armenischen Symbolums" und seine Bedeutung für die Wirkungsgeschichte der antiochenischen Synoden von 324/325 und 341–345, in: Robert F. Taft (ed.), *The Formation of a Millennial Tradition: 1700 Years of Armenian Christian Witness (301–2002)*, Rome 2004 (OCA 271), pp. 107–59

Winkler, Gabriele, 'Über die Evolution der Eingliederung von Bekenntnisformeln und des Credos in die östlichen Liturgien', in: Tinatin Khidesheli/Nestor Kavvadas (eds.), *Bau und Schrift: Studien zur Archäologie und Literatur des antiken Christentums für Hans Reinhard Seeliger*, Münster 2015 (JbAC.KR, 12), pp. 237–54

Winkler, Lorenz, *Salus: Vom Staatskult zur politischen Idee. Eine archäologische Untersuchung*, Heidelberg 1995 (Archäologie und Geschichte 4)

Winnebeck, Julia, *Apostolikumsstreitigkeiten: Diskussionen um Liturgie, Lehre und Kirchenverfassung in der preußischen Landeskirche 1871–1914*, Leipzig 2016 (AKThG 44)

Winnebeck, Julia, 'The Thompson Case', *ZNThG* 26 (2019), pp. 20–46

Wischmeyer, Oda, 'Hermeneutische Aspekte der Taufe im Neuen Testament', in: Hellholm et al. 2011, vol. I, pp. 735–63

Witkamp, Nathan, *Tradition and Innovation: Baptismal Rite and Mystagogy in Theodore of Mopsuestia and Narsai of Nisibis*, Leiden/Boston 2018 (SVigChr 149)

Wochnik, Fritz, 'Credo-Apostel in der mittelalterlichen Mark Brandenburg', in: Ulrich Kalmbach/Frank Riedel (eds.), *80. Jahresbericht des Altmärkischen Vereins für vaterländische Geschichte zu Salzwedel e.V.*, Salzwedel 2010, pp. 19–44

Wolff, Hans Julius, *Das Recht der griechischen Papyri Ägyptens in der Zeit der Ptolemäer und des Prinzipats*, 2 vols., Munich 1978 (HAW 10,5,1–2/Rechtsgeschichte des Altertums 5,1–2)

Wolter, Michael, *Paul: An Outline of His Theology*, Waco, Texas 2015

Wolter, Michael, *Der Brief an die Römer*, Teilband 2: Röm 9–16, Ostfildern/Göttingen 2019 (EKK)

Wood, D.T. Baird, '"Credo" Tapestries', *BurlM* 24 (1913/1914), pp. 247–54, 309–17

Wood, Michael, *In Search of England: Journeys into the English Past*, Berkeley/Los Angeles 1999

Woolf, Rosemary, *The English Mystery Plays*, Berkeley/Los Angeles 1972

Wordsworth, John/White, Henry J., *Nouum Testamentum Domini Nostri Iesu Christi Latine secundum editionem sancti Hieronymi*, vol. III, Oxford 1954

Wyrwa, Dietmar, '§ 94 Irenäus von Lyon', in: Christoph Riedweg/Christoph Horn/Dietmar Wyrwa (eds.), *Die Philosophie der Antike*, vol. V/1: Philosophie der Kaiserzeit und der Spätantike, Basel 2018 (Grundriss der Geschichte der Philosophie), pp. 883–896, 1087–90

Young, Frances M., *The Making of the Creeds*, London/Philadelphia 1991

Yousif, Pierre, *The Order of the Holy Qurbana in the East Syrian Tradition*, revised translation by P.Y., ed. by Johnson Chittilappilly, Kerala 2000

Zachhuber, Johannes, art. 'Physis', in: *RAC*, vol. XXVII, 2016, cols. 744–81

Zawadzki, Konrad, 'Die Anfänge des "Anathema" in der Urkirche', *Vox Patrum* 28 (2008), pp. 1323–34; 29 (2009), pp. 495–520; 30 (2010), pp. 721–66

Zwierlein, Otto, *Petrus und Paulus in Jerusalem und Rom: Vom Neuen Testament zu den apokryphen Apostelakten*, Berlin/Boston 2013 (UALG 109)

Indices

I Biblical Passages

1. Old Testament and Old Testament Apocrypha

Gen	
1:1–2	532
1:1	368
14:14	245, 388
14:19	164
Ex	
4:31	55
14:31	55
20:1–17	624
20:3	141 f.
20:11	135, 222
23:17	520
24:3	55
24:7	55
Lev	
19:18	624
Num	
21:22	401
Deut	
4:2	327
5:6–21	624
6:4	55
6:17–19	55
13:1	327
26:5–9(11)	56
30:14	59
1Sam (1Kings)	
17:51	262
2Sam (2Kings)	
7:27	254
1Chron	
8:40	388
17:24	254
2Ezra (Neh)	
15:17 (= Neh 5:17)	388

Jdt	
13:24(Vg)	164
14:10	58
2Macc	
7:28	93
7:35	254
3Macc	
6:18	254
6:28	254
Ps	
2:7	582
2:11	98
50(51)	540
61(62):13	280, 309, 314, 321
90(91)	540
109(110):1	134
109(110):3	216, 257
132(133)	543
145(146):6	135
Prov	
8	258
8:22–23	257
8:22	293, 298
8:25	257
24:12	280, 309, 314, 321
26:11	493
Eccles	
3:14	327
Job	
1:14	581
38:17	308, 310, 314, 316, 321
Wis	
1:14	93
7:25–26	269

https://doi.org/10.1515/9783110318531-023

18:20	126
23:33	103
24:4	75
24:10	75
24:30	135, 240
25:31	135, 254
25:41	135
26:64	134, 152
28:19	21, 24, 26, 70, 75, 88, 90 f., 96, 104, 120, 123, 132 f., 237 f., 254, 273 f., 618

Mk	
1:4	208
1:11	278
3:16–19	194
6:38	90
8:29	70, 84, 86
8:34–38	76
10:18	268
10:30	427
12:29–31	624
12:36	134
14:36	278
14:62	134
16:19	134, 137, 141, 254

Lk	
1:2	118
1:31	453, 455, 457
1:33	287, 370, 622
1:35	140, 166, 369
2:2	5 f.
3:3	208
3:38	532
6:31	624
9:58	374
10:17	136
10:22	223
11:50–51	98
12:1–12	76
12:8–9	65, 75 f.
12:8	66
15:12–13	254
18:39	427
20:35	188
20:42	134

22:69	134
22:70	85

Jn	
1	72
1:1–18	85
1:1–14	254, 621
1:1–9	232
1:1–5	85
1:1–3	81, 89, 99, 141, 274
1:1–2	272
1:3	94, 105, 137, 206 f., 237, 254, 272, 278, 280, 293, 308, 313, 320, 349, 449
1:4	254, 272
1:9	254, 272
1:10	621
1:14	85, 254
1:18	81, 85, 236, 254, 272, 286
1:20	65
3:13	254
3:15	62
3:16	85, 254
3:18	62, 85
3:19	94, 254
3:33	254
4:24	142
4:34	278
5:30	278
6:9	90
6:38	272
6:63	352
6:69	62, 85
6:70–71	86
8:12	254
8:42	62, 216, 257
8:44	127
9:22	64 f., 78, 86
10:15	227
10:30	139, 274
10:38	174
11:27	62, 86, 254
12:42–46	78
12:42	64 f., 82
12:45	269
13:3	62
14:9–11	139

II Ancient and Medieval Sources

https://doi.org/10.1515/9783110318531-024

III Inscriptions, Papyri, Parchments, Ostraca, Wooden Tablets

https://doi.org/10.1515/9783110318531-025

IV Manuscripts

https://doi.org/10.1515/9783110318531-026

V Numbers in FaFo

8a	52	38	52
8b	51	39a	52, 492
11	52	39b	52
14	526	43	51
14a	52	44	51, 531
14b	52 f.	47	531
15	526	61	51
15a1	51	63	502, 568
15a2	327, 527	70	568
15a3	527, 536 f., 540	74	181
15b	536	75	502, 526
16a1	52	76	526
16a2	52	81	86, 121
16c	53	82a	132
18	51 f., 193, 526 f., 537	82b	132
19	526	82c	126, 132
19a	51–3, 527, 537	82d	132
19b	51 f.	82e	132
19c	51 f.	83	121
20	53	84	133
21	52	85	52, 121
22	526	86	131
22a1	527	87a	116, 121
22a3	527, 536	87b	121
22b	52, 527, 537	88	121
22c	53, 527, 536	89	26, 174
22d	53, 527	89a1	149
22e1	51	89a2	149
22e2	527, 536	89b	XVIII, 129, 150, 166
22f	527	89c	XVIII, 129, 150, 240, 281, 369, 446 f.
22f1	52		
22f2	536	89d	148, 446
22g	51, 527, 537	89e	148, 450, 460
23	51 f., 194	89f	148, 446
27a	51	89f1	448
27b	52	89f2	447
29	52	90	131, 353
30	51 f., 527	91	131
31	526	92	52, 187
32	527	92a	52, 115, 131 f., 173, 175, 182
33	52	92b	126, 132, 182
34	51 f.	93	89
35	52 f.	94a	90
37	527	94b	90

https://doi.org/10.1515/9783110318531-027

VI Ancient and Medieval Names

https://doi.org/10.1515/9783110318531-028

VII Modern Names

https://doi.org/10.1515/9783110318531-029

VIII Credal Content

Relevant Greek and Latin terms are referenced under their respective English entries, even where not explicitly cited.

The entries are not alphabetically organized, but according to the sequence of clauses in the major creeds.

https://doi.org/10.1515/9783110318531-030